THE LAW SOCIETY'S
CONVEYANCING
HANDBOOK
1997

GW00630671

THE LAW SOCIETY'S CONVEYANCING HANDBOOK

1997

by

Frances Silverman *Solicitor*

Editorial Board

Margaret Anstey LLB *Solicitor Tozers*
Kenneth Edwards *Solicitor Burt Brill & Cardens*
Philip Freedman LLB *Solicitor Mishcon de Reya*
John Noble *Solicitor Bartlett Gregory Collins & Snow*

nominated by the Law Society's
Land Law and Succession Committee

THE LAW SOCIETY

PUBLICATIONS

1997

©The Law Society 1997

First published January 1992
Reprinted June 1992
2nd edition 1993
Reprinted April 1993
3rd edition 1994
Reprinted February 1995
4th edition 1995
5th edition 1996
Reprinted March 1997
6th edition 1997

ISBN 1 85328 452 1
ISSN 1350-1852

The material in Appendices VIII, IX, and X.1 is Crown copyright.

Published by the Law Society
113 Chancery Lane, London WC2A 1PL

Typeset by OTS Group Ltd, Caterham, Surrey
Printed by Thanet Press Ltd, Margate

Contents

CONTENTS

N.   COSTS

APPENDICES

I.   RULES AND CODES

II.   GUIDANCE

III.   MORTGAGE FRAUD

IV.   PROTOCOL

V.   STANDARD FORMS

VI.   STANDARD UNDERTAKINGS

Preface to the 1992 edition

Conveyancing is a much maligned art — an easy option in the eyes of many practitioners. If this is true, why is it that the Legal Practice Directorate and Professional Ethics Department of the Law Society have a constant stream of telephone calls and letters from practitioners anxious to know how to solve conveyancing problems? The idea of this book originated from the Law Society's Land Law and Conveyancing Committee who felt that the time had come to publish a work which attempted to deal with and resolve the many problems encountered on a daily basis by practitioners. The aim of this book, therefore, is to present in readable form a ready reference handbook of the practice of conveyancing. The book does not pretend to be a comprehensive guide to the law — for this the reader is, at various points throughout the text, referred to specialist works dealing with particular areas, but it does seek to deal fully with the practice of conveyancing and to provide guidance on resolving problems which may be encountered by practitioners. The text is, therefore, divided into sections which deal with the conveyancing transaction in chronological sequence. Chapters have been included on matters which, although peripheral to the main issue, nevertheless impinge on it, e.g. advertising, property selling, costs, undertakings and remedies. Although the book does contain some specialist sections, e.g. the purchase of licensed premises, milk quotas in agricultural land, it is intended as a handbook for the general practitioner and does not, therefore, cover in detail specialist areas pertaining to commercial transactions. It does, however, seek to gather together some information which is not found either in other conventional conveyancing texts or in some cases at all, this aspect particularly concentrating on the resolution of practical problems and provision of checklists and guidelines. Precedents are not included within the text since the practitioner has ample scope for finding precedents in many other published works. Some commonly encountered practical areas are no longer dealt with by trainee solicitors during their Finals course, and in such areas, e.g. residential security of tenure, the book aims to provide the solicitor with a brief résumé of the law with reference to a specialist work on the subject should that be required.

It is hoped that this book will form the practitioner's first point of reference and to that end extensive appendices include the text of many of the matters to which a practitioner has cause to refer during the course of each working day, e.g. HM Land Registry Practice Notes, addresses of authorities for the purpose of making searches, stamp duty tables, the Formulae for exchange of contracts.

It is of course vital that any book which purports to be an essential working tool in the hands of a busy practitioner should be up to date with both law and practice. The decision has, therefore, been taken by the Law Society that this book will be completely revised and updated regularly in order to ensure that the practitioner has available to him in one volume the very latest information relating to conveyancing.

No offence is intended to female members of the profession by references in the text to the solicitor as 'he', for which please read 'he or she' as appropriate. To include the words 'he or she' on every occasion where such reference appears would have the effect of extending the text by a considerable amount which in turn would have adverse repercussion on the publication price of the book.

I would like to acknowledge with thanks the permission of HM Land Registry and the Inland Revenue for publication of their various leaflets and guidance notes which appear in the appendices to the book.

I would also like to thank Linklaters and Paines for their help with sections on milk quotas and VAT, Withers for their assistance in preparing the text on agricultural land, Chris Jowett of the Halifax Building Society for his help in relation to mortgages, Martin Wood of HM Land Registry for his assistance with points on registered land, and Tony Donell who read through each section of the manuscript before publication.

I should also record my appreciation to the staff of the Law Society, in particular Joanna Davies-Evitt and Carl Upsall who have been responsible for the co-ordination of the text, preparation of appendices and index and eventual publication of the text itself.

Finally my thanks go to Trevor Aldridge, Margaret Anstey, Murray Ross, Philip Freedman, and Kenneth Edwards who comprised the Editorial Board for this book. They had the unenviable task of sitting through monthly meetings to discuss and correct my indecipherable manuscript. Without their constant help, support and encouragement this book might not have seen the light of day.

The law is stated as at 1 December 1991.

Frances Silverman

Rowfold Grange
West Sussex

1 December 1991

Preface to the 1997 edition

Once again there have been significant developments in the property law arena during the past year, the most radical perhaps being the Trusts of Land and Appointment of Trustees Act 1996 which came into force on 1 January 1997.

This edition of the Handbook incorporates the changes made by the Trusts of Land and Appointment of Trustees Act 1996 and by the Housing Act 1996, including a revised and expanded section on short-term residential tenancies for which grateful thanks are extended to Paul Butt for his assistance with this complex area of law. The Party Wall Act 1996 is also discussed in the context of a new chapter dealing with easements and boundaries. My thanks also go to Nicholas Lightbody for his help with the section on environmental issues which has been completely revised to take account of changes made by the Environment Act 1995.

Of great practical significance is the introduction of the new system for arbitration relating to business leases (PACT) which is referred to in the section on business leases. The Standard Mortgage Instructions are referred to in context throughout the book but, at the time of publication of this edition, they had not been finalised.

I am most grateful to Ann Humphrey for updating the sections on VAT and agricultural land, to the staff at MAFF for their advice on milk quotas, to Dr Martyn Green at NRPB for his comments on radon, and to Martin Wood and his colleagues at the Land Registry for their comments on registered land.

Trevor Aldridge who, since the inception of this project by the Law Society, has been the Chairman of the Editorial Board retired from the Board in September 1996. He will be sorely missed. His enthusiasm, commitment, erudite advice and wit managed to keep the author sane in her darkest moments of despair! Special thanks go to Trevor for his help and contributions over the past six years.

My thanks also go to the remaining members of the Editorial Board, Philip Freedman, Kenneth Edwards, John Noble and Margaret Anstey, for their continuing support, encouragement and help with this edition. I am also grateful to Sonia Purser at the Law Society for her continued hard work in updating the appendices of the book, and to the staff in the Publications Department of the Law Society who have worked very hard to turn my untidy and, in places, illegible manuscript into a polished and professional finished product. I am also indebted to Tony Donell for his indefatigable proof reading. Any errors which remain in the book are my responsibility alone.

The law is stated as at 2 April 1997.

Frances Silverman

Rowfold Grange
West Sussex

1 June 1997

Table of Cases

Table of Statutes

Table of Statutory Instruments

A. PRELIMINARY MATTERS

A.01. Taking instructions

1.1. Objectives

1.1.1. The purpose of taking instructions is to obtain sufficient information from the client to enable the solicitor to conduct the whole transaction: it will be necessary to consult the client further during the course of the transaction, but taking full instructions at an early stage will obviate the need to contact the client frequently to confirm minor details. The need constantly to check minor details with the client is not cost effective nor does it inspire the client with confidence in the solicitor's ability to do the work.

1.1.2. A further objective is to obtain an overall view of the transaction in order to to give the client full and proper advice appropriate to the circumstances: unless full instructions are taken the solicitor is in danger of overlooking matters which are relevant to the transaction, e.g. insuring the property, or the inheritance tax implications of co-ownership.

1.1.3. Taxation consequences

Regard must always be paid to the taxation consequences of the proposed transaction whether or not these are mentioned to the solicitor by the client. Failure to do so may result in an action for breach of contract or negligence by the client against the solicitor.[1]

1. See *Hurlingham Estates Ltd* v. *Wilde, The Times*, 3 January 1997.

1.2. Where have the instructions come from?

1.2.1. Instructions to act may be accepted provided there is no breach of Rule 1 Solicitors' Practice Rules 1990 (obtaining instructions). (See below, Appendix I.1.) Thus instructions must be declined *inter alia* in the following circumstances:

    (a) where to act would involve the solicitor in a breach of the law, e.g. a fraudulent conveyance;

    (b) where the solicitor would be involved in a breach of the rules of conduct, e.g. entering a contract race without disclosing the race to all prospective buyers;

(c) where a conflict of interest exists or is likely to exist;

(d) where the solicitor lacks the expertise to carry out the client's instructions competently;

(e) where the solicitor does not have sufficient time to devote to the client's affairs;

(f) where the instructions are tainted by duress or undue influence, e.g. an elderly client is 'persuaded' by her relatives to sell the family home;

(g) where the solicitor, one of his partners, employees or close relatives holds some office or appointment the holding of which might lead the client or the general public to infer that the solicitor had some influence over the outcome of the matter, e.g. a solicitor who is a member of the local planning committee should not accept instructions to act in a planning appeal against the authority of which he is a member;

(h) where another solicitor has already been instructed in the matter and that other solicitor's retainer has not been terminated;

(i) where the client's freedom of choice to instruct the solicitor of his choosing has been impaired in some way, e.g. the client has received a discount from a builder on the condition that a certain solicitor is instructed.

1.2.2. Subject to the exceptions outlined above the solicitor cannot decline to act on the basis of the colour, race, national or ethnic origins of the client[1] nor on the basis of the client's sex or sexual orientation, marital status[2] or disability.[3]

1.2.3. Instructions which have been obtained through a referral from an estate agent, mortgage broker or other third party may be accepted provided there is compliance with Rule 3 Solicitors' Practice Rules 1990 (introductions and referrals).[4]

1.2.4. If instructions are received indirectly through a third party, confirmation of the instructions must be obtained directly from the client in order to clarify the client's exact requirements and to ensure that the instructions are not tainted by duress or undue influence.

1.2.5. The solicitor should be alert to the possibilities of mortgage fraud and should adhere to the guidelines issued by the Law Society in its leaflet 'Green Card Warning on Property Fraud' (see Appendix III.2.).

1. Race Relations Act 1976, Law Society's Anti-Discrimination Code and Solicitors' Anti-Discrimination Rule 1995.
2. Sex Discrimination Act 1975 and Law Society's Code.
3. Disability Discrimination Act 1995.
4. See below, Introductions and referrals, para. A.07.

1.3. Taking instructions in person

1.3.1. Wherever possible instructions should be obtained from the client in a personal interview. This will enable the solicitor to clarify areas of doubt concerning the transaction, enable the client to ask questions about matters which worry him, and establish a confident working relationship between the solicitor and his client.

1.3.2. Where the solicitor is instructed by one person to act on behalf of that person and another, e.g. as co-sellers, the non-instructing client's authority to act and consent to the transaction should be confirmed directly with the person concerned.

1.3.3. If the interviewer is not the person who will conduct the transaction on the client's behalf, the client should be introduced to or at least told the name and status within the firm of the person who will be effecting the client's business and of the person whom he may contact should the need arise and whom the client should contact in the event of a problem or complaint arising about the solicitor's services.[1]

1.3.4. Under the terms of the Protocol, the solicitor who is acting for the seller is required to obtain his client's answers to the Seller's Property Information Form, to obtain from his client any relevant documents relating to, e.g. guarantees, building regulation consent, etc., and to ask his client to complete the Fixtures Fittings and Contents Form. He must also obtain details of all financial charges over the property (including second and subsequent mortgages, improvement grants and discounts repayable to the local authority), and ascertain the identity of all persons aged over 17 who are resident in the property in order to establish whether or not such persons have an interest in the property.

1. See Rule 15 Solicitors' Practice Rules 1990 and Practice Management Standard F4.

1.4. Identity of the client

1.4.1. Checking the client's identity serves as a precaution against mortgage fraud and money laundering and establishes that the client is the person who he says he is, thus ensuring that the solicitor has the client's authority to act in the transaction. A solicitor who purports to act on behalf of a client impliedly warrants to third parties with whom he has dealings (e.g. the other party's solicitor) that he has the client's authority to act. If he does not have the client's authority he may be liable to the third party for breach of warranty of authority.[1]

1.4.2. *Lender's requirements*

Lenders commonly require the borrower's identity to be verified by the solicitor who is acting for the borrower and lender.

1. See *Penn* v. *Bristol & West Building Society, The Times,* 19 June 1995.

1.5. Using checklists

1.5.1. Although checklists cannot be expected to cover every eventuality in every transaction they are useful in standard transactions to ensure that all necessary information is acquired during the course of the interview.

1.5.2. Checklists focus the interviewer's mind on the relevant information, which minimises preparation time and ultimately saves time in the interview itself, but do need to be used sympathetically so that the client does not feel he is being processed in an impersonal way.

1.5.3. Where checklists are used it is helpful to have them printed on a distinct colour of paper so that they are easily located in the file either by the solicitor himself or by another member of his staff who has to work on the file.

1.5.4. A reminder of the matters which will be raised at a first interview with a client is set out in paras. 1.6.—1.8. below. Standard checklists for sellers and buyers may be compiled from these guidelines to suit the individual requirements of particular firms.

1.6. Acting for the seller

1.6.1.

Item	Reason for Question	Further Reference
(a) Date instructions taken.	Record keeping.	
(b) Full names, addresses of seller(s) and buyer(s) and home and business telephone numbers.	Needed in contract and for contact with client.	
(c) Name and address of person at estate agents.	For contact.	
(d) Find out where title deeds are and obtain client's authority to obtain them if in the hands of a third party.	To deduce title.	Deducing title, D.01.
(e) Ask clients for title number (if known).	To obtain office copies.	Investigation of title, D.02.
(f) Name of other parties' solicitors or representatives.	For contact.	Dealing with non-solicitors, A.05.
(g) Do we act for the other party also?	Conflict of interest, breach of Rule 6.	Acting for both parties, A.10.
(h) Full address of property to be bought/sold.	Needed in contract.	

Item	Reason for Question	Further Reference
(i) Situation of property – position of footpaths/ railways/rivers, etc.	Need for plan or special searches.	Pre-contract searches and enquiries, B.10.
(j) Tenure: freehold/leasehold.	Needed in contract.	
(k) Price.	Needed in contract, stamp duty considerations.	
(l) Has any preliminary deposit been paid? If so, how much? Receipt obtained?	Take account in calculating deposit on exchange.	Preliminary deposits, A.12.
(m) Which fixtures are to be removed?	Needed in contract.	Fixtures and fittings, B.22.
(n) Which fittings are to remain? Additional price for fittings?	Needed in contract and may affect stamp duty. Need to supply Fixtures, Fittings and Contents Form to client.	Fixtures and fittings, B.22.
(o) Anticipated completion date.	To advise client on likely duration of transaction and to assess urgency of matter. To discuss redemption of present mortgage, i.e. interest charges up to end of month.	
(p) Present/proposed use of property.	Planning aspects / restrictive covenants.	
(q) Does the transaction attract VAT?	May be needed in contract and client may need advice.	VAT, A.16.
(r) Who is resident in the property?	Occupiers' rights, overriding interests.	Seller's investigation of title, B.03.
(s) Is the transaction dependent on the purchase/sale of another property?	Synchronisation.	Exchange, section C.

Item	Reason for Question	Further Reference
(t) Any other terms agreed between the parties?	Needed in contract.	
(u) Any correspondence between the parties?	Existence of a contract, or other terms agreed.	Form of contract, B.11.
(v) Vacant possession/ details of tenancies.	Needed in contract.	
(w) Advice as to costs.	Required by written professional standards.	Estimate for costs, A.08.
(x) Interest on deposit.	Deposit interest considerations.	Deposit, B.17.
(y) Do a financial calculation, including costs.	To ensure the client can afford the transaction.	
(z) Time taken in interview.	Time costing/recording.	
(aa) Did we act on purchase?	Look at old file prior to interview to gain relevant information.	
(bb) Are there any outstanding mortgages? How much and to whom?	Calculation of financial statement and will normally need to be redeemed on completion.	
(cc) Ask for seller's mortgage account number or reference.	Needed in order to obtain deeds from lender.	
(dd) Advise seller not to cancel mortgage repayments or insurance until completion.	So that redemption figure obtained on completion is not higher than presently anticipated.	
(ee) How much deposit required?	Advise client on dangers of reduced deposit, use of deposit in related purchase.	Deposit, B.17.
(ff) What is to happen to the proceeds of sale?	Accounting to the client, investment advice.	Financial services, A.04. Post-completion section G.

Item	Reason for Question	Further Reference
(gg) Does the sale attract CGT?	Advise the client.	Capital gains tax, A.15.
(hh) Obtain answers to Seller's Property Information Form and completion of Fixtures, Fittings and Contents Form.	To supply the buyer with this information.	Pre-contract searches and enquiries, B.10.
(ii) Check identity of client.	A precaution against mortgage fraud and money laundering.	Para. 1.4. above.

1.7.   Acting for the buyer

1.7.1.

Item	Reason for Question	Further Reference
(a) Date instructions taken.	Record keeping.	
(b) Full names and addresses of seller(s) and buyer(s) and home and business telephone numbers.	Needed in contract and for contact with client.	
(c) Name and address of person at estate agents.	For contact.	
(d) Name of other parties' solicitors or representatives.	For contact.	Dealing with non-solicitors, A.05.
(e) Do we act for the other party also?	Conflict of interest, breach of Rule 6.	Acting for both parties, A.10.
(f) Full address of property to be bought/sold.	Needed in contract.	
(g) Situation of property — position of footpaths/railways/ rivers, etc.	Need for plan or special searches.	Pre-contract searches and enquiries, B.10.
(h) Tenure: freehold/leasehold.	Needed in contract.	

Item	Reason for Question	Further Reference
(i) Price.	Needed in contract, stamp duty considerations.	
(j) Has any preliminary deposit been paid? If so, how much? Receipt obtained?	Take account in calculating deposit on exchange.	Preliminary deposits, A.12.
(k) Which fixtures are to be removed?	Needed in contract.	Fixtures and fittings, B.22.
(l) Which fittings are to remain? Additional price for fittings? Apportionment of purchase price?	Needed in contract and may affect stamp duty.	Fixtures and fittings, B.22.
(m) Anticipated completion date.	To advise client on likely duration of transaction and to assess urgency of matter. Effect of date on first payment under mortgage.	
(n) Present/proposed use of property.	Planning aspects / restrictive covenants.	
(o) Does the transaction attract VAT?	May be needed in contract and client may need advice.	VAT, A.16.
(p) Who is resident in the property?	Occupiers' rights, overriding interests.	Seller's investigation of title, B.03.
(q) Is the transaction dependent on the purchase/sale of another property?	Synchronisation.	Exchange, section C.
(r) Any other terms agreed between the parties?	Needed in contract.	
(s) Any correspondence between the parties?	Existence of a contract, or other terms agreed.	Form of contract, B.11.
(t) Vacant possession/ details of tenancies.	Needed in contract.	
(u) Advice as to costs.	Required by Rule 15 SPR.	Estimate for costs, A.08.

Item	Reason for Question	Further Reference
(v) Interest on deposit.	Deposit interest considerations.	Deposit, B.17.
(w) Do a financial calculation, including costs.	To ensure the client can afford the transaction.	
(x) Time taken in interview.	Time costing/ recording.	
(y) How will the deposit be funded?	Is bridging finance needed? Need to give notice if funds invested? Client's authority if undertaking to be given.	Deposit, B.17.
(z) How is the balance of the price to be funded? Has the client obtained a mortgage certificate or offer? Does client have outstanding mortgage on any other property?	Advice on sources of finance and/or tax relief on interest. Lenders may insist that all outstanding mortgages are repaid as a condition of the new loan.	Financial services, A.04.
(aa) Survey arrangements.	Advise the client.	Surveys, A.13.
(bb) Insurance: Property? Life? Contents? Other? e.g. employee liability.	Advise the client.	Insurance, C.03.
(cc) How is property to be held by co-owners?	Advise the client.	Joint purchasers, A.09.
(dd) Custody of deeds.	Instructions needed if property not mortgaged.	Post-completion, section G.
(ee) Client's present property?	Need to give notice to determine tenancy? Penalty on mortgage redemption.	
(ff) Check client's identity	A precaution against mortgage fraud and money laundering	Para. 1.4. above.

1.8. Instructions in special cases

1.8.1. Additional information will be required where the transaction concerns a newly constructed property, is leasehold, or is a dealing with part only of the seller's property. Further checklists to deal with these situations are contained in sections I (new properties), J (sales of part), and K (leaseholds).

1.8.2. If it appears that the property (or part of it) comprises a flying freehold, the client should be warned of the possible difficulties in obtaining finance for the property as many lenders are reluctant to accept flying freehold as security for a loan.

1.8.3. If the client is to act as a guarantor to another client's debts (e.g. on a mortgage or as surety to a lender), it may be necessary to consider separate representation for the guarantor in order to avoid any conflict of interests (see A.10.).

1.9. After the interview

1.9.1. Instructions should be confirmed to the client in writing.[1] The letter should include:

   (a) information as to costs (where appropriate, using the Estimate of Costs form published by the Law Society);

   (b) information relating to the name and status of the person who will be carrying out the work for the client and, if this person is not a partner, the name of the partner who has overall responsibility for the matter;

   (c) a résumé of the information received and advice given at the interview in order to ensure that no misunderstanding exists between solicitor and client;

   (d) confirmation of any action agreed to be taken by the solicitor;

   (e) a reminder to the client of anything which he promised to do, e.g. obtain service charge receipts;

   (f) details of who the client should contact in the event of a complaint about the solicitor's services;

   (g) a request for a payment on account in relation to disbursements; and

   (h) a copy of the Law Society's client leaflet relating to conveyancing services (where appropriate).

1.9.2. Provided that the checklist used contains a note of the time expended on the interview, and that a full written record of the interview exists in the form of a follow-up letter to the client, a detailed attendance note may be dispensed with.

1.9.3. If not already done, contact should be established with the representatives of the other parties involved in the transaction, e.g. other solicitor, estate agent, lender. If the identity of the other party's solicitor is not known, his or her status should be checked with the Law Society.

1.9.4.　For the seller:

    (a) obtain title deeds;

    (b) send for office copy entries (registered land);

    (c) ask estate agent for copy of the particulars;

    (d) requisition local search and enquiries and other searches;

    (e) investigate title before drafting contract;

    (f) prepare abstract or epitome of title (unregistered interest in land);

    (g) make Land Charges Department search against seller.

1.9.5.　For the buyer:

    (a) make search applications appropriate to the property and its location (if not to be supplied by seller);

    (b) deal with buyer's mortgage and survey arrangements if required;

    (c) obtain estate agent's particulars;

    (d) consider draft contract when received from seller.

1. See Practice Management Standard F4, Rule 15 Solicitors' Practice Rules 1990 and the Written Professional Standards. In Protocol cases the specimen letters contained in the Protocol documentation may be adapted for use in this situation.

1.10.　**Lost title deeds**

1.10.1.　If it appears that the client's title deeds to unregistered land have been lost or destroyed, it may be possible to obtain voluntary registration of the title at HM Land Registry.

1.10.2.　Where the land is already registered a replacement land or charge certificate can be obtained from HM Land Registry. HM Land Registry's requirements in relation to verifying the identity of the applicant must be complied with. These requirements are set out in Land Registry Public Information Leaflet PIL012

A.02. Property selling

See also: Advertising, para. A.03.
Introductions and referrals, para. A.07.
Estimate for costs, para. A.08.
Acting for both parties, para. A.10.

2.1. General principles

2.1.1. Property selling may be carried out by a solicitor as part of his practice either through the solicitor's own office or through a separate Property Display Centre.

2.1.2. In selling property the solicitor is still acting as a solicitor and therefore remains bound by the Solicitors' Practice Rules 1990, the Solicitors' Accounts Rules, and all other rules, regulations and principles of conduct which affect solicitors in practice.

2.1.3. A solicitor may carry out such valuation as may be necessary to give advice to the client on the price at which the property should be sold, and to prepare the sale particulars, but may not describe himself as an estate agent nor carry out any other types of surveys or valuations (see below, para. 2.3.4.).

2.1.4. The name of a firm of solicitors must comply with Rule 11 Solicitors' Practice Rules 1990. A property-selling agency may, however, be described under a subsidiary practising style provided that the subsidiary name is used in conjunction with the firm's own name and the word 'solicitor' or 'solicitors' is also used.

2.1.5. Property selling may be carried on either as part of the solicitor's business or as a separate business but in the latter case Rule 5 Solicitors' Practice Rules 1990 and the Solicitors' Separate Business Code 1994 must be observed.[1]

2.1.6.   Fees earned by the solicitor through property selling which is carried on through the solicitor's practice must be included in his gross fees return.

2.1.7.   Paragraphs 2.2.–2.13. apply where property selling is carried on as part of the solicitor's business.

1. See para. 2.14. below.

2.2.   Advertising

2.2.1.   Subject to compliance with the Solicitors' Publicity Code 1990, a solicitor may advertise that he undertakes property-selling work and/or may advertise a specific property which he has been instructed to sell.

2.2.2.   An entry or advertisement of a solicitor who undertakes a property-selling service may appear in a directory or 'Yellow Pages' under the heading of 'estate agent', but the solicitor must be described in the entry or advertisement as a solicitor.

2.2.3.   Unsolicited visits and telephone calls may be made where such a visit or call is made to publicise a specific commercial property which the solicitor has for sale or to let but are expressly prohibited by the Solicitors' Publicity Code 1990 in other cases.

2.2.4.   Solicitors may place 'for sale' boards outside properties which they have been instructed to sell provided that the boards comply with current statutory requirements and with the Publicity Code.

2.3.   Employment and remuneration of unqualified staff

2.3.1.   Unqualified, i.e. non-solicitor, staff may be employed to deal with property selling but:

    (a) they cannot enter into partnership with the solicitor;

    (b) their names may only appear on the solicitor's notepaper provided that their status is unambiguously stated, e.g. 'property negotiator' or 'non-solicitor'; the word 'associate' is ambiguous and should be avoided.

2.3.2.   Fee sharing with a genuine employee is permitted by Rule 7 Solicitors' Practice Rules 1990, but this exception to the general prohibition on fee sharing must not be used to disguise a 'partnership' by a solicitor with a non-qualified person.

2.3.3.   An estate agent who is instructed by a solicitor to act as a sub-agent for the sale of a property may be remunerated on the basis of a proportion of the solicitor's professional fee.

2.3.4.   A qualified surveyor employed by the solicitor may carry out surveys on behalf of a client or prospective client provided that the employment of the surveyor falls within Rule 14 Solicitors' Practice Rules 1990 which requires an additional premium to be paid to the Solicitors' Indemnity Fund in respect of each surveyor so employed. In such a case the survey work will be covered by the Indemnity Fund. The solicitor, as the surveyor's employer, would nevertheless remain liable for breach of duty if the surveyor carried out the survey negligently.

2.4.   Premises used for property selling

2.4.1.   A department or branch office which is used mainly for property selling may be described as an 'estate agency' or 'property centre' or by any other suitable description, provided that the description is not misleading or inaccurate.

2.4.2.   Rule 13 Solicitors' Practice Rules 1990 relating to supervision of a solicitor's office applies to premises which are used for property selling except where property selling is conducted through a Property Display Centre (see below, para. 2.5.).

2.5.   Property Display Centres

2.5.1.   A Property Display Centre is a separate 'office' or premises where a solicitor either individually, or in partnership with other firms of solicitors, displays or disseminates information relating to the selling of property, but where no other business of a normal solicitor's firm is conducted.

2.5.2.   Rule 13 Solicitors' Practice Rules 1990 (supervision of the office) applies to Property Display Centres but, under Rule 13(b)(iv), management of the office may be carried out by a chartered surveyor or person holding another qualification approved by the Council of the Law Society under Rule 14 Solicitors' Practice Rules 1990.

2.5.3.   A centre which is run jointly by several participating firms may establish a joint service company to carry out the necessary administrative functions concerned with the running of the centre, but the service company cannot carry on any legal practice nor have any dealings with the actual selling of property. The name of a service company should not appear in the name of the Property Display Centre itself, nor may it be included on the Property Display Centre's notepaper.

2.5.4.   In order to avoid conflict of interests the participating firms must operate totally independently so far as their professional business, including property selling, is concerned.

2.5.5.   Any advertising of a Property Display Centre (including the stationery or use of a logo) must include:

(a)   either the names of the participating firms or an address at which those names are available; and

(b)   the word 'solicitor' or 'solicitors'.

2.5.6. The Property Display Centre's stationery must only be used in connection with activities which a Property Display Centre may properly undertake and may not be used in connection with negotiations.

2.5.7. A prospective client of the centre may either approach an individual participating firm or the Property Display Centre itself.

2.5.8. The Property Display Centre must not accept instructions on behalf of a participating firm, but may refer a prospective client to a participating firm.

2.5.9. To ensure compliance with Rule 1 Solicitors' Practice Rules 1990 (the client's freedom of choice of solicitor), the client should be asked to make his own choice from among the participating firms.

2.5.10. Where a member of staff at the Property Display Centre is asked to recommend a firm to a client, such a recommendation must only be given on the basis of a genuine belief that the firm concerned should be recommended.

2.6. Acting for seller and buyer

2.6.1. A solicitor who sells property on behalf of a seller client may also act for the seller in the conveyancing but may not act for the buyer either in the conveyancing or in the negotiations for a mortgage for the buyer.

2.6.2. Where a solicitor is acting for a seller in the sale of the property, notwithstanding the exceptions to Rule 6 Solicitors' Practice Rules 1990 (as amended)(acting for both parties), neither he nor his partners, nor indeed any firm with whom he is associated (including one with whom the solicitor has a joint property-selling practice) may act for the buyer in the same transaction.

2.7. Written agreement as to remuneration

2.7.1. When accepting instructions to act in the sale of a property, a solicitor must give the client a written statement containing the following information:

    (a) the amount of the solicitor's remuneration, or its method of calculation;

    (b) the circumstances in which the remuneration becomes payable;

    (c) the amount of any disbursements which are to be separately charged, or the basis on which they will be calculated, and the circumstances in which they may be incurred;

    (d) whether VAT is payable and whether it is included in the estimate or fixed fee;

    (e) whether or not the solicitor is to be a sole agent;

    (f) the identity of the property to be sold;

(g) the interest to be sold;

(h) the price to be sought;

(i) an explanation of the phrases 'sole selling rights', 'ready willing and able purchaser' (or similar phrases), if used in the agreement.

2.8. Amount of remuneration

2.8.1. The amount of commission charged by the solicitor for selling a property is a matter for agreement between the solicitor and his client.

2.8.2. Unless the client signs an agreement in relation to charges under Solicitors Act 1974, s.57, the amount of the commission may be subject to the remuneration certificate procedure. The client may in any event be entitled to taxation of the bill by the court.

2.8.3. A composite fee for both property selling and conveyancing may be quoted, but the solicitor must be prepared to quote separate fees if required to do so by the client.

2.9. Application of Estate Agents Act 1979

2.9.1. Estate Agents Act 1979 does not apply to solicitors who are engaged in property selling, but Property Misdescriptions Act 1991 does. This latter Act makes it an offence for a person selling property to attach a misleading description to the property which is being sold. The liability is similar to that incurred under Trades Descriptions Act 1968. The Law Society guidance on property selling (set out in Appendix II.2.) imposes on solicitors similar duties and obligations to those to which estate agents are subject under regulations made under the 1979 Act.

2.10. Insurance

2.10.1. Property-selling activities are covered by the terms of the Solicitors' Indemnity Fund for insurance purposes.

2.11. Declining instructions to act

2.11.1. Instructions must be declined where there would be a breach of Rule 1 Solicitors' Practice Rules 1990 (obtaining instructions).

2.11.2. Where the solicitor is asked to sell a property of a type which he is unused to handling he should either decline the instructions or place the property with a sub-agent who is experienced in that type of property.

2.11.3. There may be occasions when a conflict of interest arises between the solicitor and his client when the solicitor is engaged in selling the property as well as undertaking the legal work. As in any situation where a conflict arises or is likely to arise, the solicitor must decline to act or should cease to act further in the transaction. Attention is also drawn to the Law Society's guidance relating to mortgage fraud which is set out in full in Appendix III.1.

2.12.   Introductions and referrals

2.12.1.   Provided there is compliance with Rule 3 Solicitors' Practice Rules 1990 (introductions and referrals) and with the Introduction and Referral Code a solicitor may have an arrangement with an estate agent in relation to the sale of property.

2.13.   Commissions

2.13.1.   Any commission received by a solicitor as a result of the client having entered into, e.g. an endowment mortgage is subject to Rule 10 Solicitors' Practice Rules 1990 (commissions).

2.14.   Property selling as a separate business

2.14.1.   Rule 5 Solicitors' Practice Rules 1990 permits a solicitor to control, actively participate in or operate (in each case alone, or by or with others) a separate business, including a property-selling business, provided that there is compliance with the Solicitors' Separate Business Code 1994. The Code contains some principles which are specifically applicable to property selling, which are summarised below.

2.14.2.   The property-selling (estate agency) business must be carried out from premises which are physically divided and clearly differentiated from that of any premises of the solicitor in England and Wales. If the estate agency business shares premises or reception staff with any English or Welsh practice of the solicitor, the customers of the estate agency business must be informed both by personal interview or telephone call and by subsequent written confirmation of that interview or telephone call that, as customers of the estate agency business, they do not enjoy the statutory protection afforded to clients of the solicitor.

2.14.3.   The name of any practice of the solicitor must have no substantial element in common with the name of the estate agency business and the words 'solicitor', 'attorney' or 'lawyer' must not be used in connection with the solicitor's involvement with the estate agency business.

2.14.4.   Paperwork and records relating to customers of the estate agency business must be kept separately from those relating to the solicitor's practice. Money held for the estate agency business and its customers must not be held in the client's account which relates to the solicitor's practice.

2.14.5. The solicitor (as solicitor) can only carry out conveyancing for the seller of a property where the estate agency has not provided financial or mortgage services to the buyer of that property. The solicitor must not act for the buyer of any property bought through the estate agency business.

2.14.6. All clients who are referred by the solicitor's practice to the estate agency business must be informed of the solicitor's interest in that business and that, as customers of the estate agency business, they do not enjoy the statutory protection afforded to clients of a solicitor. This latter information must be given to the customer at a personal interview or by telephone and subsequently confirmed in writing.

FURTHER REFERENCE

Property selling guidance (App. II.2.).

Estate Agents and Property Misdescriptions Acts, J.R. Murdoch, Estates Gazette.

One-Stop Property Selling: A Guide to the Legal Aspects, F.J. Silverman, Tolley.

A.03. Advertising

See also: Property selling, para. A.02.
Estimate for costs, para. A.08.

3.1. Solicitors' Publicity Code 1990

3.1.1. A solicitor may advertise his practice provided that the advertisement complies with Solicitors' Publicity Code 1990. The main points of the Code are summarised below.

3.2. Compliance with the Code

3.2.1. Advertisements must:

(a) comply with the Publicity Code and the Solicitors' Practice Rules;

(b) be in good taste;

(c) not be inaccurate or misleading;

(d) contain the name of the solicitor or his firm;

(e) comply with the British Codes of Advertising and Sales Promotion;

(f) where appropriate comply with Consumer Credit Act 1974 (licensing as a credit broker and content of advertisements), Business Names Act 1985 (address for service of process) and Companies Acts (appearance of company name on stationery).

3.2.2. The contents of advertisements relating to the provision of credit and related services must comply with Consumer Credit (Quotations) Regulations 1989 (S.I. 1989/1126) which are summarised below. These Regulations apply in circumstances where, e.g. the solicitor is advertising his services and indicates that he can obtain mortgage finance for a client. At the time of publication these regulations are still in force, although the government has recommended their repeal.

3.2.3. *Summary of the Regulations:*

1. Quotation given to client for 'credit' (including quote about cost of mortgage or life policy) must contain certain information.

2. Regulations apply where request for information is made by client either in person on credit broker's trade premises or by telephone.

3. If exact information not available, an estimate must be given. Estimate should state on what assumptions the estimate is given and give client the right to demand a further quote based on additional information supplied by client.

4. If all information is not contained in the estimate, client must be given notice in writing that this is the case and tell client that a further quote will be given if client so requests, client having supplied such additional facts as are necessary to allow the further quote to be estimated.

5. Information to be supplied (Schedule 1) (NB. Information given under the Regulations must be clear and easily legible):

   (a) APR must be specifically mentioned and given greater prominence than mention of any other charge;

   (b) name and address of person giving quotation;

   (c) statement that security for loan is or may be required;

   (d) where security comprises charge over debtor's home, a statement in the following form: *Your home is at risk if you do not keep up repayments on a mortgage or other loan secured on it*;

   (e) a statement of any contract of insurance required (not buildings or contents insurance) and details of that policy;

   (f) a statement of any requirement to place money on deposit with any person;

   (g) credit broker's fees;

   (h) the amount of credit to be provided;

   (i) nature of any security where security is *not* a charge over the debtor's home;

   (j) frequency and amount of payments;

   (k) other payments or charges;

   (l) total amount payable by debtor; and

   (m) wealth warning in the following form: *Be sure you can afford the repayments before entering into a credit agreement.*

3.3.   Matters prohibited by the Code

3.3.1.   The Publicity Code generally prohibits unsolicited visits or telephone calls to the general public and naming own clients in advertisements except with the client's consent.

3.4.   Good taste

3.4.1.   Subject to paras. 3.2. and 3.3. above, a solicitor is free to advertise his practice in any way in which he thinks fit. The overall constraint that an advertisement must be in good taste can only be judged subjectively. Advertisements should thus be designed individually for the medium or context in which they are to appear. An advertisement which may be acceptable in one context may not be regarded as in good taste if used in a different medium.

3.5.   Property selling

3.5.1.   Advertisements placed by the solicitor in relation either to his property-selling services or referring to specific property which the solicitor has been instructed to sell must comply with Solicitors' Publicity Code 1990.

3.5.2.   Unsolicited visits and telephone calls may be made where such a visit or call is made in order to publicise a specific commercial property which the solicitor has for sale or to let.

3.5.3.   The solicitor would be able to describe himself as a 'solicitor and estate agent' in an advertisement which relates to his property-selling activities, and may be listed under the heading of 'estate agent' in a directory provided that he can justify this specialist claim under the Publicity Code.

3.6.   Advertising the solicitor's charges

3.6.1.   References in an advertisement to the solicitor's charges must be clearly expressed.

3.6.2.   Paragraph 5 of the Code, which deals with solicitors' charges, draws attention to the following points:

(a) the advertisement must make clear what services are included in the quoted fee or, if no specific fee is quoted, the basis of charging;

(b) it must be clear whether disbursements and/or VAT are included in the charge;

(c) it is prohibited to state a fee as being 'from/upwards of £x';

(d) services which are advertised as being 'free' must be genuinely free and not subject to any condition;

(e) the quotation of a composite fee for two or more services, e.g. property selling and conveyancing, is permitted so long as the solicitor is prepared to undertake each of the individual services separately if the client so requires. The fee for an individual service must not be more than the solicitor would have charged for that service had he undertaken that service jointly with the other advertised service;

(f) fees quoted must be gross fees, i.e. the fee quoted must not be reduced to take into account any commission which the solicitor expects to receive as a result of the client taking out an endowment policy with his mortgage. The advertisement may state that the quoted fee may be reduced by the amount of such commission, but must not imply that endowment mortgages are appropriate in all circumstances.

3.7. Advertising placed by third parties

3.7.1. Advertisements placed by third parties which advertise the services of solicitors to whom work may be referred should contain a statement to the effect that the third party will adhere to the Solicitors' Introduction and Referral Code 1990 (see Appendix I.3.). A suggested form of wording may be found in para. (4) of the Introduction to the Code. The solicitor will remain liable for any inaccuracies in the advertisement or breaches of the Publicity Code, even though the advertisement was not drafted, placed or paid for by the solicitor. Advertisements which are placed by third parties but which contain references to the solicitor's practice should therefore be checked carefully by the solicitor before publication.

A.04. Financial services

4.1. Activities within Financial Services Act 1986

4.1.1. The following activities may involve a solicitor in investment business:

(a) advising a client about obtaining a mortgage, if this involves a life policy (endowment, unit-linked, PEP) or a pension mortgage;

(b) where a property sale is linked to the sale of a business in the form of a sale of company shares;

(c) where the sale of a property for a client leads to the client's looking for advice on how to invest the proceeds of sale.

4.1.2. It is a criminal offence to carry on 'investment business' as defined in the Act without authorisation. Solicitors' firms normally obtain authorisation from the Law Society.

4.1.3. Solicitors' Investment Business Rules 1995 (SIBR 1995) apply when solicitors who are authorised by the Law Society carry on investment business. Where the investment business constitutes 'discrete investment business' (as defined by SIBR 1995) all the rules will apply. In other cases only some of the rules will apply.

4.2. Investment business

4.2.1. 'Investment business' is defined by Financial Services Act 1986. 'Discrete investment business' is defined by SIBR 1995.

4.2.2. Advising the client on or arranging the following does not constitute investment business:

(a) a normal bank or building society account;

(b) buildings or contents insurance;

(c) a term life insurance policy, e.g. mortgage protection policy;

(d) a repayment mortgage.

4.2.3.   Generic investment advice is not within the Act. Generic advice is advice about general categories of investment, as opposed to specific investments. Recommendations to the client that 'it would be wise to invest capital in equity shares/unit trusts' or 'you should take out a life insurance policy' are both examples of generic advice. A recommendation to the client that he should 'invest £5,000 in x plc unit trusts' or to 'take out a life insurance policy for a 15-year term with y insurance company who do a very good policy' is, however, specific investment advice falling within the definition of 'investment business'.

4.2.4.   'Arranging deals in investments' is investment business within the Act, even if no advice is given. A solicitor who is involved in arrangements which lead to a client taking out a life insurance policy is likely to be carrying on investment business even if he had given no advice about the policy. However, the mere referral of the client by the solicitor to an independent intermediary is not arranging, even if the intermediary pays commission to the solicitor for the introduction.

4.3.   Trustees and personal representatives

4.3.1.   The solicitor who is a trustee or personal representative

If a solicitor buys or sells investments for the trust or estate (including making arrangements for investments for his co-trustees or personal representatives or a beneficiary) he may be exempted under the Act, provided he is acting as a principal and is not being separately remunerated for his duties as a trustee or personal representative. The extent of this exemption is, however, uncertain and it is unwise to rely on it. Any trustee or personal representative will 'manage' the investments belonging to the trust or estate unless all investment management business functions have been delegated to a third party and this aspect of the solicitor's duties may be investment business within the Act because in most cases the solicitor will be deemed to receive some separate remuneration for his management services, even where the client's bill does not show a separate item for such remuneration.

4.3.2.   Investment advice

A solicitor who gives investment advice to his fellow personal representatives or trustees will generally need to be authorised under the Act.

4.3.3.   The solicitor who is acting for trustees or personal representatives

A solicitor who buys, sells or manages investments on behalf of his trustee or personal representative clients or who makes arrangements for the trustees or personal representatives to buy or sell investments will generally be conducting investment business within the Act. If, however, the arrangements are a 'necessary' part of the solicitor's services (e.g. selling investments in order to pay inheritance tax) and are not separately remunerated, they will be exempt.

4.3.4. Investment advice given by a solicitor to his trustee or personal representative clients needs authorisation under the Act unless it can be shown that the advice was a necessary part of other advice or services given in the course of carrying on the profession of a solicitor, and it is not separately remunerated.

4.4. Mortgages

4.4.1. Arranging mortgage finance for a client or advising about the terms of a mortgage offer is not investment business within the Act nor within the SIBR 1995 so long as the mortgage does not also involve arranging a life or pension policy (whether endowment, unit-linked or PEP). Where the mortgage is linked to a life or pension policy, arranging it will be investment business within the Act. If the solicitor recommends the terms of a particular policy which is to be acquired, this is discrete investment business within SIBR 1995.

4.4.2. Where a client seeks advice about a life policy and the solicitor is not qualified to give such advice, or cannot carry on discrete investment business, the client should be referred to another adviser who must be an independent financial adviser. Solicitors may not refer clients to tied agents or to providers of financial products. This prohibition is to ensure that the client receives independent and impartial advice. Reference should be made to Principles 27.05 and 27.07 of *The Guide to the Professional Conduct of Solicitors 1996.*

4.4.3. A solicitor who is involved in obtaining mortgage finance for a client will be acting as a mortgage broker under Consumer Credit Act 1974. For this activity, the solicitor needs to hold a licence under the 1974 Act. The Law Society holds a group licence from the Director General of Fair Trading which covers all solicitors acting within the ordinary course of practice. Normally, therefore, a solicitor does not need to hold an individual licence.

4.5. Commissions

4.5.1. Life assurance companies and the providers of some other types of investment product pay commissions to intermediaries on the sale of their products. A solicitor who introduces a client to a life assurance company (or other provider) will usually receive a commission for the introduction. The referral of the client is likely to be regarded as discrete investment business requiring the holding of a category 2 certificate.

4.5.2. Any commission received by the solicitor is subject to Rule 10 Solicitors' Practice Rules 1990 (see Appendix I.1. and para. N.01.8.). Requirements for product and commission disclosure contained in Appendix 7 Solicitors Investment Business Rules 1995 must also be complied with.

4.6.   Solicitors' Financial Services

4.6.1.   Solicitors' Financial Services (SFS) is a scheme run by the Law Society which gives solicitors access to a wide range of investment advice and services, including mortgage funds, for the benefit of clients who need independent financial advice. Solicitors can provide clients with advice through this scheme, without becoming involved in discrete investment business, through the permitted third party route.

4.6.2.   Details of the scheme are available from SFS, telephone (0171) 320 5701 or fax (0171) 831 0170.

4.7.   Money laundering

4.7.1.   *What is money laundering?*

Money laundering is the process through which criminals attempt to conceal the true origin or ownership of the proceeds of their criminal activities so as to retain control over them and ultimately make it appear as though the proceeds come from a legitimate source. Solicitors should be alert to the possibilities of the client committing a money-laundering offence. Failure to report a client where there is a suspicion that a money-laundering offence may be committed can result in the solicitor being prosecuted. Solicitors are also advised to have regard to the money-laundering guidance issued by the Law Society and reproduced in Professional Standards Bulletin 12 (and further guidance in Bulletin Nos. 11 and 14).

4.7.2.   *The offences*

The offences relating to money laundering are contained in Criminal Justice Act 1988, Prevention of Terrorism Act 1989 and Drug Trafficking Act 1994. Most offences carry a penalty of between five and 14 years' imprisonment.

4.7.3.   *The conduct issues*

A solicitor may be guilty of an offence if he assists anyone in a money-laundering activity in relation to drugs or terrorism or the proceeds of criminal conduct. Having knowledge or suspicion of an offence being committed in relation to drugs or terrorism without disclosing that information to a constable may itself be an offence.

4.7.4.   Professional privilege may protect the solicitor in some circumstances. Privilege does not extend to information communicated in order to further a criminal purpose. Disclosure in accordance with the relevant statutory provision does not amount to a breach of duty of confidentiality. By Principle 16.06 of *The Guide to the Professional Conduct of Solicitors 1996,* published by the Law Society, a solicitor usually has a duty to pass on to the client all information which is material to the client's business regardless of the source of that information. The 'tipping-off' provisions (i.e. disclosure of suspicion of an offence to a constable) create an exception to this principle.

4.7.5. Although it is possible to continue to act for a client after making disclosure, the solicitor may feel that his relationship with his client is so affected as to make it necessary for the retainer to be ended.

4.7.6. Action to be taken if solicitor suspects the client may be committing an offence:

(a) The solicitor should be wary of and question clients who bring in large sums of cash and/or instructions which are out of the ordinary.

(b) If the solicitor has knowledge or suspicions, he must report to 'a constable' – the National Criminal Intelligence Service (NCIS). A solicitor's employees should report to an 'appropriate person' within the firm (see below).

4.7.7. *Money Laundering Regulations 1993*

These Regulations were passed as a result of the E.C. Council Directive 91/308 of 10 June 1991 and provide:

'[S]ince money laundering can be carried out not only through credit and financial institutions but also through other types of professions and categories of undertakings, Member States must extend the provisions of this Directive in whole or in part, to include those professions and undertakings where activities are particularly likely to be used for money laundering purposes.'

4.7.8. The Regulations came into force on 1 April 1994. They only apply if a person is carrying on 'relevant financial business' which includes investment business within the meaning of Financial Services Act 1986.

(a) **Business relationship (regulation 3)**

A business relationship exists where at least one person involved is acting in the course of a business and where:

(i) the purpose of the arrangement is to facilitate the carrying out of transactions between the persons concerned on a frequent, habitual or regular basis; and

(ii) the total amount of any payment to be made is not known or capable of being ascertained at the time the arrangement is made.

Once satisfactory evidence is obtained of the client's identity, the relationship becomes an *established business relationship*. Any transaction which is not carried out in the course of an established business relationship is regarded as a 'one-off transaction'.

(b) **Systems and training to prevent money laundering (regulation 5)**

When conducting relevant financial business, no business relationship is to be formed or one-off transaction carried out unless the solicitor maintains:

(i) identification procedures;

(ii) record-keeping procedures;

(iii) if the solicitor is an employer or in partnership, internal reporting procedures; and

(iv) such other procedures of internal control and communication as may be appropriate for the purposes of forestalling and preventing money laundering.

The solicitor must also ensure that employees who handle relevant financial business are aware of the procedures and of the law and provide employees with training in the recognition and handling of suspect transactions. The maximum penalty for failing to comply with these provisions is two years in prison.

(c) **Identifying the client (regulations 7 – 11)**

These regulations apply in all cases where the solicitor is forming a business relationship with his client. They also apply to one-off transactions where the solicitor knows or suspects the client is either himself engaged in money laundering or is acting for someone who is engaged in money laundering.

The solicitor must, as soon as is reasonably practicable after first contact, ask the client for production of satisfactory evidence of identity or take steps which will result in evidence being produced. The evidence must be reasonably capable of establishing that the client is who he says he is and the person obtaining evidence must be satisfied that it does that, e.g. current document bearing a photograph, a passport or an identity card. The client's address should also be checked. If satisfactory evidence of identity is not produced, the transaction must not proceed any further (regulation 7(l)).

(d) **Keeping records (regulations 12 and 13)**

Records must be kept for five years after completion of the transaction of the evidence obtained of identity and of all transactions carried out by the client.

(e) **Internal reporting (regulation 14)**

Internal reporting procedures are necessary where persons are employed who are handling relevant financial business or where the solicitor practices in partnership. In such cases, there must be a person within the firm to whom all information about known or suspected money launderers is to be given – 'the appropriate person' – or another designated person who has the task of deciding whether the information does amount to knowledge or suspicion and, if it is decided that it does, of reporting the matter to 'a constable'. The appropriate person or designated person will probably be a partner.

(f) **Reporting to a constable**

All reports are dealt with nationally by the National Criminal Intelligence Service (NCIS), Spring Gardens, Vauxhall, London SE11 5EN. Tel: (0171) 238 8271; 24-hour number staffed by reserve officers (0171) 238 8607; Fax: (0171) 238 8286. It is recommended that reporting is made on the standard form, examples of which are shown in the information pack available from the Law Society.

FURTHER REFERENCE

Solicitors and Financial Services: A Compliance Handbook, P. Camp, the Law Society.

The Lawyers' Financial Services Fact Book, Professional Publishing Ltd.

Financial Services: The New Core Rules, M. Blair, Blackstone Press.

A.05.   Dealing with non-solicitors

5.1.   Licensed conveyancers

5.1.1.   Guidance for solicitors dealing with licensed conveyancers is contained in *The Guide to the Professional Conduct of Solicitors 1996,* published by the Law Society, and is summarised below. See further Appendix II.4.

5.1.2.   When dealing with a licensed conveyancer who is not known personally to the solicitor, a check on the identity of the conveyancer should be made with the Council for Licensed Conveyancers.[1]

5.1.3.   The solicitor should ensure that he deals either directly with the licensed conveyancer or with a person working under the immediate supervision of such a person.

5.1.4.   Licensed conveyancers are bound by rules relating to conduct, discipline, insurance and accounts which are similar to those which bind solicitors. It is therefore possible to deal with a licensed conveyancer as if the conveyancer was a fellow solicitor.

1. For address see App. XIII.4.

5.2.   Law Society Formulae and undertakings

5.2.1.   The Protocol, the Law Society Formulae for Exchange of Contracts and the Code for Completion by Post may be used in dealings with licensed conveyancers. Licensed conveyancers have no equivalent sanction to the court's control over the conduct of solicitors, but the Law Society recommends that they are nevertheless treated by solicitors as being on an equal footing with themselves. It is therefore possible to rely on undertakings given by such persons.

5.3.   Employment of licensed conveyancers by solicitors

5.3.1.   A solicitor may employ a licensed conveyancer as a conveyancing clerk or in some other capacity. Work done by the licensed conveyancer must be done as an integral part of the solicitor's practice and is subject to all the practice rules. The licensed conveyancer may be named in the solicitor's publicity (including stationery) provided that his status is made clear. A solicitor may not enter into partnership with a licensed conveyancer nor share his fees with him (except under the exception to Rule 7 Solicitors' Practice Rules 1990 which permits fees to be shared with a genuine employee).

5.3.2.   As with any transaction, the overriding concern is for the best interests of the client. In any situation where there is doubt over the conduct of the matter, guidance should be sought from the Legal Practice Directorate of the Law Society.

5.4.   Unqualified conveyancers

5.4.1.   Under Solicitors Act 1974, s.22 (as amended), it is an offence for an unqualified person to draw up or prepare *inter alia* a contract for sale, transfer, conveyance, lease or mortgage relating to land unless that person can prove that the act was not done in expectation of fee, gain or reward.

5.4.2.   *'Qualified persons'*

The only persons who are 'qualified' under section 22 are solicitors, barristers, notaries public, licensed conveyancers, authorised practitioners, and some public officers. An unqualified person acting in breach of the section commits a criminal offence and his 'client' may be guilty of aiding and abetting the offence.

5.4.3.   A solicitor acting for the other party to the transaction could also be guilty of procuring the commission of an offence by inviting the unqualified person to submit a contract or conveyance.

5.4.4.   Courts and Legal Services Act 1990 contains provisions enabling 'authorised practitioners' (as defined in the Act) to conduct conveyancing services on behalf of their customers. Rules regulating the conduct of authorised practitioners have not yet been made.

5.5.   Dealing with unqualified persons

5.5.1.   The Law Society has published guidance for solicitors who are asked to deal with unqualified conveyancers which are summarised below. See further, Appendix II.5.

5.5.2.   A solicitor should refuse to have any dealings with an unqualified person unless he has clear evidence that no offence under section 22 will be committed.

5.5.3. At the outset of a transaction which apparently involves an unqualified person the solicitor should write to the unqualified person drawing attention to the Law Society's guidelines and asking for satisfactory evidence that no offence will be committed. The solicitor's client should also be informed of the situation.

5.5.4. Drafts of suitable letters are set out in the guidelines.

5.5.5. A letter from a qualified person confirming that he will prepare the relevant documents will be satisfactory evidence that no offence will be committed and the solicitor may proceed with the transaction.

5.5.6. The Protocol can be used with unqualified persons, but no sanctions would lie against them in the event of a breach.

5.6. Undertakings

5.6.1. Undertakings should not be accepted from unqualified persons since there is no method of enforcing them. Thus where, e.g. a seller who is represented by an unqualified person has a mortgage subsisting at completion, the buyer's solicitor must require the seller to produce a signed Form 53 (or receipted mortgage) at completion and must not accept an undertaking for its discharge. This may mean that the seller has to obtain bridging finance to repay the loan before completion or that the seller's lender will have to attend at completion. A solicitor who accepts an undertaking from an unqualified person may be in breach of his duty of care to his own client and thus liable to make good to the client any loss sustained as a result of a dishonoured undertaking.

5.7. Completions and agency work

5.7.1. There is no duty on a solicitor to undertake agency work by way of completions by post or to attend to other formalities on behalf of third parties who are not clients and who are represented by an unqualified person. A solicitor who does undertake such work should only do so after having agreed in writing with the unqualified person the precise extent of the solicitor's duties and agreed fee for such services. Where a considerable amount of work is undertaken on behalf of the unqualified person's client there is a danger of the solicitor being in breach of Rule 6 Solicitors' Practice Rules 1990 (as amended) since he may effectively be acting for both parties in the transaction.

5.8. The contract

5.8.1. It will be necessary for special provisions to be inserted in the draft contract to take account of the fact that the other party is not represented by a qualified person.

Clauses to deal with the following matters should be inserted in the contract:

(a) personal attendance by an unrepresented seller at completion to take up the deeds and purchase price because Law of Property Act 1925, s.69, only applies when a document containing a receipt for the purchase price is handed over by a qualified person or by the seller himself;

(b) payment of the deposit either to an estate agent who is a member of a recognised professional body, or to the buyer's solicitor in the capacity of stakeholder. An alternative to these arrangements would be to insert a condition in the contract providing for the deposit to be placed in a bank or building society deposit account in the joint names of seller and buyer.

5.9.   Pre-contract enquiries

5.9.1.   The answers to pre-contract enquiries and any other enquiries (including requisitions on title) given by an unrepresented seller should be signed by the seller in person. Although an unqualified person may have the seller's express authority to answer such enquiries on his behalf, an action in misrepresentation (should such become necessary) will more easily be sustained if the answers have been signed by the seller personally.

5.10.   Powers of attorney

5.10.1.   Any power of attorney which purports to give the unqualified person power to deal with a matter on behalf of his or her 'client' should be carefully checked to ensure its validity and effectiveness for its purported purpose.

5.11.   Acting for the lender

5.11.1.   A solicitor acting for a lender where the borrower is represented by an unqualified person is under no obligation to undertake work which the buyer's solicitor should normally assume (e.g. drafting the purchase deed) and should not render the unqualified person additional assistance. However, in such a situation the solicitor must bear in mind that the interests of his lender client in obtaining a good title to the property are paramount. The advance cheque should be drawn in favour of a solicitor, licensed conveyancer or person properly authorised to receive the money by the borrower. On redemption of a mortgage similar principles apply.

5.12.   Authorised practitioners

5.12.1.   Authorised practitioners are entitled to carry out conveyancing services on behalf of their clients pursuant to Courts and Legal Services Act 1990 and the regulations made under that Act (none of which have been made as yet). Conveyancing services must be carried out under the supervision of a qualified solicitor. Authorised practitioners are subject to similar rules relating to the handling of clients' money as those which affect solicitors and are also bound to honour undertakings given by them or their staff. They may, therefore, be regarded in the same light as licensed conveyancers.

NB: In cases of doubt or difficulty assistance should be sought from the Practice Advice Service at the Law Society.

A.06. In-house solicitors

6.1.	**Acting for the lay employer**	6.2.	**Acting for fellow employees**
		6.3.	**Acting for third parties**

6.1. Acting for the lay employer

6.1.1. A solicitor who is employed by a non-solicitor employer must comply with Solicitors' Practice Rules 1990 and all the other rules of professional conduct.

6.1.2. A practising certificate will be needed where the solicitor:

(a) is held out by his employer as practising as a solicitor (e.g. where the solicitor's name and qualifications appear on the employer's notepaper); or

(b) carries out any of the acts which are prohibited to unqualified persons by Solicitors Act 1974 (e.g. drawing a contract for the sale of land for fee or reward); or

(c) administers oaths.

6.1.3. If the employed solicitor uses his employer's notepaper for his professional business, the notepaper must clearly and unambiguously state the status of the solicitor.

6.1.4. Rule 4 Solicitors' Practice Rules 1990 and the Employed Solicitors Code 1990 place restrictions on the type of work which an employed solicitor may undertake. In general he is prohibited from doing work for anyone other than his employer.

6.2. Acting for fellow employees

6.2.1. An employed solicitor may carry out conveyancing on behalf of a fellow employee provided that the work is permitted by his contract of employment and is done free of charge to the fellow employee. The conveyancing must also relate to or arise out of the work of the employee client, i.e. it must be a job-related move. Before accepting the instructions to act the employed solicitor must ensure that the fellow employee does not wish to instruct another solicitor or licensed conveyancer.

6.3. Acting for third parties

6.3.1. If his contract of employment permits him to do so an employed solicitor may undertake work on behalf of private clients in his own time. In this respect he will be treated as a principal in private practice and must comply with the Practice Rules, Accounts Rules and Indemnity Rules. If he practises from home, his home may be regarded as an office which is open to the public and compliance with Rule 13 Solicitors' Practice Rules will be required. Because of the danger of conflict of interests private work must not be undertaken for clients and customers of the employer.

6.3.2. An employed solicitor may act for a joint owner/ buyer and for a lender. A lender may require an indemnity from the employer or insurance cover similar to that provided by Solicitors' Indemnity Rules.

A.07. Introductions and referrals

See also: Advertising, para. A.03.
Financial services, para. A.04.

7.1. Solicitors' Introduction and Referral Code 1990

7.1.1. A solicitor may have an arrangement with a third party for the introduction of clients to the solicitor by the third party, or the referral of clients to the third party by the solicitor. Such arrangements are permitted by Rule 3 Solicitors' Practice Rules 1990 provided that there is no breach of any of the Practice Rules and that there is compliance with the Solicitors' Introduction and Referral Code 1990. The provisions of the Code are summarised below and are set out in full in Appendix I.3.

7.1.2. The Code applies to any arrangement made by a solicitor with, e.g. an estate agent, bank, building society or mortgage broker for the introduction of clients to the solicitor from such third parties or the referral of clients to the third parties by the solicitor but not to introductions and referrals between firms of solicitors. Arrangements are forbidden where the introducer is a builder, developer or seller's estate agent where the conveyancing is to be provided for the buyer, and the buyer's costs are to be paid by the introducer.

7.1.3. Breach of the Code may amount to a breach of Rules 1 (obtaining instructions) and/or 3 (introductions and referrals) Solicitors' Practice Rules 1990 (or breach of one of the other practice rules), and may be conduct unbefitting a solicitor.

7.2. Maintaining the independence of the solicitor

7.2.1. It is of paramount importance that the solicitor should remain independent of any third party to or from whom referrals are made so that the client may be given impartial and objective advice by the solicitor.

7.2.2. To this end, the Code emphasises that Rule 1 Solicitors' Practice Rules 1990 (obtaining instructions) must be complied with at all times.

7.2.3. It should also be noted that Rule 12 Solicitors' Practice Rules 1990 prevents a solicitor from acting as an appointed representative in respect of introductions and referrals made in the field of investment business.

7.3. Reliance by the solicitor on limited sources of business

7.3.1. If a solicitor allows himself to become reliant on a limited source or sources of business from introducers there is a danger that the advice given by him to his introduced clients will be influenced by the solicitor's need to maintain his source of business, to the extent that the advice will not be impartial and may not be in the best interests of that particular client.

7.3.2. Solicitors are advised to review their sources of business at regular intervals (see below, para. 7.4.) and if it appears that more than 20% of the solicitor's income earned during the period under review has been generated from a single source of introduction, the solicitor should consider whether steps need to be taken to reduce that proportion.

7.3.3. Factors to be taken into account in deciding whether the proportion of business from a single source needs to be reduced include:

(a) the percentage of income derived from that source;

(b) the number of clients introduced by that source;

(c) the nature of the clients and the nature of the work, e.g. where the business is derived from non-commercial sources such as a charity or Law Centre it would not be so important to reduce the volume of work derived from that source as it would be if the large percentage of business was derived from a single commercial client;

(d) whether the introducer could be affected by the advice given by the solicitor to the client.

7.4. Keeping records

7.4.1. Each firm should keep a record of agreements for the introduction of work and should check at six-monthly intervals:

(a) that the provisions of the Code have been complied with;

(b) that referred clients have received impartial advice which has not been tainted by the relationship between the firm and the introducer;

(c) the amount of income arising from each agreement for the introduction of business.

Records of such reviews must be maintained for inspection by the Law Society and/or the Office for the Supervision of Solicitors.

7.5. Agreements for introductions and referrals to solicitors

7.5.1. When negotiating an agreement for the introduction of business with a potential introducer the solicitor should draw the attention of the potential introducer to the Introduction and Referral Code and also to the Publicity Code 1990. Arrangements can only be made with introducers who agree to comply with the Code.

7.5.2. Advertisements placed by introducers which advertise the services of solicitors to whom work may be referred should contain a statement to the effect that the introducer will adhere to the Code. A suggested form of wording may be found in the Code. The solicitor will remain liable for any inaccuracies in the advertisement or breaches of the Publicity Code, even though the advertisement was not drafted, placed or paid for by the solicitor. Advertisements which are placed by third parties but which contain references to the solicitor's practice should therefore be checked carefully by the solicitor before publication.

7.5.3. Potential introducers should be made aware of the terms on which the solicitor will accept instructions from an introducer and the fees which will be charged to an introduced client.

7.6. Confirming the client's instructions

7.6.1. Any instructions received from or through an introducer must be confirmed directly with the client by sending or giving the client written terms of business.

7.7. Fees and commissions

7.7.1. Although normal hospitality is permitted, a solicitor is forbidden to pay an introducer for his services, whether by commission or otherwise.

7.7.2. Any commission received by the solicitor who has referred a client to a third party is subject to Rule 10 Solicitors' Practice Rules 1990 under which rule the solicitor must normally account to the client for the amount of any commission which exceeds £20 unless the client, having been informed of the amount of the commission in writing, consents to the solicitor keeping the commission.

7.8. Referrals by the solicitor to a third party

7.8.1. A solicitor who recommends a client to a third party must do so in good faith, judging what is in the client's best interests. Any agreement entered into whereby the solicitor recommends clients to a third party must not restrict the solicitor's freedom to recommend clients to other third parties if this would be in the best interests of the client.

7.9. **Agreements to do work for customers of a third party**

7.9.1. A solicitor may enter an arrangement with a third party to provide conveyancing services for customers of the third party under which the solicitor is paid for those services by the introducer.

7.9.2. The agreement must be in writing and a copy of it must be available for inspection by the Law Society or the Office for the Supervision of Solicitors, together with records of the six-monthly reviews carried out under the Code.

7.9.3. Before making a referral the introducer must give the customer in writing:

(a) details of the conveyancing service to be provided under the terms of the referral;

(b) notification of:

    (i) the charge payable by the customer to the introducer for the conveyancing services;

    (ii) the liability for VAT and disbursements and how these are to be discharged; and

    (iii) what charge if any is to be made if the transaction does not proceed to completion or if the solicitor is unable to continue to act;

(c) notification of the amount the introducer will be paying to the solicitor for the provision of conveyancing services relating to the customer's transaction;

(d) a statement to the effect that the charge for conveyancing services will not be affected whether or not the customer takes other products or services offered (e.g. a life policy) by the introducer, and that the availability and price of other services will not be affected whether the customer chooses to instruct a solicitor under the referral or decides to instruct another solicitor or conveyancer; and

(e) a statement to the effect that the advice and service of the solicitor to whom the customer is to be referred will remain independent and subject to the instructions of the customer.

7.9.4. Publicity material of the introducer which includes reference to any service that may be provided by the solicitor must comply with the following:

(a) any reference to the charge for the conveyancing service must be clearly expressed separately from any charge for other services. Any circumstances in which the charges may be increased must be stated. It must be made clear whether disbursements and VAT are or are not included;

(b) the publicity must not suggest that the service is free, nor that different charges for the conveyancing services would be made according to whether the customer takes other products or services offered by the introducer or not;

(c) charges must not be stated as being from or upwards of a certain figure;

(d) the publicity must not suggest that the availability or price of other services offered by the introducer is conditional on the customer instructing the solicitor.

7.9.5. The solicitor may be paid by the introducer on a case-by-case basis, or on an hourly, monthly, or other appropriate basis.

7.9.6. Where the solicitor is being paid for his services by the introducer rather than by the client there is a danger of conflict of interests arising, and the solicitor must decline to act if such a conflict arises or is likely to arise.

7.9.7. A solicitor is not permitted to enter this type of agreement with a lender, builder, developer or seller or their agent, or with a life office or its tied agent, for the provision of conveyancing services for buyers or borrowers.

7.9.8. The agreement between the introducer and the solicitor must not include any provisions which would:

(a) compromise, infringe or impair any of the principles set out in Rule 1 Solicitors' Practice Rules (obtaining business) or any duties owed by the solicitor to the introducer's customer by virtue of the solicitor/client relationship and/or the requirements of professional conduct; or

(b) restrict the scope of the duties which the solicitor owes to the customer in relation to the services agreed to be provided by virtue of the professional relationship between the solicitor and client; or

(c) interfere with or inhibit the solicitor's responsibility for the control of the professional work.

FURTHER REFERENCE

Guidance – mortgages and life policies (App. II.1.).

A.08.   Estimate of costs

See also: Costs, para. N.01.

8.1.   Duty to give estimate

8.1.1.   A solicitor should, whenever possible, give a client an estimate of the likely costs of the transaction.[1]

8.1.2.   If it is not possible to give an estimate, a general forecast of the approximate costs should be given.

1. See Written Professional Standards.

8.2.   Residential conveyancing

8.2.1.   In residential conveyancing it is normally possible to give the client an estimate of the costs of the transaction. Use of the Estimate of Costs form published by the Law Society is recommended.

8.3.   Commercial transactions

8.3.1.   A precise estimate of costs may not be possible in the context of commercial transactions; nevertheless the client should still be given a general forecast of likely costs and the method of calculation of those costs at the outset of the transaction, and informed if that figure is likely to vary substantially.

8.4.   Bills payable by a third party

8.4.1.   Where the client is or will become liable to pay a bill presented by a third party, e.g. to a landlord's solicitor for consent to assignment, the solicitor should obtain an estimate of the third party's bill at the outset of the transaction and should inform the client of the amount of the estimate. If the estimate appears to be an unreasonably high figure, negotiations to attempt to reduce it should be undertaken before a substantial amount of work in the transaction has taken place. Money should be obtained from the client on account of the third party's costs before an undertaking to pay is given.

8.4.2. If the client is entitled to be indemnified by a third party, e.g. by a tenant seeking a licence to assign, an estimate of the costs should be given to the third party's solicitor. Such an estimate should be as firm as possible in the circumstances, but may be qualified by a statement to the effect that the estimate has been given on the basis that the matter proceeds without unforeseen complications.

8.5. Giving an estimate

8.5.1. In order to avoid misunderstandings it is preferable only to give an estimate in writing or, if oral, to confirm the estimate in writing either immediately or, at the latest, when the solicitor is instructed.

8.5.2. In residential conveyancing it is frequently not possible to avoid giving an estimate over the telephone. In such circumstances it should be made clear to the prospective client that the estimate is given on the basis of information supplied by the client and may be subject to variation if unknown factors later emerge which complicate the transaction.

8.5.3. The estimate should be as comprehensive as possible and should be clear as to whether VAT and/or disbursements are included in the given figure.

8.5.4. The client should be warned that if unforeseen complications arise, the estimate may be revised.

8.5.5. Minor expenses, e.g. postage and telephone are to be included in the estimate and must not be added as a disbursement.

8.5.6. In residential transactions use of the Estimate of Costs form published by the Law Society is recommended.

8.6. Change in circumstances

8.6.1. If events occur which cause the original estimate to become inaccurate the solicitor must immediately inform the client in writing of the change in circumstances and should revise his estimate accordingly.

8.6.2. Failure to advise the client of a change in the likely level of fees may render the solicitor liable to prosecution for giving misleading information relating to charges under Consumer Protection Act 1987, s.20.

8.7. Quotations for costs

8.7.1. The solicitor should make it clear to the client that an estimate for costs is not a fixed price ('a quotation') for the work unless it is the solicitor's intention to charge a fixed price which will not be altered in any circumstances.

8.7.2. Where a quotation is given the solicitor is not at liberty to charge the client more than the fixed fee even if the transaction turns out to be more difficult or complex than had been anticipated. Petty expenses such as postage and telephone must not be added as disbursements to the fixed fee.

8.7.3. It is recommended that if a fixed fee is quoted the client is informed of that fee in writing and told that the quotation will be valid for a stated period, e.g. three months. If the solicitor has not been instructed by the client within this period he will then be entitled to issue a revised quotation.

8.7.4. Money received for or on account of an agreed fee must not be paid into clients' account.[1]

8.7.5. A quotation for costs which has been accepted by the client may be subject to Solicitors Act 1974, s.57, which provides that it must:

(a) be in writing;

(b) embody all the terms of the agreement;

(c) be signed by the client or his agent;

(d) be reasonable in amount and in lieu of ordinary profit costs.[2]

8.7.6. Remuneration certificates are not available to a client where a section 57 agreement has been made, but he may seek taxation of the bill in the normal way. The agreement is enforceable by the solicitor under the ordinary principles of contract law.

1. See Solicitors' Accounts Rules 1991.
2. See *An Approach to Non-contentious Costs*, published by the Law Society.

8.8. VAT on solicitors' charges

8.8.1. Where a firm is registered, VAT will be payable by the client on the solicitors' bill and on some of the disbursements paid by the solicitor on the client's behalf.

8.8.2. When giving an estimate or quotation of costs to the client the solicitor should make it clear whether or not that estimate or quotation includes VAT. If no mention of VAT is made the client is entitled to assume that the quoted figure is inclusive of VAT.[1]

8.8.3. Where an individual or firm is registered for VAT, the firm's VAT registration number must appear on the bills issued by the firm or, if a separate tax invoice is issued, on the tax invoice.

8.8.4. Where the client's bill is reduced by the amount of commission which the solicitor has earned, e.g. on an endowment policy taken out by the client, VAT must be charged on the gross amount of the bill. Although the preceding sentence correctly represents the law in this area, in practice VAT is frequently only charged on the net sum.

1. Value Added Tax Act 1994, s.89.

FURTHER REFERENCE

An Approach to Non-contentious Costs, the Law Society.

A.09. Joint purchasers

9.1. Advising the client

9.1.1. When acting for joint purchasers, it is essential to clarify their intentions as to the method by which they are to hold the property. The solicitor should explain the different methods of co-ownership to the clients in language appropriate to their level of understanding and should advise as to the most suitable type of co-ownership to meet the particular situation. A note of the clients' wishes should be made on the file so that appropriate steps may be taken to implement the clients' instructions in the purchase deed.

9.1.2. Instructions should be obtained from both (or all) co-purchasers.[1]

9.1.3. Where the intending co-purchasers are not married to each other it may be necessary to advise each party independently about their rights in the property to be purchased. Solicitors should be alert to the possibility of a conflict of interests arising between the two clients in this situation.[2]

1. See *Penn* v. *Bristol & West Building Society, The Times*, 19 June 1995.
2. See para. 9.8. below.

9.2. Co-ownership or sole ownership?

9.2.1. In the vast majority of cases a husband and wife should be advised to hold a property jointly and this is usually a requirement of any major lending institution. The requirement by lenders for co-ownership by spouses (and cohabitees) is irrespective of the contribution which each party will make to the mortgage repayments.

9.2.2. A non-owning spouse will have rights under Family Law Act 1996 and/or an equitable interest through contribution to the purchase price of the property but neither of these methods of protection of the non-owning spouse's interest is as secure as co-ownership of the legal estate. A contra-indication to co-ownership by a married couple may exist where one or both of the parties is individually wealthy and where consideration must be given to the equalisation of estates for inheritance tax purposes.

9.2.3.   Sole legal ownership may be considered prudent if one of the parties is in a 'high-risk' category of unincorporated business where the potential consequences of bankruptcy may need to be considered.

9.2.4.   Unmarried purchasers, whether co-habitees, brother and sister or merely friends who are joining together to purchase a property, should normally be advised to hold the property jointly since the existence of an equitable or overriding interest may be costly and difficult to establish in the event of a dispute between the parties. Many lenders will insist that the legal estate is held jointly in these circumstances.

9.2.5.   Consideration should always be given to the question of taking out a joint life policy to protect the mortgage over the lives of both spouses/co-habitees even where the property is held in one name alone or where the mortgage repayments are made by one party alone. The joint lives policy will protect the repayments of the mortgage even in the event of death of the non-owning or non-earning spouse/co-habitee.

9.3.   **The options**

9.3.1.   In law co-ownership of land can usually only exist through the medium of a trust of land. The legal estate will thus be held by joint tenants on trust for themselves (and possibly other persons) in equity. The legal joint tenancy is not severable and there must be a minimum of two trustees (and maximum of four) in order to deal with the legal estate.

9.3.2.   In equity there is a choice between holding as joint tenants or as tenants in common.

9.3.3.   The capacity of the buyers, whether as joint tenants or tenants in common, must be expressly stated in the purchase deed itself or in a separate trust deed. The statement in Form 19(JP) (transfer of registered land) concerning whether a survivor can give a good receipt does not take effect as a declaration of the beneficial interests.[1]

1. See *Huntingford* v. *Hobbs* [1992] E.G.C.S. 38.

9.4.   **Joint tenants**

9.4.1.   Where co-owners hold the equitable interest as joint tenants none of the co-owners will be entitled to a distinct or separate proportion of that interest: each one owns all of it. The main distinguishing feature of the joint tenancy is the right of survivorship which leads to the interest accruing to the ultimate sole surviving joint tenant. Because no distinct part of the interest belongs to any individual tenant, no part of it will belong to the estate of a deceased joint tenant and, where the co-owners were married to each other, will not attract inheritance tax. An interest in a joint tenancy cannot be left by will, the deceased's share passing automatically to the surviving joint tenant(s). A beneficial joint tenancy can be severed which has the effect of converting it into a tenancy in common if there were only two joint tenants.

9.5. **Tenants in common**

9.5.1. Where a tenancy in common exists each co-owner holds a quantified proportion of the equitable interest which is capable of being disposed of *inter vivos* or by will or passes on the intestacy of the deceased tenant in common. The proportionate share in the property which belonged to a deceased tenant in common is subject to inheritance tax rules.

9.5.2. Unless the contrary is stated or evidence to the contrary is proved, a court will assume that tenants in common hold the equitable interest in proportion to the parties' original contributions to the property.[1] In order to avoid subsequent disputes and litigation it is desirable that the proportionate shares of each tenant in common are expressly agreed and recorded in a deed of trust (or certified copy transfer) which is signed by the co-owners and kept with the land or charge certificate. In unregistered land an express declaration as to the proportionate shares may be included in the purchase deed. If the parties cannot agree on the amount of their respective shares separate advice for one or all of them is necessary. Although HM Land Registry is not generally concerned with equitable interests, the Registry will allow the entry of a caution on the register to protect the equitable interest of a tenant in common but if a disposition is then lodged for registration which overreaches the equitable interest, the Chief Land Registrar will not permit the cautioner to prevent the registration of the disposition. This is in addition to the restriction which will be entered on the Proprietorship Register denoting the existence of a tenancy in common. Unless the proportions in which the equitable interest is held are clearly stated, it may be difficult to determine the ownership of the proceeds of sale when the property is ultimately sold. This will present problems for the solicitor if, e.g. the property is sold and the proceeds are to be divided as a result of a matrimonial breakdown.

9.5.3. One drawback to an express statement of the beneficial interest is that it cannot be changed except by deed. If, for example, a deed of trust stated that a husband owned 70% of the equitable interest and his wife 30%, but the wife subsequently paid off the whole mortgage on the house using money which she had inherited on the death of one of her parents, the wife might feel that she had become entitled to a larger proportion of the equitable interest through her contribution to the mortgage but, unless a new deed of trust is drawn up, redefining the proportionate shares of the parties, on sale of the property, the wife would still be entitled only to her original 30%. An alternative solution is that the whole or part of one joint owner's beneficial interest can be transferred to the new owner in writing, signed by the person transferring.[2]

9.5.4. A tenancy in common can be devised by will or will pass on intestacy. Where property is held by this method the parties should be advised as to the desirability of making a will.

9.5.5. Where a tenancy in common is created the deed should make specific provision relating to the appointment of a new trustee in the event of the death of one co-owner. In the absence of such a provision the provisions of Trusts of Land and

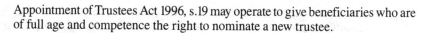

Appointment of Trustees Act 1996, s.19 may operate to give beneficiaries who are of full age and competence the right to nominate a new trustee.

1. *Springette* v. *Defoe* [1992] N.P.C. 34; *Savill* v. *Goodall* [1992] N.P.C. 153.
2. Law of Property Act 1925, s.53.

9.6. Suitability of each method

9.6.1. *Joint tenancy*

The automatic right of survivorship makes this method of co-ownership both suitable and attractive to prospective co-owners who are married to each other. Exceptionally, a joint tenancy may be unsuited to a married couple where one or both of the buyers is individually wealthy and where equalisation of estates for inheritance tax purposes is a consideration. Survivorship rights may well not be intended by co-owners who are not married to each other, and would not normally be considered suitable when dealing with partnership property.

9.6.2. *Tenancy in common*

Prospective co-owners who are not married to each other will usually be advised to hold by this method. This is also the most appropriate method by which partnership property can be dealt with. Consideration should be given to this method where the contributions made by each of the co-owners to the purchase price are in unequal proportions and where the parties are married to each other but one (or both) of them has offspring from a previous relationship who might reasonably expect to inherit on the death of their natural parent.

9.7. Gifts

9.7.1.
Where the purchase price of the property is supplied by one party alone, but the property is purchased in the joint names of the person who paid the purchase price and another, equity generally deems the property to be held on a resulting trust on behalf of the buyer, unless there is an indication to the contrary (such as an express declaration of trust in the transfer), or the circumstances are within the limited cases where a presumption of advancement applies.

9.8. Co-habitees

9.8.1.
Co-habitees may need to be advised independently about their respective rights in the property to be purchased. Solicitors should be alert to the possibility of a conflict of interests arising in this situation.

9.8.2.
It is advisable for co-habitees who are to be co-owners to enter a separate deed of trust (separate from but to be kept with the title deeds) which sets out their respective interests in the property. The rights and obligations conferred by this

document can only be altered by the execution of a further deed of trust but this disadvantage is outweighed by the advantage of having certainty as to the parties' rights and interests.

9.8.3. If the property is to be purchased in the sole name of one co-habitee, the other should be advised (where appropriate) to protect his or her interest, e.g. by lodging a caution at HM Land Registry.

9.8.4. A full discussion of the rights of co-habitees is contained in *The Family Lawyer's Handbook* (published by the Law Society, due September 1997).

FURTHER REFERENCE

Co-ownership, M.P. Thompson, Sweet & Maxwell.
The Family Lawyer's Handbook, the Law Society (due September 1997).

A.10. Acting for both parties

See also: Mortgages: acting for lender and borrower, para. A.11.
Contract races, para. B.02.

10.1. Conflict of interests

10.1.1. As a general principle of professional conduct a solicitor or firm of solicitors should not accept instructions to act for two or more clients in the same transaction where there is a conflict or a significant risk of a conflict between the interests of those clients.[1]

10.1.2. Neither should a solicitor or his firm continue to act for two or more clients if a conflict of interests arises between those clients.[2]

1. See *The Guide to the Professional Conduct of Solicitors 1996,* Principle 15.01.
2. See *The Guide to the Professional Conduct of Solicitors 1996,* Principle 15.03.

10.2. Rule 6 Solicitors' Practice Rules 1990 (as amended)

10.2.1. Subject to certain exceptions, acting for both parties in a conveyancing transaction at arm's length is generally prohibited by Rule 6 Solicitors' Practice Rules 1990 (as amended).[1]

10.2.2. In most circumstances, therefore, a solicitor who is asked to act for both parties to a transaction will decline to act for both either because of the potential conflict of interest between the parties or because of the application of Rule 6 Solicitors' Practice Rules 1990 (as amended).

10.2.3. Provided there is no conflict of interest the same solicitor may act for both seller and buyer where the transaction is not at arm's length (e.g. a transaction between parties who are related by blood, adoption or marriage).

1. See App. I.1.

10.3.   Exceptions to Rule 6

10.3.1. These exceptions, which are set out in full in Appendix I.1., will permit a solicitor to act for both seller and buyer (or landlord and tenant) in the same arm's length transaction but only apply where:

    (a)   the seller or lessor is not a builder or developer selling or leasing as such;

    (b)   the solicitor or a solicitor practising in partnership or association with him is not instructed to negotiate the sale of the property concerned;

    (c)   no conflict of interest arises;

    (d)   both parties are established clients (which expression shall include persons related by blood, adoption or marriage to established client(s));

    (e)   on a transfer of land, the consideration is less than £10,000;

    (f)   there is no other solicitor or other qualified conveyancer in the vicinity whom either party can reasonably be expected to consult; or

    (g)   two associated firms or two offices of the same firm are respectively acting for the parties, provided that:

        (i)   the respective firms or offices are in different localities; and

        (ii)   neither party was referred to the firm or office acting for him from an associated firm or from another office of the same firm; and

        (iii) the transaction is dealt with or supervised by a different solicitor in regular attendance at each firm or office; and

    (h)   both parties gave their written consent to the arrangement.

The above conditions must be satisfied for an exception to the Rule to apply.

10.4.   Mortgages

10.4.1.   *Institutional mortgages*

An institutional mortgage is one where the lender is an institution which provides mortgages on standard terms in the normal course of its activities.

A solicitor, or solicitors practising in associated practices, may act for both lender and borrower provided no conflict of interest exists or arises. Where the solicitor or a member of his immediate family is the borrower or one of two or more joint borrowers the solicitor must have given notification of the circumstance to the lender.

10.4.2.   *Private mortgage*

A private mortgage is any mortgage other than an institutional mortgage (see para. 10.4.1. above). A solicitor, or solicitors practising in associated practices, must not act for both lender and borrower unless the transaction is not at arm's length and no conflict of interest exists or arises.

10.4.3. *Acting for seller, buyer and lender*

A solicitor, or solicitors practising in associated practices, must not act for seller, buyer and lender in the same transaction unless no conflict of interest exists or arises, and, in the case of an institutional mortgage, the solicitor has given written notification of the circumstance to the lender.

10.5. **Contract races**

10.5.1. If the transaction involves a contract race the same firm may not act for two or more prospective purchasers, nor may the firm act for both seller and buyer.[1]

1. Rule 6A Solicitors' Practice Rules 1990, as amended.

10.6. **Merger of firms**

10.6.1. As a result of a merger or amalgamation a firm may find that it is acting for both seller and buyer in the same transaction. Unless the circumstances of the transaction fall within one of the exceptions to Rule 6 above the firm should cease to act for one or both of the parties from the date of the merger. It is, however, recognised that to cease to act for one client during the course of the transaction might cause hardship and inconvenience to both clients and provided that there is compliance with the guidelines set out below the firm may continue to act for both clients in order to finalise the transaction.

10.6.2. *Guidelines*

The individual solicitors within the merged firm who are representing the respective parties should, in relation to this particular transaction, regard themselves as belonging to separate firms and should not communicate with each other (except formally about the outcome of the transaction) until the transaction has been concluded. *The Guide to the Professional Conduct of Solicitors 1996* contains guidelines relating to this matter.

10.6.3. New instructions received for clients of the merged firm will be subject to the provisions of Rule 6 above.

10.7. **Solicitor who moves to another firm**

10.7.1. *Client's pending business is taken over by the new firm*

In these circumstances the solicitor may find that his new firm is already acting for the other party to the transaction and a situation analogous to that which occurs on a merger of firms pertains. The guidelines set out above should be followed.

10.7.2. On moving to the new firm the solicitor finds he is now acting for the buyer in a transaction where he had previously been acting for the seller in the same transaction (or vice versa): although in this situation there is no question of the same solicitor or same firm acting for both parties the solicitor, while working for his previous firm, will have acquired information which is confidential to his (now) former client and which may affect or prejudice the way in which he handles the transaction for the client of the new firm. In order to preserve his duty of confidentiality to his former client the solicitor should not act for the client of the new firm in this transaction, but there is no objection to the matter being handled by another fee-earner in the solicitor's new firm.

10.8. Property selling

10.8.1. As part of the solicitor's business

A solicitor who sells property on behalf of a seller client may also act for the seller in the conveyancing but may not act for the buyer either in the conveyancing or in the negotiations for a mortgage for the buyer.

10.8.2. As a separate business

The solicitor must not act for the seller where the estate agency business has provided financial or mortgage services to the buyer. The solicitor cannot act for the buyer where the property has been bought through the estate agency business.[1]

1. See Property selling, para. A.02.

10.9. Joint borrowers

10.9.1. Where joint borrowers are obtaining a mortgage for the purchase of property, there is no objection to the same solicitor advising both of them, provided that their interests coincide. Where, however, one party is acting as surety for the other's debts, e.g. a wife who is guaranteeing her husband's mortgage of the matrimonial home to secure the husband's business debts, the parties' interests will almost certainly be in conflict with each other. In these circumstances, separate and independent advice must be given to each party. It may be possible for the same solicitor to advise both clients in these circumstances, but each client should be seen separately and the advice given to each party must be consistent with that party's interests.[1]

1. See *Barclays Bank* v. *O'Brien* [1993] 4 All E.R. 417; *Midland Bank plc* v. *Serter* [1994] E.G.C.S. 45; *Clark Boyce* v. *Mouat* [1993] 3 W.L.R. 1021, P.C.; *Banco-Exterior Internacional* v. *Mann* [1995] 1 All E.R. 936 (C.A.). Also see *Bank Melli Iran* v. *Samadi Rad* [1995] 2 F.L.R. 367, where the court said that a wife who had been advised separately by a different solicitor in the firm which was also advising her husband had not received 'independent' advice.

A.11. Mortgages: acting for lender and borrower

See also: Acting for both parties, para. A.10.
Lenders, section H.
Costs, para. N.01.

11.1. General principles

11.1.1. The buyer's lender will frequently instruct the buyer's solicitor also to act for him in connection with the grant of the mortgage. The same situation commonly occurs in relation to the discharge of an existing mortgage when acting for a seller client.

11.1.2. As soon as the solicitor receives instructions to act for the lender he is acting for both parties in one transaction (i.e. for both lender and borrower) and owes a duty to both clients.[1] Their respective interests are not necessarily identical and need to be separately considered.

11.1.3. Subject to para. A.10.4. above, acting for both parties is permissible provided that no conflict of interest arises between the two clients.

11.1.4. The lender's instructions to act and (in the case of a purchase) terms of offer must be carefully scrutinised to ensure that there is no conflict or potential conflict between the interests of the lender and the buyer/seller.

1. *Mortgage Express* v. *Bowerman & Partners* [1995] 2 All E.R. 769 (C.A.).

11.2. Conflict of interests

11.2.1. If a conflict should occur the solicitor must decline to act for both parties unless he can, with the consent of one party, continue to act for the other.

11.3. Examples of conflict

11.3.1. Conflict may arise if, for example:

(a) the terms of the mortgage offer are inequitable;

(b) instructions reveal that the buyer would be in breach of one of the terms of the offer;

(c) the buyer/seller is unable to comply with the lender's terms;

(d) the buyer is offering inadequate security.

11.3.2. A conflict will also arise if the buyer's solicitor becomes aware that the buyer is misrepresenting the purchase price to the lender, e.g. where the buyer and seller have agreed that the actual purchase price of the property will be lower than that shown in the contract and purchase deed, or where the buyer receives an inducement such as a free holiday to persuade him to buy the property. Solicitors have a duty of confidentiality to their clients, but this does not affect their duty to act in the best interests of each client. Subject to the instructions received from the particular lender concerned, any information regarding variations to the purchase price should be forwarded to the lender with the consent of the buyer. If the buyer will not consent to the information being disclosed to the lender the solicitor must cease to act for the lender and must consider carefully whether he is able to continue to act for the buyer. Any attempt to defraud the lender may lead to criminal prosecutions of both the buyer and the buyer's solicitor. The solicitor would also be guilty of unprofessional conduct. If a solicitor is aware that his client is attempting to perpetrate fraud in any form he should immediately cease to act for that client. Attention is drawn to the Law Society guidelines on mortgage fraud which are set out in Appendix III.1.

11.4. Confidentiality

11.4.1. If a conflict does arise between the borrower and his lender where the same solicitor is acting for both parties it should be borne in mind that all information received by the solicitor from his client is confidential and cannot be disclosed to the lender without the client's consent. Knowledge acquired in the course of acting for the client is not imputed to the lender.[1] Where, for example, the solicitor is told by his borrower client that the client intends to breach the terms of the mortgage offer by letting the premises to a tenant, the solicitor, when informing the lender that he can no longer act for him, must tell the lender that the reason for the termination of the retainer is because a conflict of interests has arisen, but is not at liberty to disclose the nature of the conflict without the borrower client's consent.

1. *Halifax Mortgage Services Ltd.* v. *Stepsky, The Times,* 27 June 1995.

11.5. Private mortgages

11.5.1. The solicitor must not act for both lender and borrower in a private mortgage at arm's length.

11.5.2. A private mortgage is defined by Rule 6(4) Solicitors' Practice Rules 1990 as 'any mortgage other than an institutional mortgage'. An institutional mortgage is one where the lender is an institution which provides mortgages on standard terms in the normal course of its activities.

11.5.3. Subject to the general principles of conflict of interests it would be possible to act in a private mortgage which is not at arm's length (e.g. a loan between father and son), but it is advisable to ensure that the borrower receives independent advice about the terms of the loan.

11.6. Lender's costs

11.6.1. See Costs, para. N.01.

11.7. Sureties

11.7.1. Where the lender requires a surety to enter into the transaction, the surety should be advised to take independent advice before signing the security document. This is of particular importance where the intended surety is the wife of the borrower since the courts take the view that a security should not be enforced against a married woman unless the lender can show that he has taken reasonable steps to show that she understood the transaction.[1]

11.7.2. If the proceeds of a life policy fall into the deceased's estate (e.g. because the policy was not formally assigned to the lender) the surety has no claim against the deceased's estate.

1. See *Barclays Bank plc* v. *O'Brien* [1993] 3 W.L.R. 786, H.L.; *C.I.B.C. Mortgages* v. *Pitt* [1993] 3 W.L.R. 802, H.L.

11.8. Mortgage fraud

11.8.1. Mortgage fraud can occur in either a residential or commercial transaction and can assume many different guises. Solicitors must be alert to the possibility of fraud and should be careful not to participate, even unknowingly, in a transaction where such a fraud is being perpetrated. Collusion with the client in a mortgage fraud is a criminal offence and would also lead to disciplinary proceedings being taken against the solicitor involved. If ignorance of the fraud is due to the solicitor's negligence, the solicitor may also be vulnerable to an action against him in negligence.

11.8.2. The Law Society's warning on mortgage fraud is set out in Appendix III.1.[1]

11.8.3. Although a solicitor does not have a duty to investigate on his own initiative if any of the situations detailed in para. B.19.6. (or other suspicious circumstances) in which mortgage fraud may be occurring are noticed by the solicitor he should investigate those circumstances fully and if, having done so, is not satisfied as to the client's explanation, should cease to act further for the client. The solicitor remains bound by his duty of confidentiality to his client which may therefore prevent him from disclosing the suspected fraud to a third party (see para. 11.4.1. above). A solicitor who chooses to ignore the client's fraudulent intention and to continue to act may still find himself facing criminal liability even though he took no active part in the fraud and was only carrying out the solicitor's normal conveyancing work.

11.8.4. The following steps may be considered as precautions against mortgage fraud:

    (a) proper supervision of all staff;

    (b) adequate training of all staff;

    (c) staff awareness of the issues involved in mortgage fraud and the Law Society's guidance in relation to it;

    (d) close supervision of incoming post;

    (e) an instruction to the accounts department to advise the partners of any large payments made to the buyer after completion (a mortgage fraud which works by inflating the purchase price is designed to leave a large cash surplus which is paid to the buyer after completion).

1. See also Mortgage offers, para. B.19.

11.9.   Ownership of documents and confidentiality

11.9.1. The following guidance relates to the position where the same firm of solicitors acted for the buyer/borrower and for the lender on a contemporaneous purchase and mortgage and the lender asks to see documents on the 'conveyancing file'.

11.9.2. Where all the documentation is kept on one file, the solicitor will have to sort through the file to determine ownership of the various papers. Annex 12A of *The Guide to the Professional Conduct of Solicitors 1996* contains guidance on the legal subject of ownership of documents on a solicitor's file.

11.9.3. The documents which the lender will be entitled to see fall into two categories. The first category is documents prepared or received by the solicitor on behalf of the lender. The second category is documents prepared or received by the solicitor on behalf of the borrower which, it is considered, the lender is nonetheless entitled to see. The rationale is that these documents relate to that part of the solicitor's work where the lender and borrower can be said to have a common interest, i.e. the deduction of title, the acquisition of a good title to the property and ancillary legal issues, such as the use of the property. Examples of the most common items in these two categories are set out below.

11.9.4. Documents held by the solicitor on behalf of the lender are:

    (a) the lender's instructions to the solicitor;

    (b) copy mortgage deed;

    (c) copy report on title;

    (d) any correspondence between the solicitor and the lender or between the solicitor and a third party written or received on the lender's behalf.

11.9.5. Documents held by the solicitor on behalf of the borrower are:

    (a) contract for sale;

    (b) property information form /enquiries before contract;

    (c) abstract or epitome of title/office copy entries and plan;

    (d) requisitions on title;

    (e) draft purchase deed;

    (f) draft licence to assign (where appropriate);

    (g) Land Registry application forms.

11.10. Standard Mortgage Instructions[1]

11.10.1. Introduction

The Standard Mortgage Instructions (SMI) form the contract between the solicitor (or licensed conveyancer) and lender where the solicitor (or licensed conveyancer) is representing a lender who has agreed to be a party to the SMI. A number of major lenders have agreed to be parties to the SMI and other mortgage lenders may instruct solicitors to act on the terms of the SMI. The instructions apply whether or not the solicitor is acting for both borrower and lender or for the lender only.

11.10.2. Modifications of the instructions specific to the transaction in hand will be notified to the solicitor in the lender's written instructions to the solicitor.

11.10.3. It is the solicitor's responsibility to ensure that the property has a good and marketable title which can safely be accepted by the lender as security and that the property is validly charged to the lender to secure the advance made to the borrower.

11.10.4. Communications between the solicitor and the lender must be in writing (or confirmed in writing) and must quote the mortgage account or roll number, the borrower's name and initials, the address of the property and the solicitor's reference.

11.10.5. Documents contained in the 'joint file' (as defined in the SMI) must be retained by the solicitor for at least six years after completion of the mortgage.

11.10.6. The solicitor must use the lender's standard documentation the wording of which must not be varied without the lender's consent.

1. At the time of publication the SMI had not been finalised.

A.12. Preliminary deposits

12.1. General law
12.2. Payment to estate agents

12.3. New properties
12.4. Action by solicitor

See also: Deposit, para. B.17.

12.1. General law

12.1.1. There is no requirement in law for either party to pay a preliminary deposit since neither party is committed to the sale and purchase until contracts have been exchanged.

12.2. Payment to estate agents

12.2.1. An estate agent will frequently ask a prospective buyer to pay a preliminary deposit as an indication of the buyer's good intentions to proceed with negotiations. The buyer should be advised to resist pressure from the agent to make such a payment since no advantage to the buyer derives from it.

12.2.2. If a preliminary deposit is to be paid the buyer should ensure that the agent has the seller's authority to take the deposit. Without such authority the buyer has no recourse against the seller if the agent misappropriates the money.[1]

12.2.3. A signed receipt must be obtained in respect of any preliminary deposit which is paid, a copy of which should be placed on the solicitor's file for reference. The terms of the receipt should be scrutinised before signature to ensure that the deposit will be refundable if the transaction does not proceed.

12.2.4. Any preliminary deposit paid is normally fully refundable to the buyer if the transaction does not proceed.

12.2.5. Preliminary deposits are usually paid to the estate agent who will hold the money in the capacity of agent for the seller. Interest on a preliminary deposit which exceeds £500 may be payable under Estate Agents Act 1979.

12.2.6. Where a preliminary deposit is taken by a solicitor who is acting as an estate agent, consideration should be given to holding that deposit in the capacity of agent for the buyer in accordance with the Solicitors' Property Group Code of Practice.

1. See *Sorrell* v. *Finch* [1977] A.C. 728.

12.3.   New properties

12.3.1.   A seller who is a builder or developer will invariably require a prospective buyer to pay a preliminary deposit. In this situation the payment of the deposit may operate as an option to purchase a numbered plot at a stated price, the seller promising that he will not sell that plot elsewhere nor raise the price provided that contracts are exchanged within a stated period. Here the buyer may have little choice but to pay the deposit, but a receipt should always be obtained and a copy of it placed on the buyer's solicitor's file for reference. The terms of the receipt should be scrutinised to ascertain whether the deposit is refundable to the buyer if he later changes his mind and withdraws from the transaction. Since this type of preliminary deposit often buys an option on a numbered plot it is not unusual to find that the deposit is not returnable to the buyer in any circumstances, although it will be credited as part of the purchase price if the matter proceeds.

12.4.   Action by solicitor

12.4.1.   The solicitor should always enquire whether a preliminary deposit has been paid, and if so how much and to whom. A copy of the receipt should be obtained and a note of the amount of the deposit made on the file so that this may be taken into account when calculating the balance of deposit needed on exchange.

A.13. Surveys

See also: Environmental issues, para. B.25.
Other causes of action, para. M.06.

13.1. When should a survey be commissioned?

13.1.1. Ideally the buyer should always have a survey carried out before exchange of contracts, but many buyers, particularly first-time buyers for whom the expense of a survey is a major consideration, do not commission an independent survey, preferring to rely instead on the valuation undertaken by their lender. Most lenders disclose their written valuation reports to their customers.

13.1.2. In the case of commercial premises a buyer will have much more detailed concerns relating to the structure, use, and floor loading capabilities of the property. Compliance with statutory requirements must also be checked. The comments contained in the following paragraphs do not reflect the detail required in a commercial transaction.

13.2. Reasons for a survey

13.2.1. The *caveat emptor* rule places on the buyer the onus of discovering any physical faults in the property agreed to be sold. For this reason alone, a survey is always advisable in order to discover physical defects which are not readily apparent on inspection of the property by the lay client, except perhaps where a property in the course of construction is being purchased with the benefit of NHBC or similar insurance cover.

13.2.2. In addition to the above the surveyor's report should:

    (a) confirm whether or not the value of the property equates with the price agreed to be paid for it;

    (b) point out any major structural defects which exist;

    (c) give the buyer early warning of potential structural problems or major repair work which will be required in the foreseeable future so that these may be taken into account in deciding whether the buyer is able and/or prepared to undertake the responsibility for such future expenditure;

    (d) bring to the attention of the buyer's solicitor the existence of factors which may be indicative of third party rights or overriding interests over the property and which need to be the subject of further enquiries by the solicitor;

(e) point out minor matters which may need remedial work in the near future;

(f) confirm whether or not the boundaries on the ground correspond with those shown in the title deeds.

13.3. Advice to the client

13.3.1. If the client has not already instructed a surveyor, the reasons for having a survey done should be explained to the client and a note made on the file that the client was so advised and of the client's decision following the receipt of the advice. The advice given should include information relating to the different types of survey available and their relative cost.

13.3.2. The client should be advised to commission a survey as soon as a firm offer has been accepted by the seller. The results of the survey must be obtained before exchange of contracts since once exchange has taken place the client will no longer have the right to withdraw from the transaction on the grounds of a physical defect in the property. The results of the survey may reveal matters which will require further investigation by the buyer's solicitor, or even give grounds for the negotiation of a reduction in the purchase price, both of which must, where appropriate, be conducted before a binding contract is entered into.

13.3.3. Although there is no reported decision on the point, it is possible that a court might hold that a solicitor who had not advised a client to have a survey done was in breach of his duty of care towards his client or in breach of Supply of Goods and Services Act 1982, s.13 which implies an obligation to perform a contract for services with reasonable skill and care.

13.3.4. If the solicitor does go through the surveyor's report prepared for the client, he is expected to exercise his own judgment and expertise in relation to the interpretation of the report and should emphasise to the client the limitations on the advice which can be given by the solicitor about the report (i.e. that he is looking at the report as a lawyer and not as a surveyor).

13.4. Types of survey

13.4.1. In broad terms the client has three options open to him:

(a) to rely on the valuation made by his lender;

(b) to commission a 'Home Buyer's Valuation and Survey Report';

(c) to instruct an independent surveyor to do a full structural survey.

13.4.2. *Valuation*

This will be undertaken by the buyer's lender in order to establish whether the property being purchased will be adequate security for the amount of the loan. The buyer pays the cost of this valuation and is usually permitted to see the valuer's report, but the report will not necessarily reveal sufficient information about the state of the property to allow the buyer to make a reasoned judgment as to whether or not to proceed with his purchase. Where the amount required by the buyer on mortgage represents a high percentage of the purchase price of the property, the interests of the buyer and his lender in the valuation broadly coincide, in that if the value of the property does not provide adequate security for the loan, then neither does it represent a wise investment for the client. In these circumstances therefore it may be considered that a lender's valuation report alone will provide sufficient protection of the client's interests. A valuation alone may also be considered adequate in circumstances where the client is purchasing a property in the course of construction which is to be covered by the NHBC or similar scheme.

13.4.3. *Home Buyer's Valuation and Survey Report*

This option represents a compromise between the mortgage valuation and the full survey and is thus an attractive option for a client who, for reasons of expense or otherwise, is reluctant to commission a full survey. In many cases the buyer's lender will agree (for an additional fee) to instruct the lender's valuer to undertake the survey concurrently with the mortgage valuation with consequent savings in time and expense for the client. This type of survey may provide adequate information for the client who is purchasing an ordinary suburban property built within the last 100 years, but the client should not be misled into thinking that the survey result is an absolute guarantee of the state and condition of the property. Although of much more value to the client than a mere valuation, this type of survey is still relatively superficial in scope.

13.4.4. *Full survey*

The potential expense of a full survey deters many clients from choosing this option. The client might be reminded that £500 abortive expense on a survey is preferable to discovering that £30,000 worth of structural repairs needs to be done to the property he has just purchased without the benefit of a survey. This option is undoubtedly the most expensive of the three on offer, the exact expense and value to the client depending on what the surveyor has been instructed to investigate. A full survey will only reveal the true state and condition of the entire property if the surveyor is correctly instructed to investigate all aspects of the property.

13.4.5. *Guidelines*

The need for a full structural survey may be indicated by the presence of one or more of the following factors:

(a) the property is of a high value;

(b) the amount of the buyer's intended mortgage represents a low proportion of the purchase price, e.g. less than 70%;

(c) the property is more than 100 years old;

(d) the buyer intends to alter or extend the property after completion;

(e) the property is not of conventional brick and mortar construction;

(f) the proximity of the property to features which may cause subsidence or other structural problems, e.g. mines, filled-in gravel pits, rivers, vibration damage from aircraft or railways;

(g) the property is not detached.

13.4.6. Surveys in special cases

A surveyor, even when instructed to carry out a full structural survey, will not normally investigate drainage or electrical systems. A property which does not have the benefit of mains drainage will require a separate drainage survey from an expert in that field, since the cost of repair or replacement of a private drainage system can be prohibitive. Liability for escaping effluent can also involve civil and criminal penalties. If the electric wiring system in the property has not been inspected during the past five years a report on the adequacy and safety of the electrical installations may also be desirable. Where environmental issues are relevant, e.g. on purchases of development land a separate environmental survey may also be desirable to ensure that the land does not harbour any hazardous substances which may incur liability on the landowner under Environmental Protection Act 1990 or Environment Act 1995. The local authority for the area can supply information relating to the presence of radon in the area. The National Radiological Protection Board can provide more general information and has published a radon atlas of England (see para. B.25.8.).

13.4.7. Flats and other attached properties

Where the property to be purchased is a flat or is a property which is structurally attached to neighbouring property, a full survey is desirable. The structural soundness of the property being bought is in these circumstances dependent on the soundness of the neighbouring property also, and the surveyor must therefore be instructed to inspect the adjoining property (if possible) as well as the property actually being purchased.

13.4.8. Water supply pipes

The owner or occupier of land may be responsible for the maintenance of a water supply pipe which crosses privately owned land before joining the publicly maintained mains supply pipe. A full structural survey may not deal with the water supply system (particularly where the pipes supplying the property being surveyed pass through or under adjoining property). The client may be advised to obtain a separate survey of the water supply pipes from his water supply company. A fee may be payable for this service.

13.5. Surveyor's liability

13.5.1. The surveyor owes a duty of care to his client to carry out his survey with reasonable skill and care. This common law duty is reinforced by Supply of Goods and Services Act 1982, s.13 which implies into a contract for services a term that the work will be carried out with reasonable skill and care.

13.5.2. Where a client suffers loss as a result of a negligent survey an action can be sustained against his surveyor, subject to the validity of any exemption clause which may have formed part of the surveyor's terms of work. The normal rules relating to remoteness of damage apply; thus the client will not sustain a successful action unless the area of the client's complaint lies within the scope of what the surveyor was instructed to do, and hence the importance of giving full and explicit instructions when the survey is commissioned.

13.5.3. An exclusion clause which seeks to limit or to exclude the surveyor's liability in contract or tort will be subject to the reasonableness test in Unfair Contract Terms Act 1977, s.11. Where a lay client has suffered loss the burden of showing that the clause satisfies the reasonableness test will be a difficult one for the surveyor to discharge,[1] but the clause may give some protection where the client who commissioned the survey was experienced in the property field.[2]

13.5.4. Where the client suffers loss after having relied on a lender's valuer's report an action in tort may lie against the surveyor. No action in contract can be sustained because, the survey having been commissioned by the lender, there is no contractual relationship between the buyer and the surveyor. The success of such an action may again depend on the validity of any exclusion clause contained in the valuation; however, it was held by the House of Lords in *Smith* v. *Eric S. Bush (a firm); Harris* v. *Wyre Forest District Council*[3] that a valuer instructed by a lender to carry out a mortgage valuation of a modest house, in the knowledge that the buyer would rely on the valuation without obtaining an independent survey, owed a duty of care to the buyer to exercise reasonable care and skill in carrying out the valuation. Similarly in *Beresforde* v. *Chesterfield Borough Council*,[4] where the lender presented the valuer's report to the buyer on its own headed notepaper, the Court of Appeal allowed the buyer to proceed with a claim based on loss arising out of an allegedly negligent valuation directly against the lender. However, the court's decision in this case was interlocutory and as no trial took place it cannot be assumed that a lender will always be liable in such circumstances. The decisions in these cases may assist lay purchasers of ordinary modestly priced houses or small businesses,[5] but may not assist in other circumstances where it would be reasonable to assume that the buyer would commission his own independent survey.

13.5.5.   A complaint about a negligent valuation/survey made in-house by a lender may be investigated by the Building Society's Ombudsman provided the complainant is an existing borrower from that Society.[6]

1. See *Yianni* v. *Edwin Evans & Sons* [1982] 1 Q.B. 438.
2. See *Stevenson* v. *Nationwide Building Society* (1984) 272 E.G. 663.
3. [1990] 1 A.C. 831, H.L.
4. [1989] 39 E.G. 176.
5. See *Qureshi* v. *Liassides* (unreported 22 April 1994). See commentary in *Estates Gazette,* 11 November 1994, p.123.
6. *Halifax Building Society* v. *Edell* [1992] Ch. 436.

A.14. Stamp duty and stamp duty savings

14.1. Introduction

14.1.1. An estimate of the stamp duty to be incurred will need to be included in the costs estimate given to the buyer. Non-payment of stamp duty or evasion of duty gives rise to fines and penalties under Stamp Act 1891 and other statutes for which the client and his solicitor may face prosecution. A solicitor who is aware of an intention to defraud the Inland Revenue in this way, or who assists his client to do so, may also be subject to disciplinary proceedings. A document which is not properly stamped will not be accepted by HM Land Registry and cannot be used in evidence in civil proceedings. Duty is payable on the instrument of transfer (the purchase deed) within 30 days of completion.

14.1.2. Avoidance schemes

Any stamp duty avoidance scheme is vulnerable to being set aside as the courts have accepted in principle that the non-payment of stamp duty is tax evasion. Schemes which are arranged exclusively for the purpose of stamp duty avoidance may therefore prove ineffective.[1]

1. *Furniss (Inspector of Taxes)* v. *Dawson* [1984] A.C. 474; *Ingram* v. *I.R.C.* [1986] Ch. 585.

14.2. Purchase of freehold property for value

14.2.1. The transfer of freehold property for full value will attract stamp duty at the rate of 1% of the purchase price when the consideration exceeds £60,000.

14.2.2. Where the consideration is £60,000 or less, no stamp duty is payable provided that the purchase deed contains an appropriate certificate of value.

14.2.3. Form of certificate of value

'It is hereby certified that the transaction hereby effected does not form part of a larger transaction or of a series of transactions in respect of which the amount or value or the aggregate amount or value of the consideration exceeds £60,000.'

14.2.4. The wording of the certificate of value does not permit the purchase of a single piece of land to be sub-divided into separate small units with the intention of bringing the value of each small unit under the stamp duty threshold, so avoiding the payment of duty on the whole unit.

14.3. Assignment of an existing lease

14.3.1. The transfer (assignment) of an existing lease attracts stamp duty at the same rate as that applicable to freehold property.

14.4. Grant of lease

14.4.1. Stamp duty on the grant of a lease is assessed by reference to the premium paid for the grant, the rent and the length of the term. Current stamp duty tables should be consulted to inform the client of the amount of duty which will be incurred on completion. The lease itself bears full duty, a counterpart lease bears fixed duty of £0.50.[1]

14.4.2. Agreements for lease

When a lease is presented for stamping, it must either contain a certificate to the effect that there was no prior agreement for lease or be denoted with the duty paid (if any) on the agreement to which the lease gives effect. The form of certificate suggested by the Stamp Office is as follows: 'We certify that there is no agreement for lease to which this lease gives effect.' The certificate should be included in the lease itself (and not presented as a separate document) and signed by the parties who have executed the instrument. A counterpart lease does not require a certificate.

1. Tables of stamp duties are set out in App. VIII.2. Leasehold stamp duties are discussed further in section K.

14.5. Transactions at an under value

14.5.1. Unless the transfer is specifically exempt from stamp duty (e.g. under a statutory provision such as Church Building Act 1882) or falls within Stamp Duty (Exempt Instruments) Regulations 1987[1] stamp duty will be payable on the transfer, the amount to be assessed on adjudication of the transfer after completion.

1. S.I. 1987/516. See below, para. 14.7. and App. VIII.5.

14.6. Chattels

14.6.1. Stamp duty is not payable on the value of chattels which are included in the sale. For this reason it is permissible to apportion the value of the land from the value of included chattels, e.g. carpets and curtains, paying stamp duty only on the value of the land.

14.6.2. Where chattels are included in the sale and the seller has not apportioned the purchase price to reflect the value of the chattels, the buyer may wish to amend the draft contract to make such an apportionment and thus reduce his liability to stamp duty. Such an apportionment is of most value to the buyer where the purchase price of the property (including chattels) is marginally above the stamp duty threshold and the effect of the apportionment is to reduce the price of the land to bring it below the stamp duty limit. The buyer must seek the seller's permission to make an apportionment of the price. Provided the apportionment is a true reflection of the value of the chattels the seller has no reason to object to it since he will, on completion, still be receiving the full amount of the agreed price of the property.

14.6.3. The apportionment of the value of chattels must be a realistic estimate of their actual worth. Any purported over-valuation of the chattels will be a fraud on the Inland Revenue which may give rise to the sanctions mentioned above. Additionally, the effect of an over-valuation may be to render the contract illegal (and thus unenforceable) on the grounds of public policy.[1]

14.6.4. Where fixtures, fittings and stock in trade are included in a commercial sale, a professional valuation of their worth should be obtained. Although it will, in most cases, be possible to determine the value of fixtures and fittings at the outset of the transaction, stock in trade may have to be purchased at a price to be agreed pursuant to a valuation made on the day of completion, since the amount of stock held by a trading business will fluctuate from day to day.

14.6.5. In some cases the apportionment of the price of chattels may lead to a capital gains tax liability on the seller.

14.6.6. Even where the sale of the land is exempt from VAT, the sale of chattels may attract VAT.[2]

14.6.7. *Sale of a business as a going concern*

Where the contract is for the sale of the assets of a business, some of those assets may attract stamp duty while others will be exempt. Stamps Form 22[3] showing the apportionment of the price between the various assets should be completed and submitted to the Stamp Office.

1. *Saunders* v. *Edwards* [1987] 2 All E.R. 651.
2. See below, para. 14.13.
3. Form 22 is reproduced in App. VIII.4.

14.7. Exempt instruments

14.7.1. Where the document falls within one of the categories listed in Stamp Duty (Exempt Instruments) Regulations 1987 and contains an appropriate certificate, no duty is payable.[1]

14.7.2. The most commonly encountered documents which will fall within these Regulations are:

(a) conveyance or transfer to a beneficiary named in the will (or his nominee);

(b) appointment of a new trustee;

(c) conveyance or transfer to a beneficiary (or his nominee) under the intestacy rules;

(d) transfers in connection with divorce settlements;

(e) a voluntary disposition *inter vivos* for no consideration in money or money's worth.

14.7.3. The exemption conferred by the above Regulations applies provided that the document contains a certificate which specifies the category of exemption within the Regulations which is relied on.

14.7.4. *Form of certificate*

'It is hereby certified that this instrument falls within category [X] in the Schedule to Stamp Duty (Exempt Instruments) Regulations 1987'.

14.7.5. The certificate which is contained in the purchase deed must be signed by the buyer. The document does not need to be sent to the Stamp Office nor for adjudication.

14.7.6. *Exempt bodies*

The transfer of land by certain bodies (e.g. the Church Commissioners in respect of a sale of church property) is exempt from stamp duty under various statutory provisions. Where the seller is a government department or public authority the buyer's solicitor should check his client's liability to stamp duty on the transaction and inform his client accordingly. A charity is exempt from stamp duty on any lease or conveyance.[2]

14.7.7. An instrument relating to property within the U.K. but which is executed outside the U.K. does not attract stamp duty until the document is brought back to the U.K. when duty must be paid within 30 days.[3] A document executed outside the U.K. which relates to property outside the U.K. does not attract stamp duty, but a document relating to foreign property which is executed within the U.K. bears duty at the normal rate applicable to that type of document.

14.7.8. A transfer of mortgage bears no duty, but a transfer of land subject to an existing mortgage bears duty on the value of the equity of redemption. Duty is also payable on the outstanding amount of the debt if the buyer covenants to pay the debt.

14.7.9. Where the sale is of a council house with outstanding discount duty is not payable on the amount of the discount.

1. S.I. 1987/516. See App. VIII.5.
2. Finance Act 1982, s.129.
3. Stamp Act 1891, s.15(3).

14.8. Exchange of land

14.8.1. An exchange of freehold land for other freehold land attracts stamp duty at *ad valorem* rates. Duty is charged on each transfer. The duty in each case is calculated by reference to the 'consideration' (i.e. the value) given for the transfer: where the consideration consists of property, its open market value will be taken.

14.8.2. For example, if one house worth £100,000 is exchanged for another house worth £100,000, duty of £1,000 (one per cent of £100,000) is charged on each transfer. The £60,000 threshold is applied separately to each side of the exchange. For example, if there is a straightforward exchange of one house worth £50,000 for another worth £50,000, both transfers are within the threshold and so no duty would be payable on either.

14.8.3. Where the market values of the two properties being exchanged are not equal, a payment of money (or some other consideration) may often be given with the lower value property, so as to equalise the bargain. The treatment of such cases for stamp duty purposes will depend on the facts and the effect of the relevant documents.

14.8.4. *Example*

Where one house worth £100,000 is exchanged for another worth £80,000 plus £20,000 money, the conveyance for the transfer of the £100,000 house will normally say that the consideration for the transfer consists of the £80,000 house and the £20,000 money; and the conveyance will be stamped accordingly with duty on £100,000.

14.8.5.   On the conveyance of the £80,000 house, the Stamp Office charges duty by reference to the consideration expressed in the conveyance:

    (a)   where the conveyance provides that the consideration for the transfer of the cheaper property is the appropriate proportion of the value of the more expensive property, stamp duty is applied accordingly. Thus if the conveyance provides that the consideration for the £80,000 house is the appropriate proportion of the £100,000 house, the amount charged to duty on the transfer of the £80,000 house is limited to £80,000;

    (b)   more commonly the conveyance may say simply that the consideration for the transfer of the £80,000 house consists of the £100,000 house. In these circumstances, the Stamp Office will charge duty by reference to the value of the £100,000 house.

14.8.6. *Equality money*

In many cases, the wording of the conveyance of the cheaper property may not fully reflect the consideration expressed in the initial contract or agreement. Where it is clear from the contract that the intention of the parties to the transaction is that the cheaper property should be transferred for the more expensive property less the equality money, the Stamp Office will limit the charge to duty accordingly.

14.8.7.   For example, if the initial contract provided for an £80,000 house to be exchanged for a £100,000 house, and for £20,000 to be paid as equality money, the amount charged to duty on the transfer of the £80,000 property would be limited to £80,000.

14.8.8.   The result in an individual case will depend on the facts of the case and the relevant documents. The Stamp Office will need to see the relevant contract with the conveyance which is to be stamped.

14.8.9.   Where there is a multiple exchange of properties, an apportionment on similar lines may be made to determine how much of the consideration is attributable to each of the transfers. For example, two or more properties may be exchanged for one larger property, with or without a payment of equality money. Here again, the precise result will depend on the facts of each case.

14.8.10. *Application of £60,000 threshold*

Sales of property (other than shares) for a price not exceeding the £60,000 threshold are exempted from duty, provided that a 'certificate of value' is given stating that the transfer is not part of a larger transaction, or a series of transactions, for a total price of more than £60,000. The threshold is applied separately to each side of an exchange of properties.

14.8.11. *Sales*

In many cases, transactions which in the past have been structured and documented as exchanges could equally well be carried out as sales for a price which may be partly satisfied in kind.

14.8.12. For example, when a builder offers a property for sale, he may receive the price from the buyer in the form either of money, or partly of money and partly of the buyer's old house. Such a transaction can be carried out and documented (commencing with the initial contract) as a sale.

14.8.13. Stamp duty is charged on the consideration for the sale. So if, for example, the buyer is buying a new house for £100,000, and pays for it with £30,000 in cash plus his old house worth £70,000, duty of £1000 (1% of £100,000) would be charged on the transfer of the £100,000 house. The house which the builder accepts as part payment for the sale would not be regarded as a separate sale for stamp duty purposes. It would be charged only to the fixed duty of 50p. The threshold would not be of relevance to this transfer as it is not a conveyance on sale.

14.8.14. *General*

In cases of doubt about how a particular document of the types mentioned above would be treated by the Stamp Office for stamp duty purposes, the technical section, The Stamp Office, Ridgeworth House, Liverpool Gardens, Worthing BN11 1XP, will be willing to help.

14.9.   **Non-merger of freehold and leasehold interests**

14.9.1. Where the transaction comprises the purchase of an unmerged freehold and leasehold interest, and two purchase deeds are executed to transfer the respective estates in the land, the parties are entitled to decide which deed is the 'principal' instrument and that document will bear *ad valorem* stamp duty at the rates applicable to freehold land. A denoting stamp should be affixed to the other deed. This problem does not arise if a single transfer document is used, which is only suitable when both interests are either registered or registrable.

14.10.   **Sale and leaseback**

14.10.1. A sale and leaseback transaction is treated by the Inland Revenue as two separate transactions. The sale will attract *ad valorem* duty at the normal rates applicable to a transfer of freehold land, and the lease will bear the appropriate lease duty.

14.11. **Associated companies**

14.11.1. Some transfers of land between associated companies are eligible for relief from *ad valorem* stamp duty under the provisions of Finance Act 1930, s.42, as amended. This exception does not apply to the grant of a lease.

14.12. **Sub-sales**

14.12.1. See below, para. B.14.

14.13. **VAT**

14.13.1. Where the consideration for the property attracts VAT, stamp duty is payable on the whole of the consideration including the VAT element of the price.

14.13.2. Stamp duty itself does not attract a charge to VAT.

14.13.3. Where an election to waive the VAT exemption has already been exercised at the time of the transaction, stamp duty is chargeable on the purchase price premium or rent including VAT. Where, however, the election has not at that time been exercised VAT at the current rate is still to be included in any payments to which the election could still apply.[1]

1. See Inland Revenue Practice Statement 11/91, and VAT, para. A.16.

14.14. **New properties**

14.14.1. The Inland Revenue have issued a statement relating to stamp duty on new properties and building plots the text of which is set out in Appendix X.1.

14.15. **Transfers subject to a debt**

14.15.1. Where property is transferred subject to a debt (e.g. subject to an existing mortgage), the stamp duty on the debt element of the transaction is payable if the buyer expressly or impliedly undertakes an obligation to discharge the debt. If, however, the buyer passively accepts the property which is subject to the charge, no duty is payable.[1]

14.15.2. A transfer of mortgaged property between spouses may (in the absence of evidence to the contrary) be regarded as imposing on the transferee an obligation to discharge the outstanding mortgage, in which case the assumption of the debt will constitute the consideration for stamp duty purposes and the transaction is treated as a sale on which duty is payable and not as a gift. A transfer of the matrimonial home between spouses which arises out of a divorce or separation arrangement between them is usually treated by the Inland Revenue as being a transaction on which no duty is payable.[2]

1. Stamp Act 1891, s.57.
2. See Inland Revenue Statement of Practice 6/90.

14.16.   Property which is sold for unascertained price

14.16.1. Where property is sold for a price which cannot be ascertained or where a lease is granted at a premium which cannot be ascertained at the date of grant, stamp duty will be payable on the market value of the land interest transferred or lease granted immediately before the stampable document is executed. Where a lease is granted at an unascertainable rent, lease rental duty will be calculated by reference to the market rent at the time when the lease was executed.

FURTHER REFERENCE

Sergeant and Sims on Stamp Duties, Capital Duty and Stamp Duty Reserve Tax, B.J. Sims and J.F.W. Minson, Butterworths.

Stamp Duty for Conveyancers, R. Gregory, F.T. Law & Tax.

A.15. Capital gains tax

15.1. Liability to CGT

15.1.1. A liability to CGT may arise on the disposal of an interest in land. A seller's solicitor should be aware of the possibility of potential liability and advise his client accordingly. Similarly, a buyer who is purchasing property other than for use as his principal private dwelling should be made aware of potential tax liability which may be incurred in his subsequent disposal of the property.

15.1.2. The definition of 'chargeable assets' within Taxation of Chargeable Gains Tax Act 1992 includes an interest in the proceeds of sale of land held by co-owners. Thus a disposition by a beneficiary of his equitable interest in land could give rise to a charge to CGT.[1]

15.1.3. Some transactions which are incidental to the sale of land also give rise to a charge to CGT, e.g. where a separate payment is made for the release or modification of an easement or covenant.

15.1.4. For the purposes of the Act, a sale and leaseback transaction is technically treated as two separate disposals, but in practice the Inland Revenue may regard them as one, namely the part disposal of land by the seller of the freehold.

15.1.5. Subject to certain reliefs, gifts fall within the meaning of 'disposal'.

1. *Kidson* v. *Macdonald* [1974] Ch. 339.

15.2. The principal private dwelling house exemption

15.2.1. The disposal of an individual's principal private dwelling house (including grounds of up to 0.5 hectare) is exempt from CGT.[1]

15.2.2. To qualify for the exemption the seller must have lived in the dwelling house as his only or main residence throughout his period of ownership. A degree of permanence and expectation of continuity is required for the exemption to be claimable. A short period of residence (e.g. of a few months) may not qualify for relief.[2]

15.2.3. Certain periods of absence are disregarded when deciding the question of residence:[3]

(a) the last 36 months of ownership (in order to facilitate the purchase of another property);

(b) by extra-statutory concession, the first 12 months of ownership (in order to facilitate the sale of another property). If there are good reasons for this period exceeding one year, which are outside the individual's control, it will be extended up to a maximum of two years;

(c) any period(s) not exceeding three years in total throughout the period of ownership. Absence within this exception may be for any reason, e.g. an extended holiday and can be made up of several separate periods of absence provided that the total under this exception does not exceed three years;

(d) any period(s) during which the individual was working outside the U.K. This exception applies to employees only, not to self-employed persons;

(e) any period(s) not exceeding four years in total during which the individual was prevented from living in his dwelling house because he was required by his conditions of employment to live elsewhere. This exception would be applicable, e.g. to a headmaster who was required to live in accommodation provided by the school, or to an employee who was temporarily seconded to a branch office beyond commuting distance from his home.

15.2.4. The periods of absence outlined above are cumulative, and if exceeded a proportion of the exemption relative to the length of the absence in proportion to the length of ownership of the property will be lost and the non-exempt part chargeable to CGT.

15.2.5. Where a dwelling house has grounds of more than 0.5 hectare, the excess is prima facie taxable, but the Inland Revenue has a discretion to allow land in excess of 0.5 hectare to be included within the principal private dwelling house exemption if the extra land can be shown to be necessary for the reasonable enjoyment of the house.

15.2.6. The sale of land alone, where the ownership of the house is retained, enjoys the benefit of the exemption so long as the land sold does not exceed 0.5 hectare. It should be noted that if the house is sold and land retained, a subsequent sale of the land will usually attract CGT.

15.2.7. *Duality of user*

Where part of a principal private dwelling house is used for business purposes, e.g. a doctor who has a consulting room in his home, a proportion of the exemption may be lost, relative to the area of the 'business premises' in relation to the total area of the dwelling house. If, however, a 'duality of user' can be shown, the full exemption may be available. Thus a person who works from home, but who does not have a separate room for his business from which the other members of the family are prohibited from entering, may still take full advantage of the principal private dwelling house exemption.

15.2.8. Only one exemption is available to married couples. Where a married couple own more than one house an election must be made as to which property is to take the benefit of the exemption. An election in respect of one property is not irrevocable and can be switched, e.g. if it appears that one property is increasing in value at a faster rate than the other.

15.2.9. The principal private dwelling house exemption is available where the disposal is made by trustees provided that the person in occupation of the property was a person who was entitled to be in occupation under the terms of the settlement, e.g. a tenant for life.[4]

15.2.10. Tenants in common may be liable for CGT on their respective shares in the equitable interest in the property.

15.2.11. An individual who buys his dwelling house in the name of a company will not be able to claim the principal private dwelling house exemption.

1. Taxation of Chargeable Gains Act 1992, s.222.
2. *Goodwin* v. *Curtis, The Times,* 14 August 1996.
3. Taxation of Chargeable Gains Act 1992, s.223.
4. Taxation of Chargeable Gains Act 1992, s.28(1) and (2).

15.3.   **Chargeable gains**

15.3.1. Any gain which is chargeable on the disposal is subject to indexation allowances and the individual's current annual exemption. Over and above this, the gain is chargeable at the highest rate at which the individual pays income tax. Corporations pay CGT at the corporation tax rate applicable to them, subject to roll-over relief. Separate taxation is applied to married couples; each spouse therefore has his or her own annual allowance for CGT purposes.

15.3.2. *Guidelines*

When taking instructions from an individual in relation to the sale of a dwelling house, the answers to the following four questions will indicate to the solicitor whether there is likely to be a CGT liability on the property. If the client's answers to all the questions set out below match the suggested answers, there is unlikely to be a CGT liability arising out of the transaction. If any of the client's answers differ from those suggested, further enquiries should be raised with the client.

1. Question: Did you move into the house immediately after you bought it?
   Answer: Yes.

2. Question: Have you lived anywhere else since moving into this house?
   Answer: No.

3. Question: Is the garden bigger than 0.5 hectare?
   Answer: No.
   (The answer to this question may already be apparent from the estate agent's particulars of the property.)

4. Question: Do you own another house?
   Answer: No.

15.4. Business premises

15.4.1. Subject to certain reliefs, business premises are subject to CGT. The matter should be referred to the client's accountant for him to check the correct apportionment of the purchase price as between the property and any goodwill paid for the business.

15.5. Charities

15.5.1. Generally charities are exempt from CGT.

15.6. Time of disposal

15.6.1. The time of disposal of the property affects the year of assessment for the calculation of gains and losses for CGT purposes. A disposal of an interest in land is made at the time of the contract and not at the later time of completion.[1] However, no charge to tax arises unless the contract is completed, since until completion there will have been no disposal within the tax. Where a contract is conditional, the disposal is made at the time when the contract becomes unconditional.[2]

1. Taxation of Chargeable Gains Act 1992, s.28(1).
2. Taxation of Chargeable Gains Act 1992, s.28(2).

FURTHER REFERENCE

Whitehouse and Stuart-Buttle: Revenue Law — Principles and Practice, C. Whitehouse, Butterworths.

A.16. Value added tax

See also: Stamp duty and stamp duty savings, para. A.14.
Agricultural land, para. B.08.

16.1. VAT on property transactions

16.1.1. *The charge to tax*

Finance Act 1989 brought certain property transactions within the charge to VAT. Non-compliance with the legislation (where relevant) will involve the client in heavy penalties and interest payments, as well as unforeseen VAT liability. It is therefore essential that the relevance of VAT to a transaction is considered at an early stage and the client advised accordingly.

16.1.2. Generally VAT will not be of concern when dealing with residential conveyancing but may be relevant to both freehold and leasehold commercial property and to agricultural land. This chapter does not deal with problems associated with the self-supply of services.

16.1.3. *Summary checklist of application of VAT to property transactions*

Type of dealing	Rate of tax
A. Freehold sales	
Buildings designed as dwellings built or converted and sold by developer.	Zero.[1]
Communal residential buildings sold by developer.	Zero.[1]

Type of dealing	Rate of tax
A. Freehold sales	
Non-business charitable buildings sold by developer.	Zero.[1]
Domestic and other non-commercial buildings sold by others.	Exempt.
New commercial buildings.	Standard.[2]
Other commercial buildings.	Exempt subject to option.
B. Leases[3]	
New buildings or converted from non-residential buildings where dwellings, communal residential buildings or non-business charitable buildings if for more than 21 years where built by and granted by developer.	Zero on premium or first payment of rent.[1]
Similar to above but lease for 21 years or less	Exempt.
Domestic and non-commercial buildings granted by others.	Exempt.
New commercial buildings.	Exempt subject to option.
Other commercial buildings.	Exempt subject to option.
Assignments.	Exempt subject to option.
Surrenders.	Exempt subject to option.
Reverse surrenders	Exempt subject to option.
C. Listed buildings	
Approved alterations to dwellings, communal residential and non-business charitable buildings.	Zero.

Type of dealing	Rate of tax
C. Listed buildings	
Other work on similar buildings.	Standard.
Freehold sales by developer of substantially reconstructed similar buildings.	Zero.[1]
Leases for more than 21 years from developer of substantially reconstructed similar buildings.	Zero on premium or first payment of rent.[1]
Any works to commercial listed buildings.	Standard.
Sales and leases of substantially reconstructed commercial listed buildings.	Exempt subject to option.
D. Building land	
Sales and leases.	Exempt subject to option.
E. Refurbished buildings	
Sales and leases.	Exempt subject to option.
F. Conversions	
Freehold sale by developer of conversion from non-residential building into dwelling or communal residential building.	Zero.[1]
As above but grant of lease for over 21 years.	Zero.[1]
Construction services supplied to registered housing association on conversion of non-residential building into a dwelling or communal residential building.	Zero.

Type of dealing	Rate of tax
G. Building services	
Construction of new buildings designed as dwellings (including sub-contractors' services).	Zero.
Construction of communal residential and non-business charitable buildings (including sub-contractors' services) provided an appropriate certificate is obtained from the customer.	Zero.
Construction of new commercial buildings.	Standard.
Repairs and alterations.	Standard.
Demolition.	Standard.
Professional services.	Standard.
H. Civil engineering work	
New work.	Standard.
Repairs, maintenance and alteration of existing buildings.	Standard.
I. Options	
Option to undertake a transaction which itself is chargeable to VAT.	Standard on option fee.

1. Zero on first grant, subsequent sales exempt.
2. All freehold sales are taxable at standard rate while building remains 'new'.
3. In relation to leases, 'grant' includes assignment.

16.2.   Residential property

16.2.1.   The sale of an existing building (i.e. not new) which is used for a qualifying residential purpose is generally not affected by VAT.

16.2.2.   'Qualifying residential purposes' include premises which are used as a hospice; accommodation for the armed forces; a children's home; an old people's home; and the accommodation element of a residential school.

16.2.3. Supply of construction work

The construction or development of new residential property is zero-rated. A garage built at the same time as the dwelling will usually also benefit from zero-rating. Services supplied to a registered housing association for the conversion of a non-residential building are also zero-rated.

16.2.4. Time share, holiday, and other accommodation with restrictions on its use does not fall within the zero-rated category.

16.2.5. A residential developer, building new houses and flats for sale, will be able to recover his input tax (e.g. on agents, solicitors, architects and other professional fees) since the sale of a major interest in his property to a private buyer will be zero-rated. The buyer pays no VAT on his purchase.

16.2.6. Subsequent sales by private individuals will be exempt from VAT.

16.2.7. Owners of residential accommodation who did not construct the building in question, and who subsequently sell the building in the course of a business, will be making an exempt supply with no right to opt to tax.

16.2.8. Change of use

If the use of a building designed as a dwelling is subsequently changed to a non-residential use, this has no immediate VAT consequences. If, however, the use of a building intended for a qualifying residential purpose as defined above (i.e. a communal residential building) or relevant charitable (non-business) use is changed to a non-residential or non-charitable use within 10 years of its construction, a charge to VAT at the standard rate arises in order to claw back the charge which would have arisen if there had not initially been a qualifying residential or charitable use.

16.3. Mixed developments

16.3.1. Where only part of a building qualifies for zero-rating, e.g. a shop with a residential flat above, the non-zero-rated element of the building (in the example given, the shop) will either be exempt or standard rated. The proceeds received from the development must be apportioned between the two differently rated parts of the building on a fair and equitable basis. It is unclear how the apportionment of common areas of the building, e.g. foundations and roof, is to be made. As a precaution the client should be advised to seek clearance from HM Customs and Excise before development is commenced.

16.4. Land

16.4.1. The sale of a freehold interest in land (without buildings or civil engineering works on it), grant of a lease, or of a licence is generally exempt from VAT, subject to the right in most cases (except outright sales of freeholds in new buildings or civil engineering works) to exercise the option to tax. The grant of sporting rights over land, mineral rights, or the right to fell and remove standing timber and certain other freehold supplies listed in Item 1, Group 1, Schedule 9 VATA 1994 attract VAT at the standard rate.

16.5. Commercial property

16.5.1. The freehold sale of a new building is standard rated. Other dealings with commercial property are exempt subject to the option to tax. If the option to tax has been exercised and notified to Customs within 30 days or if the property is a new freehold to which the compulsory standard rate charge applies, the sale of a let property by a VAT-registered seller to a VAT-registered buyer who elects to waive the VAT exemption for the property may be treated as the sale of a business as a going concern so that VAT will not be chargeable. The election must be made by the buyer and HM Customs and Excise notified before completion of the transaction. If clearance is disallowed the seller has to account for the VAT which he should have charged on the transaction. Unless clearance is obtained before completion, it is therefore advisable for the contract to provide for a sum equivalent to the VAT payable to be placed in a joint deposit account to cover the position.

16.6. Freehold sales of new commercial buildings

16.6.1. Every freehold sale of a new commercial property (including civil engineering works) before it is completed and within the first three years after its completion attracts VAT at standard rate.

16.6.2. 'Completion' of the building is either the date of the architect's certificate of practical completion or the date when the building was first fully occupied, whichever first occurs.

16.6.3. The buyer of such a building must therefore raise additional enquiries of the seller to ascertain whether the transaction (and any subsequent disposal of the building by the buyer) will attract VAT and the parties must agree on the contractual provisions which are to be inserted relating to the payment of VAT.

16.6.4. *Guidelines*

    (a) Matters to be considered on taking instructions:

        (i) will the sale be a standard rated supply so that VAT will be chargeable?

        (ii) if not, what evidence (if any) is needed to satisfy Customs and Excise that the sale will be an exempt or zero-rated supply or a transfer of a going concern?

    (b) Additional enquiries:

[If the contract requires the buyer to pay VAT he will want to be certain that VAT is chargeable and will also wish to have evidence to establish whether or not there is a mandatory charge to VAT on a subsequent sale. If the contract does not require the buyer to pay VAT he may be inclined not to raise the issue with the seller, but he should still ensure that the supply is in fact an exempt supply and that he has sufficient evidence to establish that a future sale by him will be exempt.]

(i) why does the seller consider that the sale is a standard-rated supply?

(ii) please provide a copy of the architect's certificate of practical completion;

(iii) when was the building first fully occupied?

(iv) what evidence is available to verify the date when the building was first fully occupied?

(v) please confirm that if VAT is paid on completion the seller will at that time deliver a VAT invoice to the buyer;

(vi) has the seller previously elected to waive his exemption from VAT or does he intend to do so before completion?

(vii) if the answer to question (vi) is 'yes', please confirm that the exercise of the option to tax has been or will be notified to Customs within 30 days of its being made. The buyer's solicitor should request a copy of the option to tax document (if any) and of the letter of notification to ascertain the extent of the land to which the option will apply and to check that it is valid.

[Note that if the seller agrees not to charge VAT, the contract should either specify that the price stated is inclusive of any VAT or should expressly provide that the seller has not elected to waive the VAT exemption in respect of the property and agrees not to do so.]

(c) The deposit:

If the seller's solicitor receives the deposit in the capacity of 'agent for the seller', a VAT tax point arises on exchange of contracts in relation to the amount of the deposit. If the deposit is held as 'stakeholder' the tax point for both the deposit and the balance of the purchase price will not arise until completion.

16.6.5. A special condition on the printed version of the Standard Conditions of Sale Form provides that the sale is exclusive of VAT.

16.7. Commercial leases

16.7.1. Commercial leases are normally treated as giving rise to exempt supplies by the landlord to the tenant, and no VAT will be payable on the premium or rent unless the landlord has exercised his option to waive the VAT exemption in respect of the building on or before completion or before rent is paid (or invoiced if earlier). If the landlord exercises that option, he must account to HM Customs and Excise for VAT on the rent from all tenants of the building whether or not he obtains that VAT from the tenant. The landlord will normally want the tenant to pay the VAT, but whether the tenant will be liable to do so depends upon the date and wording of the lease. If the landlord makes the election after the grant of the lease, he can compel the tenant to pay VAT in addition to the rent unless there is anything in the lease to the contrary (and for this purpose a contrary provision must expressly refer to VAT; a general reference to the tenant not being liable to pay for tax on rent will not preclude the landlord from holding the tenant liable to pay the VAT).[1] Conversely, where a lease is granted after the landlord has elected to waive the VAT exemption for the building, the rent specified in the lease will be inclusive of VAT unless the lease states otherwise.[2] If the landlord exercises his option to tax during the term of a lease which expressly exonerates the tenant from paying VAT, or exercises his option and then grants a lease which is silent as to VAT, the landlord will have to account to HM Customs and Excise for VAT as if the rent payable by the tenant was inclusive of VAT, i.e. seven forty-sevenths of the rent will be regarded as VAT.

16.7.2. Any lease which might be subject to VAT should contain a covenant by the tenant to pay to the landlord any VAT chargeable on the rent or on any payment made under the lease in addition to the rent. The clause should also provide that in any situation where the tenant is required by the lease to reimburse the landlord for expenditure incurred by the landlord, e.g. for insurance premiums or service charge, the tenant should also reimburse any VAT paid by the landlord in respect of those payments unless VAT on those payments is recoverable by the landlord. Generally service charge follows the rent, i.e. if the rent is standard rated, so is the service charge.

16.7.3. Where in a lease a landlord has covenanted not to elect for VAT during the currency of the lease, that covenant, being personal in nature, may not be binding on a subsequent purchaser of the reversion unless a direct covenant has been entered into by that purchaser. It is therefore safer for the tenant to negotiate a lease which includes a covenant given by the landlord that he will undertake to obtain a non-opting covenant from any buyer.

16.7.4. *Exempt tenants*

If the tenant of a lease makes exempt supplies he will be seriously disadvantaged by having to pay VAT on his rent (since he will not be able to recover some or all of that VAT). An exempt tenant in a market dominated by taxable tenants should consider taking a valuer's advice about the consequences of the VAT implications in his lease.

16.7.5. *Guidelines*

(a) Options checklist for landlords:

Consider:

(i) how much irrecoverable VAT has/does the landlord incur?

(ii) the VAT status of tenants/potential tenants/purchasers;

(iii) the short- and long-term consequences of exercising an option which is only revocable in limited circumstances (generally after 20 years);

(iv) the consequences of agreeing a premium rent with an exempt tenant;

(v) the costs of any additional administration which would be incurred in collecting VAT and issuing VAT invoices;

(b) Reminders for tenants:

(i) check whether or not VAT is included in the rent;

(ii) remember that if the lease is silent section 89 could apply;

(iii) if the tenant makes taxable supplies only, the main adverse consequence of paying VAT on his rent may be a cash flow disadvantage, set against which there may also be cash benefits for the tenant, e.g. the recovery of VAT on his service charge payments;

(iv) if the tenant makes exempt or mainly exempt supplies he may be seriously disadvantaged by having to pay VAT on his rent since he will not be able to recover some or all of that VAT.

16.7.6. *Purchases subject to leases*

The leases to which the property is subject should be checked to discover whether the buyer will be able to charge VAT should he wish to exercise his option to tax. The following matters should also be considered:

(a) does the lease expressly provide that VAT is payable in addition to rent and other payments made or consideration given by the tenant or if not will section 89 apply?

(b) will the landlord be able to recover from the tenant VAT on supplies received from a third party? or

(c) is the landlord under an obligation to attempt to recover VAT from HM Customs and Excise before he can look to the tenant for indemnity?

(d) are all other sums referred to in the lease expressed to include any VAT which will be chargeable?

(e) are the rent review provisions adequate if the landlord decides to elect to tax?

1. Value Added Tax Act 1994, s.89.
2. Value Added Tax Act 1994, s.10.

16.8. The option to tax

16.8.1. Where a dealing with a building or land is exempt from VAT the seller or landlord normally has the right to elect to waive the VAT exemption for the building, with a result that VAT will be chargeable both on the rents received from lettings and on the proceeds of any sale.[1]

16.8.2. The option to tax relates to the landlord's interest in an entire building. Thus a landlord who owns a whole office block must elect to tax all his tenants or none of them. Buildings consisting of a number of units under one roof or which are linked by covered walkways are treated as one building as are complexes consisting of a number of units grouped around or fully enclosed concourse.

16.8.3. An option cannot be exercised retrospectively. When ownership of the building changes hands, the new owner can make his own election to tax. A transfer by one company to a subsidiary or holding company will be a change of ownership giving rise to a fresh election to tax so long as the transferee company is not in the same VAT group as the transferor. Normally such a transfer would have to be at the market price, that price being subject to VAT, so that the VAT on the purchase would be irrecoverable by the transferee if it did not itself make the election unless the transferee was occupying the building for the purposes of its taxable business.

16.8.4. An election which is under three months or over 20 years old can be revoked upon application to HM Customs and Excise. If the election is under three months old, no output VAT must have arisen, no input VAT must have been reclaimed and no 'transfer of a going concern' treatment applied to the land in question.

16.8.5. A buyer who has had to pay VAT on his purchase may wish to charge VAT on a letting or a subsequent disposition of the property by him in order to recover the VAT which he incurred on his purchase. VAT incurred before the date of election is irrecoverable (except with the consent of HM Customs and Excise) unless no exempt supplies have been made in the meantime; thus the buyer's election to tax must normally be made before completion, particularly where the building is bought subject to existing tenancies. Similar considerations apply to developers who have incurred substantial input tax as a result of construction work on the building.

16.8.6. Exempt or partially exempt tenants, e.g. those whose business is in the financial sector, banks, building societies, etc., will be reluctant to pay VAT on their rent because they cannot usually recover the tax in full.

16.8.7. Persons who wish to make an election may need to seek permission from Customs *before* they elect when the land or buildings concerned have *already* been the subject of an exempt supply by them, usually an exempt letting. If Customs are satisfied that there would be a 'fair and reasonable' attribution of input tax between the exempt supplies already made and the taxable supplies to be made following the election, the person will be authorised to waive exemption on the land or buildings from a current date. Alternatively, prior consent is not needed provided the conditions for automatic consent published by HM Customs and Excise are met. Under the capital goods scheme, recovery of some of the VAT incurred on the land or buildings may then follow by means of annual adjustments and, usually, a 10-year period beginning with the time the VAT was incurred. No input tax incurred before 1 August 1989 can be recovered by election under any circumstances.

16.8.8. *Finance Act 1997*

An important change has been made to the option to tax regime by Finance Act 1997. This change is intended to counter tax avoidance in this area but it can catch 'innocent' transactions. The provisions are complex and can only be summarised below. If it appears that a transaction may be caught by the provisions reference to the detail of the legislation is essential and specialist advice may be necessary. The disapplication of the option to tax could have serious effects on the viability of a development as it may result in the input tax incurred on the project being forfeited.

16.8.9. With effect from 19 March 1997 (subject to certain transitional provisions — see below) paragraph 2(3AA) of Schedule 10 VATA 1994 provides that the option to tax will not apply in situations where:

(a) an interest in, or work carried out to, property is a capital item in respect of which the input tax incurred is subject to adjustment under the capital goods scheme (see below); and

(b) the owner makes a grant in relation to the property; and

(c) at the time of the grant, it was the intention or expectation of either:

(i) the owner; or

(ii) a person funding his acquisition of the property, with a view to either of them or a person connected with either of them occupying it for ineligible purposes,

that the land would be occupied for ineligible purposes by a person falling within either (i) or (ii) above or a person connected to either of (i) or (ii) above during the capital goods scheme adjustment period applicable to it.

16.8.10. A person occupies for ineligible purposes if he is not a taxable person or, if he is a taxable person, he occupies the property other than mainly for business purposes in making supplies such that any input tax of his which was wholly attributable to those supplies would be input tax for which he would be entitled to a credit.

16.8.11. Occupation of land by a body to which section 33 applies (local authorities and various other statutory bodies) is occupation of the land for eligible purposes to the extent that the body occupies the land other than for the purposes of a business. Occupation of land by a Government department (within the meaning of VATA 1994, s.41) is also occupation of the land for eligible purposes.

16.8.12. 'Funding the acquisition of the property' includes all the following:

(a) directly or indirectly providing funds for meeting the whole or any part of the cost of the grantor's acquisition of the land or building which is a capital item;

(b) directly or indirectly procuring the provision of such funds by another;

(c) directly or indirectly providing funds for discharging, in whole or in part, any liability that has been or may be incurred by any person for or in connection with the raising of funds to meet the cost of the grantor's acquisition of the land or building which is a capital item;

(d) directly or indirectly procuring that any such liability is or will be discharged, in whole or in part, by another.[2]

16.8.13. References to the provision of funds for a purpose referred to in paragraph 3A(4) include:

(a) the making of a loan of funds that are or are to be used for that purpose;

(b) the provision of any guarantee or other security in relation to such a loan;

(c) the provision of any of the consideration for the issue of any shares or other securities issued wholly or partly for raising those funds; or

(d) any other transfer of assets or value as a consequence of which any of those funds are made available for that purpose.[3]

16.8.14. Transitional provisions

The new rules apply to supplies made on or after 19 March 1997 unless the supply arises from a 'relevant pre-commencement grant'.

16.8.15. A 'relevant pre-commencement grant' is a grant which was either made before 26 November 1996; or made after 26 November 1996 but before 30 November 1999 in pursuance of an agreement in writing entered into before 26 November 1996 on terms fixed in that agreement.

16.8.16. Capital goods scheme

The following money assets are capital items for the purposes of the scheme:

(a) land or a building or part of a building where the value of the interest supplied to the owner, by a taxable supply other than a zero-rated supply, is £250,000 or more (excluding any part of that value consisting of rent);

(b) a building or part of a building where the owner's interest in, right over or licence to occupy it is treated as self-supplied to him. The value of the supply must be £250,000 or more.

(c) a building not falling, or capable of falling, within (b) above constructed by the owner and first brought into use by him after 31 March 1990 where the aggregate of:

   (i) the value of taxable grants relating to the land on which the building is constructed made to the owner after that date, and

(ii) the value of all the taxable supplies of goods and services, other than any that are zero-rated, made or to be made to him for, or in connection with, the construction of the building after that date

is £250,000 or more;

(d) a building which the owner alters, or an extension or an annex which he constructs, where additional floor area is created in the altered building, extension or annex, of 10% or more of the original floor area before the work was carried out. The value of all taxable supplies of goods and services, other than any that are zero-rated, made or to be made to the owner after 31 March 1990 for, or in connection with, the alteration, etc., must be £250,000 or more.

1. See above, para. 16.5.1.
2. VATA 1994, Sched. 10, para. 3A(4).
3. VATA 1994, Sched. 10, para. 3A(5).

16.9.   Surrenders

16.9.1.   Surrenders in the course of a business are exempt from mandatory VAT. They may be taxable if the tenant has exercised his option to tax in respect of his leasehold interest.[1]

16.9.2.   If the tenant has exercised his option to tax in respect of his leasehold interest, and if the landlord is paying the tenant for the surrender, the tenant is making a supply of an interest in the land. Where the consideration for the surrender is other than in money VAT is payable on the value of the interest surrendered. Thus if the landlord in return for the surrender grants a long lease to the tenant, VAT is payable on the value of the surrendered lease, but a precise value may be difficult to assess. If a proposal involves a surrender by operation of law, liability to VAT should be agreed in writing before the surrender is made.

16.9.3.   In cases where the tenant has exercised his option to tax, a variation of his lease may be regarded as the surrender of this lease and the grant of another in its place. HM Customs and Excise have agreed the following Statement of Practice in relation to the variation of leases:

(a) Where there is no monetary consideration passing between landlord and tenant as a result of or in connection with the variation, HM Customs and Excise will accept that there is no surrender of the old lease for monetary consideration when:

(i)   the new lease is for the same building (or the same part of the building) but the new lease is for an extended term; or

(ii) the new lease is for a larger part of the same building than the old lease but the term is for the same or an extended term; or

(iii) the new lease is for the same land and for an extended term.

However, (i)–(iii) above do not embrace 'new for old' ground leases or building leases, i.e. leases granted on condition that the tenant will undertake development.

(b) Where there is a monetary consideration which passes between landlord and tenant, HM Customs and Excise would normally regard the monetary consideration as the sole consideration for the surrender but they would reserve the right to look at the terms of the new lease to ensure that they were not significantly more favourable than would have been expected for a tenant with no existing lease to surrender. The possibility of the surrender being for a consideration partly in money and partly in the form of the grant of the new lease has to be retained; open market valuation then comes into play. In cases of doubt, the position should be checked with HM Customs and Excise.

(c) Where there is a monetary consideration which passes to the landlord from the tenant, HM Customs and Excise would normally see this as consideration for the grant of the new lease which would be exempt subject to the landlord's election to waive exemption (option to tax) except where the circumstances indicate that it is consideration for the landlord's taxable supply of the acceptance of the surrender of an onerous lease from the tenant, sometimes known as a 'reverse surrender'. When the payment received by the landlord is seen as consideration for the grant of a new lease, there would be no surrender by the tenant.

16.9.4. Para. (c) of the above Statement of Practice may need revising following the *Lubbock Fine* decision, which on one view also exempts consideration passing from the tenant to the landlord (referred to above as a 'reverse surrender') although HM Customs and Excise do not yet accept that view.

1. *Lubbock Fine & Co.* v. *Commissioners of Customs and Excise* (Case C −63/92) [1994] S.T.C. 101.

16.10. Charities

16.10.1. The sale of a major interest in a building which is constructed or converted from non-residential use for use for a 'relevant charitable purpose' is zero-rated. Where the charity is using the premises for the purpose of a business carried on by it (e.g. a shop run by the charity where goods are sold to the public), the rules for commercial property apply as this is not a use for a relevant charitable purpose.

16.11. Conversions

16.11.1. The cost of reconstruction, alteration or enlargement of an existing building attracts VAT at the standard rate. However, the sale by a developer of a major interest in a building which has been converted to a dwelling or for residential use from a non-residential building is zero rated. A 'major' interest is a freehold sale or the grant of a lease for over 21 years.

16.12. Listed buildings

16.12.1. The reconstruction of a listed building for housing or other qualifying purposes may be zero rated. Other alterations to listed buildings attract VAT at standard rate.

16.13. Agricultural land

16.13.1. The option to tax applies to agricultural land in a broadly similar way to other kinds of land. Marshland and moorland which is used for grants of sporting rights comes within the definition of agricultural land in this context. Agricultural dwelling houses are exempt and no option to tax can be exercised in respect of them, but an apportionment of their value will have to be made where they are part of a sale of agricultural land.

16.14. Transitional provisions

16.14.1. Transitional provisions apply to transactions entered into pursuant to a legally binding obligation incurred before 21 June 1988.

FURTHER REFERENCE

Tolley's VAT on Construction Land and Property, A. Buckett, Tolley.

VAT and Property, H. Scott and D. McLellan, Butterworths.

A.17. Tax relief on mortgages

17.1. Introduction

17.1.1. The legal owner of a house is entitled to tax relief on the interest element of his mortgage repayments in certain circumstances. A buyer client should be advised about his entitlement to relief when taking instructions or when considering the terms of the client's mortgage offer.

17.1.2. Relief is only available to the legal owner, i.e. the person named in the title deeds. Therefore if, e.g. a husband transfers the ownership of the matrimonial home to his ex-wife as part of a divorce settlement, but continues to make repayments under the mortgage, he will not be able to claim tax relief on his payments as he will no longer be the legal owner of the house.

17.2. Conditions attached to relief

17.2.1. The mortgage must have been taken out in connection with the purchase by an individual of his only or main residence. Subject to this, an individual who owns more than one house may elect which one should be eligible for tax relief. A company cannot occupy a house as its 'residence'; thus no tax relief is available where an individual's home is purchased through the medium of a company.

17.2.2. Where an individual owns more than one dwelling house and has mortgages on both or all of them, he can only claim relief in respect of one house. This rule applies also to married couples who are only allowed one amount of mortgage tax relief between them and to unmarried co-owners who are only entitled to one amount of relief which will be split between them in relation to their proportionate interests in the property. Where an unmarried couple own two properties, however, each can claim full tax relief in respect of one property.

17.2.3. The maximum principal sum on which mortgage relief can be claimed is £30,000. Where the principal sum under the mortgage exceeds this sum, relief is available in respect of the first £30,000 only. Relief is available on more than one mortgage of the individual's private dwelling house provided that the loans were taken out in connection with the purchase of the property and the total sums for which relief is claimed do not exceed £30,000. Thus if an individual took out two mortgages to purchase his house, the first for £25,000, the second for £10,000, relief would be available on the interest elements of the whole of the first mortgage but only £5,000 of the second mortgage would qualify for relief.

17.2.4. Relief is available on the interest element of the mortgage repayments up to the normal commercial rates being charged for such loans. The normal commercial rate is judged by the rates prevailing on loans obtained from major lending institutions, e.g. banks and building societies. If, e.g. a borrower was paying interest at 20% on his mortgage, in circumstances where the normal commercial rate for such a loan would be judged to be 15%, tax relief would only be available on that part of the mortgage repayments which represented a repayment at a rate of 15%, the excess attracting no relief. Where an individual pays an exceptionally low rate of interest on his mortgage, e.g. he obtains a mortgage from his employer at 4% where the normal commercial rate is 15%, the difference between the actual rate being paid (4%) and the normal rate (15%) may be treated as a benefit in kind in the hands of the employee and may be taxed under Schedule E.

17.2.5. Relief is available at 15% only.

17.2.6. The principles relating to tax relief on mortgages apply equally to repayment and endowment mortgages. A self-employed individual who takes out a pension mortgage may be entitled to additional tax relief in respect of his pension contributions.

17.3. Claiming relief

17.3.1. The instructions received from the lender in connection with the grant of the mortgage will normally explain how tax relief on the mortgage is to be dealt with and the buyer's solicitor should ensure that his client understands his entitlement to relief and how that relief is obtained.

17.3.2. Where the mortgage is granted by a major institutional lender, e.g. building society or clearing bank, relief is usually dealt with under the MIRAS system. Under this system mortgage interest relief is given at source; thus the individual makes his monthly repayments to the lender net of basic rate tax, and the lender will recoup the balance direct from the government.

17.3.3. If the lender does not operate the MIRAS system, the individual makes full monthly repayments to the lender and is granted his tax relief either through coding under Schedule E (employed persons) or through an allowance on his Schedule D assessment (self-employed persons).

17.3.4. Where a married couple jointly own a house the Inland Revenue will divide the tax relief equally between the couple unless specifically asked to do otherwise.

17.4. Bridging loans

17.4.1. A bridging loan which is taken out for the purchase of land (whether just for the deposit or for the full purchase price) is eligible for tax relief on the interest element of the loan (not including any arrangement fee). The loan must not normally exceed 12 months in duration, but by concession the Inland Revenue may extend this period in justified circumstances. Relief on bridging loans is not dealt with under MIRAS and must be specifically claimed by the taxpayer. No relief is available where the loan is extended by way of overdraft on a current account. The rate of interest payable on a loan taken on overdraft may be less than that chargeable on a separate bridging loan and the client must balance the advantages of paying a lower rate of interest against the benefit of receiving tax relief on a bridging loan, bearing in mind that in calculating the cost of the bridging loan, account must also be taken of the arrangement fee on which no tax relief is available.

17.5. **Business premises**

17.5.1. Tax relief on the principles outlined above applies only in respect of an individual's sole or main residence.

17.5.2. Where a loan is taken out in respect of the purchase or improvement of business premises that loan may qualify as an allowable expense of the business for tax purposes and thus some element of tax relief will be obtained against an individual's income tax liability or a company's corporation tax liability.

17.6. **Companies**

17.6.1. A company which takes out a loan for the purchase or improvement of business premises may obtain corporation tax relief on the interest element of the loan provided it is an allowable business expense.

A.18. Transfers on breakdown of marriage

See also: Stamp duty and stamp duty savings, para. A.14.
Capital gains tax, para. A.15.
Tax relief on mortgages, para. A.17.
Pre-contract searches and enquiries, para. B.10.

18.1. Introduction

18.1.1. Special considerations apply to the transfer of property between husband and wife on the breakdown of a marriage. This chapter does not deal with giving advice on the terms of the settlement between husband and wife, only on its implementation.

18.1.2. Conflict of interests

Even in cases where the settlement is amicable and is not made pursuant to a court order in matrimonial proceedings, the parties must be independently advised because of the inevitable risk of conflict of interests which arises in this situation.

18.2. Acting for the transferor

18.2.1. Mortgages

The solicitor acting for the transferor should ascertain the extent of existing mortgages over the property to be transferred. It must be decided whether the property is to be transferred free of the mortgage to the other spouse, and if so, whether the transferring spouse will redeem the mortgage or will continue to make repayments. If the property is to be transferred free of the mortgage, steps must be taken to discharge those charges before completion of the transfer. This may involve advising the transferor about refinancing and taking a new loan secured over another property in order to discharge his indebtedness over the property to be transferred. The lender's consent to the transfer will be required if either the mortgage deed requires it or if the borrower—spouse is to be released from his or her covenant under the mortgage. The borrower's continuing liability under the mortgage may affect his or her ability to obtain another loan on a different property. Arrangements must be made for the continuation of payments under the mortgage. Any life policy taken out in connection with an existing mortgage should be checked to ascertain the name(s) of the person(s) insured under the policy. If the property is to be transferred free of the mortgage to which the policy related, a re-assignment of the policy should be effected on discharge of the mortgage. If the benefit of the policy is to be transferred, the consent of the lender should be obtained and the insurance company notified of the change. The transfer of the benefit of the policy may attract CGT liability.

18.2.2. Outstanding discount on purchased local authority housing

A disposal of property which had been bought from a local authority under the provisions of Housing Act 1985, Pt. V made in pursuance of an order under Matrimonial Causes Act 1973, s.24 does not trigger the repayment of discount provisions under the Housing Act 1985.[1] Thus no discount is repayable where the property is transferred under a court order for the transfer or a property adjustment order made under section 24. Where the court order is for the sale of the property under Matrimonial Causes Act 1973, s.24A a proportion of the discount may be repayable if the property is sold within three years after its purchase from the local authority.

18.2.3. Tax relief on mortgages

Income tax relief on the interest element of the mortgage repayments is only available to the legal owner of the property. If the transferor is to continue to make mortgage repayments after the transfer of the legal ownership to the other spouse, the transferor will lose his or her right to tax relief. An adjustment in maintenance payments to the other spouse may be required to reflect the loss of the transferor's tax relief. Where the property is secured by a pension mortgage, specialist advice about the consequences of the transfer should be obtained.

1. Housing Act 1985, s.160(1)(*c*).

18.3. Acting for the transferee

18.3.1. The transferee's solicitor should undertake the normal pre-contract searches and enquiries to ensure that no adverse entries exist which might adversely affect the property or its value.

18.3.2. Any charge which had been registered to protect the spouse's rights of occupation under Family Law Act 1996 ceases to be effective on issue of a divorce decree absolute.

18.3.3. In appropriate cases advice should be given in relation to raising finance to purchase the share in the property to be transferred.

18.3.4. If the property is to be transferred subject to an existing mortgage, the lender's consent to the transfer must be obtained if the borrower is to be released from the covenant and/or if the mortgage so requires and arrangements made for the continuance of payments under the mortgage. If the benefit of a life policy is to be transferred, notice of the transfer must be given to the insurance company after completion.

18.3.5. Where the transferred property is mortgaged, consideration should be given to the protection of the mortgage by either an endowment policy or a mortgage protection policy. A lender may also insist that a policy to insure against the transferor's subsequent insolvency is acquired.

18.3.6. Transfers made in connection with divorce settlements do not attract stamp duty on the purchase deed provided that the requirements of Stamp Duty (Exempt Instruments) Regulations 1987 are met.

18.3.7. A transfer of land between spouses for which 'value' is not given, that is, full consideration or something like it, in some form may be set aside by the court, under Insolvency Act 1986, ss.339-342 at the request of the trustee in bankruptcy if the transferring spouse becomes bankrupt within five years of the transfer. The solvency of the transferring spouse at the time of the transfer may be a material factor in the decision whether the transfer can or should be set aside, so the transferee spouse may want to get a declaration of solvency from the transferor at the time when the transfer is made. The transferee might also want to consider the possibility of insuring against the risk of the transferor's becoming bankrupt within five years. Should the transferee want to mortgage or sell the property within five years, this should not cause difficulties because of the amendments made to the 1986 Act by Insolvency (No.2) Act 1994 – see para. D.2.10.4.

18.4. Legal aid

18.4.1. The cost of conveyancing work necessary to give effect to the terms of a court order will usually be covered by the client's legal aid certificate. This applies equally to consent orders and the work which is undertaken to implement such orders.[1]

1. See *S* v. *S. (Legal Aid Taxation)* [1991] Fam. Law 271; *Copeland* v. *Houlton* [1955] 3 All E.R. 178.

A.19. The National Protocol ('TransAction')

19.1. Aim of the Protocol

19.1.1. The Protocol for domestic conveyancing was introduced in March 1990 in an attempt to standardise and streamline the procedures involved in domestic transactions.

19.2. Domestic transactions

19.2.1. Solicitors are recommended to use the Protocol in domestic transactions and should agree with the other party's solicitor at the outset of each transaction whether or not the Protocol will be used in that transaction.

19.2.2. Developers

Not all of the Protocol procedures will be appropriate for use when a developer is selling individual houses on an estate but, as far as possible, developers who have chosen to use the Protocol should adhere to the Protocol procedures, having notified the buyer's solicitors of any changes which have been made.

19.2.3. Local authority transactions

The Law Society's Local Government Group recommends that a local authority which is selling property should consider whether or not the transaction is one where it is appropriate to use the Protocol in whole or in part. In cases where the authority dispenses with a formal contract of sale use of the Protocol may not be appropriate.

19.3. Departure from the Protocol

19.3.1. If the Protocol is not being used in a residential transaction, or is to be substantially varied, the solicitor who intends to depart from the Protocol must inform the solicitor acting for the other party of this fact at the earliest opportunity. For the avoidance of doubt, variations to the Protocol should be recorded in writing between the parties. A departure from the Protocol when it has been agreed that it should be used in the transaction, or a failure to notify the other party of a departure from the Protocol, may be professional misconduct.

19.4. Standard Conditions of Sale

19.4.1. The Standard Conditions of Sale will be used to form the basis of the contract of sale in transactions which are regulated by the Protocol. The drafting of the Standard Conditions reflects the requirements of the Protocol, and thus an amendment to the Standard Conditions may itself be a departure from the Protocol which will need to be notified to the other party.

19.5. Disclosure of related transactions

19.5.1. When a solicitor is instructed to buy or sell a residential property on behalf of his client he will explain the use of the Protocol to the client and will discuss with him the advantages and disadvantages of disclosing information to the other party about the progress of any related sale or purchase transaction. Disclosure of such information may be helpful to the other party but might not be helpful to the solicitor's own client if, e.g. the client was experiencing difficulties in selling his own property. Disclosure of information about related transactions can only be made with the client's consent, and the client's refusal to give such consent is not deemed to be a departure from the Protocol.

19.6. Non-solicitors

19.6.1. *Licensed conveyancers*

Where it is in the interests of a client that the Protocol procedures are followed, a licensed conveyancer acting for the other party should be invited to adopt them. Licensed conveyancers are to be regarded in the same light as solicitors; it is therefore possible to rely on a licensed conveyancer's agreement to use the Protocol in a transaction.

19.6.2. *Unqualified persons*

There is no reason why an unqualified person should not agree to comply with the Protocol procedures and use the related standard forms in the course of a transaction but no sanction would lie against such a person who departed from the

Protocol. Not all of the standard forms are available to unqualified persons. Since undertakings cannot be accepted from unqualified persons it follows that an exchange of contracts using the Law Society formulae and completion using the Code for Completion by Post (both required under the Protocol) cannot be used when dealing with an unqualified person.[1]

1. See Dealing with non-solicitors, para. A.05.

19.7. Text of the Protocol

19.7.1. The full text of the Protocol (and accompanying Council statement) is set out in Appendix IV, and the procedures referred to in the Protocol are dealt with in context in other sections of this book.

19.8. Use of forms

19.8.1. Where the Protocol is used the Standard Conditions of Sale should be used to form the basis of the agreement between the parties. While the Standard Agreement for Sale may be reproduced on a solicitor's word processor, the text of the Conditions themselves, for copyright reasons, may not.[1]

19.8.2. Pre-contract enquiries under the Protocol are conducted using the Seller's Property Information Form; Part I of which (to be completed by the client) is subject to copyright and may not be reproduced on a solicitor's word processor. Part II of the form (to be completed by the solicitor) may be reproduced as may the Fixtures, Fittings and Contents Form and the Completion Information and Requisitions on Title Form.

19.8.3. Any form which is reproduced under the general licence outlined above, which applies to solicitors only, must be presented in a format as close as possible to the original form with no textual alterations and must state in a prominent position 'This form is part of the Law Society's TransAction Scheme'. The forms may not be photocopied except for the purpose of taking a file copy.

1. See para. B.26.1.1.

A.20. Interest on clients' money

20.1. Solicitors' Accounts Rules 1991

20.1.1. A solicitor who holds money on behalf of a client may be required to pay the client interest on the money he is holding. The circumstances when the client is entitled to interest and the amount of that interest are governed by Solicitors' Accounts Rules 1991, a summary of which is set out below. The text of Part III of the Rules appears in Appendix I.2.

20.1.2. The Rules can be varied by agreement in writing between the solicitor and his client.

20.1.3. If a solicitor pays a lender's cheque into his client's account in anticipation of completing the mortgage and completion is postponed, he may be liable to pay interest at the mortgage rate if the money is not returned to the lender within the time stipulated in the lender's instructions.

20.2. Deposits in conveyancing transactions

20.2.1. The Rules apply to all money held by a solicitor on behalf of a client, including a deposit held by a solicitor whether as agent for the seller or as stakeholder.

20.2.2. Where the Rules apply, interest must be paid to the client irrespective of whether the money was held on deposit or current account.

20.3. Stakeholder deposits

20.3.1. A deposit which is held in the capacity of stakeholder does not belong to either client until completion, but an entitlement to interest on that deposit arises under Rule 24 Solicitors' Accounts Rules 1991.

20.3.2. In the absence of express agreement to the contrary the interest will follow the stake.

20.3.3. Standard Condition 2.2.3. provides for the seller to receive the interest earned on a stakeholder deposit, provided the contract is completed (but not if it is rescinded).

20.4. Designated accounts

20.4.1. Where clients' money is held in a separate designated account, the solicitor must account to the client for the interest actually earned on that account. A separate designated account must be a deposit account.

20.5. General clients' account

20.5.1. If the money is held in a general clients' account the duty to pay interest depends on the amount of money held and the period for which it is held.

20.5.2. *Table of minimum balances*

Interest must be paid when the money is held for as long or longer than the number of weeks set out in the table below, and the minimum balance held during that period equals or exceeds the amounts set out in the table below.

No. of weeks	Minimum balance
8	£1,000
4	£2,000
2	£10,000
1	£20,000

20.6. Sums exceeding £20,000

20.6.1. If a sum exceeding £20,000 is held for less than a week and it is fair and reasonable to do so, the solicitor must pay interest on that sum to the client. Although this part of the rule allows some discretion to be exercised by the solicitor in deciding whether or not to pay interest, such discretion should be exercised in the client's favour. Thus, if a sum of £1,000,000 were held on behalf of a client for two days, the considerable amount of interest which would accrue during that short time should be paid to the client.

20.7. Intermittent amounts

20.7.1. There will be occasions when the solicitor either holds money intermittently for the client, or when the amount being held varies from time to time. In these circumstances the solicitor must account to the client for interest where it would be fair and reasonable to do so, having regard to the amounts of money held and to the length of time for which it is held. The discretion permitted by this rule should be exercised in favour of the client.

20.8. Rate of interest

20.8.1. The rate of interest (for money not held in a separate designated account) is the same rate as would have been payable if the money had been kept in a separate designated account. Where money is held in a separate designated account (which should be a deposit account with a building society or major clearing bank) the amount of interest payable is the sum actually earned on that money while on deposit.

20.8.2. Interest on a contractual deposit held under the terms of the Standard Conditions of Sale is governed by Standard Condition 1.1.1.(a).

20.9. Trustees

20.9.1. The Rules do apply to money held by a solicitor which belongs to a trust (not being a controlled trust) of which the solicitor is a trustee, where the solicitor is acting for the trust. If interest arises under a controlled trust, all of the interest must be paid to the beneficiaries.

20.10. Client's right to certificate

20.10.1. A client who feels that he ought to have been paid interest on money held on his behalf by his solicitor may apply to the Law Society for a certificate as to whether or not interest ought to have been paid and, if so, the amount of that interest.

20.11. Tax on interest

20.11.1. In some circumstances deduction of tax at source may be applicable to interest which is paid on clients' money. The Law Society guidance on this matter is set out in full in Appendix II.6.

A.21. Gifts of property by elderly clients

21.1. Introduction

21.1.1. Elderly people or those nearing retirement may seek advice from solicitors as to the advantages and disadvantages of transferring their home, or other property to relatives, even though in some cases they still intend to live in the home. The solicitor's advice will, of course, vary according to the individual circumstances of the client, their motivation for making such a gift, and what they are hoping to achieve by it.

21.1.2. The following guidelines have been drawn up by the Law Society's Mental Health and Disability Sub-Committee to assist solicitors, both to ensure that their clients fully understand the nature, effects, benefits, risks and foreseeable consequences of making such a gift, and also to clarify the solicitor's role and duty in relation to such transactions.

21.2. Who is the client?

21.2.1. The solicitor must be clear as to who he is acting for, especially where relatives purport to be giving instructions on behalf of an elderly person. In most cases, it will be the elderly person who owns the home and is therefore the client. It is important to recognise that there is a potential conflict of interest between the elderly person and anyone who stands to gain from the transaction, so the elderly person should receive independent advice (see also para. A.10.).

21.2.2. The solicitor acting for the elderly person should see the client alone to satisfy himself that the client is acting freely, to confirm the client's wishes and to gauge the extent, if any, of family or other influence. If the client is not already known to the solicitor, it may be necessary to spend some time with the client, talking about wider issues, in order to get to know him, to be clear about the family circumstances, and also to assess whether the client has the mental capacity to make the gift.

21.2.3. It may also be advisable to check whether another solicitor has previously acted for the client and, if so, to seek the client's consent to contact that solicitor, in case there are factors to be taken into account which are not immediately apparent.

21.3.   **The client's understanding**

21.3.1.   It is important to ensure that the client understands the nature and effect of making the gift. Before making the gift the client should understand:

     (a)   that the money or property intended to be given away belongs absolutely to the client;

     (b)   why the gift is being made;

     (c)   whether it is a single transaction or part of a series of gifts;

     (d)   the extent of the gift in relation to the rest of the client's money and property;

     (e)   that the client is making an outright gift rather than, for example, a loan or acquiring a share in a business or property owned by the recipient;

     (f)   whether the client expects to receive anything in return and, if so, how much, or on what terms? (For example: someone who is giving away their house might expect to be able to carry on living there rent free for the rest of their life, but who pays for the insurance and upkeep?);

     (g)   whether the gift is intended to take effect immediately, or at a later date − perhaps when the client dies, or goes into residential care;

     (h)   that, if the gift is outright, the client cannot ask for the money or property to be returned to him;

     (i)   the effect that making the gift could have on the client's future standard of living;

     (j)   the effect that the gift could have on other members of the family who might have expected eventually to inherit a share of the money or property;

     (k)   the possibility that the recipient could die first, or become involved in divorce or bankruptcy proceedings, in which case the money or property given away could end up belonging to somebody else;

     (l)   that the donor and recipient could fall out, and even become quite hostile to one another;

     (m)   whether the client has already made gifts to the recipient or other people; and

     (n)   any other foreseeable consequences of making or not making the gift (some of which are considered below).

21.3.2.   *The client's objectives*

The solicitor should establish why the gift of property is being contemplated, and whether the client's objectives will in fact be achieved by the making of the gift or could be achieved in some other way.

In establishing the client's objectives, the following matters may be relevant:

(a) If the objective is to ensure that a particular relative (e.g. a child or children) inherits the client's home rather than someone else, this can be achieved equally as well by making a will.

(b) If the objective is to avoid inheritance tax on the death of the client, an approximate calculation should be made of the client's likely estate to assess the amount of tax which may be payable, and whether other tax-saving measures could be considered. For example, the value of the property, together with the remainder of the client's estate, may not exceed the level at which inheritance tax becomes payable.

The client may also not be aware that if he intends to continue living in the home, there may be no inheritance tax saving because of the 'reservation of benefit' rules unless a complicated scheme is put into effect, involving 'carving out' a leasehold interest and transferring the freehold reversion to the recipient. The result might also be to increase the liability to inheritance tax on the death of the relative to whom the gift has been made if he dies before the client. Again, other schemes to mitigate these effects should be considered.

(c) If the objective is to relieve the elderly client of the worry and responsibility of home ownership, other ways of achieving this should be discussed, such as making an Enduring Power of Attorney.

(d) If the objective is to try to avoid the value of the house being taken into account in various forms of means-testing or to gain some other benefit, the advantages and disadvantages should be discussed with the client in order to assess whether the potential risks of the arrangement are justified, according to the client's individual circumstances, future needs and desires.

21.4. The solicitor's duty

21.4.1. The solicitor's role is more than just drawing up and registering the necessary deeds and documents to effect the making of the gift. He has a duty to ensure that the client fully understands the nature, effect, benefits, risks and foreseeable consequences of making the gift. The solicitor has no obligation to advise the client on the wisdom or morality of the transaction, unless the client specifically asks.

21.4.2. The Professional Ethics Division of the Law Society has advised that the solicitor should follow the client's instructions, provided that by doing so the solicitor will not be involved in a breach of the law or a breach of the principles of professional conduct. Reference is made to Principle 12.02 of *The Guide to the Professional Conduct of Solicitors 1996,* which indicates when instructions must be refused. Solicitors will want to satisfy themselves in each individual case that no breach of the law is involved in the proposed transaction. Having advised the client as to the implications and possible consequences of making the gift, the decision of whether or not to proceed remains with the client.

21.4.3. Solicitors must also be aware of the possible conflict of interest, or significant risk of such a conflict, between the donor and recipient of a gift. While there is no general rule of law that a solicitor should never act for both parties in a transaction where their interests might conflict, Principle 15.01 of *The Guide to the Professional Conduct of Solicitors 1996* states: 'A solicitor or firm of solicitors should not accept instructions to act for two or more clients where there is a conflict or a significant risk of a conflict between the interests of the clients'. Given the potentially vulnerable position of an elderly client, the solicitor will have to consider carefully whether he can act for the donor and the recipient or whether there is an actual or significant risk of conflict. If the solicitor has initially advised the donor alone as to all the implications of the gift and is satisfied that there is no undue influence and that the donor has capacity, the solicitor may be able to act for both clients in the conveyancing.

21.4.4. If the solicitor is asked to act for both parties, the solicitor should make them both aware of the possibility of a conflict of interest and advise one of them to consider taking independent advice. He should also explain that as a result of any conflict of interest, a solicitor acting by agreement for both parties may be unable to disclose all that he knows to each of them or to give advice to one of them which conflicts with the interests of the other and may have to cease acting for both. Both parties must be content to proceed on this basis, and give their consent in writing. However, if any doubt remains, the solicitor would be advised not to act for both parties.

B.   PRE-EXCHANGE
B.01.   Pre-contract negotiations

1.1.   Effect of 'subject to contract'

1.1.1. The phrase 'subject to contract' may no longer be of great importance in view of the fact that Law of Property (Miscellaneous Provisions) Act 1989, s.2, requires the contract for the sale of land to be in writing and signed by both parties. It is unlikely that a contract would inadvertently be entered into by correspondence between the parties.[1]

1.1.2. The inclusion of the phrase 'subject to contract' will normally act as a suspensory condition which will prevent the formation of a binding contract until such time as the effect of the condition is removed, e.g. on exchange.

1.1.3. Once introduced, the phrase will continue to govern subsequent correspondence until its effect is expressly or impliedly removed. It is thus not essential that every item of pre-contract correspondence carries the suspensory condition.

1. See para. 1.6.4. below.

1.2.   A contract already exists

1.2.1. The phrase 'subject to contract' can only give protection to the parties where no contract exists. If a contract has already come into existence the phrase cannot invalidate or eradicate that contract.

1.3.   Removal of suspensory condition

1.3.1. The condition will normally remain in effect until removed with the consent of both parties on exchange. It cannot be removed unilaterally.[1]

1.3.2. However, care should be taken to ensure that the wording of correspondence or telephone conversations does not imply the current existence of a contract which will negate the effect of the 'subject to contract' formula.[2]

1.3.3. The phrase should thus be used with care and not regarded as a magic formula which will protect the parties in all circumstances.

1. *Sherbrooke* v. *Dipple* (1980) 255 E.G. 1203.
2. See *Griffiths* v. *Young* [1970] Ch. 675; *Michael Richards Properties Ltd.* v. *Corporation of Wardens of St. Saviour's Parish Southwark* [1975] 3 All E.R. 416.

1.4.   Protracted negotiations

1.4.1. In *Cohen* v. *Nessdale*,[1] it was held that the phrase 'subject to contract' continued to govern negotiations despite an interval of some eight months; however, it is unwise to rely on this decision as the continued protection of the phrase cannot be guaranteed in all circumstances.

1.4.2. Where negotiations for the property have become interrupted or protracted a solicitor should not rely on the continued effect of the phrase 'subject to contract'. When negotiations recommence after an interval the 'subject to contract' formula should be repeated in all subsequent correspondence to ensure its continued protection pending the resolution of the negotiations.

1. [1982] 2 All E.R. 97.

1.5.   Contract denied

1.5.1. Difficulties have in the past arisen over the use of the phrase 'subject to contract'[1] and some solicitors prefer to use the words 'contract denied' in preference to 'subject to contract'. However, there is no reported decision on the effect of the phrase 'contract denied' and the phrase should therefore, for safety's sake, be regarded as being similar in operation and effect to the words 'subject to contract'.

1. See *Law* v. *Jones* [1974] Ch. 112; *cf. Tiverton Estates* v. *Wearwell Ltd.* [1975] 1 Ch. 146.

1.6.   Need for written contract

1.6.1. In most cases the requirement for a written contract for the sale of land will be satisfied by the formal exchange of contracts by the parties, following negotiations conducted by their respective solicitors.

1.6.2. To ensure that no contract inadvertently comes into existence before the parties are ready to exchange it is customary to qualify all pre-contract correspondence with the words 'subject to contract' or 'contract denied'.

1.6.3. In exceptional cases an exchange of correspondence may satisfy the requirements of section 2 Law of Property (Miscellaneous Provisions) Act 1989, but only where:

(a) the letters set out or incorporate all the terms of the agreement; and

(b) there is an intention that the exchange of letters will result in a binding contract.[1]

Correspondence which is headed 'subject to contract' cannot fulfil the above conditions.[2]

1. *Commission for New Towns* v. *Cooper* [1995] 26 E.G. 129 (C.A.)
2. *Commission for New Towns* v. *Cooper* [1995] 26 E.G. 129 (C.A.)

1.7. **Lock-out agreements**

1.7.1. A lock-out agreement where the seller agrees not to negotiate with any third party for a specified period of time is capable of being a valid collateral contract and does not need to satisfy the requirements of Law of Property (Miscellaneous Provisions) Act 1989, s.2.[1] A lock-in agreement, i.e. to negotiate with these parties only, is never valid.[2]

1. *Pitt* v. *PHH Assett Management Ltd.* [1993] E.G.C.S. 127; *Walford* v. *Miles* [1992] 2 A.C. 128, H.L.
2. *Courtney & Fairburn Ltd.* v. *Tolaini Bros Ltd.* [1975] 1 W.L.R. 297.

B.02. Contract races

2.1. Solicitors' Practice Rules 1990 (as amended)

2.1.1. Where a seller's solicitor is asked by his client to deal simultaneously with more than one prospective buyer he is required to comply with Rule 6A Solicitors' Practice Rules 1990 (as amended), the text of which is summarised below. The full text of the Rule is reproduced in Appendix I.1.

2.1.2. Compliance with the Rule is mandatory and breach thereof can lead to disciplinary action being taken against the solicitor.

2.1.3. The Rule applies irrespective of whether the prospective buyers are supplied with their contracts simultaneously or whether contracts are issued to different prospective buyers one after the other. The supply of documentation such as a plan of the land or Land Registry title number in order to facilitate the transfer of the premises to a buyer is covered by the Rule. It is not necessary for each prospective buyer to be supplied with a 'contract', nor need each contract be in identical terms. The Rule applies to both domestic and commercial transactions. The Rule also applies where the seller's solicitor knows that the second (and subsequent) buyer(s) are being dealt with directly by the seller without the solicitor's involvement.

2.1.4. Where, having supplied a prospective buyer with a draft contract or other documentation, the seller later receives a further offer for the property which later offer he would prefer to accept, the seller may accept the second offer but his solicitor should give notice of withdrawal to the first prospective buyer's solicitor prior to dealing with the second prospective buyer and submitting draft papers to him. If notice of withdrawal is given, Rule 6A does not apply. Similarly, if the first prospective buyer's solicitor returns the papers to the seller's solicitor before papers are submitted to the second prospective buyer, only one buyer would be in possession of draft papers at any given time, thus a contract race does not exist and Rule 6A does not apply.

2.2. Solicitor acting for seller

2.2.1. Where a solicitor is acting for the seller he must explain to his client that the solicitor is required to comply with the Practice Rule referred to above, and if the seller refuses to allow the solicitor to notify all the prospective buyers of the contract race the solicitor must decline to act. The duty to notify the buyers only arises if a contract race situation exists.

2.2.2. Since buyers are themselves wary of entering into contract races, the seller should also be warned of the danger of losing the prospective buyers altogether if a race is commenced. It is normally preferable to avoid a contract race if at all possible.

2.3. Disclosure of race to buyers

2.3.1. Having obtained his client's authority, the solicitor must at once disclose the seller's decision to conduct a contract race direct to the solicitor acting for each prospective buyer or (where no solicitor is acting) to the prospective buyer(s) in person. Such disclosure, if made face to face, or by telephone, must at once be confirmed in a letter, or by fax.

2.3.2. When the seller's solicitor informs the prospective buyers of the race, he must make it clear to each of them the precise terms of the race, i.e. what has to be done by a buyer in order to secure the property. Commonly the terms of the race are that the first buyer who presents a signed contract and deposit cheque at the seller's solicitor's office will secure the property.

2.4. Acting for seller and buyer

2.4.1. Even where a solicitor would normally be entitled to act for both the seller and buyer, e.g. because the situation falls within one of the exceptions to Rule 6(2) Solicitors' Practice Rules 1990 (as amended), the contract race gives rise to a significant risk of conflict of interests between the two clients and the solicitor must not continue to act for both.

2.5. Acting for more than one buyer

2.5.1. Where forms of contract are submitted to more than one prospective buyer, a solicitor must not accept instructions to act for more than one such buyer.

2.6. Licensed conveyancers

2.6.1. Licensed conveyancers may be regarded in the same light as solicitors; thus, for the purpose of the Rule, disclosure of a contract race to a licensed conveyancer can be treated as disclosure of the race to the client of the conveyancer. Disclosure of the existence of the race must, however, be made directly to the buyer if that buyer is represented by an unqualified person.

2.6.2. Authorised practitioners may be regarded in the same light as licensed conveyancers.

B.03. Seller's investigation of title

See also: Seller's title awaiting registration, para. B.04.
Seller's duty of disclosure, para. B.05.
Defective title and restrictive covenant insurance, para. B.06.
Form of contract, para. B.11.
Investigation of title, para. D.02.

3.1. Seller's investigation of title

3.1.1. Having obtained office copies of the register of title (registered land) or the seller's title deeds or a copy of them (unregistered land), the seller's solicitor should investigate title before drafting the contract for sale. The manner and method of such investigation is dealt with in para. D.02.

3.2. Reasons for investigation

3.2.1. The investigation of the title by the seller's solicitor at this stage of the transaction is a precautionary measure to ensure that:

(a) the seller is the owner of or is otherwise entitled to sell the whole of the estate in accordance with the instructions given to his solicitor;

(b) any incumbrances on the title can be revealed in the draft contract in order to satisfy the seller's duty of disclosure;

(c) any defects in the title may be spotted and appropriate steps taken to rectify them before exchange of contracts;

(d) any consents which may be necessary from third parties may be obtained;

(e) any requisitions on title by the buyer can be anticipated.

3.3.   **Registered land**

3.3.1.   Obtain up-to-date office copies of the register of title and check to ensure that no entries have been made which will affect the seller's right to sell the property as instructed, e.g. there may be a caution against dealings on the register which will have to be cleared off. On first registration of the title positive covenants may have been omitted from the register; in such a case the seller will need to take an indemnity covenant from the buyer and provide the buyer with a copy of the transfer which imposed the covenants in order to prove the need for indemnity. This latter will involve the inspection of pre-registration title deeds.

3.4.   **Unregistered titles**

3.4.1.   Check when the compulsory registration order came into force in the area and that no dealings which would have induced registration have occurred since that date.

3.4.2.   In many cases the land will require registration after completion of this transaction. Although this will primarily be the responsibility of the buyer, this factor should be borne in mind by the seller's solicitor in his pre-contract investigation of title so that any areas of difficulty which might be the subject of a requisition by HM Land Registry may be clarified.

3.4.3.   If it transpires that the land should have been registered on a previous disposition, an immediate application for late registration must be made by the seller's solicitor, a full disclosure of the situation being made to both the seller and the buyer's solicitor. Title will then need to be dealt with as if the seller's title was awaiting registration at HM Land Registry (see para. B.04.).

3.4.4.   An index map search should be made to ensure that no part of the land has already been registered without the owner's knowledge.

3.4.5.   A Land Charges Department search should be made against the name of the seller to ensure that no incumbrances exist other than those revealed by the title deeds.

3.4.6.   *Freeholds*

(a) Decide which document is to be used as the root of title, and check the validity of the chain of title forwards from that time.

(b) Does the root document refer to any earlier documents which the buyer may be entitled to call for?

(c) Are there any pre-root covenants which need to be disclosed to the buyer?

(d) Are all documents within the chain correctly stamped and executed?

(e) Watch for change of names, e.g. on marriage or change of a company name. Obtain evidence of the changes if necessary.

(f) If in doubt as to the effectiveness of restrictive covenants, options or third party rights revealed by the title a Land Charges Department search should be made to clarify the position.

(g) Obtain copies of any necessary death certificates or grants of representation.

3.4.7. Existing leaseholds

The entitlement to title of a buyer of an existing lease is dealt with by Law of Property Act 1925, s.44 which does not allow the buyer to call for the deduction of the title to the freehold. In most cases, however, the buyer's (or his lender's) solicitor will require the deduction of the freehold title and frequently standard contractual conditions will also so provide unless amended to exclude this provision (see Standard Condition 8). Unless the lease is for a short period with little or no premium payable for its assignment the buyer is likely to insist on deduction of the freehold title.

3.4.8. Problems may, however, arise if the title to the freehold was not called for on the original grant of the lease. The following points should be checked:

(a) Is a marked copy of the freehold title available or can it be obtained? If not, check that the contract excludes the buyer's right to deduction of the freehold.

(b) Check the chain of title from the lease (or sub-lease) including evidence of surrenders and copies of any necessary consents, e.g. to assignments or alterations.

(c) Is consent to this assignment required? If so, obtain the names of referees from the buyer's solicitor and forward them to the landlord's solicitor. Obtain a firm estimate from the landlord's solicitor before giving an undertaking for costs.

(d) Is the freehold or superior leasehold title registered? Whether or not this is so can be ascertained by making an index map search. Where the freehold or superior title is registered office copies of the title can be obtained by the buyer. This may overcome the limitation posed by the seller being unable to deliver the freehold or superior leasehold title.

3.5. Title in name of sole owner

3.5.1. Instructions will have revealed whether anyone other than the seller is living at the property. If there is, consideration should be given to the question of whether the occupants have any rights in the property which may impede the seller's intention of selling with vacant possession.

3.5.2. *Is the seller married?*

The seller's spouse may have statutory rights of occupation the under Family Law Act 1996 and/or an equitable interest in the property through a contribution to the purchase price. Enquiries should also be made to ascertain whether the non-owning spouse has the benefit of an occupation order under Family Law Act 1996.

3.5.3. *Matrimonial homes rights*

Current registration of such rights can be verified by inspecting office copies of the title (registered land) or by making a Land Charges Department search against the seller (unregistered land). Even if such rights are not presently protected by registration the spouse may still effect a registration at any time until actual completion.

3.5.4. *Rights are already registered*

It will be a condition of the contract that such registration is removed before completion.[1] Negotiations must be entered into with the spouse's solicitors for the removal of the charge and a satisfactory solution obtained before exchange of contracts.

3.5.5. *Rights in existence but not registered*

It is unsafe to assume that the spouse will not exercise the right to register a charge under Family Law Act 1996 and instructions should be obtained directly from the spouse (through a separate solicitor if there is any possibility of conflict of interests) to confirm the spouse's acquiescence in the proposed sale. A formal release of rights and agreement not to enforce any such rights against the seller should be prepared for signature before exchange by the non-owning spouse.

3.5.6. A registration under Family Law Act 1996 can be removed on production of:

(a) an application made by the person with the benefit of the rights;

(b) a divorce decree absolute;

(c) a court order to that effect;

(d) the death certificate of the spouse.

3.5.7. *Equitable interests*

If it is thought that the spouse may also be entitled to an equitable interest in the property it should be assumed that the property is held by the seller on constructive trust for himself and his spouse. The spouse's independent confirmation of agreement to the sale must be obtained and the spouse joined as a party to the contract. A solicitor would be well advised to explain to the spouse that his/her written consent to the sale is required, that giving such consent may affect his/her legal rights and that the spouse should obtain independent advice before signing the release. The dangers of negligence and undue influence should also be noted where the owning spouse 'persuades' the non-owning spouse to consent to the transaction.

3.5.8. Suggested form of wording for release of rights:

(a) 'In consideration of the buyer entering this agreement I (*name of spouse*) agree:

    (i) to the sale of the property on the terms of this agreement; and

    (ii) that I will not register rights in relation to the property, whether under Family Law Act 1996 or otherwise, and that I will procure before completion the removal of any registration made by me; and

    (iii) that I will vacate the property by the completion date'.[2]

or

(b) 'In consideration of your today entering into a contract with (*name of owning spouse*) for the purchase of the property known as (*insert address of property to be sold*), I agree:

    (i) to release any equitable interest which I may have in the property (such interest, if any, being transferred to the proceeds of sale of the property), such release to be effective from the date of completion of the sale of this property;

    (ii) to procure the cancellation of any registration which may have been effected by me or on my behalf on or before completion, including any registration in respect of rights of occupation which I may have under Family Law Act 1996; and

    (iii) to vacate the property by the completion date.'[3]

3.5.9. Sharers and co-habitees

Sharers and co-habitees may be able to establish an equitable interest in the property through contribution to the purchase price. Investigation must be made of the exact status of each occupier. If necessary a release of rights should be obtained, or they may be joined as parties to the contract. The solicitor should advise the sharer/co-habitee in similar terms to those suggested in para. 3.5.8. above. Enquiries should also be made to ascertain whether the non-owning occupier has the benefit of an occupation order under Family Law Act 1996, s.33.

3.5.10.   *Overriding interests*

Persons in actual occupation of registered land may have overriding interests by virtue of Land Registration Act 1925, s.70(1)(*g*). A formal release of such rights should be obtained. The occupiers may also be joined as contracting parties.

3.5.11.   *Tenants*

If vacant possession is to be given of the property on completion effective steps must be taken to terminate the tenancies.

If vacant possession is not to be given on completion full details of the tenancies must be obtained since disclosure of the tenancies must be made in the draft contract. Accurate information will be required by the buyer in relation to the amount of rent payable by the tenants, the dates of rent reviews, and the effect of any security of tenure legislation on the tenancies.

1. Family Law Act 1996, Sched.4, para. 3(1).
2. This clause should be included in the contract of sale.
3. This clause may either be incorporated in the contract or drawn up as a separate document and attached to the contract. In either case the clause should be signed by the non-owning spouse.

3.6.   **Death of a joint proprietor**

3.6.1.   *Registered land*

3.6.1.1.   Registration of restriction

A restriction in Form 62 registered in the proprietorship register indicates that the equitable interest was held on a tenancy in common and two trustees will be needed to transfer the legal estate. If the survivor is entitled to the whole of the property it is possible to obtain the grant of representation to the deceased's estate and execute an assent in favour of the survivor who may then sell in the capacity of beneficial owner. It is, however, safer for the buyer to insist that the seller obtains the removal of the Form 62 restriction before taking a transfer from him. If he does not do this then, on lodging his application for registration of the transfer, the buyer would need to produce to HM Land Registry evidence of the seller's entitlement to the entire equitable interest in accordance with Rule 214 Land Registration Rules 1925. The evidence which is usually acceptable is a statutory declaration by the sole survivor that in stated circumstances the declarant has become entitled legally and beneficially to the registered land, that he has not encumbered his undivided share, and that he has not received notice of any incumbrance upon the undivided share of the deceased proprietor. A certificate by the seller's solicitor will be accepted in place of a declaration if the solicitor is able to speak from his knowledge of all the relevant facts.

3.6.1.2. Appointment of second trustee

The seller's solicitor may be appointed as the new trustee provided that there is no conflict of interest between the instructing client and the other person(s) now entitled to the remainder of the property. The appointment of the second trustee should be dealt with as a matter of urgency so that there are two trustees named in the contract. If there is difficulty over the appointment of a second trustee the contract may include a clause providing that a second trustee will be appointed prior to execution of the purchase deed, the existing trustee contracting alone at this stage of the transaction. This latter situation should be avoided if possible because it is less satisfactory to the buyer who in contracting with one trustee alone has no guarantee that the matter will proceed smoothly to completion.

3.6.1.3. No restriction registered

Where no restriction is registered the equitable interest may be presumed to have been held under a joint tenancy and the sole surviving joint tenant may sell as beneficial owner on production of the death certificate of the deceased.

3.6.2. *Unregistered land*

Check the document under which the joint owners acquired the property to ascertain whether it was held on a joint tenancy or tenancy in common.

3.6.2.1. Tenancy in common

The existence of two trustees of the legal estate gives the buyer the assurance that any subsisting beneficial interests will be overreached on completion, thus removing any doubt which may exist as to whether the deceased had disposed of his interest in the property during his lifetime (see above).

3.6.2.2. Joint tenancy

Check the deed by which the joint tenants bought the property to ensure that no memorandum of severance is endorsed on it and make a bankruptcy search in the Land Charges Department to establish that no bankruptcy proceedings were or are pending against either joint tenant. Provided that these conditions are satisfied, the sole survivor may sell with a certificate that he is a sole beneficial owner on production of the death certificate of the deceased joint tenant. Again, provided that these conditions are satisfied, the personal representatives of a last surviving joint tenant can convey the land on production of the grant so long as the conveyance contains a statement that the survivor was solely and beneficially entitled to the property. If the joint tenancy has been severed or if bankruptcy proceedings are pending the tenancy must be treated as a tenancy in common and dealt with by the appointment of a second trustee (see above).

3.7.   Breach of restrictive covenant/other defect in title

3.7.1.   Restrictive covenants

If the breach cannot be remedied, e.g. by obtaining belated consent of the person entitled to the benefit of the covenant, consider obtaining restrictive covenant indemnity insurance in an appropriate sum.

3.7.2.   Other defects in title

Defects which can be remedied, e.g. the appointment of a new trustee or missing stamp duties should be rectified as soon as possible and in any event before exchange of contracts. Defects which are irremediable will have to be revealed in the draft contract and insurance cover obtained as appropriate.

3.8.   Planning

3.8.1.   Although not strictly a matter of title, the seller's solicitor should check at this stage that any necessary planning or building regulation consents have been obtained and complied with. If not with the deeds copies of such consents should be requisitioned from the local authority for the buyer's use.

3.9.   Donatio mortis causa

3.9.1.   It is possible, although extremely rare, for the seller to have acquired the land through a *donatio mortis causa*.[1] In such a case there will be no documentary evidence of the devolution of title from the deceased to the present seller. Proof of the validity of the seller's title will have to be shown to the buyer; it may be possible to do this by means of a statutory declaration made by the seller.

1. See *Sen* v. *Headley* [1991] 2 All E.R. 636.

3.10.   Action after investigation of title

3.10.1.   Registered land

Office copies of the register entries and any other supporting documentation, e.g. evidence of tenancies or overriding interests should be prepared for delivery to the buyer with the draft contract.

3.10.2.   Unregistered land

An epitome of title should be prepared for delivery to the buyer with the draft contract.

B.04. Seller's title awaiting registration

4.1.	The nature of the problem	4.5.	Contractual condition for deduction of title
4.2.	Seller's right to deal with land	4.6.	Provision for payment of interest by buyer
4.3.	Buyer's entitlement to title	4.7.	Protection of the buyer
4.4.	Delay	4.8.	Protection of the lender

4.1. The nature of the problem

4.1.1. Where the seller, after completion of a recent purchase of registered land, seeks to sell the land to a third party before registration of his own transfer has been completed at HM Land Registry, he will be unable to deduce title to his buyer under the usual provisions of Land Registration Act 1925, s.110, since he will not at that stage be the registered proprietor of the land. A similar problem exists where, having bought unregistered land which is subject to compulsory registration, the seller wishes to sell that land before his application for first registration has been completed. In this latter situation he should not sell on his unregistered title to the buyer, leaving the buyer to apply for registration on completion of his purchase, since the seller's title will become void if no application for registration is made by the seller within two months of the completion of his own purchase.[1] A safer course of action is for the seller to submit his application to the registrar for first registration and then to sell on with registration of title pending.

1. *Pinekerry* v. *Needs (Contractors)* (1992) 64 P. & C.R. 245.

4.2. Seller's right to deal with land

4.2.1. The seller is entitled to deal with the land pending his own registration as proprietor.[1]

1. Land Registration Act 1925, s.37 and Rule 72 Land Registration Rules 1925.

4.3. Buyer's entitlement to title

4.3.1. A buyer of registered land is entitled to insist that the seller either procures his own registration before completion of the sale to the buyer, or procures a transfer to the buyer from the present registered proprietor.[1] This provision applies regardless of any condition to the contrary in the contract, but is not considered to apply where the seller's pending application is for first registration of title.[2]

1. Land Registration Act 1925, s.110(5).
2. *Re Evans' Contract* [1970] 1 All E.R. 1236.

4.4.   Delay

4.4.1.   In practice, if the buyer was to insist that completion of his purchase be delayed until the seller became the registered proprietor of the land through completion of the pending application for registration, the transaction might be delayed by several months which would result in adverse practical and financial consequences for both parties. The buyer will normally agree to complete provided that the seller's own title to the land is registered at some time before the buyer's application for registration is completed.

4.4.2.   The buyer's lender must be informed of the position and his requirements observed.

4.5.   Contractual condition for deduction of title

4.5.1.   The seller must, however, prove to the buyer's satisfaction that the seller is a person who is entitled to be the registered proprietor of the land concerned. This is normally achieved by producing to the buyer a copy of the register entries (which will show the seller's predecessor as registered proprietor), together with a copy of the stamped transfer from the registered proprietor to the seller, a clear Land Registry search against the title, and evidence that the seller lodged a correct application for registration preferably within the priority period afforded by his own search.

4.5.2.   Where the land is presently unregistered, the buyer will insist on deduction of the unregistered title together with evidence that the seller has lodged a properly completed application form for first registration of the title. Deduction of title by this method requires the insertion of a special condition to this effect in the contract.

4.5.3.   The seller should be required to assist the buyer in answering any requisitions which might be raised by HM Land Registry in relation to the pending registration.

4.5.4.   If the contract requires the buyer to purchase the seller's existing equitable interest in the property (the seller does not have the legal estate until registration is complete), the seller must be required to give an undertaking to transfer the legal estate to the buyer on completion of the seller's registration of title.

4.6. Provision for payment of interest by buyer

4.6.1. In order to discourage the buyer from delaying completion by insisting on the seller actually becoming registered as proprietor it is not uncommon to find a contractual provision to the effect that if the buyer does insist on the seller completing his own registration before completion of the sale to the buyer, the buyer will pay interest on the balance of the purchase price at the contract rate for the period between the agreed contractual completion date and actual completion. Such a provision cannot be enforced since the buyer has a legal entitlement to insist that the seller procures his own registration.[1]

1. Land Registration Act 1925, s.110(5).

4.7. Protection of the buyer

4.7.1. The buyer may insist that the seller includes a provision in the contract whereby he agrees to expedite his application for registration by paying the appropriate expedition fee, and that he will assist the buyer by answering any requisitions relating to the pending application which are raised by HM Land Registry. Such a condition should be expressed so that it remains extant after completion of the buyer's contract and does not merge with the transfer on completion. Some risks are inherent in this situation and the buyer should protect his contract by registration.

4.8. Protection of the lender

4.8.1. The mortgage, until registration, takes effect only as a charge on the equitable interest and will not comply with the provisions of Building Societies Act 1986. The borrower would, however, be estopped from denying the validity of the charge.[1]

1. *First National Bank plc* v. *Thompson* [1995] NPC 130.

B.05. Seller's duty of disclosure

5.1. Reasons for disclosure

5.1.1. It is an implied term of a contract for the sale of land that the seller is selling free from incumbrances. If this is not to be so the seller must reveal the incumbrances to which the property is subject. Failure to disclose incumbrances may give the buyer the right to rescind the contract and to claim damages.

5.2. What must the seller disclose?

5.2.1. As an exception to the *caveat emptor* principle the seller is under a duty to disclose to the buyer latent incumbrances and defects in his title. This duty exists irrespective of whether the buyer raises enquiries about such matters.

5.2.2. *Meaning of latent*

Legally a defect is latent if it is not apparent, but the distinction between latent and patent defects is, in practice, unclear: see, e.g. *Yandle & Sons* v. *Sutton*[1] where a right of way which was apparent on inspection of the property was nevertheless held to be a latent defect. A seller should err on the side of caution and make a full disclosure of defects and incumbrances.

5.2.3. *Law of Property Act 1969, s.24*

Although a defect is not latent if the buyer has constructive notice of it under Law of Property Act 1925, s.198, the effect of Law of Property Act 1969, s.24 is to place a duty on the seller to reveal matters which are registered at the Land Charges Department. A buyer who enters into a contract knowing of an irremovable incumbrance impliedly agrees to take subject to that incumbrance (i.e. cannot rescind because of it), but the effect of section 24 is that mere registration under Land Charges Act 1972 is not knowledge for this purpose.

5.2.4. Occupiers

A buyer who inspects the property will be deemed to have notice of the rights of occupiers.[2] This provision apart, it is uncertain whether the rights of occupiers fall within the duty of disclosure. Following *Williams & Glyn's Bank Ltd.* v. *Boland*[3] the accepted view is that a full disclosure of occupiers' rights should be made.

5.2.5. Local land charges

Unless the contract provides to the contrary, the duty of disclosure includes matters which would be revealed by a local land charges search. Where the contract does not contain an effective clause excluding such matters from the duty of disclosure the seller should make a local land charges search before drafting the contract.[4]

5.2.6. Matters outside the seller's knowledge

It was held in *Re Brewer & Hankin's Contract*[5] that the seller's duty of disclosure may extend even to matters of which he was unaware. However, standard contractual conditions will normally exclude the seller's liability for non-disclosure in these circumstances (see Standard Condition 3). Knowledge acquired by the seller's solicitor in the course of acting for his client is imputed to the seller.[6]

5.2.7. Overriding interests

The seller is under a duty to disclose latent overriding interests. In practice a disclosure of all overriding interests known to the seller should be made.

1. [1922] 2 Ch. 199.
2. *Hunt* v. *Luck* [1902] 1 Ch. 428.
3. [1981] A.C. 487.
4. *Rignall Developments Ltd.* v. *Halil* [1988] Ch. 190.
5. (1889) 80 L.T. 127.
6. *Strover* v. *Harrington* [1988] Ch. 390.

5.3. Matters falling outside the duty of disclosure

5.3.1. Matters known to the buyer

There is no duty to disclose matters which are already known to the buyer, but the seller must ensure that the buyer has actual knowledge of such matters and cannot assume that a matter is within the buyer's knowledge. Even where an incumbrance is contained within one of the title deeds (or appears on the register in registered land) supplied to the buyer with the draft contract, the buyer's knowledge of the incumbrance cannot be assumed and the seller should take steps, whether by inclusion of a contractual condition or otherwise, specifically to draw the defect to the buyer's attention.

5.3.2. *Matters apparent on inspection*

Matters which can readily be discovered on an inspection of the property do not fall within the duty of disclosure.[1]

5.3.3. *Physical defects*

Physical defects, whether latent or patent, do not generally fall within the duty of disclosure, but the buyer may seek a remedy in misdescription if the contractual description of the land is rendered inaccurate through this omission.[2] Rescission may also be available to a buyer who, through the non-disclosure of a physical defect, is unable to use the land for the specific purpose for which it was sold.[3] The deliberate concealment of a known physical defect may give rise to an action in the tort of deceit.[4]

5.3.4. *Planning matters*

Planning matters are not matters of 'title' and are therefore not strictly within the duty of disclosure. It is, however, considered good practice to make disclosure of such matters.

1. But see *Yandle & Sons* v. *Sutton* [1922] 2 Ch. 199.
2. *Re Puckett & Smith's Contract* [1902] 2 Ch. 258.
3. *Re Puckett & Smith's Contract* [1902] 2 Ch. 258.
4. *Gordon* v. *Selico Co. Ltd.* (1986) 278 E.G. 53.

5.4. Non-disclosure by buyer

5.4.1. As a general rule a prospective buyer who is not already in a fiduciary relationship with his seller owes no duty of disclosure to his seller. Exceptionally such a duty may exist, e.g. *English* v. *Dedham Vale Properties*,[1] where the buyer was held liable to account to the seller for profit ultimately received from an undisclosed planning application made by the buyer.

1. [1978] 1 W.L.R. 93.

5.5. Consequences of non-disclosure

5.5.1. The buyer's remedies for non-disclosure will be rescission of the contract if the non-disclosure is judged to be substantial. If the non-disclosure is not substantial the buyer can be forced to complete and will obtain his remedy through an abatement in the purchase price. A substantial non-disclosure is one where its effect is substantially to deprive the buyer of his bargain. A remedy may also lie in misrepresentation since non-disclosure effectively amounts to a misrepresentation by silence.

5.6.   **Contractual exclusion clauses**

5.6.1.   Clauses which purport to exclude liability for non-disclosure and misrepresentation are common, e.g. Standard Condition 7.1, and as far as the latter is concerned
are subject to the reasonableness test in Unfair Contract Terms Act 1977. Their
effectiveness in protecting the seller cannot therefore be guaranteed. Some
restriction of the seller's duty of disclosure may be felt desirable but a total exclusion
of liability would probably not be upheld by the courts save in exceptional
circumstances.

5.7.   **Conclusion**

5.7.1.   Despite the various recognised exceptions to the duty of disclosure outlined above,
a prudent seller will make a full disclosure of all defects and incumbrances to the
buyer, protecting himself where necessary by the inclusion of appropriate
contractual clauses to prevent the buyer from exercising a right to rescind in respect
of the disclosed matters. Some restriction of the seller's duty of disclosure may be
incorporated by way of an exclusion clause in the contract, but care must be
exercised to ensure that the clause is reasonable in the light of the circumstances
of the particular transaction.

B.06. Defective title and restrictive covenant insurance

See also: Seller's investigation of title, para. B.03.
Seller's duty of disclosure, para. B.05.

6.1. Discovery of defects

6.1.1. The seller's solicitor should make a full investigation of the seller's title prior to drafting the contract for sale. Any potential defects in that title must be disclosed to the buyer in the contract and accepted by him, otherwise the seller may be called upon to remove the incumbrance.

6.1.2. Where it appears that a defect in title exists which is not remediable, the seller's solicitor may consider obtaining defective title insurance to cover liability arising out of the defect. Many, but not all, defects can be insured against in this way.

6.1.3. Before obtaining the policy the seller's instructions should be obtained, authorising the solicitor to proceed with this course of action. The seller should be fully advised of the problem and of the likely cost of a policy.

6.1.4. Some lenders insist on the borrower obtaining an indemnity policy against the seller's insolvency, for example where it is apparent that a voluntary transaction has been effected within the past five years. A typical policy will cost a minimum of £175.

6.2. Obtaining a policy

6.2.1. Some major insurance companies will issue policies to cover defects in title. To ensure that a proper premium, commensurate with the risk involved, is paid, quotations should be obtained from more than one company. Countrywide Legal Indemnities offer a policy which has been negotiated by the Law Society (for address see Appendix XIII.4.).

6.2.2. The defect in title is the seller's responsibility because he will be contractually bound to prove a good title to his buyer. The seller should therefore normally expect to meet the costs of obtaining the policy. If the policy is obtained at the request of the buyer it may be possible to negotiate to share the expense with him. In any event the contract should deal with the liability for the expense of obtaining such a policy.

6.2.3. The policy will be a single premium policy the benefit of which will attach to the land. The policy should be mentioned in the contract (if the policy is available at that time) and handed over to the buyer on completion to be kept in a safe place with the documents of title.

6.3. Information needed by insurance company

6.3.1. Before issue of the policy the insurance company will need to assess the risk involved. As a general rule, defects which have occurred in the recent past, e.g. during the last 15 years will be more expensive and difficult to insure against than those which occurred many years ago. The seller's solicitor should be prepared to provide the insurance company with the following information or documents:

   (a) the precise nature of the defect;

   (b) where relevant, a copy of the document in which the defect appears;

   (c) the date when the defect arose, or date when the problem giving rise to the defect occurred;

   (d) what steps (if any) have been taken to remedy the defect;

   (e) whether any third party has taken steps to assert rights against the land because of the defect;

   (f) an approximate estimate of the amount of cover needed.

6.4. Restrictive covenants

6.4.1. The breach of a restrictive covenant affecting the title is a common reason for needing defective title insurance. In some cases the need for the policy will arise, not because a covenant has been broken, but because some contemplated action with or on the land will cause a breach. For example, it is common to find a restrictive covenant which prevents use of the property except as a single private dwelling house and the client wishes now to convert the property into flats, which action would cause a breach of covenant. In such a case it may be possible to obtain an insurance policy which will cover liability for the future breach of covenant. Where the seller is contracting to sell with planning permission for development, he should obtain and bear the cost of the policy; in other cases this matter will be the buyer's responsibility.

6.4.2. Apart from the matters listed above in para. 6.3., the insurance company will also need the following information or documents:

   (a) a copy of the document imposing the covenant or, if this is not available, a copy of the exact wording of the covenant;

(b) the exact nature of the breach which has occurred or details of the action which is contemplated which will cause the breach;

(c) the date when the covenant was imposed;

(d) whether or not the covenant is registered on the charges register of the title (or as a Class D(ii) charge in unregistered land where the covenant was imposed after 1925);

(e) the nature of other properties in the immediate neighbourhood. This is to enable the insurance company to assess the risk of enforcement of the covenant more precisely. Taking the example given above of a potential breach being caused by a conversion of a dwelling into flats, if many of the neighbouring properties have already been converted into flats, the likelihood of this particular covenant being enforced if breached is more remote than if the surrounding properties remain in single ownership. A plan which shows the property in the context of the surrounding locality is often useful;

(f) a copy of any planning permission which permits the development to be undertaken by the client and copies of any objections which were lodged in respect of the application;

(g) what steps have been taken (if any) to trace the person(s) with the benefit of the covenant and the results of those enquiries. The identity of the person who has the benefit of the covenant should be revealed if known, but steps should not be taken to approach that person without the prior consent of the insurance company since such an approach may have an adverse effect on the outcome of the situation and the consequent insurance risk;

(h) details of any complaints which have been received from persons with the benefit of the covenants.

6.5. Accepting the policy when acting for the buyer

6.5.1. Where a buyer is asked to accept a policy taken out by the seller or his predecessor which purports to cover liability for a defect or breach consideration should be given to the following matters:

(a) ensure that the policy enures to the benefit of successors and is not restricted to a named person;

(b) check that the policy covers the defect or breach in question;

(c) check that the amount of cover offered by the policy appears to be adequate;

(d) if the policy is already in existence enquire whether any claims have been made under the policy and the result of those claims;

(e) ensure that the original policy will be handed over on completion. Where the policy has been taken out by a developer to cover the building of several properties, an examined or certified copy of the policy should be handed over on completion;

(f) where a policy already exists, consideration should be given to taking an express assignment of the benefit of the policy from the seller and, after completion, giving notice of the assignment to the insurance company;

(g) obtaining any proposed lender's approval to the policy terms and amount of cover.

6.6. Positive covenants

6.6.1. Since positive covenants are not directly enforceable, insurance against their breach is unlikely to be obtainable.

6.7. Standard Mortgage Instructions[1]

Under the Standard Mortgage Instructions (SMI) where a property has been built or altered or is used in breach of a restrictive covenant the solicitor will only report that the property has a good marketable title if he is satisfied either that the covenant is unenforceable or that indemnity insurance has been arranged.

1. At the time of publication the SMI had not been finalised.

B.07. Capacity

7.1.   Introduction

7.1.1.   In general a seller cannot convey a legal estate unless that estate is vested in him, although in very limited cases he may, under a power, convey a legal estate vested in some other person, e.g. a lender exercising a power of sale.

7.1.2.   Although the nature of the seller's capacity no longer affects the extent of the covenants which are implied in the buyer's favour in the purchase deed, certain points relating to the seller's capacity to deal with the interest in land which he is purporting to dispose of still need to be addressed. These points are outlined in the paragraphs below. Implied covenants are discussed in para. M.09.[1]

7.1.3.   In general, a buyer of registered land will, subject to very limited exceptions, be concerned only to ensure that any restrictions on the register are complied with. The seller will in any event be bound to comply with any fiduciary duties he has, but a buyer is not concerned with them unless they are reflected in a restriction on the register. Where the title to the property is registered with title absolute, and there is no restriction placed on the proprietorship register, the seller is deemed to have the capacity to transfer the land (subject to the provisions relating to rectification of the register) and further enquiry into the seller's capacity is in such cases unnecessary.

1. See Law of Property (Miscellaneous Provisions) Act 1994 and para. M.09.

7.2. Provision for capacity in the contract

7.2.1. For contracts entered into on or after 1 July 1995, it is no longer necessary to state the seller's capacity in the contract.[1]

1. See Law of Property (Miscellaneous Provisions) Act 1994 and para. M.09.

7.3. Beneficial owner

7.3.1. A beneficial owner is a single estate owner who owns the whole of the legal and equitable interest in the property for his own benefit. Either an individual or a corporation may satisfy this requirement. No other person must have any beneficial interest in the interest in land if the capacity of beneficial owner is to apply. Co-owners cannot satisfy this requirement since they hold the property on trust for sale.[1]

7.3.2. If it appears that someone other than the seller named in the contract is in occupation of the property, the buyer must make full enquiries about the status of such occupier in order to establish what interest he has in the property and to establish whether or not the seller is in fact a beneficial owner.

7.3.3. An occupier may claim a beneficial interest in the property through, e.g. contributing to the purchase price. In such a case, it will be necessary for a second trustee to be appointed to act with the seller in order to overreach the beneficial interest of the occupier.[2] Alternatively (or additionally) it may be thought desirable for the occupier to sign a release of his or her rights. Such a release may be included as a contractual term, in which case the occupier will need to sign the contract before exchange. The validity of such disclaimers seems to have met with the court's approval.[3]

7.3.4. In registered land the rights of occupiers will usually be overriding interests within Land Registration Act 1925, s.70(1)(g). Thus the buyer will take subject to these rights (including those which are capable of registration but which are not in fact registered) unless enquiry is made of the occupier and the interest is not revealed, or the sale is by trustees, in which case the rights arising under the trust will be overreached provided the capital money arising is paid to at least two trustees or a trust corporation.

7.3.5. In unregistered land a buyer is deemed to buy with notice of occupiers' rights, other than those capable of registration but which are not registered as land charges;[4] thus the buyer needs to inspect the property and to make full enquiries about the rights of any occupiers.

7.3.6. A surviving co-owner may be a beneficial owner.[5]

1. See *Re Robertson's Application* [1969] 1 All E.R. 257.
2. See *City of London Building Society* v. *Flegg* [1988] A.C. 54; *Lloyds Bank* v. *Rossett* [1991] 1 A.C. 107.
3. *Appleton* v. *Aspin* [1988] 1 W.L.R. 410.
4. *Hunt* v. *Luck* [1902] 1 Ch. 428.
5. See below, para. 7.4.

7.4. Trustees of land

7.4.1. Where land is held on a trust of land any conveyance or transfer of the land must be made by the trustees, being at least two individuals or a trust corporation, in order to overreach the equitable interests of the beneficiaries.

7.4.2. Co-owners hold land on a trust of land.[1]

7.4.3. Where a trust of land exists, whether expressly created or arising under statute (e.g. on intestacy), the trustees are under a duty to consult with, and, so far as is consistent with the general interests of the trust, give effect to the wishes of the adult competent beneficiaries who are entitled to a beneficial interest in possession of the land, when exercising their powers under the trust (e.g. to sell the land).[2] A trust which is created by an *inter vivos* disposition (but not by will) can expressly exclude the duty to consult.[3] A buyer is not concerned to check compliance with the obligation to consult.[4]

7.4.4. Where the trust was expressly created, a power to postpone the sale is implied and cannot be excluded by contrary provision in the trust instrument.[5]

7.4.5. Where the trust arises under statute (e.g. on intestacy), the trustees have a power (but not a duty) to sell the land.[6]

7.4.6. Difficulties may arise if there are only two acting trustees who disagree over the decision to sell, since one trustee alone cannot transfer the legal estate. It may therefore be necessary in these circumstances to apply to the court under Trusts of Land and Appointment of Trustees Act 1996, s.14 to resolve the dispute. On an application under this section the court may make any order it thinks fit (including an order for sale), and thus may, but is not obliged to, order the sale of the property.

7.4.7. In making such an order the court must have regard to the factors listed in section 15 of Trusts of Land and Appointment of Trustees Act 1996 including the purpose of the trust and the interests of any secured creditor or beneficiary.

7.4.8. If a disposition creating a trust of land requires the trustees to obtain the consents of a person or persons before exercising their power of sale, the buyer is only concerned to see that a maximum of two consents have been obtained (even if the trust deed requires a greater number) and is never concerned with the consents of persons suffering mental incapacity. Where a person whose consent is required is not of full age, the buyer is not concerned to see that such consent has been obtained, but the trustees must obtain the consent of a parent or guardian of the under age beneficiary.[7] In registered land the buyer is only concerned to see that the terms of any restriction on the register are complied with.

7.4.9. Trustees' powers to sell, mortgage, and grant leases are the same as those of an absolute owner but they must exercise those powers having regard to the rights of the beneficiaries.[8] Trustees must, however, sell under a fixed price contract unless otherwise authorised by the court under Trustee Act 1925, s.57.

7.4.10. Trusts of Land and Appointment of Trustees Act 1996 has converted existing trusts for sale into 'trusts of land'. From 1 January 1997, co-owners will hold land on a trust of land (formerly trust for sale).

7.4.11. Where the purpose of the trust is to sell the land an expressly created trust for sale can still be created. The requirement for the trustees to sell must however be expressly stated since it is no longer implied under the general law.

1. Law of Property Act 1925, ss.34 and 36.
2. Trusts of Land and Appointment of Trustees Act 1996, s.11.
3. *Ibid.* s.11(2).
4. *Ibid.* s.16(1).
5. *Ibid.* s.4(1).
6. *Ibid.* Sched 2.
7. *Ibid.* s.10.
8. *Ibid.* s.6.

7.5. Personal representatives

7.5.1. Personal representatives have all the powers of trustees of land but are only entitled to exercise those powers during the administration.[1] They are not, however, subject to ss.10, 11 and 14 of Trusts of Land and Appointment of Trustees Act 1996 (duties to obtain consents, consultation with beneficiaries and the court's power of sale).[2]

7.5.2. Their powers are joint as to land, whether freehold or leasehold; therefore all proving personal representatives must be made parties to the contract and purchase deed (conveyance, lease, etc.).[3] A single proving personal representative may, however, act on his own.

1. Administration of Estates Act 1925, s.39.
2. Trusts of Land and Appointment of Trustees Act 1996, s.18.
3. Law of Property (Miscellaneous Provisions) Act 1994, s.16.

7.6. Settled land

7.6.1. The following sub-paragraphs should be read in the light of Trusts of Land and Appointment of Trustees Act 1996 which abolishes the creation of new strict settlements (with very limited exceptions) on or after 1 January 1997. The Act is not retrospective in effect and existing strict settlements are unaffected by the legislation. Land which is held under Universities and Colleges Estates Act 1925 will continue to be settled land and is unaffected by the 1996 Act.

7.6.2. The tenant for life is the person in whom the legal estate in settled land is vested via the vesting instrument. Where there is no tenant for life, or he is a minor, the legal estate is vested in statutory owners who are usually the trustees of the settlement. The tenant for life (or, if none, the statutory owners) will therefore be the seller of settled land, but the trustees of the settlement must be joined as parties to the purchase deed in order to give a valid receipt for capital moneys arising and thus to overreach the interests of the beneficiaries.

7.6.3. The trust deed itself is generally 'behind the curtain' and thus of no concern to a buyer. The buyer is bound and entitled to assume that the person in whom the legal estate is vested by the vesting instrument is the person rightfully entitled to the legal estate and that the persons named as trustees are the properly constituted Settled Land Act trustees.

7.6.4. A sale or other disposition of settled land can only be made for the purposes of the settlement and must be made for the best consideration in money reasonably obtainable.[1] Unless expressly extended by the terms of the settlement certain restrictions on dispositions are imposed by Settled Land Act 1925. The main restrictions relate to mortgages and leases, e.g. the Act permits leases for building or forestry to be granted for a term not exceeding 999 years, for mining, not exceeding 100 years, and for agricultural or occupational purposes, not exceeding 50 years. Powers to grant options to purchase or to take a lease and to grant easements are limited by Settled Land Act 1925, s.51. A disposition which is not authorised either by the Act or by the terms of the settlement is void, even if the buyer was unaware of the settlement.[2]

7.6.5. Where settled land is registered, the tenant for life (or statutory owners) will be registered as proprietor and appropriate restrictions are entered on the proprietorship register.

1. Settled Land Act 1925, s.39(1).
2. *Weston* v. *Henshaw* [1950] Ch. 510; *cf. Re Morgan's Lease; Jones* v. *Norsesowicz* [1972] Ch. 1.

7.7. **Mortgagees**

7.7.1. In order to sell the property the lender must have an express or implied power of sale and that power must have arisen and become exercisable. A power of sale is implied in every mortgage made by deed unless expressly excluded.[1] A legal mortgage must be made by deed.[2] It therefore follows that a lender who has taken a legal mortgage will always have a power of sale unless (exceptionally) that power has been expressly excluded. An equitable mortgage need not be made by deed;[3] it will therefore be necessary to check carefully the existence of the lender's power to sell. In some cases an equitable mortgage may give the lender an irrevocable power of attorney which would give the lender power to convey the legal estate vested in the borrower in exercise of the power of sale. Under Land Registration Act 1925, s.34(1) the proprietor of a registered charge has and may exercise all the powers conferred by law on the owner of a legal mortgage. Conversely, the owner of a charge which is not substantively registered has no power of sale.

7.7.2. As far as a buyer is concerned, he need only check the existence of the power of sale and that it has arisen. The power of sale arises on the legal date for redemption of the mortgage which is usually specified to be a date early on in the mortgage term (e.g. one month after creation of the mortgage).

7.7.3. A lender who is exercising his power of sale must ensure that:

(a) his power of sale exists;

(b) the power has arisen; and

(c) the power has become exercisable.

7.7.4. The lender's power becomes exercisable if one of the three following conditions is met:[4]

(a) notice requiring payment of the principal money has been served on the borrower and default has been made in payment of the principal money for three months; or

(b) some interest under the mortgage is in arrears and unpaid for two months after becoming due; or

(c) there has been breach of some other provision contained in the mortgage deed or Law of Property Act 1925.

7.7.5. A lender who sells in a situation where his power has arisen but not become exercisable will nonetheless pass good title to the buyer but may be liable in damages to the borrower.

7.7.6. *Borrowers*

Subject to any contractual restriction in the mortgage (e.g. restricting further the limited statutory power to grant leases of the property) which may be reflected by a restriction on the register of the title, a borrower may be treated as a beneficial owner.

1. Law of Property Act 1925, s.101.
2. Law of Property Act 1925, s.85.
3. But must be in writing and signed by both parties to satisfy Law of Property (Miscellaneous Provisions) Act 1989, s.2.
4. Law of Property Act 1925, s.103.

7.8. Charities

7.8.1. If there is no restriction on the proprietorship register, a buyer may safely deal with the charity as if it were an absolute owner. If there is a restriction on the register, the following sub paragraphs should be considered. Reference should also be made to Land Registry Practice Advice Leaflet No.1, 'Charity Land Transactions'.

7.8.2. Unless a charity is exempt, no disposition (this word includes a contract as well as conveyance/transfer/lease, etc.) can be made by the charity without an order of the court or Charity Commissioners unless all the following conditions are satisfied:[1]

(a) the trustees must obtain a written report about the proposed disposition from a qualified surveyor (FRICS, ARICS, SVA or ASVA);

(b) the property is advertised for the period and in the manner advised by the surveyor;

(c) the trustees decide that in the light of the surveyor's report they are satisfied that the terms of the disposition are the best that can be obtained;

(d) prescribed words are inserted in both the contract and purchase deed.

7.8.3. The prescribed words referred to state that:

(a) the land is held by or on trust for the charity;

(b) the charity is/is not an exempt charity; *and if not exempt*

(c) whether paras. (a), (b) or (c) of Charities Act 1993 s.36(9) applies; and

(d) if not, that the conditions in para. 7.8.2. above apply.[2]

7.8.4. Where the prescribed words are included in the disposition, the buyer and persons who subsequently acquire the property for money or money's worth are entitled to rely on the conclusiveness of the facts stated and rely on a certificate in the purchase deed that the trustees have power under the trusts of the charity to effect the disposition and that they have complied with the provisions of Charities Act 1993, s.36 so far as applicable to it. The buyer may also rely on such a certificate where the land is registered with a restriction in Form 62.[3]

7.8.5. *Dealing with land owned by a charity*

When dealing with land owned by a charity the following points should be checked:

(a) Is the transaction authorised by the statute or deed which governs the charity?

(b) Is the charity exempt? If so, the transaction can proceed without delay; if not an exempt charity:

(c) Can the trustees give the certificate referred to in para. 7.8.4. above?

(d) If not has an order of the court or the Charity Commissioners been obtained?

7.8.6. Where an order is needed it must either be obtained before exchange of contracts or the contract must be made conditional on the order being obtained.[4]

7.8.7. The purchase deed containing the certificate must be signed by the charity trustees, or by two or more of them acting under an authority given by the trustees.[5] In the case of a corporate charity this means the directors. It is not sufficient for the deed to be sealed by the company in the presence of two directors.

7.8.8. Land held by charitable, ecclesiastical and public trusts ceased to be settled land on 1 January 1997 (with the exception of land held under Universities and Colleges Estates Act 1925).[6]

1. Charities Act 1993, ss.36–40.
2. Land Registration Rules 1996 (S.I. 1996/2925) prescribe the form of wording for use in connection with a registered land transaction.
3. See Schedule to Land Registration Rules 1925 (1925/1093).
4. See Conditional contracts, para. B.13.
5. See Charities Act 1993, s.82.
6. Trusts of Land and Appointment of Trustees Act 1996.

7.9. Companies

7.9.1. A company which is regulated by the Companies Acts may deal with land so long as the transaction is within the scope of the objects clause of its memorandum of association. In favour of a person dealing with a company the validity of an act done by a company shall not be called into question on the ground of lack of capacity by reason of anything in the company's memorandum. The good faith of the buyer is irrelevant and it is no longer necessary to make a company search to ensure that the power to conduct the transaction exists.[1] A company may hold property jointly with another company or individual.[2] Where a company applies to become the proprietor of registered land, details of the company's powers must be supplied to the registrar and, if those powers are limited, an appropriate restriction will be entered on the register.

7.9.2. The powers of a company incorporated by Royal Charter are not restricted by the terms of its Charter; it may therefore be regarded as having the same powers as an individual.

7.9.3. The powers of a company which is incorporated by some other statute are governed by the enabling statute which should in each case be checked and the requisite procedures followed. A transaction outside the terms of the statute will be void.

7.9.4. The powers of a foreign company should be expressly checked and the requisite procedures followed. Enquiries should be made of HM Land Registry as to their requirements for execution of a document by a foreign company. Such requirements may include confirmation from a lawyer entitled to practise in the jurisdiction in which the foreign company was incorporated that the company exists in law and has power to buy, sell and hold land, etc.

7.9.5. Transactions between a company and one of its directors

Companies Act 1985, s.320, applies to arrangements under which a director acquires an asset from the company. The word 'arrangement' covers freehold and leasehold transactions and options made between the director and the company. Transactions under which the company purchases assets from one of its directors are also covered by section 320(1)(*b*). Under these provisions, a transaction to which the section applies must be sanctioned by the company in general meeting.

The company's approval should be obtained before exchange of contracts, but a retrospective approval, obtained before completion, will validate the transaction. The resolution should identify the property, the buyer and the price and may approve the transaction on such other terms as the board of directors may agree. A private company may pass a written resolution (without holding a formal meeting) provided that the vote is unanimous. Where a formal meeting is held, a bare majority will suffice to pass the resolution. Minor transactions, defined as those which are below £2,000 in value or those with a value of between £2,000 and £100,000 where the value represents less than 10% of the company's assets, do not need approval. The term 'director' includes persons connected with the director so that a transfer by a company to a director's wife or to another company with which the director is associated will invoke the provisions of the section. The consequences of failure to comply with section 320 are contained in section 322: broadly, the transaction is voidable at the instance of the company. The company is entitled to be compensated for any loss it has suffered as a result of the unapproved transaction and to account for any gain.

1. Companies Act 1989, s.108.
2. Bodies Corporate (Joint Tenancy) Act 1899, s.1.

7.10. Minors

7.10.1. A person aged under 18 years cannot hold a legal estate in land but may hold an equitable interest. If, however, there is no restriction on the register of the title, the buyer is entitled to assume that the seller has full capacity. A conveyance to a minor alone takes effect as an agreement to create a trust of land and in the meantime to hold the land on trust for him. A contract for sale to a minor is binding on him unless repudiated by him during minority or within a reasonable time after attaining majority.[1]

1. See Minors' Contracts Act 1987.

7.11. Persons suffering from mental disability

7.11.1. A contract for the sale or purchase of land, entered into by a person who is suffering from mental incapacity sufficient to deprive him of understanding of the nature of the transaction, is voidable at the option of the incapacitated party, provided he can prove that at the time of the transaction the other contracting party was aware of the disability.[1]

7.11.2. Once a receiver is appointed under Mental Health Act 1983, s.99, the patient loses all contractual capacity and any purported *inter vivos* disposition by him is void. The receiver has power, subject to the court's approval, to deal with the patient's property.[2]

7.11.3. On the appointment of a receiver a restriction is not normally entered on registered land unless the receiver or other authorised person requests its entry and, on a dealing with registered land, the registrar will require a copy of the order which provides the receiver's authority to act. Where the receiver is registered as proprietor a restriction is automatically entered.

7.11.4. See also para. D.02.8.6.

1. *Broughton* v. *Snook* [1938] Ch. 505.
2. See Mental Health Act 1983, ss.95 and 96.

7.12. Universities and colleges

7.12.1. Universities and Colleges Estates Act 1925 confers powers to sell and exchange land and to purchase land as an investment on the universities of Oxford, Cambridge and Durham (and their respective colleges) and on Winchester and Eton Colleges and restrictions are entered in registered land reflecting the limitations on their powers under the statutes governing them. Other universities and colleges may be educational charities and are subject to the rules on charities outlined above.

7.13. Local authorities

7.13.1. A local authority may acquire land, inside or outside its own area, for the purpose of any of its functions under any Public General Act or for the benefit, improvement or development of its area. Power to acquire land for the provision of accommodation is given by Housing Act 1985, s.17. Powers of compulsory purchase of land are conferred by many statutes.[1]

7.13.2. Ministerial consent is required for certain disposals of land by a local authority. In such a case, consent must be obtained before contracts are exchanged, or alternately the contract made conditional on such consent being forthcoming. A conveyance made without the requisite consent may be void. In certain cases a buyer is entitled to assume that the transaction is within the powers of the local authority and does not have to investigate whether or not ministerial approval has been given. Under Housing Act 1988, s.44 (which does not apply to right to buy sales and leases), any disposal of residential property by a local authority for which the consent of the Secretary of State for the Environment is required is void if made without consent unless:

(a) the disposal is in favour of an individual or two or more individuals; and

(b) the disposal comprises only a single house or flat.

7.13.3. The protection afforded by Local Government Act 1972, s.128 does not apply in respect of residential premises unless both these conditions are satisfied. Accordingly on the application to register a transfer or lease of residential premises by a local authority the relevant consent must be lodged unless both conditions (a) and (b) above are satisfied. No restriction will appear on the register of title to reflect these requirements.

1. Compulsory purchase is outside the scope of this book.

7.14. Parish and community councils

7.14.1. Land may be acquired by such a council (whether inside or outside its own area) for the purposes of any of its functions under Local Government Act 1972 or any other Public General Act.

7.14.2. Ministerial consent is required for disposals of land, but buyers from parish and community councils are protected against breach of the consent provisions.[1]

1. Local Government Act 1972, s.128.

7.15. Building societies, friendly societies, trade unions

7.15.1. A building society may acquire and hold land for the purpose of its business or for commercial purposes under Building Societies Act 1986, ss. 16 and 17. It will also have power to sell land as a lender where it has lent money on mortgage and the lender's power of sale has become exercisable.[1]

7.15.2. Registered friendly societies and industrial and provident societies have power to buy, sell and hold land, subject to the rules of each individual society.

7.15.3. Property belonging to a trade union is usually vested in trustees on trust for the union. Powers of acquisition and disposition are subject to the rules of the union, the general law relating to trustees, and some special provisions contained in Trade Union and Labour Relations Act 1974, s.2.

1. See above, para. 7.7.

7.16. Fiduciary relationships

7.16.1. Where a fiduciary relationship exists between the parties to the transaction, there is a presumption of constructive fraud which is rebuttable on proof (by the dominant party to the relationship) that the transaction was at a fair price (an independent valuation is highly desirable), that all the circumstances of the transaction were known to the subordinate party, and that each party received, or was given a proper opportunity to take, independent legal advice. The transaction is prima facie voidable at the instance of the subordinate party.

7.16.2. A fiduciary relationship is deemed to exist in dealings between the following persons:

    (a) solicitor and client;

    (b) trustee and beneficiary;

    (c) parent and child (where the influence of the parent over the child may be held to have endured beyond the child's majority);

    (d) doctor and patient;

    (e) religious advisor and disciple;

    (f) teacher and pupil;

    (g) fiancés (but not between husband and wife).

7.16.3.   A fiduciary relationship may exist in circumstances other than those listed above, but is not presumed to exist, and the dominance of one party over the other would have to be proved before the court would apply the doctrine of constructive fraud.[1]

7.16.4.   If a solicitor is asked to act in dealings between any of the parties listed above, in para. 7.16.2., or in any other situation where he feels that the relationship between the contracting parties may be classed as fiduciary, he should ensure that:

    (a) an independent valuation of the property is obtained;

    (b) all the facts pertaining to the transaction are known by and understood by both parties;

    (c) the parties are separately represented.[2]

1. See, e.g. *Lloyds Bank* v. *Bundy* [1975] Q.B. 326 (fiduciary relationship proved to have existed between bank manager and customer).
2. See Acting for both parties, para. A.10.

7.17.   **Death and insolvency**[1]

7.17.1.   The death of one of the contracting parties between contract and completion does not affect the validity of the contract. The party's personal representatives step into the shoes of the deceased and are obliged to continue with the transaction.

7.17.2.   Where one of the contracting parties has a bankruptcy order made against him between contract and completion, his capacity to contract is transferred to his trustee in bankruptcy who, subject to his power to disclaim the contract, will take over the rights and obligations of the bankrupt under the contract. Where the seller is bankrupt a disclaimer of the contract by the trustee can only be made if the trustee also disclaims the property.

1. See Death and insolvency, para. E.06.

7.18.   **One-man companies**

7.18.1.   It is permitted for a company to have only one shareholder. That shareholder may also be a director of the company. If he is the only director a second person must be appointed to act as company secretary.

7.19. **Administrative receiver**

7.19.1. An administrative receiver must be a qualified insolvency practitioner and must accept his appointment to act by the business day following the receipt by him of his appointment.

7.19.2. When buying a property from an administrative receiver the validity of the receiver's appointment should be checked, including:

(a) the validity of the floating charge under which the appointment was made;

(b) that the charge covered the whole or substantially the whole of the company's property;

(c) that the charge is not likely to be invalidated, e.g. for want of registration, or fraudulent preference;

(d) that the receiver's appointment does not exceed any powers in the charge;

(e) that the receiver has power to conduct the transaction in question;

(f) in a case where two receivers have been appointed, whether they are able to act jointly and severally or jointly only.

7.19.3. A certified copy of the receiver's appointment should be obtained by the buyer since this document will have to be produced to HM Land Registry on registration of the transfer.

7.19.4. As a matter of practice the receiver may decline to give any warranties or covenants and may seek to exclude his personal liability. A buyer may, where appropriate, prefer to take a transfer from the lender in exercise of his power of sale where the buyer will benefit from the limited covenants given by lenders and will also have the guarantee of overreaching subsequent incumbrances.

B.08. Agricultural land

8.1. Introduction

8.1.1. The procedure when buying agricultural land will be similar to that employed when buying any piece of freehold or leasehold land (as appropriate). The following paragraphs merely draw attention to some matters to which particular attention needs to be paid because of the nature of agricultural land. For more detailed information reference should be made to a specialist text on the subject.

8.1.2. Where the Standard Mortgage Instructions (SMI) apply the special provisions of the SMI relating to agricultural land and/or land subject to an agricultural restriction must be complied with.[1]

1. At the time of publication the SMI had not been finalised.

8.2. Plans

8.2.1. The boundaries of agricultural land need to be checked carefully so that both parties understand clearly and precisely which land is to be the subject of the sale. The seller and buyer and/or their respective surveyors should inspect the land and agree the boundaries which should be marked on a plan to be attached to the contract. The plan should be of sufficiently large scale, e.g. 1:2500, and dimensions to clearly identify the land and its salient features. A large scale Ordnance Survey map may be used for this purpose. The route of any public footpaths, services and easements which cross the land should be identified.

8.2.2. Where possible 'T' marks should be marked on the plan to indicate the future responsibility for maintenance of boundaries. Where no definite indications as to boundaries exist, reference may be made to the common law presumptions, e.g. where there is a hedge and ditch boundary, the boundary lies on the far side of the ditch from the hedge. At common law the *ad medium filum* rule applies to roads and rivers.

8.2.3. Rights of way and access to the property should be checked and marked on the plan.

8.3. Pre-contract searches

8.3.1. The situation of the land may indicate that some of the less usual pre-contract searches should be undertaken, e.g. rivers, railways.[1] A commons registration search should always be undertaken. It will also be necessary for the buyer's solicitor to require the local authority to answer some of the questions on Part II of Enquiries of Local Authority Search Form.

8.3.2. If only part of land which enjoys rights of common is being sold, an apportionment of those rights between the two parcels of land may be considered.

8.3.3. A search should be made against sites of special scientific interest where the local search replies indicate that such a site is included in the land to be bought.

8.3.4. A search may be made with the owning authority where it is necessary to establish the routes of pipelines and cables passing under, through or over the property.

8.3.5. A corn rent and corn annuity or chancel repairs search may be necessary where the land is near an ancient parish church.

8.3.6. Geological workings may necessitate searches, e.g. for coal, oil, sand and gravel.

8.3.7. *Enquiries of the seller*

In addition to the normal pre-contract enquiries, a form of agricultural tenancy enquiries may be required where the land to be bought includes tenanted property and some of the following additional enquiries may be relevant to the purchase:

(a) planning enquiries concerning agricultural buildings and whether or not they fall within Agricultural General Development Order;

(b) enquiries concerning listed buildings and scheduling under Ancient Monuments and Archaeological Areas Act 1979;

(c) confirmation should be sought that all grant or subsidy schemes relating to the property have expired, that the conditions applicable to them have been met and that no money will become repayable;

(d) enquiries concerning crop and other quotas which may benefit the property and whether they are transferable to the buyer;

(e) enquiries concerning boundaries and their maintenance;

(f) enquiries relating to services benefiting the property (especially water supplies);

(g) questions relating to potential chancel repair liability;

(h) enquiries relating to sites of special scientific interest if these come to light in answer to a local search;

(i) enquiries relating to discharge licences granted by the Environment Agency under Water Act 1989, Environmental Protection Act 1990 or Environment Act 1995;

(j) enquiries as to the history of the occurrence of notifiable diseases on the property;

(k) specific enquiries relating to sporting rights;

(l) enquiries relating to the existence of standing timber felling licences and grant conditions.

1. See Pre-contract searches and enquiries, para. B.10.

8.4.   Planning

8.4.1.   The authorised use of the land under the Town and Country Planning Act 1990 should be ascertained. This information will be revealed in answer to enquiries of the local authority. Any restrictions on the use of the property should be discussed by the buyer's solicitor with his client to ensure that they do not conflict with the client's requirements. The seller should only give a warranty in the contract relating to the authorised use of the property if he is sure that the information which he is warranting is correct.

8.4.2.   A change of use to agricultural use needs no consent. In some cases the erection of agricultural buildings does not require consent.

8.5.   Taxation consequences

8.5.1.   If the transaction involves the sale of a business as a going concern, value added tax should not be paid where both the seller and the buyer are registered for VAT. The VAT rules for a going concern transaction are more rigorous where land is included. If the buyer is not registered but the seller is, the seller must charge VAT on the assets which are subject to VAT at the standard rate. This may include the agricultural land if the option to tax has effect in relation to it.[1] In other cases value added tax may be payable on the transaction, in which case an appropriate clause to this effect needs to be included in the contract.

1. Value Added Tax Act 1994, s.40 and VAT (Special Provisions) Order 1995 (S.I. 1995/1268).

8.5.2. This type of transaction can raise taxation issues in relation to, e.g. capital gains tax, inheritance tax and/or corporation tax.

8.6. Grants and subsidies

8.6.1. The buyer should enquire of the seller whether any grants or subsidies have been received or are payable in respect of the land. If any part of these grants or subsidies is repayable on sale of the land, the seller should be required to fulfil this obligation before completion.

8.7. Growing crops, livestock, machinery

8.7.1. The seller must agree with the buyer which items of livestock and/or plant and machinery are to be included in the sale. A valuation of these items may be required and a schedule of items to be included in the sale should be annexed to the contract.

8.7.2. Similarly agreement must be reached between the parties relating to growing crops, i.e. whether the seller is to be entitled to return to the property after completion in order to harvest his crops, or whether the benefit of the growing crops will pass to the buyer. Where the buyer is to take over responsibility for livestock and/or growing crops he may require the seller to give a warranty in the contract that the seller will use his best (or reasonable) endeavours to maintain standards of good husbandry over the land until completion. The buyer may consider it prudent to employ a veterinary surgeon to inspect livestock and to certify their state of health. The seller may be required to produce current vaccination certificates for livestock (where appropriate). It should be noted that a contract to fell and remove standing timber is a contract for the sale of an interest in land which is, by Law of Property (Miscellaneous Provisions) Act 1989, s.2, required to be in writing.

8.8. Water

8.8.1. If the land currently has a water abstraction licence under Water Act 1989, enquiries should be raised to confirm that the benefit of the licence is assignable; a condition providing for the licence to be assigned to the buyer must then be included in the contract. The buyer must then notify the water authority of the change of ownership of the licence within 15 months of completion. Failure to do so results in the licence becoming void and there is no guarantee that a new licence would be granted. Form CON46G (in duplicate and accompanied by a plan of the land) may be used to notify the authority of the assignment. Following completion the buyer has 15 months to apply to the water company for the transfer of the licence. Failure to apply for the transfer makes the licence void with no guarantee of the issue of a new licence. Assignment of a licence is only possible where the buyer takes over the whole of the land to which the licence applies. If the licence relates to only part of the land sold, no assignment is possible and the buyer will need to apply for a new licence in relation to the land acquired by him.

8.8.2. Where the water supply to the property is metered, the water authority must, in addition to being notified of the change of ownership, be asked to read the meter on the day of completion, in order that apportioned accounts can be sent to seller and buyer.

8.8.3. Some or all of the following enquiries may need to be raised in connection with the water supply to the property:

(a) does the property have a mains water supply?

(b) if there is a mains water supply, does the mains pipe (which is maintained by the water company) run through the property or immediately adjacent to the property in a public highway?

(c) if there is no direct access to the mains water pipe, how is the property connected to the mains, who owns and is liable for the private spur, and does the property have the benefit of private easements for the continued use of the pipe, its maintenance repair and replacement and the taking of water through it?

(d) where is the mains water meter?

(e) if the property has a private water supply its source should be identified and enquiries raised as to whether the source supplies this property exclusively;

(f) are special water uses required, e.g. for spray irrigation?

(g) if the property is supplied by a private water source from an adjoining property enquiries should be raised to ascertain the contractual rights and obligations of the parties.

8.9.   Tenancies

8.9.1. In order to fulfil his duty of disclosure the seller must give the buyer full details of any tenancies which affect the property. Such details having been supplied, the buyer is, by Standard Condition 3.2.2(a), deemed to enter the contract knowing and accepting the tenancy terms. By Standard Condition 3.2.2(e), it is the buyer's responsibility to check the effects of any security of tenure legislation affecting such tenancies. Some tenant farmers may have some protection under Agricultural Holdings Act 1986 or Agricultural Tenancies Act 1995,[1] and farm workers living in tied accommodation may be protected by Rent (Agriculture) Act 1976 or Housing Act 1988.[2]

8.9.2. If the property is sold subject to existing tenancies the buyer should covenant with the seller to observe and perform those conditions which remain to be observed and performed by the landlord and to indemnify the seller against them.

1. See Agricultural holdings, para. K.08.
2. See Long-term residential tenancies, para. K.06.

8.10. **Wayleave agreements**

8.10.1. Any wayleave agreements which affect the property (e.g. for pylons, pipelines, etc.) should be expressly assigned to the buyer with the consent of the appropriate authority. Wayleave payments need only be apportioned if they are of substance. Generally a plan of the property sold is sent to the utility board after completion and they will apportion the wayleave and issue refunds and demands as appropriate.

8.11. **Quotas**

8.11.1. Milk quota must be expressly assigned to the buyer. This topic is further considered in para. B.09. The sale of milk quotas is a standard-rated supply of services for VAT purposes if it is done in the course of a business and the seller is VAT registered. If the quota is sold together with the land, Customs have indicated that they will treat it as a simple supply of the land. The position is different where the quota is sold with a grazing licence.

8.11.2. Contracts with British Sugar plc for the growing of sugar beet are delivery contracts made with the individual grower (contract holder), which cannot be assigned with land. Any significant changes to contract details must be notified to British Sugar. Changes may (as defined in the Inter-Professional Agreement) result in the contract tonneage automatically reverting to British Sugar. In this case, British Sugar exercises its reasonable discretion in deciding how to handle the change. Assignment of the right to receive income from such a sugar beet contract must be approved by British Sugar.[1]

8.11.3. There are no formal restrictions on the assignment of potato quota. The Potato Guarantee and Quota Areas have now been ended by the bringing into force of Agriculture Act 1993, ss.55 and 59.[2]

1. For address see App. XIII.4.
2. Agriculture Act 1993 (Commencement No.1 Order) (S.I. 2038/1993).

8.12. **Agricultural credits search**

8.12.1. A fixed or floating charge made by a farmer in favour of a bank over agricultural stock or assets is void against anyone other than the farmer himself unless the charge is registered within seven days of its execution.[1]

8.12.2. A person who is buying farming stock or assets or a mortgagee who is lending money on the security of such items should make an agricultural credits search in order to check the existence and validity of subsisting charges. The search should be made by the buyer before contracts are exchanged in order to find out whether any charges affect the property; in such a case the seller must be required to provide evidence of their discharge at completion. A further search is advised, to be made just before completion, to ensure that no further charges have been registered since the date of the earlier search.

8.12.3. The search is made by submitting Form AC6 in duplicate to The Superintendent, Agricultural Credits Department, Burrington Way, Plymouth. No personal or telephone search facilities currently exist. Current search fees are listed in Appendix IX.4.

8.12.4. A certificate of search is conclusive but affords no priority period in favour of the searcher. Copies of the register entries can be obtained on application on Form AC5.

1. Agricultural Credits Act 1928, s.9.

8.13. Post-exchange matters

8.13.1. Company search

If buying or leasing land from a limited company or granting a mortgage to a limited company, a company search will normally be desirable. If preferred, this search can be made before exchange of contracts and updated before completion.

8.13.2. Mortgages

The Agricultural Mortgage Corporation plc, which was incorporated under Agricultural Credits Act 1928, provides finance for any agricultural or forestry purpose, including the purchase of land, working capital and the replacement of existing borrowing. The security required is a first charge on agricultural property. The maximum sum advanced cannot exceed two-thirds of the mortgage valuation of the security.

8.13.3. Where a floating charge is discovered against a company seller, a certificate of non-crystallization should be obtained from the lender.

8.13.4. Duplicate purchase deed

When a part only of agricultural land is sold, it is advisable to have the purchase deed drawn up in duplicate, the duplicate being kept by the seller as evidence of, e.g. restrictive covenants imposed on the buyer.

8.13.5. Completion statement

In addition to the normal requirements for a completion statement (see Preparing for completion, para. E.04.) the following may need to be considered on a dealing with agricultural land:

(a) VAT on vatable supplies, e.g. sporting or fishing rights or quota;

(b) apportionment of agricultural rents, cottage rents, wayleave payments, sporting or fishing rents;

(c) payment for fittings being purchased;

(d) payment for any seeds, cultivations or labour at valuation (plus VAT if applicable);

(e) allowance for any agreed retentions for holdover;

(f) where VAT is payable, a separate VAT invoice should be supplied with the completion statement on receipt of the VAT from the buyer.

8.14. Post-completion matters

8.14.1. On the sale of the whole or part of a freehold which is subject to an agricultural tenancy, written notice of the change of ownership should be served on the tenant including details of the rent apportionment.

8.14.2. Transfer forms for transfer of milk quota must be registered with the Intervention Board within 28 days of the change of occupation.[1]

8.14.3. If the benefit of a grant is taken over with the granting authority's consent, registration of the new owner must be made in accordance with the granting authority's requirements.

8.14.4. Notice of transfer of a water abstraction licence must be given to the water authority within 15 months of the transfer.

1. See para. B.09.

8.15. Environmental aspects

8.15.1. Any discharge which may pollute controlled waters will require a licence/consent from the Environment Agency under Water Act 1989. Discharge from slurry tanks or yard washing may be sufficiently contaminated to require such a consent.[1]

8.15.2. Enquiries should be made as to whether the agricultural processes carried out on the property fall within the scope of the regulations made under Environmental Protection Act 1990 as amended or other statutes governing the environment.

8.15.3. Enquiries should be raised as to whether the property has been the subject of a past land use which has left residual contamination likely to interfere with the buyer's proposed use of the property or which may cause pollution.

1. See Control of Pollution (Silage, Slurry and Agricultural Fuel Oil) Regulations (S.I. 1991/324).

8.16. Sporting and other rights

8.16.1. Often sporting rights are reserved by the seller. These include game under Ground Game Acts, deer (not included in Ground Game Acts) and fishing rights for the seller and his licensees. The rights will include rights of access both to exercise the sporting rights and to retrieve fallen game, any damage caused being made good by the seller. The terms of the contract should be checked to see which, if any, of such rights are being reserved by the seller.

8.16.2. If it is likely that minerals are contained under the land being sold, consideration should be given to their reservation to the seller, including, where appropriate, rights to work and take away the minerals. A bare reservation of minerals does not allow either seller or buyer to work them. Alternatively, a restrictive covenant may be imposed on the buyer preventing him from working any minerals in the land. If this is done a buyer who wished in the future to work the minerals would have to seek a release of the covenant from the seller (or his successor in title), but no further transfer of the mineral rights would be needed.

8.16.3. Unless there is a specific reservation in the purchase deed, most incorporeal hereditaments (including a lordship of the manor) will pass with the land. Lordships and manorial rights are frequently reserved to the seller when land is sold since they are saleable commodities in themselves.

B.09. Milk quotas

9.1.	**General principles**	9.5.	**Tenancies**
9.2.	**Buying land with quota attached**	9.6.	**Compensation payable to tenants for loss of quota**
9.3.	**Sales of part of land**		
9.4.	**Selling land with the benefit of quota**	9.7.	**Quota transfers without land**

See also: Agricultural land, para. B.08.

9.1. General principles

9.1.1. Milk quotas were introduced in the U.K. on 2 April 1984 to regulate the quantity of milk and milk products being produced in the E.U. Farms producing milk and other milk products have an allocation (a quota) the amount of which is normally based on their production levels in 1983. A levy is payable if a producer exceeds his quota. Quota attaches to the land and will thus pass to a buyer or tenant of the land.

9.2. Buying land with quota attached

9.2.1. Pre-contract enquiries

Additional pre-contract enquiries will be necessary to establish:

(a) the exact amount of quota attaching to the land;

(b) the composition of the quota (i.e. does it include direct sales, or SLOM quota);

(c) that the seller is the freehold owner of the whole holding to which the quota attaches;

(d) that the quota does not attach to any land outside the land agreed to be sold;

(e) that if the seller is not the freehold owner of the entire quota, all other persons with an interest in the holding, such as landlords or lenders, who will be affected by the disposal of the quota have signified their agreement to the disposal on Form MQ1; or

(f) if an apportionment of the quota has been made within the previous six months and notified to the Intervention Board Executive Agency by means of Form MQ8.

9.2.2. If a third party, other than persons referred to in (d) above, has an interest in the land (e.g. lender or trustee) that person's consent to the transfer of the quota should be required on Form MQ1.

9.2.3. The seller should be required to supply the buyer with his most recent computer print-out from the Intervention Board Executive Agency [1] which will show the allocation of quota and the registration of the quota in the seller's name. The seller will also need to produce his latest statement from his purchaser(s) of milk, showing deliveries to date, to assess the used/unused element of the quota to be sold.

9.2.4. To assist the buyer in dealing with future transfers of quota or claims for compensation from tenants the seller's records relating to livestock cropping in 1983 and details of the use of the land and buildings, tenant's improvements and rent paid in 1983 should be produced to the buyer and handed over to him on completion.

9.2.5. A seller who sells milk direct to the public must have a licence, a copy of which should be supplied to the buyer and arrangements made for the transfer of the licence to the buyer on completion. Farmhouse cheesemakers are classified as direct sellers in so far as they use their own milk for cheese production. If a farmhouse cheesemaker buys milk directly from a producer, the cheesemaker must be approved by the Intervention Board Executive Agency to act as a purchaser. The producer will need to ensure that the quota is registered with the farmhouse cheesemaker to cover deliveries.

9.2.6. *The contract*

The contract must contain a clause dealing with the transfer of the quota to the buyer. Wording similar to that set out below will be appropriate for this purpose:

> 'The seller is the proprietor of wholesale /direct sales quota for … litres of milk per annum. On completion the seller shall hand over to the buyer an application form for the transfer of the said quota duly signed and completed so far as the seller is able together with a signed statement as required by the Intervention Board Executive Agency and thereafter shall use his best endeavours to obtain the transfer of the said quota to the buyer by providing any further evidence as the Board shall require.'

9.2.7. *The purchase deed*

The purchase deed must contain a clause assigning the benefit and burden of the specified amount of quota to the buyer.

9.2.8. *Completion*

On completion (in addition to normal completion requirements) the buyer must ensure that such of the following documents as are relevant to the transaction are handed over:

(a) completed Form MQ1 (consent to transfer of quota);

(b) any documentation relevant to an apportionment of quota;

(c) the quota notification from the Intervention Board Executive Agency;

(d) the seller's records for 1983;

(e) a direct seller's licence.

9.2.9. *Post-completion*

Within 28 days of completion the buyer must give notice of change of occupation to the Intervention Board Executive Agency on a quota transfer form (Form MQ1). The buyer should also be advised to keep accurate records of his milk production, use of land, tenant's improvements, etc., for use in future transfers or disputes relating to a tenant's right to compensation.

1. For address see App. XIII.4

9.3. **Sales of part of land**

9.3.1. Where a buyer buys part of the seller's land he will become entitled to a proportionate amount of the quota attaching to the holding. If the parties (including interested parties) cannot agree on the apportionment of the quota taking account of areas used for milk production within 28 days then the matter must be referred to arbitration.

9.3.2. *Arbitration*

If after 28 days the parties cannot agree on an apportionment then the matter must be referred by the Intervention Board to the President of the Royal Institution of Chartered Surveyors (RICS) who will, for a fee of £115, appoint an arbitrator to decide the apportionment. The arbitrator must base his award on the pattern of milk production on the area of land being transferred over the last five-year period during which production took place. One or all of the parties may decide to refer the matter to arbitration within the 28 days referred to above if it becomes apparent that agreement is not possible.

9.3.3. The provisions in para. 9.2. above will also be relevant to a sale of part of a holding. In particular the contract must contain a clause to deal with the transfer of the quota. Provisions similar to those set out below will be appropriate:

'(a) in addition to the property the seller shall transfer on completion ... litres of wholesale/direct sales quota;

(b) on completion the seller shall hand over to the buyer's solicitors an application form for the transfer of the said quota duly signed and completed (so far as the seller is able) together with a signed statement the contents of which are in accordance with the provisions of S.I. 1994/672, The Dairy Produce Quotas Regulations 1994 which documentation shall be submitted to the Intervention Board forthwith;

(c) if the seller fails to hand over the requisite forms the buyer may rescind the contract and the seller shall repay the deposit money to the buyer;

(d) the seller shall supply the buyer and the Intervention Board (or as appropriate) with all necessary evidence required to substantiate the amount of quota transferred with the property and shall use the seller's best endeavours to obtain a transfer of that share of the quota.'

9.4. Selling land with the benefit of quota

9.4.1. The seller should be prepared to supply the buyer with the information specified in para. 9.2.1. above and, on completion, such of the documents listed in para. 9.2.8. above as are relevant. The contract and purchase deed must contain a clause dealing with the transfer of the quota (see above, para. 9.2.6.).

9.5. Tenancies

9.5.1. Clauses to deal with the following matters should be considered for inclusion in any tenancy agreement which relates to land which has the benefit of quota:

(a) prohibition of alienation of the quota by the tenant;

(b) maintenance of production on the land to prevent loss of quota;

(c) the benefit of the quota on termination of the tenancy;

(d) tenant's rights to compensation for loss of quota at the end of the tenancy.

9.5.2. The quota will revert to the landlord on termination of the tenancy but the tenant may be entitled to compensation for the loss of the quota. Where the quota reverts to the landlord Form MQ1 needs to be completed and sent to the Intervention Board.

9.6. Compensation payable to tenants for loss of quota

9.6.1. Agriculture Act 1986 provides for payment by the landlord to certain agricultural tenants on termination of a tenancy which is subject to the provisions of Agricultural Holdings Act 1986. Agricultural Tenancies Act 1995 applies to farm business tenancies entered into or after 1 September 1995. The 1995 Act entitles a tenant to compensation at the end of a tenancy for physical improvements made to a holding and for intangible advantages which increase the value of the holding, provided they are left behind by a departing tenant and the landlord's written consent to the improvements has been obtained. Intangible advantages include milk quota obtained during the course of a tenancy. For tenancies covered by the 1995 Act the milk quota provisions in section 13 and Schedule 1 Agriculture Act 1986 do not apply.

9.6.2. *Eligible tenants*

To be eligible for compensation under Agriculture Act 1986 a tenant must:

(a) have the quota registered in his own name (not in the name of a company or partnership through which the tenant carries on business); and

(b) have been in occupation of the land as tenant on 2 April 1984; or

(c) have succeeded to a tenancy since 2 April 1984 under the succession provisions of Agricultural Holdings Act 1986, so long as the party from whom the tenant succeeded was himself in possession on 2 April 1984.

9.6.3. Assignors of tenancies assigned after 2 April 1984 are not eligible, but the assignee is, subject to satisfying the qualifications outlined above.

9.6.4. The statutory entitlement to compensation relates to only one transfer of occupation. There is no entitlement on subsequent transfers. It is therefore open to a landlord to determine the terms under which new tenants can enjoy the quota attached to the holding, i.e. whether they will be charged for quota at the beginning of the tenancy and whether or not they will be entitled to any payment at the end of the tenancy. If the land being vacated comprises only part of the tenant's holding there is an apportionment of the quota for compensation purposes.

9.6.5. *Calculation of payment*

Payment is calculated by taking:

(a) the value of the allocated quota in excess of the standard quota for the land (or if allocated quota is less than the standard quota a proportionate reduction is made); and

(b) the value of the tenant's fraction of the standard quota; and

(c) the value of the transferred quota (this will be the entire value where the tenant has borne the whole cost of the transfer and proportionately where the tenant has only borne part of the cost).

9.6.6. *Valuation of quota*

Value=value at the termination of the tenancy taking into account available evidence of the value of the quota including the value of the land with and without quota.

9.6.7. Standard quota is calculated by multiplying the relevant number of hectares by the prescribed quota per hectare.

9.6.8. Prescribed quota is defined by Milk Quota (Calculation of Standard Quota) (Amendment) Order 1992 (S.I. 1992/1225) as 7,140 litres per hectare. There is a lower figure for land in less favoured areas (areas eligible for hill livestock compensatory allowance) and different figures apply for different breeds.

9.6.9. The relevant number of hectares is the average number of hectares used during the relevant period (the period to which allocated quota was determined, normally 1983) for feeding of dairy cows kept on the land.

9.6.10. *Method of assessing quantum*

The quantum of compensation (called the 'tenant's fraction') is ascertained by comparing the annual rental value of the tenant's dairy improvements and fixed equipment with the rent paid for the land during the relevant period.

9.6.11.   The formula used is $\dfrac{r}{r+R}$

where $r=$ the annual rental value at the end of the relevant period of the tenant's dairy improvement and fixed equipment and $R=$ the rent of the land.

9.6.12.   Liability for compensation does not arise until the termination of the tenancy but either landlord or tenant may at any time prior to termination seek determination of the standard quota or the tenant's fraction by agreement or arbitration.

9.6.13.   The procedure for claiming compensation is similar to that for claiming tenant right under Agricultural Holdings Act 1986.

9.7   Quota transfers without land

9.7.1.   An application may be made to the Intervention Board to transfer quota without land 'to improve the structure of milk production at the level of the holding'.[1] The transferor must need to dispose of the quota because he is scaling down or winding down dairy production *permanently* on the land to which the quota is attached. The transferee must need to acquire additional quota because his milk production business has expanded or will be expanding.

9.7.2.   WARNING: Transferor and transferee must comply with the following restrictions, on transferring *any* quota to or from their holding after they have been involved in a transfer without land:[2]

9.7.3. *The seller*

Sellers or 'transferors' must get permission from everyone with a legitimate interest in their holding before they apply to transfer quota without land. (A holding is all the land and production units operated by a quota holder.) They must declare on the form MQ/2 (*Application for approval to transfer quota without land*) that they will not buy or lease in quota between the date of submission of the application for approval (MQ/2) and the end of the quota year following the quota year in which the transfer takes place.

9.7.4   They must also declare that they have not:

    (a)   bought or leased in quota under the 'transfer without land' provisions during the quota year in which the application was made;

    (b)   bought or leased in quota under the 'transfer without land' provisions during the previous quota year.

9.7.5. *The buyer*

The buyer or 'transferee' must declare on the form MQ/2 (*Application for approval to transfer quota without land*) that they will not lease or transfer out quota between:

    (a)   the date of submission of the application for approval (MQ/2); and

(b) the end of the quota year following the quota year in which the transfer takes place.

9.7.6. *Applying for approval*

The transfer must not go ahead until written approval has been obtained from the Intervention Board. An application for approval is made:

(a) using form MQ/2 (*Application for approval to transfer quota without land*);

(b) at least 10 working days before the intended date of transfer.

The Intervention Board will assess the application and write to the transferor:

(a) to approve the proposed transfer of quota; or

(b) to ask for more information; or

(c) to explain why approval cannot be given.

9.7.7. *Applying to register an approved transfer*

If the Intervention Board approves the transfer, they will send form MQ/2a (*Application to register an approved transfer of quota without land*) on which an application may be made to register the transfer. This form must be received by the Intervention Board, via the transferee or his agent, within 28 days of the transaction. If the transfer happens at the end of the quota year, the form must be sent within seven working days of the start of the next quota year. Approval for the transfer may be withdrawn if the form is not received on time.

9.7.8. *Used and unused quota*

The transferor and transferee must agree how much quota is used or unused. When calculating how much of the original wholesale quota is used it is necessary to take into account deliveries which have already been made with the butterfat adjustment, and without the butterfat adjustment. The higher figure must be used.

9.7.9. If used quota is transferred, the Intervention Board will:

(a) permanently transfer the quota to the new owner (the transferee);

(b) recalculate their ongoing and permanent butterfat bases to take account of the newly-acquired quota;

(c) temporarily return the used quota to the transferor, for the rest of the current quota year, at the transferor's own permanent butterfat base.

9.7.10. The producer taking over the used quota cannot produce against it until the beginning of the next quota year. The quota will remain registered with the original purchaser or producer group until the end of the current quota year.

9.7.11. *Geographical restrictions on transfers*

Quota cannot be transferred to or from any of these groups of Scottish islands:

(a) the Shetlands;

(b) the Orkneys;

(c) the Kintyre Peninsula south of Tarbert and the islands of Islay, Jura, Gigha, Arran, Bute, Great Cumbrae, Little Cumbrae;

(d) the islands in the Inner and Outer Hebrides not listed above.

9.7.12. These groups of islands form separate units of production and are known as 'ring-fenced areas'. Quota may be transferred to any other producer in the U.K., provided that the general transfer requirements are met.

9.7.13. *Butterfat*

9.7.13.1. Changes in butterfat base after a permanent transfer

'Permanent' butterfat base is the figure attached to permanent quota, after being adjusted for transfers, permanent conversions and special allocations. If the butterfat base of any wholesale quota transferred in is higher or lower than the transferor's ongoing or permanent butterfat base, the new ongoing or permanent butterfat base will be recalculated as the weighted average of the butterfat base of the quota transferred in and the transferor's existing quota and butterfat base.

9.7.14. *Confirmation of transfer*

The Intervention Board will write to the transferor to confirm:

(a) that the transfer has been entered on the quota register;

(b) the changes to the transferor's quota and permanent and ongoing butterfat bases (where applicable);

(c) the details of the producers and purchaser(s) involved.

They will also write to the purchaser giving the same information.

1. See Council Regulation (EEC) 3950/92, Art. 8, as amended, and Dairy Produce Quotas Regulations 1994, reg. 13(1) (S.I. 1994/672).
2. Dairy Produce Quotas Regulations 1994 (S.I. 1994/672) (S.I. 1994/672). reg. 13(2).

FURTHER REFERENCE

Dairy Produce Quotas Regulations 1994 (S.I. 1994/672).

Council Regulation (EEC) 3950/92 (O.J. L.405, 31.12.92, p.1), as amended.

Commission Regulation (EEC) 536/93 (O.J. L.57, 10.3.93, p.12), as amended.

Punknowle Farmers Ltd. v. *Kane* [1985] All E.R. 790.

MAFF explanatory leaflet on the provisions relating to the end of tenancy compensation for milk quotas in England and Wales (MSQ2).

The 'Guide to Milk Quotas' available from the Intervention Board.

B.10. Pre-contract searches and enquiries

See also: Seller's duty of disclosure, para. B.05.
Planning, para. B.24.
Reproduction of standard forms, para. B.26.
Pre-completion searches, para. E.02.

10.1. Reason for making searches

10.1.1. Subject to the seller's duty of disclosure,[1] it is up to the buyer to make sure of his bargain. Thus the buyer needs to find out as much about the property as possible before he commits himself to a binding contract to purchase the property. At common law the seller is generally under no obligation to disclose physical defects in the property to the buyer; therefore if the seller does not reveal information about the physical aspects of the property the buyer must obtain such information from other sources, much of which can be obtained through making proper pre-contract searches and enquiries. Failure to make these searches may give rise to liability in negligence to the buyer if as a result the buyer suffers loss.[2]

1. Discussed in para. B.05. The common law duty of disclosure is often modified by contractual condition, e.g. Standard Condition 3.
2. *Cooper* v. *Stephenson* (1852) Cox M. & H. 627.

10.2. Who should make the searches and enquiries?

10.2.1. The onus of making searches rests with the buyer, but in some cases the seller may make all appropriate pre-contract searches and pass the results of these searches to the buyer as part of the pre-contract package. It will frequently assist the progress of the transaction if the seller chooses to instigate pre-contract searches on behalf of the buyer and thus gives the buyer a complete package of documentation at an early stage in the transaction, but he is not obliged to do so.

In any case where the seller does not make all the appropriate pre-contract searches, the buyer should do so. Since the risk of buying the property subject to undiscovered defects broadly rests with the buyer, it is up to the buyer to ensure that all necessary pre-contract searches have been made, whether by the buyer himself, or by the seller on the buyer's behalf.

10.3. When should searches be made?

10.3.1. Where the searches are being undertaken by the seller's solicitor, they should be put in hand in sufficient time to ensure that their results will be available to send to the buyer with the draft contract. Where it is anticipated that delay in receiving the search result will be experienced this may mean that it is necessary to submit a search application as soon as instructions for the sale of the property are received notwithstanding that a buyer has not at that time been found for the property. In other cases the search application need not be submitted until a buyer for the property has been found since, the more recent the date of the search result, the more benefit it will be to the buyer. If the buyer's solicitor is to make searches, he should put his searches in hand as soon as firm instructions to proceed are received from his client. In Protocol cases, the buyer's solicitor, on receipt of the pre-contract package from the seller's solicitor, should check which searches (if any) have been made by the seller, and immediately submit additional search forms if he considers that any additional searches need to be made to meet the requirements of the particular transaction. Search applications should always be submitted without delay since some authorities take a long time to reply to them. It is unwise for a buyer to exchange contracts before having analysed the results of his pre-contract searches; thus delay in submitting search applications may result in delay in the transaction itself.

10.4. Which searches should be made?

10.4.1. Details of the searches listed below are contained in para. 10.5.

10.4.2. *All transactions*

The following searches are regarded as 'usual' and should be undertaken in every transaction:

  (a) search of the local land charges register;

  (b) enquiries of the local authority and, if appropriate, additional enquiries;

  (c) pre-contract enquiries of the seller.

10.4.3.   *Registered land*

Depending on the circumstances of the transaction the following searches may need to be undertaken in addition to obtaining office copies of the register of the title:

    (a) commons registration search;

    (b) mining search;

    (c) index map search if dealing with an unregistered interest in registered land;

    (d) any of the less usual searches which may be applicable in the circumstances.[1]

10.4.4.   *Unregistered land*

In addition to the searches listed in the preceding two paragraphs, it is recommended that a Land Charges Department search against the name of the seller should be undertaken in every transaction.

10.4.5.   *Standard Mortgage Instructions*

Where the Standard Mortgage Instructions (SMI) apply para. 3.6. of the SMI requires the solicitor to make certain searches during the course of the transaction.[2]

1. See below, para. 10.6.
2. At the time of publication the SMI had not been finalised.

10.5.   **Summary of searches listed in para. 10.4.**

10.5.1.   *Local land charges search*

10.5.1.1. When to make: in every transaction.

10.5.1.2. Form: LLC1 in duplicate.

10.5.1.3. Plan: needed if land cannot be clearly identified from postal address.

10.5.1.4. Send to: District or London Borough Council: see Appendix XIII.2.

10.5.1.5. Fee: yes − VAT is payable on a personal search but not on one made by post.

10.5.1.6. Approximate return time: within approximately two weeks at present.

10.5.1.7. Summary of information to be obtained from search: the most important are: some planning decisions, compulsory purchase orders, financial charges affecting the property, tree preservation orders.

10.5.1.8. **Protection given by search:** none: search result only shows state of register at time when search is made but warning of impending land charges can sometimes be obtained by making an Enquiries of Local Authority search on Form CON29 (para. 10.5.2. below). Third party can take benefit of search made by someone else (e.g. seller can make search to pass result to buyer or his lender). Local Land Charges Act 1975, s.10 provides compensation in limited circumstances where there is an error in search certificate or where a matter is binding on the land but is not revealed by the search because it was not registered at the time of the search, but an entry is binding on the land whether or not it is revealed by the search.

10.5.1.9. **Personal search facility:** there is a statutory right to make a personal search, but local authorities do not guarantee the accuracy of the result; should only be undertaken where time does not permit an official search to be made.

10.5.1.10. **Computer or fax search:** available with some authorities.

10.5.1.11. **Special points:** can be made personally or by agent, but result not guaranteed. Insurance available if exchange has to take place before result of search received. Search validation scheme can be used if result of search made by seller to be handed to the buyer or his lender.

10.5.2. *Enquiries of local authority and additional enquiries*

10.5.2.1. **When to make:** in every transaction.

10.5.2.2. **Form:** CON29 in duplicate.

10.5.2.3. **Plan:** insisted on by some authorities, always needed if land cannot be clearly identified from postal address.

10.5.2.4. **Send to:** District or London Borough Council: see Appendix XIII.2.

10.5.2.5. **Fee:** yes – see the Law Society's booklet, 'Local Search fees: England and Wales'. VAT is payable on a personal search but not on one made by post.

10.5.2.6. **Approximate return time:** within approximately two weeks at present.

10.5.2.7. **Summary of information to be obtained from search:** planning applications, pending compulsory purchase orders, public maintenance of highways and drains, smoke control orders, planning policy of council, breaches of planning control, roadworks affecting the property. In some cases Form CON29 will reveal information relating to matters which will in the future become registered as local land charges.

10.5.2.8. **Protection given by search:** buyer is bound by matters even if not discovered by search. Local authority accepts liability in negligence for incorrect replies but disclaimer on application form may protect them. Local Land Charges Act 1975, s.10 does not apply.

10.5.2.9. Personal search facility: some authorities permit personal searches, but do not guarantee the accuracy of the result; it should only be undertaken where time does not permit an official search to be made. Even where facilities are granted for personal searches, these may not cover all the matters normally covered by Form CON29 and may not be acceptable to the buyer's lender.

10.5.2.10. Computer or fax search: available with some authorities.

10.5.2.11. Special points: can be made personally or by agent, but result not guaranteed. Insurance available if exchange has to take place before result of search received. Search validation scheme can be used if result of search made by seller to be handed to the buyer or his lender. Important to list in search application all roads, footpaths, etc., which abut the property in order to discover whether authority is liable for their maintenance — this is of particular relevance to properties which are on the corner of two adjoining roads. Answers to Part I enquiries only are included in search fee. Additional fee payable for each Part II enquiry raised. Consider which, if any of these, are relevant to the transaction. Some authorities permit additional questions to be asked if submitted in duplicate on separate sheet of paper, but charge extra fee for replies. Where property is close to authority's boundary, consider whether some enquiries (e.g. in relation to road widening) should also be submitted to adjoining authority. Where a local authority refuses to answer a question relating to whether or not a property abuts a public highway consideration should be given to undertaking a commons registration search (see para. 10.5.5. below) and to making an inspection of the property.

N.B. 1. Both the local search and enquiries of the local authority contain questions relating to planning matters. In most cases the local authority to whom the search application is submitted will also be the planning authority for the area who will therefore answer the planning enquiries on the standard forms. In a few cases, e.g. new town development corporations, the planning authority is separate from the local authority and planning enquiries have to be separately addressed to the planning authority. If in doubt, telephone the local authority prior to submitting the search application in order to check the position.

N.B. 2. In general, the information revealed by both the local search and enquiries of the local authority relates only to the property being searched against. Matters which affect neighbouring properties are not disclosed in the search replies.

N.B. 3. Some local authorities decline or are unable to answer questions relating to water and drainage. In such cases, these enquiries must be raised separately with the appropriate water authority.

N.B.4. In view of local government boundary changes, care should be exercised to ensure that the search forms are sent to the correct local authority.

N.B.5. Some local authorities have specific requirements in relation to the submission of forms and plans (e.g. Cornwall County and District Councils). Non-compliance with these procedures may result in delay in receiving the answers to enquiries.

10.5.2.12. The Association of District Councils has recently promulgated a Code of Practice relating to local searches. The following extract from the Code demonstrates how the solicitor can assist the local authority to avoid delays and difficulties with search applications.

'The obligations of the searcher

Searchers will wish to assist local authorities to avoid unnecessary delays and difficulties. Good professional practice should ensure that the following principles are observed:

1. On the Search Form LLC1 and the Enquiry Form CON29 to give sufficient description and location of the property to be searched to include wherever possible a good and sufficient location plan. "Description and location" is particularly important since there are many properties, such as flats, that are searched which form part of a larger building. It may, for example, be prudent with some Enquiries such as Equiry 7 of CON29 relating to Planning that not only the flat itself but the building of which the flat forms part is searched.

2. To ensure that the current correct fee charged by the Local Authority is paid at the time of submitting the Search.

3. To ensure that box C of CON29 is completed to identify by a description and if necessary by marking on the accompanying location plan any other roadways, footpaths and footways that are relevant to the Search. It is recognised that if the searcher has identified all of these points of information when submitting the Search, there is less likelihood of having to return to the Local Authority following the result of the Search to raise further Enquiries which in itself is time consuming on the part of the Local Authority.

4. To correctly identify the Part II optional Enquiries that should be raised relevant to the type of property and the area within which it is situated.

5. To ensure that the correct name and address and DX number if appropriate, telephone number, reference and all other details of the searcher are accurately set out on the Form LLC1 and the CON29 and that the appropriate editing of the Form LLC1 is carried out so that at first glance the Local Authority Officer can identify the parts of the Local Land Charges Registers that have to be searched.

6. All correspondence subject to the search should quote the Search Number and the address of the property.'

10.5.2.13. Personal search guidelines: The following extract from the Association of District Councils Code of Practice relates to personal searches.

'Any person may make a personal search of the Local Land Charges Register upon payment of the prescribed fee, currently £6.00. The Council require the following information:

the name of the person or company carrying out the personal search and the address/area of land against which the personal search is to be made.

A map based index showing an area containing the property will be made available for inspection. "Charges" affecting the property will be either plotted directly over the property in red, or noted generally on or at the top, side or bottom of the index board, i.e. smoke control areas, conservation areas, conservation and advert control areas.

It is the searcher's responsibility to identify and request sight of any applicable entries on the Register and to make any other relevant enquiries. Rule 7 Local Land Charges Rules 1977 states that other public records maintained by the Local Authority may have to be consulted as part of the Local Land Charges Register, an example of this is the information contained on the planning register. Details of conditional planning permission are not held on the Local Land Charges Register, but may be inspected in the Planning Section.

A Local Land Charges Officer may not be available to assist, therefore a basic knowledge of the personal search system is required.

Listed below are some of the Council's Statutory Registers which are open for public inspection, any or all of these may be inspected during reasonable office hours. Please note, these **DO NOT** form part of the personal search and an appointment may be necessary. A charge may be levied for additional information.

> Register of Maintainable Highways
> Public Sewer Maps
> Register of Planning Applications/Decisions
> Stop & Enforcement Notice Register
> Hazardous Substances Register.'

10.5.3. *Pre-contract enquiries of seller*

10.5.3.1. When to make: in every transaction.

10.5.3.2. Form: in Protocol cases SPIF (and Seller's Leasehold Information Form); in other cases a standard form of preliminary enquiries (in duplicate) should be submitted (additional forms available for leaseholds, agricultural property or tenanted property).

10.5.3.3. Plan: no.

10.5.3.4. Send to: seller's solicitor.

10.5.3.5. Fee: no.

10.5.3.6. Approximate return time: seller may supply replies as part of pre-contract package, in which case it is unnecessary for buyer to send form to seller. In other cases buyer should send forms to seller as soon as possible at the start of the transaction, and seller should reply as quickly as possible.

10.5.3.7. Summary of information to be obtained from search: ownership of boundaries, disputes about the property, occupiers' interests, planning requirements, guarantees affecting the property, approximate completion date, fixtures and fittings, details of notices received by the seller which affect the property.

10.5.3.8. Protection given by search: none: seller may be liable in misrepresentation for inaccurate replies.

10.5.3.9. Personal search facility: N/A.

10.5.3.10. Computer or fax search: if both parties have compatible equipment.

10.5.3.11. Special points: enquiries additional to those on the printed forms should only be raised where relevant and necessary to the particular transaction. Do not raise additional enquiries about matters which can be resolved by a survey or personal inspection of the property. Seller's replies should be factual and accurate and not based on statements of opinion. Seller's solicitor must take his client's instructions before answering the enquiries. In leasehold cases, both the SPIF and the SLIF must be submitted; the information on these two forms does not overlap and answers to both sets of enquiries will be needed by the buyer.

10.5.4. *Office copy entries*

10.5.4.1. When to make: in every registered land transaction.

10.5.4.2. Form: 109 for office copy entries, 110 for copies of filed documents (other than leases or mortgages).

10.5.4.3. Plan: no.

10.5.4.4. Send to: District Land Registry: see Appendix XIII.1.

10.5.4.5. Fee: £5 per title for register entries, £5 for a plan, £5 for each document or set referred to.

10.5.4.6. Approximate return time: normally within a week.

10.5.4.7. Summary of information to be obtained from search: up-to-date copy of entries affecting seller's title.

10.5.4.8. Protection given by search: none.

10.5.4.9. Personal inspection facility: available (Form 111).

10.5.4.10. Computer or fax application: available subject to HM Land Registry's Direct Access Conditions of Use.

10.5.4.11. Telephone application: application can be made by a credit account holder between 9.30 a.m. and 5.00 p.m. by telephoning any one of six telephone numbers (for numbers, see Appendix XIII.1.). These numbers deal with all telephone applications irrespective of where the land is situated.

10.5.4.12. Special points: application usually made by seller who supplies results to buyer.

10.5.5. Commons registration search

10.5.5.1. When to make: in any case where the property to be purchased abuts a village green or common land, where property is to be built on previously undeveloped land, where a verge strip, not owned by the property, separates the property from the public highway.

10.5.5.2. Form: CR1 in duplicate.

10.5.5.3. Plan: large-scale plan needed.

10.5.5.4. Send to: County Council: see Appendix XIII.2.

10.5.5.5. Fee: £6.

10.5.5.6. Approximate return time: approximately two weeks.

10.5.5.7. Summary of information to be obtained from search: whether any land is registered under Commons Registration Act 1965.

10.5.5.8. Protection given by search: none.

10.5.5.9. Personal search facility: not available.

10.5.5.10. Computer or fax search: not advisable because of need for accurate plan.

10.5.5.11. Special points: where land has been registered under the 1965 Act it is difficult to remove that land from the register and not possible to obtain planning permission for development over the land. Third parties may have rights over the land which is registered, e.g. rights to graze cattle. Registers relating to land in East Sussex were destroyed by fire in 1994. Reconstituted registers have been validated under Commons Registration (East Sussex) Act 1994.

10.5.6. Mining search

10.5.6.1. When to make: in any case where the property is situated in an area in which coal mining takes place or has done so in the past. Reference should be made to the Law Society's directory on mining searches and the Law Society's guidance on mining searches, reproduced at para. 10.14. below.

10.5.6.2. Form: CON29M.

10.5.6.3. Plan: Yes.

10.5.6.4. Send to: The Coal Authority: see Appendix XIII.4.

10.5.6.5. Fee: £23.50.

10.5.6.6. Approximate return time: approximately two weeks.

10.5.6.7. Summary of information to be obtained from search: whether the property is in an area where mining has or is likely to take place, the existence of underground workings which may cause problems with subsidence, whether compensation for subsidence has been paid in the past or any claim is pending.

10.5.6.8. Protection given by search: none.

10.5.6.9. Personal search facility: none.

10.5.6.10. Computer or fax search: not available at present.

10.5.6.11. Special points: disused mines exist in many areas where coal mining has not been carried on within living memory. The dangers of subsidence exist in any area where mining has at some time taken place. A search for the sites of abandoned mines or disused workings may be made at HM Mines Inspectorate Office at Bootle. Provisions for compensation for subsidence are complex: in some cases, once a sum has been paid in compensation, no further claim can be sustained despite further subsidence damage to the land.

10.5.7. *Land Charges Department search*

10.5.7.1. When to make: in all cases when dealing with unregistered land. Strictly not relevant to land registered with an absolute title but sensible for seller's solicitor to make search against his own client's name to ensure no bankruptcy proceedings pending.

10.5.7.2. Form: K15 (full search), K16 (bankruptcy only).

10.5.7.3. Plan: N/A: search is made against correct names of owners of the land.

10.5.7.4. Send to: Land Charges Department, Plymouth: see Appendix XIII.4.

10.5.7.5. Fee: £1 per name for written applications, £2 per name for telephone, fax and computer searches.

10.5.7.6. Approximate return time: within approximately seven days.

10.5.7.7. Summary of information to be obtained from search: this is the quickest method of checking that no bankruptcy proceedings are registered against a client (although it must be borne in mind that bankruptcy entries are normally cancelled automatically after five years). In addition in unregistered land information relating to incumbrances over the land, e.g. post-1925 restrictive covenants, second and subsequent mortgages, estate contracts, and matrimonial home rights.

10.5.7.8. **Protection given by search:** full search: 15 working days from date of official search certificate provided completion takes place within this period. Where an entry is revealed which appears to be irrelevant to the transaction in hand, the seller's solicitor may be asked to certify that the entry does not apply to the transaction (by endorsing the search certificate to this effect). Such endorsement does not alter the legal significance of the search result, but an unqualified endorsement by the seller's solicitor would commit him to personal liability if loss were subsequently suffered by the buyer resulting from that particular entry.

10.5.7.9. **Personal search facility:** at Land Charges Department, Plymouth only but no protection given by personal search.

10.5.7.10. **Computer or fax search:** applications for searches and/or office copies may be delivered by computer (subject to HM Land Registry's Direct Access Conditions of Use) or fax. The result and/or office copies are issued by Document Exchange (DX) or post.

10.5.7.11. **Special points:** the effect of Law of Property Act 1969, s.24 (by displacing the 'registration is notice' rule contained in Law of Property Act 1925, s.198) is to place the burden of disclosure of incumbrances on the seller and thus renders this search strictly unnecessary at the pre-contract stage of the transaction. Since the search needs to be made against all estate owners of the land whose names are revealed in the evidence of title, it is only possible for a buyer to make proper searches if title is deduced to him before exchange. These points notwithstanding it is advisable for the buyer to make a search at least against the seller's name at this stage in order to ensure that no bankruptcy or other financial charges are pending against the seller and that no Class F charge protecting the seller's spouse's matrimonial home rights have been registered at that time. Additionally, if the documentation supplied by the seller reveals the existence of restrictive covenants which if valid would impede the buyer's proposed use of the land, a check may be made against the name of the person on whom the burden of the covenants was imposed to check whether the covenants were registered as Class D(ii) land charges (if not the covenants are not enforceable against a subsequent purchaser if entered into after 1925). To take advantage of the protection period afforded by the search it will usually need to be repeated shortly before completion. In registered land, bankruptcy entries or a notice or caution protecting a spouse's matrimonial home rights will be entered on the register and so revealed by office copies of the register so long as those copies are up to date.

10.5.8. Index map search

10.5.8.1. **When to make:** in all cases when buying an interest in unregistered land.

10.5.8.2. **Form:** Form 96 (96B for copies of index map sections).

10.5.8.3. **Plan:** yes — a large-scale (limited to A4 size if delivered by fax) plan showing the property in context with the surrounding area if the land cannot be identified by the postal description.

10.5.8.4. **Send to:** District Land Registry for the area: see Appendix XIII.1.

10.5.8.5. **Fee:** None if no more than 10 titles disclosed, otherwise £4 per title disclosed in excess of 10.

10.5.8.6. **Approximate return time:** within approximately seven days.

10.5.8.7. **Summary of information to be obtained from search:** whether the land is already registered or is subject to a pending application or caution against first registration or priority notice, existence of registered rentcharges.

10.5.8.8. **Protection given by search:** none: if search result is inaccurate, compensation from the Land Registry indemnity fund is available.

10.5.8.9. **Personal search facility:** no.

10.5.8.10. **Computer or fax search:** fax available at all District Registries. Applicant must be a credit account holder. Delivery by computer available (subject to HM Land Registry's Direct Access Conditions of Use) provided the land can be adequately defined by reference to its postal address. The result is issued by document exchange (DX) or post.

10.5.8.11. **Special points:** if it is discovered that the land is already registered or that a compulsory registration order came into force before the date of the most recent conveyance on sale on the title the seller must be asked to rectify the situation before this transaction proceeds.

10.5.9. *Sewerage enquiries*

In some areas the local authority no longer maintains complete information about sewerage and enquiries should be raised directly with the water authority (for addresses see Appendix XIII.4.). Detailed information relating to drainage matters may be obtained direct from the water services company. Application should be made by letter to the customer services manager at the appropriate divisional office requesting a drainage search. A fee is payable for this service.

10.5.10. *Road widening schemes*

Apart from schemes relating to subways and dual carriageways road widening schemes are not revealed in response to the standard question on Form CON29. In appropriate cases the client should be advised to make additional enquiries about such matters.

10.6.   Less usual searches

10.6.1.   The buyer's solicitor must in all cases be alert to the need to make additional searches since his client will normally be bound by any matters which those searches would have revealed if made. If a less usual search is not made, in circumstances where it would have been relevant, and as a result of this omission the client suffers loss, the buyer's solicitor will be liable in negligence.[1] In some cases the seller's solicitor may make the appropriate searches and supply the results to the buyer's solicitor, but it remains the buyer's solicitor's duty to ensure that all the correct searches have been undertaken and that their results are satisfactory. A summary of some of the less usual pre-contract searches appears below.

10.6.2.   *Railways*

10.6.2.1.   When to make: land adjoins railway, railway passes through land, property built close to underground railway network.

10.6.2.2.   Form: letter.

10.6.2.3.   Plan: yes.

10.6.2.4.   Send to: appropriate railway area surveyor or underground authority: see Appendix XIII.4.

10.6.2.5.   Fee: yes.

10.6.2.6.   Approximate return time: delay should not be experienced.

10.6.2.7.   Summary of information to be obtained from search: ownership of track, routes of underground tunnels.

10.6.2.8.   Protection given by search: none.

10.6.2.9.   Personal search facility: none.

10.6.2.10. Computer or fax search: not available.

10.6.2.11. Special points: Railtrack will answer queries relating to track ownership and infrastructure (but not boundaries). Queries relating to track usage need to be addressed to the operating company.

10.6.3.   *Waterways*

10.6.3.1.   When to make: river, stream or canal passes through or adjoins property.

10.6.3.2.   Form: letter.

10.6.3.3. Plan: yes.

10.6.3.4. Send to: Environment Agency: see Appendix XIII.4.

10.6.3.5. Fee: yes.

10.6.3.6. Approximate return time: no delay should be experienced.

10.6.3.7. Summary of information to be obtained from search: ownership of river banks, fishing rights, licences to abstract water, drainage rights.

10.6.3.8. Protection given by search: none.

10.6.3.9. Personal search facility: none.

10.6.3.10. Computer or fax search: not available.

10.6.3.11. Special points: the Environment Agency is responsible for most rivers and inland waterways. The local authority has responsibility for smaller waterways within its own area.

10.6.4. *Tin mining*

10.6.4.1. When to make: mainly applicable to land to be purchased in West Devon or Cornwall.

10.6.4.2. Form: letter.

10.6.4.3. Plan: yes.

10.6.4.4. Send to: Cornwall Consultants: see Appendix XIII.4.

10.6.4.5. Fee: yes.

10.6.4.6. Approximate return time: no delay should be experienced.

10.6.4.7. Summary of information to be obtained from search: presence of disused underground workings which could cause subsidence damage.

10.6.4.8. Protection given by search: none.

10.6.4.9. Personal search facility: not available.

10.6.4.10. Computer or fax search: not available.

10.6.4.11. Special points: none.

10.6.5. Clay mining

10.6.5.1. When to make: mainly applicable to land to be purchased in West Devon or Cornwall.

10.6.5.2. Form: letter.

10.6.5.3. Plan: yes.

10.6.5.4. Send to: English China Clays: see Appendix XIII.4.

10.6.5.5. Fee: yes.

10.6.5.6. Approximate return time: no delay should be experienced.

10.6.5.7. Summary of information to be obtained from search: presence of workings which could cause subsidence damage.

10.6.5.8. Protection given by search: none.

10.6.5.9. Personal search facility: not available.

10.6.5.10. Computer or fax search: not available.

10.6.5.11. Special points: none.

10.6.6. Brine

10.6.6.1. When to make: land to be purchased in Cheshire or Greater Manchester, Droitwich (Hereford or Worcester).

10.6.6.2. Form: letter.

10.6.6.3. Plan: yes.

10.6.6.4. Send to: Cheshire Brine Subsidence Compensation Board: see Appendix XIII.4.

10.6.6.5. Fee: yes.

10.6.6.6. Approximate return time: no delay should be experienced.

10.6.6.7. Summary of information to be obtained from search: presence of disused workings which could cause subsidence damage, an indication of whether there have been any claims for damage made by the owner or a previous owner against the Brine Board for past or suspected past damage, whether the Board has made a once and for all payment commuting the property from any further claim for compensation: such a commutation will usually result in the value of the property being reduced and making it difficult to mortgage. If the search result reveals that a claim for compensation has been lodged but not yet adjudicated the buyer must after completion give notice of the change of ownership to the Board.

10.6.6.8. **Protection given by search:** none.

10.6.6.9. **Personal search facility:** not available.

10.6.6.10. **Computer or fax search:** not available.

10.6.6.11. **Special points:** none.

10.6.7. *Limestone*

10.6.7.1. **When to make:** land to be purchased in Dudley, Sandwell, Walsall or Wolverhampton.

10.6.7.2. **Form:** letter.

10.6.7.3. **Plan:** yes.

10.6.7.4. **Send to:** local, district or metropolitan council: see Appendix XIII.2.

10.6.7.5. **Fee:** yes.

10.6.7.6. **Approximate return time:** no delay should be experienced.

10.6.7.7. **Summary of information to be obtained from search:** presence of disused underground workings which could cause subsidence damage.

10.6.7.8. **Protection given by search:** none.

10.6.7.9. **Personal search facility:** not available.

10.6.7.10. **Computer or fax search:** not available.

10.6.7.11. **Special points:** none.

10.6.8. *Rent registers*

10.6.8.1. **When to make:** land to be purchased is subject to a Rent Act tenancy.

10.6.8.2. **Form:** letter.

10.6.8.3. **Plan:** no.

10.6.8.4. **Send to:** office of local rent officer.

10.6.8.5. **Fee:** no, but copies of entries on the register (Form RR25) are charged for.

10.6.8.6. **Approximate return time:** no delay should be experienced.

10.6.8.7. **Summary of information to be obtained from search:** whether a rent is registered, its amount and date of registration.

10.6.8.8. **Protection given by search:** none.

10.6.8.9. **Personal search facility:** available.

10.6.8.10. **Computer or fax search:** not available.

10.6.8.11. **Special points:** if a rent is registered, it is an offence for the landlord to charge more than the registered rent for the property. Rent charged in excess of the registered amount is recoverable by the tenant. Registration of a revised rent can normally only be made after two years have elapsed since the last registration.

10.6.9. *Chancel repairs*

10.6.9.1. **When to make:** chancel repair liability can only affect land within a Church of England parish which has a vicar (not a rector) and has a church dating from the mediaeval period or earlier.

10.6.9.2. **Form:** personal search only.

10.6.9.3. **Plan:** yes.

10.6.9.4. **Send to:** Public Records Office, Hayes, Middlesex: see Appendix XIII.4.

10.6.9.5. **Fee:** no.

10.6.9.6. **Approximate return time:** N/A.

10.6.9.7. **Summary of information to be obtained from search:** potential liability to contribute to cost of repairs to chancel of a church.

10.6.9.8. **Protection given by search:** none.

10.6.9.9. **Personal search facility:** available on Tuesdays and Thursdays only provided telephone appointment made: 0181 573 3831.

10.6.9.10. **Computer or fax search:** not available.

10.6.9.11. **Special points:** it is not easy to define with certainty those properties which are affected by liability since the records held at the Public Record Office are not complete. If it appears that liability may exist, a buyer should consider taking out insurance to cover this liability.

1. *G. & K. Ladenbau (U.K.) Ltd.* v. *Crawley & De Reya* [1978] 1 All E.R. 682.

10.7. **Results of searches**

10.7.1. On receiving the results of searches the buyer's solicitor must check the answers given to ensure that the information supplied complies with his client's instructions. Any reply which is unclear must be pursued with the appropriate authority (or seller in the case of pre-contract enquiries) until a satisfactory explanation is received. Failure to pursue an unsatisfactory reply which results in loss being suffered by the client may result in the buyer's solicitor being liable to his own client in negligence.[1] Any reply which is for any reason not satisfactory must be referred to the client for further instructions. Contracts should not be exchanged until satisfactory results of all searches have been received. A summary of the information received from the searches should be communicated to the buyer by his solicitor.

1. *Computastaff Ltd.* v. *Ingledew Brown Bennison Garrett & Co.* (1983) 133 N.L.J. 598.

10.8. **Checklist**

10.8.1. *Making searches*

(a) Decide which searches need to be made.

(b) Is a plan required, is it accurate, and is it on a sufficiently large scale to clearly identify the property and the surrounding area?

(c) What questions (in addition to those on the printed form) need to be asked?

(d) Correct application form and fee?

(e) Correct address for submission of the search?

(f) Diarise the file and chase up delayed responses.

10.8.2. *Search replies*

(a) Analyse the answer to each question − does it accord with what you would expect to find and with what the client wants?

If it does − place a tick in the margin against that question.

If it does not − place a cross in the margin by the question, pursue the question with the relevant authority until a satisfactory reply is received, then replace the cross with a tick, take the client's further instructions if the ultimate reply is not satisfactory.

(b) Where an answer contains information which should be communicated to the client or on which the client's further instructions are needed, place a 'C' in the margin beside that question and contact the client.

(c) Do not exchange contracts until all search replies have been received and all answers are marked with a tick.

10.9. Liability on searches

10.9.1. Local land charges

Where a person suffers loss as a result of an error in an official certificate of search, compensation may be payable under Local Land Charges Act 1975, s.10.

10.9.2. Pre-contract enquiries of the seller

An incorrect reply to pre-contract enquiries may lead to liability in misrepresentation. A reply expressed in terms such as 'the seller is not aware (etc.)' may impart a warranty that the seller has made reasonable enquiries relating to the matter in question.[1] Any exclusion clause purporting to avoid or minimise liability for misrepresentation will be subject to the reasonableness test in Unfair Contract Terms Act 1977, s.11 and cannot therefore be guaranteed to afford protection to the seller.[2] Where the erroneous reply stems from the seller's solicitor's negligence he will be liable to his own client;[3] he may also owe a duty of care to the buyer under *Hedley Byrne* v. *Heller* principles.[4] Knowledge acquired by the solicitor while acting on his client's behalf is imputed to the client (regardless of whether the client had actual knowledge of the matter in question); thus a seller may be liable in misrepresentation to the buyer for a statement made by his solicitor without his knowledge. In such a case indemnity against the seller's liability could be sought from the seller's solicitors.[5] Where the answers to the enquiries are to be completed by the seller personally (and not by his solicitor), e.g. the SPIF in Protocol cases, the seller's solicitor should advise his client to complete the form with care, since an inaccurate or misleading reply could lead to liability in misrepresentation. The seller should also be advised of the need to notify the buyer if circumstances change, thus rendering inaccurate the original reply given to a question on the search form.

1. *William Sindall* v. *Cambridgeshire County Council, The Times*, 8 June 1993.
2. See Standard Condition 7.1. Some forms of pre-contract enquiries also contain an exclusion clause. See also *Walker* v. *Boyle* [1982] 1 All E.R. 634.
3. *Cemp Properties* v. *Dentsply* [1989] 35 E.G. 99.
4. *Hedley Byrne & Co. Ltd.* v. *Heller and Partners Ltd.* [1964] A.C. 465 and see *Wilson* v. *Bloomfield* (1979) 123 S.J. 860.
5. See *Strover* v. *Harrington* [1988] Ch. 390.

10.10. Relying on searches made by a third party

10.10.1.
The results of searches are not personal to the searcher; thus their benefit may be transferred to a third party. Where the seller makes pre-contract searches and passes their results to the buyer, the buyer and his lender may take the benefit of the results. The buyer must check that the seller has undertaken all the searches and enquiries which the buyer deems necessary for the transaction in hand and, if not, he must effect the additional searches himself. If the buyer is not satisfied with the results of the searches made by the seller because, e.g. he considers that they are out of date, or that insufficient questions have been raised, he should repeat the search himself.

10.10.2. *Search validation insurance scheme*

Where a local search has been effected by a seller on domestic property with a purchase price not exceeding £500,000 the Law Society's Search Validation Insurance Scheme may be used to provide the buyer and his lender with an indemnity in respect of the difference in the market value of the property at exchange of contracts caused by an adverse entry being registered against the property in the period between the date of the search certificate and the date of exchange. It is up to the parties to decide who is to bear the cost of paying for cover under this scheme. Commercial property and properties with a purchase price of over £500,000 are not covered by the scheme but a similar type of insurance may be available from other insurers.

10.11. Inspection of the property

10.11.1. Inspection of the property should be undertaken by the client in all cases. There is no obligation on the solicitor, either in law or conduct, to carry out an inspection in every transaction, but he should do so if his client so requests or if matters reported by the client's inspection give rise to suspicion on the part of the buyer's solicitor. The client should be advised to look for (and to report their existence to his solicitor) any of the following matters:

(a) a discrepancy or uncertainty over the identity or boundaries of the property;

(b) evidence of easements which adversely affect the property;

(c) the existence and status of non-owning occupiers;

(d) discrepancy between the fixtures and fittings which the client understood to belong to the property and those actually existing.

10.11.2. It is useful for the client to take a plan of the property with him in order to check its accuracy. An appointment to inspect should be arranged with the seller. The client's surveyor may be able to obtain the necessary information whilst carrying out a survey, but must be instructed to do so.

10.11.3. A solicitor who carries out an inspection on behalf of his client may be liable in negligence if he fails to discover a matter which he ought reasonably to have discovered,[1] e.g. the existence of a right of way crossing the property, but the solicitor should stress to the client that the inspection has been carried out by the solicitor in his role as solicitor, and that he does not profess to have the same knowledge about, e.g. structural defects in the property as possessed by a surveyor.

1. *Barclay-White* v. *Guillame & Sons* [1996] E.G.C.S. 123.

10.12. Tithes

10.12.1. Tithes were abolished in 1936. The 60-year annuities which replaced them were themselves extinguished by Finance Act 1977. There is therefore no need to consider any search for tithes.

10.13. Company search

10.13.1. Where either the seller or buyer is a corporate body a company search prior to exchange should be undertaken in order to check that the company actually does exist. Company searches are discussed under Pre-completion searches, para. E.02.

10.14. Mining searches

10.14.1. A coal mining search in the form approved by the Law Society and the Coal Authority should be made on the occasion of any dealing with land in coal mining areas ('affected areas'), including purchase, mortgage, further advance or before any development takes place. The search should be made before the exchange of contracts or any binding obligation is entered into.

10.14.2. Affected areas

Most of England and Wales are not affected areas. A coal mining search is necessary only if the property is within an area which may be affected by previous, current or proposed underground working of coal. The practitioner should not rely upon his own "local knowledge" in determining whether or not a search should be made.

10.14.3. No coal mining search is required to be made in respect of property in any of the following counties of England: Bedfordshire, Buckinghamshire, Cambridgeshire, Cornwall, Devon, Dorset, East Sussex, Essex, Greater London, Hampshire, Hertfordshire, Norfolk, Suffolk, Surrey, West Sussex, Wiltshire, and of Wales: Gwynedd but excluding Anglesey.

10.14.4. In other areas a coal mining search may need to be made. Reference should be made to the current edition of the Law Society directory on coal mining searches.

10.14.5. Other minerals

A coal mining search relates only to coal and minerals worked in association with coal. The replies will not necessarily disclose the presence of workings of tin, limestone, sand, brine and other minerals, etc., in respect of which separate enquiries may be required in certain areas.

10.14.6. Preliminary enquiries

If the property is in an affected area a buyer's solicitor should, in addition to making a coal mining search of the Coal Authority, ask as a preliminary enquiry of the seller, whether during the ownership of the seller, or to the seller's knowledge his predecessors in title, the property has sustained coal mining subsidence damage and if so how any claim was resolved (by repair or payment in respect of the cost of remedial, merged or redevelopment works or otherwise).

10.14.7. If the replies to the search disclose a current stop notice or the withholding of consent to a request for preventive works affecting the property, a buyer's solicitor should ask preliminary enquiries of the seller as to the present position.

10.14.8. *Search enquiries*

The search contains Standard Enquiries relating to:

(a) past, present and future underground coal mining;

(b) shafts and adits;

(c) surface geology;

(d) past, present and future opencast coal mining;

(e) subsidence (damage notice/claim/method of discharge of remedial obligation or claim/stop notice/request for preventive works).

10.14.9. The search form also contains optional Special Enquiries. The practitioner should consider whether in the circumstances of the case these Special Enquiries should be used in particular if the transaction affects non-domestic property or where development of the property is intended or where a claim against the responsible person is being contemplated for remedial works payment or compensation in respect of coal mining subsidence damage. An additional fee is payable if replies to the Special Enquiries are required. The Special Enquiries relate to:

(a) withdrawal of support;

(b) working facilities orders;

(c) payments to owners of former copyhold land.

10.14.10. *Procedure*

The requisition for a search must be completed by insertion of the full postal address and also the post code of the property, then the name and Document Exchange (DX) number (or address if the practitioner is not a member) of the practitioner to whom the reply should be sent and the practitioner's file reference and telephone number. The requisition contains provision for the optional Special Enquiries to be made and for the search to be expedited − each on payment of an additional fee. A plan of the property should be enclosed (see para. 10.14.17. below).

10.14.11. The search should be sent to the Coal Authority, Mining Reports, DX 29281 Bretby or by post to the Coal Authority, Mining Reports, Ashby Road, Stanhope Bretby, Burton-upon-Trent, Staffordshire DE15 0QD, together with payment of the fee (and any additional fee) and the plan of the property which will be retained.

10.14.12. No covering letter is required to be sent nor is it necessary to sign the search. A copy of the search, enquiries and notes and of the plan should be retained and affixed to the replies when received.

10.14.13. A separate search is required to be made in respect of each individual property.

10.14.14. *Reproduction of forms*

The search form and enquiries are the copyright of the Law Society which has granted to its members a non-exclusive licence to reproduce them. However, any such form must follow precisely and in all respects the printed version (1994 edition). Paper quality of not less than 80gsm must be used on international A4 size and the printing must be by a non-impact printer at a resolution of not less than 300 dpi or an equivalent process.

10.14.15. Any reproduction of the search form which does not comply with these requirements will be rejected by the Coal Authority.

10.14.16. It is important that both sides of the search form should be reproduced for retention and annexing to the reply when received.

10.14.17. *Plans*

Practitioners are recommended to submit a plan with every search as it is likely to be replied to sooner than a search without a plan. If a plan is not submitted there may be difficulties and delays in identifying the property or its extent, in which circumstances, the Coal Authority may request that a plan be supplied with consequent delay in replying to the search. If a search without an accompanying plan of the property is replied to the reply will normally contain a disclaimer to the effect that the coal Authority will not accept any liability for the consequences of incorrect property identification.

10.14.18. *Fees*

The current fee for the Standard Enquiries is £20.00 plus £3.50 VAT, a total of £23.50. The current fee for the Special Enquiries (with the Standard Enquiries) is £30.00 plus £5.25 VAT, a total of £35.25. The fees charged in respect of searches, the Special Enquiries and for expedition are reviewed from time to time. The Law Society will be consulted when there is any increase proposed.

10.14.19. The fee is payable when the search is made and should accompany the form. The reply will contain a VAT receipt for the fee. The VAT element of the fee should be treated by the practitioner as an input for VAT purposes and VAT must be charged to the client. It should not be necessary to retain the receipted reply (nor a copy) for VAT purposes.

10.14.20. If by mistake a practitioner makes a coal mining search in respect of property outside the affected areas, the Coal Authority will reply but the fee will not be refunded. In these circumstances the practitioner should not claim reimbursement from his client of the abortive fee.

10.14.21. Replies

Replies to the enquiries will be provided in accordance with Coal Authority's duties under Coal Industry Act 1994. The replies will be given in the belief that they are in accordance with the information at present available to the Coal Authority but on the distinct understanding that the Coal Authority is not legally responsible for them, except for negligence.

10.14.22. The Coal Authority's licencees are required by section 58 of the 1994 Act to exercise all due diligence to secure the provision of full and accurate information to the Coal Authority in accordance with the conditions of the licence.

10.14.23. Any liability of the Coal Authority for negligence in giving replies to enquiries pursuant to the Law Society's Scheme shall extend for the benefit of not only the person by or for whom the search is made but also of a person (being a purchaser for the purposes of section 10(3) Local Land Charges Act 1975) who or whose agent had knowledge, before the relevant time (as defined in that section), of the replies to the search. Such extension of liability to another (who did not make the search), is limited to a purchaser lessee or mortgagee of the property and not others (e.g. other recipients of reports on title, etc.).

10.14.24. Whether a practitioner's client can rely on a previous search (of his own or another's) depends upon all the circumstances of the case including how recently it was made, the content of the replies, whether the person making the search indicated an intention to develop the property, the nature of the property and the client's intentions in relation to it. If there is any doubt as to whether the previous replies remain valid, a new search should be made.

10.14.25. Upon receipt of the replies the practitioner should copy them (with the copy enquiries) to and/or discuss the results with the client and where appropriate report on them to the client's valuer/surveyor. The searches, plans and replies should be kept with the title deeds or land registry certificate.

10.14.26. Expedited replies

In urgent cases a practitioner may make a search by fax and receive replies by fax. The fee for this service is £57.80 plus £10.12 VAT, a total of £67.92, in addition to the basic fee payable for the Standard and Special Enquiries.

10.14.27. In order to obtain expedited search replies the requisition form should be completed as normal but also completing the request for expedition of the reply (which involves an undertaking to pay the expedition fee). The form and plan should then be faxed to the Coal Authority on 01283 551233. The practitioner should on the same day send the requisition form with the fee (including the additional fee for expedition) to the Coal Authority by post or DX.

10.14.28. In normal circumstances the replies will be returned by fax the same day or the next working day. The Coal Authority will then on receipt of the confirmatory requisition and fee send the confirmatory replies with the VAT receipt for the fee.

10.14.29. *Mining surveys and site investigation*

A coal mining search is not a substitute for a site investigation nor a mining survey. Clients will have to assess whether such a site investigation or mining survey is required having regard (amongst other relevant factors) to the content of the replies and whether the property is to be developed and, if so, the nature and extent of the development.

10.14.30. Practitioners should explain to clients that in most affected areas there are experienced mining surveyors and structural engineers able to advise as to what further enquiries, mining surveys or site investigations should be made. If a lender is involved in the transaction, the practitioner should establish that the surveyor or engineer selected is acceptable to the lender.

10.14.31. *Shafts and adits*

The reply to the enquiry as to shafts and adits and other entries to underground coal mine workings (within 20 metres of the boundary of the property) will be prepared only from the records in the possession of the Coal Authority. These records may not be complete.

10.14.32. Disclosure of a disused mine shaft or adit should be a matter of particular concern to the client. The approximate location of the shaft or adit will be identified on a plan with the replies at no extra cost unless several shafts and adits are identified on a larger (non-domestic) site when an extra fee may be payable. Practitioners should in these circumstances explain to clients that in most affected areas there are experienced mining surveyors and structural engineers able to advise as to what further enquiries, surveys or investigations should be made.

10.14.33. Practitioners are reminded that with effect from 31 October 1994 British Coal's interests in unworked coal and coal mines became vested in the Coal Authority. In most cases any shaft or adit will be owned by the Coal Authority and not the adjacent surface landowner and clients should be advised accordingly.

10.14.34. *Dealing with lenders*

If domestic property, the subject of a coal mining search is to be charged as security for a loan, a copy of the Coal Authority's replies should be sent to the lender as soon as received. The practitioner should not comment substantively on the replies to the Standard Enquiries but should recommend that they are referred to the lender's valuer to review.

10.14.35. Provided that a copy of the replies to a coal mining search has been so provided, practitioners are not expected to make any further reference to the replies in any Report on Title to a lender save to refer to the existence of the search and replies thereto.

10.14.36. With regard to non-domestic property a similar procedure should be adopted. Practitioners should, however, refer to the replies to any Special Enquiries (if these have been made) as these deal with legal matters, namely the withdrawal of support, the existence of working facilities orders and payments to owners of former copyhold land.

10.14.37. In all cases, practitioners, when also acting for the lender, should, however, check whether the instructions from that lender require the practitioner to deal with the replies to the coal mining search in any other manner. If so, the practitioner should explain to the lender the basis upon which the practitioner is recommended by these paragraphs to proceed. It is important that practitioners should not attempt to perform the function of the client's valuer or surveyor with regard to the replies to the search.

10.14.38. *Time validity*

There is no time protection afforded by replies to coal mining searches. Licensed operators' plans for mining may change as may the other relevant information available to the Coal Authority. If there is any doubt as to whether previous replies remain valid, a new search should be made.

10.14.39. *Law Society's Coal Mining Search*

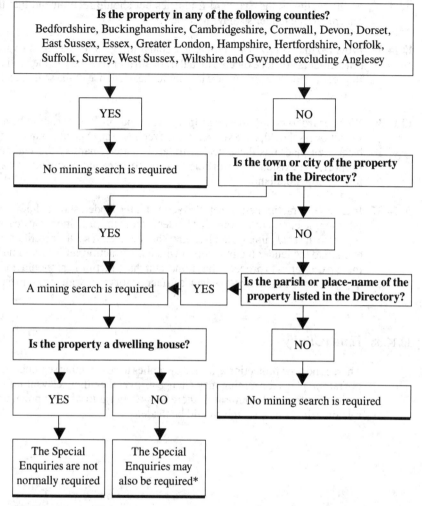

This flow chart should always be used in conjunction with the Law Society's Guidance Notes and Directory.

* The Special Enquiries should only be used in relation to transactions affecting non-domestic property or where a development of the property is intended or where a claim against the Coal Authority is being contemplated.

10.15. **Assignment of guarantees**

Where the answers to pre-contract enquiries reveal that the property has the benefit of a structural defects policy (e.g. NHBC) or other guarantee (e.g. for woodworm or damp treatment) the benefit of which will pass to the buyer on completion, consideration should be given to whether a formal assignment of the benefit of the policy or guarantee will be needed. NHBC will normally honour a policy without evidence of formal assignment but not all other insurers adopt this practice.

10.16. **Properties without mains drainage**

10.16.1. Some rural properties may not have the benefit of mains drainage. The client's surveyor should be asked to ascertain the type of drainage provided at the property and if necessary a drainage survey may need to be undertaken to ensure that the system is functional and adequate to meet the needs of the property and its occupants. In some cases it will be necessary to obtain the consent of the National Rivers Authority for the operation of the drainage system (because the system may discharge effluent into the land or into an adjacent watercourse). The seller should be asked to supply a copy of any such consents in his possession. It may be necessary to transfer such consents to the buyer on completion.

10.16.2. *Cesspools*

A cesspool is a covered watertight tank used for receiving and storing sewage. It has no outlet but must be regularly emptied either by the local authority or by a private contractor. The tank must be and remain impervious to the ingress of groundwater or surface water and to leakage. No consent from the National Rivers Authority is required for a cesspool.

10.16.3. *Septic tanks*

A septic tank is a sewage system (usually consisting of two or three chambers) in which the sewage is retained for sufficient time to allow it to partially break down (anaerobic decomposition) before the contents are discharged. Discharge may be by soakage into the ground. The effluent cannot be discharged into a watercourse without further treatment. National Rivers Authority consent may be required for discharge into the ground.

10.16.4. *Package sewage treatment plants*

Package sewage treatment plants are similar to septic tanks but treat the sewage to a higher standard than the former before discharging the effluent. National Rivers Authority consent is required for the discharge.

10.16.5. *National Rivers Authority consent*

Under Water Resources Act 1991, National Rivers Authority consent is required for any discharge of sewage effluent into a watercourse, lake or pond, and may also be required for any discharge into or onto land. Separate consent is required under Land Drainage Act 1991 if the discharge is made into a main river. An administration charge is made by the National Rivers Authority for an application for consent together with an annual fee to cover monitoring and other costs.

FURTHER REFERENCE

Enquiries of Local Authorities: A Practical Guide, K.M. Pugsley, Tolley.

Searches and Enquiries: A Conveyancer's Guide, F.J. Silverman, Butterworths.

B.11. Form of contract

See also: Standard Conditions of Sale, para. B.12.
Plans, para. B.21.

11.1. Statutory provisions

11.1.1. Law of Property (Miscellaneous Provisions) Act 1989 repealed Law of Property Act 1925, s.40. The 1989 Act requires all contracts for the sale or other disposition of land or an interest in land to be made in writing and signed by the parties. The writing must incorporate all the terms which been expressly agreed by the parties and the document must then be signed by or on behalf of all the parties. Where contracts are to be exchanged each part of the contract must contain all the agreed terms and be signed by the appropriate party. It is possible for the signed document to refer to another document which itself contains the agreed terms. If the document does not contain all the agreed terms an order for rectification may be sought.[1]

11.1.2. The requirement for a written contract does not apply to contracts:

(a) to grant a lease for a term not exceeding three years taking effect in possession without a fine;

(b) made at public auction;

(c) regulated under Financial Services Act 1986.

11.1.3. Joining two documents together to satisfy the section

Where the signed document does not itself contain all the agreed terms it is possible to join two (or more) documents together in order to constitute a complete contract and thus satisfy the statutory requirements. Little case law yet exists under the 1989 Act, but the rules which applied to the joining of documents under Law of Property Act 1925, s.40 (predecessor to section 2) will not necessarily be applied to actions brought under the new section.[2] It is possible, e.g. to draft a contract which incorporates the Standard Conditions of Sale by reference without setting out the full text of those conditions. In such a case the Standard Conditions will be deemed to be incorporated as part of the contract although contained in a different document from that which was signed by the parties. Since the court's interpretation of this aspect of section 2 is as yet unknown, it is not possible to speculate in what circumstances the court will allow documents to be joined together to form a contract. It should be borne in mind that failure to satisfy the requirements of section 2 results in there being no contract at all between the parties, and the court has no equitable jurisdiction to allow the enforcement of a contract which does not meet the statutory requirements. Care should therefore be taken to ensure that the contract does satisfy section 2 and to this end it is recommended that the full text of the general conditions of sale which are being used (e.g. the Standard Conditions of Sale) is set out in the contract itself.[3]

1. *Wright* v. *Robert Leonard Developments Ltd.* [1994] E.G.C.S. 69.
2. See *Firstpost Homes Ltd.* v. *Johnson* [1995] 1 W.L.R. 1567.
3. See *B. Ltd.* v. *T. Ltd.* [1991] N.P.C. 47 where it was held that incorporation of the National Conditions of Sale by reference did satisfy s.2 of the Act. See also *Commission for New Towns* v. *Cooper, The Independent,* 15 March 1995 (C.A.) where it was held that an exchange of letters did not satisfy s.2.

11.2. Satisfying the statutory requirements

11.2.1. The statutory requirements are normally satisfied by the preparation by the seller's solicitor of a formal contract. The contract is usually prepared in two identical parts based on the Standard Conditions of Sale as amended to fit the particular circumstances of the transaction. A summary of the Standard Conditions is contained in para. B.12. The contract comes into being when exchange of contracts takes place. For signature and exchange of contracts see section C.

11.2.2. *Collateral contracts*

To be enforceable, options, equitable mortgages[1] and side letters issued in connection with sale of land transactions also need to satisfy the requirements of section 2. This will mean that these documents need to be in writing and signed by both parties. An agreement not to negotiate with any other buyer (a 'lock-out' agreement) can be enforceable as a separate collateral contract provided good consideration is given. This type of agreement does not fall within the scope of section 2.[2] A 'lock-in' agreement (i.e. to negotiate with these buyers only) is not an enforceable contract.[3]

11.2.3. *Variation of contract*

A variation of a contract to which section 2 applies must itself comply with the section.[4]

1. *United Bank of Kuwait* v. *Sahib* [1996] N.P.C. 12.
2. *Pitt* v. *PHH Asset Management Ltd.* [1993] E.G.C.S. 127.
3. *Courtney & Fairburn* v. *Tolaini Bros.* [1975] 1 W.L.R. 297.
4. *McCausland* v. *Duncan Lawrie* [1996] N.P.C. 94.

11.3. **Contents of the contract**

11.3.1. In addition to the formal parts, i.e. date, parties, signature, the contract comprises two main elements:

    (a) the particulars, which describe the physical extent of the property to be sold and its tenure; and

    (b) the conditions which set out the terms on which the seller is prepared to sell the property.

11.4. **The particulars**

11.4.1. These must contain a clear description of the physical extent of the property to be sold and whether the estate to be sold is freehold or leasehold. The title number of a parcel of registered land is its sole distinguishing feature and thus must be referred to in the particulars. The class of title under which the land is registered (e.g. absolute) must also be included in order to give the buyer an accurate description of the estate which is being sold. Where the boundaries are well defined and the property has a regular postal address, the postal address may suffice to describe the land itself. In other cases a more detailed description may be necessary, referring where appropriate to the measurements of the property and/or a plan (see para. B.21.). Any inaccuracy in the particulars may give rise to an action in misdescription or misrepresentation (see Delay and remedies, section M).

11.5. **Conditions of sale**

11.5.1. *Open contract rules*

Where a contract makes no reference to a particular matter the contract is said to be 'open' on this point and is thus governed by the open contract rules which are laid down either by common law or by statute. Some of the open contract rules are satisfactory in operation, e.g. the rules for deduction of title on the sale of unregistered freeholds, and are invariably used without alteration. Others, e.g. the time for completion, which under the open contract rules is set at 'a reasonable time after the contract', are less satisfactory and are frequently altered by special condition in the contract itself. The Standard Conditions of Sale normally vary the open contract rules, but may themselves require amendment to suit the particular circumstances of the transaction.

11.5.2. Assuming that the Standard Conditions of Sale have been used to form the basis of the contract, special conditions will still be needed to deal with any variations which are required to the Standard Conditions, and any features peculiar to the particular transaction. Even in the most straightforward transaction special conditions will invariably be required to deal with the matters listed below.

11.5.3. *Checklist of usual special conditions*

Condition to deal with	Reason for inclusion	Standard Condition	Further reference
Title	Buyer is entitled to know what title is being offered.	4.2	Section D.
Deposit	No provision at common law, variation of general conditions may be required.	2.2	B.17.
Interest on deposit	Interest is payable under Solicitors' Accounts Rules.	2.2.3	A.20.
Completion date	Open contract rule and general conditions not satisfactory.	6.1	
Title guarantee	Defines scope of implied covenants for title.	4.5.2	M.09.
Incumbrances	Seller's duty of disclosure.	3	B.05.
Fixtures and fittings	To create an obligation and to avoid disputes between the parties.	9	B.22.
Vacant possession	Implied by common law unless stated to the contrary. Normally included for certainty and must deal with requirement for completion to take place at the property if so required.		B.03.

11.6. Covenants for title

11.6.1. With effect from 1 July 1995, it is no longer necessary to include the seller's capacity in the contract, because it will have no legal effect to include it. Implied covenants for title, previously given to the buyer by virtue of Law of Property Act 1925, s.76 (as modified by Land Registration Act 1925, s.24, in registered land), the extent of which was dependent on the nature of the seller's capacity, are now governed by Law of Property (Miscellaneous Provisions) Act 1994, as outlined in the following sub-paragraphs.

11.6.2. Law of Property (Miscellaneous Provisions) Act 1994 repeals Law of Property Act 1925, s.76, and associated legislation relating to covenants for title and replaces them with 'statutory guarantees' which will be implied in a transfer document by the use of the key words 'with full guarantee' or 'with limited guarantee' (or their Welsh equivalents). An indication of whether full or limited guarantee is being given to the buyer (or no guarantee) must be included in the contract. Standard Condition 4.5.2 provides that the seller will sell with full title guarantee and will therefore need to be amended by special condition in the contract if this is not intended to be the case. If the key words are omitted from the contract, no guarantee will be implied. The extent of the guarantee can also be altered by express agreement. The guarantees apply not only on the transfer of freehold or leasehold property but can also apply on the grant of a lease and on the transfer of personal property, including intellectual property and rights in shares. The extent of the guarantees given under the 1994 Act is discussed under Covenants for title, para. M.09.

11.6.3. Transitional provisions

Transactions which are completed before 1 July 1995 are not affected by Law of Property (Miscellaneous Provisions) Act 1994 and Law of Property Act 1925, s.76 (as amended) continues to apply to them. Where a contract is entered into before 1 July 1995 but completion takes place after this date, section 76 will apply to the disposition where:

(a) the contract contained a term to which section 76 would have applied (e.g. a statement that the seller was selling as 'beneficial owner' or in some other capacity);

(b) the existence of the contract and the relevant term is apparent on the face of the purchase deed, i.e. the purchase deed contains express reference to these matters; and

(c) there has been no intervening disposition which was made 'with full title guarantee'.

11.6.4. Law of Property (Miscellaneous Provisions) Act 1994, s.11(3), defines an 'intervening disposition' as a disposition made after 1 July 1995 to, or to a predecessor in title of, the person making the disposition. If, for example, prior to 1 July 1995 L had granted a lease to T, giving T an option to purchase the freehold in which L had agreed to transfer the freehold as 'beneficial owner' and after 1 July 1995 sold the freehold to P, subject to T's lease, the sale of the freehold from L to P is an intervening disposition and the subsequent exercise of the option by T will take the benefit of the full title guarantee given by the 1994 Act; Cases which do not fall within the above exception will be governed by the 1925 Act.

11.6.5. If after 1 July 1995 a contract dated before 1 July 1995 but taking effect after that date contains a reference to the seller's capacity but does not refer to full or limited title guarantee, a purported disposition by a beneficial owner is deemed to include the full title guarantee provisions under the 1994 Act; a disposition in some other capacity (e.g. trustee, personal representative) is deemed to include limited title guarantee provisions.

11.6.6. By Law of Property (Miscellaneous Provisions) Act 1994, s.13, where there is an option, the contract for the disposition is deemed to have been entered into on the grant of the option; the nature of the title guarantee will therefore be governed by the date of the option agreement itself.

11.7. Drafting the contract

11.7.1. Although drafting the contract is the prerogative of the seller, the relative bargaining strength of the parties rarely permits the seller to draft a contract which is entirely to his own satisfaction. Contract drafting is therefore an exercise in the art of compromise. The seller must seek to preserve his own interests without misleading the buyer, but will frequently have to include or concede some terms which favour the buyer in order to achieve a prompt conclusion to the transaction. A solicitor, whether acting for seller or buyer, who obstinately insists on the total protection of his own client's interests in the contract terms will at best prolong the transaction unnecessarily or at worst find that negotiations break down entirely and in neither case can he be said to be providing a proper service to his client.

11.8. Style of drafting

11.8.1. The contract must clearly state what the seller is offering to sell and on what terms including price. Use of anachronistic language should be avoided but clarity must not be sacrificed for brevity. Conditions should only be included where they are relevant and necessary and not through force of habit. Bearing in mind that it is the solicitor's duty to draft a contract which will avoid disputes or litigation between the parties, it becomes a matter of judgment as to the extent of the inclusion of clauses which cater for unforeseen eventualities.

11.8.2. *Guidelines*

    (a) Does the contract describe clearly what is to be sold?
    (b) Is a plan necessary?
    (c) Does the contract accord with the client's instructions as to the conditions on which the property is to be sold?
    (d) Are the conditions concise and unambiguous?

11.9. Looking at the contract from the buyer's point of view

11.9.1. No two draftsmen will ever produce identically worded contracts for the sale of the same property. Drafting is a personal skill and the draftsman's choice of words must be respected by the buyer's solicitor. Amendments should not be made to suit the individual whim of the buyer's solicitor but should be confined to those which are necessary and relevant to the particular transaction. The primary questions in looking at the contract from the buyer's point of view are:

(a) does the clause accord with the client's instructions? and

(b) does the clause do what it is intended to do?

11.9.2. If the answers to these questions are in the affirmative – leave the wording alone. If not, alter the clause until it does meet the above criteria.

11.9.3. Amendments should be clearly inserted on both copies of the draft contract in a distinctive colour.

11.10. National Conditions of Sale

11.10.1. Prior to the introduction of the Standard Conditions of Sale in 1990 there were two standard forms of contract in common use in England and Wales: The Law Society's Conditions of Sale (1984 revision) and the National Conditions of Sale (20th edition). The Standard Conditions of Sale (1st edition) represented a merger of these two popular forms and the current (3rd edition) of the Standard Conditions describes itself in a sub-title as 'National Conditions of Sale 23rd edition, Law Society's Conditions of Sale 1995'. The National Conditions are therefore no longer published as an independent set of conditions and many former Nationals users have adopted the Standard Conditions as the basis of contracts drafted by their firms, but a few firms continue to base their contracts on the 20th edition of the National Conditions.

11.10.2. In view of the number of changes in both law and practice which have occurred since the last independent revision of the National Conditions in 1981, it is considered unwise to base a contract on these conditions which, as time goes by, become increasingly out of date.

11.11. Unfair Terms in Consumer Contracts Regulations 1995

11.11.1. Unfair Terms in Consumer Contracts Regulations 1995[1] affect all contracts (oral or written) made between a seller or supplier and a consumer (this latter expression applies to individuals only). Unlike Unfair Contract Terms Act 1977, the new regulations apply to land contracts, including mortgages and tenancy agreements. Agreements for financial services made between an individual and his broker are also potentially within the Regulations. The E.U. Directive from which the English Regulations derive may have intended land contracts to be included within its scope and some national versions of the Regulations do apply to land (e.g. France), but the English Regulations use the expression 'goods' (although land is not specifically excluded in the list of exclusions from the Regulations). There is therefore some doubt as to the application of the Regulations to contracts affecting land, but the Department of Trade and Industry has issued a statement which indicates that, in their view, the Regulations do apply to land contracts.

The English Regulations could be amended in future to clarify the position, or could be challenged by application to the European Court of Justice on the basis that the English Regulations do not correctly implement the E.U. Directive. Practitioners should therefore be aware of the Regulations and of their possible effects on land transactions.

11.11.2. *Situations in which the Regulations apply*

The Regulations do not apply to a contract for sale made between two private individuals but catch contracts made between a corporate or business seller and a private individual. Thus contracts for new houses or plots on a building estate where the seller is a developer and the buyer a private individual are potentially affected since in these circumstances the contract is usually in standard form and there is little or no freedom for the buyer to negotiate terms. Similarly mortgages, where the lender is in business and the borrower is not, are caught, as also are sales by mortgagees.

Tenancy agreements and contracts for financial services are potentially within the scope of the Regulations.

11.11.3. *Effect of the Regulations*

If a term is held to be unfair, that term is to be treated as void, but the rest of the contract remains binding on the parties, so long as it is capable of continuing without the offending term.

A term will be regarded as unfair if, contrary to the requirement of good faith, it causes a significant imbalance in the parties' rights and obligations arising under the contract to the detriment of the consumer. Various factors, similar to those contained in Unfair Contract Terms Act 1977, are contained in the Regulations to act as guidelines as to whether 'good faith' exists, e.g. the strength of the bargaining position of the parties, the circumstances surrounding the contract, and whether the consumer has received any special inducement, such as a discount, to agree to the term.

The burden of proof will lie on the consumer to show that a term included in the contract which was not individually negotiated between the parties is unfair.

The Regulations also require all contracts to be drafted in plain intelligible language.

1. S.I. No. 1994/3159.

B.12. Standard Conditions of Sale

See also: The National Protocol ('TransAction'), para. A.19.
Form of contract, para. B.11.

12.1. Standard Conditions of Sale

12.1.1. Most contracts for the sale of land will be made either on the Standard Conditions of Sale Form or by reference to the Standard Conditions.[1]

12.1.2. The text of the Standard Conditions of Sale (3rd edition) with accompanying notes for guidance is set out in Appendix V.1. Individual conditions are referred to in context in the text of this book.

1. The Standard Conditions of Sale (1st edition) came into force on 21 March 1990 and replaced the Law Society Conditions of Sale (1984 revision) and the National Conditions of Sale (20th edition). The third edition came into force on 1 July 1995.

12.2. Incorporating the Standard Conditions of Sale

12.2.1. To satisfy Law of Property (Miscellaneous Provisions) Act 1989, s.2 a contract for the sale or other disposition of land must be in writing, incorporating all the terms which have been agreed between the parties. These terms will normally include the Standard Conditions of Sale. Where a solicitor prepares a contract on a word processor or by other duplicated means incorporation of the Standard Conditions by reference may satisfy the requirements of section 2 (but see above, para. B.11.1.3.). Failure to satisfy section 2 means that no contract exists between the parties.[1]

1. See *B. Ltd.* v. *T. Ltd.* [1991] N.P.C. 47.

12.3. Using the Standard Conditions of Sale

12.3.1. Not all of the Standard Conditions will be appropriate for use in every transaction. Solicitors should, in every transaction, give careful thought to the application of the conditions and expressly amend those which are inappropriate to the particular circumstances of the current transaction. As in all cases, amendments should be restricted to those which are essential to meet the circumstances of an individual case.

12.4. **The Protocol**

12.4.1. The Standard Conditions of Sale are one of the standard documents forming part of the Protocol. The proposed use by the seller's solicitor of a different form of conditions would be a departure from the Protocol which would need to be disclosed to the buyer's solicitor at the commencement of the transaction. The drafting of the Standard Conditions mirrors the requirements of the Protocol; thus an amendment to the Standard Conditions may itself be a departure from the Protocol requiring notification to the other party. Since the aim of the Protocol is to simplify and speed up the conveyancing process it is recommended that in transactions where the Protocol is being used, solicitors alter the Standard Conditions as little as possible, subject to their paramount duty of acting in the best interests of their client.

FURTHER REFERENCE

Standard Conditions of Sale: A Conveyancer's Guide, F.J. Silverman, Tolley.

B.13.   Conditional contracts

See also: Capacity, para. B.07.

13.1.   When are conditional contracts appropriate?

13.1.1.   Conditional contracts carry with them some risks and uncertainties which make them inappropriate for everyday use, but they may be considered for use in the following circumstances:

    (a)   where the buyer has not had the opportunity before exchange of contracts to make searches and enquiries or to conduct a survey or where his mortgage arrangements have not been finalised;

    (b)   where the contract is dependent on planning permission being obtained for the property;

    (c)   where the sale requires the consent of the Charity Commissioners under Charities Act 1993 (see para. B.07.8.);

    (d)   where the sale is dependent on permission being obtained from a third party, e.g. ministerial consent, landlord's consent;

    (e)   where the parties wish to be bound to a contract but there is some other unresolved matter which prevents commitment to an unconditional contract for the time being, e.g. the seller has to get in part of the legal estate.

13.2.   Desirability of conditional contracts

13.2.1.   Conditional contracts are generally not desirable since they leave an element of doubt as to the very existence and validity of the contractual obligations between the parties. Most of the situations in which conditional contracts are proposed for use benefit the buyer more than the seller (e.g. 'subject to planning permission'), and the seller should resist the suggestion of entering a conditional contract if at all possible. A conditional contract may, however, be inevitable where the seller needs the consent of the Charity Commissioners to the sale under Charities Act 1993 since an unconditional contract which is entered into without such consent is not lawful.

13.2.2. Conditional contracts should never be used where one or both of the parties has an unconditional sale or purchase contract which is dependent on the conditional contract. In this situation, if the conditional contract were to be rescinded for non-fulfilment of the condition, this would give rise to great difficulties in the fulfilment of the linked unconditional contract and may result in a breach of that contract.

13.2.3. Before agreeing to enter a conditional contract the seller should consider whether there are any viable alternative solutions. Where it has been suggested that the sale is 'subject to planning permission', it may be preferable to delay exchange until the results of the planning application have been received by the buyer, rather than enter into a hastily drafted conditional contract. An alternative solution may be to grant the buyer for a nominal consideration an option to purchase the property to be exercised within a stated period.

13.3. Conditions precedent and subsequent

13.3.1. Conditions precedent

A condition precedent has the effect of suspending the operation of the contract until the terms of the condition have been met. If the condition has not been fulfilled by the appropriate time-limit, the party with the benefit of the condition may withdraw and the contractual obligations of the parties never come into existence.

13.3.2. Conditions subsequent

Where the contract is subject to a condition subsequent, the contractual obligations of the parties arise on the creation of the contract and continue to exist until terminated by the party with the benefit of the condition on its non-fulfilment.

13.3.3. If the wording of the condition reads 'subject to x', this indicates a condition precedent.

13.3.4. If the wording of the condition reads 'until x', this indicates a condition subsequent.

13.4. Requirements for a valid conditional contract

13.4.1. Certainty

The terms of the condition must be clear and certain. In *Lee Parker* v. *Izzett* (*No. 2*),[1] an agreement to sell a freehold house 'subject to the buyer obtaining a satisfactory mortgage' was held to be void because the word 'satisfactory' was too nebulous and there was thus no certainty regarding the circumstances in which the buyer would validly be able to withdraw from the contract. It should be noted, however, that not all 'subject to mortgage' clauses will suffer the same fate. A similarly worded clause in *Janmohamed* v. *Hassam*[2] was held to be valid.

13.4.2. *Time for performance*

It was held in *Aberfoyle Plantations Ltd.* v. *Cheng*[3] that the time for performance of the condition is of the essence and cannot be extended either by agreement between the parties or by the court. The same case also laid down the rules relating to the time for performance of the condition which are summarised as follows:

(a) where the contract contains a completion date, the condition must be fulfilled by that date, irrespective of whether time was of the essence of the contractual completion date;

(b) if a time is stated for the fulfilment of the condition, that time-limit must be complied with or the contract will fail;

(c) if no time-limit is specified the condition must be fulfilled within a reasonable time. This provision is patently unsatisfactory since it leaves room for argument about what is a reasonable time.

1. [1972] 2 All E.R. 800.
2. (1976) 241 E.G. 609.
3. [1960] A.C. 115.

13.5. Withdrawal from the contract

13.5.1. Only the party with the benefit of the condition may withdraw from the contract, and only for reasons connected with the condition. No other reason will justify withdrawal, although there is no obligation on the resiling party to prove that he is being reasonable in exercising his rights to withdraw. It is a question of construction of the condition itself as to whether a party may withdraw before performance of the condition.[1]

1. *Tesco Stores Ltd.* v. *William Gibson & Co. Ltd.* (1970) 214 E.G. 835.

13.6. Waiver of the condition

13.6.1. Where the condition benefits one party only, it may be waived unilaterally. In other cases the waiver amounts to a variation of the contract and requires the consent of both parties. If to remove the condition takes away the whole purpose of the contract, the whole contract will fail for uncertainty.

13.7. Drafting

13.7.1. The drafting of a condition requires extreme care to ensure that the requirements outlined above in para. 13.4. have been satisfied. No such provision is included in the Standard Conditions of Sale although a contract to asssign a lease may be conditional on the landlord's consent being obtained under Standard Condition 8.3.

13.7.2. Guidelines

(a) Consider the precise event(s) on which the contract is to be made conditional.

(b) By what time must the condition be fulfilled? (Bear in mind that the specified time-limit cannot be extended.)

(c) Consider the precise terms on which the party with the benefit of the condition may rescind.

(d) Ensure that there are no loopholes which would enable one party to escape from the contract other than for the non-fulfilment of the event(s) contemplated in (a) above.

(e) Use an established precedent, tailoring it to fit your exact requirements.

(f) Take your time: a condition which is hastily drafted may contain unforeseen errors.

(g) Having drafted your 'perfect' condition, leave it on the desk overnight and review the wording objectively in the cold light of day. Does the condition achieve its objectives? Is it clear and certain? Do any unforeseen or unwanted consequences flow from the wording?

13.7.3. Precise terms for rescission

13.7.3.1. 'Subject to searches'

(a) Which searches?

(b) Which adverse entries will give rise to the right to rescind?

(c) By when must the search result(s) be received?

(d) Can buyer rescind if he changes his mind and never makes search applications?

13.7.3.2. 'Subject to mortgage'

(a) Specify name of lender(s) to whom application made.

(b) Specify amount of required advance.

(c) Specify acceptable interest rates.

(d) Should the buyer be entitled to rescind if the mortgage offer is subject to conditions or a retention — what conditions attached to the offer would be acceptable/unacceptable?

(e) Time-limit by which application must be determined?

(f) Can buyer rescind if he changes his mind and never puts in an application for a mortgage?

13.7.3.3. 'Subject to survey'

(a) Named surveyor?

(b) What type of survey?

(c) Which defects revealed by survey report will entitle buyer to withdraw?

(d) Should a financial limit be placed on the entitlement to rescind? e.g. buyer can rescind if survey reveals defects which exceed £x in total — if so who assesses the value?

(e) Time-limit for obtaining result of survey.

(f) Can buyer rescind if he changes his mind and never instructs the surveyor?

13.7.3.4. 'Subject to planning permission'

(a) Form of application to be agreed between the parties.

(b) What conditions attached to the consent would entitle the buyer to rescind?

(c) Can buyer rescind if he changes his mind and never puts in a planning application?

(d) Time-limit for result of application.

(e) Which party is to make the application and pay the fee?

(f) The non-applying party should agree in writing not to oppose the application and to support it.

(g) Is the application to be for outline or detailed permission?

(h) Which party is to pay the architect's and other professional fees in connection with the application?

B.14. Sub-sales

14.1. Definitions

14.1.1. In this section of the text only, the following expressions have the meanings set out below:

   (a) 'the buyer' means the person who has contracted to buy land and who is selling the land under a sub-sale contract before completion of his own purchase;

   (b) 'the seller' means the person from whom the buyer (as defined above) is purchasing the land and in whom the legal title to the property will be vested pending completion;

   (c) 'the third party' means the person who is buying the land from the buyer (as defined above) under the sub-sale contract.

14.2. Buyer's position pending completion

14.2.1. A buyer who has exchanged contracts for the purchase of property is the owner of the beneficial interest in the land, but does not obtain the legal estate until registration of the transfer to him (or completion in the case of unregistered land). However, in the case of registered land the buyer is nevertheless empowered to deal with the land as if he was registered as proprietor.

14.3. Contractual restriction on sub-sales

14.3.1. Where a buyer intends to sell the property to a third party by way of sub-sale he must ensure that his existing contract to purchase the land contains no restriction which would prevent the sub-sale. The Standard Conditions of Sale do not restrict sub-sales of freehold land nor assignments of existing leases, but Condition 8.2.5 does prevent a sub-sale where the contract is for the grant of a new lease. A seller should resist a buyer's request to remove Condition 8.2.5 from the contract, because its presence ensures that the seller will take the benefit of the covenants given by the first tenant. Covenants given by an original tenant endure throughout the term of the lease notwithstanding its assignment to an assignee.

B

14.3.2. If a restriction against sub-sales is included in the buyer's contract, he will be able to contract to resell the land to a third party, but will have to complete this second transaction separately and subsequent to his own purchase.

14.3.3. Provided there is no such restriction, the buyer may enter a contract for sale with a third party, prior to completion of his own purchase. In such a case, the buyer may, if he wishes, draft the transfer document to reflect the sub-sale (i.e. the seller transfers direct to the sub-purchaser with the original buyer joining in as a party to transfer his beneficial interest in the estate being transferred). Provided the buyer's transfer is technically correct, the seller cannot refuse to sign even if he had previously been unaware of the sub-sale.

14.3.4. Where there is a restriction on sub-sales in the contract it may be possible for the buyer to assign the benefit of his contract with the seller to the third party and then to complete the purchase as nominee for the third party. The subsequent transfer of the property from the buyer (as nominee) to the third party will not attract *ad valorem* stamp duty.

14.4. Special conditions in the sub-sale contract

14.4.1. Special conditions may need to be inserted in the sub-sale contract to deal with the following matters:

(a) **The contract**

When drafting the sub-sale contract, care must be taken to take account of any relevant provisions in the principal contract, e.g. as to length of a notice to complete; the buyer needs to be in a position to give the third party a notice to complete expiring not later than the date of expiry of any notice to complete which the buyer receives from the seller.

(b) **Title**

In registered land the buyer cannot deduce his own title to the third party under Land Registration Act 1925, s.110 since he is not at the time of contract the registered proprietor of the land. The third party must be required by contractual condition to accept title shown by the production of copies of the seller's registered title, and the contract between seller and buyer. In unregistered land the buyer, having investigated title with his own seller, can usually satisfy Law of Property Act 1925, s.44 by supplying a good root of title and subsequent documentation, but will need to produce his own purchase contract to the third party as evidence that he can compel the seller to convey the legal estate.

(c) **The purchase deed**

The purchase deed will usually consist of a transfer or conveyance from the seller direct to the third party. The buyer will need to be made a party to the document in order to transfer his equitable interest in the property to the third party. In the case of a sub-sale the buyer must be in a position to obtain a transfer direct from the seller to the third party in order to be able to compel the third party to complete the purchase.[1]

(d) Apportionment of the price

Where the amount payable by the third party exceeds the consideration due from the buyer to the seller, the purchase deed will need to contain an apportionment of the price as between buyer and seller, with a receipt for their respective portions being given by each.

1. See Land Registration Act 1925, s.110(5).

14.5. Completion

14.5.1. Depending on the arrangements which have been made between the parties, special provisions may need to be considered in relation to actual completion of the transaction, e.g.

(a) where completion is to take place;

(b) transmission of the money;

(c) custody of deeds;

(d) undertakings for the discharge of the seller's mortgage(s) over the property.

14.6. Stamp duty

14.6.1. Provided that the transfer or conveyance is made directly between the seller and the third party, the two transactions are regarded as one, thus incurring only one amount of stamp duty which will be borne by the third party. If two purchase deeds are executed, one from the seller to the buyer and a second from the buyer to the third party, two transactions will have taken place and stamp duty will be payable by both the buyer and the third party on their respective purchase deeds. Where there is a restriction on sub-sales in the contract it may be possible for the buyer to assign the benefit of his contract with the seller to the third party and then to complete the purchase as nominee for the third party. The subsequent transfer of the property from the buyer (as nominee) to the third party will not attract stamp duty.

14.7. Registration of third party

14.7.1. Whether the transaction proceeds by way of a direct transfer from the seller to the third party or by two separate purchase deeds, the third party will still be able to effect registration of his own title at HM Land Registry without needing to insist that the buyer obtains a registered title in his own name first. Where two purchase deeds have been executed, the third party will need to produce the transfer or conveyance from the seller to the buyer to the Registry as proof of the devolution of title.[1]

1. See Seller's title awaiting registration, para. B.04.

14.8. Protection of sub-sale contract

14.8.1. The third party is in a more vulnerable position than a normal buyer since completion of his contract is dependent on the buyer's completion of his own contract with the seller. It may therefore be advisable for the third party to protect his contract by registration. Registration of a contract for sale can only be effected against the owner for the time being of the legal estate, i.e. the seller.[1] When the title is registered the registration is against the land itself rather than against the owner.

1. See Protection of the contract, para. C.05.3.

14.9. Notice to complete

14.9.1. The buyer cannot serve a notice to complete on the third party unless and until he has completed his own contract with the seller. Until this happens the buyer is not 'ready able and willing' to complete within the terms of Standard Condition 6.8.2.[1] This problem can be overcome by the insertion of a special condition in the contract which allows the buyer to serve a notice notwithstanding that he has not yet completed his own contract. Once a notice to complete is served, time will be of the essence of the contract; the buyer should therefore not serve such a notice unless he is confident that he can complete his own purchase (from the seller) within the time-limit which he has imposed on the third party.

1. See generally *Cole* v. *Rose* [1978] 3 All E.R. 1121.

14.10. Capital gains tax

14.10.1. Where a capital gains tax liability is incurred by either the seller or buyer as a result of the sale(s) the Inland Revenue treats a sub-sale transaction as being two separate sales (even if completed by one deed), the sale from seller to buyer being regarded as having taken place before the transaction between the buyer and the third party.

14.11. VAT

14.11.1. The VAT implications of a sub-sale will also need to be considered and provision made in the contract for the responsibility for payment of VAT where applicable.[1]

1. See VAT, para. A.16.

B.15. Supply of abstract before exchange

| 15.1. **Supply of abstract** | 15.2. **Registered land** |
| before exchange | 15.3. **Unregistered land** |

See also: Seller's investigation of title, para. B.03.
Deducing title, para. D.01.

15.1. Supply of abstract before exchange

15.1.1. Having investigated title prior to drafting the contract it will be possible in most cases for the seller to supply the buyer with evidence of title concurrently with the draft contract. Where the Protocol is being used, the seller is obliged to supply his evidence of title to the buyer at this stage of the transaction (Protocol, para. 4.3).

15.1.2. The supply of such evidence of title before exchange is recommended as it will enable the buyer to obtain a comprehensive view of the property which he is buying and will obviate delays after exchange since problems which arise on the title will be brought to light and dealt with at an early stage in the transaction.

15.1.3. Where this is done, it is common for the seller to include a contractual condition which precludes the buyer's right to raise requisitions on the evidence of title. Such a condition does not bind the buyer's lender. Such a condition will exclude the normal contractual condition allowing requisitions to be raised within a certain time after exchange of contracts (see Standard Condition 4.1.1). Where such a condition is included in the contract the buyer must obtain satisfactory answers to his queries on the evidence of title before exchange of contracts. He will not be able to rescind the contract after exchange if he discovers a defect arising out of the evidence of title which was supplied to him prior to exchange. The buyer should ensure that any condition excluding his right to raise requisitions should be limited to requisitions upon the evidence of title actually supplied by the seller prior to exchange of contracts. It should not prohibit requisitions being raised on undisclosed matters which are only revealed by pre-completion searches at HM Land Registry or the Land Charges Department.

15.2. Registered land

15.2.1. Up-to-date office copies of the register entries together with supporting documents, e.g. evidence of overriding interests, tenancies, filed plan, etc., should be supplied by the seller at his own expense. The copies supplied to the buyer must be *original* office copies. Photocopies of the land or charge certificate or photocopies of office copies do not satisfy this requirement.

15.3. Unregistered land

15.3.1. An epitome of title together with clear photocopies of the documents referred to in it should be supplied to the buyer.

B.16. Undertakings for bridging finance

16.1. General points on undertakings

16.1.1. An undertaking is a promise by a solicitor (or a member of the solicitor's staff) to do, or to refrain from doing, something. The promise is enforceable against the solicitor personally, even where the promise was given by a member of staff and not by the solicitor himself. An undertaking given in the firm's name binds all the partners. Undertakings are binding because they are given and no other considerations impinge on their enforceability; thus the normal period of limitation of actions imposed by the Limitation Acts does not apply and an undertaking may be enforced against the giver irrespective of the fact that the normal limitation period has expired.[1]

16.1.2. Failure to honour an undertaking is professional misconduct.[2]

16.1.3. Because of the personal liability which attaches to undertakings it is important that both the giver and recipient of the promise understand precisely what the terms of the promise are. To avoid any misunderstanding it is recommended that undertakings are always given in writing. Any ambiguity in the terms of the promise is construed against the giver of the undertaking. The guidelines contained in the Law Society's warning card 'Undertakings' should be observed.

16.1.4. An undertaking is enforceable because it has been given and thus needs no consideration for its validity, although in practice consideration will often be present.

16.1.5. A promise to give an undertaking is enforceable as an undertaking.

16.1.6. A solicitor is responsible for honouring any undertaking given by his staff. In order to ensure that no undertaking is given which is outside the control of the solicitor to perform it is recommended that undertakings should only be given by partners in the firm, or by other staff with the prior consent of a partner.

16.1.7. Where an undertaking is given by a member of staff without having obtained or exceeding the requisite authority from a partner, the firm will still be bound to honour that undertaking unless the recipient was aware of the lack of authority on the part of the giver.

16.1.8. Any exclusion of the personal liability of the giver of the undertaking must be clear and explicit. Such undertakings should be regarded with great caution since the primary value of the undertaking, i.e. its enforceability may have been seriously eroded by the exclusion clause. A solicitor may give an undertaking on behalf of a client provided that the wording of the undertaking makes it clear that the primary responsibility for performance of the promise lies with the client and not with the solicitor.

16.1.9. The solicitor must ensure that whatever is promised by the undertaking is capable of performance and is totally within his own control to perform. An undertaking will be enforceable even if the circumstances which prevailed at the time when the undertaking was given subsequently change. Any change in circumstances which potentially affects the fulfilment of an undertaking must be notified to the recipient and, if necessary, the terms renegotiated to ensure that whatever promise has been given is capable of performance.

16.1.10. An undertaking to do something which is not within the direct control of the giver should, if it is appropriate to give such an undertaking at all, only be given in qualified form, e.g. an undertaking to procure the client's signature to a document is not totally within the solicitor's own control since he cannot force the client to sign; thus the undertaking should be worded on the basis that the solicitor will use his best (or reasonable) endeavours to procure the required signature.

16.1.11. Undertakings given by licensed conveyancers or authorised practitioners are enforceable as if they were given by solicitors.

16.1.12. Undertakings given by unqualified persons who are not acting through a solicitor's practice are only enforceable under the ordinary law of contract and should never be accepted.

16.1.13. *Guidelines*

(a) Obtain the client's irrevocable written authority before giving an undertaking.

(b) Ensure the wording of the undertaking is clear, unambiguous, and totally capable of performance.

(c) Only give written undertakings, signed or authorised by a partner.

(d) Mark the client's file conspicuously to ensure that the undertaking is not overlooked.

(e) When the undertaking has been fulfilled obtain a written release from the recipient.

1. *Bray* v. *Stuart West & Co.* [1989] E.G.C.S. 60.
2. *The Guide to the Professional Conduct of Solicitors 1996*, Principle 18.05.

16.2. **Bridging finance for the deposit**

16.2.1. Where bridging finance is being extended for the deposit on the client's purchase the bank or other lender will normally require the solicitor to give an undertaking to repay the loan, usually out of the proceeds of sale of the client's existing property.

16.2.2. Such an undertaking should only be given where:

(a) the solicitor is sure that sufficient funds will be available on completion to repay the loan with interest;

(b) the solicitor knows the client well enough to feel confident of making a binding commitment on that client's behalf;

(c) the client has given his irrevocable authority for the undertaking to be given. If in doubt, obtain the authority in writing.

16.3. **When should the undertaking be given?**

16.3.1. Until contracts have been exchanged on the client's related sale transaction there is no guarantee that any funds will be available to repay the loan. Ideally, therefore, such an undertaking should not be given until contracts have been exchanged on the sale. In practice it may be necessary to give the undertaking shortly before exchange in order to ensure the availability of funds for a simultaneous exchange on both sale and purchase contracts. The undertaking should not be given until negotiations for the sale contract are close to the point of exchange, with no outstanding unresolved problems.

16.4. **Terms of the undertaking**

16.4.1. The Law Society has agreed a form of wording for use by solicitors when giving undertakings to banks for bridging finance. The full form of this undertaking is set out in Appendix VI.1.

16.4.2. Even where an undertaking is presented to the solicitor in the standard form or a familiar and frequently used form of wording, the entire wording should be read carefully in the light of the particular transaction to ensure that the wording is appropriate for those circumstances. If the wording is not wholly appropriate to the circumstances in hand, the undertaking should be amended to reflect the particular requirements of the transaction.

16.4.3. Confine the terms of the undertaking to repayment:

(a) of a stated figure, plus interest on that sum if so instructed;

(b) from a defined source, e.g. the proceeds of sale of a named property;

(c) of the net proceeds of sale, having defined what is understood by the word 'net', i.e. after deduction of specified loans, estate agents' commission, solicitor's fees, disbursements on the sale and purchase, and any other known and defined liabilities which will reduce the amount available to repay the loan;

(d) when the proceeds of sale are actually received by the solicitor. This protects the solicitor against having to honour the undertaking in circumstances where the sale of the property is completed but for some reason the funds are never received by him, e.g. the client intercepts the money and absconds with it.

16.5. Change of circumstances

16.5.1. If, having given an undertaking, the circumstances of the client's sale and purchase transactions change, e.g. the consideration for the sale is reduced to take account of a structural defect, the terms of the undertaking must be considered carefully to ensure that they are still capable of performance. The recipient of the undertaking must be informed of the changed circumstances irrespective of whether they affect the obligations covered by the undertaking. Where the undertaking has become impossible of performance because of the changed circumstances the solicitor must re-negotiate the undertaking to obtain either a release of his obligations or a form of wording which is capable of performance in the light of the current situation.

16.6. Checklist

16.6.1. (a) Do I know the client well enough to feel confident about giving the undertaking?

(b) Have I got the client's irrevocable written authority to give the undertaking?

(c) Has the client disclosed all subsisting mortgages and liabilities which will or might affect the amount of money which will be available to discharge the loan?

(d) Is there sufficient equity to repay the loan with interest?

(e) Are the terms of the undertaking totally acceptable?

(f) Are negotiations for the client's sale sufficiently firm and advanced to make it safe to give the undertaking?

(g) Has the undertaking been authorised by a partner?

(h) Has the cover of the client's sale file been clearly marked to show that an undertaking has been given, to whom, and for what amount?

16.7. Loan guarantees

16.7.1. A solicitor who gives an undertaking which is effectively a guarantee of a loan being taken out by the client will be bound by that undertaking even if it is not given 'in the normal course of practice'. Such an undertaking may, however, be outside the scope of the Solicitors' Indemnity Fund.

B.17. Deposit

See also: Dealing with non-solicitors, para. A.05.
Preliminary deposits, para. A.12.
Interest on clients' money, para. A.20.
Form of contract, para. B.11.
Standard Conditions of Sale, para. B.12.
Undertakings for bridging finance, para. B.16.

17.1. Is a deposit necessary?

17.1.1. In law a deposit is unnecessary and neither common law nor statute provides for such to be payable. The payment of a deposit is a purely customary arrangement which is expressly incorporated into the contract for the benefit of the seller.

17.1.2. Purpose of deposit

The payment of a deposit acts as part payment of the purchase price, demonstrates the buyer's good intentions of completing the contract, and gives the seller leverage to ensure the fulfilment of the contract since he is usually able to forfeit the deposit if the buyer defaults, thereby recouping part or all of the loss occasioned by the buyer's default.

17.2. How much deposit?

17.2.1. No deposit at all is payable unless the contract expressly makes provision for one.

17.2.2. A deposit of 10% of the purchase price has until recently been standard practice and is the figure provided by the Standard Conditions of Sale unless specifically amended.

17.2.3. In recent years deposits of less than 10% have become more widespread due in part to the increase in 95% or 100% mortgage offers to buyers, and to the fact that high property prices, with consequently high deposits, place an unfair financial burden on the buyer whilst over-compensating a seller who forfeits that deposit on the buyer's default.

17.2.4. It is clearly to the seller's advantage to demand a 10% deposit; if, however, he is asked by the buyer to accept a reduced amount the following factors should be considered:

    (a) the risk of the sale going off, with the consequent need to forfeit the deposit to compensate for loss;

    (b) the buyer's mortgage arrangements – are they firm and settled? Is the offer of advance for the whole of the purchase price (taking into account the amount of the reduced deposit)?

    (c) the likely amount of loss which the seller would suffer if the buyer were to default, e.g. cost of bridging finance or interest needed to complete a related purchase, length of time and costs of resale of the property.

17.2.5. The seller's solicitor must explain the consequences of taking a reduced deposit to his client and obtain his client's express authority before agreeing the reduction with the buyer's solicitor or representative. *Morris* v. *Duke Cohan*[1] suggests that it may be professional negligence for a solicitor to accept a reduced deposit without the client's express authority.

17.2.6. If a reduced deposit is taken on exchange, the contract should provide for the balance of the 10% to become immediately payable on service of a notice to complete.[2]

17.2.7. Only in exceptional circumstances should the transaction proceed without any deposit being taken. Examples might include family transactions or sales to sitting tenants.

17.2.8. Deposits in excess of 10% are very rare, and cannot be justified in normal circumstances.[3]

17.2.9. The amount of the deposit actually payable on exchange will take into account any preliminary deposit already paid, but, unless the contract provides otherwise, is calculated exclusive of the value of chattels which are to be paid for in addition to the purchase price of the land.

1. (1975) 119 S.J. 826.
2. See Standard Condition 6.8.4.
3. See *Dojap Investments Ltd.* v. *Workers Trust and Merchant Bank Ltd.* [1993] A.C. 573 where the forfeiture of a 24% deposit was held to be a penalty.

17.3. How is the deposit to be funded?

17.3.1. The answer to this question should be obtained when initial instructions are taken from the client. It is safest to assume at this stage that the seller will require a full 10% deposit, and if the buyer wishes to pay a reduced deposit the matter will have to be raised during negotiations with the seller's solicitor.

17.3.2. *From an investment account*

(a) How much notice does the buyer need to give to withdraw his funds without losing a significant amount of interest?

(b) Ensure sufficient money is transferred to a short-term investment account in time for it to be immediately available on exchange.

17.3.3. *Bridging finance*

Bridging finance from a bank or other lender will often be needed in a situation where the purchase is dependent on a related sale:

(a) It should be apparent at an early stage in the transaction that bridging finance will be required and arrangements should be made as soon as possible so that the money is immediately available when required on exchange.

(b) An undertaking to repay the bridging loan out of the proceeds of sale of the client's existing property will often be required from the solicitor. Should an undertaking be given and, if so, are its terms acceptable?

(c) Has the client been properly advised about the costs and risks of bridging finance, e.g. high interest rate payable over an uncertain period if the sale goes off, arrangement fees?

(d) Tax relief on the amount of the bridging finance is available where the loan is taken on a separate loan account, but not where the loan is taken by way of overdraft on a current account. If the client has a high cash flow passing through his current account it may be more cost effective to forego the tax relief and take advantage of the lower interest rates payable on the current account.

17.3.4. *Deposit guarantee*

Check buyer's eligibility – the conditions of the scheme may provide, e.g. that the scheme is not available for first-time buyers, or that the deposit must not exceed either 10% of the purchase price or £15,000, or that the completion date in the contract must not be more than six weeks from the date of exchange.

17.3.5. The seller's agreement to use of the scheme must be obtained as soon as possible and arrangements put in hand to obtain the guarantee so that it is available to be handed to the seller on exchange of contracts.

17.3.6. Before agreeing to accept deposit by way of guarantee the seller should consider:

(a) the fact that he may not be able to use the deposit towards the deposit on his own purchase (depending on the scheme used) although this factor will be of no consequence if a deposit guarantee is to be used in that transaction also;

(b) the consequences (including costs and delay) of attempting to enforce payment through the scheme if the reasons for the buyer's ultimate default are either disputed or not covered by the scheme.

17.3.7. *Lenders' deposit-free schemes*

The terms of these schemes vary from lender to lender. The terms of the particular scheme should be considered carefully by both parties before a decision to use them is taken. In particular the seller should have regard to the possible consequences (including costs and delay) if the reasons for the buyer's ultimate default are either disputed or not covered by the scheme.

17.4. **Clearing funds**

17.4.1. The seller will normally require the deposit to be paid either by solicitor's cheque or banker's draft.[1] The buyer's solicitor must therefore ensure that he receives the amount of the deposit from his own client in sufficient time to allow the client's cheque to be cleared through the solicitor's clients' account before drawing the cheque in favour of the seller for the deposit.

1. See Standard Condition 2.2.1.

17.5. **Capacity in which deposit is held**

17.5.1. The deposit is held in one of the three capacities listed below:

(a) agent for the seller;

(b) agent for the buyer;

(c) stakeholder.

17.5.2. In the absence of contrary agreement solicitors and estate agents hold in the capacity of agent for the seller, but an auctioneer holds as stakeholder.[1] This general rule may be varied by express contractual condition.

17.5.3. The capacity of agent for the buyer is rarely used since in most situations the seller will be reluctant to agree to the deposit being held in this way. It may, however, be necessary to use this capacity where the seller is represented by an unqualified person.

17.5.4. If the deposit is held as agent for the seller, the agent may hand the money over to the seller before completion. In this situation the seller can use the money towards the deposit on his own purchase, but where this occurs the buyer may have difficulty in recovering the money if the seller defaults on completion. The buyer should be advised of the risks involved in agreeing to the deposit being held in the capacity of agent.

17.5.5. A stakeholder is the principal for both parties and where this capacity is used the money can be handed to either party without the consent of the other provided the stakeholder is confident that circumstances exist which justify his decision to make payment.

17.5.6. Most deposits are paid to the seller's solicitor in the capacity either of agent for the seller or stakeholder.

17.5.7. The Standard Conditions of Sale (Condition 2.2.1) generally provide for the deposit to be held as stakeholder and this is the capacity recommended by the Law Society.[2] The capacity of agent for the seller will, however, apply if the seller is to use all or part of the deposit towards the deposit on his related residential transaction in England and Wales (Condition 2.2.2), and may be necessary in some circumstances where an exchange under the Law Society's Formula C is contemplated.

17.5.8. Where the seller is represented by an unqualified person the buyer's solicitor should ensure that he or a reputable estate agent holds the deposit (in either case in the capacity of stakeholder) or that it is placed in a deposit account in a bank or building society in the joint names of seller and buyer.

17.5.9. Fiduciary vendors

Where the sellers are selling as trustees the money arising from the sale will be trust money and should never be outside the control of the trustees.[3] This requirement will be satisfied if the deposit is paid to some person in the capacity of agent for the seller.

17.5.10. Where the deposit or any part of it is proposed to be held as agents of the seller, it is recommended that the buyer client should be advised of the risks involved in agreeeing to this.

1. *Edgell* v. *Day* (1865) L.R. 1 C.P. 80; *Ryan* v. *Pilkington* [1959] 1 All E.R. 689.
2. [1975] *Gazette*, 184.
3. [1957] *Gazette*, 327.

17.6. Solicitor holding the deposit

17.6.1. The money is clients' money and must be placed in a clients' account in accordance with Solicitors' Accounts Rules 1991.

17.7. Interest on the deposit

17.7.1. Whether the money is held in the capacity of agent for the seller or stakeholder interest may be payable under Solicitors' Accounts Rules 1991.

17.7.2. Where the money is held as stakeholder interest is payable on the stake money under the provisions of Solicitors' Accounts Rules 1991. It is up to the parties to decide which of them should be entitled to the interest on the stake money and an appropriate clause must be included in the contract to deal with the payment of interest in these circumstances. The Law Society's recommended form of wording for such a clause is as follows: 'The stakeholder shall pay to the seller/buyer a sum equal to the interest the deposit would have earned if placed on deposit (less costs of acting as stakeholder).'

17.7.3. Standard Condition 2.2.3 provides that where the deposit, or part of it, is held in the capacity of stakeholder, interest on the deposit will be payable to the seller on completion. If the buyer negotiates an agreement that he is to be credited with interest on the deposit, a special condition must be inserted in the contract to that effect.

17.8. Deposits paid to estate agents

17.8.1. At common law an estate agent holds the deposit as agent for the seller, but this capacity may be changed to stakeholder by express contractual provision.

17.8.2. In whichever capacity the deposit is held the risk of its loss through the default of the agent generally falls on the buyer.[1]

17.8.3. This risk has been minimised by Estate Agents Act 1979, s.16 which requires agents to carry insurance to cover clients' money. 'Clients' money' is defined by section 12 of the 1979 Act to include any contract or pre-contract deposit.

17.8.4. The money must be placed in a clients' account (*ibid.* s.14), and is held on trust by the agent for the person who is or who will become entitled to the money. Since the money is trust money it will not vest in a trustee in bankruptcy should the agent be made bankrupt.[2]

17.8.5. An estate agent who holds in the capacity of agent for the seller is under a duty to account to the client for interest on any deposit exceeding £500.[3] It is not clear whether an estate agent who holds in the capacity of stakeholder is subject to the provisions relating to the payment of interest.

1. *Sorrell* v. *Finch* [1977] A.C. 728.
2. Estate Agents Act 1979, s.13(1).
3. Estate Agents (Accounts) Regulations 1981 (S.I. 1981/1520), reg.7.

17.9.   **Contractual terms relating to the deposit**

17.9.1.   Standard contractual conditions will normally provide for the seller's solicitor to hold a 10% deposit as stakeholder, the deposit to be paid by banker's draft or solicitor's cheque (see Standard Condition 2.2.1).

17.9.2.   The standard clauses represent the safest method both of payment and of holding the deposit. Variations of these provisions by express contractual term is possible but should only be done where the substituted term is necessary to meet the circumstances of the individual transaction and sufficiently safeguards the interests of both parties.

17.9.3.   Variation of the standard provisions may be required where the seller is represented by an unqualified person, or where a less than 10% deposit is being taken. In the latter case provision should be included in the contract for the balance of the 10% to become immediately payable in the event of a notice to complete being served so that the seller is able to forfeit the full 10% sum should it become necessary to do so. (See Standard Condition 6.8.4.)

17.9.4.   Any preliminary deposit which was paid to an estate agent before exchange should be handed over to the solicitor who is holding the deposit once exchange has taken place. If this does not occur the seller will technically be in breach of contract because the contract requires the solicitor to hold 'the deposit', and this may in turn cause problems for a buyer who seeks the recovery of his deposit on the seller's default. In practice estate agents are reluctant to part with the preliminary deposit, seeking to retain it in part payment of their commission.

17.9.5.   *Checklist for contract terms*

      (a) How much deposit is required in total?

      (b) Has a preliminary deposit been paid − if so, how much and to whom?

      (c) Who is to hold the deposit and in which capacity?

      (d) Method of payment?

      (e) If in cash, provide for payment by banker's draft or equivalent.

      (f) If less than 10%, provide for balance to be immediately payable on service of a completion notice.

17.9.6.   The Protocol and the Standard Conditions of Sale recognise the existing practice in many areas for the deposit received on the sale of the property to be used to pay the deposit on the purchase of another property.

17.9.7.   The presence of Condition 2.2.3 may mean that a special condition will be necessary if the Law Society's Formula C is used on exchange of contracts and the person at the end of the chain will not agree to the deposit being held as stakeholder. In this event, it would be necessary for all parties in the chain to be notified and a special condition would be required only in the last contract in the chain. It is suggested that this should be:

'The deposit shall be paid to the seller's solicitor as agent for the seller and Standard Condition 2.2.3 is varied accordingly.'

17.10. Methods of payment of deposit

17.10.1. The seller may insist on the payment of the deposit in cash unless he has agreed to accept some other method of payment.[1] Standard Condition 2.2.1 requires payment to be made by banker's draft or solicitor's cheque only, except where the contract is made at auction.

17.10.2. If a cheque taken in payment of the deposit bounces, this constitutes a fundamental breach of contract which gives the seller the option either of keeping the contract alive for the benefit of both parties, or of treating the contract as discharged by the breach, and in either event of suing for damages.[2] A separate cause of action arises out of the cheque itself. The contract should be drafted to indicate precisely what the rights of the parties are in the event of the dishonour of the deposit cheque.

17.10.3. The option of treating the contract as discharged is of little consolation to a seller who, on the strength of his sale contract, has exchanged contracts for the purchase of another property. Provision should therefore be made in the contract to ensure that the deposit is only payable by a method which will be honoured on presentation, e.g. banker's draft or solicitor's clients' account cheque.

1. *Johnston* v. *Boyes* (1898) 14 T.L.R. 475.
2. *Millichamp* v. *Jones* [1983] 1 All E.R. 267, and see Standard Condition 2.2.4.

17.11. Using the deposit to fund another transaction

17.11.1. A seller who is a builder or developer, or one who is involved in the purchase of another property, may wish to use part or all of the deposit received from his sale before completion of that transaction takes place.

17.11.2. The deposit may only be used by the seller in this way if it is held in the capacity of agent for the seller.

17.11.3. Although totally satisfactory for the seller, this situation is less than satisfactory for the buyer who may find that he has difficulty in recovering his money if the sale is not completed through the default of the seller or if the seller goes bankrupt or absconds with the money. The buyer should be advised of these risks.

17.11.4. Before agreeing to allow the seller to have use of the deposit pending completion the buyer should try to ensure that the contract contains some protection for him against the seller's default. In an exceptional case it would be possible for the buyer to secure the deposit by taking an equitable charge over the seller's existing and new properties. Such a charge would need to be registered as a notice or caution (registered land) or Class C(iii) land charge (unregistered land) to bind a purchaser and could only be enforced by a court order for the sale of the property.

17.11.5. Standard Condition 2.2.2 allows the seller to use all or part of the deposit to fund his own deposit on a related residential transaction in England and Wales but for no other purpose.

17.12. Buyer's lien

17.12.1. From the moment when he pays the deposit to the seller in the capacity of agent (but not stakeholder) the buyer has a lien over the property for the amount of the deposit. The lien is only enforceable by a court order for sale of the property and must be protected as a notice or caution (registered land) or Class C(iii) land charge (unregistered land) in order to bind a purchaser. If the buyer is in occupation his lien will be an overriding interest in registered land under Land Registration Act 1925, s.70(1)(*g*).

17.12.2. If the buyer defaults on completion he has no right to the return of his deposit. This is subject to the court's discretion to order the return of a deposit under Law of Property Act 1925, s.49(2).

17.12.3. If the contract is terminated for any other reason the buyer has a lien which may be enforced either by the buyer himself or by a person claiming under him.[1]

17.12.4. When the reason for non-completion of the sale is a defect in the seller's title the lien extends to the deposit, interest, and the costs of investigating title, and where the sale is by auction under the direction of the court, costs incurred by the buyer in connection with the auction are also included.[2]

17.12.5. A buyer who pays a deposit to a stakeholder is not entitled to recover through his lien the costs of an unsuccessful action for specific performance brought against him by the seller.[3]

1. *Levy* v. *Stogdon* [1898] 1 Ch. 478.
2. *Holliwell* v. *Seacombe* [1906] 1 Ch. 426.
3. *Combe* v. *Lord Swaythling* [1947] Ch. 625.

17.13. Deposits paid direct to the seller

17.13.1. A buyer's solicitor should be wary of a situation in which the buyer has apparently paid a deposit directly to the seller. This may indicate the existence of a mortgage fraud.

17.13.2. The Protocol envisages the deposit being passed by the buyer's solicitor to the seller's solicitor. Solicitors are reminded of the Law Society's guidance on mortgage fraud. In many cases of such fraud, the deposit is allegedly paid direct between the parties.

17.13.3. A solicitor should not confirm to another solicitor that deposit payments have been made or received unless the moneys have been paid into that solicitor's client account or that solicitor has actual evidence that the payment has been made or received by a third party.

17.13.4. Solicitors are reminded of Principle 16.01 in *The Guide to the Professional Conduct of Solicitors 1996.* Any solicitor with a query about a suspected mortgage fraud should contact the Law Society Practice Advice Service on (0171) 242 1222.

B.18. Liquor licensing and food safety

18.1. **Pre-contract enquiries**
18.2. **Checking the current licences**
18.3. **The premises**
18.4. **Transfer of licence**
18.5. **The buyer**
18.6. **Food Safety Act 1990**

18.1. Pre-contract enquiries

18.1.1. Additional enquiries of the seller should be made in relation to the following matters:

(a) to require copies of all current licences and certificates applicable to the premises;

(b) to ascertain whether notice has been received by the seller for revocation of the licence or the imposition of a restriction order;

(c) to find out whether any alterations have been made to the premises (see below);

(d) to require copies of all correspondence relevant to the licence between the licensee and the court, police, fire and environmental health authorities since the date of the last renewal.

18.2. Checking the current licences

18.2.1. The licences supplied by the seller should be checked to see:

(a) that they are valid and subsisting;

(b) what (if anything) they cover in addition to a justices licence, e.g. restaurant certificate under Licensing Act 1964, s.68 or public entertainment licence;

(c) what restrictions they impose on the use of the premises;

(d) the date of the next licensing session at which renewal will be required.

18.3. The premises

18.3.1. The premises themselves must be inspected to establish that they accord with the plan deposited with the licensing justices which defines the physical limits of the licence, e.g. a pub garden may be outside the licensed area. The client may be advised to instruct a chartered surveyor to carry out this inspection. On inspection it should also be noted whether any alterations have been made to the premises because unauthorised alterations (in addition to planning penalties) may lead to the forfeiture of the licence under Licensing Act 1964, s.20. The client's intentions in relation to future alterations of the property should also be noted and their feasibility in relation to any restrictions imposed by the licence considered. Enquiries should also be made as to the extent (if any) of security of tenure enjoyed by present tenants of the premises.

18.4.   Transfer of licence

18.4.1.   A licence cannot be transferred unless its transfer is approved by the justices who meet at approximately monthly intervals. In the interim, a temporary transfer order (a protection order) should be obtained.

18.4.2.   A corporation cannot hold a licence. Therefore an individual must be nominated by the corporation to hold the licence on its behalf. Some multiple owners (e.g. supermarkets and breweries) prefer to hold all their licences in the name of one central nominee, but this practice is not favoured by all licensing panels.

18.4.3.   Informal enquiries should be made of the clerk to the local licensing justices to obtain a copy of their procedural guidelines (if any) relating to the grant and transfer of licences.

18.4.4.   Applications for transfer of the relevant licences must be made. Except where the transfer can be synchronised with the completion of the purchase, an application for a temporary licence (protection order) will have to be made.

18.4.5.   The buyer's solicitor must ascertain how much notice of the application is required by the justices. Seven days' notice is the minimum required in normal circumstances, but some courts do not sit on every day of the week. The dates of the following licensing sessions must also be ascertained because an application for a full transfer of the licence, following grant of the protection order, must be made at the latest at the second session following the grant of the protection order, failing which the protection order expires.

18.4.6.   If a protection order cannot be obtained before contracts are exchanged, the contract will need to be made conditional on such an order being obtained and should contain a clause stating that the seller consents to the buyer's application for a protection order and to the transfer of the licence. It should be noted that the grant of a protection order does not guarantee the grant of a transfer of the licence.

18.5.   The buyer

18.5.1.   The buyer should be fully advised about the extent of the licence which he is proposing to take over, the items which are permitted by it, restrictions on hours, and its next renewal date (licences are renewable every three years).

18.5.2.   The buyer's solicitor should check that his client is eligible to take a transfer of the licence and that no order has been made under Licensing Act 1964, s.100 disqualifying the client from holding a licence. A number of licencing districts prefer the applicant to hold a British Institute of Innkeeping certificate.

18.5.3.   Enquiries should be made as to whether the licencing justices have made any regulation under Licencing Act 1964, s.8(4) determining the time which must elapse between the grant of a transfer and another application for transfer.

18.6.   Food Safety Act 1990

18.6.1.   Regulations made under Food Safety Act 1990 (currently Food Premises (Registration) Regulations 1991, S.I. 1991/2825) make it an offence to carry on a food business from unregistered premises.

18.6.2.   Application for registration must be made on a prescribed form to the appropriate local authority at least 28 days before the commencement of the business.

18.6.3.   There is no fee for registration, and no requirement for renewal of registration once registered, but any changes in the information supplied must be notified to the registering authority.

18.6.4. *Need to register*

The following must be registered:

    (a) premises where a food business is carried on for five or more days (whether or not consecutive) in any period of five consecutive weeks;

    (b) premises where two or more food businesses carried on by the same or different individuals or organisations are carried on for five or more days (whether consecutive or not) within a consecutive five-week period.

18.6.5.   A building where several different food businesses are carried on (e.g. the food court of an airport terminal) may not need to be registered but the individual food businesses must be registered.

18.6.6.   Where moveable stalls, barrows, etc., are used for a food business in a market, the individual stall holders will usually have to register.

18.6.7.   Moveable premises, e.g. an ice cream van or mobile food stall are exempt from registration, but the premises where the van or stall are kept may be subject to the regulations.

18.6.8.   Staff canteens, directors' dining rooms and their kitchens attract registration under the regulations.

18.6.9. Exemptions from registration:

    (a) slaughterhouses;

    (b) dairies;

    (c) milk distribution centres;

    (d) cold stores;

    (e) meat product plants approved for export to the E.U.;

    (f) grouse moors and river banks;

    (g) places where crops are harvested, stored and/or packed except where the crops are wrapped in the way in which they will be sold to the consumer;

    (h) honey harvesting;

    (i) egg production or packing;

    (j) livestock farms and markets;

    (k) kitchens used only for washing up;

    (l) private cars, aircraft and ships;

    (m) some religious ceremonies;

    (n) some domestic premises where food is prepared for another food business;

    (o) houses where bed and breakfast is provided in not more than three bedrooms.

18.6.10. Part I of the register maintained by the local authority is open to public inspection. Copies of this part of the register which contains the name and address of the premises and the name and nature of the business may be obtained. The local authority may charge a fee for copies. Part II of the register contains the information set out in the application form with the name of the proprietor and (if different) the manager of the premises together with other information collected by the authority about the premises. This part of the register is open to inspection by the police and authorised officers under section 6 of the Act but is not open to public inspection.

18.6.11. Clients may be advised to obtain Code of Practice 11 published by HMSO (ISBN: 0-11-321478-2) which deals with the application and enforcement of these regulations.

FURTHER REFERENCE

Licensing Law for Conveyancers, A. Pendlebury, F.T. Law & Tax.

Paterson's Licensing Acts, M. Pink, Butterworths.

B.19. Mortgage offers

19.1. **Acceptance of offer**
19.2. **Conditions attached to offer**
19.3. **Duty of confidentiality**

19.4. **Consumer Credit Act 1974**
19.5. **Discharge of existing mortgage**
19.6. **Mortgage fraud**

See also: Financial services, para. A.04.
Acting for both parties, para. A.10.
Mortgages: acting for borrower and lender, para. A.11.

19.1. Acceptance of offer

19.1.1. Where the client is purchasing a property with the aid of mortgage finance, the solicitor must ensure that the client has received and (where necessary) accepted a satisfactory offer of a mortgage before advising the client to exchange contracts. Advice given to the client about the terms of a mortgage offer may be 'investment business' within the terms of Financial Services Act 1986.[1]

1. See Financial services, para. A.04.

19.2. Conditions attached to offer

19.2.1. Before acceptance of the offer or committing his client to the purchase, the solicitor should ensure that the client understands the conditions attached to the mortgage offer and the terms of the mortgage and will be able to comply with them. Conditions may be general, e.g. a condition that the property must not be let without the lender's consent, or special, having application to this offer only, e.g. a condition that the buyer obtains an endowment policy as security for the mortgage. The mortgage offer, if formally accepted, may constitute a contract between the buyer and his lender, and the lender may not be able to withdraw his offer once accepted. The solicitor should check the offer to see whether this is the case and whether or not the lender requires a formal acceptance of the offer.

19.2.2. If the conditions attached to the mortgage offer are not wholly acceptable to the client, e.g. the offer requires the client to take out a new endowment policy when the client would be better advised to extend and re-assign an existing policy, an attempt should be made to renegotiate the terms with the lender. Such a term may be invalid under Part IV Courts and Legal Services Act 1990. In extreme cases an alternative source of finance may need to be investigated.

19.2.3. In this situation, where the buyer's solicitor has also been instructed to act for the lender, a conflict exists between the interests of the buyer client and the lender client. Unless such conflict can be resolved to the satisfaction of both clients, the solicitor cannot continue to act for either, unless with the consent of one client he is permitted to continue to act for the other. The solicitor's duty of confidentiality towards his client may prevent him from continuing to act for either client in this situation.

19.2.4. If it comes to the notice of the solicitor that the client will be in breach of the terms of the mortgage offer, e.g. where the purchase price for the property has been misrepresented to the lender, the lender must be informed of the problem.[1] The duty to inform the lender exists throughout the transaction, not just at the time when the offer is being considered. Failure to inform the lender of circumstances in which it appears that the buyer client is attempting to perpetrate a fraud on the lender may lead to the criminal prosecution of the solicitor and to disciplinary proceedings being taken against him. This gives rise to a conflict of interests between the buyer client and the lender client since the lender may, in the light of the information received, choose to adjust the terms of the mortgage offer to the detriment of the buyer client. Attention is drawn to the Law Society's guidelines on mortgage fraud which are reproduced in Appendix III.

1. See also Mortgages: acting for lender and borrower, para. A.11.

19.3.   Duty of confidentiality

19.3.1. In any of the above circumstances where a conflict of interests exists between the buyer client and the lender client the solicitor, acting in his capacity of adviser to the buyer, may only disclose the nature of the conflict to the lender with the consent of the buyer client. Disclosure of information without the buyer client's consent will be a breach of the solicitor's duty of confidentiality.

19.4.   Consumer Credit Act 1974

19.4.1. Consumer Credit Act 1974, s.58 may be applicable if the mortgage is:

    (a)   for a sum less than £15,000; and

    (b)   to be granted to an individual or partnership by a non-exempt lender; and

    (c)   is not a loan for the *purchase* of land.

19.4.2. Consumer Credit Act 1974 does not generally apply to loans exceeding £15,000 and, by regulations made under the Act,[1] loans granted by most major banks, building societies and insurance companies are exempted from the provisions of the Act.

19.4.3. The requirements of section 58 will thus not normally be relevant in circumstances where the buyer client is purchasing land with the assistance of a first mortgage from an institutional lender. Where, however, the client already owns the land in question and is refinancing or taking out a second or subsequent mortgage the provisions of section 58 should be borne in mind, particularly where the solicitor is acting also for the lender.

19.4.4.   Section 58 provides that the borrower must be given a 'cooling-off' period (normally of 14 days) after the mortgage documentation has been sent to him by the lender. The purpose of this period is to allow the borrower to reflect on and to take independent advice on the terms of the loan without being subjected to pressure from the lender or anyone acting on behalf of the lender. During the 'cooling off' period neither the lender nor anyone acting on his behalf (which includes the solicitor acting for the lender) may make contact with the borrower, whether by letter, telephone or any other means of communication. During this time the solicitor may speak or write to his borrower client if the client approaches him, but client contact should not be initiated by the solicitor whilst the consideration period is running. Failure to comply with this provision will render the mortgage unenforceable except with leave of the court, which will not automatically be granted. Thus a solicitor who is acting for a lender in circumstances where section 58 applies must establish precisely when the consideration period begins to run and must not prejudice the enforceability of the loan by voluntarily contacting his client during this period.

1. Consumer Credit (Exempt Agreements) Order 1989/869.

19.5.   Discharge of existing mortgage

19.5.1.   It is usually a term of a mortgage offer for a first mortgage over property that any existing mortgage which the client has should be discharged on or before completion of the new loan. The solicitor must ensure the buyer client is aware of and can comply with this condition.

19.5.2.   Some lenders charge interest on an existing loan until the end of the calendar month notwithstanding that the mortgage is repaid earlier. Since this extra amount of interest can add up to a considerable sum, the solicitor should enquire of the lender whether such interest will be charged on the discharge of the existing mortgage and advise his client accordingly.

19.6.   Mortgage fraud

19.6.1.   Solicitors need to be alert to the possibility of a mortgage fraud. The Law Society's guidance on mortgage fraud is set out in Appendix III. The following subparagraphs outline the most common types of fraud and the solicitor's duty in relation to a suspected fraud.

19.6.2. *Solicitor's duty*

The Law Society's guidance on mortgage fraud (set out in Appendix III.) states that if a solicitor is aware that his or her client is attempting to perpetrate fraud in any form, he or she must immediately cease acting for that client.

19.6.3. Principle 12.02 of *The Guide to the Professional Conduct of Solicitors 1996* states that a solicitor must not act or, where relevant, must cease acting further where the instructions would involve the solicitor in a breach of the law or a breach of the principles of professional conduct, unless the client is prepared to change his or her instructions appropriately.

19.6.4. Failure to comply with the above principles carries with it the risk of criminal prosecution (for having aided and abetted a fraud) and/or civil action (breach of contract or negligence by, e.g. a lender who suffers loss) and of being disciplined for breach of the principles of professional conduct.

19.6.5. A solicitor may be guilty of conspiracy to defraud by undertaking the conveyancing work for a client who is himself engaged in a fraudulent transaction. The solicitor's active knowledge of or participation in the fraud is not necessary; if the work involved in the conveyancing falls below the standard expected of a normal solicitor, this may indicate that the solicitor had no genuine belief in the transaction in which he was acting and imply that the solicitor was involved in the conspiracy. A solicitor who is found guilty of fraud is likely to be struck off the Roll.

19.6.6. *Types of fraud*

(a) **Status**

(i) Income
The borrower overstates his income in the mortgage application, usually with the sole aim of securing a higher mortgage. A solicitor who knows that his client is unemployed or that there are substantial arrears owing on the client's current mortgage owes a duty to the lender to inform him of these facts.

(ii) Identity
The borrower conceals his true identity, perhaps to disguise the fact that he has another subsisting mortgage. Fraud can also occur where a husband forges his wife's signature (or vice versa). An indication of this type of fraud is where the solicitor is asked to contact the husband at his business address rather than his home address. Another example in this category is the sale at an inflated price to an individual by a company controlled by him. This device is used to raise additional finance for the company. This type of fraud is sometimes carried out on a large scale and often involves other fraud, e.g. tax, improvement grants. Instructions to purchase or transfer the property into the name of nominees may indicate a fraud of this type. In all cases where the client is not personally known to the solicitor, it may be prudent to

check the identity of the client. Where there are co-buyers (e.g. husband and wife), instructions must be confirmed from both of them.[1]

(b) **Property**

(i) Price reduction

The price to be shown in the purchase deed is less than that agreed to be paid by the buyer, or situations where the client instructs that a reduced price has been agreed to take account of an allowance for 'repairs to the property'. In some cases, the amounts shown in the contract and purchase deed will be identical but fraud occurs because the full amount of the purchase price is never in fact paid, e.g. the buyer says he has paid money directly to the seller, or that part of the price has been set off by the buyer against money owed to him by the seller.

(ii) Fraudulent valuations

Where it appears that the valuation of the property is higher than might be expected for a property of that type or is considerably higher than the figure in a recent (say within the last 12 months) disposal of the property. A solicitor is not an expert in valuations and cannot be expected to advise on the accuracy of a valuation obtained by the client; nevertheless; a valuation which is patently out of line with the apparent value of the property may give rise to suspicion.

(iii) Roll-over fraud

This occurs where the borrower sells a property to an associate at an inflated price. As a result, the associate is able to obtain a higher mortgage. No repayments are made under the mortgage. Before the lender is able to repossess the property, it is sold to another associate for a higher figure, and so on.

(iv) Use of sub-sales

A client instructs a solicitor in the purchase of a property for, say, £100,000. The solicitor is told that the property is to be bought in the name of B who is selling to C at a price of £160,000. B and C are either the same person (using assumed identities) or associated persons. A may also be a party to the fraud, although in some cases he may be an innocent seller. C obtains a mortgage of £150,000 based on the higher value and secures an immediate profit of £50,000. The balance between the original sale price and the higher sub-sale price is never paid, or is said to be paid direct by B to C, or is allegedly set off by B against money owed to him by C. A simultaneous exchange of contracts followed by a quick completion is often a feature of these transactions. The lender is then left with a property worth only £100,000 as security for the loan.[2] A variation on this theme is where A grants a lease to B at a ground rent; B then assigns the lease to C at a premium. The purpose of this type of transaction is to give C a legal interest on which he can then obtain a mortgage.

(v) Money paid direct

A deposit or balance of the purchase price which is paid (or said to be paid) direct to the seller from the buyer may indicate a mortgage fraud.

19.6.7. The conduct issues

A solicitor must act in the best interests of the client. Where he is acting for both the buyer and his lender, he owes a duty to both. There is a duty to report to the lender any alteration in the purchase price and any other information relevant to the lending decision.[3]

19.6.8.   The solicitor's duty of confidentiality means that the buyer/borrower must consent to disclosure being made to the lender. This situation may give rise to a conflict of interests between the lender client and the buyer client. The solicitor cannot then continue to act for both clients and cannot continue to act for one client without the consent of the other. The safest course of action to adopt is to cease to act for both clients in these circumstances. Where the solicitor is obliged to cease to act for the lender, he should return the papers to the lender, stating that they are returned on the grounds of conflict of interests.

1. *Penn* v. *Bristol & West Building Society, The Times,* 19 June 1995.
2. *Bristol & West Building Society* v. *Kramer, The Independent,* 26 January 1995.
3. *Alliance & Leicester Building Society* v. *Edgestop Ltd.* [1994] 2 E.G.L.R. 229; *Bristol & West Building Society* v. *May, Merriman* [1996] E.G.C.S. 69.

FURTHER REFERENCE

Mortgage Planning: Guidance for Solicitors Marketing Financial Services, M. MacCormack, the Law Society.

B.20. Auctions

See also: Conditional contracts, para. B.13.

20.1. Acting for the seller

20.1.1. Where property is to be sold by auction the contract generally consists of particulars, describing the land to be sold, conditions stating the terms of the sale, and a memorandum of the sale which will be signed by or on behalf of the buyer at the auction itself.

20.1.2. The special conditions of the contract are normally prepared by the seller's solicitor in conjunction with the auctioneer who will prepare the particulars of sale. The contract will frequently incorporate the Standard Conditions of Sale.

20.2. Preparing the contract

20.2.1. In addition to the usual contractual clauses particular attention should be paid to the matters listed below. Most of these matters are normally dealt with by the Standard Conditions of Sale, but it is advisable to check their relevance to the particular property concerned and to ensure that any necessary amendments or additions to the Standard Conditions are included in the special conditions of the contract. Some, but not all, of the matters listed below are included in Standard Condition 2.3:

(a) **Reserve price**

By Sale of Land by Auction Act 1867, s.5 the contract must state whether or not the property is subject to a reserve price. Unless a reserve is placed on the property the auctioneer will be bound to sell to the highest bidder.

(b) **Right to bid**

Where the property is subject to a reserve price the seller may, under Sale of Land by Auction Act 1867, reserve the right to bid at the auction. This right when reserved by special condition in the contract may be exercised by the seller or his agent.

B

(c) The auctioneer's control over the bidding

In order to avoid uncertainty the contract should make it clear whether the auctioneer has the right to refuse a bid; or to fix the amount of bids; and should contain provisions whereby the auctioneer may settle any dispute which arises over the bidding.

(d) Payment of deposit

The contract should provide for the amount of the deposit to be paid, the time when it is to be paid, and the methods of payment which are acceptable. It is usual at an auction to provide for a full 10% deposit to be paid. At common law the deposit must be tendered in cash.[1] Standard Condition 2.2.1 provides for a 10% deposit to be payable but does not limit the methods of payment (e.g. to solicitor's cheque); therefore unless this condition is amended the seller would have to accept payment by the buyer's own cheque with the attendant risks of that cheque not being honoured on presentation.

(e) Seller's right to withdraw from auction

In the absence of a special condition it is uncertain whether the seller is entitled to withdraw the property from auction once bidding has commenced unless the sale is subject to a reserve price.

(f) Retraction of bids by buyer

It is common to include a condition precluding the retraction of a bid once made. Such a condition is probably unenforceable at common law under the general principles of offer and acceptance.[2] A bid made at auction is an offer, and the offeror (buyer) is free to withdraw his offer at any time until acceptance by the auctioneer. Acceptance takes place with the fall of the hammer. It should be noted that auction contracts are excluded from the provisions of Law of Property (Miscellaneous Provisions) Act 1989, s.2 (requiring a contract for the sale of land to be in writing); an auction contract will therefore be binding and enforceable even if oral and no memorandum is signed.

(g) Division of property into lots

If required, an express right to divide the property into separate lots should be included in the contract.

(h) Buyer's right to rescind

Where the buyer has not been given the opportunity to make searches or to inspect copies of searches made by the seller prior to the auction, it may be felt appropriate to include a provision which allows the buyer to rescind within a certain time if the results of his searches are not satisfactory. The inclusion of such a condition will introduce an element of uncertainty into the contract, which is not primarily in the interests of the seller. Any such condition must be carefully drafted to ensure that it will not render the contract void for uncertainty and will not allow the buyer to escape from the contract except in precisely worded given circumstances.

(i) **Tenancies**

The seller's duty of disclosure requires that accurate details of all tenancies to which the property is subject must be revealed in the contract.

(j) **Inspection of title deeds and searches**

It is common to include a clause in the auction particulars which entitles any prospective buyer to inspect the title deeds and any searches which have been made by the seller. The clause should provide for a time and place for the inspection.

1. *Johnston* v. *Boyes* (1898) 14 T.L.R. 475.
2. See *Cheshire, Fifoot & Furmston's Law of Contract*, M.P. Furmston, Butterworths.

20.3. **Other preparatory steps by the seller**

20.3.1. In addition to the preparation of the contract the seller's solicitor should, before the auction, undertake the following preparatory steps.

20.3.2. *Searches*

A buyer will frequently not have sufficient time before the auction in which to make the usual searches and enquiries. In order to avoid having to include a clause in the contract entitling the buyer to rescind if the results of searches are not satisfactory, it is preferable for the seller to undertake such searches himself and to make them available for inspection by prospective buyers both before the auction and at the sale itself. A local authority search and enquiries may be requisitioned by the seller's solicitor, as well as any other searches which are relevant to the particular transaction. The seller's solicitor should also prepare and make available answers to standard enquiries before contract.

20.3.3. *Title*

As with the preparation of any draft contract, the seller's solicitor should investigate his client's title prior to drafting the contract so that any imperfections may either be disclosed in the contract or put right before the auction takes place. Particular care is needed to ensure that full details of any existing tenancies are obtained.

20.3.4. *Inspection of deeds*

It is helpful to the buyer if the seller can allow a prospective buyer an opportunity to inspect the title deeds and search results at the seller's solicitors' office or other named place at a convenient time prior to the auction. The deeds and search results should also be available for inspection at the auction itself.

20.4. **Attending the auction**

20.4.1. The seller's solicitor should attend the auction in order to make the title deeds and search results available for inspection to prospective buyers and to answer any queries which may arise.

20.5. **Memorandum of sale**

20.5.1. The memorandum of sale is usually annexed to the printed auction particulars and conditions. It is common to include a condition that the buyer will sign the memorandum immediately after the sale. The auctioneer has implied authority to sign on behalf of both seller and buyer. An auctioneer's clerk has no such implied authority but may be expressly authorised to sign for one or both of the parties. As far as the buyer is concerned, the auctioneer's authority is limited to 'the time of the sale' which expression has no legal definition but must be taken to mean either at the sale itself or within a short time afterwards. In *Chaney* v. *Maclow*[1] the auctioneer's signature, effected at the auctioneer's own offices some two hours after the sale, was held to bind the buyer; *cf. Bell* v. *Balls*[2] where a signature made one week after the sale was not effective to bind the buyer. If the buyer refuses to sign and the auctioneer will not sign as the buyer's agent the seller cannot force the buyer to sign, because an oral agreement to put a contract into writing and to sign it cannot be enforced by specific performance, but it seems that damages may be recovered for breach of such a condition.[3] It should be noted that auction contracts are excluded from the provisions of Law of Property (Miscellaneous Provisions) Act 1989, s.2 (requiring a contract for the sale of land to be in writing); an auction contract will therefore be binding and enforceable even if oral and no memorandum is signed.

1. [1929] 1 Ch. 461.
2. [1897] 1 Ch. 663.
3. See *Wood* v. *Midgely* (1854) 5 De M.& G. 41.

20.6. **Acting for the buyer**

20.6.1. *Searches*

The buyer will frequently not be aware of the auction and/or instruct his solicitor in sufficient time to permit the usual searches and enquiries to be undertaken. If there is time, then searches should be made in the usual way. If not, the buyer's solicitor should at least attempt to make a local authority search and enquiries either in person or through an agent unless up-to-date search results are available for inspection from the seller's solicitor or the auctioneer.

20.7. Survey

20.7.1. Where time permits the buyer should be advised to have the property surveyed prior to the auction.

20.8. Contract and title

20.8.1. A copy of the auction particulars, containing the contract terms, should be obtained and scrutinised prior to the auction. Where searches have not been made by the buyer it should be ascertained whether the contract contains a provision allowing the buyer to rescind if the results of searches undertaken after the auction are adverse. If no such provision is included, the buyer should be advised of the consequences of entering a contract without having made searches and enquiries.

20.8.2. The seller's solicitor will often allow the buyer the opportunity to inspect the title deeds (and sometimes also searches which he has undertaken) before the auction. The buyer's solicitor should inspect the deeds and make such further enquiries as are relevant to the property at the earliest possible opportunity. The buyer may take the benefit of searches requisitioned by the seller, but reliance on such searches is inadvisable if the search results are more than two months old. If inspection of the deeds is not possible prior to the auction the buyer's solicitor should attend the auction and make such inspection before the bidding commences.

20.8.3. The terms of an auction contract are often less favourable to the buyer than would be the case in a sale by private treaty. Auction contract terms are generally non-negotiable as far as the buyer is concerned and therefore the terms of the contract need to be carefully scrutinised before the auction and the buyer advised about the consequences of any adverse terms. Occasionally, the special conditions of the contract will be altered by an oral statement made at the time of the auction itself and the buyer should be advised to listen carefully and note the effect of any such amendments. Examples of terms which might be onerous to the buyer include the following:

(a) terms precluding the buyer's right to raise enquiries or requisitions after the auction;

(b) restrictions on sub-sales by the buyer;

(c) obligations on the buyer to pay the arrears of rent or service charge on a leasehold property;

(d) terms requiring the buyer to reimburse the seller for search fees and/or the cost of supplying an engrossment of the transfer deed;

(e) on the sale of a freehold reversion of a block of flats, terms excluding any warranty by the seller that the provisions of Landlord and Tenant Act 1987 have been complied with. This statute is discussed in para. K.09.

20.9.   Finance

20.9.1.   The buyer should be warned of the possibility of abortive expenditure if his bid is not successful. As the contract to purchase will come into existence at the time of the auction itself it is essential that the buyer's financial arrangements have been finalised prior to the auction. Arrangements must be made for the deposit to be available at the auction, in cash (banker's draft) if this is required by the auction particulars.

20.10.   Insurance

20.10.1.   The buyer should also make arrangements for the property to be placed on insurance cover from the moment of the fall of the auctioneer's hammer since, depending on the terms of the contract, risk in the property may pass to him at this time.

20.11.   Rights of first refusal

If the property to be sold at auction is affected by Landlord and Tenant Act 1987 which gives the tenants of some leasehold flats the right to purchase the landlord's reversionary interest (see para. K.09.) the landlord must comply with section 5B Landlord and Tenant Act 1987 (as amended by Housing Act 1996). This section requires the landlord to serve notice on at least 90% of the qualifying tenants between four and six months before the auction. Failure to comply with the Act is a criminal offence.

B.21. Plans

21.1. When is a plan necessary?	**21.3. Showing features on the plan**
21.2. Preparing the plan	**21.4. Referring to the contract plan**

See also: Form of contract, para. B.11.

21.1. When is a plan necessary?

21.1.1. Before drafting the contract the seller's solicitor should consider whether it is necessary to identify or describe the property by reference to a plan. On receipt of the draft contract from the seller's solicitor, the buyer's solicitor should also consider whether a plan is required. The buyer is entitled to demand a plan on the purchase deed (at the seller's expense) only if the description of the property through the contract and evidence of title is inadequate without one; therefore this matter must be addressed at the pre-contract stage. In other circumstances the buyer might be able to insist on the inclusion of a plan provided that he offered to prepare and pay for it. The buyer's solicitor may need a plan of the property in order to make pre-contract searches and enquiries.[1]

21.1.2. A plan must be used on a sale of part of land (which includes the grant of leases of flats) and may be desirable in other cases, e.g. where the boundaries of the property are not self-evident, but should not be used indiscriminately. The sale of the whole of a freehold registered title in a suburban area can usually be described adequately by reference to its postal address and title number.

21.1.3. Rule 79 Land Registration Rules 1925 usually requires the instrument of transfer to be accompanied by a plan where the disposition is of part of a registered estate. The seller should normally submit his estate layout plan to HM Land Registry for their approval before the sale of the individual plots is commenced. Any changes in the approved estate layout plan should be notified by the seller to HM Land Registry.

21.1.4. Whatever type of plan is used it must be of sufficient size and scale to enable the boundaries and other features of the property to be readily identified.[2] A plan on a scale of 1:1,250 will suffice for most cases, but a larger scale will usually be required for sales of flats or the division of buildings into separate units.

21.1.5. Boundaries shown on plans prepared by HM Land Registry are general boundaries only and may not therefore show the precise line of the boundaries.[3] It is possible to ask the Land Registry to show fixed boundaries on a filed plan, but this procedure is rarely used in practice.[4]

THE LAW SOCIETY'S CONVEYANCING HANDBOOK 1997

21.1.6. A plan will be required where the sale is by reference to a fence line or where the boundaries of the property are otherwise unclear. In such a case the parties should be asked to agree the boundaries (if necessary by a site inspection and with the co-operation of the owner of neighbouring property) and the fence line or boundary should be staked out on the site.

1. See Pre-contract searches and enquiries, para. B.10.
2. See *Scarfe* v. *Adams* [1981] 1 All E.R. 843.
3. Land Registration Rules 1925, r.278.
4. Land Registration Rules 1925, rr.276, 277.

21.2. Preparing the plan

21.2.1. The use of scale plans is recommended but they must be entirely accurate and should show the scale used on the plan itself.

21.2.2. A hand-drawn plan which is not to scale may be adequate in simple transactions, e.g. the sale of part of a garden, but is inappropriate for use in a sale of flats or of a commercial property. Such a plan must be referred to as being 'for identification purposes only' (see below, paras. 21.3. and 21.4.).

21.2.3. An existing plan in the title deeds may be used as the starting point for the preparation of the plan but should not be photocopied and re-used owing to the distortion which occurs on reproduction.

21.2.4. A filed plan obtained with office copy entries may not be drawn on a sufficiently large scale to enable it to be utilised.

21.2.5. Large-scale Ordnance Survey maps are obtainable through The Stationery Office and may be reproduced provided that the solicitor holds a licence from Copyright Branch, Ordnance Survey, Romsey Road, Maybush, Southampton.

21.2.6. The British Library (Map Library, Great Russell Street, London WC1) will supply large-scale maps on request. The fee charged depends on the size and quality of the reproduction required.

21.2.7. Where the value or complexity of the transaction justifies the expense, an architect or surveyor may be instructed to prepare a plan. The client's authority should be obtained prior to incurring such expenditure.

21.2.8. Where the transaction is for the sale or lease of flats or of part of a commercial property a floor and/or section plan may be required in addition to a site plan.

21.2.9. The property should not be drawn in isolation. Adjoining land or buildings should be shown on the plan so that the site of the property in relation to its neighbours may be established.

21.2.10. If there is any doubt as to the size or extent of the property an inspection should be carried out and measurements taken.

21.2.11. Units of measurement must be shown in metric values. Imperial measurements alone can no longer be used.[1]

21.2.12. Guidance on the preparation of plans can be found in HM Land Registry Practice Advice Leaflet No. 8 (Land Registry Plans).

1. Units of Measurement Regulations 1986, as amended (in force 1 October 1995). See also HM Land Registry Practice Leaflet No.11 (Metrication).

21.3. Showing features on the plan

21.3.1. The plan must be clearly drawn so that it is capable of being read in isolation from the accompanying contract or purchase deed. The wording of the contract or purchase deed will, however, need to make reference to the plan and its various features and this point should be borne in mind when the plan is drawn, e.g. a right of way may be more easily described in words in the contract if its beginning and end points are marked 'A' and 'B' on the plan in addition to the demarcation of the route.

21.3.2. *Points to note*

(a) Markings should be clear and precise.

(b) Land to be sold should be outlined or coloured in red.

(c) Retained land (if any) should be outlined or coloured in blue.

(d) Other land referred to should be coloured or hatched in distinct colours other than red or blue. If possible it is best to avoid the use of green on a plan where red has already been used since the most common form of colour blindness relates to the inability to distinguish between these two colours. Reference should also be made to Land Registry practice leaflets (see Appendix IX.1.) in relation to the Registry's preferred practice for colouring plans.

(e) The ownership of boundaries should be indicated by 'T' marks with the 'T' on the side of the boundary line within the land which bears responsibility for the maintenance of the boundary.

(f) Rights of way and routes of services should be tinted or marked with broken or dotted lines of a distinct colour, with each end of the route being additionally identified with separate capital letters.

(g) Where the plan is to scale the scale should be shown.

(h) If the plan is not to scale, metric measurements should be shown along each boundary.

(i) A compass point indicating the direction of North should be shown.

(j) A key should be included to explain the meaning of the various colours and
     lines used on the plan.

21.4.   Referring to the contract plan

21.4.1. The contract (and subsequent purchase deed) may refer to the plan as being 'for
identification purposes only', or will describe the land as being 'more particularly
delineated on the plan'. These two phrases are mutually exclusive and a
combination of the two serves no useful purpose.[1]

21.4.2. 'Identification purposes only'

Where there is a discrepancy between the land shown on the plan and the contract
description and the plan has been described as being for identification purposes
only, the verbal description of the land will normally prevail over the plan. The
court may, however, refer to such a plan to define the boundaries of the property
where the verbal description is unclear.[2] This type of plan is unacceptable for use
in connection with registered land and will be returned by HM Land Registry.

21.4.3. 'More particularly delineated'

In the event of a discrepancy between the verbal description of the land and the plan,
the plan will prevail over the words where the phrase 'more particularly delineated'
has been used. This phrase should not be used unless the plan is to scale.

21.4.4. A plan which is included in the purchase deed but which is not referred to by use
of one of the above phrases may be looked at in order to identify the land only if
the description of the property as afforded by the purchase deed and other available
evidence (e.g. title deeds) is unclear.[3]

1. *Neilson* v. *Poole* (1969) 20 P. & C.R. 909.
2. See *Wiggington & Milner Ltd.* v. *Winster Engineering Ltd.* [1978] 3 All E.R. 436.
3. *Leachman* v. *L. & K. Richardson Ltd.* [1969] 3 All E.R. 20.

B.22. Fixtures and fittings

22.1. **Distinction between fixtures and fittings**
22.2. **Need for certainty in contract**
22.3. **Apportionment of purchase price**
22.4. **The Protocol**
22.5. **Guidelines**

See also: Form of contract, para. B.11.

22.1. Distinction between fixtures and fittings

22.1.1. Fixtures

Fixtures are generally items which are attached to and form part of the land and which will therefore be included as part of the property on sale of the land unless the seller expressly reserves the right to remove them.

22.1.2. Fittings

Fittings or chattels do not form part of the land and so are not included as part of the property on sale of the land unless the seller expressly agrees to leave them behind.

22.1.3. Practical distinction

The legal distinction between fixtures and fittings as outlined in the above sub-paragraphs is quite clear. The practical distinction between the two categories is sometimes less obvious. Movable objects which are not attached to the land, e.g. carpets, curtains and free-standing furniture clearly fall within the definition of fittings, but items which are attached to the land such as gas boilers and satellite dishes are not always classified as fixtures. Case law in this area is unclear and there have been reported cases where items such as greenhouses, garden ornaments, plumbed-in kitchen appliances and even freezers have been held to be fixtures, and other cases where the same items have been held to be fittings.[1]

1. See *TSB Bank* v. *Botham* [1996] E.G.C.S. 149.

22.2. Need for certainty in contract

22.2.1. In view of the uncertainty of the status of some items in law it is essential that in appropriate circumstances the contract deals expressly with:

(a) fixtures which the seller intends to remove on or before completion (including, where appropriate, the tenant's right to remove tenant's trade fixtures);

(b)   compensation for the buyer if the seller causes damage in the course of the removal of fixtures;

(c)   fittings which are to remain at the property;

(d)   any additional price which the buyer is to pay for the fittings;

(e)   the apportionment of the purchase price to exclude from the total the price paid for the fittings;

(f)   deferment of passing of title to fittings until completion because in the absence of such a condition Sale of Goods Act 1979, s.18 will provide that title to the fittings passes to the buyer on exchange;

(g)   a warranty that fittings are free of incumbrances (e.g. subsisting hire-purchase agreements). Although Sale of Goods Act 1979, s.12 will imply such a warranty its express inclusion in the contract prevents the matter from being overlooked by the seller (see Standard Condition 9).

22.2.2.   Disputes over the unexpected removal of fixtures and fittings are common and frequently cost more to resolve than the value of the disputed items. The buyer may require the seller to supply written confirmation that fixtures and fittings which were seen by the buyer on inspection of the property will not be removed from the property and are included in the sale, or in appropriate cases the contract may contain a warranty given by the seller that he has not removed any fixtures from the property since a stated date.

22.2.3.   The estate agent's particulars should be scrutinised to see which items are listed as being included or excluded from the sale, and checked with the client to ensure their accuracy.

22.2.4.   When taking instructions it will be necessary to ascertain from the client which items are to be removed, which items he expects to remain at the property, and whether any price in addition to the price of the land is required for the fittings.

22.3.   **Apportionment of purchase price**

22.3.1.   *No stamp duty on chattels*

The sale of chattels does not attract *ad valorem* stamp duty. The value of chattels which have been included in the purchase price of the land may therefore be subtracted from the total purchase price, thereby effecting a reduction in the value of the land and a possible consequent reduction in the amount of *ad valorem* stamp duty payable by the buyer.

22.3.2.   This apportionment of the purchase price between the land and the chattels is of most value to the buyer when the value of the land and chattels together is marginally above the current stamp duty threshold.

22.3.3. *Consequences of over-valuation*

Only the true value of the chattels may be deducted from the purchase price for this purpose. Any over-valuation of the price of the chattels is a fraud on the Inland Revenue which may render both the solicitor and his client liable to criminal sanctions. Such conduct would also be conduct unbefitting the solicitor which could result in disciplinary proceedings being brought against him. A further consequence of the over-valuation is that the contract for the sale of the land would be unenforceable by court action since it could be construed by the courts as being a contract to defraud the Inland Revenue, such contracts being unenforceable on the grounds of public policy.[1]

22.3.4.   If the draft contract does not make provision for the apportionment of the purchase price in a situation where such apportionment would be appropriate, the buyer should, as a matter of courtesy, seek the seller's consent before making the necessary adjustment to the contract.

1. See *Saunders* v. *Edwards* [1987] 2 All E.R. 651.

22.4. **The Protocol**

22.4.1.   Paragraph 2.8 of the Protocol requires the seller's solicitor to obtain information relating to fixtures and fittings from the seller, using the standard Fixtures, Fittings and Contents Form. The completed form should then be sent to the buyer's solicitors with the draft contract (Protocol, para 4.3).

22.5. **Guidelines**

22.5.1.   In order to avoid future disputes between the parties the solicitor is advised to check with the client which items are included/excluded from the sale and whether any additional price is payable for the included items. Items which would normally be considered to be fixtures (e.g. fitted wardrobes) should not be charged for in addition to the contract price nor removed from the property unless there is an express reservation of the right to do so in the contract. Items which are normally removable as fittings, e.g. carpets will not be included in the contract unless the parties agree to their inclusion, possibly at a price additional to the sum payable for the land. Where there are items which may be regarded either as fixtures or fittings depending on the circumstances, e.g. a greenhouse, the solicitor will need to make further enquiries of his client and should consider express mention of these items in the contract for the avoidance of doubt. In residential transactions use of the Fixtures, Fittings and Contents Form is strongly recommended. This form, the contents of which will be agreed by the parties, will be annexed to and form part of the contract.

B.23. Powers of attorney

See also: Title, section D.

Completion, section F.

23.1. When is a power needed?

23.1.1. The solicitor should consider the preparation of a power of attorney for his client if the client:

(a) is elderly and/or physically infirm; or

(b) is likely to be unavailable at the time when it will be necessary to obtain his signature to documents.

23.2. What type of power?

23.2.1. *General power under Powers of Attorney Act 1971*

This type of power will give the attorney authority to deal with all of the donor's assets including the sale or purchase of property.

23.2.2. *Special power under Powers of Attorney Act 1971*

A special power will give the attorney authority to deal only with the matters specified in the power and thus may be limited to, e.g. the sale of a named property. Except where it is intended to allow the attorney to assume complete control of the donor's affairs this type of power would be more appropriate than a general power in the context of the sale or purchase of land.

23.2.3. *Trustee power*

Neither of the above types of power can be used to vest authority in an attorney where property is subject to a trust. This includes property which is held on trust for sale by co-owners. Where property is held on trust a trustee power under Trustee Act 1925, s.25, as amended by Powers of Attorney Act 1971, s.9 must be used. Such a power enables a trustee to delegate his duties as trustee to the attorney for a period not exceeding 12 months. A trustee cannot appoint his sole co-trustee as attorney.

23.2.4. *Enduring power under Enduring Powers of Attorney Act 1985*

This type of power must be executed in the form prescribed by the Regulations made under the 1985 Act[1] and is not revoked on the subsequent mental incapacity of the donor. It may also be used by a trustee to confer power on his sole co-trustee and thus is useful where, e.g. a property is jointly owned by husband and wife and one party wishes to appoint the other as his or her attorney during a period of absence abroad.

23.2.5. *Jointly owned property*

Property which is held by co-owners (e.g. a matrimonial home held in the joint names of husband and wife) must be held on trust for sale. A trustee power or enduring power must be used in this situation. Except where an enduring power is used, a trustee cannot appoint his sole co-trustee as attorney.

23.2.6. *Security powers*

A security power under Powers of Attorney Act 1971, s.4 may be taken by a lender who has taken an equitable mortgage in order to give him a power to sell the property if the borrower defaults on the mortgage. This type of power is irrevocable and may be incorporated in the mortgage document or given by separate deed.

1. See Enduring Powers of Attorney (Prescribed Forms) Regulations 1990 (S.I. 1990/1376). A power which is executed under a prescribed form which is not current at the time of execution is probably not valid and a new power using the form prescribed by the current regulations must be executed. Acts done by the attorney under an invalid power can be ratified by execution of a deed of ratification by the donor, provided the donor is still mentally capable.

23.3. **Who should be the attorney?**

23.3.1. The client should be advised of the consequences of giving a power of attorney, i.e. that the attorney will (depending on the terms of the power) have a wide authority and discretion to deal with the client's affairs. Only a person whom the client trusts absolutely should be considered for appointment as attorney. The solicitor may be appointed as attorney provided that no conflict of interests exists between himself and his client(s). The solicitor should advise the client of his charges in relation to so acting. The limitations on the appointment of an attorney in the case of trust property have been noted above.

23.4. When should the appointment be made?

23.4.1. The power of attorney should be drawn up and executed as soon as the decision to appoint an attorney has been made. This is necessary because it is courteous to inform the other party to the transaction at the earliest opportunity that the documents will be signed under a power of attorney.

23.5. The client who already has a power

23.5.1. Where a client comes to the solicitor with an existing power of attorney, the solicitor should examine the power to ascertain its type and validity for the transaction proposed.

23.6. Informing the other party of the appointment

23.6.1. It is courteous to inform the other party to the transaction at the earliest opportunity that the documents will be signed under a power of attorney. A copy of the power should be supplied to the other party as soon as possible so that its validity and suitability for the transaction in progress may be confirmed.

23.6.2. Except in the case of a security power or an enduring power which has been registered with the Court of Protection, if the power will be more than 12 months old at the date when it is purportedly exercised, the person who buys from the attorney will need to make a statutory declaration immediately after completion stating that he believed the power to be valid and had no knowledge of its revocation at the time of its exercise.[1]

1. See Powers of Attorney Act 1971, s.5.

B.24. Planning

See also: Conditional contracts, para. B.13.
Environmental issues, para. B.25.

24.1. Relevance of planning to the transaction

24.1.1. Heavy penalties may ensue from breach of planning legislation; it is therefore important to check at the start of a transaction that any necessary planning requirements have been or will be complied with. It may also be necessary to check whether any restrictive covenants on the property conflict with the present structure(s) and/or use, and if so whether consent to the buildings and/or their current use/or a release or indemnity insurance has been obtained.

24.1.2. The development of land will normally require the grant of planning permission. Development is defined by Town and Country Planning Act 1990 (as amended) as 'the carrying out of building, engineering, mining or other operations in, on, over or under land, or the making of any material change in the use of any buildings or other land'. This definition encompasses the erection of new buildings, the demolition of and alterations and additions to existing buildings, fish farming and in certain circumstances changing the use of a building.

24.2. Acting for the seller

24.2.1. Although planning matters do not necessarily fall within the seller's duty of disclosure, the buyer's solicitor will raise various enquiries about planning matters and will be reluctant to proceed with the transaction unless he can be reassured that the buildings and use of the property satisfy current planning regulations. In Protocol cases, a number of matters pertaining to planning will be revealed by the seller on the Seller's Property Information Form which is supplied to the buyer. The following matters should therefore be checked either from the documents in the solicitor's possession, from information obtained from the client, or from the local planning authority (usually the district council):

    (a)   the date when the property was first built;

    (b)   whether any additions, alterations or extensions have been made to the property or within its grounds since the property was first built and, if so, the date of each addition, etc.;

(c) if the property has been built or any alteration to it has been made within the past four years, either that planning consent was obtained (either expressly or by virtue of General Permitted Development Order) or was not required. Any conditions attached to the planning consent should, if possible, be checked to ensure that they have been complied with. Proceedings to enforce planning restrictions in respect of development which consists of 'building works' must normally be taken within four years of the breach;

(d) if the property is leasehold, in addition to (c) above, whether any additions, alterations, etc., have been made since the date of the grant of the lease and, if so, whether any restriction on development contained in the lease has been complied with;

(e) what the property is used for, whether any material change of use to the property has occurred during the past 10 years and, if so, whether the appropriate consent has been obtained. There is a 10-year time-limit on the enforcement of breach of planning control through change of use. If no enforcement proceedings are taken within the 10-year period the previously unlawful use becomes an authorised use. The change of use from one use class to another requires consent, as does the change from use as a single dwelling house to use of the premises for multiple occupation or sub-division into separate units;

(f) where alterations or additions to the property have been made within the past 12 months, whether building regulation consent has been obtained and complied with (see below, para. 24.6.);

(g) whether the property is a listed building or in a conservation area. Special provisions apply to such buildings and areas and the restrictions on development are more stringent than those applied in other cases. Where a building is listed, separate listed building consent may be required.

24.2.2. Any irregularity in the planning situation should ideally be corrected by the seller before contracts are exchanged. Realistically this may not always be possible and the seller may have to reveal the irregularity to the buyer who, depending on the nature of the problem, may be prepared to proceed with the transaction subject to a reduction in the price or an indemnity against liability given by the seller in the contract.

24.2.3. Paragraph 2.4 of the Protocol requires the seller's solicitor to obtain copies of all relevant planning decisions and to submit these to the buyer's solicitor as part of the pre-contract documentation.

24.3. Acting for the buyer

24.3.1. The matters itemised above in para. 24.2.1. should be raised as pre-contract enquiries with the seller. Any irregularity revealed by the seller's answers should either be corrected at the seller's expense or, depending on the nature of the breach, an indemnity taken from the seller in the contract. Liability for breach of planning legislation enures with the land; thus any breach which exists on completion will become the responsibility of the buyer.

24.3.2. Instructions should be taken from the buyer in relation to the following matters:

(a) Does the buyer's intended use of the property correspond with its present authorised use? If not, will planning permission be required for the buyer's intended use and is it realistic to expect that consent from the local planning authority would be forthcoming?

(b) Is it apparent on inspection of the property that new buildings or alterations have been made within the last four years? If so, check with the seller whether planning consent for the new buildings was needed/obtained/ complied with.

(c) Does the buyer intend to alter the property in any way after completion? If so, will the proposed alterations require planning consent or consent from the person with the benefit of an existing restrictive covenant against development and is it realistic to expect that such consent(s) will be forthcoming?

24.3.3. The answers to the local search and enquiries should be checked carefully to ensure that no breach of planning law is revealed in those answers. Any matters of doubt should be clarified with the local authority and the seller before the matter proceeds to exchange of contracts.

24.3.4. Where the client's instructions reveal that his proposals for the property will require planning permission to be obtained it should first be ascertained whether or not the client would wish to proceed with his purchase in the event of an application for permission being refused by the local authority. If the client would not wish to pursue his purchase in such circumstances, he should be advised either to delay exchange until planning permission for his proposed development is obtained, or to ask the seller to make the contract conditional on obtaining such consent.[1] Even where the client is prepared to take the risk of planning permission ultimately being refused, he should be advised about the procedure for making such application (including the costs) and the consequences of developing the land without permission. The register of planning applications maintained by the local authority under Town and Country Planning Act 1990 may be inspected to obtain an insight into the authority's policy for the area, and thus the likelihood of obtaining permission for the proposed development. Generally an authority will not permit development which conflicts with its local plan for the area, e.g. industrial development would not be permitted in an area designated for residential use or vice versa.

24.3.5. Even where the client's proposals will not require planning permission, consideration should still be given to the necessity for building regulation consent (for building works of any description) and compliance with or insurance against any restrictive covenants on the property which would prevent the client's intended development.

1. See Conditional contracts, para. B.13.

24.4. Matters which do not require specific planning permission

24.4.1.   Certain matters which would otherwise fall within the definition of development (and thus require planning permission) are specifically excluded from that definition by the Act itself or by General Permitted Development Order. A summary of the main cases where permission is not required either by the statute or by regulation is listed below. In any case of doubt, the Act and the various regulations made under it should be checked, and/or advice sought from the planning department of the local authority:

(a)   maintenance works to buildings, e.g. painting the exterior;

(b)   internal works which do not materially affect the appearance of the exterior, e.g. sub-dividing a room by the erection of a non-load-bearing partition wall;

(c)   the use of buildings or land within the curtilage of a dwelling house for any purpose incidental to the use of the dwelling house, e.g. using an existing outhouse as a playroom. The 'curtilage' of a dwelling house is the land immediately surrounding the house and except where the grounds are large will normally encompass the whole of the garden area;

(d)   change of use within the same use class as specified by Town and Country Planning (Use Classes) Order 1987, e.g. changing from use as a newsagent's shop to an ironmonger's shop. Changing a single dwelling house into two or more units is a material change of use which requires planning permission, as is a change from one use class to another, e.g. changing from use as a shop to use as an office;

(e)   development which falls within Town and Country Planning (General Permitted Development) Order 1995, e.g. erection of fences (subject to a height restriction), some demolition works, development within the curtilage of a dwelling house. This latter provision will permit the building of a small extension to an existing dwelling house without the need for express planning permission but is subject to strict conditions on the extent and siting of the extension; once the size limit for extensions under General Permitted Development Order has been used, all further extensions to the house require express permission. The conditions attached to General Permitted Development Order must be strictly observed, and if they cannot be complied with express permission for the development is needed. The local authority has power to restrict General Permitted Development Order in whole or in part in relation to its area. Before the client proceeds to effect works which ostensibly fall within the Order it should be confirmed that the relevant part of the Order is in force in the area concerned.

24.4.2.   Enquiries of the local authority, which will be undertaken in every transaction, contain several questions relating to planning matters. The answers to these questions should be analysed carefully by the buyer's solicitor.

24.4.3. Special rules apply to listed buildings and the provisions outlined above may not apply.

24.5. Planning rules which apply in special cases

24.5.1. If the land is covered by a Special Development Order, or is within an enterprise zone or a simplified planning zone, special rules apply which alter the general law.

In some cases the rules relating to the need for planning permission are relaxed within these special zones, in others parts of General Permitted Development Order may be restricted. The replies to enquiries of the local authority will reveal whether or not the property is affected by any of these special zonings. If so, the provisions of the relevant Order should be checked before advice is given to the client on the need for planning permission.

24.6. Building Regulations

24.6.1. The Building Regulations 1991 came into force on 1 June 1992, replacing Building Regulations 1984. Building Regulations compliance is necessary wherever building works are to be undertaken. The need for this is separate from planning consent and is required even where the development falls within General Permitted Development Order and so does not require express planning permission. A person who intends to undertake building works must serve notice on and deposit plans with the local authority before works are commenced. On completion of the works, a certificate of compliance ('a final certificate') should be obtained from the local authority. Proceedings for breach of the Building Regulations must be taken within 12 months of the infringement.[1]

1. Building Act 1984, s.36(1) and Public Health Act 1936, s.65.

24.7. Environmental issues

24.7.1. Where a planning application is made for 'environmentally sensitive development' as defined in Town and Country Planning (Assessment of Environmental Effects) Regulations 1988 (S.I. 1988/1199) the local planning authority may require the applicant to submit an environmental statement with his application. Some local authorities ask for an environmental assessment to be submitted in connection with all applications for major development irrespective of the above Regulations.

FURTHER REFERENCE

Butterworths Planning Law Service, Butterworths.

Encyclopedia of Planning Law and Practice, Sweet & Maxwell.

Planning Law for Conveyancers, C.M. Brand and D.W. Williams, F.T. Law & Tax.

An Outline of Planning Law, Sir Desmond Heap, Sweet & Maxwell.

Planning Controls and their Enforcement, A.J. Little, Shaw & Sons.

Practical Approach to Planning Law, V. Moore, Blackstone.

Planning Law and Procedure, A.E. Telling, Butterworths.

The Building Regulations Explained and Illustrated, V. Powell-Smith, Blackwell Publishers.

B.25. Environmental issues

25.1. Introduction

25.1.1. The responsibility for polluting substances in or on land rests on the owner or occupier for the time being of the land under Environmental Protection Act 1990 (E.P.A.) and Environment Act 1995 (E.A.). Civil liability may also exist in tort.[1] Future statutory guidance may attribute liability to the original polluter, if it can be found.

25.1.2. E.A. inserts detailed provisions regarding liability for contaminated land into E.P.A. Those provisions are to be implemented by extensive Statutory Guidance which is presently at an advanced consultative stage. It is expected to come into force in 1998.

25.1.3. A lender who has taken possession of land (but not a receiver) is liable as an owner or occupier under these provisions which enable a local authority to require polluted land to be cleaned up.

25.1.4. The cost of compliance with the Act is potentially a major liability in connection with land and polluted land may be difficult to sell or to mortgage. A perception of pollution, even if incorrect, may lead to similar difficulties.

25.1.5. When buying property in an urban area, whether residential or commercial, remember that many newer developments are on land previously used for a potentially contaminative use such as: petrol station; sewage farm; light industrial; brickworks; railway sidings; town gas works.

25.1.6. Potential buyers should be made aware of the consequences of past contaminating activities on the land that they want to purchase. Although it is not possible to be certain of contamination of a site, or non-contamination, without a fairly expensive investigation, including soil tests, it is possible to be reasonably certain of the likelihood of contamination occurring based on the historic use of the site. Certain past uses have been shown to consistently result in contamination with certain substances. Whether possible contamination of a site poses a significant risk to the potential buyer will also depend on the geological structure of the ground, the height and flow of ground-water, whether the site is over an aquifer which is abstracted for drinking purposes or other sensitive types of consumption and what is the current and proposed new use of the site by the buyer. Sites can be contaminated by leaching of contaminants from neighbouring land.

B

Some substances will leach in ground-water. Methane will leach up to 300 metres or more from its source in an old landfill, through soil strata above the water-table.

25.1.7. Inspection of old plans and maps forming part of the title deeds and pre-registration deeds can prove invaluable in identifying earlier contaminative uses. There are presently three companies (see para. 25.1.8. below) selling site-specific environmental data in England and Wales. A search from one of these, ranging in cost from approximately £55 − £300 will identify whether there may be cause for concern based on past use. It is more difficult, and expensive, to accurately assess the risk where there is possible cause for concern.

25.1.8. To obtain information about past historic land use of both the property and surrounding land the following options are presently available:

(a) consider the title deeds, including pre-registration deeds, going back to a green field site, if possible;

(b) search old trade directories and old Ordnance Survey Maps for details of previous occupiers and obvious features or activities;

(c) make personal enquiries of local authority and Environment Agency personnel who may know of the site's history: make use of the Access to Environmental Information Regulations 1992 (S.I. 1992/3240) where information exists but is not shown on public register;

(d) employ an environmental auditor to undertake a 'desk-top' study or Phase 1 audit which will comprise the three preceding areas of enquiry with others that the consultant may be able to access (typical cost £750−£1500);

(e) purchase an environmental data search from any of the following:

Environmental Auditors Limited
Unit 2, Red House Farm
London Road
New Timber
Hassocks
West Sussex BN6 9BS

Tel: 01273 857500
Fax: 01273 857550
e-mail: envauditepavilion.co.uk

Product: Contamicheck: typical cost £55 with two working days delivery.

ICC Site Search
Nutmeg House
3rd Floor
60 Gainsford Street
London SE1 2NY

Tel: 0171-357 6757
Fax: 0171-357 6181

Product: Search for Contaminative Uses Report.

Landmark Information Group Limited
7 Abbey Court,
Eagle Way,
Exeter EX2 7HY

Tel: (01392) 441 700
Fax: (01392) 441 709

Product: Sitecheck: typical cost £195 with a 7 day service.

British Geological Survey
Kingsley Dunham Centre
Nottingham NG12 5GG

Tel: 0115-936 3100
Fax: 0115-936 3593

Product: ALGI 'housebuyers report'.

25..1.9. Each of the above search services will provide the data which they think most suitable for a potential purchaser's needs. The more expensive products include maps, the cheaper provide data by reference to grid-referenced location. Some services are developing risk-rating protocols. If in doubt, you may need to seek advice on the significance of the search report that you have obtained.

25.1.10. Part II of Enquiries of Local Authority Search Form contains a few questions relating to some environmental matters which should be raised in appropriate circumstances. These Enquiries are to be revised to provide more appropriate enquiries on relevant matters.

25.1.11. Draft European legislation proposes to make the contamination of land a civil offence of strict liability where directors and other individuals concerned with the running of a company or organisation will suffer personal liability.

25.1.12. Under E.A. the Environment Agency has responsibility for the enforcement of environmental matters under both E.P.A. and E.A.

1. See *Scott-Whitehead* v. *National Coal Board* (1987) 53 P. & C.R. 263; *cf. Cambridge Water Co.* v. *Eastern Counties Leather plc* [1994] 1 All E.R. 53, H.L.

25.2. Advising buyers and lenders

25.2.1. Prospective buyers who are contemplating buying or leasing development land or land which is to be used for an industrial use where chemicals are involved may consider taking certain precautions before completing the transaction. They may consider having an environmental audit undertaken, setting up, maintaining and regularly reviewing a policy for the control of pollution on the land and taking out an insurance policy to cover liability against contamination of the land, if such a policy is available (environmental impairment liability policy). As protection against future liability it may be useful to have a Phase 2 audit carried out, including soil tests, to establish existing contamination.

25.2.2. Similar enquiries should be undertaken on behalf of a prospective lender.

25.2.3. A full environmental investigation is also necessary in support of any planning application where the local authority believes that the land may be contaminated. If the result of the investigation is in the local authority's view unsatisfactory, they may require remediation of the land at the applicant's expense as a condition of the planning consent.

25.2.4. Prospective buyers of land which is being acquired for development and their lenders may consider making full enquiries relating to neighbouring land as well as the land which they are buying. Contaminating chemicals and gases, especially methane and radon, may leach from neighbouring land and contaminate the land being purchased.

25.2.5. The contract to purchase the land might contain warranties from the seller relating to the lack of actions which may otherwise have contaminated the land during the period of the seller's ownership. The seller should not give such warranties unless he is fully aware of the commercial risks involved in giving them. They should in any event be limited to the period of the seller's use of the land.

25.2.6. Lenders and landlords may consider taking covenants from their borrowers/tenants to cover some or all of the following matters:

(a) not to bring hazardous material on to the property;

(b) to comply with environmental law;

(c) to remedy any breach of environmental law, with power reserved for the lender/landlord to remedy the breach himself and recoup the resulting cost from the borrower/tenant;

(d) to notify the lender/landlord of any circumstances which could give rise to liability for environmental damage;

(e) to provide periodical environmental investigations and audits (in each case specifying the detail required to be covered by the investigation or audit);

(f) reservation of a right for the lender/landlord to enter to inspect the property.

25.2.7. A Phase 1 environmental audit consists of documentary evidence only; an investigation, or Phase 2 audit, may include geological and chemical data obtained from, e.g. soil samples.

25.3. Pre-contract enquiries

25.3.1. Additional pre-contract enquiries may be raised with the seller/borrower in relation to some or all of the following matters, most of which are relevant only to commercial and industrial property and property previously used for industrial or waste disposal purposes:

(a) whether to the seller's knowledge there is now or has been carried out at the property a process controlled under E.P.A.;

(b) whether to the seller's knowledge there is now or has been kept or deposited at the property any substance controlled under E.P.A.;

(c) whether there is or ever has been on the property the disposal, storage, deposit, treatment, recycling or transportation of controlled waste as defined by E.P.A., s.75;

(d) permission for the buyer or his authorised agent to take samples of air, water and soil from the property;

(e) whether there are any old storage tanks on, or under, the site;

(f) whether the seller or its predecessor has had any environmental audit or investigation into the site, if so please provide a copy;

(g) whether the seller has any reason to believe, or does believe, that the site is contaminated with any noxious, toxic or dangerous substances.

25.3.2. Control of Pollution (Silage, Slurry and Agricultural Fuel Oil) Regulations 1991[1] will also be of concern when acting in a matter where any of these items are to be used or stored on land. Escape of these substances will be an offence under the Regulations.

25.3.3. Environmental Protection (Prescribed Processes and Substances) Regulations 1991[2] give details of the business activities for which a licence is required under IPC (see below). Enquiries should be raised with a seller as to whether such a licence is required and/or has been obtained.

1. S.I. 1999/324.
2. S.I. 1991/1472, as amended by S.I. 1992/614.

25.4. Contravention

25.4.1. The Environment Agency has the task of enforcing the rules made by the Secretary of State for the Environment relating to the regulation system under E.P.A. The Agency works through regional offices. Some enforcement procedures are carried out by the local authority for the area. The Local Authority retains responsibility for Air Pollution Control. Contravention of environmental law will generally result in committing an offence leaving the committer open to a criminal charge. Some penalties can be heavy. Some company directors have been imprisoned for repeated flagrant breaches of environmental law.

25.4.2. Certain specified industrial processes must be licensed under the Integrated Pollution Control Regime (IPC) before they can be carried out. The Environment Agency maintains registers of information relating to applications for authorisations under E.P.A. and E.A. These registers are open to public inspection.

25.4.3. Activities which fall into the following general categories should be checked to ensure that any necessary licence has been obtained and its terms have been complied with. The Agency has power to enforce the terms of a licence and to prosecute for breach:

    (a) production of fuel and power;

    (b) metal production;

    (c) mineral industries;

    (d) chemical industries;

    (e) waste disposal and recycling.

25.5. Contaminated water

25.5.1. The Environment Agency has power under Water Resources Act 1991, s.161 to clean up polluted water and to recover the expenses reasonably incurred from the party who caused or knowingly permitted the pollution to occur. The meaning of 'caused or knowingly permitted' is well established and includes those who fail to take reasonable precautions against the occurrence of a contaminating event; those who fail to take reasonable steps which would have alerted them to the need to take reasonable precautions and those who deliberately fail to find out about their possible liabilities.

25.5.2. Most instances of contaminated land involve contaminated controlled water – ground and surface water. Whether or not contamination of a site is likely to cause the owner problems is closely linked to whether or not ground water used for drinking and other purposes is affected.

25.6. Statutory nuisance

25.6.1. Under E.P.A., ss.79–82, statutory nuisances include the following:

    (a) any premises in such a state as to be prejudicial to health or a nuisance;

    (b) emission of smoke, fumes or gases which are prejudicial to health or a nuisance;

    (c) dust, steam or other effluvia arising on trade or industrial premises which are prejudicial to health or a nuisance;

    (d) any accumulation or deposit which is prejudicial to health or a nuisance;

    (e) noise emitted from premises so as to be prejudicial to health or a nuisance.

25.6.2. Local authorities have a duty to inspect their areas to detect statutory nuisances and to take steps to investigate complaints made by individuals.

25.6.3. Where an authority is satisfied that a statutory nuisance exists or is likely to occur or recur it is under a duty to serve an abatement notice on the person responsible for the nuisance or, if that person cannot be found, on the owner or occupier of the premises. Non-compliance with an abatement notice is a criminal offence penalised by a maximum fine of £20,000 and/or an injunction.

25.7 Contaminated land

25.7.1. Plans to introduce registers of contaminated land are contained in E.A., s.57 which inserts sections 78A−78YC into E.P.A. When it is brought into force, E.P.A., s.78R will require every enforcing authority to maintain a register containing prescribed particulars of, or relating to, *inter alia:*

  (a) remediation notices;

  (b) remediation statements or declarations;

  (c) designation of special sites;

  (d) termination of designation as a special site;

  (e) notifications of claimed remediation;

  (f) convictions for offences for failure to comply with a remediation notice.

E.P.A. ss.78B−78E, gives local authorities power to inspect land and if they find land to be contaminated to serve notice to that effect on the Environment Agency and the owner. The local authority also has power to serve a remediation notice requiring the land to be remediated to a specified extent.

25.8. Radon

25.8.1. Radon is a naturally occurring radioactive gas which is present in the ground and is found at low levels in all buildings. In some areas high levels, which can increase the lifetime risk of lung cancer, occur in some dwellings. A radon Affected Area is declared when the estimated percentage of dwellings with high levels exceed 1%.

25.8.2. Measurements are available from the National Radiological Protection Board (NRPB)[1] and are made over three months to average out short-term variations. In Affected Areas, NRPB recommends that dwellings are measured. Letters, offering a measurement at Government expense, have been sent to householders in the areas of greatest risk. At the date of writing, the time-limit of this offer had expired. There may be similar offers in some areas in the future. Measurements on a repayment basis are available at the request of the householder or landlord. The cost, including analysis, the reporting of the result and VAT is about £36.

25.8.3. The result of the survey is confidential and NRPB will advise the householder of the result and, if necessary, what steps can be taken to reduce the radon level. NRPB will not reveal the survey result or the fact a survey has been undertaken to a prospective buyer or his solicitor. The seller's solicitor should be asked for a copy of the survey result.

25.8.4. The majority of dwellings requiring remedial measures are concentrated in the radon Affected Areas. In England, these are the shaded 5 km squares of the Ordnance Survey grid shown on a map contained in formal advice from NRPB to the Government published in May 1996 and available from HMSO (reference: Documents of the NRPB, volume 7, no.2, 1996. ISBN: 0-85951-396-3). A larger version of this map was published in September 1996 and is available from HMSO or NRPB (reference NRPB-R290, Radon Atlas of England, ISBN 0-85951-400-5). Parts of Aberdeenshire and Highland in Scotland and the southeast of Northern Ireland (reference: Documents of the NRPB, volume 4, no.6, 1993. ISBN: 0-85951-396-3) and parts of Wales (reference: Documents of the NRPB, volume 7, no.2, 1996. ISBN: 0-85951-396-3) have also been declared radon Affected Areas.

25.8.5. Special requirements under the Building Regulations are also in force for new homes in some parts of the Affected Areas. Optional enquiry 36 on Part II Enquiries of Local Authority Form can be raised in appropriate cases. It is known at the time of writing that the guidance document associated with these regulations will be revised to take account of the formal advice published by NRPB in 1996. These revisions are expected to come into force in the summer of 1997 following consultations with interested parties.

25.8.6. An information pack on radon is available from NRPB. Private householders can also obtain background information by leaving their name, address and postcode on the 24 hour radon free phone 0800 614529. For postal and e-mail addresses and telephone and fax numbers see App. XIII.4. A web site (www.nrpb.org.uk) is in preparation.

1. For address see App. XIII.4.

FURTHER REFERENCE

Proceedings of the Radon 2000 Conference, March 1992 organised by NRPB. *New Law Journal,* 19 July 1996, p.1052.

The Law Society's Environmental Law Handbook (2nd ed.), Trevor Hellawell, the Law Society.

B.26. Reproduction of standard forms

26.1. **Standard Conditions of Sale**
26.2. **Protocol forms**

26.3. **Enquiries of Local Authority Form**
26.4. **HM Land Registry forms**

26.1. Standard Conditions of Sale

26.1.1. Solicitors may reproduce on their own word processors the agreement for sale which incorporates the Standard Conditions of Sale by reference but are not permitted to reproduce (whether on a word processor or by other means of reproduction) the text of the Standard Conditions themselves (General Conditions of Sale) without express permission from the copyright holder. Enquiries relating to copyright should, in the first instance, be addressed to the Publications Department of the Law Society (for address see Appendix XIII.4.).

26.2. Protocol forms

26.2.1. It is in the interests of both the solicitor and his client that uniformity of presentation should be maintained where forms form part of the TransAction scheme. For this reason some of the Protocol forms remain Law Society copyright and are not permitted to be reproduced on a solicitor's word processor (or by any other means of reproduction) without express permission first being obtained from the Publications Department of the Law Society.

26.2.2. The following forms are Law Society copyright and may not be reproduced by a solicitor (except by means of taking a photocopy to keep on his client's file):

(a) Seller's Property Information Form, Part I;

(b) Seller's Leasehold Information Form, Part I.

26.2.3. Other TransAction forms, e.g. Seller's Property Information Form, Part II, may be reproduced on a solicitor's word processor but must be reproduced in a version which resembles the printed form as closely as possible. No additions, deletions, adaptations or alterations of the text of the printed version must be made. Additionally each word-processed copy must bear in a prominent position the following phrase 'This form is part of the Law Society's TransAction Scheme' in order to indicate to a person who reads the form that the document is a genuine reproduction of a Protocol form.

26.3. Enquiries of Local Authority Form

26.3.1. A general licence has been granted to solicitors to reproduce Form CON29 on word processors provided that the quality of the form produced is of a standard acceptable to local authorities.

26.3.2. As a general guideline, reproduction on paper which weighs no less than 80gsm, at a resolution of no less than 300 dpi, in 12 point Roman typeface should satisfy these requirements. The local authority has the right to reject a form which does not meet an acceptable standard of reproduction.

26.3.3. The form may be reproduced on separate sheets of A4 paper. Permission has been granted for practitioners to reproduce and submit to the local authority only the front page of the printed Form CON29. The local authority may insist that the format of the printed form is followed as closely as is possible and in particular that the boxes which appear on the front page of the printed form are reproduced in the word-processed version.

26.4. HM Land Registry forms

26.4.1. HM Land Registry has given permission for solicitors to reproduce some of their forms on a word processor. The forms to which this permission applies are listed in Appendix IX.2.

26.4.2. The layout of the forms must follow the HMSO printed versions and not those printed by other companies. All HMSO official publishing and printing imprint must be omitted from the word processed version. Only notes prescribed by the Rules need to be reproduced on the form (e.g. the instruction on the front of Form 109 must be reproduced but not the notes for guidance on the reverse of the form).

26.4.3. A solicitor's word-processing equipment must be programmed to display the following acknowledgement on the entry screen each time the system is accessed: 'Crown copyright forms are reproduced with the permission of the Controller of HMSO'.

26.4.4. The word-processed forms may only be used by the applicant and may not be sold to a third party in hard copy or machine readable format. Neither may the forms be transmitted electronically except in-house or, where the Rules permit, by fax to HM Land Registry or its Land Charges Department.

26.4.5. Out-of-date forms must be erased from the database.

26.4.6. *Quality of printing*

Black print on white A4 size paper of no less than 80gsm weight (100 gsm for transfers) at a resolution of no less than 300 dpi from a non-impact printer.

B.27. Easements and boundaries

27.1. Checking boundaries

27.1.1. The burden of discovering the identity and ownership of boundaries usually lies with the buyer since Condition 4.3.1 Standard Conditions of Sale will (unless excluded from the contract) relieve the seller of the obligation to define precisely their route or to prove title to their ownership.

27.1.2. The buyer's solicitor should therefore check the boundaries as shown on the title deeds, accompanying plans, and (where supplied) the estate agent's particulars. Where from investigation of the above documents the boundaries are unclear or a discrepancy exists, further enquiries should be undertaken to clarify the position.

27.1.3. The client should be asked to check the boundaries by a site inspection or the client's surveyor should specifically be asked to undertake this task in the course of his own inspection of the property. The solicitor is not generally under an obligation to inspect the property but may need to do so where a discrepancy or query over the boundaries exists which is not resolved by inspection of the deeds and plans or by other enquiries made by the solicitor. An inspection may be required in the case of the purchase of a newly constructed property to ensure that the site plans accord with the property as it stands on the ground. Where the solicitor does accept the obligation of inspecting the property he will be liable in negligence if he does not carry out that duty with proper care.[1]

27.1.4. The following enquiries and investigations may also assist to determine the extent and ownership of boundaries:

(a) specific pre-contract enquiries of the seller;

(b) application of the common law presumptions (see para. 27.2.2 below);

(c) a site inspection of the property;

(d) an inspection of pre-root or pre-registration title deeds (if available);

(e) an Index Map search at HM Land Registry (see para B.10 (Pre-contract searches and enquiries));

(f) inspection of Ordnance Survey Maps.

1. See *Barclay-White* v. *Guillame & Sons* [1996] E.G.C.S. 123.

27.2. Evidence of boundaries

27.2.1. Registered land

Provided that provisions relating to the ownership of boundaries were clearly set out in the documentation which was filed with the application for first registration, this will be recorded on the register of the title and the ownership shown by a 'T' mark on the filed plan. This evidence can normally be relied on as showing the true position relating to ownership. However, the extent of the boundaries shown on the plan may not in all cases show the exact position since boundaries shown on plans drawn by H.M. Land Registry are general boundaries only unless fixed boundaries have been registered under the provisions of Rule 278 Land Registration Rules 1925. This is not commonly done and where it is done a note to this effect will appear on the register of the title.

27.2.2. Common law presumptions as to boundaries

The ad medium filum rule

A person who owns land abutting on a private or public highway is presumed to own the soil or sub-soil respectively of the highway up to the middle line. The surface of a public highway is vested in the highway authority. Registered titles do not show ownership of the sub-soil to the centre of a road even where there has been an express transfer including these rights.

The hedge and ditch rule

Where two properties are separated by a hedge and an artificial ditch, the boundary line is presumed to lie on the far side of the ditch from the hedge.

Foreshore

In the absence of contrary evidence, the boundary of land adjoining the sea lies at the top of the foreshore. The foreshore is that part of the shore lying between the ordinary high and low water marks. Land below the medium line of the foreshore belongs to the Crown.

Non-tidal rivers and streams

The *ad medium filum* rule applies so that the owners of properties on either bank of the stream or river own the bed up to the middle of the stream or river. The owner of the river is also presumed to own the right to fish in the river but this presumption may be rebutted and it is common to find that fishing rights have been separately sold to third parties.

Tidal rivers and sea inlets

The bed and foreshore of a tidal river is prima facie vested in the Crown subject to the public's rights of navigation and fishing. The Crown's rights extend to that point in the river where the tide ebbs and flows, beyond which point the *ad medium filum* rule applies.

Trees

A tree belongs to the owner on whose land it was planted even if its trunk, roots or branches extend on to a neighbouring property. Where it cannot be established who planted the tree (e.g. because the trunk straddles the boundary of the land) ownership may be inferred from the circumstances. Regular maintenance (e.g. lopping or topping) by one person may be indicative of ownership by that person.

27.2.3. *Ordnance survey maps*

It is the practice of ordnance survey maps to show the centre line of boundary features as the boundary. These maps may therefore give a general indication of the placing of a boundary but will not always show the precise delineation of the boundary. For example, an ordnance survey map will show a boundary line as running through the centre of a hedge whereas if the boundary is a hedge and artificial ditch the actual boundary will lie on the far side of the ditch from the hedge since, in the absence of evidence to the contrary, the common law presumptions prevail over the ordnance survey maps.

27.3. **Party walls**

27.3.1. *Party Wall Act 1996*

Party Wall Act 1996 in substance re-enacts London Building Acts (Amendment) Act 1939 which previously only applied to London. The 1996 Act applies its provisions throughout England and Wales.

27.3.2. *New party structures*

Section 1 requires a building owner to give at least one month's notice if he wishes to build a party structure where none exists. If the adjoining owner consents within 14 days, the wall is to be built half on the land of each owner or in such position as they agree. The expense of building is agreed between them or in an appropriate proportion considering the use and the cost of labour and materials. If consent is not forthcoming, the building owner may only build on his land. He may, subject to certain conditions, place footings below the land of the adjoining owner. He must compensate the adjoining owner and any occupier for any damage caused. Any dispute which arises is to be determined in accordance with the dispute resolution procedure in section 10.

27.3.3. Existing party structures

Section 2 gives a building owner wide powers to deal with party structures. Rebuilding may be to a height of not less than two metres where the wall is not used by the adjoining owner. A building owner may not cause unnecessary inconvenience and must compensate the adjoining owner and occupier for any loss or damage caused. If he opens any part of the adjoining land or building, he must maintain hoarding or shoring for its security. He must usually make good all damage caused to adjoining premises, internal furnishings and decorations, and may be required to pay expenses in lieu. He must also pay a fair allowance for disturbance and inconvenience.

27.3.4. Procedure

Section 3 requires a building owner to serve the adjoining owner with a party structure notice stating the building owner's name and address, details of the proposed work and the date on which it is to start at least two months before any proposed work is to start. Section 20 defines 'owner' to include anyone with a tenancy for more than a year and any purchaser under an agreement for purchase or lease. The notice ceases to have effect if work is not started within 12 months and if it does not proceed with due diligence. If an adjoining owner does not consent to the notice within 14 days, a dispute arises and section 10 applies. An adjoining owner may serve a counter notice within one month requiring the owner to build chimney breasts, recesses or other such works. The works must be specified and plans, sections and particulars must accompany the counter notice. The counter notice may require the existing height of the wall to be maintained if a building owner proposes to reduce it to not less than two metres. A building owner must comply with a counter notice unless this would injure him, cause unnecessary inconvenience or delay. If he does not consent to the counter notice within 14 days, section 10 applies. The procedure differs where a building owner wants to construct special foundations. If the adjoining owner does not consent, they may not be put in.

27.3.5. Dispute resolution procedure

Where a dispute arises, it is to be settled by surveyors (section 10). Both parties must agree on the appointment of a surveyor or appoint their own surveyor and the two surveyors must select a third surveyor. Either of the other two may then call on him to settle the matter. All appointments must be in writing and cannot be rescinded. Provision is made to deal with the situation where a surveyor dies, becomes incapable of acting, or refuses or neglects to act effectively. An award cannot authorise interference with an easement of light or rights in the party wall but may deal with the right, time and manner of carrying out work and any other matter arising from the dispute. The surveyor's award is conclusive, subject to the right of either party to appeal to the county court within 14 days of the date of the award. The court may rescind or modify the award.

27.3.6. *Payment for the work*

The building owner generally pays for all work. Where work is due to lack of repair, required by the adjoining owner or the latter makes use of the work, he must pay or contribute to the cost of the work. The building owner must serve him with an account within two months of completion. If the adjoining owner objects within one month, the matter is to be settled under section 10. Security for costs may be required before any work starts.

27.3.7. *Miscellaneous*

A building owner who proposes to excavate and construct a building or structure within three to six metres of any building or structure of the adjoining owner may, and must if required by the adjoining owner, strengthen or safeguard at his own expense the foundations of the adjoining owner if certain conditions are met. Finally, the Act gives rights to enter and remain on land for carrying out works and an occupier who refuses to permit this may be guilty of an offence.

27.4. **Access to neighbouring land**

27.4.1. Access to Neighbouring Land Act 1992 allows the court to grant the applicant a temporary right of access to another person's land for the purpose of carrying out basic preservation work, i.e. work necessary to protect, repair or maintain (but not to improve) the applicant's property. The fact that the repairs would be substantially more expensive to carry out without access to the neighbour's land is not itself a ground for making the order. For an order to be made, the proposed works must be either impossible or substantially more difficult to carry out without an access order. The applicant need not be the owner of the land in question.

27.4.2. The county court must refuse an access order where it is satisfied that the respondent or any other person would suffer interference with or disturbance of his use or enjoyment of the land to such a degree that it would be unreasonable to make the order.

27.4.3. An order, if made, will be binding on successors in title of the respondent, provided it is registered. Although the applicant need not own the land, if he does the Act does not seem to provide for the benefit of the order to enure for the benefit of successors in title to the applicant's land. An application under the Act is registrable as a pending action, an order as a writ and order.

27.4.4. The Act contains provisions for compensation for loss of privacy, inconvenience, pecuniary loss, damage or injury. Except where the dominant land concerned is residential payment of a fee for the access may be ordered by the court.

27.4.5. Pre-completion searches at HM Land Registry (or HM Land Charges Department in the case of unregistered land) will identify cases where access orders have been registered under the Act.

27.4.6. It is not possible to contract out of the provisions of the Act.

C. EXCHANGE
C.01. Preparing to exchange

1.1.	**Introduction**	1.3.	**Reporting to the buyer**
1.2.	**Checklist**		

See also: Surveys, para. A.13.
Pre-contract searches and enquiries, para. B.10.
Undertakings for bridging finance, para. B.16.
Deposit, para. B.17.
Mortgage offers, para. B.19.
Fixtures and fittings, para. B.22.
Signature of contract, para. C.02.
Insurance, para. C.03.

1.1. Introduction

1.1.1. On exchange a binding contract will come into existence, after which time neither party will normally be able to withdraw from the contract without incurring liability for breach. It is therefore essential to check that all outstanding queries have been resolved and that both parties' financial arrangements are in order before the client is advised to commit himself to the contract.

1.2. Checklist

1.2.1. Although the checklist below largely reflects matters which are of concern to a buyer, many of the items will also be of concern to a seller. The seller should pay particular attention to those items marked with an asterisk.

1.2.2. *Searches*

    (a) Have all necessary searches and enquiries been made?

    (b) Have all the replies to searches and enquiries been received?

    (c) Have all search and enquiry replies been checked carefully to ensure that the replies to individual questions are satisfactory and accord with the client's instructions?

    * (d) Have all outstanding queries been resolved satisfactorily?

1.2.3. *Survey*

    (a) Has a survey of the property been undertaken?

    (b) Is the result of that survey satisfactory?

1.2.4.   *Mortgage arrangements*

(a) Has a satisfactory mortgage offer been made and (where necessary) accepted by the client?

(b) Are arrangements in hand to comply with any conditions attached to the advance, e.g. in relation to an endowment policy?

(c) Taking into account the deposit, the mortgage advance (less any retention) and the costs of the transaction (including stamp duty and Land Registry fees), has the client sufficient funds to proceed with the purchase?

* (d) Are arrangements in hand to discharge the seller's existing mortgage(s)?

* (e) If the transaction is a sale of part, has the seller's lender (if any) agreed to release the property to be sold from the mortgage?

1.2.5.   *Deposit*

* (a) How much (if any) preliminary deposit has been paid?

* (b) How much money is needed to fund the deposit required on exchange?

(c) Has a suitable undertaking been given in relation to bridging finance?

* (d) To whom is the deposit to be paid?

NB: where Formula C is to be used for exchange, the deposit may have to be paid to someone other than the immediate seller.

(e) Have the deposit funds been obtained from the client and cleared through clients' account?

NB: Contractual conditions (e.g. Standard Condition 2.2) normally require that payment is to be made only by banker's draft or solicitor's cheque.

1.2.6.   *The contract*

* (a) Have all outstanding queries been satisfactorily resolved?

* (b) Have all agreed amendments been incorporated clearly in both parts of the contract?

* (c) Has the approved draft been returned to the seller?

* (d) Is a clean top copy of the contract available for signature by the client?

* (e) Have the terms of the contract been explained to the client?

* (f) Has the list of fixtures and fittings been agreed between the parties?

1.2.7. *Insurance*

    (a) Have steps been taken to insure the property?

  * (b) If the buyer is to rely on the seller's insurance policy, has the buyer's interest been noted on that policy?

    (c) Have steps been taken to obtain any life policy required under the terms of the buyer's mortgage offer?

1.2.8. *Completion date*

  *   Has a completion date been agreed?

1.2.9. *Method of exchange*

  *   Which method of exchange is most suitable to be used in this transaction?

1.2.10. *Synchronisation*

  *   Where the client requires a simultaneous exchange on both sale and purchase contracts, ensure that both transactions are ready to proceed and that all related transactions in the chain are also ready.

1.2.11. *Signature of contract*

  *   Has the client signed the contract?

1.2.12. *Occupiers*

  *   Has the concurrence of all non-owning occupiers been obtained?

1.3.   Reporting to the buyer

1.3.1.   When the buyer's solicitor has completed his investigations into the property (including having finalised any amendments to the draft documentation) he should consider preparing and sending or giving to his client a report on the proposed purchase which should explain to the client (in language appropriate to the client's level of understanding) the nature of the solicitor's investigations into the property and its legal title, the results of these investigations, and a summary of conclusions or advice to the client.

1.3.2.   An example of such a report is set out below. The precise content of the report will vary from transaction to transaction and in the case of commercial property a more detailed report may be desirable. A report on leasehold property should explain the terms of the lease to the client (see Acting for the tenant, para. K.03.).

REPORT ON PROPOSED PURCHASE

of the property known as

15 High Hill, Harkley, Herts

prepared for Mr and Mrs Harvey Hart

1. **The Property**

   The Property is known as 15 High Hill, Harkley, Herts HH1 2ZZ. A copy of the Land Registry plan is attached [*not produced in this book*] showing the extent of the property edged in red.

   Land Registry plans are to a small scale and are not intended to show the precise location of each boundary; these should be checked on site and any significant discrepancies referred to us so that we can seek clarification from the sellers.

2. **Title**

   The Property is freehold. The title number is HH123456. It is registered at the Land Registry with "absolute" title, which means that freehold ownership is guaranteed by the Registry. You should inspect the property to ensure that it is only occupied by the seller and his immediate family and let us know if this is not the case. The property is being sold to you with full vacant possession on completion.

3. **Rights passing with the Property**

   The Property has the benefit of a right of way over the alleyway at the rear of the Property, marked in blue on the Land Registry plan, leading to the road known as Hall Hollow. This right is on foot only, so there is no right to drive vehicles (or ride bicycles or horses) along it. The deeds do not make provision for any person to be responsible for maintaining or clearing the alleyway but do provide for the owner of the Property to pay a fair contribution towards any expenditure on such matters. The sellers state that they are not aware of anyone carrying out such works and have not been asked to pay anything in this regard. If the alleyway needs maintaining so that you can walk along it, as a matter of general law the right of way would give you the right to do necessary maintenance, but wholly at your own cost.

4. **Rights over the Property**

   The owner of the property known as 13 High Hill has a right of way on foot across the south-west corner of the rear garden of the Property, to enable him to pass between the end of his garden and the alleyway. The route is marked in yellow on the Land Registry plan. This right was apparently granted because the alleyway stops level with the west boundary of the Property and does not run behind the garden of number 13. The sellers state that the neighbour has never exercised this right during their 8 years of ownership of the Property; however, this does not mean that the right has legally lapsed.

5.   **Covenants**

A number of restrictive covenants were imposed on the owner of the Property when the plot was sold to the original house builder in 1898. It appears that similar covenants were imposed on all the plots in the street, and these covenants may still be enforceable by one house owner against another; if you purchase the Property, you may be obliged to observe them, and you may be entitled to require the neighbouring owners to observe them. The following is a summary of those that may still be relevant:

(1)   not to park any caravan or similar vehicle on the Property;

(2)   not to erect more than one single house on the Property, apart from a greenhouse or other usual outbuilding;

(3)   not to use any house for business use but only as a private dwelling;

(4)   not to cause nuisance or annoyance to neighbours.

Even if these covenants are not strictly enforceable in law, planning restrictions imposed by the local authority may in practice have a similar effect.

A positive covenant was also imposed in 1898, requiring the owner of the Property to maintain the fence on the east boundary of the Property. We have marked this fence with the letter "T" on the attached copy of the Land Registry plan. Whilst it is unlikely that anyone could legally enforce compliance with this covenant, in practice you should be prepared to maintain this fence, and the other fences bounding the Property, at your own cost.

6.   **Information from the Sellers**

The solicitors acting for the sellers, Henry and Hetty Hodgson, have supplied us with a package of information under the Law Society TransAction scheme. We attach copies of the following items supplied to us in that package:

(a)   **Seller's Property Information Form**
      This gives information about boundaries, disputes, notices, guarantees, services, rights and other matters. Our comments are:

      (1)   the information on boundaries must be read subject to our comment about the eastern fence, in paragraph 5 of this Report;

      (2)   the building work mentioned in reply to question 10.3 of the Form did not need planning permission, but future enlargement of the building might.

(b) **List of Fixtures Fittings and Contents**

This indicates which items at the Property are included in the sale and which are not. Please let us know if anything stated to be excluded was in fact supposed to be included, or if you reach agreement with the sellers to buy any of the excluded items.

We understand that this sale is dependent upon the sellers buying another property, but their solicitors tell us that this is progressing well and they hope to be in a position to exchange contracts on both transactions at the end of next month.

7. **Information from the Local Authority etc**

We have made a search in the Register of Local Land Charges and have raised enquiries with the local council, and have obtained the following information which relates to the property which you are intending to buy. A separate search would be needed to obtain information relating to neighbouring properties:

(1) High Hill and Hall Hollow are publicly maintained roads, but the rear alleyway is not;

(2) there are no current plans for road improvements or new roads within 200 metres of the Property;

(3) foul drainage is believed to be connected to the public sewer but the means of connection is not known (a drain running between a house and the public sewer is not maintained at public expense and you should consult your surveyor as to the likelihood of your having to repair or maintain any drain connected to the property).

None of the other replies by the council to our enquiries need to be drawn to your attention.

Because of the location of the Property, we have also made a search with British Coal in order that you or your surveyor can assess the risk of future subsidence due to coal extraction beneath the Property. A statutory compensation scheme is available if you suffer damage as a result of mining works. British Coal has given the following response:

(1) Two seams of coal have been mined at an approximate depth of 200 metres under or near the Property, the last working being in 1990.

(2) There are presently no workings taking place within influencing distance of the Property.

(3) Although coal exists unworked, British Coal states that the possibility of future working is considered unlikely.

8. **Outgoings**

The property is in band F for council tax purposes. The annual water charge (currently £XXX) is payable to Hartford Water Company, The water supply at the property is not metered.

9.   The Purchase Contract

This is in a form incorporating the Standard Conditions of Sale, which are widely used for this type of transaction. The main provisions of the contract are:

(1)   The purchase price is £XXX,XXX. (No VAT will be payable on this.) The price includes the items shown on the list attached to the contract, which corresponds with the list of Fixtures, Fittings and Chattels mentioned above.

(2)   On exchange of contracts, you must pay a deposit of £XX,XXX. If we cannot complete your purchase of the Property due to the Hodgsons' default, you will become entitled to the return of the deposit (and may be able to claim damages for your loss). However, under the Standard Conditions of Sale, all or part of the deposit money can be used by Mr and Mrs Hodgson to pay the deposit on their new property, and only the remainder, if any, will be retained by their solicitors as "stakeholder" until we satisfactorily complete the purchase. Whilst this arrangement has become common practice, we must warn you that in the event of the matter not completing, it may be more difficult to obtain repayment of deposit money which has been used by the Hodgsons in that way, than if the whole deposit was retained by their solicitors until completion; on the other hand, very few house purchases totally fail to complete (though completion is occasionally delayed), and you may be prepared to take this risk rather than insisting that the Hodgsons incur the expense of obtaining separate bridging finance for the deposit on their new property. Please discuss this with us if you are concerned about it.

(3)   The completion date will be inserted just before contracts are exchanged. We will discuss it with you at that time so that a date acceptable to both you and the Hodgsons can be fixed. This date will then be the date on which the transaction is to be completed: the Hodgsons must vacate the Property on that date, if they do not vacate earlier, and we must send the completion money to their solicitors to reach their bank account by 2pm, that afternoon. You will be liable to pay daily interest at X per cent per year above bank base rate if cleared funds are not made available to us in time to remit the completion money early enough, so we will need to receive the funds (other than the loan from your Building Society, mentioned below) from you either by cheque in favour of this firm reaching us at least five working days before the completion date, or by bank transfer into this firm's bank account preferably on the day before the completion date. Nearer the time, we will let you know how much we require; this will include a sum to cover our fees, disbursements paid or payable by us (including stamp duty of £X,XXX and registration fees of £XXX) and VAT.

(4)   You are buying the Property in its actual state and condition. You must be satisfied about this from your own inspection of the Property and from your surveyor's report. If you expect the sellers to remedy (or pay for the remedy of) any defects, this will have to be agreed with them before contracts are exchanged and special provisions added to the contract.

(5) The Property remains at the sellers' risk until completion, and the sellers must hand it over in its present condition, except for fair wear and tear. You would be entitled to withdraw from the transaction, with the return of your deposit, if the Property was so badly damaged before the completion date to make it unusable, and the sellers would have a similar right if the damage was caused by a risk against which they could not have been expected to insure.

10. Mortgage

We have received instructions from the Highland Building Society to act for them on a mortgage loan to assist you in buying the Property. We have to report to them on the result of our investigations about the Property and also on any discrepancies between the details of the transaction known to us and the details you gave the Society with your mortgage application (e.g. as to the purchase price). So far, the documents supplied to us do not show any such discrepancies.

The main terms of the proposed mortgage are:

(1) The loan will be £XX,XXX.

(2) Interest is variable at the discretion of the Society, but will initially be at the rate of X per cent per year.

(3) The loan is repayable, with interest, over XX years, by monthly instalments comprising a mixture of capital and interest. Initially the instalments will be £XXX per month, but this is variable and the Society will recalculate the amount as a result of changes in the rate of interest. You will be required to pay the instalments by bank standing order. Failure to pay any instalments will entitle the Society to call for immediate repayment of the entire loan.

(4) The loan will be to both of you, and you will both be individually legally responsible for ensuring that the instalment payments are duly made and that the other provisions of the mortgage, mentioned below, are observed.

(5) The loan and interest will be secured on a first legal mortgage over the Property. This will give the Society various rights if you fail to pay the instalments, including the right to apply to the court to evict you and your family so that the Society can sell the Property in order to recoup the outstanding loan and any unpaid interest. If the sale proceeds exceed the amount due to the Society, the surplus will be paid to you (or to any second lender), but if there is a shortfall the Society can sue you for it.

(6) The mortgage will impose a number of standard obligations and restrictions, the most important being:

(a) you must keep the Property in good repair;

(b) you must insure the Property with insurers agreed between you and the Society;

(c) you must not alter the Property, or change its use, without the Society's prior consent;

(d) you must not let any part of the Property without the Society's prior consent;

    (e) no second or subsequent mortgage must be taken out without the Society's prior consent.

  (7) The mortgage will be security for any future loans you may borrow from the Society, as well as for the loan mentioned above.

The full text of the mortgage terms are set out in the enclosed book from the Society, and we recommend that you read them.

11.   Environmental matters

We have/have not made enquiries relating to environmental matters affecting the property. [Our enquiries revealed the following information (*set out details*)].

Please ask us if you have any queries about this report or on any other aspect of this transaction.

(Name of Solicitors)

C.02. Signature of contract

2.1. Requirement for signature

2.1.1. Both parties must sign the contract (or each must sign one of two identical copies) in order to satisfy Law of Property (Miscellaneous Provisions) Act 1989, s.2. Such signature need not be witnessed.

2.2. Signature by the client

2.2.1. Ideally the client should be asked to sign the contract in the presence of his solicitor, the solicitor first having ensured that the client understands and acquiesces in the terms of the contract.

2.2.2. In cases where it is not practicable for the client to sign in the solicitor's presence, the contract may be sent to the client for signature with an accompanying letter which clearly explains where and how the client is required to sign the document. If not already done, the letter should explain the terms of the contract in language appropriate to the client's level of understanding, and also request a cheque for the deposit indicating by which date the solicitor needs to be in receipt of cleared funds. The client should be asked to return the signed contract to the solicitor as soon as possible.

2.3. Signature by solicitor on behalf of client

2.3.1. A solicitor needs his client's express authority to sign the contract on behalf of the client.[1]

2.3.2. Unless the solicitor holds a valid power of attorney, it is recommended that such an authority be obtained from the client in writing, the client previously having been informed of the legal consequences of giving such authority (i.e. signature implies authority to proceed to exchange, and exchange creates a binding contract). Failure to obtain authority may render the solicitor liable in damages for breach of warranty of authority.[2]

1. *Suleman v. Shahsavari* [1989] 2 All E.R. 460.
2. *Suleman v. Shahsavari* [1989] 2 All E.R. 460.

2.4. **Special cases**

2.4.1. *Co-owners*

One co-owner may sign the contract on behalf of all the co-owners, but the solicitor should ensure that all co-owners have voluntarily given their consent to the transaction and have authorised the signature of the contract.

2.4.2. *Trustees*

One trustee alone may sign the contract for sale on behalf of his co-trustees. The solicitor should ensure that all co-trustees have voluntarily given their consent to the transaction and have authorised the signature of the contract.

2.4.3. *Partners*

Provided that the transaction has been authorised by the partnership, one partner may be given authority to sign the contract on behalf of the partners.

2.4.4. *Companies*

Provided that the transaction has been authorised by the company, an officer of the company (usually a director or the secretary) may be authorised to sign on behalf of the company.

2.4.5. *Attorneys*

A person who holds a valid power of attorney on behalf of another may sign the contract on behalf of the donor of the power. The attorney may sign either in his own name or that of the donor. The solicitor acting for the other party should be notified that the contract will be signed by an attorney and a properly certified copy of the power supplied to him so that he may satisfy himself as to the validity of the power and that it contains proper authority for the conduct of the particular transaction.

2.4.6. *Personal representatives*

All proving personal representatives must be parties to the contract and purchase deed.[1]

2.4.7. *Occupiers*

A non-owning occupier may be joined as a party to the contract in order to give a release of his or her purported interest in the property. Where this occurs the non-owning occupier must sign the contract.[2]

1. Law of Property (Miscellaneous Provisions) Act 1994, s.16.
2. See para. B.03.5.8. above for an appropriate form of wording to release rights.

C.03. Insurance

See also: Financial services, para. A.04.
After exchange, para. C.05.

3.1. Risk in the property

3.1.1. At common law and unless the contract provides otherwise, the risk in the property passes to the buyer from the moment of exchange; the buyer thus bears the risk of loss or damage, except where it can be shown that the loss or damage is attributable to the seller's lack of proper care.[1] The buyer should therefore normally insure the property from exchange of contracts onwards. A solicitor who fails to advise his client of the consequences of failure to insure, or who fails to carry out his client's instructions to insure the property, will be liable in negligence if the client suffers loss as a result of the lack of insurance.

3.1.2. Since it is impossible to predict at which precise moment exchange will occur, it is essential that the buyer's insurance arrangements have been made in advance of actual exchange so that the policy will be effective immediately upon exchange.

1. *Clarke* v. *Ramuz* [1891] 2 Q.B. 456; *Phillips* v. *Lamdin* [1949] 2 K.B. 33.

3.2. Insuring the property

3.2.1. Where the buyer's solicitor has in force a block policy which covers all properties currently being handled by the firm, the property should be noted on the policy in accordance with the firm's standard procedures and, at the latest, by the morning of the day on which it is anticipated that exchange will occur.

3.2.2. If the buyer is financing his purchase with the assistance of a building society mortgage, the lender will normally attend to the insurance arrangements on being requested to do so by the buyer's solicitor. The building society's standing instructions to solicitors should be checked to ensure that:

(a) the amount of cover will be adequate;

(b) the property will be put on cover from the time of exchange;

(c) the lender's insurance requirements do not conflict with the terms of the contract or of any lease to which the property is subject.

3.2.3. If neither of the preceding subparagraphs apply the buyer must obtain a policy which will cover the property from exchange.

3.3. The terms of the policy

3.3.1. The terms of the policy should be checked to ensure that:

(a) the amount of cover is adequate;

(b) the sum insured is index linked;

(c) the risks insured against are adequate, e.g. is flood damage covered where the property is situated in a low-lying area?

(d) particular features of the property have been disclosed to the insurance company and are adequately insured, e.g. thatched roofs, garden walls, interior decorative plasterwork;

(e) where the property consists of a flat within a larger building, or is otherwise attached to adjoining property, the insurance cover extends to damage to neighbouring property where practicable.

3.3.2. The client should be alerted to possible exclusions under the policy. In particular damage caused by terrorist activity may not be covered; in a leasehold context damage caused to the property by, e.g. a terrorist bomb would not be an insured risk; nevertheless the tenant or prospective tenant would remain liable under the terms of the lease, including the covenant to pay rent. Similarly, some policies will not cover damage to empty properties (or to blocks of flats where a resident is claiming social security benefits).

3.4. Property at seller's risk

3.4.1. In some cases, and commonly with property which is in the course of construction, the contract will provide that the property is to remain at the seller's risk until completion. Standard Condition 5.1 also provides for the seller to bear the risk in the property until completion and permits rescission if the property is substantially damaged between exchange and completion. Except in certain cases applicable to the sale of leaseholds, the seller is not obliged by the condition to maintain his own insurance policy after exchange. Where the risk in the property remains with the seller the buyer need not take out his own policy until completion but should ensure, before exchange, that:

(a) the seller will maintain his policy until completion and the terms of that policy provide sufficient protection for the buyer;

(b) the buyer receives written confirmation that his interest has been noted on the seller's policy;

(c) the contract contains a provision requiring the seller to transfer the property in substantially the same physical condition as it was in at the time of exchange, failing which the buyer is entitled to rescind the contract (Standard Condition 5.1 contains this type of provision). This type of clause is not necessary where the property is in the course of construction because the contract for such a property will normally contain provisions requiring the seller to complete the building in accordance with specifications, failing which the buyer is under no obligation to complete.

3.4.2. Where the property is in the course of construction and the risk is to remain with the seller until completion, the buyer should clarify with the seller whether the word 'completion' is intended to refer only to completion of the building works, or whether it is intended that the seller will retain the risk in the property until actual completion of the transaction.

3.5. Standard contractual conditions

3.5.1. Standard Condition 5.1 permits the seller to cancel his insurance policy (except in certain cases related to the sale of an existing lease), thus implicitly obliging the buyer to insure. This condition also excludes Law of Property Act 1925, s.47 which would otherwise give the buyer the right, in certain circumstances, to claim off the seller's policy in the event of damage to the property. The seller must transfer the property in the same physical condition as it was in at the date of the contract, failing which a right to rescind exists.

3.6. Maintenance of seller's policy

3.6.1. Except where the seller is obliged by a condition of his mortgage or lease to maintain his policy, the seller could, with little risk, cancel his insurance policy on exchange of contracts, but in practice he would be ill advised to do so, e.g. in case the buyer failed to complete.

3.6.2. In practice the seller will not usually cancel his policy until after completion; thus for the period between exchange and completion there will often be two policies in force (one having been taken out by the buyer on exchange), both covering the same property against the same risks.

3.6.3. Should the property be damaged or destroyed during the period when the two policies subsist difficulty may sometimes be experienced in obtaining payment from the insurer, since each insurer may maintain that the responsibility for payment lies with the other. This difficulty may be resolved by including a special condition in the contract which requires the buyer to complete, subject to an abatement in the purchase price, leaving the seller to resolve the dispute with his own insurers. For a suitable form of wording see the Law Society Conditions of Sale (1984 revision), Condition 11(1).

3.7.   **Damage to the property**

3.7.1.   Under the common law the buyer will have to bear the cost of any damage caused to the property after exchange unless one of the provisions outlined below can be utilised. Additionally, the buyer's solicitor may be liable to his client in negligence.

3.7.2.   Law of Property Act 1925, s.47 provides that a buyer may claim his loss from the policy maintained by the seller provided that:

   (a)   the contract does not exclude the operation of the section;

   (b)   the buyer pays a proportionate part of the insurance premium; and

   (c)   the insurance company consents to noting the buyer's interest in the policy.

3.7.3.   The contract will normally exclude the operation of section 47, rendering the section ineffective so far as the buyer is concerned. (See Standard Condition 5.1.)

3.7.4.   Fires Prevention (Metropolis) Act 1774, s.83 allows a person interested in or entitled to a property to require an insurance company to apply the proceeds of the policy towards the reinstatement of the property in the event of its damage by fire. Despite its title, the operation of the Act is not confined to London, but there is no direct authority for the proposition that a buyer under a contract for sale is a 'person interested' under the section.[1]

1. *Rayner* v. *Preston* (1881) 18 Ch. 1 suggests *obiter* that a buyer can claim under the Act.

3.8.   **Other types of insurance**

3.8.1.   In appropriate cases the buyer should be advised to take out insurance to cover other risks, e.g. house contents, as well as life insurance in accordance with the terms of the mortgage offer.

3.8.2.   Steps should be taken before or immediately after exchange to put such policies on foot although they will not normally need to be effective until completion. Advice given by the solicitor to his client about the terms of a life insurance policy will in most cases be subject to the provisions of Financial Services Act 1986.[1] The seller should be advised not to cancel his house contents or other policies (including life policies linked to his mortgage) until completion.

1. See para. A.04.

FURTHER REFERENCE

Insurance in Domestic Conveyancing, C. Mitchell and J.T. Farrand Q.C. (Hon.), F.T. Law & Tax.

C.04. Exchange of contracts

4.1.	The practice of exchange	4.3.	Methods of exchange
4.2.	Authority to exchange	4.4.	The Protocol
		4.5.	Standard Conditions of Sale

See also: Acting for both parties, para. A.10.
Undertakings for bridging finance, para. B.16.
Preparing to exchange, para. C.01.

4.1. The practice of exchange

4.1.1. The physical exchange of contracts between the parties is not a legal requirement for a contract for the sale of land but where a contract is drawn up by solicitors acting for the parties it is usual for the contract to be prepared in two identical parts, one being signed by the seller, the other by the buyer. When the two parts are physically exchanged, so that the buyer receives the part of the contract signed by the seller and vice versa, a binding contract comes into existence. The actual time when the contract comes into being depends on the method which has been employed to effect the exchange.[1]

4.1.2. The practice of exchange was given legal recognition in *Eccles* v. *Bryant and Pollock*[2] where Lord Greene in his judgment stated in relation to the then existing law under Law of Property Act 1925, s.40[3] that the three essential ingredients of a contract for the sale of land were:

(a) compliance with the requirements of Law of Property Act 1925, s.40;[4]

(b) certainty in respect of the existence of the contract; and

(c) certainty in respect of the terms of the contract.

4.1.3. All three of the above requirements are satisfied by the practice of exchange of contracts, because where a contract is to come into existence through exchange both parties have the assurance of knowing that no contract exists until that time, i.e. either party is free to change his mind and withdraw from the negotiations until exchange. In the same way, once exchange has taken place, there is certainty for both parties as to the existence of an enforceable contract, and also certainty over the terms which have been agreed since each party retains a copy of the contract signed by the other in identical form to the one which he himself signed. Where contracts are to be exchanged both parts of the contract must be identical. This includes the filling in of the date of the contract and the date of completion. If this requirement is not met no contract will come into existence whether or not the exchange takes place.[5]

4.1.4.   Since exchange is not a legal necessity there is no reason why the contract should not be embodied in a single document which is signed by both parties. In such a case the contract becomes binding and enforceable as soon as the second signature has been put on the document.[6] This situation will not frequently occur and in any event the same solicitor is usually forbidden from acting for both parties by Rule 6 Solicitors' Practice Rules 1990.

4.1.5.   An exchange of faxes is not an exchange of contracts to satisfy section 2 Law of Property (Miscellaneous Provisions) Act 1989.[7] In *Commission for the New Towns* v. *Cooper (Great Britain) Ltd*[8] an exchange of letters was held not to satisfy section 2.

1. See below, para. 4.3.
2. [1948] Ch. 93.
3. [1948] Ch. 93 at 99.
4. Now replaced by Law of Property (Miscellaneous Provisions) Act 1989, s.2.
5. *Harrison* v. *Battye* [1975] 1 W.L.R. 58.
6. *Smith* v. *Mansi* [1963] 1 W.L.R. 26.
7. *Milton Keynes Development Corporation* v. *Cooper (Great Britain) Ltd.* [1993] E.G.C.S. 142.
8. [1995] 2 All E.R. 929 (C.A.).

4.2.   Authority to exchange

4.2.1.   A solicitor who exchanges contracts without his client's express or implied authority to do so will be liable to the client in negligence. In *Eccles* v. *Bryant and Pollock*[1] Lord Greene said that where a contract was to come into existence using the standard form of contract (now the Standard Conditions of Sale), it was implicit that the contract would come into existence on exchange, and that the client therefore impliedly authorised his solicitor to effect an exchange. In *Domb* v. *Isoz*[2] it was held that, once the solicitor has his client's authority to exchange, he has the authority to effect the exchange by whichever method the solicitor thinks most appropriate to the situation.

4.2.2.   Although *Eccles* v. *Bryant and Pollock*[3] suggests that a solicitor's authority to exchange may be implied, it is better practice to obtain express authority from the client at the time of signature of the contract. Where an exchange of contracts by telephone is contemplated, it is suggested that, for the avoidance of doubt, express authority to use this method should be obtained. Where Formula C is to be used, it is a requirement of that Formula that express authority be obtained, preferably in writing. The Formula contains a suggested form of wording to meet this situation.[4]

1. [1948] Ch. 93.
2. [1980] Ch. 548.
3. [1948] Ch. 93.
4. Formula C is set out in full with notes for guidance in App. VII.1.

4.3. Methods of exchange

4.3.1. Whichever method is chosen the exchange is usually initiated by the buyer indicating to the seller that he is now ready to commit himself to a binding contract. Once contracts have been exchanged neither party will be able to withdraw from the contract; it is therefore essential that the parties' solicitors have checked that all necessary arrangements are in order before proceeding to exchange. Also, where the purchase of one property is dependent on the sale of another the solicitor must ensure that the exchange of contracts on both properties is synchronised to avoid leaving his client either owning two houses or being homeless. Failure to synchronise the exchange where the client has instructed that his sale and purchase transactions are interdependent is professional negligence.

4.3.2. *Telephone*

Exchange by telephone is now the most common method of effecting an exchange of contracts. Legal recognition of the practice was given by the Court of Appeal in *Domb* v. *Isoz*.[1] With the exception of personal exchange this method represents the quickest way of securing an exchange of contracts and is thus particularly useful in a chain of transactions. The method is not, however, risk free. Where exchange is effected by telephone, the contract between the parties becomes effective as soon as the parties' solicitors agree in the course of a telephone conversation that exchange has taken place. The telephone conversation is usually followed by a physical exchange of documents through the post in the normal way, but the existence of the contract is not dependent on this physical exchange; the contract already exists by virtue of the telephone conversation. If one party were subsequently to change his mind about the contract there is ample scope with this method for disputing the contents of the telephone conversation and thus the existence of the contract itself. To avoid the uncertainties arising out of this method of exchange the parties' solicitors must agree prior to exchange that the telephonic exchange will be governed by one of the Law Society's Formulae which were drawn up by the Law Society in response to the decision in *Domb* v. *Isoz*. The text of these Formulae appears in Appendix VII.1. An accurate attendance note recording the telephone conversation must also be made as soon as practicable.

4.3.3. *Using the Formulae*

(a) The text of the Formulae with their accompanying guidance notes is set out in Appendix VII.1.

(b) Whichever Formula is used, the client's express authority to exchange must be obtained before the procedure to exchange is commenced.

(c) If any variation to a Formula is to be made, such variation must be expressly agreed and noted in writing by all the solicitors involved before exchange takes place. Any agreement relating to the payment of a less than 10% deposit should be finalised at the preliminary enquiries stage of the transaction and not left until exchange is imminent. Any agreed variation to the Formula which has been made orally must be confirmed in correspondence between the solicitors.

(d) Subject to (c) above, the conditions attached to the Formula being used must be strictly adhered to. In particular, where an undertaking is given to remit a deposit cheque and/or contract to the solicitor acting for the other party, such undertaking must be complied with on the day on which exchange takes place or, if compliance on the same day is not practicable, e.g. because exchange takes place after normal working hours, at the earliest opportunity on the next working day.

(e) To ensure compliance with the conditions attaching to the Formulae it is recommended that only qualified staff be authorised to effect an exchange by telephone.

(f) The Formulae may be used where the other party to the transaction is represented by a licensed conveyancer. The Formulae must never be used where the other party is represented by an unqualified person whose undertaking is not enforceable in the same way as those given by solicitors and licensed conveyancers.

(g) Extreme care needs to be exercised when using Formula C (for use in chain transactions) where, in certain circumstances, a solicitor is required to give an undertaking, the performance of which is outside his direct control, e.g. solicitor A undertakes to solicitor B that solicitor C will send the deposit cheque to solicitor B. The Standard Conditions of Sale only permit a deposit to be used for an exchange of contracts along the chain if that contract contains similar provisions as to the deposit. This almost inevitably means that the second contract must also be made by reference to the Standard Conditions.

(h) Under Formula C the ultimate recipient of the deposit must hold as stakeholder. No other capacity is permitted.

(i) An attendance note recording full details of the exchange by telephone must be made immediately exchange has taken place.

(j) A solicitor's failure to honour an undertaking given in relation to use of one of the Formulae (e.g. failure to send the deposit cheque on the same day as exchange takes place) is professional misconduct but probably does not affect the validity of an otherwise valid contract.[2]

(k) Fax can be used to activate the Formulae.

4.3.4. *Personal exchange*

By this method the solicitors for the parties meet, usually at the seller's solicitor's office, and the two contracts are physically exchanged. A contract exists from the moment of exchange. Although this type of exchange represents the safest and most instantaneous method of exchange it is frequently not possible to use personal exchange because the physical distance between the offices of the respective solicitors make it impractical to do so. Personal exchange is little used today, but it should be considered for use when the parties' solicitors are located in sufficient geographical proximity to make personal exchange feasible. A personal exchange has the benefit not only of being instantaneous, and thus leaving no uncertainty over the timing of the creation of the contract, but also of enabling both parties to see the other party's part of the contract before exchange actually takes place, so that both may be reassured that the parts of the contract are identical in form and have been properly signed.

4.3.5. Postal exchange

Where exchange is to take place by post the buyer's solicitor will send his client's signed contract and the deposit cheque to the seller's solicitor who on receipt of these documents will post his client's signed contract back to the buyer. Generally a contract does not come into being until the buyer has *received* the seller's contract. Exchange of contracts by post forms an exception to this rule and the contract is made when the seller *posts* his part of the contract to the buyer.[3] Posting the contract means that the seller must actually place the letter in the letter box. Handing the letter to a third party with instructions that it should be posted is not sufficient.[4] The postal rules of acceptance may be displaced by contrary intention in the contract itself.[5] It follows from the above that a contract will be formed even if the seller's part of the contract is lost in the post and is thus never received by the buyer. Using the post as a method of exchange is reasonably satisfactory when dealing with a single sale or purchase which is not dependent on another related transaction, but even in this simple scenario some dangers exist. There will inevitably be a delay between the buyer sending his contract to the seller and the seller posting his part back, during which time the buyer is uncertain of whether he has secured the contract. There is also no guarantee that the seller will complete the exchange by posting his part of the contract back to the buyer. Until he actually does so he is free to change his mind and withdraw from the transaction. Although these dangers are minimal where a single sale or purchase is being undertaken, the risks assume a much greater importance where a chain of transactions is involved; thus, the use of postal exchange is not to be advocated in linked transactions.

4.3.6. Document exchanges

A document exchange would be used to effect an exchange of contracts in a similar way to the normal postal service and is subject to the same risks as are outlined in the preceding subparagraph. The court has approved the use of document exchanges for the service and delivery of documents in non-contentious matters in *John Wilmot Homes* v. *Reed.*[6] The rules on postal acceptance do not apply to document exchanges and unless the contract contains a contrary provision the contract will come into existence when the seller's part of the contract is received by the buyer.[7] Where the Standard Conditions of Sale are used, Condition 2 provides that the contract is made when the last copy of the contract is deposited at the document exchange. If the Standard Conditions of Sale do not form the basis of the contract, the contract probably comes into existence when the last part of the contract is placed in the solicitor's box at the document exchange. There is no decided case on the making of a contract for the sale of land where a document exchange has been used to effect an exchange, and the proposition outlined above would be subject to the rules of the particular document exchange which was being used.

4.3.7. Telex

The use of telex as a method of exchanging contracts has largely been superseded by telephone and more recently by fax. In operation the use of telex for exchange is very similar to the telephone and the Law Society's Formulae have equal application to this situation.[8] It is suggested that the contract comes into existence when the seller's telex message activating the Law Society's Formulae is received on the buyer's telex terminal.[9] The advantage of telex over the telephone is that the actual message transmitted between the parties' solicitors is reduced into writing, thus eliminating any possibility that one party might later deny the existence of the contract. A physical exchange of contracts should follow the telex messages but is not essential since the contract will already be in existence. It should be noted, however, that if the physical exchange is not made, and one party subsequently refuses to complete, without the documentary evidence supplied by the contract itself, the party seeking to enforce the contract will have difficulty in demonstrating that the requirements of Law of Property (Miscellaneous Provisions) Act 1989, s.2 have been satisfied.

4.3.8. Fax

Exchange of contracts by using facsimile transmission is similar in operation to telex but is probably to be preferred to telex in that with facsimile transmission a copy of the contract signed by the buyer is transmitted to the seller's terminal and may thus be verified by him before he transmits his copy of the contract in return. A physical exchange of documents must follow the faxed messages; if this were never to happen a party seeking enforcement of the contract would have difficulty in demonstrating that the requirements of Law of Property (Miscellaneous Provisions) Act 1989, s.2 have been satisfied.[10] The main use of fax is to transmit the messages which activate the Law Society's Formulae. In this context fax is merely a substitute for using the telephone. Standard Condition 1.3.3 does not permit fax to be used as a valid method of service of a document where delivery of the original document is essential (as it is with the contract), thus effectively ruling out an *exchange* by this method, although there is no objection to the parties using fax in order to activate the Law Society's Formulae.[11]

1. [1980] Ch. 548.
2. See *Khan* v. *Hamilton* [1989] E.G.C.S. 128.
3. Despite doubts expressed about these rules in *Eccles* v. *Bryant and Pollock* (above), it is generally accepted that the postal rules as established in *Adams* v. *Lindsell* (1818) 1 B. & Ald. 681 do apply.
4. *Re London and Northern Bank, ex p. Jones* [1900] Ch. 220.
5. *Holwell Securities* v. *Hughes* [1974] 1 All E.R. 161.
6. (1985) 51 P. & C.R. 90.
7. See Standard Conditions 1 and 2.

8. See above, para. 4.3.2.
9. *Entores Ltd.* v. *Miles Far East Corporation* [1955] 2 Q.B. 327.
10. *Milton Keynes Development Corporation* v. *Cooper (Great Britain) Ltd.* [1993] E.G.C.S. 142. An exchange of faxes was held not to be an exchange of contracts.
11. See *Hastie & Jenkerson* v. *McMahon* [1991] 1 All E.R. 255 where the court, in a contentious case, approved Fax as a valid method of service of a document but said that, to be valid as a method of service, the onus was on the sender of the document to prove that the document, in complete and legible form, had arrived at the recipient's terminal.

4.4. The Protocol

4.4.1. Paragraph 6 of the Protocol provides as follows:

'On exchange the buyer's solicitor shall send or deliver to the seller's solicitor:

6.1 The signed contract with all names, dates and financial information completed.

6.2 The deposit provided in the manner prescribed in the contract. Under the Law Society's Formula C the deposit may have to be sent to another solicitor nominated by the seller's solicitor.

6.3 If contracts are exchanged by telephone, the procedures laid down by the Law Society's Formulae A, B or C must be used and both solicitors must ensure (unless otherwise agreed) that the undertakings to send documents and pay the deposit on that day are strictly observed.

6.4 If contracts are exchanged in the post the seller's solicitor shall, once the buyer's signed contract and deposit are held unconditionally, having ensured that details of each contract are fully completed and identical, send the seller's signed contract on the day of exchange.'

4.5. Standard Conditions of Sale

4.5.1. Condition 2.1 governs the making of the contract and allows contracts to be exchanged by document exchange, by post, or by telephone using the Law Society's Formulae.

C.05. After exchange

See also: Insurance, para. C.03.

5.1.   The effects of exchange

5.1.1.   A binding contract exists from which normally neither party may withdraw without incurring liability for breach.

5.1.2.   The beneficial ownership in the property passes to the buyer who becomes entitled to any increase in value of the property, but also bears the risk of any loss or damage; hence the need to ensure that insurance of the property is effective from the moment of exchange.[1] However, Standard Condition 5.1 states that the risk in the property is to remain with the seller until completion.

5.1.3.   The seller retains the legal title to the property until completion, but holds the beneficial interest on behalf of the buyer. During this period the seller is entitled to remain in possession of the property and to the rents and profits (unless otherwise agreed). He must also discharge the outgoings, e.g. water rates until completion. He owes a duty of care to the buyer and will be liable to the buyer in damages if loss is caused to the property through neglect or wanton destruction.[2] This duty continues so long as the seller is entitled to possession of the property and does not terminate because the seller vacates the property before completion.[3]

5.1.4.   From the moment that a binding contract exists between the parties two equitable liens arise, enforceable only through a court order for sale of the property. The seller's lien on the buyer's equitable interest is for the balance of the purchase price and if this is not paid in full on completion the lien attaches to the legal estate in the hands of the buyer. The buyer's lien is on the seller's legal estate for any deposit paid to the seller in the capacity of agent (but not as stakeholder), and in the case of unregistered land would not bind another buyer from the seller unless registered as a Class C(iii) land charge under Land Charges Act 1972. In the case of registered land the lien could be protected by a caution, although this would not be necessary if the buyer was already in occupation of the property as the lien would then constitute an overriding interest within Land Registration Act 1925, s.70(i)(g).[4] Protection of the lien by registration is not normally considered to be necessary, but should be undertaken immediately if problems arise between the parties in the period between contract and completion.

1. In *National Carriers Ltd.* v. *Panalpina (Northern) Ltd.* [1981] A.C. 675 it was held that the doctrine of frustration can, in exceptional cases, apply to leases. Thus if a leasehold property were to be totally destroyed between exchange and completion, it is arguable that the buyer could not be forced to complete. The same case contains

dicta to the effect that the doctrine may also be applicable to freehold land, but to date there has been no decided case where the doctrine has been held to apply, and it is therefore unsafe to assume that the buyer will be discharged from his obligations following total destruction of the property.

2. *Clarke* v. *Ramuz* [1891] 2 Q.B. 456; *Phillips* v. *Lamdin* [1949] 2 K.B. 33.
3. *Lucie-Smith* v. *Gorman* [1981] C.L.Y. 2866.
4. *London & Cheshire Insurance Co. Ltd.* v. *Laplagrene Property Co. Ltd.* [1971] Ch. 499.

5.2. After exchange

5.2.1. *The seller*

(a) Inform the client and estate agent that exchange has taken place and enter completion date in diary or file prompt system.

(b) Where, immediately after exchange, the seller is in possession of both copies of the contract, the seller's solicitor should check that both parts of the contract have been dated and bear the agreed completion date. The copy of the contract signed by the seller should immediately be sent to the buyer's solicitor to fulfil any undertaking given in the course of an exchange by telephone.

(c) Any deposit received must immediately be paid into an interest-bearing clients' deposit account.

(d) If any preliminary deposit has been held by an estate agent, the agent should be asked to remit such sum to the seller's solicitor who is normally required under the contract to hold 'the deposit', i.e. the whole of the amount specified in the contract as the contractual deposit (see Standard Condition 2.2). The agent may be reluctant to part with the money, preferring to hold it on account for any commission due to him.

(e) If not already done, the seller should deduce title to the buyer.

5.2.2. *The buyer*

(a) Inform the client and his lender that exchange has taken place and enter completion date in diary or file prompt system.

(b) Where exchange has taken place by telephone, immediately send to the seller (or as directed by him) the signed contract and deposit cheque in accordance with the undertaking given, having first checked that the contract is dated and bears the agreed completion date.

(c) Where appropriate, protect the contract by registration. (See below, para. 5.3.)

5.3. Protection of the contract

5.3.1. *Registered land*

The contract constitutes a minor interest which, in order to be binding on future buyers of an interest in the land, needs to be protected by entry of a notice or caution on the register of the title. Where the seller has a subsisting mortgage on the property, so that the land certificate is already held by HM Land Registry, it is possible to enter a notice on the charges register which will bind all comers except the subsisting lender. In other cases, unless the seller is willing to place his Land Certificate on deposit at the Registry, it is only possible to enter a caution which does not give quite such good protection to the buyer because of the need to take further action to substantiate the buyer's claim if and when the caution is 'warned off'. The contract, once protected on the register, will bind all future buyers of interests in the land, but would not take priority over another buyer who had made an official search before registration of the contract and who lodged his own application for registration within the priority period afforded by his search. A buyer who is in possession of the property could establish that the contract constituted an overriding interest within Land Registration Act 1925, s.70(1)(*g*), in which case protection of the contract by registration would seem to be unnecessary.

5.3.2. *Unregistered land*

The contract is an estate contract within the Class C(iv) category of land charge and will be void against a buyer of the legal estate for money or money's worth if not registered. Registration must be made against the name of the legal estate owner for the time being.[1] Care needs to be exercised when effecting the registration of sub-contracts, where the buyer under the sub-contract needs to register his C(iv) against the current owner of the legal estate who will not be his immediate seller.

> Example:
> A contracts to sell to B.
> Before completion of this contract B contracts to sell to C.
> If C seeks to protect his estate contract, he must register his Class C(iv) land charge against A who will be the owner of the legal estate until completion of the contract between himself and B.

5.3.3.
Options to purchase and rights of pre-emption also require registration within this category.

5.3.4. *Registration of the contract*

Since the contract is capable of registration, a solicitor who fails to register, thereby causing loss to his client, may be liable in negligence to the client. However, since completion of most contracts occurs within a very short period following exchange, in practice registration of the contract is uncommon.

Consideration should always be given to the question of whether or not a particular contract requires protection by registration and the contract should always be registered if any of the circumstances listed below in para. 5.3.5. apply.

5.3.5. *Guidelines*

Registration of the contract is desirable in any of the situations listed below. The following is not an exhaustive list of all the circumstances in which registration is desirable. If the solicitor is in any doubt, he should err on the side of caution and register the contract in order to protect his client's interests:

(a) there is to be a long interval (e.g. more than two months) between contract and completion;

(b) there is reason to doubt the seller's good faith;

(c) a dispute arises between the seller and buyer;

(d) the seller delays completion beyond the contractual date;

(e) the purchase price is to be paid by instalments, the conveyance or transfer to be executed after payment of the final instalment;

(f) the transaction is a sub-sale.

1. *Barrett* v. *Hilton Developments Ltd.* [1975] Ch. 237.

D. TITLE
D.01. Deducing title

See also: Seller's investigation of title, para. B.03.
Defective title and restrictive covenant insurance, para. B.06.
Acting on grant of lease, para. K.01.
Assignment of leases, para. K.11.

1.1. Time for deduction of title

1.1.1. Traditionally the seller deduces title to the buyer after exchange of contracts. The practice of delaying deduction of title until after exchange is purely historical in its origins; since the preparation of an abstract in traditional form was both time-consuming and expensive, the seller was reluctant to engage in this exercise until he was sure of the buyer's commitment to the transaction. This traditional practice has become disadvantageous to the buyer because it results in the buyer having to commit himself to a binding contract to purchase the land without knowing whether the seller can in fact make good title. If the seller were unable to show a good title to the land the buyer would be able to withdraw from the contract and sue the seller for breach (subject to the seller's right to rescind under a contractual term), but this remedy would be little consolation to a buyer who was involved in a chain of transactions, who might therefore find himself able to withdraw from his contract to buy the property, but still committed to sell his own house to a third party.

1.1.2. Only in exceptional cases should deduction of title be delayed until after contracts have been exchanged.

1.1.3. Where the Protocol is used, by para. 4.3, the seller is required to send evidence of his title to the buyer with the draft contract and other pre-contract documentation.

1.1.4. Standard Condition 4.1.1, in requiring evidence of title to be supplied 'immediately after making the contract', reflects the traditional practice of supplying the evidence of title after exchange of contracts. Despite this condition, in most cases deduction of title will in practice take place before exchange of contracts.

1.2. Seller's obligations

1.2.1. The seller's obligation in relation to the deduction of his title is to supply sufficient documentary evidence to the buyer to prove that the seller is either the outright owner of the land he has contracted to sell or, if not, that he is in a position to compel someone else to transfer the land to the buyer or is a lender whose power of sale has arisen and become exercisable, thus entitling him to sell the land. It is not enough to show that the seller is able to ask a third party to transfer the land to the buyer; the seller must be able to force or oblige the third party to execute the purchase deed, e.g. where the land is held in the name of a company, the seller would need to own a controlling shareholding in that company in order to be able to compel the company to convey to the buyer.[1]

1. See *Re Bryant and Barningham's Contract* (1890) 44 Ch. 218; *cf. Elliott* v. *Pierson* [1948] Ch. 452.

1.3. Method of deduction in registered land

1.3.1. Land Registration Act 1925, s.110 provides that the seller shall supply the buyer with:

    (a) a copy of the entries on the register of title;

    (b) a copy of the filed plan;

    (c) an abstract or other evidence of matters as to which the register is not conclusive, e.g. overriding interests; and

    (d) copies or abstracts of any document(s) noted on the register (except charges or incumbrances to be discharged or overridden at completion).

1.3.2. The items listed in (a), (b) and (d) above cannot be excluded by contractual condition. Where the sale is *inter alia* of part of the seller's land on a building estate, a certificate in Form 102 may be substituted for the copy of the filed plan.

1.3.3. Although not required by the statute, both the Protocol and Standard Condition 4.2.1 require the seller at his own expense to supply office copies of his title to the buyer. Office copies should always be supplied since they usually show the up-to-date position of the register − ordinary photocopies of the land or charge certificate may not have been updated by the Land Registry for several years and may therefore not reflect the true state of the register. The office copies supplied to the buyer must be originals (not photocopies) and of recent date. Later, when making a search at HM Land Registry, the buyer will need to search from the date of an office copy issued within the previous 12 months.

1.4. Method of deduction in unregistered land

1.4.1. The seller will prove his ownership of unregistered land by supplying the buyer with an abstract or epitome of the documents comprising the title. In some cases the evidence supplied will be made up of a combination of these two styles of presentation.

1.4.2. An abstract of title is in essence a summary of all the documents comprised in the title. The preparation of an abstract in traditional form is a skilled and time-consuming task which has largely been superseded by the practice of supplying an epitome of the title supported by photocopies of all the documents referred to.

1.4.3. An epitome of title is a schedule of the documents comprising the title. The documents should be numbered and listed in chronological order, starting with the earliest in time. Each document should be identified as to its date, type (e.g. conveyance, assent, etc.), the names of the parties to it, whether a copy of the document is supplied with the epitome, and whether or not the original of the document will be handed to the buyer on completion. Photocopies of the documents which accompany the epitome must be of good quality, marked to show the document's corresponding number on the list shown by the epitome, and any plans included in the documents must be coloured or marked so that they are identical to the original document from which the copy has been made. Before the epitome and copy documents are sent to the buyer the seller's solicitor should check that all the copies are legible and bear the appropriate markings as outlined in the preceding sentence, and that all pages are complete and assembled in the correct sequence. The paper on which the epitome is supplied must be sufficiently permanent and durable to last in a clearly legible state throughout the likely period of its need as evidence of the title. An epitome which is supplied by means of a faxed copy may not at present satisfy these requirements unless the originals of all the documents referred to are to be handed over on completion. Thus if a seller delivers the epitome by fax, in a situation where all of the original documents will not be handed over on completion, he should deliver a further copy of the abstract to the buyer, by post or document exchange, such further copy being produced on non-glossy A4 size durable paper.

1.4.4. *Documents to be included in the epitome*

1.4.4.1. Root of title

The epitome must commence with a good root of title, as specified by a special condition in the contract. A good root of title is a document which, at the date of the contract:

(a) is at least 15 years old;[1]

(b) deals with or shows the ownership of the whole legal and equitable interest contracted to be sold;

(c) contains an adequate description of the property; and

(d) contains nothing to cast any doubt on the title.

1.4.4.2. A conveyance on sale or legal mortgage which satisfies the above requirements is generally acknowledged to be the most acceptable root of title because it effectively offers a double guarantee on the title. The buyer in the present transaction will be investigating the seller's title for a minimum period of 15 years;

the buyer under the root conveyance would similarly have investigated title over a period of at least 15 years when he bought the property. Thus the present buyer is provided with the certainty of the soundness of the title over a period of at least 30 years. If there is no conveyance on sale on the title which satisfies the requirements of a good root, a legal mortgage provides an acceptable alternative. Since a lender will not lend money on the security of a property without investigating the title, a legal mortgage used as a root document provides a similar double guarantee of the title to that afforded by a conveyance on sale. In the absence of both a conveyance on sale and a legal mortgage, title may be commenced with either a voluntary conveyance or an assent dated after 1925.[2] Since both of these documents effect gifts of the land, no investigation of prior title would have taken place at the time when they were executed, and they do not therefore provide the double check on the title which is given by the conveyance on sale or the legal mortgage and for this reason are less satisfactory to a buyer when offered as roots of title. They should therefore only be offered as roots of title (and accepted as such by the buyer) where, after investigation of all the title documents available to the seller, no better root can be found. The nature of the root document will be specified by special condition in the contract, and if the buyer does not consider the root being offered to be adequate he must raise this problem with the seller before contracts are exchanged; once contracts have been exchanged, it is too late to vary the terms of the contract. If, however, it transpired that the seller was ultimately unable to prove his title to the property, the buyer could withdraw from the contract.

1.4.4.3. Less than statutory minimum title is offered

Only in very rare cases will it be found that the seller cannot provide the buyer with a root of title which satisfies the statutory minimum period of 15 years prescribed by Law of Property Act 1925, s.44 (as amended). A buyer who is offered a short title should not accept the situation until he has received a satisfactory explanation for the reasons for the short root from the seller and should be advised that, in accepting less than his statutory entitlement under Law of Property Act 1925, he is also assuming the risk of being bound by incumbrances on the title which he has had no opportunity of discovering or investigating. The risk of being bound by undiscovered incumbrances stretches backwards in time, not just to the statutory 15-year period, but to the date of the first document on the title (however old) which would satisfy the requirements for a good root. A short root should not be accepted by the buyer without a full investigation of the circumstances, the concurrence of his lender, and investigation of the possibility of obtaining defective title insurance, preferably at the seller's expense. The acceptance by the buyer of a short root of title may also affect his ability to obtain registration with an absolute title at HM Land Registry.

1.4.4.4. Documents to be included in the abstract or epitome

From the root of title, all dealings with the legal and equitable interests in the land down to and including the interests of the present seller must be shown, thus constituting an unbroken chain of ownership stretching from the seller named in the root document to the present day. This includes the following:

(a) evidence of devolutions on death (death certificates, grants of representation, assents);

(b) change of name of an estate owner, e.g. marriage certificate, deed poll or statutory declaration;

(c) discharge of legal mortgages;

(d) documents prior to the root which contain details of restrictive covenants which affect the property;

(e) memoranda endorsed on documents of title, e.g. recording a sale of part, assent to a beneficiary, or severance of a beneficial joint tenancy;

(f) powers of attorney under which a document within the title has been executed.

1.4.4.5. Documents which need not be included in the abstract or epitome

Certain documents need not be included in the abstract or epitome, although in some cases their inclusion will be helpful to the buyer and may forestall queries on the title raised by the buyer. They include:

(a) documents of record and Land Charges Department search certificates (but it is good practice to include these so that the buyer can see which searches have been correctly made in the past, in which case he need not repeat the search during his own investigation of the title). It is recommended that documents of record should always be abstracted so that the buyer receives a complete picture of the title and one on which he can act immediately. Failure to supply such documents may lead to delay while, e.g. the buyer obtains a document which was not supplied by the seller;

(b) documents relating to equitable interests which will be overreached on completion of the current transaction (the buyer may discover these charges when he makes his pre-completion searches and if he has already been supplied with information about them he will not need to raise last-minute queries with the seller or to delay completion while he investigates them; therefore as a matter of good practice some notice of their existence should be given to the buyer);

(c) leases which have expired by effluxion of time (but if the tenant is still in possession of the property, possibly with the benefit of security of tenure, evidence of the terms on which the tenant enjoys the property should be supplied). Although leases which have been surrendered should be abstracted, together with evidence of the surrender, it is common practice not to provide evidence of leases which no longer affect the title;

(d) documents which pre-date the root of title except where a document within the title refers to the earlier document[3] (note that where a document within the title has been executed under a power of attorney, the power must be abstracted whatever its date);

(e) documents relating to discharged equitable interests in the land, e.g. receipted equitable mortgages.

1.4.4.6. Standard Condition 4.2.3 requires the seller to produce to the buyer (at the seller's expense) the original of every relevant document, or an abstract, epitome or copy with an original marking by a solicitor of examination either against the original or against an examined abstract or an examined copy.

1.4.4.7. If the title documents produced by the seller do not adequately show the physical extent of the property or its title, the seller may have to supplement the evidence of title with a statutory declaration. By Standard Condition 4.3 the seller is relieved of the obligation to define precisely the boundaries of the property, or to show the ownership of fences, hedges, ditches or walls, or to identify separately parts of the property with different titles, further than he is able to from information in his possession, but the buyer may, if reasonable, call for a statutory declaration as to the facts of these matters. If the land cannot be properly identified or described from its description in the title deeds and contract, the buyer is entitled to call for a plan, to be prepared at the seller's expense. In other cases if the buyer insists on describing the property by means of a plan, he must bear the cost of preparation of the plan himself.

1.4.4.8. Documents which will not be handed over on completion

The epitome must specify which documents will be handed to the buyer on completion and which will be retained by the seller. The buyer is entitled on completion to take the originals or marked abstracts or marked copies of all the documents within the title except those which relate to an interest in the land which is retained by the seller, e.g. on a sale of part the seller will retain the title deeds in order to be able to prove his ownership of the land retained by him. Similarly, a general power of attorney will be retained because the donee of the power needs to keep the original document in order to deal with other property owned by the donor, and personal representatives will retain their original grant in order to administer the remainder of the deceased's estate.

1. Law of Property Act 1925, s.44, as amended by Law of Property Act 1969.
2. Before 1926 there was no requirement for an assent to be in writing, and an oral assent alone would not have been capable of satisfying the definition of a good root of title.
3. Law of Property Act 1925, s.45.

1.5. **Sub-sales**

1.5.1. Neither Law of Property Act 1925, s.44 nor Land Registration Act 1925, s.110 appears to apply to a contract for a sub-sale. The buyer will require his immediate seller to deduce title to him as if these sections (whichever is relevant) did apply to the transaction, otherwise the buyer will not be sure of purchasing a good title, but the seller, until he completes his own purchase, may not be in a position to deduce such a title to the buyer. In any event the requirements for the deduction of title in these circumstances must be specifically dealt with by a special condition in the contract since there are no common law rules applicable to this situation.[1]

1.5.2. Land Registration Act 1925 s.110(5), which cannot be excluded by the contract provides that a seller who is not registered as proprietor will, at the seller's expense, either procure such registration or procure a disposition from the proprietor to the buyer.

1. See also paras. B.04. and B.14.

1.6.   Leaseholds

1.6.1.   Deduction of title to leaseholds is discussed in section K.

D.02. Investigation of title

See also: Mortgages: acting for lender and borrower, para. A.11.
Seller's investigation of title, para. B.03.
Defective title and restrictive covenant insurance, para. B.06.
Requisitions on title, para. D.03.
Pre-completion searches, para. E.02.
Lenders, section H.

2.1. Purpose of investigation

2.1.1. The seller having supplied the buyer with evidence of his title, the buyer's task is to investigate that evidence to ensure that the seller is able to transfer that which he has contracted to sell and that there are no defects in that title which would adversely affect the interests of the buyer or his lender.

2.1.2. Any matters which are unclear or unsatisfactory on the face of the documentary evidence supplied by the seller may be raised as queries (requisitions) with the seller within the time-limits specified in the contract for raising requisitions.[1]

2.1.3. Investigation will be carried out by the solicitor on behalf of his buyer and/or lender client. Where the same solicitor is acting for both the buyer and his lender in a simultaneous transaction investigation is carried out only once, bearing in mind the particular requirements of each client.[2]

2.1.4. If ultimately the seller cannot show a good title, the buyer is entitled to withdraw from the contract. Prima facie the seller's inability to show title is a breach of contract entitling the buyer to a remedy in damages, but in practice the buyer's right to damages may, in certain circumstances, be curtailed or precluded by express provision in the contract.[3]

1. See Requisitions on title, para. D.03.
2. See Mortgages: acting for lender and borrower, para. A.11.; The buyer's mortgage, para. E.03.; Lenders, section H.
3. See Requisitions on title, para. D.03.; Delay and remedies, section M.

2.2.   Time for investigation

2.2.1.   Conventionally investigation of title follows deduction of title as a procedure which is undertaken after exchange of contracts and is subject to time-limits imposed by the contract.[1]

2.2.2.   In practice the seller will usually supply his evidence of title at the draft contract stage of the transaction (and in Protocol cases must do so) and may, by inclusion of a contractual provision to such effect, prevent the buyer from raising his requisitions after exchange, thus compelling the buyer to carry out his investigation at that stage of the transaction.

1. See Standard Condition 4.1.

2.3.   Registered land

2.3.1.   Investigation of title comprises:

(a)   an examination of the office copy entries and filed plan supplied by the seller (including a copy of the lease where the title is leasehold and documents which are referred to on the register and evidence relating to matters as to which the register is not conclusive);[1]

(b)   checking for evidence of overriding interests since these cannot be entered on the register but are binding on the buyer irrespective of notice; and

(c)   pre-completion searches.[2]

2.3.2.   Particular points which may arise out of the examination of the office copy entries are dealt with below and in paras. 2.6. *et seq.*

2.3.3.   The existence of most overriding interests can be discovered through:

(a)   pre-contract enquiries of the seller under which the seller will normally be asked to reveal details of adverse interests and occupiers' rights. A seller who did not disclose such matters might be liable to the buyer for non-disclosure;[3]

(b)   a local land charges search (local land charges are overriding interests);

(c)   inspection of the property before exchange which may reveal, e.g. occupiers, easements, or adverse possession. The buyer may also be advised to reinspect immediately prior to completion.

2.3.4.   The examination of office copy entries in registered land is a relatively quick and simple process. So long as a note is made of any matters on which requisitions need to be raised the method of investigation to be employed with a registered title is a matter to be decided by the solicitor concerned.

2.3.5. *Office copy entries*

The following points should be checked:

   (a) on the property register:

      (i)   the description of the land accords with the contract description;

      (ii)   the title number corresponds with that given on the contract;

      (iii) the estate — is it freehold or leasehold?

      (iv) easements enjoyed by the property (if they are entered on the register);[4]

      (v)   has any land been removed from the title? If so, does this affect the land being purchased?

   (b) on the proprietorship register:

      (i)   is the class of title correct?

      (ii)   is the seller the registered proprietor? If not, who has the ability to transfer the land?

      (iii) the existence and effect of any entries (cautions, restrictions, or inhibitions);[5]

   (c) on the charges register:

      (i)   are there any incumbrances?

      (ii)   how do these affect the buyer?

      (iii) which of them will be removed or discharged on completion and how will their removal be effected?

   (d) on the filed plan:

      (i)   is the land being bought included within the title?

      (ii)   check any colourings/hatchings which may indicate rights of way, the extent of covenants or land which has been removed from the title;

   (e) the date of issue of the office copies — they must be less than 12 months old at the date of the buyer's pre-completion search.

2.3.6. *Adverse entries on the proprietorship register*

The most commonly found entry on the proprietorship register will be a restriction which usually indicates that the beneficial interest in the land may not belong to the registered proprietor. The wording of the restriction will indicate what procedure must be followed in order to conduct a valid disposition of the land. The buyer must therefore either follow that procedure (e.g. payment of money to two trustees in the case of land held on trust for sale) or require the seller to procure the removal of the restriction from the register on or before completion. In some cases an inhibition will be found on the proprietorship register (usually only in connection with the bankruptcy of the proprietor) which will prevent any disposition of the land until it is removed. A third party who asserts rights in the land may place a caution on the proprietorship register which means that no dealing with the land can be registered until the cautioner has been given the opportunity by the Chief Land Registrar to show cause why the dealing to the buyer should not proceed.

1. See Standard Condition 4.2.1.
2. See Pre-completion searches, para. E.02.
3. See Seller's duty of disclosure, para. B.05.
4. See also Access to neighbouring land, para. B.27.4.
5. See para. 2.3.6.

2.4. Unregistered land

2.4.1. Investigation of title comprises:

    (a) an examination of the documents supplied in the abstract or epitome to check that:

        (i) the root document is as provided for by the contract or, if none is specified, complies with Law of Property Act 1925, s.44.[1] The root document will usually have been specified by special condition of the contract. Once contracts have been exchanged it is too late to object to the date or nature of the deed being offered as a root of title. If the wrong document has been supplied, the buyer is entitled to insist on the correct document being supplied in its place. Both parties may agree to substitute a different document as the root of title;

        (ii) there is an unbroken chain of ownership beginning with the seller in the root document and ending with the present seller;

        (iii) there are no defects in the title which will adversely affect the buyer's title or the interests of his mortgagee;

    (b) verification, i.e. inspection of the original deeds;[2]

    (c) checking for evidence of occupiers (this is normally done by inspection of the property);

    (d) pre-completion searches.[3]

1. See Deducing title, para. D.01.
2. See below, para. 2.13.
3. See Pre-completion searches, para. E.02.

2.5. Method of investigation (unregistered land)

2.5.1. Examination of an unregistered title can be a complex and time-consuming business. It is essential that each of the documents within the abstract or epitome is carefully scrutinised to ensure that it is in order and a note made of any irregularities which need to be clarified by way of requisitions with the seller.

2.5.2.   To ensure that nothing is overlooked on investigation it is recommended that the solicitor adopts and follows a systematic and thorough method of investigation of an unregistered title and allows himself sufficient time in which to carry out this procedure at an unhurried pace. Except in the simplest cases, written notes of the title should be made while carrying out the investigation so that these notes can be used as the basis for framing requisitions and, if needed, will be available for reference at a later stage of the transaction.

2.5.3.   *Method*[1]

     (a)   Check each document chronologically starting with the root.

     (b)   Is the root as provided for in the contract?[2]

     (c)   Is there an unbroken chain of title from the root to the present day?

Then, in each document within the abstract or epitome, check the following points, making written notes of any matter which needs to be clarified or rechecked:

     (d)   **Date**

         A deed is not invalid because it is not dated or is wrongly dated, but the date of the document will:

         (i)   establish whether a root document is a good root;[3]

         (ii)   affect the amount of stamp duty payable;

         (iii)   affect its vulnerability under the Insolvency Act 1986 in the case of a voluntary disposition;

         (iv)   assist in making a reasoned judgment on an apparent defect in title, e.g. a technical defect in a document which is over 15 years old may be less detrimental to the title than one contained in a more recent document.

     (e)   **Stamp duties**

         Ad valorem duties and particulars delivered stamp. The amount of duty will depend on the nature of the document, the value of the consideration and the date of the document. The seller must be required to rectify any irregularities of this nature. If no certificate of value is included in the document, stamp duty at full rate should have been paid on the conveyance.

     (f)   **Parties**

         For example, are the seller's names as shown on the previous document?

     (g)   **Description of the property**

         Does it accord with what the buyer is purchasing?

(h) **Acknowledgments for production of earlier deeds?**

(i) **Execution**

Have all formalities been observed?

(j) **Powers of attorney**

Is the disposition by the attorney valid and are subsequent buyers protected?

(k) **Endorsements on deeds**

Are those that are necessary present, and are there any adverse memoranda?

(l) **Incumbrances**

What are they? Are they as expected? Is there a chain of indemnity covenants where required?

(m) **Easements and rights**

Are these as expected? Do they follow down the chain? Have any been added or taken away?[4]

(n) **Receipt clause**

This is evidence (although not necessarily conclusive evidence) that the seller's lien for the unpaid purchase price has been extinguished.[5]

(o) **Searches supplied with the abstract**

Have searches against all previous estate owners been abstracted or are there gaps? Are the names and periods searched against correct? Did completion take place within the priority period?

(p) **Compulsory registration**

Check that there has been no conveyance on sale since the area became one of compulsory registration. The date of the compulsory registration order can be checked from HM Land Registry Explanatory Leaflet No.9. If necessary the seller should be required to register before completion.

1. Particular points which may arise out of the examination of the abstract or epitome are dealt with in paras. 2.6. *et seq.*
2. See above, para. 2.4.1.
3. See above, para. 2.4.1.

4. See also Access to neighbouring land, para. B.27.4.
5. See *London & Cheshire Insurance Co. Ltd.* v. *Laplagrene Property Co. Ltd.* [1971] Ch. 499.

2.6.   **Root of title**

2.6.1.   Documents which are capable of being used as a good root of title are listed in para. D.01.4.4.1.

2.6.2.   The document which is to constitute the root will be specified by a special condition in the contract and once contracts have been exchanged cannot be changed except with the consent of both parties (and, where relevant, the buyer's lender).

2.6.3.   Generally the buyer cannot require evidence of title prior to the root except:[1]

(a)   he is always entitled to a copy of a power of attorney under which any abstracted document is executed;

(b)   where an abstracted document refers to an earlier document, he may call for that earlier document, e.g. where an abstracted document refers to restrictive covenants imposed by a pre-root conveyance, the document imposing the covenants may be called for;

(c)   where an abstracted document describes the property by reference to a plan which is attached to or referred to in an earlier document, that earlier document may be called for so that the plan may be examined;

(d)   any document creating any limitation or trust by reference to which any part of the property is disposed of by an abstracted document may be called for even if dated pre-root.

1. Law of Property Act 1925, s.45.

2.7.   **Conveyance by trustees to themselves**

2.7.1.   If on the title there is a conveyance by trustees or personal representatives to one of themselves, enquiry must be made into the circumstances of the transaction since, on the face of it, such a conveyance is in breach of trust and is voidable by the beneficiaries without enquiry as to fairness.

2.7.2.   Such a transaction can be justified if one of the following situations exists:

(a)   there is proof of a pre-existing contract to purchase, an option or right of pre-emption in favour of the trustee or personal representative;

(b)   the personal representative was a beneficiary under the will or intestacy of the seller;

(c)   the consent of all the beneficiaries being legally competent was obtained to the transaction;

(d)   the conveyance was made under an order of the court;

(e)   the transaction was sanctioned by the trust instrument.

2.8.   Particular capacities

2.8.1.   Trustees of land

2.8.1.1. Registered land

In registered land, a restriction may be entered on the proprietorship register which will indicate to the buyer what must be done to overreach the beneficiaries' interests. Provided the terms of the restriction are complied with the buyer will get good title. Where trustees hold the land on trust for themselves as joint tenants in equity, no restriction is placed on the register and the buyer may safely deal with the survivor on proof of death of the other trustee.

2.8.1.2. Unregistered land

(a) Such trustees have a wide power of sale,[1] and if consents are required to a sale a buyer is not concerned to see that the consents of more than two persons are obtained and is never concerned with the consents of persons under disability (i.e. minors, persons under mental incapacity).

(b) A buyer paying his money to the trustees, being at least two individuals or a trust corporation, will take the land free from the equitable interests of the beneficiaries, but not otherwise.[2] Thus a conveyance on the title by a sole individual trustee will require investigation.

2.8.2.   Personal representatives

2.8.2.1. Registered land

On production of the grant, personal representatives may become registered as proprietors of the land, in which case, provided the buyer deals with the registered proprietors and complies with any restriction on the register, he will get good title. Personal representatives would not normally register themselves as proprietors unless they intended to hold on to the land without disposing it for some period of time, e.g. during the minority of a beneficiary. In other cases the personal representatives will produce their grant of representation to the buyer as proof of their authority to deal with the land. Provided the buyer takes a transfer from all the proving personal representatives and submits an office copy or certified copy of the grant with his application for registration, he will obtain a good title. An assent made by personal representatives to a beneficiary must be in the form prescribed under Land Registration Rules 1925.

2.8.2.2. Unregistered land

(a) Personal representatives have the wide powers of trustees of land. If there is only one proving personal representative he has all the powers of two or more personal representatives and consequently (unlike a sole individual trustee) can convey the land on his own and give a valid receipt for the proceeds of sale. If, however, the grant is made to two or more personal representatives, they must all join in the assent or conveyance, but a sole proving personal representative is entitled to act on his own. A buyer must therefore call for the grant to see who have been appointed as personal representatives, and must insist that all the personal representatives named in the grant join in the assent or conveyance, or call for evidence of the death of any personal representative who will not be a party to the purchase deed.

(b) An assent made by personal representatives must be in writing in order to pass the legal estate in the land to the beneficiary. The beneficiary who is to take the land must be named in the document, which must be signed by the personal representatives. If the document contains covenants given by the beneficiary (e.g. indemnity in respect of existing restrictive covenants) it must be by deed. Even where the beneficiary is also the sole personal representative (as may be the case where a widow is her deceased husband's sole personal representative and sole beneficiary) a written assent is required.[3]

(c) The effect of Administration of Estates Act 1925, s.36 is that an assent in favour of a beneficiary may be defeated by a later sale of the land by the personal representatives in favour of a buyer who takes from them a written statement that they have made no previous assent or conveyance of the land. However, this will not be the case if either there was an endorsement of a previous assent on the grant or there had been a previous sale by the assentee. It follows that a conveyance on sale by personal representatives should contain a section 36(6) statement and that an assentee (and a buyer) should require an endorsement on the grant. This may be done at the cost of the estate. Where the transaction induces first registration an endorsement on the grant is not required.

(d) A disposition by personal representatives should contain an acknowledgment of the right to production of their grant of representation as this is a document of title the inspection of which may be required by subsequent buyers of the land. The grant should be inspected to check for endorsements which have been made on it.

(e) An assent or conveyance by personal representatives of a legal estate is sufficient evidence in favour of a buyer that the person in whose favour it is made is the person entitled to have the legal estate conveyed to him, unless there is a memorandum of a previous assent or conveyance on the grant. This in effect means that a buyer from an assentee of land, having checked the grant and found no adverse endorsements, does not have to look at the deceased's will to check that the assentee was rightly entitled to the land, but this provision will not protect the buyer if it is apparent from some other source (e.g. the assent itself) that it was made in favour of the wrong person.[4]

(f) On a sale by the personal representatives of the survivor of beneficial joint tenants, a statement should be included in the conveyance to the effect that the survivor was solely and beneficially entitled so that the buyer has the protection of Law of Property (Joint Tenants) Act 1964. If such personal representatives did not sell the land but made an assent in favour of a beneficiary, the assent should properly include the above statement in order to protect a buyer from the assentee. If the statement was missing from the assent, consideration should be given to joining the personal representatives of the survivor into the conveyance by the assentee in order to give the statement.

(g) If a sole or sole surviving trustee of a trust of land dies in a case where a buyer cannot rely on the 1964 Act (because the survivor was not solely and beneficially entitled), his personal representatives can exercise all the powers of that trustee. If a sole personal representative is appointed in such a situation, he can act on his own in dealing with the deceased's private property (including land), but he must act jointly with another trustee in making a disposition of the trust property under which capital money arises.

2.8.3. Co-owners

2.8.3.1. Co-owners hold land on a trust of land and the remarks relating to trustees in para. 2.8.1. above apply.

2.8.3.2. Registered land

If the co-owners are tenants in common in equity, a restriction will be entered on the proprietorship register to the effect that a disposition of the land under which capital money arises must be conducted by two trustees or by a trust corporation. In the event of the death of one or more of the co-owners, so that at the time of sale there is only one surviving trustee, a second trustee must be appointed to join with the survivor in the transfer. Alternatively, the buyer can deal with the survivor alone provided that the restriction is removed from the register, or the survivor provides the buyer with documentary evidence which will enable the restriction to be removed on the buyer's application for registration. Such proof would consist of a certified or office copy of the grant of representation, an assent made in favour of the survivor and a statutory declaration by the survivor that he has not encumbered or dealt with his own half share nor has he received notice of any incumbrance on or dealing with the deceased's half share. In practice, it is better either for the seller to procure the removal of the restriction or to appoint a second trustee to act with the seller.

2.8.3.3. If the co-owners are joint tenants in equity, no restriction is placed on the register and a buyer may deal with the survivor of them on proof of the death of the deceased co-owner.

2.8.3.4. Unregistered land

(a) Inspection of the conveyance under which the co-owners bought the land will reveal whether they held as joint tenants or tenants in common in equity.

(b) The sole survivor of tenants in common does not automatically become entitled to the whole equitable estate in the land since a tenancy in common is capable of passing by will or on intestacy. The trust therefore still subsists and a buyer from the survivor should insist on taking a conveyance only from two trustees in order to overreach any beneficial interests which may subsist under the trust. Alternatively, if the survivor has become solely and beneficially entitled to the whole legal and equitable interest in the land, he may convey alone on proof to the buyer of this fact. Such proof would consist of the death certificate of the deceased, a certified or office copy of the grant of representation and an assent made in favour of the survivor.

(c) The survivor of beneficial joint tenants becomes entitled to the whole legal and equitable interest in the land but a buyer from him will only accept a conveyance from the survivor alone if he can be satisfied that he will gain the protection of Law of Property (Joint Tenants) Act 1964. This Act (which is retrospective in operation to 1925) allows the buyer to assume that no severance of the joint tenancy (turning it into a tenancy in common) had occurred before the death of the deceased joint tenant. To gain the protection of the Act the following three conditions must all be satisfied:

(i) there must be no memorandum of severance endorsed on the conveyance under which the joint tenants bought the property;

(ii) there must be no bankruptcy proceedings registered against the names of either of the joint tenants;

(iii) the conveyance by the survivor must contain a recital stating that the survivor is solely and beneficially entitled to the land.

If any of the above conditions is not met, the survivor must be treated as a surviving tenant in common and the procedure in para. (b) above followed.

2.8.4. Settled land

2.8.4.1. Section 2 of Trusts of Land and Appointment of Trustees Act 1996 prohibits the creation of new strict settlements (except in limited circumstances). The following sub-paragraphs will generally be relevant only to settlements which were in existence on 1 January 1997.

2.8.4.2. Registered land

The tenant for life (or, if none, the statutory owners) will be registered as proprietor of the land and a restriction entered on the register which will usually require capital money arising on a transaction to be paid to the trustees of the settlement. Provided the buyer complies with the terms of the restriction he will take a good title.

2.8.4.3. Unregistered land

(a) Where land is settled land within Settled Land Act 1925, the legal estate in the land will be vested in the tenant for life under the Act by a vesting instrument, which will be a vesting deed in the case of an *inter vivos* settlement and may be a vesting assent by the personal representatives of the deceased where the settlement arises under a will. In exceptional cases, e.g. where the person who would otherwise be tenant for life is a minor, the legal estate will be vested in the trustees of the settlement as statutory owners. Both the tenant for life and the statutory owners have a wide power of sale under the Act (which can be extended by the terms of the settlement itself) but it is provided by Settled Land Act 1925, s.18 that where the land is the subject of a vesting instrument and the trustees of the settlement have not been discharged, any disposition which is not authorised by the Act or by the settlement is void. Further, where capital money arises on a disposition of the land, the disposition is of no effect for the purposes of the Act unless the money is paid to the trustees of the settlement, being at least two individuals or a trust corporation.

(b) A vesting instrument under Settled Land Act 1925 must describe the land, name the person in whose favour it is vested and name the trustees of the settlement for the purposes of the Act. Except in exceptional circumstances, a buyer is bound and entitled to rely on these statements and cannot call for the trust instrument.

2.8.5. Lenders

2.8.5.1. A power to sell the legal estate vested in the borrower, subject to prior incumbrances but discharged from subsequent ones, is given by Law of Property Act 1925, s.101 to every lender whose mortgage is made by deed. Thus unless expressly excluded the power is available to a lender who has taken a legal mortgage and to one whose equitable mortgage is made by deed. In order actually to convey the legal estate of the borrower to the buyer an equitable lender whose mortgage is not made by deed must adopt some conveyancing device such as an irrevocable power of attorney granted by way of security in his favour by the borrower. An equitable lender whose mortgage is not made by deed can apply to the court under Law of Property Act 1925, s.90 for an order for sale and an order appointing a person to convey the land. In relation to registered land, only the registered proprietor of a charge has a power of sale.

2.8.5.2. The power of sale arises when the mortgage money becomes due under the mortgage, i.e. on the legal date for redemption which is usually set at an early date in the mortgage term. The power only becomes exercisable by the lender when one of the events specified in Law of Property Act 1925, s.103 has occurred.[5] A buyer from the lender must check (by looking at the mortgage deed) that the power of sale has arisen, but is not concerned to enquire whether the power has become exercisable.

2.8.5.3. The sale must be genuine; a sale to the lender's nominee or to a company controlled by him will not be treated as a valid exercise of the power of sale.

2.8.6. Attorneys

2.8.6.1. The buyer is entitled to a copy of any power of attorney which affects the title (even if in unregistered land the power is dated earlier than the root of title). A general power of attorney under Powers of Attorney Act 1971, s.10 cannot be used by trustees or co-owners to deal with the legal estate. By checking the terms of the power itself the buyer should ensure that the transaction was authorised by the power.[6]

2.8.6.2. Registered land

The original or a certified copy of the power must be submitted when an application is made to register a disposition made in exercise of the power. If the transaction between the attorney and the buyer is not made within 12 months of the grant of the power a statutory declaration made by the buyer to the effect that he had no knowledge of the revocation of the power must accompany the application for registration. For Land Registry purposes a certified copy of a power of attorney must be certified on every page. Where the power is an enduring power an office copy of the power may be lodged at HM Land Registry. A certificate signed by the buyer's solicitor may be accepted by HM Land Registry in place of a statutory declaration. However, such certificate, to be acceptable to HM Land Registry, must be unqualified. Unless the buyer's solicitor has actual knowledge of the non-revocation of the power he cannot give an unqualified certificate.

2.8.6.3. Unregistered land

(a) Security powers under Powers of Attorney Act 1971, s.4
A buyer from an attorney holding such a power will take good title provided that he had no actual knowledge that the power had been revoked.

(b) Other non-enduring powers
A person who buys directly from the attorney will take good title under Powers of Attorney Act 1971, s.5(2) provided he buys in good faith without knowledge of the revocation of the power. Death revokes such a power; thus the buyer cannot take good title if he is aware of the death of the donor. A subsequent purchaser gains the protection of Powers of Attorney Act 1971, s.5(4) if either:

(i) the dealing between the attorney and his immediate purchaser took place within 12 months of the grant of the power; or

(ii) the person who buys directly from the attorney makes a statutory declaration within three months of completion of his transaction to the effect that he had no knowledge of the revocation of the power.

Where a person buys directly from an attorney more than 12 months after the date of the grant of the power, the buyer's solicitor should require his client immediately on completion of the transaction to make the requisite statutory declaration, since this document will be required as evidence of non-revocation on a subsequent disposition of the property. If not made immediately, and the buyer client dies before making the declaration, there will be a defect in title, since the subsequent buyer will not be able to take the protection of Powers of Attorney Act 1971, s.5(4).

(c) Enduring powers
An enduring power of attorney under Enduring Powers of Attorney Act 1985 must be in the form prescribed by the Act. Until the incapacity of the donor the power takes effect as an ordinary power and the Act contains provisions to protect buyers which are similar to those outlined above. On the incapacity of the donor the attorney's authority to act becomes limited to such acts as are necessary for the protection of the donor and his estate until such time as the power is registered with the Court of Protection. Once registered, the power is incapable of revocation and the attorney's full authority to act is restored. Where a person is buying from an attorney who holds an enduring power he should conduct a search at the Court of Protection to ensure that no application for registration of the power is pending. If the power has already been registered, the attorney should produce the registration certificate to the buyer. An office copy of the power can be produced as evidence both of the contents of the power and of its registration.

(d) Trustees
Unless an enduring power is used, one trustee cannot validly act as attorney for his sole co-trustee to deal with the legal estate.

(e) Powers granted before 1 October 1971
Such powers are governed by Law of Property Act 1925, ss.126−128 and not by Powers of Attorney Act 1971.

1. Trusts of Land and Appointment of Trustees Act 1996, s.6.
2. Law of Property Act 1925, ss.2 and 27.
3. *Re Kings Will Trusts* [1964] Ch. 542.
4. Administration of Estates Act 1925, s.36.
5. See above, para. B.07.7.4.
6. See Powers of attorney, para. B.23.

2.9. Discharged mortgages

2.9.1. Registered land

A mortgage over registered land which has been discharged will be deleted from the charges register of the title and is thus of no further concern to the buyer. As far as the seller's existing mortgage is concerned the buyer should raise a requisition requiring this to be removed on or before completion.

2.9.2. Unregistered land

(a) Discharged legal mortgages should be abstracted by the seller and checked by the buyer's solicitor to ensure that the discharge was validly effected. Discharged equitable mortgages will not normally be abstracted and once discharged no longer affect the title.

(b) Where a sale has been effected by a lender in exercise of his power of sale, the mortgage deed will not bear a receipt.

(c) Building society mortgages

Provided that the receipt (usually endorsed on the mortgage deed) is in the form of wording prescribed by Building Societies Act 1986, and is signed by a person authorised by the particular society, the receipt may be treated as an effective discharge of the mortgage without further enquiry being made.

(d) Other mortgages

By Law of Property Act 1925, s.115 a receipt endorsed on the mortgage deed (even if the receipt is not executed as a deed) operates to discharge the mortgage provided it is signed by the lender and names the person making repayment. However, where the money appears to have been paid by a person not entitled to the immediate equity of redemption, the receipt will usually operate as a transfer by deed of the mortgage. Thus if the person making repayment is not the borrower named in the mortgage or a personal representative or trustee acting on his behalf, the receipt should make it expressly clear that the receipt is to operate as such and is not intended to be a transfer of the mortgage to the person making payment. If the borrower makes repayment of the mortgage debt, but the receipt is dated later than the date of the conveyance by the borrower to a buyer of the land charged, at the date of the receipt the borrower will not be the person immediately entitled to the equity of redemption under the mortgage, because the mortgage had not been discharged at the date of completion of the sale of the land; thus the buyer will technically have bought the land subject to this incumbrance. In these circumstances the receipt operates to transfer the mortgage to the borrower (and not as a receipt) and it is, in theory, undischarged. In reality, any rights which the borrower has under the mortgage are unlikely to be enforced since he may be estopped from setting up the mortgage against the buyer. The borrower's position is at best that of a puisne mortgagee, since the title deeds will have passed to the buyer on completion of the sale, and unless registered as a Class C(i) or C(iii) land charge would be unenforceable against a subsequent buyer of the land for valuable consideration.[1] A buyer should therefore check the mortgage receipt to see who made repayment and also check that the receipt is dated no later than the date of the next transaction in the chain. If the mortgage receipt appears inadvertently to have transferred the mortgage and not discharged it a requisition should be raised to ensure that the seller or his lender is in possession of the title deeds (so that no mortgage supported by deposit of deeds can have come into existence as a result of the transfer) and the buyer should make a Land Charges Department search against the name of the person who bought from the borrower to ensure that no land charge has been registered against his name. Provided that the present seller or his lender has the deeds and the result of the land charges search reveals no adverse entries the defect can be ignored.

1. See *Cumberland Court (Brighton) Ltd.* v. *Taylor* [1964] Ch. 29.

2.10.   **Transactions at an undervalue**

2.10.1.   Dispositions which are made by way of gift or at an undervalue (whether *inter vivos* or by assent) are not generally acceptable as roots of title in unregistered land because no investigation of title would have been made by the donee at the time of the transaction. They do not therefore provide the double check on title which is afforded by an arm's length conveyance.

2.10.2.   Where a prospective buyer or mortgagee of land, whether registered or not, has notice that the land has been the subject of an undervalue transaction, it may be necessary to consider whether the courts' powers to set aside, under Insolvency Act 1986, s.238 or s.339, apply. An undervalue transaction may be the result of a gift, a partial gift (made for a consideration but a substantially below market value one), financial arrangements following a marriage breakdown, or a deed of variation in relation to an inheritance. If sections 238 or 339 do apply, it will then be necessary to see whether the protection provided by Insolvency (No.2) Act 1994 operates. The courts' sections 238 and 339 powers are exercisable for periods of two or five years, respectively, from the date of the transaction (depending on whether the transferor was a company or an individual), but the 1994 Act's provisions protect a person acquiring in good faith and for value during those periods – see para. D.2.10.4. below.

2.10.3.   *Disposition by an individual*

Provided the buyer from the donee takes in good faith and for value, he will obtain a good title. It is no longer necessary for the buyer to show that he bought without notice of the undervalue transaction. However, in two situations good faith is presumed *not* to exist unless the contrary is proved:

(a)   where the buyer is an 'associate' of the donee. The word 'associate' is widely defined in Insolvency Act 1986, s.435 to include the donor's spouse, ex-spouse, partner, partner's relatives, employers and employees; or

(b)   where the buyer had notice of the relevant proceedings (the bankruptcy) *and* of the relevant transaction (the undervalue transaction).

2.10.4.   *Notice*

Insolvency (No.2) Act 1994 was passed to deal with difficulties caused by those provisions of Insolvency Act 1986 which apply to undervalue transactions. Various questions had arisen about its effect since it came into force in July 1994. As a result, the Law Society obtained the opinion of leading counsel, Gabriel Moss Q.C., on certain points. This paragraph sets out his views.

Section 339 of the 1986 Act gives the court power, on the application of the trustee in bankruptcy, to set aside an undervalue transaction, i.e. a gift or transfer for significantly low consideration, should the maker of the gift or transfer become bankrupt within five years after the date of the undervalue transaction. Section 342 provides protection, in certain conditions, against the use of section 339 powers. However, in its 1986 form, it was too restrictive. It left exposed to the risk of section 339 proceedings not only those who had benefited from undervalue transactions, but also those who had subsequently acquired, in good faith and for value, by way of genuine open market purchases, any property which had previously been the subject of an undervalue transaction. The 1994 Act overcame this problem by removing the 1986 Act's requirement that a buyer of − or, strictly, the acquirer of an interest in − property had to acquire not only in good faith and for value, but also without notice of the previous undervalue transaction, in order to get a title unchallengeable under section 339. With most types of property, a subsequent good faith buyer is unlikely to have notice of a previous undervalue transaction affecting it, and this generally applies to land as long as its title is registered. However, where title is unregistered, a buyer will inevitably have notice of a previous undervalue transaction. There is still a substantial amount of unregistered land in the U.K. and difficulties caused by section 339 are common. To the extent that the 1994 Act brought about protection for the good faith and for value acquirer, its effect was wholly beneficial. Unfortunately, as the price paid for removing the 'without notice' requirement, section 2(2) of the Act (which inserted new subsection (2A) into section 342 of the 1986 Act) made two exceptions to the improved protection. One of these is of little significance since it applies to an acquirer who is an 'associate of', or is 'connected with' (both terms are defined by the 1986 Act) either the undervalue transferor or transferee. However, the other exception, the 'dual notice' exception, gives rise to the main question which has been raised about the 1994 Act. These are counsel's views on this and other questions about the Act's effect.

Question 1

What is the effect of the 'dual notice' exception on the person who will for convenience be called the 'subsequent acquirer' (i.e. a person acquiring on the open market from the undervalue transferee, and also any further person who later acquires on the open market from that person)? The dual notice exception (section 342(2A) of the 1986 Act as amended by the 1994 Act) says that, where a subsequent acquirer of an interest in property has notice both of a previous undervalue transaction and of bankruptcy proceedings (i.e. a petition which leads to a bankruptcy order; or an actual bankruptcy order) against the undervalue transferor, the acquirer will be presumed to acquire other than in good faith, until he or she shows otherwise. The problem which this exception causes arises thus: A transfers a property at an undervalue to B; B sells on the open market to C who buys in good faith; C, some time later, wants to sell to D, another open market and good faith buyer. C knew of the undervalue transaction between A and B (though, with current land registration rules, this is perhaps unlikely to happen very often) but, at the time when he or she bought, there were no bankruptcy proceedings against A, so C acquired an unquestionably good title. However, by the time C sells to D, bankruptcy proceedings have begun against A, and D knows of the previous undervalue transaction (though this is even more unlikely under the current land registration regime). What is D's position as to possible section 339 proceedings? Counsel's view is that D is, in practice, at no risk if he acquires in these circumstances (provided that, in reality, he acts in good faith. Counsel says that this is an issue which must be looked at in context. The underlying purpose of the legislation is to protect the *bona fide* buyer in good faith and for value, i.e. the buyer in the ordinary course of buying and selling property, while preventing creditors being cheated. Counsel is also confident that no court would deprive D of an interest bought in good faith and for value, for the benefit of the creditors of A, since it would be outrageously unfair to do so. Counsel is also confident that the courts would be concerned to interpret the legislation so as to achieve a fair result. He refers to the observation of Sir Donald Nicholls V-C in *Paramount Airways Ltd (No. 2)* [1992] 3 All E.R. 1 (C.A.) in support of the view that 'the court will ensure that it does not seek to exercise oppressively or unfairly the very wide jurisdiction conferred by the sections' (in that case, sections 238 to 241). In fact, counsel thinks it highly unlikely that, in practice, any trustee in bankruptcy would even consider trying to challenge D since it would be a waste of the assets of the bankrupt's estate to do so. However, should this unlikely situation occur, counsel's view is that there are three bases on which an application should be resisted.

(i) Under the 'shelter' rule: this rule, which is not widely known, is illustrated in *Wilkes* v. *Spooner* [1911] 2 K.B. 473 (C.A.). It says, broadly, that a person who acquires property in good faith and for value can pass on as good a title as he or she has to another person who also acquires in good faith. In *Wilkes* v. *Spooner,* a person acquired land which was subject to various covenants. However, as he had acquired without notice of them, but in good faith and for value, he was not bound by them. By the time he came to sell, the covenants had come to light, but he claimed that, because of the 'shelter' principle, he could sell free of them to another good faith buyer. The Court of Appeal agreed. In counsel's view, this principle applies equally to property in the undervalue transaction context – and, indeed, some of the drafting of section 342 may, he thinks, be a somewhat clumsy attempt to reflect the 'shelter' rule.

(ii) On the grounds that D's title is 'derived' from that of C section 342(2)*(a)* of the 1986 Act (as amended) says that no order made under section 339 shall prejudice an interest acquired in good faith and for value, nor any interest 'derived' from that interest. What 'derived' means in this context is unclear, but counsel thinks that its use may have been intended to replicate the 'shelter' rule. If this is the effect of the term, D's interest would be protected by reason of being 'derived' from that of C. It is possible, however, that interests such as those of subsequent buyers were not intended to be treated as 'derived' interests and that the term was meant to cover only interests such as those acquired by inheritance.

(iii) On the grounds, simply, that he or she had acquired in good faith and for value. In a normal open market transaction, there would be no question that the buyer had acquired his or her interest in this way. However, new subsection (2A) of section 342 (inserted by the 1994 Act) creates an artificial presumption against good faith where the dual notice exception applies, even in relation to such a transaction. Counsel's view, however, is that a court would ask no more of D, in order to displace this presumption, than to show that his purchase was at arm's length and for value, i.e. that it was a normal, open market purchase. Thus, in the highly unlikely event of a challenge, the presumption against good faith would be easily rebutted. Only where there was actual evidence calling D's good faith into question could there be any prospect of a serious challenge by a trustee. If D had bought on the open market, this would be a highly unusual situation – indeed, it is difficult to imagine its arising.

Question 2

What does 'notice' mean in this context (i.e. as to notice of a previous undervalue transaction but, in particular, notice of bankruptcy proceedings)? Counsel's view is that actual notice is notice in this context, both as to bankruptcy proceedings and previous undervalue transactions. As to statutory notice of bankruptcy proceedings, an acquirer of an interest in unregistered land will have notice of any information recorded either in the register of pending actions or in the register of writs and orders − sections 5 and 6 Land Charges Act 1972. Although there is some question (because of the wording of sections 5 and 6, and also of section 198 Law of Property Act 1925) as to whether this notice would be effective against an acquirer, because it would not be recorded against the name of a bankrupt with any present connection with the property concerned, the prudent view is to assume that it would do so. As to registered land, the acquirer will have notice only of what appears on the land register. Section 59 Land Registration Act 1955 says that a writ, order, etc. has effect against registered land only if lodged as provided by that Act, so that it is shown on the registered title; and section 14 Land Charges Act 1972 excludes that Act's effect as to any matter relating to registered land. Nevertheless, counsel suggests that, where a prospective buyer of registered land has notice of an undervalue transaction − but only then − it would be prudent to carry out a bankruptcy search against the undervalue transferor, if known, as failure to do so might cause difficulties in rebutting the presumption against good faith (section 342 (2A)) should the issue arise.

Question 3

What is the effect of the 1994 Act on mortgagees? In counsel's view, exactly the same as on the acquirer of any other kind of interest. A mortgagee acquires an interest in property. In a normal mortgage of domestic property to a bank or building society, the mortgagee clearly acquires its interest in good faith and gives value. The mortgagee's interest is thus protected by section 342(2)*(a)* as amended. This applies regardless of whether the mortgagor is B, the undervalue transferee; or C, the first subsequent good faith and for value buyer; or D, the next subsequent good faith and for value buyer. Similarly, a mortgagee exercising its power of sale would be able to pass good title to a subsequent acquirer, for the same reasons that a subsequent freehold buyer (C or D) can do so. The Law Society has received queries about the effect of section 339 and the 1994 Act where property which is the subject of an undervalue transaction is transferred subject to an existing mortgage. In this situation, no section 339 issue arises at all, as far as the mortgaged interest is concerned, because the mortgage agreement was entered into before the undervalue transaction took place. Though the trustee in bankruptcy could apply under section 339 for the return of the property itself − in practice, the equity which would have been the subject of an undervalue transaction − the mortgagee's interest would remain intact (as it would have had the mortgage been created after the undervalue transaction, in the event of section 339 proceedings).

Question 4

Where A transfers property at an undervalue to A (self) and B jointly or in common; or A and B transfer jointly either to A or B alone, does the section 342(2)*(a)* protection operate in relation to C, the subsequent acquirer, or is it disapplied by the exclusion contained in section 342(2)*(a)* of an interest acquired from 'that individual', i.e. the undervalue transferor. Counsel's view is that C is not excluded from the protection given by section 342(2)(a) because of having acquired from 'that individual'. Where A, as sole owner, transfers to himself and B jointly, what happens is that A transfers the whole of the legal estate in the property, but only that part of his beneficial interest which passes to B. In this context, what Insolvency Act 1986 is concerned with is the beneficial, not the legal, interest in the property which is the subject of an undervalue transaction. Thus, when A and B then sell to C (a good faith and for value buyer), what C acquires is A's beneficial interest which has not been the subject of an undervalue transaction, and B's beneficial interest which has been but which C obviously does not acquire from 'that individual'). Thus, the interest acquired by C comes within the section 342(2)(a) protection to the extent that it is acquired from B, and is outside section 339 altogether to the extent that it is acquired from A. Simiarly, when A and B transfer jointly owned property to B, and B then sells to C, the same principle applies. That is, since the only transfer to which section 339 and section 342(2)(a) are material is that of A's beneficial interest to B and, as C is acquiring from B and not A, he or she is not affected by the 'other than that individual' exclusion.

2.10.5. Disposition by a company

Sections 238-241 of Insolvency Act 1986 are the equivalents of sections 339-342 as to undervalue transfers by companies. The same principles apply. The only difference of substance is that the period during which the courts' set aside powers may be exercised is two, instead of five, years. The Insolvency (No.2) Act 1994 amends the 1986 Act as to companies in the same way as it does as to individuals – see para. D.2.10.4. above. In relation to companies, the term 'connected person' includes a director – see section 249 of the 1986 Act; and 'associate' includes an associated company – see section 435.

2.10.6. Company search

A company search should be made against the transferor company to ensure that no liquidation or administration proceedings have begun.

2.10.7. Registered land

The difficulties which sections 238 and 339 cause arise more often in relation to unregistered than regsistered land, because a registered title will not usually show that land has previously been the subject of an undervalue transaction and a buyer is unlikely to have notice of it. However, Land Registry practice is at present to enter a note, on first registration, that the land may be affected by sections 238 or 339, either where the transfer to the applicant appears to be an undervalue transaction; or where an undervalue transaction appears in the title deduced, unless it is shown that the two or five-year period (company or individual transferor) had expired by the time the transaction took place, or that the applicant is protected by the 1994 Act.

2.11. Effect of failure to register land charges (unregistered land)

2.11.1. Charges of Classes C(i), C(ii), C(iii) and F are void against a purchaser of any interest in the land for valuable consideration (including marriage).

2.11.2. Charges of Classes C(iv) and D are void only against a purchaser of a legal estate for money or money's worth.

2.12. Checking stamp duties

2.12.1. *Registered land*

Once the buyer has become registered as proprietor, the transfer and/or pre-registration deeds no longer concern a subsequent buyer and in any event are not generally available to be checked.

2.12.2. *Unregistered land*

(a) Unstamped or incorrectly stamped documents are not good roots of title, nor good links in the chain. They cannot be produced in evidence in civil proceedings and will not be accepted by the Chief Land Registrar on an application to register the title.

(b) A buyer is entitled to insist that all documents within the title are properly stamped at the expense of the seller. If, therefore, on examination of the title stamping defects are found, the buyer should raise a requisition requiring the seller to remedy the deficiency at his own expense.[1]

(c) Stamp duty may be *ad valorem* or fixed duty, the rates of which vary from time to time. Each document in the title should be checked against a table of stamp duties to ensure that it bears the correct duty in relation to the nature of the instrument, its date, and the amount of its consideration. The presence of a certificate of value in a document may have the effect of reducing the liability to duty or of exempting it from duty altogether. Where VAT has been paid on the consideration, stamp duty is payable on the VAT element of the price.

(d) In addition to stamp duty, conveyances on sale (including registered land transfers) and leases granted for a term of seven years or more and assignments of such leases must be produced to the Inland Revenue under Finance Act 1931. On production a Produced Stamp (Particulars Delivered Stamp) is affixed to the document. The consequences of failure to produce a document are the same as for lack of stamp duty and the seller must be required to rectify any deficiency at his own expense.

1. Stamp Act 1891, s.117.

2.13.   **Verification of title**

2.13.1. Verification of title consists of checking the evidence of title supplied by the seller against the original deeds.

2.13.2. In registered land this procedure is strictly unnecessary since the land or charge certificate in the seller's possession is itself only a copy of the register at the Land Registry. The true state of the register can be confirmed by the buyer when making his pre-completion search at HM Land Registry. It is, however, usual to check the contents of the seller's land or charge certificate on completion of a sale of the whole of the seller's title, if only to ensure that the correct certificate is handed over at that time.

2.13.3. In unregistered land, the abstract or epitome should be checked against the seller's original deeds. The buyer's time-limit for making this inspection expires with his time-limit for raising requisitions. Verification should therefore be carried out as part of the investigation of title procedure. In most cases, where the title is not complex, and the photocopy documents supplied by the seller are of good quality, the buyer's solicitor postpones his verification until actual completion. If, however, he then finds an error on the title it will be too late to query the error since his time-limit for raising requisitions will have expired. If there is any doubt over the validity of the title, or it is of a complex nature, verification should be carried out at the proper time. Unless the contract provides to the contrary the costs of verification are borne by the buyer. Standard Condition 4.2.3 requires the seller to produce to the buyer (without cost to the buyer) the original of every document within the title or, if the original is not available, an abstract, epitome or copy with an original marking by a solicitor of examination either against the original or against an examined abstract or an examined copy.

2.14.   **Standard Mortgage Instructions[1]**

2.14.1. Where the Standard Mortgage Instructions (SMI) apply it is the solicitor's duty to ensure that the property has a good and marketable title which may safely be accepted by the lender as security.

2.14.2. The lender may not be prepared to accept as security any property which is registered with a title other than absolute or any property which is a flying freehold.

1. At the time of publication the SMI had not been finalised.

D.03. Requisitions on title

See also: Investigation of title, para. D.02.
Delay and remedies, section M.

3.1. Purpose of requisitions

3.1.1. The purpose of requisitions on title is to require the seller's solicitor to clarify and if necessary to rectify matters on the title supplied which the buyer's solicitor finds unsatisfactory. In practice they are commonly used also to resolve administrative queries relating to the arrangements for completion.

3.2. Time for raising requisitions

3.2.1. By Standard Condition 4.1.1, written requisitions on the title supplied must be raised within six working days after either the date of the contract or the day of delivery of the seller's evidence of title, whichever is the later. The buyer will lose his right to raise requisitions if he does not do so within the time-limits prescribed by this condition. If the evidence of title is incomplete and this fact is pointed out to the seller within the above period, under Standard Condition 4.1.1 the buyer's solicitor has six working days from the supply of additional evidence to raise requisitions on that additional evidence. By Standard Condition 4.1.4, this time-limit may be adjusted *pro rata* to fit a completion date which is less than 15 working days from the date of the contract.

3.3. Standard form requisitions

3.3.1. Most law stationers produce a standard form of requisitions on title which includes many commonly asked questions, e.g. confirmation that the seller's mortgage on the property will be discharged on or before completion. A standard form of requisitions (the Completion Information and Requisitions on Title Form) is published for use in Protocol transactions. The seller's solicitor should be asked to confirm that the answers given to enquiries before contract or information volunteered on the Seller's Property Information Form remain correct. Additionally the printed questions frequently deal with the administrative arrangements for completion itself, e.g. method of payment of money. Queries which are specific to the title under consideration may be added to the end of the standard form or typed on a separate sheet. The buyer's solicitor should send two copies of the form to the seller's solicitor who will return one copy with his answers appended, keeping the other copy on his own file for reference. Standard Condition 4.1.1 requires the seller's solicitor to reply to requisitions within four working days after receiving them from the buyer's solicitor.

3.4. Further queries

3.4.1. On receipt of replies from the seller's solicitor, the buyer's solicitor should ensure that the answers given to his queries are satisfactory both in relation to the title and to the client's interests. Any replies which are unsatisfactory should be taken up with the seller's solicitor and further written queries raised until the matter is resolved. Standard Condition 4.1.1 governs the time-limits for raising observations on the seller's replies to requisitions. In some cases the replies given to requisitions may be construed as undertakings, e.g. to discharge the seller's outstanding mortgage on the property. Where such an undertaking is given the seller's solicitor should ensure that he has only committed himself to do what is within his power to do; an undertaking to discharge the seller's mortgage(s) on the property or one which is simply worded 'confirmed' or 'noted' will be interpreted as meaning that *all* subsisting charges will be removed. The seller's solicitor should therefore ensure that he is fully aware of the details of all such charges before committing himself to such an undertaking. Alternatively, the seller's solicitor or licensed conveyancer may prefer to undertake to discharge certain named charges only. From the buyer's point of view, the buyer's solicitor should ensure that he asks the seller's solicitor to supply a list of all outstanding charges and obtains a specific undertaking in relation to each of them. He should only accept an undertaking from a solicitor or licensed conveyancer, such undertaking being in the form approved by the Law Society, failing which the buyer's solicitor should raise a requisition requiring the mortgages actually to be discharged on or before completion.

3.5. Restrictions on subject matter of requisitions

3.5.1. The buyer's solicitor is only entitled to raise requisitions on the title which he has, by contractual condition, agreed to accept. Except where Law of Property Act 1925, s.45 applies, he cannot in the case of unregistered land require production of documents prior to the root of title.[1] The buyer's right to raise requisitions may be curtailed or excluded by a condition in the contract.[2] Such a restriction only takes effect on exchange of contracts and does not preclude the buyer from raising queries in relation to that particular matter before contracts are exchanged. If the seller wishes to curtail or exclude the buyer's right to raise requisitions he must make a full disclosure of all defects in his title. In strict theory, the seller is only obliged to answer requisitions which relate to title, and not those which relate to, e.g. the form of the purchase deed. In practice the distinction between true requisitions on title and those relating to other matters is largely ignored and the seller's solicitor will answer all reasonable queries raised by the buyer's solicitor. Contractual conditions may also require the buyer in certain circumstances to waive a defect in title. At common law the buyer is deemed to accept the seller's title (and thus loses his right to raise requisitions or further requisitions) when he delivers a draft purchase deed to the seller. In practice the draft purchase deed is usually submitted to the seller simultaneously with requisitions and the buyer's right to raise requisitions will be expressly preserved by a contractual condition, e.g. Standard Condition 4.5.1.

1. See above, para. D.02.6.
2. Special Condition 2 of the Standard Conditions of Sale Form excludes requisitions in relation to the matters defined in the contract as 'incumbrances'.

3.6. Vendor and purchaser summons

3.6.1. If the seller's solicitor refuses to answer a proper requisition, the buyer can compel an answer by means of the vendor and purchaser summons procedure under Law of Property Act 1925, s.49 which provides a summary method of resolving disputes between the parties. This procedure is intended to be used to resolve an impasse between the parties where agreement cannot be reached over a specific point in relation to the title and not as a general sounding-board to test the validity of the whole title or of the contract.

3.7. Seller's right to rescind

3.7.1. The Standard Conditions of Sale (3rd edition) no longer contains a clause entitling the seller to rescind the contract where the buyer raises a requisition with which the seller is unable or unwilling to comply.

E.   PRE-COMPLETION
E.01.   The purchase deed

See also: Plans, para. B.21.

1.1.   Who prepares the deed?

1.1.1.   It is normally the buyer's duty to prepare the purchase deed, although the seller may, by Law of Property Act 1925, s.48(1), reserve the right by contractual condition to prepare the deed himself. This right is usually only used in estate conveyancing where the seller commonly supplies an engrossment of the purchase deed in standard form, a draft of the deed having been annexed to the contract. If the seller charges a fee for the engrossment, such fee must be reasonable and is deemed to include VAT unless stated otherwise.

1.2.   Time for preparation of deed

1.2.1.   Conventionally the purchase deed is prepared after completion of the buyer's investigation of title, but in practice the deed is usually prepared shortly after exchange of contracts and submitted to the seller for his approval with the buyer's requisitions on title. At common law the buyer is deemed to have accepted the seller's title when he submits the purchase deed for approval, and thus the submission of the purchase deed simultaneously with requisitions would preclude the buyer's right to raise requisitions on the seller's title. This problem is surmounted by Standard Condition 4.5.1 which preserves the buyer's right to raise requisitions in such circumstances. By Standard Condition 4.1.2, the buyer is required to submit the draft purchase deed to the seller at least 12 working days before the contractual completion date. Under para. 7.1 of the Protocol the buyer's solicitor is required to submit the draft purchase deed simultaneously with his requisitions on title as soon as possible after exchange of contracts and in any case within the time-limits specified in the contract.

1.3.   **Form of the deed**

1.3.1.   The purchase deed must be a deed in order to transfer the legal estate in the land to the buyer.[1]

1.3.2.   The purchase deed puts into effect the terms of the contract and so must reflect its terms.

1.3.3.   Where the property being transferred is registered land the form of the purchase deed is prescribed by rules made under Land Registration Act 1925 and, subject to permitted variations, the prescribed form of wording must be used. Many of the standard Land Registry forms are reproduced by law stationers, and in simple cases these may be used as the basis of the purchase deed. In more complex cases it will be necessary to produce an individually drafted deed, but in either case the form of wording prescribed by the rules should be followed as closely as circumstances permit. The Swansea District Land Registry will accept a document which is prepared in Welsh and do not require a translation to be supplied.

1.3.4.   No prescribed form of wording exists for a conveyance of unregistered land. The buyer is thus free to choose his own form of wording subject to the seller's approval and provided that it accurately reflects the terms of the contract. Instead of using a traditional conveyance the buyer may prepare his purchase deed as a Land Registry transfer under Rule 72 Land Registration Rules 1925.

1. Law of Property Act 1925, s.52.

1.4.   **Drafting the deed**

1.4.1.   When drafting the purchase deed the buyer's solicitor needs to have access to:

(a)   the contract — because the purchase deed must reflect the terms of the contract;

(b)   the office copy entries/title deeds — because the contract may refer to matters on the title which need to be repeated or reflected in the purchase deed;

(c)   except in straightforward cases, a precedent on which to base the deed under preparation.

1.4.2.   *Using a precedent*

Except in the simplest cases it is advisable to refer to a precedent if only to focus the mind on the types of clause which will be required in the draft deed. Use the precedent as a guide and not as a model to be followed slavishly. Consider whether a clause is really necessary before copying it from a precedent and check that the law has not altered since the precedent was published.

1.5. Seller's approval of draft deed

1.5.1. When the draft has been prepared two copies should be submitted to the seller's solicitor for his approval. A further copy of the draft should be retained by the buyer's solicitor so that amendments can be agreed over the telephone if required. By Standard Condition 4.1.2 one of the copies submitted to the seller's solicitor can be of engrossment quality enabling the seller to use this as a top copy for signature in cases where no amendments are needed and where the buyer does not need to sign the deed.

1.5.2. On receipt of the draft, the seller's solicitor should check it carefully to ensure that the document accurately reflects the terms of the contract. Amendments should be confined to those which are necessary for the fulfilment of the document's legal purpose, bearing in mind that the choice of style and wording is the buyer's prerogative. Minor amendments may be agreed with the buyer's solicitor by telephone in order to save time. More substantial amendments should be clearly marked in a distinct colour on both copies of the draft, one copy being returned to the buyer's solicitor for his consideration, the other being retained in the seller's solicitor's file for reference. By Standard Condition 4.1.2 the seller's solicitor is to approve or return the revised draft document within four working days after delivery of the draft transfer by the buyer's solicitor.

1.6. Engrossment

1.6.1. When amendments (if any) to the draft deed have been finalised, the buyer's solicitor should prepare an engrossment of the deed on good quality paper. A deed which is to be submitted to HM Land Registry should be engrossed on paper of no less quality than 100gsm.

1.6.2. The engrossment must be checked carefully (if necessary by comparing the draft document with the engrossment) to ensure the accuracy of the typing and that all agreed amendments have been incorporated. A copy of the engrossment should be kept on the buyer's solicitor's file for reference.

1.6.3. The completed engrossment should then be sent to the seller's solicitor for execution by his client. Where the buyer is required to execute the deed it is common practice for the buyer to execute the deed prior to delivery of the deed in escrow to the seller for his signature. The condition attached to the escrow should be defined. By Standard Condition 4.1.2 the buyer must deliver the engrossment of the purchase deed to the seller at least five working days before completion.

1.7. Execution

1.7.1. To be valid in law a deed must be clear on the face of it that it is a deed, signed by the necessary parties in the presence of a witness, and delivered.[1] Use of a seal is no longer required either by individuals or bodies corporate. A company seal may, however, still be used and is a valid method of execution of a document.

1.7.2. Signature by the seller is always required in order to transfer the legal estate. [2]

1.7.3. The buyer is required to execute the deed if it contains a covenant or declaration on his behalf. Thus execution by the buyer will be needed where the document contains an indemnity covenant in respect of existing restrictive covenants or a declaration by the buyers relating to the trusts on which they hold the property.

1.7.4. Where other parties are joined in the deed, e.g. to release the property from a mortgage or to give a valid receipt for money paid under the deed, they should also sign the document.

1.7.5. Signature by an individual must be made by him in person, preferably in ink.

1.7.6. Where an individual is incapable of signing the document himself, e.g. because he is blind or illiterate, another person may execute it on his behalf. In such a situation the document should be read over to the individual, or its contents clearly explained to him, before signature. Two witnesses are required to the signature. [3]

1.7.7. Any responsible person may be a witness to the signature of an individual. There is no legal restriction on one party to a document being a witness to the other party's signature nor on one spouse being a witness to the signature of the other spouse, but an independent witness is preferable since if the validity of the document was ever challenged in court, the independent witness would provide a stronger testimony. The witness should sign his name, and add underneath the signature his address and occupation. If the name of the witness is not clear from the signature it is sensible to ask the witness also to write his full name in block capitals after his signature. Two witnesses are required whenever the document is signed by one person on another's behalf.

1.7.8. A solicitor should always be satisfied before submitting a document for signature that the client understands the nature and contents of the document. Where the solicitor invites his client to sign the purchase deed in the solicitor's presence the deed can be explained to the client before signature, and actually signed in the presence of the solicitor who can then act as a witness to the signature. If this is not possible, the purchase deed may be sent to the client for signature and return. The letter which accompanies the purchase deed should:

    (a) explain the purpose and contents of the document;

    (b) contain clear instructions relating to the execution of the deed;

    (c) specify a date by which the signed document must be returned to the solicitor;

    (d) request that the client leaves the document undated.

1.7.9. *Attorneys*

A person who holds a power of attorney on behalf of another may execute a deed on that person's behalf. The attorney may sign either in his own name or in that of the person on behalf of whom he is acting, e.g. 'X by his attorney Y' or 'Y as attorney on behalf of X'.

1.7.10. Companies

A company will normally execute a deed by using its common seal which is impressed on the document in the presence of a director of the company and its secretary (who for this purpose must be two separate individuals) or two directors who will then sign the document to witness the execution by the company. Alternatively, the document may simply be signed by a director and the secretary or by two directors on behalf of the company. Use of a common seal is no longer compulsory but the document must make it clear on the face of it that it is a deed.[4] If either of these methods is used, due execution by the company may be presumed under Companies Act 1985, s.36A(6) and a buyer need not investigate whether the manner of execution is authorised by the company's articles. In some cases a company's articles may permit execution of a document by a method different to those outlined above, e.g. signature by an authorised person acting alone. In such a case the procedure prescribed by the articles should be followed and a copy of the signatory's authorisation attached to the deed to prove the validity of its execution. The requirements for execution of documents by companies incorporated outside the U.K. are dealt with in para. E.07. below.

1.7.11. Other bodies

The requirements for execution of deeds by other bodies, e.g. corporations sole (e.g. a bishop), district councils, government departments or statutory undertakings, will vary depending on the body concerned. The precise procedure for execution should be checked well in advance of execution. The document should then be executed in accordance with the prescribed method, and a copy of the authority of the signatory to sign attached to the deed to prove the validity of its execution. The relaxation on the use of corporate seals which was granted to registered companies by Companies Act 1989 does not extend to these bodies.

1.7.12. Patients

Following Court of Protection Rules 1994, deeds affecting sale and purchase transactions are no longer required to be sealed by the Court of Protection.

1.7.13. In addition to signature a deed must be delivered. A deed takes effect on its delivery. When the buyer delivers the engrossment to the seller for execution by him, he does not normally intend the deed to become effective at that time. It is therefore common practice for the buyer to deliver the deed to the seller in escrow, i.e. conditionally, so that the operation of the deed is postponed until completion. In the case of a company, delivery is presumed at the date of execution unless the contrary is proved.[5]

1. Law of Property (Miscellaneous Provisions) Act 1989, s.1. See also Land Registration (Execution of Deeds) Rules 1990 (S.I. 1990/1010).
2. Law of Property Act 1925, s.52.
3. Law of Property (Miscellaneous Provisions) Act 1989, s.1.
4. Companies Act 1989, s.130.
5. Companies Act 1985, s.36A(5).

1.8.   Plans

1.8.1.   If the contract provides for the use of a plan the purchase deed will also refer to the plan. In other cases the buyer is not entitled to demand that a plan is used with the purchase deed unless the description of the property as afforded by the contract and title deeds is inadequate without one. If the buyer wishes to use a plan in circumstances where he is not entitled to demand one, he may do so with the seller's consent but will have to bear the cost of its preparation.

1.8.2.   Where the sale is of the whole of the seller's property use of a plan is not normally considered necessary, and unless very clearly drawn may confuse rather than clarify the deed as well as adding unnecessary expense.

1.8.3.   On a sale of part (including flats and office suites) a plan is highly desirable and where the land is registered generally must be used.

1.8.4.   The plan(s) to be used with the purchase deed should be checked for accuracy, including all necessary colourings and markings, and firmly bound into the engrossment of the deed which should in its wording refer to the use of the plan(s). Measurements must be expressed in metric values.

1.8.5.   All parties who execute the deed must, in registered land cases, also sign the plan as an acknowledgement of its inclusion as an integral part of the document. In unregistered land signature of the plan is not compulsory but is highly desirable. Such signatures need not be witnessed. Where a company seals the purchase deed, it should also seal the plan.

1.8.6.   The preparation and use of plans is further discussed in para. B.21.

1.9.   Parties

1.9.1.   Anyone whose concurrence is necessary in order to transfer the legal estate or who is to give a valid receipt for capital money arising out of the transaction must be joined as a party to the deed.

1.9.2.   The seller and buyer will usually be the only parties to the deed, but in view of the principle outlined in para. 1.9.1. above it may be necessary to join, e.g. the trustees of a Settled Land Act settlement or a non-owning occupier.

1.9.3.   Where the seller is bankrupt, his trustee in bankruptcy will transfer the property and the seller is not a party to the deed.

1.9.4. If the seller is a company which is in liquidation or under receivership, the company itself transfers the property with the receiver or liquidator joining in the deed to give a receipt for the purchase price. In such a case the liquidator actually executes the deed. Exceptionally, if an order has been made by the court under Companies Act 1989 vesting the legal estate of the company's property in the liquidator, the liquidator will be the seller and the company will not be a party to the deed.

1.9.5. In a sub-sale transaction, the seller transfers the property directly to the sub-purchaser, but the original buyer will join in the document to direct the seller to convey and also to release his equitable interest to the sub-purchaser, to give implied covenants and, where appropriate, to give a receipt for part of the purchase price.

1.9.6. On a sale of part of registered land which is subject to a mortgage, it is not necessary for the lender to be a party to the purchase deed since he can release the part sold from his charge by using Form 53. In the same situation in unregistered land the lender may join in the conveyance in order to release the part sold from the mortgage and, where appropriate, to give a receipt for such part of the purchase price as is paid to him. Alternatively, a lender of unregistered land may give a separate deed of release to the buyer. The seller must ascertain from his lender which of these methods of release the lender wishes to employ and inform the buyer accordingly so that the buyer can, if necessary, include appropriate clauses relating to the lender in the draft purchase deed.

1.10.   Transfer of whole

1.10.1. This will usually follow Land Registry Form 19, which is available in several different versions dependent on the capacity of the contracting parties.

1.10.2. Any Land Registry document will commence with the county and district or London borough of the property being sold, its title number, and a short description of the property, i.e. its postal address, all of which information may be taken from the office copy entries supplied by the seller.

1.10.3. The date of the document is inserted on actual completion.

1.10.4. The amount of consideration must be stated[1] and is usually set out in both words and figures. The purchase price in the deed should exclude the amount of any consideration attributable to chattels for which a separate receipt should be prepared.[2]

1.10.5. A receipt clause is normally included in the document since its inclusion renders any other form of receipt for the purchase price unnecessary and acts as a sufficient discharge to the buyer.[3] The presence of this clause also gives the buyer authority to pay the purchase price to the seller's solicitor.[4] The receipt clause is also evidence, but not necessarily conclusive evidence, that the seller's lien over the property for the unpaid purchase price has been extinguished.

1.10.6. The seller's name and address should be inserted, as they appear on the proprietorship register of the title. If the seller is not the current registered proprietor, the seller's full name and present address should be inserted.

1.10.7. A statement of the seller's title guarantee, which will imply covenants for title under Law of Property (Miscellaneous Provisions) Act 1994,[5] e.g. 'I, [AB] of [address] transfer [description of property transferred] with full title guarantee to …' Any modification of the covenants must be set out expressly on the face of the transfer and must refer to the section of the 1994 Act which is being modified or excluded.

1.10.8. The buyer's full name and address should be inserted. The address given for the buyer in the Transfer Form or A4 Application for Registration Form will be placed on the proprietorship register on registration of the buyer's interest and is the address which will be used by the Chief Land Registrar should it become necessary for him to contact the registered proprietor of the land, e.g. to serve notices on him. The address given should therefore be one at which it is certain that the buyer can be contacted. In the case of residential property where the buyer will be moving into the property on completion, the address should therefore be the address of the property being purchased and not the address at which the buyer is currently living.

1.10.9. Where the sale is subject to existing incumbrances the contract will usually provide for the purchase deed to include an indemnity covenant to be given by the buyer.[6] An indemnity covenant will be required in respect of positive covenants and restrictive covenants which are not limited to seisin.[7] Where such a covenant is necessary it should be added expressly to the transfer form, there being no such covenant included on the printed versions of the form. A covenant which gives indemnity only is enforceable in breach by an action for damages. One which is 'to observe perform and indemnify' is enforceable by injunction and damages and thus provides fuller protection for the seller. Standard Condition 4.5.3 provides for the full form of covenant to be given. Where there are joint purchasers, the covenant should be given by both or all of them.

1.10.10. Co-owners should indicate in the transfer the capacity in which they hold the equitable interest in the property, i.e. as joint tenants or tenants in common and should additionally indicate whether or not the survivor of them is able to give a valid receipt for capital money arising on a disposition.[8] A statement indicating that the survivor is able to give a valid receipt is appropriate to a beneficial joint tenancy. A statement that the survivor is unable to give a valid receipt is appropriate to a beneficial tenancy in common and on registration of the buyers as proprietors a restriction in Form 62 will automatically be entered on the register. Instructions as to the method in which the beneficial ownership is to be held should have been taken by the buyer's solicitor at an early stage in the transaction, and those instructions will now be effected in the transfer. Where the buyers have decided to hold as tenants in common, instructions should also have been obtained in relation to the proportionate shares which each co-owner holds in the equitable interest. In the absence of evidence to the contrary it will be assumed by the court that they hold the equity in proportion to their original contributions to the property.[9] In order to avoid costly and time-consuming litigation at a later date, it is recommended that the beneficial interests of the co-owners are recorded in writing at the time of their purchase. When dealing with registered land a separate document should be drawn up to record the respective beneficial interests, signed by all the co-purchasers and kept safely with the land or charge certificate for future reference. A short deed of trust may be drawn up to give effect to the buyers' wishes, but a less formal document or letter, provided it is signed by all concerned, would suffice.

1.10.11. Where the consideration for the transaction is below the current stamp duty threshold, a certificate of value should be included in the deed.[10]

1.10.12. The document should then provide for execution by all parties in the presence of a witness. The form of attestation clause will vary dependent on the identity of the signatory. Reference should be made to Land Registry Practice Leaflet No. 17 (Appendix IX.1.) which sets out HM Land Registry's requirement in relation to the execution of deeds.

1.10.13. Additional clauses may be required in the body of the deed in accordance with special conditions of the contract.

1. Stamp Act 1891, s.5.
2. The amount of the consideration affects the amount of stamp duty payable on the document and, since chattels are not subject to stamp duty, any sum payable for them does not need to be included in the purchase deed. Where VAT is payable the amount of the consideration stated should include the VAT element of the price.
3. Law of Property Act 1925, s.67.
4. Law of Property Act 1925, s.69.
5. See below, Delay and remedies, section M.
6. See Standard Condition 4.5.3.
7. See *Rhone* v. *Stephens, The Times,* 18 March 1994, H.L.; *Austerberry* v. *Oldham Corporation* (1885) 29 Ch.D. 750.
8. *Huntingford* v. *Hobbs* [1992] E.G.C.S. 38.
9. *Springette* v. *Defoe* (1993) 65 P. & C.R. 1 (C.A.)
10. See below, Stamping documents, para. G.02.

1.11.   Transfer of part

1.11.1. Law stationers' forms for a transfer of part are available but since these are more complex documents than a transfer of whole, they are often individually prepared by the solicitor. All of the clauses referred to above in para. 1.10. will be relevant to a sale of part but the following will also be required either in addition to or in substitution for the above.

1.11.2. At this stage the sale is made by reference to the seller's existing title number. A new title number for the part being sold will be allocated by HM Land Registry on registration of the transaction.

1.11.3. A clear description of the land being sold must be included with reference to the plan annexed to the transfer. The land retained by the seller should be expressly defined and identified on the plan.

1.11.4. Where the contract made provision for the grant of easements to the buyer or reservations in favour of the seller, these contractual provisions must be expressly inserted into the transfer.

1.11.5.   The contract will usually provide for the exclusion of rights of light and air from the transfer. This contractual provision (see Standard Condition 3.3.2) must be implemented by a declaration to this effect in the transfer.

1.11.6.   New restrictive covenants are frequently imposed in a contract for the sale of part of land; these too must be expressly set out in the transfer. Except where the land forms part of a building scheme, to be enforceable against subsequent owners of the land sold, the covenants must be taken for the benefit of land retained by the seller and the burden annexed to the land sold. Express words to give effect to these principles are advisable.

1.11.7.   To avoid confusion and verbosity in the body of the transfer consideration may be given to including only a short reference to easements, covenants, etc., in the body of the deed, the detail of such matters being included in numbered schedules at the end. Schedules should appear after the main body of the deed but above the attestation clauses to ensure that they are incorporated as part of the signed document and that there cannot be any argument about them having been added to it at a later stage.

1.12. Conveyance

1.12.1.   A conveyance of unregistered land fulfils the same purpose as a Land Registry transfer and contains similar information but is presented in a different manner and consequently looks, on its face, entirely different from a registered land transfer. Each conveyance of unregistered land has slightly different requirements and thus each has to be individually drafted to fit the situation in hand. Although not all of the clauses which are mentioned below will be relevant to every trans-action, where they are required they will normally be inserted in the deed in the order in which they are given in the following paragraphs. It is not obligatory to insert the clauses in this particular order but by convention they do so appear and it is of assistance to another solicitor who looks at the document at a later date to be able to locate a particular clause quickly because it has been placed in the recognised order. Where the current transaction induces first registration a registered land transfer under Rule 72 Land Registration Rules 1925 may be used instead of a conveyance.

1.12.2.   The conveyance will start with the words 'This conveyance' followed by the date (which is inserted on actual completion) and the full names and addresses of all the parties to the deed.

1.12.3. *Recitals*

Recitals are not included in Land Registry forms nor by draftsmen who favour a modern approach to drafting. If a traditional approach to drafting is taken, recitals may be used in the conveyance. These do not form part of the body of the deed but are more by nature of a preamble, the function of which is to introduce the nature of and to set the scene for the deed which follows, e.g. by explaining the recent history of the title. Although recitals do not form an operative part of the deed, where they are included they must still be drafted with care and accuracy since a party is estopped from later denying the accuracy of a statement of fact made in a recital. Recitals of fact which are contained in a deed which is 20 years old are by Law of Property Act 1925, s.45(6) deemed to be correct. Where there is an ambiguity in an operative part of the deed, recitals may be looked at and used to clarify that ambiguity.[1] Where personal representatives are required to give a statement under Administration of Estates Act 1925, s.36(6) that they have not made any previous assent or conveyance, such statement is usually dealt with by way of recital. Similarly a statement that the survivor of joint tenants is solely and beneficially entitled to the property (required under Law of Property (Joint Tenants) Act 1964) is commonly dealt with in this way.

1.12.4. A consideration and receipt clause will be included. See above, paras. 1.10.4. and 1.10.5.

1.12.5. The operative word ('convey(s)') is followed by a statement of title guarantee which imports covenants for title.[2]

1.12.6. The parcels clause must clearly and adequately describe the land being sold. An adaptation of the description of the land in the particulars of the contract may be used for this purpose. Where the sale is of part of the seller's land, reference must be made to the land which is retained by the seller, such land being identified on the plan annexed to the deed.

1.12.7. Express reference should be made to benefits previously enjoyed by the land which are to pass to the buyer.

1.12.8. Clauses should be included to deal with exceptions, i.e. those matters which are excluded from the land and which do not therefore pass to the buyer, and to reservations, i.e. those matters which (usually on a sale of part) are being regranted by the buyer for the benefit of the seller. If reservations are to be reserved, a clause in the contract will have specified which rights were to be reserved to the seller in the purchase deed and those clauses are now activated by inclusion in the purchase deed itself.

1.12.9. Easements which are to be expressly granted to the buyer (usually only on a sale of part) will have been set out in the contract and are now included in the purchase deed to give effect to them.

1.12.10. The habendum ('to hold') is followed by express references to the estate conveyed (fee simple) and existing incumbrances, e.g. existing restrictive covenants subject to which the property is sold.

1.12.11. Declarations may be inserted, e.g. on a sale of part to negate the implied grant rules especially in respect of rights of light and air following a contractual provision to this effect.[3] Declarations may also be used to define the ownership of party walls.

1.12.12. Where the property is bought by co-owners a statement of their capacity must be included, i.e. as joint tenants or tenants in common. Where the co-owners are tenants in common the division of the beneficial interest between them may be specified either in the purchase deed or by separate deed of trust.[4] It is no longer necessary to include a clause to extend the powers of the trustees to make them co-extensive with those of an absolute owner because these powers are implied by Trusts of Land and Appointment of Trustees Act 1996, s.6.

1.12.13. On a sale of part, new restrictive covenants may be imposed and these should be inserted following the contractual provision to this effect. See above, para. 1.11.

1.12.14. Where existing positive covenants or restrictive covenants which are not limited to seisin will continue to bind the land after completion of the sale to the buyer an indemnity covenant will be required in fulfilment of the contractual obligation to that effect.[5]

1.12.15. If any of the documents of title which the seller has are not to be handed over to the buyer on completion, e.g. a grant of probate or all the title deeds on a sale of part, an acknowledgment for their production and undertaking for safe custody should be included in the document. By Law of Property Act 1925, s.64 the acknowledgment gives a right to production of the named document(s) at the cost of the person requiring production. Production may be required, e.g. to prove title to a subsequent buyer. The undertaking gives a right to damages (but no other remedy) if the named document(s) is lost or destroyed otherwise than by fire or inevitable accident. These rights are reiterated by Standard Condition 4.5.4. The rights given in the statute run with the land, so that once given they will benefit all subsequent purchasers of the land (except a lessee at a rent) and do not need to be repeated in respect of the same document(s). The burden of production and safe custody runs with the person who, for the time being, has custody of the relevant deeds and is enforceable against him without repetition of the obligation in a subsequent deed. All sellers will give an acknowledgment for production (where relevant), but only a seller selling as a beneficial owner gives the undertaking for safe custody. Such an undertaking is not appropriate in a situation where the seller is not the true owner of the deeds. If the title deeds which are being retained are not in the seller's possession at the time of completion, e.g. on a sale of part, they may be in the hands of his lender; the seller may be asked to give a covenant that he will give an undertaking for safe custody as and when the title deeds come into his possession.

1.12.16. In appropriate circumstances a certificate of value should be included in the document (see above, para 1.10.11.).

1.12.17. The document concludes with schedules (if any), e.g. of covenants, etc., testimonium (in witness) and attestation clauses. The attestation clause should contain the words 'signed as a deed' to comply with Law of Property (Miscellaneous Provisions) Act 1989, s.1.

1. The converse situation is not true. An ambiguous recital cannot be clarified by a statement in the operative part of the deed.
2. See below, Delay and remedies, section M.
3. See Standard Condition 3.3.2.
4. See above, para. 1.10.10.
5. See Standard Condition 4.5.3 and above, para. 1.10.9.

1.13. **Assent**

1.13.1. Where personal representatives transfer land to a beneficiary they will use an assent. If they sell land to a third party the purchase deed will be a transfer or conveyance depending whether or not the land is registered.

1.13.2. One exception to the rule that a legal estate can only be conveyed by a deed is an assent by personal representatives which must be in writing but need not be by deed unless it contains a covenant by the assentee, e.g. for indemnity in respect of restrictive covenants.

1.13.3. An assent of registered land must be in the form prescribed by Land Registration Rules 1925. An assent of unregistered land is not subject to any restraints on its form or contents except that it must be in writing and must name the person(s) in whose favour it is given.

1.13.4. On a sale or assent by personal representatives all proving personal representatives must be parties to the document.

1.13.5. In unregistered land the assent may contain recitals, and will otherwise be similar to an unregistered conveyance. Signature by the beneficiary is required if he gives a covenant. A memorandum of the assent should be noted on the grant after completion.

1.14. **Assignment**

1.14.1. An assignment of an existing registered lease is the transfer of a registered estate and the purchase deed will be a Land Registry transfer form. The form prescribed under Land Registration Rules 1925 for the transfer of a leasehold (Form 32) is the same as for the transfer of a freehold but adding the words 'for the residue of the term granted by the lease'. An assignment of an unregistered lease is similar in form to a conveyance of unregistered land, subject to some modifications.

1.14.2. Frequently the contract contains provision modifying the effect of the implied covenants for title in leasehold cases (e.g. Standard Condition 3.2.2) and the purchase deed will contain a clause giving effect to this contractual term.

1.14.3. An express indemnity covenant will be inserted if required by the contract (if any) (see Standard Condition 4.5.3). No indemnity covenant is implied by statute in new leases (granted after 1 January 1996).[1] In leases granted before this date an indemnity covenant is implied except where in unregistered land value is not given by the assignee for the transaction.

1.14.4. In addition, an unregistered assignment may contain recitals relating to the recent history of the lease, the agreement to sell and, where appropriate, the fact that the landlord has consented to the assignment. The estate transferred will be the unexpired residue of the term, subject to the terms and conditions of the lease itself. The benefit of options should be expressly assigned to ensure that their benefit is transferred to the buyer.

1. Landlord and Tenant (Covenants) Act 1995, s.14.

1.15.   Sellers' cashback schemes

1.15.1. These schemes appear to be operated by brokers who, in conjunction with a small number of lenders, participate in enabling a seller to offer an incentive to a buyer. In essence the seller and lender state that, e.g. the property is to be sold for £40,000 but that on completion the seller agrees to pay £5,000 to the buyer. Traditionally the contract discloses the arrangement, but the price inserted in the transfer will be the higher figure, e.g. £40,000 rather than £35,000, which is the net price the seller receives from the buyer.

1.15.2. In these schemes the lender is normally aware of the circumstances, and so the schemes do not, in fact, involve a fraud on the lender in the usual sense. Solicitors (whether acting for sellers or buyers) should always check that the lender is aware of the proposed cashback.

1.15.3. As the transfer is a matter of public record, it is a solicitor's duty not to be a party to any mis-statement of the sale price. Inserting the higher price would be a mis-statement. If solicitors are instructed in relation to such schemes, they should make it clear from the outset that the figure they will insert in the transfer will be the net figure, and should decline to act if the client instructs otherwise.

1.15.4. These schemes should be distinguished from cases where the lender gives an incentive 'cashback' to borrowers, as such cashbacks do not affect the price paid to the seller.

FURTHER REFERENCE

Precedents for the Conveyancer, Sweet & Maxwell.

The Encyclopedia of Forms and Precedents, Vol. 36, Butterworths.

Practical Conveyancing Precedents, T.M. Aldridge, F.T. Law & Tax.

Parker's Modern Conveyancing Precedents, Butterworths.

E.02. Pre-completion searches

See also: Pre-contract searches and enquiries, para. B.10.

2.1. Who makes the searches?

2.1.1. In accordance with the *caveat emptor* principle it is up to the buyer to make sure of his bargain. Therefore it is the buyer's solicitor's responsibility to ensure that such pre-completion searches as are relevant to the transaction are carried out and that the results of those searches are satisfactory to his client.

2.1.2. Where the buyer is purchasing with the assistance of a mortgage, his lender also has an interest in the soundness of the title to the property and some or all of the pre-completion searches may be carried out by the lender's solicitor acting at this stage on behalf of both the lender and the buyer.

2.2. Reason for making searches

2.2.1. The principal reason for making pre-completion searches is for the buyer's solicitor to confirm that information obtained about the property prior to exchange remains correct. In some situations searches additional to those which were made before exchange of contracts will also be undertaken at this stage either to verify information received after exchange or where the circumstances were such that the buyer did not have sufficient time to make the relevant search before contracts were exchanged.

2.3. When to make searches

2.3.1. The searches must be done in sufficient time to guarantee that the results are received by the buyer's solicitor in time for completion to take place on the contractual completion date.

2.3.2. Pre-completion searches should generally be made about seven days before the contractual completion date but may be left until closer to the completion date if, e.g. a telephone, computer or fax search is to be made. Searches will need to be done earlier than seven days before completion if some delay in the receipt of replies, e.g. through industrial action is anticipated.

2.3.3. The principal searches which are made at this stage of the transaction (Land Registry and/or Land Charges Department searches) generally confer protection on the searcher against later entries (i.e. they give a priority period); thus a balance has to be drawn between making the search at the latest moment before completion in order to gain the benefit of a long priority period after completion, and the risk, if a search is submitted at the last moment, of completion being delayed (and compensation payable by the buyer for the delay) because the search result has not been received by the date of completion.

2.4. Which searches to make

2.4.1. The following searches should be made:

(a) for registered land, search against title number at the District Land Registry (see below, para. 2.5.);

(b) for unregistered land, including an unregistered reversion to a lease, search at Land Charges Department against names of estate owners of the land (land registered with non-absolute title and unregistered land: see below, para. 2.6.);

(c) if acting for a lender, a bankruptcy search against the name of the borrower (see below, para. 2.8.);

(d) such other of the searches listed below in paras. 2.9.−2.13. as are applicable to the transaction.

2.5. Land Registry search

2.5.1. When taking an interest in a registered estate in land, a pre-completion search should be made at the appropriate District Land Registry. A fee of £4 per title is payable.[1] Fees can be paid by cheque or credit account, provided in the case of the latter that the applicant's solicitor's key number is quoted on the application form. Prescribed forms of wording should be followed when requesting a search by fax. Telephone searches confer immediate priority. If the search is 'clear', a guaranteed result will be given over the telephone. In all cases, a proper result will be issued by post or Document Exchange (DX). The telephone search procedure is only available for searches of whole titles and must be made by telephoning dedicated numbers at the Croydon, Durham, Gloucester, Lytham and Stevenage Registries only (see Appendix XIII.1 for numbers). All district registries will accept applications by fax for priority searches for a whole title or part of a title (but only where the search is in respect of a plot number on an approved estate plan) (see below, para. 2.5.9.).

2.5.2.   Where the search is made in Form 94A the result is supplied in Form 94D; this form contains the applicant's name but where, for example, the clients are both the chargor and chargee and the applicant is the chargee, the chargor's name will not be shown. Further, Form 94D does not contain the address of the property. Without this information it may be difficult to match the incoming search result with the correct file in the solicitor's office. However, an applicant's reference of not more than 25 digits (including oblique strokes and punctuation) can be reproduced on Form 94D. It is therefore suggested that the applicant's reference stated on Form 94A should include sufficient detail (e.g. applicant's or chargor's name and the address of the property or solicitor's file number) to ensure that the incoming search can be returned to its proper file without delay.

2.5.3.   *Search of whole title*

Where the interest being purchased, leased or mortgaged concerns the whole of a registered title, the search application should be made on Form 94A. The application will give details of the title number of the property to be searched, a brief description of its situation, i.e. postal address, county and district, and the names of the registered proprietors. The applicant's name must also be given together with his reason for making the search, i.e. he intends to purchase/lease/ take a charge on the land. Where a solicitor is acting both for a buyer and his lender the search application should be completed in the name of the lender client. If this is done the buyer may take the benefit and protection of the search and a separate search in the buyer's name is unnecessary. The search application form requests the registrar to provide information relating to any fresh entries which have been made on the register since a stated date which will be the date of the office copy entries supplied to the buyer. The office copy must have been issued not more than 12 months before the date of the search application. An official certificate of search made on this form confers on the searcher a priority period of 30 working days from the date of the certificate.[2]

2.5.4.   *Search of part of the title*

Where the interest being acquired comprises only part of a registered title, the search application is made on Form 94B and must identify the part of the land against which the search is to be made either by the submission of a clearly marked plan of the land or by its plot number where HM Land Registry has already approved an estate layout plan. In other respects the application is similar to that made on Form 94A.

2.5.5.   *Non-priority search on Form 94C*

The searches made on Forms 94A and 94B are only available for use by a person who intends in good faith and for valuable consideration to purchase, lease or take a mortgage over a legal estate in registered land. In situations which are not covered by these two forms an application for a search of the register must be made on Form

94C. The application form is similar to those outlined above but the result of the search does not confer any priority period on the applicant. Form 94C must be used in the following circumstances, e.g.

(a) when acting for a buyer of an equitable interest in the land;

(b) by a lender who seeks to protect his charge by a notice of deposit;

(c) a lender who is releasing land from a mortgage or who is selling under a power of sale should make a search to discover subsequent incumbrances (if any).

2.5.6. Search where application for first registration pending

Where an applicant has applied for first registration of his title and has contracted to resell the land to a third party before completion of the first registration, the third party will make a search on either Form 94A or 94B (FR) (as appropriate). The purpose of the search, in relation to a pending first registration, is to ascertain whether any adverse entry has been made in the daylist (i.e. list of applications received by HM Land Registry) since the date of the pending first registration application. The date of the pending first registration application does not have to be specified by the searcher. The effect of the certificate of search will be to give the searcher priority against any other intervening application if he lodges his own application before the expiry of the priority period. Guidance on making these searches can be found in Land Registry Practice Advice Leaflet No. 5.

2.5.7. Sub-sales

Where A has contracted to sell to B, and before B completes his purchase he contracts to resell to C, the sub-purchaser (C) will need to make a search against the title quoting A's name as proprietor since at the time of C's application B will not be the registered proprietor of the land.

2.5.8. Mortgagee's search on Form 106

This search is of limited application and may only be used by the proprietor of a charge whose interest is already protected by an entry on the register of the title. The purpose of the search is for the chargee of a dwelling house to ascertain whether any entry has been made on the register to protect a non-owning spouse's matrimonial homes rights under Family Law Act 1996. A chargee is required to serve notice on such a person before taking action to enforce his security.

2.5.9. Applications for priority searches made by telephone

An application can be made (through the Croydon, Durham, Gloucester, Lytham and Stevenage registries) by an applicant who is or who acts for an intending buyer (including lessee and chargee) and must be for a search of the whole title or of a pending first registration of land in England and Wales. The telephone search procedure is not restricted to the areas covered by the registries who operate the telephone service. The telephone call, using the special number allocated for this service (see Appendix XIII.1.), will only be accepted between the hours of 11 a.m. and 5.00 p.m. on any day Monday to Friday (inclusive) which is not Christmas Day, Good Friday or a statutory bank holiday. The application can only be made by a credit account holder. Office copies entries can be obtained by this procedure. On telephoning the registry the following information must be supplied in the order given below:

(a) the applicant's key number;

(b) name and address of firm holding the account;

(c) if different from (b) above, the name and address to which the result of search is to be sent;

(d) title number of the land;

(e) the name of the registered proprietor (or applicant for first registration);

(f) the county and district or London borough in which the land is situated;

(g) where the land is already registered, the date from which the search is to be made;[3]

(h) the name of the applicant (i.e. buyer, lessee or chargee);

(i) whether the search is intended to protect a purchase lease or charge;

(j) the name and telephone number of the person making the search telephone call.

2.5.10. A paper result of the search is normally despatched to the applicant's solicitor on the following working day. The priority period commences from the time of the telephone call. If the search is 'clear', a guaranteed result will be given over the telephone. Several search applications may be made during the course of the one telephone call. Informal disclosure of entries revealed by the search can be made over the telephone if so requested by the applicant. Such information is not, however, guaranteed by the Registry.

2.5.11. *Applications lodged by fax*

This facility is available at all district registries but only to credit account holders. Applications may be faxed between the hours of 10 a.m. on one day and 8 a.m. on the next but, if the second day is not a working day, applications will only be accepted until 4 p.m. on the first day. The search must be either a search of whole on Form 94A (no duplicate form required) or of a pending first registration. Applications must be completed in black ink or black type and, where the facility is available, sent in fine mode. No additional fee is charged for this service. The result of the search cannot be sent by fax but is posted to the applicant in the normal way.

1. For fee see App. VIII.3. and for address see App. XIII.1.
2. See below, para. 2.15.
3. This must be taken from an office copy issued not more than 12 months before the date of the search or, where the solicitor has on-line access to the Registry's computer file, a Register View in the same 12-month period.

2.6.   Land Charges Department search

2.6.1.   This search is only of relevance to unregistered land.

2.6.2.   The search is made by submitting Form K15 to the Land Charges Department at Plymouth with the appropriate fee.[1] Fees can be paid by credit account provided the applicant's solicitor's key number is stated on the application form. An official certificate of result of search confers a priority period of 15 working days on the applicant.[2] The search application can be made by post, or by telephone, telex or fax by a credit account holder. A personal search of the register can be made but it confers no protection or priority period on the applicant.

2.6.3.   The register comprises a list of the names of estate owners of land, with details of charges registered against those names. The search is therefore made not against the land itself but against the names of the estate owners. In the case of unregistered land it is necessary for the search to be made against the names of all the estate owners whose names appear on the abstract or epitome of title supplied by the seller, including those who are merely referred to in the bodies of deeds (as opposed to being parties to the deeds themselves) or in schedules attached to deeds which form part of the title. There is no need to repeat searches where a proper search certificate made against previous estate owners has been supplied with the abstract of title.

2.6.4.   The register is maintained on a computer which will only search against the exact version of the name as shown on the application form. It is therefore important to check that the name inserted on the application form is identical to that shown on the title deeds and that if any variations of that name appear in the deeds, e.g. if Frederick Brown is variously referred to as 'Frederick Brown', 'Frederick Browne' and 'Fred Brown', all the given variations of the name are separately entered on the search form and a separate fee paid in respect of each. Guidance on filling in the application form together with a list of accepted abbreviations and variations which the computer will search against is given in Land Charges Department Practice Leaflet No. 2.

2.6.5.   It is only possible for an effective entry to be made against a name in relation to that person's (or company's) period of estate ownership of the land in question. Except as below it is therefore only necessary to search against a name for the period during which the estate owner owned the land. For the purposes of the search form, periods of ownership must be stated in whole years and can be ascertained by looking at the abstract or epitome of title supplied by the seller. If the estate owner's period of ownership is not known, as will be the case when searching against the name of the person who was the seller in the document forming the root of title, the search is in practice made from 1926 (the year when the register was opened). Where there is a voluntary disposition on the title which is, at the date of the contract, less than five years old, it is necessary to search against the donor's name for a period up to and including the fifth year after the date of the voluntary disposition to ensure that no bankruptcy of the donor occurred during this period. The bankruptcy of the donor during this period could lead to the disposition being set aside by the trustee in bankruptcy. Since it is possible to register a land charge against a deceased estate owner after his death, it is necessary to extend the period of search against the deceased to cover the period between his death and the current date.

2.6.6. Unless a description of the land is inserted on the search application form, the computer will produce entries relating to every person of the given name in the whole of the county or counties specified. In order to avoid having to read through and then reject multiple search entries revealed by the certificate of search, a brief description of the land which is sufficient to clearly identify it should be included on the application form. Although the intention of describing the land is to curtail the number of irrelevant entries produced by the computer, care should be taken in supplying the description, since an inaccurate description of the land may result in a relevant entry not being revealed by the search. Particular care is needed when the abstract shows that the land was formerly part of a larger piece of land, e.g. is one plot on a building estate, since the land may previously have been known by a different description to its current postal address. If the search is limited to the present postal address, entries registered against its former description will not be revealed by the search. In such a case both the present address and former description of the land should be entered on the search application form. Similarly, there is a possibility that the land was previously situated in a different administrative county to that in which it is now situate. For the reasons given above, both the present and former county must be included in the description of the land given on the search application form. In some cases the postal address of the property differs from its actual address, e.g. the village of Rogate is in the administrative county of West Sussex, but its postal address is Hampshire. In such cases the search must be made against the actual address of the property and not its postal address.

2.6.7. The buyer is not concerned to search against estate owners who held the land prior to the date of the root of title supplied to him except in so far as the names of such persons have been revealed to him in documents supplied by the seller.

2.6.8. An official certificate of search is conclusive in favour of the searcher provided that the search has been correctly made, i.e. it extends over the whole period of the title supplied by the seller and has been made against the correct names of the estate owners for this period, against the correct county or former county, and for the correct periods of ownership of each estate owner. In order to ensure that the buyer gains the protection afforded by the search, and the accompanying priority period, it is vital to check that the search application form is accurately completed.

2.6.9. Where the seller provides previous search certificates as part of the evidence of title, it is not necessary to repeat a search against a former estate owner provided that the search certificate supplied by the seller reveals no adverse entries and was made:

(a)   against the correct name of the estate owner as shown in the deeds;

(b)   for the correct period of ownership as shown in the title deeds; and

(c)   against the correct description of the property as shown in the deeds,

and the next disposition in the chain of title took place within the priority period afforded by the search certificate. If any of the conditions outlined above cannot be met, a further search against the previous estate owner must be made.

2.6.10. Sub-sales

Where A has contracted to sell to B, and before B completes his purchase he contracts to sub-sell to C, the sub-purchaser (C) will need to make a search against A's title since at the time of C's search application B will not be the estate owner of the land. B's name should be included on the search (although B will not be an estate owner in the land within the terms of Land Charges Act 1972) because the search may reveal bankruptcy entries against him. If, however, B does become an estate owner before completing the second sale to C, B's name must also be searched against.

1. For fee see App. IX.4. and for address see App. XIII.4.
2. See below, para. 2.15.

2.7.   **Acting for the lender**

2.7.1.   The lender is, like the buyer, concerned to ensure that the property being purchased has a good and marketable title.

2.7.2.   Where the same solicitor is acting both for the buyer and his lender, pre-completion searches in HM Land Charges Department are normally carried out once on behalf of both clients each of whom is able to claim the protection (if any) afforded by the search certificate.

2.7.3.   Where a Land Registry search is being made the buyer is able to take the protection of the search if it is made in the name of the lender but not vice versa. It is therefore important in this situation to remember to complete the search application form in the name of the lender client. If the application form is completed in the name of the buyer client a second search must be made on behalf of the lender.

2.7.4.   If the buyer and his lender are separately represented, subject to para. 2.7.3. above, the lender will frequently accept the results of searches made by the buyer's solicitor, but in some cases may insist on carrying out the pre-completion searches himself. The lender's requirements in relation to this matter should be ascertained in good time to avoid the duplication of work and expense involved in making two separate sets of searches.

2.7.5.   No lender will lend money to a buyer who is bankrupt. The lender will therefore always insist that his solicitor obtains a clear result of a bankruptcy search against the buyer (see below, para. 2.8.) before releasing the advance.

2.7.6.   Some lenders may also insist that a search is also made against the buyer's name in the Register of Voluntary Arrangements.

2.7.7.   Where the Standard Mortgage Instructions (SMI) apply the solicitor is required to make certain searches during the course of the transaction. The procedure for certifying a search result is also outlined in the SMI.[1]

1. At the time of publication the SMI had not been finalised.

2.8.   **Bankruptcy search**

2.8.1.   Irrespective of whether the transaction relates to registered or unregistered land, a lender will require a clear bankruptcy search against the name of the buyer before releasing the advance.

2.8.2.   Unless a full search of the register has been made on Form K15 (see above, para. 2.6.) the lender's solicitor should submit Form K16 to the Land Charges Department, completed with the full and correct names of the borrower(s).[1]

2.8.3.   A search certificate will be returned by the Department.

2.8.4.   In the event of there being an adverse entry revealed by the search, the solicitor should seek to establish without delay whether or not his client is the person to whom the search entry relates. For this purpose he can obtain an office copy entry, and enquiries of the Official Receiver's office may assist in this investigation. The lender must be informed immediately if the search entry does relate to the borrower client. If there is any doubt about whether the entry does relate to the borrower, the lender's instructions should be obtained. The solicitor should only certify the search entry as not relating to the borrower if he is absolutely certain that this is the case. A certification is tantamount to a warranty given by the solicitor. The client's self-certification of the entry may not satisfy a lender client.

2.8.5.   Where a mortgage is being taken out independently from the purchase of unregistered land the lender's solicitor should make a full search on Form K15 (see above, para. 2.6.) against the names of the borrowers to ensure that there are no bankruptcy entries or priority notices registered against them. A bankruptcy only search will not reveal priority notices or deeds of arrangement under Insolvency Act 1986. In respect of the latter a search should be made at the Register of Voluntary Arrangements. This register is maintained by the Insolvency Practitioners Control Unit and a search can be undertaken, without fee, by letter or by telephone.[2]

1. For fee see App. IX.4. and for address see App. XIII.4.
2. For fee see App. IX.4. and for address see App. XIII.4.

2.9. **Probate and administration**

2.9.1. Where a grant of representation is relevant to the title and it appears from replies given to requisitions on title that the seller cannot produce the original or a marked copy of the grant on completion, the buyer should consider making a pre-completion search at the Principal Probate Registry to ensure that the grant has not been revoked or, in the case of a limited grant, that it has not expired. Alternatively, where the grant forms a link in the chain of title to unregistered land, the buyer's solicitor may ask the seller's solicitor to produce written evidence (i.e. a clear probate search) on or before completion that the grant was valid at the time of the purported disposition. Where the grant was issued by a District Registry there may be some delay before it is noted at the Principal Registry. Therefore a clear search result may not be conclusive. There is a case for saying that the search should be made in all cases where a grant forms a link in the title but in practice this is not the case.

2.9.2. The protection given to a buyer by Administration of Estates Act 1925, s.27(2) that the payment of money to a personal representative in good faith acts as a good discharge to the payer only operates where the grant is valid and had not been revoked at the time of payment. A probate search confers no priority period on the searcher and if where the buyer is buying directly from personal representatives there is doubt as to the validity of a grant, the buyer may consider whether he should require the seller to insist on the registration of the personal representatives as proprietors at HM Land Registry before completion takes place.

2.9.3. The search may be made in person by searching the year book for the year of the issue of the grant. If the grant has been revoked, a note of this fact will be recorded next to the entry recording the issue of the grant.

2.9.4. Alternatively an application may be made by letter for a postal search enclosing the appropriate fee.[1] The application should specify the full names of the deceased, the date of death, and the last known address of the deceased.

1. For fee see App. VIII.3. and for address see App. XIII.3.

2.10. **Company search**

2.10.1. The effect of Land Registration Act 1925, s.60 is that a buyer is not bound by a charge created by a company over a registered estate unless that charge is registered at HM Land Registry, regardless of whether the charge is also registered under Companies Act requirements. Therefore when buying registered land from a company it is prima facie unnecessary to make a company search in addition to a Land Registry search. However, floating charges and impending insolvency will not always be revealed by a Land Registry search and it is suggested that a company search should still be made even in the case of registered land. Additionally, the company search might reveal, e.g. that the company had been struck off the register and therefore no longer exists in law.

2.10.2. When buying unregistered land from a company, a company search ought to be undertaken in order to ensure that there are no adverse entries which would affect the buyer. Adverse entries would include, e.g. fixed or floating charges, or the appointment of a receiver or liquidator.

2.10.3. No official search procedure exists for making a company search which must be made either in person or through an agent by attendance at the Companies Registration office.[1]

2.10.4. The search is made by requisitioning the company's filed documents and examining them through a microfiche reader. The information obtained from the search is thus dependent on both the extent of the instructions given to the searcher and his diligence in carrying out those instructions. The search will only reveal matters registered against companies which are registered in England and Wales (not foreign companies). Equivalent facilities are available in Scotland for Scottish companies. Since company charges need only be registered within 21 days of creation, and are valid in the intervening period, a company search may not reveal a very recently created charge.[2]

2.10.5. Where the search is carried out through an agent care must be taken to instruct the agent fully as to the information which it is desired to obtain from the search.

1. For fee see App. VIII.3. and for address see App. XIII.4.
2. See *Burston Finance* v. *Speirway* [1974] 3 All E.R. 735.

2.11. Enduring powers of attorney

2.11.1. Where the purchase deed is to be executed by a person who is acting under the authority of an enduring power of attorney a search should be made at the Court of Protection on Form EP4[1] to check whether or not registration of the power has been effected or is pending.

2.11.2. If no registration has been made or is pending the transaction may proceed to completion.

2.11.3. If the power has been registered the attorney may deal with the land and thus, provided the donor is still alive, completion may proceed, since the power is no longer capable of revocation without notification to the Court of Protection.

2.11.4. While registration is pending the transaction may only proceed it if is within one of the limited categories permitted by Enduring Powers of Attorney Act 1985.

1. For fee see App. VIII.3. and for address see App. XIII.4.

2.12. Local land charges search and enquiries

2.12.1. These searches are invariably made before exchange of contracts and are discussed above at para. B.10. Although the local land charges search only shows the state of the register at the time of issue of the search certificate and neither search confers a priority period on the buyer, a repeat of these searches before completion is not normally considered to be necessary provided that completion takes place within a short time after receipt of the search results or (in the case of the local land charges search) adequate insurance has been taken out. Delay in receipt of the replies to these searches also frequently makes it impracticable for them to be repeated at this stage of the transaction.

2.12.2. These searches should, however, be repeated prior to completion if:

(a) there is to be a period of two months or more between exchange of contracts and completion and the search has not been covered by insurance or replaced by insurance;

(b) information received by the buyer's solicitor suggests that a further search may be advisable in order to guard against a recently entered adverse entry on the register;

(c) the contract was conditional on the satisfactory results of later searches.

2.12.3. In the absence of a special condition in the contract the discovery of a late entry on such a search is not a matter of title and will not thus entitle the buyer either to raise requisitions about the entry or to refuse to complete. Where there is to be a long gap between exchange of contracts and the contractual completion date, the buyer should try to negotiate a special condition enabling him to raise requisitions prior to completion in respect of any local land charges or adverse schemes and proposals revealed by a local search and enquiries made prior to completion and not revealed by the searches and enquiries made before exchange. Such a condition may be resisted by the seller.

2.13. Other searches

2.13.1. The buyer's solicitor should check to ensure that all other searches which are relevant to the circumstances of the transaction have been carried out and that their results are satisfactory. A checklist of the most common pre-contract searches appears above at para. B.10. These searches should normally have been carried out before exchange of contracts but may be required at this stage of the transaction if either there was insufficient time to make them before exchange or since that time additional information has come to light which indicates that a particular search may be relevant. Inspection of the property is dealt with in para. E.04. below.

2.14. Results of searches

2.14.1. The results of searches must be received by the date when completion is due to take place. Completion cannot proceed until these results have been received and are deemed to be satisfactory to the interests of the client.

2.14.2. In the majority of cases the results of searches will either show no subsisting entries or will merely confirm information already known, e.g. an entry on the register protecting the contract between the buyer and the seller or, in the case of unregistered land, the registration of existing restrictive covenants. In such circumstances no further action on the search results is required from the buyer's solicitor.

2.14.3. If an unexpected entry (other than a Class D(ii) protecting restrictive covenants, which cannot generally be removed) is revealed by the search result the buyer's solicitor should:

(a) find out exactly what the entry relates to;

(b) if the entry appears adversely to affect the property, contact the seller's solicitor as soon as possible to seek his confirmation that the entry will be removed on or before completion;

(c) in the case of a Land Charges Department search, apply for an office copy of the entry using Form K19.[1] The office copy consists of a copy of the application form which was submitted when the charge was registered and will reveal the name and address of the person with the benefit of the charge who may have to be contacted to seek his consent to its removal;

(d) keep the client, his lender and, subject to the duty of confidentiality, other solicitors involved in the chain of transactions informed of the situation since negotiations for the removal of the charge may cause a delay in completion.

2.14.4. An application form for the removal of an entry from the register in either registered or unregistered land will generally only be accepted by the Chief Land Registrar if it is signed by the person with the benefit of the charge or a person acting on his behalf. An application form signed by the seller's solicitors or an undertaking given by them on completion to secure the removal of the charge may not therefore suffice unless the seller is the person with the benefit of the charge.[2] In the case of registered land, an application for the removal of a registered charge is normally made on Form 53. Withdrawals of cautions and restrictions are effected on Forms 71 and 75 respectively. There is no specific form for the withdrawal of a notice which will be cancelled provided the Chief Land Registrar is satisfied that the notice no longer affects the land. As to bankruptcy entries, evidence needs to be lodged that the bankruptcy no longer affects the property. In the case of inhibitions (other than bankruptcy inhibitions) the Registry needs to be satisfied that the inhibition no longer serves a useful purpose or that the interests of the parties would be better served by entering a notice or restriction on the register. When an inhibition is entered pursuant to a court order, the application for its cancellation must be made to the court.

2.14.5. Charges which are registered at the Land Charges Department can only be entered against the name of an estate owner in relation to the period during which he was the owner of the land in question. Thus an entry which was made before or after this time cannot prejudice the buyer. The computerised system which is used to process these searches will sometimes throw up entries which are clearly irrelevant to the transaction in hand, particularly where the name searched against is a very common one, e.g. John Smith. Having checked that the entry is irrelevant, it may either be disregarded or the seller's solicitor may at completion be asked to certify the entry as being inapplicable to the transaction. Certification by a solicitor is tantamount to a warranty, the consideration for it being completion of the transaction.

2.14.6. The court has a discretion to remove entries which are redundant but which cannot be removed from the register because the person with their benefit will not consent to their removal or cannot be contacted.

2.14.7. Entries protecting a spouse's matrimonial homes rights under Family Law Act 1996 can be removed on production of the death certificate of the spouse or a decree absolute or by an order of the court. In the absence of these items, the charge can only be removed with the consent of the spouse who has the benefit of the charge.

2.14.8. An official certificate of search issued by HM Land Registry is not conclusive in favour of the searcher who will thus take his interest in the land subject to whatever entries are on the register irrespective of whether or not they were revealed by the search certificate.[3] However, where a person suffers loss as a result of an error in an official certificate of search he may be able to claim compensation under Land Registration Act 1925, s.83(3), as amended.

2.14.9. An official certificate of search issued by the Land Charges Department is conclusive in favour of the searcher who will thus take his interest in the land free of any entries which are on the register but which were not revealed by the search certificate. Where a person suffers loss as a result of an error in an official certificate of search he may be able to claim compensation from the Chief Land Registrar, but there is no statutory right to compensation in these circumstances. No liability will attach to the solicitor who made the search provided that a correctly submitted official search was made.[4]

1. For fee see App. VIII.3. and for address see App. XIII.4.
2. See *Holmes* v. *Kennard & Son* (1985) 49 P.& C.R. 202.
3. *Parkash* v. *Irani Finance Ltd*. [1970] Ch. 101.
4. Land Charges Act 1972, s.12.

2.15. Priority periods

2.15.1. An official certificate of search issued by HM Land Registry following a search made on Form 94A or 94B gives a priority period to the searcher of 30 working days. A buyer will also take advantage of this protection where a search was made on his behalf in the name of his lender. The searcher will take priority over any entry made during the priority period provided that completion takes place and a correct application for registration of the transaction is received by the appropriate District Land Registry by 9.30 a.m. on the day when the priority period given by the search expires.

2.15.2. An official certificate of search issued by the Land Charges Department gives a priority period of 15 working days from the date of the certificate: in that time the searcher will take free of any entries made on the register between the date of the search and the date of completion (except pursuant to a priority notice) provided that completion takes place during the priority period given by the search.

2.15.3. The date of expiry of the priority period is shown on the search certificate and should be marked on the outside of the client's file and entered in the solicitor's diary or file prompt system to ensure that it is not overlooked.

2.15.4. The priority period given by these searches cannot be extended. If completion is delayed and cannot take place within the priority period given by the search, a new search application will have to be made. The new search certificate will give another priority period but does not extend the original priority period from the first search. This means that if a third party has made a search in the intervening period, the third party may have priority and entries made in the intervening period may be binding.

FURTHER REFERENCE

Searches and Enquiries: A Conveyancer's Guide, F.J. Silverman, Butterworths.

E.03.   The buyer's mortgage

See also: Mortgages: acting for lender and borrower, para. A.11.
Investigation of title, para. D.02.
Pre-completion searches, para. E.02.
Post-completion, section G.
Lenders, section H.
Costs, para. N.01.

3.1.   Instructions from lender

3.1.1. Instructions from the lender to act will usually be received at the same time as an offer of mortgage is made to the buyer, i.e. shortly before exchange of contracts. Since each lender's requirements will differ slightly from another, the precise instructions of the lender for whom the solicitor is acting in the present transaction must be noted and strictly observed. Any queries which arise in relation to those instructions, whether at the outset of the transaction or during its course, must be immediately clarified with the lender. Where the solicitor is acting also for the buyer, the problems of conflict of interests and confidentiality must be borne in mind. Where the same solicitor is acting for both borrower and lender he owes a duty to both clients.[1] These issues are further discussed in para. A.11. Some lenders require their solicitors to obtain evidence of the client's identity (e.g. a passport) and to keep a copy of the evidence of identity on file.

3.1.2.   *Standard Mortgage Instructions*

The Standard Mortgage Instructions[2] (SMI) form the contract between the solicitor (or licensed conveyancer) and lender where the solicitor (or licensed conveyancer) is representing a lender who has agreed to be a party to the SMI. A number of major lenders have agreed to be parties to the SMI and other mortgage lenders may instruct solicitors to act on the terms of the SMI. The instructions apply whether or not the solicitor is acting for both borrower and lender or for the lender only.

3.1.3. Modifications of the instructions specific to the transaction in hand will be notified to the solicitor in the lender's written instructions to the solicitor. Communications between the solicitor and the lender must be in writing (or confirmed in writing) and must quote the mortgage account or roll number, the borrower's name and initials, the address of the property and the solicitor's reference.

3.1.4. The solicitor must use the lender's standard documentation the wording of which must not be varied without the lender's consent.

1. See *Mortgage Express* v. *Bowerman & Partners* (1994) 34 E.G. 116; and *Bristol & West Building Society* v. *May, Merriman* [1996] E.G.C.S. 69.
2. At the time of publication the SMI had not been finallised.

3.2. Investigation of title

3.2.1. When instructed to act both for the buyer and his lender, investigation of title on behalf of both clients will be carried out simultaneously, but the particular requirements (if any) of the lender must be considered when carrying out this procedure. Any queries which arise during the course of the investigation should immediately be clarified with the mortgagee client since if they are deferred until a later stage in the transaction some delay in completion may result.

3.2.2. When acting only for the lender, the lender's solicitor should request the buyer's solicitor to send him copies of the following documents as soon as the buyer's solicitor has completed his own investigation of title:

    (a) all pre-contract searches and enquiries with their results;

    (b) the contract;

    (c) evidence of title;

    (d) requisitions on title with their answers;

    (e) the draft and subsequently the approved purchase deed;

    (f) at a later stage, all pre-completion searches with their results;

    (g) any other documents which are relevant to the acquisition of a good title by the lender or which are specifically required by the lender's instructions.

3.2.3. On receipt of these documents from the buyer's solicitor, the lender's solicitor should conduct his own investigation of the title in accordance with instructions received from his client. Any queries on the title should be raised with the buyer's solicitor who will in turn seek an answer from the seller's solicitor. Investigation must be carried out as quickly as possible so that no delay in completion occurs.

3.3. Report on title

3.3.1. Investigation of title having been completed, the solicitor will be required to make a report on title to his lender client certifying that he has carried out a full investigation in accordance with the lender's instructions and that the title to the property is good and marketable and safe for the lender to accept as security. At the stage when the Report on Title Form is submitted to the lender, there should be no remaining queries on the title, any such queries having been clarified during the course of investigation of title. Notification of queries at this late stage may well result in completion being delayed pending their resolution. If a plan has been supplied by the lender for verification this must be carefully checked before certification. The solicitor may also be asked to advise whether a further inspection of the property by the lender's surveyor before completion will be required. This is usually only required in connection with property which is in the course of construction.

3.3.2. A number of lenders have a policy of requesting that borrowers, or their solicitors, certify that all planning conditions have been complied with and that there are no breaches of building regulations.

3.3.3. Solicitors will rarely be in a position to give an unqualified certificate. Breaches of building regulations are unlikely to be detectable, even by surveyors. Likewise, compliance with planning conditions may only be ascertained by inspection.

3.3.4. Local land charge searches on Form LLC1 will reveal if there are any planning charges and proceedings for building regulation breaches. The reply to question 6 of CON 29 (1994) should reveal if proceedings have been authorised for any infringement of building regulations.

3.3.5. Enquiries of the seller's solicitors, or the borrower himself if he is in occupation, should reveal whether any notices have been received from the local authority complaining of building regulation or planning breaches.

3.3.6. Any certificate by the borrower's solicitor should be limited to matters revealed by the usual local searches and by their enquiries of the seller/borrower. It is suggested that reporting solicitors should decline to certify that they are not aware of any matters which would give rise to a breach of planning conditions or building regulation control. Such a statement might lead a lender to assume that the solicitor has undertaken more extensive enquiries than a solicitor would reasonably be expected to make.

3.3.7. A reporting solicitor can properly go no further than confirm to the lender that searches and enquiries do not reveal evidence of any breach.

3.3.8. Where the Standard Mortgage Instructions[1] (SMI) apply the reports on title must be in the standard form and signed by a solicitor holding a current practising certificate, a licensed conveyancer or a fellow of the Institute of Legal Executives.

1. At the time of publication the SMI had not been finalised.

3.4. Searches before completion

3.4.1. Searches before completion are an integral part of the investigation of title procedure and should be strictly carried out before a report on title is submitted to the lender. If time does not permit this, the report on title should be qualified by a statement saying that the report is given subject to the results of such searches being satisfactory. The searches which need to be undertaken are identical to those which are conducted on behalf of a buyer, subject to the following modifications, and when the same solicitor is acting both for the buyer and his lender will be carried out once on behalf of both clients. Where two separate solicitors are acting for the buyer and his lender, the lender's solicitor should indicate to the buyer's solicitor whether he will accept the results of pre-completion searches made by the buyer, or whether he wishes to conduct his own searches. Where the title being purchased is registered, the buyer may take the benefit and protection of a search made in the name of the lender; thus only one search application is necessary. The converse is not true, so that if the search application is made in the name of the buyer, a second application must be submitted in the name of the lender. Whether or not the land is registered, the lender will invariably instruct his solicitor to make a Land Charges Department search for bankruptcy against the name of the borrower(s) and to obtain a clear result to that search before releasing the mortgage funds into the buyer's hands. Where the borrower is a company a company search should be made against the borrower both as a safeguard against liquidation, receivership or administration and also for potential incumbrances, e.g. debentures which charge after-acquired property.

3.5.   **Life policies**

3.5.1.   The lender's instructions in relation to any life policy which is to protect or act as collateral security to the mortgage must be carried out before completion. In a case where a solicitor is acting both for the buyer and his lender, in his capacity as buyer's solicitor and irrespective of whether the lender requires an endowment policy to be on foot by actual completion, or whether his instructions permit the policy to be obtained within a certain period after completion has taken place, the solicitor owes a duty to the buyer to ensure that the policy is on foot at the date of actual completion,[1] failing which the solicitor might be liable to the buyer or his personal representatives in negligence for any resulting loss, e.g. if the buyer died after completion so that the mortgage had to be repaid before the policy became effective. It is also usual in the case of a new policy to check that the first premium has been paid and that it states that the age of the insured is admitted. If age is not admitted and the age of the policy holder turns out to be wrong, this could have the effect either of invalidating the policy or of reducing the proceeds which are payable under the policy.

3.5.2.   Some lenders require a formal assignment to them of the benefit of the policy, in which case such assignment must be prepared (usually on a standard form supplied by the lender) and executed by the borrower. The assignment should be kept with the title deeds to the mortgaged property and after completion sent to the lender for safe custody. The deed of assignment is not submitted to HM Land Registry when an application for registration of title is made. Where the lender does not require a formal mortgage or deposit of the policy, the proceeds of the policy will fall into the deceased's estate on his death, and may not therefore be available to pay off the mortgage debt. This problem is particularly relevant where one of two unmarried co-owners dies, and the policy taken out by the deceased will fall into his estate and not into the hands of the surviving co-owner. The consequences of non-assignment or non-deposit of the policy should be explained to the policy holder and to potential beneficiaries under the policy at the time when the policy is taken out.

3.5.3. To preserve the priority of the lender's claim to the benefit of the policy moneys, notice of the assignment of the benefit of the policy should, after completion, be given to the insurance company in accordance with Policies of Assurance Act 1867. If the lender does not supply a standard form on which to make this notification, a letter may be sent to the insurance company informing them of the assignment, the name of the assignee (the lender), and the details of the policy which has been assigned. Two copies of this letter or standard form notice should be sent to the insurance company, requesting them to sign one copy in acknowledgement of its receipt and to return it to the solicitor. The receipted copy must then be placed with the title deeds of the property for safe custody.

3.5. The lender may require under the Standard Mortgage Instructions [2] (SMI) that an endowment policy is put on risk on or before completion of the mortgage.

1. But see *Lynne* v. *Gordon Doctors & Walton* (1991) 135 S.J. (L.B.) 29.
2. At the time of publication the SMI had not been finalised.

3.6. The mortgage deed

3.6.1. Where the mortgage is granted by an institutional lender, e.g. a bank or building society, drafts and engrossment copies of the lender's standard form of mortgage will be supplied to the solicitor for completion and execution by the borrower. In other cases the lender's instructions (if any) as to the form and contents of the mortgage must be followed and his approval obtained to the draft deed before engrossment. A legal mortgage must be made by deed to comply with Law of Property Act 1925, s.87. Form 45 is prescribed for use in registered land cases, but use of this form is not compulsory. The mortgage deed must, however, identify the registered land which is to be charged, i.e. by its title number.

3.6.2. The mortgage deed will be prepared simultaneously with the purchase deed and will be executed by the borrower prior to completion. The borrower is required to execute the deed in the presence of a witness, but in the case of a legal mortgage the lender does not usually sign the deed. If the mortgage is equitable it will generally be a contract for a disposition of an interest in land within Law of Property (Miscellaneous Provisions) Act 1989, s.2 which is required to be in writing and signed by both contracting parties.

3.6.3. The contents and effect of the mortgage deed should be explained to the borrower before signature to ensure that, e.g. the borrower understands that the lender will be entitled to sell the property if the borrower defaults in his repayments. Any prohibitions contained in the mortgage, e.g. as to letting the property or particular conditions attached to it, should also be explained to the borrower and where the charge is an all-moneys charge the effect of this type of charge should be explained to the client.[1]

3.6.4. The solicitor acting for the lender owes a duty to his lender client to ensure that the security effected over the property will be valid and enforceable. Problems can arise where, e.g. a 'friend' of one of the co-borrowers ostensibly pretending to be the co-borrower's wife signs the mortgage deed in the wife's place thus vitiating the security. It would appear that a solicitor does not generally have a duty to ensure that the mortgage deed is validly executed by the named borrower(s) but he should be alert to the issues involved and should do what he can to ensure proper execution by the correct persons. Execution by the borrower(s) in the solicitor's presence is a sensible precaution to take, although even this will not guard against forgery where the identity of the borrowers is not known personally to the solicitor.[2]

3.6.5. The lender's instructions will frequently also require the solicitor to discuss repayment of the mortgage with the borrower and may require the solicitor to obtain a signed banker's standing order for repayments from the borrower. The borrower should also be advised as to the tax consequences of the mortgage and the availability of tax relief on the interest elements of his repayments.[3]

1. Under the Standard Mortgage Instructions (SMI) the solicitor must explain the terms of the mortgage deed with the borrower client. At the time of publication the SMI had not been finalised.
2. See the Law Society's guidance on mortgage fraud, App. III.1.
3. See Tax relief on mortgages, para. A.17.

3.7. Mortgage funds

3.7.1. The effect of any retentions from the mortgage advance must be explained to the buyer in advance of completion and, if necessary, the buyer should be advised to seek estimates for any works which are to be effected on the property.

3.7.2. The lender will not release the mortgage advance to the solicitor until he is satisfied that all conditions attached to the advance have been complied with and he has been requested to release the funds by the solicitor acting for him. Such request is commonly made on the Report on Title Form, or on a separate form supplied by the lender. The solicitor should ensure that he is in receipt of cleared funds (in order to avoid any breach of Solicitors' Accounts Rules) by the morning of the day of actual completion. The mortgage advance is clients' money and must be placed in a clients' account. If completion does not take place on the anticipated date, the amount of the mortgage advance must be returned to the lender or dealt with in accordance with his instructions, and a further cheque requested for the re-arranged completion date. If the solicitor pays the advance cheque into his clients' account and completion is delayed the solicitor may be liable to pay interest on the amount of the advance if the cheque is not returned to the lender within the time specified in the lender's instructions. The mortgage advance is held by the solicitor (pending completion) on trust for the lender. If the solicitor deals with the funds during this time, except in accordance with the lender's instructions, a breach of trust will occur.[1]

3.7.3. Any conditions relating to the discharge of the borrower's existing mortgage over the same or another property must be complied with before the mortgage advance is released for his use.

3.7.4.   If it is not possible to synchronise a sale and purchase transaction or in any other situation where it becomes apparent that the mortgage funds will not be available in time to complete the purchase, the buyer must be advised of the consequences of a delayed completion and of any decision to use bridging finance in order to complete the purchase on the due date.

3.7.5.   Where different solicitors are acting for the buyer and his lender, it will be necessary for the two solicitors to liaise in order to ensure that the mortgage funds reach the seller's solicitor's bank account in time for completion.

1. *Target Holdings* v. *Redferns (a firm)* [1995] N.P.C. 136 (H.L.) and see *Bristol & West Building Society* v. *May Merriman* [1996] E.G.C.S. 69.

3.8.   Duty to lender

3.8.1.   Solicitors who are in breach of their instructions from a lender to notify it of any matters which prejudice the lender's security or which were at variance with the offer of advance are liable contractually to repay the advance. The advance is held on trust to apply in accordance with the lender's instructions.[1] Where the lender instructs that separate advice must be given to joint borrowers, the joint borrowers must be seen separately (although advice may be given to both by the same solicitor). Where the solicitor signs a certificate saying that he has independently advised the borrowers, the lender is not under a duty to enquire as to the nature of the advice given.[2]

1. *Bristol & West Building Society* v. *A. Kramer & Co.*, *The Independent*, 26 January 1995, Ch. D.; *Target Holdings* v. *Redferns (a firm)* [1995] N.P.C. 136 (H.L.).
2. In *Bank Melli Iran* v. *Samadi Rad* [1995] 2 F.L.R. 367 the court suggested that advice given by a separate solicitor in the same firm was not considered to be 'independent'.
3. *Bank of Baroda* v. *Rayorel* [1995] N.P.C. 6, and see Acting for both parties, para. A.10.

3.9.   Completion of the mortgage

3.9.1.   Since it is not possible for the buyer to mortgage a property which he does not own, it follows that formal completion of the mortgage cannot take place until after completion of the purchase, irrespective of the fact that the mortgage funds will have been released to the use of the borrower on completion of the earlier purchase. As soon as completion of the purchase of the property has taken place, the mortgage deed can be completed by insertion of the date of completion and any other formalities which have to be entered in it, e.g. date of first repayment. The lender client may require to be informed that completion has taken place. There is no danger that occupiers in the property will gain an overriding interest in the property which will take priority over the lender's interest unless the occupier was in occupation before completion of the purchase took place.[1] If there is any doubt over whether vacant possession will be given the client should be advised to inspect the property immediately prior to completion.

3.9.2.   Following completion of the mortgage, the lender's charge must be protected by registration on the charges register of the title. The solicitor acting for the lender should take possession of all the necessary documents on completion and should effect the registration on behalf of his client. Where separate solicitors are acting for the buyer and the lender, it is usual for the lender's solicitor to require the buyer's solicitor to hand over on completion completed and signed Land Registry application forms and PD forms as appropriate.

3.9.3. Charges created by companies must, in addition to any registration at HM Land Registry, be registered at the Companies Registry within 21 days of their creation in accordance with Companies Act requirements. The practice now is to file a memorandum of the charge with the appropriate form at Companies House. Additionally evidence must be lodged at HM Land Registry that the charge has been registered at Companies House.[2]

1. See *Abbey National Building Society* v. *Cann* [1991] 1 A.C. 56; *Lloyds Bank plc* v. *Rosset* [1991] 1 A.C. 107.
2. See Post-completion, section G.

3.10. Custody of deeds

3.10.1. On completion of the post-completion formalities, i.e. registration, the charge certificate or title deeds and any other relevant documents, e.g. life policy and assignments and notices relating to it, should be sent to the lender for safe custody. The documents to be sent should be listed in triplicate, one copy of the list being retained on the solicitor's file, the remaining two being sent to the lender with the deeds with a request that one copy of the list is signed by the lender and returned to the solicitor as an acknowledgement of their receipt. The deeds should be despatched by a method which ensures their safe arrival at their destination, e.g. registered post, document exchange or insured post. If there is to be any delay in the despatch of the deeds, e.g. because of delays in registration at HM Land Registry, the lender should be informed of the delay, the reason for it and its likely duration.

3.11. Costs

3.11.1. The lender's costs in relation to the grant of the mortgage are primarily the lender's responsibility since he is the client who has instructed the solicitor, but the lender commonly seeks indemnity for those costs from the buyer who should be informed of this fact and their likely amount at the outset of the transaction. Where the lender is a building society, the charges should be made according to the guidelines agreed between the Law Society and the Council of Mortgage Lenders. In other cases the amount to be charged must be agreed between the solicitor and his lender client.[1]

1. See below, Costs, para. N.01.

E.04. Preparing for completion

See also: Undertakings for bridging finance, para. B.16.
The purchase deed, para. E.01.
Pre-completion searches, para. E.02.
The buyer's mortgage, para. E.03.
The buyer in occupation, para. E.05.
Completion, section F.
Acting on grant of lease, para. K.01.
Delay and remedies, section M.
Costs, para. N.01.

4.1. Introduction

4.1.1. In order to ensure that completion proceeds smoothly, both parties need to undertake a number of preparatory steps. Most of these steps have been examined in depth in other areas of this book. The following paragraphs therefore concentrate on summarising the matters to be dealt with at this stage of the transaction by way of checklists with some additional commentary.

4.2. Seller's checklist

4.2.1. (a) Ensure purchase deed has been approved and requisitions answered.

(b) Receive engrossed purchase deed from buyer – has buyer executed the deed (where appropriate) and plan (if used), or has an acceptable undertaking been given that he will execute after completion?

(c) Get seller to execute purchase deed and return it to solicitor in time for completion.

(d) Obtain redemption figure(s) for seller's mortgage(s) and check that they are correct and ensure that the seller's solicitor is aware of *all* the mortgages which need to be redeemed.

(e) Obtain last receipts, etc., where apportionments are to be made on completion.

(f) Prepare completion statement (where necessary) and send two copies to buyer in good time before completion.

(g) Remind client to organise final readings of meters at the property.

(h) Prepare forms for discharge of land charges where necessary (unregistered land).

(i) Approve any memorandum which the buyer has requested be placed on retained title deeds or grant of representation (unregistered land).

(j) Place land or charge certificate on deposit at HM Land Registry and obtain deposit number (sale of part or grant of registrable lease of registered land).

(k) Prepare any undertaking which needs to be given on completion (e.g. for discharge of seller's mortgage if also acting for the lender).

(l) Contact lender to confirm final arrangements for discharge of seller's mortgage, method of payment, etc.

(m) Prepare authority addressed to tenants relating to payment of future rent (tenanted property).

(n) Check through file to ensure all outstanding queries have been dealt with.

(o) Prepare list of matters to be dealt with on actual completion.

(p) Locate deeds and documents which will need to be inspected/handed over on completion and prepare certified copies for the buyer of those documents which are to be retained by the seller.

(q) Prepare two copies of schedule of deeds to be handed to buyer on completion.

(r) Prepare inventory of chattels and receipt for money payable for them.

(s) Check arrangements for vacant possession and handing over keys.

(t) Receive instructions from buyer's solicitor to act as his agent on completion and clarify instructions with him if necessary.

(u) Make final arrangements with buyer's solicitor for time and place of completion.

(v) Ensure estate agents are aware of completion arrangements.

(w) Prepare bill for submission to client.

4.3. Buyer's checklist

4.3.1.
(a) Ensure purchase deed has been approved and requisitions satisfactorily answered.

(b) Engross purchase and mortgage deeds.

(c) Get buyer to execute mortgage deed, purchase deed and plan (if necessary) and return it to solicitor.

(d) Send (executed) purchase deed to seller's solicitor for his client's execution in time for completion. The submission of the deed should be in escrow subject to the express condition that the buyer may withdraw if the seller fails to complete.[1]

(e) Make pre-completion searches and ensure their results are satisfactory.

(f) Make report on title to lender and request advance cheque in time for completion.

(g) Receive completion statement (where necessary) and copies of last receipts in support of apportionments and check it is correct.

(h) Remind client of arrangements for completion.

(i) Prepare forms for discharge of land charges where necessary (unregistered land).

(j) Obtain seller's approval of the wording of any memorandum which the buyer has requested be placed on retained title deeds or grant of representation (unregistered land).

(k) Prepare and agree the form of wording of any undertaking which needs to be given or received on completion.

(l) Contact lender to confirm final arrangements for completion.

(m) Ensure that any life policy required by the lender is on foot and check with client that any other insurances required for the property (e.g. house contents insurance) have been taken out. Prepare and engross assignments of other insurance policies to the buyer (e.g. for damp treatment) if appropriate.

(n) Check through file to ensure all outstanding queries have been dealt with.

(o) Prepare statement of account and bill for client and submit together with a copy of the completion statement, requesting balance due from client be paid in sufficient time for the funds to be cleared before completion.

(p) Receive advance cheque from lender, pay into clients' account and clear funds before completion.

(q) Receive balance of funds from client and clear through clients' account before completion.

(r) Arrange for final inspection of property if necessary.

(s) Prepare list of matters to be dealt with on actual completion.

(t) Check arrangements for vacant possession and handing over keys.

(u) Instruct seller's solicitor to act as agent on completion if completion not to be by personal attendance.

(v) Make final arrangements with seller's solicitor for time and place of completion.

(w) Ensure estate agents are aware of completion arrangements.

(x) Make arrangements for transmission of completion money to seller's solicitor (or as he has directed).

1. Under Companies Act 1985, s.36A execution by a company is deemed to be delivery of the deed: this re-emphasises the need for execution subject to an express condition in such cases.

4.4. Apportionments

4.4.1. Where completion does not take place on a date when outgoings on the property fall due, outgoings which attach to the land may be apportioned between the parties on completion, the calculations of the apportioned sums being shown on the completion statement.

4.4.2. Uniform business rate and water rates can be apportioned but it is normally considered better practice to inform the relevant authority after completion of the change of ownership and request them to send apportioned accounts to seller and buyer.

4.4.3. Where applicable rent and service charge payments may have to be apportioned. These matters are further dealt with in paras. K.01. and K.05.

4.4.4. Standard Condition 6.3 deals with apportionments and allows a provisional apportionment to be made where exact figures are not available at completion (e.g. in respect of service charges).

4.4.5. The seller must be asked to produce the last demands or receipts for all sums which are to be apportioned so that the calculations of the amounts due or to be allowed on completion may be made. Copies of these receipts should be sent to the buyer with the completion statement to enable him to check the accuracy of the calculation.

4.5. Completion statement

4.5.1. A completion statement, to be prepared by the seller's solicitor, showing the amount of money required to complete the transaction and how that figure is calculated, will be requested by the buyer when he submits his requisitions on title.

4.5.2. It is only necessary to provide the buyer with a completion statement where the sum due on completion includes apportionments or other sums in excess of the balance of the purchase price.[1]

4.5.3. If not sent to the buyer with the answers to his requisitions on title, the completion statement should be supplied in good time before completion to enable the buyer to check its accuracy and to make arrangements for the amount due to be available.

4.5.4. The statement should show clearly the total amount due on completion, and how that total sum is made up. Depending on the circumstances it may be necessary to take account of some or all of the following items:

    (a) the purchase price, giving credit for any deposit paid;

    (b) apportionments of outgoings;

    (c) money payable for chattels;

    (d) compensation if completion is delayed;

(e) a licence fee if the buyer has been in occupation of the property.

4.5.5. Two copies of the completion statement should be sent to the buyer together with copies of any receipts or demands on which apportioned figures have been based.

1. *Carne* v. *Debono* [1988] 3 All E.R. 485.

4.6. Statement to client

4.6.1. The buyer's solicitor should prepare and submit to his client a financial statement which shows clearly the total sum which is due from him on completion and how that sum is calculated.

4.6.2. In addition to the matters dealt with on the completion statement, the financial statement should also take account of such of the following matters as are relevant to the transaction:

   (a) the mortgage advance and any costs and/or retentions made in respect of it;

   (b) disbursements, e.g. stamp duty, Land Registry fees, fees payable for registration of notices or search fees;

   (c) the solicitor's costs.

4.6.3. The financial statement, accompanied by a copy of the completion statement and the solicitor's properly drawn bill, should be sent to the client in sufficient time before completion to allow the client to forward the required balance of funds to the solicitor in time for those funds to be cleared by completion.

4.7. Money – the buyer

4.7.1. On being informed of the amount required to complete, the buyer's solicitor should check the figures for accuracy, verifying any apportionments made against the copy receipts or demands supplied by the seller. Any discrepancies must be clarified as a matter of urgency.

4.7.2. The solicitor should then make a final calculation of the sums due on completion, preparing his financial statement and bill for submission to the client.

4.7.3. If at this stage it appears that there is any shortfall in funds the client must immediately be informed and steps taken to remedy the shortfall. If bridging finance or a further loan are necessary in order to complete the transaction arrangements must be made to effect such arrangements without delay. An undertaking given by the solicitor to repay bridging finance must only be given where the promise given by the solicitor is wholly capable of performance by him.[1]

4.7.4. The mortgage advance requested by the solicitor from the lender should be received in sufficient time to permit the funds to be cleared through clients' account before completion.

4.7.5. The client must be asked to put the solicitor in funds for the balance of the completion money (over and above the mortgage advance) in sufficient time to permit the funds to be cleared through clients' account before completion. On receipt of the funds from the client, the cheque should be credited to a ledger account in the name of that client.

4.7.6. On the day of completion arrangements must be made to remit the amount due to the seller's solicitor in accordance with his instructions.

1. See Undertakings for bridging finance, para. B.16.

4.8. Completion checklist

4.8.1. When preparing for completion the buyer's solicitor should make a checklist of the matters which need to be dealt with on actual completion to ensure that nothing is overlooked. Where the transaction is complex, the list should be submitted to the seller's solicitor for his agreement as to its contents. Where the buyer instructs a person to act as his agent on completion he should, when instructing the agent, send him a copy of the checklist so that the agent is fully informed as to the matters which need to be dealt with.

4.8.2. Some or all of the items in the following checklist will need to be attended to on actual completion.

4.8.3. The list should contain an itemised list of the documents which need to be inspected/marked/handed over/ received at completion.

    (a) **Documents to be available at completion**

        (i)   contract;

        (ii)   evidence of title;

        (iii) copy purchase deed;

        (iv) answers to requisitions;

        (v)   completion statement.

    (b) **Documents to be inspected by buyer**

        (i)   title deeds where in unregistered land these are not to be handed over on completion (e.g. on a sale of part);

        (ii) general or enduring power of attorney;

        (iii) grant of administration;

        (iv) receipts/demands for apportionments if not previously supplied.

(c) **Documents, etc., to be handed to buyer on completion**

   (i)   land or charge certificate(s)/title deeds;

   (ii)   original lease;

   (iii)   executed purchase deed;

   (iv)   undertaking to deposit land certificate or actual deposit number if known (sale of part of registered land);

   (v)   schedule of deeds;

   (vi)   Form 53/discharged mortgage or undertaking in respect of discharge of mortgage(s);

   (vii)   receipt for money paid for chattels;

   (viii) authority addressed to tenants relating to payment of future rent and original tenancy agreements/leases (tenanted property);

   (ix)   keys of the property (if these are not available the seller's solicitor should be asked to telephone the key holder to request the release of the keys);

   (x)   certified copy of any memorandum endorsed on retained deeds;

   (xi)   landlord's licence.

(d) **Documents, etc., to be handed to seller on completion**

   (i)   banker's draft for amount due on completion;

   (ii)   executed duplicate purchase deed/counterpart lease/licence (where appropriate);

   (iii)   receipted schedule of deeds received from seller;

   (iv)   release of deposit if held by third party in capacity of stakeholder.

(e) **Endorsements on documents if required by buyer**

   (i)   endorsement of assent or conveyance on grant of representation (unregistered land);

   (ii)   endorsement of sale on most recently dated retained document of title (sale of part of unregistered land);

   (iii)   mark up abstract or epitome as compared against the original deeds (unregistered land in respect of any document the original of which is not handed over on completion).

E.05.   The buyer in occupation

See also: Licence or tenancy, para. K.12.
Delay and remedies, section M.

5.1.   Introduction

5.1.1.   In many cases the seller will be in actual occupation of the property until completion and thus the question of the buyer taking possession before completion does not arise. The seller is entitled to retain possession until completion unless otherwise agreed.

5.1.2.   The buyer's request to enter and occupy the premises before completion should be regarded with some caution by the seller since once the buyer takes up occupation he may lose his incentive to complete on the contractual completion date and, if ultimately he does not complete the transaction at all, it may be difficult to evict the buyer from the property. Where the seller has a subsisting mortgage on the property, his lender's consent should be obtained before the buyer is allowed into occupation.

5.1.3.   It is essential that the nature of the buyer's occupation is a licence and not a tenancy in order to avoid the possibility of the buyer claiming security of tenure against the seller.[1] Even where a licence is granted a court order will always be necessary to remove a residential occupier who does not voluntarily vacate the property,[2] and may be necessary in non-residential cases where the tenant will not peaceably surrender his occupation.

1. See below, Licence or tenancy, para. K.12. An outline of the major statutes affecting security of tenure is given in section K.
2. Protection From Eviction Act 1977, s.2.

5.2.   Conditions to be imposed on buyer

5.2.1.   Where it is agreed to allow the buyer into possession the seller may consider imposing some restrictions or conditions of occupation on the buyer. If the contract does not make provision for occupation by the buyer (e.g. Standard Condition 5.2), the terms of the occupation should be agreed in writing and signed by both parties prior to the commencement of the buyer's occupation.

5.2.2.   Some or all of the following conditions may be considered:

        (a) the occupation shall be a licence and not a tenancy;[1]

        (b) payment of a further instalment of the purchase price as a pre-condition of occupation;

        (c) payment of a licence fee during occupation (frequently this is calculated by reference to the rate at which compensation for late completion is payable under the general conditions of the contract);

        (d) the licence should be non-assignable;

        (e) restrictions on who may occupy the property;

        (f) restrictions on the use of the property during the buyer's occupation (including an obligation to comply with the terms of the lease in the case of leasehold property);

        (g) payment by the buyer of all outgoings on the property;

        (h) the buyer to be responsible for insuring the property and/or paying the insurance premium;

        (i) the buyer to be responsible for repairs and maintenance;

        (j) prohibition on alterations and improvements;

        (k) provisions for termination of the licence by either party;

        (l) entitlement to the income of the property (if any).

5.2.3.   Some but not all of the above conditions are provided by Standard Condition 5.2 which restricts the occupation of the property to the buyer and his household.

5.2.4.   Alternatively, the seller may consider granting the buyer a licence for access only, e.g. for measuring up for alterations, such licence to be restricted to access at specified times and for a specific purpose.

1. But see below, Licence or tenancy, para. K.12. Where the terms of the original contract do not provide for the buyer's occupation, care must be exercised in drawing up the terms of the licence agreement. Such an agreement does not fall within Law of Property (Miscellaneous Provisions) Act 1989, s.2 but for certainty should be in writing and signed by both parties.

5.3.   **Delay**

5.3.1.   Where there is a delay in completion and the seller sues for specific performance, the court usually gives the buyer the option either of paying the balance of the purchase price with interest into court or of giving up possession.[1] This provision is, however, thought not to apply where the buyer takes possession under a provision to that effect contained in the contract to purchase the property, e.g. Standard Condition 5.2.[2]

5.3.2.   The seller has an equitable lien over the property which endures until the purchase price is paid in full.[3]

1. This order is known as a 'Greenwood and Turner' order after the case of that name: *Greenwood* v. *Turner* [1891] 2 Ch. 144.
2. *Attfield* v. *D.J. Plant Hire and General Contractors Ltd.* [1987] Ch. 141.
3. See below, Delay and remedies, section M.

5.4.   Common law provisions

5.4.1.   The seller's position as quasi-trustee of the property on behalf of the buyer, from which stems the seller's duty to take care of the property pending completion, is not affected by the buyer's occupation. Therefore the seller should expressly pass this duty of care (and to do repairs) on to the buyer as part of the licence to occupy.

5.4.2.   The buyer becomes entitled to receive the income of the property and is responsible for outgoings.

5.4.3.   Unless the contract provides to the contrary, the buyer, by taking possession, will be deemed to have accepted the seller's title and thus loses his right to object to any defects of which he knew at that time.[1] Standard Condition 5.2.7 reverses this common law rule by providing that the buyer's right to raise requisitions is unaffected by his occupation of the property.

1. See above, After exchange, para. C.05.

5.5.   The buyer

5.5.1.   Since the terms of the occupation agreement will normally be construed as a licence and not a tenancy the buyer's position as occupier is somewhat tenuous and he will face certain eviction if he does not ultimately complete the purchase. The buyer should therefore be advised not to spend money on altering or improving the property until completion has taken place. The terms of the occupation agreement will often prohibit the buyer from altering or improving the property pending completion.

5.5.2.   If delay in completion is anticipated, the buyer may seek to protect his contract by registration as a notice or caution (a Class C(iv) estate contract in unregistered land) although this may strictly be unnecessary in registered land cases since by being in occupation the buyer would be able to establish an overriding interest under Land Registration Act 1925, s.70(1)(g).[1]

5.5.3.   The terms of the occupation agreement should be fully explained to the buyer. In particular his attention should be drawn to the financial provisions since the buyer is often required to pay a further instalment of the purchase price together with a daily licence fee as one of the terms of his occupation. Where the purchase is being financed by a mortgage, the lender's consent to the terms of the occupation agreement should be obtained.

1. See above, After exchange, para. C.05.

5.6. **Sitting tenants**

5.6.1. Where the property is being sold to a sitting tenant there is ample justification for accepting a less than 10% deposit on exchange of contracts, or even for dispensing with the deposit altogether.[1]

5.6.2. Although the tenant will already be familiar with the physical condition and structure of the property, he should still consider the merits of a survey of the property. In cases where the landlord is responsible for repairs, the tenant will on completion become responsible for the maintenance and upkeep of the property and will thus need to be aware of any major structural defects in it which might affect his decision to proceed with the purchase or his ability to resell the property at a later date. Even in cases where the tenant is currently responsible for repairs he may still consider it wise to have a survey of the property made.

5.6.3. Even where the tenant is not raising a mortgage to finance his purchase, full deduction of title by the landlord should be required to ensure that the tenant will become registered with an absolute freehold title and thus able to resell the property should he wish to do so. If the title to the tenant's lease is already registered, an application for merger of the freehold and leasehold titles may be made after completion. If the tenant's leasehold interest in the property is subject to a mortgage which is not discharged on completion of the purchase of the reversion, the freehold and leasehold titles cannot be merged.[2]

5.6.4. The landlord should include a contractual provision to the effect that the tenant will remain liable on the tenant's covenants contained in the lease until actual completion. Without such a clause it could be argued that the lease under which the tenant currently holds the property comes to an end on the contractual completion date irrespective of whether actual completion occurs then or later. This would mean that the landlord would be unable to enforce covenants or to recover any rent from the tenant during the period between the contractual completion date and actual completion. Alternatively a contractual condition may be inserted to the effect that the sale of the property is subject to the terms of the lease, the lease merging with the freehold on completion. The landlord should consider the effect of the contract for sale on his insurance policy covering the property. Where the tenant enjoys the protection of a statutory tenancy under Rent Act 1977 or other statutory provision, he may lose his security of tenure on exchange of contracts since after that time he is in occupation of the property pursuant to the terms of his contract to buy and not by virtue of the statute; if therefore the contract to purchase was rescinded before completion, such a tenant might have no security of tenure.

5.6.5.   Standard Condition 5.2 (occupation before completion) does not apply to a sale to a sitting tenant.

1. See above, Deposit, para. B.17. Standard Condition 2.2.1 provides for payment of a 10% deposit.
2. See below, Registration of title, para. G.03.

E.06. Death and insolvency

See also: Delay and remedies, section M.

6.1. Death of a contracting party

6.1.1. The death of one of the contracting parties between contract and completion does not affect the validity of the contract; the benefit and burden of the contract passes to the deceased's personal representatives who are bound to complete.

6.2. Death of sole seller

6.2.1. The seller's personal representatives are bound to complete the contract, but cannot actually do so until issue of the grant of representation. Executors derive their authority from the will, administrators from the grant, but in either case the grant is necessary in order to make title to the buyer. Even in the case of executors, it is unsafe for a person dealing with them to rely on evidence of their appointment other than by production of the grant.

6.2.2. If completion does not take place on the contractual completion date, a breach of contract will occur (irrespective of whether time was of the essence of the completion date) and remedies, e.g. compensation or damages, will be available to the innocent party.[1]

6.2.3. A delay in obtaining the grant of representation will have adverse consequences for a buyer who is involved in a chain of transactions since he may be forced to complete his sale, but unable to complete his purchase simultaneously because of the death of the seller and delay in the issue of the grant of representation. Loss suffered by the buyer, e.g. the cost of temporary accommodation may be claimable as a head of damage against the seller's personal representatives.

6.2.4. If time was not originally of the essence of the completion date, it can be made so by service of a notice to complete. Such a notice can be served on the executor(s) named in the seller's will (if any) and a separate copy of the notice served on the Public Trustee.

6.2.5. The practical answer to the problem of the seller's death is for the seller's solicitor immediately to inform the solicitors for the other party (or parties in a chain of transactions) and (with the authority of those concerned) to apply for an expedited grant of probate or letters of administration. Obviously the closer the death to the date of completion, the more acute the problem, but even in a chain transaction the parties may agree in the circumstances to postpone completion until a grant is obtained if assured that this can be done with expedition. In any circumstances where delay in completion is likely, consideration should be given to the protection of the contract by registration by the buyer's solicitor of a notice or caution (registered land) or a Class C(iv) land charge (unregistered land).

6.2.6. Although generally probate cannot issue within seven days of death (administration within 14 days), there is an exception in case of emergency with leave of two registrars. It is considered that leave would normally be granted in this situation where there is a possibility of damages being awarded against the estate and the Probate Registry will assist with quick responses and advice in such a situation.

6.2.7. A possible solution to the problems caused by the death of the seller before completion is for the executors named in the will to negotiate to allow the buyer into possession pending formal completion. On taking possession the buyer would normally be required to pay a licence fee under the terms of the contract[2] which could be offset against the compensation payable by the personal representatives for late completion.

1. See below, Delay and remedies, section M.
2. Standard Condition 5.2. See above, The buyer in occupation, para. E.05.

6.3.   **Death of co-owner**

6.3.1. Property owned by beneficial co-owners is held on trust and all the trustees must join in any conveyance of the legal estate.[1] The death of one trustee between contract and completion does not, however, affect the validity of the contract.

6.3.2. Where following the death there still remain at least two trustees of the legal estate, the transaction can proceed to completion without delay. It will be necessary to produce the death certificate of the deceased in order to provide the buyer with evidence of the death. The purchase deed will need to be redrawn to reflect the change of parties to the transaction.

6.3.3. Frequently the legal estate is held by only two trustees (e.g. husband and wife) and the death of one of them will leave only one trustee of the legal estate which will prima facie be insufficient to satisfy Law of Property Act 1925, s.27. If the trustees held the property as joint tenants in equity, the surviving joint tenant will become entitled to the deceased's equitable interest through the law of survivorship (*jus accrescendi*) and can deal with the property as a beneficial owner provided that there is no restriction on the proprietorship register of a registered title or, in unregistered land, that the requirements of Law of Property (Joint Tenants) Act 1964 are satisfied.

6.3.4. *Surviving beneficial joint tenant*

Where the sole surviving joint tenant is to transfer registered land the buyer should:

(a) check that no restriction is entered on the proprietorship register of the title;

(b) redraft the transfer to reflect the change of parties and capacity of the seller;

(c) require the seller to hand over a certified copy of the death certificate of the deceased co-owner on completion.

6.3.5. Where thc land is unregistered the buyer should:

(a) check the conveyance under which the co-owners *bought* the property to ensure that no memorandum of severance of the joint tenancy has been endorsed on it;

(b) redraft the purchase deed to reflect the change in parties. The conveyance should recite the death and state that the sole seller has become solely and beneficially entitled to the property;

(c) make a Land Charges Department search against the names of both the deceased and the survivor to ensure that no bankruptcy proceedings have been registered against either name.

6.3.6. Steps (a) and (c) immediately above would be done as a matter of course during the normal investigation of title procedure and thus do not put the buyer to extra inconvenience or expense.[2]

6.3.7. If these conditions are not satisfied, another trustee should be appointed to act with the survivor. Where the survivor has become solely and beneficially entitled to the property, delay in completion should be minimal, but normal remedies for delay would in any event be available.[3]

6.3.8. *Surviving beneficial tenant in common*

In all circumstances another trustee should be appointed to act with the surviving tenant in common. This appointment can be effected either by separate deed of appointment or by including the appointment in the purchase deed. In either case the purchase deed will have to be redrafted to reflect the change in parties. The seller's solicitor may act as the second trustee provided that there is no potential conflict of interests between the survivor and other beneficiaries (if any). Alternatively, the other beneficiary (or one of them, being of full age and competence) may be appointed as second trustee of the legal estate.[4] If a dispute arises between the trustees in relation to the sale, delay may occur. The contract is, however, binding and such delay will incur liability to the buyer[5] and the refusal of the new trustee to, e.g. sign the purchase deed will not frustrate the transaction since the buyer could seek specific performance of the contract or serve a notice to complete.

6.3.9.   *Settled land*

On the death of a sole tenant for life under Settled Land Act 1925 the position depends on whether the land remains settled land after the death. If it does, the trustees of the settlement are entitled to a grant of probate or administration limited to the settled land, and they will be the persons with capacity to make good title. If, however, the settlement ends on the death, the former settled land is included in the grant made to the deceased's ordinary personal representatives who will perform the contract.

1. Law of Property Act 1925, s.27.
2. See Investigation of title, para. D.02.
3. See Delay and remedies, section M.
4. See Trusts of Land and Appointment of Trustees Act 1996, s.19 in relation to the appointment of new trustees.
5. See Delay and remedies, section M.

6.4.   Death of sole buyer

6.4.1.   The personal representatives step into the shoes of the deceased and will be bound to complete the contract. Even in the most straightforward case some delay in completion may be experienced because the purchase deed will have to be re-drafted to reflect the change in parties and the personal representatives cannot complete until they obtain the grant of representation. Where the purchase was due to be financed by a mortgage, the death of the borrower (the buyer) will usually mean that the offer of mortgage is revoked and the personal representatives may therefore find themselves with insufficient funds to complete unless an alternative source of finance can be found. Where the deceased buyer intended to purchase the house for his own sole occupation the personal representatives may feel that since the purpose of the transaction has been defeated they no longer wish to proceed with the transaction. Unless they can negotiate a written release with the seller they will, however, be bound to complete (and may then attempt to resell the property) or face an action in damages from the seller.

6.5.   Death of joint buyer

6.5.1.   The survivor remains bound by the contract and can be forced to complete. The joint buyers obtained an equitable interest in the property on exchange of contracts and it is possible that the deceased's share in the property may on his death have passed to a third party (not to the co-purchaser) under his will or intestacy. In order to avoid delay while this matter is resolved it may be advisable to transfer the property into the names of two trustees on completion. In any event the purchase deed will have to be redrafted to reflect the change in parties. Finance may have to be rearranged and a new mortgage deed prepared. Some delay seems to be inevitable and the seller will have a claim against the buyer for loss caused by the delay.[1] In cases where the surviving buyer (being solely entitled to the benefit of the contract) decides that he/she no longer wishes to proceed with the purchase, an attempt may be made to negotiate a written release with the seller, but he is under no obligation to accede to this request. Failing a negotiated release the buyer will have to proceed with the purchase and then attempt to resell the property.

1. See Delay and remedies, section M.

6.6.   Service of notices on deceased estate owner

6.6.1.   If the person serving the notice is at the time of service unaware of the death, service on the deceased at his last known address is valid.

6.6.2.   If at the time of service the person serving the notice was aware of the death, notice should be served on the deceased and his personal representatives at the deceased's last known address and a copy of the notice served on the Public Trustee.[1]

1. Law of Property (Miscellaneous Provisions) Act 1994, ss.10−14.

6.7.   Bankruptcy of seller

6.7.1.   A buyer will usually only be affected by the bankruptcy of the seller if there is a bankruptcy entry shown on the result of his official search or on office copy entries. Such entry may reveal either the presentation of the petition and/or the making of a bankruptcy order. On the bankruptcy of an individual who is the sole proprietor of the land, the legal estate in the property owned by him passes to his trustee in bankruptcy and the buyer must from that time deal only with the trustee and not the seller. The trustee may be forced to complete the sale by an action for specific performance, subject to his right to disclaim under section 315 of Insolvency Act 1986. Under that section the trustee may, by the giving of a prescribed notice, disclaim any onerous property, which is defined as 'any unprofitable contract, and any other property comprised in the bankrupt's estate which is unsaleable or not readily saleable or is such that it may give rise to a liability to pay money or perform any other onerous act'. 'Onerous' does not in this context extend to disclaiming the contract simply because the trustee can realise more money by entering into some other contract. The trustee might in an appropriate case take the view that the contract constituted a transaction at an undervalue or a preference, in which event he might refuse to complete the transaction on this ground. Assuming the matter proceeds to completion, the purchase deed will have to be redrafted to show the trustee as the seller and the bankrupt will not be a party to the deed. Between the making of a bankruptcy order and the time at which the bankrupt's estate vests in a trustee, the Official Receiver is the receiver and manager of the bankrupt's estate, but under section 287 of Insolvency Act 1986 his powers in this period are very limited and it is doubtful whether in most cases he would be entitled to complete the transaction. The Official Receiver has, under section 293 of Insolvency Act 1986, 12 weeks following the bankruptcy order in which to decide whether to convene a meeting of creditors to appoint a trustee. If the Official Receiver decides not to summon such a meeting then he must give notice of his decision to the court and to every creditor of the bankrupt known to him or identified in the bankrupt's statement of affairs and as from the giving to the court of such notice the Official Receiver becomes the trustee of the bankrupt's estate (section 293(3)). If a creditors' meeting is held then a trustee may be appointed at such a meeting. Trust property, which includes property held by co-owners, does not vest in a bankrupt's trustee. The making of a bankruptcy order effects a severance of a joint tenancy. The bankrupt's beneficial interest in the property will vest in the trustee in bankruptcy. Consequently on the bankruptcy of one co-owner the legal estate is unaffected and completion may proceed, the bankrupt and the co-owner being entitled to convey the legal estate. If the bankrupt will not co-operate it is open to his or her co-trustee to replace the bankrupt on the grounds of the bankruptcy under the provisions of Trustee Act 1925. A buyer should attempt to get the trustee in bankruptcy to join in the purchase deed to give his consent to the sale of the beneficial interest and preferably to give a receipt for the part of the purchase money attributable to the beneficial interest, but cannot insist on this happening, nor can the trustee insist on joining in the deed.

6.8. Bankruptcy of buyer

6.8.1. The benefit of the contract passes to the buyer's trustee in bankruptcy who may complete the transaction subject to his right to disclaim onerous contracts. Where the transaction was to be financed by a mortgage the buyer's mortgage offer will have been revoked by the bankruptcy, and there will obviously be no other available funds to complete the purchase. The trustee is in this situation more likely to disclaim, although he would in so doing forfeit the deposit already paid and be subject to an action brought by the seller against the bankrupt's estate to recover loss suffered. Some delay is inevitable pending the appointment of the trustee and while waiting for his decision whether or not to disclaim. Where one of two or more co-purchasers goes bankrupt, the bankrupt's equitable interest will pass to his trustee. The remaining buyer(s) may have difficulty in completing on the contractual completion date, or at all, since a joint mortgage offer may have been vitiated by the co-purchaser's bankruptcy. If the non-bankrupt buyer can refinance his purchase he may complete the purchase on his own (he is contractually bound to do so) but would hold the bankrupt's equitable interest in the property on trust for the trustee who might at a later stage wish to sell the property in order to realise this asset for the benefit of the bankrupt's creditors. A seller who wished to force completion on a buyer's trustee in bankruptcy must give written notice to the trustee requiring him within a period of 28 days (or such longer period specified by the court) in which to perform or disclaim the contract and the property. If the trustee does not disclaim within this period the right to disclaim is lost. The seller may at all times pursue the remedies open to a seller where a buyer defaults, including bringing an action for specific performance. If the seller completes the transaction with the buyer between the presentation of a petition but before the bankruptcy order is made, but having effected a priority search on which no bankruptcy entry appears, the trustee cannot reclaim the purchase price from the seller: this is probably the case even if he is able to prove that after the making of the priority search the seller became aware of the presentation of a bankruptcy petition.

6.9. Appointment of liquidator

6.9.1. Every disposition of a company's property after presentation of a winding-up petition to the court is void if a winding-up order is subsequently made unless sanctioned by the court. Accordingly where a petition for the compulsory winding-up of a company is presented the buyer must insist on obtaining the sanction of the court to the completion of the transaction or he must await the result of the petition. In the case of a voluntary liquidation the directors' powers cease on the appointment of a liquidator whether the liquidation is a members' voluntary liquidation or a creditors' voluntary liquidation. A liquidator can complete a sale on behalf of the company and can bring proceedings to force a buyer to complete a transaction. In the case of a compulsory winding up the liquidator will require the sanction of the court to bring proceedings, but in the case of a voluntary winding up no such sanction is required. When a seller company goes into liquidation the liquidator will normally complete the transaction. The company will normally remain as 'seller' and the liquidator will attest the deed on the company's behalf. The liquidator will only become the 'seller' in the purchase deed if an order vesting the legal estate in him has been made by the court, which happens only very rarely. The formalities of a liquidator's appointment are dealt with by Insolvency Rules 4.100−4.105 and a buyer from a liquidator should ensure that those formalities have been complied with. Where a liquidator is appointed to a company which is buying land, the liquidator has the power to complete or to disclaim an onerous contract in which latter case the position is the same as already discussed under para. 6.7.1. in the case of an individual buyer becoming insolvent. Non-availability of funds may present practical problems in proceeding to completion. Where the buyer company is in liquidation and does not complete the seller may exercise his contractual rights, including the ability to forfeit any deposit, and in the converse situation the buyer has the right to recover his deposit from any stakeholder. If the matter does not proceed to completion then any damages will be a proveable debt in the liquidation.

6.10.   **Appointment of administrative receiver**

6.10.1.   The appointment of an administrative receiver does not affect the validity of the transaction. The powers of the receiver will be those contained in the instrument under which he was appointed and in addition he will have the powers conferred upon him by Schedule 1 Insolvency Act 1986. Most of the powers of the directors will be suspended by virtue of the appointment of the administrative receiver. The appointment of a receiver has the effect of crystallising floating charges created by the company and a buyer from a company in receivership will have to take steps to obtain the release of the property from the now fixed charge. The receiver may join in the purchase deed on sale to give a receipt for the purchase price and will execute the purchase deed on behalf of the company. The company normally remains the 'seller' under the contract or purchase deed since if the receiver enters the transaction in his own name he will assume personal liability for it. For this reason, any contract entered into by the receiver in the name of the company will normally contain a clause excluding the receiver's personal liability and excluding the effect of any implied covenants for title from the purchase deed. Where the company is buying land, the receiver will execute the purchase deed on behalf of the company, but in this situation the financing of the purchase may have to be re-arranged and this may result in some delay. A certified copy of the document appointing the receiver should be handed over on completion.

6.11.   **Signature of documents**

6.11.1. *Trustee in bankruptcy*

A trustee in bankruptcy should sign a contract using the following wording: 'trustee in bankruptcy of XY a bankrupt [without personal liability]'.

6.11.2.   The attestation clause of the purchase deed can be expressed in the following way: 'signed as a deed by CD in the presence of.............(trustee of the estate of XY, a bankrupt)'.

6.11.3.   Many insolvency practitioners seek to limit their liability by adding the words 'without personal liability' to the attestation clause. It is understood that these words imply that the trustee can still be sued *qua* trustee, but that liability in him in his personal capacity is excluded. These words do not preclude negligence liability for which most insolvency practitioners will carry indemnity insurance.

6.11.4. *Supervisor of voluntary arrangement*

The company, individual or mortgagee will execute the document in the normal way unless the scheme is such that the land has been vested in the supervisor or trustee. If this occurs the supervisor must transfer and execute as a trustee.

6.11.5.   A contract signed or transfer executed by a supervisor may use the following wording: 'Supervisor of XY acting in the voluntary arrangement of XY [without personal liability]'.

6.11.6.   The words 'without personal liability' have the same effect as is noted in para. 6.11.3. above.

6.11.7. *Law of Property Act receiver*

A Law of Property Act receiver can sign a contract or execute a transfer provided that the appointing lender delegates this power. The authority from the lender should be in writing but under section 1 of Law of Property (Miscellaneous Provisions) Act 1989 does not need to be under seal. A receiver signs a contract as agent for the borrower. It is normal practice in these circumstances for the appointing lender to sign the contract and execute the transfer using his power of sale. The capacity in which the lender sells will affect the nature of the implied covenants for title given to the buyer in the purchase deed.

6.11.8. *Debenture holder*

A debenture holder can sign in the name of the company provided that he holds a valid power of attorney from the company.

6.11.9. *Administrative receiver*

In the absence of any provision to the contrary, Insolvency Act 1986, s.42 and Sched. 1 gives power to an administrative receiver to execute deeds and other documents in the name of and on behalf of the company using the company's seal.

6.11.10. *Company in administration*

A deed should be executed using the common seal of the company in the presence of the administrator.

6.11.11. *Administrative receiver of company in liquidation*

The following form of wording is accepted by HM Land Registry:

'Signed as a deed by Z Limited   (Signature: Z Limited)
in liquidation by CD its receiver
pursuant to powers granted to him   by its receiver
in clause n of a debenture dated   (or liquidator as
[   ] in favour of   appropriate)
MM Bank plc in the presence of: (Signature: CD)'

6.11.12. The receiver should provide evidence of his appointment and acceptance of office.

6.11.13. *Execution on behalf of insolvent company*

(a) **Execution by receiver (whether or not the company is in liquidation)**

The following form of execution is acceptable to HM Land Registry:

'Signed as a deed by Z Limited   (Signature: Z Limited
[in liquidation] acting by CD,   [in liquidation])
its receiver pursuant to powers
granted to him in clause n
of a debenture dated   by its receiver
[   ] in favour of
MM Bank plc in the presence of: (Signature: CD)

(Signature, name and address
of witness)'

(b) **Execution by administrative receiver (whether or not the company is in liquidation)**

As for receiver (above).

(c) **Execution by administrator**

Using the common seal of the company in the presence of the administrator:

'The common seal of ABC Limited
was affixed to this deed in   Signature of administrator
the presence of: (Seal)'

(d) **Execution by liquidator**

Using the common seal of the company in the presence of the liquidator:

'The common seal of ABC Limited
(in liquidation) was affixed   Signature of liquidator
to this deed in the presence of: (Seal)'

6.11.14. *Transfer by Law of Property Act receiver*

The powers of administrative receivers do not extend to receivers appointed under section 101(1)(iii) of Law Property Act 1925. Therefore, even if sales are arranged by receivers appointed under Law of Property Act 1925, it is better practice to arrange for the appointing lender to sign the contract once his power of sale has arisen and thereafter for the lender to execute the conveyance or to transfer as lender.

6.11.15. Although the case of *Windsor Refrigeration Co. Ltd.* v. *Branch Nominees Ltd.* [1] states that if a receiver uses a power of attorney to sell under a contractually extended power, his appointment should be by deed rather than under hand, conventionally administrative receivers are appointed under hand and the appointment is regarded as merely identifying the receiver upon whom the debenture confers the power of attorney.

6.11.16. In *Phoenix Properties Ltd.* v. *Wimpole Street Nominees Ltd.* [2] one of the questions addressed by the court was whether a receiver appointed by a debenture holder *in writing* and not under seal had the power to bind a borrower to a conveyance of the legal estate in the property charged by the debenture. It was held that, since the irrevocable appointment of the receiver as attorney for the company was contained in a debenture executed as a deed by the company itself, the common law rule requiring that a receiver should be appointed under seal was satisfied. In other words, provided that the company has executed the debenture under seal, the receiver can then validly be appointed by the debenture holder in writing alone.

6.11.17. If a receiver sells with a power of attorney in place of a lender, he will not be able to sell the property free of incumbrances and a deed of release will also need to be executed by the lender and any other charge holders. In this instance, care should be taken to ensure the deed of release is executed by the lender after the execution of the transfer, as otherwise there is a risk that the receiver has no power to sell the property due to the determination of his power of sale and power of attorney under the debenture. However, if the lender sells as outlined above, the property will automatically be sold free of the mortgage and will remove subsequent charges from the title.

6.11.18. *Transfer by debenture holder*

A debenture holder can sign in the name of the company provided he holds a valid power of attorney from the company. The attestation clause should read as follows:

'Executed as a deed by ABC COMPANY acting by JOHN SMITH duly appointed to execute as an officer of XYZ Bank pursuant to clause [ ] of a debenture dated [ ] in the presence of:	ABC LIMITED by JOHN SMITH duly appointed officer of XYZ Bank by a resolution of XYZ Bank plc dated [ ] Signature: John Smith'

6.11.19. *Signature of contracts*

Due to the doubt cast by Lord Reading in the case of *Brandt (H.O.) & Co.* v. *Morris (H.N.) & Co.*[3] the better view is that agreements should be signed by including the extra words 'without personal liability' in order to ensure that a signatory signs as agent and not principal. The following is a suggested example of how agreements should be signed:

'Signed as agent for ABC LIMITED without personal liability	Signature of supervisor/ administrator/ administrative receiver/ liquidator/trustee'

6.11.20. After winding up, or after the presentation of a winding-up petition, a better wording may be:

'Signed in the name of ABC LIMITED by its [administrator/ administrative receiver] JOHN SMITH ESQ. Without personal liability'	Signature: ABC LIMITED [in liquidation]

1. [1961] Ch. 88.
2. [1989] Ch. 737.
3. [1917] 2 K.B. 784.

E.07.   Foreign companies

7.1.   What is the status of the foreign company?

7.1.1.   If it is recognised as a corporation under its foreign law it will be treated as such by English law.

7.1.2.   If the status of the company is not clear from its documents, further evidence of status will be needed before an application for registration of title can be made. This will consist either of an unequivocal certificate by the company's solicitors that it is a corporation validly incorporated under the law of its country of origin or a letter from a lawyer practising in the foreign country confirming that the applicant is a corporation under that law. Confirmation should also be obtained of the corporation's power to enter the particular transaction and of the authenticity of a named person or persons to sign the contract/purchase deed on the corporation's behalf.

7.1.3.   The information in para. 7.1.2. above does not apply to companies incorporated in Scotland. Companies registered in the Channel Isles or Isle of Man are foreign companies.

7.1.4.   Solicitors acting for the foreign company should ensure that any local consent needed for the transaction is obtained . The documents relating to the transaction should also make it clear which jurisdiction is applicable to the transaction.

7.1.5.   If the original documents are not in English or Welsh a certified translation should be supplied with an application to register at HM Land Registry.

7.2.   What are the powers of the company?

7.2.1.   This question is not relevant in the case of companies incorporated in the European Union nor where there is evidence that the law of the country of origin contains provisions equivalent to the powers conferred by the Companies Acts on trading companies. In other cases any limitation on the power of the company will be reflected on the register of title by an appropriate restriction. The constitution of the company will be perused to see what its powers are and, if not clear, evidence of the powers will be requested.

7.3.   **Execution of documents**

7.3.1.   Land Registration (Execution of Deeds) Rules 1994 (S.I. 1994/1130) which came
into force on 16 May 1994 and Foreign Companies (Execution of Documents)
Regulations 1994 (S.I. 1994/950) have the effect of making Companies Act 1985,
s.35(A) (as amended) apply to foreign companies. Section 35(A) abolished the
requirement for a company to execute a deed by using its company seal. This
section was until now of little use to foreign companies, which in many cases did
not have company seals of the type used in England and Wales. Although the
intention of the Rules is to allow foreign companies to execute deeds by the same
method as applies to English companies, thus dispensing with the need for proof
of due execution under the jurisdiction of incorporation, the Rules actually deem
a deed to be correctly executed by a foreign company if the execution complies with
the rules of execution under the jurisdiction of the company's incorporation. It may
still therefore be necessary to provide proof that the execution of the document
complies with foreign law. A new Form 19 has been introduced under the Rules
to deal with execution by foreign companies. The prescribed form of execution is
as follows:

'Signed as a deed on behalf of AB,
a corporation in [name of territory
in which AB is incorporated] by EF [and   Signature(s) of EF [and GH]
GH] being [a] person[s] who, in
accordance with the laws of this
territory, [is *or* are] acting under
the authority of the company   Authorised Signatory [Signatories]'

7.4.   **Disposals by foreign companies**

7.4.1.   When a foreign company is disposing of property which it owns the following
question is relevant: does the company have power to make the disposition? This
will only be of concern where a restriction is already on the register. Provided the
terms of the restriction can be complied with the transaction can proceed.

FURTHER REFERENCE

Land Registry Practice Leaflet No. 17, section on foreign companies and
corporations.

F. COMPLETION

F.01. Date and time of completion

1.1. **Date**   1.2. **Time**

See also: Delayed completion, para. M.01.

1.1.   **Date**

1.1.1.   The date of completion will be agreed between the solicitors for the parties (after consultation with their respective clients) shortly before exchange of contracts.

1.1.2.   Where the buyer's purchase is dependent on his sale of another property the completion dates in both contracts must be synchronised. It follows that the completion dates in all transactions in a chain of transactions must also be synchronised if the chain is not to break.

1.1.3.   In residential transactions a completion date 28 days or less from the date of exchange is common. Sufficient time must be allowed between exchange and completion for the respective solicitors to undertake the pre-completion steps in the transaction. If it is anticipated that the clients will wish to complete very quickly after exchange, arrangements can usually be made for some of the pre-completion steps in the transaction to be effected before exchange, e.g. preparation of the purchase deed.

1.1.4.   In the absence of express agreement Standard Condition 6.1.1 provides that completion shall take place on the twentieth working day after exchange.

1.1.5.   Under Standard Condition 6.1.1, time is not of the essence of the completion date; thus although a delay in completion beyond the date fixed in the contract would give rise to an action in damages at the instigation of the innocent party and would activate the compensation provisions of Standard Condition 7.3, the delay would not of itself entitle the innocent party to withdraw from the contract at that stage.[1] In the absence of this provision time would be of the essence of the completion date (thus enabling the innocent party to withdraw from the contract if delay occurs) where the common law so provides, e.g. in the case of the sale of a business as a going concern. Since delay in completion can occur for reasons beyond the control of the contracting parties, e.g. postal delays, it is not generally a good idea to make time of the essence of the completion date. If exceptionally it is desired to make time of the essence, this may be done by inserting an express provision to this effect in the contract, e.g. by adding the words 'as to which time shall be of the essence' alongside the insertion of the contractual completion date.

1. See Delayed completion, para. M.01.

1.2. **Time**

1.2.1. Where a buyer's purchase is dependent on the receipt of money from a related sale transaction, the solicitor must ensure that arrangements are made to complete the sale before the purchase and with a sufficient interval between the two transactions (e.g. a minimum of half an hour depending on the circumstances) to allow funds received from the sale to be transferred and utilised in the purchase transaction. Such arrangements will be made when final completion arrangements are made shortly before completion.

1.2.2. Where the transaction is part of a long chain, such arrangements may be complex since inevitably the transaction at the bottom of the chain (which will usually involve a buyer who is not selling in a related transaction) must complete first, the money then progressing upwards through the chain. Such a transaction will frequently have to be completed early in the morning of completion day to allow all the subsequent transactions to take place within the same working day. A completion time earlier than 10 a.m. is often difficult to comply with, unless the money is remitted to the seller on the previous day, because of restrictions on banking hours.

1.2.3. Even where a seller has no related purchase, he should ensure that the completion time agreed allows sufficient time for the proceeds of sale to be banked on the day of completion. If the money is not banked or remitted to the mortgagee until the following working day the seller will suffer loss of interest on his money. To this end a completion time later than 2.30 p.m. is inadvisable.

1.2.4. In the absence of contrary provision Standard Condition 6.1.2 provides that if completion does not take place by 2 p.m. on the day of completion interest for late completion becomes payable. This condition does not impose a time-limit for completion (in respect of which a special condition needs to be added to the contract), but merely imposes financial penalties. For the reasons given above, this time-limit may need to be amended (either in the contract or by subsequent agreement between the parties) to provide an earlier time for completion where the transaction forms part of a chain. Non-compliance with this condition is deemed a late completion which invokes the compensation provisions of Standard Condition 7.3 requiring payment of compensation at the contractual interest rate for the delay. Standard Condition 6.1.2 does not apply where the sale is with vacant possession and the seller has not vacated the property by 2 p.m. on the date of actual completion.

F.02. Place of completion

2.1. Place of completion

2.1.1. By Standard Condition 6.2 completion is to take place in England and Wales, either at the seller's solicitor's office or at some other place which the seller reasonably specifies.

2.1.2. This condition mirrors the convention that the money goes to the deeds.

2.1.3. Where the seller has an undischarged mortgage over the property and the seller's solicitor is not also acting for the lender, completion may be required to take place at the offices of the seller's lender's solicitors.

2.1.4. Where there is a complex chain of transactions it may sometimes be convenient for some or all of the solicitors for the parties involved in the chain to meet at a mutually convenient location in order to complete several of the transactions in the chain within a very short interval.

2.1.5. Under Standard Condition 6.2 the choice of venue for completion is given to the seller. If completion is not to take place at the seller's solicitor's office he should give the buyer's solicitor sufficient notice of the chosen venue to allow the buyer's solicitor to make his arrangements for attendance at completion and/or transmission of funds. If possible, the buyer's solicitor should be informed of the venue for completion in the answers given to his requisitions on title.

2.1.6. Although traditionally the buyer's solicitor attends the seller's solicitor's office in person to effect completion, it is more common today (especially in residential transactions) for completion to be effected by using the Law Society's Code for Completion by Post[1] with the transmission of funds being made directly to the seller's solicitor's bank account. In such cases the actual place of completion is of little significance to the transaction so long as both parties' solicitors are able to contact each other by telephone or fax to confirm the transmission and receipt of funds on the day of completion itself.

2.1.7. If the sale is with vacant possession and the buyer is in doubt whether or not the seller will comply with this condition (e.g. because of the presence of tenants or other non-owning occupiers in the property) he may consider the benefits of insisting on completion taking place at the property itself following an inspection of the property. The buyer may also wish to complete at the property if he, for other reasons, needs to inspect the property or its contents before completion, e.g. to check an inventory of stock or fittings. In such cases the buyer should have included a special condition in the contract stating that completion shall take place at the property, or, if this was not possible, make his request to the seller's solicitor in adequate time before completion to permit the necessary arrangements to be made. Unless such a term is included as a contractual condition, the seller is under no obligation to accede to the buyer's request since the choice of location for completion is, by Standard Condition 6.2, given to the seller.

1. The text of the Code is set out in full below in App. VII.2.

F.03. The money

See also: Financial services, para. A.04.
Preparing for completion, para. E.04.
Completion, para. F.04.

3.1. Method of payment

3.1.1. Standard Condition 6.7 provides that the buyer is to pay the money due on completion in one or more of the following ways:

(a) legal tender;

(b) a banker's draft drawn by and on a clearing bank (defined as meaning a bank which is a member of CHAPS Ltd);

(c) a direct credit to a bank account nominated by the seller's solicitor;

(d) an unconditional release of a deposit held by a stakeholder.

3.1.2. In the absence of agreement to the contrary, the seller's solicitor is entitled to refuse payment tendered by any method other than those mentioned in the contract. A special condition in the contract is required if payment is to be made in foreign currency or out of the jurisdiction.

3.1.3. Notes and gold coins are legal tender up to any amount,[1] but other coins are subject to the limits imposed in Coinage Act 1971, s.2. Currently these limits restrict payment by cupro-nickel or silver coins with a value exceeding 10p (including £1 coins) to a maximum face value of £10. Payment by cupro-nickel or silver coins with a face value not exceeding 10p are limited to a maximum of £5, and bronze coins to a maximum of £0.20.

3.1.4. Provided the parties agree, payment of money on completion may be made by a solicitor's clients' account cheque or building society cheque, but in practice payment by such methods is uncommon since there is the danger that the cheque could in theory be stopped. A 'stop' on a building society cheque would in practice be very rare and is generally confined to cases of theft, forgery, or fraud.

---

1. Currency and Bank Notes Act 1954, s.1.

3.2. Banker's draft

3.2.1. Where completion is to take place in person payment by banker's draft is the most common method of payment.

3.2.2. The buyer's solicitor may have the draft drawn in favour of the seller's solicitor (or as he has directed) or may prefer to have the draft drawn to show the buyer's solicitor as payee. In the latter case, the draft will be endorsed in favour of the seller's solicitor at actual completion, but can easily be paid back into the buyer's solicitor's clients' account should completion for some reason not take place on the due date. The draft should not be marked 'account payee only' or 'not negotiable' since the seller's solicitor may wish to endorse the draft to a third party, e.g. to use towards payment in another transaction.

3.2.3. A banker's draft can be regarded as being analogous to cash. It is therefore sensible to take precautions against forgery and theft of a draft. For this reason it may be considered to be unwise to send a banker's draft through the post and, where completion is to take place through the post or through the attendance of an agent, some other method of transmission of funds should be used.

3.3. Telegraphic transfer of funds

3.3.1. Frequently completion will take place using the Law Society's Code for Completion by Post. In such a case the parties will normally agree to transfer the amount of money needed to complete the transaction through the telegraphic transfer (or similar) system.

3.3.2. The seller's solicitor should inform the buyer's solicitor of the amount needed to complete the transaction and of the details of the account to which the funds are to be remitted. This information is normally given in response to the buyer's requisitions on title.

3.3.3. The buyer's solicitor should instruct his bank to remit funds from the buyer's solicitor's clients' account to the account nominated by the seller's solicitor. Instructions to the bank must be given sufficiently early on the day of completion to ensure that the funds arrive at their destination before the time-limit for receipt of funds, as specified in the contract, expires. Some delay in the transmission of funds may be experienced where the funds are to be transmitted from one bank to another as opposed to transfers between different branches of the same bank.

3.3.4. The seller's bank should be asked to telephone the seller's solicitor to inform him of the receipt of the funds immediately they arrive. Completion may proceed as soon as the seller's solicitor is satisfied as to the arrival of the funds in his clients' account, and it is courteous for him to confirm the safe arrival of the funds to the buyer's solicitor.

3.4.   Cleared funds

3.4.1.   In order to avoid breach of Solicitors' Accounts Rules 1991, payment of completion money should only be made from cleared funds in clients' account. This means that the buyer's solicitor must ensure that he is put in funds by his client in sufficient time for those funds to clear through clients' account before it becomes necessary to draw against them.

3.5.   Time for payment

3.5.1.   Standard Condition 6.1.2 encourages the payment of money on the day of completion by 2 p.m. in default of which payment is treated (for compensation purposes only) as having been received on the next following working day which may result in the buyer becoming liable to pay compensation for late completion under Condition 7.3. Condition 6.1.2 does not apply where the sale is with vacant possession and the seller has not vacated the property by 2 p.m. on the date of actual completion.

3.5.2.   Where the transaction forms part of a chain of transactions it may be necessary to insert a time-limit for the payment of completion money imposing a contractual obligation to complete by this specified time. If this is not done, there is a danger that the seller will not receive the funds from his sale in sufficient time to allow him to meet the time-limit in his related purchase transaction.

3.6.   Chain transactions

3.6.1.   As noted in para. 3.5.2. above, it will frequently be necessary to insert a special condition relating to the time of completion in order to allow sufficient time for funds to be received by the seller's solicitor and then utilised to complete a purchase transaction later on the same day.

3.6.2.   Where it is known that the transaction forms part of a chain arrangements may be made by the solicitors involved for the funds to be sent directly to their ultimate destination. Thus if A is selling to B and buying from C, he may need to use part of the proceeds of sale (to be paid by B) towards payment for his purchase from C. In this case A's solicitor may ask B's solicitor to send a specified part of the sale money direct to C's solicitor, the remainder being sent to A's solicitor in the normal way. C's solicitor must be asked to telephone A's solicitor when he receives the funds from B's solicitor so that the transaction between A and B can be completed. C's solicitor will also be asked to undertake to hold the funds received from B's solicitor to A's order until completion of the transaction between A and C is ready to proceed. Such an arrangement can help to avoid delays in the transmission of funds, since fewer telegraphic transfers are required (particularly in a long chain), and thus it ultimately helps to ensure that all transactions within the chain are completed within their relevant time-limits. The solicitors involved must nevertheless be careful to obtain the written authority of the parties since the protection given by Law of Property Act 1925, s.63, only applies where the money is paid to the seller's solicitor. It is a breach of trust for the buyer's solicitor to part with the money without having the title deeds in his possession or without knowing that the seller's solicitor is holding the deeds to the buyer's solicitor's order.

3.7.   Discharge of seller's mortgage

3.7.1.   The seller's existing mortgage over the property being sold will frequently be discharged immediately after completion of the sale using part of the proceeds of sale to make payment to the lender.

3.7.2.   The seller's solicitor may choose to ask the buyer to draw separate banker's drafts for completion, one in favour of the lender for the amount needed to discharge the mortgage and the other, for the balance of the money due, in the seller's solicitor's favour.

3.7.3.   Alternatively, where payment is to be made by telegraphic transfer, the seller's solicitor may request that a direct transfer is made to the separately represented mortgagee's solicitor, and a second transfer, for the balance of funds due, to the seller's solicitor. The method for achieving this is broadly similar to the method described in para. 3.6.2. above.

3.8.   Undertakings to remit funds

3.8.1.   In some circumstances the seller's solicitor may be prepared to complete the transaction against the buyer's solicitor's undertaking to remit funds within a specified time, the actual transfer of the money occurring after completion has taken place. The seller's solicitor should only do this if he has his client's authority to do so, and the client understands the consequences of completing against an undertaking. In such circumstances the seller should consider protecting his lien against the property for the unpaid purchase price by the registration of a caution against the title. It should, however, be noted that Standard Condition 6.5.1 has the effect of removing the seller's lien over documents of title. He may, however, have an equitable lien over the property for money not paid. Since it is not possible to register a caution against a property already owned by the cautioner, it is in practice difficult to protect the lien by registration until after the buyer has become registered as proprietor. If the land is unregistered a priority notice should be lodged before completion.

3.8.2.   Such an undertaking given by the buyer's solicitor is binding on him and should therefore not be given unless the buyer's solicitor is absolutely certain that he will be put in funds in sufficient time to comply with his promise to the seller's solicitor.

3.8.3.   If completion does take place on the strength of the buyer's solicitor's undertaking, the seller is bound to complete and may not retain possession of the title deeds and other documents even if the money does not arrive when promised. The common law lien which the seller may exercise over documents of title until he receives payment in full would be overridden by the seller's solicitor's acceptance of an enforceable undertaking from the buyer's solicitor. Standard Condition 6.5.1 removes the seller's lien over documents of title.

3.9. Release of deposit

3.9.1. A deposit which is held in the capacity of agent for the seller belongs to the seller and does not need to be released on completion.

3.9.2. Where a deposit is held by some person in the capacity of stakeholder, the buyer's solicitor should on completion provide the seller's solicitor with a written release addressed to the stakeholder, authorising payment of the deposit to the seller or as he directs. Where the deposit is being held by the seller's solicitor as stakeholder, a written release is often neither asked for nor provided, the release being given orally once completion has taken place. If the deposit is being held by a third party, e.g. an estate agent in the capacity of stakeholder, a written release will be required. In the absence of a written release the stakeholder, on being satisfied that the conditions under which he holds the money have been fulfilled, may pay the stake money to the party whom he considers entitled to receive it, subject to his becoming liable to account to the other party if he makes the wrong judgment in relation to the handing over of the money.[1]

1. *Hastingwood Property Ltd.* v. *Saunders Bearman Anselm* [1991] Ch. 114.

3.10. Retentions from the purchase price

3.10.1. Where it has been agreed that a retention should be deducted from the purchase price on completion, e.g. to cover the cost of outstanding works to be done by the seller, the agreement should be expressly clear as to whether interest is payable on the retained sum and to whom, and whether the buyer is to withhold the sum on completion or, e.g. to pay the full purchase price to the seller's solicitor with the amount of the agreed retention being held by the seller's solicitor in a deposit account opened in the joint names of the seller and buyer until the matter is resolved. It is also desirable to agree that if the obligation secured by the retention money has not been performed by a particular date, the retention money would be remitted back to the buyer to deal with the matter instead, and if it costs more than the retention money to do so, the buyer can claim the deficit from the seller.

3.11. Money laundering

3.11.1. Where a transaction is being funded by the client in cash, or via a third party (other than a recognised lender) or from a foreign bank, the solicitor should be alert to the possibilities of money laundering and should take appropriate steps to check the identity of the client and the source of the funds. More detailed notes on money laundering are set out in Financial services, para. A.04.

F.04. Completion

See also: Preparing for completion, para. E.04.
Date and time of completion, para. F.01.
Place of completion, para. F.02.
The money, para. F.03.
After completion, para. G.01.
Delayed completion, para. M.01.

4.1. Introduction

4.1.1. The date and time of actual completion will be specified in the contract but may be varied by subsequent agreement between the parties. Similarly the place and method of completion will previously have been agreed by the parties.

4.1.2. Completion may take place by personal attendance by the buyer's solicitor or his agent or through the post using the Law Society's Code for Completion by Post.

4.2. Completion by personal attendance

4.2.1. Personal attendance by the buyer's solicitor on the seller's solicitor or seller's lender's solicitor is the traditional method by which completion takes place but is not commonly used in uncomplicated transactions where, particularly in residential conveyancing, it is now more common for completion to take place through the post.

4.2.2. If the transaction is complex or of a high value, consideration should be given to the benefits of completing the matter in person since, when this method is employed, the buyer's solicitor is able physically to inspect all the relevant documents prior to handing over the purchase price; he takes possession of those documents immediately completion has taken place instead of having to rely on the seller's solicitor's undertaking to forward the documents to him, and there is therefore absolute certainty that all the documents are in order and that completion has taken place at a specific time. Against these benefits may be set the time and expense involved in the buyer's solicitor having to travel to the seller's solicitor's office in order to attend personally at completion.

4.2.3. A few days before the date arranged for completion the buyer's solicitor should telephone the seller's solicitor to arrange a mutually convenient appointment for completion.

4.2.4. On the morning of completion a banker's draft for the amount required to complete the transaction should be drawn by the buyer's solicitor and kept in a safe place until it is needed.[1]

4.2.5. The representative from the buyer's solicitors who is to attend completion should take with him to the seller's solicitor's office the following items:

    (a) the contract (queries which arise may sometimes be resolved by checking the terms of the contract);

    (b) evidence of title (in order to verify the title);

    (c) a copy of the approved draft purchase deed and of any other documents which are to be executed by the seller and handed over on completion (in case there is any query over the engrossments);

    (d) answers to requisitions on title (some queries which arise, e.g. over who has the keys may be resolved by the answers previously given to requisitions);

    (e) the completion checklist and completion statement;[2]

    (f) banker's draft;

    (g) any documents which are required to be handed over to the seller's solicitor on completion, e.g. release of deposit.

4.2.6. Verifying title

The buyer's time-limit for verifying title, i.e. comparing the original deeds against the evidence of title supplied by the seller, expires with the time-limit for raising requisitions.[3] Strictly therefore the buyer has no right to verify at this stage. In practice verification is not normally carried out at the requisitions on title stage of the transaction unless the transaction is complicated and the buyer's solicitor will check the evidence of title against the original deeds at completion itself. It should, however, be remembered that since the time-limit for verification has now expired, the buyer will have no right to query any defect which he discovers on verification, nor to refuse to complete because of a defect discovered at this stage. In the case of registered land verification is strictly unnecessary since the office copies supplied by the seller's solicitor will show the true up-to-date position of the register and so may be more accurate as to the state of the register than the land or charge certificate in the seller's possession. It is, however, still worthwhile checking the land or charge certificate which the seller is to hand over, if only to ensure that it is the one relating to the correct title to be purchased. Since all land and charge certificates look very similar on the outside it is easy for the wrong certificate to be handed over by mistake. Where there is more than one mortgage registered against the title, the buyer's solicitor must ensure that he obtains charge certificates relating to all the mortgages. The outside cover of non-computerised charge certificates specifies the number of the entry to which the particular certificate relates. On a sale by a lender under his power of sale, it is not essential to obtain the charge certificates, or discharges relating to subsequent mortgages which will be overreached on the completion of the sale by the selling lender.

4.2.7.   When the buyer's solicitor is satisfied as to the title, he should ask the seller's solicitor to hand over the documents necessary to complete the transaction. These documents including the land or charge certificate or title deeds (in unregistered land) will have been previously agreed in a list drawn up between the parties and itemised on the completion checklist. Except where these documents have recently been checked by verification, the buyer's solicitor should check each document to ensure it is as he expects to find it, and tick each off on his list as he receives it. The purchase deed will be among the documents to be received by the buyer's solicitor and should be dated at completion after being checked by the buyer's solicitor to ensure it has been validly executed and has not been altered since the buyer last saw the document. The seller's solicitor will have prepared a schedule of deeds in duplicate, one copy of which will be handed to the buyer's solicitor to keep; the other should be signed by the buyer's solicitor when he is satisfied that he has received all the documents listed on it, and returned to the seller's solicitor as evidence for his file of the handing over of the deeds.

4.2.8.   Depending on the circumstances it may be necessary for the buyer's solicitor to inspect receipts for, e.g. last payment of outgoings where such items have been apportioned on the completion statement. Copies of these receipts should have been supplied to the buyer's solicitor with the completion statement in order to allow him to check the amount of the apportionments. By Standard Condition 6.6 the buyer is required to assume that whoever gave any receipt for the payment of rent, rentcharge or a service charge which the seller produces was the person or agent of the person then entitled to that rent or service charge. In the absence of this condition from the contract Law of Property Act 1925, s.45(2) requires the buyer to make the same assumptions in respect of rent and rentcharges.

4.2.9.   Where the sale includes fittings or chattels, a separate receipt for the money paid for those items should be signed by the seller's solicitor and handed to the buyer's solicitor. A copy of the receipt should be retained by the seller's solicitor. The receipt clause in the purchase deed only operates as a receipt for the money paid for the land; therefore a separate receipt for the money paid for chattels is necessary.

4.2.10. *Discharge of seller's mortgage*

Arrangements for the discharge of the seller's mortgage(s) over the property will have been agreed between the parties at the requisitions on title stage of the transaction. Where the mortgage is a first mortgage of the property in favour of a building society lender, the parties will frequently have agreed to permit the seller to discharge his mortgage after completion takes place by using part of the proceeds of sale to make payment to the lender. In such a case it will have been agreed that the seller's lender's solicitor should hand to the buyer's solicitor on completion an undertaking in the form of wording recommended by the Law Society to discharge the mortgage (para. 4.2.11. below) and to forward the receipted deed or Form 53 to the buyer's solicitor as soon as this is received from the lender. An undertaking to discharge the seller's mortgage should only be accepted from a solicitor or licensed conveyancer because of the difficulties of enforcement of undertakings against unqualified persons. The undertaking should also be in the form of wording approved by the Law Society. Since there can be difficulties with the discharge of mortgages by lenders who do not belong to the Council of Mortgage Lenders, e.g. disagreements over the amount needed to repay the loan, it may be sensible not to accept an undertaking in respect of such a mortgage but to insist on the mortgage actually being discharged on or before completion. In such a case it may be necessary for completion to take place at the lender's solicitors' offices (not the seller's solicitors' offices) or for the lender's solicitor to attend personally at completion in order to discharge the mortgage. The buyer's solicitor must ensure that any undertaking given mentions every subsisting mortgage on the title.

4.2.11. The form of wording recommended by the Law Society for undertakings to discharge building society mortgages is as follows:

> 'In consideration of you today completing the purchase of [*insert description of property*] we hereby undertake to pay over to [*insert name of lender*] the money required to discharge the mortgage/legal charge dated [*insert date of charge*] and to forward the receipted mortgage/Form 53 to you as soon as it is received by us from [*insert name of lender*].'

4.2.12. When the buyer's solicitor is satisfied as to the documents received from the seller's solicitor and the documents which he has inspected, he should hand to the seller's solicitor any documents which the seller's solicitor requires in accordance with the list agreed prior to completion, e.g. release of deposit, and a banker's draft for the amount specified on the completion statement or otherwise notified to the buyer's solicitor by the seller's solicitor.

4.2.13. Where the banker's draft has been made out in the name of the buyer's solicitor it will have to be endorsed over to the seller's solicitor or as he directs. An endorsement may be general or special. To effect a general endorsement the buyer's solicitor simply signs the reverse of the draft using the payee's name as shown on the front of the draft. To effect a special endorsement the buyer's solicitor writes on the reverse of the draft 'pay to the order of [*name of seller's solicitor or as he directs*]' and then signs the endorsement. In either case the buyer's solicitor must ensure that his signature is in an identical form of wording to that used on the front of the draft where the payee is named. In default of this the endorsement may not be accepted by the bank when the draft is presented for payment.

4.2.14. *Release of deposit*

An unconditional written release of deposit should be supplied in any situation where the deposit under the contract has been held in the capacity of stakeholder. In practice, where the deposit has been held by the seller's solicitor in that capacity, an oral release will suffice. A written release is only therefore necessary where the deposit has been held by a third party, e.g. an estate agent as stakeholder.

4.2.15. *Endorsement of memoranda*

Where in unregistered land a document affecting the title is not to be handed over on completion, the buyer may want the seller to endorse a memorandum of the transaction on the deed(s) retained by the seller. The endorsement of such a memorandum protects the buyer against a subsequent mistaken or fraudulent re-conveyance of the same property. This is most likely to be needed on the sale of part of unregistered land where the buyer is entitled to insist on the endorsement of the memorandum on the most recent in date of the seller's retained title deeds under Law of Property Act 1925, s.200 (where the seller enters into new restrictive covenants), or where the purchase is from personal representatives of a deceased seller where Administration of Estates Act 1925, s.36(4) gives the buyer the right to insist on the endorsement of a memorandum on the grant of representation. The form of wording to be used for the endorsement should be drafted by the buyer's solicitor and agreed with the seller's solicitor at the requisitions on title stage of the transaction. A copy of the endorsement should be given to the buyer's solicitor for retention by him as evidence that this has been done. In registered conveyancing this procedure is not necessary since once the buyer is registered as proprietor of the land, previous documents relating to the title become irrelevant.

4.2.16. If in unregistered land the seller is entering into new restrictive covenants he should either retain a copy of the conveyance which imposes those covenants or a copy of the covenants themselves. The covenants will be contained in the purchase deed which will be handed to the buyer on completion and unless a copy is retained by the seller, he will have no documentary evidence of the covenants to produce to a buyer on a subsequent sale of the retained land. An alternative is for the conveyance or transfer to be prepared and executed in duplicate, the seller's solicitor retaining the duplicate on completion (or the buyer's solicitor having it denoted for stamp duty when he stamps the original part, and then sending the duplicate to the seller's solicitor).

4.2.17. In some cases the buyer will only be entitled to have copies of documents relating to the seller's title and not the originals. Chiefly this will occur on a sale of part of unregistered land where the seller is entitled to retain the title deeds which relate to the land retained by him. Other examples would include purchases from personal representatives where they are entitled to retain the original grant and purchases from attorneys who hold a general or enduring power. Where a power is a special power, relating only to the sale of this property, the buyer is entitled to the original power. In any case where an original document relevant to the title is not being handed over, the buyer's solicitor should call for the original document and examine his copy against the original. The copy should then be marked to show that it has been examined against the original and is a true copy of the original document. On a sale of part of unregistered land all the documents contained in the abstract or epitome of title will have to be so marked and each examined document should bear the wording 'examined against the original at the offices of [*insert name of* *seller's solicitors or as appropriate*] signed [*by buyer's solicitor's representative either in his own name or in the name of the firm*] and dated [*insert date of examination*]'. Where a certified copy of a document will be required, e.g. by HM Land Registry, of a grant of representation or power of attorney, the certification should be carried out by a qualified solicitor or licensed conveyancer by writing on the document clearly and in a conspicuous position the words 'I certify this to be a true copy of the [*insert type of document*] dated [*insert date of document being certified*] signed [*signature of solicitor*] and dated [*insert date of certification*]'. The addition of the address of the signatory would assist in the event of the certification later having to be checked in a subsequent transaction. It should be noted that under Powers of Attorney Act 1971, s.3(1)(*b*)(ii), a copy of a power of attorney must be certified on every page.

4.2.18. On a sale of part of registered land the seller will be required to deposit the land or charge certificate relating to the seller's title at HM Land Registry to await the buyer's application for registration of the land purchased. The buyer's solicitor should have requested the seller's solicitor to do this by means of a requisition on title. If not previously supplied, the seller's solicitor should now inform the buyer's solicitor of the deposit number allocated to the deposited certificate by HM Land Registry.

1. See above, The money, para. F.03.
2. See above, Preparing for completion, para. E.04.
3. Under Standard Condition 4.1.1 the buyer must raise his requisitions within six working days after the date of the contract or delivery of evidence of title by the seller, whichever is later. In practice, where title is deduced before exchange of contracts, the right to raise requisitions on certain matters after exchange may be precluded by special condition.

4.3. Completion through the post

4.3.1. In many cases, particularly with simple residential transactions, the buyer's solicitor will not wish to attend completion personally. In such a case arrangements may be made with the seller's solicitor to complete the transaction through the post.

4.3.2. Arrangements to complete through the post should be made at the latest at the requisitions on title stage of the transaction, although it is courteous for the buyer's solicitor to ask the seller's solicitor whether this method of completion will be convenient at an earlier stage so that the seller can if necessary obtain the consent of his lender's solicitor to this procedure.

4.3.3. The Law Society's Code for Completion by Post should be used.[1] The buyer's solicitor should agree any variations to the Code in writing with the seller's solicitor well before completion is due to take place. He should also send written instructions to the seller's solicitor specifying precisely what the buyer's solicitor requires the seller's solicitor to do on the buyer's solicitor's behalf at completion and agreeing a time on the day of completion itself when completion will take place.

4.3.4. The seller's solicitor will effectively act as the buyer's solicitor's agent for the purpose of carrying out the completion procedure. The instructions given by the buyer's solicitor should therefore encompass such of the matters detailed in para.

4.2. above as the buyer's solicitor would have carried out had he attended personally at completion. If the seller's solicitor perceives any difficulty or ambiguity in the instructions received from the buyer's solicitor, he must resolve that query or ambiguity before completion is due to take place.

4.3.5. The buyer's solicitor must either send the banker's draft to the seller's solicitor to arrive in time for completion and to be held by the seller's solicitor to the buyer's solicitor's order until completion takes place, or, more commonly, remit the necessary funds by telegraphic transfer to the seller's solicitor's nominated bank account to arrive there in time for completion to take place at the agreed time.

4.3.6. On being satisfied as to the proper payment of the completion money, either by draft or telegraphic transfer, the seller's solicitor must carry out the buyer's instructions and effect completion on his behalf. He should then immediately telephone (or fax) the buyer's solicitor to inform him that completion has taken place and post to the buyer's solicitor, by first class post or document exchange, the documents which the buyer is entitled to receive on completion. Where documents are required to be marked, certified or endorsed, the seller's solicitor will carry out these operations on behalf of the absent buyer's solicitor.

4.3.7. Under the Law Society's Code, the seller's solicitor is not entitled to make a charge to the buyer's solicitor for acting as his agent in carrying out completion.

1. The text of the Code is set out in App. VII.2.

4.4. Using an agent

4.4.1. If the buyer's solicitor is unable to attend personally at completion, but does not wish to complete through the post, he may appoint another solicitor to act as his agent, the agent attending completion in person and carrying out the same procedures that the buyer's solicitor would have done had he been present.

4.4.2. The agent will generally be a solicitor who practises within the vicinity of the office where completion is due to take place and should be given instructions to act in good time before actual completion day.

4.4.3. The instructions given to the agent should be full and explicit so that the agent is in no doubt as to what he is required to do. Copies of all the documents which the buyer's solicitor would normally take to completion with him should be supplied with the instructions and the agent should be put in funds either by banker's draft or telegraphic transfer so that he has cleared funds in his own clients' account against which to draw the draft for the completion money.

4.4.4. The agent is entitled to charge a reasonable sum for carrying out his duties as agent. The fee should be agreed in advance between the agent and the buyer's solicitor to avoid any later dispute. The buyer's solicitor is then bound to pay the agent's fee after completion irrespective of whether he has received reimbursement from his own client. It should be made clear to the client at the outset of the transaction that if the employment of an agent is required in order to attend completion, the agent's fee will be added as a disbursements on the client's bill.[1]

4.4.5. The agent should attend completion in person and carry out the buyer's solicitor's instructions. As soon after completion as possible he should telephone (telex or fax) the buyer's solicitor to confirm that completion has taken place and should send the documents which he has received at completion to the buyer's solicitor by first class post or document exchange.

1. See above, Estimate for costs, para. A.08.

4.5. Synchronisation

4.5.1. Where the client is to complete a sale and purchase of property on the same day, it is essential that the sale actually takes place before the purchase so that the proceeds of sale can be utilised in the later purchase transaction. Sufficient time should be allowed between the times of completion of sale and purchase to permit the funds received from the sale transaction to be transmitted to and received by the seller's solicitor in the purchase transaction within the time-limits specified in the purchase contract.

4.6. Deemed late completion

4.6.1. By Standard Conditions 6.1.2 and 6.1.3, where the sale is with vacant possession and the money due on completion is not paid by 2 p.m. on the day of actual completion (or such other time as may have been agreed by the parties), for compensation purposes completion is deemed to have taken place on the next following working day unless the seller had not vacated the property by 2 p.m. (or other agreed time). The buyer's solicitor must therefore instruct his bank to remit the completion money in sufficient time to ensure its arrival at its destination bank within the time-limit specified in the contract. In default the buyer may find himself liable to pay compensation to the seller under Standard Condition 7.3.[1]

1. Standard Condition 7.3 is discussed below in para. M.01.

4.7. Lender's requirements

4.7.1. The buyer's solicitor will often also be acting as solicitor for the buyer's lender. In such a case the buyer's solicitor should check the lender's requirements for completion when he is preparing his checklist and making arrangements for completion. In most cases the lender's requirements will be identical to the buyer's solicitor's own requirements, but a check on the lender's instructions should always be made to ensure that nothing is overlooked.

4.8. Problems with vacant possession

4.8.1. If the buyer's solicitor suspects that there may be practical problems in obtaining vacant possession, he should deal with this matter at an early stage in the transaction. Taking a written release of rights from an occupier and/or joining the occupier as a party to the contract will in most cases resolve the problem, but a signed release is of little comfort if on the day of completion the occupier refuses to vacate the property. If it is suspected that this might happen, the buyer's solicitor may take the precaution of inserting a contractual condition specifying that completion shall take place at the premises themselves so that an inspection of the property can be carried out immediately before completion takes place. Such a condition would have to be inserted into the contract before exchange and it is too late to try and impose such a term just before completion. Standard Condition 6.2 gives the seller the right to decide where completion will take place.

4.8.2. In the absence of a term allowing completion to take place on the premises themselves, the buyer's solicitor may, in appropriate cases, either inspect the property himself on the day of completion, or ask the client or the client's surveyor to do so and then to telephone the buyer's solicitor to confirm that the premises are vacant before completion proceeds. An inspection will also be necessary if the lender's instructions require the solicitor acting for the lender to ensure that vacant possession is obtained. Such an instruction places a heavy responsibility on the lender's solicitor who should seek to delete this term from his instructions.

4.9. Effect of completion

4.9.1. In unregistered land, title in the property passes to the buyer on completion.

4.9.2. In registered land, technically title does not pass until the buyer has become registered as proprietor of the land. The buyer will therefore take the property subject to any overriding interests which subsist or are created before the date of his registration except those which are protected under Land Registration Act 1925, s.70(1)(g), where in order to bind a buyer or his lender, occupiers' rights must have been in existence before completion took place.[1]

4.9.3. On completion the contract merges with the purchase deed in so far as the contract and purchase deed cover the same ground; thus after completion it is not possible to bring an action which arises out of one of the terms of the contract unless that provision has been expressly left extant by a term of the contract itself. For this reason it is common for the contract to contain a non-merger clause. Standard Condition 7.4 says that the provisions within the contract do not merge on completion in so far as there is outstanding liability under these provisions.

4.9.4. In the absence of a non-merger provision an action on the contract may not be possible after completion has taken place, but an action in tort or for misrepresentation would still be available since neither of these actions is based on the contract.

4.9.5. The principal remedy available to the buyer after completion is an action on the title guarantee or covenants for title, which is further discussed below in para. M.09.

1. *Abbey National* v. *Cann* [1991] 1 A.C. 56; *Lloyds Bank* v. *Rossett* [1991] 1 A.C. 107.

THE LAW SOCIETY'S CONVEYANCING HANDBOOK 1997

G. POST-COMPLETION
G.01. After completion

See also: Undertakings for bridging finance, para. B.16.
Stamping documents, para. G.02.
Registration of title, para. G.03.

1.1. Seller's checklist

1.1.1. Where appropriate to the transaction the following steps should be taken by the seller's solicitor as soon as possible after completion has taken place:

(a) Where completion has taken place by post, telephone the buyer's solicitor to inform him that completion has taken place.

(b) Telephone the estate agent to inform him of completion and to direct him to release the keys to the buyer.

(c) Inform client that completion has taken place.

(d) Where completion has taken place by post, send purchase deed, land or charge certificate or title deeds and other relevant documents to buyer's solicitor by first class post or document exchange.

(e) If part of the proceeds of sale are to be used towards the purchase of another property on the same day, make arrangements for the transmission of these funds in accordance with instructions received.

(f) Deal with the discharge of the seller's existing mortgage(s) by sending a clients' account cheque for the amount required (as per redemption statement previously obtained) to the lender together with the engrossment of the Form 53 (or deed of release relating to unregistered land) requesting him to discharge the mortgage and to forward the receipted Form 53 to you as quickly as possible. If the mortgage is over unregistered land, the lender will, instead of using a Form 53, complete the receipt clause on the reverse of the mortgage deed and forward the receipted deed to the seller's solicitor. If in unregistered land the lender is not a building society, the lender should be requested to date the receipt with the date of completion in order to avoid the risk of a transfer of the mortgage under Law of Property Act 1925, s.115. Where necessary, the reassignment of collateral security, e.g. a life policy, should also be dealt with, and a lender who has insured the property will also need to be told to cancel the property insurance cover.

(g) If instructed to do so, pay the estate agent's commission and obtain a receipt for the payment.

(h) Account to the seller's bank for the proceeds of sale in accordance with any undertaking given to them.

(i) Account to the client for the balance of the proceeds of sale in accordance with his instructions.

(j) If not already done, draft and remit bill of costs to the client.

(k) Where money is being held by the solicitor on account of costs, it may be transferred to office account provided that the client has expressly or impliedly agreed to this being done.

(l) If the land is to remain unregistered after completion of this transaction (e.g. on a voluntary conveyance, assent or grant or assignment of a lease having 21 years or less to run) make application for registration of land charges at the Land Charges Department, e.g. new restrictive covenants on a gift of part.

(m) On receipt of the completed Form 53 or receipted mortgage from the lender, check the form or receipt to ensure it is correct, then send it to the buyer's solicitor and ask to be discharged from the undertaking given on completion.

(n) If the land or charge certificate relating to the seller's title has been placed on deposit at HM Land Registry, make a diary or file prompt entry noting the anticipated date for return of the document and send a reminder to the Registry if the certificate has not been returned by that time.

(o) Remind the client of the need to notify the local and water authorities of the change of ownership of the property.

(p) Remind the client to cancel insurance cover over the property (and associated insurances if relevant).

(q) Advise the client about the payment of capital gains tax on assessment.

(r) Deal with the custody of deeds in accordance with the client's instructions. Most, if not all, original deeds will have passed to the buyer's solicitor on actual completion, but the seller will have retained custody of such deeds on a sale of part, or may have, e.g. an original grant of representation or power of attorney.

(s) Check through the file to ensure that all outstanding matters have been dealt with before sending the file for storage.

1.2. Buyer's checklist

1.2.1. Where appropriate to the transaction the following steps should be taken by the buyer's solicitor as soon as possible after completion has taken place:

(a) Inform client and his lender that completion has taken place.

(b) Complete the mortgage deed by insertion of the date and any other information which still has to be completed, e.g. date when first repayment is due.

(c) Complete file copies of the mortgage, purchase deed and other relevant documents.

(d) Attend to payment of stamp duty on purchase deed and other appropriate documents.

(e) Submit purchase deed for production to the Inland Revenue (PD stamp).

(f) Register any charge created by a company at Companies House within 21 days of its creation in accordance with Companies Act requirements. This time-limit is absolute and cannot be extended without an order of the court. Failure to register within the time-limit may prejudice the lender's security and will be an act of negligence on the part of the defaulting solicitor.

(g) Account to the buyer's bank for any bridging finance in accordance with any undertaking given to them and ask to be released from that undertaking.

(h) If not already done, draft and remit bill of costs to the client.

(i) Where money is being held by the solicitor on account of costs, it may be transferred to office account provided that the client has expressly or impliedly agreed to this being done.

(j) If the seller's land is to remain unregistered after completion of this transaction make application for registration of land charges at the Land Charges Department within the period given by the previously lodged priority notice, e.g. new restrictive covenants on a sale of part.

(k) On receipt of the completed Form 53 or receipted mortgage from the seller's lender's solicitor, check the form or receipt to ensure it is correct, acknowledge its receipt and release the sender from the undertaking given on completion.

(l) Make copies of all documents which are to be sent to HM Land Registry to ensure that file copies exist in case requisitions are raised by the Registry or the documents are lost or damaged before registration is complete.

(m) Make copies of any documents of which HM Land Registry require copies, e.g. the buyer's mortgage, a transfer or conveyance of part which imposes new restrictive covenants.

(n) Certify copy documents which are to be sent to HM Land Registry.[1]

(o) Make application for registration of title within the relevant priority period (land already registered) or within two months of completion (application for first registration).

(p) Make diary or file prompt entry recording the approximate date when the new land or charge certificate may be expected to be received from HM Land Registry and send a reminder if the certificate is not received by that time.

(q) Send notice of assignment of a life policy to the insurance company and place their acknowledgement of receipt with the title deeds.

(r) Give notice to the landlord's solicitors of an assignment, mortgage, etc., in accordance with a requirement to that effect in the lease or in the mortgagee's instructions and place their acknowledgement of receipt with the title deeds.

(s) Notify tenants of the change of ownership of the property.

(t) Make application for the discharge of any entry which was lodged to protect the contract.[2]

(u) If the land is to remain unregistered consider lodging a caution against first registration at HM Land Registry to protect the client's interest.

(v) On receipt of the land or charge certificate from HM Land Registry, check its contents carefully and ask the Registry to correct any errors which have been made.

(w) Deal with the custody of deeds in accordance with the client's instructions.

(x) Check through the file to ensure that all outstanding matters have been dealt with before sending the file for storage.

NB: Where a separate solicitor has been instructed to act for the buyer's lender, the lender's solicitor will normally have taken custody of the purchase deed and other title deeds on completion and he will assume responsibility for the stamping and registration of the documents in place of the buyer's solicitor.

1. See above, para. F.04.2.17.
2. In registered land this will be combined with any application for registration.

1.3. Undertakings

1.3.1. Failure to honour an undertaking is professional misconduct. Any undertaking given must therefore be honoured and the obligations promised must be fulfilled without delay.

1.3.2. A solicitor who has performed his undertaking should formally ask the recipient to release the giver from his undertaking so that the giver has written evidence of the fulfilment of the undertaking. The recipient may either acknowledge the giver's release by letter, or return the original undertaking to the giver, and in either case the evidence of release is to be kept on the giver's file.

1.4. Stamping documents

1.4.1. Documents should be submitted for stamping as soon as possible after completion has taken place to ensure that they will be returned to the buyer's solicitor in sufficient time for an application for registration of title to be made within the appropriate time-limits.

1.4.2. If it is anticipated that there will be delay in the return of the documents from the Inland Revenue, an application for registration of title should be made before the documents are stamped or adjudicated, thus ensuring that the relevant time-limits for registration are complied with. A letter accompanying the application for registration should explain that the documents have not yet been stamped and enclose certified copies of the documents which are to be stamped. The Registry will expect the solicitor to give an undertaking to send the duly stamped documents to them on completion of the stamping requirements. This procedure is necessary because HM Land Registry will not accept unstamped documents for registration, but nevertheless ensures that relevant time-limits for the application for registration are met. It is not possible to delay the initial application for registration until the documents have been correctly stamped because in so doing the client might lose the protection of the priority period afforded to him by his pre-completion search. A certified copy of the document to be stamped should be submitted with the application, pending submission of the properly stamped document to the Registry.

1.4.3. Where a document has to be produced to the Inland Revenue under Finance Act 1931, but is otherwise exempt from stamp duty, the completed Form LA451 (PD) may be sent to HM Land Registry with the application for registration of title and the Registry will act as agents for the Inland Revenue in attaching the PD stamp to the document. This procedure circumvents any delay which might otherwise be experienced in separate submission of the document for stamping prior to registration. New leases must be presented to the Stamp Office even if no duty is payable.

1.4.4. Depending on the nature of his instructions and report on title, a mortgagee's solicitor may be under a duty to stamp documents and register at HM Land Registry even if the buyer has not put him in funds to do so.

1.5.   Registration of title

1.5.1. It is essential that the relevant time-limits for submission of an application for registration of the client's title are complied with. Failure to make an application for first registration within two months of completion results in the transfer of the legal estate becoming void. Failure to make an application for a registration of a dealing within the priority period of 30 working days given by a pre-completion Land Registry search may have the consequence of the client's interest losing priority to another application. In either case, if the client suffered loss as a result of the late application, the solicitor would be liable in negligence.

1.5.2. Delays caused by late return of the documents from the Inland Revenue following an application for stamping or registration at the Companies Registry can be avoided if the procedure outlined in para. 1.4.2. above is followed.

1.5.3. Registration of title is further dealt with in para. G.03.

1.6. Registration of company charges

1.6.1. Fixed charges created by a company are registrable at HM Land Registry (or the Land Charges Department in the case of a charge over unregistered land which is not supported by a deposit of title deeds) and, as a separate obligation in relation to any charge on land, at the Companies Registry under Companies Act requirements. Failure to register the charge under the Companies Act 1985 within the 21 days following its creation renders the charge void against a liquidator or another creditor of the company. This time-limit can only be extended by an order of the court which is not automatically granted. Floating charges must also be noted on the register if they are to affect registered land.

1.7. Notices of assignment

1.7.1. Where following completion notice has to be given to a landlord of an assignment or mortgage, or notice given to an insurance company of the assignment of a life insurance policy, such notice should be given in duplicate. The recipient of the notice should be requested to sign one copy of the notice in acknowledgement of its receipt, and to return the receipted copy to the sender. The receipted copy will then be kept with the title deeds as evidence of compliance with this requirement.

1.7.2. In the case of the assignment of a life policy, the notice of assignment should be given as soon as possible after completion, since the giving of the notice establishes the priority of charges and is required to be given by Policies of Assurance Act 1867.

1.7.3. Where notice is being given under the terms of a lease, it should be delivered within the time-limits specified in the lease together with the appropriate fee.

1.8. Certifying documents

1.8.1. Where a document is required to be certified as a true copy of its original, the certification should be carried out by a qualified solicitor or licensed conveyancer. The words 'I/we certify this to be a true copy of the [transfer] (*or as the case may be*) dated the [*insert date*]' should be placed in a conspicuous position on the copy document. The certification is then signed by the solicitor or licensed conveyancer in his own name or in the name of his firm.[1] In the case of a power of attorney each page must be individually certified.

1. See above, para. F.04.2.17.

1.9. Custody of deeds

1.9.1. Instructions relating to custody will have been obtained from the client at an earlier stage in the transaction.

1.9.2. In many cases the client's lender will require custody of the deeds after completion or, if this is not the case, the client may have been advised to deposit the deeds with his bank or in the solicitor's strongroom.

1.9.3. Where the original deeds are not to be sent to the client himself, it is courteous to photocopy the land or charge certificate (or principal title deeds in the case of unregistered land) and to send these copies to the client who will thus have immediate access to the relevant information in the case of, e.g. a dispute over a right of way or restrictive covenant.

1.9.4. Before deeds are sent to a mortgagee (or other third party) for custody, they should be checked for accuracy and a schedule of deeds drawn up in duplicate. The recipient should be asked to acknowledge the receipt of the deeds by signing and returning one copy of the schedule. This signed acknowledgement will then be placed on the buyer's solicitor's file as evidence that the deeds have been sent to the recipient.

1.9.5. Deeds should normally be sent by recorded delivery, insured post or document exchange to ensure their safe arrival at their destination.

1.9.6. If deeds are to remain in the solicitor's own strongroom, a schedule of the deeds should be drawn up in duplicate, one copy being placed with the deeds, the other remaining in the solicitor's file. In no circumstances should original deeds be left in the solicitor's file when the file is sent for storage. If deeds are kept in the solicitor's strongroom, the solicitor owes a duty of care to his client and, if the deeds are lost, the solicitor may not charge the client with the cost of replacement.

G

G.02. Stamping documents

2.1. **Introduction**
2.2. **Particular instruments**
2.3. **Value added tax**

2.4. **Particulars Delivered stamp**
2.5. **Adjudication**
2.6. **Payment of duty**

See also: Stamp duty and stamp duty savings, para. A.14.
After completion, para. G.01.
Registration of title, para. G.03.

2.1. Introduction

2.1.1. Stamp duty must be paid on certain documents within 30 days of execution or, if a document is delivered subject to conditions, within 30 days of the date when the conditions are fulfilled.

2.1.2. There is no legislation which sets out who is responsible for bearing the stamp duty. The convention is that it is the transferee or lessee who pays the duty.

2.1.3. A document can be stamped outwith the 30-day period mentioned at 2.1.1. above on payment of a penalty for late stamping.[1]

2.1.4. HM Land Registry will not accept unstamped or incorrectly stamped documents for registration. Duty must therefore normally be paid before an application for registration of title is submitted. Nor may an unstamped or incorrectly stamped document be used in evidence in civil proceedings; such a document is not therefore a good root or link in the chain of title to unregistered land.

2.1.5. It is a criminal offence to avoid the payment of duty, and an agreement to avoid the payment of the correct duty on a document may be a fraud on the Inland Revenue which could result in the transaction being declared void as being illegal on the grounds of public policy.[2]

2.1.6. The buyer's potential liability to pay stamp duty on the transaction must be discussed with him when instructions are taken. Details of the rates of duty on various instruments are set out in para. A.14. above and the following paragraphs contain only a summary of the information given in the earlier paragraph referred to.[3]

2.1.7. The stamp duty cheque should be made payable to 'Inland Revenue – Stamp Duties' and should include the firm's reference number where such a number has been allocated.

1. See Stamp Office Leaflet SO10
2. See *Saunders v. Edwards* [1987] 2 All E.R. 651.
3. See above, para. A.14.

2.2. Particular instruments

2.2.1. Conveyance or transfer on sale

Duty is payable at the rate of 1% of the consideration where the consideration exceeds £60,000. No duty is payable where the consideration is £60,000 or less provided an appropriate certificate of value is included in the document.

2.2.2. Voluntary conveyance or transfer

No duty is payable provided the document bears an appropriate certificate under Stamp Duty (Exempt Instruments) Regulations 1987.[1]

2.2.3. Assent under hand

No duty.

2.2.4. Assent under seal

No duty is payable provided the document bears an appropriate certificate under Stamp Duty (Exempt Instruments) Regulations 1987.[2]

2.2.5. Mortgages and vacating receipts

No duty.

2.2.6. Powers of attorney

No duty.

2.2.7. Leases

Duty is assessed in relation to the length of the term, amount of rent and premium paid for grant. An agreement for lease is liable to the same duty as if it were the actual lease. Under the terms of Finance Act 1994, s.240 all leases must either contain a statement that there is no agreement for lease to which the lease gives effect or they must be denoted to show that the proper stamp duty has been paid on the relevant agreement.

2.2.8. Assignments of existing leases

These are treated as conveyances and bear the same duty as a conveyance.

2.2.9. Duplicate and counterpart leases

Fixed duty of £0.50 is payable.

2.2.10. Agreements to surrender leases

Under Finance Act 1994, s.243, an agreement to surrender a lease may be liable to stamp duty as if it were a conveyance or transfer of the interests surrendered.

2.2.11. Declaration of trust

Fixed duty of £0.50 is payable. Certain declarations of trust are liable to *ad valorem* duty as a conveyance or transfer on sale.

2.2.12. Transfer in consideration of a debt

Where a conveyance or transfer is made so that the transferee takes over liability for a debt without there being any other money consideration for the transfer, e.g. a transfer of property subject to a mortgage, the Inland Revenue may treat the transfer as a sale of property and *ad valorem* duty will be payable on the amount of the debt.[3]

1. S.I. 1987/516. See below, App. VIII.5.
2. S.I. 1987/516. See below, App. VIII.5.
3. See Inland Revenue Statement of Practice 6/90.

2.3. Value added tax

2.3.1. Where the consideration paid for an interest in land includes value added tax, the tax is treated as part of the value of the land and attracts stamp duty. Duty is therefore payable on the whole of the consideration including the value added tax element of the price. Stamp duty itself is not however taxable.

2.4. Particulars Delivered stamp

2.4.1. Under Finance Act 1931 certain instruments are required to be produced to the Inland Revenue within 30 days of their execution. Failure to comply with this requirement where applicable results in the same penalties and consequences as for lack of stamp duty.

2.4.2. These provisions apply to a conveyance (or transfer) on sale of freeholds, leases which are granted for a term exceeding seven years and to assignments of such leases.

2.4.3. To comply with Finance Act 1931, the relevant document must be produced to the Inland Revenue with a completed Form LA451 (PD). The Inland Revenue will stamp the document (a Particulars Delivered or 'PD' stamp) to show that this requirement has been complied with. A plan showing the land should be submitted with the Form LA451 if the postal description of the land is not adequate to identify it clearly.

2.4.4. Where the transfer being produced does not require stamp duty and registration of title is required, the document, with its completed Form LA451, may be sent direct to HM Land Registry as part of an application for registration of the title and HM Land Registry will deal with the production of the document as agents for the Inland Revenue. Separate submission of the document to the Inland Revenue is in such cases unnecessary. Leases which need to be produced must be sent to the Inland Revenue irrespective of whether stamp duty is also payable.

2.5. Adjudication

2.5.1. The presence of stamp duty on a document is not conclusive proof that the correct duty has been paid. If conclusive proof of payment of the correct duty is needed, the document must be submitted for adjudication by the Inland Revenue. An adjudication stamp placed on the document will then be conclusive as to the payment of duty.

2.6. Payment of duty

2.6.1. The client should be asked to pay his solicitor the amount necessary to cover the stamp duty before completion, so that the solicitor has funds available to make this payment on behalf of the client immediately following completion. Where the solicitor is acting also for the buyer's mortgagee, the documents must be stamped within the relevant period, regardless of whether the buyer client has paid his solicitor the amount required to discharge the stamp duty. Failure to do so would put the solicitor into breach of his duty to the mortgagee.

2.6.2. It is important that payment of stamp duty is made as soon as possible following completion, not only in order to comply with the 30-day period for payment of duty, but also so that the stamped documents may be submitted to HM Land Registry for registration within the relevant time-limits applicable. Where the application is for registration of a dealing (i.e. the land is already registered), the application for registration must be received by HM Land Registry within 30 working days of the date of the official certificate of search issued prior to completion. If stamping is not carried out with reasonable expedition, it is likely that this latter time-limit will not be complied with.[1]

2.6.3. Documents to be stamped may either be taken to an Inland Revenue stamping office or, if this is not convenient, delivered by post to the Inland Revenue.[2] A cheque for the correct amount of duty must accompany the documents. The cheque should be made payable to 'Inland Revenue—Stamp Duties' and bear the solicitor's registered number where such a number has been allocated.

2.6.4.   If the amount of duty payable is not known by the solicitor presenting the document, he may ask the Inland Revenue to assess the duty, 'mark' the document accordingly and return it to the solicitor who will then resubmit the document for stamping with a cheque for the assessed duty. This course of action will inevitably delay the date when the document can be submitted to HM Land Registry and re-emphasises the necessity to deal with the stamping of documents at the earliest possible opportunity.

1. For the consequences of making a late application for registration see below, Registration of title, para. G.03.
2. For addresses see below, App. XIII.4.

G.03. Registration of title

See also: After completion, para. G.01.
Rectification and indemnity, para. M.07.

3.1. Introduction

3.1.1. The extension of compulsory registration to the whole of England and Wales became effective on 1 December 1990 under Registration of Title Order 1989.[1]

3.1.2. Failure to make an application for first registration within the requisite time-limits in circumstances where the transaction falls within the scope of the compulsory registration order has the effect of revesting the legal estate of the interest in the seller. The transfer of the legal estate becomes void so far as the buyer is concerned. An application for late registration can be made pursuant to an order of the registrar or the court, but the client would have to take his interest subject to any other interest which had been registered prior to his own.

3.1.3. Failure to register a registrable lease may result in the tenant having an equitable lease.

1. S.I.1989/1347.

3.2. Compulsory registration

3.2.1. An application for first registration of title must be made following the completion of one of the transactions listed below:

    (a) conveyance on sale of the freehold;

    (b) grant of a lease for a term of more than 21 years;

    (c) assignment on sale of a lease having more than 21 years left to run.

3.2.2.   The acquisition of land through an assent made by personal representatives or by a voluntary conveyance or assignment does not induce compulsory registration.

3.2.3.   The grant of a lease for a term of 21 years certain or less, or the assignment of a lease which at the date of its assignment has 21 years or less to run, does not induce compulsory registration. Such leases will either be minor interests which are protected by noting against the reversionary title or may take effect as overriding interests under Land Registration Act 1925, s.70(1)(*g*), if the tenant is in possession, and/or under section 70(1)(*k*).[1]

3.2.4.   A lender is not entitled to become registered as proprietor of the borrower's interest in the land unless and until the borrower's equity of redemption has been extinguished, e.g. by foreclosure. Until such time, the lender's interest must be protected by registration of an entry on the charges register of the title.[2]

3.2.5.   Once an estate in land is registered, all devolutions from that title, e.g. grant of leases and sub-leases, must follow the registered system of conveyancing.

1. See below, para. 3.15. Note that the word 'possession' in this context includes possession of the rents and profits as well as physical possession.
2. See below, para. 3.14.

3.3.   **Voluntary registration**

3.3.1.   Voluntary registration of a registrable interest is possible, e.g. following devolution of the land by an assent or voluntary conveyance.

3.3.2.   The benefits of the registered system of conveyancing, e.g. simplified methods of deduction of title, are such that a client should be encouraged to make an application for voluntary registration in appropriate circumstances. This might be particularly appropriate where, e.g. an unregistered title is complex or has minor defects in it, since on first registration the registrar has a discretion to 'cure' such defects under Land Registration Act 1925, s.13(*c*).

3.4.   **Registration of dealings**

3.4.1.   Where registered land is transferred, an application for registration of the dealing must be made, preferably on the appropriate application form, accompanied by the correct documentation and fee, and received by the District Land Registry for the area[1] within the priority period of 30 working days given by the Land Registry search made before completion.

3.4.2.   The registration must be made at the District Land Registry for the geographical area in which the land is situated. Care must be taken to send the application to the correct registry in cases where the geographical county differs from the property's postal address. Lodging documents at the wrong registry may result in loss of priority for the application or at worst no registration at all.

3.4.3.   The application must be received by the District Land Registry by 9.30 a.m. on the day on which protection under the applicant's search expires in order to preserve the applicant's priority over the registration of other interests. The period of protection under the search cannot be extended (although a second search conferring a separate priority period can be made) and failure to lodge the client's application within the priority period may result in his interest ceding priority to another application.

3.4.4.   Except as noted in para. 3.4.5. below, HM Land Registry will not accept documents for registration unless they are correctly stamped with stamp duty and/or a Particulars Delivered stamp as appropriate.[2]

3.4.5.   Where a document other than a lease is required to be produced to the Inland Revenue under Finance Act 1931 (for a PD stamp) but does not otherwise attract stamp duty, the document, with its completed Form LA451, may be sent direct to HM Land Registry as part of an application for registration of the title and HM Land Registry will deal with the production of the document as agents for the Inland Revenue. Separate submission of the document to the Inland Revenue is in such cases unnecessary.

3.4.6.   Where at the time of the application for registration the applicant has not received from the seller's solicitor the completed Form 53 in respect of the seller's discharged mortgage, the applicant should nevertheless apply for registration of his client's title and discharge of the old mortgage within the appropriate time-limits. The list of documents accompanying the application should state that Form 53 will follow within a stated number of days. This comment on the application form ensures that HM Land Registry is aware that the omission of the Form 53 is not merely an oversight by the applicant's solicitor, and thus saves the time and expense of a requisition being raised by the Registry. If it appears that the estimate of time stated on the application form for delivery of the Form 53 will not be complied with, the applicant's solicitor should inform the Registry of this fact, giving a revised estimate of time and the reason for the delay. On receipt of the correct Form 53 from the seller's solicitor (or from his mortgagee) the form should be sent immediately to HM Land Registry. All communications with HM Land Registry must refer to the title number which is the subject of the application.

1. A list of the District Land Registries, their addresses and areas covered is in App. XIII.1. below.
2. See above, para. G.01.4.2. which deals with avoiding delays in stamping documents.

3.5.   Transfer of whole

3.5.1.   The following points relate to any transfer of the whole of the seller's registered title, irrespective of whether the interest transferred is freehold or leasehold.

3.5.2. Application for registration of the dealing on Form A4 accompanied by the following documents should be lodged within 30 working days of the date of issue of the applicant's pre-completion official search certificate:

    (a) land or charge certificate relating to the title;

    (b) transfer (generally no copy of this document is required);

    (c) appropriate fee unless to be paid by credit account.[1]

3.5.3. In addition, such of the documents listed below as are appropriate to the circumstances of the transaction should be submitted with the application:

    (a) completed Form 53 (to show the discharge of the seller's mortgage);

    (b) mortgage deed relating to the buyer's new mortgage and certified copy;[2]

    (c) office copy or certified copy grant of representation where the seller was personal representative of the deceased proprietor;

    (d) original power of attorney if transfer has been executed under a special power which is limited to the disposal of this property;

    (e) certified copy power of attorney if the transfer has been executed under a power of attorney other than as in (g) above;

    (f) completed PD form where the purchase deed has to be produced to the Inland Revenue under the Finance Act 1931, but only if the deed is not liable to stamp duty and is not a lease;

    (g) if the applicant's solicitor wishes to have the receipt of his application acknowledged by the registry, a self-addressed postcard in Form C4B should be enclosed with the application;

    (h) where relevant, an application to withdraw a caution which was lodged after exchange of contracts to protect the contract.

1. See below, App. VIII.3. for table of current fees.
2. For certification of documents see above, para. G.01.8.

3.6. **Transfer of part**

3.6.1. The following points relate to any transfer of a part of the seller's registered title, irrespective of whether the interest transferred is freehold or leasehold.

3.6.2. Application for registration of the dealing on Form A5 accompanied by the documents listed in paras. 3.5.2. – 3.5.3. above (or those of them which are relevant to the transaction and subject to the variations noted below) must be made within 30 working days of the date of issue of the applicant's pre-completion official search certificate.

3.6.3. The transfer should incorporate a plan which must be signed by both parties. A solicitor can sign the plan on behalf of his buyer client.

3.6.4. Where the transfer imposes fresh restrictive covenants a certified copy of it must also be supplied.[1]

3.6.5. The seller's land or charge certificate will have been placed on deposit at HM Land Registry prior to submission of the buyer's application for registration. The deposit number issued by the Registry should be referred to in the buyer's application so that the certificate and application for registration can be brought together to effect the registration of the sale of part and the removal of the land sold from the seller's certificate. The seller's certificate will be amended and returned to him on completion of the registration of the sale of part.

1. For certification of documents see above, para. G.01.8.

3.7. Application for first registration

3.7.1. An application for first registration of title (freehold or leasehold) must be made within two months of completion of the transaction which induces the registration. The application must be made to the District Land Registry which serves the geographical area in which the property is located. Care must therefore be exercised where the geographical county and postal address of the property differ.

3.7.2. Different application forms are available for registrations of freeholds and leaseholds, the precise form to be used depending on the class of title being applied for. The correct application form appropriate to the circumstances of the transaction must be used. This point should be checked carefully before submission of the application.

3.7.3. *Table of forms for use in first registration*

Form number	Description
1A	Application by owner for first registration of freehold (no solicitor acting).
1B	Application by solicitor for first registration of freehold.
2A	Application by owner for first registration of leasehold land on behalf of an applicant other than an original lessee (no solicitor acting).
2B	Application by solicitor for first registration of leasehold land on behalf of an applicant other than an original lessee.
3A	Application by owner for first registration of leasehold land on behalf of an original lessee (no solicitor acting).
3B	Application by solicitor for first registration of leasehold land on behalf of an original lessee.

1F	Application for first registration of a rentcharge (form obtainable on request from District Land Registry).
1K	Application for registration of a rentcharge where no solicitor is acting.

3.7.4. The application form and fee accompanied by the documents listed in para. 3.7.6. below should be sent to the District Land Registry for the area.

3.7.5. Documents accompanying the application must be listed in triplicate. One copy of this form will be returned to the applicant's solicitor in acknowledgement of receipt of the application. The acknowledgement copy will also give an estimate of the likely time which the registry expects to take to deal with the application. This anticipated time should be noted in the solicitor's diary or file prompt system and a reminder sent to the registry if the land or charge certificate has not been received within that period.

3.7.6. *Documents to be submitted on application for first registration of title*

The registrar needs to investigate title on an application for first registration in order to decide which class of title can be allocated to the title. He therefore needs to have access to all the documents which formed the evidence of title supplied to the applicant by the seller's solicitor. These documents should be individually numbered in chronological sequence and listed in the same sequence (Form A13 may be used for this purpose):

(a) an itemised list of all the documents which formed the evidence of title supplied by the seller's solicitor;

(b) all the buyer's pre-contract searches and enquiries with their replies (including any variations or further information contained in relevant correspondence);

(c) the contract;

(d) requisitions on title with their replies;

(e) all pre-completion search certificates;

(f) the purchase deed with a certified copy;

(g) the seller's mortgage, duly receipted;

(h) the buyer's mortgage with a certified copy;

(i) where the transaction is leasehold, the original lease and a certified copy;

(j) PD form, where no stamp duty is payable.

3.7.7. *Rentcharges*

An application for registration of a rentcharge must be made on the appropriate form (Form 1F, obtainable on request from a District Land Registry), accompanied by a certified copy of the document creating the rentcharge. This application is usually made by the seller by arrangement with the buyer. A separate rentcharge land certificate is issued on completion of the registration.

3.8. Copies of documents sent to the registry

3.8.1. There is a case for retaining copies of all documents which are to be submitted to the registry on the applicant's solicitor's file pending completion of the registration. The registrar may need to raise requisitions on an application (particularly for first registration) and it assists in the speedy reply to those requisitions if the solicitor has retained copies of the documents which may contain information relevant to the query raised by the registry. Delay is often experienced, especially with applications for first registration. A further reason for retaining copies of the documents is so that any queries which arise in relation to the land pending completion of the registration, e.g. over boundaries or the exercise of a right of way, can be resolved from the copies in the solicitor's possession.

3.9. Joint buyers

3.9.1. Joint buyers are required to state on their application for registration whether they will hold the land as beneficial joint tenants or beneficial tenants in common. Only in the latter case will a restriction in Form 62 be entered on the proprietorship register of the title. Where the parties are to hold as tenants in common, a separate document may have been drawn up prior to completion indicating the proportionate shares which each tenant in common holds in the property because the register will not record the beneficial interests. This document is not submitted to the registry with the application for registration of the title but should be placed with the land or charge certificate on its receipt from the registry to avoid later disputes over the shares in the beneficial interests in the property.[1]

1. See above, The purchase deed, para. E.01.

3.10. Corporate buyers registered in England and Wales

3.10.1. The solicitor to the company is required to certify on the application form for registration that the transaction (including any charge) is within the capacity of the company. Alternatively a certified copy of the memorandum and articles of the company may be lodged with the application.

3.10.2. In other situations the solicitor may have to satisfy the registrar as to the capacity of the applicant to enter the transaction, e.g. housing associations, charities, building societies.

3.11.   Return of land or charge certificate

3.11.1.   The anticipated date for completion of the application for registration as shown on the acknowledgement card returned by the registry on receipt of the application (or on Form A13 in the case of applications for first registration) should be noted in the solicitor's diary or file prompt system. If the land or charge certificate has not been returned by the anticipated date a reminder should be sent to the registry.

3.11.2.   On return of the certificate, its contents should be carefully checked to ensure that the entries accurately record the transaction which has taken place. Any error should be immediately notified to the registry and the certificate returned to them for correction.

3.11.3.   The application form for registration gives the applicant the choice of having the new land or charge certificate sent directly to a third party for custody, e.g. a lender instead of being returned to the applicant's solicitor. It is preferable for the applicant's solicitor to have the certificate returned to him and not to a third party, so that the certificate can be checked for accuracy before being sent to a third party for custody. In some cases a lender's solicitor may require the buyer's solicitor to sign the certificate as to capacity on the application form, and then direct that the new land or charge certificate is returned direct to the lender's solicitor.

3.11.4.   On being satisfied that the certificate received from the registry is correct, custody of the deeds should be dealt with in accordance with the client's instructions.

3.11.5.   When a lease is registered, it is not attached to the land or charge certificate, but is stamped by the registry to show that they have seen it, and returned to the applicant on completion of the registration. The lease should be kept with the land or charge certificate since it will be needed on any disposal of the land or if any problem arises over its terms or renewal.

3.11.6.   Pre-registration title deeds will be returned by the registry on completion of an application for first registration. These may have been stamped by the registry both to show that they have been seen by the registry and to prevent any subsequent fraudulent resale of the same land. Subject to any specific instructions issued by a lender, these deeds should be kept with the new land or charge certificate since they may in future be needed to resolve a problem which arises in circumstances where the register does not provide a conclusive solution, e.g. as to boundaries or the existence and effect of positive covenants. Where the title granted to the land is less than absolute the pre-registration title deed should always be kept with the land or charge certificate.

3.11.7.   Where custody of the deeds is with someone other than the buyer client, e.g. with a mortgagee, it is courteous to make a copy of the charge certificate and to send it to the client who will then have ready access to this document should he need to resolve a problem relating to the land, e.g. over the existence or extent of a right of way.

3.12.　**Classes of title**

3.12.1.　On first registration the registrar will decide which class of title should be allocated to the interest which is being registered. The class of title which has been given to the interest is shown on the proprietorship register of the title.

3.12.2.　*Absolute title*

The vast majority of registered titles are classed as 'absolute', which in effect connotes an unassailable title. This class of title can be given to either a freehold or a leasehold interest in the land. The proprietor of an interest which is registered with an absolute title has vested in him the legal estate together with all appurtenant rights and subject only to:

- (a)　entries on the register;
- (b)　overriding interests;
- (c)　where the proprietor is a trustee, minor interests of which he has notice, e.g. the interests of the beneficiaries under the trust; and
- (d)　where the land is leasehold, the express and implied covenants and obligations under the lease.

3.12.3.　*Possessory title*

Registration with a possessory title has the same effect as registration with absolute title except that the proprietor is also subject to all adverse interests existing at the date of first registration. Where, e.g. an application for first registration shows that the applicant's title to the land is based on adverse possession it is likely that the registrar will initially only grant a possessory title to the land, the applicant taking subject to the rights of any person who has a superior interest in the land. Registration will only be effected where the land has identifiable boundary features or is fenced. This class of title can be given to either a freehold or a leasehold interest in the land. If the title deeds have been lost, HM Land Registry may register only a possessory title even if the seller can show that he has been in undisputed possession of the property for more than 15 years.

3.12.4.　*Qualified title*

A qualified title, which is in practice very rare, is granted where the title submitted for registration shows a specific identified defect which the registrar deems to be of such a nature that he cannot use his discretion to overlook the defect and grant an absolute title. The registration has the same effect as registration with an absolute title except that the state guarantee of the title does not apply to the specified defect. Such a title might be awarded where, e.g. the title submitted for first registration showed that a transaction within the title had been carried out in breach of trust. In this situation the proprietor would take his interest in the land subject to the interests (if any) of the beneficiaries under the trust. This class of title can be given to either a freehold or a leasehold interest in the land.

3.12.5. *Good leasehold title*

A good leasehold title (applicable only to leaseholds) will be awarded where the registrar is satisfied that the title to the leasehold interest is sound but, having no access to the title to the superior reversionary interest, he is not prepared to guarantee the lease against defects in the freehold title or to guarantee that the freeholder had the right to grant the lease. Such a title will therefore generally only result where the title to the freehold reversion is unregistered and where the applicant for registration of the leasehold interest does not submit evidence of title to the freehold reversion when making his application. A good leasehold title is regarded by some mortgagees as being unsatisfactory, and for this reason is sometimes difficult to sell or mortgage.[1]

1. The problems of a good leasehold title are discussed in para. K.01. See also Standard Condition 8.2.4 which requires a seller on the grant of a new lease for over 21 years to deduce to a buyer such evidence of title as will enable the buyer to obtain registration of his title with an absolute title.

3.13.   **Upgrading title**

3.13.1.   A possessory title may be upgraded to an absolute title (or in the case of leasehold land to a good leasehold title) if either the registrar is satisfied as to the title or the land has been registered with possessory title for at least 15 years (freehold transactions, 10 years for leasehold) and the registrar is satisfied that the proprietor is in possession.[1]

3.13.2.   A qualified title may be upgraded to an absolute title (or in the case of leasehold land to a good leasehold title) if the registrar is satisfied as to the title.

3.13.3.   A good leasehold title may be converted to an absolute title if the registrar is satisfied as to the reversionary freehold title and any intermediate leasehold title. This could occur after, e.g. registration of the reversion or of a superior lease.

3.13.4.   The registrar may upgrade a title on his own initiative or the proprietor may make application for upgrading on Land Registry Form 6.[2]

1. Section 77 of Land Registration Act 1925 (as substituted by Land Registration Act 1986) provides for a period of 12 years to be substituted for the current period of 15 years, but this provision does not apply to any title before 1 January 1999.
2. See Land Registration Act 1925, s.77, as amended by Land Registration Act 1986.

3.14.   **Lenders on mortgage of registered land**

3.14.1.   By far the best way of protecting a lender of registered land is by substantive registration of the charge when it will be registered in the charges register of the mortgaged land. Second and subsequent lenders are issued with their own charge certificates which will show their own charges on the charges register in addition to those belonging to prior lenders. The priority of lenders in registered land is governed by the relevant date of registration of the charges,[1] subject to any contrary entry on the register or in the charges.

3.14.2. Alternatively, a caution could be entered. While a registered charge subsists, the land certificate is held at HM Land Registry, a charge certificate being issued to the lender. However, this will only give the cautioner the right to be notified of future dealings with the title and the right to object to the registration of such dealings. It does not confer any priority on the cautioner. A charge can also be noted on the Register under Land Registration Act 1925, s.49 and any future purchaser of the land would take subject to a charge noted in this way. However, this protection is not as effective as substantive registration because no charge certificate is issued to the chargee and the chargee cannot exercise his power of sale until his charge is registered substantively (see para. 3.14.2. below).

3.14.3. Land Registration Act 1925, s.106 provides that a proprietor of registered land may mortgage the land in any manner which would have been permissible if the land had not been registered and with like effect.[2] The section also provides that unless and until the mortgage becomes a registered charge, it takes effect only in equity and unless protected by notice under section 49, a caution under section 54 or any other such notice as may be prescribed, it shall be capable of being overridden as a minor interest. Land Registration Rules 1995[3] revoke Rules 240−243 Land Registration Rules 1925, so that as from 3 April 1995 it is no longer possible to protect an equitable mortgage of registered land by a notice of deposit or notice of intended deposit. Existing notices of deposit and intended deposit will remain on the register until cancelled but the validity of the interest they purport to protect will need to be considered in the light of Law of Property (Miscellaneous Provisions) Act 1989, s.2. In any case where a charge is not a registered charge, in order to exercise a lender's power of sale, the chargee would need either to register the charge substantively (if it is capable of being registered in its own right), or to obtain an order of the court under Law of Property Act 1925, s.90 and obtain substantive registration pursuant to that order, so that he would then have the powers of a legal mortgagee pursuant to section 34.[4]

3.14.4. Where a lender wishes HM Land Registry to note on the register an obligation to make further advances, a request to HM Land Registry to do so must either be incorporated in the charge document itself or a separate application for noting in Form 113 must be lodged when the charge is lodged for registration. The Registry will not note an obligation to make further advances unless one of these steps is taken by the lender. No fee is payable for noting if the application for noting accompanies an application on which a scale fee is payable: otherwise a fee of £40 is payable. Where any charge is lodged for registration and incorporates by reference any other separate document (e.g. standard mortgage clauses), that other document must also be lodged at HM Land Registry if it is intended to be part of the terms and conditions of the charge unless:

    (a)   the other document is a standard form approved by the Registry; or

(b) the other document is of a type approved by the Registry and an undertaking has already been given to lodge the document if required; or

(c) an undertaking is given to and accepted by the Registry to deliver a copy of the other document when so directed, e.g. a debenture trust deed.[5]

3.14.5. Land Registry fees are payable on the substantive registration of a charge which is not contemporaneous with a purchase of the mortgaged land.

3.14.6. Note that charges created by companies need to have been registered at the Companies Registry under the Companies Acts.

1. See *Mortgage Corporation Ltd.* v. *Nationwide Credit Corporation Ltd.* [1994] Ch. 49, C.A., where a second charge was created before registration of the first charge. Priority was given to the first in time to be to be created.
2. *United Bank of Kuwait plc* v. *Sahib* [1996] N.P.C. 12.
3. S.I. 1995/140. Commencement date is 3 April 1995.
4. See below, para. H.03.2.3.
5. Land Registration Charges Rules 1990, rr. 139A and 139.

3.15. Protection of third party rights

3.15.1. Third party rights in registered land (other than mortgages) will be protected either as overriding interests or as minor interests.

3.15.2. Overriding interests, as defined in Land Registration Act 1925, s.70(1), bind a buyer of the land irrespective of whether he has notice of them or of whether or not they are entered on the register of the title.

3.15.3. The main types of overriding interest likely to be encountered are as follows (the numbering given below reflects the appropriate subparagraph numbers from section 70(1)):[1]

(a) legal easements and profits created before first registration of the land;

(f) rights acquired or in the course of acquisition under Limitation Act 1980;

(g) the rights of every person in actual occupation of the land or in receipt of the rents and profits except where enquiry is made of such person and he fails to disclose those rights;

(h) rights excepted from the effect of registration where the title is other than absolute;

(i) local land charges;

(k) leases granted for a term not exceeding 21 years.

3.15.4. A spouse's matrimonial homes rights under Family Law Act 1996 are not overriding even though the spouse will be in occupation of the land.

3.15.5. To be binding on a subsequent purchaser overriding interests within para. (g) above must be in existence at the date of completion. There is therefore little danger of a lender being subjected to an overriding interest claimed by a non-owning spouse unless the spouse was lawfully in occupation of the property before completion of the purchase and the related mortgage.[2] The date at which the existence of other types of overriding interest are to be judged is the date of registration of the proprietor. If therefore an overriding interest was created between the date of completion and the later date when the proprietor's title is registered, the proprietor will take subject to that interest.

3.15.6. Minor interests are all third party interest in registered land which are not overriding and thus include, e.g. equitable easements, restrictive covenants, and estate contracts. Minor interests must be protected by some entry on the register and if not so protected will not bind a buyer irrespective of whether he has notice of them.

3.15.7. An interest which would normally be classified as minor, such as an option, can also take effect as an overriding interest if, e.g. the person with its benefit is in occupation of the land. Where there is a choice of treatment of the third party interest it is safer to regard it as a minor interest and to secure a protecting entry on the register which will constitute notice to all parties of the existence of the right.[3]

3.15.8. Most minor interests are protected by entry of a notice on the charges register of the title. This method of protection is suitable for, e.g. estate contracts and restrictive covenants. An application for noting should be made on Form A4, and the land or charge certificate relating to the title must generally accompany the application to denote the registered proprietor's consent to the entry being made. The charge certificate need only be lodged if the chargee is a party to the deed or if the application is made by or with the concurrence of the chargee. The certificate need not be separately submitted if the matter giving rise to the entry of the notice arises on a dealing with the land, or where the land certificate is already held by the registry. New restrictive covenants which arise on a dealing with the land are automatically noted on the register and no separate application is required. The protection of a spouse's matrimonial homes rights under Family Law Act 1996 is made by notice entered on the proprietorship register and does not have to be accompanied by the land certificate.

3.15.9. Where it is not possible to protect a minor interest by notice, e.g. where the proprietor does not consent to the application being made, a caution should be entered on the proprietorship register of the title. This will provide temporary protection for the owner of the minor interest but, on a subsequent application by a third party for registration of his interest, the cautioner will be warned off by the registrar and will be given a limited period in which to establish his rights by substantive registration, failing which the third party will take free of the caution.[4] A caution is entered by applying on Form 63 with a statutory declaration in the form printed on the reverse of Form 63, or separately on Form 14. An application for a caution intended to be lodged in the name of a partnership must be made in the names of the individual partners (or some of them) and not in the name of the firm.

3.15.10. Entries which restrict the registered proprietor's powers of disposition of the land are made by restriction on the proprietorship register. Typically such an entry is made where co-owners hold as beneficial tenants in common, where the land is held on trust or strict settlement or where the proprietor is a limited company or charity which is subject to Charities Act 1993, ss.36−40.[5] In some cases the Chief Land Registrar is under a duty to enter a restriction. The most common example is the Form 62 restriction. There are other restrictions in respect of which the applicant is under a duty to apply for entry; still other restrictions are purely voluntary. Where it is wished to enter a restriction in either of the last two categories, specific application must be made for it either in Form 75 or in the body of the transfer or other document presented for registration.

3.15.11. Notice of the proprietor's insolvency is given by entry of an inhibition on the proprietorship register where the proprietor is an individual.

3.15.12. Positive covenants, which do not run with the land, are personal obligations affecting only the proprietor who entered into the covenants. They are commonly noted on the proprietorship register of the title and are deleted on a subsequent dealing. Such covenants may, however, be enforceable through a chain of indemnity covenants and, to give a subsequent buyer of the land notice of the existence and wording of the covenants, a separate copy of the deed imposing the covenants should be kept with the title deeds.

1. This is not a comprehensive list: for others see Land Registration Act 1925, s.70(1).
2. See *Abbey National* v. *Cann* [1991] 1 A.C. 56 and *Lloyds Bank* v. *Rosset* [1991] 1 A.C. 107.
3. See, e.g. *Webb* v. *Pollmount Ltd.* [1966] Ch. 584, where an option, which should have been registered as a minor interest but was not so registered, was allowed to take effect as an overriding interest under s. 70(1)(*g*) − but only after lengthy and expensive litigation to establish the point.
4. See *Clarke* v. *Chief Land Registrar, Chancery plc* v. *Ketteringham, The Times,* 10 May 1994, C.A.
5. For capacity generally, see above, Capacity, para. B.07.

3.16. Death of applicant while registration pending

3.16.1. If the applicant dies while an application for first registration of title is pending, the application may be continued by any person who would be entitled to apply for registration, e.g. the deceased's personal representatives.[1] The application may be continued either in the name of the deceased or of his successor in title. This procedure can be followed even in cases where the death occurs before the application for registration is lodged.

3.16.2. If the transferee of registered land dies before registration of his interest has been completed, the deceased's equitable interest in the property passes to his personal representatives who may continue the application in their names on production of the grant of representation to the registrar.

1. Land Registration Rules 1925, r. 305.

H. LENDERS
H.01. Acting for the lender

See also: Mortgages: acting for lender and borrower, para. A.11.

1.1. Introduction

1.1.1. Matters relating to the solicitor who is acting for a lender client are dealt with in context in other sections of this book. The following paragraphs draw together some of those points in the form of checklists for ready reference.

1.1.2. In many cases the solicitor acting for the lender will also be acting for the borrower in a related sale or purchase transaction. In such a case the principles of conduct relating to conflict of interests and confidentiality must at all times be observed.[1]

1.1.3. *Standard Mortgage Instructions*

The Standard Mortgage Instructions[2] (SMI) form the contract between the solicitor (or licensed conveyancer) and lender where the solicitor (or licensed conveyancer) is representing a lender who has agreed to be a party to the SMI. A number of major lenders have agreed to be parties to the SMI and other mortgage lenders may instruct solicitors to act on the terms of the SMI. The instructions apply whether or not the solicitor is acting for both borrower and lender or for the lender only.

1.1.4. Modifications of the instructions specific to the transaction in hand will be notified to the solicitor in the lender's written instructions to the solicitor.

1.1.5. Communications between the solicitor and the lender must be in writing (or confirmed in writing) and must quote the mortgage account or roll number, the borrower's name and initials, the address of the property and the solicitor's reference.

1.1.6. The solicitor must use the lender's standard documentation, the wording of which must not be varied without the lender's consent.

1. See above, Mortgages: acting for lender and borrower, para. A.11.
2. At the time of publication the SMI had not been finalised.

1.2. **Instructions to act**

1.2.1. Even where instructions are received from a lender for whom the solicitor acts frequently, it should not be assumed that the instructions in the current transaction are identical to those issued on previous occasions.

1.2.2. Instructions to act must be carefully checked in each particular case and any queries clarified with the lender. If at any time during the course of the transaction it appears that compliance with the lender's instructions will not be possible, further instructions must immediately be sought.

1.3. **Creation of new mortgage – checklist**

1.3.1.
(a) Check instructions to ensure that all conditions attached to the advance can be complied with by both the solicitor and the borrower.

(b) If the lender is not a building society, confirm with him the rate of charging for acting for him and who is to be responsible for payment of the solicitor's bill.

(c) Check that the terms of the contract to purchase are acceptable – does the purchase price in the contract accord with that shown on the lender's instructions?

(d) If the mortgage is being granted to a sole borrower, what are the lender's instructions relating to non-owning occupiers? Has any relevant consent form been signed?

(e) Have adequate enquiries been made to ensure that there are no overriding interests over the property which will adversely affect the lender's security?

(f) Inform lender of exchange of contracts and of contractual completion date if necessary.

(g) Check that the property will be properly insured from the moment of exchange or completion (as appropriate).

(h) Has investigation of title been completed satisfactorily (including the results of pre-contract searches and enquiries) – have all the lender's specific requirements been met?

(i) Engross mortgage deed and obtain borrower's signature(s) to it. Where there are joint borrowers one or more of whom is not known personally to the solicitor, precautions should be taken to verify the signature of the unknown borrower(s) in order to guard against forgery, e.g. by requiring the document to be signed in the presence of the solicitor.

(j) Engross and obtain borrower's signature to assignment of life policy (where appropriate).

(k) Ensure that life policy in terms which comply with lender's instructions is in existence.

(l) Are results of pre-completion searches satisfactory, including a clear result of a bankruptcy search against the names of the borrower(s) and a company search against a company seller?

(m) Make a report on title to the lender and request the advance cheque.

(n) On receipt of advance cheque pay it into clients' account — ensure funds have been cleared before completion.

(o) Make arrangements for completion.

(p) If required, arrange for inspection of property immediately before completion to ensure vacant possession will be given.

(q) Arrange for transmission of funds on day of completion.

(r) Inform lender of completion.

(s) Obtain purchase deed and land/charge certificate/title deeds from borrower's solicitor on completion with cheque for stamp duty and Land Registry fees.

(t) Date and fill in blanks in mortgage deed and related documents.

(u) Send notice of assignment of life policy (in duplicate) to insurance company.

(v) Give notice to prior lender(s) (if second or subsequent mortgage).

(w) Attend to stamping of purchase deed (*ad valorem* and PD stamp as appropriate).

(x) Submit application for registration of title within relevant priority period.

(y) Keep lender informed of the reason for any delays at HM Land Registry.

(z) On receipt of charge certificate from HM Land Registry, check its contents for accuracy and return to HM Land Registry if any errors need to be corrected.

(aa) Prepare schedule of deeds for lender.

(bb) Send deeds to lender (or as instructed) and request return of receipted schedule of deeds.

1.4.   Redemption of mortgage – checklist

1.4.1.   (a) Request charge certificate/title deeds from lender with redemption figure.

(b) Make a search to check if there is a subsequent chargee to whom the title deeds should be handed on completion.

(c) Check instructions from lender on their receipt.

(d) In the case of a related sale prepare epitome of title and send to borrower's solicitor (if unregistered land and lender's solicitor is not also acting for borrower).

(e) In the case of a related sale keep in touch with borrower's solicitor about arrangements for completion.

(f) Prepare Form 53 (or receipt in unregistered land) for signature by lender.

(g) Prepare reassignment of life policy (where relevant).

(h) Prepare undertaking for discharge of mortgage to be given to buyer's solicitor on completion.

(i) Prepare forms for discharge of land charges entries (second and subsequent mortgages of unregistered land).

(j) Obtain final redemption figure from lender and inform borrower's solicitor of the figure.

(k) Arrange with borrower's solicitor for actual payment on completion.

(l) On receipt of repayment money, clear draft through clients' account and account to lender in accordance with redemption statement.

(m) Hand over undertaking for discharge of mortgage to buyer's solicitor.

(n) Send Form 53 (or receipt in unregistered land) and deed of reassignment of life policy to mortgagee for execution and return. In the case of non-building society lenders, request that documents are dated with the date that completion of the mortgagor's sale took place to avoid problems over inadvertent transfer of the mortgage.[1]

(o) On receipt of executed Form 53 (or receipt), check it before sending to buyer's solicitor and request to be released from the undertaking given on completion.

(p) Return life policy to borrower.

1. See above, para. D.02.9.2.

1.5. Mortgage not simultaneous with purchase – checklist

1.5.1.
(a) Obtain office copy entries/title deeds.

(b) Make relevant pre-contract searches and enquiries including a search to find out whether prior mortgages exist.[1]

(c) Make enquiries about non-owning occupiers and obtain signature of consent form/release of rights in accordance with lender's instructions.

(d) Investigate title to the property.

(e) Check the state of the prior mortgage account (if relevant).

(f) Ensure compliance with Consumer Credit Act 1974, s.58 where applicable.[2]

(g) Draft, then engross mortgage deed.

(h) Send report on title to lender with request for advance cheque.

(i) Obtain borrower's signature to mortgage deed.

(j)   Make pre-completion searches, including bankruptcy search against name of borrower, and obtain clear results to searches.

(k)   Ensure any conditions attached to offer of advance have been complied with.

(l)   Arrange to complete.

(m) On completion hand advance money to mortgagor, date and fill in any blanks in mortgage deed.

(n)   Protect lender's security by registration.

(o)   Give notice to a prior lender (where relevant).

(p)   Send charge certificate/title deeds to lender.

1. See above, para. B.10.
2. See Second and subsequent mortgages, para. H.03.

1.6.   Incorrect redemption statements

1.6.1.   The guidance set out below has been issued jointly by the Law Society and Council of Mortgage Lenders in connection with problems arising out of incorrect redemption statements supplied by lenders.

1.6.2.   *Guidance notes*

Problems relating to mortgage redemption statements have caused difficulties for lenders and solicitors (this expression to include licensed conveyancers) for a number of years. In 1985 the Building Societies Association and the Law Society issued detailed advice to their respective members on this subject because of the difficulties which were apparent at that time.

The advice comprised paras. 9 to 13 of BSA circular No. 3155. Those paragraphs are now replaced by the new guidance set out below.

In recent months, the Council of Mortgage Lenders (CML) has received a number of enquiries in respect of redemption statements provided by lenders to solicitors acting for the lender (who will often also act for the seller). This guidance refers to some of the circumstances which can produce errors and problems, and the consequences which this can have for the solicitor in the conveyancing transaction. It also suggests certain practical measures designed to reduce problems in this area. Accordingly, it is of importance to all lenders and covers:

(a)   the function and importance of solicitors' undertakings;

(b)   the general principle that lenders should seal a discharge where a redemption statement was incorrect;

(c)   ways in which lenders might overcome the difficulty caused when the borrower prematurely stops payments;

(d)   similar proposals as to the problem of dishonoured cheques;

(e) suggestions for overcoming difficulties sometimes presented by multiple mortgage accounts;

(f) information to be provided to banks for inclusion in telegraphic transfers; and

(g) the importance of returning the sealed discharge promptly.

Terms of reference

This guidance applies to England and Wales; separate guidance for Scotland and Northern Ireland will follow, if necessary.

Redemption on sale

The guidance applies primarily to redemption of a mortgage on sale of the security and, consequently, the lender's/seller's solicitor is required to give an undertaking to the buyer's solicitor that the charge will be discharged.

Remortgages

It is appreciated that an undertaking will also be given on a remortgage and that, accordingly, the guidance should be interpreted as including this situation.

Simple redemption

Much of the guidance is inapplicable to a straightforward redemption (without sale or remortgage) as no undertaking is given. However, even in redemption *per se*, solicitors and lenders will no doubt wish to provide accurate information and deal promptly with their respective responsibilities.

Solicitors' undertakings

The solicitor acting for the seller will need, on completion, to satisfy the buyer's solicitor that the mortgage on the property being sold has been or will be discharged. In theory the buyer's solicitor will wish to see the mortgage discharged before the purchase money is paid. However, where the monies to repay the mortgage are being provided wholly or partly by the proceeds of sale, then the mortgage cannot be paid off until after completion.

Most lenders will not seal the discharge (this expression to include sealing the vacating receipt on a mortgage deed or sealing of Form 53) until they receive the redemption money. This leaves the buyer's solicitor with a problem in that he or she has to be satisfied that the mortgage will be discharged and that he or she will obtain the receipted mortgage or Land Registry Form 53. This problem is solved by the use of the solicitor's undertaking.

On completion, the seller's/lender's solicitor will provide the buyer's solicitor with a written undertaking to redeem the mortgage(s) in a form recommended by the Law Society similar to that set out below:

'In consideration of your today completing the purchase of . . . . we hereby undertake forthwith to pay over to . . . . [the lender] the money required to redeem the mortgage/legal charge dated . . . . and to forward the receipted mortgage/legal charge [Form 53] to you as soon as it is received by us from . . . . [the lender].'

Incorrect redemption statements

Before completion of a sale, the lender's seller's solicitor will obtain a redemption statement calculated to the date of redemption. He or she will sometimes request the daily figure for interest which will be added if completion is delayed. If the lender supplies an incorrect redemption statement, the solicitor is likely to forward insufficient money to redeem the mortgage. The lender might be unwilling to discharge the mortgage and, if the solicitor is not holding more funds on behalf of the borrower, the solicitor would be in breach of his or her undertaking.

Problem areas

Problems with redemption statements can arise for a number of reasons:

    (a)   a lender might simply make a mistake in calculating the redemption figure;

    (b)   difficulties could be caused by the cancellation of standing orders or direct debit payments or by borrowers' cheques being dishonoured; and

    (c)   there might be misunderstanding between a lender and the solicitor.

Some of the more common practical problems are outlined below.

Cancellation

A difficulty arises if the mortgage payments are made by standing order and, shortly before completion, the borrower stops the payments without notice to the lender. There will be a shortfall if the lender assumed, without making this assumption clear, that the next payment would be paid and made the redemption figure calculation accordingly.

If this is the case, and the solicitor has acted in good faith and with no knowledge that a payment has been or is likely to be cancelled, the view of the CML is that the lender should seal the discharge. This is to avoid the solicitor being in breach of his or her undertaking to the buyer's solicitor. (The lender would then have to recoup the money from the borrower.)

This difficulty is less likely to arise where payments are made by direct debit because the lender is the originator of the debit and therefore has control over the raising of any future direct debits from the borrower's bank account.

However, there is no guarantee that direct debits will be honoured and they may be returned on the grounds of insufficient funds or that the customer has closed his or her account or instructed his or her bank to cancel the direct debit.

Some lenders overcome this problem by excluding any future payments due when calculating the redemption figure. In other words, they 'freeze' the account balance at the day of the redemption calculation. The disadvantages of this are that (if the payment has not been cancelled) the borrower has to pay a higher redemption figure and the lender has to make a refund to the borrower after redemption.

An alternative is for the lender on the redemption statement to make it clear to the solicitor that it is assumed that the next payment will be made and that, if it is not paid, the mortgage will not be discharged until the balance is received. This gives the solicitor an early chance to address his or her and his or her borrower client's mind to this situation and to ensure that sufficient monies will be available to redeem the mortgage. Indeed, this would also serve as a reminder to the solicitor to warn the borrower client of the importance of continuing the payments in the normal way up to completion.

Uncleared cheques

This is a very similar situation to that of standing orders and direct debits. The CML's view is that if the lender does not notify the solicitor that it is assumed that the borrower's cheque will clear then, provided that the solicitor acts in good faith and without knowledge that the cheque would be or is likely to be dishonoured, the lender should seal the discharge. Exceptions to this are if the lender:

(a) prepares the redemption statement on the assumption that the cheque will not clear and informs the solicitor of this, probably, in a note on the statement. This has the disadvantages described above, or

(b) notifies the solicitor that a cheque has been received and that, if it does not clear by the date of redemption, the mortgage will not be discharged until the balance is received.

Separate loan account

The lender may have more than one loan secured on the property. For example, in addition to the principal mortgage, there could be a secured personal loan which is a regulated agreement under Consumer Credit Act 1974 and/or a further advance conducted on a separate account basis. In such cases, there will be more than one account number.

On a sale, as all mortgage accounts will be repaid, multiplicity of accounts should not present a problem unless the solicitor does not know and is unable to specify every account and has no notice or cause to query the matter and the lender fails to cross-check the matter internally.

However, it is possible, for example, on certain remortgages, that it is the intention of the borrower and the lender that not all mortgages will be discharged and replaced. If so, when requesting the redemption statement, the solicitor should make it clear to the lender which mortgages the borrower wishes to redeem. The solicitor should inform the lender of any mortgages of which he or she is aware which are outstanding with the lender but which are not being redeemed. The solicitor should also quote all relevant account numbers if known as far as possible and ensure that the redemption statement received from the lender includes all the mortgages which are intended to be redeemed.

The lender should have its own internal cross-checking system but it is vital that the solicitor (who will, after all, be acting for the lender in most cases) is as clear as possible about the mortgage account(s) being redeemed. It is suggested that the solicitor should if possible, and time permits, send a copy of the redemption statement to the borrower to check agreement on the amount shown as due to the lender. Solicitors should be encouraged to ask for a statement at the earliest possible date.

Telegraphic transfers

Lenders could request that solicitors adopt procedures to assist in the identification of telegraphic transfers. When mortgages are being redeemed the telegraphic transfer which a lender receives is often difficult to identify and to match to a particular account.

The administrative difficulties which are caused by the inability to identify the money would be overcome if solicitors provided to the bank the information to be included in the telegraphic transfer, i.e. the borrower's mortgage account number and the firm's name and address.

Delay

Lenders are sometimes criticised for delay in providing a form of discharge after redemption of the mortgage. It is recognised that most lenders can and do return the receipted mortgage or Form 53 promptly and that solicitors can apply for registration to protect priority. However, unless there is good reason for the delay, e.g. a solicitor sending the form to the wrong office of the lender, lenders will no doubt deal promptly with this important procedure.

It is suggested that lenders should aim to return the receipted mortgage or Form 53 within seven days, and if there is likely to be a delay beyond that period they should notify the seller's solicitor. This would enable the buyer's solicitor to lodge an application with the Land Registry pending receipt of receipted mortgage or sealed Form 53, although it is hoped that this would only be necessary in exceptional circumstances.

The CML view

Many of the difficulties described above would be reduced if as a matter of course solicitors gave lenders correct information about the borrower, the property, the account number(s), etc., and lenders, in turn, operated internal cross-checking systems and provided accurate and complete redemption statements showing clearly the last payment to be taken into account and, systems permitting, details of all the borrower's accounts relating to the property which represent mortgages to be discharged.

If the solicitor, relying on an incorrect redemption statement provided by the lender, sends insufficient money to redeem a mortgage, the lender should discharge the mortgage. (However, the lender might wish to make it clear that the release was not intended to discharge the borrower from his or her outstanding personal liability. This might prevent the borrower from successfully claiming estoppel against the lender.)

Such cases do not occur frequently; when they do, it is generally because of a clerical or administrative error on the part of the lender, such as by omitting one month's interest or an insurance premium, and the amount is usually small. Nevertheless, where it appears that there has been an error, the solicitor should immediately draw this to the lender's notice and should pursue his or her borrower client actively for any shortfall.

Very rare cases could arise where general guidance of this kind is inapplicable, for example, if there is such a major discrepancy in the redemption figure that the borrower, and, perhaps, his or her solicitor, could not reasonably have believed in the accuracy of the statement.

Conclusion

Where there is an incorrect redemption statement, which is clearly due to an error by the lender or lack of clarification, it is unreasonable that a solicitor should be put in breach of his or her undertaking. The undertaking given to the buyer's solicitor is a vital part of the conveyancing process. It is the CML's view, in such cases, that the lender should seal the discharge.

The Law Society and the Council for Licensed Conveyancers agree with the views expressed in these paragraphs. It is hoped that some of the practical measures referred to above will be implemented to avoid difficulties on redemption.

H.02. Sales by lenders

2.1.	**Power of sale**	2.5.	**Proceeds of sale**
2.2.	**Possession**	2.6.	**Administrative**
2.3.	**Price**		**receivers**
2.4.	**The sale transaction**	2.7.	**Receiver appointed by lender**

See also: Capacity, para. B.07.

2.1. Power of sale

2.1.1. A lender may sell property over which he enjoys a power of sale and convey in his own name provided his power has both arisen and become exercisable. The existence and exercise of the power are discussed above in para. B.07.7.

2.1.2. A first lender sells free of all charges registered subsequent to his own; thus a buyer is not concerned with the discharge of second and subsequent mortgages when a power of sale is exercised by a first lender.[1]

2.1.3. If a second or subsequent lender wishes to sell he must either sell the property subject to any prior charges, or redeem them (thus becoming a first lender) but will overreach all charges which are subsequent to his own.

2.1.4. The lender must exercise his power in good faith for the purpose of obtaining repayment; subject to this, he can exercise his powers even if the exercise is disadvantageous to the borrower.[2] There is no wider duty in negligence.[3]

2.1.5. A lender must not sell to himself or to his nominee.[4] There is no rule that he cannot sell to a person connected with him[5] but the correctness of the price must plainly be beyond doubt, and the lender must have taken and acted on expert advice as to the best method of selling, what steps should reasonably be taken to make the sale a success, and what reserve price should be fixed.

2.1.6. It is usually inadvisable for the sale contract to be conditional or for an option to be granted, since there is a risk that the loan might be repaid and the borrower would then be entitled to a discharge of the mortgage. The borrower's equity of redemption, and his ability to redeem, is only destroyed when there is a binding unconditional contract for sale.[6]

2.1.7. If the mortgage is only over the beneficial interest of a joint owner, the lender will have to make application to the court under section 14 of Trusts of Land and Appointment of Trustees Act 1996 for an order for sale. This order will not necessarily be granted by the court.

1. Law of Property Act 1925, s.104 and Land Registration Act 1925, s.34.
2. *Kennedy* v. *De Trafford* [1897] A.C. 180.
3. *Downsview Nominees* v. *First City Corp.* [1993] 3 All E.R. 626.
4. *Farrar* v. *Farrars Ltd.* (1888) 40 Ch. 395.
5. *Tse Kwong Lam* v. *Wong Chit Sen* [1983] 3 All E.R. 54, P.C.
6. *Property & Bloodstock Ltd.* v. *Emerton* [1968] Ch. 94.

2.2. Possession

2.2.1. Before selling the lender will normally take possession in order to be able to sell with vacant possession (or subject to any tenancies which bind him).

2.2.2. In the case of residential property it will be necessary to obtain a court order for possession unless the occupier leaves the premises voluntarily.[1]

2.2.3. A buyer from the lender is not concerned to see the court order authorising possession.

1. Protection from Eviction Act 1977, s.2.

2.3. Price

2.3.1. Building societies are under a statutory duty to obtain the best price for the property.[1]

2.3.2. Other lenders must take reasonable precautions to obtain a proper price for the property.[2] Although there is a theoretical distinction between building societies and other lenders in relation to the price which they must obtain for the property, in practice the courts appear to apply similar criteria when applying each test.

2.3.3. Sales by lenders commonly take place by auction but there is no legal requirement to this effect. A sale by auction does not necessarily constitute evidence that the lender has obtained the best possible price for the property,[3] and the lender's duty in this respect is not discharged by placing the property for sale in the hands of reputable agents.[4]

2.3.4. A sale at a sum which is sufficient only to pay off the mortgage would be looked at carefully by the court.[5]

2.3.5. The fact that the property is resold to a third party shortly after the sale by the lender and at a substantially higher price than that obtained by the lender would also be viewed with suspicion by the court.[6]

2.3.6. The borrower can challenge the amount of costs claimed by the mortgagee by making an application to the court for the taxation of the lender's costs.[7]

1. Building Societies Act 1986, s.13(7).
2. *Cuckmere Brick Co. Ltd.* v. *Mutual Finance Ltd.* [1971] Ch. 949.
3. *Tse Kwong Lam* v. *Wong Chit Sen* [1983] 3 All E.R. 54.
4. *Cuckmere Brick Co. Ltd.* v. *Mutual Finance Ltd.* [1971] Ch. 949.
5. *Midland Bank Ltd.* v. *Joliman Finance Ltd.* (1967) 203 E.G. 612; *Predeth* v. *Castle Phillips Finance Co. Ltd.* [1986] 2 E.G.L.R. 144, C.A.
6. *Bank of Cyprus (London) Ltd.* v. *Gill* [1980] 2 Lloyd's Rep. 51.
7. *Gomba Holdings (U.K.) Ltd.* v. *Minories Finance (No. 2)* [1992] 4 All E.R. 588.

2.4.   The sale transaction

2.4.1.   The sale follows the normal procedures for the sale of land, subject to any specific requirements or instructions given by the mortgagee client.

2.4.2.   Since the lender will have taken possession of the property (if at all) only shortly before exercising his power of sale, he will have little or no knowledge of the condition of the property and may not therefore be able to answer pre-contract enquiries as fully as the buyer would wish. The buyer should be advised of this fact and of any other special conditions attaching to the sale, e.g. requirement for payment of a full 10% deposit. A selling lender will commonly require the buyer to exchange contracts within a stated period, reserving the right to withdraw from the sale if this condition is not met. This type of condition is imposed because of the lender's duty to obtain the best price for the property. If exchange of contracts became delayed, property values might in the interim period have altered and the lender might find himself liable in an action for breach of trust if he continued with a prospective sale in circumstances where the market price of the property had risen and a better price would be obtainable elsewhere.

2.4.3.   The lender's duty to both the borrower and to subsequent lenders to obtain the best or proper price means that the lender is under an implicit duty to preserve the value of the property by ensuring that it remains in good physical order. For this reason, the buyer should not be allowed access or entry into possession before completion. Standard Condition 5.2 (occupation by the buyer) or any similar provision should therefore normally be excluded from the contract. If not so excluded a buyer does not have a *right* to occupy; he may only do so with the seller's consent.

2.4.4.   The buyer can demand to see the mortgage deed under which the power of sale is being exercised in order to check the existence of the power and that it has arisen, but is not concerned to enquire whether circumstances exist which entitle the lender to exercise the power.

2.4.5.   In the case of registered land, the transfer must be in Form 31.

2.4.6.   The lender will need to consider which covenants for title (if any) he is prepared to give to the buyer in the purchase deed.

2.4.7.   On completion of a sale by a lender, the mortgage under which the power is exercised is not 'discharged' although the buyer takes free from it. The buyer will therefore receive the charge certificate (mortgage deed and other title deeds in unregistered land) but will not receive a Form 53 (or mortgage receipt in unregistered land) in respect of the mortgage. Charge certificates and/or Forms 53 (mortgage deeds and/or receipts in unregistered land) relating to subsequent mortgages (if any) do not need to be handed over on completion since the sale by the lender overreaches these subsequent charges.

2.5. Proceeds of sale

2.5.1. The selling lender will discharge the debt owing to him, including interest and the costs of the sale, from the proceeds of sale.

2.5.2. If any surplus then remains, the selling lender holds the surplus on behalf of and must account to a subsequent lender. It is therefore essential that the selling lender makes a search at HM Land Registry (registered land) or the Land Charges Department (unregistered land) to discover whether or not subsequent mortgages exist before accounting to the borrower for the surplus proceeds of sale. The buyer from the lender is not concerned to see that the lender deals properly with the surplus.

2.6. Administrative receivers

2.6.1. A properly appointed administrative receiver of a company (this person must be a licensed insolvency practitioner) has power to sell a company's property but is personally liable on all contracts he enters into, unless the contract otherwise provides. He owes a duty to both borrower and lender to take reasonable care to obtain the best price which circumstances permit when selling the assets.[1]

1. *Gosling* v. *Gaskell* [1897] A.C. 575.

2.7. Receiver appointed by lender

2.7.1. The receiver need not be a licensed insolvency practitioner unless his position is classified as that of an administrative receiver (i.e. his responsibilities extend to substantially the whole of the company's assets and he is appointed under floating as well as fixed charges). The receiver is agent for the borrower company and is personally liable on his contracts unless the contract otherwise provides. The receiver will not automatically take possession of the company's property but is entitled to collect income accruing from it. He must apply that income as directed by section 109 of Law of Property Act 1925. Rent collected by and in the hands of the borrower's managing agent may strictly not be classified as 'income' to which the receiver is entitled. To overcome this difficulty the receiver should as soon as practicable after his appointment give notice to all tenants and to the managing agent advising that all rent should be paid to the receiver as from that time. The receiver owes a duty to the borrower to carry out all rent reviews, lease renewals and other acts that a prudent landlord would do.[1] Where a receiver contracts to sell property owned by the borrower, the contract should provide for the purchase deed to be signed by the lender under his power of sale; this procedure will ensure that other interests in the property are overreached on completion.

1. See *Knight* v. *Lawrence* [1991] 1 E.G.L.R. 143.

FURTHER REFERENCE

Fisher and Lightwood's Law of Mortgage, E.L.G. Tyler, Butterworths.

H.03. Second and subsequent mortgages

3.1.	**Introduction**	3.4.	**Consumer Credit Act 1974**
3.2.	**Registration of charges**	3.5.	**Tacking**
3.3.	**Power of sale**	3.6.	**Consolidation**

See also: Mortgages: acting for lender and borrower, para. A.11.
Capacity, para. B.07.
Sales by lenders, para. H.02.

3.1. Introduction

3.1.1. The creation of a second or subsequent mortgage will not necessarily occur simultaneously with the purchase of the property over which the mortgage is taken.

3.1.2. The solicitor acting for the borrower may also be instructed to act for the lender but not infrequently separate solicitors are instructed to act in this situation.

3.1.3. The procedures to be followed by the lender's solicitor broadly follow the steps to be taken in a normal purchase transaction (except that there is no contract) since full enquiries about the property and its title must be made on the lender's behalf to ensure that he will obtain a viable security for his loan.

3.1.4. A checklist of the steps to be taken when acting on a mortgage which is not simultaneous with a purchase is set out above in para. H.01.5.

3.1.5. Mortgages sometimes contain a condition prohibiting the borrower from creating further charges over the property without that lender's consent. In such a case the requisite consent should be sought and obtained at an early stage in the transaction. A mortgage created in breach of such a condition is not itself invalid but will render the borrower vulnerable to repayment of the first charge.

3.2. Registration of charges

3.2.1. On completion of a mortgage of registered land the charge must be protected by registration at HM Land Registry within the priority period afforded by the lender's search. On registration, a second (or as appropriate) charge certificate will be issued to the lender.

3.2.2. The priority of registered charges in registered land depends on the order in which the charges are registered on the title; therefore registration within the priority period given by a pre-completion search certificate is essential.[1]

3.2.3. An equitable mortgage must be in writing and signed by both parties in order to satisfy Law of Property (Miscellaneous Provisions) Act 1989, s.2.[2]

3.2.4. An equitable mortgage of registered land should be protected by registration of a notice or caution at HM Land Registry. If not so protected the lender is at risk of losing his priority to the holder of a subsequently created charge. It is no longer possible to protect an equitable mortgage of registered land by notice of deposit.[3]

3.2.5. A charge created by a company, whether fixed or floating and whether over registered or unregistered land, must be registered at the Companies Registry under Companies Act requirements within 21 days of its creation.

3.2.6. In unregistered land a mortgage which is not accompanied by the deposit of title deeds must be protected by registration at the Land Charges Department by entry of a Class C(i) (for a legal mortgage) or Class C(iii) (for an equitable mortgage) land charge. By Law of Property Act 1925, s.198 registration constitutes actual notice to a third party for all purposes connected with the land; further, the date of registration governs the priority of mortgages. In order to effect registration at the earliest possible opportunity, a priority notice should be lodged at the Land Charges Department at least 15 working days before completion and the application for registration made within 30 working days of lodging the priority notice. This will ensure that registration is effective from the date of completion itself.

3.2.7. Notice of the mortgage should also be given to prior lenders in order to ensure that they are actually aware of the existence of the new charge.

1. See *Mortgage Corporation Ltd.* v. *Nationwide Credit Corporation Ltd.* [1994] Ch. 49, C.A.
2. *United Bank of Kuwait plc* v. *Sahib* [1996] N.P.C. 12.
3. Land Registration Rules 1995, S.I. 1995/140.

3.3.   **Power of sale**

3.3.1. Provided that he has a power of sale and that it has both arisen and become exercisable[1] there is no legal reason why a second or subsequent lender should not sell the property in order to realise his security.

3.3.2. In practical terms he may experience difficulty in selling the property. Although he will sell free of incumbrances ranking in priority subsequent to his own, he cannot sell free of prior incumbrances (although he may be able to redeem these on completion if the proceeds of sale are sufficient). He should therefore make a search at HM Land Registry (registered land) or the Land Charges Department (unregistered land) to establish which incumbrances, if any, have priority over his own.

3.3.3. The sale of a property which is subject to a subsisting mortgage is not an attractive marketable proposition and the price attainable on such a sale may be low as a reflection of the existence of the mortgage over the property. The selling lender may therefore either have to persuade his prior lender to join with him in exercising the power of sale (assuming that the price obtainable would then be sufficient to discharge both debts) or discharge the prior mortgage out of his own funds before selling thus placing himself in the position of first lender. A contract for sale by a subsequent lender cannot prevent the prior lender selling the property in the meantime. This would put the second lender in breach of his sale contract. He needs to come to an arrangement with the first lender before exchanging contracts. That could either involve him redeeming the first mortgage beforehand out of his own money, or agreeing to discharge it on completion out of the proceeds of sale.

1. See above, para. B.07.7.

3.4. Consumer Credit Act 1974

3.4.1. Section 58 of Consumer Credit Act 1974 is primarily of concern when dealing with the creation of second or subsequent mortgages in favour of finance houses.

3.4.2. The section applies where:

(a) a mortgage is created over land;

(b) the mortgage is not taken out to finance the purchase of the land which is being mortgaged, i.e. a bridging loan or mortgage which is simultaneous with the purchase of land is not within this section;

(c) the lender is not exempt under Consumer Credit Act 1974, s.16 (most building societies, banks and insurance companies are exempt lenders);[1]

(d) the sum secured by the mortgage does not exceed £15,000.

3.4.3. Where this section applies the creditor (lender) must supply the debtor (borrower) with a copy of the prospective mortgage agreement and related documents, e.g. assignment of life policy. Having done this, he must allow seven days to elapse before sending a further copy of the agreement and related documents to the debtor for signature by him. A further period of seven days must then elapse before the creditor is permitted to contact the debtor for any reason. Thus the debtor is given a 14-day 'consideration period' which runs from the date when the first copies of the agreement and related documents are sent to him in which to consider the prospective transaction free of influence from the creditor and if desired to take legal advice. During the whole of this time the creditor must not contact the debtor except to send him the signature copies of the agreement and related documents, although he may speak to or otherwise communicate with the debtor if the debtor contacts him first. Any communication between the creditor and debtor during this period must only be at the instigation of the debtor.

3.4.4. The consideration period can come to an end before the expiry of the 14 days if within that time the debtor signs and returns the agreement to the creditor.

3.4.5. For the purposes of this section, communications sent to or made with the debtor by the creditor's solicitor would be treated as being communications made by the creditor himself.

3.4.6.   Failure to comply with the section or breach of its provisions renders the agreement improperly executed. This means that it cannot be enforced without a court order under Consumer Credit Act 1974, s.127. Such a court order would not necessarily be granted.

3.4.7.   Because of the seriousness of the consequences of non-compliance with section 58, it is imperative that creditors and their solicitors comply with its requirements and do not contact the debtor while the consideration period is running.

3.4.8.   Where it appears that the loan will be subject to the provisions of section 58, it is best for the parties to be represented by separate solicitors in order to avoid the problems outlined in this paragraph. The section causes particular difficulty where the same solicitor is acting for both parties to the transaction since it means that during the consideration period the solicitor is unable to contact his debtor client, even to advise him about the terms of the loan agreement. It is uncertain whether in such circumstances contact made by the solicitor with the debtor about a matter unrelated to the loan would infringe the terms of the section, but it would seem advisable not to contact the debtor client at all during this period.

3.4.9.   Where the loan is subject to Consumer Credit Act 1974 a proper default notice under section 87 of the Act must be served before enforcement of the security. The court may then make a time order under sections 129–130 of the Act (these sections are similar in their effect to Administration of Justice Act 1970, s.36).[2]

1. See Consumer Credit (Exempt Agreements) (No. 2) Order 1985 (S.I. 1985/757), as amended.
2. See *Southern & District Finance* v. *Barnes* [1995] N.P.C. 52.

3.5.   Tacking

3.5.1.   Tacking is the name given to the process by which a lender makes a further advance to the borrower and claims priority for repayment of both the original loan and the further advance over intervening lenders whose mortgages were created after the first loan but before the further advance.

3.5.2.   *Registered land*

Registered charges rank for priority in the order in which they are entered on the register. However, this general rule is affected by two provisions contained in Land Registration Act 1925, s.30 as amended:

(a)   where the proprietor of a charge is under an *obligation* which is noted on the register to make a further advance, a subsequent registered charge takes effect subject to any further advance made pursuant to the obligation;

(b)   where a registered charge is made for securing further advances, the registrar, before registering a subsequent charge, has to give notice of the intended entry to the proprietor of the earlier charge. In such a case, the latter, in respect of any further advance, is not affected by the entry of the notice of the subsequent charge unless the further advance was made after the date when the notice should have been received by him in due course of post.

3.5.3. *Unregistered land*

Section 94 of Law of Property Act 1925 allows a mortgagee to tack a further advance in three cases:

(a) where the intervening lender agrees;

(b) where his mortgage imposes on him an *obligation* to make a further advance;

(c) where he had no notice of the intervening mortgage at the time of making the further advance. The registration of the intervening mortgage (whether legal or equitable) under Land Charges Act is notice for this purpose, except that if the first mortgage was made to secure a current account or other further advances, the mere registration of the intervening mortgage as a land charge is not of itself notice to the first lender to prevent tacking.

3.5.4. It follows from (c) above that a second or subsequent lender of unregistered land should (as well as registering his mortgage as a land charge) give express notice of his mortgage to any prior lender in order to prevent the tacking of further advances by the prior lender.

3.5.5. A further reason for giving such notice is to compel a first (or prior) lender to hand the title deeds to the later lender when the earlier mortgage is discharged. The earlier lender is bound to do this where he has notice of the later mortgage, but the mere registration of the mortgage as a land charge is not notice for this purpose.

3.6. **Consolidation**

3.6.1. Consolidation is the right of a lender to refuse to allow a mortgage on one property to be redeemed unless a mortgage on another property (or properties) is also redeemed. It is an equitable doctrine, based on the principle that it would be unfair to allow a borrower to redeem a mortgage over a valuable property and leave the lender with security on another property which was not worth the amount of the loan.

3.6.2. As it is an equitable doctrine, the borrower must be seeking to exercise his equitable right to redeem, i.e. the legal date for redemption on all the mortgages sought to be consolidated must have passed, and all the mortgages must originally have been created by the same borrower. At least one of the mortgages must expressly reserve the right to consolidate, i.e. it must expressly exclude the effect of Law of Property Act 1925, s.93 which restricts consolidation.

3.6.3. Provided the conditions set out in the preceding subparagraph are satisfied, a lender may consolidate provided that all the equities of redemption are in one hand (i.e.

owned by the same person) and all the mortgages in another, or, that state of affairs having existed in the past, the equities (only) have become separated.

3.6.4.   Because a second mortgage of land is in principle a mortgage of the equity of redemption of the first mortgage, the right, where it exists, can be exercised not only against the transferees of the land, but also against subsequent lenders.

3.6.5.   A buyer who is taking land subject to an existing mortgage, or a subsequent lender of the land, should make enquiry as to the existence of mortgages on other land created by the same borrower, since the doctrine operates independently of notice and even the subsequent uniting of mortgages in one hand could cause prejudice to such a person.

H.04. Certificates of title

4.1. Definition

4.1.1. A certificate of title is written confirmation given by a solicitor or other person qualified in the law of the country in which the property is situated as to the ownership of land or any interest in land.

4.2. When will a certificate of title be required?

4.2.1. A certificate of title may be used in any case where confirmation as to the title to property is required but is unusual in the case of residential properties situated in the U.K. It may be appropriate to require that a certificate of title be given by or on behalf of the person who owns the land. As an alternative to a certificate it may be possible to deal with the title to the property by means of warranties given by the person owning the property or an investigation and report on the title by lawyers acting on behalf of the person who is seeking to ascertain the quality of the title.

4.2.2. Examples of situations where a certificate may be appropriate:

    (a) the purchase of shares in a company;

    (b) the purchase of assets from a company;

    (c) flotation, mortgage, debenture or other security arrangements made by companies;

    (d) occasionally on a straightforward house purchase.

4.3. Contents of certificate

4.3.1. The person to whom the certificate is addressed is entitled to rely on its contents; thus the person giving the certificate can be held liable for inaccuracies in its contents. It is therefore important for the person giving the certificate to identify the recipient of the certificate and to know for what purpose the certificate is required. The giver may seek to limit his liability on the certificate to named recipients and/or to limit the validity of the certificate for a specified period, e.g. three months from its date.

4.3.2. The object of certification is not to give evidence of a perfect title but to provide an accurate description of the legal character of the property in question. Any material information or irregularities affecting the property should be stated in a schedule to the certificate.

4.3.3. To be of practical use to the recipient the certificate should deal with the following matters:

    (a) ownership of the property;

    (b) an adequate description of the property;

    (c) its tenure with relevant details;

    (d) the name of the current owner of the estate in land;

    (e) whether the title to the land is good, marketable and unencumbered;

    (f) whether there are any statutory orders, schemes or provisions detrimental to the property or its use;

    (g) where appropriate, provisions relating to planning, highways, public health, etc., should be referred to;

    (h) appropriate searches which have been made at HM Land Registry, the Land Charges Department and the district council, and other relevant searches;

    (i) which searches have not been carried out in order to give the recipient a complete picture of the title which he is accepting.

4.3.4. Although the certificate should be positive, a solicitor should qualify it to suit the circumstances where it has not been possible to obtain or to verify all the relevant information.

4.3.5. Where land is being purchased under right to buy legislation, HM Land Registry is bound to accept a certificate of title supplied by the seller, the seller being obliged to indemnify the Registry if the certificate turns out to be inaccurate.

I. NEW PROPERTIES
I.01. New property

See also: Value added tax, para. A.16.
Pre-contract searches and enquiries, para. B.10.
Plans, para. B.21.
Planning, para. B.24.
Sales of part, para. J.01.

1.1. Introduction

1.1.1. A sale of a new property is a more complex transaction than the sale of an existing house or building, and some matters additional to those relevant to a sale of an existing house or building must be considered. The following paragraphs only deal with those matters which are exclusive to new properties.

1.1.2. Where the Standard Mortgage Instructions (SMI) apply the specific requirements in relation to new properties must be observed.[1]

1. At the time of publication the SMI had not been finalised.

1.2. The contract

1.2.1. Where the property comprises a plot on a new building estate the contract will often be in standard form and the seller will be reluctant to allow substantial amendments to that form[1]. The buyer's solicitor should ensure that the contract does not impose unnecessarily burdensome terms on the buyer, sufficiently protects his client's interests and complies with any conditions required by the buyer's lender. The seller may require the deposit to be paid to him as 'agent' and not as 'stakeholder'. The consequences of this requirement should be explained to the buyer and the lender's consent to such a contractual condition obtained.

1.2.2. A contract for the sale of a new property will frequently be a sale of part of the seller's existing property and may comprise a plot on a new building estate. In either case adequate provision must be made in the contract for the grant and reservation of easements to the parties and the property being sold will usually be described by reference to a plan which should be coloured in accordance with HM Land Registry requirements.[2]

1.2.3. The contract should require the seller to complete the building works in accordance with the agreed specifications, planning permissions and plans submitted to the buyer. It may also contain a 'long stop' completion date requiring the builder to use his reasonable endeavours to complete the building works within a specified period so that, e.g. in the event of a prolonged strike by the workmen on site the buyer has the opportunity to rescind the contract. The buyer and his lender may wish to have a right to inspect the property during and at the completion of the building works.

1.2.4. Where the property being sold is in the course of construction it may not be possible for the seller to agree a definite completion date at the time of exchange since he will not be able to guarantee that the building works will be completed by a specified time. In such a case he may prefer to include a condition in the contract providing for completion of the transaction to take place within a specified number of days after completion of the building works.[3] This type of condition may give rise to difficulties from the buyer's point of view since if he is involved in a chain of transactions such a condition will make it difficult to synchronise the chain, unless similar conditions relating to completion are imposed in every transaction in the chain. The buyer should therefore be advised of this difficulty and warned of the possibility that in the event of the transactions not being synchronised the buyer may either have to complete his dependent sale first and move into temporary accommodation pending completion of the new property, or be prepared to use bridging finance for the completion of the new property pending sale of the old one. Where completion is to take place within a specified number of days of completion of the building works, the buyer's solicitor should also ensure that the number of days provided by the contract gives the buyer's solicitor sufficient time in which to carry out his pre-completion searches and to arrange for the purchase price to be obtained and for a final inspection of the building by the buyer's lender's surveyor.

1.2.5. Provision may be made for the seller to rectify minor defects in the building within a specified time after completion, although where the property is to be covered by a structural defects policy (see below, para. 1.5.) this matter will usually be covered by such a policy. A contract to build a building is a contract for services within Supply of Goods and Services Act 1982 which implies a condition that the builder will provide his services to a reasonable standard and within a reasonable time if no time is specified in the contract.

1.2.6. The buyer should consider whether the contract should provide for the builder to remove all builder's rubbish from the site before completion, to leave the property in a clean and tidy condition, for the erection of boundary fences, and if appropriate for the landscaping of the gardens and surrounding areas.

1.2.7. New restrictive covenants will frequently be imposed on the buyer by the contract. From the seller's point of view, the imposition of the covenants will be done to allow the seller to maximise his ability to sell the remainder of the houses in the development. From the buyer's point of view, the imposition of such covenants provides the buyer with the certainty that the estate will be developed and will remain in a saleable condition without having to worry about unsightly or undesirable alterations carried out by neighbours to their properties. The wording of the covenants should be checked to ensure that they do not impose an unnecessary or burdensome restriction on the buyer's use and enjoyment of the property and their significance explained to the buyer.[4]

1.2.8. The plan attached to the purchase deed should be signed by the seller and by or on behalf of the buyer.

1.2.9. Where there is to be a long delay between exchange of contracts and completion, the buyer's contract should be protected by registration.[5]

1. The terms of the contract may be subject to Unfair Terms in Consumer Contracts Regulations 1995 S.I. 1994/3159, see para. B.11.11. above.
2. See below, Sales of part, para. J.01. and Plans, para. B.21. above.
3. The building works will be 'complete' on the issue of a certificate of practical completion or on certification by the seller's architect. Habitation certificates are not generally now issued on completion of a building.
4. See above, The purchase deed, para. E.01.
5. See above, After exchange, para. C.05.

1.3. Planning permission

1.3.1. The erection of a new building will normally require both express planning permission and building regulation consent. Copies of the relevant documents should be supplied to the buyer's solicitor prior to exchange of contracts and should be checked by the client or his surveyor to ensure (as far as possible) that the erection of the building complies with the permissions and with any restrictions or conditions attached to them. If on the face of the planning permission there are reserved matters requiring the further consent of the planning authority, compliance with such matters should be checked by the buyer's solicitor. Where there is a short-term condition attached to the permission which affects the right to occupy the property (e.g. the property shall not be occupied until all estate roads have been completed) the contract must be checked to ensure that the completion date specified in the contract can, if necessary, be adjusted to take account of this restriction on occupation. The contract may contain a warranty given by the seller to the effect that he has complied with all restrictions and conditions attached to the planning permission.

1.3.2. In relation to work completed after 1 June 1992 it may be possible to obtain a certificate of completion of the building works from the local authority. The buyer should enquire whether such a certificate is available.

1.4. Roads and drains

1.4.1. Roads

The buyer's solicitor will need to check whether the roads and street lighting adjoining the property are publicly maintained or are intended to be so. Where the property forms part of a new building estate the seller (or developer) will frequently have entered into an agreement with the local highway authority under Highways Act 1980, s.38 whereby the highway authority will, after a certain period of time, adopt the highway and thereafter maintain it at public expense. Such an agreement should be supported by a bond which will guarantee sufficient money to allow the making up of the road to the proper standards required by the highway authority in case of default by the developer. Where appropriate a copy of the section 38 agreement and bond should be supplied to the buyer's solicitor with the draft contract and the buyer's solicitor should ask his client whether he wants his surveyor to check the bond to ensure that the amount guaranteed by it is adequate to cover the cost of the outstanding roadworks. In practice it is difficult to estimate the cost of the outstanding works and the buyer's solicitor may have to accept the bond which is offered without further investigation. The contract should contain provisions allowing the buyer and his employees, and others authorised by him, a right of access over the road pending its adoption. If no agreement and bond has been entered into, the road will remain in private ownership, maintainable at the expense of the owner. In such a case the buyer's solicitor must ensure that his client is given adequate rights of way to provide access to the property, and should ascertain that proper provisions are being made for the maintenance of the road and the likely cost of maintenance. The buyer and his lender must be advised accordingly. Where the property forms part of a small new estate it is common for the roads to remain in the ownership of the seller (or developer). From the buyer's point of view, the contract should then contain a covenant for maintenance by the road owner (at the shared cost of the buyer and owners of other houses on the estate), with provision for the house owners to carry out the work and recover any charges from other liable contributors in the event of default by the road owner. Such a provision may be dealt with by the imposition of an estate rentcharge under Rentcharges Act 1977.[1] In appropriate cases the client should be advised of any potential liability to road charges arising out of section 219 of Highways Act 1980 (where advance payments procedure has not been correctly followed by builder and local authority) or arising from the situation where (as is not uncommon) the local authority has released the builder from his bond in relation to part of the development but without formally adopting the roads in the part released.

1.4.2. Drains

Except where the property is being built in a rural area, the seller will normally have entered into an agreement and bond with the water authority under Water Industry Act 1991, s.104 for the ownership and maintenance of the drains to be transferred to the water authority within a certain time after completion of the building works. Similar considerations apply here as in relation to the maintenance of highways (see above, para. 1.4.1.). If the drainage system is to remain in private ownership a drainage survey may be desirable to ensure that the system under construction will be adequate to service the property.

1. See below, para. K.15.

1.5.   Insurance against structural defects

1.5.1.   Most new residential properties will be offered with the benefit of the NHBC 'Buildmark' or similar scheme which provides the buyer and his successors in title with insurance against structural defects in the property for the first 10 years (NHBC) after completion of the building. The contract will normally provide for such cover to be obtained by the seller without cost to the buyer and the appropriate insurance policy and other documentation should be supplied to the buyer on or before completion. Municipal Mutual Insurance Co. Ltd. (MMI), underwriters to the Foundation 15 scheme, ceased to write new business under that scheme on 1 October 1992 but existing initial or final certificates issued before that date continue in force and are accepted by lenders. The Newbuild scheme from Zurich Municipal offers an initial 10-year cover period which may be extended by a further five years. This scheme is accepted by most lenders. A summary of the scheme appears in Appendix X.4.

1.5.2.   The absence of such insurance cover may present the buyer with problems since it will frequently be a condition of the mortgage offer that cover is obtained. Even where the present buyer is not financing his purchase with the assistance of a mortgage, a subsequent buyer who buys the property within the first 10 years after its construction will expect to take the benefit of the policy, and thus the absence of such cover will restrict the potential both to mortgage and to resell the property.

1.5.3.   The NHBC scheme and Newbuild apply to newly constructed dwellings and to conversions, but the terms of the policy and its limitations should be examined in each case and their effect explained to the client. The explanatory note furnished with the scheme documentation should be handed to the client.

1.5.4.   NHBC 'Buildmark' scheme

A builder who is registered with NHBC will receive from NHBC a sealed 'Buildmark' pack which should be handed to the builder's solicitor for onwards transmission to the buyer's solicitor on exchange of contracts. The tear-off outer cover of the pack constitutes the Buildmark offer form. This should be completed by the buyer's solicitor and returned to NHBC on exchange of contracts. The remaining sealed envelope containing the policy and copy offer should be passed to the buyer. The 10-year notice will be sent to the buyer by NHBC after completion. NHBC documents should be kept safely by the buyer and not lodged with the title deeds. The buyer's lender will require only the duplicate of the 10-year notice as proof of cover under the scheme. The buyer should be told to keep the NHBC documents safely as he is under a duty to hand them to a subsequent buyer on a further sale of the property. Cover commences in respect of the builder's warranty and for loss caused by the builder's insolvency before completion as soon as the offer form is received by NHBC. It is therefore important that this matter be dealt with by the buyer's solicitor immediately after exchange has taken place.

1.5.5.   The extent of the cover provided by the scheme is summarised in Appendix X.2. It should be noted that subsidence is not generally covered by the scheme and so must be covered by the buyer's buildings insurance policy. The builder's liability under the scheme is limited to the first two years after completion. After that time, the policy only covers structural defects. A structural survey of the property may be desirable at the end of the two-year period.

1.5.6. Special provisions relate to retirement schemes under the NHBC Sheltered Housing Code. In such a case the buyer's solicitor will also receive from the seller's solicitors a copy of the management agreement and the residents' information pack.

1.5.7. Where a property is to be covered by NHBC or a similar scheme a full survey may not be necessary, particularly if the property is still in the course of construction so that there is very little for the surveyor actually to survey. In some cases a surveyor may be asked to look at the plans for the prospective building to ensure that as far as can be ascertained the building is to be erected in accordance with the client's wishes and expectations.

1.5.8. *Assignment of policy*

The benefit of the policy can be assigned to a subsequent buyer of the property. NHBC will honour the policy in favour of a subsequent buyer irrespective of whether a formal assignment has taken place between the original and subsequent buyers. A formal assignment of the benefit of the policy may be desirable in other cases.

1.5.9. Where the property is being constructed under the supervision of an architect (e.g. under a JCT contract), a lender may accept an architect's certificate of completion of the building in place of an NHBC or similar policy, although in such a case it may be desirable from the buyer's point of view for the contract to contain warranties given by the seller as to the proper design and construction of the building. The insurance cover carried by architects will only provide indemnity if the architect has a valid current policy at the time when liability is notified to the insurers. If therefore the architect has died or ceased to practise since completion of the building and before liability is discovered there may be no insurance policy in force to meet the claim and the architect's own assets or estate may be insufficient to cover the liability.

1.5.10. Defective Premises Act 1972 implies a term into a contract to purchase a building in the course of construction that the building when built will be habitable. Buildings constructed under the NHBC scheme are not exempted from Defective Premises Act.

1.6. **Payment of purchase price**

1.6.1. The contract should state clearly whether the buyer is required to pay an additional price for extras (e.g. a coloured bathroom suite) and, if so, how much.

1.6.2. Some builders require the purchase price to be paid in stages as the building works progress. In such a case the buyer's lender must be informed of this fact and his agreement sought to release the mortgage advance in accordance with the builder's requirements. For the buyer's protection, he may seek an equitable charge over the property to the extent of the instalments paid by him. Such a charge must be registered and the contract to purchase should also be protected by registration as an estate contract since completion is unlikely to follow quickly after exchange of contracts in this situation. The lender's consent should be obtained to the form of the contract prior to exchange.

1.6.3. Any retention made by the buyer's mortgagee, e.g. in respect of outstanding roadworks must be discussed with the buyer and arrangements made to cover the resulting shortfall in time for completion.

1.6.4. Where the new property is a single building, i.e. not part of an estate development, it may be advantageous for the buyer initially to enter a contract to buy the site alone, and then to have a second contract for the builder to build the house or other building. In such a case the builder would expect to take a charge over the site to secure payment for the building works. There are possible stamp duty savings for the buyer if the two stages of the development are separated in this way.[1]

1. See below, Inland Revenue Practice Statement, App. X.1.

1.7.   **Building estates**

1.7.1. This paragraph does not deal in detail with site acquisition and development for which the reader should refer to a specialist work on the subject.[1]

1.7.2. *Checklist for seller's solicitor*

(a) Has the site been inspected to ascertain the boundaries of each plot and the extent of easements and reservations?

(b) Has planning permission been obtained?

(c) Has a section 38 agreement and bond been obtained in respect of the roads?

(d) Has a section 104 agreement and bond been obtained in respect of sewers?

(e) Who is responsible for building regulation control and who will issue the certificate of completion of the building?

(f) Is the seller to make (and regularly update) pre-contract searches or will this be each buyer's responsibility?

(g) In residential cases will the Protocol be used; if so what variations to it are necessary to meet the present transactions? Remember to notify the buyer's solicitor of such variations.

(h) Will the property be covered by NHBC or similar scheme? Has the builder registered and handed to his solicitor the appropriate documentation? (See above, para. 1.5.4.). Ensure that an unqualified (i.e. unconditional) certificate will be issued.

(i) Has a site plan been prepared and approved by HM Land Registry?

(j) Has the form of transfer been approved by HM Land Registry? This is not essential but may save time and requisitions from the Land Registry at a later stage.

(k) Has all the necessary pre-contract documentation been prepared and duplicated for each plot? (See below, para. 1.7.3.)

(l) Have arrangements been made with the seller's lender to release the plots from the charge?

(m) Has the builder complied with Construction (Design and Management) Regulations 1994, S.I. 1994/3140 (e.g. the appointment of a planning supervisor)?

1.7.3. Documents to be prepared and sent to the prospective buyer's solicitor for each plot on receipt of instructions:

(a) Pre-contract enquiries with answers.

(b) Pre-contract searches with replies (where the seller is to undertake this task).

(c) Draft contract in duplicate (with buyer's name left blank).

(d) Draft transfer in duplicate with plan attached (annexed to contract, buyer's name left blank).

(e) Evidence of title.

(f) Requisitions on title with answers.

(g) Copies of relevant planning permissions and building regulation approval.

(h) Copies of relevant section 104 and section 38 agreements and bonds.

(i) NHBC or equivalent documentation where appropriate.

(j) A copy of the plan of the property properly marked and coloured in accordance with HM Land Registry requirements, with a spare copy for search purposes.

(k) If desired, a general information sheet for the buyer containing *inter alia* address of local authorities and other bodies with whom searches may need to be conducted, explanation of the contract terms (including arrangements for deposit and completion), notification of whether the Protocol will be used (residential transactions) and of any variations to it.

(l) Covering letter.

FURTHER REFERENCE

Housing Development Conveyancing, P.J. Palmer, F.T. Law & Tax.

I.02. Defects in new commercial buildings

2.1.   Introduction

2.1.1.   The owner or tenant of a new commercial building,[1] not being the party for whom the building was constructed or refurbished, will only be in a position to recover the cost of remedying defects to the building from the contractor or professional team (architect, engineer, etc.) if he has a contractual relationship with them.[2] He would, however, be able to sue the contractor or other professional in negligence for damages arising out of personal injury or damage to other property. To enable the subsequent owner to be able to sue the contractor or other professional for the cost of remedial works to the building, he needs to establish an enforceable contractual relationship with the contractor or professional who is to be sued.[3] This can be achieved either by creating new contracts between the subsequent owner/tenant and the contractor/professionals (these are usually called 'collateral warranties') or, where practical, by taking an assignment from the original owner of the building of his original contract(s) with the contractor/ professionals. The subsequent owner/tenant might additionally seek a warranty from the original owner as to the condition of the building even in the current market, which may be difficult to obtain; sellers and landlords of new buildings understandably prefer the liability for defects to rest with the contractor/ professionals.

2.1.2.   *Collateral warranties*

A buyer or tenant of a new commercial building should, as a term of the contract, require the seller or landlord to procure that on completion collateral warranties in favour of the buyer/tenant are provided by the contractor and all professionals in the form approved by the buyer/tenant. In these the contractor/professionals warrant that they have to date exercised reasonable skill and care and (where work is unfinished at the time of the contract) agree to continue to do so. Other terms are generally included dealing with professional indemnity insurance, the limitation period, assignment and limitations on the warrantor's liability, for example where the defect was partly his fault and partly the fault of other parties.[4]

2.1.3. Assignment of original contracts

Where the whole development is being sold or let the buyer/tenant should consider requiring an assignment of the original contracts with the contractor/professionals with a view to putting the buyer/tenant in a position to recover under these contracts for any breaches by the contractor/professionals.

2.1.4. In the following paragraphs references to 'A' are to the contractor, architect or other professional, 'B' is the original owner of the building who entered the construction (or as the case may be) contract with A (the 'A−B' contract), and C is the subsequent owner of the building who, having purchased from B, seeks to enforce a term of the A−B contract.

1. i.e. not covered by NHBC or similar structural insurance policy.
2. *Murphy* v. *Brentwood District Council* [1991] 1 A.C. 398; *Department of the Environment* v. *Thomas Bates & Son Ltd.* [1991] 1 A.C. 499.
3. *Murphy* v. *Brentwood District Council* [1991] 1 A.C. 398; *Department of the Environment* v. *Thomas Bates & Son Ltd.* [1991] 1 A.C. 499.
4. See, e.g. the precedents produced by the British Property Federation.

2.2. Method of assignment

2.2.1. The object of the assignment is a chose in action which, by section 136(1) of Law of Property Act 1925 must be in writing (between B and C) and notice of the assignment must be given to A. Notice of the assignment could be given by either B or C, but it is clearly in C's interests to ensure that it is done. A should be asked to sign and return one copy of the notice of assignment served on him in duplicate by C so that tangible evidence exists of the fact that notice was correctly given.

2.3. Types of assignment

2.3.1. The object of the exercise is to enable the benefit of the contract between A and B to be transferred to and enforced by C against A.

2.3.2. Novation

Where it is intended that obligations under the A−B contract should be assigned, a novation must take place. The assignment of one party's burdens or obligations can only be done with the consent of the other original contracting party. Therefore, for this to occur, a new contract, made between A, B, and C, will have to be entered into.

2.3.3. Sub-contract

A might enter a sub-contract with D (the sub-contractor) under which D agreed with A to perform some or all of A's obligations to B under the A−B contract. This is effectively an assignment of A's obligations without B's consent, but in this situation A always remains liable to B since the original contract between A and B has been neither novated nor discharged. Any defect in D's performance can therefore be remedied by an action by B against A. The main issue in this situation is whether B is bound to accept D's performance of the contract in A's place. Where the obligations to be performed by A are construed as 'personal services', B cannot be forced to accept performance from anyone other than the original contracting party, i.e. he is entitled to reject D's performance and treat A as being in breach of contract. An obligation to carry out building works has been held to be within the concept of personal services.[1]

2.3.4. *Assignment of benefits or rights*

Where there is a prohibition against the assignment of the benefit of the contract, that prohibition is effective to prevent the assignment unless the party with the burden of performance consents to it. Thus an assignment by A to C of the benefit of the A−B contract would require B's consent. This applies irrespective of whether the assignment is of accrued rights (e.g. existing breaches committed by B) or of future rights (e.g. the right to sue for breaches as and when they occur in the future).[2]

2.3.5. If assignment is not possible (because B will not consent) C's remedy lies in persuading A to take direct action against B. The contract between A and C should contain warranties to this effect given by A. The damages recoverable by A on C's behalf are not restricted to A's losses (which may be nominal since he will no longer have an interest in the property) but can include reimbursement of losses suffered by C.[3] The contract between A and C should also contain a warranty given by A to hold any damages recovered on behalf of C.

1. See *Southway Group Ltd.* v. *Wolff* [1991] E.G.C.S. 82 (C.A.).
2. *Linden Gardens Trust Ltd.* v. *Lenesta Sludge Disposals Ltd.; St Martins Property Corporation Ltd.* v. *Sir Robert McAlpine Ltd.* [1993] 3 W.L.R. 408. See also *Darlington Borough Council* v. *Wiltshier Northern Ltd.*, *The Times*, 4 July 1994 (C.A.).
3. *Ibid.*

2.4. **Protection of subsequent owners**

2.4.1. In view of the uncertainty demonstrated by the general law a subsequent owner of a building needs to ensure that he will have the right to recover his losses in the event of a later defect being discovered.

2.4.2. In residential property transactions, the property will normally be covered by NHBC or a similar insurance policy which should provide adequate protection for the buyer.

2.4.3. In commercial situations a buyer from the original owner should ensure that his contract to purchase contains warranties given by the original owner, and that a valid novation or assignment with the contractor's consent takes place. Protection of the subsequent owner is a matter to which attention should be paid when the original owner is entering the original A−B contracts. If at that stage he can ensure that there is no prohibition against assignment in the A−B contract, the benefit of the A−B contract may more easily be assigned to C at a later stage.

2.4.4.   The distinction between the assignment of obligations and fruits of performance should not, however, be overlooked since the court seems to apply different rules to these two types of benefit.

J. SALES OF PART
J.01. Sales of part

See also: Plans, para. B.21.
The purchase deed, para. E.01.

1.1. Introduction

1.1.1.   A sale of part is a more complex transaction than the sale of the whole of the seller's interest in a particular piece of land, and some matters additional to those relevant to a sale of whole must be considered. The following paragraphs only deal with those matters which are exclusive to sales of part.

1.2. Description of the land

1.2.1.   The description of the land in the seller's existing land or charge certificate (or title deeds) will not suffice to describe the land being sold and a new, accurate description of the property must be devised to describe the land in the particulars of sale of the contract. It will be necessary to describe the land by reference to a plan and, if that plan is not drawn to scale, to include the measurements of the land within the verbal description.[1] There may be circumstances in which it is useful for the seller's solicitor to inspect the property prior to drafting the contract.

1.2.2. *Retained land*

Reference will usually have to be made to the land which is to remain in the ownership of the seller after the sale off, e.g. in relation to easements and reservations; such land must therefore also be defined verbally in the contract and marked clearly on the plan attached to the contract.

1.2.3.   Where the sale is of part of a registered title and comprises a plot on a building estate, the seller will frequently have deposited a site plan at HM Land Registry and the office copies which are issued will give a certificate in Form 102 in lieu of a filed plan. Where the estate plan procedure is used it is important that it is strictly adhered to in order to avoid difficulties. In addition the solicitor should emphasise to his builder client that if revisions are made on the ground to the layout shown on the approved estate plan, the builder should notify the solicitor immediately so that the solicitor can inform the Registry and submit a revised estate plan.

1. See above, Plans, para. B.21.

1.3.   Grants and reservations

1.3.1. On a sale of part of land Law of Property Act 1925, s.62 and the rule in *Wheeldon* v. *Burrows*[1] may give the buyer as easements certain rights over the land which are continuous and apparent, are necessary for the reasonable enjoyment of the land sold, and which had been and are at the time of the sale used by the seller for the benefit of the part sold. Although Law of Property Act 1925, s.62 and the rule in *Wheeldon* v. *Burrows*[2] will give the buyer such easements and quasi-easements as were previously enjoyed by the land before its division, the existence and extent of these implied rights may not be entirely clear and, for certainty, such matters should be dealt with expressly in the contract. Easements which pass by the operation of these provisions cannot give the buyer any right which the seller had no power to grant, and do not create any better title to any right than the seller is able to transfer. It will therefore usually be necessary to grant new express easements to the buyer, e.g. for a right of way or drainage. Express easements which are to arise in the future must comply with the perpetuity rule.

1.3.2. Section 62 of Law of Property Act 1925 and the rule in *Wheeldon* v. *Burrows*[3] only operate in the buyer's favour. There is no reciprocal section or case which entitles the seller to easements over the land being sold off (other than easements of necessity). For this reason it is important to consider what rights the seller will need to exercise over the land being sold, e.g. passage of cables, drainage, etc., and to reserve these expressly in the contract.

1.3.3. Rights of light and air may pass to the buyer under either Law of Property Act 1925, s.62 or the rule in *Wheeldon* v. *Burrows*.[4] The acquisition of such rights by the buyer may have adverse consequences for the seller since the buyer might be able by exercising such rights to prevent the seller from building on his retained land. It it therefore usually considered necessary to exclude the buyer's right to easements of light and air by an express condition in the contract which provides for the insertion of a provision to this effect in the purchase deed.[5] Standard Condition 3.3.2 contains a provision to this effect.

1.3.4. Standard Condition 3.3.2 provides for the mutual grant of easements and reservations on a sale of part, but the rights given by this condition are limited and will in most cases be inadequate to deal effectively with the parties' requirements on a sale of part of land.

1. (1879) 12 Ch. 31.
2. *Ibid.*
3. *Ibid.*
4. *Ibid.*
5. See *Emmet on Title*, Chap. 15.

1.4. Imposition of new covenants[1]

1.4.1. In many cases the seller will wish to impose new covenants on the buyer, e.g. restricting the future use of the land. Provision for the imposition of new restrictions must be made expressly in the contract.

1.4.2. Covenants which are imposed on the sale of a new house on a building estate will usually comply with the terms of a building scheme.[2] In other cases, the enforceability of such restrictions against a subsequent purchaser of the land depends on their being negative in substance, expressly taken for the benefit of the seller's retained land, and registered on the charges register of the title (or as class D(ii) land charges in unregistered land).[3] Positive covenants may be indirectly enforced through a chain of indemnity covenants but their burden does not run with the land.

1. See above, The purchase deed, para. E.01.
2. See *Re Dolphin's Conveyance* [1970] 1 Ch. 654.
3. *Tulk* v. *Moxhay* (1848) 2 Ph. 774.

1.5. Consent of seller's lender

1.5.1. Where the land to be sold comprises part of the land which is mortgaged to the seller's lender, the seller must, at the earliest possible opportunity, obtain his lender's consent to the transaction. It should be ascertained from the lender whether the lender requires repayment of the whole or any part of the principal sums owing out of the proceeds of the sale of part and, if part, how much. Arrangements must be made for the lender to discharge the land being sold from the mortgage. In registered land this will be effected by a Form 53 (accompanied by a plan to show the extent of the land being released). In unregistered land the lender may either give a deed of release, or he may prefer to be joined as a party to the conveyance in order both to release the land being sold and to give a receipt for the money being paid to him. If the lender has taken a mortgage by way of deposit of the title deeds, he will give a consent to dealing on completion; no formal release or Form 53 is necessary in these circumstances.

1.6. The purchase deed

1.6.1. Registered land

A transfer of part will be drawn up to reflect the contract terms. The seller's title number is used at the head of the transfer form, a new title number being allocated to the land sold off on registration of the sale of part. A plan must be attached to the transfer. The transfer should be executed and the plan signed by both parties. The buyer's pre-completion search at HM Land Registry should be made on Form 94B and accompanied by a plan or should refer to a Land Registry approved plan or plot number supplied by the seller. The plan must be signed by the seller personally but a third party (e.g. solicitor) can sign a plan on behalf of the buyer.

1.6.2. *Unregistered land*

The conveyance will reflect the terms of the contract. Although a plan is not essential in unregistered land, it is highly desirable in cases where only part of the seller's estate is being sold and should be signed by both parties. Since the seller will be retaining the documents of title an acknowledgement for production and undertaking for safe custody (where appropriate) of the deeds should be included in the conveyance.[1] Where the seller is selling other than as beneficial owner, only an acknowledgement will be given. The undertaking is not given by owners who are selling in a fiduciary capacity. Where the land is subject to a mortgage the seller may be required to give a covenant that he will give the statutory undertaking for safe custody of the deeds as and when they come into his possession. Where the buyer is entering into a covenant in the deed (whether for indemnity or to observe fresh restrictive covenants) he must execute the purchase deed.

1.6.3. Commonly the draft purchase deed will be prepared by the seller and annexed to the draft contract so that the buyer in fact has no discretion over its contents.

1. See Law of Property Act 1925, s.64 and Standard Condition 4.5.4.

1.7. **Completion and post-completion**

1.7.1. Where the land is unregistered, the seller will not be handing over his title deeds to the buyer on completion; the buyer should therefore verify his abstract or epitome against the original deeds and mark his abstract or epitome as examined against the original.[1] Where the Protocol is used the seller is required to mark the abstract as examined against the original title deeds before sending it to the buyer. Even where the title to the land bought is to be registered immediately after completion this procedure is necessary so that the buyer can produce proper evidence of the title to HM Land Registry with his application for first registration. Additionally, a memorandum of the sale off should be noted on the most recent of the seller's retained title deeds to prevent a second sale of the same land by the seller.[2] A note of any restrictive covenants imposed by the conveyance to the buyer (or a copy of that conveyance) should also be retained by the seller. New restrictive covenants will automatically be entered on the register of the new title on first registration.

1.7.2. Where the seller's title is already registered it is not strictly necessary to provide for an acknowledgement for production of the deeds nor for a memorandum to be endorsed on the seller's deeds since the buyer will obtain his own title number on registration of the sale of part. An acknowledgement is needed where the sale is of part only of a lease or where the purchase deed is to be executed in duplicate. New restrictive covenants imposed or rights reserved by the transfer of part will automatically be entered on the charges register of the new title on registration. Since no entry except a caution can generally be made against the seller's title without his consent (including removing part of his land from the register) it is necessary under Land Registration Act 1925, s.64(1) for him to lodge his land certificate at HM Land Registry to await the buyer's incoming application for registration. The seller should deposit his certificate prior to completion, accompanied by Form A15 and stating the reason for the deposit. On receipt of the certificate the Land Registry will issue the seller with a deposit number which should be communicated to the buyer who will make reference to this number on his application for registration. Where a charge subsists over the property, the Land Registry already has the land certificate in its custody (a charge certificate being issued to the lender) and it is technically not necessary for the charge certificate to be deposited to meet the buyer's application for registration, but will be needed if the land sold is to be discharged from the seller's existing mortgage.

1.7.3.   A lender who has custody of the title deeds will give an acknowledgement for their production. Such an acknowledgement may be contained in the deed of release supplied by the lender but is not necessary when dealing with registered land.

1.7.4.   In some cases where new covenants are being imposed the contract will require the buyer to prepare the purchase deed in duplicate, the duplicate copy to be stamped and denoted at the buyer's expense and then handed to the seller as a record of the transaction. An acknowledgement for production is required in this situation.[3]

1. See Completion, section F.
2. See Law of Property Act 1925, s.200.
3. See Standard Condition 4.5.3(b).

1.8.   Checklist of matters to be considered on sale of part

1.8.1.   Easements in the buyer's favour

    (a) To what extent will Law of Property Act 1925, s.62 and/or the rule in *Wheeldon* v. *Burrows* imply easements in the buyer's favour?[1]

    (b) Is it necessary to extend the implied easements by granting express rights to the buyer?[2]

    (c) What does the buyer need, for example:

        (i)   rights of way;

        (ii)   right to lay new cables/pipelines/drains;

        (iii) right to use/maintain existing or new pipelines/cables/drains?

1.8.2.   Rights of way

    (a) Will the right be to pass over the land in both directions or should it be restricted to one way only?

    (b) Should the right be restricted, e.g. to a particular class of user, e.g. pedestrian only?

(c) Is the exercise of the right to be restricted, e.g. use only for a particular purpose or only at a specified time of day?

1.8.3. All easements

(a) Is the route of the right of way/drain, etc., specified on the plan?

(b) Who is liable for maintenance/repairs?

(c) Will it be necessary for the buyer to enter the seller's land to inspect the state of repair and/or to maintain?

(d) Should the buyer's access to inspect be restricted, e.g. a right to inspect on 24 hours' notice except in case of emergency?

(e) Should the buyer be under an obligation to cause no unnecessary damage and to make good any damage done while inspecting/maintaining?

(f) Where the buyer is to construct a new pipeline/cable, etc., should he be required to finish the construction works within a specified period after completion?

1.8.4. Reservations

(a) Remember the seller generally gets nothing under the implied grant rules.

(b) After completion will the seller need to continue to use a right of way/drain/pipeline/cable passing through the land being sold?

(c) If so, express reservations must be included in the contract by way of special condition. The same considerations in drafting apply as in paras. 1.8.2. and 1.8.3. above.

(d) Additionally, to protect the seller, it may be considered necessary to include a general reservations clause in his favour dealing with all easements, quasi-easements, etc., presently enjoyed by the land as a whole.

(e) Should rights of light and air be expressly reserved in order to preserve the seller's freedom to use the retained land in the future?[3]

1.8.5. Existing covenants

Is an indemnity clause required?[4]

1.8.6. New covenants[5]

(a) Should new restrictive covenants be imposed?

(b) If so, what type of restrictions will serve to protect the seller's land without imposing unnecessary constraints on the buyer?

(c) Consider:

(i) erection of new buildings on the land;

(ii) use of the land;

(iii) repair/maintenance of buildings or land;

(iv) general covenant against nuisance.[6]

(d) Will the covenants be negative in nature?

(e) Do the words used ensure that the covenants will create an enforceable obligation?

1.8.7. *Description of the property in the contract*

(a) Does the wording of the particulars accurately describe the land being sold?

(b) Has the seller's retained land been precisely defined?[7]

(c) Is there reference in the particulars to a plan?

(d) Is the plan of sufficient size and scale to be able to delineate accurately both the area of land being sold and the routes of easements, etc.?

(e) Is a scale plan needed; if so is it accurate?

(f) If the plan is not to scale, do the particulars refer to the plan as being for identification purposes only?

1.8.8. *Seller's lender*

(a) Will it be necessary to obtain the lender's consent to the sale − if so has this been obtained?

(b) How will the lender deal with the release of the land being sold from the mortgage?

1. Section 62 of Law of Property Act 1925 may operate to create easements over retained land where at the time of sale the two tenements are in separate occupation. Further, the rule in *Wheeldon* v. *Burrows* (1879) 12 Ch. 31 will impliedly grant to the buyer as easements all rights which are continuous and apparent and reasonably necessary to the reasonable enjoyment of the property sold. These provisions will normally have the effect of giving the buyer fewer easements than he requires, but in some cases may give him more than the seller intends. It is therefore considered safer to negate the effect of these rules in the contract and to deal with easements by way of express grant.
2. Since the extent of the implied easements created by the implied grant rules is not always clear, these matters are better dealt with by way of express condition. Standard Condition 3.3.2 deals briefly with easements but does not normally give adequate rights to the buyer; hence the need for express special conditions.
3. Standard Condition 3.3.2 reserves rights of light and air to the seller.
4. Standard Condition 4.5.3 requires indemnity covenants but it is common to include an indemnity clause by way of special condition in order specifically to draw the requirement to the buyer's attention. See above, The purchase deed, para. E.01.

5. See above, The purchase deed, para. E.01.

6. Nuisance is a tort actionable at common law; therefore the imposition of such a covenant may strictly be unnecessary.

7. Inspection of the property may assist with these matters. It may also be desirable to peg out the boundaries to the property or to ask a surveyor to confirm that it is possible to plot the site.

K. LEASEHOLDS

This section deals only with those matters where the considerations applicable to leasehold property differ from the requirements outlined in other sections of this handbook relating to freehold land.

Some problem areas, e.g. licences to assign, are confined exclusively to the context of leaseholds and these are discussed within this section of the handbook.

A summary of the law relating to security of tenure is included, but the handbook does not contain a comprehensive guide to this topic.

The first group of paragraphs within this section deal with matters which are applicable to most leases, whether short or long and whether of business or residential premises. Then follow paragraphs dealing with specific types of lease or tenancy and, finally, paragraphs on specific points which affect leasehold land such as the right to buy, options, and liability on covenants. A short paragraph on rentcharges is also included in this section.

The Standard Mortgage Instructions (SMI) contain specific requirements in relation to dealing with leasehold property which must be observed. At the time of publication the SMI had not been finalised.

K.01. Acting on grant of lease

1.1. Taking instructions

1.1.1. There are a number of key issues upon which thought, advice and instructions will be needed when acting on the grant or acceptance of a lease. There can be no standard approach; instead the details of the property and letting in question must be carefully considered.

1.1.2. Subject to the above, much of the information required by the landlord's solicitor from his client will be similar to that required from the seller in the case of a freehold transaction.

1.1.3. When acting for a landlord or tenant, a solicitor should draw his client's attention to, and explain, lease provisions which may be of importance to the client and influence the client's decision whether or not to accept the proposed terms.

1.1.4. *Code of Practice for Commercial Leases*

In appropriate cases, the client's attention should be drawn to the Code of Practice for Commercial Leases.

1.2.   **Demised premises**

1.2.1.   The lease must clearly define the extent of the demised premises. A detached building standing in its own ground should cause no problems of description but care is needed when letting parts of a building, e.g. flats or suites of offices.

1.2.2.   As far as possible express provision should be made relating to the ownership of walls, floors, ceilings, etc. In the absence of express provision the following presumptions apply:

(a) external walls − these are included in the demise even if the landlord is responsible for their repairs;[1]

(b) internal walls − there is no presumption in respect of the internal boundary walls dividing one flat from another or the flat from common parts;

(c) floors and ceilings − the flat includes the ceiling at least to the underside of the floor joists to which the ceiling is attached;

(d) the ownership of the roof area should also be specifically dealt with since if this is not done it may be possible for the tenant of a top floor flat to claim occupation of the roof space and to carry out alterations to the roof space against the landlord's wishes.[2]

1. *Sturge* v. *Hackett* [1962] 3 All E.R. 166.
2. See *Davies* v. *Yadegar* [1990] 09 E.G. 67 and *Haines* v. *Florensa* [1990] 09 E.G. 70.

1.3.   **Easements**

1.3.1.   Consideration must then be given to whether the tenant will require easements over the landlord's adjoining property in order to use the demised premises. The tenant might, e.g. need the right to use a private road in order to gain access to the premises or to use conducting media on the landlord's adjoining land to bring services from the mains supply to the demised premises. The tenant of a flat or suite of offices will certainly need such rights over the remainder of the building.

1.4.   **Exceptions**

1.4.1.   The landlord will need to consider if he or others claiming title under him will wish to exercise rights over the demised premises because, if so, an express reservation should be included. An example would be a driveway (part of) which is included within the demised premises but which is required to be used by the landlord and his other tenants.

1.5.   **Length of the term to be granted**

1.5.1.   Apart from the parties' wishes, consideration must be given to the the stamp duty consequences of the length of the term and also to the possible effect of security of tenure legislation on the lease which may affect the seller's ability to recover possession at the end of the term.[1] Where a short lease of a dwelling is to be granted the effect of the landlord's implied repairing obligations under Landlord and Tenant Act 1985, ss.11–14 must also be borne in mind (para. 1.7.2. below). The term created must be of certain duration but, subject to security of tenure legislation, it may be made determinable on a certain event.[2]

1.5.2.   Where a premium is paid on the grant of a lease not exceeding 50 years the landlord is treated as receiving rent calculated by reference to a formula involving a multiplication of the premium and the length of the term.[3]

1. See paras. K.05., K.07. and K.08.
2. *Prudential Assurance Co. Ltd.* v. *London Residuary Body* [1992] 3 All E.R. 504.
3. Income and Corporation Taxes Act 1988, s.34; and see *Hurlingham Estates Ltd* v. *Wilde, The Times,* 3 January 1997.

1.6.   Amount of rent and frequency of reviews

1.6.1.   Some statutory limitations on the amount of rent recoverable may be applicable where the lease is an assured shorthold tenancy or a protected or statutory tenancy (see below, para. K.05.).

1.6.2.   Rent review provisions should be carefully checked by both landlord and tenant. In commercial leases reviews every three to five years are common. In long residential leases fixed increment reviews every 25–30 years are more usual. Without an enforceable rent review provision the landlord will not be able to increase the rent during the term of the lease. Rent review provisions are complex, but they must specify the period at which each review is to take place, and a formula for determining the amount of rent to be paid after each review date with a fall-back procedure (e.g. arbitration with a named office holder as the arbitrator) in case of dispute. A landlord prefers a clause which provides for 'upwards review' only so that the rent payable after the review date can never be less than that which was payable before the review date. It is also common to provide that the new rent, whenever determined, shall be payable from the review date in question so that where a rent review goes to arbitration and the new rent is not determined until some time after the actual review date, the tenant should be advised to place some money in a deposit account on each rent day so that he will be able to meet the cost of the reviewed rent when it is finally determined. Some leases will have break clauses which are operative in the tenant's favour at review dates, thus enabling the tenant to bring the lease to an end before the contractual term date if the rent payable after the review is more than he can afford to pay.

1.7.   Common express covenants

1.7.1.   *To pay rent*

The covenant should be clear as to the amount of rent, the intervals of payment, whether payable in advance or in arrear, whether the rent includes outgoings on the property, provisions for increase of the rent and payment of VAT.[1]

1.7.2. *To repair*

In certain cases the landlord will be obliged by statute to keep the structure and exterior of the premises in repair.[2] An express covenant to repair should precisely identify the obligations required of the party responsible for undertaking the repairs including, in the case of redecoration obligations, the intervals at which the work is to be undertaken. Where the demised premises form part of a larger building the landlord (or in the case of a flat perhaps a management company) will usually covenant to keep the structure and common parts of the building in repair. See the Law Society Standard Business Leases, of whole clause 5, of part clause 6.

1.7.2.1. Gas Safety (Installation and Use) Regulations 1994 (as amended by Gas Safety (Installation and Use) (Amendment) Regulations 1996) require gas appliances to be installed and maintained by competent personnel and regularly inspected. Landlords of residential premises only are under an obligation to carry out an annual inspection of such appliances (even where the lease places full repairing obligations on the tenant). Where an existing lease does not deal specifically with the responsibillity for maintenance of such appliances, the landlord should ask the tenant to confirm in writing that the tenant will be responsible for ensuring that the installations are inspected each year. Where a new lease is being drafted, it should include a specific provision in the lease dealing with this responsibility. A full tenant's repairing covenant in the lease will not implicitly remove this obligation from the landlord. These provisions apply to leases for a term of less than seven years (including periodic tenancies). A lease which contains a landlord's break clause, exercisable within the first seven years of the term, falls within these provisions but a lease which contains a tenant's option to renew which, if exercised, would extend the term beyond seven years does not.

1.7.3. The extent of the repairing obligations imposed by the lease will vary from lease to lease but the following general principles are relevant:

(a) the wording of the clause must cover every part of the building and of the estate which it is intended to be covered. Usually this will mean that the clause(s) must cover five main areas (which may overlap): the demised premises, the structure (including roof, main walls and foundations), the common parts, the common conduits, and the exterior;

(b) the operative words of the clause(s) must be sufficient to cover all foreseeable repair activities. In this respect the wording of the clause should provide for the main areas of maintenance: repairing, cleaning, and decorating. Improvements to the property or major rebuilding effected by the landlord will not necessarily be covered by the wording of a covenant 'to repair' and thus, unless expressly included in the wording of the covenant, a landlord may be unable to recover their cost from the tenants;[3]

(c) the wording of the covenant(s) must leave no grey areas where liability for repair is uncertain, and should not have areas of overlap. Care should be taken with the liability for repair, etc., of walls, ceilings, floors and joists. Clarity in these areas is largely dependent on the clarity of the definition of the ownership of the various parts of the walls, floors, ceilings, etc., in the description of the property demised. The obligation to repair can then be defined in relation to ownership of the various parts. The lease should make it expressly clear whether the windows are part of the structure or of the demise;[4]

(d) the wording of the clause must clearly specify the apportionment of liability for repairs, etc., between landlord and tenant.

1.7.4. Not to make improvements or alterations

Such a covenant is commonly included in short leases of residential premises and leases of business premises in order to allow the landlord to retain control over his property and to ensure that no alterations are effected in breach of restrictive covenants on the landlord's title, or in breach of planning law or building regulation consent. Some improvements made by a tenant of business premises or agricultural land may commit the landlord to the payment of compensation when the tenant leaves the premises. The covenant may be absolute, in which case the tenant is totally prohibited from making improvements or alterations unless the landlord grants a deed of variation of the lease. A qualified covenant means that the tenant must seek the landlord's prior consent to the alterations or improvements, such consent, in the case of improvements, not being unreasonably withheld by the landlord.[5] The landlord must not unreasonably withold his consent where alterations to the premises are required by the tenant to adapt the premises for the needs of a disabled person.[6] Even in the case of an absolute covenant a tenant may seek the court's consent to the proposed improvements or alterations; in this respect the court's discretion will override an absolute covenant. An absolute covenant is usually considered inappropriate in the context of the grant of a long lease (i.e. exceeding 21 years) of a house. See the Law Society Standard Business Leases, of whole clause 5, of part clause 6.

1.7.5. Covenant restricting user

Some restriction on the tenant's user of the premises is usually considered desirable for the same reasons as are cited in para. 1.7.4. above. The covenant may be absolute, in which case the tenant is totally prohibited from changing the use of the property unless the landlord grants a deed of variation of the lease. A qualified covenant means that the tenant must seek the landlord's prior consent to change of use, no premium being payable for giving consent.[7] There is no implied statutory proviso that the landlord's consent will not be unreasonably withheld. In the context of the lease of a dwelling house it may be appropriate to include an absolute covenant against any use except that as a private residence. In the case of business premises a very restrictive user clause (e.g. a clause which permits one specific type of business only) may have an adverse effect on the saleability of the premises and the amount of rent chargeable for them.

1.7.6. *Covenant against alienation*

A covenant restricting the tenant's right to dispose of the property must be carefully drafted since such covenants are construed narrowly by the courts, e.g. a covenant preventing assignment alone will not prevent the tenant from granting a sub-lease of the property. The covenant may be absolute in form, in which case no alienation of the property will be possible unless the landlord specifically grants consent or grants a deed of variation of the lease. A qualified covenant is subject to the statutory restrictions and modifications which are explained in para. K.11. below.[8] Except where the lease provides for payment of a premium as a condition of the granting of consent, no premium is payable for such consent.[9] In the context of the long lease of a dwelling house it is unusual to include a general restriction against alienation except during the last few years of the term. In other cases such a restriction is common and desirable to ensure that the landlord retains some control over the occupiers of his property. See the Law Society Standard Business Leases, of whole clause 6, of part clause 7.

1.7.7. *Covenant to give notice of dealings to landlord*

Such a covenant is normally included in order to give the landlord notice of all dealings by the tenant with the property. The obligation for the tenant to give notice of dealings should specify the occasions on which the covenant is to operate, e.g. notice of assignment, sub-lettings, mortgage, change of ownership on death or bankruptcy of the tenant. The tenant is usually required to pay a small registration fee to the landlord with each notice served. See the Law Society Standard Business Leases, of whole clause 6, of part clause 7.

1.7.8. *Landlord's covenant for quiet enjoyment*

Such a covenant will be implied into the lease by the common law, but it is usual to find an express covenant to this effect. See the Law Society Standard Business Leases, of whole clause 10, of part clause 11. Damages for mental distress are not recoverable for breach of this covenant.[10]

1. See para. A.16.7. above.
2. See Landlord and Tenant Act 1985, ss.11−14. Exceptionally a landlord may be under a common law implied duty to repair: see *Liverpool City Council* v. *Irwin* [1977] A.C. 239; *King* v. *South Northamptonshire District Council* [1992] 1 E.G.L.R. 53, C.A.
3. See *Mullaney* v. *Maybourne Grange (Croydon) Management Ltd.* [1986] 1 E.G.L.R. 70; *cf. Sutton (Hastoe) Housing Association* v. *Williams* [1988] 16 E.G. 75.
4. See *Holiday Fellowship Ltd.* v. *Hereford* [1959] 1 All E.R. 433.
5. Landlord and Tenant Act 1927, s.19(2).
6. Disability Discrimination Act 1995, s. 22
7. Landlord and Tenant Act 1927, s.19(2).
8. See Landlord and Tenant Act 1927, s.19(1), as amended by Landlord and Tenant Act 1987, and Landlord and Tenant (Covenants) Act 1995.
9. Law of Property Act 1925, s.144.
10. *Branchett* v. *Beaney* [1992] 3 All E.R. 910.

1.8. Service charge

1.8.1. Leases of flats and of commercial premises will frequently require the tenant to pay a service charge for services, e.g. heating or cleaning and repair of the building of which the demised premises form part and the decoration of the common parts, provided by either the landlord or a management company. The service charge is usually expressed to be payable as 'additional rent', thus allowing the landlord to distrain for its non-payment. This device also enables the landlord to recover the sum due without the necessity of serving a section 146 notice. The tenant should ensure that the proportion of the charge which he is required to pay is fair in relation to the amount of the building which he occupies or enjoys rights over, and should ensure that the clause specifies precisely what services are to be supplied in return for the charge. A landlord may wish to provide for an estimate of the service charge to be payable in advance for there to be a reconciliation at the end of the year. The landlord may also contemplate setting up a sinking fund to cater for major expenditure on the property. The tenant of a flat may be required to become a member of a residents' association or management company which will have responsibility for effecting the landlord's repairing covenants under the lease, but which also allows the tenants to control the expenditure to which they are committing themselves. Membership of a management company is normally restricted to the tenants of the block or estate and the covent will require the tenant on assignment of his lease to require his assignee to take a transfer of the tenant's share in the management company. The landlord should be required to assume responsibilities for the management company's responsibilities under the lease until the company is set up and shares have been allotted to all the tenants. Statutory controls over service charges on dwellings are discussed in para. K.06. See the Law Society Standard Business Lease of part clause 3.

1.8.2. Tenants are only obliged to pay for items agreed in the lease. The landlord should therefore be careful to include in the service charge provisions all the necessary expenditure which he may incur on the building. The clause must therefore encompass all the obligations which are covered by the landlord's covenants in the lease, e.g. repairs and decoration, insurance, services such as lifts, cleaning common parts, garden maintenance, etc. If the landlord may need in the future to make improvements to the property, this too should be covered by the clause. Provision for the tenants to contribute to a reserve fund or sinking fund will assist in the financing of major works and eliminate the burden of imposing a very large service charge in one particular year when major items such as a central heating system need to be renewed. The landlord's expenditure on bank interest and bank charges can only be recovered if the lease so permits.[1] Management charges need only be included where either the landlord will be carrying out his obligations himself or employing independent managing agents to so do. Professional fees are only recoverable under a service charge clause where they are properly incurred in respect of items which are chargeable under the service charge provisions.[2] It is advisable to include a sweeping-up clause to cover any omissions of specific items and to take account of any higher expectations in standards which were not anticipated at the commencement of the term.

1.8.3. In appropriate cases, the client's attention should be drawn to *The Guide to Good Practice relating to Service Charges in Commercial Properties.*

1. Frobisher (Second Investments) Ltd. v. Kiloran Trust Co. Ltd. [1980] 1 All E.R. 488.
2. Holding & Management Ltd. v. Property Holding & Investment Trust plc [1988] 2 All E.R. 702.

1.9. Proviso for forfeiture or re-entry

1.9.1. The landlord's right to forfeit the lease for the tenant's breach of covenant is a valuable remedy which must be expressly included in the lease since such a right is not implied by the common law unless, exceptionally, the lease is made conditional on the due observance of the covenants. Without such a clause the landlord will be unable to remove the tenant from the premises during the currency of the lease term. It is usual to include a clause which gives the landlord the right to forfeit the lease on non-payment of rent by the tenant after a stated period (e.g. 21 days) and for breach of any other covenant in the lease. Forfeiture for the tenant's insolvency is common in non-residential leases but should not be included in the long lease of a dwelling house since such a provision is unacceptable to most mortgagees. Forfeiture for breach of a covenant other than to pay rent must generally be preceded by service of a notice under Law of Property Act 1925, s.146 and may in certain cases be affected by Leasehold Property (Repairs) Act 1938. Repossession of an occupied dwelling house requires a court order.[1] In other cases a court order will be required if re-entry cannot be made peaceably.

1.9.2. Forfeiture may also occur (even in the absence of an express proviso) where the tenant denies the landlord's title to the property. If a tenant makes a specific allegation that the landlord does not own the property or that a third party has better rights to the property than the landlord, this may be construed as a denial of the landlord's title and result in forfeiture.[2] A general denial of the landlord's title contained in a defence to proceedings brought by the landlord will not have this effect.[3]

1.9.3. A tenant may not apply for relief against forfeiture for breach of covenant other than for non-payment of rent after a landlord has forfeited a lease by issuing and serving a writ and has entered into possession of the property pursuant to the judgment obtained in those proceedings. Where, however, entry is regained peaceably, the tenant retains his right to apply for equitable relief against forfeiture even after the landlord has taken possession of the property.[4] An equitable tenant may claim relief against forfeiture.[5]

1.9.4. If possession is resisted by the tenant when the landlord seeks to re-enter, there is a danger that a criminal offence under Criminal Law Act 1977, s.6 may be committed.

1.9.5. Where the landlord seeks to forfeit following breach of a covenant against alienation by the tenant, any section 146 notice must be served on both the assignor (tenant) of the lease and on the purported assignee (person currently in possession).[6] This rule is complied with if the lease makes provision for the notice to be served on 'the tenant at the property' where the word 'tenant' is defined to include successors in title.

1.9.6. A notice under Law of Property Act 1925, s.146 is not required before forfeiting for non-payment of rent, and no formal demand is needed if the re-entry clause states that the landlord can re-enter if rent is in arrears 'whether or not formally demanded' or similar wording. Where the tenant is in breach of a repairing covenant and the landlord (acting under a power expressly given to him by the lease) effects the repairs himself and then seeks to recover the cost of the repairs from the tenant, it is not necessary to serve a section 146 notice and Leasehold Property (Repairs) Act 1938 does not apply. The action is for recovery of a liquidated sum only.[7]

1.9.7. If the landlord forfeits by legal proceedings, he can include a claim for arrears of rent, mesne profits, and interest (see below). The county court will have jurisdiction if the amount claimed does not exceed £50,000.

1.9.8. Where the landlord is forfeiting by action (i.e. legal proceedings) in the county court, the tenant can apply to the court for relief against forfeiture under County Courts Act 1984, s.138:

    (i) automatic relief if the tenant pays all arrears and costs of the action into court not less than five clear days before the return day of the landlord's proceedings;

    (ii) if relief is not obtained as above the court makes an order for possession on a future date (minimum four weeks) unless the tenant pays into court all arrears and costs by that date;

    (iii) even if a possession order is made and the landlord re-enters, the tenant or any person with an interest under the lease derived from the tenant's interest can apply to the court for relief within six months from the landlord's recovery of possession and the court may grant relief on terms it thinks fit.

1.9.9. These rules only apply to forfeiture for non-payment of rent and the court has a wider discretion in cases of other breaches of covenant.

1. Protection from Eviction Act 1977, s.2.
2. *W.G. Clarke (Properties) Ltd.* v. *Dupre Properties Ltd.* [1992] Ch. 297.
3. *Warner* v. *Sampson* [1959] 1 Q.B. 297.
4. *Billson* v. *Residential Apartments* [1992] 1 A.C. 494, H.L.
5. *High Street Investments* v. *Bellshore* [1996] N.P.C. 20.
6. *Fuller* v. *Judy Properties* [1992] 1 E.G.L.R. 75 but see *Old Grovebury Manor Farm Ltd.* v. *Seymour Plant Sales & Hire Ltd. (No. 2)* [1979] 3 All E.R. 504.
7. *Jervis* v. *Harris The Times,* 14 November 1995.

1.10. Insurance

1.10.1. If the landlord is to insure the property (as would generally be the case in a lease of commercial premises) he should ensure that he is able to recover the amount of the premiums from the tenant and the tenant should be permitted to inspect the landlord's policy and the receipt for the last premium due. If the tenant is to insure the covenant should specify the risks against which the landlord wishes the policy to be effected and should give the landlord the right to inspect the policy, to see the receipt for the last premium due, and to insure in the case of the tenant's default. Where the premises comprise part of a building, the whole of which is owned by the landlord, the landlord will normally covenant to insure the structure and common parts of the building.

1.10.2. The lease must provide for both the unit and the common parts of the building to be properly insured. The lease may make provision for each tenant to insure his individual unit and for the landlord to insure the common parts of the building, but such an arrangement is not popular with tenants since it can lead to situations where not all tenants are insured for the same amounts or against the same risks with consequent difficulties in enforcing claims where it has become necessary for one tenant to claim against another. A more modern solution is for the landlord to covenant to insure all the units and the common parts together under a block policy, with a right to recover a proportionate part of the premium from each tenant.

1.10.3. The insurance covenant in the lease should provide for an adequate level of cover and of risk to be maintained over the units and common parts, including the full costs of rebuilding or reinstatement and related professional fees, with reputable insurers. Damage caused by terrorist activities is often excluded from cover. Absolute covenants to insure are strictly construed so that, for example, where a landlord is under an absolute duty to insure against fire risks, he would have to reinstate the property even if the property burns down as a result of an excluded cause such as terrorist action.[1] The Law Society Standard Business Leases deal with this point. The tenants should have the right to a copy of the insurance policy or reasonable evidence of its existence and validity, and to inspect the original policy and the receipt (or reasonable evidence of payment) for the last premium due.

1.10.4. A tenant will wish the lease to provide for the landlord to use the proceeds of the policy to reinstate the premises in the event of their damage or destruction by an insured risk. Provision should also be made for the application of the policy money in the event of reinstatement not being possible.

1.10.5. From the tenant's point of view it is also desirable that the landlord should maintain an occupiers' liability insurance policy in a situation where the landlord retains the ownership of common parts of the building.

1.10.6. It is preferable for the landlord to obtain a policy which cannot be vitiated by act or default of the tenants.

1. See *Enlayde Ltd.* v. *Roberts* [1917] 1 Ch. 109; *Moorgate Estates Ltd.* v. *Trower* [1940] 1 All E.R. 195.

1.11.   **Certificate of value**

1.11.1. A certificate of value should be included in the lease where the premium does not exceed the current stamp duty threshold and the annual rent does not exceed £600.

1.11.2. Form of certificate of value:

> 'It is hereby certified that the transaction hereby effected does not form part of a larger transaction or of a series of transactions in respect of which the amount or value or the aggregate amount or value of the consideration other than rent exceeds [£60,000].'

1.12. Underleases

1.12.1. Most of the matters which are relevant when acting for the seller or buyer on grant of a lease will also be applicable to the grant of a sub-lease.

1.12.2. The head-tenant will be liable to his own landlord (the freeholder) on the covenants contained in his lease irrespective of whether the breach is committed by the head- or sub-tenant. To protect himself against liability for a breach committed by the sub-tenant, the head-tenant should impose on the sub-tenant obligations which are at least as onerous as those contained in the head-lease.

1.12.3. A sub-tenant will be directly liable to the freeholder in respect of breach of restrictive covenants which are contained in the head-lease since he will be deemed to know of those covenants through his entitlement to call for the head-lease as part of the evidence of title. Apart from this, the freeholder may choose as a term of the head-lease or by a condition attached to the grant of any necessary consent to the sub-lease to require the sub-tenant to enter into a direct covenant with the freeholder. This will put the freeholder in a strong position in relation to the enforcement of covenants contained in the head-lease because it has the effect of establishing the relationship of privity of contract between the freeholder and the sub-tenant, but such a requirement may be contrary to Landlord and Tenant Act 1988.

1.12.4. The existence and validity of a sub-lease is dependent on the existence and validity of the head-lease out of which it is derived. If, therefore, the head-lease is forfeited, the sub-lease is also automatically forfeited although the sub-tenant may have the right to apply directly to the freeholder for relief against forfeiture even in circumstances where the head-tenant is unable to apply for relief. A lender (of the tenant or sub-tenant) has the same right to apply for relief against forfeiture as a sub-tenant.

1.12.5. Where the head-lease requires the prior consent of the freeholder to the grant of a sub-lease, the head-tenant should seek such consent at an early stage in the transaction and should not enter a binding contract for the grant of the sub-lease until it is certain that such consent will be forthcoming. The head-tenant's lender's consent may also be required to the grant of the sub-lease and this too should be obtained at an early stage in the transaction. Obtaining a landlord's consent to a sub-lease or assignment is discussed in para. K.11.

1.12.6. Standard Condition 8.3 requires the seller to apply for and pay for any necessary licence, the buyer (sub-tenant) supplying references and other information. In certain circumstances either party may rescind the contract if the consent is not forthcoming.

1.13. **Title**

1.13.1.   Under an open contract the tenant is not entitled to call for deduction of the freehold reversionary title on the grant of a lease.[1] This rule is unsatisfactory, particularly where the lease is to be granted for a term in excess of 21 years, where a premium is to be paid for the grant of the lease or where a tenant is paying a significant rent for commercial premises. A lender who has taken a mortgage of a dwelling house will frequently not accept a lease as security for a loan unless the freehold title has been satisfactorily deduced, and the absence of the freehold title will preclude the tenant and his successors from obtaining an absolute leasehold title on the subsequent registration of the lease unless the freehold is already registered or the 'title shown' procedure has been used. The landlord should therefore be prepared to deduce his freehold title to the tenant in exactly the same way as if he were selling the freehold[2] and should include a condition in the contract to this effect. Standard Condition 8.2.4 requires the landlord to deduce such title to the tenant as would enable the tenant to obtain an absolute title at HM Land Registry where the grant in question is to be for a term which will exceed 21 years. This condition effectively means that the landlord is under an obligation in all circumstances to deduce his freehold reversionary title to the tenant.

1.13.2.   In the case of sub-letting the sub-tenant is entitled to call for the head-lease out of which his sub-lease is to be derived and all subsequent assignments under which the lease has been held for the last 15 years. In the absence of a contractual condition to the contrary he is not entitled to call for production of the freehold title.[3] The sub-tenant's inability at common law to call for the deduction of the freehold title may cause problems if, e.g. a premium is being demanded for the grant of the sub-lease, or the sub-lease is to be mortgaged or requires registration with its own title. It should be noted that the sub-lease will not contain an implied covenant that any user clause in the sub-lease is either lawful or complies with a restriction on user in a superior title.[4] A solicitor who accepts a lease or sub-lease without checking the validity of the user clause would be liable to his client in negligence if, as a result, the client suffered loss. Standard Condition 8.2.4 requires the head-tenant to deduce a title to the sub-tenant which will enable the sub-tenant to acquire registration of his sub-lease with an absolute title at HM Land Registry where the sub-lease will exceed 21 years. This condition therefore requires the head-tenant to produce the title to the freehold reversion to the sub-tenant on grant of the sub-lease. A head-tenant who did not call for deduction of the freehold title when he took his own lease may not be able to comply with this condition and will have to exclude it by special condition in the contract.

1.13.3.   If the head-lease out of which the sub-lease is to be derived is registered with a separate title the sub-tenant is entitled to call for production of the head-lease but is not entitled to inspect copies of the registered title itself since the grant of a sub-lease is not covered by Land Registration Act 1925, s.110. The sub-tenant will normally require the head-tenant to supply office copies of his registered title and the contract should contain a special condition to this effect.[5] Production of the title to the freehold is unnecessary if the head-lease is registered with an absolute title. In other cases, unless excluded by special condition, Standard Condition 8.2.4

will apply to the contract and the head-tenant may be obliged to deduce the reversionary title to the sub-tenant.

1. See Standard Condition 8.2.4 and Law of Property Act 1925, s.44.
2. See Standard Condition 4.5.3.
3. Law of Property Act 1925, s.44.
4. *Hill* v. *Harris* [1965] 2 Q.B. 601.
5. Inspection of the registered title is now possible since the Land Register is open to the public.

1.14. **Registration**

1.14.1.   A lease for 21 years or less is not capable of being registered with its own title at HM Land Registry,[1] but the lease will normally take effect as an overriding interest under Land Registration Act 1925, s.70(1)(*g*) or (*k*) (para. (*g*) only applies where the tenant is in occupation). If there is concern about protecting the tenant's interest in the property a caution may be lodged against the landlord's title. In unregistered land a purchaser of the reversion is deemed to purchase with knowledge of the rights of occupiers, but an agreement for a lease may be registered as an estate contract Class (C(iv) land charge) and a caution against first registration registered against the property at HM Land Registry.

1.14.2.   Where on completion of the grant the tenant will make application for registration of the lease with a separate title, a landlord whose own freehold title is registered should take steps to place his land certificate on deposit at HM Land Registry and inform the tenant of the deposit number. Where the landlord's freehold title is subject to a mortgage, his lender will be in possession of the charge certificate (which may therefore not be available to be placed on deposit); in any event, in this situation the land certificate is already held by the Registry and thus there is no need to require deposit of the charge certificate except where the consent of the chargee was required to the grant of the lease.

1. Except leases granted under Housing Act 1985, Part V, see K.9.1.5. below.

1.15. **Surety**

1.15.1.   The landlord may require a surety to the lease as a condition of its grant. Where the proposed tenant is a small private company it is common to find that the directors of the company are asked to guarantee the company's obligations under the lease. This gives the landlord additional protection under the lease since the sureties' obligations will be co-extensive with those of the principal debtor. If it is intended to enter a contract prior to the grant of the lease, the sureties should be made parties to that contract.

1.15.2.   A buyer's solicitor who is also acting for the sureties to the lease must consider whether any conflict of interests exists or is likely to arise between the interests of his buyer client and the interests of the sureties. It may be in the best interests of the buyer to obtain a lease of the premises, which he can only do if he provides sureties to the lease (a pre-condition imposed by the landlord), but it may not be in the best interests of the sureties to enter into covenants with the landlord to guarantee performance of the buyer's obligations under the lease, e.g. as to payment of rent, repairs, etc., where the enforcement of the sureties' covenants would put the sureties' personal assets, such as a matrimonial home, at risk. Where such a conflict exists or is likely to arise, the sureties should receive independent advice about their potential liability.

1.16. Mortgages

1.16.1. If the freehold reversion is subject to a mortgage, the mortgage deed should be checked to see whether it requires the lender's consent to be obtained prior to the grant of a lease. If so, steps should be taken to obtain the lender's consent before a binding contract to grant the lease is created.[1] Failure to obtain such consent, where necessary, will put the seller into breach of his mortgage covenants, with the consequence that the principal sum under the mortgage will become due immediately. If consent is not required it should be checked that the lease is within the borrower's powers under Law of Property Act 1925, s.99.

1. The borrower's powers of leasing can be extended by or excluded from the mortgage by agreement (Law of Property Act 1925, s.99) except in the case of a mortgage of an agricultural holding where they cannot be excluded and the mortgage cannot exclude the court's power to order a new tenancy of business premises under Pt. II Landlord and Tenant Act 1954.

1.17. Sub-sales

1.17.1. By Standard Condition 8.2.5 sub-sales are not permitted where the contract is for the grant of a lease. A landlord will be reluctant to allow amendment of this condition since by doing so he will lose the benefit of the continuing liability on the lease obligations which he obtains from the covenants given by an original tenant.

1.18. Searches and enquiries before contract

1.18.1. When acting for a tenant on a long lease for a premium or on a commercial lease the same searches and enquiries as are relevant to a freehold purchase should be made. Searches are discussed above in para. B.10.

1.18.2. Where a commercial lease is for a very short term at a low rent, or on short-term lettings of residential property, it is not usual for searches and enquiries to be made since the low risk attached to these lettings does not justify the expense of making the searches. In the latter case, however, the prospective tenant may feel it is prudent to make enquiries about the prospective landlord's solvency, particularly where the property is mortgaged, to avoid the risk of the landlord's lender seeking a possession order against the tenant if the landlord does not pay the mortgage.

1.19.   **The contract**

1.19.1.   A contract for the grant of the lease is normally entered into in the case of a purchase for a premium of a long-term residential lease but is not generally entered into on short-term lettings of residential premises nor on commercial leases where in both cases the parties directly enter negotiations on the draft lease. The only exception to this in the case of commercial lettings is where in order to achieve quickly a binding commitment a contract is entered into which is expressed to be subject to some contingency, e.g. landlord's consent or grant of planning permission.

1.20.   **Drafting the lease**

1.20.1.   A lease for a term of over three years must be granted by deed to vest the legal estate in the tenant. A lease for three years or less, taking effect in possession at the best rent without a fine, may be granted orally or in writing.[1] To ensure certainty of terms between the parties it is recommended that all leases, no matter how short the term, should be in writing.

1.20.2.   The lease is drafted by the seller's (landlord's) solicitor and annexed to the draft contract submitted to the buyer's (tenant's) solicitor. Except where the lease is to be for a term not exceeding three years, taking effect in possession and with no premium payable for its grant, the contract for the lease must satisfy Law of Property (Miscellaneous Provisions) Act 1989, s.2. Standard Condition 8.2 provides for the lease to be in the form annexed to the draft contract and for the seller to engross the lease and supply the buyer with the engrossment at least five working days before completion date. The length of the term and its commencement date must be expressly stated in the draft lease in order to satisfy Law of Property (Miscellaneous Provisions) Act 1989, s.2, or either or both could be stated in the contract.

1.20.3.   Leases which are granted by the same landlord to different tenants of separate units all of which are in the common ownership of the landlord (e.g. flats within a block owned by the landlord) should be uniform in content. If this is not so, difficulty may subsequently be experienced in the enforcement of covenants against individual tenants. Subject to this, given the diversity of circumstances in which leases are granted, no two leases will ever be identical, and it is recommended that the seller's solicitor refers to a suitable precedent before embarking on the drafting of the lease.[2]

1.20.4.   Where the lease is of business premises the Law Society Standard Business Leases for the whole or part of premises may be used. The texts of these are set out in Appendix V.2.

1.20.5.   Consideration should be given to whether the landlord should give covenants for title on the grant of the lease.[3]

1. Law of Property Act 1925, ss.52−54 and Law of Property (Miscellaneous Provisions) Act 1989, s.2.
2. See, e.g. *Encyclopaedia of Forms and Precedents (Vol. 22), Drafting and Negotiating Commercial Leases* by Murray Ross, *Practical Lease Precedents* by Trevor Aldridge.
3. Covenants can now be given on the grant of a lease: Law of Property (Miscellaneous Provisions) Act 1994, and see Covenants of title, para. M.09.

1.21. **The Protocol**

1.21.1. The Protocol does not specifically refer to procedures on the grant of a lease. Since the procedure on grant of a lease is very similar to that applicable to a freehold transaction it is recommended that in appropriate cases when dealing with residential property the Protocol procedures are adhered to as closely as circumstances permit.

1.22. **Side letters**

1.22.1. A side letter (or letter of comfort) may take effect as a collateral contract. Such a letter may bind an assignee of the reversion, even if the assignee did not know of the letter or its contents.[1]

1. *System Floors* v. *Ruralpride* [1994] E.G.C.S. 162.

FURTHER REFERENCE

The Encyclopaedia of Forms and Precedents, Butterworths.

Practical Lease Precedents, T.M. Aldridge, F.T. Law & Tax.

Drafting Business Leases, K.Lewison, F.T. Law & Tax.

Drafting and Negotiating Commercial Leases, M.J. Ross, Butterworths.

Drafting and Negotiating Rent Review Clauses, M. Kemp F.T. Law & Tax.

K.02. Acting for the landlord

2.1. **Taking instructions**	2.5. **Completion and post-**
2.2. **Drafting the lease**	**completion**
2.3. **Preparing the package**	2.6. **Apportionment of rent**
2.4. **Engrossment and**	
execution of lease	

See also: Taking instructions, para. A.01.
Acting on grant of lease, para. K.01.
Acting for the tenant, para. K.03.
Long-term residential tenancies, para. K.06.
Business premises, para. K.07.
Right to buy, para. K.09.

2.1. Taking instructions

2.1.1. Much of the information required by the landlord's solicitor from his client will be similar to that required from the seller in the case of a freehold transaction. These matters are considered in paras. A.01. and K.01. above.

2.2. Drafting the lease

2.2.1. The lease is drafted by the seller's (landlord's) solicitor and annexed to the draft contract submitted to the buyer's (tenant's) solicitor. Except where the lease is to be for a term not exceeding three years, taking effect in possession and with no premium payable for its grant, the contract for the lease must satisfy Law of Property (Miscellaneous Provisions) Act 1989, s.2. Standard Condition 8.2 provides for the lease to be in the form annexed to the draft contract and for the seller to engross the lease and supply the buyer with the engrossment at least five working days before completion date. The length of the term and its commencement date must be expressly stated in the lease in order to satisfy Law of Property (Miscellaneous Provisions) Act 1989, s.2.

2.2.2. Where the lease is of business premises the Law Society Standard Business Leases for the whole or part of premises may be used. The texts of these are set out in Appendix V.2.

2.3. Preparing the package

2.3.1. *The contract*

The particulars of sale must state that the property is leasehold and give details of the term to be vested in the tenant. The draft lease should be drafted and annexed to the contract. It is usual to include a condition requiring the tenant to accept the lease in the form annexed to the contract.[1] Incumbrances affecting the freehold title must be disclosed and indemnity taken from the tenant in respect of future breaches.[2] The landlord's solicitor should consider whether or not it is appropriate for his client to offer covenant for title to the tenant.[3]

2.3.2. Checklist

The landlord's solicitor should send to the tenant's solicitor the following documents:

(a) draft contract with draft lease annexed;

(b) evidence of the freehold title;

(c) any relevant planning consents;

(d) answers to pre-contract searches and enquiries (including in Protocol cases the Seller's Property Information Form and Seller's Leasehold Information Form);

(e) where appropriate, evidence of the lender's consent to the grant of the lease;

(f) the memorandum and articles of any management company.

1. See Standard Condition 8.2.3.
2. See Standard Condition 4.5.3.
3. See para. M.09.

2.4. Engrossment and execution of lease

2.4.1. The lease is normally prepared in two parts (lease and counterpart) both engrossed by the landlord's solicitor.[1] If the landlord requires the tenant to pay a fee for the preparation of the engrossment this must be dealt with by special condition in the contract.

2.4.2. The landlord will sign the lease itself in readiness for completion; the counterpart should be sent to the tenant's solicitor at least five days before contractual completion date[2] for execution by the tenant. The requirements for execution of a deed are dealt with in section E above. The landlord's execution of the lease should expressly be made subject to a condition that the landlord can withdraw from the transaction if the tenant fails to complete.

1. Standard Condition 8.2.6.
2. Standard Condition 8.2.6.

2.5. **Completion and post-completion**

2.5.1. On completion in addition to or in substitution for the matters relevant to a freehold transaction the landlord will receive:

(a) the counterpart lease executed by the tenant;

(b) any premium payable for the grant (less any deposit paid on exchange of contracts);

(c) an apportioned sum representing rent payable in advance under the lease and interim service charge. If the commencement date of the term precedes the date of the lease itself, no rent can be recovered in respect of the period from the start of the term until the date of the grant.

2.5.2. The landlord should give to the tenant:

(a) the lease executed by him;

(b) if not already done, properly marked or certified copies of the freehold title deeds (unregistered land);

(c) where the landlord's title is registered, the deposit number relating to the landlord's land or charge certificate;

(d) where relevant and if not already done, a certified copy of the consent of the landlord's lender to the transaction;

(e) share certificate relating to the management company.

2.5.3. After completion the counterpart lease should be stamped with the appropriate duty. The landlord may receive notice in duplicate from the tenant, in accordance with the tenant's covenant to so do in the lease, of the tenant's mortgage of the property. One copy of the notice should be placed with the landlord's title deeds, the other receipted on behalf of the landlord and returned to the tenant's solicitor.

2.6. **Apportionment of rent**

2.6.1. The Standard Conditions of Sale do not provide for the apportionment of rent on completion of the grant of a lease; therefore an express special condition is required to deal with this matter.

2.6.2. Where the rent reserved by the lease is an annual rent payable quarterly in advance on the usual quarter days and the rent commencement date does not coincide with either the term commencement date or the usual quarter days, the apportionment of rent on completion of the grant of the lease should be made in accordance with the recommended method of calculation set out below.

2.6.3. Where completion takes place at a date within a rent quarter (and where the lease remains in place), any apportionment of the quarter's rent should be treated as falling outside the scope of VAT, notwithstanding that an election to tax the rent has been, or will be, made.

2.6.4. *Recommended method of calculation*

The following formula applies where the term year runs from a date which is a rent payment date.

2.6.5. The method of calculation is based on the view that, where a lease or tenancy agreement reserves an annual rent, the usual direction to pay the rent by equal quarterly payments will have been inserted for estate management convenience only and will not have been intended to convert the annual rent into a quarterly rent. This is important because the traditional quarters are of unequal duration and hence the daily amount of rent would differ between one quarter and another if it were calculated quarter by quarter.

2.6.6. The example used below to illustrate the methods is for a lease dated 8 March 1990 expressed to grant a term of 'ten years commencing on 29 September 1989' and expressed to reserve 'a rent of £36,500 per annum payable by equal quarterly payments in advance on the usual quarter days (the first payment being a due proportion thereof for the period from the date hereof to the following quarter day to be paid on the execution hereof)'.

Initial payment

Step 1

Ascertain the 'term year'. In the example, the term year will begin on 29 September in one year and end on 28 September in the following year. If, instead, the term had been expressed as 'a term commencing on the date hereof and expiring on 28 September 1999', the 'term year' would probably (although it is a matter of intention evidenced by the wording used in the lease) commence on 8 March in one year and end on 7 March in the following year. If the term was expressed to run 'from' a particular date, it would be necessary to consider whether under the particular lease the term began on that date or on the next day, a question discussed in most of the reference books on leases.

Step 2

Count the number of days for which the tenant is liable to pay rent during the first term year. In the example, this would be from 8 March 1990 to 28 September 1990 inclusive, namely 205 days.

Step 3

Calculate the rent payable for that number of days on an annual basis. In our example, this would be 205/365 × £36,500 = £20,500.

Step 4

Calculate the rent that the tenant will have to pay on those rent payment days which will fall between the grant of the lease and the end of the first term year. In our example, there would be two such rent payment days, 25 March 1990 and 24 June 1990, on each of which the tenant will have to pay one quarter's rent (£9125) and therefore the total rent payable on those days will be 2 × £9125 = £18,250.

Step 5

Deduct the sum calculated at step 4 from the sum calculated at step 3. The difference is the amount that the tenant must pay on the grant of the lease. In our example, this is £20,500 − £18,250 = £2250. (Contrast this with the figure of £1700 that would have been calculated by simply taking the number of days from 8 March to 24 March inclusive at a daily rate of £100 (calculated on an annual basis) or the figure of £1723.61 that would have been calculated by taking those days as a fraction of the current quarter.)

Assignment of lease

Assume that the lease is assigned on 31 March 1991. The apportionment as between the assignor and the assignee is to be calculated as follows:

Step 1

Ascertain the term year.

Step 2

Count the number of days for which the present tenant is liable to pay the rent during the current term year down to the date of the assignment. In our example, this is from 29 September 1990 to 31 March 1991, namely 184 days.

Step 3

Calculate the rent payable for that number of days on an annual basis. In our example, this would be 184/365 × £36,500 = £18,400.

Step 4

Ascertain the amount of rent that will have been paid by the present tenant in respect of the current term year. In our example, the present tenant will have paid rent for the current year on 29 September 1990, 25 December 1990 and 25 March 1991, namely 3 × £9125 = £27,375.

Step 5

Compare the figures calculated at steps 3 and 4. If the former exceeds the latter, the present tenant must make an allowance of the difference to the assignee. If the latter exceeds the former, the assignee must make an allowance in favour of the present tenant. In our example, the present tenant has paid more rent than relates to his period of occupation during the current term year by the figure £27,375 − £18,400 = £8975. This is the amount for which he is to be reimbursed by his assignee. (Contrast this with the sum of £8400 that would have been calculated by simply applying the daily rate of £100 to the number of days between 31 March and the end of that quarter.)

On sale of reversion

Using our example, suppose that the landlord's interest was transferred to a new landlord on 30 April 1991. The apportionment of rental income between the old landlord and the new landlord is to be calculated as follows:

Step 1

Ascertain the term year.

Step 2

Count the number of days for which the old landlord is entitled to retain the rent received from the tenant in respect of the current term year. In our example, the old landlord is entitled to the rent for the period from 29 September 1990 to 30 April 1991, namely 214 days.

Step 3

Calculate the rent receivable for that number of days on an annual basis. In our example, this would be 214/365 × £36,500 = £21,400.

Step 4

Calculate the amount of rent actually received by the old landlord from the tenant in respect of the current term year. In our example, this rent should have been received on 29 September 1990, 25 December 1990 and 25 March 1991, namely 3 × £9125 = £27,375.

Step 5

Compare the figures calculated at steps 3 and 4. If the former exceeds the latter, the new landlord must make an allowance of the difference to the old landlord. If the latter exceeds the former, the old landlord must make an allowance of the difference to the new landlord. In our example, the old landlord has received more rent than relates to his period of ownership by the sum of £27,375 − £21,400 = £5975. This is the amount which the old landlord must allow to the new landlord on transferring the reversion. (Contrast that with the sum of £5400 that would have been calculated simply by taking the number of days between 30 April and the end of the current quarter and applying the daily rate of £100.)

2.6.7. For consistency, where the term expires by effluxion of time on a date other than the last day of a term year, the amount of the tenants' final payment of rent should be calculated on a basis similar to the apportionment of his initial payment on the grant of the lease.

2.6.8. Apportionment of rent where the term date does not commence on a rent payment date cannot be made according to the formula explained in para. 2.6.6. In most cases the most appropriate method of calculation in this situation will be what is sometimes called the 'surveyor's method'. This involves simply counting the days to immediately before the next payment date, and applying a daily rate computed on a yearly basis.

2.6.9. The illogicality of this approach is obvious. A daily rate for rent payable by, e.g. equal quarterly instalments is being calculated on a yearly basis and then applied to the residue of a particular quarter, which does not comprise exactly one-fourth of a year. A variation would be to calculate the daily rate for the particular quarter by reference to the total number of days in that quarter.

2.6.10. On either basis, it will be apparent that, should it be necessary to calculate an apportionment at a later date (e.g. when the lease is assigned or surrendered, or the reversion is transferred), to achieve a fair result it would be necessary to ascertain how much rent was actually paid under the apportionment at the grant of the lease and carry the calculation forward on that basis. This will usually be impractical, and the parties will have to be prepared to adopt each time a more rough and ready approach, such as the 'surveyor's method'.

2.6.11. However, since that method is entirely arbitrary and bears no logical relationship to the term/rent structure of the lease, it is recommended that leases should be drafted so that the term year commences on one of the recurring rent payment dates. Thus if rent is to be payable on the usual quarter days, the term year should commence on a quarter day. This will enable apportionments to be computed on a logical basis as set out in the standard formula above.

K.03. Acting for the tenant

3.1. **Before exchange**	3.3. **Post-completion**
3.2. **Pre-completion and completion**	

See also: Taking instructions, para. A.01.
Acting on grant of lease, para. K.01.
Acting for the landlord, para. K.02.
Long-term residential tenancies, para. K.06.
Business premises, para. K.07.
Right to buy, para. K.09.

3.1.   Before exchange

3.1.1.   Taking instructions

The information required by the buyer's (tenant's) solicitor from his client will be similar to that required in a freehold transaction.[1] The client should be advised about the effect of any security of tenure provisions which may be applicable in the circumstances.[2]

3.1.2.   The draft lease

The draft lease, prepared by the seller's (landlord's) solicitor, will be supplied to the tenant's solicitor with the draft contract. The contract will normally require the tenant to accept the draft in the form annexed to the contract;[3] therefore any queries or observations which are to be raised in connection with the lease must be finalised before contracts are exchanged. Even where the lease appears to contain 'usual' clauses appropriate to the particular transaction in hand, the document must be carefully examined by the tenant's solicitor to ensure that it does contain provisions which are adequate to protect his client's interests and contains no onerous clauses (e.g. in relation to repairing obligations or rent review) which may adversely affect the client. The length of the term will affect the amount of stamp duty payable on the lease by the tenant and this also should be considered.

3.1.3.   Checklist

When checking the lease particular attention should be paid to the provisions relating to the following matters:

(a)   the property to be demised;

(b) easements and reservations (particularly in the case of flats or other non-detached property: see para. K.01. above);

(c) repairing obligations;

(d) rent and rent review provisions (too low a ground rent may act as a disincentive to the landlord to carry out his repairing obligations to the property);

(e) provisions relating to service charges (see para. K.01.);

(f) insurance (who is to insure: landlord or tenant? do the insurance provisions accord with the tenant's mortgagee's instructions? what is covered by the policy both in terms of premises, amount of cover and risks insured against?);

(g) forfeiture clauses;

(h) covenants restricting alienation of the property;

(i) covenants restricting the use of the property;

(j) provisions relating to a management company or residents' association (is the tenant required to become a member of a management company which is limited by guarantee? will his liability to the management company terminate on assignment of the lease?);

(k) requirements for a surety or rent deposit scheme;

(l) are any of the covenants onerous?

(m) do the covenants adequately protect the tenant and his lender?

(n) are covenants for title being offered?

NB: A brief summary of the most common express covenants found in leases is contained above in para. K.01.

3.1.4. Searches

The tenant's solicitor should usually undertake the same searches and enquiries as if he were buying the freehold.[4] Exceptionally, where a short tenancy agreement is being granted, it may be considered unnecessary to do such searches.

3.1.5. Lender's requirements

The tenant's lender's requirements, contained in the instructions given to the solicitors acting for the lender, must be observed. The tenant's lender will frequently be concerned to see that the following conditions have been satisfied:

(a) the consent of the landlord's lender to the transaction has been obtained (where relevant);

(b) the length of the term to be granted provides adequate security for the loan (terms of less than 60 years are often unacceptable for mortgage purposes in the case of residential leases);

(c) the lease contains adequate insurance provisions relating both to the premises themselves and (where relevant) to common parts of the building and that the insurance provisions coincide with the lender's own requirements for insurance;

(d) title to the freehold reversion is deduced, enabling the lease itself to be registered with an absolute title at HM Land Registry;

(e) the lease contains proper repairing covenants in respect both of the property itself and (where relevant) the common parts of the building;

(f) in the case of residential leases, that there is no provision for forfeiture on the insolvency of the tenant;

(g) where the lease is of part of a building or is, e.g. of one house on an estate comprising leasehold houses all owned by the same landlord, that the lease provides for mutual enforceability of covenants as between the tenants;

(h) the landlord is giving appropriate covenants for title.

3.1.6. Advising the client

The tenant's obligations under the lease, which are often complex and extensive, should be clearly explained to him. In particular, the tenant (where relevant) should be warned of his continuing liability on the covenants in the lease notwithstanding the subsequent sale of the residue of the term to a third party[5] and of the danger of losing the lease through forfeiture for breach of covenant. A pre-contract report may be prepared and given to the client (as in freehold transactions).[6] The report should explain the main provisions of the terms of the lease and their effect on the tenant.

3.1.7. The Protocol

The Protocol does not specifically refer to procedures on the grant of a lease. Since the procedure on grant of a lease is very similar to that applicable to a freehold transaction it is recommended that in appropriate cases when dealing with residential property the Protocol procedures are adhered to as closely as circumstances permit.

1. See above, Taking instructions, para. A.01.
2. See below, paras. K.06., K.08. and K.10.
3. See Standard Condition 8.2.3.
4. See above, para. B.10. and section E.
5. See below, Liability on covenants in leases, para. K.10.
6. See Preparing to exchange, para. C.01.

3.2. **Pre-completion and completion**

3.2.1. The engrossment of the lease and counterpart will usually be prepared by the landlord's solicitor. The tenant, if the contract so provides, may be required on completion to pay a fee to the landlord for the preparation of the engrossment. By Standard Condition 8.2.6 the landlord is to deliver the engrossment of the counterpart lease to the tenant at least five working days before completion and by Standard Condition 8.2.7 the tenant is to execute the counterpart lease and deliver it to the landlord on completion. Execution should be made in escrow. Exccution of the purchase deed (lease) is discussed in section E above.

3.2.2. The tenant's solicitor should make pre-completion searches in the same way as if he were buying the freehold.[1]

3.2.3. Apportionments on completion may include amounts in respect of rent and service charge payable in advance under the provisions of the lease.

3.2.4. On completion the tenant should give to the landlord:

    (a) the duly executed counterpart lease;

    (b) any money due on completion, e.g. balance of premium (less deposit paid on exchange), apportioned sums payable in respect of rent and service charge, landlord's fee for engrossment of the lease.

3.2.5. The tenant should on completion receive from the landlord:

    (a) the duly executed lease;

    (b) where the landlord's title is registered, the deposit number relating to deposit of the landlord's land or charge certificate at HM Land Registry;

    (c) where the landlord's title is unregistered, a marked abstract of the freehold title;

    (d) where appropriate, consent to the dealing given by the landlord's mortgagee;

    (e) share certificate and management company documents.

1. See Pre-completion, section E above.

3.3. **Post-completion**

3.3.1. *Stamp duty*

The lease must be lodged for stamping with duty at the appropriate rate within 30 days of completion but should in practice be presented for stamping at the earliest opportunity because other time-limits (e.g. in relation to registration of the lease itself) may also have to be complied with. Stamp duty on leases is assessed by reference to the amount of the premium, the length of the term and the rent payable.[1] Where rent payable after a rent review is of an ascertainable amount, this rent will attract duty. A service charge for a fixed sum attracts duty in relation to its amount, but a service charge of an amount to be ascertained by reference to the application of a formula contained within the lease attracts a fixed duty only. No duty is payable on a service charge which is payable to a third party, e.g. a management company. No stamp duty is payable where the premium on the lease does not exceed the current stamp duty threshold and the average annual rent does not exceed £600 provided that an appropriate certificate of value is included in the lease.[2]

3.3.2. If the lease is granted for a term of seven years or more, it falls within Finance Act 1931, s.28 and must be produced to the Inland Revenue in accordance with the requirements of that section.[3]

3.3.3. Registration of the lease

Where applicable the lease must be registered at HM Land Registry within the relevant priority period, or on first registration within two months of completion. The requirements for registration of a lease are outlined in para. K.01. above.

3.3.4. Notice to landlord

The lease will usually contain a covenant requiring the tenant to notify the landlord within a stated period of all dealings with the lease and to pay a fee to the landlord for registration of the notice. The creation of a mortgage by the tenant, depending on the wording of the covenant, may fall within this obligation. Where the tenant is obliged to give notice of dealings, this should be done by sending two copies of the notice, together with a cheque for the appropriate fee, to the landlord's solicitor or other person named in the covenant. The landlord should be asked to sign one copy of the notice and to return it to the tenant so that the receipted notice may be placed with the tenant's title deeds as evidence of compliance with this requirement.

3.3.5. A tenant's lender may require a signed but otherwise blank stock transfer form and the tenant's share certificate to be lodged with him to ensure that the lender will be able to transfer the tenant's share in the management company in the event of the lender exercising his power of sale.

1. See the table of stamp duties in App. VIII.2.
2. For form of certificate of value see para. K.01.11. Also see Stamp duty and stamp duty savings, para. A.14.
3. See Post-completion, section G above.

K.04. Acting for both parties

See also: Acting for both parties, para. A.10.
Mortgages: acting for lender and borrower, para. A.11.
Acting on grant of lease, para. K.01.

4.1.   Conflict of interests

4.1.1.   A solicitor must not act where there is a conflict of interest between himself and his clients or between two of his clients.

4.2.   Rule 6 Solicitors' Practice Rules 1990 (as amended)

4.2.1.   Specifically in relation to conveyancing Rule 6 Solicitors' Practice Rules 1990 (as amended) prohibits a solicitor from acting for both landlord and tenant in the grant or assignment of a lease at arm's length. This rule and its exceptions are further discussed in para. A.10. above.

4.3.   Acting for the client's lender

4.3.1.   Generally, a solicitor may act for his landlord or tenant client and that client's lender provided that no conflict of interests exists or is likely to arise. See Mortgages: acting for lender and borrower, para. A.11.

4.4.   Sureties

4.4.1.   A buyer's solicitor who is also acting for the sureties to the lease must consider whether any conflict of interest exists or is likely to arise between the interests of his buyer client and the interests of the sureties. It may be in the best interests of the buyer to obtain a lease of the premises, which he can only do if he provides sureties to the lease (a pre-condition imposed by the landlord), but it may not be in the best interests of the sureties to enter into covenants with the landlord to guarantee performance of the buyer's obligations under the lease, e.g. as to payment of rent, repairs, etc., where the enforcement of the sureties' covenants would put the sureties' personal assets, such as a matrimonial home, at risk. Where such a conflict exists, or is likely to arise, the sureties should receive independent advice about their potential liability.

K.05. Short-term residential tenancies

5.1. Grant of lease

5.1.1. A lease for a term of over three years must be granted by deed to vest the legal estate in the tenant. A lease for three years or less, taking effect in possession at the best rent without a fine, may be granted orally or in writing.[1] To ensure certainty of terms between the parties it is recommended that all leases, no matter how short the term, should be in writing.

5.1.2. A contract for the grant of the lease is not generally entered into on short-term lettings of residential premises.

5.1.3. On short-term lettings of residential property it is not usual for searches and enquiries to be made since the low risk attached to these lettings does not justify the expense of making the searches. However, the prospective tenant may feel it is prudent to make enquiries about the prospective landlord's solvency, particularly where the property is mortgaged, to avoid the risk of the landlord's lender seeking a possession order against the tenant if the landlord does not pay the mortgage.

5.1.4. Where the lease is to be granted for a short term, or is merely a tenancy agreement, some of the considerations outlined in paras. K.01., K.02. and K.03. above will not be relevant. Frequently a formal contract for the grant of the lease is dispensed with and the landlord's solicitor simply submits a draft lease or tenancy agreement for approval by the tenant's solicitor. When the form of the lease or agreement is finalised and signed, the tenant will take possession of the premises. No premium is normally taken (and in some cases is not permitted by law) but a deposit which must not exceed one-sixth of the annual rent may be taken as security against damage to fixtures and fittings.

5.1.5. Where the premises are furnished, an inventory of the contents should be prepared by the landlord and agreed by the tenant.

5.1.6. If the rent is to be payable weekly, a rent book must be provided to the tenant.

5.1.7. The tenant's solicitor will not normally investigate title on his client's behalf, but the risks of omitting this step must be considered in each individual case. The terms of the tenancy agreement must be carefully scrutinised and their effect explained to the client. Particular attention should be paid to the effects of any security of tenure legislation on the tenancy.

5.1.8. A lease for 21 years or less is not capable of being registered with its own title at HM Land Registry,[2] but providing the tenant is in occupation of the property will take effect as an overriding interest under Land Registration Act 1925, s.70(1)(g) or otherwise under section 70(1)(k). If there is concern about protecting the tenant's interest in the property a caution may be lodged against the landlord's title. In unregistered land a purchaser of the reversion is deemed to purchase with knowledge of the rights of occupiers, but the agreement for a lease may be registered as an estate contract (C(iv) land charge) and a caution against first registration registered against the landlord at HM Land Registry.

1. See below, para. 5.3.3.
2. Except leases granted under Housing Act 1985, Part V, see K.9.1.5.below.

5.2. **Public sector tenants**

5.2.1. Security for public sector tenants is provided by Part IV Housing Act 1985 (as amended by Housing Act 1988) under what are called 'secure tenancies'.

5.2.2. Subject to:

    (a) a number of exceptions set out in Schedule 1 (e.g. tenancies granted for over 21 years and business tenancies within Part II Landlord and Tenant Act 1954);

    (b) tenancies ceasing to be secure tenancies after the death of the tenant; and

    (c) tenancies ceasing to be secure tenancies in consequence of an assignment or sub-letting,

a tenancy under which a dwelling house is let as a separate dwelling is a secure tenancy at any time when the 'landlord condition' and the 'tenant condition' are both satisfied.

5.2.3. The provisions apply to most licences as well as to tenancies.

5.2.4. The 'landlord condition'

The 'landlord condition' is that the interest of the landlord belongs to one of a number of bodies specified in Housing Act 1985, s.80, as modified by Housing Act 1988, s.35. These include local authorities and housing associations.

5.2.5. The 'tenant condition'

The 'tenant condition' is that the tenant is an individual and occupies the house as his only or principal home or, where the tenancy is a joint tenancy, that each of the joint tenants is an individual and at least one of them occupies the house as his only or principal home.

5.2.6. Where a secure tenancy for a term certain ends by effluxion of time or by an order terminating the tenancy in pursuance of a right of forfeiture, a periodic tenancy arises. A secure tenancy which is either a periodic tenancy or for a term certain but subject to termination by the landlord cannot usually be brought to an end by the landlord except by obtaining a court order for possession. The grounds for possession are set out in Schedule 2 Housing Act 1985.

5.2.7. A secure tenancy ends on the death of the tenant, although provisions for succession to the tenancy after the death of the tenant are contained in Housing Act 1985, ss.87–90.

5.2.8. A secure tenancy cannot generally be assigned, but there are limited exceptions to this rule, e.g. an assignment with the landlord's consent by way of exchange. A secure tenant cannot, without the landlord's consent, sub-let or part with the possession of part only of the house. In this case, the landlord must not unreasonably withhold his consent to the alienation and, if consent is unreasonably withheld, it is treated as having been given. If, however, the tenant parts with the possession of the whole house, or sub-lets the whole, the tenancy ceases to be a secure tenancy and cannot later revert to being one.

5.2.9. Introductory tenancies

A local housing authority or housing action trust is empowered by Housing Act 1996, s.124 to operate an introductory tenancy regime.

5.2.10. New periodic tenancies or licences granted by such authorities will be 'introductory tenancies'. A new tenancy is one granted to a person (or persons) who immediately before its grant was not a secure tenant of the same or different premises and was not an assured tenant of a registered social landlord of the same or another dwelling house.

5.2.11. An introductory tenancy remains such for a trial period of one year subject to certain earlier termination provisions contained in Housing Act 1996, s.125.

5.2.12. The landlord can bring an introductory tenancy to an end, after serving notice on the tenant, by obtaining a court order under Housing Act 1996, s.127. The tenant has the right to ask for a review of the landlord's decision to end the tenancy within 14 days of notice of possession proceedings being served on him. Subject to this, the possession ground is mandatory.

5.2.13. Provisions for succession to an introductory tenancy are contained in Housing Act 1996 ss.131–133. An introductory tenancy is not capable of assignment except under court order (e.g. Matrimonial Causes Act 1973, s.24).

5.3. Rent Act tenancies

5.3.1. A tenancy under which a dwelling house (including part of a house) was let as a separate dwelling before 15 January 1989 was (and will until termination of the tenancy continue to be) a protected tenancy under Rent Act 1977, unless that tenancy was excluded from the Act.[1] Since 14 January 1989 no new Rent Act tenancies have come into being because on that date Rent Act 1977 was superseded by Housing Act 1988.[2]

5.3.2. On the termination of a protected tenancy (e.g. by forfeiture or notice to quit), the person who at that time was the protected tenant will become a statutory tenant if and so long as he occupies the house as his residence. Although the terms of the protected tenancy apply to the statutory tenancy so far as they are consistent with the nature of the statutory tenancy, there are a number of differences between the two types of tenancy, such differences deriving from the fact that a protected tenancy is a proprietary right, while a statutory tenancy is merely a personal right of residence. A protected tenancy will vest in a tenant's trustee in bankruptcy and can be disclaimed by him (so ending the tenant's right of residence as against his landlord) but a statutory tenancy does not vest in a trustee in bankruptcy.

5.3.3. Exclusions from protection

These include:[3]

(a) tenancies of high rateable value dwellings;

(b) tenancies at low rents;

(c) holiday lettings;

(d) lettings by resident landlords;

(e) lettings by local authorities and housing associations;

(f) business tenancies within Part II Landlord and Tenant Act 1954; and

(g) licences.

5.3.4.   *Rent control*[4]

Unless a rent is registered with the rent officer, a landlord who granted a protected tenancy can initially lawfully recover whatever amount of rent has been agreed between the parties. Such rent can be increased provided that the conditions in the Act relating to the making of a rent agreement are followed. It is open to the tenant to apply to the rent officer for the determination and registration of a 'fair rent', in which case the fair rent will be the maximum legally recoverable amount. An application for revision of the fair rent cannot normally be made within two years of the previous registration.

5.3.5.   *Recovery of possession*

A court order is necessary in order to recover possession from a tenant who has security of tenure under Rent Act 1977.[5] Such an order can only be made where the court[6] is satisfied either that suitable alternative accommodation is available to the tenant or that one or more of the grounds for possession set out in Schedule 15 Rent Act 1977 has been established. Some of the grounds under Schedule 15 are mandatory and others are discretionary, i.e. the landlord must not only prove the existence of the ground, he must also satisfy the court that it is reasonable in all the circumstances to make an order for possession.

5.3.6.   *Protected shorthold tenancies*

These were introduced by Housing Act 1980, enabling landlords to grant fixed-term tenancies for a minimum period of one year and a maximum period of five years giving the landlord the guaranteed right to possession at the end of the term provided certain conditions were satisfied. The fair rent provisions of Rent Act 1977 apply to such tenancies. No new protected shorthold tenancies have come into existence since 14 January 1989 when these provisions were superseded by Housing Act 1988.

5.3.7.   *Death of tenant*

A protected tenancy is capable of devolution on the death of the tenant, subject to the rights to transmission of the tenancy to a member of the tenant's family. A statutory tenancy cannot pass by will or on intestacy since it is neither an estate in land nor a proprietary right. The transmission provisions contained in the Act apply equally to statutory tenancies.[7] On transmission the tenancy is converted into an assured tenancy.[8]

5.3.8.   *Assignment and sub-letting*

Whether or not a protected tenant can assign or sub-let the house or part of it depends on the terms of the tenancy. A statutory tenant cannot assign or sub-let the whole house without the consent of the landlord, although he may sub-let part unless he has agreed not to do so or the remainder is already sub-let.

5.3.9.   Premiums

There is a general prohibition on the taking of a premium as a condition of or in connection with the grant, renewal, continuance or assignment of a protected tenancy. In relation to long tenancies, these rules are substantially modified by Rent Act 1977, s.127, as amended by Housing Act 1980, s.78 and Housing Act 1988, s.115.

1. See para. 5.3.3.
2. See below, para. 5.4.
3. See Rent Act 1977, ss.4−16.
4. Parts III and IV Rent Act 1977, as amended by Housing Act 1980.
5. Rent Act 1977, s.98.
6. The county court has jurisdiction over all matters under Rent Act 1977.
7. Rent Act 1977, Sched. 1, Pt. 1, as amended by Housing Act 1980, s.76 and Housing Act 1988, s.39.
8. See below, para. 5.4.

5.4.   **Assured tenancies**

5.4.1.   Introduction

The definition of an assured tenancy is set out in Housing Act 1988, s.1. A tenancy under which a dwelling house is let as a separate dwelling will be an assured tenancy, if and so long as all of the following requirements are met:

   (a) the tenant or each of joint tenants is an individual; and

   (b) the tenant or at least one of joint tenants occupies the dwelling house as his only or principal home; and

   (c) the tenancy is not specifically excluded by other provisions of the Act.

5.4.2.   From the commencement date of Housing Act 1996, most new lettings will be assured shorthold tenancies (see para. 5.5.) and NOT assured tenancies. However, a shorthold is merely a type of assured tenancy and so must comply with the definition of an assured tenancy as well as the extra requirements which make it a shorthold.

5.4.3.   Tenancies which do NOT satisy the definition of an assured tenancy (and so cannot be shortholds either) will not be subject to the provisions of Housing Act 1988. Instead, ordinary common law rules as to termination, etc., will apply. They will, however, be subject to Protection From Eviction Act 1977 (see para. K.12.5.1.).

5.4.4. *Constituent elements of an assured tenancy*

5.4.4.1. Tenancy

There must be a 'tenancy'; licences to occupy dwelling houses are excluded from protection.

5.4.4.2. Dwelling house

There is no statutory definition of 'dwelling house', and it will be a question of fact whether premises are a house or not, but any building designed or adapted for living in is capable of forming a dwelling house for these purposes.

5.4.4.3. Let as a separate dwelling

The premises, as well as being a dwelling house, must be let as a dwelling. So the purpose of the letting is relevant; thus if a building that would otherwise qualify as a dwelling house is let for business purposes, the tenant cannot claim that it is let on an assured tenancy merely because he decides to move in and live there.

5.4.4.4. There must be a letting as a dwelling. It has been established that this only permits of a singular construction (notwithstanding Interpretation Act 1978). So if the let property comprises two or more residential units, each intended for separate occupation (e.g. the letting of the whole of a house converted into several flats), that tenancy cannot be an assured tenancy. The sub-letting of each of the individual flats could, however, be within the definition.

5.4.4.5. There must be a separate dwelling. This is intended to exclude lettings of accommodation which lacks some essential feature of a dwelling, such as a kitchen. However, Housing Act 1988, s.3 makes special provision for the situation where the tenant shares some of the essential features of a dwelling with others. Such a letting is deemed to be an assured tenancy (assuming that all the other conditions are met) even though the absence of essential facilities in the demised property would normally prevent the tenancy from fulfilling the statutory requirements. The tenant must, however, have the exclusive occupation of at least one room (otherwise it cannot be a tenancy), and if the other accommodation is shared with the landlord, the tenancy will be excluded from the definition of an assured tenancy for different reasons. Arrangements where each tenant is given exclusive occupation of his own bed-sitting room, but shares bathroom and kitchen with other tenants, will be deemed to be capable of being assured tenancies.

5.4.4.6. 'If and so long as'

The status of the tenancy is not to be determined once and for all at the commencement of the letting. Whether a tenancy is an assured tenancy can fluctuate according to changed circumstances. For example, one requirement of the definition is that the tenant must be occupying the house as his only or principal home. This may have been the case at the start of the tenancy, and so the tenancy would be assured, but if subsequently the tenant ceases to reside, the tenancy will no longer be assured. The tenant will thuse lose his security of tenure.

5.4.4.7. The tenant must be an individual

Lettings to companies are excluded from the definition, even though an individual (e.g. a director or employee of the company) may be in occupation of the house. Any sub-letting by a company tenant could, however, qualify as an assured tenancy.

5.4.4.8. The tenant must occupy as his 'only or principal home'

It is possible for a person to have more than one 'home'. If that is the case, then it is a question of fact as to which is the tenant's principal home. Only a tenancy of the principal home can be an assured tenancy. Although the provision requires 'occupation', this does not mean continuous occupation. A mere temporary absence will not deprive a tenancy of its status as an assured tenancy.

5.4.5. Tenancies excluded from the definition

5.4.5.1. Tenancies entered into before the commencement of Housing Act 1988

Only lettings entered into on or after 15 January 1989 can be assured tenancies. Any pre-existing tenancy will, if it has any protection at all, still remain subject to the provisions of Rent Act 1977. There are, however, exceptions to this rule in some cases where a succession has taken place in relation to a pre-existing tenancy.

5.4.5.2. High value properties

For tenancies granted before 1 April 1990, a tenancy of a dwelling house with a rateable value in excess of £750 (£1,500 in Greater London) cannot be an assured tenancy. If the tenancy was granted on or after 1 April 1990, it cannot be an assured tenancy if the rent payable is £25,000 or more per annum.

5.4.5.3. Tenancies at a low rent

Lettings made before 1 April 1990 cannot be assured if the annual rent is less than two-thirds of the rateable value of the property. For tenancies granted on or after 1 April 1990, the exclusion applies to tenancies in which the rent does not exceed £250 per annum (£1,000 per annum in Greater London).

5.4.5.4. Business tenancies

A tenancy to which Part II of Landlord and Tenant Act 1954 applies cannot be an assured tenancy.

5.4.5.5. Licensed premises

Premises licensed for the sale of alcohol for consumption on the premises, e.g.

a public house, are excluded from the definition of an assured tenancy even if the tenant is residing on the premises.

5.4.5.6. Tenancies of agricultural land

A tenancy under which agricultural land exceeding two acres is let together with the house cannot be an assured tenancy.

5.4.5.7. Tenancies of agricultural holdings

A tenancy under which a dwelling house is comprised in an agricultural holding (within the meaning of Agricultural Holdings Act 1986) and is occupied by the person responsible for the control of the farming of the holding cannot be an assured tenancy.

5.4.5.8. Lettings to students

Lettings to students by specified educational bodies are outside the definition of an assured tenancy. This exception does not apply to lettings to students by landlords other than the specified universities and colleges.

5.4.5.9. Holiday lettings

A letting for the purpose of a holiday cannot be an assured tenancy.

5.4.5.10. Lettings by resident landlords

A letting by a resident landlord is excluded from the definition of an assured tenancy provided that certain conditions are satisfied (see para. 5.4.14. below).

5.4.5.11. Crown, local authority and housing association lettings

Crown, local authority and housing association lettings are excluded from the definition of an assured tenancy.

5.4.6. *Rents under assured tenancies*

5.4.6.1. The initial rent

There is no restriction on the amount of rent which can initially be charged on the grant of an assured tenancy. However, if the landlord subsequently wishes to increase the rent, he may not be able to do so unless he follows the correct procedure.

5.4.6.2. Statutory increases for assured periodic tenancies

Statutory increases for assured periodic tenancies are governed by Housing Act 1988, ss.13 and 14 which lay down a complicated procedure requiring the landlord to serve a notice (in the prescribed form) on the tenant. This can then be referred to the Rent Assessment Committee for arbitration if agreement as to the new rent cannot be reached between the parties. The Rent Assessment Committee must determine the rent at which the premises might reasonably be let in the open market. If there is an express term in the tenancy agreement permitting rent increases, this avoids the need to rely on the statutory procedure.

5.4.6.3. Rent increases for fixed-term assured tenancies (including shortholds)

There are no statutory provisions allowing an increase for fixed-term assured tenancies. In the absence of any express provision in the tenancy agreement, the landlord will be unable to increase the rent during the fixed term without the agreement of the tenant. Once the fixed term has ended and the tenant continues in possession as a statutory periodic tenant, then the above provisions of Housing Act 1988 ss. 13 and 14 will apply to enable the landlord to increase the rent, even if there is no express provision on the lease.

5.4.7. Prohibition of assignment without consent

If there is no such express provision against assignment in the lease, Housing Act 1988, s.15 may assist the landlord. The section only applies to periodic assured tenancies (including statutory periodic tenancies). It does not apply to fixed-term assured tenancies (including shortholds).

5.4.8. The term implied into a periodic assured tenancy is that the tenant must not without the consent of the landlord:

    (a) assign the tenancy; or

    (b) sub-let or part with possession of all or part of the property.

Landlord and Tenant Act 1927, s.19 does not apply to this implied term.

5.4.9. In the case of a periodic tenancy which is not a statutory periodic tenancy, these prohibitions do not apply if a premium was paid on the grant or renewal of the tenancy. 'Premium' is defined to include any pecuniary consideration in addition to rent and also includes returnable deposits exceeding one-sixth of the annual rent.

5.4.10. Succession on death

On the death of one of joint tenants, the tenancy will vest in the survivor(s). On the death of a sole tenant the tenancy will pass under his will or intestacy. Housing Act 1988, however, contains specific provisions in section 17 dealing with the succession to an assured periodic tenancy on the death of a sole tenant which will override these normal rules.

5.4.11. On the death of a sole periodic tenant the tenancy will vest in the tenant's spouse, notwithstanding the terms of the deceased's will, provided that immediately before the deceased tenant's death the spouse was occupying the dwelling house as his or her only or principal home. 'Spouse' is defined to include a person who was living with the tenant as his or her wife or husband as well as persons who were lawfully married. There can be no succession, however, in favour of a person of the same sex who may have been co-habiting with the deceased tenant. This provision will not apply if the deceased tenant was himself a 'successor', as defined, i.e. the tenancy became vested in him:

    (a) by virtue of this section; or

    (b) under the will or intestacy of a former tenant; or

    (c) he is the sole survivor of joint tenants; or

    (d) he succeeded to the tenancy under the provisions of Rent Act 1977.

5.4.12. Only one statutory succession is possible. If there is no statutory succession, e.g. because there is no qualifying 'spouse', or there has already been a succession, or the tenancy is for a fixed term, the tenancy will then pass under the will or intestacy of the deceased in the normal way. However, on the death of a periodic assured tenant in such a situation, the landlord would be able to make use of one of the mandatory grounds in order to obtain possession.

5.4.13. Sub-lettings

Housing Act 1988, s.18 provides that in the case of a house lawfully sub-let on an assured tenancy, on the ending of the head lease, the sub-tenancy will still continue. The assured sub-tenant will then become the direct tenant of the head landlord with full security of tenure. However, this only applies to lawful sub-lettings. In the case of an unlawful sub-letting, the sub-tenant will have no security once the head lease has been determined and the head landlord will thus have an absolute right to possession.

5.4.14. Lettings by resident landlords

5.4.14.1. Qualifying conditions

The following qualifying conditions apply:

    (a) the dwelling house which is let forms only part of a building; and

    (b) the building is not a purpose-built block of flats; and

    (c) the tenancy was granted by an individual (i.e. not a limited company) who at the time of the grant occupied another part of the same building as his only or principal home; and

    (d) at all times since the tenancy was granted, the interest of the landlord has continued to belong to an individual who continued so to reside.

5.4.14.2. Continuity of residence

It is not sufficient for the landlord merely to have been in residence at the commencement of the tenancy; he must be in occupation throughout the tenancy. If he ceases to reside then the exception will cease to apply and the letting will once again be capable of being an assured tenancy with full security of tenure. But if the tenancy was entered into on or after the commencement date of Housing Act 1996, the letting will become an assured shorthold tenancy. However, if the interest of the landlord is vested in two or more individuals, only one of those persons need be in residence at any one time.

5.4.14.3. Periods of absence disregarded

Certain periods of absence will be disregarded when deciding whether the landlord's occupation has been continuous:

(a) a period of 28 days beginning with the date on which the interest of the landlord becomes vested at law and in equity in a new owner. If, during this 28 days, the new owner notifies the tenant in writing of his intention to occupy another part of the building as his only or principal home, the disregard will be extended up to six months from the change of ownership; and

(b) any period not exceeding two years during which the interest of the landlord becomes and remains vested in:

(i) trustees as such; or

(ii) the Probate Judge under Administration of Estates Act 1925, s.9; or

(iii) personal representatives of a deceased person acting in that capacity.

Throughout any period during which absence is disregarded (except in a situation where the house is vested in personal representatives), no order for possession can be made except one which might have been made if the tenancy were an assured tenancy. In other words, during these periods of deemed residence the letting becomes a quasi-assured tenancy and possession can only be obtained against the tenant if assured tenancy grounds can be established. However, as an exception to that rule, personal representatives of a deceased resident landlord will be able to recover possession without proving assured tenancy grounds, provided that the contractual term can be terminated.

5.4.14.4. Purpose-built blocks of flats

The resident landlord exception does not apply if the building is a purpose-built block of flats and the landlord occupies one flat in the block and lets one (or more) of the others. Such lettings are therefore capable of being assured tenancies.

A building is a purpose-built block of flats if *as constructed* it contained, and still contains, two or more flats.

'Flat' means a dwelling house which forms only part of a building and is separated horizontally from another dwelling house which forms part of the same building.

Housing Act 1988 makes it clear, however, that if the landlord occupies one flat in a purpose-built block and lets part of that flat, then the resident landlord exception can still apply.

5.4.14.5. Exceptions

A tenancy will be excluded from the resident landlord provisions if two conditions are both fulfilled:

(a) it was granted to a person who immediately before the grant was an assured tenant of the same house or of another house in the same building; and

(b) the landlord under the new tenancy and under the former tenancy is the same person. If either of the tenancies was granted by two or more persons, it is sufficient for this condition that the same person is the landlord or one of the landlords under each tenancy.

This is an anti-avoidance provision designed to ensure that a landlord does not deprive existing tenants of their protection as assured tenants by taking up possession himself and then granting a new tenancy to those existing tenants.

5.4.15.   *Security of tenure*

5.4.15.1. Restriction on termination by landlord

An assured tenancy cannot be brought to an end by the landlord otherwise than by obtaining a court order for possession. Thus, in the case of a periodic assured tenancy, a notice to quit is of no effect. On the ending of a fixed-term assured tenancy (including a shorthold) otherwise than by an order of the court or by surrender, the tenant is entitled to remain in possession as a statutory periodic tenant. This statutory periodic tenancy will be on the same terms as the previous fixed-term tenancy.

5.4.15.2. Obtaining a court order

The landlord will only obtain a court order for possession if he follows the correct procedure and can establish one or more of the grounds for possession set out in Schedule 2 Housing Act 1988. Although some of these grounds are mandatory grounds, i.e. the court must order possession if the ground is established, many of them are discretionary grounds. With these, the court, on proof of the ground, may order possession only if it considers it reasonable to do so. The landlord must serve a notice on the tenant (a 'section 8 notice') in the prescribed form specifying the ground(s) upon which the landlord intends to rely and must give two weeks' notice of the landlord's intention to commence possession proceedings. (Sometimes two months' notice has to be given.) However, from the commencement of Housing Act 1996, if ground 14 is specified (whether or not with any other ground), then the proceedings can be commenced as soon as the section 8 notice has been served. The proceedings must then be commenced not earlier than the date specified and not later than 12 months from the date of service of the notice. It is possible for the court to dispense with the requirement for a section 8 notice (unless ground 8 is being relied upon), but only if it considers it just and equitable to do so.

5.4.15.3. In the case of a fixed-term assured tenancy, the landlord cannot normally obtain possession until after the end of the contractual fixed term (assuming that a ground for possession can then be established). However, as an exception to this, certain of the grounds for possession will be available to the landlord during the fixed term provided that the tenancy agreement contains a provision for it to be brought to an end on the ground in question. This provision can take any form at all, including a proviso for re-entry or a forfeiture clause. The grounds on which the landlord can obtain possession in this way during the fixed term are grounds 2, 8 and 10 to 15.

5.5.   **Shorthold tenancies**

5.5.1.   *Introduction*

A distinction must be drawn between 'old' shortholds, i.e. those entered into before the commencement of Housing Act 1996 and 'new' shortholds, i.e. those entered into on or after the commencement date of the Act.

5.5.2. An old shorthold is a fixed-term tenancy of at least six months' duration with no security of tenure. Thus, once the fixed term has expired the landlord has an absolute right to recover possession, provided that he complies with the correct procedure. Prior to the grant of the tenancy, however, the landlord must have served a notice on the tenant, in the prescribed form, warning him of the lack of security of tenure. This notice cannot be dispensed with.

5.5.3. From the commencement of Housing Act 1996, however, all new lettings (with certain exceptions) are deemed to be shortholds. The old conditions need no longer be complied with; the letting need not be for a fixed term, there is no need for a warning notice, etc. However, the landlord still has the same absolute right to possession as in an old shorthold.

5.5.4. Note, that 'old' shortholds continue as before and if one fails due to the conditions not having been complied with, e.g. no warning notice was served, the tenancy will still become a fully protected assured tenancy. This means that the conditions for the grant of an old shorthold are still of considerable practical importance even after the introduction of new shortholds.

5.5.5. The only disadvantage of a shorthold (whether new or old) from a landlord's point of view is the right given to the tenant to refer the rent initially payable to the Rent Assessment Committee. However, such Committee can only reduce the rent if it is 'significantly higher' than the rents under other comparable assured tenancies.

5.5.6.   Old shortholds

Section 20 Housing Act 1988 sets out the qualifying conditions for shortholds entered into before the commencement date of Housing Act 1996. It provides that an assured shorthold tenancy is an assured tenancy which:

(a)   is a fixed-term tenancy granted for a term of not less than six months; and

(b)   contains no power for the landlord to terminate it during the first six months; and

(c)   was preceded by the giving to the tenant of the prescribed shorthold notice.

5.5.6.1.   An assured tenancy

An assured shorthold tenancy is merely a type of assured tenancy. It must, therefore, comply with all the requirements of an assured tenancy (see para. 5.4. above). There must be a letting of a dwelling house to an individual who occupies the house as his only or principal home. Equally, none of the specific exclusions from the definition of an assured tenancy must apply. For example, high rental tenancies and lettings by resident landlords cannot be assured shortholds as they fall outside the definition of an assured tenancy.

5.5.6.2.   A shorthold cannot be granted to an existing tenant under an ordinary assured tenancy (or to one of joint tenants) if it is granted by the landlord under that existing tenancy. This is so even if the lettings are not of the same premises.

5.5.6.3.   Minimum six-month fixed term

The initial grant of a shorthold cannot be for a periodic term. It must be for a fixed term and for a minimum duration of six months. A letting for 'six months and then from month to month' is not a letting for a term certain and so cannot be a shorthold, even though it is for longer than the minimum six months. There is, however, no maximum length. Many shortholds are granted for the minimum six-month period and, in such a case, care must be taken to ensure that the tenant is given a right to occupy for the minimum period. The six-month period will run from the date on which the tenancy is entered into; it cannot be backdated. So a tenancy granted 'from and including 1 January 1994 until 30 June 1994' but not actually executed until 15 January 1994 would not give the tenant the requisite six months' occupation from the date of grant and so could not be a shorthold.

5.5.6.4.   Problems are likely to arise where a tenancy agreement is drawn up containing a fixed termination date and there is then a delay in the agreement being executed so that by the time that it is executed there then remains less than six months until the prescribed termination date. Such a letting would amount to an ordinary assured tenancy giving the tenant full security of tenure.

5.5.6.5. No power for landlord to terminate during first six months

Even if a minimum period of six months is granted, any power, however expressed, which would or might allow the landlord to terminate the tenancy within the first six months of the tenancy will prevent the tenancy from amounting to a shorthold. Break clauses exercisable outside that period are not prohibited, but care must be taken with such clauses to ensure that they are only exercisable outside the initial six months; otherwise an ordinary assured tenancy will be created giving the tenant full security of tenure. Note, however, that a forfeiture clause or a clause allowing termination on assured tenancy grounds 2, 8 and 10 to 15 will not breach this requirement even though it is exercisable during the first six months of the term. A term allowing the tenant to terminate during the first six months can be validly included. Such a provision, however, will not be implied. A tenant entering into a shorthold will, therefore, normally be contractually bound to pay the rent and perform the other obligations under the tenancy agreement for the full term entered into.

5.5.6.6. Preceded by the giving of the prescribed shorthold notice

As the tenant under an assured shorthold has no security of tenure, he has to be served with a notice prior to the grant of the tenancy warning him of this fact. This notice must be in the prescribed form.

5.5.6.7. The notice must be served before the tenancy agreement is entered into and not at the same time. Thus, it cannot be included in the tenancy agreement itself. It is best to ensure that there is an adequate interval between the service of the notice and the signing of the tenancy agreement to give the tenant the opportunity of digesting the contents of the notice. However, it appears from *Bedding v. McCarthy* [1994] 41 E.G. 151 that an interval of a few hours between the service of the section 20 notice and the tenancy agreement being entered into would be sufficient. In the case of joint tenants, all of the prospective tenants should be served. Common law rules as to service will apply (and not section 196 of Law of Property Act 1925) and so it is necessary to show that the notice actually came into the tenant's hands. It is advisable for a landlord to serve the notice in duplicate and to require all the prospective tenants to endorse one copy with an acknowledgement of receipt, and the date and time of receipt, and return this to the landlord before the tenancy agreement is entered into. Correct service of the current version of the shorthold notice is vital. The court has no power to dispense with these notice requirements even though it might be just and equitable to do so.

5.5.7. *New shortholds*

5.5.7.1. Definition

Shortholds entered into on or after the commencement date of Housing Act 1996 (otherwise than pursuant to a contract made before that date) are governed by Housing Act 1988, s.19A (as inserted by Housing Act 1996). This provides that any assured tenancy entered into on or after the commencement date will be a shorthold unless it falls within one of the specified exceptions.

5.5.7.2. There is no longer any need for a shorthold to be preceded by a prescribed form of notice. There is no need for a shorthold to be for a fixed term, it can be periodic; there is no need for a minimum period of six months; it can be for any period, no matter how short. However, although there is no prohibition on the landlord being able to terminate during the first six months, no order for possession using the shorthold ground can be made earlier than six months from the start of the tenancy, whether the tenancy is for a fixed term or is a periodic tenancy. However, this does not stop possession being obtained during the first six months using an assured tenancy ground, e.g. ground 14; a new shorthold, like an old shorthold, is merely a type of assured tenancy.

5.5.7.3. As a new shorthold is a type of assured tenancy, it must still comply with all the requirements of an assured tenancy (see para. 5.4.). A tenancy which falls outside the definition of an assured tenancy (e.g. due to the resident landlord rule) cannot be a shorthold either. Such a tenancy will be subject to ordinary common law rules as to termination.

5.5.7.4. Which lettings will not be new shortholds?

All new assured tenancies granted on or after the commencement date of Housing Act 1996 (other than those granted pursuant to a contract made before that date) will be shortholds subject to certain exceptions. These exceptions are set out in Schedule 2A to Housing Act 1988 as inserted by Housing Act 1996. The following lettings will be excluded and will thus take effect as ordinary assured tenancies:

(1) Tenancies excluded by notice.

The Schedule allows the landlord to serve a notice on the tenant either before or after the grant of the tenancy stating that the letting is not to be a shorthold. There is no prescribed form for this notice.

(2) Tenancies containing a provision stating that the tenancy is not to be a shorthold.

(3) Lettings to existing assured tenants.

A letting to an existing assured (i.e. not shorthold) tenant (whether alone or with others) by a person who is the landlord (or one of the landlords) under the existing tenancy will not be a shorthold unless the tenant serves notice on the landlord before the new tenancy is entered into that he wants it to be a shorthold. This notice must be in the prescribed form.

5.5.8. *Duty of landlord to provide a statement of the terms of a shorthold tenancy*

Under Housing Act 1988, s.20A (as inserted by Housing Act 1996), the landlord is placed under a duty in certain circumstances to provide a tenant with written details of the following terms provided that they are not already evidenced in writing:

(a) the commencement date of the tenancy;

(b) the rent payable and the dates on which it is payable;

(c) any terms providing for rent review;

(d) the length of a fixed term tenancy.

The tenant must make a request to the landlord in writing for this information.

5.5.9. It is a criminal offence to fail to provide the information within 28 days, unless the landlord has reasonable excuse. On summary conviction, the penalty is to be a fine not exceeding level 4.

5.5.10. The right only exists where the terms are not already evidenced in writing. The provision will only apply to tenancies granted orally, or those granted in writing which makes no reference to one or more of the specified matters.

5.5.11. A statement provided by the landlord is not to be regarded as conclusive evidence as to what was agreed between the parties. The statement is the landlord's version of what was agreed; it is still open to the tenant to allege that any particular term was not agreed to by him.

5.5.12. These provisions only apply to new shortholds, i.e. those to which Housing Act 1988, s.19A applies. They do not apply to old shortholds. However, on the ending of an old shorthold any new letting between the same parties will be a new shorthold, and these provisions will then apply.

5.5.13. *Rent Control*

The protection given differs depending upon whether the tenant has a new shorthold or an old shorthold, but the general principles are the same for both.

5.5.14. On the granting of the tenancy, the landlord can charge such rent for the premises as the market will bear. There is no statutory restriction on the amount of rent chargeable. Any existing registration of a 'fair rent' under the provisions of Rent Act 1977 can be ignored, as can any rental figure previously determined by the Rent Assessment Committee under these provisions. However, an assured shorthold tenant can apply to the local Rent Assessment Committee for the determination of the rent which, in the Committee's opinion, the landlord might reasonably be expected to obtain under the shorthold tenancy.

5.5.15. If the tenant has an old shorthold, he can apply at any time during the tenancy.

5.5.16. If the tenant has a new shorthold, whether for a fixed term or a periodic letting, he cannot apply if more than six months have elapsed since the beginning of the tenancy. If the tenancy is a 'replacement tenancy', i.e. a second or subsequent shorthold between the same parties and of the same property, the application cannot be made if more than six months have elapsed from the commencement of the first shorthold between the parties.

5.5.17. *The effect of a determination by the Rent Assessment Committee*

If a rent is determined by the Committee, the effect again differs between old and new shortholds.

5.5.18. In the case of old shortholds and fixed-term new shortholds, the rent as assessed will become the maximum rent chargeable for the property throughout the remainder of the fixed term. This is despite anything to the contrary in the tenancy agreement. There is no provision for this figure to be increased during the fixed term, no matter how long the unexpired term of the tenancy.

5.5.19. In the case of a new shorthold which is a periodic tenancy, again the rent once fixed will, in theory, remain fixed throughout the tenancy. However, in practice, once 12 months have expired, the landlord will then be able to make an application under Housing Act 1988, ss.13 and 14 to increase the rent.

5.5.20. With both old and new shortholds, once the rent has been determined by the Committee no further application for the fixing of a different figure can be made by either landlord or tenant. However, the rent determined by the Committee only has relevance to the particular tenancy in question. It will not limit the amount of rent chargeable under any subsequent letting, even if this is between the same parties. Further, in the absence of a further grant, on the ending of a fixed-term shorthold (whether old or new), a statutory periodic tenancy will arise and the provisions of Housing Act 1988 ss.13 and 14 will again apply to allow the landlord to increase the rent.

5.5.21. *When is an application to the Rent Assessment Committee not possible?*

The restrictions on tenants with new shortholds applying have been dealt with in para. 5.5.16. above.

5.5.22. As far as old shorthold tenants are concerned, it is not possible for the tenant to refer the rent to the Rent Assessment Committee once the original term of the shorthold has expired. This is so even if a new letting is entered into between the same parties and irrespective of whether an application was made during the original shorthold.

5.5.23. With both old and new shortholds, only one application to the Committee can be made. Once the rent has been determined by the Committee, it cannot be resubmitted for a further determination, even if the original determination was many years before and open market rents have fallen in the meantime.

5.5.24. *What happens when a shorthold expires?*

On the expiry of a fixed-term tenancy, the tenant is allowed to remain in possession as a statutory periodic tenant. However, the tenant still has no security of tenure.

Under Housing Act 1988, s.21(1) the court must still make an order for possession if the landlord follows the correct procedure. This involves the service on the tenant of not less than two months' notice stating that the landlord requires possession.

5.5.25. *What happens if a new tenancy is granted?*

Although there are differences between new and old shortholds, the basic principle remains the same; if the parties are the same, any new tenancy of the same (or substantially the same) premises will be deemed to be a shorthold unless the landlord serves notice on the tenant that the new letting is not to be a shorthold.

5.5.26. In the case of an old shorthold, the effect of this deeming provision is that the new tenancy will be a shorthold even though it does not comply with the normal requirements for an old shorthold. So no shorthold notice need have been served, the letting need not be for a fixed term, i.e. a periodic shorthold is permissible, and any fixed term need not be for a minimum period of six months. However, the new tenancy must still comply with the normal requirements for an assured tenancy, e.g. the tenant must still be occupying the house as his only or principal home.

5.5.27. A further feature of a deemed shorthold following an old shorthold is that there is no right to refer the rent to the Rent Assessment Committee. This is the case whether or not an application was made to the Committee during the initial shorthold term. In the case of a tenancy following a new shorthold, the second tenancy will be a 'replacement tenancy' and an application to the Rent Assessment Committee cannot be made more than six months from the commencement of the original tenancy. So in the unlikely event of a new shorthold granted for three months, followed by a replacement tenancy granted for (say) six months, an application to the Rent Assessment Committee could be made during the first three months of that replacement tenancy.

5.5.28. In any event, if a rent was determined by the Committee during the initial term this will not limit the amount of rent chargeable by the landlord under the new tenancy agreement.

5.5.29. *How does the landlord obtain possession?*

Unless the tenant leaves voluntarily, the landlord must apply to the court and obtain an order for possession. The court must order possession provided that the landlord follows the correct procedure. This involves the landlord serving a notice on the tenant (the 'section 21 notice') giving the tenant at least two months' notice that he requires possession.

5.5.30. Possession cannot be obtained using this shorthold procedure during the continuance of a fixed term; possession is only available after its expiry (although the procedure can be set in motion during the fixed term so that possession can be obtained as soon as it has ended). Note also that in the case of a new shorthold possession cannot be obtained within six months of the commencement of the term using the shorthold procedure. This is so whether the tenancy is a fixed term or is periodic.

5.5.31. *Grounds for possession*

A shorthold is a type of assured tenancy and so, during the term, the mandatory and discretionary grounds which apply to ordinary assured tenancies can also apply. Mandatory ground 8 and discretionary grounds 10 and 11 (all of which relate to rent arrears) can be used during the subsistence of the shorthold should the landlord be faced with a defaulting tenant. However, in the case of a fixed-term letting, as with other assured tenancies, these grounds can be used during the fixed term only if the tenancy agreement so provides.

5.5.32. In the case of a shorthold which is a periodic tenancy, the ordinary assured tenancy grounds will be available to a landlord without the need for any such provision in the tenancy agreement.

5.5.33. In the case of a fixed-term shorthold, however, it is always sensible to insert a provision allowing the landlord to terminate the tenancy on the specified grounds. In the case of an old shorthold, this is permissible despite the usual rule that there must be no power for the landlord to terminate within the first six months of the tenancy. This rule does not apply to termination because of a breach of the terms of the tenancy, e.g. non-payment of rent. Similarly, in the case of new shortholds, although possession cannot be obtained using the shorthold procedure within six months of the commencement, possession can be obtained during that period using the ordinary assured grounds provided that they are satisfied.

5.5.34. When the landlord is seeking to obtain possession on one of the ordinary assured grounds, then the procedure relevant to an ordinary assured tenancy should be followed, and not the shorthold procedure. In particular, this will mean that a section 8 notice will have to be served on the tenant before proceedings can be commenced, and not a section 21 notice.

5.6. Long tenancies at low rents

5.6.1. Rent Act 1977 (as with previous Rent Acts) gave no protection to the tenant where the rent payable under the tenancy was less than two-thirds of the rateable value of the dwelling on the appropriate day (as defined in the Act), with the result that most tenants of dwellings under long tenancies at ground rents had no security of tenure when their contractual tenancies expired. Part I Landlord and Tenant Act 1954 extended to many such tenants the protection of Rent Act 1977 (and its predecessors) when their tenancies expired. Part I applied to a tenancy granted for over 21 years at a rent of less than two-thirds of the rateable value of the property where 'the circumstances (as respects the property comprised in the tenancy, the use of the property, and all other relevant matters) are such that on the coming to an end of the tenancy ... the tenant would, if the tenancy had not been one at a low rent, be entitled by virtue of the Rent Acts to retain possession of the whole or part of the property comprised in the tenancy'.

5.6.2. *Security of tenure*

A long tenancy within Part I Landlord and Tenant Act 1954 is continued by Rent Act 1977 until determined in accordance with the statute. The landlord may terminate by notice expiring on or after the term date of the tenancy, but his notice must either propose a Rent Act statutory tenancy or state that he is seeking a court order for possession. The grounds on which an order for possession can be made are contained in section 12 and Schedule 3 Landlord and Tenant Act 1954, as amended by Leasehold Reform Act 1967, s.38.

5.6.3. The Rent Act regime applicable on the termination of these long tenancies (unless the landlord obtains possession) is eventually to be replaced by the assured tenancy regime under section 186 and Schedule 10 Local Government and Housing Act 1989.

5.7. **Agricultural employees**

5.7.1. Security of tenure for farm workers living in accommodation provided by their employers is governed by either Rent (Agriculture) Act 1976 or Housing Act 1988, depending on the date of the grant of the tenancy.

5.7.2. To gain the protection of the 1976 Act, the employee must generally have spent two years whole time in agriculture; he then becomes a protected occupier of the house. If as a result of a notice to quit or otherwise he ceases to be a protected occupier, he becomes a statutory tenant of the house under terms laid down by the Act.

5.7.3. The court cannot make an order for possession of a house subject to a protected occupancy or statutory tenancy under the 1976 Act except on the grounds set out in the Act. Special provisions apply to the rehousing of agricultural employees. The provisions for rent control in the Act apply only to statutory tenancies.

5.7.4. Farm workers who enjoyed the protection of Rent Act 1977 (e.g. because they were tenants paying an economic rent) were equated to those protected by the 1976 Act by Rent Act 1977, s.99.

5.7.5. Farm workers with tenancies or licences granted before 15 January 1989 retain their protection under the 1976 Act. Tenancies or licences granted on or after that date are governed by Housing Act 1988. This Act introduced the assured agricultural occupancy, which qualifies for protection if it is an assured tenancy or would be such except for the fact that the rent (outside London) is less than £250 per annum or the fact that the house forms part of an agricultural holding and is occupied by the person responsible for the control of the farming. A licence to occupy which confers exclusive occupation and which fulfils the requisite conditions will also qualify. An assured shorthold is excluded from the definition, thus enabling the owner to create a tenancy giving a mandatory right to possession.

5.7.6. In the case of tenancies or licences governed by Housing Act 1988, the main change is in regard to rent. The provisions of the Act in regard to the increase of rents under assured tenancies apply to assured agricultural occupancies, so that on a reference of a notice of increase of rent to a Rent Assessment Committee an open market rent can be fixed.

5.7.7. An occupier of agricultural land may apply to the housing authority concerned (i.e. the local housing authority as defined by Housing Act 1985) to rehouse a tenant on the ground that the land occupier requires the dwelling house to provide accommodation for an agricultural employee, the land occupier being unable to provide the present tenant with suitable alternative accommodation. The housing authority in reaching its decision on whether to rehouse the tenant must have regard to the advice tendered to them by the Agricultural Dwelling-House Advisory Committee.[1]

1. See Rent (Agriculture) Act 1976, ss.27–29.

FURTHER REFERENCE

Drafting Residential Leases, C. Bennett, F.T. Law & Tax.

Woodfall's Law of Landlord and Tenant, Sweet & Maxwell.

Residential Landlord and Tenant, P. Butt, Jordans.

Manual of Housing Law, A. Arden and C. Hunter, Sweet & Maxwell.

K.06. Long-term residential tenancies

6.1. Grant of lease

6.1.1. The grant or assignment of a long lease of a house or flat is similar to the grant or assignment of a lease of other premises. The matters to which particular attention needs to be paid when dealing with this type of lease are merely highlighted here.

6.1.2. The lease of a flat is frequently a complex document which should be specifically drafted to suit the individual requirements of the site. Except in the most straight-forward cases, copying a precedent directly from a book or the reuse of a lease drafted for another development will not suffice. The client's attention should be directed to the need for a site inspection before drafting of the lease is commenced so that the following points can be correctly dealt with in the lease:

(a) What is the structure of the building composed of? Repairing covenants must be drafted appropriately so that a covenant, e.g. 'to repair main walls and timbers' will be inappropriate where the building is of concrete construction.

(b) Access: the lease must deal with easements of access, e.g. is there a right of way over the drive from the public highway to the entrance of the flats, how does each tenant get from the door of the building to the door of his own flat, is there to be a lift, does each tenant require access to the dustbin area, etc.?

(c) Where do the mains services run? Which tenants need easements for pipes, cables, etc., to pass through another flat or common parts on the way to or from their own flat?

(d) Amenities: who is to have a garage or parking space, are these to be a part of the demise (i.e. a specific allocated space) or is there to be just a licence to use a garage/parking space (with no guarantee that a space will actually be available), use of gardens, is there communal central heating, is there an entry-phone system, is there a communal television or satellite aerial, are individual aerials to be permitted, is there a caretaker's flat?

(e) Service charges: what services are to be included in the charge, will all tenants have the benefit of all the services supplied, should the service charge be split equally between all the tenants or should some pay a greater proportion than others or should different proportions apply to different services?

(f) Check site and floor plans against the physical extent of the building both in relation to the whole building and individual flats, are they accurate, which tenants need which plans, are they coloured in accordance with HM Land Registry recommendations?

6.1.3. *Checklist of items to be sent to buyer's solicitor*

NB: Not all of the following will be relevant in every transaction:

(a) draft contract in duplicate;

(b) draft lease in duplicate;

(c) copy head lease;

(d) other evidence of superior and reversionary titles;

(e) draft agreement between landlord and management company for transfer of reversion to management company;

(f) copy memorandum and articles of management company;

(g) copy local authority search and enquiries with replies;

(h) copy planning permissions and building regulation consents;

(i) copy indemnity insurance policy covering defects in title, restrictive covenants, etc;

(j) copy of approved estate layout plan as deposited at HM Land Registry;

(k) copy replies to enquiries before contract (Seller's Property Information Form and Additional Property Information Form in Protocol cases);

(l) copy insurance policy and schedules;

(m) copy guarantees, e.g. for repairs to structure;

(n) documentation relating to insurance against structural defects, e.g. NHBC or similar;

(o) estimated service charge calculation;

(p) audited accounts of the management company.

6.2. **Enforcement of covenants in flats**

6.2.1. The landlord for the time being can almost always enforce covenants in the lease against the tenant for the time being of each flat, because he enjoys privity of estate and in many cases also privity of contract with each tenant. Prima facie there is neither privity of contract nor of estate between the tenants and, although they will each be bound by identical covenants in their leases, without some device in the leases they cannot sue each other directly for breach of the tenants' covenants in their respective leases. It is advisable that the lease contains some method of allowing mutual enforceability of covenants between the tenants, particularly in relation to covenants concerning use, structural repair and noise.

6.2.2. This can be achieved either by taking a covenant in each lease that the landlord will if so requested by a tenant take action to enforce a breach of covenant committed by another tenant in the same block. Such a covenant usually requires the requesting tenant to provide a complete indemnity to the landlord against the costs of the action and provides an effective although cumbersome method of mutual enforceability of covenants. Alternatively, the tenant can enter a direct covenant in the lease with the landlord and the *other tenants*. By so doing, one tenant can directly sue another tenant without having to invoke the landlord's covenant to sue. Although this type of covenant does provide direct enforceability between tenants, it depends for its validity against a successor in title of the original tenant upon a covenant in the lease that the outgoing tenant will require an assignee to enter a direct deed of covenant with the landlord that he will observe all the covenants in the lease, and the assignee actually executing such a deed.

6.2.3. As an alternative the building scheme principle may be used.[1] The result of an effective scheme is to make restrictive covenants enforceable by and against all present and future tenants. The requirements of such a scheme are:

    (a) a common landlord;

    (b) an intention to impose the same restrictions on all the flats;

    (c) an intention that all the tenants should benefit from these restrictions;

    (d) the flats are acquired on the basis that the restrictions are for the benefit of other flats;

    (e) the area affected by the scheme is clearly defined.

6.2.4. To show that the covenants are intended to be mutually enforceable an appropriate clause expressing this intention should be included in the lease. This type of scheme only works for restrictive and not for positive covenants.

6.2.5. Where a management company is to perform the landlord's obligations under the lease it should give a direct covenant to the tenants (in each lease) to undertake performance of these obligations, the landlord remaining liable if the management company defaults. The lease should provide that on assignment a direct deed of covenant is entered into between the assignee and the management company. This clause will be recorded as a restriction on the register of title. There is some doubt as to whether such a covenant in the lease touches and concerns the land; the benefit and burden may not therefore pass under the principles of privity of estate.

1. *Elliston* v. *Reacher* [1908] 2 Ch. 865.

6.3. Management schemes

6.3.1. Any management scheme must ensure that the rights and obligations of both the landlord and the tenants under the lease are always enforceable. The landlord's objectives in setting up such a scheme are to provide for the maintenance and repair of the block. The type of scheme employed will depend on the landlord's particular requirements in relation to the flats concerned.

6.3.2. If the landlord is to retain the reversion of the block he may choose to carry out the landlord's functions personally or through a managing agent. From the landlord's point of view this arrangement has the disadvantage of the work involved and from the tenants' point of view it has the disadvantage that the tenants have no control over the way in which their block is managed.

6.3.3. Another type of arrangement is for the tenants to covenant with each other by separate deed of covenant to perform the obligations of repairing, etc., the common parts. Such a scheme is not binding on future assignees unless the lease obliges them to enter into similar deeds of covenant as a condition of their assignment.

6.3.4. Alternatively, the landlord may vest the reversion (with its obligations) in trustees (who would be representatives of the tenants) on trust for the tenants as a whole. This type of scheme is only suitable for the management of small blocks and saves the expense in that situation of setting up and running a management company.

6.3.5. Most larger blocks have schemes which entail the use of a management company. The landlord will transfer his reversion to the management company which will then assume the responsibility for performance of the landlord's covenants in the lease. Until transfer the landlord will be responsible for the management company's duties and should ideally expressly covenant to this effect in the lease. A management company can either be limited by shares or guarantee and is commonly purchased as a ready-made company. The management company should be a party to the lease and enter into direct covenants with the tenant for the performance of the maintenance obligations. Each tenant must be required to become a member of the company and to transfer his share in the company to an assignee on sale of the lease. Such a scheme allows the tenants to have absolute control over the management of their block, but carries with it the responsibility of performance of the maintenance obligations and duties in relation to the company itself under the Companies Acts. The landlord may reserve the right to take over the management company's responsibilities in the event of default by the company.

6.3.6. If maintenance is to be carried out by a maintenance trustee company, the tenant's solicitor should be satisfied as to the integrity of the trustee company. If this has been set up by a third party, the tenant will have no control over the company, and thus needs to be assured that the trustees (and any potential successors to the original trustees) are sound and responsible.

6.4. Other matters to be considered

6.4.1. The landlord may wish to reserve the right to prepare the engrossment of the lease himself. Such right must be expressly reserved in the contract and any fee payable by the tenant for the engrossment must be reasonable.

6.4.2. Where the landlord is to retain the reversion (and the liability for performance of the landlord's covenants in the lease) consideration may be given by the landlord to the appointment of reliable managing agents to carry out the landlord's duties under the lease.

6.4.3. On completion apportionments of the rent and service charge will have to be made. Apportionments of service charge will at this stage have to be made on an estimated basis and settled at the end of the first accounting period. The Standard Conditions of Sale do not provide for apportionments to be made on completion of the grant of a new lease and a special condition to such effect is necessary.

6.4.4. Where a management company is to perform the landlord's covenants under the lease, the company must be set up and share certificates and the company books prepared in readiness for completion.

6.4.5. The term dates of all the leases should commence on the same date (irrespective of the dates of completion of the various leases) otherwise it becomes very difficult to know precisely when performance of the covenants to decorate is due.

6.4.6. Apportionment of rent

This should be done by the method recommended by the Law Society explained in paras. K.02.6.4.–K.02.6.7. above.

6.5. Maisonettes

6.5.1. Where a maisonette is being purchased, particular care needs to be exercised to ensure that the lease is quite specific as to the ownership and rights over the various parts of the property (especially common parts). Each tenant may be the freeholder of the other tenant's property; they will thus be jointly responsible for the maintenance and upkeep of the structure and common parts. Such a demise will create a flying freehold of part of the upper maisonette. A maintenance trustee company may be set up to deal with maintenance and repair.

6.6. Lenders' requirements

6.6.1. Apart from any particular conditions contained in the mortgage offer or instructions to the solicitor, a lender is usually concerned with the following matters:

(a) to ensure that the lease contains proper provision for the mutual enforceability of covenants between tenants;

(b) to ensure that the property is leasehold and that the lease contains adequate repairing covenants relating to the flat itself, the exterior structure and the common parts of the building;

(c) that the lease contains adequate provision for the insurance of the whole building;

(d) that the length of the term of the lease (or unexpired residue in the case of an assignment) is sufficient to permit a resale of the premises on the open market. A term which will have less than 20 years unexpired after the end of the mortgage term may be considered inadequate in the context of normal residential conveyancing;

(e) that the lease contains no provision for forfeiture on the insolvency of the tenant;

(f) that the lease contains no restrictions on alienation which may hinder a sale on the open market;

(g) that the lease is or will be registered at HM Land Registry with an absolute leasehold title;

(h) where the tenant is to become a member of a management company, the mortgagee sometimes requires that a blank form of share transfer (signed by the mortgagor) and the tenant's share certificate is deposited with the lender to enable the lender to transfer that share to a buyer should he need to exercise his power of sale. A copy of the management company's memorandum and articles may also have to be deposited with the lender;

(i) that notices have been given to the landlord of any previous assignments or mortgages;

(j) that the lease reserves an adequate ground rent to ensure that the landlord has a sufficient financial interest in the building for him to have the incentive to perform his obligations under the lease and that there will be no shortfall in the service charge fund should another lease in the block be forfeited;

(k) if the property being purchased is held under a sub-lease (so that the landlord's own interest is leasehold), it is desirable that the aggregate ground rents payable by the flats in the block should exceed the amount of rent payable by the landlord to the freeholder. If this is not the case the landlord will have little incentive to pay his own rent, and thus the sub-tenants of the flats would be put at risk from forfeiture of the head-lease. For this reason it is desirable that in any situation where sub-letting is permitted the tenant should be required to enter a covenant with his landlord not to sub-let the whole at a rent lower than that payable under his own lease.

6.6.2. *Standard Mortgage Instructions*

Where the Standard Mortgage Instructions (SMI) apply, specific requirements in relation to the mortgage of leasehold property must be observed.[1]

1 At the time of publication the SMI had not been finalised.

6.7. **The Protocol**

6.7.1. The Protocol makes no direct reference to the grant of a lease.

6.7.2. On the sale of an existing lease paragraph 2.8 requires the seller's solicitor to ask his client to produce, if possible:

    (a) a receipt or evidence from the landlord of the last payment of rent;

    (b) the maintenance charge accounts for the last three years, where appropriate, and evidence of payment;

    (c) details of the buildings insurance policy.

6.7.3. If any of these are lacking and are necessary to the transaction the solicitor should obtain them from the landlord. Investigation should also be made as to the necessity for a licence to assign, and whether, in the case of a retirement scheme, any charge is payable to the management company on the change of ownership. The documents and information obtained in relation to the above matters should be given or communicated to the buyer's solicitor when the pre-contract documentation is sent to him (paragraph 4.3).

6.8. **Service charges**

6.8.1. Service charge accounts must be examined carefully and the buyer advised as to his potential liability under the lease.

6.8.2. Statutory provisions relating to service charges are now contained in Landlord and Tenant Act 1985, ss.18–30, as amended. For the purposes of these provisions, a service charge is an amount payable by a tenant as part of or in addition to rent:

    (a) which is payable, directly or indirectly, for services, repairs, maintenance or insurance or the landlord's costs of management; and

    (b) the whole or part of which varies or may vary according to the relevant costs.

6.8.3. The statutory provisions now apply to a lease of any dwelling (including houses as well as flats) except that they do not apply to lettings by certain bodies such as local authorities unless the tenancy is a long tenancy as defined in Landlord and Tenant Act 1985, s.26(2).

6.8.4. The statutes impose certain limitations and obligations on landlords which are not set out in detail here but which relate to the following:

    (a) limitations on the amount recoverable;

    (b) estimates for work to be done and the giving of notices;

    (c) time-limits on making demands for service charges;

    (d) the tenant's right to apply for a summary of costs incurred and to inspect the landlord's accounts;

    (e) the landlord's duty to pass on requests for a summary of the relevant costs to a superior landlord;

    (f) service charge contributions to be held in trust.

6.8.5. A buyer of the reversion on a lease reserving a service charge and a buyer of a lease subject to such a charge should be aware of the following matters:

    (a) the statutory provisions outlined above;

    (b) that the obligation to pay a service charge can arise only from an express provision in the lease and the extent of the obligation depends on the wording of such provision. Whether or not the landlord can recover from non-defaulting tenants his legal costs incurred in recovering rent and service charge contributions depends on the wording of the tenant's covenant, and the same is true in respect of a landlord's interest payments on money borrowed to finance the provision of works and services;

    (c) ideally the landlord's obligation should match with the service charge provisions. If the obligations are not matched the landlord may find that he is obliged to provide more services than he can charge for or conversely that the tenants cannot force the landlord to, e.g. carry out repairs because the landlord's covenant does not extend to this matter;

    (d) the manner in which the total service charge is to be apportioned between the various tenants;

    (e) whether or not the landlord can require payment of a charge in advance of expenditure;

    (f) the statutory provisions do not apply to contribution covenants concerned with improvements as distinct from repairs;

    (g) where premises are let wholly or mainly as a dwelling for less than seven years, a service charge provision cannot cast on the tenant the cost of matters falling within the landlord's repairing obligation under Landlord and Tenant Act 1985, ss.11–16;

    (h) a provision in the lease enabling the landlord to make an interim service charge is desirable. In the absence of such a provision a landlord may be disinclined to carry out expensive repairs or to provide services since he would have to bear the cost of these matters himself seeking recovery of the sums from the tenants at a later date.

6.8.6. The amount of service charge payable will be of particular concern to the buyer of a lease. The Protocol requires production of the maintenance accounts for the last three years which should give some indication of the amounts involved, although sums expended will frequently vary from year to year. A substantial sum recently spent on repairs and redecoration of the exterior of a building may indicate that a similar item should not recur for some time. In each case enquiry should be made of the particular circumstances relating to the building.

6.8.7. The apportionment of a service charge on a sale may create a problem as the amounts payable may not be determined at the time of completion. Standard Condition 6.3.5 provides that when any sums to be apportioned are not known or easily ascertainable a provisional apportionment is to be made on completion according to the best estimate available. As soon after completion as the amount is known, a final apportionment is to be made and notified to the other party and any resulting balance paid no more than 10 working days later, interest calculated at the contract rate being chargeable for late payment.

6.8.8. Sections 45–51 of the Housing Act 1985 (as amended by Landlord and Tenant Act 1987, s.41) contain restrictions on service charges where a house has been disposed of by a public sector authority other than under a long lease.

6.8.9. A landlord may not forfeit the lease of a dwelling house for failure to pay a service charge unless the amount of the service charge is agreed or admitted by the tenant or has been determined by a court or tribunal.[1]

1. Housing Act 1996, s.81.

6.9. **Appointment of manager**

6.9.1. Where a landlord has not complied with his obligations under the terms of the lease, a tenant of a flat may, after serving a preliminary notice on his landlord (and the landlord's lender where relevant), apply to the court under Part II Landlord and Tenant Act 1987 (as amended by Housing Act 1996) for the appointment of a manager to carry out the landlord's management functions. These provisions apply to premises where the building or part of a building consists of two or more flats except *inter alia* where the landlord is an exempt or resident landlord as defined in para. K.09.3. below.

FURTHER REFERENCE

Law of Flats, T.M. Aldridge, F.T. Law & Tax.

The Sale and Management of Flats: Practice and Precedents, J. Cawthorn, Butterworths.

The Sale of Flats, E.F. George and J.P. George, Sweet & Maxwell.

K.07. Business premises

See also: VAT, para. A.16.
Acting on grant of lease, para. K.01.
Assignment of leases, para. K.11.

7.1.   Business tenancies

7.1.1.   Part II Landlord and Tenant Act 1954 (as amended) established a comprehensive code of security of tenure for business tenants. The following paragraphs provide only an introduction to this very complex subject. At the time of publication the Law Commission have published a report[1] which, if implemented, would make some minor changes to the law contained in the following paragraphs.

7.1.2.   The Act applies to a tenancy where the property comprised in the tenancy is or includes premises which are occupied by the tenant and are so occupied for the purposes of a business carried on by him or for those and other purposes.

7.1.3.   The word 'business' is widely defined to include a trade, profession or employment and includes any activity carried on by a body of persons, whether corporate or unincorporate.

1. Law Comm. No. 208.

7.2.   Exclusions from the Act

7.2.1.   These include:

(a)   agricultural holdings;

(b)   mining leases;

(c)   written service tenancies;

(d)   tenancies at will;

(e)   tenancies granted for a term certain not exceeding six months (unless the tenancy contains provisions for renewing the term or for extending it beyond six months or the tenant has been in occupation in any capacity for over one year);

(f) tenancies for a term certain where the court's approval to the exclusion from protection has been obtained prior to the commencement of the tenancy.

7.2.2. Subject to para. 7.2.1.(f) above, where a tenancy is within the provisions of the Act it is not possible to exclude the operation of the Act by agreement between the parties.

7.3. Termination of tenancy

7.3.1. A tenancy within the Act can only be determined by one of the methods prescribed by the Act. These include:

(a) forfeiture;

(b) notice to quit given by the tenant;

(c) immediate surrender;[1]

(d) service by the landlord of a notice under Landlord and Tenant Act 1954, s.25;

(e) a tenant's request for a new tenancy under Landlord and Tenant Act 1954, s.26;

(f) notice served under section 27 of the Act.

7.3.2. Where the tenant has a periodic tenancy, his notice to quit will be of the length appropriate to the period of his tenancy (e.g. one month's notice for a monthly tenancy). In the case of a fixed-term tenancy, the tenant may serve a three-month notice under section 27 of the Act to expire on the term date or on any quarter day after the term date.

7.3.3. A tenancy which is not determined by one of the above methods continues to run (despite expiry of a fixed term) on the same terms until terminated by one of these methods.

1. An agreement for the tenant to surrender his tenancy at some future time is void under Landlord and Tenant Act 1954, s.38 except if authorised by the court.

7.4. Landlord's notice

7.4.1. A notice to terminate a tenancy served by a landlord under Landlord and Tenant Act 1954, s.25 must be in a prescribed form and must specify a date (not earlier than the term date and not less than six nor more than 12 months ahead) on which the tenancy is to end. The notice must require the tenant to notify the landlord whether or not the tenant is willing to give up possession and must state whether the landlord would oppose the application to the court for a new tenancy and, if so, on what ground(s).[1]

7.4.2. If the tenant wants a new tenancy, he must notify the landlord to this effect within two months of the landlord's notice and should apply to the court for a new tenancy not less than two nor more than four months after service of the landlord's notice. A tenant's application to the court is a pending land action and should be protected by a caution in registered land (or by an entry in the register of pending land actions in the case of unregistered land). If the tenant is in occupation of registered land, his application will be protected as an overriding interest under Land Registration Act 1925, s.70(1)(*g*).

7.4.3. The landlord's grounds for opposing the grant of a new tenancy are contained in Landlord and Tenant Act 1954, s.30 and are briefly as follows:

(a) breach of repairing obligations by the tenant;

(b) persistent delay in paying rent;

(c) substantial breaches of other obligations under the tenancy;

(d) alternative accommodation;

(e) possession of whole property required where tenant has a sub-tenancy of part;

(f) landlord's intention to demolish or reconstruct the property;

(g) landlord requires possession for his own purposes.[2]

7.4.4. The time-limits specified in the Act for service of notices and application to the court are construed strictly and in general no extension of those limits is permitted. Thus if a tenant fails to serve a counter-notice on the landlord within the prescribed period he will lose his right to a new tenancy. Similarly, the right to a new tenancy will be lost if the tenant does not make his application to the court *between* two and four months after service of the original notice terminating the tenancy.

1. See above, para. 7.4.3.
2. This ground is not available to a landlord whose interest was purchased or created within the five years preceding the termination date of the tenancy as specified in the notice terminating the tenancy (provided that the tenancy or series of tenancies was existing at the time of creation and has continued uninterrupted since that time).

7.5. Tenant's request for a new tenancy

7.5.1. A tenant's request for a new tenancy can be made only if the tenant originally had a tenancy for a term of years certain exceeding one year. It must be in prescribed form and must specify a date (not earlier than the term date and not less than six nor more than 12 months ahead) for the start of the new tenancy. If the landlord wishes to oppose the grant of a new tenancy, he must notify the tenant within two months, stating on which ground(s) he will rely.[1] The tenant must then apply to the court for a new tenancy not less than two months and not more than four months from the service of his request.[2] A tenant's application to the court is a pending land action and should be protected by a caution in registered land (or by an entry in the register of pending land actions in the case of unregistered land). If the tenant is in occupation of registered land, his application will be protected as an overriding interest under Land Registration Act 1925, s.70(1)(*g*).

1. See above, para. 7.4.3.
2. See above, para. 7.4.4.

7.6. Application to the court

7.6.1. Unless the landlord can establish one or more of the grounds for possession within section 30(1) of the Act,[1] a new tenancy must be ordered by the court comprising such holding (i.e. the part of the property occupied by the tenant), at such rent and on such other terms as the court orders (in the absence of agreement between the parties), although the new tenancy cannot, in the absence of agreement, exceed 14 years in length.[2]

1. See above, para. 7.4.3.
2. See ss.32−35 of the Act.

7.7. Compensation

7.7.1. If the landlord succeeds in obtaining possession, based on a ground which involves no fault on the part of the tenant (other than the alternative accommodation ground), the tenant is entitled to compensation for giving up his tenancy.

7.7.2. In certain circumstances a tenant of business premises may also be entitled to compensation for improvements effected by him under Landlord and Tenant Act 1927.

7.8. Rent control

7.8.1. There are no statutory limitations on the rent recoverable on the original grant of a tenancy of business premises, but on a renewal the court can fix a new rent failing agreement by the parties. The court also has power, on application, to fix an interim rent pending the outcome of proceedings.

7.9. Buying a business lease

7.9.1. A prospective purchaser of a lease of business premises should (in addition to the usual matters to be considered on the assignment of a lease) pay careful attention to the following matters:

    (a) the rent review provisions contained in the lease;

    (b) the repairing obligations imposed by the lease;

    (c) any service charge provisions in the lease;

    (d) the VAT implications of the transaction;

    (e) whether the existing tenant has committed any breach of covenant which would give the landlord the right to determine the lease or to refuse a renewal of it;

    (f) the likelihood of a lease renewal being opposed by a landlord on other grounds, e.g. redevelopment;

    (g) the provisions relating to alienation of the lease.

7.10. **Covenants restricting assignment**

7.10.1. Where the lease being assigned was granted before 1 January 1996 or was granted after that date but is not classified as a 'new' tenancy under Landlord and Tenant (Covenants) Act 1995 (e.g. is granted pursuant to an option dated before 1 January 1996), the following provisions apply.

7.10.2. Where a lease contains a covenant prohibiting assignment without the landlord's consent, that consent is not to be unreasonably withheld (section 19(1) Landlord and Tenant Act 1927). Guidelines for testing reasonableness are set out in the Court of Appeal decision in *International Drilling Fluids Ltd* v. *Louisville Investments (Uxbridge) Ltd*[1]:

    (a) the purpose of the covenant is to protect the landlord from an undesirable tenant or from an undesirable use being made of the premises;

    (b) a landlord cannot, therefore, refuse consent on grounds which have nothing to do with the relationship of landlord and tenant;

    (c) as long as the landlord's conclusions were those which a reasonable man might reach he does not have to prove they were justified;

    (d) it may be reasonable for a landlord to withhold consent on the grounds of the proposed use of the premises even though the proposed use of the premises is not prohibited by the lease;

    (e) normally a landlord need have regard only to his own interests but it may be that the detriment caused to the tenant by withholding consent so outweighs the advantage to the landlord that it is unreasonable for consent to be withheld.

Subject to these considerations, whether a landlord is acting reasonably is a question of fact in each case. A lease cannot set out what is to be considered reasonable, although a condition precedent can be imposed.[2] Under Landlord and Tenant Act 1988, a landlord must give consent within a reasonable time unless there is a reason for withholding it. Reasons for refusal must be given within a reasonable time. The burden of proving that the withholding of consent is reasonable is on the landlord.

7.10.3 The above provisions have been amended[3] in relation to assignments of new tenancies (granted on or after 1 January 1996) of commercial premises and provides as follows:

7.10.4. A landlord may agree in advance with his tenant:

    (a) any circumstance in which he may withhold consent to a proposed assignment; or

    (b) any conditions subject to which his consent will be granted, and if he withholds consent for these reasons he is not acting unreasonably. The agreement has to be made before the application for consent but does not have to be contained in the lease nor made at the same time as the lease.

The 1995 Act distinguishes between factual matters, for example:

    (a) the assignee must be a plc;

    (b) the assignee must have net assets equal to a specified multiplier of the rent;

    (c) the assignee must provide a rent deposit; or

    (d) the assignor must enter an A.G.A.,

and discretionary matters, for example the assignee is, in the opinion of the landlord, of equal financial standing to the assignor.

In the latter case, the landlord's decision has to be arrived at reasonably, or the tenant must have the right to have the decision reviewed by an independent third party who is identifiable from the agreement and whose decision is conclusive.

7.10.5. The imposition of stringent conditions may have an adverse effect on the assessment of a revised rent or a subsequent review and/or may make it difficult for the tenant to assign the lease.

1. [1986] 1 All E.R. 321.
2. See *Bocardo S.A.* v. *S & M Hotels* [1980] 1 W.L.R. 17; *Vaux Group plc* v. *Lilley* [1991] 04 E.G. 136.
3. Landlord and Tenant (Covenants) Act 1995.

7.11.   Professional adjudication on court terms (PACT)

7.11.1. The Royal Institution of Chartered Surveyors (RICS) and the Law Society have jointly agreed to offer a service providing private determination of lease renewals under the provisions of Landlord and Tenant Act 1954. This should provide a faster, cheaper and more efficient method of settling lease renewal disputes than in the courts by professionals who have the expertise to make decisions on technical matters.

7.11.2. The scheme is voluntary with referral by mutual agreement of the landlord and the tenant. Appointments of arbitrators and experts, experienced in landlord and tenant matters, is made by the President of the RICS or the President of the Law Society. The parties will need to protect their position under the Act and an application to the court will be made in the usual way to be followed by a consent order. Model consent orders are provided to be adapted to cover the needs of the particular case.

7.11.3. The nature of the dispute will dictate the expertise required. Sufficient information on the issue in dispute will be requested from the parties to enable the appropriate President to determine whether the services of a surveyor or solicitor or indeed both are required.

7.11.4. The primary aim is to settle rents where other terms have already been agreed.

Other disputes can be referred to the scheme on matters of principle or drafting of a lease.

7.11.5. The tenant will retain the right to reject the tenancy which at present exists under the Act.

7.11.6. Parties will have the option of excluding or retaining a right of appeal to the court from the arbitrator's decision.

7.11.7. The system is designed to be flexible, giving the parties the right to settle their own procedure for determination of a dispute in a way not open to them in litigation.

7.11.8. *Using PACT - a summary of key issues*

1. Decide with the other party whether it would be advantageous to refer aspects of the lease renewal to a third party solicitor or arbitrator rather than a judge.

2. Identify which aspects of the renewal (if any) are agreed.

3. Decide which aspects to refer to the third party:
   (a) the interim rent;
   (b) the new rent;
   (c) other terms of the lease;
   (d) the detailed drafting of terms;
   (e) a combination of these.

4. Choose which aspects are to be resolved by a third party solicitor and which by a third party surveyor.

5. Choose the third party's capacity - arbitrator or expert?

6. Draft court application making use of or adapting PACT model orders.

7. Apply to court for consent.

8. Apply for appointment of person adjudicating (if not agreed).

9. Proceed with adjudication.

10. Receive award subject only to 'cooling off' rights and, in arbitration, any right of appeal.

FURTHER REFERENCE

Hill and Redman's Law of Landlord and Tenant, Butterworths.

Woodfall's Law of Landlord and Tenant, Sweet & Maxwell.

Leasehold Law, T.M. Aldridge, F.T. Law & Tax.

Drafting Business Leases, K. Lewison, F.T. Law & Tax.

Drafting and Negotiating Commercial Leases, M.J. Ross, Butterworths.

K.08. Agricultural tenancies

See also: Agricultural land, para. B.08.

8.1. Definitions

8.1.1. Many tenants of agricultural holdings which were created before 1 September 1995 enjoy security of tenure under Agricultural Holdings Act 1986. As from 1 September 1995, it is no longer possible to create a new agricultural tenancy which has the protection of the 1986 Act.[1] Paragraphs 8.2.–8.5. only appy to tenancies which were created before 1 September 1995.

8.1.2. The expression 'agricultural holding' is defined as the aggregate of land (whether agricultural land or not) comprised in a contract of tenancy which is a contract for an agricultural tenancy (not being a service tenancy).

8.1.3. In general, 'agricultural land' means land used for agriculture and so used for the purpose of a trade or business.

8.1.4. 'Contract of tenancy' means a letting of land or an agreement for letting land, for a term of years or from year to year.

1. See para. 8.5. below.

8.2. Protection of short-term tenants and licensees

8.2.1. Under Agricultural Holdings Act 1986, s.2 an agreement under which any land is let to a person for use as agricultural land for an interest less than a tenancy from year to year or under which a person is granted a licence to occupy land for use as agricultural land (in circumstances such that if his interest were a tenancy from year to year he would be the tenant of an agricultural holding) takes effect (with the necessary modifications) as an agreement for the letting of land for a tenancy from year to year. This is not so, however, if the agreement was approved before its commencement by the Minister, or if the letting agreement or licence is made in contemplation of the use of the land only for grazing or mowing (or both) during some specified period of the year.

8.3.   Security of tenure

8.3.1.   Subject to a provision dealing with the death of the tenant before the term date[1] and a contracting-out provision with the consent of the Minister,[2] a tenancy of an agricultural holding for two years or more continues as a tenancy from year to year unless written notice to quit is given by either party at least one year and not more than two years before the end of the tenancy.[3]

8.3.2.   In consequence of Agricultural Holdings Act 1986, ss.2 and 3 (above), a notice to quit is normally necessary to determine an agricultural letting for an interest less than a tenancy from year to year, a licence to occupy agricultural land, and a tenancy for two years or more. The importance of this is that the security of tenure provisions of Agricultural Holdings Act 1986 come into operation where notice to quit (the method of determination of periodic tenancies) is given to the tenant. If no notice to quit is necessary — as in the case of a fixed-term tenancy for a term between one and two years (e.g. 18 months) which is caught by neither section 2 nor section 3[4] — the tenant has no security of tenure under either Agricultural Holdings Act or Landlord and Tenant Act 1954.[5]

8.3.3.   In general, if a notice to quit an agricultural holding or part of a holding is given to the tenant he has the right to serve a counter-notice on the landlord, requiring the landlord to obtain the consent of the Agricultural Land Tribunal to the operation of the notice to quit, which consent can only be given on certain grounds. The tenant's right to serve a counter-notice is excluded if the notice to quit is given and is expressed to be given on one of a number of grounds specified in Schedule 3 Agricultural Holdings Act 1986.

1. Agricultural Holdings Act 1986, s.4.
2. Agricultural Holdings Act 1986, s.5.
3. Agricultural Holdings Act 1986, s.3.
4. *Gladstone* v. *Bower* [1960] 2 Q.B. 384.
5. *E.W.P. Ltd.* v. *Moore* [1992] 1 Q.B. 460, C.A.

8.4.   Other matters dealt with by Agricultural Holdings Act 1986

8.4.1.   Agricultural Holdings Act 1986 deals with a large number of matters regulating the relationship between landlord and tenant, including the right of succession on the death or retirement of the tenant, the tenant's right to compensation for improvements, and arbitration as to rent.

8.5.   Agricultural Tenancies Act 1995

8.5.1.   Agricultural Tenancies Act 1995 applies to all agricultural tenancies granted after the commencement of the Act.[1] It is not retrospective in effect and does not affect existing tenancies (or successions to those tenancies) granted under Agricultural Holdings Act 1986.

8.5.2.   The words 'agriculture' and 'agricultural' have the same meaning as under the 1986 Act.

8.5.3.   Tenancies created under the 1995 Act are called 'farm business tenancies'. Certain conditions must be satisfied for a tenancy to fall within this definition:

(a) **Business**

All or part of the land is farmed for the purposes of a trade or business and has been so farmed since the start of the tenancy.

(b) **Agriculture**

Having regard to a number of matters specified in the Act, the character of the tenancy is primarily or wholly agricultural.

(c) **Notice**

As an alternative to the agriculture condition, the parties can, before the grant of the tenancy, exchange written notices identifying the land and stating that the person giving the notice intends that the proposed tenancy is to be and remain a farm business tenancy. Even where such notices are exchanged at the start of the tenancy, the character of the tenancy must be primarily or wholly agricultural.

8.5.4.   To be a farm business tenancy, condition (a) above must be satisfied, together with either (b) or (c). If (c) is used, the tenancy will remain a farm business tenancy so long as some part of the land is farmed, but other parts of the land may later be used for other business and non-agricultural purposes.

8.5.5. *Exclusions*

The following tenancies are excluded:

(a) tenancies granted before the commencement of the Act;

(b) tenancies granted under the succession on death provisions;

(c) tenancies granted to an existing tenant who is protected under the 1986 Act where a variation of the previous tenancy has the effect of an implied surrender.

8.5.6. *Termination of tenancies*

There is no security of tenure or right of renewal given to the tenant under the 1995 Act (other than as provided for in the agreement itself).

8.5.7. *Preparation of the agreement*

If the tenancy agreement is to be for a fixed term of three years or more, it must be made by deed[2] and can only be prepared by 'accredited persons' (a barrister, solicitor, notary public, licensed conveyancer, a full member of the Central Association of Agricultural Valuers, or an Associate or Fellow of ISVA or RICS)[3].

8.5.8. *Rent and rent review*

There are no statutory controls on rent. In relation to rent review, section 10 of the 1995 Act provides for a rent review to take place in accordance with the provisions of that section except where the provisions of section 9 are complied with. Section 9 applies to a tenancy which:

(a) expressly states that the rent is not to be reviewed during the term of the tenancy; or

(b) provides for a rent review at specified times, either:

    (i) by or to a specified amount; or

    (ii) in accordance with a specified formula (not upwards only) assessed by objective criteria.

8.5.8.1. Statutory review under section 10:

(a) either party can call for a review by notice to the other;

(b) the review date must not be less than 12 nor more than 24 months from service of a 'statutory review notice';

(c) if the parties have agreed a specified review date, the review date must be a date as from which rent could be varied under the agreement;

(d) if the parties have agreed in writing that the review date is to be a specified date, the review must be on that date;

(e) if there is no agreement as to the date of the review, the date is the anniversary of the beginning of the tenancy;

(f) there is no review during the first three years of the tenancy and thereafter reviews must take place at no less than three-yearly intervals.

An independent expert or arbitrator is to be appointed to fix the reviewed rent. In default of agreement, the President of RICS is to appoint the arbitrator.

The reviewed rent on a statutory review is assessed on an open market formula (section 13). Tenant's improvements are broadly disregarded.

8.5.9. *Assignment*

The 1995 Act does not restrict assignment but section 19 of Landlord and Tenant Act 1927 does not apply to these tenancies.

8.5.10. *Agricultural covenants*

No agricultural covenants are implied by the 1995 Act. Such covenants must be expressly included in the agreement if required.

8.5.11. *Repairs and insurance*

The 1995 Act does not deal with these matters, thus appropriate clauses to deal with them must be included in the agreement.

8.5.12. *Termination*

   (a) A fixed-term agreement for two years or less will expire automatically.

   (b) Common law rules apply to periodic tenancies except that a yearly tenant needs to be given not less than one year's, and not more than two years' notice, expiring at the end of a year.

   (c) For a fixed-term tenancy of more than two years, not less than 12 months' and not more than 24 months' notice to terminate on the term day must be given (otherwise the tenancy continues as a tenancy from year to year).

   (d) Notices must be in writing.

8.5.13. *Compensation*

Compensation is payable for the tenant's improvements. These provisions cannot be excluded by the agreement. Improvements are categorised as follows:

   (a) **intangible advantages**

Something which attaches to the holding and which the tenant has brought to the holding at his own expense, e.g. unimplemented planning permission or a water abstraction licence;

   (b) **physical improvements**

     (i) non-routine, e.g. building a shed,

     (ii) routine (section 19(10) of the 1995 Act), e.g. 'tenant's right' (growing crops, etc.)

8.5.13.1. Conditions for claiming compensation

The landlord's consent must have been obtained (generally before or after the improvement was made). Appeal against the landlord's refusal of consent lies to an arbitrator (but in respect of non-routine physical improvements an appeal can only be lodged before the improvement has been made). There is no appeal against the landlord's refusal of consent to an application by the tenant for planning permission. The arbitrator cannot vary any conditions imposed by the landlord.

8.5.13.2. Amount of compensation (sections 20–27 of the 1995 Act)

The amount of compensation is the amount attributable to the improvement in the value of the holding at the termination of the tenancy. Appeal lies to an arbitrator under section 22 of the 1995 Act.

8.5.14. *Fixtures*

Tenant's fixtures can be removed by the tenant at the end of the tenancy. The tenant is under an obligation not to cause damage and to rectify any damage caused. The tenant need not give notice to the landlord of his intention to remove fixtures. If consent to an improvement was obtained, the tenant could alternatively claim compensation for the fixture as an improvement. The agreement should specify which fixtures are/are not tenant's fixtures.

8.5.15. *Dispute resolution*

The 1995 Act contains specific provisions for arbitration on rent review, improvements and compensation (see above). Other disputes are to be referred to arbitration unless the parties agree to a different procedure. The arbitrator is appointed with the consent of the parties (either on a joint reference or four weeks' notice by one party unchallenged by the other). In default of agreement, the President of RICS is to appoint the arbitrator. The court's jurisdiction is not excluded. The Arbitration Act 1996 applies to arbitrations under the 1995 Act.

1. Commencement date: 1 September 1995.
2. Law of Property Act 1925, s.52.
3. Agricultural Tenancies Act 1995, s.35.

FURTHER REFERENCE

Scammell and Densham's Law of Agricultural Holdings, H.A.C. Densham, Butterworths.

Agricultural Holdings, J. Muir Watt, Sweet & Maxwell.

K.09. Right to buy

9.1. Public sector

9.1.1. Subject to certain conditions, a secure tenant normally has a right to buy.[1]

9.1.2. 'Right to buy' means:

   (a) if the dwelling is a house, and the landlord or a public sector head-landlord owns the freehold, the right to acquire the freehold;

   (b) if the landlord does not own the freehold or the dwelling is a flat, to be granted a lease of the premises.

9.1.3. To qualify, the tenant must usually have occupied the house or flat as a secure tenant for two years, although there are special provisions in Schedule 4 Housing Act 1985 relating to spouses and children. Schedule 5 Housing Act 1985 (as amended) contains a number of exceptions to the right to buy.

9.1.4. The price payable on exercise of the right is the price which the house would realise if sold on the open market by a willing seller, less any discount to which the buyer is entitled. The amount of the discount depends on the length of occupation of the secure tenant, but cannot usually be less than 32% nor more than 60% in the case of a house, or less than 44% or more than 70% in the case of a flat. This is subject to a limitation on the amount of the discount imposed by Housing Act 1985, s.131 and related to costs incurred in respect of the house.

9.1.5. If a tenant who has received a discount sells the property within three years, he will (except in certain specified cases) be required to repay to the landlord a proportionate part of the discount. This liability takes effect as a legal charge on the property. There are provisions in the legislation governing the form and effect of the conveyance/transfer or lease. There are service charge limits which the buyer can expect to see set out in the conveyance or lease. Where the title to the landlord's property is unregistered, the tenant does not need to examine a landlord's title because the landlord is required to supply the tenant with a certificate of title in the prescribed form, which certificate HM Land Registry is bound to accept for the purposes of registration of the tenant's title. A lease taken by a tenant under the right to buy provisions needs to be registered even if for a term of 21 years or less since Land Registration Act 1925, s.123(1) applies to it. If application for registration is not made within two months, the lease will be void as regards the grant of the legal estate and accordingly section 70(1)(*k*) would not then apply as there would no longer be a lease. In such circumstances the tenant would presumably have an equitable interest in the property which would be protected by section 70(1)(*g*) so long as the tenant was in occupation.

1. Housing Act 1985, as amended by Housing and Planning Act 1988.

9.2.   **Leasehold Reform Act 1967**

9.2.1.   Part I Leasehold Reform Act 1967 gives certain tenants the right compulsorily to buy out the landlord's freehold interest (enfranchisement) or to take an extended lease for an additional 50 years. The right to enfranchise can still be exercised after the grant of an extended lease so long as the original term has not expired. These provisions have been modified by Leasehold Reform Housing and Urban Development Act 1993 and Housing Act 1996 (see below, para. 9.3.).

9.2.2.   *Qualifying conditions*

For the tenant to qualify, the following conditions must be satisfied:

(a) at the time when the tenant seeks to exercise the right he must be occupying a leasehold house as his residence;

(b) his tenancy must be a long tenancy;

(c) the property had a rateable value other than nil at the date of commencement of the tenancy or otherwise at any time before 1 April 1990;

(d) the house must fall within the definition of that word in the 1967 Act;

(e) the tenant must have been tenant of the house under a long tenancy at a low rent, and occupying the house as his residence, for the last three years or for periods amounting to three years in the last 10 years.

(f) in the case of leases for a term not exceeding 35 years, the tenancy must be at a low rent.

9.2.3.   *Long tenancy*

A long tenancy is one granted for a term certain exceeding 21 years; but there are certain exceptions where shorter leases which have been extended beyond 21 years through renewal will qualify.

9.2.4.   *Low rent*

Low rent is defined by Leasehold Reform Act 1967, s.4, and means either:

(a) there was no rent payable during the initial year of the tenancy; or

(b) where the tenancy was entered into before 1 April 1963, the rent did not exceed two-thirds of the letting value of the property on the date of the commencement of the tenancy; or

(c) where the tenancy was entered into on or after 1 April 1963 but before 1 April 1990 and the property had a rateable value either at the date of the tenancy or else at any time before 1 April 1990, the rent did not exceed two-thirds of the rateable value at the date of the commencement of the tenancy; or

(d) if (a)−(c) above do not apply, the rent did not exceed £1,000 in Greater London or £250 elsewhere.[1]

9.2.5. The rent is assessed at the date when the tenancy is entered into.[2]

9.2.6. *House*

A 'house' within the Act includes any building designed or adapted for living in and reasonably so called. The fact that part of the building is used for business purposes may not exclude the application of the Act. Where a building has been converted into flats or maisonettes, it depends on the structure of the conversion as to whether the converted units fall within the scope of the Act. If the result of the conversion is to produce a building which is divided horizontally, so that each tenant occupies the whole or part of one floor of the building, the units will be classed as flats which do not enjoy the benefit of the Act. If, however, the conversion has been made vertically, so that each tenant occupies a part of each floor of the building from the ground upwards, the individual units will be classed as houses, each of which may utilise the provisions of the Act. Flats, whether purpose built or otherwise, are not within the Act.

9.2.7. *Residence qualification*

The residence qualification applies only where the tenant is an individual and occupies the house as his only or main residence. The condition is not satisfied at any time when the house is let to and occupied by him with other land or premises to which it is ancillary or if it is comprised in an agricultural holding.

9.2.8. A member of the tenant's immediate family (e.g. spouse, child) who resided with the tenant and who succeeds to the tenancy on the tenant's death may be able to include his period of residence with the tenant before the death to make up the residential qualification. Where a house is owned by trustees and occupied by a beneficiary under the trust, the trustees may exercise rights under the Act so long as the occupying beneficiary satisfies the residence qualification.

9.2.9. A notice served by a qualifying tenant on his landlord of his desire to purchase the freehold or to take an extended lease creates a contract between the parties capable of registration as a notice or caution in registered land or a Class C(iv) land charge in unregistered land. The tenant's rights under the contract, even though he is in occupation, do not constitute an overriding interest in registered land.

9.2.10. The benefit of a notice served by a tenant under a lease within the Act can be assigned, but only with the lease itself. A buyer who is buying a lease to which the Act applies should enquire whether the seller satisfies the qualifications under the Act. If he does so and the buyer wishes to enfranchise, the buyer should ask the seller to serve a notice on the landlord, and then to assign the benefit of such notice with the lease itself. In this way the buyer will be able to exercise his rights under the Act without having to establish his own period of residential qualification. Such a provision must be dealt with by special condition in the contract to purchase the lease.[3]

9.2.11. Details of the rights and obligations of the parties under the notice and of the procedures to be followed (e.g. form of transfer, etc.) are set out in the Act, which also contains provisions dealing with the acquisition of intermediate reversions where the immediate landlord is not the freeholder. In many cases, however, the strict procedures under the Act are not followed and the procedure following service of the desire notice follows the ordinary steps in a normal purchase transaction. The payment of a deposit is often dispensed with although by written notice the landlord can demand a deposit not exceeding three times the annual rent or £25 whichever is greater. Since the service of notice by the tenant creates a contract between the parties it is not open to the landlord subsequently to draw up a contract on, e.g. the Standard Conditions of Sale Form and to require the tenant to agree to the terms included in the landlord's contract. Where not agreed by the parties the terms of the contract are governed by Leasehold Reform (Enfranchisement and Extension) Regulations 1967.[4] Section 10 of the Act regulates the terms of the conveyance to the tenant. The tenant will take the property subject to legal easements and restrictive covenants of which he has notice, e.g. by registration. The general words implied by Law of Property Act 1925, s.62 cannot be excluded without the tenant's consent and certain more extensive rights as to support and access are implied. The purchase deed must also make reasonable provision for rights of way over and for the benefit of other property belonging to the landlord (where relevant). The landlord is only obliged to give one covenant for title; namely that he has not himself incumbered the property and must give the statutory acknowledgement relating to retained title deeds (in unregistered land) but need not give an undertaking for safe custody.[5]

9.2.12. The price payable on enfranchisement is the subject of two formulae, depending on the rateable/ rental value of the property. Failing agreement between the parties the price is settled by the Lands Tribunal. Where premises have been brought into the Act by virtue of Leasehold Reform Housing and Urban Development Act 1993, the tenant must pay compensation to the landlord for loss of development value.

9.2.13. Where an extended lease is taken, the rent under the extended term represents a ground rent for the property and may be subject to upwards revision after 25 years of the extension.

9.2.14. The tenant is responsible for payment of the landlord's costs, e.g. of valuation, deduction of title and the purchase deed.

9.2.15. Where the landlord's interest is subject to a mortgage, the lender must, on payment of the purchase price to him, release the property from the mortgage.

9.2.16. Where the Act applies it is non-excludable, although in certain limited circumstances a landlord may be able to defeat a tenant's claim to an extended lease because he intends to redevelop the premises, or to defeat a claim to enfranchise or to take an extended lease on the ground that he reasonably requires the property for occupation as the only or main residence of himself or an adult member of his family. In each case compensation is payable to the tenant by the landlord.

1. S.I. 1990/434, as amended by S.I. 1990/701.
1. *Ibid.*
3. See Assignment of leases, para. K.11.
4. S.I. 1967/1879.
5. See Covenants for title, para. M.09.

9.3. Leasehold Reform Housing and Urban Development Act 1993

9.3.1. *Introduction*

This Act, the main provisions of which came into force on 1 November 1993, extends the rights to enfranchise/acquire an extended lease to the owners of flats and removes the rateable value limits which previously applied to houses under Leasehold Reform Act 1967. The Act also deals with some matters relating to public sector housing which are not dealt with in this book.

9.3.2. *Collective enfranchisement*

(a) The right

The right is given to the tenants of a block of flats collectively to acquire the freehold of the block . The freehold is to be conveyed into the name of a nominee nominated by the tenants. The conveyance can take place without the landlord's consent (subject to certain defences – see below). Certain qualifying conditions must be fulfilled (see 9.3.3. below). Qualifying tenants (as defined) must hold at least two-thirds of the total number of flats in the premises. Not all the flats in the block need to be let on long leases, nor need all the premises be let exclusively for residential purposes for the Act to apply.

(b) Nature of the collective right

The nature of the collective right is for the tenants to have the freehold of the premises acquired on behalf of the participating qualifying tenants by a person or persons appointed by them at a price to be determined in accordance with the Act.

(c) **Exercise of the collective right**

Two-thirds of the flats in the block must be held by 'qualifying tenants' (but not all the qualifying tenants in the block have to join in). Notice must be served on the reversioner by two-thirds of the qualifying tenants of whom at least one-half must satisfy the residence condition (below). The number of tenants who sign the 'initial notice' must represent at least one-half of the total number of flats in the block. If, therefore, a block consists of 12 flats, at least eight of those flats must be occupied by qualifying tenants for the block to qualify under the Act (two-thirds of the total number of flats). Two-thirds of those eight tenants (six) need to join in the initial notice, and of those six who join in the notice at least one-half (three) need to satisfy the residence qualification. Finally the number of tenants who sign the notice must represent at least one-half of the total number of flats in the block, i.e. six. These conditions must be met at the time when the intial notice is served.

(d) **Landlord's grounds of opposition**

The landlord can oppose the tenants' bid to enfranchise if the qualifying conditions are not met by the tenants. He may also oppose on the grounds that he wants to redevelop the whole or a substantial part of the premises but this ground is only available where not less than two-thirds of the long leases in the block are due to terminate within five years and the landlord cannot reasonably carry out the redevelopment without gaining possession.

(e) **Qualifications**

   (i) Qualifying tenant
   To qualify the tenant must be a 'tenant' of a 'flat' under a 'long lease' at a 'low rent'.

   (ii) Tenant
   Tenant includes a person holding a lease or tenancy, or an agreement for a lease or tenancy, and includes sub-leases/tenancies. Joint leaseholders are treated as one tenant.

   (iii) Flat
   A flat is defined as a separate set of premises but need not necessarily be all on the same floor level. The premises must form part of a building and be constructed or adapted for use as a dwelling. Additionally, either the whole or some material part of the premises must lie above or below some other part of the building. This definition includes flats above shops, but may not apply to extensions, e.g. granny flats.

   (iv) Long lease
   A long lease is one which is granted for a term of years certain exceeding 21 years. Provisions for determination within that period by either party do not affect this. The definition also includes most perpetually renewable leases, leases terminable by death or marriage,

and leases granted under right to buy provisions and shared ownership leases where the tenant's total share is 100%, and new leases (of whatever length) granted on the expiry of an old long (i.e. 21 years plus) lease, and continuations under Landlord and Tenant Act 1954, Pt. I. Leases for less than 21 years which have been renewed without payment of a premium, taking the total term over 21 years, are also included within this definition.

(v) Rateable value
The property must have had a rateable value other than nil at the commencement of the tenancy or otherwise at any time before 1 April 1990.

(vi) Residence
To qualify, a tenant must satisfy a residence qualification by showing that he has occupied (or one of the joint tenants has occupied) the premises for the past 12 months or for periods totalling three years out of the past 10 years. A company cannot satisfy the residence qualification.

(f) **Excluded tenants**

The following tenancies are excluded from the Act:

(i) business tenancies;

(ii) where the immediate landlord is a charitable housing trust;

(iii) unlawful sub-lease out of non-qualifying superior lease;

(iv) tenants who do not satisfy the residence qualification.

(g) **Interests included in the collective right**

Tenants who enfranchise will obtain the freehold of the premises in which the flats are situated and:

(i) certain other property owned by the same freeholder ('appurtenant property'), e.g. garage, garden;

(ii) intermediate leasehold interests.

(h) **Interests excluded from the collective right**

Mineral rights owned by the freeholder are excluded from the collective right.

(i) **Interests to be leased back**

The Act contains provisions relating to certain interests which may (or in certain cases must) be leased back to the reversioner. They include the following:

(i) flats let by the freeholder on secure tenancies;

(ii) flats let by housing associations on tenancies other than secure tenancies;

(iii) units which are not flats let to qualifying tenants;

(iv) flat occupied by a resident landlord.

The items in (i) and (ii) above are subject to mandatory leaseback; (iii) and (iv) need only be leased back if the freeholder requires them. Schedule VIII of the Act contains detailed provisions dealing with the terms of the leaseback. Broadly this is to be a 999-year term at a peppercorn rent and will include the usual covenants but there will be no restrictions on alienation where the premises are residential.

(j) **Price**

The price which the tenants are to pay for the freehold comprises three elements:

(i) market value;

(ii) one-half of marriage value;

(iii) compensation;

plus landlord's reasonable costs. Where intermediate leases are also to be acquired, the price of each interest has to be separately calculated. A valuer's advice must be sought in relation to this matter.

(k) **Market value**

Market value is the price which might reasonably be expected to be paid if the property was sold on the open market by a willing seller to an arm's length buyer. The following assumptions also apply:

(i) the seller is selling the freehold subject to any leases subject to which the freeholder's interest is to be acquired by the buyer, but subject to any intermediate or other leases which are to be acquired by the buyer;

(ii) that the Act does not apply;

(iii) any increase in value caused by the participating tenant's improvements to the premises are to be disregarded.

(l) **Marriage value**

Marriage value is the increase in the value of the unencumbered freehold over the aggregate values of the freehold and any intermediate leasehold interest when held by the persons from whom they are to be acquired.

(m) **Compensation**

Compensation is payable to the freeholder for any loss or damage he may suffer as a result of the enfranchisement. It includes any diminution in the value of any other property owned by the landlord, including loss of development value. Schedule 11 Housing Act 1996 also provides for the tenant to pay compensation to the landlord if an unsuccessful claim is made within two years of the original term date of the lease. This provision comes into effect on 15 January 1999.

(n) **Premises**

The flat must be in premises which either consist of a self-contained building or a self-contained part of a building whether or not the freehold of the whole building or of that part is owned by the same person. Self-contained means structurally detached. Buildings which are divided vertically may qualify under the Act. Premises where more than 10% is occupied or intended to be occupied for non-residential purposes are excluded. This last exclusion means that many flats above shops will not qualify under the Act. Resident landlords are excluded only if there are less than four flats in the block or the block is not a purpose-built block.

9.3.3. *Individual acquisition of a long lease*

(a) **Nature of the right**

The tenant has the right to be granted new lease to expire 90 years after expiry of the existing lease. The rent under the new lease is to be a peppercorn. A premium is payable for the grant. The new lease takes effect immediately in substitution for the tenant's existing lease. This right is available irrespective of the rights to collective enfranchisement.

(b) **Entitlement to extension**

The right to an extension applies to a qualifying tenant (as defined above) who has occupied the flat as his only or main residence for the past three years or for periods totalling three years out of the past 10 years. Companies cannot satisfy the residence requirement. Only one joint tenant need satisfy the residence requirement.

(c) **Landlord's defences**

The landlord can oppose the tenant's request on the following grounds:

(i)   that the tenant's existing lease is due to expire within five years; and

(ii) that the landlord intends to demolish/reconstruct the property and would be unable to do so without being given possession of the premises.

(d) **Terms of new lease**

The terms of the new lease will be the same as the existing lease except that the new rent is a peppercorn. The new lease takes effect immediately and is for a period which comprises the residue remaining on the old lease plus a further 90 years. Service charge provisions are to be included. The new lease will also contain a statement that the lease has been granted under the Act. Options which were included in the original lease will not be included in the new lease. The new lease will also contain a modification of the landlord's liability under his covenants and modifications to reflect defects in the existing lease. The new lease will include the landlord's right to apply to the court for possession for redevelopment purposes during the last 12 months of the original term or the last five years of the extension, subject to compensation being payable to the tenant.

(e) **Premium**

The amount of the premium payable by the tenant is the aggregate of:

(i) the diminution in the value of the landlord's interest;

(ii) the landlord's share of the marriage value;

(iii) compensation to landlord.

(f) **Effect of grant of new lease**

The grant of a new lease does not preclude a later application for collective enfranchisement. A further claim for another new lease can be brought in relation to any lease granted; subject to this, no security of tenure provisions apply once the original term date has passed.

9.3.4. *Advising in relation to collective enfranchisement*

(a) The first step is for the solicitor to find out whether the tenants and the building qualify under the Act. Information relating to these matters can be obtained by the service of various notices under section 11 of the Act:

(i) on the immediate landlord (or person receiving rent on his behalf) to obtain the name and address of the freeholder and any superior leasehold interest;

(ii) on the freeholder to obtain the name and address of every person who is a tenant of the whole or any part of the building;

(iii) on the freeholder and/or other tenants to acquire information reasonably required in relation to the enfranchisement claim (e.g. as to how many other tenants qualify).

Service of these notices does not commit the tenant(s) to proceed and apart from payment for copies of documents the tenants are not required to pay for the provision of this information by the landlord. The landlord must respond to this request for information within 28 days. The tenants have a right to inspect and take copies of documents which might reasonably be required in connection with the enfranchisement claim (e.g. the landlord's title deeds). The landlord is obliged to disclose to the tenant(s) whether he has received initial notices under the Act from any other person.

(b) **Costs of enfranchisement**

Taking any further steps towards enfranchisement is inevitably going to commit the tenants to the payments of their own solicitor's costs and also the reasonable costs of the landlord. Other expenses, e.g. in connection with the preparation of plans, valuation of the premises, the setting up of a company to purchase the freehold and possibly the expense of a court action to enforce the tenants' rights, will also be incurred. The tenants should be fully advised of the potential liability to costs and an arrangement for the payments of these costs by the qualifying tenants should be made before the matter proceeds further.

(c) **Plans**

If the tenants decide to proceed with their claim, a plan of the premises will be needed to accompany their initial notice (see (c) below). It may be necessary to have this plan prepared by a surveyor.

(d) **Valuation**

The provisions for assessment of the price which the tenants have to pay for the freehold are complex and advice will be needed from a surveyor. An estimate of the price which the tenants may have to pay to acquire the freehold should be obtained from a suitably qualified surveyor at an early stage in the transaction to ensure that the tenants collectively will be able to afford to proceed with the transaction.

(e) **The initial notice**

To exercise rights under the Act the qualifying tenants must serve an initial notice on the reversioner under section 13 of the Act (as revealed in answer to the enquiries noted in (a) above). The notice must be in writing and may be served by post. The Act prescribes the contents of the notice but not its form. Printed forms are available from law stationers. It must:

(i)   specify the premises with a plan;

(ii) contain a statement of the grounds on which eligibility rests;

(iii) specify other freehold or leasehold interests (if any) to be acquired;

(iv) state which flats (if any) are subject to mandatory leaseback provisions;

(v)   specify the proposed purchase price of the freehold and any other interest specified in the notice;

(vi) give the full names of all the qualifying tenants together with details of their leases;

(vii) specify which tenants satisfy the residence qualification and how this is achieved;

(viii) give the name and address of the nominee purchaser;

(ix) specify a date by which the landlord must respond with his counter-notice (not less than two months).

The initial notice must be registered as an estate contract against the reversioner's title. A second notice cannot be served while a previously served notice is in force. If the notice is withdrawn (or is deemed to be withdrawn) no further notice can be served for 12 months. Once given, the notice remains in force until a binding contract is entered into or the notice is withdrawn or deemed to be withdrawn. Schedule 3, para. 15 of the Act contains provisions to overcome technical defects in the notice.

(f) **Nominee purchaser**

The initial notice must specify the name and address of a nominee purchaser through whom negotiations for the acquisition of the freehold interest will be conducted and in whose name the freehold interest will ultimately be vested. In the first instance it may be acceptable for the nominee purchaser to be one of the qualifying tenants, but if the matter proceeds beyond the initial notice serious consideration should be given to the setting up of a corporate body to fulfil this role. Alternatively, in the case of small blocks (e.g. consisting of four flats only), the freehold might be vested in the names of trustees.

(g) **Landlord's rights and obligations when an initial notice is served**

Once notice has been served on the reversioner he has the immediate right to access to the premises for the purposes of valuation and to require evidence from the nominee purchaser of title to the lease. The nominee purchaser must respond to this request from the landlord within 21 days in default of which the notice is deemed to be withdrawn. The landlord is required to serve a counter-notice on the nominee purchaser within the time-limit specified in the initial notice (not less than two months). The counter-notice must either admit or deny the tenants' claim and, if the claim is denied, give the grounds of opposition.

(h) **Subsequent procedure**

After service of the landlord's counter-notice, and assuming that the matter is to proceed, negotiations will then ensue between the nominee purchaser and the reversioner for the completion of the acquisition. The form of the conveyance is prescribed by section 34 and Schedule 7. Provided the purchase price is paid to the landlord's lender, the property is discharged from the landlord's mortgage. If the landlord fails to respond to the tenant's initial notice, after two months the tenants can apply to the court to determine the validity of the claim and the terms on which the freehold is to be acquired. If negotiations do not proceed, the initial notice is deemed to be withdrawn by the tenants after a period of six months (or eight months after service by the landlord of his counter-notice).

(i) The Act contains no provisions enabling the time-limits prescribed within it to be extended.

9.3.5. *Acting for a buyer of an individual flat*

When acting for a buyer who is buying an existing lease which potentially qualifies under the Act, consideration should be given to raising enquiries of the seller to establish:

    (a) whether the flat and the lease qualify under the Act;

    (b) how many qualifying flats and qualifying tenants there are in the block;

    (c) whether and when any initial notice has been served by the tenants and if so how far negotiations have reached (a copy of the notice should be requested if not already supplied by the seller's solicitor);

    (d) whether any steps have been taken by the seller to acquire an extension of his lease under the Act.

9.4. Landlord and Tenant Act 1987

9.4.1. Landlord and Tenant Act 1987 (as amended) gives the tenants of certain premises the right of first refusal where the landlord intends to dispose of his interest in the premises. The Act applies where the landlord of premises which contain two or more flats held by qualifying tenants proposes to make a relevant disposal of the premises and provides that the landlord must first offer to make a disposal to a nominee of the qualifying tenants.

9.4.2. *Premises*

The provisions of the Act apply to premises consisting of the whole or part of a building which contains two or more flats held by qualifying tenants provided that the number of such flats exceeds 50% of the total number of flats in the building. The definition of a flat includes maisonettes and houses which have been converted into flats as well as purpose-built blocks. Premises which are used partly for non-residential purposes may be within the Act subject to a measurement limit. Thus premises which consist of a shop on the ground floor with two or more flats on the upper floors may qualify under the Act provided that the internal floor area of the shop represents less than 50% of the internal area of the whole building[1] and a nominee of the qualifying tenants who purchased the reversion of the flats would also therefore become the landlord of the shop. Where a landlord owns several blocks of flats with communal grounds on an estate development, each block is probably regarded as a separate building, the reversion of which may therefore be sold independently of the remainder of the estate.

9.4.3. *Landlord*

For the purposes of the Act a landlord is the immediate landlord of the qualifying tenants, or the superior landlord if the immediate landlord is himself a tenant under a tenancy for less than seven years or one terminable by his landlord within the first seven years.[2] Certain landlords are exempt and the provisions of the Act do not apply to, e.g. local authorities, urban development corporations or registered housing associations.[3] Resident landlords are also exempted from the provisions of the Act where the three following conditions are satisfied:

(a) the premises are not a purpose-built block of flats;

(b) the landlord occupies a flat in the premises as his only or principal residence;

(c) the landlord has been in occupation for the last 12 months.

9.4.4. Qualifying tenants

A tenant of a flat (including a company tenant) is a qualifying tenant unless his tenancy is:

(a) a protected shorthold tenancy;

(b) a business tenancy within Part II Landlord and Tenant Act 1954;

(c) an assured tenancy or an assured agricultural occupancy;

(d) a tenancy terminable on the cessation of the tenant's employment;

(e) of the flat and by virtue of one or more non-excluded tenancies he is also the tenant of at least two other flats contained in the same building;

(f) a sub-tenancy and his landlord is a qualifying tenant of the flat in question.

9.4.5. Relevant disposal

The word 'disposal' is defined in Landlord and Tenant Act 1987, s.4(3) as meaning a disposal whether by the creation or the transfer of an estate or interest. It includes the surrender of a tenancy and the grant of an option or right of pre-emption but excludes a disposal by will or under the intestacy rules.

9.4.6. A 'relevant disposal' is defined by Landlord and Tenant Act 1987, s.4(1) as a disposal by the landlord of any estate or interest (legal or equitable) in premises to which the Act applies, including a disposal of an interest in any common parts of the premises, other than the grant of a tenancy of a single flat with or without any appurtenant premises and subject to certain exceptions which are listed below in para. 9.4.8.

9.4.7. Since a contract to sell creates an equitable interest in favour of a buyer, a contract to sell is itself capable of being a relevant disposal. Further a disposal includes a disposal by the landlord's lender in selling or leasing the property, but not the creation of a mortgage.

9.4.8. Exceptions to 'relevant disposal'

By Landlord and Tenant Act 1987, s.4, the following are excluded from the definition of a relevant disposal:

    (a) a disposal:

        (i)   of an interest of a beneficiary in settled land;

        (ii) by way of the creation of a mortgage;

        (iii) of any incorporeal hereditament;

    (b) a disposal to a trustee in bankruptcy or liquidator;

    (c) a disposal in pursuance of an order under Matrimonial Causes Act 1973, s.24 or 24A, or Inheritance (Provision for Family and Dependents) Act 1975, s.2;

    (d) a disposal in pursuance of a compulsory purchase order or agreement in lieu;

    (e) a gift to a member of the landlord's family as defined in section 4(5) or to a charity;

    (f) a disposal of functional land by one charity to another as defined in section 60;

    (g) a disposal of trust property in connection with the appointment or discharge of a trustee;

    (h) a disposal between members of the same family provided that at least one of the original owners still retains an interest;

    (i) a disposal in pursuance of an option or right of pre-emption irrespective of the date of grant or of any other obligation created before 1 February 1988;

    (j) a surrender of a tenancy in pursuance of any obligation contained in it;

    (k) a disposal to the Crown;

    (l) where the landlord is a body corporate, a disposal to an associated company.

9.4.9. *The landlord's offer*

Where a landlord proposes to make a relevant disposal of premises to which the Act applies, he must follow the procedure set out in section 5 of the Act which requires him to serve notice on the qualifying tenants of the flats in the premises. The notice must:

    (a) set out the principal terms proposed including the property and the estate or interest to be disposed of (the 'protected interest') and the consideration required;

    (b) state that it constitutes an offer to dispose of the property on those terms which may be accepted by the requisite number of qualifying tenants (the offer is deemed by the Act to be 'subject to contract');

(c) specify a period for acceptance being at least two months beginning with the date of service; and

(d) specify a further period of at least two months beginning with the end of the period of acceptance within which a person or persons may be nominated to take the landlord's interest.

9.4.10. The tenant's acceptance

(a) The landlord's offer can be accepted by a simple majority of the qualifying tenants on the basis of one vote per flat let to qualifying tenants in the building. The tenants must nominate a person to deal with the landlord within the periods for acceptance and nomination specified in the landlord's notice.

(b) If a management company structure run by the tenants is already in place in the building, the management company may be nominated to purchase the landlord's interest. In other cases the tenants may consider the nomination of two of their number to hold the reversion on trust for the remainder of the qualifying tenants.

(c) Acceptance by the qualifying tenants must be by written notice served on the landlord within the period specified in the offer. A single notice is served on behalf of all the accepting tenants which specifies the names and addresses of all the persons serving the notice.

(d) When the title is registered the acceptance notice is not protected as an overriding interest and should be protected by applying for a notice or caution.

9.4.11. Effects of acceptance

Once the acceptance notice has been served the landlord cannot dispose of the interest described in his offer to anyone other than the tenants' nominees during the relevant period. The procedure by which the tenants acquire their landlord's interest is not specified by the Act and will follow a normal conveyancing procedure. The 'relevant period' is the period beginning with the date of service of the acceptance notice and expiring at the end of the period for nominating a transferee specified in the offer notice plus three months if a transferee is nominated. If no nomination is made the landlord may dispose of his interest during the 12 months following expiry of the nomination period provided that the price is not less than that stated in the offer notice and the other terms of the disposal correspond with the terms of the offer to the tenants. Such a disposal may be by auction provided the reserve price is set to equate with the offer price. If no disposal occurs within this 12-month period, the landlord must serve a new offer notice on the tenants before attempting to dispose of the property. Acceptance of the offer does not create a binding contract since the offer itself is only subject to contract.

9.4.12. *Rejection or counter-offer*

If the tenants do not serve an acceptance notice or counter-offer within the period specified for acceptance in the landlord's offer notice, the landlord may dispose of his interest during the 12 months following the expiry of that period subject to the same conditions outlined in para. 9.4.11. above.

9.4.13. *Disposals in breach of the Act*

A new landlord who acquires a reversionary interest in flats from a seller who is in breach of the provisions of the Act can be required (on request made by a majority of the qualifying tenants) to supply details of the transaction to a nominee of the qualifying tenants. The qualifying tenants, by serving a purchase notice on the new landlord, can require him to dispose of his interest to a nominee of the qualifying tenants on the same terms as he acquired his interest. If the new landlord's interest is mortgaged, the property is discharged from the mortgage provided that the nominee pays the purchase price to the lender (even if the purchase price is less than the amount of the mortgage). A landlord who disposes of provisions in breach of the Act is also guilty of a criminal offence under Housing Act 1996.

9.4.14. *Advice to proposed buyers of reversionary interests*

A person who intends to purchase a reversionary interest direct from a landlord must before exchange of contracts check:

(a) whether or not the premises fall within the scope of the Act; and if they do

(b) whether the landlord has served notice on the qualifying tenants as required by the Act; and if so

(c) that either the tenants have rejected the landlord's offer or that the time-limits for acceptance have expired and the purchase transaction to the buyer can be completed within 12 months of the expiry of the acceptance period; and

(d) the terms on which the buyer is buying are similar to the terms of the offer which was made to the tenants.

9.4.15. Section 18 of Landlord and Tenant Act 1987 enables a prospective buyer to serve notice on tenants to ensure that rights of first refusal do not arise where it appears to the buyer that the disposal might be a relevant disposal of premises to which the Act applies. The notice must:

(a) set out the principal terms of the proposed disposal;

(b) invite the recipient to serve a notice stating:

    (i) whether an offer notice has been served;

    (ii) if not, whether he is aware of any reason why he is not entitled to such a notice, and

(iii) whether he would wish to exercise any right of first refusal; and

(c) set out the effect of section 18(3) which says that, provided notices have been served on at least 80% of the tenants, and not more than 50% have replied within 28 days, or more than 50% have indicated that they do not regard themselves as entitled to an offer notice or would not wish to exercise a right of first refusal, the premises shall be treated as premises to which the Act does not apply.

1. This percentage is subject to alteration by Landlord and Tenant Act 1987, s.1.
2. Landlord and Tenant Act 1987, s.2.
3. Landlord and Tenant Act 1987, s.58.

9.4.16. Auctions

The notice procedures set out in para. 9.4.9. above are modified where the landlord intends to dispose of the property at auction. Such notice must be served on 90% of the tenants between four to six months before the auction, giving the tenants at least two months to respond to the notice.

9.5. Compulsory acquisition by tenants of landlord's interest

9.5.1. Where a receiver or manager has been appointed under Part II Landlord and Tenant Act 1987 but this remedy proves to be inadequate, the majority of the qualifying tenants may in certain circumstances apply to the court under Part III Landlord and Tenant Act 1987 for an acquisition order which allows them to acquire their landlord's interest without his consent.

9.6. Registered social landlords

9.6.1. A tenant of a registered social landlord has the right to acquire the dwelling of which he is tenant under Housing Act 1996, s.16. The purchase price may be discounted by the landlord and similar provisions relating to the repayment of discount apply as to public sector tenants (para. 9.1. above).

FURTHER REFERENCE

Woodfall's Law of Landlord and Tenant, Sweet & Maxwell.

A Guide to the Leasehold Reform Housing and Urban Development Act 1993, R. Matthews & D. Millichap, Butterworths.

K.10. Liability on covenants in leases

10.1. Introduction

10.1.1. The general rule that an original tenant remains liable under his covenants throughout the term of the lease has been abolished by Landlord and Tenant (Covenants) Act 1995 but only in respect of new tenancies (as defined by the 1995 Act, see para. 10.1.2. below).

10.1.2. *New tenancies*

A new tenancy is one which is granted on or after 1 January 1996, except those tenancies granted pursuant to:

(a) an agreement made before 1 January 1996; or

(b) a court order made before 1 January 1996; or

(b) an option granted before 1 January 1996.

A reversionary lease (e.g. granted to a former tenant who has discharged the liability of a subsequent assignee) takes its status from that of the original lease.

Some leases granted on or after 1 January 1996 will not be new tenancies. Such a lease should make this clear by including a statement that the lease is not a new lease within the provisions of the 1995 Act.

A variation of a lease sometimes results in a deemed surrender and re-grant, e.g. where:

— extra land is included in the tenancy in return for additional rent;[1] or

— there is an extension of the term;[2]

but probably only in these situations.[3] The date of the variation will determine whether the lease deemed to be re-granted is a new one.

10.1.3.   Paras. 10.2.–10.5. inclusive deal with old leases (i.e. those to which the 1995 Act does not apply). Para. 10.6. applies to all leases whenever granted. Paras. 10.7. onwards deal with new leases to which the provisions of the 1995 Act apply.

1. *Jenkin R. Lewis* v. *Kerman* [1971] Ch.477.
2. *Baker* v. *Merckel* [1960] 1 Q.B. 657.
3. *Friends Provident Life Office* v. *Bristol Railways Board, The Times,* 31 July 1995 (C.A).

10.2. Liability of original landlord and tenant

10.2.1.   Unless released by the landlord the original tenant is liable on all the express and implied covenants in the lease for breaches committed at any time during the term of the lease. His liability is to the landlord for the time being since on a transfer of the reversion all rights of action attached to the reversion pass to the transferee including the right to sue for an existing breach of covenant.[1] The liability of the original tenant to the transferee of the reversion exists even though the tenant assigned the lease before the transfer of the reversion.[2]

10.2.2.   The continuing liability of the original tenant may have serious consequences for him if an assignee of the lease cannot meet his obligations to the landlord. The original tenant remains liable for rent due after disclaimer of the lease on an assignee's insolvency,[3] and the release by the landlord of an assignee's surety does not release the original tenant since the latter is not in the position of a surety.[4] Although the landlord will normally only pursue the original tenant when the current assignee is unable to fulfil his commitments under the lease, the landlord's right of action against the original tenant is not confined to this situation.[5] The original tenant's liability does not, however, extend to arrears of rent accrued by an assignee during a statutory continuation of the term under Landlord and Tenant Act 1954, Pt. II unless the original tenant's covenant is expressed widely enough to cover this liability.[6]

10.2.3.   The original landlord remains contractually bound to the original tenant throughout the term of the lease.[7] If an original landlord is unable through his own act or default (e.g. by transferring the reversion to a third party) to carry out an obligation imposed on him by the lease the landlord may be liable in damages to the tenant.[8]

10.2.4.   Insurance against an original tenant's contingent liability under the covenants in the lease is available from a few major insurance companies but is neither easy nor cheap to obtain because of the difficulty in quantifying the insurable risk.

1. Law of Property Act 1925, s.141 and see *Re King* [1963] Ch. 459; *London and County (A. and D.) Ltd.* v. *Wilfred Sportsman Ltd.* [1971] Ch. 764.
2. *Arlesford Trading Co. Ltd.* v. *Servansingh* [1971] 3 All E.R. 113.
3. *Warnford Investments* v. *Duckworth* [1979] Ch. 127.
4. *Allied London Investments Ltd.* v. *Hambro Life Assurance Ltd.* (1985) 50 P. & C.R. 207.
5. *Norwich Union Life Assurance Society* v. *Low Profile Fashions Ltd.* [1992] 21 E.G. 104.
6. *London City Corporation* v. *Fell; Herbert Duncan* v. *Cluttons (A Firm)* [1992] N.P.C. 150, C.A.
7. *Stuart* v. *Joy* [1904] 1 K.B. 362.
8. See, e.g. *Eagon* v. *Dent* [1965] 3 All E.R. 334 where a landlord sold the reversion to a third party and the original tenant who failed in his attempt to exercise an unregistered option against the buyer of the reversion recovered damages from the original landlord for breach of covenant.

10.3.   Landlord and tenant for the time being

10.3.1.   The relationship between a transferee of the reversion and the tenant for the time being and between an assignee of the lease and the landlord for the time being rests on the doctrine of privity of estate. Liability under this doctrine extends to breaches of covenants which touch and concern the land committed by a transferee of the reversion while he holds the reversion and by an assignee of the lease while the lease is vested in him. This means that an assignee may be liable to the landlord for a breach of covenant giving rise to continuing liability, committed by the assignor.

10.3.2.   The doctrine embraces those covenants in the lease which affect the land demised and which also govern the landlord and tenant relationship as such, e.g. payment of rent, repairing covenants. While most covenants in leases will fall within the doctrine, including an option to renew the lease, it does not extend to purely personal obligations or to collateral obligations such as an option to purchase the reversion.[1]

10.3.3.   An assignee of the lease will not be liable to the landlord for breaches of covenant committed after the date of an assignment of the lease by him to a third party unless, as is commonly required, he has entered into direct covenants with the landlord, in which case his liability will continue throughout the remainder of the term. In this respect the liability of an assignee is no different from that of an original tenant.

10.3.4.   *Indemnity*

Irrespective of para. 10.3.3. above, an assignee of the lease may be called upon to indemnify his assignor in respect of any breach of covenant committed after the date of the assignment to him regardless of whether he has parted with the lease. On the transfer of a registered lease such an indemnity covenant is implied whether or not value was given for the assignment.[2] A similar indemnity provision is implied on the assignment of an unregistered lease, but only where value has been given for the assignment.[3] If the assignment of an unregistered lease is to be made for no valuable consideration an express indemnity covenant will be required by the assignor. At common law an original tenant who is sued by the landlord for a breach of covenant committed by an assignee can pursue a direct claim against that assignee.[4] Standard Condition 4.5.4 requires the purchase deed to contain an express indemnity covenant except where one is implied by law. The contractual exclusion of Law of Property Act 1925, s.77 does not negate the underlying common law obligation to reimburse.[5]

1. The benefit of an option to purchase the reversion may, however, pass to an assignee of the lease by assignment: see para. K.13.
2. Land Registration Act 1925, s.24.
3. Law of Property Act 1925, s.77.
4. *Moule* v. *Garrett* (1872) L.R. 7 Exch. 101.
5. *Re Healing Research Trustee Co. Ltd.* [1992] 2 All E.R. 481.

10.4. Liability between head-landlord and sub-tenant

10.4.1. No privity of estate exists between a head-landlord and a sub-tenant although a contractual relationship will exist between them if the sub-tenant has entered into direct covenants with the head-landlord (e.g. in a licence to sub-let). The sub-tenant will in any event be directly liable to the head-landlord on restrictive covenants in the head-lease of which the former had notice when he took his sub-lease. The sub-tenant is entitled to call for production of the head-lease on grant of the sub-lease to him (Law of Property Act 1925, s.44) and will be deemed to have notice of the contents of the head-lease even if he does not exercise his right under Law of Property Act 1925, s.44 to inspect it. Although it is very likely that an assignee of the sub-lease will have actual notice of restrictive covenants contained in the head-lease (and so assume liability on them), he is not fixed with constructive notice of the contents of the head-lease because, on the assignment to him, he is not entitled under the general law to call for production of the head-lease as part of his title.

10.5. Guarantors and sureties

10.5.1. The liability of a person who guarantees the performance of the tenant's obligations under the lease only arises if the original debtor defaults, but that liability may be extended by the terms of the guarantee which may also impose on the guarantor a continuing liability even though the lease has been disclaimed and the tenant's obligations terminated.

10.5.2. The benefit of a tenant's surety's covenant passes automatically to a buyer of the reversion,[1] as does the benefit of a surety's covenant to accept a lease to replace one disclaimed on the tenant's insolvency.[2]

10.5.3. Where an assignee of the lease goes into liquidation and the landlord sues the original tenant for arrears of rent, the latter can pursue an action against the assignee's surety for reimbursement. Although both are liable to the landlord the surety's obligation is prior to that of the original tenant.[3]

1. *P. & A. Swift Investments (A firm)* v. *Combined English Stores Group plc* [1989] A.C. 643.
2. *Coronation Street Industrial Properties* v. *Ingall Industries plc* [1989] 1 All E.R. 979.
3. *Becton Dickinson U.K. Ltd.* v. *Zwebner* [1989] Q.B. 208.

10.6. Restriction on liability of former tenant or guarantor for rent or service charge

10.6.1. Where a landlord seeks to recover a 'fixed charge' from a former tenant or guarantor he must serve a written notice on the tenant within six months of the charge becoming due and in it inform the tenant that the charge is now due, and that the landlord intends to recover the sum specified in the notice plus, where payable, interest. The notice must comply with the Notices Regulations made pursuant to Landlord and Tenant (Covenants) Act 1995.[1]

10.6.2. Fixed charge

A fixed charge is rent, or a service charge as defined by section 18 of Landlord and Tenant Act 1985 (but without the statutory restrictions applicable to residential property) or any other liquidated sum payable in the event of a breach of covenant.

10.6.3. Effect of failure to comply

A landlord who fails to comply will not be able to recover the amounts from either the former tenant or a guarantor.

10.6.4. Amount of fixed charge unknown

The landlord can only recover the amount stated in the notice. If the rent is in the process of being reviewed, the notice must state that the liability may be greater than that specified, and once the amount is known a further notice must be served claiming the increased amount within three months.

10.6.5. Restriction of liability of former tenant or his guarantor where tenancy subsequently varied

(a) **The effect of variations at common law**
A variation was thought to bind the original tenant – *Centrovincial Estates plc* v. *Bulk Storage,* but see now *Friends Provident Life Office* v. *British Railways Board.*[2] If an assignee agrees a variation with the landlord, the variation does not alter the terms of the contract between the original parties to the lease. The original tenant is not released from liability, but the liability remains governed by the terms of the contract which he entered when he was granted the lease.

(b) **Section 18 of Landlord and Tenant (Covenants) Act 1995**
Section 18 relieves a former tenant of liability for any amount which is referable to a relevant variation made on or after 1 January, 1996. A relevant variation need not be contained in a deed. It is a variation which occurs where either a landlord has an absolute right to refuse it, or the lease has

been altered after the assignment so as to deprive the landlord of a right of absolute refusal (e.g. a lease which prohibits a change of use without consent). To the extent that the guarantor remains liable despite the variation he will nevertheless not be liable to pay any amount referable to a relevant variation.

10.6.6.   *Right of former tenant to overriding lease*

A person discharging a fixed charge has a right to require the landlord to grant him an overriding lease (concurrent lease). An overriding lease is a reversionary lease granted for the remainder of the term usually plus a short term (e.g. a few days). Its terms are broadly identical to those of the relevant tenancy. It does not contain personal covenants or covenants which are spent, and covenants framed by reference to the beginning of the tenancy, e.g. repairing covenants, should be adjusted. To obtain an overriding lease the tenant must serve on the landlord a written request specifying the payment and claiming the right to the lease. The request must be made at the time of making the payment or within 12 months. The landlord must grant the lease within a reasonable time. The tenant has to deliver a counterpart and is liable for the landlord's reasonable costs. There is no obligation to grant an overriding lease if the original tenancy has been determined, or if an overriding lease has been granted or a request for one is still outstanding. Two or more requests for overriding leases made on the same day are dealt with in the sequence in which the liability was incurred with a tenant having prior right to a guarantor. A tenant may withdraw his request or may fail to respond to a request from the landlord to take a lease within a reasonable time. In either case, the tenant will be liable for the landlord's costs. A request is registrable as a notice or caution in registered land (or as an estate contract in unregistered land). It is possible to have tiers of overriding leases. Whether an overriding lease is a new lease or an old one depends upon the status of the original lease. It should state that it is an overriding lease granted under section 19 of Landlord and Tenant (Covenants) Act 1995 and whether or not it is a new tenancy for the purpose of section 1. Where the lease is registrable at HM Land Registry, it must comply with Land Registration (Overriding Leases) Rules 1995.[3] A landlord who fails to grant a reversionary lease may face a claim in tort for breach of statutory duty. A tenant who fails to deliver a counterpart lease cannot exercise rights under the overriding lease. These provisions are binding on mortgagees.

1. S.I. 1995/2964.
2. *The Times*, 31 July 1995 (C.A.).
3. S.I. 1995/3154. The statement required by these regulations is as follows: 'This lease is granted under section 19 of Landlord and Tenant (Covenants) Act 1995 and is (not) a new tenancy for the purposes of section 1 of that Act.'

10.7.   Covenants to which Landlord and Tenant (Covenants) Act 1995 applies

10.7.1.   The 1995 Act applies to all covenants whether they are express, implied or imposed by law and whether or not they 'touch and concern the land', but not to those imposed pursuant to section 35, 155 or paragraph 1 of Schedule 6A Housing Act 1985, or paragraph 1 or 3 of Schedule 2 Housing Associations Act 1985. Most covenants in a lease do touch and concern the land, but see, for example, *Hua Chiao Commercial Bank Ltd* v. *Chiaphua Industries Ltd.*[1]

10.7.2.   *Transmission of the benefit and burden*

An assignee now acquires the benefit and takes the burden of all the covenants. The assignor remains liable, and can sue, for breaches occurring before the assignment is made.[2] An assignor may, however, assign the benefit of a right.[3] The covenants are enforceable by and against any person entitled to the rents and profits and also by and against a mortgagee in possession.

10.7.3.   *Exceptions*

    (a)   Personal covenants.

    (b)   A covenant which does not bind the assignor immediately before the assignment, for example, one that is of limited duration or which has been released.

    (c)   A covenant which relates to a part of the demised premises which is not included in the assignment.

    (d)   A covenant which needs to be protected by registration and has not been so protected (e.g. an option).

10.7.4.   *The Landlord's right of re-entry*

A landlord's right of entry attaches to the reversion and passes on an assignment of it.[4]

1. [1987] A.C. 99 (P.C.).
2. *cf.* Law of Property Act 1925, s.141; and *Re King: Robinson* v. *Gray* [1963] Ch. 459.
3. Landlord and Tenant (Covenants) Act 1995, s.23(2).
4. Landlord and Tenant (Covenants) Act 1995, s.4.

10.8.   Tenant's release from covenants

10.8.1.   A tenant who assigns the lease will be released from the burden and deprived of the benefit of the covenants from the moment the assignment is made. His guarantor is also released to the same extent. The release is only from future observance of the covenants.

10.8.2. *Exceptions*

(a) An assignment in breach of covenant or by operation of law (e.g. devolution to PR's) is an 'excluded assignment'. The assignor is not released until the next assignment as long as it is not another excluded one.

(b) A tenant who has entered an authorised guarantee agreement is similarly not released until the next non-excluded assignment.[1]

1. See below, para. 10.9.

10.9. **Authorised guarantee agreements**

10.9.1. Where a lease contains a restriction on assignment, the landlord can, as a condition of his granting consent to the assignment, require the tenant to enter into an agreement which guarantees the performance of the lease covenants by the immediate assignee (called an 'authorised guarantee agreement'). The terms of the proposed agreement should be set out in the lease.

10.9.2. The agreement:

(a) can only guarantee the liability of the assignee;

(b) must cease when that assignee assigns the lease;

(c) may impose a primary liability;

(d) is void to the extent that it imposes obligations beyond those permitted[1];

(e) may require the tenant to accept a new lease where the old one is disclaimed as long as the tenancy is for no longer a period than the original term and its covenants are no more onerous.

10.9.3. *Effect of disclaimers, vesting orders and reversionary leases*

Where a tenant is granted a lease following disclaimer, or has a vesting order made in his favour under Insolvency Act 1986, or is granted a reversionary lease, he may be required to enter a further A.G.A. on its assignment.

1. Landlord and Tenant (Covenants) Act 1995, s.16(4)(a) and (b), and s.25.

10.10. **Landlord's release from covenants**

10.10.1. *Need to serve notice*

The landlord who assigns the reversion may apply for a release by serving a notice on the tenant either before or within four weeks beginning with the date of the assignment.

10.10.2. *Contents of notice*

The tenant must be told about the proposed assignment or the fact that it has occurred and that the landlord is seeking a release from his covenants.

10.10.3. *Tenant's response*

A tenant may object to the landlord's release by serving a notice on the landlord within four weeks beginning with the date of service of the landlord's notice.

10.10.4. *Role of the court*

Unless the objection is withdrawn, the county court will decide whether it is reasonable for the landlord to be released.

10.10.5. *Date of release*

A landlord's release takes effect from the date of the assignment. Section 3(3A) Landlord and Tenant Act 1985 still applies: the liability of an assigning landlord is preserved until the tenant is notified of the change of landlord.

10.10.6. *Subsequent release*

A landlord who has not been released may make a fresh application on the next assignment of the reversion. He should, therefore, take an indemnity covenant from his buyer together with a covenant that the buyer will notify the landlord of his intention to re-sell the reversion.

10.10.7. Notices must comply with the Notices Regulations made pursuant to Landlord and Tenant (Covenants) Act 1995.[1]

1. S.I. 1995/2964.

10.11. **Assignment of part**

10.11.1. The release of the assignor is only in respect of covenants which relate to the part sold except where the assignment is an excluded assignment.

10.11.2. *Apportionment of liability*

The assignor and the assignee remain bound by 'non-attributable' covenants, e.g. a covenant to pay rent or a service charge which is charged on the whole property, but they can agree between them how the liability is to be borne. The apportionment may bind the other party to the lease if a notice[1] is served either before or within four weeks beginning with the date of the assignment in question on the other party to the lease. The notice must inform him of the proposed assignment or the fact that it has occurred, the prescribed particulars of the agreement, and the request that the apportionment becomes binding on him. The apportionment will be binding if the recipient fails to serve a written notice[1] of objection within four weeks. If he does object, the parties to the agreement may apply to the county court for a declaration that it is reasonable for the apportionment to bind the other party to the lease. The recipient may also indicate consent to the apportionment or may withdraw a notice of objection. An apportionment which becomes binding does so from the date of the assignment.

10.11.3. *Forfeiture or disclaimer limited to part only of demised premises*

Where the landlord has a right to forfeit or there is a right for a liquidator or trustee in bankruptcy to disclaim a lease and where part only of the demised premises is affected, the forfeiture or disclaimer relates only to that part vested in the defaulting or insolvent tenant and not to the whole lease.

1. The notices must comply with Landlord and Tenant (Covenants) Act 1995 (Notices) Regulations 1995 S.I. 1995/2964.

10.12. **Exclusion of the 1995 Act**

10.12.1. An agreement to exclude, modify or otherwise frustrate the operation of provisions in the 1995 Act is void.

K.11. Assignment of leases

See also:

NB: In this section the word 'lease' should be read to include the word 'sub-lease' where appropriate to the context.

11.1. Taking instructions

11.1.1. The information required by the seller's solicitor and buyer's solicitor will be similar to that needed in a freehold transaction[1] with the addition of details of the lease to be sold or bought. Of particular importance is the question of whether the landlord's consent to the transaction will be required.[2] The seller's solicitor should check his own title, in particular to ensure that no outstanding breaches of covenant exist, before drafting the contract for sale.

11.1.2. The length of the residue of the term should be checked. Where the buyer is to obtain a mortgage on the property his lender will usually require that a minimum stated length of the term remains unexpired at the date of acquisition of the buyer's interest in order to provide the lender with adequate security for his loan. A lease with only a few years left unexpired is a wasting asset in the hands of the tenant and particularly in the case of residential property may prove difficult to sell unless the lease can be extended or enfranchised.[3]

11.1.3. *Seller's solicitor*

The seller's solicitor should obtain from his client or, if not available from the client, from the landlord:

(a) the receipt for the last rent due under the lease;

(b) where relevant, evidence of payment of service charge over the past three years including the receipt for the last payment due;

(c) details of the insurance of the property including the receipt for the last premium due;

    (d) details of any fee payable to a management company on the transfer of the lease (mainly applicable to retirement schemes);

    (e) a copy of the memorandum and articles of association of any management company together with a copy of the seller's share certificate;

    (f) copies of any side letters made between landlord and tenant which affect the terms of the lease.

11.1.3.1. Seller's checklist

Does the seller's solicitor have in his possession:

    (a) evidence of the freehold title?

    (b) licence permitting the current assignment and/or use of the property?

    (c) insurance policy?

    (d) latest rent review memo?

11.1.3.2. What consents are needed:

    (a) from landlord?

    (b) from lender?

11.1.3.3. Consider what statutes affect the current letting and the proposed sale. What impact does this legislation make on the proposed transaction?

11.1.3.4. Consider the terms of the existing lease, e.g. as to repairs, user, alterations, alienation, forfeiture, because the buyer's solicitor may raise points on these clauses.

11.1.3.5. Will it be necessary to obtain a release of the current sureties' liability from the landlord, or to obtain a deed of variation of the lease to reflect the current situation as between landlord and tenant?

11.1.3.6. If the lease to be assigned commenced before 1 January 1996, the assignor should be reminded of his continuing liability under the covenants in the lease.

11.1.3.7. If the lease to be assigned commenced after 1 January 1996, its terms should be checked to see whether the landlord requires the outgoing tenant to enter into an authorised guarantee agreement on assignment.

11.1.4. Buyer's solicitor

11.1.4.1. Checking the lease

On receipt of a copy of the lease from the seller's solicitor, the buyer's solicitor should check the lease carefully and advise his client about his responsibility under the various covenants in the lease. The lease may require an assignee to enter into direct covenants with the landlord which will create a contractual relationship between the landlord and the assignee and will make the assignee liable on all of the lease covenants for the remainder of the term, notwithstanding subsequent assignment of the lease to a third party.[4]

11.1.4.2. Landlord's consent

If the landlord's consent to the transfer will be needed the buyer should be asked to supply his solicitor with the names and addresses of potential referees so that this information may be passed on to the seller's solicitor as quickly as possible in order to avoid any delay in obtaining the licence. References are commonly required from all or some of the following sources:

    (a) a current landlord;

    (b) the buyer's bankers;

    (c) the buyer's employer;

    (d) a professional person, e.g. accountant or solicitor;

    (e) a person or company with whom the buyer regularly trades;

    (f) three years' audited accounts in the case of a company or self-employed person.

11.1.4.3. A solicitor should only give a reference on behalf of his client if he knows the client well and trusts him. The landlord will rely on the information given in the reference in assessing the suitability of the buyer as a potential tenant and a misstatement made by a solicitor in the course of giving a reference may lead to liability to the landlord under the principles in *Hedley Byrne & Co. Ltd.* v. *Heller and Partners Ltd.*[5] It is thus common practice for a reference given by a solicitor to exclude liability or responsibility for its contents.

11.1.4.4. Surety

The landlord may also require a surety to the lease as a condition of the grant of a licence to assign. Consideration should be given as to who should stand surety under the lease. Where the proposed assignee is a company it is common to find that the directors of the company are asked to guarantee the company's obligations under the lease. Although the directors may be happy to do this since, unless they agree, they are unlikely to secure the landlord's consent to the assignment, they should be advised of the considerable personal liability which they are assuming by accepting such a role. This is particularly so if the assignee, by entering direct covenants with the landlord, will be assuming a contingent liability under the lease since the sureties' obligations will be co-extensive with those of the principal debtor. In this situation there may be a conflict between the interests of the company client (the prospective assignee) and those of the sureties (the company directors) and it may be advisable for the sureties to receive independent advice about their responsibilities in relation to the guarantee of the lease obligations.

11.1.4.5. Buyer's lender

The terms of the lease should be checked to ensure that it will be acceptable to the buyer's lender.[6]

1. See above, Taking instructions, para. A.01.
2. See below, para. 11.2.
3. See above, Right to buy, para. K.09.
4. See above, Liability on covenants in leases, para. K.10.
5. [1964] A.C. 465.
6. See above, para. K.01.

11.2. Covenants against alienation

11.2.1. Covenants against alienation take many forms; they may restrict all or any of the following acts: assignment of the lease, sub-letting, parting with possession of the whole or any part of the property, creating a mortgage over the property. Such covenants are construed strictly by the courts so that when drafting a covenant it is essential that the covenant is worded to cover precisely the acts which it is intended to restrict, e.g. a covenant which prevents assignment will not restrict sub-letting and vice versa.

11.2.2. Long residential leases

A covenant which restricts assignment of a long lease of a house, except during the final years of its term (e.g. during the last seven years of a 99-year lease), is not generally favoured by either buyers or their lenders since it unnecessarily restricts the saleability of the property and thus has an adverse effect on its market value. For this reason such a covenant is uncommon in such a lease and a buyer's solicitor should seek to remove such a restriction from the lease on grant.

11.2.3. Except in long residential leases the inclusion of some type of covenant against alienation is usual and acceptable and provides the landlord with some measure of control over the occupiers of his property. The precise effect of any covenant depends on its wording. The effect of Landlord and Tenant Act 1927, s.19(1)(*b*) on building leases should be noted.[1]

11.2.4. Absolute covenants

If the covenant is absolute, e.g. 'the tenant shall not assign or part with possession of the property', any assignment (or other dealing depending on the wording of the restriction), although effective, will be a breach of covenant by the tenant and may lead to forfeiture of the lease. An absolute covenant is not subject to any statutory restrictions on its operation except those imposed by Sex Discrimination Act 1975, Race Relations Act 1976 and Disability Discrimination Act 1995, and thus gives the landlord total control over the tenant's dealings with the lease, but is not popular with tenants since there is no guarantee that the tenant will be able to sell the lease should the need or desire to do so arise. The presence of an absolute covenant may therefore have a deflationary effect on the rent obtainable for the property. Where an absolute covenant exists, there is no objection to the tenant asking the landlord's permission to grant him a variation of the lease to permit assignment (or as the case may be), but there is no obligation on the landlord to accede to the tenant's request or to give reasons for his refusal.

11.2.5. *Qualified covenants*

A qualified covenant permits the tenant to assign provided that the tenant obtains the prior consent of the landlord to the dealing. This type of covenant is more acceptable to prospective tenants than an absolute covenant but does not give the landlord total control over the occupiers of his property since his discretion to refuse consent to a proposed assignee may be tempered by the application of statutory provisions which, where they apply, are non-excludable.

11.2.6. *Consent not to be unreasonably withheld*

In the case of a qualified covenant contained in a lease dated before 1 January 1996 or in a lease of residential property granted after that date, Landlord and Tenant Act 1927, s.19 adds to the covenant the non-excludable proviso that consent shall not be unreasonably withheld by the landlord.[2] The question of whether a landlord in refusing consent is acting 'unreasonably' presents problems for the tenant. If the tenant does apply for consent and the landlord unreasonably withholds his consent, the tenant may go ahead and assign (or as the case may be) without consent and the dealing will not constitute a breach of covenant by the tenant. The difficulty lies in knowing what is 'unreasonable' since a refusal which may appear to be unreasonable from the tenant's point of view may look very different when considered from the landlord's side. If the landlord does refuse consent the prospective assignee (or as the case may be) is unlikely to wish to proceed with the transaction without consent because he runs the risk of the lease being forfeited against him. One solution is for the tenant to seek a declaration from the court to the effect that the landlord is being unreasonable in withholding his consent but such a course of action is costly and time-consuming. Landlord and Tenant Act 1988 attempts to resolve some of the problems associated with the application of section 19 by providing that the landlord must, after having received a written request for consent, give his consent within a reasonable time unless it is reasonable for him to withhold his consent. He must serve written notice of his decision on the tenant within a reasonable time stating what conditions (if any) are attached to the consent or, if consent is refused, stating his reasons for withholding his consent. Breach of the landlord's duty under the Act is actionable in tort as a breach of statutory duty, giving a remedy to the tenant in damages.

11.2.7. *Offer to surrender*

Attached to some covenants against assignment is a proviso that should the tenant wish to assign he should first offer to surrender his lease to the landlord. Such a proviso (commonly known as an 'Adler clause' after the case of that name[3]) was held to be valid in *Bocardo S.A.* v. *S. & M. Hotels,*[4] but the effect of such a clause and the terms of any surrender need to be considered carefully by the tenant, especially since, in the case of business tenancies within Landlord and Tenant Act 1954, Pt. II, section 38 of the 1954 Act makes void an agreement which has the effect of precluding the tenant from making an application for a new tenancy under the Act. It may therefore be necessary in a commercial lease for landlord and tenant to obtain the consent of the court to an agreement to surrender.[5] Since Law of Property (Miscellaneous Provisions) Act 1989, s.2 requires a contract for the disposal of an interest in land to be in writing, it is arguable that to create an effective surrender landlord and tenant must both sign a single document incorporating all the terms of the surrender.[6]

11.2.8. *Landlord and Tenant (Covenants) Act 1995*

In relation to new tenancies (i.e. generally those granted on or after 1 January 1996) of commercial property the provisions of section 19 of Landlord and Tenant Act 1927 are modified so that a landlord may agree in advance with his tenant:

(a) any circumstances in which the landlord may withhold his licence or consent to a proposed assignment; or

(b) any conditions subject to which such licence or consent may be granted.

A landlord who withholds consent because of the existence of any such circumstance or who imposes any such condition is not acting unreasonably.

The 1995 Act distinguishes between factual matters, for example:

(a) the assignee must be a plc;

(b) the assignee must have net assets equal to a specified multiplier of the rent;

(c) the assignee must provide a rent deposit; or

(d) the assignor must enter an A.G.A.,

and discretionary matters, for example, the assignee is, in the opinion of the landlord, of equal financial standing to the assignor.

In discretionary matters, the landlord's decision has to be arrived at reasonably, or the tenant must have the right to have the decision reviewed by an independent third party, who is identifiable from the agreement, and whose decision is conclusive.

11.2.9. *Demanding a premium for consent*

Unless the lease specifically allows the landlord to charge a premium for giving his consent (an uncommon provision in modern leases) the landlord may not attach a condition to his consent requiring a premium to be paid by the tenant.[7]

11.2.10. *Undertaking for landlord's costs*

The landlord is entitled to ask the tenant to pay the landlord's solicitors' reasonable charges in connection with the preparation of the deed of consent (licence) but may not demand a premium. Overcharging by the landlord's solicitor is unprofessional conduct. When the tenant's solicitor approaches the landlord's solicitor asking for consent to be given he should require the landlord's solicitor to provide a firm estimate of the costs of the application which should indicate whether or not VAT and disbursements are included in the estimate and should give a maximum fee which will be charged by the landlord in any event.[8] It may be difficult for the landlord's solicitor to quote a fixed figure at the outset of the transaction, but he should try to give the tenant's solicitor an accurate estimate of the likely costs and there is no objection to his qualifying the estimate by saying that it is given on the understanding that the matter proceeds to completion without any unforeseen difficulties or delays. The estimate should make it clear whether the tenant is to be responsible for the landlord's costs in any event, i.e. whether or nor consent is forthcoming and whether or not the proposed assignment (or as the case may be) proceeds to completion. To assist the landlord in giving an accurate estimate the tenant's solicitor should be prepared to supply the landlord with such information as he requires, e.g. references about the proposed assignee (or as the case may be) as quickly as possible and preferably at the time when the application for consent is first made. A tenant's solicitor must advise his client of his potential liability to meet the landlord's costs and should not give an unqualified undertaking to meet the landlord's solicitors' costs of preparing the consent since he may be committing his client to an unquantified sum. An undertaking may be given, provided that the landlord has provided an estimate of costs, and subject to the prior approval of the tenant client.[9] Where an undertaking has been given, the tenant's solicitor should obtain money on account from his client to ensure that he will be able to fulfil the undertaking. However, since Landlord and Tenant Act 1988 renders the landlord liable to the tenant in damages if an application for consent is not dealt with within a reasonable time, the landlord's solicitor should be wary of refusing to deal with the matter until such time as he receives an undertaking in respect of his costs.

11.2.11. *Standard Conditions of Sale*

Standard Condition 8.3 requires the seller to apply for the landlord's consent at his own expense and to use his best endeavours to obtain such consent, the buyer providing all information and references reasonably required. Unless in breach of these obligations, either party may rescind the contract by notice if the consent has not been given three working days before completion date or if, by that time, consent has been given subject to a condition to which the buyer reasonably objects. The condition does not require the assignee to enter into a direct covenant with the landlord. If the lease provides for the assignee to enter into a direct covenant, the contract should contain a special condition to this effect.

11.2.12.   In view of the difficulties attached to covenants against alienation, contracts for a disposition which is dependent on consent being obtained should not be exchanged until it is certain that the landlord's consent will be forthcoming.

1. See *Vaux Group plc* v. *Lilley* [1991] 04 E.G. 136.
2. Section 19 does not apply to agricultural holdings.
3. *Adler* v. *Upper Grosvenor Street Investments* [1957] 1 All E.R. 229.
4. [1980] 1 W.L.R. 17.
5. Landlord and Tenant Act 1954, s.38(4)(*b*) (added by Law of Property Act 1969, s.11).
6. *Proudread Ltd.* v. *Microgen* (1995) N.P.C. 120, C.A.
7. Law of Property Act 1925, s.144.
8. See above, Estimate for costs, para. A.08.
9. See above, Undertakings for bridging finance, para. B.16.

11.3. Preparing the package

11.3.1. The seller's solicitor should supply the buyer's solicitor with the following documents or information:

(a) the draft contract;

(b) a copy of the lease/sub-lease being purchased;

(c) a plan of the property (where appropriate);

(d) evidence of the seller's title;

(e) replies to pre-contract searches;

(f) details of the insurance of the property (including the receipt for the last premium due);

(g) details of any management company, including copies of the memorandum and articles of association;

(h) service charge accounts for the last three years including the receipt for the last sum payable (where appropriate);

(i) information about what steps have been taken to obtain the landlord's consent to the transaction (where appropriate);

(j) a request for references or such other information about the buyer as the landlord has indicated that he requires (where appropriate).

11.4. The Protocol

11.4.1. The Protocol applies as in the case of a freehold transaction, but the seller should be asked to produce, if possible, a receipt or evidence from the landlord of the last payment of rent, the maintenance charge accounts for the last three years (where appropriate) and evidence of payment, and details of the buildings insurance policy. If a licence to assign is required, enquiry should be made of the landlord as to what references from the assignee are necessary. A copy of the lease, together with such of the above information as has been obtained and is relevant to the transaction, should be sent to the buyer's solicitor as soon as possible.

11.5. Title

11.5.1. *Lease registered with absolute title*

The buyer is entitled to call for copies of the registered title and other documents specified in Land Registration Act 1925, s.110. By Standard Condition 4.2.1 copies supplied must be office copies. Since the title to the lease is guaranteed by HM Land Registry there is no need for the buyer to investigate the title to the freehold or superior leases.

11.5.2. *Lease registered with good leasehold title*

The buyer is entitled to call for copies of the registered title and other documents specified in Land Registration Act 1925, s.110. By Standard Condition 4.2.1 copies supplied must be office copies. Registration with a good leasehold title provides no guarantee of the soundness of the title to the freehold reversion and thus, although not entitled under the general law to do so, the buyer should insist on deduction of the superior title to him. Without deduction of the reversionary title the lease may be unacceptable to the buyer and/or his lender.[1] The reversionary title will be deduced by the appropriate method applicable to unregistered land.[2] Now that the registers of title are open to public inspection a prospective tenant will in practice be able to find out a great deal about his proposed landlord's title (assuming it is registered), but he will not be able to inspect or obtain copies of any registered leases from which his landlord's title is derived. The Standard Conditions of Sale do not require a seller to deduce the reversionary title in these circumstances.

11.5.3. *Unregistered lease*

Under the general law contained in Law of Property Act 1925, s.44 the buyer is entitled to call for the lease or sub-lease which he is buying and all assignments under which that lease or sub-lease has been held during the last 15 years, but is not entitled to call for evidence of any superior title. Without deduction of the superior title, unless the reversion is already registered with absolute title, the assignee on registration of the lease at HM Land Registry following completion would only obtain a good leasehold title which may be unacceptable to him and/or to his lender.[3] A special condition should in appropriate cases be added to the contract requiring the seller to deduce the reversionary title to the buyer by the method appropriate to unregistered land.[4] The Standard Conditions of Sale do not require the seller to deduce a reversionary title in these circumstances.

1. See above, para. K.01. for the reasons why a good leasehold title is considered to be inadequate.
2. See Title, section D.
3. See above, para. K.01. for the reasons why a good leasehold title is considered to be inadequate.
4. See Title, section D.

11.6. Preparing for completion

11.6.1. *The purchase deed*

The purchase deed (an assignment in unregistered land) will be prepared by the buyer's solicitor. Even where the lease was granted informally the assignment (transfer) must be by deed in order to transfer the legal estate in the land to the buyer.[1] The form of transfer is broadly similar to that used in freehold transactions.[2] An assignment of an unregistered lease will normally recite the brief history of the lease and the granting of any necessary consent to the present transaction, but is otherwise similar to a conveyance of freehold land.[3] Execution of the purchase deed is discussed above in para. E.01.

11.6.2. *Indemnity*

If the assignor is to remain liable on the covenants in the lease after completion of the assignment, the purchase deed should include an express indemnity covenant from the buyer. Where Landlord and Tenant (Covenants) Act 1995 applies so as to release the assignor from future liability, no indemnity covenant is necessary. If on an assignment of the reversion the assignor is not to be released from his covenants by the tenant (or there is a possibility that the tenant may refuse to give consent to the landlord's release), the assignor may wish to consider taking an express indemnity covenant from the buyer together with a covenant by the buyer to notify the assignor of the buyer's sale of the reversion to a third party within a specified time of completion of that further sale. This is to enable the first assignor to serve notice on the tenant renewing his request to be released from liability under the landlord's covenants in the lease. The assignor must serve notice on the tenant before or within four weeks after completion of an assignment if he wishes to be released from the landlord's covenants in the lease. The buyer should therefore be required to notify the assignor within seven days of completion of a further sale in order to give the assignor sufficient time to serve his notice on the tenants within the four-week period. Alternatively, the assignor could take an option from his buyer to re-purchase the reversion from the buyer if the buyer does not notify the assignor of a subsequent sale of the reversion. The option would need to be limited to 21 years (perpetuities) but would be registrable as a notice or caution against the reversionary title.

11.6.3. *Modification of covenants for title*

If a seller is in breach of a repairing covenant in the lease, the lack of repair could involve him in liability to the buyer after completion under the covenants for title which will be implied in the purchase deed.[4] Since liability under the covenants is strict, and it is usual for the contract to contain a provision requiring the buyer to accept the property in its existing state of repair,[5] the contract should also provide for modification of the covenants for title in this respect. Such a contractual condition must be reflected by an express modification of the covenants in the purchase deed itself, if the Standard Conditions of Sale have not been used in the transaction.[6] A buyer who accepts a condition which restricts the seller's liability under the covenants for title must ensure that he is fully aware of the actual state of repair of the property (e.g. by inspection or survey) before contracts are exchanged since the effect of such a contractual condition is to take away the buyers right to sue the seller in respect of a breach of repairing covenant.

11.6.4. Pre-completion searches

Where the lease is registered with an absolute title the buyer will make a pre-completion search at HM Land Registry in the same way as if he were buying the freehold. Any other searches which would be appropriate to the purchase of a registered freehold should also be undertaken.[7] Where the title to the lease is unregistered a Land Charges Department search against the names of the estate owners of the leasehold title should be made together with any other searches appropriate to the circumstances of the transaction.[8] Where the freehold or other reversionary title has been deduced the names revealed through investigation of that title should also be included in the land charges search application. If the lease is registered with a good leasehold title, a search at HM Land Registry must be made in respect of the registered title and a Land Charges Department search against the estate owners of an unregistered reversion. A company search should be carried out against the management company.

11.6.5. Landlord's consent

The landlord's solicitor will supply the engrossment of the licence which must be by deed if it is to contain covenants. If the licence requires the buyer to enter into a direct covenant with the landlord (and/or a management company) to observe and perform the covenants in the lease, the licence is usually drawn up in two parts, the landlord executing the original licence which will be given to the seller on completion for onwards transmission to the buyer, the buyer executing the counterpart which will be given to the landlord on completion.

11.6.6. Apportionments

Since it is unlikely that completion will take place on a day when rent and/or service charge become due under the lease it will be necessary for these sums to be apportioned on completion and the seller should supply the buyer with a completion statement which shows the amounts due and explains how they have been calculated. Copies of the rent and service charge receipts or demands should be supplied to the buyer with the completion statement so that the buyer can check the apportioned sums. In many cases it will not be possible to make an exact apportionment of service charge since the figures required in order to make this calculation will not be available. In such a case a provisional apportionment of the sum should be made on a 'best estimate' basis in accordance with Standard Condition 6.3.5.[9] This condition, although of most relevance to the apportionment of service charges, is not confined in its application to service charges alone and can be used to make a provisional apportionment of any sums where the amount to be apportioned is not known or easily ascertainable. Where the seller's liability for unascertained service charges may be substantial and there is concern about enforcing his obligation to pay (e.g. where the seller is emigrating), it may be appropriate to negotiate a retention to be held by his solicitors pending the ascertainment of the service charge.

11.6.7. *Shares in management company*

Where appropriate the solicitor for the buyer should prepare a stock transfer form to be signed by the seller before completion in order to transfer the seller's management company share(s) to the buyer. If the management company is limited by guarantee (not shares) there will be no share certificate to transfer to the buyer but the buyer will need to write to the company and apply for membership after completion. If the amount of the guarantee is more than nominal the seller's liability under the guarantee continues for a year after he ceases to be a member and he should in such a case take an appropriate indemnity from the buyer.

1. Short leases do not have to be made by deed (Law of Property Act 1925, s.54), but the transfer of a legal estate in land must be by deed by Law of Property Act 1925, s.52. This includes the assignment of a short lease. See *Crago* v. *Julian* [1992] 1 All E.R. 744.
2. See above, The purchase deed, para. E.01.
3. *Ibid.*
4. Land Registration Act 1925, s.24; Law of Property Act 1925, s.76: see above, Capacity, para. B.07.
5. See Standard Condition 3.2.2.
6. See Standard Condition 4.5.3.
7. See above, Pre-completion searches, para. E.02.
8. *Ibid.*
9. See section F.

11.7. **Completion**

11.7.1. The procedure on completion follows closely that in a freehold transaction.[1]

11.7.2. The seller will hand to the buyer such of the following documents as are relevant to the transaction in hand:

    (a) the lease/sub-lease;

    (b) the purchase deed;

    (c) the landlord's licence;

    (d) land or charge certificate (registered lease);

    (e) marked abstract or other evidence of superior titles in accordance with the contract (lease not registered or not registered with absolute title);

    (f) Form 53 or undertaking in respect of of the seller's mortgage;

    (g) copies of duplicate notices served by the seller and his predecessors on the landlord in accordance with a covenant in the lease requiring the landlord to be notified of any dispositions;

(h) insurance policy (or copy if insurance is effected by the landlord) and receipt (or copy) relating to the last premium due;

(i) rent and service charge receipts;

(j) management company memorandum and articles;

(k) seller's share certificate and completed stock transfer form.

11.7.3. The buyer should hand to the seller such of the following items as are appropriate to the transaction:

(a) money due in accordance with the completion statement;

(b) duly executed counterpart licence to assign;

(c) a release of deposit.

11.7.4. *Rent receipts*

Law of Property Act 1925, s.42 provides that on production of the receipt for the last rent due under the lease or sub-lease which he is buying a buyer must assume, unless the contrary appears, that the rent has been paid and the covenants performed under that and all superior leases. The buyer's solicitor should inspect the receipts on completion and also, where appropriate, receipts for payment of service charge. Standard Condition 6.6 entitles a buyer to assume that the correct person gave the receipt.

1. See above, section F.

11.8. **Post-completion**

11.8.1. *Stamp duty*

If the consideration for the sale does not exceed the current stamp duty threshold and a certificate of value is included in the purchase deed, no *ad valorem* duty will be payable on the deed. In other cases the purchase deed will bear duty at the same rates applicable to a conveyance of the freehold.[1] The licence to assign and its counterpart (whether or not made by deed) do not attract stamp duty provided that, in the case of a licence granted by deed, it contains an appropriate certificate under Stamp Duty (Exempt Instruments) Regulations 1987.[2] The stock transfer form must be stamped with the appropriate duty.

11.8.2. *Particulars delivered*

Irrespective of whether the the purchase deed attracts stamp duty, the transfer of a lease or sub-lease which was granted for seven years or more must be produced to the Inland Revenue in accordance with Finance Act 1931, s.28.[3]

11.8.3. Registered lease

Where the lease is already registered at HM Land Registry with separate title an application for registration of the transfer to the buyer should be made within the priority period afforded by the buyer's pre-completion search.

11.8.4. Unregistered lease

An unregistered lease or sub-lease which, at the date of the transfer to the buyer, still has over 21 years unexpired will need to be registered at HM Land Registry within two months of the assignment. An application for registration with absolute title can be made where the buyer can produce to the Registry satisfactory evidence relating to the superior title(s); in other cases only good leasehold title can be obtained. An application for first registration of title should therefore be made within this time-limit. If the title to the reversion is already registered, the lease will be noted against the superior title. In other cases the buyer may consider lodging a caution against first registration against the freehold title in order to protect his interests against a subsequent buyer of the reversion. If the lease has 21 years or less unexpired it is incapable of registration with separate title but will in many cases take effect as an overriding interest under section 70(1)(g) Land Registration Act 1925 against a superior title which is itself registered,[4] although registration of a notice or caution against the superior title may be considered prudent.

11.8.5. Notice to landlord

The buyer's solicitor should give notice of the transfer (and of the buyer's mortgage if required) in accordance with any covenant to that effect in the lease. Two copies of the notice together with the appropriate fee should be sent to the landlord's solicitor (or other person specified in the covenant) and the landlord's solicitor should be asked to sign one copy of the notice as an acknowledgement of its receipt and to return the signed copy to the buyer's solicitor. The receipted notice should be kept with the buyer's title deeds as evidence of compliance with this covenant. The fee payable for service of the notice should have been included in the statement of account sent by the buyer's solicitor to his client before completion.

11.8.6. Share transfer

The duly stamped stock transfer form and seller's share certificate should be sent by the buyer's solicitor to the management company who will register the transfer of the share and issue a new share certificate in the buyer's name. The new share certificate should be kept with the buyer's title deeds. Where the management company is limited by guarantee the buyer should write to the company and apply for membership.

11.8.7. *Outstanding apportioned sums*

As soon as the figures are available the parties' solicitors should make an adjustment of the provisional apportionments which were made on completion. By Standard Condition 6.3.5 such outstanding sums must be settled within 10 working days of notification by one party to the other of the adjusted figures. The liability to account for the apportioned sums remains outstanding despite completion having taken place under Standard Condition 7.4.[5]

1. See above, Stamping documents, para. G.02.
2. S.I. 1987/516. See para. A.14.7.4. for form of certificate.
3. See above, para. G.02.
4. Land Registration Act 1925, s.70(1)(g), (k).
5. See also above, para. 11.6.6.

FURTHER REFERENCE

Privity of Contract − A Practitioner's Guide, The College of Law.

K.12.   Licence or tenancy

12.1.   Importance of the distinction

12.1.1.   The principal reason for distinguishing between a licence and a tenancy is that in general a licencee will not enjoy the benefit of security of tenure, whereas a tenant may be protected from eviction at the end of his contractual term by the operation of some statutory provision. A licensee is not protected under:

  (a)   Rent Act 1977;

  (b)   Housing Act 1988 (assured tenancies);

  (c)   Landlord and Tenant Act 1954, Pt. I (long tenancies);

  (d)   Local Government and Housing Act 1989, Sched. 10;

  (e)   Landlord and Tenant Act 1954, Pt. II (business tenancies).

12.1.2.   Conversely, licensees do enjoy protection from eviction in the following situations:

  (a)   where the licensee would otherwise be a secure tenant under Housing Act 1985, s.79;

  (b)   under Rent (Agriculture) Act 1976; and

  (c)   generally where a person is granted a licence to occupy land for use as agricultural land under Agricultural Holdings Act 1986, s.2.

12.2.   Licences

12.2.1.   It is not always easy to determine whether an arrangement between two parties constitutes a licence or a tenancy. The modern starting point is usually accepted to be *Street* v. *Mountford*[1] where it was held as a general rule that if exclusive possession is given for a term at a rent (although the reservation of a rent is not essential to a tenancy), a tenancy will come into being, whatever the parties chose to call the arrangement and whatever they intended to be the result of that arrangement.

12.2.2.   The giving of exclusive possession is essential to the creation of a tenancy, so that if the agreement genuinely denies this to the grantee, no tenancy will come into being. If, therefore, a clause is inserted into an agreement for the occupation of business premises, enabling the grantor to move the location of the grantee's occupied space or stall, such a right, being inconsistent with the creation of a tenancy, would generally ensure that the grantee became a licensee and not a tenant.[2]

12.2.3. The ability of the grantor to move the location of the grantee has more realism in the case of a business arrangement than in the context of residential premises, but in residential cases grantors have sometimes succeeded in denying the existence of a tenancy by using the device of requiring the grantee to share the accommodation either with other tenants or with the grantor himself (i.e. denying exclusive possession to the grantee). The courts will, however, not accept these devices at their face value, and will look into the reality of the situation; thus if a sharing arrangement is patently a sham in order to deprive the grantee of security of tenure, it is unlikely to succeed.[3]

1. [1985] A.C. 809.
2. *Dresden Estates Ltd.* v. *Collinson* (1988) 55 P. & C.R. 47.
3. See *Antoniades* v. *Villiers* [1988] 3 All E.R. 1058; *Aslan* v. *Murphy (Nos. 1 & 2)* [1989] 3 All E.R. 130; *Duke* v. *Wynne* [1989] 3 All E.R. 130; *A.G. Securities* v. *Vaughan* [1988] 3 All E.R. 1058; *Mikeover Ltd.* v. *Brady* [1989] 3 All E.R. 618; *Westminster City Council* v. *Clarke* [1992] 2 A.C. 288, H.L.

12.3. Lodgers

12.3.1. A genuine lodger is a recognised licensee and (apart from the denial of exclusive possession) special circumstances such as a family arrangement may negative a tenancy.

12.4. Possession before completion

12.4.1. In most circumstances a buyer who is let into occupation of the property before completion would be treated as a licensee.[1] Standard Condition 5.2 provides that the buyer takes occupation as a licensee and not as a tenant.

1. But see *Bretherton* v. *Paton* [1986] 1 E.G.L.R. 172.

12.5. Notice to terminate

12.5.1. The length of notice necessary to determine a licence which is not protected by statute will normally be settled by agreement between the parties. In the absence of such agreement, reasonable notice must be given. Notice should always be given in writing so that it will be possible, if a dispute arises, to prove the existence and contents of the notice. Some record of posting or delivery should for the same reason be kept. Even where the licensee does not have the benefit of security of tenure, it may still be necessary to obtain a court order if the grantor seeks to regain possession.[1]

1. See, e.g. Protection from Eviction Act 1977, s.2 in the case of residential premises and Housing Act 1988, s.32.

K.13. Options

See also: Form of contract, para. B.11.
Right to buy, para. K.09.

13.1. Introduction

13.1.1. An option for the tenant to renew the lease or to purchase the reversion may be included in some leases or may be granted to the tenant independently of the grant of the lease.

13.1.2. It is important that the price or rent to be paid on the exercise of the option is either fixed by the lease itself or is otherwise ascertainable by the operation of some effective formula (e.g. by reference to 'open market value at the time of the exercise of the option') in the absence of which the option may fail for uncertainty.

13.1.3. If the lease is a registrable lease granted out of a registered title, when the lease is registered and notice of the lease is entered on the landlord's title, HM Land Registry will, as a matter of course, enter notice of any option included in the lease. If the option is included in a separate document (i.e. not in the body of the lease itself) specific application would need to be made for it to be protected. If the lease is an overriding interest under Land Registration Act 1925, s.70(1)(k), the option will not be an overriding interest and should be protected on the landlord's title by notice or caution. If the tenant is in occupation, the option will be protected by Land Registration Act 1925, s.70(1)(g), but it would be unwise to rely on its protection as an overriding interest because if the tenant went out of occupation for any reason, that protection would cease.

13.1.4. In unregistered land an option will not bind the buyer of the landlord's reversionary interest unless registered as an estate contract under Land Charges Act 1972. Where an option cannot be enforced against a buyer of the reversion through lack of registration, the tenant may be able to sue the original landlord for damages for breach of contract, who in turn may seek indemnity from the buyer under a contractual provision, e.g. Standard Condition 3.2.2. To protect his own interests the tenant should ensure that his option is registered as soon as possible after completion of its grant (the priority notice procedure may be used to ensure the date of registration is backdated to the date of grant). A landlord may choose to draft the option so that its validity is dependent on its registration within a stated period. Where a lease is granted out of an unregistered reversion, the option must be protected by registration under Land Charges Act 1972 even if the lease granted will itself be registered under the Land Registration Acts 1925.

13.1.5. The grant of an option is a disposition of an interest in land within Law of Property (Miscellaneous Provisions) Act 1989, s.2 and so must satisfy the requirements for writing specified by that section.[1]

13.1.6. It is unusual to find options contained in long leases of dwellings which are granted at a low rent because, provided the qualifying conditions are satisfied, Leasehold Reform Act 1967 (as amended) or Leasehold Reform Housing and Urban Development Act 1993 will frequently give the tenant the right to an extended lease and/or to purchase the freehold reversion.[2]

1. See above, Form of contract, para. B.11.
2. See above, Right to buy, para. K.09.

13.2. Options to purchase the reversion

13.2.1. The perpetuity rule does not apply to an option to purchase the reversion provided that the option is contained in the lease itself and its exercise is restricted to the tenant and his successors in title either during the term of the lease or no later than one year after the end of the term. Any option which does not satisfy these requirements will fail for perpetuity unless confined within or exercised within 21 years from the date of the grant.[1]

13.2.2. An option to purchase the reversion is not within the doctrine of privity of estate, so that the mere fact that such a relationship exists between the landlord and an assignee of the lease does not automatically mean that the assignee can enforce the option. However, unless the lease restricts the assignability of the option, its benefit may be assigned to a third party,[2] so that an unrestricted option to purchase the reversion at any time during a term in excess of 21 years would fail for perpetuity after 21 years. In such a case the exercise of the option should be restricted to the tenant and his successors in title.

13.2.3. Although the benefit of such an option can be expressly assigned to an assignee of the lease (even after the assignment of the lease itself) and may pass to him by operation of law without express words of assignment,[3] it is recommended that in order to avoid doubt express words assigning the benefit of the option should be included in the document under which the benefit of the lease is transferred to the assignee.

1. Perpetuities and Accumulations Act 1964. Different rules apply to leases granted before this Act came into force.
2. *Re Button's Lease* [1964] Ch. 263.
3. *Griffith* v. *Pelton* [1958] Ch. 205.

13.3. Options to renew

13.3.1. An option to renew a lease is not subject to the rule against perpetuities but a contract (which by definition includes an option) to renew a lease for a term exceeding 60 years is invalidated by Law of Property Act 1922.

13.3.2. Care must be taken in drafting such an option to ensure that it does not create a perpetually renewable lease, such leases being converted by Law of Property Act 1922 into terms for 2,000 years which are not terminable by a landlord's notice. To avoid creation of a perpetually renewable lease, the option to renew should be drafted to permit the tenant to renew 'on terms identical to those contained in the present lease *with the exception of the covenant to renew'*. Unless the words which are italicised in the previous sentence are included in the option clause, the new lease will also have to contain a further option to renew, thus creating a perpetually renewable lease.

13.3.3. An option to renew is within the doctrine of privity of estate so that provided the terms of exercise are complied with it can be enforced by the assignee who is in possession of the lease at the date when the option becomes exercisable.

13.3.4. If the exercise of the option is conditional on the tenant's performance of his covenants under the lease, the landlord can insist on strict compliance with the covenants and can refuse to grant the renewal even where the tenant's breach of covenant is merely technical and causes no loss to the landlord.[1]

1. See *West Country Cleaners (Falmouth) Ltd.* v. *Saly* [1966] 3 All E.R. 210. See also *Little* v. *Courage Ltd.*, *The Times*, 6 January 1995 (C.A).

13.4. **Exercise of option**

13.4.1. Time is automatically of the essence of the exercise of an option.

13.4.2. Following initial uncertainty Law of Property (Miscellaneous Provisions) Act 1989 has been interpreted as permitting the exercise of an option by a single document signed by the grantee only.[1]

13.4.3. The exercised option is itself an estate contract capable of protection by registration as a notice or caution in registered land or as a Class C(iv) land charge in unregistered land.

1. *Spiro* v. *Glencrown Properties Ltd.* [1991] 1 All E.R. 600.

K.14.   Variation of leases

14.1. Variation of lease
14.2. Flats

14.3. Surrender and re-grant
14.4. Effect of variation on former tenant

14.1.   Variation of lease

14.1.1.   In some cases an informal variation of the terms of the lease (e.g. as to user) to be effective as between the landlord and tenant for the time being will be agreed between the parties. Such a variation is commonly effected by a letter or informal agreement, leaving the terms of the lease itself unaltered. The variation may fall within the definition of the disposition of an interest in land within Law of Property (Miscellaneous Provisions) Act 1989, s.2 in which case it must be in writing and signed by both parties. The letter must make express reference to exactly which terms of the lease are being varied and to what effect and should state whether the variation is for the benefit only of the signatories to the letter or is intended to bind and benefit their successors in title. The precise status of such informal variations is uncertain in law.[1] The formal variation of a lease which is made by deed must itself be made by deed and submitted to HM Land Registry for entry against the leasehold registration and the title to the reversion.

1. See *Kleinwort Benson Ltd.* v. *Malaysia Mining Corporation Berhad* [1989] 1 All E.R. 785; and see *McCausland* v. *Duncan Lawrie* [1996] N.P.C. 94.

14.2.   Flats

14.2.1.   Any party to a long lease of a flat may apply to the court under Part IV Landlord and Tenant Act 1987 for an order for the variation of the lease where the lease fails to make satisfactory provision for:

    (a)   repair or maintenance of the flat or building;

    (b)   insurance of the premises;

    (c)   repair or maintenance of installations;

    (d)   provision for maintenance of services;

    (e)   recovery by one party to the lease from another party of expenditure incurred for the benefit of the other party;

    (f)   computation of service charges under the lease.

14.2.2.   The list of provisions which can be varied seemingly only applies to applications under section 35 of the 1987 Act, i.e. individual applications. It appears that applications under section 37, made by a majority of tenants, are not restricted to the items listed above.

14.2.3. Similar but more limited provisions apply to leases of dwellings other than flats in relation to insurance provisions only.

14.3. Surrender and re-grant

Where the variation of the lease extends or exchanges the premises contained in the original demise or extends the length of the original term (but probably only in these situations), it may be deemed to be a surrender of the original lease and a re-grant of a new lease on the varied terms.[1] The new lease created by the variation will be a 'new' lease and will therefore be subject to the provisions of Landlord and Tenant (Covenants) Act 1995. It is preferable in these circumstances to execute a new lease rather than a deed of variation. In the new lease the landlord may need to consider whether he should include provisions (in a lease of commercial premises) dealing with the terms on which he will be prepared to consent to an assignment of the lease (including provision for an authorised guarantee agreement) by the tenant.[2]

1. See *Friends Provident Life Office* v. *British Railways Board* [1995] 38 E.G. 106.
2. See Landlord and Tenant (Covenants) Act 1995 and K.10. above.

14.4. Effect of variation on former tenant

Where there has been a variation of a lease which variation the landlord has an absolute right to refuse or where the lease has been altered after an assignment so as to deprive the landlord of an absolute right of refusal (called a 'relevant variation' under section 18 of Landlord and Tenant (Covenants) Act 1995), a former tenant is not liable to pay any amounts under the covenants in the lease which are referable to the relevant variation. If, for example, a lease is varied after an assignment and the rent payable under the lease is increased, a former tenant who is sued by the landlord for rent unpaid by the assignee will only be liable for the amount of rent which was payable by the tenant before the variation and the former tenant cannot be held liable for the whole of the increased rent. A guarantor's liability under a variation is co-extensive with that of the tenant whose liability is being guaranteed.

K.15. Rentcharges

15.1. Definition

15.1.1. A rentcharge is generally defined as being a periodic sum issuing out of land which arises other than out of a landlord/tenant relationship.

15.1.2. Since 22 August 1977 rentcharges have not been able to be created (with limited exceptions).[1]

15.1.3. If a rentcharge is created in fee simple or for a fixed term of years it is a legal interest which is binding on a subsequent buyer of the land charged irrespective of notice.

15.1.4. A rentcharge for life (e.g. created under a settlement) is equitable only.

1. Rentcharges Act 1977, s.2.

15.2. Title

15.2.1. On a sale of unregistered land subject to a rentcharge, in the absence of a provision to the contrary in the contract, the document creating the rentcharge must be abstracted in addition to a 15-year-old good root of title and subsequent documentation.

15.2.2. On registration of land which is subject to a rentcharge, a rentcharge is noted in the charges register of the title to the land and a rentcharge land certificate is issued to the rentcharge owner where the rentcharge owner has made application for the registration of the rentcharge.

15.3. Transfer

15.3.1. The benefit of an existing rentcharge must be transferred by deed. In the case of a registered rentcharge, HM Land Registry prescribe a form of transfer for use in such circumstances.[1] The benefit of a covenant for payment of the rentcharge must be expressly assigned.[2] In the absence of express assignment, the obligation to pay remains, but would be unenforceable by action for its recovery other than by distress or re-entry.

1. Form 19 R.1., which incorporates the necessary assignment of the benefit of the covenant for payment.
2. *Grant* v. *Edmondson* [1931] 1 Ch. 1.

15.4. Extinction

15.4.1. The three main ways in which a rentcharge can come to an end are:

(a) by release by the owner of the rentcharge to the owner of the land charged;

(b) by merger when the owner of the rentcharge and the owner of the land charged become the same person;

(c) by redemption under Law of Property Act 1925, s.191 or under the Rentcharges Act 1977.

15.4.2. Except for rentcharges which are created under Rentcharges Act 1977 (para. 15.5. below), the 1977 Act provides that every rentcharge will be extinguished at the expiry of the period of 60 years from 22 August 1977 or on the date when it first becomes payable, whichever is later.

15.4.3. On compulsory redemption of a rentcharge and on proof that an applicant has paid the rentcharge price either to the person entitled to payment or into court, the Secretary of State will issue a redemption certificate. Where a rentcharge is redeemed by agreement or surrender, a deed of release should be drawn up and signed by the parties. Where the land subject to the rentcharge is registered, it is necessary to register at HM Land Registry the deed which ends the liability under the rentcharge.

15.5. Creation of new rentcharges

15.5.1. Rentcharges Act 1977 prevents the creation of new rentcharges after 22 August 1977, except in the following circumstances:

(a) where the creation of the charge has the effect of making the land on which it is charged settled land or land held on trust for sale, or where the creation of the charge would have that effect if the land were not already settled land or held on trust for sale;

(b) creation of an estate rentcharge;

(c) a rentcharge created under any Act in connection with works on land;

(d) a rentcharge created under an order of the court.

15.6. Estate rentcharges

15.6.1. An estate rentcharge is a rentcharge created for the purposes either:

(a) of making covenants to be performed by the owner of the land affected enforceable by the rent owner against the owner for the time being of the land; or

    (b) of meeting the costs of performance by the rent owner of covenants for the provision of services, the carrying out of maintenance or repairs, or effecting insurance or the making of a payment for the benefit of the land affected by the charge.

15.6.2. Rentcharges created under (a) above represent one method of providing for the effective enforcement of positive covenants.[1] Rentcharges under (b) above are a useful method of reserving service charges out of freehold sales, e.g. where a management company covenants to maintain amenity areas or to provide services, although some lenders may be reluctant to lend money on the security of a property which is subject to such a charge.

15.6.3. The rentcharge must represent a payment for the performance by the rent owner of a covenant (e.g. for insurance, etc., under (b) above) which is reasonable in relation to that covenant. If this provision is not complied with, the rentcharge will not be a valid estate rentcharge unless the amount reserved is only nominal.

1. See above, The purchase deed, para. E.01.

15.7. Apportionment

15.7.1. By Rentcharges Act 1977, s.4, the owner of land affected by a rentcharge which also affects other land not owned by him may in certain circumstances apply to the Secretary of State for a certificate apportioning the rent between the two parcels of land. A similar procedure exists for the apportionment of a rentcharge on a sale of part of land.

15.7.2. By Standard Condition 4.4 the buyer is not entitled to object to an informal apportionment of a rentcharge as being a defect in title.

15.8. Registration of rentcharges

15.8.1. If a rentcharge capable of subsisting as a legal interest is granted out of a registered title, then, in accordance with the fundamental principles of registration of title, the disposition must be completed by registration to be legally effective. In other cases the compulsory registration provisions do not apply to rentcharges. They may, however, be registered voluntarily.

K.16. Commonhold

16.1. Introduction

It is expected that a Bill to introduce commonhold will be introduced in the current session of Parliament. This follows from the Law Commission's recommendations (CM 1345) that a new type of tenure should be introduced *inter alia* to overcome the present difficulties and deficiencies associated with leasehold titles. The main provisions of the draft Bill are summarised below. The parliamentary progress of any Bill is unpredictable, but solicitors who are acting for developers may wish to advise their clients of the new proposals and to consider whether it may be advantageous to develop future estates on a commonhold, rather than on a leasehold, basis. The proposals are intended to apply both to commercial and residential developments.

16.2. The nature of commonhold

A commonhold will be a freehold development of two or more units which share services and facilities and so require a system for communal management and for the ownership of common parts. Commonhold will thus exist as an entirely new type of tenure, intended in part to resolve the problems which are commonly encountered with the enforcement of covenants in relation to leasehold flats and/or freehold flats.

The provisions contained in the draft Bill are not however restricted to residential property, nor to the horizontal division of units. Existing leaseholds could be converted into commonholds, but all commonholds, whether of existing or newly constructed buildings, must be created from a structurally detached building.

16.3. Rights and obligations

A 'commonholder' will own the freehold in the unit *plus* the right to essential services, e.g. gas, water, etc., the right to communal services *and*, where appropriate, the right to use communal facilities, e.g. parking, recreational facilities, etc. Commonhold Regulations, to be prescribed by statute in standard form, will impose mutual obligations on all unit holders. A service charge will be payable by each unit holder for the services provided to him.

16.4.   Creation

Creation of a commonhold will be by standard documentation prescribed by the enabling Act, and all commonholds will be subject to compulsory registration at HM Land Registry.

16.5.   Management

A commonhold Association (a corporate body run exclusively by the unit owners and having 'restricted liability' *cf.* limited liability) will own and manage the common parts of the building and run the facilities and services. This association will have the benefit of a charge against each unit for arrears of service charge.

16.6.   Termination

On termination of a commonhold, e.g. for redevelopment of the site, each individual unit owner's interest will be converted into a proportionate share in the proceeds of sale.

L. TENANTED PROPERTY
L.01. Sale of tenanted property

1.1.	**Introduction**	1.4.	**Buyer's solicitor**
1.2.	**Disclosure of tenancies**	1.5.	**Completion**
1.3.	**Tenancy terminates**	1.6.	**After completion**
	before completion		

See also: Long-term residential tenancies, para. K.06.
Business premises, para. K.07.
Right to buy, para. K.09.

1.1. Introduction

1.1.1. Where a sale is subject to a tenancy, the procedure and steps to be taken equate with those of a vacant possession transaction, but a number of additional matters need to be considered.

1.2. Disclosure of tenancies

1.2.1. It is an implied (and frequently express) term of a contract for the sale of land that vacant possession will be given to the buyer on completion. If this is not to be the case, the contract must include an express term saying that the sale is subject to a tenancy or tenancies, and a copy of the relevant lease(s) or tenancy agreement(s) should be supplied to the buyer with the draft contract. An express condition will also provide that the buyer, having been supplied with copies of the relevant agreements, shall be deemed to purchase with full knowledge of their contents. Standard Condition 3.2.2(a) makes provision to this effect.

1.3. Tenancy terminates before completion

1.3.1. If the tenancy to which the sale is subject comes to an end between contract and completion, the seller should not re-let the property without first consulting the buyer and obtaining his instructions. To re-let the property without the buyer's permission would frequently put the seller in breach of his fiduciary duty to the buyer. Standard Condition 3.2.2(b) provides that the seller is to inform the buyer without delay if any tenancy ends; the seller is then to act as the buyer directs, provided the latter agrees to indemnify the seller against all loss and expense. Standard Condition 3.2.2(c) provides that after the contract is made, the seller is to inform the buyer without delay of any change in the tenancy terms.

1.4.   Buyer's solicitor

1.4.1.   The buyer's solicitor should check:

    (a) the terms of the lease(s) or agreement(s) supplied by the seller's solicitor;

    (b) the effect of any security of tenure legislation on the tenant(s);

    (c) details of the landlord's obligations under the lease(s) or agreement(s), and in particular whether or not the seller has complied with such obligations;

    (d) whether the tenant has complied with all his obligations under the lease or agreement (e.g. as to payment of rent and service charge) and, if not, what steps the seller has taken to enforce the agreement against the tenant;

    (e) what variations have been made to the agreements and/or licences granted;

    (f) details of any renewal applications or the exercise of an option made by the tenant.

1.4.2.   The buyer should be informed of the matters listed above and advised accordingly. If it is discovered that the landlord is in breach of any of his obligations (e.g. breach of a repairing covenant) the buyer's solicitor should require the seller to remedy the breach before completion. Alternatively the buyer may insist that the contract contains an express term providing that the seller will indemnify the buyer against liability for such breach since, on completion, the buyer will assume the seller's role as landlord and will thus be liable to the tenant for breaches of the landlord's covenants, even though such breach was committed before the buyer became the owner of the property. In the absence of an express provision for indemnity given by the seller, Standard Condition 3.2.2(d) will prevent the buyer from seeking indemnity from the seller in respect of a breach of covenant committed by the latter.

1.4.3.   If the tenant has the benefit of security of tenure legislation, consideration should be given to the question of whether the buyer, on termination of the contractual tenancy, would be able to recover vacant possession of the property if he so wished. In certain circumstances the buyer may be precluded from relying on some of the statutory grounds for possession, e.g. a landlord who purchases premises which are subject to a business tenancy within Landlord and Tenant Act 1954, Pt. II will be unable to regain possession under section 30(1)(*g*) of that Act until he has owned his interest in the property for a period of five years. On termination of some tenancies the landlord may also be liable to pay compensation to the outgoing tenant, and this contingency should also be discussed with the buyer.

1.4.4.   Full enquiries must be made in relation to the amount of rent payable by the tenant, any statutory restrictions on the amount of rent recoverable, and the provisions for review or increase of that rent. Enquiries should also be made to ensure that the rent payable under the lease or agreement has been paid to the date of completion and that no arrears exist. Standard Condition 3.2.2(e) provides that it is for the buyer to satisfy himself whether and how any legislation affects any tenancy and what rent is legally recoverable.

1.4.5. In certain circumstances a landlord who wishes to dispose of his reversionary interest in a block of flats must, before contracting to sell to a third party, first offer the reversion to the 'qualifying tenants'. Where these provisions apply, the buyer must ensure that the seller has correctly fulfilled his obligation to notify the qualifying tenants of their right to purchase the reversion, and that the time-limit for the tenants' right to exercise this option has elapsed. See also Right to buy, para. K.09. above.

1.4.6. Where a tenancy is of a dwelling, and the lease is for a term not exceeding seven years, the landlord may be responsible for repairing the structure and exterior of the premises under Landlord and Tenant Act 1985, ss.11–14. Where these sections apply, they are generally non-excludable and in appropriate cases the buyer should be advised of his potential liability under these provisions.

1.5. Completion

1.5.1. In addition to the usual requirements on completion of the purchase of a freehold property, the buyer should receive:

    (a) the original lease(s) or tenancy agreement(s);

    (b) an authority signed by the seller and addressed to the tenant(s), authorising the tenant(s) to pay future rent to the buyer.

1.6. After completion

1.6.1. Where the premises which have been purchased consist of a dwelling, Landlord and Tenant Act 1985, s.3 requires the new landlord (the buyer) to give written notice of the assignment and of his name and address to the tenant not later than the next day on which rent is payable, or if that is within two months of the date of the assignment, the end of the period of two months. The seller remains liable for breaches of covenant occurring until written notice of the assignment is given to the tenant by either the seller or the buyer.

1.6.2. Landlord and Tenant Act 1987, s.48 also requires the landlord to provide the tenant with an address in England and Wales for service of notices. This section applies where the premises consist of or include a dwelling (including an agricultural holding[1]) but not to premises to which Landlord and Tenant Act 1954, Pt. II applies. Further, until such notice is given, any rent or service charge under the lease is treated as not being due, and is thus not recoverable by action by the buyer. It is therefore in the interests of both seller and buyer to ensure that such notice is given promptly after completion. Notice should be given to the tenant in duplicate, the tenant being requested to sign one copy and return it to the landlord who will, on receipt of the tenant's signed copy notice, have evidence of compliance with this provision.

1.6.3. Section 47 of Landlord and Tenant Act 1987 requires the landlord's name and address to be given on all demands for rent or any other sums payable under the tenancy. This will not satisfy the requirements of section 48.

1.6.4. Section 48 notices should be drafted in terms along the following lines:

> Notification by landlord of address for service of notices.
> To: (tenant's name)
> (tenant's address)
>
> Landlord and Tenant Act 1987, s.48
>
> We (landlord's solicitors' or agents' name and address), on behalf of your landlord (landlord's name and address) hereby give you notice pursuant to section 48(1) of the Landlord and Tenant Act 1987 that your landlord's address for service of notices (including notices in proceedings) is as follows:
>
> (landlord's address for service)
>
> Signed
> Dated this   day of   199

1.6.5. However, the Act does not make it clear to whom and at what point the notice should be given. The safest course is to give a section 48 notice to the original tenant on the grant of a new lease and to the assignee following every assignment of the lease.

1.6.6. Since most leases contain a covenant by the tenant to give the landlord a notice of assignment within a specified time after the disposition, the section 48 notice should be given to the new assignee as soon as the change of tenant becomes known. Alternatively managing agents or landlords should print the notice on every rent or service charge demand.

1.6.7. Section 48 notices do not have to be served personally on the tenant; delivery by post should be sufficient to meet the requirement that the landlord 'furnishes' the tenant with the information by notice.[2]

1. *Dallhold Estates (U.K.) Pty. Ltd.* v. *Lindsey Trading Properties Inc.*, *The Times*, 15 December 1993 (C.A.).
2. Draft notice supplied by Tom Lumsden.

M. DELAY AND REMEDIES

This section contains a brief summary of the matters which are relevant when there is either a delay in completion or a breach of contract. If court proceedings are contemplated reference should be made to a more detailed text which deals with such matters and the advice of a litigation specialist sought without delay.

M.01. Delayed completion

1.1. **Breach of contract**	**1.4.** **Compensation for**
1.2. **Time of the essence**	**delay**
1.3. **Anticipating delay**	**1.5.** **Service of a notice to**
	complete

See also: Breach of contract, para. M.03.
Specific performance, para. M.04.

1.1. Breach of contract

1.1.1. Any delay in completion beyond the contractual date will be a breach of contract entitling the innocent party to damages for his loss, but will not entitle him immediately to terminate the contract unless time was of the essence of the completion date.[1]

1. *Raineri* v. *Miles* [1981] A.C. 1050.

1.2. Time of the essence

1.2.1. At common law time is impliedly of the essence of the completion date where the subject matter of the contract makes it so, e.g. on the sale of a business as a going concern, or the sale of a wasting asset.[1] In such cases time will therefore be of the essence unless this implication is expressly negatived by a condition to the contrary in the contract.

1.2.2. By Standard Condition 6.1 time is not of the essence of the contract (but can be made so by express contractual condition) unless a notice to complete has been served.

1. See *Pips (Leisure Productions) Ltd.* v. *Walton* (1982) 43 P. & C.R. 415 (sale of a 21-year lease). It was also stated *obiter* in *Raineri* v. *Miles* [1981] A.C. 1050 that time might be considered to be of the essence in chain transactions.

1.3. Anticipating delay

1.3.1. Delay may occur owing to events outside the immediate control of the parties and their solicitors, e.g. postal delays or late receipt of funds from a lender. In such cases there is usually little doubt that completion will take place but it may be postponed for a few days beyond the contractual completion date.

1.3.2. Where delay is anticipated the client, his mortgagee and the other party's solicitor should be informed of the anticipated delay as soon as possible, and of its likely duration and, subject to the solicitor's duty of confidentiality, of the reason for the delay. This is particularly important in chain transactions where the delay in completion of one link in the chain may have serious consequences on the remainder of the transactions in the chain.

1.3.3. Any delay in completion may result in an adjustment being made to the repayment figure due on a seller's existing mortgage. This matter must, therefore, be resolved with the solicitors acting for the lender or the lender himself. Similarly, an advance cheque issued by the buyer's lender is usually delivered subject to the condition that it is used to complete the transaction within a stated number of days of its issue, failing which it must be returned to the lender and a fresh advance cheque issued in time for the rearranged completion date. Such an instruction must be observed by the solicitor acting for the buyer's lender.

1.3.4. Delay in completing one transaction may affect the client's ability to complete a related sale or purchase. If, e.g. completion of the client's sale becomes delayed, he will not have the necessary funds available with which to complete his synchronised purchase transaction, and failure to complete that purchase on the contractual date for completion will be a breach of contract involving the client at the very least in the payment of compensation for the delay. The client should be advised of the delay and of its consequences. Although the solicitor should do his best to ensure that any breach of contract is avoided, e.g. by arranging bridging finance so that the purchase transaction can be completed on time, he is also under a duty to act in his own client's best interests, and in these circumstances completion of the purchase with the assistance of bridging finance may not always represent the best course of action for the client to take. In the example under discussion, the client would probably not be able to utilise the advance cheque from his new mortgage to complete the purchase since there will commonly be a condition attached to it that the advance is conditional on the client's existing mortgage first being discharged. Not being able to utilise the new mortgage advance may result in a large sum being needed by way of bridging finance with a possible consequent heavy commitment to interest on the loan. Alternatively the client may choose to use bridging finance to pay off his first mortgage, thus releasing the mortgage funds for his purchase. Secondly, the client will be in the position of owning two houses until the sale of the first is completed, and if the sale transaction is not completed within a short space of time, this too will represent an onerous commitment for the client. The reason for the delay on the sale transaction and the likely period of delay in its completion must be taken into account when advising the client whether to complete the purchase on time, or to delay completion of the purchase thereby putting himself into breach of that contract. In the converse situation, where the sale can proceed but the purchase is delayed, completion of the sale transaction on the due date will result in the client becoming homeless for an uncertain length of time with consequent problems relating to alternative accommodation for the period of the delay, storage of furniture and other similar problems.

1.3.5. Any delay in completion will be a breach of contract for which the innocent party could recover damages but, where the delay is short, the amount of loss sustained by the breach is unlikely to justify the time and expense of an action for breach of contract. Compensation provisions under the contract may provide adequate redress for the innocent party in these circumstances. If not, an action for breach may be brought, but the amount of compensation received under the contract has to be credited against the amount claimed as damages.

1.4. Compensation for delay

1.4.1. The application of the common law provisions relating to payment of compensation for delay might not provide the innocent party with sufficient financial compensation for his loss and are usually replaced by specific contractual provisions providing for compensation. In default of a specific contractual clause dealing with the matter, the common law provisions as set out below would apply.

1.4.2. *Common law provisions*

In addition to any action for damages, where the delay is the buyer's fault:

(a) the buyer pays the outgoings on the property from the contractual date for completion;

(b) the buyer is entitled to keep the income from the property (if any) from the date of completion;

(c) from the contractual date of completion, the buyer pays interest to the seller on the balance of the purchase price at the general equitable rate.[1]

1.4.3. Where the delay is the seller's fault:

(a) the seller remains responsible for the outgoings on the property;

(b) he is entitled to keep whichever sum is the lesser of:

(i) the net income of the property; or

(ii) the amount of interest payable by the buyer, calculated as under (c) above.

1.4.4. Since there will be no income generated by a property which is being sold with vacant possession, the application of these rules effectively means that the buyer has to pay interest when the delay is his fault, but not when the delay is caused by the seller.

1.4.5. Standard Condition 7.3 provides for the payment of compensation at the 'contract rate' which is defined by Condition 1.1.1(g) as being 'the Law Society's interest rate from time to time in force' (as published weekly in the Law Society's *Gazette*), although the parties are free to substitute a different rate by special condition if they so wish.

1.4.6. Under this condition, compensation is assessed using the 'concept of relative fault', so that whoever is most at fault for the delay pays the compensation; it is not simply a matter of the party who delayed in actual completion being liable to pay compensation. To calculate the liability for compensation, it is necessary to refer back to the timetable of events contained in Conditions 4.1.1 and 4.1.2 in order to establish whether the delay in completion has been caused by a delay in carrying out a procedural step earlier in the transaction. Delay occurring before completion is assessed by reference to the definition of a 'working day' contained in Condition 1.1.1(n) but this definition ceases to apply once completion date has passed, after which every day's delay counts towards the liability for compensation. Having apportioned the delay between the parties, the party who is most at fault for the delay pays compensation to the other for the period by which his delay exceeds the delay of the other party. Compensation under this provision is neither additional to nor in substitution for common law damages, but merely on account.

1.4.7. By Standard Conditions 6.1.2 and 6.1.3, where the sale is with vacant possession and the money due on completion is not paid by 2 p.m. on the day of actual completion (or such other time as may be have been agreed by the parties), for the purposes of the compensation provisions only, completion is deemed to have taken place on the next following working day unless the seller had not vacated the property by 2 p.m. (or other agreed time). If this time-limit is not complied with the buyer may find himself liable to pay compensation to the seller under Standard Condition 7.3.

---

1. According to *Esdaile* v. *Stephenson* (1822) 1 Sim. & St. 122, the general equitable rate is a mere 4% per annum, but more recently in *Bartlett* v. *Barclays Bank Trust Co. Ltd.* [1980] Ch. 515 interest was awarded based on the rate allowed on the court's short-term investment account under the Administration of Justice Act 1965.

1.5. Service of a notice to complete

1.5.1. Where it appears that the delay in completion is not likely to be resolved quickly (or at all), consideration may be given to the service of a notice to complete which will have the effect of making time of the essence of the contract so that if completion does not take place on the new completion date specified in the notice the aggrieved party may then terminate the contract forthwith, forfeit or recover his deposit (as the case may be)with accrued interest and commence an action for damages to recover his loss. This then gives the aggrieved party the certainty of knowing that on a stated date he can make a definite decision either to look for a new property to purchase (if a buyer), or resell the property elsewhere (as a seller). It must, however, be remembered that making time of the essence imposes a condition which binds both parties. If, therefore, between the date of service and new date for completion as specified by the notice, unforeseen events occur which result in the previously aggrieved party being unable to complete on the new date, the previously defaulting party could turn round and terminate the contract, leaving the aggrieved party in breach of contract himself. For this reason a notice to complete should never be served as an idle threat. The server must be sure that he will be able to comply with the new completion date himself before serving the notice.

1.5.2. At common law, the service of a valid notice to complete can only be achieved where the notice specifies a 'reasonable time' for the new completion date, and the party serving the notice is himself ready, able and willing to complete. Both of these conditions present considerable difficulties for the server since it is difficult to assess the 'reasonable time' for the new completion date — a few days ahead may seem quite reasonable to a seller who is anxious to complete the sale, but a few weeks may seem more reasonable to a buyer whose mortgage arrangements have just fallen through. A seller may not be 'ready, able and willing' to complete if he has not discharged his subsisting mortgage over the property.[1] Since it is common practice for a seller to discharge his mortgage after completion, using part of the proceeds of sale with which to make repayment, this condition presents particular difficulties for a seller who wishes to serve a notice on a defaulting buyer. Since the decision in *Behzadi* v. *Shaftesbury Hotels Ltd*[2] it seems that a notice to complete (making time of the essence) can be served immediately contractual completion date passes — there is no need for there to have been 'unreasonable delay'.

1.5.3. The contract normally provides specifically for the service of a notice to complete, such clause being drafted to circumvent the common law problems outlined in the preceding paragraph. Standard Condition 6.8 is such a condition, and provided that the notice expressly refers to the fact that it is served under the provisions of this condition, its service will be valid, the common law requirements being ousted by the specific contractual provisions.

1.5.4. Standard Condition 6.8 provides that on service of a notice to complete, completion must take place within 10 working days (exclusive of the date of service) and makes time of the essence of the contract.

1.5.5. Standard Condition 6.8.4 requires a buyer who has paid less than a 10% deposit to pay the balance of the the full 10% immediately on receipt of a notice to complete.

1.5.6. The parties' rights and obligations where a valid notice has been served but not complied with are governed by Standard Conditions 7.5 and 7.6.

1.5.7. Once served, a notice to complete cannot be withdrawn.

1.5.8. If compliance with a first notice to complete is waived there is no reason why a second notice to complete, specifying an extended period for compliance should not be served on expiry of the initial notice, or why the period for compliance, with a first notice should not be extended by mutual agreement, but there is some doubt whether time would remain of the essence in such circumstances.

1.5.9. Non-compliance with a notice to complete gives the aggrieved party the right to terminate the contract, but is not in itself an automatic termination of the contract.

1.5.10. If it is necessary to serve a notice in a situation where the delay is caused by the death of one of the contracting parties, the notice should be addressed to the deceased and his personal representatives at the deceased's last known address. A further copy of the notice should be served on the Public Trustee.

1. *Cole* v. *Rose* [1978] 3 All E.R. 1121.
2. [1992] Ch. 1.

M.02. Rescission

See also: Conditional contracts, para. B.13.
Misrepresentation, para. M.05.

2.1. Introduction

2.1.1. The word rescission is used here in the context of contracts which involve a vitiating element, e.g. misrepresentation, fraud, mistake, and refers to the remedy which is available in these circumstances.

2.1.2. Rescission denotes the restoration of the parties to their pre-contract position by 'undoing' the contract and balancing the position of the parties with the payment of compensation by one party to the other. Damages in the conventional sense of that word are not payable since there will have been no breach of contract.

2.1.3. Since rescission is an equitable remedy, its operation is subject to the general equitable bars which are set out in more detail in para. M.04.2.

2.2. Contractual right to rescind

2.2.1. No right to rescind exists except where there is a vitiating element in the contract or a specific contractual right to rescind. Therefore, unless there is a breach of contract entitling one party to terminate his obligations under it, the contract must be performed.

2.2.2. A right to rescind may be given by a specific contractual condition which will specify the circumstances in which the right is to operate and the parties' rights and obligations in the event of rescission taking place. Such a right may be granted, e.g. where the contract is conditional on the fulfilment of a condition.

2.2.3. Under the Standard Conditions of Sale, the right to rescind is available in three situations:

    (a) where risk in the property remains with the seller and the property is rendered unusable between contract and completion (Condition 5.1);

(b) for misrepresentation (Condition 7.1);

(c) where a licence to assign is not forthcoming (Condition 8.3).

2.2.4. Where the right to rescind is exercised under one of the Conditions referred to in para. 2.2.3. above, the parties' rights on rescission are governed by Condition 7.2 which provides for the repayment of the deposit to the buyer with accrued interest, the return of documents to the seller and the cancellation of any registration of the contract at the buyer's expense.

2.3. Restrictions on the use of contractual rescission clauses

2.3.1. The most commonly encountered type of contractual rescission clause is one which gives the seller the right to rescind if he is unable or unwilling to answer a requisition raised by the buyer. This type of clause is narrowly construed by the courts who will only permit the seller to rescind where the requisition reveals an incumbrance of which the seller was previously unaware and which he is unable to discharge. They thus provide an emergency escape route for a seller in the event that an unforeseen difficulty with the title arises, and cannot be relied on by a seller who had not taken proper care to investigate his own title before drafting the contract, nor where the seller changes his mind after exchange and decides not to go ahead with the contract.[1] The Standard Conditions of Sale (3rd edition) do not, however, contain this type of clause.

2.3.2. This type of clause was examined by the court in *Selkirk* v. *Romar Investments*[2] from which case it appears that the conditions set out below must be satisfied before the court will allow the seller to rely on the clause:

(a) the seller can show some title; if he can show no title at all his withdrawal from the contract will be a breach entitling the buyer to damages;

(b) at the date of the contract the seller was unaware of the defect of which the buyer complains;

(c) the defect is either irremovable or only removable at disproportionate expense;

(d) the seller relies on the condition definitely and within a reasonable time;

(e) the seller is reasonable in exercising his right to withdraw.

2.3.3. The right to rescind under this type of clause can only be exercised in response to requisitions which are raised on the title itself and not in relation to, e.g. the form of the purchase deed or administrative matters relating to completion. Law of Property Act 1925, ss. 42, 45 and 125 gives the buyer non-excludable rights to raise requisitions about certain matters affecting the title and a contractual rescission clause would not be effective in circumstances affected by one of these sections.[3]

1. See *Day* v. *Singleton* [1899] 2 Ch. 320.
2. [1963] 3 All E.R. 994.
3. See above, Investigation of title, para. D.02.

2.4. Misrepresentation

2.4.1. In certain circumstances rescission may be available for misrepresentation. This remedy is further discussed below in para. M.05.

2.5. Misdescription

2.5.1. Misdescription results from an error in the particulars of sale, e.g. misdescribing the tenure of the property or the physical extent of the land to be sold.

2.5.2. If the misdescription is substantial the buyer may ask for rescission of the contract and compensation. A misdescription is substantial if its effect is substantially to deprive the buyer of his bargain.[1]

2.5.3. If the misdescription is not substantial the buyer can be forced to complete but may seek compensation by way of an abatement from the purchase price.

2.5.4. A misdescription of the property will usually also amount to a misrepresentation and it is more common nowadays to pursue a remedy under Misrepresentation Act 1967 than for misdescription.

1. See generally *Watson* v. *Burton* [1957] 1 W.L.R. 19.

2.6. Non-disclosure

2.6.1. Non-disclosure arises out of the seller's failure to comply with his duty of disclosure. The seller's duty of disclosure is discussed above in para. B.05.

2.6.2. Where the effect of the non-disclosure is substantial, i.e. its effect is substantially to deprive the buyer of his bargain, the buyer may seek rescission of the contract.

2.6.3. If the non-disclosure is not substantial the buyer can be forced to complete but may seek compensation by way of an abatement to the purchase price.

2.7. Mistake

2.7.1. Where the parties have entered a contract under a fundamental mistake of fact, the contract is void at common law. The transaction will be set aside by the court and the buyer is entitled to recover any money paid. Examples of this principle are mainly confined to situations where the subject matter of the contract had been destroyed before the contract was made[1] or where the buyer unknowingly contracts to buy property which he already owns.[2]

2.7.2. A mistake as to the quality of the subject matter of the contract will not normally have the effect of making the contract void at common law, although equity may in such circumstances refuse specific performance. If the effect of the mistake is to make the subject matter of the contract something entirely different from that which the parties thought it to be, the contract may be avoided.[3]

2.7.3. A mistake as to the identity of the contracting parties seems not to affect a written contract for the sale of land. The court treats the parties named in the contract as being the correct parties to it and will enforce the contract on that basis.[4]

1. I.e. *res extincta*: see, e.g. *Hitchcock* v. *Giddings* (1817) 4 Price 135.
2. I.e. *res sua*: see, e.g. *Cooper* v. *Phibbs* (1865) 17 I. Ch. R. 73.
3. See generally *Bell* v. *Lever Bros Ltd.* [1932] A.C. 161.
4. *Hector* v. *Lyons* (1989) 58 P. & C.R. 156. The principles relating to mistaken identity outlined in *Lewis* v. *Averay* (*No. 2*) [1973] 2 All E.R. 229 are inapplicable in this situation.

2.8. Limitation periods

2.8.1. Where the right to rescind arises out of a contractual provision, it must be exercised within the time-limits given within the condition, or if no time is specified within a reasonable time. An action based on a contractual rescission clause is subject to the normal six-year limitation period under Limitation Act 1980 unless the contract was by deed when a 12-year limitation period would be available.

2.8.2. Actions for rescission arising out of the general law principles, e.g. for misdescription are subject to the equitable doctrine of laches.

M.03. Breach of contract

See also: Delayed completion, para. M.01.
Specific performance, para. M.04.
Misrepresentation, para. M.05.
Covenants for title, para. M.09.

3.1. Introduction

3.1.1.   This section is intended as a brief overview of the subject under discussion. It is not intended to be used as a substitute for the advice of an experienced litigation solicitor. Prompt action by someone knowledgeable in the area of litigation is often required where problems arise in relation to a breach of contract.

3.1.2.   Remedies for breach of contract depend on whether the breach is of a condition in the contract, entitling the aggrieved party to terminate the contract and/or claim damages, or of a warranty, entitling the aggrieved party to claim damages only.

3.1.3.   A term of the contract will be a 'condition' if it is a major or fundamental term. Minor terms are classified as 'warranties'. In some cases it is not possible to classify a term as specifically falling into one or other of these categories until the consequences of the breach can be seen. Where the consequences are serious or far reaching, the unclassified term will be treated as a condition. In the converse situation it will be a warranty only. The terminology or labelling which the parties themselves have attached to the various terms of the contract is not conclusive as to their classification. In conveyancing contracts all terms are usually called 'conditions', but in law some of those terms would only have the status of warranties.[1]

3.1.4.   An action on a simple contract, i.e. one not made by deed, has a limitation period under Limitation Act 1980 of six years running from the date of the breach. A limitation period of 12 years applies where the contract was made by deed. A three-year limitation period applies where the amount claimed includes damages for personal injury or death. In some cases, Latent Damage Act 1986 may extend the limitation period.

3.1.5. On completion the terms of the contract merge with the purchase deed in so far as the two documents cover the same ground, and an action on the contract is no longer sustainable after completion except where it is based on a contract term which remains extant despite completion taking place. For this to happen the contract would generally have to contain a non-merger clause which expressly allowed a particular clause or clauses to remain alive after completion,[2] although sometimes the court may imply such an intention from the subject matter of the clause. If an action on the contract cannot be maintained, the buyer may have to attempt to pursue a remedy under the covenants for title or title guarantee.[3]

3.1.6. In any situation where the buyer suspects that the seller will or may default, consideration should be given to protecting the buyer's contract by registration as a caution (in registered land) or as a Class C(iv) land charge (if the seller's title is unregistered).

1. See *Cehave* v. *Bremer* [1976] Q.B. 44.
2. See Standard Condition 7.4.
3. See below, Covenants for title, para. M.09.

3.2. Specific performance

3.2.1. In sale of land cases an action for specific performance may provide an alternative remedy to an action for damages. This remedy is discussed below in para. M.04.

3.3. Exclusion clauses

3.3.1. An exclusion clause which purports to exclude liability under the contract must be incorporated in the contract if it is to be valid. In the case of a written contract, an exclusion clause contained within the writing is deemed to be incorporated whether or not the parties have read the document or were capable of reading it. In such circumstances illiteracy or inability to read English is no defence.[1]

3.3.2. Exclusion clauses must be specifically drafted to fit the breach which has occurred; thus a clause which excludes liability for breach of condition will not protect against a breach of warranty and vice versa.[2]

3.3.3. Any ambiguity in the wording of the clause will be construed against the party who is seeking to rely on the clause.

3.3.4. The clause normally only affords protection to the parties to the contract. Therefore an action in tort may be brought against a third party who caused the loss of which the plaintiff complains. He will be unable to shelter behind the protection of the clause since he does not enjoy privity of contract with the plaintiff.[3]

3.3.5. Exclusion clauses contained in contracts for the sale of land (except those relating to the exclusion of liability for misrepresentation) are not subject to the reasonableness test in Unfair Contract Terms Act 1977.

1. See *L'Estrange* v. *Graucob* [1934] 2 K.B. 394; *Thompson* v. *LMS Railway* [1930] 1 K.B .41.

2. See *Curtis* v. *Chemical Cleaning Co.* [1951] 1 K.B. 805.
3. See *Adler* v. *Dickson* [1955] 1 Q.B. 158.

3.4.   Delayed completion

3.4.1.   Unless time was of the essence of the completion date, or had been made so by service of a notice to complete, a completion which takes place later than the date specified in the contract does not of itself entitle the aggrieved party to terminate the contract.

3.4.2.   Late completion will, however, be a breach of warranty entitling the aggrieved party to recover damages for any loss suffered as a result of the delay.[1]

1. *Raineri* v. *Miles; Wiejski (Third Party)* [1981] A.C. 1050 and see above, para. M.01.4.

3.5.   Damages for breach

3.5.1.   Damages for breach of a contract for the sale of land are assessed under the normal contractual principles established in *Hadley* v. *Baxendale*.[1] Thus, subject to establishing causation, damages for losses naturally flowing from the breach may be claimed and in addition reasonably foreseeable consequential loss.

3.5.2.   The quantum of damages under the consequential loss head are limited to loss which was reasonably foreseeable by the defaulting party in the light of the facts known by him (or by his agent) at the date when the contract was made (not at the date of the breach of contract).

3.5.3.   The starting point for damages for breach of a contract for the sale of land is the difference between the contract and market prices of the property at the date of the breach. To this may be added actual financial loss suffered as a result of the breach, e.g. wasted conveyancing costs, legal costs involved in the purchase of another property, interest payable on a mortgage or bridging loan, costs of removal or storage of furniture, costs of alternative accommodation pending purchase of another property.[2]

3.5.4.   Loss of development profit, or loss of profit on a sub-sale, can only be claimed if the defendant was aware of the plaintiff's proposals for the property at the time the contract was made.[3]

3.5.5.   Where the buyer defaults and the seller makes a loss on the resale, that loss can be claimed as damages but, if the seller makes a profit on the resale, he would have to give credit for the amount of the profit in his action since he is only entitled to recover his financial loss and is not entitled to benefit from the buyer's breach. The purpose of contractual damages is to place the parties in the position in which they would have been had the contract been duly performed. There is no punitive element in the assessment of damages.

3.5.6.   As a general principle of contractual damages, it is only possible to recover for financial loss, and no claim can be made in respect of mental distress suffered as a result of the defendant's breach. The practice of awarding a nominal sum in respect of damages for mental distress established by *Jarvis* v. *Swans Tours*[4] seems to be confined to leisure and pleasure contracts, e.g. holiday contracts and contracts for leisure activities.

3.5.7.   Damages can normally only be claimed in respect of losses which have occurred since the contract was made; thus there is generally no possibility of recovering expenses incurred at the pre-contract stage of the transaction, e.g. for a wasted surveyor's report or search fees.[5]

3.5.8.   The plaintiff must have attempted to mitigate his loss, e.g. by trying to purchase another similar property (as disappointed buyer) or by attempting to resell the property (as disappointed seller). The attempt to mitigate should be made; otherwise the award of damages may be reduced because of the failure to mitigate. If the plaintiff attempts to mitigate and in so doing increases his loss, the defendant will be liable for the increased loss.

3.5.9.   Credit must be given in the claim for damages for any compensation received under Standard Condition 7.3 (or similar provision)[6] or for any deposit forfeited by the seller.

3.5.10.   Actions claiming a sum under £50,000 will be brought in the county court; above that limit, the High Court has jurisdiction. Actions brought in the county court for sums not exceeding £1,000 may be referred to arbitration (but not if there is a dispute over a point of law) in which case no costs are normally awarded in the action. In other county court cases, a successful litigant may be penalised as to costs if he does not recover more than £1,000 in his judgment, or does not recover more than the amount paid into court by the defendant prior to the hearing. The question of costs must be fully discussed with the client before the decision to start proceedings is taken, since in some cases the action for breach of contract may not be cost effective for the client.

1. (1854) 9 Exch. 341.
2. See, e.g. *Beard* v. *Porter* [1948] 1 K.B. 321.
3. *Diamond* v. *Campbell-Jones* [1961] Ch. 22; *cf. Cottrill* v. *Steyning and Littlehampton Building Society* [1966] 2 All E.R. 295.
4. [1973] Q.B. 233; and see *Bliss* v. *South-East Thames Regional Health Authority* [1987] I.C.R. 700.
5. But see *Lloyd* v. *Stanbury* [1971] 2 All E.R. 267 where pre-contract expenditure including money spent on repairs to the property was recovered.
6. See above, Delayed completion, para. M.01.

3.6.   Action in tort

3.6.1.   If an action in contract is not possible, e.g. a valid exclusion clause prevents the claim, an action in tort may be considered. The limitation period for such an action will usually be six years from the time the tort was committed, but a three-year limitation period applies where the claim includes damages for personal injury or death. Actions in tort may also be considered where it is desired to sue a third party who was not privy to the contract. Most actions of this type will lie in negligence which imposes a fairly onerous burden of proof on the plaintiff. The quantum of damages is assessed using different principles and in general damages for pure economic loss cannot be claimed.[1]

1. Damages are awarded following the principles laid down in *The Wagon Mound* [1961] A.C. 388. See *Junior Books* v. *Veitchi* [1983] 1 A.C. 520 and *Murphy* v. *Brentwood District Council* [1991] 1 A.C. 398 relating to economic loss.

3.7.   Misrepresentation

3.7.1.   Where an action on the contract cannot be sustained an action in misrepresentation may still be viable. This remedy is further discussed below in para. M.05.

3.8.   Mareva injunction

3.8.1.   Although not a conventional sale of land remedy, a Mareva injunction could be obtained if it was suspected that the defendant was intending to remove his assets from the jurisdiction in order to avoid liability. Such an injunction would not provide a direct remedy but would protect the plaintiff's position as an interim measure. Prompt action is required.

3.9.   Frustration

3.9.1.   Where the contract has become impossible of performance due to an unforeseen act which is beyond the control of both parties, the contract is frustrated and the parties' rights and obligations are terminated without there being liability for breach on either side. The parties' rights in this situation are, in the absence of specific contractual provision, governed by Law Reform (Frustrated Contracts) Act 1943 which aims to restore the parties to their pre-contract position without imposing penalties. Frustration is usually raised as a defence to an action for breach of contract and, if successfully pleaded, provides an absolute defence to the defendant.

3.9.2.   Although the general view is that the doctrine of frustration does not apply to contracts for the sale of land, dicta from the House of Lords in *National Carriers Ltd.* v. *Panalpina (Northern) Ltd.*[1] suggest otherwise. It is therefore possible that the defence of frustration might be allowed in a situation where, e.g. the land which was the subject of the sale was totally destroyed by landslip into the sea between the dates of contract and completion. If the land was destroyed before the date of the contract, the contract would be void for common mistake. Frustration would not apply where the property burned down between contract and completion. Neither does it apply where the property is subject to a compulsory acquisition order.[2]

1. [1981] A.C. 675.
2. *E. Johnson & Co (Barbados) Ltd.* v. *NSR Ltd* [1996] E.G.C.S. 133.

3.10. **Return of deposit**

3.10.1. Where the buyer defaults on completion, the seller will wish to forfeit the deposit, but Law of Property Act 1925, s.49(2) gives the court an absolute discretion to order the return of the deposit to the buyer. A contractual clause attempting to negate the provisions of section 49 is of no effect.[1]

3.10.2. Where the seller defaults on completion the buyer will have to bring an action under Law of Property Act 1925, s.49(2) to recover his deposit.

3.10.3. Under section 49, the court appears to have power to return all of the deposit or none of it to the buyer. There is no discretion to order the return of part of the deposit even where this course of action would represent the most equitable way of dealing with the position between the parties. It seems, however, that the court may be prepared to order the return of the whole deposit to the buyer on condition that the buyer reimburse certain expenses to the seller, which would seem to be a fair way round the restrictions imposed by section 49.[2]

1. *Country & Metropolitan Homes Surrey Ltd.* v. *Topclaim Ltd.* [1996] 3 W.L.R. 525.
2. See *Universal Corporation* v. *Five Ways Properties* [1979] 1 All E.R. 552; *James Macara Ltd.* v. *Barclay* [1945] K.B. 148; *cf. Dimsdale Developments (South East) Ltd.* v. *De Haan* (1984) 47 P. & C.R. 1.

3.11. **Trade Descriptions Act 1968**

3.11.1. Under Trade Descriptions Act 1968, it is an offence to make a false statement in a contract for the supply of services (including land). The Act applies where the seller is acting in the course of a business and so would be applicable where, e.g. a buyer was purchasing land from a builder, but not in an ordinary residential purchase between private individuals. If an action in contract or misrepresentation cannot for some reason be sustained, it may be worth considering reporting a 'false statement', e.g. a misrepresentation about the quality of the property, to the local trading standards office and asking them to pursue a prosecution under the Act. Such a prosecution does not afford a direct remedy for the client. On conviction for the offence it would, however, be possible for the client to ask the court for a compensation order under Powers of Criminal Courts Act 1973, s.35. Where the conviction is obtained in the magistrates' court, the compensation order cannot exceed £2,000 in respect of each offence.[1]

1. See *Breed* v. *Cluett* [1970] 2 Q.B. 459 where such an order was obtained following a builder's conviction under this Act for making false statements about the availability of NHBC protection on a new house.

3.12. **Property Misdescriptions Act 1991**

3.12.1. This Act which came into force on 4 April 1993 creates a criminal offence which is committed where a false or misleading description is applied to certain aspects of the property as listed in regulations made under the Act in the course of an estate agency or property development business. The offence is of strict liability and can be committed by publishing a misleading photograph of property as well as by misdescribing property orally or in writing. An action must generally be brought within three years of the alleged offence. Enforcement of the Act is through criminal proceedings brought by the Trading Standards Department for the area. Some estate agents are now seeking an indemnity from the seller in respect of liability under this Act. The seller should be advised not to accept such a clause.

3.13. MIG policies

3.13.1. A lender who benefits from the proceeds of a MIG policy does not need to five credit for this sum when quantifying damages.[1]

1. *Europe Mortgage v. Halifax Estate Agencies* [1996] N.P.C. 68.

3.14. Checklist

3.14.1. A client who is encountering problems with a property transaction will probably first seek the advice of the person who is advising him in the sale or purchase. A checklist of the main points to be considered when discussing the client's problems is set out below. These matters should be taken into consideration when deciding whether and how to pursue a remedy for breach of contract and cover the main points of information which will be needed by the litigation department if the matter is handed to them for further action. In addition to the matters listed below, the person taking instructions should obtain a complete history of the conveyancing transaction from the client, including a detailed timetable of the events leading to the present dispute, and should obtain from the client either the original documents relevant to the matter, or copies of them.

3.14.2. The following is a checklist of the main points to be considered:

    (a) Has there been a breach of contract?

    (b) If so, what type of breach, i.e. of condition or warranty?

    (c) What remedy does the client want, e.g. damages or specific performance?

    (d) Is there a valid exclusion clause which might prevent the claim?

    (e) When did the limitation period start to run?

    (f) What (approximately) is the total of the client's financial loss?

    (g) How much of that loss would be recoverable, bearing in mind the rules on remoteness of damage?

    (h) Would the costs of an action be justified?

    (i) Who should be sued, e.g. other party to the contract, solicitor, surveyor?

    (j) If a claim cannot be made in contract, is there a viable alternative action, e.g. in tort or for misrepresentation?

M.04. Specific performance

4.1. **Introduction**
4.2. **General bars to the award**
4.3. **Delay**

4.4. **Damages in lieu**
4.5. **Standard Conditions of Sale**

See also: Breach of contract, para. M.03.

4.1. Introduction

4.1.1. Although this is an equitable remedy which is granted at the discretion of the court, an order for specific performance is not uncommon in sale of land cases where, since no two pieces of land are identical, an award of damages would be inadequate compensation for the injured party's loss.[1]

4.1.2. The claim can be made either on its own, or in conjunction with a claim for damages or rescission, depending on the circumstances.

4.1.3. Specific performance cannot generally be awarded for breach of a contract to grant a loan (whether secured or unsecured).[2] It would not therefore be available where a lender, in breach of contract, withdrew his offer of mortgage.

1. *Hall* v. *Warren* (1804) 9 Ves. 605.
2. *Rogers* v. *Challis* (1859) 27 Beav. 175.

4.2. General bars to the award

4.2.1. As an equitable remedy, the award of a decree of specific performance is subject to the usual principles of equity. It will not therefore be awarded where:

    (a) an award of damages would adequately compensate for the loss sustained by the breach;

    (b) one of the contracting parties lacks full contractual capacity;

    (c) the contract contains a vitiating element, e.g. mistake, fraud, illegality;

    (d) the enforcement of the order would require the constant supervision of the court;

    (e) a third party has acquired an interest for value in the property;

    (f) the award would cause exceptional hardship to the guilty party;

    (g) the seller cannot make good title.

4.3. **Delay**

4.3.1. The Limitation Acts do not usually apply to equitable remedies, but the doctrine of laches (lapse of time) does. The remedy may therefore be barred if the innocent party is dilatory in seeking an award.[1]

4.3.2. Unlike a common law action for breach of contract, the injured party can apply for a decree before a breach of contract has actually occurred (i.e. before contractual completion date) provided that he can show that a serious breach is likely to take place if the court does not intervene.[2]

4.3.3. Laches will not bar the application where the buyer is already in possession of the property.[3]

1. *Lazard Brothers & Co. Ltd.* v. *Fairfield Properties Co. (Mayfair) Ltd.* (1977) 121 S.J. 793.
2. *Marks* v. *Lilley* [1959] 2 All E.R. 647; *Hasham* v. *Zenab* [1960] A.C. 316, P.C.
3. *Williams* v. *Greatrex* [1957] 1 W.L.R. 31.

4.4. **Damages in lieu**

4.4.1. Subject to the above principles the injured party always has the right to apply for a decree of specific performance, but there is no guarantee that an award will be forthcoming in any given circumstances. If, in a situation where specific performance would otherwise be available to the injured party, the court decides not to make such an order, it may award damages in lieu of specific performance under Supreme Court Act 1981, s.50. Such damages are assessed using normal contractual principles as outlined above in para. M.03.

4.4.2. Where an award of specific performance has been made but has not been complied with, the injured party may return to the court asking the court to withdraw the order and to substitute the decree of specific performance with an award of damages.[1]

1. *Johnson* v. *Agnew* [1980] A.C. 367.

4.5. **Standard Conditions of Sale**

4.5.1. Where a notice to complete has been served by the seller under Standard Condition 6.8 and is not complied with, by Standard Condition 7.5 and 7.6, the innocent party's right to apply for a decree of specific performance is not excluded.

M.05. Misrepresentation

5.1. Definition

5.1.1. A misrepresentation is an untrue statement of fact which is relied on by the aggrieved party, which induces him to enter the contract, and as a result of which he suffers loss.

5.1.2. The statement must be of fact, not law.[1] A statement of opinion is not actionable unless it can be proved that the opinion was never genuinely held.[2]

5.1.3. A misrepresentation may be fraudulent, i.e. deliberately dishonest within the definition of fraud laid down in *Derry* v. *Peek*,[3] negligent, i.e. made carelessly without having checked the facts, but not necessarily negligent within the tortious meaning of that word, or innocent, i.e. a genuine and innocently made mistake.

1. The distinction between fact and law is not always clear; see *Solle* v. *Butcher* [1950] 1 K.B. 671.
2. *Edgington* v. *Fitzmaurice* (1885) 29 Ch. 459.
3. (1889) 14 App. Cas. 337.

5.2. Fraudulent misrepresentation

5.2.1. Where the misrepresentation has been made fraudulently, the aggrieved party may bring an action in tort for deceit which may result in rescission of the contract and damages.

5.2.2. The party who alleges fraud must prove fraud. This places a very onerous burden of proof on the plaintiff in the action and, except where the evidence of fraud is indefeasible, it is more usual to treat the misrepresentation as having been made negligently and to pursue a remedy under Misrepresentation Act 1967.

5.3. Actions under Misrepresentation Act 1967

5.3.1. The plaintiff must show that he has an action in misrepresentation as defined in para. 5.1. above, after which the burden of proof shifts to the defendant who, in broad terms, has to disprove negligence.

5.3.2. A misrepresentation is negligent if the defendant cannot prove that he had grounds for belief and did believe the statement he made was true up to the time the contract was made. There is therefore a duty to correct a statement which, although being true at the time when it was made, subsequently becomes untrue.

5.3.3. The remedies for a negligent misrepresentation are rescission of the contract and damages.

5.3.4. If the defendant successfully establishes the defence of grounds and belief outlined in para. 5.3.2. above, thus showing that the misrepresentation was truly innocent, rescission is available, but not damages.

5.3.5. Although Misrepresentation Act 1967 allows a party to ask for rescission of the contract, the award of the remedy remains within the equitable jurisdiction of the court and is thus discretionary and subject to the equitable bars.[1]

5.3.6. If none of the equitable bars applies, but nevertheless the court decides not to grant rescission, it may instead award damages in lieu of rescission to the plaintiff.[2]

5.3.7. Damages under Misrepresentation Act 1967 are awarded on a tortious basis[3] under Misrepresentation Act 1967, s.2(2).

5.3.8. An award of damages can be made under both the subsections of section 2, i.e. an award in lieu of rescission and an award to compensate the plaintiff for his loss, subject to the overriding principle that the plaintiff cannot recover more than his actual loss; thus the awards under the two subsections are not cumulative.

5.3.9. Rescission is only likely to be awarded where the result of the misrepresentation is substantially to deprive the plaintiff of his bargain.[4]

5.3.10. An action in misrepresentation does not arise out of the contract, since the misrepresentation is a non-contractual statement which has the effect of inducing the contract. Neither does it arise out of tort. The limitation periods prescribed by Limitation Act 1980 do not therefore apply in this situation and it seems that the limitation period for an action based on misrepresentation relies on the equitable doctrine of laches.

5.3.11. Where a misrepresentation has become incorporated as a minor term of the contract it is possible by Misrepresentation Act 1967, s.1 to treat the statement as a mere representation and to pursue a remedy under Misrepresentation Act 1967. This option would benefit the plaintiff by giving him the right to ask for rescission of the contract as well as damages. If his action were confined to breach of a minor contractual term his only available remedy would be damages.

1. The equitable bars are listed above in para. M.04.2.
2. Misrepresentation Act 1967, s.2(1).
3. *Chesneau* v. *Interhome, The Times,* 9 June 1983, C.A.; and see *Royscott Trust* v. *Rogerson* [1991] 2 Q.B. 297.
4. See *Gosling* v. *Anderson, The Times,* 8 February 1972; *cf. Museprime Properties Ltd.* v. *Adhill Properties Ltd.* (1990) 61 P. & C.R. 111.

5.4.   Imputed knowledge

5.4.1.   Knowledge gained by a solicitor in the course of a transaction is deemed to be known by the solicitor's client whether or not this is in fact the case. Thus where a solicitor makes an incorrect reply to pre-contract enquiries, basing his reply on an erroneous assessment of the title deeds, the solicitor's knowledge and also his misstatement is attributable to the client who will be liable to the buyer in misrepresentation.[1] In such a situation the solicitor would be liable to his own client in negligence.

5.4.2.   The converse situation is also true. If, for example, the seller makes a misrepresentation to the buyer personally, but the misrepresentation is later corrected in correspondence between the seller's solicitors and the buyer's solicitors, the buyer is deemed to know of the correction (even if not actually told by his solicitor) and would not in these circumstances be able to sustain an action for misrepresentation against the seller.[2]

1. *Cemp Properties* v. *Dentsply* [1989] 35 E.G. 99.
2. *Strover* v. *Harrington* [1988] Ch. 390.

5.5.   Exclusion clauses

5.5.1.   By Misrepresentation Act 1967, s.3, as amended by Unfair Contract Terms Act 1977, s.8, any clause which purports to limit or exclude liability for misrepresentation is only valid in so far as it satisfies the reasonableness test laid down in section 11 and Schedule 2 Unfair Contract Terms Act 1977.

5.5.2.   The reasonableness test is applied subjectively, in the light of the circumstances which were known to the parties at the time when the contract was made. It therefore depends on the circumstances of each particular case as to whether the exclusion clause is valid in that situation. There is no guarantee that any given form of wording will satisfy the test unless and until the clause is subjected to the scrutiny of the court. Such clauses therefore require great care in drafting.

5.5.3.   Standard Condition 7.1 purports to limit the seller's liability for, *inter alia*, misrepresentation. The validity of this clause is subject to its satisfying the reasonableness test on the facts of each particular case.

5.5.4.   The majority of misrepresentation actions arising out of property transactions appear to result from erroneous replies to pre-contract enquiries. Some standard forms of pre-contract enquiries (but not the Seller's Property Information Form used in Protocol transactions) have an exclusion clause printed on them. This exclusion clause is also subject to the reasonableness test.[1]

1. See *Walker* v. *Boyle* [1982] 1 All E.R. 634 where an exclusion clause contained in a then current edition of a standard form of pre-contract enquiries failed the reasonableness test. In the same case, the exclusion clause contained in the 19th edition of the National Conditions of Sale was held to be invalid for the same reason.

M.06.   Other causes of action

See also: Rectification and indemnity, para. M.07.
Solicitor's negligence, para. M.10.

6.1.   Introduction

6.1.1.   In certain circumstances it may be possible or necessary to seek a remedy from someone other than a party to the contract. Such action will normally have to be brought in tort since no privity of contract will exist between the potential parties to the action.

6.1.2.   A non-exhaustive list of suggestions of alternative sources of action which might be relevant if an action on the contract was unavailable is included here.

6.2.   Solicitor's liability

6.2.1.   A solicitor who is guilty of bad professional work may be reprimanded by the Office for the Supervision of Solicitors who additionally may order the solicitor to rectify a mistake at his own expense or to waive his costs or repay costs to the client. The Bureau can also order the solicitor to pay compensation of up to £1,000 to the client.

6.2.2.   A solicitor who has been negligent in the conduct of a client's affairs can be sued in negligence.

6.2.3.   If a client has suffered loss as a result of default by a solicitor which loss cannot be recovered from any other source, the Solicitors' Compensation Fund may be able to assist.

6.2.4.   A solicitor's duty of care is owed not only to his own client, but in certain circumstances to third parties as well.[1] It may therefore be possible in some circumstances for an aggrieved buyer to sue his seller's solicitor in negligence[2] although the court has held that in a normal conveyancing transaction the seller's solicitor does not owe a duty of care to the buyer.[3]

6.2.5.   Where the solicitor's own client had been held liable for, e.g. breach of contract in circumstances where the breach was caused by the party's solicitor, the solicitor can be required to indemnify the client against his liability for damages.[4]

1. See *Ross* v. *Caunters* [1980] 1 Ch. 297 but see *Murphy* v. *Brentwood District Council* [1991] 1 A.C. 398.
2. See, e.g. *Wilson* v. *Bloomfield* (1979) 123 S.J. 860 (C.A).
3. *Gran Gelato Ltd.* v. *Richcliff Ltd.* [1992] Ch. 560.
4. E.g. *Cemp Properties* v. *Dentsply* [1989] 35 E.G. 99.

6.3.   **Breach of warranty of authority**

6.3.1.   Where an agent acts outside the scope of his authority he will be liable to the third party for breach of warranty of authority.[1]

6.3.2.   A solicitor or estate agent who exceeds his client's authority may thus be sued by a third party.[2]

1. *Yonge* v. *Toynbee* [1910] 1 K.B. 215.
2. *Suleman* v. *Shahsavari* [1989] 2 All E.R. 460; *Penn* v. *Bristol and West Building Society* [1995] Ch. 938.

6.4.   **Estate agents**

6.4.1.   An estate agent may be liable for misrepresentation occurring in the particulars of sale of the property.

6.4.2.   Liability may also exist if the agent exceeds his authority as under para. 6.3. above.

6.4.3.   An estate agent who is authorised to *sell* the property (but not one who is merely empowered to procure a buyer) may have authority to receive the contract deposit.[1]

6.4.4.   As far as pre-contract deposits are concerned, unless there is express authority from the seller to take and hold a pre-contract deposit, such sum must be held on behalf of the buyer. If the pre-contract deposit is lost, e.g. where an estate agent absconds with the money, the loss falls on the buyer except where the agent was expressly authorised to take the pre-contract deposit.[2]

6.4.5.   The estate agent's duty to the seller is similar to the common law duties which exist between an agent and his principal.[3]

6.4.6.   The estate agent's duty is owed to his principal, i.e. the seller client, and generally he owes no duty to the buyer.[4] There may also in some circumstances be a liability in relation to the pre-contract deposit, or in negligence under *Hedley Byrne* v. *Heller* principles.[5]

6.4.7.   Similar remedies to those afforded under Trade Descriptions Act 1968 lie under the Property Misdescriptions Act 1991 against an estate agent (including a solicitor who is acting as an estate agent) who misdescribes a property which he is selling. This Act creates a criminal offence which is committed where a false or misleading description is applied to property in the course of an estate agency or property development business. The offence is of strict liability and can be committed by publishing a misleading photograph of property as well as by misdescribing property orally or in writing. An action must generally be brought within three years of the alleged offence. Enforcement of the Act is through criminal proceedings brought by the Trading Standard Department for the area.

1. *Boote* v. *R.T. Shiels & Co.* [1978] 1 N.Z.L.R. 445.
2. *Sorrell* v. *Finch* [1977] A.C. 728.
3. But see *Luxor* v. *Cooper* [1941] A.C. 108; *cf. Prebble (P.G.) & Co.* v. *West* (1969) 211 E.G. 831.
4. *McCulloch* v. *Lane Fox, The Times,* 22 December 1995 (C.A).
5. [1964] A.C. 465.

6.5.   Surveyors

6.5.1.   A surveyor owes his client a duty to perform his contract with reasonable skill and care. This common law duty has been replaced by the implied term to the same effect under Supply of Goods and Services Act 1982, s.13 but the surveyor's duty, and thus his liability, are necessarily limited by the extent of the instructions given to him.

6.5.2.   If the problem with the survey stems from the results of a valuation report, the surveyor will generally have been instructed by the client's lender, and so there will probably be no contractual relationship between the client and the surveyor; thus any liability which does exist will necessarily be in tort.

6.5.3.   In other cases a contractual relationship between the client and the surveyor will or may exist, giving the choice of action under either contract or tort.

6.5.4.   An exclusion clause purporting to exclude liability for the survey will be construed narrowly against the party seeking to rely on it and will only be valid in so far as it is fair and reasonable in the context of the particular contract in which it is included.[1]

6.5.5.   A surveyor who prepares a valuation report for a lender in the knowledge (express or implied) that the buyer will see the report and may rely on it in deciding whether or not to proceed with his purchase owes a duty of care to the buyer.[2] This duty will not, however, apply in every case. Where, for example, it is reasonable for the surveyor to assume that the buyer would be obtaining his own independent survey — which may be a fair assumption for him to make where the property is at the top end of the property market — or where the buyer is experienced in property matters, the surveyor may be entitled to shelter behind the protection of his exclusion clause and thus avoid liability.[3]

6.5.6. Where a surveyor is sued, the quantum of damages is usually limited to the difference between what the property was actually worth at the date of the contract and what it would have been worth if the survey report had been accurate (not what the client paid for the property, or the cost of repairs). Thus, in some circumstances, the amount of damages recoverable will not equate with the client's loss. For example, the difference in value may be only a few thousand pounds, but the cost of repairs to put the property right at the date of the action may be huge, and the client can only recover the smaller sum representing the difference in value.[4] Loss in value to the property which is attributable to the fall in value of the property market is not generally recoverable as a head of loss.[5] The lender's contributory negligence (e.g. in relying on the valuation without checking it) may reduce the award made against the surveyor.[6]

6.5.7. There is no doubt that a valuer owes a duty to the seller to provide a valuation which is as accurate as circumstances allow — a duty of skill and care is owed to the seller. If the valuer's error results in there being an undervalue of the property, the measure of damages will usually be the difference between the sale price and the market value of the property. If on the other hand an over-valuation is given, full contractual damages within *Hadley* v. *Baxendale*[7] principles will be payable to the seller, including loss caused by his inability to sell the property within a reasonable time, if this has been a consequence of the over-valuation.

6.5.8. The cause of action by a lender in respect of a negligent valuation arises when the loss crystallises, i.e. at the date when the security is sold.[8]

6.5.9. The RICS appraisal and valuation manual ('The Red Book') contains mandatory guidelines for surveyors to follow when undertaking surveys and valuations of all types of property. Non-observance of these guidelines may be evidence of negligence.

1. The reasonableness test in Unfair Contract Terms Act 1977, s.11 must be satisfied.
2. *Smith* v. *Eric Bush* [1990] 1 A.C. 831; and see *Qureshi* v. *Liassides* (unreported) (1995) E.G. 123 (case comment).
3. *Stevenson* v. *Nationwide Building Society* (1984) 272 E.G. 663.
4. *Philips* v. *Ward* [1956] 1 All E.R. 874; and see *Watts* v. *Morrow, The Independent,* 20 August 1991.
5. *Banque Bruxelles Lambert S.A.* v. *Eagle Star Insurance,* [1995] 12 E.G. 144, C.A. reversed on appeal to the House of Lords *sub nomine South Australia Asset Management (Pty) Ltd.* v. *York Montague* [1996] N.P.C. 100.
6. *Ibid.*
7. (1854) 9 Exch. 341.
8. *First National Commercial Bank* v. *Humberts, The Times,* 27 January 1995, C.A.

6.6. Dangerous substances

6.6.1. There may be heavy liability (in financial terms) to third parties in tort, in negligence[1] or under Environmental Protection Act 1990 if, e.g. untreated sewage escapes into a waterway and pollutes the water.

1. Subject to foreseeability: *Cambridge Water Company* v. *Eastern Counties Leather plc* [1994] 1 All E.R. 53.

6.7. **Local searches**

6.7.1. In certain circumstances compensation may be claimed under Local Land Charges Act 1975, s.10, where there has been an error in an official search.[1]

1. See above, Pre-contract searches and enquiries, para. B.10.

6.8. **HM Land Registry**

6.8.1. In certain circumstances compensation may be claimed from HM Land Registry where loss is suffered as a result of an error on the register or an error in an official search.[1]

1. See below, Rectification and indemnity, para. M.07.

6.9. **Covenants in freehold land**

6.9.1. Where restrictive covenants have been validly annexed to land, the person with the benefit of those covenants (who may be a successor in title of the original covenantee) will be able to enforce the covenants by injunction and/or damages against either the present estate owner of the land which bears the burden of the covenants or the original covenantor. The original covenantor may, in turn, be able to recover his loss from his immediate successor in title through an indemnity covenant.

6.9.2. In certain circumstances it may be possible to make an *ex parte* application to the Lands Tribunal under Law of Property Act 1925, s.84 for the modification or release of an obsolete restrictive covenant and so remove the potential liability under it.

6.9.3. The burden of positive covenants does not run with freehold land and can only be enforced directly between the original contracting parties.[1] An original covenantor who is held liable in this way may seek to recoup his own loss if an indemnity covenant was taken from his immediate successor in title.[2]

1. *Rhone* v. *Stephens, The Times,* 18 March 1994, H.L.
2. See Rentcharges, para. K.15. above and *Preston and Newsom: Restrictive Covenants Affecting Freehold Land.*

6.10. **Covenants in leasehold land**

6.10.1. Although both positive and restrictive covenants are enforceable, liability is limited by the doctrines of privity of contract and of estate. It may not therefore always be possible for a head-landlord to take direct action against a sub-tenant since neither privity of contract nor of estate exist in this situation.

6.10.2.   Similarly, in the absence of special provisions in the lease, it is not generally possible for one tenant directly to sue a fellow tenant for breach of one of the covenants contained in their leases, and the enforcement of the covenant against the offending tenant frequently has to be brought by the landlord at the request of the injured tenant.

6.10.3.   Liability on leasehold covenants is further discussed in paras. K.06. (Long-term residential tenancies) and K.10. (Liability on covenants in leases).

6.11.   **Estate agent's commission**

6.11.1.   The following points are relevant to the estate agent's entitlement to his commission and when it becomes payable.

6.11.2.   The contract between the agent and the seller must be absolutely clear as to what is included in the price. For example does the fee quoted include, e.g. advertising, valuation, agent's expenses, VAT, or are these to be added to the bill?

6.11.3.   In the absence of express provision in the contract no charge can be made for abortive work.[1]

6.11.4.   As a general principle, an agent's entitlement to his fee depends on his introduction of a ready, able and willing buyer. This means someone who is prepared and able to go ahead to completion not merely a 'subject to contract' offer.[2]

6.11.5.   It is in the estate agent's interests to ensure that the contract is quite specific as to the time when his fee for the estate agency work becomes due, and that the fee becomes payable as soon as a binding contract is entered into with the buyer − not on condition that completion takes place. This type of provision (commonly found in estate agent's contracts) ensures that the commission is still payable even if the contract is terminated between exchange and completion or completion fails to take place.[3]

6.11.6.   The courts interpret the expressions 'the agent is to find a buyer' or 'the agent is to introduce a buyer' as meaning that the buyer must actually sign the contract before the commission becomes due.[4]

6.11.7.   Three conditions must all be satisfied before the agent can claim his commission:

     (a)   the agent must introduce a person who enters a valid binding contract. This means a contract which satisfies the requirements of Law of Property (Miscellaneous Provisions) Act 1989, s.2 and the contract is not otherwise voidable for mistake, fraud, etc.;

     (b)   the buyer must be willing and able (financially) to complete. The buyer's ability in this respect is judged at contractual date for completion, so if there is a dispute about the agent's entitlement to his fee the contractual completion date must be allowed to pass before proceedings for the commission are commenced. This is so even if, under the contract with the seller, commission became payable on exchange of contracts;

(c) the agent must be the effective cause of the sale. This means that he must be able to show that his introduction of the buyer led to the formation of the contract of sale between the seller and buyer.

6.11.8. If the buyer fails to complete the contract and is in breach of his contract with the seller, unless commission was expressly due on exchange, no completion means no commission. If, however, the seller successfully claims damages from the buyer for breach, the agent may be entitled to recover a *quantum meruit* out of the seller's damages.[5]

6.11.9. Where two agents are instructed by the seller, there is frequently an argument about which of the agents is entitled to the commission for the sale. The principle here is that commission is payable to the first agent to secure a buyer who enters a binding contract.[6]

6.11.10. If it is the seller who withdraws from the sale, no contract means no commission, unless the contract contains express provision to the contrary. It makes no difference in this situation if the seller rescinds after the contract is made (even if the seller is in breach).

6.11.11. If a sole agency is agreed with the client, it is important that the terms of that agreement are fully and clearly explained to the client so he cannot complain of being misled if things go wrong. The danger as far as the client is concerned is that he does not understand what a sole agency means, instructs a second agent who sells the property and then feels aggrieved because both agents claim to be entitled to commission. If a sole agency agreement is expressed in terms using the phrase 'sole agent', the seller is not entitled to instruct another agent to sell the property, but there is nothing to prevent him from contracting a private sale and in that way depriving the agent of his commission. On the other hand, if the expression 'sole right to sell' is used this prohibits the seller from contracting a private sale on his own initiative. This latter phrase is therefore much more restrictive of the seller's rights than the former and would merit explicit explanation of its implications to the client. The term 'sole selling agent' is construed as meaning 'sole agent', so the seller is not prevented from contracting a private sale if this phrase is used.

6.11.12. If the seller withdraws his instructions from the agent before a sale contract is entered into, this is not a breach of the sole agency contract (the seller is entitled to change his mind and this is a normal and acceptable risk attached to estate agency) but a *sale* contracted elsewhere will be and the sole agent can then claim damages for the breach.

6.11.13. An agent who is himself in breach of his duty to his client may forfeit his right to commission.

6.11.14. Estate Agents (Provision of Information) Regulations 1991 require estate agents to inform their clients in writing of the terms of the agreement between themselves and their clients including, where appropriate, the meaning of 'sole agency' and 'sole selling rights'. The Regulations have adopted definitions of these two phrases which are similar to the explanations contained in para. 6.11.11. above.

1. *Lott* v. *Outhwaite* (1893) 10 T.L.R. 76.
2. *Luxor* v. *Cooper* [1941] A.C. 108.
3. *Poole* v. *Clarke & Co.* [1945] 2 All E.R. 445; *cf. Midgely Estates Ltd.* v. *Hand* [1952] 2 Q.B. 432.
4. *Jones* v. *Lowe* [1945] K.B. 73.
5. *Boots* v. *E. Christopher & Co.* [1952] 1 K.B. 89.
6. *A.A. Dickson & Co.* v. *O'Leary* (1979) 254 E.G. 731 suggests that the seller cannot be made liable to pay commission twice over.

6.12. Timeshare properties

6.12.1. The Timeshare Act 1992 gives the prospective buyer of a timeshare property a 14-day 'cooling off' period during which he has the right to cancel the contract. The Act only applies where the buyer is buying from the developer and not to 'secondhand' timeshares.

6.12.2. Notice of the buyer's right to cancel must be given by the seller in prescribed form. Failure to give the correct notice renders the contract unenforceable and the seller is guilty of a criminal offence punishable by a fine. Enforcement of the Act is the responsibility of the local weights and measures office.

6.12.3. The publication of a draft E.U. Directive on Timeshare is likely to lead to the repeal of the existing legislation and its replacement with regulations in accordance with such Directive.

6.13. Squatters

6.13.1. A summary procedure for the eviction of squatters exists under Order 24 of County Court Rules or under Criminal Justice and Public Order Act 1994, ss.72–75. The 1994 Act applies to both residential and commercial property.

FURTHER REFERENCE

Preston and Newsom: Restrictive Covenants Affecting Freehold Land, G.L. Newsom, Sweet & Maxwell.

M.07. Rectification and indemnity

7.1. **Rectification of the contract**	**7.3.** **Rectification of the register**
7.2. **Rectification of the purchase deed**	**7.4.** **Indemnity**

7.1. Rectification of the contract

7.1.1. Where the parties have reached agreement over a particular matter, but in error that matter is either omitted from the written contract, or is wrongly recorded in the written agreement, an application for rectification of the contract in order to correct the error can be made.[1] Under Law of Property (Miscellaneous Provisions) Act 1989, s.2(4) where rectification is ordered the court has a discretion to determine the date on which the contract comes into operation. If a term is missing from the contract, there is no contract.

1. See *Wright* v. *Robert Leonard Developments Ltd.* [1994] E.G.C.S. 69.

7.2. Rectification of the purchase deed

7.2.1. Where a term of the contract is either omitted from, or inaccurately represented in, the purchase deed an application for rectification of the deed may be made to the court. Rectification relates back to the date when the original document was executed and there is no need to draw up an amended deed. The order granting rectification is often endorsed on the affected deed.[1] Rectification is an equitable remedy and is thus subject to the equitable bars.

1. For examples of the court's discretion to rectify see, e.g. *Craddock Bros* v. *Hunt* [1923] 2 Ch. 136; *Wilson* v. *Wilson* [1969] 3 All E.R. 945; *Riverlate Properties Ltd.* v. *Paul* [1975] Ch. 133.

7.3. Rectification of the register

7.3.1. The grounds for an application for rectification of the register at HM Land Registry are set out in Land Registration Act 1925, s.82 (as amended), and include the following:

    (a) rectification is ordered by the court;

    (b) all parties concerned consent to the order being made;

    (c) the court or registrar is satisfied that an entry on the register has been obtained by fraud;

    (d) where two or more persons have by mistake been registered as the owners of the same interest in land or charge;

    (e) where by reason of any error in the register it is deemed just to order rectification;

7.3.2.   An order for rectification is always in the discretion of the court or registrar. Establishing one of the grounds for rectification does not entitle the applicant to the order.[1]

7.3.3.   Except where the effect of the order is to give effect to an overriding interest or an order of the court, rectification cannot be ordered against a registered proprietor who is in possession of the land unless either the registered proprietor has caused or substantially contributed to the error on the register by fraud or lack of proper care or it would be unjust not to order rectification against him. The word possession seems to be limited to physical possession. A proprietor who is in possession of the rents and profits of the land or who exercises acts of ownership over the land may not be within the scope of the word possession.[2]

---

1. For examples of the court's discretion to order rectification see *Chowood* v. *Lyall (No. 2)* [1930] 1 Ch. 426; *Re 139 High St Deptford* [1951] Ch. 884; *Re Sea View Gardens; Claridge* v. *Tingey* [1966] 3 All E.R. 935; *Epps* v. *Esso Petroleum Co. Ltd.* [1973] 2 All E.R. 465; *Norwich & Peterborough Building Society* v. *Steed (No. 2)* [1993] 1 All E.R. 330.
2. Despite *obiter* comment to the contrary in *Freer* v. *Unwins Ltd.* [1976] Ch. 288.

7.4.   Indemnity

7.4.1.   Subject to the qualifications contained in Land Registration Act 1925, s.83 (as amended) indemnity may be claimed from the Chief Land Registrar by any person who has suffered loss by reason of:

    (a) any rectification of the register;

    (b) any error or omission which has occurred in the register, but where the register is not rectified;

    (c) the loss or destruction of any document lodged at the Registry for inspection or safe custody;

    (d) an error in any official search or office copy issued by the Registry.

7.4.2.   Indemnity is not payable where the applicant or a person from whom he derives title (except under a disposition for valuable consideration which is registered or protected on the register) has caused or substantially contributed to the loss by fraud or lack of proper care.

7.4.3.   There are special provisions limiting indemnity in relation to mines and minerals.

7.4.4.   Indemnity may be claimed for reasonable costs and expenses properly incurred.

7.4.5.   If it is proposed to take or defend legal proceedings on any matter in respect of which a claim for indemnity might arise, the Registry should be approached for consent to take the proceedings, since no indemnity is payable in respect of proceedings taken without consent. In any event, whenever a dispute or question arises involving the possibility of an error in the register, the Registry should be contacted as soon as possible since it is frequently able to assist in resolving such problems. Conversely, where substantial costs are incurred in relation to a dispute before the Registry is contacted, it is unlikely to regard all such costs as reasonable and properly incurred where the dispute could have been resolved quickly with its assistance.

7.4.6. Where the claim for indemnity arises as a consequence of the registration of an absolute or good leasehold title, the claim must be made within six years of the date of registration. In other cases the time-limit of six years starts to run when the claimant knows or ought to know of his claim.

7.4.7. A claim for indemnity should initially be made to the registrar, and referred to the court if the registrar refuses the claim. The court has power to decide on any question as to the claimant's right to indemnity and its amount.

7.4.8. Where the register is not rectified, the amount of indemnity payable cannot exceed the value of the estate or interest at the time when the error or omission which caused the loss was made. Where the register is rectified, the amount of indemnity is limited to the value of the estate or interest immediately before rectification.

M.08. Liens

8.1. **Seller's lien**
8.2. **Buyer's lien**

8.3. **Solicitor's lien**
8.4. **Abortive transactions**

8.1. Seller's lien

8.1.1. The seller has an equitable lien over the property being sold to the extent of the unpaid purchase price.[1]

8.1.2. The lien arises immediately there is a binding contract for sale and is discharged on completion to the extent that the purchase price is paid at that time.[2]

8.1.3. By Law of Property Act 1925, s.68 the presence of a receipt clause in the purchase deed is evidence (but not conclusive evidence) of the discharge of the seller's lien. In registered land, in the absence of an adverse entry on the register of the title (or protection of the lien as an overriding interest) a subsequent purchaser of the land will take free from the lien irrespective of section 68.[3]

8.1.4. To protect the lien against a subsequent buyer, it should be registered as a notice or caution on the register of the title in registered land, or as a Class C(iii) land charge in unregistered land pursuant to a priority notice. The lien may take effect as an overriding interest in registered land if (unusually) the person with its benefit is in occupation of the land under Land Registration Act 1925, s.70(1)(g). An unpaid seller who is in actual occupation may be estopped from claiming that the lien is an overriding interest if he has warranted, in answer to pre-contract enquiries, that vacant possession will be given on completion.[4]

8.1.5. The lien is enforceable by foreclosure[5] or by a court order for sale of the property.[6]

8.1.6. If the seller has agreed to permit the buyer to leave part of the purchase price outstanding on mortgage, the purchase deed should not contain a receipt clause. The buyer should enter a covenant to pay the money to the seller and to enter a formal mortgage if required. If, in the case of registered land, it appears from the transfer that further moneys are payable by the buyer to the seller, and it therefore appears that a seller's lien has arisen, HM Land Registry will enter the lien on the register unless it is established that the lien has been waived. If the seller has taken a mortgage to secure the outstanding moneys, this will displace the lien. Where it appears from the transfer that further moneys are payable by the buyer to the seller but it is intended that the seller should not have a lien on the property, it is desirable for an express waiver to be included in the transfer so that no entry of the lien is made on the register. Where the buyer is entering another mortgage to assist with his purchase of the property, care needs to be exercised to ensure that the priorities of the lender's and seller's charges are correctly maintained; a lender will not normally cede priority to the seller's lien. It may be preferable to include a receipt clause in the document and to execute a formal mortgage in the seller's favour.

8.1.7.   If the transfer cites the non-payment and contains a provision for a charge over the land this charge will take priority over a formal mortgage created by the buyer in favour of a third party immediately after completion.

8.1.8.   By Standard Condition 6.5.1 the seller is not entitled to a lien over the title deeds after completion. If the seller wishes to reserve such a lien this provision must be expressly excluded by contractual condition.

1. *Mackreth* v. *Symmons* (1808) 15 Ves. 329.
2. *London & Cheshire Insurance Co. Ltd.* v. *Laplagrene Property Co. Ltd.* [1971] Ch. 499.
3. *Ibid.*
4. *UCB Finance* v. *France* [1995] N.P.C. 144.
5. *Hughes* v. *Griffin* [1969] 1 All E.R. 460.
6. *Williams* v. *Aylesbury & Buckingham Rail Co.* (1874) 9 Ch. App. 684.

8.2.   Buyer's lien

8.2.1.   The buyer has a similar lien over the property to the extent of any deposit paid by him. This lien can be registered as a notice or caution in registered land or as a Class C (iii) land charge in unregistered land.[1]

1. See above, para. B.17.12.

8.3.   Solicitor's lien

8.3.1.   At common law a solicitor has a lien over his client's property until his costs are paid. He may also ask the court to direct that property recovered by the solicitor in an action brought on the client's behalf should be retained by the solicitor as security against the solicitor's costs.

8.3.2.   The common law lien attaches to all deeds, papers and other personal property of the client which comes into the solicitor's possession with the client's consent. Such property must have been received by the solicitor in his capacity as solicitor. No lien attaches to a client's will. A buyer's solicitor must have received documents over which he exercises his lien in his capacity as buyer's solicitor and not, e.g. as lender's solicitor.

8.3.3.   The lien is restricted to costs due to the solicitor in respect of work done on the client's instructions. The solicitor is entitled to retain the client's property until his costs are paid in full.

8.3.4.   The existence of the lien does not entitle the solicitor to sell or otherwise dispose of the client's property.

8.3.5.   Despite the existence of a lien the Law Society has power to order a solicitor to hand over papers to one of its officers where there is an intervention in a solicitor's practice under Solicitors Act 1974, Sched. 1 and the court also has power to order papers to be delivered.[1]

8.3.6.   On termination of the retainer where the client has instructed another solicitor to act for him, the first solicitor should hand over papers and documents to the second solicitor, subject to obtaining a satisfactory undertaking from the second solicitor in respect of payment of the first solicitor's costs.

8.3.7.   A solicitor has no lien against the official receiver or a trustee in bankruptcy.[2]

8.3.8.   A further type of lien exists by virtue of Solicitors Act 1974, s.73 which empowers the court to make a charging order over real or personal property belonging to the client as security for the solicitor's taxed costs.[3]

8.3.9.   No lien can be exercised over property which is held by the solicitor in the capacity of stakeholder.[4]

1. Solicitors Act 1974, s.68.
2. See *Re Toleman and England, ex p. Bramble* (1880) 13 Ch. 885.
3. See below, Costs, para. N.01.
4. *Rockeagle Ltd.* v. *Alsop Wilkinson* [1992] Ch. 47.

8.4.   Abortive transactions

8.4.1.   A draft contract and other papers supplied by the seller's solicitor to the buyer's solicitor belong to the seller until contracts for the transaction are exchanged. If therefore the transaction is aborted before exchange takes place the buyer's solicitor should comply with a request for return of those papers made by the seller's solicitor. This is notwithstanding any contrary instructions issued by the buyer to his own solicitor. For the avoidance of doubt the seller's solicitor may choose to indicate in his covering letter to the buyer's solicitor that he expects such papers to be returned to him on request if the transaction does not proceed to exchange.

M.09. Covenants for title

See also: Capacity, para. B.07.
The purchase deed, para. E.01.

9.1. Introduction

9.1.1. On completion of the transaction the contract merges with the purchase deed in so far as the two documents cover the same ground, and in general an action arising out of the contract is not possible after completion has taken place. The principle post-completion remedy available to the buyer after completion lies in an action for breach of the implied covenants for title or title guarantee.

9.1.2. As an exception to the general rule outlined in the preceding paragraph, an action arising out of the contract is sustainable after completion in circumstances where a clause or clauses of the contract have been expressed in such a way that they do not merge with the purchase deed on completion.[1] In appropriate circumstances an action in misrepresentation would also be available since this action does not derive from the contract itself.

9.1.3. For transfers entered into and completed before 1 July 1995, the appropriate law is contained in Law of Property Act 1925, s.76 (as modified by Land Registration Act 1925, s.24). The nature of the covenants which will be implied into the purchase deed depends on the capacity in which the seller has transferred the land. These provisions are explained in paras. 9.2.–9.9. below.

9.1.4. For transfers entered into before 1 July 1995 but completed after that date and for all transfers entered into or after 1 July 1995 the provisions of Law of Property Act 1925, s.76 (as amended) cease to apply and are replaced by the provisions relating to title guarantee which were introduced by Law of Property (Miscellaneous Provisions) Act 1994. These provisions are set out in para. 9.10. below.

1. See Standard Condition 7.4.

9.2. **Beneficial owner covenants**

9.2.1. On a conveyance or transfer (but not on the grant of a lease) for valuable consideration by a seller who conveys and is expressed to convey as beneficial owner the following four covenants are implied into the purchase deed by section 76(1)(*a*) and Part I of Schedule 2 Law of Property Act 1925:

(a) good right to convey;

(b) quiet enjoyment;

(c) freedom from incumbrances;

(d) further assurance.

9.2.2. On the sale of an existing lease for valuable consideration by a beneficial owner two additional covenants are implied:

(a) that the lease is valid and subsisting;

(b) that the rent has been paid and the covenants in the lease performed up to the date of completion.

9.2.3. The benefit of these covenants is only given to the buyer in a situation where the seller is as a matter of law the beneficial owner of the property and is expressed in the purchase deed to be transferring the land in that capacity.

9.2.4. Co-owners, who in law hold the property as trustees, do not therefore give the benefit of the beneficial owner covenants even where they are expressed to convey in that capacity.[1]

9.2.5. Except where the transaction is the creation of a mortgage by a beneficial owner (where the effect of the covenants outlined above are absolute), the covenants given by the seller are qualified in their effect, i.e. the covenants are limited to defects arising since the last transaction for value with the land.

9.2.6. If the seller has no title to the land which he purports to sell, he will obviously be in breach of the 'good right to convey' covenant, and in all probability the 'quiet enjoyment' and 'freedom from incumbrances' covenants will also be broken in these circumstances because a third party will have better title to the land than the seller. An action would therefore lie for breach of all three of these covenants provided that it was brought within the relevant limitation period of 12 years. Time starts to run against the buyer for breach of the good right to convey covenant from the date of completion, but time does not start to run in respect of the other breaches until, in the case of the 'quiet enjoyment' covenant, quiet enjoyment is interrupted or possibly, in the case of 'freedom from incumbrances', the incumbrance is discovered. There may, therefore, be circumstances when an action for breach of one of the covenants is available but an action on another covenant (although the covenant has been breached) is statute barred. Actions on the covenants are not common but will most frequently occur in the circumstances described above where the effect of breach of the 'good right to convey' covenant is to create subsequent breaches of the other covenants as well. It is, however, possible for there to be breach of one covenant alone, e.g. the seller has good title, but has failed to disclose an overriding interest affecting registered land. This might give rise to a breach of the 'freedom from incumbrances' covenant, and possibly also the 'quiet enjoyment' covenant, but not of the 'good right to convey' covenant.

9.2.7. Where registered land is transferred, the covenants outlined above will be implied even in the absence of valuable consideration. A modification of the covenants for title is only effective if noted on the register of the title.

1. *Re Robertson's Application* [1969] 1 All E.R. 257.

9.3.   Fiduciary owners

9.3.1. Where a person conveys as 'trustee', 'mortgagee', 'personal representative', or under an order of the court, a single covenant to the effect that the grantor has not himself incumbered the land is implied.

9.3.2. Co-owners, who hold the land on trust for sale, convey in the capacity of trustees, giving only the one covenant outlined above.

9.3.3. On a transfer of land to a tenant under the Leasehold Reform Act 1967, the freeholder is entitled to transfer in the capacity of 'trustee' irrespective of the fact that he is actually a beneficial owner.[1]

9.3.4. A transfer of leasehold land by the seller as fiduciary owner implies only the single covenant outlined above.

1. Leasehold Reform Act 1967, s.10(1).

9.4.   Settlors

9.4.1. Where a conveyance or transfer creates a Settled Land Act settlement, the settlor gives only a covenant for further assurance.

9.5.   No covenants for title

9.5.1. Covenants for title are not normally given on a voluntary disposition nor where the seller has only a possessory title.

9.5.2. It is uncertain whether covenants for title can be called for in a transfer made under powers of compulsory purchase, but there is some authority to suggest that covenants can be required in this situation.[1]

9.5.3. If a seller purports to convey in a capacity other than that which he in fact possesses, e.g. a trustee purports to convey as beneficial owner, probably no covenants for title at all will be implied into the purchase deed.

9.5.4.   Receivers and liquidators who are selling land generally exclude the covenants for title by express contractual condition.

1. *Re King; Robinson* v. *Gray* [1963] Ch. 459.

9.6.   **Modification and extension of the covenants**

9.6.1.   It will not normally be in the seller's interest to give more covenants than those implied by law, but a buyer may consider that he wishes to have the protection of the full beneficial owner covenants in circumstances where such covenants are not automatically accorded to him. If the seller agrees, the covenants can be extended by express contractual condition, such condition being given effect by express clause in the purchase deed.[1] An extension of the covenants is commonly requested by a buyer who is purchasing from co-owners who would otherwise only give the single trustee covenant. Conversely, a seller who does not wish to give the full covenants to which the buyer would otherwise be entitled may limit his liability by express condition in the contract, such condition being given effect by express words of limitation in the purchase deed itself.

9.6.2.   In leasehold land the 'covenants performed' covenant can cause problems for the seller. Liability under the covenants is strict; thus a seller could be held liable for such a breach even if the breach of the lease covenant complained of was merely technical. For example, if a lease contains an obligation for the seller to paint the exterior of the premises in every third year of the term, and he had not complied with that obligation, the buyer could complain of a breach of the covenant for title even if the premises were in fact in good condition and did not need to be repainted. For this reason it is common practice for this particular covenant to be modified on a sale of leasehold land. Such a modification, to release the seller from liability under this covenant, must be expressly set out as a term of the contract and repeated as a clause of the purchase deed. Standard Condition 8.1.4 contains a provision to this effect.

1. See Capacity, para. B.07.

9.7.   **Benefit and burden of the covenants**

9.7.1.   The benefit of the covenants, once given, is annexed to and passes with the estate of the covenantee. Therefore a covenant given in a transfer by A to B can be enforced by B's successors in title against A provided that the action is brought within the relevant limitation period. A lender, however, cannot enforce the covenants against his borrower's predecessors in title. Since the nature of the covenants given by the borrower is absolute, this limitation is of little practical consequence.

9.7.2.   Except in the case of a borrower, whose liability is absolute, a seller who gives covenants for title only assumes liability for his own acts and omissions and those of certain people for whom he is responsible. Thus his liability covers:

       (a)   his own acts and omissions;

(b)   those of any person through whom he claims otherwise than for value (in this context 'value' does not include marriage);

(c)   those of any person claiming a derivative interest by, through or under the seller, e.g. a tenant or mortgagee;

(d)   those of any person claiming in trust for the seller.

9.8.   Enforcement of the covenants

9.8.1.   In the case of unregistered land, liability on the covenants is strict.[1] Rule 77(1) Land Registration Rules 1925 provides that any covenant implied by virtue of Law of Property Act 1925, s.76 in a disposition of registered land shall take effect as though expressly made subject to, *inter alia*, any overriding interests of which the buyer has notice and subject to which it would have taken effect had the land been unregistered.[2]

9.8.2.   The limitation period of 12 years runs from the date of completion in the case of the 'good right to convey' covenant, and usually from the date of actual breach in other cases.

9.8.3.   The only remedy available for breach of the covenants is damages.

1. *Page* v. *Midland Railway Co.* [1894] 1 Ch. 11.
2. See *Hissett* v. *Reading Roofing* [1970] 1 All E.R. 122.

9.9.   Registered land

9.9.1.   The covenants for title have equal application to registered and unregistered land. The state guarantee of a registered title means that in practice actions on the covenants are less likely to occur with the transfer of registered land.

9.9.2.   The covenants implied on the transfer of a registered leasehold estate apply even where no value was given for the transaction.[1]

9.9.3.   Liability on the covenants is not strict.[2]

9.9.4.   The existence of the covenants for title implicitly reaffirms the seller's duty to disclose incumbrances, including overriding interests. The commonly held view that an action on the covenants in registered land could only be sustained where there had been a failure to disclose overriding interests was shown to be incorrect by *A. J. Dunning* v. *Sykes* where an action based on a breach of the 'good right to convey' covenant was successful.[3]

1. Land Registration Act 1925, s.24 and see above, para. 9.2.2.
2. *Hissett* v. *Reading Roofing* [1970] 1 All E.R. 122 and see above, para. 9.8.1.
3. [1987] Ch. 287.

9.10. **Title guarantee**

9.10.1. *Introduction*

Law of Property (Miscellaneous Provisions) Act 1994 enacts Law Commission Report No. 199 relating to covenants for title and title on death. It applies to all contracts made on or after 1 July 1995 and contains transitional provisions relating to contracts which were made before that date but not completed until after 1 July 1995.

9.10.2. *Key words*

The Act repeals the previous law on covenants for title contained in Law of Property Act 1925, s.76 (as modified) and replaces them with 'statutory guarantees' which will be implied in a transfer document by the use of the key words 'with full guarantee' or 'with limited guarantee' (or their Welsh equivalents).

9.10.3. *Seller's capacity*

The title guarantees are not dependent on the capacity in which the seller transfers the land. Although matters relating to the seller's capacity are still relevant to the buyer (e.g. on a sale by a surviving joint owner, it will still be necessary to check whether the survivor is entitled to sell on his own or whether a second trustee needs to be appointed), the nature of the seller's capacity will no longer be stated in the contract.

9.10.4. *Modification and exclusion of the guarantees*

The extent of the title guarantee depends on the use of the key phrases 'with full guarantee' or 'with limited guarantee' in the contract. The extent of the guarantees given by these phrases can be modified by express words in the contract, or excluded altogether.

9.10.5. *Standard Conditions of Sale*

Where the contract is silent (i.e. neither key phrase is used) no title guarantee will be implied. Standard Condition 4.5.2 provides that where the contract contains no provision as to title guarantee, the seller is to transfer with full title guarantee.

9.10.6. *Application of guarantee*

The guarantee applies to the transfer of freehold or leasehold property including the grant of a lease and on the transfer of personal property including intellectual property and rights in shares.

9.10.7. *Full guarantee*

Where the phrase 'full guarantee' is used the transferor warrants that:

(a) he has the right to dispose of the property in the manner purported;

(b) he will at his own cost do all he reasonably can to give his transferee the title he purports to give;

(c) he disposes of the whole interest where that interest is registered;

(d) he disposes of the whole lease where the interest is leasehold;

(e) he disposes of a freehold where it is unclear from the face of the documents whether the interest is freehold or leasehold;

(f) in the case of a subsisting lease he gives covenants that the lease is still subsisting and that there is no subsisting breach which might result in forfeiture;

(g) in the case of a mortgage of property which is subject to a rentcharge or lease, the mortgagor will observe and perform the obligations under the rentcharge or lease;

(h) the person giving the disposition is disposing of it free from all charges and incumbrances (whether monetary or not) and from all other rights exercisable by third parties, not being rights which the transferor does not and could not reasonably be expected to know about.

9.10.8. Note that (h) above it will extend to matters which pre-date the transferor's ownership of the property. Unlike the previous covenants contained in Law of Property Act 1925, s.76, the new covenants do not include a covenant for quiet enjoyment.

9.10.9. *Limited guarantee*

Where limited title guarantee is given, the above covenants apply except for (h) above, which is replaced by the following:

'(h) the transferor has not charged or incumbered the property by a charge or incumbrance which still exists, that he has not granted any third party rights which still subsist and that he is not aware that anyone else has done so since the last disposition for value.'

9.10.10. *Transferee's knowledge*

Whichever guarantee is given, the transferor is not liable for anything to which the disposition is expressly made subject or which, at the time of the disposition, is within the actual knowledge of the transferee or which is a necessary consequence of facts then within the actual knowledge of the transferee. Knowledge imputed by Law of Property Act 1925, s.198, is expressly excluded from the definition of the word 'knowledge' within the Act.

9.10.11. *Assignment of guarantee*

The title guarantees run with the land and are enforceable by the buyer's successors in title against his immediate predecessor.

9.10.12. *Leases*

As noted above, the title guarantees apply on both the grant and assignment of a lease. Where either full or limited title guarantee is given in the case of a subsisting lease, the seller gives covenants that the lease is still subsisting and that there is no subsisting breach which might result in forfeiture. Unless expressly modified, this provision could render a seller liable under the covenants for a technical breach of, e.g. a repairing covenant under the lease being sold. Standard Condition 3.2.2 modifies this implied covenant by providing that a leasehold property is sold subject to any subsisting breach of a condition or tenant's obligation relating to the physical state of the property which renders the lease liable to forfeiture. Standard Condition 3.2.3 contains a similar provision relating to sub-leases. This modification of the covenants should be expressly repeated in the transfer.

9.10.13. *Remedies*

A breach of the covenants is actionable as a breach of contract. Once completion has taken place, or a third party, e.g. a lender, has acquired an interest in the property, it is unlikely that rescission would be granted. Damages will therefore be the most usual remedy for breach, but a seller could be required, e.g. to execute a further document to perfect the title.

9.10.14. *Transitional provisions*

(a) **Transactions completed before 1 July 1995**

Law of Property Act 1925, s.76 (as modified) continues to apply to these transactions.

(b) **Transactions where contract entered into before 1 July 1995 but completed after that date**

Where the contract contains a term to which Law of Property Act 1925, s.76 would have applied (e.g. a statement that the seller sells as beneficial owner) and the existence of the contract and the relevant term is apparent on the face of the instrument effecting the disposition (e.g. contained expressly in the transfer) and there has been no intervening disposition (see below), section 76 continues to apply to that disposition.

(c) If the conditions in (b) above are not satisfied, the 1994 Act applies to the transaction in that a disposition by a seller who transfers in the capacity of beneficial owner will give the buyer the benefit of full title guarantee, and dispositions made in other capacities (e.g. trustee or personal representative) will import the limited title guarantee.

(d) **Intervening dispositions**

Where there has been an intervening disposition, as defined below, the 1994 Act applies in place of Law of Property Act 1925, s.76. An intervening disposition is defined by section 11(3) of the 1994 Act as being a disposition (i.e. completion of a transaction) made after 1 July 1995 to, or to a predecessor in title of, the person making the disposition. If, for example, L grants a lease to T giving T an option to purchase the freehold which L has agreed to transfer as beneficial owner, and after 1 July 1995 L disposed of the freehold to P, subject to T's lease, the sale by L to P is an 'intervening disposition' and the subsequent exercise of the option by T will contain full title guarantee covenants under the 1994 Act and is not subject to Law of Property Act 1925, s.76.

M.10. Solicitor's negligence

10.1. Introduction

10.1.1. Where a solicitor has been negligent the client must seek redress through a civil action against the solicitor.

10.1.2. Where a client or third party makes a claim against a solicitor (or gives notice of intention to make such a claim) and the claim is one in respect of which indemnity is provided by the Solicitors' Indemnity Fund the solicitor must as soon as practicable notify the Solicitors' Indemnity Fund and co-operate with them in order to enable the claim to be dealt with in the appropriate manner. Where top-up indemnity cover is maintained the terms of that policy should also be considered.

10.2. Action to be taken by solicitor

10.2.1. If a solicitor discovers an act or omission which would justify a claim by a client (or third party) against him he should:

    (a) contact his insurers;

    (b) inform the client (or third party) in order to enable him to take independent legal advice;

    (c) seek the advice of his insurers as to any further communication with the client (or third party); and

    (d) confirm any oral communication in writing.

10.2.2. If a client makes a claim against his solicitor or notifies his intention of doing so, or if the solicitor discovers an act or omission which would justify such a claim, the solicitor is under a duty to inform his client that he should seek independent advice.

10.2.3. If the client refuses to seek independent advice the solicitor should decline to act further for the client unless he is satisfied that no conflict of interest exists.

10.2.4. The solicitor should not admit liability or settle a claim without the consent of his insurers.

10.2.5. Where the solicitor is asked to hand papers over to another solicitor who is giving independent advice to the client about the claim, the solicitor should keep copies of the original documents for his own reference. If the first solicitor has a lien over the client's papers he may, as an alternative to taking copies, ask the second solicitor to give an undertaking for the production of the papers should they be required.

N. COSTS
N.01. Costs

See also: Estimate for costs, para. A.08.

1.1. The basis of charging

1.1.1. Costs in non-contentious matters including conveyancing are governed by Solicitors' (Non-Contentious Business) Remuneration Order 1994.[1]

1.1.2. Rule 3 Solicitors' (Non-Contentious Business) Remuneration Order 1994 provides that the remuneration shall be 'such sum as may be fair and reasonable having regard to all the circumstances of the case'. The following matters must be taken into account:

(a) the complexity of the matter or the difficulty or novelty of the questions raised;

(b) the skill, labour, specialised knowledge and responsibility involved;

(c) the time spent on the business;

(d) the number and importance of the documents prepared or perused, without regard to length;

(e) the place where and the circumstances in which the business or any part thereof is transacted;

(f) the amount or value of any money or property involved;

(g) whether any land involved is registered land;

(h) the importance of the matter to the client; and

(i) the approval (express or implied) of the entitled person or the express approval of the testator to:

(i) the solicitor undertaking all or any part of the work giving rise to the costs; or

(ii) the amount of the costs.

1.1.3. On taking instructions the solicitor should give his client the best information he can about the likely cost of the matter including when costs will be charged and whether or not such costs will be deducted from money held by the solicitor on the client's behalf. Where possible an estimate should be given to the client; in other cases the solicitor should give the client a general forecast of the approximate costs to be incurred. Where no estimate has been given and the solicitor has not arranged an agreed fee for the work, the client must be told how the solicitor's charges are to be calculated, e.g. on an hourly rate basis or as a percentage of the value of the transaction. Information should also be given to the client about the nature and cost of disbursements.

1.1.4. The Law Society's Written Professional Standards on costs and Practice Management Standards should also be followed. Failure to observe these standards is regarded as inadequate professional services by the Solicitors' Complaints Bureau.

1.1.5. By Supply of Goods and Services Act 1982, s.15 the contract between solicitor and client contains an implied term that the client will pay the solicitor a reasonable sum for his services; however, the matter of costs should be dealt with expressly. It is the solicitor's duty to raise the issue of costs if the client does not enquire.

1.1.6. When confirming the client's instructions the solicitor should record whether a fee has been agreed, and if so what it covers and whether it includes VAT and disbursements.

1.1.7. Where the client has imposed an upper limit on costs, a solicitor who exceeds that limit without the client's authority will not be able to recover his costs in so far as they exceed the agreed maximum sum. The client must be informed as soon as possible if it appears that the limit imposed on the costs will be insufficient and instructions obtained as to whether the client wishes the solicitor to continue with the matter. If the solicitor continues to act and exceeds the limit imposed by the client on the costs to be incurred the amount of the bill in excess of the agreed amount will be disallowed if the client applies for a remuneration certificate or taxation. The solicitor may also be guilty of professional misconduct in these circumstances.

1.1.8. The amount of costs being incurred on a client's behalf should be reviewed regularly. It is recommended that the client should be informed at least every six months of the amount of costs incurred to date and where appropriate an interim bill should be delivered.

1.1.9. A solicitor may, at the outset of the retainer, require the client to make a payment on account of costs and disbursements to be incurred. The solicitor must make his acceptance of the instructions conditional on the client's advance payment. Unless he does this the solicitor will not be able to justify the termination of the retainer if the client does not make the interim payment.

1.1.10. A solicitor may charge interest on the whole or outstanding part of an unpaid bill with effect from one month after delivery of the bill, provided that notice has been given to the client informing him of his right to apply for a remuneration certificate and taxation of the bill. The rate of interest chargeable is that which is payable on judgment debts.

1.1.11. A solicitor must not take advantage of the client by overcharging for work done or to be done. Overcharging the client may be professional misconduct. If a taxing officer allows less than one-half of the sum charged he is under a duty to report the matter to the Law Society. The solicitor is responsible for ensuring that the amount of the bill is fair and reasonable and cannot escape liability by delegating the preparation of the bill to a costs draftsman.

1.1.12. Unless there is an agreement to the contrary, a solicitor is personally responsible for paying the proper costs of any professional agent or other person whom he instructs on behalf of his client, whether or not he receives payment from his client.

1.1.13. Costs which are taken by way of deduction from money which the solicitor is holding on the client's behalf cannot be transferred from clients' account to office account without the consent of the client.

1.1.14. In the absence of agreement to the contrary a solicitor will charge on a *quantum meruit* basis (or for a reasonable sum under Supply of Goods and Services Act 1982, s.15) for abortive work.

1. The 1994 Order applies to bills delivered on or after 1 November 1994 (even if the bill covers work done before that date). Solicitors' Remuneration Order 1972 applies to bills delivered before that date.

1.2. Agreements for charges

1.2.1. Solicitors Act 1974, s.57 allows a solicitor to make an agreement with a client for costs in a non-contentious matter.

1.2.2. In order to be enforceable under the Act, the agreement must fully comply with the provisions of section 57. Thus the agreement must:

    (a) be in writing;

    (b) embody all the terms of the agreement;

    (c) be signed by the party to be charged or his agent, i.e. the client;

    (d) be reasonable in amount and be in lieu of ordinary profit costs.

1.2.3. Remuneration may be by a gross sum, commission, percentage, salary or otherwise, and should state whether the agreed remuneration is to be inclusive of disbursements and VAT. The agreement should specifically set out the method by which the remuneration is to be calculated.

1.2.4. An agreement which complies with section 57 is enforceable under the ordinary principles of contract law.

1.2.5. If the costs are ultimately taxed and the client raises an objection to the agreement on the grounds that it is unfair or unreasonable, the taxing officer may enquire into the facts and the court may set the agreement aside or reduce the amount payable and give such consequential directions as it thinks fit.

1.3. **Value added tax**

1.3.1. When giving an estimate or quotation for costs the solicitor should make it clear to the client whether or not VAT is included in the quoted sum.

1.3.2. If VAT is not mentioned it is presumed that the quotation or estimate is VAT inclusive.

1.3.3. Where an individual or firm is registered for VAT the firm's VAT registration number must appear on the bills issued by the firm or, if a separate tax invoice is issued, on the tax invoice.

1.3.4. The VAT registration number is also required to appear on any bill or fee note produced on a taxation of costs *inter partes.*

1.3.5. Stamp duties are exempt from VAT.

1.3.6. Where the client's bill is reduced by the amount of commission which a solicitor has earned, e.g. on an endowment policy taken out by the client, VAT should be charged on the gross amount of the bill but in practice is sometimes only charged on the net sum.

1.3.7. Fees for telegraphic transfers, when passed on by a solicitor to his or her client, must bear VAT at the standard rate.

1.4. **Delivery of bill**

1.4.1. A solicitor is under a duty to render a bill of costs to his client within a reasonable time of concluding the matter to which the bill relates.

1.4.2. It is recommended practice to submit a bill to the client as soon as possible after the conclusion of the transaction and is particularly important to do so where the solicitor is already holding sums of money on his client's behalf and is waiting for the client's approval of the bill before deducting his costs and accounting to the client for the balance, or where the client has asked for the papers and the solicitor is claiming a lien over them until his costs are met.

1.4.3. In residential conveyancing purchase transactions the bill is usually submitted to the client before completion on the understanding that the solicitor's charges are paid in full before completion. In sale transactions, the solicitor's costs are usually deducted from money held by the solicitor on the client's behalf before the balance is remitted to the client. If the client refuses to allow payment of costs by deduction the solicitor must nevertheless complete the transaction since he is obliged to fulfil his retainer.

1.4.4. A solicitor's bill of costs should contain sufficient information to identify the matter to which it relates and the period covered.

1.4.5. The form of the bill should comply with Solicitors Act 1974, s.69 and must be signed by the solicitor personally or by one of the partners in the firm. The signature may be either that of the solicitor signing the bill or made in the name of the firm. Alternatively the letter which accompanies and refers to the bill should be so signed. Unless this provision is complied with the solicitor will be unable to sue on the bill. A form of signature such as, e.g. 'signed A. Smith, a partner in A. Smith & Co.' is recommended to ensure that it can be proved in evidence (should it be necessary to sue) that the bill was signed by a solicitor and not merely by an unqualified assistant. Disbursements should be separately itemised in the bill.

1.4.6. A solicitor must not sue or threaten to sue unless he has first informed the client in writing of his right to require a remuneration certificate and of his right to seek taxation of the bill. The form of notice to be given to the client should be in the following wording:

> 'This constitutes notice of your right under paragraph 1 of Article 3 of the Solicitors' Remuneration Order 1972 to require me within one month of the receipt hereof to obtain a certificate from the Law Society stating that in their opinion the costs charged are fair and reasonable or, as the case may be, what lesser sum would be fair and reasonable. Also there are provisions in sections 70, 71, and 72 of the Solicitors Act 1974 relating to taxation of costs which give you the right to have the bill checked by an officer of the High Court.'

1.4.7. This notice must be given even where costs are payable by deduction from money already held by the solicitor on behalf of the client.

1.5. Remuneration certificate

1.5.1. A client or residuary beneficiary of an estate where all the personal representatives are solicitors who is dissatisfied with his solicitor's bill may require the solicitor to apply to the Law Society for a remuneration certificate which will either state that in the opinion of the Law Society the sum charged by the solicitor is fair and reasonable, or what lesser sum would be fair and reasonable. If the sum stated in the remuneration certificate is less than the amount of the bill, the client need only pay the amount stated in the certificate. An application for a remuneration certificate is free of charge to the client. A client applying for a remuneration certificate must pay half the costs plus paid disbursements and VAT unless the solicitor agrees to waive this requirement.

1.5.2. The client is not entitled to require a remuneration certificate where:

    (a) a period of more than one month has expired after the date on which he was notified of his right to such a certificate; or

    (b) a bill has been delivered and paid (otherwise than by deduction without authority); or

    (c) the High Court has ordered the bill to be taxed; or

    (d) the bill exceeds £50,000, exclusive of VAT and disbursements.

1.5.3. In addition to or as an alternative to a remuneration certificate the client may apply to have his bill taxed by the High Court.

1.5.4. Except as below, the right to a remuneration certificate applies to the client in relation to his own solicitor's costs; it is not therefore available to a third party who has agreed to be responsible for another person's solicitor's costs. Where a third party is to pay the solicitor's bill, e.g. where a tenant is to pay his landlord's solicitor's costs, the tenant's solicitor should agree the fee to be paid at the outset of the transaction. Alternatively the third party can apply for a third party taxation within three months of delivery of the bill (see below, para. 1.6.). A residuary beneficiary of an estate where the personal representatives are all solicitors may apply for a remuneration certificate.

1.6. Taxation of costs

1.6.1. The right to taxation of the bill by the High Court is in addition to or may be used by the client as an alternative to an application for a remuneration certificate. The costs of an application for taxation must be borne by the client.

1.6.2. If in a non-contentious matter a taxing officer allows less than one-half of the sum charged to the client by the bill, he is under a duty to bring the facts of the case to the attention of the Law Society.

1.6.3. A third party who is responsible for paying the costs of another can apply for a third party taxation within three months of delivery of the bill.

1.7. Lender's costs

1.7.1. When acting under the terms of the Standard Mortgage Instructions (SMI), charges should be made in accordance with the appropriate scale of charges.[1]

1.7.2. In other cases the solicitor should agree his charges with the lender client at the outset of the transaction in the normal way.

1. At the time of publication the SMI had not been finalised.

1.8. Commissions

1.8.1. Under Rule 10 Solicitors' Practice Rules 1990, a solicitor must normally account to his client for any commission received by him which exceeds £20. Thus where the solicitor introduces a client to an insurance company for the purposes of the client obtaining an insurance policy, and as a result of that introduction the solicitor receives commission from the insurance company, that commission will be subject to Rule 10. The solicitor is only entitled to keep a commission which exceeds £20 if, having disclosed its receipt and the amount to the client, the client agrees that the solicitor may keep the money. If the amount is not known, the solicitor must have disclosed the basis of the calculation of the commission to the client.

1.8.2. The rule does not apply where the solicitor acts as agent for a building society or other financial institution and a member of the public, whom the solicitor has not advised as a client about the investment of the money, deposits money with the solicitor.

1.8.3. Stock Exchange commissions fall within the scope of the rule.

1.8.4. The amount of any commission earned by the solicitor should be shown on the client's bill.

1.9. Recovery of charges

1.9.1. A solicitor may sue a client who does not pay his solicitor's bill provided that the conditions in the following paragraphs have been complied with.

1.9.2. A bill of costs in the proper form must have been delivered to the client.

1.9.3. In a non-contentious matter, a solicitor may not sue the client until the expiration of one month from the delivery of the bill, unless the solicitor had been given leave to do so on the grounds set out in Solicitors Act 1974, s.69. A solicitor must not sue or threaten to sue unless he has first informed the client in writing of his right to require a remuneration certificate and of his right to seek taxation of the bill. A statutory demand in bankruptcy can, however, be made within one month of an unpaid bill being presented.[1]

1.9.4. A lien exists by virtue of Solicitors Act 1974, s.73 which empowers the court to make a charging order over real or personal property belonging to the client as security for the solicitor's taxed costs.

1. *Re A Debtor (No. 88 of 1991)* [1992] 4 All E.R. 301.

1.10. Court of Protection work

1.10.1. Fixed costs are payable for all conveyancing matters in the Court of Protection.

1.10.2. Two elements will be allowable, as follows:

    (a) a sum of £146 in every case to cover correspondence with the Court of Protection, the preparation of the certificate or affidavit of value, and all other work solely attributable to the Court of Protection; together with

    (b) a value element of 0.5% of the consideration up to £400,000 and 0.25% thereafter, with a minimum sum for this element of £291.

1.10.3. As well as a fee for both the above elements, VAT and disbursements will be allowed.

1.10.4. Fixed costs will apply to conveyancing of all types of property.

1.10.5.   If solicitors wish, they may choose to have their costs taxed, rather than to accept fixed costs. It should, however, be emphasised that agreed costs will not be an option, save in exceptional circumstances.

FURTHER REFERENCE

An Approach to Non-contentious Costs, the Law Society.

Non-contentious Costs, A. Barrett, F.T. Law & Tax.

APPENDICES

I.   RULES AND CODES

I.1.   Solicitors' Practice Rules 1990[1]

Rules dated 18th July 1990 made by the Council of the Law Society with the concurrence of the Master of the Rolls under section 31 of the Solicitors Act 1974 and section 9 of the Administration of Justice Act 1985, regulating the English and Welsh practices of solicitors, registered foreign lawyers and recognised bodies and, in respect of Rule 12 only, regulating the English and Welsh and overseas practices of such persons in the conduct of investment business in or into any part of the United Kingdom.

Rule 1 (Basic principles)

A solicitor shall not do anything in the course of practising as a solicitor, or permit another person to do anything on his or her behalf, which compromises or impairs or is likely to compromise or impair any of the following:

(a)   the solicitor's independence or integrity;

(b)   a person's freedom to instruct a solicitor of his or her choice;

(c)   the solicitor's duty to act in the best interests of the client;

(d)   the good repute of the solicitor or of the solicitors' profession;

(e)   the solicitor's proper standard of work;

(f)   the solicitor's duty to the Court.

Rule 2 (Publicity)

Solicitors may at their discretion publicise their practices, or permit other persons to do so, or publicise the businesses or activities of other persons, provided there is no breach of these rules and provided there is compliance with a Solicitors' Publicity Code promulgated from time to time by the Council of the Law Society with the concurrence of the Master of the Rolls.

Rule 3 (Introductions and referrals)

Solicitors may accept introductions and referrals of business from other persons and may make introductions and refer business to other persons, provided there is no breach of these rules and provided there is compliance with a Solicitors' Introduction and Referral Code promulgated from time to time by the Council of the Law Society with the concurrence of the Master of the Rolls.

Rule 4 (Employed solicitors)

(1)   Solicitors who are employees of non-solicitors shall not as part of their employment do for any person other than their employer work which is or could be done by a solicitor acting as such, save as permitted by an Employed Solicitors Code promulgated from time to time by the Council of the Law Society with the concurrence of the Master of the Rolls.

---

1. With consolidated amendments to 1 June 1996.

(2) Solicitors who are employees of multi-national partnerships shall not be regarded as "employees of non-solicitors" for the purpose of this rule.

Rule 5 (Providing services other than as a solicitor)

Solicitors must comply with the Solicitors' Separate Business Code in controlling, actively participating in or operating (in each case alone, or by or with others) a business which

    (a) provides any service which may properly be provided by a solicitor's practice, and

    (b) is not itself a solicitor's practice or a multi-national partnership.

Rule 6 (Avoiding conflicts of interest in conveyancing)

(1) (Transfers and leases of land)

A solicitor, or solicitors practising in associated practices, must not act for both seller and buyer on a transfer of land for value at arm's length, or for both lessor and lessee on the grant of a lease for value at arm's length, except as permitted by paragraph (2).

Notes

    (i) For the interpretation of "solicitor" and "associated practices", see paragraph (6).

    (ii) It is a principle of professional conduct that a solicitor shall not act for two or more clients where there is a conflict of interest between those clients. Paragraph (1) goes further and prohibits the solicitor from acting for both parties in a conveyancing transaction, even if there is no actual conflict at the time of acting.

    (iii) The fact that a transaction is at market value, or is stated to be on arm's length terms, does not necessarily mean that it is "at arm's length" for the purpose of the rule. Whether a transaction is "at arm's length" will be determined by the relationship between the parties and the context of the transaction. For example, the transaction would not usually be at arm's length where the parties are:

      — *persons related by blood, adoption or marriage;*

      — *the settlor of a trust and the trustees;*

      — *the trustees of a trust and its beneficiary or the beneficiary's relative;*

      — *personal representatives and a beneficiary;*

      — *the trustees of separate trusts for the same family;*

      — *a sole trader or partners and a limited company set up to enable the business to be incorporated;*

      — *associated companies;*

      — *a local authority and a related body within the meaning of paragraph 6(b) of the Employed Solicitors' Code 1990.*

    In such a case, it would be possible, subject to there being no conflict of interest, to act for both parties.

    (iv) Two companies are "associated" where one is a holding company and the other is its subsidiary within the meaning of the Companies Act 1985, or both are subsidiaries of the same holding company.

    (v) Land includes an interest in land, for example the assignment of a lease or grant of a right of way.

(2)   (Exceptions)

A solicitor, or solicitors practising in associated practices, may act for both seller and buyer on a transfer of land for value at arm's length, or for both lessor and lessee on the grant of a lease for value at arm's length, if all the following conditions are satisfied:

(a)   no conflict of interest exists or arises; and

(b)   neither the solicitor, nor any solicitor practising in an associated practice, is instructed to negotiate the sale of the property; and

(c)   the seller or lessor is not a builder or developer selling or leasing as such; and

(d)   one or more of the following applies:

    (i)   both parties are established clients; or

    (ii)   on a transfer of land, the consideration is £10,000 or less; or

    (iii)   there is no other solicitor or other qualified conveyancer in the vicinity whom either party can reasonably be expected to consult; or

    (iv)   the parties are respectively represented by two associated practices or two offices of the same practice, provided that:

        (A)   the respective practices or offices are in different localities; and

        (B)   neither party was referred to the practice or office acting for him or her from an associated practice or from another office of the same practice; and

        (C)   the transaction is conducted or supervised by different solicitors, each in regular attendance at the practice or office concerned; and

(e)   both parties give their written consent to the arrangement.

Notes

(i)   A builder or developer is not selling or leasing "as such" when selling without development a property originally acquired in part exchange.

(ii)   The test of whether a person is an "established client" is an objective one; that is, whether a reasonable solicitor would regard the person as an established client. A seller or buyer who is instructing the solicitor for the first time is not an established client.

(iii)   A person related by blood, adoption or marriage to an established client may be treated as an established client.

(iv)   Where only one of two joint sellers or buyers is an established client, the solicitor may act as if both are established clients.

(v)   In determining whether the consideration is £10,000 or less, the value of any property given in exchange or part exchange must be taken into account.

(3)   (Institutional mortgages)

A solicitor, or solicitors practising in associated practices, may act for both lender and borrower on the grant of an institutional mortgage of land, if both the following conditions are satisfied:

(a) where the solicitor or a member of his or her immediate family is the borrower, or one of two or more joint borrowers, the solicitor has given written notification of the circumstances to the lender; and

(b) no conflict of interest exists or arises.

Notes

(i) *The rule relates to mortgages of land and does not cover, for example, mortgages of ships and aircraft. "Mortgage" includes first and subsequent mortgages, and remortgages.*

(ii) *An "institutional mortgage" is one where the lender is an institution which provides mortgages on standard terms in the normal course of its activities.*

(iii) *It is essential that the lender is fully informed of the circumstances where the solicitor, or a member of his or her immediate family, is the recipient of the loan. The lender is then in a position to decide whether or not to instruct the solicitor to act for it as well. "Immediate family" means the solicitor's spouse, children, parents, brothers and sisters.*

(iv) *"Solicitor" in paragraph (3) (a) means all the principals in a practice, as well as the solicitor conducting or supervising the transaction (who may be a principal or may be employed by the practice as, for example, an assistant solicitor).*

(v) *Although the rule requires notification in a limited number of circumstances only, it should be borne in mind that a lender's instructions may require a wider disclosure. The solicitor also needs to assess in each case whether the circumstances give rise to a conflict. There will, for instance, be a conflict between lender and borrower in cases where the solicitor becomes involved in negotiations relating to the terms of the loan. A conflict may also arise from many types of relationship which a solicitor has with a borrower; for example, where the borrower is a debtor or creditor of the solicitor, or has a business association with the solicitor, or lives with but is not married to the solicitor.*

(4)   (Private mortgages)

A solicitor, or solicitors practising in associated practices, must not act for both lender and borrower on the grant of a private mortgage of land, unless both the following conditions are satisfied:

(a) the transaction is not at arm's length; and

(b) no conflict of interest exists or arises.

Note

A "private mortgage" is any mortgage other than an institutional mortgage.

(5)   (Acting for seller, buyer and lender)

A solicitor, or solicitors practising in associated practices, must not act for seller, buyer and lender in the same transaction, unless both the following conditions are satisfied:

(a) if the mortgage is an institutional mortgage, the solicitor has given written notification of the circumstances to the lender; and

(b) no conflict of interest exists or arises.

(6) (Interpretation)

(a) This rule is to be interpreted in the light of the explanatory notes.

(b) "Solicitor" includes a recognised body.

(c) "Associated practices" are practices with at least one common principal. In relation to a recognised body, "principal" means a director, or a member of that body, or the beneficial owner of any share in the body, or the body itself.

Note

The rule affects the solicitor conducting or supervising the transaction, and all principals in the practice.

Rule 6A (Seller's solicitor dealing with more than one prospective buyer)

(1) This rule applies to the conveyancing of freehold and leasehold property. The rule is to be interpreted in the light of the notes.

Notes

(i) *Rule 6A replaces the Council Direction of 6th October 1977 and Principle and Commentary 24.04 in the 1993 edition of "The Guide to the Professional Conduct of Solicitors" with effect from 1st March 1995. As was the case with the Council Direction, it appplies to all conveyancing of land, whether the transaction is of a "commercial" or "domestic" nature.*

(ii) *The Council Direction did not and Rule 6A does not set terms for a contract race. It lays down requirements which must be met when a solicitor is instructed to deal with more than one prospective buyer. The rule imposes no obligation on the seller's solicitor to exchange contracts with the first buyer to deliver a signed contract and deposit. It will be a matter of law whether or not the seller has entered into a contractual obligation to exchange with the buyer "first past the post", or whether the whole matter remains "subject to contract".*

(iii) *References to "solicitor" throughout the rule include a firm of solicitors, a multi-national partnership or a recognised body.*

(2) Where a seller instructs a solicitor to deal with more than one prospective buyer, the solicitor (with the client's consent) shall immediately disclose the seller's decision, if possible by telephone or fax, to the solicitor or other conveyancer acting for each prospective buyer or direct to the prospective buyer if acting in person. Such disclosure, if made by telephone, shall at once be confirmed by letter or fax. If the seller refuses to authorise disclosure, the solicitor shall immediately cease to act. Each prospective buyer must be notified each time a decision is taken to deal with any further prospective buyer.

Notes

(i) *It is the seller's decision to deal with more than one prospective buyer which must be notified. The seller's solicitor must not wait until contracts are actually submitted but must notify the appropriate parties immediately upon receiving instructions to deal with a prospective buyer (other than the first).*

(ii) *A solicitor will have been instructed to deal with a prospective buyer where the solicitor is asked to submit a draft contract or to provide any other documentation or information (e.g. a plan or a note of the Land Registry title number) in order to facilitate the conveyancing of the premises to the prospective buyer. The rule does not, however, cover activities normally performed by an estate agent, such as issuing particulars of sale, showing prospective buyers round the property, and negotiating the price.*

(iii) The rule will apply where the contracts are to contain non-identical terms (e.g. where one contract is to include additional land). It will also apply where the contracts are to relate to different interests in the same property where the sale of one such interest would affect the sale of the other. For example, a party negotiating to take a lease of premises will be affected by another party negotiating to buy the freehold with vacant possession, since the sale of one precludes the sale of the other. On the other hand, the rule would not apply where the seller is proposing to grant a lease and to effect a simultaneous sale of the freehold reversion subject to that lease, since neither transaction precludes the other.

(iv) Where a prospective buyer has retained an unqualified conveyancer, solicitors are reminded to consult the Council guidance on dealing with unqualified conveyancers (Annex 25A in the 1996 edition of "The Guide to the Professional Conduct of Solicitors"). However, so far as Rule 6A is concerned, the obligations in paragraph (2) will be met by disclosure either to the prospective buyer direct or to the unqualified conveyancer.

(3)   The obligations in paragraph (2) of this rule apply where a seller client, to the solicitor's knowledge, deals (whether directly or through another solicitor or other conveyancer) with another prospective buyer (or with that buyer's solicitor or other conveyancer).

Note

"Deals with another prospective buyer" should be interpreted in the light of note (ii) to paragraph (2).

(4)   A solicitor shall not act for more than one of the prospective buyers.

Notes

(i)   "Prospective buyers" should be interpreted in the light of note (ii) to paragraph (2).

(ii) This part of the rule recognises the inevitable conflict of interest which makes it impossible for a solicitor to act for more than one of the prospective buyers.

(5)   A solicitor shall not act for both the seller and one of the prospective buyers, even in a case which would fall within Rule 6(2) of these rules.

Notes

(i)   "Prospective buyers" should be interpreted in the light of note (ii) to paragraph (2).

(ii) Clearly a solicitor must not act for both where it is known at the time of taking instructions on behalf of the buyer that there is more than one prospective buyer. In addition, this part of the rule does not permit a solicitor to continue to act for both in a case falling within Rule 6(2), where another prospective buyer is introduced during the course of the transaction because of the significant inherent conflict; the solicitor would find it impossible to reconcile the interests of both clients if, for example, it was in the seller's best interests to exchange with the other prospective buyer.

(6)   For the purposes of this rule a prospective buyer shall continue to be treated as such until either the prospective buyer or the seller gives written notice (either by letter or by fax) of withdrawal from the transaction, such notice to be between solicitors or other conveyancers save where such notice is given by or to a prospective buyer acting in person.

Notes

(i)   *Solicitors should take particular care where a contract has been submitted but nothing has been heard from the prospective buyer's solicitor for some time. If the seller decides to deal with another buyer, the rule must still be complied with unless the seller's solicitor has already given notice of withdrawal.*

(ii)   *Where a prospective buyer has retained an unqualified conveyancer, the provisions of paragraph (6) should be interpreted in the light of note (iv) to paragraph (2).*

(7)   This rule does not apply to a proposed sale by auction or tender. The rule does, however, apply to require disclosure to a prospective buyer by private treaty of instructions to offer the property by auction or tender.

Rule 7 (Fee sharing)

(1)   A solicitor shall not share or agree to share his or her professional fees with any person except:

    (a)   a practising solicitor;

    (b)   a practising foreign lawyer (other than a foreign lawyer whose registration in the register of foreign lawyers is suspended or whose name has been struck off the register);

    (c)   the solicitor's **bona fide** employee, which provision shall not permit under the cloak of employment a partnership prohibited by paragraph (6) of this rule; or

    (d)   a retired partner or predecessor of the solicitor or the dependents or personal representatives of a deceased partner or predecessor.

(2)   Notwithstanding paragraph (1) of this rule a solicitor who instructs an estate agent as sub-agent for the sale of properties may remunerate the estate agent on the basis of a proportion of the solicitor's professional fee.

(3)   The exceptions set out in paragraphs 2 to 9 of the Employed Solicitors Code shall where necessary also operate as exceptions to this rule but only to permit fee sharing with the solicitor's employer.

(4)   A solicitor who works as a volunteer in a law centre or advice service operated by a charitable or similar non-commercial organisation may pay to the organisation any fees or costs that he or she receives under the legal aid scheme.

(5)   For the purposes of sub-paragraph (1)(d) above, the references to a retired or deceased partner shall be construed, in relation to a recognised body, as meaning a retired or deceased director or member of that body, or a retired or deceased beneficial owner of any share in that body held by a member as nominee.

(6) (a)   A solicitor shall not enter into partnership with any person other than a solicitor, a registered foreign lawyer or a recognised body.

    (b)   A recognised body shall not enter into partnership with any person other than a solicitor or a recognised body.

    (c)   In this paragraph, "solicitor" means a solicitor of the Supreme Court of England and Wales.

(7)   A solicitor shall not practise through any body corporate except a recognised body, or save as permitted under Rule 4 of these rules.

Rule 8 (Contingency fees)

(1)   A solicitor who is retained or employed to prosecute or defend any action, suit or other contentious proceeding shall not enter into any arrangement to receive a contingency fee in respect of that proceeding.

(1A)   Paragraph (1) of this Rule shall not apply to a conditional fee agreement relating to specified proceedings as defined in section 58 of the Courts and Legal Services Act 1990, provided the agreement complies with all the requirements of that section and any order made thereunder.

(2)   Paragraph (1) of this rule shall not apply to any arrangement in respect of an action, suit or other contentious proceeding in any country other than England and Wales to the extent that a local lawyer would be permitted to receive a contingency fee in respect of that proceeding.

Rule 9 (Claims assessors)

(1)   A solicitor shall not, in respect of any claim or claims arising as a result of death or personal injury, either enter into an arrangement for the introduction of clients with or act in association with any person (not being a solicitor) whose business or any part of whose business is to make, support or prosecute (whether by action or otherwise, and whether by a solicitor or agent or otherwise) claims arising as a result of death or personal injury and who in the course of such business solicits or receives contingency fees in respect of such claims.

(2)   The prohibition in paragraph (1) of this rule shall not apply to an arrangement or association with a person who solicits or receives contingency fees only in respect of proceedings in a country outside England and Wales, to the extent that a local lawyer would be permitted to receive a contingency fee in respect of such proceedings.

Rule 10 (Receipt of commissions from third parties)

(1)   Solicitors shall account to their clients for any commission received of more than £20 unless, having disclosed to the client in writing the amount or basis of calculation of the commission or (if the precise amount or basis cannot be ascertained) an approximation thereof, they have the client's agreement to retain it.

(2)   Where the commission actually received is materially in excess of the amount or basis or approximation disclosed to the client the solicitor shall account to the client for the excess.

(3)   This rule does not apply where a member of the public deposits money with a solicitor who is acting as agent for a building society or other financial institution and the solicitor has not advised that person as a client as to the disposition of the money.

Rule 11 (Name of a firm)

(1)   The name of a firm of solicitors shall consist only of the name or names of one or more solicitors, being present or former principals together with, if desired, other conventional references to the firm and to such persons; or a firm name in use on 28th February 1967; or one approved in writing by the Council of the Law Society.

(1A) The firm name used by a multi-national partnership shall consist only of the name or names of one or more lawyers, being present or former principals of *either* the multi-national partnership *or* a predecessor legal practice, together with, if desired, other conventional references to the firm and to such persons; or a name approved in writing by the Council as the name of the multi-national partnership or of a predecessor legal practice.

(2) This rule shall not apply to the name of a recognised body.

Rule 12 (Investment business)

(1) Without prejudice to the generality of the principles embodied in Rule 1 of these rules, solicitors shall not in connection with investment business:

(a) be appointed representatives; or

(b) have any arrangements with other persons under which the solicitors could be constrained to recommend to clients or effect for them (or refrain from doing so) transactions in some investments but not others, with some persons but not others, or through the agency of some persons but not others; or to introduce or refer clients or other persons with whom the solicitors deal to some persons but not others.

(2) Notwithstanding any proviso to Rule 5 of these rules, solicitors shall not by themselves or with any other person set up, operate, actively participate in or control any separate business which is an appointed representative.

(3) Where a solicitor, authorised to conduct investment business, is required by the rules of the relevant regulatory body to use a buyer's guide, the solicitor shall use a buyer's guide in a form which has been approved by the Council of the Law Society.

(4) This rule shall have effect in relation to the conduct of investment business within or into any part of the United Kingdom.

(5) In this rule "appointed representative", "investment" and "investment business" have the meanings assigned to them by the Financial Services Act 1986.

Rule 13 (Supervision and management of an office)

(1) Solicitors shall ensure that every office where they or their firms practise is and can reasonably be seen to be properly supervised in accordance with the following minimum standards:

(a) Every such office shall be attended on each day when it is open to the public or open to telephone calls from the public by:

(i) a solicitor who holds a practising certificate and has been admitted for at least three years; or

(ii) in the case of an office from which no right of audience or right to conduct litigation is exercised and from which no exercise of any such right is supervised, a registered foreign lawyer who is a principal of the firm and who has been qualified in his or her own jurisdiction for at least three years;

who shall spend sufficient time at such office to ensure adequate control of the staff employed there and afford requisite facilities for consultation with clients. In the case of a firm in private practice such solicitor may be a principal, employee or consultant of the firm, provided that the firm must have at least one principal who is a solicitor who has been admitted for at least three years, or alternatively, in the case of a firm none of whose principals exercise any right of audience or right to conduct litigation or supervise or assume responsibility for the exercise of any such right, a registered foreign lawyer who has been qualified in his or her own jurisdiction for at least three years;

(b) Every such office shall be managed by one of the persons listed below who shall normally be in attendance at that office during all the hours when it is open to the public or open to telephone calls from the public:

   (i) a solicitor holding a current practising certificate;

   (ii) a Fellow of the Institute of Legal Executives confirmed by the Institute as being of good standing and having been admitted as a Fellow for not less than three years;

   (iia) in the case of an office from which no right of audience or right to conduct litigation is exercised and from which no exercise of any such right is supervised, a registered foreign lawyer who is a principal of the firm;

   (iii) in the case of an office dealing solely with conveyancing, a licensed conveyancer; or

   (iv) in the case of an office dealing solely with property selling and surveying, a chartered surveyor or person holding another professional qualification approved by the Council under Rule 14 of these rules.

(2)   In determining whether or not there has been compliance with the requirement as to supervision in paragraph (1) of this rule, account shall be taken of, inter alia, the arrangements for principals to see incoming mail.

(3)   Where daily attendance or normal attendance in accordance with sub-paragraphs (1)(a) or (1)(b) of this rule is prevented by illness, accident or other sufficient or unforeseen cause for a prolonged period, suitable alternative arrangements shall be made without delay to ensure compliance.

(4)   A solicitor's employee who would not otherwise qualify under sub-paragraph (1)(b) of this rule to manage an office and who was 50 years of age or more on 9th May 1975 and had at that date been continuously employed in connection with the practice of that solicitor for not less than 20 years shall, provided he or she exercised the duty of management at that date, be entitled to continue to do so until retiring or attaining the age of 70 years, whichever first happens.

(5)   In this rule:

   (a)   references to a principal shall be construed, in relation to a recognised body, as references to a director of that body;

   (b)   in paragraph (2) of this rule, "principals" shall be construed, except in relation to a firm none of whose principals exercise any right of audience or right to conduct litigation or supervise or assume responsibility for the exercise of any such right, as referring to principals who are solicitors; and

   (c)   "right of audience" and "right to conduct litigation" shall be construed in accordance with Part II and section 119 of the Courts and Legal Services Act 1990.

Rule 14 (Structural surveys and formal valuations)

Solicitors may not provide structural surveys or formal valuations of property unless:

    (a) the work is carried out by a principal or employee who is a chartered surveyor or who holds another professional qualification approved by the Council; and

    (b) the appropriate contribution has been paid to the Solicitors' Indemnity Fund.

Rule 15 (Client care)

(1) Every principal in private practice shall operate a complaints handling procedure which shall, inter alia, ensure that clients are informed whom to approach in the event of any problem with the service provided.

(2) Every solicitor in private practice shall, unless it is inappropriate in the circumstances:

    (a) ensure that clients know the name and status of the person responsible for the day to day conduct of the matter and the principal responsible for its overall supervision;

    (b) ensure that clients know whom to approach in the event of any problem with the service provided; and

    (c) ensure that clients are at all relevant times given any appropriate information as to the issues raised and the progress of the matter.

(3) Notwithstanding Rule 19(2) of these rules, this rule shall come into force on 1st May 1991.

Rule 16 (Cross-border activities within the European Community)

(1) In relation to cross-border activities within the European Community solicitors shall, without prejudice to their other obligations under these rules or any other rules, principles or requirements of conduct, observe the rules codified in articles 2 to 5 of the CCBE Code of Conduct for Lawyers in the European Community adopted on 28th October 1988, as interpreted by article 1 (the preamble) thereof and the Explanatory Memorandum and Commentary thereon prepared by the CCBE's Deontology Working Party and dated May 1989.

(2) In this Rule:

    (a) "cross-border activities" means:

        (i) all professional contacts with lawyers of member states of the European Community other than the United Kingdom; and

        (ii) the professional activities of the solicitor in a member state other than the United Kingdom, whether or not the solicitor is physically present in that member state; and

    (b) "lawyers" means lawyers as defined in Directive 77/249 of the Council of the European Communities dated 22nd March 1977 as amended from time to time.

Rule 16A (Solicitors acting as advocates)

Any solicitor acting as advocate shall at all times comply with the Law Society's Code for Advocacy.

Rule 16B (Choice of advocate)

(1)   A solicitor shall not make it a condition of providing litigation services that advocacy services shall also be provided by that solicitor or by the solicitor's firm or the solicitor's agent.

(2)   A solicitor who provides both litigation and advocacy services shall as soon as practicable after receiving instructions and from time to time consider and advise the client whether having regard to the circumstances including:

    (i)   the gravity, complexity and likely cost of the case;

    (ii)   the nature of the solicitor's practice;

    (iii)   the solicitor's ability and experience;

    (iv)   the solicitor's relationship with the client;

the best interests of the client would be served by the solicitor, another advocate from the solicitor's firm, or some other advocate providing the advocacy services.

Rule 17 (Waivers)

In any particular case or cases the Council of the Law Society shall have power to waive in writing any of the provisions of these rules for a particular purpose or purposes expressed in such waiver, and to revoke such waiver.

Rule 18 (Application and interpretation)

(1)   (Application to solicitors)

These rules shall have effect in relation to the practice of solicitors whether as a principal in private practice, or in the employment of a solicitor or of a non-solicitor employer, or in any other form of practice, and whether on a regular or on an occasional basis.

(1A)   (Application to registered foreign lawyers)

    (a)   For the avoidance of doubt, neither registration in the register of foreign lawyers, nor anything in these rules or in any other rules made under Part II of the Solicitors Act 1974 or section 9 of the Administration of Justice Act 1985, shall entitle any registered foreign lawyer to be granted any right of audience or any right to conduct litigation within the meaning of Part II and section 119 of the Courts and Legal Services Act 1990, or any right to supervise or assume any responsibility for the exercise of any such right.

    (b)   A registered foreign lawyer shall do nothing in the course of practising in partnership with a solicitor which, if done by a solicitor would put the solicitor in breach of any of these rules or any other rules, principles or requirements of conduct applicable to solicitors.

    (c)   A registered foreign lawyer shall do nothing in the course of practising as the director of a recognised body which puts the recognised body in breach of any of these rules, or any other rules, principles or requirements of conduct applicable to recognised bodies.

(2) (Interpretation)

In these rules, except where the context otherwise requires:

(a) "arrangement" means any express or tacit agreement between a solicitor and another person whether contractually binding or not;

(b) "contentious proceeding" is to be construed in accordance with the definition of "contentious business" in section 87 of the Solicitors Act 1974;

(c) "contingency fee" means any sum (whether fixed, or calculated either as a percentage of the proceeds or otherwise howsoever) payable only in the event of success in the prosecution or defence of any action, suit or other contentious proceeding;

(d) "firm" includes a sole practitioner or a recognised body;

(da) "foreign lawyer" means a person who is a member, and entitled to practise as such, of a legal profession regulated within a jurisdiction outside England and Wales;

(db) "multi-national partnership" has the meaning given in section 89 of the Courts and Legal Services Act 1990;

(e) "person" includes a body corporate or unincorporated association or group of persons;

(ea) "principal in private practice" includes a recognised body;

(f) "recognised body" means a body corporate for the time being recognised by the Council under the Solicitors' Incorporated Practice Rules from time to time in force;

(fa) "registered foreign lawyer" means a person registered in accordance with section 89 of the Courts and Legal Services Act 1990; and "register" and "registration" are to be construed accordingly;

(g) "solicitor" means a solicitor of the Supreme Court of England and Wales and, except in Rules 7(6) and 15(2A)(b) of these rules, also includes a firm of solicitors or a recognised body; and

(h) words in the singular include the plural, words in the plural include the singular, and words importing the masculine or feminine gender include the neuter.

Rule 19 (Repeal and commencement)

(1) The Solicitors' Practice Rules 1988 are hereby repealed.

(2) These rules shall come into force on 1st September 1990.

1.2. Solicitors' Accounts Rules 1991: Part III – Interest[1]

PART III–INTEREST

20.(1) Subject to rule 26 of these rules, a solicitor who holds money for or on account of a client shall account to the client for interest or an equivalent sum in the following circumstances:

    (i) where such money is held on deposit in a separate designated account the solicitor shall account to the client for the interest earned on that money;

    (ii) where such money is not so held on deposit, the solicitor shall, subject to rule 21 of these rules pay to the client out of the solicitor's own money a sum equivalent to the interest which would have accrued if the money received had been so kept on deposit, or its gross equivalent if the interest would have been net of tax.

(2) In paragraph (1) of this rule, for the avoidance of doubt, the reference to a solicitor who holds money for or on account of a client includes the solicitor holding money in his or her capacity as solicitor on account of the trustees of a trust (other than a controlled trust) of which the solicitor is a trustee.

21. A solicitor shall only be required to account in accordance with rule 20(1)(ii) of these rules where:

    (i) the solicitor holds the money for as long as or longer than the number of weeks set out in the left hand column of the table below and the minimum amount held equals or exceeds the corresponding figure in the right hand column of the table:

TABLE

No. of weeks	Minimum amount
8	£1,000
4	£2,000
2	£10,000
1	£20,000

or

1. With consolidated amendments to 1 June 1992.

(ii)   the solicitor holds a sum of money exceeding £20,000 for less than one week and it is fair and reasonable to so account having regard to all the circumstances; or

(iii) the solicitor holds money continuously which varies significantly in amount over the period during which it is held and it is fair and reasonable so to account having regard to any sum payable under paragraph (i) of this rule and to the varying amounts of money and length of time for which these are held; or

(iv)   the solicitor holds sums of money intermittently during the course of acting and it is fair and reasonable so to account having regard to all the circumstances including the aggregate of the sums held and the periods for which they are held notwithstanding that no individual sum would have attracted interest under paragraph (i) of this rule; or

(v)   rule 22 of these rules applies.

22. Where money is held by a solicitor for or on account of a client for a continuous period and the money is held on deposit in a separate designated account for only part of that period, and no interest would be payable for the rest of the period under rule 21(i) to (ii) of these rules, the solicitor shall:

(i)   for the part of the period during which the money was so held on deposit, account for interest in accordance with rule 20(1)(i) of these rules; and

(ii)   for the rest of the period, pay interest where it is fair and reasonable to do so having regard to all the circumstances including the interest which would have been payable under rule 21(i) to (iii) if the money had been kept off deposit for the whole of the period.

23. For the purposes of rule 20(1)(ii) of these rules the sum payable to the client shall be calculated by reference to the interest payable on a separate designated account:

(i)   at the bank or building society where the money is held; or

(ii)   where the money, or part of it, is held in successive and concurrent accounts maintained at different banks or building societies, at whichever of those banks or building societies was offering the highest rate of interest on such account on the day when the sum payable under rule 20(1)(ii) commenced to accrue; or

(iii) where, contrary to the provisions of Parts I and II of these rules, the money is not held in a client account, at any bank or building society nominated by the client.

24. Subject to Rule 26(c) of these rules, where a solicitor holds money as a stakeholder (whether or not such money is paid by a client of the solicitor) the solicitor shall pay interest in accordance with Part III of these rules save that such interest shall be paid to the person to whom the stake is paid.

25. Without prejudice to any other remedy which may be available to him or her, any client who feels aggrieved that interest or a sum equivalent thereto has not been paid to him or her under Part III of these rules shall be entitled to apply to the Law Society for a certificate as to whether or not interest ought to have been earned for him or her and, if so, the amount of such interest: and upon the issue of such a certificate the sum certified to be due shall be payable by the solicitor to the client.

26. Nothing in Part III of these rules shall:

    (a) affect any arrangement in writing, whenever made, between a solicitor and his or her client as to the application of the client's money or interest thereon;

    (b) apply to money received by a solicitor:

        (i)   being money subject to a controlled trust; or

        (ii) in his capacity as trustee rather than as solicitor, on account of the trustees of any other trust of which the solicitor is a trustee;

    (c) affect any agreement in writing for payment of interest on stakeholder money held by a solicitor.

I.3. Solicitors' Introduction and Referral Code 1990[1]

Code dated 18th July 1990 promulgated by the Council of the Law Society with the concurrence of the Master of the Rolls under Rule 3 of the Solicitors' Practice Rules 1990, regulating the introduction of clients to and by solicitors, registered foreign lawyers and recognised bodies practising in England and Wales.

Introduction

(1)   This code states the principles to be observed in relation to the introduction of clients by third parties to solicitors or by solicitors to third parties.

(2)   The code does not apply to introductions and referrals between solicitors, between solicitors and barristers or between solicitors and lawyers of other jurisdictions.

(3)   Non-compliance, evasion or disregard of the code could represent not only a breach of Practice Rule 3 (introductions and referrals) but also a breach of Practice Rule 1 (basic principles) or one of the other practice rules, and conduct unbefitting a solicitor.

(4)   Those wishing to advertise the services of solicitors to whom they refer work should be encouraged to publicise their adherence to the code by means of a notice on the following lines:

> "We comply with the Solicitors' Introduction and Referral Code published by the Law Society, and any solicitor to whom we may refer you is an independent professional from whom you will receive impartial and confidential advice. You are free to choose another solicitor."

(5)   In this code all references to individual practice rules are references to the Solicitors' Practice Rules 1990 and all words have the meanings assigned to them in Rule 18 of those rules.

(6)   The code will come into force on 1st September 1990.

Section 1: The basic principles

(1)   Solicitors must always retain their professional independence and their ability to advise their clients fearlessly and objectively. Solicitors should never permit the requirements of an introducer to undermine this independence.

(2)   In making or accepting introductions or referrals, solicitors must do nothing which would be likely to compromise or impair any of the principles set out in Practice Rule 1:

(a)   the solicitor's independence or integrity;

(b)   a person's freedom to instruct a solicitor of his or her choice;

(c)   the solicitor's duty to act in the best interests of the client;

1. With consolidated amendments to 1 January 1992.

(d)   the good repute of the solicitor or the solicitors' profession;

(e)   the solicitor's proper standard of work;

(f)   the solicitor's duty to the Court.

(3)   Practice Rule 9 prevents a solicitor from entering into any arrangement with a claims assessor for the introduction of personal injury clients to the solicitor.

(4)   Practice Rule 12 makes provision in respect of introductions and referrals in the field of investment business. In particular the rule prevents a solicitor from acting as an appointed representative as defined in the Financial Services Act 1986.

Section 2: Introduction or referral of business to solicitors

(1)   Solicitors may discuss and make known to potential introducers the basis on which they would be prepared to accept instructions and the fees they would charge to clients referred.

(2)   Solicitors should draw the attention of potential introducers to the provisions of this code and the relevant provisions of the Solicitors' Publicity Code.

(3)   Solicitors must not reward introducers by the payment of commission or otherwise. However, this does not prevent normal hospitality. A solicitor may refer clients to an introducer provided the solicitor complies with Section 4 below.

(4)   Solicitors should not allow themselves to become so reliant on a limited number of sources of referrals that the interests of an introducer affect the advice given by the solicitor to clients.

(5)   Solicitors should be particularly conscious of the need to advise impartially and independently clients referred by introducers. They should ensure that the wish to avoid offending the introducer does not colour the advice given to such clients.

(6)   Where a tied agent refers to a solicitor a client who is proposing to take out a company life policy, the solicitor should, where necessary, have regard to the suitability of that policy in each particular case.

(7)   Solicitors must ensure that they alone are responsible for any decisions taken in relation to the nature, style or extent of their practices.

(8)   This code does not affect the need for the solicitor to communicate directly with the client to obtain or confirm instructions, in the process of providing advice and at all appropriate stages of the transaction.

(9)   Each firm should keep a record of agreements for the introduction of work.

(10)   Each firm should conduct a review at six-monthly intervals, which should check:

(a)   that the provisions of this code have been complied with;

(b)   that referred clients have received impartial advice which has not been tainted by the relationship between the firm and the introducer; and

(c)   the income arising from each agreement for the introduction of business.

(11)   Where, so far as can be reasonably ascertained, more than 20 per cent of a firm's income during the period under review arises from a single source of introduction of business, the firm should consider whether steps should be taken to reduce that proportion.

(12)   Factors to be taken into account in considering whether to reduce the proportion include:

    (a)   the percentage of income deriving from that source;

    (b)   the number of clients introduced by that source;

    (c)   the nature of the clients and the nature of the work; and

    (d)   whether the introducer could be affected by the advice given by the solicitor to the client.

Section 3: Solicitor agreeing to be paid by a third party to do work for the third party's customers other than conveyancing work

(1)   In addition to the other provisions of this Code the following requirements should be observed in relation to agreements for the introduction of clients' business to solicitors under which the solicitor agrees with the introducer to be paid by the introducer to do work other than conveyancing work for the introducer's customers.

(2)   The terms of the agreement should be set out in writing and a copy available for inspection by the Law Society or the Solicitors Complaints Bureau.

(3)   The solicitor may agree to be remunerated by the introducer either on a case by case basis or on an hourly, monthly or any other appropriate basis.

(4)   The solicitor should ensure that any agreement between the introducer and customer for the provision of services under this section includes:

    (a)   express mention of the independence of the solicitor's professional advice;

    (b)   a provision that control of the professional work should remain in the hands of the solicitor subject to the instructions of the client; and

    (c)   a provision that information disclosed by the client to the solicitor should not be disclosed to the introducer unless the client consents.

Section 3A: Contractual referrals for conveyancing

(1)   In addition to the other provisions of this code the following requirements must be observed in relation to agreements for the introduction of clients/business to solicitors under which the solicitor agrees with the introducer to be paid by the introducer to provide conveyancing services for the introducer's customers.

Agreements for referrals

(2)   Solicitors may enter into agreements under this section for referrals for conveyancing services only with introducers who undertake in such agreements to comply with the terms of this code.

(3)   Referrals under this section must not be made where the introducer is a seller or seller's agent and the conveyancing services are to be provided to the buyer.

(4)   The agreement between the solicitor and the introducer must be set out in writing. A copy of the agreement and of records of the six monthly reviews carried out under paragraph 10 of Section 2 of this code in relation to transactions under the agreement must be retained by the solicitor for production on request to the Law Society or the Solicitors Complaints Bureau.

(5)   If the solicitor has reason to believe that the introducer is breaching terms of the agreement required by this section the solicitor must take all reasonable steps to procure that the breach is remedied . If the introducer persists in breaches the solicitor must terminate the agreement in respect of future referrals.

(6)   The agreement between the introducer and the solicitor must not include any provisions which would:

    (a)   compromise, infringe or impair any of the principles set out in Rule 1 of the Solicitors' Practice Rules or any duties owed by the solicitor to the introducer's customer by virtue of the solicitor/client relationship and/or the requirements of professional conduct; or

    (b)   restrict the scope of the duties which the solicitor owes to the customer in relation to the services agreed to be provided by virtue of the professional relationship between solicitor and client; or

    (c)   interfere with or inhibit the solicitor's responsibility for the control of the professional work.

Publicity as to conveyancing services

(7)   Publicity material of the introducer which includes reference to any service that may be provided by the solicitor must comply with the following:

    (a)   Any reference to the charge for the conveyancing service must be clearly expressed separately from charges for other services. Any circumstances in which the charges may be increased must be stated. It must be made clear whether disbursements and VAT are or are not included.

    (b)   The publicity must not suggest that the service is free, nor that different charges for the conveyancing services would be made according to whether the customer takes other products or services offered by the introducer or not.

    (c)   Charges must not be stated as being from or upwards of a certain figure.

    (d)   The publicity must not suggest that the availability or price of other services offered by the introducer are conditional on the customer instructing the solicitor.

Notice to customer

(8)   Before making a referral the introducer must give the customer in writing:

    (a)   details of the conveyancing service to be provided under the terms of the referral;

    (b)   notification of:

        (i)   the charge payable by the customer to the introducer for the conveyancing services;

        (ii)   the liability for VAT and disbursements and how these are to be discharged; and

        (iii)   what charge if any is to be made if the transaction does not proceed to completion or if the solicitor is unable to continue to act;

    (c)   notification of the amount the introducer will be paying to the solicitor for the provision of conveyancing services relating to the customer's transaction;

    (d)   a statement to the effect that the charge for conveyancing services will not be affected whether or not the customer takes other products or services offered by the introducer, and that the availability and price of other services will not be affected whether the customer chooses to instruct a solicitor under the referral or decides to instruct another solicitor or conveyancer; and

(e)   a statement to the effect that the advice and service of the solicitor to whom the customer is to be referred will remain independent and subject to the instructions of the customer.

Solicitor's terms of business

(9)   Where a solicitor accepts instructions on referral under this section the solicitor must provide the client with written terms of business which must include:

(a)   details of the conveyancing service to be provided under the referral and if appropriate any other services the solicitor is to provide and on what terms;

(b)   a statement that any advice given by the solicitor will be independent and that the client is free to raise questions on all aspects of the transaction;

(c)   confirmation that information disclosed by the client to the solicitor will not be disclosed to the introducer unless the client consents; but that where the solicitor is also acting for the introducer in the same matter and a conflict of interest arises, the solicitor might be obliged to cease acting.

Definition

(10)   In this section references to a conveyancing service or services include services to be provided to the introducer if the solicitor is also to be instructed to act for the introducer.

Section 4: Referral of clients by solicitors

(1)   If a solicitor recommends that a client use a particular firm, agency or business, the solicitor must do so in good faith, judging what is in the client's best interest. A solicitor should not enter into any agreement or association which would restrict the solicitor's freedom to recommend any particular firm, agency or business.

(2)   The referral to a tied agent of a client requiring life insurance would not discharge the solicitor's duty to give his client independent advice. In such circumstances, any referral should be to an independent intermediary.

(3)   If the best interests of the client require it, a solicitor may refer a client requiring a mortgage to a tied agent, provided that the client is informed that the agent offers products from only one company.

(4)   In relation to commission received for the introduction of clients' business to third parties, Practice Rule 10 applies.

I.4. Solicitors' Separate Business Code 1994 (extracts)

Rules dated 4th February 1994 made by the Council of the Law Society with the concurrence of the Master of the Rolls under Section 31 of the Solicitors Act 1974 and Section 9 of the Administration of Justice Act 1985, regulating the circumstances in which practising solicitors, registered foreign lawyers and recognised bodies may provide certain services other than through their practices.

5. Safeguards and exceptions – particular businesses

(2) Estate agency

Requirements:

A solicitor who has a separate business providing estate agency must ensure

  (a) that the requirements of Section 4(2)(a), (b), (c) and (f) are observed;

  (b) that the separate business is conducted from accommodation physically divided and clearly differentiated from that of any practice of the solicitor in England and Wales; and

  (c) that the solicitor does not carry out conveyancing for the seller of a property if the separate business provides (or has provided) financial or mortgage services to the buyer of that property; and

  (d) that the solicitor does not carry out conveyancing for the buyer of any property bought through the separate business; and

  (e) that all clients referred by any practice of the solicitor to the separate business are informed of the solicitor's interest in the business and that, as customers of the separate business, they do not enjoy the statutory protections attaching to clients of a solicitor (or recognised body or multi-national partnership, as the case may be) by the following steps:

    (i) in a personal interview or telephone call and

    (ii) in writing confirming the contents of that interview or call; and

  (f) that (without prejudice to (b) above) where the separate business shares premises or reception staff with any English or Welsh practice of the solicitor, all customers of the separate business are informed that, as customers of the separate business, they do not enjoy the statutory protections attaching to clients of a solicitor (or a recognised body or multi-national partnership, as the case may be) by the following steps:

    (i) in a personal interview or telephone call and

    (ii) in writing confirming the contents of that interview or call.

4. Safeguards and exceptions – separate businesses generally

Requirements:

(2) A solicitor who has a separate business must ensure:

   (a) that the name of any practice of the solicitor has no substantial element in common with the name of that separate business;

   (b) that the words "solicitor(s)", "attorney(s)" or "lawyer(s)" are not used in connection with the solicitor's involvement with that separate business;

   (c) that paperwork and records relating to customers of the separate business are kept separately from paperwork and records relating to clients of the solicitor (whether or not those customers are also clients of the solicitor);

   (d) that all clients referred by any English or Welsh practice of the solicitor to the separate business are informed in writing of the solicitor's interest in the business and that, as customers of the separate business, they do not enjoy the statutory protections attaching to clients of a solicitor (or a recognised body or multi-national partnership, as the case may be);

   (e) that where the separate business shares premises, office accommodation or reception staff with any English or Welsh practice of the solicitor, all customers of the separate business are informed in writing that, as customers of the separate business, they do not enjoy the statutory protections attaching to the clients of a solicitor (or a recognised body or multi-national partnership, as the case may be); and

   (f) that the solicitor does not hold on the client account of the solicitor's practice money held for customers of the separate business as such; or money held for the separate business.

II. GUIDANCE

II.1. Guidance – mortgages and life policies[1]

Solicitors should refer a client who is likely to need an endowment policy, or similar life insurance with an investment element, to an independent intermediary authorised to give investment advice.

1.   Where clients may need life insurance, solicitors should either act as independent intermediaries themselves, or introduce the client to another independent intermediary. The duty to give independent advice is not normally discharged by referring a client to an appointed representative, i.e. a tied agent. See also section 4 of the Solicitors' Introduction and Referral Code 1990 (Annex 11B at p.209).

2.   Although a mortgage of land is not an investment under the Financial Services Act 1986, solicitors who advise on or make arrangements in respect of mortgages where an endowment policy or pension policy is to be used as additional security may be caught by the Act. A mere referral to an independent intermediary is not caught by the Act, but solicitors should assess the client's needs and consider factors such as speed and reliability of administration, availability, interest rates and general terms. Referral to a mortgage provider who is a tied agent may result in the client not receiving independent investment advice. If the client's interests dictate a referral to a tied agent, the client should be informed that the agent can offer investment products from a single company only.

3.   Solicitors should be aware of the Financial Services Act status of persons to whom clients are referred, as many banks, building societies, estate agents and insurance agents are appointed representatives of particular insurance companies and are unable to offer independent advice.

4.   A client who is proposing to take out a company life policy or other financial product without independent advice may be referred to a solicitor by the life office, bank, building society or other tied agent. It is not a solicitor's duty to force clients to take independent advice, if they do not wish to do so. However, solicitors should be prepared to make enquiries of a client if the proposed policy seems unsuitable and, if appropriate, provide independent advice, or refer the client to an independent intermediary. The solicitor will need to consider and discuss with the client whether obtaining independent advice will involve additional cost or delay or prejudice the proposed purchase. See also section 2(6) of the Solicitors' Introduction and Referral Code 1990 (Annex 11B at p.206).

5.   Similar considerations arise where the referral is by an independent financial adviser who has persuaded the client to enter into an obviously inappropriate scheme. Whilst a solicitor is not under a duty to re-advise, or to offer investment business advice as part of a conveyancing retainer, there may be a general duty in relation to the conveyancing retainer to give advice on the legal implications. See also **25.10** note 5, p.404.

---

1. The following text is taken from Chapter 25, 25.09 of *The Guide to the Professional Conduct of Solicitors 1996*, published by the Law Society.

6.   All home income or equity release schemes, whereby homes are mortgaged to raise a capital sum for investment, carry an element of risk. Two home income plans sold to the elderly a few years ago have given rise to a number of claims against advisers, including solicitors. Reference may be made to *Using Your Home as Capital* by Cecil Hinton, published by Age Concern, for an account of these schemes - the 'investment bond income scheme' and the 'roll-up loan scheme'. So far as they can, solicitors should dissuade clients from entering into any scheme of this kind without expert and independent advice.

7.   Rule 12 of the Solicitors' Practice Rules 1990 (see **27.20**, p.457) provides that solicitors shall not, in connection with investment business, be appointed representatives or operate any separate business which is an appointed representative. Solicitors' agency arrangements with building societies or other financial institutions which are tied agents, and the business transacted at the solicitor's agency office, must be confined to non-investment business. A solicitor operating a building society agency, etc., if asked about mortgages, should consider whether the customer needs independent advice.

8.   The Society has a group licence covering credit brokerage by solicitors, limited to activities arising in the course of practice. Solicitors who arrange mortgages will be carrying on credit brokerage within the meaning of the Consumer Credit Act 1974 and should take care to comply with the Consumer Credit (Quotations) Regulations 1989 (S.I. 1989 no. 1126) when giving quotations.

9.   Solicitors who advertise that they are able to arrange mortgages must comply with the Consumer Credit (Advertisements) Regulations 1989 (S.I. 1989 no. 1125). Such an advertisement, provided it contains no details of amounts due in repayment of the mortgage, will be an intermediate credit advertisement for the purpose of the regulations which provide that the following information must be contained in the advertisement:

     (a)   the name of the solicitors and a postal address or telephone number;

     (b)   a statement in the following form:

         'Your home is at risk if you do not keep up repayments on a mortgage or other loan secured on it.'

         This statement must be in capital letters and afforded no less prominence than the statement relating to the ability to arrange mortgages;

     (c)   the amount of any arrangement fee payable or a statement of its methods of calculation;

     (d)   a statement that individuals may obtain on request a quotation in writing about the terms on which the solicitors are prepared to do business, e.g. 'written details on request'.

II.2. Property selling guidance[1]

26.01 Solicitors selling property

Property selling as part of practice

1. Property selling is work which a solicitor may properly carry on in the course of his or her professional practice. Section 1(2)(a) of the Estate Agents Act 1979 exempts from that Act 'things done in the course of his profession by a practising solicitor or a person employed by him'. A solicitor's property selling work is covered by the Solicitors' Indemnity Rules, and the solicitor's earnings from property selling must be included in his or her gross fee returns.

2. If a solicitor sells property as part of his or her practice, the seller will be his or her client. The solicitor's relationship with and the work carried out for the client will be subject to the same law and professional rules binding on solicitors in relation to their other work. (This contrasts with the situation where a solicitor sells property through a separate business − see **26.16**).

3. A solicitor may sell property either as an activity of his or her general practice or through a separate practice formed for that purpose, and either alone or with other firms of solicitors (but see practice rule 14 at **26.10**). The property selling practice may be conducted in the same office used for the rest of the solicitor's practice. If two or more solicitors from separate practices form a new partnership for the purpose of property selling, it will be a new practice for all purposes, including the Indemnity Rules, the Accounts Rules, the Practice Rules and conflict of interests.

Fee sharing with estate agents

4. Rule 7(6) of the Practice Rules prohibits solicitors from entering into partnership with non-solicitors, other than registered foreign lawyers and recognised bodies. Rule 7(1) prohibits solicitors from otherwise sharing their fees with non-solicitors (other than foreign lawyers and recognised bodies), although there are exceptions (see **26.03** note 1). Rule 7(2) permits a solicitor who instructs an estate agent as his or her sub-agent for the sale of a property to remunerate the sub-agent on the basis of a proportion of the solicitor's professional fee. Conversely, a solicitor may be instructed as the sub-agent of an estate agent. Rule 7 is set out at **14.02**, p.234.

Incorporated practices

5. A solicitor may undertake a property selling business through a company (recognised body). The guidance in this chapter applies equally to an incorporated practice and its directors, employees and shareholders.

Competence

6. A solicitor who is asked to sell property of a value or character not usually handled

---

1. The following text is taken from Chapter 26 of *The Guide to the Professional Conduct of Solicitors* 1996, published by the Law Society. Cross-references to paragraphs in the *Guide* , other than Chapter 26, include page references from the *Guide*.

by his or her practice must, as in the case of any work which the solicitor does not feel competent to handle, decline instructions and advise the client to consult another property seller, possibly a specialist agent.

26.02 Description of property selling work

1. A designation may be used in addition to the name of a solicitor's practice but the word 'solicitor' or 'solicitors' must be included and the designation must not be misleading. A practice may be designated 'solicitor and estate agent', provided that the firm can justify a claim to specialism or particular expertise in the field of estate agency. See paragraph 6 of the Solicitors' Publicity Code 1990 (Annex 11A at p.196).

2. A solicitor may advertise that he or she undertakes property selling work. Provided that the description is not misleading or inaccurate, the relevant part of a practice (e.g. the property selling department or a branch office conducting only or mainly property selling) may be described as an estate agency, a property centre, a property selling department, or by any other suitable description. For appearance under 'Estate Agents' in a directory, see **26.06** note 5.

3. Practice rule 11 (see **3.10**, p.56) provides that the name of a firm of solicitors must be in traditional form. However, paragraph 9 of the Publicity Code (see Annex 11A at p.201) permits the use of a subsidiary practising style, of a type other than that used as the name of a firm of solicitors, in relation to a firm or a part of a firm provided that it is used in conjunction with the firm's name and the word 'solicitor(s)' is also used.

26.03 Staff

1. In property selling, a solicitor may employ staff experienced in estate agency. Rule 7(1) of the Practice Rules (see **14.02**, p.234) allows a solicitor to share fees with his or her *bona fide* employee, whether or not a solicitor. Thus, property selling negotiators may be paid on a commission basis.

2. Paragraph 7 of the Publicity Code (see Annex 11A at p.200) allows any member of staff to be named in publicity (including on stationery), but the status of a staff member who is not a solicitor with a current practising certificate must be unambiguously stated.

26.04 Supervision

A solicitor may open a branch office with, for example, a street-level window purely for the purpose of property selling. A branch office must be staffed and supervised in accordance with practice rule 13 (supervision and management of an office—see **3.02**, p.48). Rule 13(1)(b)(iv) makes special provision for an office dealing solely with property selling and surveying. An application for a waiver will also be considered in the case of an office at which the only work carried out is property selling. See also **26.13** notes 4−5 as regards a property display centre.

26.05 Conflict of interests

Connected persons

1. The requirements in notes 4 and 8−11 below are similar to those imposed on estate agents by the Estate Agents (Provision of Information) Regulations 1991 (S.I. 1991 no. 859) and the Estate Agents (Undesirable Practices)(No. 2) Order 1991 (S.I. 1991 no. 1032).

2.   Reference throughout **26.05** to a connected person includes:

   (a)   any of the solicitor's family meaning a spouse, former spouse, reputed spouse, brother, sister, uncle, aunt, nephew, niece, direct descendant, parent or other direct ancestor;

   (b)   any employee of the solicitor and any family of an employee;

   (c)   any partner in an associated firm as defined in rule 6 of the Practice Rules (i.e. where two or more firms have at least one common principal), any employee of that firm and any family of an employee;

   (d)   any company of which the solicitor is a director or employee or in which the solicitor, either alone or with any other connected person or persons is entitled to exercise, or control the exercise of, one-third or more of the voting power at any general meeting;

   (e)   any company of which any of the persons mentioned in (a), (b) and (c) above is a director or employee or in which any of them, either alone or with any other connected person or persons is entitled to exercise, or control the exercise of, one-third or more of the voting power at any general meeting;

   (f)   any other associate of the solicitor as defined in section 32 of the Estate Agents Act 1979.

3.   Reference throughout **26.05** to a solicitor's partners includes those with whom he or she carries on a joint property selling practice, and partners in an associated firm (see note 2(c) above for meaning of associated firm).

Notification to client when connected person has interest in property

4.   A solicitor must always place the client's interests first. In addition to the requirements of **15.04**, p.276, the solicitor should promptly inform the client in writing whenever the solicitor or, to his or her knowledge, any connected person has, or is seeking to acquire, a beneficial interest in the property or in the proceeds of sale of any interest in the property.

Avoiding conflicts of interest

5.   A solicitor and his or her partners who act in the sale of a property may be faced with insuperable problems of conflict of interests. In accordance with the general principles of professional conduct, a solicitor must not act (or continue to act) if a conflict of interests arises or is likely to arise.

Prohibitions on acting for buyer

6.   In particular, because of the likelihood of conflicting interests, the solicitor who or whose partners act in the sale, even if not in the conveyancing, must not act also for the buyer, either in the negotiations or in respect of a mortgage (but see note 14 below) or in the subsequent conveyancing. None of the exceptions to rule 6 of the Practice Rules (see **25.01**, p.392) apply where a solicitor or a solicitor practising in partnership or association with him or her is instructed to negotiate the sale of the property concerned. The solicitor who acts in the sale is free to act for the seller in the conveyancing as well, or the seller may choose to instruct different solicitors.

7.   Even where a solicitor acting for the seller in the conveyancing has not acted in the sale of the property, rule 6 would, subject to its exceptions, prevent any firm with whom that solicitor practises in partnership or association (including one with whom he or

she has a joint property selling practice) from acting for the buyer in the conveyancing of the property.

Notification to client of sale instructions from prospective buyer

8. Besides cases governed by rule 6, questions of conflict may arise where the solicitor and his or her partners act also for parties in related transactions. Where a prospective buyer has made an offer for a client's property, the solicitor must promptly inform the client in writing if, to the solicitor's knowledge, he or she or any connected person has also been instructed by the buyer to sell an interest in land, and that sale is necessary to enable the buyer to buy from the client or results from that prospective purchase.

Notification of offers to client

9. A solicitor must promptly send to the client written accurate details (other than those of a description which the client has indicated in writing he or she does not wish to receive) of any offer the solicitor has received from a prospective buyer in respect of an interest in the property.

Duties to buyers

10. In addition to the general requirements of **17.01**, p.308 (a solicitor must not use his or her position as a solicitor to take unfair advantage either for the solicitor or another person), a solicitor must promptly and in writing inform any person negotiating to acquire or dispose of any interest in the property whenever the solicitor or, to his or her knowledge, any connected person has a beneficial interest in the property or in the proceeds of sale of any interest in it. The solicitor should not enter into negotiations with a prospective buyer until that disclosure has been made.

11. A solicitor must not discriminate against a prospective buyer because he or she has not or is unlikely to instruct the solicitor to sell an interest in land, which sale is necessary to enable the buyer to buy from the solicitor's client or results from that prospective purchase.

12. A solicitor acting for a seller of property may need to contact the buyer direct but the communication should be restricted to the solicitor's estate agency function. Communications about legal matters should so far as possible be through the buyer's solicitor, and the buyer should not be led to believe that he or she is receiving legal advice from the seller's solicitor.

Mortgages for buyers

13. In order to facilitate the sale of properties, solicitors sometimes wish to assist buyers to obtain mortgages. A solicitor who or whose partners (for 'partners' see note 3 above) act in the sale of a property may not also act (which includes giving advice) for the buyer in respect of a mortgage.

14. A solicitor may, acting as solicitor for the seller, arrange (in a particular case or as part of a scheme) with a building society or other financial institution that a mortgage will be available on a property (subject to the buyer's status). The solicitor may inform a prospective buyer of the availability of the mortgage but must make it clear in writing that the solicitor cannot advise or act for the prospective buyer in respect of the mortgage, that the mortgage may not be the only one available and that he or she should consult his or her own solicitor.

15. Where a solicitor wishes to advise on mortgages linked with a life policy, the solicitor will have to ensure compliance with the Financial Services Act 1986. It is likely that in order to give such advice the solicitor would require authorisation under that Act (see Chapter 27, p.447).

26.06 Publicity

1. A solicitor may publicise his or her property selling service or properties for sale, subject to the provisions of the Solicitors' Publicity Code 1990 (see Annex 11A, p.196). For the effect of the Publicity Code on the description of property selling work and the naming of staff in publicity, see **26.02** and **26.03** note 2.

2. Paragraph 3 of the Publicity Code (at p.197), which contains the prohibition on unsolicited visits or unsolicited telephone calls, nevertheless permits an unsolicited visit or telephone call to publicise a specific commercial property or properties the solicitor has for sale or to let.

3. Paragraph 4 of the Publicity Code (at p.198) permits the naming or identification of a client in advertisements with the client's written consent where the naming or identification is not likely to prejudice the client's interests. Subject to these provisions therefore, a solicitor may name a client in advertising property for sale or to let on that client's behalf.

Composite fees

4. Where a solicitor publicises a composite fee for a package of property selling and conveyancing (and/or some other service) paragraph 5(d) of the Publicity Code (at p.198) provides that he or she must be willing if required:

    (a) to quote separate fees for the individual services (not totalling more than the composite fee), and

    (b) to carry out any one only of those services on the basis of the separate fee.

    A solicitor is 'required' for this purpose if he or she has a clear indication that a prospective client may wish to give instructions in respect of only one service in the package.

Directories

5. An entry or advertisement of a solicitor who provides a property selling service may appear in a directory, such as the Yellow Pages, under the classification 'Estate Agents', provided that 'solicitor(s)' appears *either* in the heading of the directory or listing *or* in a designation of the practice appearing in the entry or advertisement itself. See paragraph 8 of the Publicity Code (at p.201).

Flag advertising

6. A reference may be made in publicity to the solicitor's membership of an organisation or association of solicitors, but if an advertisement does not name the solicitor's firm it must comply with paragraph 10 of the Publicity Code (at p.202).

Arranging mortgages

7. A solicitor may advertise the ability to arrange mortgages but will need to comply with relevant consumer credit regulations. See **25.09** note 9 (p.402) and also **26.05** note 15.

26.07 Introductions and referrals

1. Rule 3 of the Practice Rules (see **11.04**, p.192) allows solicitors to enter into arrangements for the introduction and referral of clients to and from the solicitor's practice subject to compliance with the Solicitors' Introduction and Referral Code 1990 (see Annex 11B, p.205). The code provides *inter alia* that a solicitor may not reward an introducer by the payment of commission or otherwise (see section 2(3) of the code).

Investment business and mortgages

2. Rule 12 of the Practice Rules (see **27.20**, p.457) places conditions on the ability of a solicitor to enter into arrangements for introductions and referrals in the field of investment business. In particular, a solicitor cannot act as an appointed representative as defined in the Financial Services Act 1986.

3. In accepting or making referrals in the field of mortgages or investment business, solicitors must comply with **25.09**, p.401.

26.08 Remuneration

Statement as to remuneration

1. When accepting instructions to act in the sale of a property, a solicitor must give the client a written statement setting out their agreement as to the amount of the solicitor's fee or the method of its calculation, the circumstances in which it is to become payable, the amount of any disbursements to be charged separately (or the basis on which they will be calculated) and the circumstances in which they may be incurred, and as to the incidence of VAT. It should state the identity of the property, the interest to be sold and the price to be sought. This requirement is similar to that imposed on estate agents by the Estate Agents Act 1979 and enables the client to be clear as to the proposed basis of charging.

2. The statement should also deal with whether or not the solicitor is to have 'sole agency' or 'sole selling rights' and, if so, explain the intention and effect of those terms (or any similar terms used) in the following manner:

   (a) **Sole selling rights**

   'You will be liable to pay a fee to us, in addition to any other costs or charges agreed, in each of the following circumstances:

   - if unconditional contracts for the sale of the property are exchanged in the period during which we have sole selling rights, even if the buyer was not found by us but by another agent or by any other person, including yourself; or

   - if unconditional contracts for the sale of the property are exchanged after the expiry of the period during which we have sole selling rights but to a buyer who was introduced to you during that period or with whom we had negotiations about the property during that period.

   (b) **Sole agency**

   'You will be liable to pay a fee to us, in addition to any other costs or charges agreed, if unconditional contracts for the sale of the property are exchanged at any time:

   - with a buyer introduced by us with whom we had negotiations about the property in the period during which we have sole agency; or

- with a buyer introduced by another agent during the period of our sole agency.

These requirements and those in notes 3−5 below are similar to the obligations imposed on estate agents by the Estate Agents (Provision of Information) Regulations 1991.

3. If reference is made to a 'ready, willing and able' buyer (or similar term), the statement should contain the following explanation:

   'A buyer is a "ready, willing and able" buyer if he or she is prepared and is able to exchange unconditional contracts for the purchase of your property. You will be liable to pay a fee to us, in addition to any other costs or charges agreed, if such a buyer is introduced by us in accordance with your instructions and this must be paid even if you subsequently withdraw and unconditional contracts for sale are not exchanged, irrespective of your reasons.'

4. If, by reason of the provisions of the statement in which any of the terms referred to above appear, any of the prescribed explanations is in any way misleading, the content of the explanation should be altered so as accurately to describe the liability of the client to pay a fee in accordance with those provisions. Subject to this requirement, the prescribed explanations should be reproduced prominently, clearly and legibly without any material alterations or additions and should be given no less prominence than that given to any other information in the statement apart from the heading, practice names, names of the parties, numbers or lettering subsequently inserted.

5. The statement must be given at the time when communication commences between the solicitor and the client or as soon as is reasonably practicable thereafter, provided that this is before the client is committed to any liability towards the solicitor.

Commission − remuneration certificates and taxation

6. The Society does not make any recommendation about property selling commissions. Commission charged on property sales is, however, subject to the Society's remuneration certificate procedure, unless the client signs a non-contentious business agreement in accordance with section 57 of the Solicitors Act 1974 (see Annex 14A, p.242), and to taxation by the Court.

Commission from third party

7. Commission paid by a third party, e.g. by an insurance company where the client takes out an endowment policy, is distinct from the remuneration paid by the client to the solicitor in relation to the property transaction. The solicitor must deal with commission from a third party in accordance with rule 10 of the Practice Rules (see **14.14**, p.240). An exception is where commission has been received for the referral of a prospective buyer who is merely browsing; rule 10 only comes into operation when a buyer expresses interest in a specific property.

Composite fees

8. A solicitor may quote a composite fee for property selling and conveyancing but should be prepared to quote separate fees if asked. For the more onerous requirement where a composite fee is quoted in publicity, see **26.06** note 4.

26.09 Interest earned on preliminary deposits

A preliminary deposit is usually held on behalf of and is fully refundable to the buyer. Part III of the Solicitors' Accounts Rules 1991 (deposit interest) applies only to interest arising on client's and stakeholder money. However, as a matter of good practice, solicitors should consider, when refunding a preliminary deposit, whether it is appropriate to pay interest to the buyer. Regulation 7 of the Estate Agents (Accounts) Regulations 1981(S.I. 1981 no.1520) provides that estate agents must account to the buyer where the preliminary deposit exceeds £500, and the interest actually earned on it, or which could have been earned if it had been kept in a separate deposit account, is at least £10. In that case, the agent must account for all interest earned, or for the interest which could have been earned in a separate deposit account. Solicitors could follow these regulations themselves. Alternatively, they could refer to the Accounts Rules (see **28.22**, p.597 *et seq.* ,and Annexes 28B at p.620 and 28E, p.634).

26.10 Practice rule 14 (structural surveys and formal valuations)

'Solicitors may not provide structural surveys or formal valuations of property unless:

(a) **the work is carried out by a principal or employee who is a chartered surveyor or who holds another professional qualification approved by the Council; and**

(b) **the appropriate contribution has been paid to the Solicitors' Indemnity Fund.'**

Solicitors Practice Rules 1990, rule 14

26.11 Structural surveys and formal valuations – additional guidance

A solicitor may carry out structural surveys and formal valuations of property as part of his or her practice. Rule 36.2 of the Solicitors' Indemnity Rules 1995 (see Annex 29A at p.648) details the additional contribution payable and provides that any practice intending to undertake this work must immediately notify Solicitors Indemnity Fund Limited.

26.12 Joint property selling practice

1. Where a number of firms of solicitors undertake property selling jointly, those firms will be carrying on a joint property selling practice. The professional rules applicable to such a joint practice are the same as those generally applicable to a solicitor's firm.

2. Severe constraints for firms in a joint property selling practice are presented by the principles on conflict of interests and rule 6 of the Practice Rules (see Chapter 15, p.274, **25.01**, p.392 and **26.05**.

26.13 Property display centre

1. Rather than carrying on a joint property selling practice with the resultant constraints referred to in **26.12** above, a number of independent firms of solicitors (the participating firms) may join together to carry on a joint property display centre (PDC) to publicise properties in the sale of which an individual participating firm is instructed.

2. A PDC which observes the requirements set out in note 3 below is regarded as an administrative extension of the practices of the participating firms. It is not regarded either as a department or branch office of all or any of the participating firms, or as

a joint property selling practice. The address of a PDC should be notified to Records Centre (PSD) under section 84(1) of the Solicitors Act 1974 (see **2.09**, p.22) as a business address of all the participating firms. Although it may involve a partnership for administrative purposes between participating firms, a PDC is not a partnership for the purposes of carrying on a solicitor's practice.

Characteristics and functions of a PDC

3. (a) A PDC can have no clients; it may merely carry out certain activities on behalf of the participating firms. Only individual participating firms may be instructed in the sale of a property.

   (b) A PDC is a place where the principal activity carried on is the display and dissemination of information about properties which the individual participating firms have for sale.

   (c) No part of a solicitor's professional practice may be carried on at a PDC. In particular no negotiations may be conducted there; prospective buyers must be referred to the individual participating firm instructed in the sale of the property in question. Instructions to sell a property may only be accepted at offices of participating firms. To avoid problems with conflict of interests (see **26.05**) the participating firms must operate totally independently so far as their professional business, including property selling, is concerned.

   (d) A PDC is inherently an administrative extension of the practices of the participating firms, not a separate entity.

   (e) The participating firms may wish to establish a joint service company to carry out support functions connected with the running of the PDC, e.g. hiring premises and equipment. The service company (as with a service company established by an individual firm of solicitors) cannot carry on any legal practice or have any dealings with the property selling or property buying public (see **3.19**, p.66).

   (f) Having regard to rule 1(b) and (c) of the Practice Rules (see **1.01**, p.1), a participating firm may not make it a condition that a prospective buyer instructs another participating firm in his or her conveyancing or any other matter.

Supervision and management

4. As no part of a solicitor's practice is carried on at a PDC, rule 13 of the Practice Rules (supervision and management of an office) does not apply. Note that the participating firms are nevertheless responsible for the activities of the PDC staff and have a duty to supervise them.

A single firm PDC

5. A single firm of solicitors could establish its own PDC where no negotiations or any other part of the firm's practice was conducted. Rule 13 would not apply to such a PDC. The firm would nevertheless be responsible for the activities of its PDC staff and would have a duty to supervise them. Note that rule 13 (see **3.02**, p.48 and **26.04**) applies to a branch office (as opposed to a PDC).

26.14 Joint property display centre – publicity

1. Paragraph 10 of the Solicitors' Publicity Code 1990 governs 'flag advertising' (see Annex 11A at p. 202). This term includes any advertising by a joint PDC which does not name the firm or firms whose services are being advertised.

2. Any advertising under the logo of or in the name of a joint PDC, if it does not name the firm or firms whose services are being advertised, must include the word 'solicitor(s)' (or, as an additional option in the case of publicity conducted outside England and Wales, the word 'lawyer(s)') and the PDC's address (or some other address at which the names of all the participating firms are available). A name such as 'Solicitors' Property Centre' or 'Solicitors' Property Centre, Craxenford' (provided it is not misleading or inaccurate) may appear on the PDC premises, advertisements or stationery.

3. On the PDC premises the PDC name must be accompanied by the names of the participating firms (either outside or visible from outside the premises) and the word 'solicitor(s)'. The PDC stationery must be used only in connection with activities which a PDC may properly undertake in accordance with **26.13** note 3. In particular it must not be used in connection with negotiations.

4. For the reasons stated in **26.13** note 3 the name of a service company (e.g. 'Solicitors' Property Centre Ltd') should not appear on the PDC itself or in its advertisements or on its stationery.

5. An individual participating firm advertising in its own name may refer to its membership of the PDC or include the PDC logo in its advertisements. The firm's stationery may include the PDC logo or refer to the firm's membership of the PDC. Notepaper used for a solicitor's professional business, including notepaper used in negotiating a sale of property, must include the name of the firm and not merely the name of the PDC.

6. 'For Sale' boards and particulars of properties for sale may, at the discretion of the participating firms, either be the boards and particulars of an individual participating firm or the boards and particulars of the PDC. Boards and particulars of the PDC must comply with notes 2–4 above. An individual participating firm may use the PDC name and/or logo on its boards or particulars in addition to the firm's own name.

26.15   Joint property display centre – referrals

In practice a prospective client may either first approach an individual participating firm or the PDC itself. A joint PDC must not accept instructions on behalf of participating firms. However, rule 3 of the Practice Rules (see **11.04**, p.192) allows a PDC to refer prospective clients to the participating firms. In the light of rule 1(b) of the Practice Rules (see **1.01**, p.1) a prospective client should be asked to make his or her own choice from amongst the participating firms. If he or she decides not to make a choice, the method whereby a participating firm is selected for a referral is a matter for the participating firms. Note, however, that if a member of the PDC staff is asked for a recommendation (rather than for a referral), the recommendation must only be given on the basis of a genuine belief that the firm concerned should be recommended.

26.16   Selling property as a separate business

1. Rule 5 of the Practice Rules and the Solicitors' Separate Business Code 1994 (see **3.20**, p.66 and Annex 3D, p.102) permits a solicitor to conduct property selling through a separate business, subject to the provisions of section 5(2) of the code at p.105.

2. In practice, these provisions may make property selling unattractive as a separate business, except where the separate business is geographically remote from the solicitor's practice, or where the solicitor's practice does not undertake conveyancing.

II.3. Seller's solicitor dealing with more than one prospective buyer

The new Practice Rule 6A approved by the Council in October 1994 came into effect on 1 March 1995.

It replaces the Council direction on submitting draft contracts to more than one prospective purchaser.

There is no change to the scope of the rule, which applies to all conveyancing of land, whether the transaction is of a commercial or domestic nature. The rule therefore continues to affect, for example, vending agreements where part of the assets to be sold consist of freehold or leasehold property.

The following main changes should be noted:

* The rule applies to the solicitor who knows that the seller client is dealing with another prospective buyer without the solicitor's involvement.

* There is now an absolute prohibition on continuing to act for both buyer and seller (even in a case falling within the exceptions to Practice Rule 6) where a further prospective buyer is introduced during the course of the transaction.

* A fax need no longer be confirmed by letter.

The text of the rule is set out in Appendix I.1.

II.4. Guidance – dealing with licensed conveyancers[1]

A solicitor may normally deal with a licensed conveyancer as if the conveyancer were a solicitor, subject to the best interests of the solicitor's client.

Licensed conveyancers are permitted to practise in partnership with other licensed conveyancers, or with other persons (although not with solicitors). Licensed conveyancers may also practise through the medium of a 'recognised body', i.e. a body corporate recognised by the Council for Licensed Conveyancers.

The identity of firms of licensed conveyancers can be checked in the *Directory of Solicitors and Barristers.* In cases of doubt contact the Council for Licensed Conveyancers [16 Glebe Road, Chelmsford, Essex CM1 1QG. DX: 121925 Chelmsford 6. Tel: 01245 349599].

Licensed conveyancers are subject to conduct and accounts rules similar to those which apply to solicitors. They are covered by compulsory indemnity insurance and contribute to a compensation fund. In dealings with licensed conveyancers, it should normally be possible to proceed as if the licensed conveyancer were a solicitor and bound by the same professional obligations. For example, if it is agreed to use the Law Society's code for exchange of contracts by telephone, it is understood that any failure to respect the code would expose the licensed conveyancer to disciplinary proceedings; this also applies to the Society's code for completion by post, and reliance on undertakings. Since licensed conveyancers may practise in partnership or association with others, it is important to ensure that the other party's representative is a licensed conveyancer, or a person working immediately under the supervision of a licensed conveyancer.

1. The following text appears as principle 25.06 in *The Guide to the Professional Conduct of Solicitors 1996*, published by the Law Society.

II.5. Guidance – dealing with unqualified conveyancers[1]

Effect of section 22 of the Solicitors Act 1974

1.   Section 22 of the Solicitors Act 1974 (see Annex 2A at p.27 in the Guide) makes it an offence for an unqualified person to draw or prepare, *inter alia,* a contract for sale or a transfer, conveyance, lease or mortgage relating to land in expectation of fee, gain or reward. Qualified persons under this section are solicitors, barristers, notaries public, licensed conveyancers, some public officers and, for unregistered conveyancing, Scottish solicitors.

2.   It is inevitable that an unqualified person who undertakes a conveyancing transaction in the course of a conveyancing business will commit an offence under section 22, unless the drawing or preparation of the relevant documents is undertaken by a qualified person. In such circumstances, the unqualified conveyancer's client is likely, albeit unwittingly, to be guilty of aiding and abetting the offence. The solicitor acting for the other party could also be guilty of procuring the commission of an offence by inviting or urging the unqualified person to provide a draft contract or transfer or to progress the transaction.

3.   Solicitors should therefore refuse to have any dealings with any unqualified person carrying on a conveyancing business unless there is clear evidence that offences under section 22 will not be committed.

4.   It is recommended that, at the outset of any transaction, the solicitor should write to the unqualified conveyancer drawing attention to this guidance and saying that the solicitor cannot enter into any dealings with him or her unless there is clear evidence that no offences will be committed. An example of satisfactory evidence would be a letter from a qualified person confirming that he or she will prepare the relevant documents. The solicitor should also immediately report to his or her own client and explain why he or she cannot deal with the unqualified conveyancer unless clear evidence is forthcoming.

Draft letter to unqualified conveyancer

'We are instructed to act for the seller/buyer in connection with the above transaction and understand that you have been instructed by the buyer/seller. Please confirm that you are a solicitor or licensed conveyancer. If not, please state who will prepare the contract/conveyance/transfer for you; we need to receive written confirmation from a qualified person that he or she will personally settle the contract/conveyance/transfer.

As you know, it is an offence for an unqualified person to prepare a contract for sale or a transfer, conveyance or mortgage relating to land in expectation of fee, gain or reward. We have been advised by the Law Society that we should not deal with an unqualified person carrying on a conveyancing business unless clear evidence is provided that offences under section 22 of the Solicitors Act 1974 will not be committed. The written confirmation referred to above, if explicit and unequivocal, could provide such evidence.

We regret that unless you are a solicitor or licensed conveyancer, we cannot deal with you until the evidence required above is provided.'

1.   The following text appears as Annex 25A in *The Guide to the Professional Conduct of Solicitors 1996,* published by the Law Society.

Draft letter to client of solicitor

'Thank you for your instructions relating to the above transactions. There is unfortunately a problem. The buyer/seller appears to have instructed an unqualified conveyancer to act for him/her and this could lead to the conveyancer, his/her client and myself being involved in the commission of criminal offences under the Solicitors Act 1974. The Law Society, my professional body, has advised solicitors not to deal with unqualified conveyancers because of the possibility of committing criminal offences.

I have therefore written to the firm acting for the buyer/seller asking for confirmation whether or not they are unqualified conveyancers and, if they are, whether they will be making arrangements to prevent the commission of such offences. If they cannot satisfy me about this, the buyer/seller will have to instruct a solicitor or licensed conveyancer, or deal with me direct.

Further help

1.   Solicitors should first check with the Council for Licensed Conveyancers whether a person is a licensed conveyancer, since a licensed conveyancer can normally be dealt with as if a solicitor (see **25.06**, p.399 in the Guide).

2.   The Society can help practitioners dealing with unqualified conveyancers if the above guidance and the practice notes below do not cover the situation. Telephone calls and written requests for guidance should be made to the practice advice service.

3.   The Professional Adviser has responsibility for investigating and prosecuting non-solicitors who appear to be in breach of the Solicitors Act 1974. Solicitors are asked to report (without submitting their files) any case where there is *prima facie* evidence of breaches of the Solicitors Act.

4.   For assistance in those cases where the solicitor has clear evidence that no offences under section 22 will be committed, there is set out below a series of practice notes relating to the problems which might arise in a transaction in which the other party is represented by an unqualified conveyancer. These practice notes give advice only and it is for solicitors to decide for themselves what steps should properly be taken in any particular situation.

PRACTICE NOTES
(applicable only where evidence is provided of compliance with section 22)

General

1.   Any undertaking which unqualified agents may offer in the course of a transaction is not enforceable in the same way as an undertaking given by a solicitor or licensed conveyancer. Solicitors should therefore never accept such undertakings.

2.   Solicitors are under no duty to undertake agency work by way of completions by post on behalf of unqualified persons, or to attend to other formalities on behalf of third parties who are not clients, even where such third parties offer to pay the agent's charges.

3.   The Council also suggests that in cases where a solicitor is dealing with an unqualified conveyancer, the solicitor should bear in mind the line of decisions starting with *Hedley Byrne* v. *Heller*]1964] A.C. 465, which extends the duty of care owed by a solicitor to persons who are not clients, but who rely and act on the solicitor's advice to his or her knowledge.

4.   Solicitors must decide in each case whether special provisions should be incorporated in the draft contract to take account of the problems which arise by reason of the other party

having no solicitor or licensed conveyancer, e.g. that the seller should attend personally at completion if represented by an unqualified agent. All such matters must be considered prior to exchange of contracts since contractual conditions cannot, of course, be imposed subsequently.

5. The protection provided by section 69 of the Law of Property Act 1925 only applies when a document containing a receipt for purchase money is handed over by a solicitor or licensed conveyancer or the seller himself or herself. Thus it should be considered whether the contract should provide either for the seller to attend personally at completion, or for an authority signed by the seller, for the purchase money to be paid to his or her agent, to be handed over on completion.

Acting for the seller: buyer not represented by a solicitor or licensed conveyancer

Completion

6. It is important to ensure that the deeds and keys are passed to the person entitled to receive them, i.e. the buyer. If an authority on behalf of the buyer is offered to the seller's solicitor, it is for the solicitor to decide whether or not to accept it, bearing in mind that no authority, however expressed, can be irrevocable. Again it is worth considering at the outset whether the point should be covered by express condition in the contract (see practice note 4 above).

Acting for the buyer: seller not represented by a solicitor or licensed conveyancer

Preliminary enquiries and requisitions on title

7. It may be prudent to require and ensure that replies to all preliminary enquiries and requisitions are signed by the seller.

Payment of deposit

8. Difficulties may arise in connection with payment of the deposit where there is no estate agent involved to whom the deposit may be paid as stakeholder in the ordinary way. The deposit may be paid direct to the seller, but this cannot be recommended since it is equivalent to parting with a portion of the purchase money in advance of investigation of the title and other matters.

9. Some unqualified agents insist that the deposit be paid to them. The Council does not recommend this. If a solicitor is obliged to pay the deposit to unqualified agents, he or she should inform the client of the risks involved, and obtain specific instructions before proceeding.

10. An alternative is for the deposit to be paid to the buyer's solicitor as stakeholder. The buyer's solicitor should insist on this where possible. If the seller will not agree to this, it may be possible to agree to place the deposit in a deposit account in the joint names of the buyer's solicitor and the seller, or in a deposit account in the seller's name, with the deposit receipt to be retained by the buyer's solicitor.

Payment of purchase money

11. As referred to in practice note 5 above, the buyer's solicitor should ensure that all the purchase money, including any deposit, is paid either to the seller or to the seller's properly authorised agent.

Matters unresolved at completion

12.   Whilst it is unusual to leave any issues revealed by searches and other enquiries outstanding at completion, undertakings relating to their discharge or resolution may on occasions be given between solicitors or licensed conveyancers. Such undertakings should not be accepted from unqualified agents for the reason mentioned in practice note 1 above.

Power of attorney

13.   Unqualified agents sometimes obtain a power of attorney to enable themselves or their employees to conduct certain aspects of the transaction. It is clearly important to ensure that such powers are valid, properly granted, and effective for all relevant purposes.

Acting for the lender: borrower not represented by a solicitor or licensed conveyancer

14.   The lender's solicitor often finds himself or herself undertaking much of the work which a borrower's solicitor would do. Whilst the client's interests are paramount, the solicitor must ensure that he or she does not render the unqualified agent additional assistance in a way which might establish a solicitor/client relationship either with the unqualified conveyancer or with the borrower, or leave the solicitor open to a negligence claim either from the solicitor's lender client or from the borrower.

Advances

15.   As regards the drafting and preparation of the instrument of transfer by the borrower's representative, the lender's solicitor is not obliged to undertake work which would normally be done by the borrower's solicitor. Solicitors are reminded, however, that it is of paramount importance to their lender client that good title is conveyed to the borrower.

16.   The importance of paying mortgage advances only to those properly entitled to receive them is a reason for insisting either that the borrower attends personally on completion, or that a signed authority from the borrower in favour of his or her agent is received on completion. Section 69 of the Law of Property Act 1925 is a relevant consideration in this context (see practice note 5 above).

Redemptions

17.   On completion, cheques or drafts should be drawn in favour of solicitors or licensed conveyancers or their clients, and not endorsed over to some intermediate party. The deeds should normally be handed over to the borrower personally, unless he or she provides a valid authority for them to be handed to a third party.

18.   Any issues of doubt or difficulty must be referred to the lender/client for detailed instructions. Where the lender is a building society and its solicitor considers that the totality of the work involved justifies a charge in excess of the building society's guideline fee, he or she should seek the approval of the lender/client, supported if necessary by a bill of costs containing sufficient detail of the work and the time spent on it.

16 March 1988, revised December 1995

II.6.　Tax on bank or building society interest – practice information[1]

On 6th April 1991 the system of taxing interest paid to UK individuals by banks and building societies changed. Composite rate tax was abolished and replaced by deduction of basic rate tax at source. This article, which has been discussed with the Inland Revenue, explains the effect of this change on interest arising after 5th April 1991 on clients' money. The position in relation to interest arising before then is described in an article which appeared in [1987] *Gazette,* 1st July, 1960 and which was reprinted in the 1990 edition of the *Guide to the Professional Conduct of Solicitors.*

The Solicitors' Accounts Rules 1991, Part III

Under this part of the rules ("the deposit interest provisions"), a solicitor who is required to account for interest to a client may do so by either of two methods. He or she may:

(a)　account to the client for the interest earned on the client's money in a separate designated account; or

(b)　pay to the client a sum equivalent to the interest which would have accrued for the benefit of the client if the money had been deposited in a separate designated account pursuant to the rules. This will usually follow the deposit of the money in a general client deposit account.

These two procedures are referred to as Method A and Method B respectively. The tax position under the Solicitors' Accounts (Deposit Interest) Rules 1988, which operated prior to 1st June 1992, was identical.

Deduction of tax at source

The tax deduction at source rules apply, broadly, to designated client accounts which, before 6th April 1991, were subject to composite rate tax, e.g. accounts held for individuals who are ordinarily resident in the UK, and, where held with a building society, clients' accounts on which the society was required to account for a sum representing basic rate tax, e.g. investments by companies, discretionary and accumulation trusts.

Interest on general client accounts, whether with a bank or (since 6th February 1989) a building society, is paid gross.

When opening any designated account the solicitor must provide the necessary information for the bank or building society to decide whether or not deduction of tax at source is appropriate.

Tax treatment of interest – Method A

Method A applies to designated accounts. Where tax is deducted at source by the bank or building society interest will be received by the solicitor net, and he or she will simply pass it on to the client net – no tax deduction certificate is required. The client, when making

1. 4 March 1992 (updated January 1993).

his or her tax return, will declare the interest as having been received under deduction of tax, and will only be liable to be assessed in relation to higher rate tax in respect of it (since he or she will have a tax credit for basic rate tax). If the client is for any reason not liable to income tax, he or she can recover any tax deducted from the interest. In those circumstances the solicitor must, on being required by the client, obtain a certificate of deduction of tax from the bank or building society and deliver this to the client. The client's position is, therefore, for practical purposes, the same as that which arises where he or she receives interest from a building society or bank on a deposit of his or her own.

Where the client is not liable to tax or is not ordinarily resident (NOR) in the UK the bank or building society will pay the interest gross provided that it holds the relevant declaration. Declarations of non-ordinary residence can be completed by either the solicitor or the client but declarations of non-liability by UK residents will normally be completed by the client. However, in view of the difficulty of obtaining complete information about an overseas client, solicitors may feel that it is more appropriate for the client concerned to make the declaration, especially since it contains an undertaking to notify the bank or building society should circumstances change.

Where the tax deduction at source rules do not apply, the solicitor will receive interest from the bank or building society gross and may account to the client for it gross, even if the client is non-resident. The client will be assessed on his gross receipt (but a non-resident client may, by concession, not be assessed) and, (unless the solicitor has been acting as the client's agent for tax purposes – see below under 'Solicitors as agents'), the solicitor himself or herself will not be assessed in respect of the interest.

Tax treatment of interest – Method B

Where Method B is used, a deduction of tax at source does not apply to the solicitor's general client deposit account at either a bank or building society, and interest is therefore paid to the solicitor gross. When making a payment to the client of an equivalent sum under the deposit interest provisions the solicitor should make the payment gross even if the client is not ordinarily resident. The payment is of compensation in lieu of interest, and is not itself interest. The client will be assessed to income tax on his or her receipt, but a non-resident may, by concession, not be assessed.

Wherever payments are made by solicitors to clients under Method B they can, in practice, be set off against the solicitor's Case III assessment on gross interest received on general client account deposits; if the payments exceed the interest received, a Case II deduction can be claimed for the excess.

Stake money

(a) Position until 1st June 1992

The existing law in relation to interest on stake money is generally agreed to be that the interest belongs to the stakeholder. However at [1986] *Gazette,* 23rd July, 2292, there was a recommendation by the Council that contracts should make provision for the interest on any stake held by a solicitor; the following clause was suggested:

> 'The stakeholder shall pay to the vendor/purchaser a sum equal to the interest the deposit would have earned if placed on deposit (less costs of acting as stakeholder).'

It was further recommended that, in default of such a provision, interest on stakes should normally be treated as if it were covered by the Solicitors' Account (Deposit Interest) Rules 1988 where the stake is paid to the stakeholder's client. The tax treatment of interest on stake money will depend on which, if either, recommendation has been followed.

Where the stake was held in a general client account interest will be paid gross by the bank or building society. The solicitor is assessable under Schedule D Case III in the normal way but any payment to the client in accordance with the Law Society's recommendation can be set-off in full. If there is insufficient available a Case II deduction would have to be claimed.

Where the stake is held in a designated client deposit account the tax position is slightly more complicated. Because in law the interest belongs to the stakeholder/solicitor it will be paid by the bank or building society under deduction of basic rate tax. But when making an equivalent payment in accordance with the Law Society's recommendation, the solicitor will have to account to the client on a gross basis since the amount received by the client will be treated by the Revenue as a taxable receipt in his or her hands. The solicitor will, however, be able to set-off the whole amount paid to the client in respect of the interest, as above. In either case the situation can arise where the solicitor is unable to make a payment to the client in the same tax year in which interest is received, for example, if stake money is held pending the outcome of litigation. Because the solicitor remains assessable throughout the period for which the stake deposit is held, there is a possible loss in terms of cashflow if the tax liability cannot be met out of the interest arising. It is essential to bear this in mind when making provision for interest in any contract or undertaking to the Court. It would not be prudent for a solicitor in such circumstances to agree a term which precluded him or her resorting to the interest arising to satisfy the taxation liability.

(b) Position from 1st June 1992

Under the Solicitors' Accounts Rules 1991 (which came into force on 1st June 1992) stake money is expressly brought within the definition of 'client's money'. Interest will be payable to the person to whom the stake is paid using either Method A or B above. But there will still be circumstances in which payment is not possible until a later tax year. Where this situation looks likely to arise, e.g. if the stake is held pending the outcome of litigation, the deposit would normally be placed in a general client account until it is established to whom the stake is to be paid. Because, in the meantime, interest will be included in the solicitor's Case III assessment it is again important to make provision for the tax liability to be met out of the interest as it arises.

Tax treatment of interest – money paid into court

The position of moneys paid into court is covered by the Supreme Court Funds Rules as amended. Where any order for payment out of moneys in court is made, the order should provide for the disposal of any interest accrued to the date of the judgment or order, and for interest accruing thereafter up to the date the moneys are paid out in accordance with the order. In the absence of such provision interest accruing between the date of the payment into court, and its acceptance or the judgement or order for payment out, goes to the party who made the payment in, and interest from the date of the judgement or order follows the capital payment.

Where interest is paid to a party to proceedings in respect of money held in court, it should be paid to the client gross, even if he or she is non-resident. The client will normally be assessable under Case III, but the solicitor will not, unless exceptionally he or she is assessable as the client's agent.

Solicitors as agents

Where a solicitor acts for tax purposes as agent for a non-resident client, the solicitor will remain liable to be assessed on behalf of the client in relation to interest earned in a designated deposit account, where Method A is used, unless he or she is an agent without management or control of the interest, in which case, under Extra Statutory Concession B13, no assessment will be made on him or her. Where the solicitor is assessable, the charge may, if appropriate, be to higher rate tax, so the solicitor will need to retain tax at the client's marginal rate of income tax from interest received gross from a bank or building society before remitting it to the client. This is the case even though the account would not be subject to deduction of tax at source since the client would have completed a declaration of non-liability due to his or her non-residence. No question of the solicitor being taxed as an agent will arise where the interest in question has been earned in a general client deposit account, or on stake money, but it could very exceptionally do so in relation to money held in court.

Determination of whether a solicitor has management or control for the purposes of the extra statutory concession will depend on the nature of the solicitor's relationship with his client. Under section 78 of the Taxes Management Act 1970, a person not resident in the UK is assessable and chargeable to income tax in the name of an agent if the agent has management or control of the interest. Acting as a solicitor in giving advice or in conducting a transaction on the client's instructions will not of itself give management or control nor usually would the holding of a power of attorney on behalf of the client for a specific purpose, e.g. concluding a specified purchase or sale. If a client had no fixed place of business in the UK, and his or her solicitor had, and habitually exercised, an authority to conclude contracts on behalf of the client, this would give rise to the client having a permanent establishment in the UK, and accordingly the client would be taxable. In essence, the solicitor would be deemed to have management and control if he or she were effectively carrying on the client's business in the UK, rather than merely acting as a solicitor, even regularly. Therefore, in order for the agency principle to apply, the solicitor/client relationship would normally have to go beyond a solicitor's usual representative capacity. It should be noted that where interest arises in connection with the receipt of rents on behalf of the non-resident, the solicitor would be chargeable as agent in relation to the rent.

For a more detailed analysis of when solicitors can be taxed as agents, see [1991] *Gazette* 1st May, 15 (article by John Avery Jones).

If a solicitor is assessable on behalf of his client, he or she has a general right to reimbursement out of the monies of the client coming into his or her hands, for any tax for which the client is liable and in respect of which the solicitor has been charged. For the exercise of this right see sections 82 and 84 of the Taxes Management Act 1970.

Trusts

Deduction of tax at source may apply depending upon the type of trust and where the investment is held. But it can only apply where money is held in a designated account. The income of trusts where none of the beneficiaries is ordinarily resident in the UK will not be subject to deduction of tax at source, even if a designated account is used, provided that the appropriate declaration has been made.

Administration of estates

Interest on money held for UK resident personal representatives will, if placed in a designated account, be subject to deduction of tax at source unless a declaration is made by the solicitor or the personal representatives that the deceased was not resident in the UK immediately before his death.

[See also aide-memoire on next page.]

AIDE-MEMOIRE OF NORMAL SITUATIONS

Type of Account	Payment of interest by bank or building society	Consequences
A Designated – where subject to tax deduction.	Net	Pay net to client, who gets basic rate tax credit. No further tax deductions for residents (unless the solicitor is assessable as an agent).
B Designated – where paid gross (client money generally).	Gross	Pay gross to client who is assessable on payment as gross income. No deduction of tax for non-residents (unless the solicitor is assessable as agent).
C Bank and building society general client account deposit – always paid gross (client money generally and stake money).	Gross	Pay gross to client who in turn is assessable on payment as gross income; in practice solicitor assessed on interest after setting-off this payment. No deduction of tax for non-residents.

II.7. Extracts from *Client Care* booklet (Rule 15)

Rule 15 (Client care)

(1)   Every principal in private practice shall operate a complaints handling procedure which shall, *inter alia,* ensure that clients are informed whom to approach in the event of any problem with the service provided.

(2)   Every solicitor in private practice shall, unless it is inappropriate in the circumstances:

    (a)   ensure that clients know the name and status of the person responsible for the day to day conduct of the matter and the principal responsible for its overall supervision;

    (b)   ensure that clients know whom to approach in the event of any problem with the service provided; and,

    (c)   ensure that clients are at all relevant times given any appropriate information as to the issues raised and the progress of the matter.

(3)   Notwithstanding rule 19(2) of these rules, this rule shall come into force on 1st May 1991.

EXAMPLE LETTER

Conveyancing and Financial Services

Dear [   ]

Sale of [   ] at £ .00
Purchase of [   ] at £ .00

Thank you for instructing this firm to handle your house sale/purchase/sale and purchase. I and everyone here at [   ] will do our best to see that everything proceeds as smoothly as possible.

Responsibility for the work

I shall carry out most of the work in this matter personally, but you can also contact [   ] who is and will be familiar with the file. If s/he is unable to help you her/himself, s/he will be able to take a message for you.

The partner of this firm with ultimate responsibility for this matter is [   ]. We aim to offer all our clients an efficient and effective service and I am confident that we will do so in this case. However, should there be any aspect of our service with which you are unhappy, and which we cannot resolve between ourselves, you may raise the matter with [   ].

Conveyancing

(A)   I am enclosing a copy of the Law Society's Guide "Buying and Selling your Home". This explains the work we do.

or

(B)   A broad outline of our work is:

Supplying information to your buyers and obtaining it from your sellers;
Checking that the sellers have good title;
Agreeing the terms of the contracts for sale and purchase;
When everyone is ready, and the same moving date has been agreed with sellers and buyers, exchanging contracts on both transactions at once; this is the stage at which you are committed to the move;
Making the pre-completion legal arrangements and checks;
Getting the mortgage money from your new lender and any balance we will need from you;
On moving day:

> Receiving the purchase money from your sale;
> Paying off your old mortgage;
> Paying for your new house;
> Sending any surplus to you;

Registering your ownership at the Land Registry which may take some months – although that makes no difference from your point of view – and we will let you know when we receive your Certificate of Ownership;
Acting for your lenders to make sure that their interests are properly protected.

You will get the deed of the house (or we can store them for you) unless you have a mortgage; in that case the lenders will keep them; they may, however, let you keep the old deeds which are no longer needed for conveyancing but which might be of interest to you.

Financial Services

We have already discussed your new mortgage and we [have already obtained] [shall obtain] quotations and advice from
which will enable us to ensure that you have the most appropriate mortgage arrangements
This usually includes advice on, for example, a suitable endowment policy [policies]. This aspect of the work requires us to be authorised under the Financial Services Act, and we confirm that we hold a current investment business certificate from the Law Society.

Fees

A.   The fees my firm will charge for the work will be as follows:

or

B.   The estimated fees my firm will charge for the work will be as follows:

      Conveyancing
        £
      Financial Services Advice
        £

Total Fees	£	+VAT
Total	£	

      We shall also have to pay out
      disbursements as follow:

Search Fees	£
Stamp Duty	£
Land Registration Fees	£
Total Disbursements	£

Should any of the above transactions fail to proceed to completion then [my firm's charges for that transaction will be such lesser sum as is reasonable having regard to the amount of work done by that stage in the transaction together with VAT and any disbursements incurred] [my firm will make no charge for the work which has been done in that transaction but will require you to pay any disbursements which have been incurred].

Commission

As I mentioned to you, I expect to receive a commission from [   ].

[Our brokers will retain [   ] % of the commission as their remuneration.] Unlike other advisers, solicitors do not simply inform clients when they receive a commission in these circumstances; they are effectively obliged to pay it to the client unless there is an agreement for the solicitor to keep it. I estimate that the commission payable to this firm will come to about £[   ], and the amount received will be credited to you against my firm's fees.

[This will have the effect of reducing the net amount payable on my firm's bill from £[   ] plus VAT (as set out above) to £[   ] plus VAT.]

and/or

[This would mean that there will be no separate payment required of you as my firm's fees (as set out above) would be wholly met by the commission.]

or

[This would mean that my firm's fees (as set out above) would be wholly met by the commission and we would repay to you the amount by which the commission exceeds those fees.]

and/or

[However you would still have to pay disbursements.]

and/or

[I should mention that if you surrender the policy within four years I may have to refund part of the commission to [   ]. If this happens I will have to ask you to repay the amount involved.]

Agreement

A.   As confirmation that you would like us to proceed on this basis, I should be grateful if you would sign the extra copy of this letter enclosed and return it to me. We will then have entered into an agreement which will mean that the firm's fees as set out above will be fixed. Given this agreement, your rights in law to challenge the amount of my firm's fees will be restricted.

or

B.   As confirmation that you would like us to proceed on this basis I should be grateful if you would sign the enclosed extra copy of this letter and return it to me. The charges set out above are an estimate based on the information that I have at present and I will inform you in writing if any difficulties arise or if anything occurs which makes it necessary to revise this estimate.

Yours sincerely

III. MORTGAGE FRAUD

III.1. Guidance – mortgage fraud – variation in purchase price[1]

This guidance deals with the solicitor's duty in conduct when acting for lender and borrower when there is some variation in the purchase price.

Professional Ethics is frequently asked to advise on a solicitor's duty to the lender in conduct when there is some variation in the purchase price of a property of which the lender may be unaware. The Standards and Guidance Committee has therefore prepared the following guidance (which is supported by the Council of Mortgage Lenders) on the professional conduct issues involved.

Solicitors acting contemporaneously for a buyer and a lender should consider their position very carefully if there is any change in the purchase price, or if the solicitors become aware of any other information which they would reasonably expect the lender to consider important in deciding whether, or on what terms, it would make the mortgage advance available. In such circumstances the solicitor's duty to act in the best interests of the lender would require him or her to pass on such information to the lender.

Solicitors have a duty of confidentiality to clients, but this does not affect their duty to act in the best interests of each client. Therefore any such information concerning variations to the purchase price should be forwarded to the lender with the consent of the buyer. If the buyer will not agree to the information being given to the lender, then there will be a conflict between the solicitor's duty of confidentiality to the buyer and the duty to act in the best interests of the lender. Solicitors must therefore cease acting for the lender and must consider carefully whether they are able to continue acting for the buyer, bearing in mind 15.02, note 1, p.275 in the Guide and also 12.01, note 1 referred to below.

Solicitors must not withhold information relevant to a transaction from any client. Where the client is a lender this includes not only straightforward price reductions but may also include other allowances (e.g. for repairs, payment of costs, the inclusion of chattels in the price and incentives of the kind offered by builders such as free holidays and part-subsidisation of mortgage payments) which amount to a price reduction and which would affect the lender's decision to make the advance. Solicitors should not attempt to arbitrate on whether the price change is material but should notify the lender. It is recommended that solicitors advise their clients as soon as practicable that it would be regarded as fraud to misrepresent the purchase price and that a solicitor is under a duty to inform the lender of the true price being paid for a property.

Solicitors who are party to an attempt to deceive a lender may be exposing both the buyer and themselves to criminal prosecution and/or civil action and will be liable to be disciplined for having breached the principles of professional conduct (see 12.01, note 1, p. 211 in the Guide). If a solicitor is aware that his or her client is attempting to perpetrate fraud in any form he or she must immediately cease acting for that client.

1. 12 December 1990, revised January 1996.

III.2. 'Green card' warning on property fraud – practice information[1]

Could you be involved or implicated?

Could you be unwittingly assisting in a fraud? The general assumption is that if there has been a property fraud a solicitor *must* have been involved. Solicitors should therefore be vigilant to protect both their clients and themselves. Steps can be taken to minimise the risk of being involved or implicated in a fraud (see below).

Could you spot a property fraud?

The signs to watch for include the following (but this list is not exhaustive):

● **Fraudulent buyer or fictitious solicitors** – especially if the buyer is introduced to your practice by a third party (for example a broker or estate agent) who is not well known to you. Beware of clients whom you never meet and solicitors not known to you.

● **Unusual instructions** – for example a solicitor being instructed by the seller to remit the net proceeds of sale to anyone other than the seller.

● **Misrepresentation of the purchase price** – ensure that the true cash price actually to be paid is stated as the consideration in the contract and transfer and is identical to the price shown in the mortgage instructions and in the report on title to the lender.

● **A deposit or any part of purchase price paid direct** – a deposit or the difference between the mortgage advance and the price, paid direct, or said to be paid direct, to the seller.

● **Incomplete contract documentation** – contract documents not fully completed by the seller's representative, i.e. dates missing or the identity of the parties not fully described or financial details not fully stated.

● **Changes in the purchase price** – adjustments to the purchase price, particularly in high percentage mortgage cases or allowances off the purchase price, for example, for works to be carried out.

● **Unusual transactions** – transactions which do not follow their normal course or the usual pattern of events:

    (a)   client with current mortgage on two or more properties;

    (b)   client using alias;

    (c)   client buying several properties from same person or two or more persons using same solicitor;

1. March 1991, revised January 1996.

(d)   client reselling property at a substantial profit, for which no explanation has been provided.

What steps can I take to minimise the risk of fraud?

Be vigilant. If you have any doubts about a transaction, consider whether any of the following steps could be taken to minimise the risk of fraud:

(1)   Verify the identity and bona fides of your client and solicitors' firms you do not know – meet the clients where possible and get to know them a little. Check that the solicitor's firm and office address appear in the *Directory of Solicitors and Barristers* or contact the Law Society's Records Centre (PSD) (Tel: 0171-242 1222).

(2)   Question unusual instructions – if you receive unusual instructions from your client discuss them with your client fully.

(3)   Discuss with your client any aspects of the transaction which worry you – if, for example, you have any suspicion that your client may have submitted a false mortgage application or references, or if the lender's valuation exceeds the actual price paid, discuss this with your client. If you believe that the client intends to proceed with a fraudulent application you must refuse to continue to act for the buyer and the lender.

(4)   Check that the true price is shown in all documentation – check that the actual price paid is stated in the contract, transfer and mortgage instructions. Where you are also acting for a lender, tell your client that you will have to cease acting unless the client permits you to report to the lender all allowances and incentives. See also the guidance printed in [1990] *Gazette,* 12 December, 16 [See Annex 25F, p.426 in the Guide].

(5)   Do not witness pre-signed documentation – no document should be witnessed by a solicitor or his or her staff unless the person signing does so in the presence of the witness. If the document is pre-signed ensure that it is re-signed in the presence of a witness.

(6)   Verify signatures – consider whether signatures on all documents connected with a transaction should be examined and compared with signatures on any other available documentation.

(7)   Make a company search – where a private company is the seller, or the seller has purchased from a private company in the recent past, and you suspect that the sale may not be on proper arm's length terms, you should make a search in the Companies Register to ascertain the names and addresses of the officers and shareholders, which can then be compared with the names of those connected with the transaction and the seller and buyer.

Remember that, even where investigations result in a solicitor ceasing to act for a client, the solicitor will still owe a duty of confidentiality which would prevent the solicitor passing on information to the lender. It is only where the solicitor is satisfied that there is a strong prima facie case that the client was using the solicitor to further a fraud or other criminal purpose that the duty of confidentiality would not apply.

Any failure to observe these signs and to take the appropriate steps may be used in court as evidence against you if you and your client are prosecuted, or if you are sued for negligence.

Further guidance can be obtained from the Law Society's Practice Advice Service (Tel: 0171-242 1222).

IV. PROTOCOL

IV. National Protocol (3rd edition) for domestic freehold and leasehold property

COUNCIL STATEMENT

1. The Council recommend that solicitors follow the procedures set out in the Protocol in all domestic conveyancing transactions.

2. The procedures set out in the Protocol include the use of standardised documentation. This will simplify the checking of variables and will enable departures from the recommended format to be readily identified. The Protocol does not preclude the use of printed or typed contracts produced by firms themselves, although it may be thought desirable that the full text of the Conditions of Sale are reproduced rather than merely included by reference.

3. The introduction of a National Protocol is designed to streamline conveyancing procedures. Experience has shown that where local protocols have been implemented, these have speeded up the completion of pre-contract formalities and have improved communications between solicitors and their clients.

4. The Protocol is a form of 'preferred practice' and its requirements should not be construed as undertakings. Nor are they intended to widen a solicitor's duty save as set out in the next paragraph. The Protocol must always be considered in the context of a solicitor's overriding duty to his or her own client's interests and where compliance with the Protocol would conflict with that duty, the client's wishes must always be paramount.

5. A solicitor acting in domestic conveyancing transactions should inform the solicitor acting for the other party at the outset of a transaction, whether or not he or she is proposing to act in accordance with the Protocol in full or in part. If the solicitor is using the Protocol he or she should give notice to the solicitor acting for the other party if during the course of the transaction it becomes necessary to depart from Protocol procedures.

6. A solicitor is, as a matter of professional conduct, under a duty to keep confidential client's business. The confidentiality continues until the client permits disclosure or waives the confidentiality (16.01, note 3 of *The Guide to the Professional Conduct of Solicitors 1996*). With reference to paragraphs 4.5 and 5.3 of the National Protocol, the disclosure of information about a client's position is strictly subject to obtaining that client's authority to disclose. In the absence of such authority, a solicitor is not deemed to be departing from the terms of the Protocol and, as such, is not required to give notice as set out in paragraph 5 of this Statement.

THE NATIONAL PROTOCOL (THIRD EDITION)

Acting for the Seller

1. **The first step**

   The seller should inform the solicitor as soon as it is intended to place the property on the market so that delay may be reduced after a prospective purchaser is found.

2. **Preparing the package: assembling the information**

   On receipt of instructions, the solicitor shall then immediately take the following steps, at the seller's expense:

   2.1 Locate the title deeds and, if not in the solicitor's custody, obtain them.

   2.2 Obtain a copy of the O.S Map, if necessary, where deeds do not have a suitable plan.

Preparing the package: information from the seller

   2.3 Obtain from the seller details to complete the Seller's Property Information Form.

   2.4 Obtain such original guarantees with the accompanying specification, planning decisions and building regulation approvals as are in the seller's possession and copies of any other planning consents that are with the title deeds or details of any highway and sewerage agreements and bonds.

   2.5 Give the seller the Fixtures, Fittings and Contents Form, with a copy to retain, to complete and return prior to the submission of the draft contract.

   2.6 Obtain details of all mortgages and other financial charges of which the seller's solicitor has notice including where applicable improvement grants and discounts repayable to a local authority. Redemption figures should be obtained at this stage in respect of all mortgages on the property so that cases of negative equity can be identified at an early stage.

   2.7 Ascertain the identity of all the people aged 18 or over living in the dwelling and ask about any financial contribution they or anyone else may have made towards its purchase or subsequent improvement. All persons identified in this way should be asked to confirm their consent in the sale proceedings.

   2.8 In leasehold cases, ask the seller to produce, if possible:

   (1) A receipt or evidence from the landlord of the last payment of rent.

   (2) The maintenance charge accounts for the last three years, where appropriate, and evidence of payment.

   (3) Details of the buildings insurance policy.

   If any of these are lacking, and are necessary for the transaction, the solicitor should obtain them from the landlord. At the same time investigate whether a licence to assign is required and if so enquire of the landlord what references are necessary and, in the case of some retirement schemes, if a charge is payable to the management company on change of ownership.

3. **Preparing the package: the draft documents**

As soon as the title deeds are available, the solicitor shall:

3.1 If the title is *unregistered:*

(1) Make a Land Charges Search against the seller and any other appropriate names.

(2) Make an Index Map Search in the Land Registry in order to verify that the seller's title is unregistered and ensure that there are no interests registered at the Land Registry adverse to the seller's title.

(3) Prepare an epitome of title. Mark copies or abstracts of all deeds which will not be passed to the buyer as examined against the original.

(4) Prepare and mark as examined against the originals copies of all deeds, or their abstracts, prior to the root of title containing covenants, easements etc., affecting the property.

(5) Check that all plans on copied documents are correctly coloured.

3.2 If the title is *registered,* obtain office copy entries of the register and copy documents incorporated into the land certificate.

3.3 Prepare the draft contract and Seller's Property Information Form Part II using the standard forms.

4. **A buyer's offer is accepted**

When made aware that a buyer has been found the solicitor shall:

4.1 Inform the buyer's solicitor in accordance with paragraph 5 of the Council Statement that the Protocol will be used.

4.2 Ascertain the buyer's position on any related sale and in the light of that reply, ask the seller for a completion date.

4.3 Send to buyer's solicitor as soon as possible as many of the following items as are available:

(1) Draft contract.

(2) Office copy entries, or a photocopy of the land or charge certificate if they are not available, or the epitome of title (including details of any prior matters referred to but not disclosed by the documents themselves). The Index Map Search. A photocopy of the land or charge certificate should have marked on it the date that the certificate was last examined by the Land Registry.

(3) The Seller's Property Information Form with copies of all relevant planning decisions, guarantees etc.

(4) The completed Fixtures, Fittings and Contents Form. Where this is provided it will form part of the contract.

(5) In leasehold cases, a copy of the lease with all the information about maintenance charges and insurance which has so far been obtained and about the procedure (including references required) for obtaining the landlord's consent to the sale.

(6) The seller's target date for completion.

The remaining items should be forwarded to the buyer's solicitor as soon as they are available.

4.4 Ask the buyer's solicitor if a 10% deposit will be paid and, if not, what arrangements are proposed.

4.5 If and to the extent that the seller consents to the disclosure, supply information about the position on the seller's own purchase and of any other transactions in the chain above, and thereafter, of any change in circumstances.

Acting for the Buyer

5. The buyer's response

On receipt of instructions, the buyer's solicitor shall promptly:

5.1 Confirm to the seller's solicitor in accordance with paragraph 5 of the Council Statement that the Protocol will be used.

5.2 Ascertain the buyer's position on any related sale, mortgage arrangements and whether a 10% deposit will be provided.

5.3 If and to the extent that the buyer consents to the disclosure, inform the seller's solicitor about the position on the buyer's own sale, if any, and of any connected transactions, the general nature of the mortgage application, the amount of the deposit available and if the seller's target date for completion can be met, and thereafter, of any change in circumstances.

5.4 Make local search with the usual Part I Enquiries and any additional enquiries relevant to the property.

5.5 Make Commons Registration Search if appropriate.

5.6 Make Mining Enquiries if appropriate and any other relevant searches.

On receipt of draft documents:

5.7 Confirm approval of the draft contract and return it approved as soon as possible, having inserted the buyer's full names and address, subject to any outstanding matters.

5.8 At the same time ask only those specific additional enquiries which are required to clarify some point arising out of the documents submitted or which are relevant to the particular nature or location of the property or which the buyer has expressly requested omitting any enquiry, including those about the state and condition of the building, which is capable of being ascertained by the buyer's own enquiries or survey or personal inspection. Additional duplicated standard forms should not be submitted; if they are, the seller is under no obligation to deal with them nor need answer any enquiry seeking opinions rather than facts.

5.9 Ensure that buildings insurance arrangements are in place.

6. Exchange of contracts

On exchange, the buyer's solicitor shall send or deliver to the seller's solicitor:

6.1 The signed contract with all names, dates and financial information completed.

6.2 The deposit provided in the manner prescribed in the contract. Under the Law Society's Formula C the deposit may have to be sent to another solicitor nominated by the seller's solicitor.

6.3 If contracts are exchanged by telephone, the procedures laid down by the Law Society's Formulae A, B or C must be used and both solicitors must ensure (unless otherwise agreed) that the undertakings to send documents and pay the deposit on that day are strictly observed.

6.4 If contracts are exchanged in the post the seller's solicitor shall, once the buyer's signed contract and deposit are held unconditionally, having ensured that details of each contract are fully completed and identical send the seller's signed contract on the day of exchange.

7. Between exchange and the day of completion

As soon as possible after exchange and in any case within the time limits contained in the Standard Conditions of Sale:

7.1 The buyer's solicitor shall send to the seller's solicitor, in duplicate:

(1) Completion Information and Requisitions on Title Form.

(2) A draft conveyance, transfer or assignment.

(3) Other documents e.g. draft receipt for fixtures, fittings and contents.

7.2 As soon as possible after receipt of these documents, the seller's solicitor shall send to the buyer's solicitor:

(1) Replies to Completion Information and Requisitions on Title Form.

(2) Draft conveyance, transfer or assignment approved.

(3) If appropriate, completion statement supported by photocopy receipts or evidence of payment of apportionments claimed.

(4) Copy of licence to assign obtained from the landlord if appropriate.

7.3 The buyer's solicitor shall then:

(1) Engross the approved draft conveyance, transfer or assignment, obtain the buyer's signature to it (if necessary) and send it to the seller's solicitor in time to enable the seller to sign it before completion without suffering inconvenience.

(2) Take any steps necessary to ensure that the amount payable on completion will be available in time for completion.

(3) Dispatch the Land Registry and Land Charges Searches and, if appropriate, a company search.

7.4 The seller's solicitor shall request redemption figures for all financial charges on the property revealed by the deeds/office copy entries.

8. Completion: the day of payment and removals

8.1 If completion is to be by post, the Law Society's Code for Completion shall be used, unless otherwise agreed.

8.2 As soon as practicable and not later than the morning of completion, the buyer's solicitor shall advise the seller's solicitor of the manner of transmission of the purchase money and of the steps taken to dispatch it.

8.3 On being satisfied as to the receipt of the balance of the purchase money, the seller's solicitor shall authorise release of the keys and notify the buyer's solicitor of release.

8.4 The seller's solicitor shall check that the seller is aware of the need to notify the local and water authorities of the change in ownership.

8.5 After completion, where appropriate, the buyer's solicitor shall give notice of assignment to the lessor.

9. Relationship with estate agents

Where the seller has instructed estate agents, the seller's solicitor shall take the following steps:

9.1 Inform them when draft contracts are submitted.

9.2 Inform them of any unexpected delays or difficulties likely to delay exchange of contracts.

9.3 Inform them when exchange has taken place and the date of completion.

9.4 On receipt of their commission account send a copy to the seller and obtain instructions as to arrangements for payment.

9.5 Inform them of completion and, if so instructed, pay the commission.

V.   STANDARD FORMS
V.1.   Standard Conditions of Sale (3rd edition)

AGREEMENT
(Incorporating the Standard Conditions of Sale (Third Edition))

Agreement date   :

Seller   :

Buyer   :

Property   :
(freehold/leasehold)

Root of title/Title Number   :

Incumbrances on the Property   :

Title Guarantee   :
(full/limited)

Completion date   :

Contract rate   :

Purchase price   :

Deposit   :

Amount payable for chattels   :

Balance   :

The Seller will sell and the Buyer will buy the Property for the Purchase price.

The Agreement continues on the back page.

WARNING	**Signed**
This is a formal document, designed to create legal rights and legal obligations. Take advice before using it.	Seller/Buyer

STANDARD CONDITIONS OF SALE (THIRD EDITION)
(NATIONAL CONDITIONS OF SALE 23rd EDITION, LAW SOCIETY'S
CONDITIONS OF SALE 1995)

1.   GENERAL

1.1   Definitions

1.1.1   In these conditions:

    (a)   "accrued interest" means:

        (i)   if money has been placed on deposit or in a building society share account, the interest actually earned

        (ii)   otherwise, the interest which might reasonably have been earned by depositing the money at interest on seven days' notice of withdrawal with a clearing bank

    less, in either case, any proper charges for handling the money

    (b)   "agreement" means the contractual document which incorporates these conditions, with or without amendment

    (c)   "banker's draft" means a draft drawn by and on a clearing bank

    (d)   "clearing bank" means a bank which is a member of CHAPS Limited

    (e)   "completion date", unless defined in the agreement, has the meaning given in condition 6.1.1

    (f)   "contract" means the bargain between the seller and the buyer of which these conditions, with or without amendment, form part

    (g)   "contract rate", unless defined in the agreement, is the Law Society's interest rate from time to time in force

    (h)   "lease" includes sub-lease, tenancy and agreement for a lease or sub-lease

    (i)   "notice to complete" means a notice requiring completion of the contract in accordance with condition 6

    (j)   "public requirement" means any notice, order or proposal given or made (whether before or after the date of the contract) by a body acting on statutory authority

    (k)   "requisition" includes objection

    (l)   "solicitor" includes barrister, duly certificated notary public, recognised licensed conveyancer and recognised body under sections 9 or 32 of the Administration of Justice Act 1985

    (m)   "transfer" includes conveyance and assignment

    (n)   "working day" means any day from Monday to Friday (inclusive) which is not Christmas Day, Good Friday or a statutory Bank Holiday.

1.1.2   When used in these conditions the terms "absolute title" and "office copies" have the special meanings given to them by the Land Registration Act 1925.

1.2 Joint parties

If there is more than one seller or more than one buyer, the obligations which they undertake can be enforced against them all jointly or against each individually.

1.3 Notices and documents

1.3.1 A notice required or authorised by the contract must be in writing.

1.3.2 Giving a notice or delivering a document to a party's solicitor has the same effect as giving or delivering it to that party.

1.3.3 Transmission by fax is a valid means of giving a notice or delivering a document where delivery of the original document is not essential.

1.3.4 Subject to conditions 1.3.5 to 1.3.7, a notice is given and a document delivered when it is received.

1.3.5 If a notice or document is received after 4.00pm on a working day, or on a day which is not a working day, it is to be treated as having been received on the next working day.

1.3.6 Unless the actual time of receipt is proved, a notice or document sent by the following means is to be treated as having been received before 4.00pm on the day shown below:

(a) by first-class post: two working days after posting

(b) by second-class post: three working days after posting

(c) through a document exchange: on the first working day after the day on which it would normally be available for collection by the addressee.

1.3.7 Where a notice or document is sent through a document exchange, then for the purposes of condition 1.3.6 the actual time of receipt is:

(a) the time when the addressee collects it from the document exchange or, if earlier

(b) 8.00am on the first working day on which it is available for collection at that time.

1.4 VAT

1.4.1 An obligation to pay money includes an obligation to pay any value added tax chargeable in respect of that payment.

1.4.2 All sums made payable by the contract are exclusive of value added tax.

2. FORMATION

2.1 Date

2.1.1 If the parties intend to make a contract by exchanging duplicate copies by post or through a document exchange, the contract is made when the last copy is posted or deposited at the document exchange.

2.1.2 If the parties' solicitors agree to treat exchange as taking place before duplicate copies are actually exchanged, the contract is made as so agreed.

2.2 **Deposit**

2.2.1 The buyer is to pay or send a deposit of 10 per cent of the purchase price no later than the date of the contract. Except on a sale by auction, payment is to be made by banker's draft or by a cheque drawn on a solicitors' clearing bank account.

2.2.2 If before completion date the seller agrees to buy another property in England and Wales for his residence, he may use all or any part of the deposit as a deposit in that transaction to be held on terms to the same effect as this condition and condition 2.2.3.

2.2.3 Any deposit or part of a deposit not being used in accordance with condition 2.2.2 is to be held by the seller's solicitor as stakeholder on terms that on completion it is paid to the seller with accrued interest.

2.2.4 If a cheque tendered in payment of all or part of the deposit is dishonoured when first presented, the seller may, within seven working days of being notified that the cheque has been dishonoured, give notice to the buyer that the contract is discharged by the buyer's breach.

2.3 **Auctions**

2.3.1 On a sale by auction the following conditions apply to the property and, if it is sold in lots, to each lot.

2.3.2 The sale is subject to a reserve price.

2.3.3 The seller, or a person on his behalf, may bid up to the reserve price.

2.3.4 The auctioneer may refuse any bid.

2.3.5 If there is a dispute about a bid, the auctioneer may resolve the dispute or restart the auction at the last undisputed bid.

3. **MATTERS AFFECTING THE PROPERTY**

3.1 **Freedom from incumbrances**

3.1.1 The seller is selling the property free from incumbrances, other than those mentioned in condition 3.1.2.

3.1.2 The incumbrances subject to which the property is sold are:

(a) those mentioned in the agreement

(b) those discoverable by inspection of the property before the contract

(c) those the seller does not and could not know about

(d) entries made before the date of the contract in any public register except those maintained by HM Land Registry or its Land Charges Department or by Companies House

(e) public requirements.

3.1.3 After the contract is made, the seller is to give the buyer written details without delay of any new public requirement and of anything in writing which he learns about concerning any incumbrance subject to which the property is sold.

3.1.4 The buyer is to bear the cost of complying with any outstanding public requirement and is to indemnify the seller against any liability resulting from a public requirement.

3.2   **Physical state**

3.2.1   The buyer accepts the property in the physical state it is in at the date of the contract, unless the seller is building or converting it.

3.2.2   A leasehold property is sold subject to any subsisting breach of a condition or tenant's obligation relating to the physical state of the property which renders the lease liable to forfeiture.

3.2.3   A sub-lease is granted subject to any subsisting breach of a condition or tenant's obligation relating to the physical state of the property which renders the seller's own lease liable to forfeiture.

3.3   **Leases affecting the property**

3.3.1   The following provisions apply if the agreement states that any part of the property is sold subject to a lease.

3.3.2   (a) The seller having provided the buyer with full details of each lease or copies of the documents embodying the lease terms, the buyer is treated as entering into the contract knowing and fully accepting those terms.

        (b) The seller is to inform the buyer without delay if the lease ends or if the seller learns of any application by the tenant in connection with the lease; the seller is then to act as the buyer reasonably directs, and the buyer is to indemnify him against all consequent loss and expense.

        (c) The seller is not to agree to any proposal to change the lease terms without the consent of the buyer and is to inform the buyer without delay of any change which may be proposed or agreed.

        (d) The buyer is to indemnify the seller against all claims arising from the lease after actual completion; this includes claims which are unenforceable against a buyer for want of registration.

        (e) The seller takes no responsibility for what rent is lawfully recoverable, nor for whether or how any legislation affects the lease.

        (f) If the let land is not wholly within the property, the seller may apportion the rent.

3.4   **Retained land**

3.4.1   The following provisions apply where after the transfer the seller will be retaining land near the property.

3.4.2   The buyer will have no right of light or air over the retained land, but otherwise the seller and the buyer will each have the rights over the land of the other which they would have had if they were two separate buyers to whom the seller had made simultaneous transfers of the property and the retained land.

3.4.3   Either party may require that the transfer contain appropriate express terms.

4.   **TITLE AND TRANSFER**

4.1   **Timetable**

4.1.1   The following are the steps for deducing and investigating the title to the property to be taken within the following time limits:

Step	Time Limit
1. The seller is to send the buyer evidence of title in accordance with condition 4.2	Immediately after making the contract
2. The buyer may raise written requisitions	Six working days after either the date of the contract or the date of delivery of the seller's evidence of title on which the requisitions are raised whichever is the later
3. The seller is to reply in writing to any requisitions raised	Four working days after receiving the requisitions
4. The buyer may make written observations on the seller's replies	Three working days after receiving the replies

The time limit on the buyer's right to raise requisitions applies even where the seller supplies incomplete evidence of his title, but the buyer may, within six working days from delivery of any further evidence, raise further requisitions resulting from that evidence. On the expiry of the relevant time limit the buyer loses his right to raise requisitions or make observations.

4.1.2   The parties are to take the following steps to prepare and agree the transfer of the property within the following time limits:

Step	Time Limit
A. The buyer is to send the seller a draft transfer	At least twelve working days before completion date
B. The seller is to approve or revise that draft and either return it or retain it for use as the actual transfer	Four working days after delivery of the draft transfer
C. If the draft is returned the buyer is to send an engrossment to the seller	At least five working days before completion date

4.1.3   Periods of time under conditions 4.1.1 and 4.1.2 may run concurrently.

4.1.4   If the period between the date of the contract and completion date is less than 15 working days, the time limits in conditions 4.1.1 and 4.1.2 are to be reduced by the same proportion as that period bears to the period of 15 working days. Fractions of a working day are to be rounded down except that the time limit to perform any step is not to be less than one working day.

4.2   Proof of title

4.2.1   The evidence of registered title is office copies of the items required to be furnished by section 110(1) of the Land Registration Act 1925 and the copies, abstracts and evidence referred to in section 110(2).

4.2.2   The evidence of unregistered title is an abstract of the title, or an epitome of title with photocopies of the relevant documents.

4.2.3   Where the title to the property is unregistered, the seller is to produce to the buyer (without cost to the buyer):

(a)   the original of every relevant document, or

(b)   an abstract, epitome or copy with an original marking by a solicitor of examination either against the original or against an examined abstract or against an examined copy.

4.3   Defining the property

4.3.1   The seller need not:

(a)   prove the exact boundaries of the property

(b)   prove who owns fences, ditches, hedges or walls

(c)   separately identify parts of the property with different titles

further than he may be able to do from information in his possession.

4.3.2   The buyer may, if it is reasonable, require the seller to make or obtain, pay for and hand over a statutory declaration about facts relevant to the matters mentioned in condition 4.3.1. The form of the declaration is to be agreed by the buyer, who must not unreasonably withhold his agreement.

4.4   Rents and rentcharges

The fact that a rent or rentcharge, whether payable or receivable by the owner of the property, has been or will on completion be, informally apportioned is not to be regarded as a defect in title.

4.5   Transfer

4.5.1   The buyer does not prejudice his right to raise requisitions, or to require replies to any raised, by taking any steps in relation to the preparation or agreement of the transfer.

4.5.2   If the agreement makes no provision as to title guarantee, then subject to condition 4.5.3 the seller is to transfer the property with full title guarantee.

4.5.3   The transfer is to have effect as if the disposition is expressly made subject to all matters to which the property is sold subject under the terms of the contract.

4.5.4   If after completion the seller will remain bound by any obligation affecting the property, but the law does not imply any covenant by the buyer to indemnify the seller against liability for future breaches of it:

(a)   the buyer is to covenant in the transfer to indemnify the seller against liability for any future breach of the obligation and to perform it from then on, and

(b)   if required by the seller, the buyer is to execute and deliver to the seller on completion a duplicate transfer prepared by the buyer.

4.5.5   The seller is to arrange at his expense that, in relation to every document of title which the buyer does not receive on completion, the buyer is to have the benefit of:

(a)   a written acknowledgement of his right to its production, and

(b)   a written undertaking for its safe custody (except while it is held by a mortgagee or by someone in a fiduciary capacity).

5. PENDING COMPLETION

5.1 Responsibility for property

5.1.1 The seller will transfer the property in the same physical state as it was at the date of the contract (except for fair wear and tear), which means that the seller retains the risk until completion.

5.1.2 If at any time before completion the physical state of the property makes it unusable for its purpose at the date of the contract:

(a) the buyer may rescind the contract

(b) the seller may rescind the contract where the property has become unusable for that purpose as a result of damage against which the seller could not reasonably have insured, or which it is not legally possible for the seller to make good.

5.1.3 The seller is under no obligation to the buyer to insure the property.

5.1.4 Section 47 of the Law of Property Act 1925 does not apply.

5.2 Occupation by buyer

5.2.1 If the buyer is not already lawfully in the property, and the seller agrees to let him into occupation, the buyer occupies on the following terms.

5.2.2 The buyer is a licensee and not a tenant. The terms of the licence are that the buyer:

(a) cannot transfer it

(b) may permit members of his household to occupy the property

(c) is to pay or indemnify the seller against all outgoings and other expenses in respect of the property

(d) is to pay the seller a fee calculated at the contract rate on the purchase price (less any deposit paid) for the period of the licence

(e) is entitled to any rents and profits from any part of the property which he does not occupy

(f) is to keep the property in as good a state of repair as it was in when he went into occupation (except for fair wear and tear) and is not to alter it

(g) is to insure the property in a sum which is not less than the purchase price against all risks in respect of which comparable premises are normally insured

(h) is to quit the property when the licence ends.

5.2.3 On the creation of the buyer's licence, condition 5.1 ceases to apply, which means that the buyer then assumes the risk until completion.

5.2.4 The buyer is not in occupation for the purposes of this condition if he merely exercises rights of access given solely to do work agreed by the seller.

5.2.5 The buyer's licence ends on the earliest of: completion date, rescission of the contract or when five working days' notice given by one party to the other takes effect.

5.2.6 If the buyer is in occupation of the property after his licence has come to an end and the contract is subsequently completed he is to pay the seller compensation for his continued occupation calculated at the same rate as the fee mentioned in condition 5.2.2(d).

5.2.7 The buyer's right to raise requisitions is unaffected.

6. COMPLETION

6.1 Date

6.1.1 Completion date is twenty working days after the date of the contract but time is not of the essence of the contract unless a notice to complete has been served.

6.1.2 If the money due on completion is received after 2.00pm, completion is to be treated, for the purposes only of conditions 6.3 and 7.3, as taking place on the next working day.

6.1.3 Condition 6.1.2 does not apply where the sale is with vacant possession of the property or any part and the seller has not vacated the property or that part by 2.00pm on the date of actual completion.

6.2 Place

Completion is to take place in England and Wales, either at the seller's solicitor's office or at some other place which the seller reasonably specifies.

6.3 Apportionments

6.3.1 Income and outgoings of the property are to be apportioned between the parties so far as the change of ownership on completion will affect entitlement to receive or liability to pay them.

6.3.2 If the whole property is sold with vacant possession or the seller exercises his option in condition 7.3.4, apportionment is to be made with effect from the date of actual completion; otherwise, it is to be made from completion date.

6.3.3 In apportioning any sum, it is to be assumed that the seller owns the property until the end of the day from which apportionment is made and that the sum accrues from day to day at the rate at which it is payable on that day.

6.3.4 For the purpose of apportioning income and outgoings, it is to be assumed that they accrue at an equal daily rate throughout the year.

6.3.5 When a sum to be apportioned is not known or easily ascertainable at completion, a provisional apportionment is to be made according to the best estimate available. As soon as the amount is known, a final apportionment is to be made and notified to the other party. Any resulting balance is to be paid no more than ten working days later, and if not then paid the balance is to bear interest at the contract rate from then until payment.

6.3.6 Compensation payable under condition 5.2.6 is not to be apportioned.

6.4 Amount payable

The amount payable by the buyer on completion is the purchase price (less any deposit already paid to the seller or his agent) adjusted to take account of:

(a) apportionments made under condition 6.3

(b) any compensation to be paid or allowed under condition 7.3.

6.5   **Title deeds**

6.5.1   The seller is not to retain the documents of title after the buyer has tendered the amount payable under condition 6.4.

6.5.2   Condition 6.5.1 does not apply to any documents of title relating to land being retained by the seller after completion.

6.6   **Rent receipts**

The buyer is to assume that whoever gave any receipt for a payment of rent or service charge which the seller produces was the person or the agent of the person then entitled to that rent or service charge.

6.7   **Means of payment**

The buyer is to pay the money due on completion in one or more of the following ways:

(a)   legal tender

(b)   a banker's draft

(c)   a direct credit to a bank account nominated by the seller's solicitor

(d)   an unconditional release of a deposit held by a stakeholder.

6.8   **Notice to complete**

6.8.1   At any time on or after completion date, a party who is ready able and willing to complete may give the other a notice to complete.

6.8.2   A party is ready able and willing:

(a)   if he could be, but for the default of the other party, and

(b)   in the case of the seller, even though a mortgage remains secured on the property, if the amount to be paid on completion enables the property to be transferred freed of all mortgages (except those to which the sale is expressly subject).

6.8.3   The parties are to complete the contract within ten working days of giving a notice to complete, excluding the day on which the notice is given. For this purpose, time is of the essence of the contract.

6.8.4   On receipt of a notice to complete:

(a)   if the buyer paid no deposit, he is forthwith to pay a deposit of 10 per cent

(b)   if the buyer paid a deposit of less than 10 per cent, he is forthwith to pay a further deposit equal to the balance of that 10 per cent.

7.   **REMEDIES**

7.1   **Errors and omission**

7.1.1   If any plan or statement in the contract, or in the negotiations leading to it, is or was misleading or inaccurate due to an error or omission, the remedies available are as follows.

7.1.2   When there is a material difference between the description or value of the property as represented and as it is, the injured party is entitled to damages.

7.1.3   An error or omission only entitles the injured party to rescind the contract:

(a)   where it results from fraud or recklessness, or

(b)   where he would be obliged, to his prejudice, to transfer or accept property differing substantially (in quantity, quality or tenure) from what the error or omission had led him to expect.

7.2 Rescission

If either party rescinds the contract:

(a)   unless the rescission is a result of the buyer's breach of contract the deposit is to be repaid to the buyer with accrued interest

(b)   the buyer is to return any documents he received from the seller and is to cancel any registration of the contract.

7.3 Late completion

7.3.1   If there is default by either or both of the parties in performing their obligations under the contract and completion is delayed, the party whose total period of default is the greater is to pay compensation to the other party.

7.3.2   Compensation is calculated at the contract rate on the purchase price, or (where the buyer is the paying party) the purchase price less any deposit paid, for the period by which the paying party's default exceeds that of the receiving party, or, if shorter, the period between completion date and actual completion.

7.3.   Any claim for loss resulting from delayed completion is to be reduced by any compensation paid under this contract.

7.3.4   Where the buyer holds the property as tenant of the seller and completion is delayed, the seller may give notice to the buyer, before the date of actual completion, that he intends to take the net income from the property until completion. If he does so, he cannot claim compensation under condition 7.3.1 as well.

7.4 After completion

Completion does not cancel liability to perform any outstanding obligation under this contract.

7.5 Buyer's failure to comply with notice to complete

7.5.1   If the buyer fails to complete in accordance with a notice to complete, the following terms apply.

7.5.2   The seller may rescind the contract, and if he does so:

(a)   he may

(i)   forfeit and keep any deposit and accrued interest

(ii)   resell the property

(iii)   claim damages

(b) the buyer is to return any documents he received from the seller and is to cancel any registration of the contract.

7.5.3   The seller retains his other rights and remedies.

7.6   Seller's failure to comply with notice to complete

7.6.1   If the seller fails to complete in accordance with a notice to complete, the following terms apply.

7.6.2   The buyer may rescind the contract, and if he does so:

(a)   the deposit is to be repaid to the buyer with accrued interest

(b)   the buyer is to return any documents he received from the seller and is, at the seller's expense, to cancel any registration of the contract.

7.6.3   The buyer retains his other rights and remedies.

8.   LEASEHOLD PROPERTY

8.1   Existing leases

8.1.1   The following provisions apply to a sale of leasehold land.

8.1.2   The seller having provided the buyer with copies of the documents embodying the lease terms, the buyer is treated as entering into the contract knowing and fully accepting those terms.

8.1.3   The seller is to comply with any lease obligations requiring the tenant to insure the property.

8.2   New leases

8.2.1   The following provisions apply to a grant of a new lease.

8.2.2   The conditions apply so that:
"seller" means the proposed landlord
"buyer" means the proposed tenant
"purchase price" means the premium to be paid on the grant of a lease.

8.2.3   The lease is to be in the form of the draft attached to the agreement.

8.2.4   If the term of the new lease will exceed 21 years, the seller is to deduce a title which will enable the buyer to register the lease at HM Land Registry with an absolute title.

8.2.5   The buyer is not entitled to transfer the benefit of the contract.

8.2.6   The seller is to engross the lease and a counterpart of it and is to send the counterpart to the buyer at least five working days before completion date.

8.2.7   The buyer is to execute the counterpart and deliver it to the seller on completion.

8.3   Landlord's consent

8.3.1   The following provisions apply if a consent to assign or sub-let is required to complete the contract.

8.3.2   (a)   The seller is to apply for the consent at his expense, and to use all reasonable efforts to obtain it.

(b)   The buyer is to provide all information and references reasonably required.

8.3.3   The buyer is not entitled to transfer the benefit of the contract.

8.3.4   Unless he is in breach of his obligation under condition 8.3.2, either party may rescind the contract by notice to the other party if three working days before completion date:

(a)   the consent has not been given or

(b)   the consent has been given subject to a condition to which the buyer reasonably objects.

In that case, neither party is to be treated as in breach of contract and condition 7.2 applies.

9.   CHATTELS

9.1   The following provisions apply to any chattels which are to be sold.

9.2   Whether or not a separate price is to be paid for the chattels, the contract takes effect as a contract for sale of goods.

9.3   Ownership of the chattels passes to the buyer on actual completion.

SPECIAL CONDITIONS

1.   (a)   This Agreement incorporates the Standard Conditions of Sales (Third Edition). Where there is a conflict between those Conditions and this Agreement, this Agreement prevails.

(b)   Terms used or defined in this Agreement have the same meaning when used in the Conditions.

2.   The Property is sold subject to the Incumbrances on the Property and the Buyer will raise no requisitions on them.

3.   Subject to the terms of this Agreement and to the Standard Conditions of Sale, the Seller is to transfer the Property with the title guarantee specified on the front page.

4.   The chattels on the Property and set out on any attached list are included in the sale.

5.   The Property is sold with vacant possession on completion.

(or) 5.   The Property is sold subject to the following leases or tenancies:

Seller's Solicitors   :

Buyer's Solicitors   :

V.2. The Law Society standard business leases (of whole and of part)

Licences

The Law Society will hold the copyright in the leases and will grant licences to print the documents. The printed forms will be available from law stationers and from the Law Society's shop. However, it is intended that solicitors who wish to do so will be licensed to produce the leases on their word processors but it is on the understanding that:

1. The format of the standard leases is adopted as closely as practicable in the form of the printed lease.

2. No alterations or additions whatsoever are to be made to the text of the standard clauses. This means that cll 1 to 14.6 of the lease of the whole building and cll 1 to 17.6 of the lease of part of the building are to be reproduced without any amendment whatsoever.

3. The lease must contain a statement that it is in the form of the Law Society Business Lease.

4. All variations, whether being amendments or additional clauses, must be set out at the end of the document in an additional page to be attached to the lease which will deal with all alterations and variations to the standard clauses and any additional provisions required. It is essential that neither alterations nor deletions are made to the text itself.

5. The licence to reproduce the lease does not extend to printing the lease. Local law societies will be granted a licence to print both forms of the leases on favourable terms should they wish to do so.

6. Photocopies of the leases must not be used other than as file copies.

The Law Society business leases (whole and part of building are set out on the following pages. The business leases are sold in packs of 10.

THE LAW SOCIETY

THE LAW SOCIETY BUSINESS LEASE (WHOLE OF BUILDING)

DATE _____

LANDLORD _____

OF _____

LETS TO _____

TENANT _____

OF _____

_____

THE PROPERTY KNOWN AS

PROPERTY _____

RESIDENTIAL
ACCOMMODATION   [WHICH INCLUDES _____

_____]

FOR THE PERIOD STARTING ON

LEASE PERIOD _____

AND ENDING ON _____

FOR USE (EXCEPT ANY RESIDENTIAL ACCOMODATION) AS

USE ALLOWED _____

OR ANY OTHER USE TO WHICH THE LANDLORD CONSENTS (AND THE LANDLORD IS

NOT ENTITLED TO WITHHOLD THAT CONSENT UNREASONABLY)

THE TENANT PAYING THE LANDLORD RENT AT THE RATE OF

RENT _____ POUNDS

(£ _____) _____

A YEAR BY THESE INSTALMENTS:

(A) ON THE DATE OF THIS LEASE, A PROPORTIONATE SUM FOR THE PERIOD

STARTING ON

_____ TO

_____ AND THEN

(B) EQUAL MONTHLY INSTALMENTS IN ADVANCE ON THE

RENT DAYS   _____ DAY OF EACH MONTH

THE RENT MAY BE INCREASED (UNDER CLAUSE 8) WITH EFFECT FROM EVERY

RENT REVIEW DATES   ANNIVERSARY OF THE START OF THE LEASE PERIOD

This lease is granted on the terms printed on pages 2 to 4, as added to or varied by any terms appearing on any attached continuation page

© The Law Society   **L.S.2 (Whole) 5/96**

1

TENANT'S OBLIGATIONS

1 PAYMENTS

1. The Tenant is to pay the Landlord:

1.1 the rent

1.2 the amount of every premium which the Landlord pays to insure the property under this lease, to be paid within 14 days after the Landlord gives written notice of payment (and this amount is to be paid as rent)

and the following sums on demand:

1.3 a fair proportion (decided by a surveyor the Landlord nominates) of the cost of repairing maintaining and cleaning:

party walls, party structures, yards, gardens, roads, paths, gutters, drains, sewers, pipes, conduits, wires, cables and things used or shared with other property

1.4 the cost (including professional fees) of any works to the property which the Landlord does after the Tenant defaults

1.5 the costs and expenses (including professional fees) which the Landlord incurs in:

(a) dealing with any application by the Tenant for consent or approval, whether or not it is given

(b) preparing and serving a notice of a breach of the Tenant's obligations, under section 146 of the Law of Property Act 1925, even if forfeiture of this lease is avoided without a court order

(c) preparing and serving schedules of dilapidations either during the lease period or recording failure to give up the property in the appropriate state or repair when this lease ends

1.6 interest at the Law Society's interest rate on any of the above payments when more than fourteen days overdue, to be calculated from its due date

and in making payment under this clause:

(a) nothing is to be deducted or set off

(b) any value added tax payable is to be added.

2

2. The Tenant is also to make the following payments, with value added tax where payable:

2.1 all periodic rates, taxes and outgoings relating to the property, including any imposed after the date of this lease (even if of a novel nature), to be paid promptly to the authorities to whom they are due

2.2 the cost of the grant, renewal or continuation of any licence or registration for using the property for the use allowed, to be paid promptly to the appropriate authority when due

2.3 a registration fee of £20 for each document which this lease required the Tenant to register, to be paid to the Landlord's solicitors when presenting the document for registration

3 USE

3. The Tenant is to comply with the following requirements as to the use of the property and any part of it and is not to authorise or allow anyone else to contravene them:

3.1 to use the property, except any residential accommodation, only for the use allowed

3.2 to use any residential accommodation only as a home for one family

3.3 not to do anything which might invalidate any insurance policy covering the property or which might increase the premium

3.4 not to hold an auction sale in the property

3.5 not to use the property for any activities which are dangerous, offensive, noxious, illegal or immoral, or which are or may become a nuisance or annoyance to the Landlord or to the owner or occupier of any neighbouring property

3.6 not to display any advertisements on the outside of the property or which are visible from the outside unless the Landlord consents (and the Landlord is not entitled to withhold that consent unreasonably)

3.7 not to overload the floors or walls of the property

3.8 to comply with the terms of every Act of Parliament, order, regulation, bye-law, rule, licence and registration authorising or regulating how the property is used, and to obtain, renew and continue any licence or registration which is required

4 ACCESS

4. The Tenant is to give the Landlord, or anyone authorised by him in writing, access to the property:

4.1 for these purposes:

(a) inspecting the condition of the property, or how it is being used

(b) doing works which the Landlord is permitted to do under clause 5.8(c)

(c) complying with any statutory obligation

(d) viewing the property as a prospective buyer or mortgagee or, during the last six months if the lease period, as a prospective tenant

(e) valuing the property

(f) inspecting, cleaning or repairing neighbouring property, or any sewers, drains, pipes, wires, cables serving neighbouring property

4.2 and only on seven days' written notice except in an emergency

4.3 and during normal business hours except in an emergency

4.4 and the Landlord is promptly to make good all damage caused to the property and any goods there in exercising these rights

5 CONDITION AND WORK

5. The Tenant is to comply with the following duties in relation to the property:

5.1 to maintain the state and condition of the property but the Tenant need not alter or improve it except if required under clause 5.7

5.2 to decorate the inside and outside of the property:

(a) in every fifth year of the lease period

(b) in the last three months of the lease period (however it ends) except to the extent that it has been decorated in the previous year

and on each occasion the Tenant is to use the colours and the types of finish used previously

5.3 but the Tenant need only make good damage caused by an insured risk to the extent that the insurance money has not been paid because of any act or default of the Tenant

5.4 not to make any structural alterations, external alterations or additions to the property

5.5 not to make any other alterations unless with the Landlord's consent in writing (and the Landlord is not entitled to withhold that consent unreasonably)

5.6 to keep any plate glass in the property insured for its full replacement cost with reputable insurers, to give the Landlord details of that insurance on request, and to replace any plate glass which becomes damaged

5.7 to do the work to the property which any authority acting under an Act of Parliament requires, even if it alters or improves the property. Before the Tenant does so, the Landlord is to:

(a) give his consent in writing to the work

(b) contribute a fair proportion of the cost of the work taking into account any value to him of the work

5.8 if the Tenant fails to do any work which this lease requires him to do and the Landlord gives him written notice to do it, the Tenant is to:

(a) start the work within two months, or immediately in case of emergency, and

(b) proceed diligently with the work

(c) in default, permit the Landlord to do the work

5.9 any dispute arising under clause 5.7(b) is to be decided by arbitration under clause 14.5

6 TRANSFER ETC.

6. The Tenant is to comply with the following:

6.1 the Tenant is not to share occupation of the property and no part of it is to be transferred, sublet or occupied separately from the remainder

L.S.2(Whole)/2

2

6.2 the Tenant is not to transfer or sublet the whole of the property unless the Landlord gives his written consent in advance, and the Landlord is not entitled to withhold that consent unreasonably

6.3 any sublease is to be in terms which are consistent with this lease, but is not to permit the sub-tenant to underlet

6.4 within four weeks after the property is transferred mortgaged or sublet, the Landlord's solicitors are to be notified and a copy of the transfer mortgage or sublease sent to them for registration with the fee payable under clause 2.3

6.5 if the Landlord requires, a tenant who transfers the whole of the property is to give the Landlord a written guarantee, in the terms set out in the Guarantee Box, that the Transferee will perform his obligations as Tenant

7 OTHER MATTERS

7. The Tenant:

7.1 is to give the Landlord a copy of any notice concerning the property or any neighbouring property as soon as he receives it

7.2 is to allow the Landlord, during the last six months of the lease period, to fix a notice in a reasonable position on the outside of the property announcing that it is for sale or to let

7.3 is not to apply for planning permission relating to the use or alteration of the property unless the Landlord gives written consent in advance

8 RENT REVIEW

8.1 On each rent review date, the rent is to increase to the market rent if that is higher than the rent applying before that date

8.2 The market rent is the rent which a willing tenant would pay for the property on the open market, if let to him on the rent review date by a willing landlord on a lease on the same terms as this lease without any premium and for a period equal to the remainder of the lease period, assuming that at that date:

(a) the willing tenant takes account of any likelihood that he would be entitled to a new lease of the property when the lease ends, but does not take account of any goodwill belonging to anyone who had occupied the property

(b) the property is vacant and had not been occupied by the Tenant or any sub-tenant

(c) the property can immediately be used

(d) the property is in the condition required by this lease and any damage caused by any of the risks insured under clause 11 has been made good

(e) during the lease period no tenant nor sub-tenant has done anything to the property to increase or decrease its rental value and "anything" includes work done by the Tenant to comply with clause 5.7, but nothing else which the Tenant was obliged to do under this lease

8.3 If the Landlord and the Tenant agree the amount of the new rent, a statement of that new rent, signed by them, is to be attached to this lease

8.4 If the Landlord and the Tenant have not agreed the amount of the new rent two months before the new rent review date, either of them may require the new rent to be decided by arbitration under clause 14.5

8.5

(a) The Tenant is to continue to pay rent at the rate applying before the rent review date until the next rent day after the new rent is agreed or decided

(b) Starting on that rent day, the Tenant is to pay the new rent

(c) On that rent day, the Tenant is also to pay any amount by which the new rent since the rent review date exceeds the rent paid, with interest on that amount at 2% below the Law Society's interest rate.

9 DAMAGE

9. If the property is damaged by any of the risks to be insured under clause 11 and as a result of that damage the property, or any part of it, cannot be used for the use allowed:

9.1 the rent, or a fair proportion of it, is to be suspended for three years or until the property is fully restored, if sooner

9.2 if at any time it is unlikely that the property will be fully restored within three years from the date of the damage, the Landlord (so long as he has not delayed the restoration) or the Tenant can end this lease by giving one month's notice to the other during the three year period, in which case

(a) the insurance money belongs to the Landlord and

(b) the Landlord's obligation to make good damage under clause 11 ceases

9.3 a notice given outside the time limits in clause 9.2 is not effective

9.4 the Tenant cannot claim the benefit of this clause to the extent that the insurers refuse to pay the insurance money because of his act or default

9.5 any dispute arising under any part of this clause is to be decided by arbitration under clause 14.5

LANDLORD'S OBLIGATIONS AND FORFEITURE RIGHTS

10 QUIET ENJOYMENT

10. While the Tenant complies with the terms of this lease, the Landlord is to allow the Tenant to possess and use the property without lawful interference from the Landlord or any trustee for the Landlord

11 INSURANCE

11. The Landlord agrees with the Tenant:

11.1 the Landlord is to keep the property (except the plate glass) insured with reputable insurers to cover:

(a) full rebuilding, site clearance, professional fees, value added tax and three years' loss of rent

(b) against fire, lightning, explosion, earthquake, landslip, subsidence, heave, riot, civil commotion, aircraft, aerial devices, storm, flood, water, theft, impact by vehicles, damage by malicious persons and vandals and third party liability and any other risks reasonably required by the Landlord

so far as cover is available at the normal insurance rates for the locality and subject to reasonable excesses and exclusions

11.2 and to take all necessary steps to make good as soon as possible damage to the property caused by insured risks except to the extent that the insurance money is not paid because of the act or default of the Tenant

11.3 and to give the Tenant at his request once a year particulars of the policy and evidence from the insurer that it is in force

11.4 and that the Tenant is not responsible for any damage for which the Landlord is compensated under the insurance policy

12 FORFEITURE

12. This lease comes to an end if the Landlord forfeits it by entering any part of the property, which the Landlord is entitled to do whenever:

(a) payment of any rent is fourteen days overdue, even if it was not formally demanded

(b) the Tenant has not complied with any of the terms in this lease

(c) the Tenant if any individual (and if more than one, any of them) is adjudicated bankrupt or an interim receiver of his property is appointed

(d) the Tenant if a company (and if more than one, any of them) goes into liquidation (unless solely for the purpose of amalgamation or reconstruction when solvent), or has an administrative receiver appointed or has an administration order made in respect of it

The forfeiture of this lease does not cancel any outstanding obligation of the Tenant or a Guarantor

13 END OF LEASE

13. When this lease ends the Tenant is to:

13.1 return the property to the Landlord leaving it in the state and condition in which this lease required the Tenant to keep it

13.2 (if the Landlord so requires) remove anything the Tenant fixed to the property and make good any damage which that causes

L.S.2(Whole)/3

3

GENERAL

14 PARTIES' RESPONSIBILITY

14.1 Whenever more than one person or company is the Landlord, the Tenant or the Guarantor, their obligations can be enforced against all or both of them jointly and against each individually

LANDLORD
14.2

(a) The obligations in this lease continue to apply to the Landlord until he is released by the Tenant or by a declaration of the court

(b) The current owner of the Landlord's interest in the property must comply with the Landlord's obligations in this lease

TENANT
14.3

(a) A transfer of this lease releases the Tenant from any future obligations under it. This does not apply in the case of a transfer made without the Landlord's consent or as a result of the Tenant's death or bankruptcy

(b) After a transfer, the Tenant's successor must comply with the Tenant's obligations in this lease

SERVICE OF NOTICES

14.4 The rules about serving notices in Section 196 of the Law of Property Act 1925 (as since amended) apply to any notice given under this lease

ARBITRATION

14.5 Any matter which this lease requires to be decided by arbitration is to be referred to a single arbitrator under the Arbitration Acts. The Landlord and the Tenant may agree the appointment of the arbitrator, or either of them may apply to the President of the Royal Institution of Chartered Surveyors to make the appointment.

HEADINGS

14.6 The headings do not form part of this lease

STAMP DUTY

15. This lease has not been granted to implement an agreement for a lease

Signed as a deed by/on behalf of the
Landlord and delivered in the presence of:

....

Witness

....

Witness's occupation and address

Signed as a deed by/on behalf of the
Tenant and delivered in the presence of:

....

Witness

....

Witness's occupation and address

Signed as a deed by/on behalf of the
Guarantor and delivered in the presence of:

....

Witness

....

Witness's occupation and address

GUARANTEE BOX

The terms in this box only take effect if a guarantor is named and then only until the Tenant transfers this lease with the Landlord's written consent. The Guarantor must sign this lease.

'Guarantor':

of

agrees to compensate the Landlord for any loss incurred as a result of the Tenant failing to comply with an obligation in this lease during the lease period or any statutory extension of it. If the Tenant is insolvent and this lease ends because it is disclaimed, the Guarantor agrees to accept a new lease, if the Landlord so requires, in the same form but at the rent then payable. Even if the Landlord gives the Tenant extra time to comply with an obligation, or does not insist on strict compliance with terms of this lease, the Guarantor's obligation remains fully effective.

THIS DOCUMENT CREATES LEGAL RIGHTS AND LEGAL OBLIGATIONS. DO NOT SIGN IT UNTIL YOU HAVE CONSULTED A SOLICITOR. THERE IS A CODE OF PRACTICE CONCERNING COMMERCIAL LEASES IN ENGLAND AND WALES PUBLISHED UNDER THE AUSPICES OF THE DEPARTMENT OF THE ENVIRONMENT.

....

Landlord

....

Tenant

....

Guarantor

THE LAW SOCIETY

4

L.S.2(Whole)/4

THE LAW SOCIETY

DATE

LANDLORD

OF

LETS TO

TENANT

OF

THE PROPERTY KNOWN AS

PROPERTY

WHICH IS PART OF

BUILDING

(WHICH, WHEN REFERRED TO IN THIS LEASE, INCLUDES ITS GROUNDS) FOR THE
PERIOD STARTING ON

LEASE PERIOD   AND ENDING ON

FOR USE AS

USE ALLOWED

OR ANY OTHER USE TO WHICH THE LANDLORD CONSENTS (AND THE LANDLORD IS

NOT ENTITLED TO WITHHOLD THAT CONSENT UNREASONABLY)

THE TENANT PAYING THE LANDLORD RENT AT THE RATE OF

RENT   POUNDS

(£   )

A YEAR BY THESE INSTALMENTS:

(A) ON THE DATE OF THIS LEASE, A PROPORTIONATE SUM FOR THE PERIOD

STARTING ON

TO

AND THEN

(B) EQUAL MONTHLY INSTALMENTS IN ADVANCE ON THE

RENT DAYS   DAY OF EACH MONTH

THE RENT MAY BE INCREASED (UNDER CLAUSE 9) WITH EFFECT FROM EVERY

RENT REVIEW DATES   ANNIVERSARY OF THE START OF THE LEASE PERIOD

This lease is granted on the terms printed on pages 2 to 5, as added to or varied by any terms appearing on page 6 or any attached
continuation page

© The Law Society   **L.S.1 (Part) 5/96**

1

THE LAW SOCIETY BUSINESS LEASE (PART OF BUILDING)

TENANT'S OBLIGATIONS

1   PAYMENTS

1. The Tenant is to pay the Landlord:

1.1 the rent

1.2 the service charge in accordance with clause 3 (and this is to be paid as rent)

and the following sums on demand:

1.3 a fair proportion (decided by a surveyor the Landlord nominates) of the cost of repairing maintaining and cleaning:

party walls, party structures, yards, gardens, roads, paths, gutters, drains sewers, pipes, conduits, wires, cables and things used or shared with other property

1.4 the cost (including professional fees) of any works to the property which the Landlord does after the Tenant defaults

1.5 the costs and expenses (including professional fees) which the Landlord incurs in:

  (a) dealing with any application by the Tenant for consent or approval, whether or not it is given

  (b) preparing and serving a notice of a breach of the Tenant's obligations, under section 146 of the Law of Property Act 1925, even if forfeiture of this lease is avoided without a court order

  (c) preparing and serving schedules of dilapidations either during the lease period or recording failure to give up the property in the appropriate state of repair when this lease ends

1.6 interest at the Law Society's interest rate on any of the above payments when more than fourteen days overdue, to be calculated from its due date

and in making payments under this clause:

  (a) nothing is to be deducted or set off

  (b) any value added tax payable is to be added

2

2. The Tenant is also to make the following payments, with value added tax where applicable:

2.1 all periodic rates, taxes and outgoings relating to the property, including any imposed after the date of this lease (even if of a novel nature), to be paid promptly to the authorities to whom they are due

2.2 the cost of the grant, renewal or continuation of any licence or registration for using the property for the use allowed, to be paid promptly to the appropriate authority when due

2.3 a registration fee of £20 for each document which this lease requires the Tenant to register to be paid to the Landlord's solicitors when presenting the document for registration

3   SERVICE CHARGE

3. The Landlord and the Tenant agree that:

3.1 the service charge is the Tenant's fair proportion of each item of the service costs

3.2 the service costs:

  (a) are the costs which the Landlord fairly and reasonably incurs in complying with his obligations under clauses 12 and 13

  (b) include the reasonable charges of any agent contractor consultant or employee whom the Landlord engages to provide the services under clauses 12 and 13

  (c) include interest at no more than the Law Society's interest rate on sums the Landlord borrows to discharge his obligations under clauses 12 and 13

3.3 the Tenant is to pay the Landlord interim payments on account of the service charge within 21 days of receiving a written demand setting out how it is calculated

3.4 an interim payment is to be the Tenant's fair proportion of what the service costs are reasonably likely to be in the three months following the demand

3.5 the Landlord is not entitled to demand interim payments more than once in every three months

3.6 the Landlord is to keep full records of the service costs and at least once a year is to send the Tenant an account setting out, for the period since the beginning of the lease period or the last account as the case may be:

  (a) the amount of the service costs

  (b) the service charge the Tenant is to pay

  (c) the total of any interim payments the Tenant has paid

  (d) the difference between the total interim payments and the service charge

3.7 within 21 days after the Tenant receives the account, the amount mentioned in clause 3.6(d) is to be settled by payment between the parties except that the Landlord is entitled to retain any overpayment towards any interim payments he has demanded for a later accounting period

3.8 the Landlord is either:

  (a) to have the account certified by an independent chartered accountant, or

  (b) to allow the Tenant to inspect the books records invoices and receipts relating to the service costs

3.8 disagreements about the amounts of the service charge or the service costs are to be decided by arbitration under clause 17.5

4   USE

4. The Tenant is to comply with the following requirements as to the use of the building and any part of it, and is not to authorise or allow anyone else to contravene them:

4.1 to use the property only for the use allowed

4.2 not to obstruct any part of the building used for access to the property or any other part of the building

4.3 not to do anything which might invalidate any insurance policy covering any part of the building or which might increase the premium

4.4 not to hold an auction sale in the property

4.5 not to use any part of the building for any activities which are dangerous, offensive, noxious, illegal or immoral, or which are or may become a nuisance or annoyance to the Landlord or to the owner or occupier of any other part of the building or of any neighbouring property

4.6 not to display any advertisements on the outside of the property or which are visible from outside the property unless the Landlord consents (and the Landlord is not entitled to withhold that consent unreasonably)

4.7 not to overload the floors or walls of the property

4.8 to comply with the terms of every Act of Parliament, order, regulation, bye-law, rule, licence and registration authorising or regulating how the property is used, and to obtain, renew and continue any licence or registration which is required

5   ACCESS

5. The Tenant is to give the Landlord, or anyone authorised by him in writing, access to the property:

5.1 for these purposes:

  (a) inspecting the condition of the property, or how it is being used

  (b) doing works which the Landlord is permitted to do under clauses 6.11(c) or 13

  (c) complying with any statutory obligation

  (d) viewing the property as a prospective buyer, tenant or mortgagee

  (e) valuing the property

  (f) inspecting, cleaning or repairing neighbouring property, or any sewers, drains, pipes, wires, cables serving the building or any neighbouring property

5.2 and only on seven days' written notice except in an emergency

5.3 and during normal business hours except in an emergency

5.4 and the Landlord is promptly to make good all damage caused to the property and any goods there in exercising these rights

L.S.1/2

2

6　CONDITION AND WORK

6. The Tenant is to comply with the following duties in relation to the property:

6.1 to maintain the state and condition of the inside of the property but the Tenant need not alter or improve it except if required in clause 6.10

6.2 to decorate the inside of the property:

(a) in every fifth year of the lease period

(b) in the last three months of the lease period (however it ends) except to the extent that it has been decorated in the previous year

6.3 where the property has a shop front to maintain and decorate it

6.4 when decorating, the Tenant is to use the colours and the types of finish used previously

6.5 but the Tenant need only make good damage caused by an insured risk to the extent that the insurance money had not been paid because of any act or default of the Tenant

6.6 the inside of the property is to include all ceilings, floors, doors, door frames, windows, window frames and plate glass and the internal surfaces of all walls but is to exclude joists immediately above the ceilings and supporting floors

6.7 not to make any structural alterations or additions to the property

6.8 not to make any other alterations unless with the Landlord's consent in writing (and the Landlord is not entitled to withhold that consent unreasonably)

6.9 to keep any plate glass in the property insured for its full replacement cost with reputable insurers, to give the Landlord details of that insurance on request, and to replace any plate glass which becomes damaged

6.10 to do the work to the property which any authority acting under an Act of Parliament requires even if it alters or improves the property. Before the Tenant does so, the Landlord is to:

(a) give his consent in writing to the work

(b) contribute a fair proportion of the cost of the work taking into account any value to him of that work

6.11 if the Tenant fails to do any work which this lease requires him to do and the Landlord gives him written notice to do it, the Tenant is to:

(a) start the work within two months, or immediately in case of emergency, and

(b) proceed diligently with the work

(c) in default, permit the Landlord to do the work

6.12 any dispute arising under clause 6.10(b) is to be decided by arbitration under clause 17.5

7　TRANSFER ETC.

7. The Tenant is to comply with the following:

7.1 the Tenant is not to share occupation of the property and no part of it is to be transferred, sublet or occupied separately from the remainder

7.2 the Tenant is not to transfer or sublet the whole of the property unless the Landlord gives his written consent in advance, and the Landlord is not entitled to withhold that consent unreasonably

7.3 any sublease is to be on terms which are consistent with this lease, but is not to permit the sub-tenant to underlet

7.4 within four weeks after the property is transferred mortgaged or sublet, the Landlord's solicitors are to be notified and a copy of the transfer mortgage or sublease sent to them for registration with the fee payable under clause 2.3

7.5 if the Landlord requires, a Tenant who transfers the whole of the property is to give the Landlord a written guarantee, in the terms set out in the Guarantee Box, that the Transferee will perform his obligations as Tenant

8　OTHER MATTERS

8. The Tenant:

8.1 is to give the Landlord a copy of any notice concerning the property or any neighbouring property as soon as he receives it

8.2 is to allow the Landlord, during the last six months of the lease period, to fix a notice in a reasonable position on the outside of the property announcing that it is for sale or to let

8.3 is not to apply for planning permission relating to the use or alteration of the property unless the Landlord gives written consent in advance

9　RENT REVIEW

9.1 On each rent review date, the rent is to increase to the market rent if that is higher than the rent applying before that date

9.2 The market rent is the rent which a willing tenant would pay for the property on the open market, if let to him on the rent review date by a willing landlord on a lease on the same terms as this lease without any premium and for a period equal to the remainder of the lease period, assuming that at that date:

(a) the willing tenant takes account of any likelihood that he would be entitled to a new lease of the property when the lease ends, but does not take account of any goodwill belonging to anyone who had occupied the property;

(b) the property is vacant and had not been occupied by the Tenant or any sub-tenant;

(c) the property can immediately be used;

(d) the property is in the condition required by this lease and any damage caused by any of the risks insured under clause 12 has been made good;

(e) during the lease period no Tenant or Sub-Tenant has done anything to the property to increase or decrease its rental value and "anything" includes work done by the Tenant to comply with clause 6.10, but nothing else which the Tenant was obliged to do under this lease

9.3 If the Landlord and the Tenant agree the amount of the new rent, a statement of that new rent, signed by them, is to be attached to this lease

9.4 If the Landlord and the Tenant have not agreed the amount of the new rent two months before the rent review date, either of them may require the new rent to be decided by arbitration under clause 17.5

9.5

(a) The Tenant is to continue to pay rent at the rate applying before the rent review date until the next rent day after the new rent is agreed or decided

(b) Starting on that rent day, the Tenant is to pay the new rent

(c) On that rent day, the Tenant is also to pay any amount by which the new rent since the rent review date exceeds the rent paid, with interest on that amount at 2% below the Law Society's interest rate

10　DAMAGE

10. If the property is or the common parts are damaged by any of the risks to be insured under clause 12 and as a result of that damage the property, or any part of it, cannot be used for the use allowed:

10.1 the rent, or a fair proportion of it, is to be suspended for three years or until the property or the common parts are fully restored, if sooner

10.2 if at any time it is unlikely that the property or the common parts will be fully restored within three years from the date of the damage, the Landlord (so long as he has not wilfully delayed the restoration) or the Tenant may end this lease by giving one month's notice to the other during the three year period, in which case

(a) the insurance money belongs to the Landlord and

(b) the Landlord's obligation to make good damage under clause 12 ceases

10.3 a notice given outside the time limits in clause 10.2 is not effective

10.4 The Tenant cannot claim the benefit of this clause to the extent that the insurers refuse to pay the insurance money because of his act or default

10.5 any dispute arising under any part of this clause is to be decided by arbitration under clause 17.5

LANDLORD'S OBLIGATIONS AND FORFEITURE RIGHTS

11　QUIET ENJOYMENT

11. While the Tenant complies with the terms of this lease, the Landlord is to allow the Tenant to possess and use the property without lawful interference from the Landlord, anyone who derives title from the Landlord or any trustee for the Landlord

L.S.1/3

3

12 INSURANCE

12. The Landlord agrees with the Tenant:

12.1 the Landlord is to keep the building (except the plate glass) insured with the reputable insurers to cover

(a) full rebuilding, site clearance, professional fees, value added tax and three years' loss of rent

(b) against fire, lightning, explosion, earthquake, landslip, subsidence, heave, riot, civil commotion, aircraft, aerial devices, storm, flood, water, theft, impact by vehicles, damage by malicious persons and vandals and third party liability and any other risks reasonably required by the Landlord

so far as cover is available at the normal insurance rates for the locality and subject to reasonable excesses and exclusions

12.2 and to take all necessary steps to make good as soon as possible damage to the building caused by insured risks except to the extent that the insurance money is not paid because of the act or default of the Tenant

12.3 and to give the Tenant at his request once a year particulars of the policy and evidence from the insurer that it is in force

12.4 and that the Tenant is not responsible for any damage for which the Landlord is compensated under the insurance policy

13 SERVICES

13. The Landlord is to comply with the following duties in relation to the building:

13.1 to maintain the state and condition (including the decorations) of:

(a) the structure, outside, roof, foundations, joists, floor slabs, load bearing walls, beams and columns of the building

(b) those parts of the building which tenants of more than one part can use ("the common parts")

13.2 to decorate the common parts and the outside of the building every five years, using colours and types of finish reasonably decided by the Landlord

13.3 to pay promptly all periodic rates, taxes and outgoings relating to the common parts, including any imposed after the date of this lease (even if of a novel nature)

13.4 to pay or contribute to the cost of repairing, maintaining and cleaning party walls, party structures, yards, gardens, roads, paths, gutters, drains, sewers, pipes, conduits, wires, cables and other things used or shared with the other property

13.5 to provide the services listed on page 5, but the Landlord is not to be liable for failure or delay caused by industrial disputes, shortage of supplies, adverse weather conditions or other causes beyond the control of the Landlord

14 FORFEITURE

14. This lease comes to an end if the Landlord forfeits it by entering any part of the property, which the Landlord is entitled to do whenever:

(a) payment of any rent is fourteen days overdue, even if it was not formally demanded

(b) the Tenant has not complied with any of the terms in this lease

(c) the Tenant if an individual (and if more than one, any of them) is adjudicated bankrupt or an interim receiver of his property is appointed

(d) the Tenant if a company (and if more than one, any of them) goes into liquidation (unless solely for the purpose of amalgamation or reconstruction when solvent), or had an administrative receiver appointed or had an administration order made in respect of it

The forfeiture of this lease does not cancel any outstanding obligation of the Tenant or a Guarantor

15 END OF LEASE

15. When this lease ends the Tenant is to:

15.1 return the property of the Landlord leaving it in the state and condition in which this lease requires the Tenant to keep it

15.2 (if the Landlord so requires) remove anything the Tenant fixed to the property and make good any damage which that causes

PROPERTY RIGHTS

16 BOUNDARIES

16.1 This lease does not let to the Tenant the external surfaces of the outside walls of the property and anything above the ceilings and below the floors

FACILITIES

16.2 The Tenant is to have the use, whether or not exclusive, of any of the following facilities:

the right for the Tenant and visitors to come and go to and from the property over the parts of the building designed or designated to afford access to the property, the rights previously enjoyed by the property for shelter and support and for service wires, pipes and drains to pass through them, and the right to park vehicles in any designated parking area subject to any reasonable rules made by the Landlord

16.3 The Landlord is to have the rights previously enjoyed over the property by other parts of the building for shelter and support and for service wires, pipes and drains to pass through it, and the right for the Landlord and his tenants and their visitors to come and go to and from the other parts of the building over the parts of the property designated for that purpose

GENERAL

17 PARTIES' RESPONSIBILITY

17.1 Whenever more than one person or company is the Landlord, the Tenant or the Guarantor, their obligations can be enforced against all or both of them jointly and against each individually

LANDLORD

17.2

(a) The obligations in this lease continue to apply to the Landlord until he is released by the Tenant or by a declaration of the court

(b) The current owner of the Landlord's interest in the property must comply with the Landlord's obligations in this lease

TENANT

17.3

(a) A transfer of this lease releases the Tenant from any future obligations under it. This does not apply in the case of a transfer made without the Landlord's consent or as a result of the Tenant's death or bankruptcy

(b) After a transfer, the Tenant's successor must comply with the Tenant's obligations in this lease

SERVICE OF NOTICE

17.4 The rules about serving notices in Section 196 of the Law of Property Act 1925 (as since amended) apply to any notice given under this lease

ARBITRATION

17.5 Any matter which this lease requires to be decided by arbitration is to be referred to a single arbitrator under the Arbitration Acts. The Landlord and the Tenant may agree the appointment of the arbitrator, or either of them may apply to the President of the Royal Institution of Chartered Surveyors to make the appointment

HEADINGS

17.6 The headings do not form part of this lease

18 STAMP DUTY

This lease has not been granted to implement an agreement for a lease

L.S.1/4

4

SERVICES

These are the services mentioned in clause 13.5
(delete or add as required)

Cleaning of the common parts

Lighting of the common parts

Heating of the common parts

Lift maintenance

Hot and cold water to wash hand basins in the common parts

Porterage

Fire extinguishers in the common parts

Heating in the property

Window cleaning for the building

Furnishing the common parts

GUARANTEE BOX

The terms in this box only take effect if a guarantor is named and then only until the Tenant transfers this lease with the Landlord's written consent. The Guarantor must sign this lease.

'Guarantor':

of

agrees to compensate the Landlord for any loss incurred as a result of the Tenant failing to comply with an obligation in this lease during the lease period or any statutory extension of it. If the Tenant is insolvent and this lease ends because it is disclaimed, the Guarantor agrees to accept a new lease, if the Landlord so requires, in the same form but at the rent then payable. Even if the Landlord gives the Tenant extra time to comply with an obligation, or does not insist on strict compliance with terms of this lease, the Guarantor's obligation remains fully effective.

THIS DOCUMENT CREATES LEGAL RIGHTS AND LEGAL OBLIGATIONS. DO NOT SIGN IT UNTIL YOU HAVE CONSULTED A SOLICITOR. THERE IS A CODE OF PRACTICE CONCERNING COMMERCIAL LEASES IN ENGLAND AND WALES PUBLISHED UNDER THE AUSPICES OF THE DEPARTMENT OF THE ENVIRONMENT.

Signed as a deed by/on behalf of the
Landlord and delivered in the presence of:

....

Landlord

....

Witness

....

Witness's occupation and address

Signed as a deed by/on behalf of the
Tenant and delivered in the presence of:

....

Tenant

....

Witness

....

Witness's occupation and address

Signed as a deed by/on behalf of the
Guarantor and delivered in the presence of:

....

Guarantor

....

Witness

....

Witness's occupation and address

L.S.1/5

5

VI.   STANDARD UNDERTAKINGS
VI.1.   Agreed form of wording with banks for undertaking for bridging finance

FORM No. 4 (BRIDGING FINANCE)

Undertaking by solicitor (with form of authority from client) to account to bank for net proceeds of sale of the existing property, the bank having provided funds in connection with the purchase of the new property.

Authority from client(s)

. . . . . 19 . . . . .

To . . . . (name and address of solicitors)

I/We hereby irrevocably authorise and request you to give an undertaking in the form set out below and accordingly to pay the net proceeds of sale after deduction of your costs to . . . . Bank plc . . . . Branch.

Signature of client(s) . . . .

Undertaking

. . . . .19 . . . . .

To: . . . . **Bank plc**
If you provide facilities to my/our client . . . .
for the purchase of the freehold/leasehold property (the new property)
. . . . (description of property)

pending the sale by my/our client of the freehold/leasehold property (the existing property)
. . . . (description of property)

I/We undertake:

1.   That any sums received from you or your customer will be applied solely for the following purposes:

    (a)   *in discharging the present mortgage(s) on the existing property* [*delete if not applicable*];

    (b)   in acquiring a good marketable title to the new property, *subject to the mortgage mentioned below* [*delete if not applicable*];

    (c)   in paying any necessary deposit, legal fees, costs and disbursements in connection with the purchase.

The purchase price contemplated is £ .... gross.

I/We are informed that a sum of £ .... is being advanced on mortgage by .... [*delete if not applicable*]. The amount required from my/our client for the transaction including the deposit and together with costs, disbursements and apportionments is not expected to exceed £ ....

2. To hold to your order when received by me/us the documents of title of the existing property pending completion of the sale (unless subject to any prior mortgage(s) and of the new property (unless subject to any prior mortgage(s)).

3. To pay to you the net proceeds of sale of the existing property when received by me/us. The sale price contemplated is £ .... and the only deductions which will have to be made at present known to me/us are:

    (i)   the deposit (if not held by me/us),

    (ii)   the estate agents' commission,

    (iii) the amount required to redeem any mortgages and charges, which so far as known to me/us at present do not exceed £ ....

    (iv) the legal fees, costs and disbursements relating to the transaction.

4. To advise you immediately of any subsequent claim by a third party upon the net proceeds of sale of which I/we have knowledge.

NOTES

(1) If any deductions will have to be made from the net proceeds of sale other than those shown above, these must be specifically mentioned.

(2) It would be convenient if this form of undertaking were presented in duplicate so that a copy could be retained by the solicitor.

VI.2. Recommended form of undertaking for discharge of building society mortgages

'In consideration of your today completing the purchase of . . . .

WE HEREBY UNDERTAKE forthwith to pay over to the . . . .

Building Society the money required to redeem the mortgage/legal charge dated . . . . .

. . . . and to forward the receipted mortgage/legal charge to you as soon

as it is received by us from the . . . . Building Society.'

VI

VI.3. 'Pink card' warning on undertakings – practice information[1]

Cost to the profession

The giving of sloppy or negligent undertakings is a considerable drain on the Solicitors' Indemnity Fund and the Compensation Fund. SIF estimate that such undertakings cost in excess of £5 million per annum. However, many undertakings may result in a liability within the deductible (i.e. excess) – exposing solicitors to considerable personal liability. Your work is made easier because people know they can rely on a solicitor's undertaking. However, it can be a two-edged sword. The wide and routine use of undertakings can result in a lack of care. The profession can no longer afford to underwrite the bill!

Remember – there is **no** obligation on a solicitor to give an undertaking, even to assist the progress of a client's matter.

Financial guarantees

Think twice before standing guarantor for a client – you could be personally liable for a substantial sum. There can be cases where SIF provides no cover if an undertaking is given which amounts to a bare guarantee of the financial obligations of a client or third party. Moreover, you would have no cover from SIF if you give an undertaking to a lender to repay money which you have borrowed and which you then re-lend to a client who subsequently defaults.

Be **SMART** when giving undertakings – make sure they are:

S Specific

Undertakings should refer to a particular task or action which has been clearly identified and defined. Do not give general or open-ended undertakings, such as an undertaking to discharge "all outstanding mortgages on a property" or the "usual undertaking". Make sure that any undertaking to pay monies out of a fund is qualified by the proviso that the fund comes into your hands, **and** that it is sufficient.

M Measurable

Undertakings should include agreed measures or steps which are understood by both parties and can easily be monitored or checked, so that there can be no dispute as to whether an undertaking has been fully discharged. If an undertaking involves the payment of a sum of money, make sure the amount is clear or that it is easy to calculate. Ambiguous undertakings will be construed in favour of the recipient.

A Agreed

Undertakings should be expressly agreed by both the person giving and the person receiving

---

1. May 1993.

them and should be confirmed in writing. They may be given orally or in writing and need not necessarily include the word "undertake" − beware of inadvertent undertakings.

R Realistic

Undertakings should be achievable. Before giving an undertaking consider carefully whether you will be able to implement it. If any events must happen before you will be able to implement your undertaking, it is good practice to spell out those events on the face of the undertaking. An undertaking is still binding even if it is to do something outside your control. As **you** give the undertaking − you **can** stay in control.

T Timed

Undertakings should indicate when, or on the happening of which event, they will be implemented. In the absence of an express term, there is an implied term that an undertaking will be performed within a reasonable time, having regard to its nature.

General points

Costs

- Don't ask other solicitors to provide an undertaking in terms you wouldn't give yourself. This applies particularly to undertakings as to costs: it's unfair to expect another solicitor to give an open-ended undertaking to pay your costs. Be prepared to give an upper limit or agree a basis of charging.

- An undertaking to pay another party's costs is generally discharged if the matter does not proceed to completion. If you intend some other arrangement, make this clear.

Conveyancing

- The Law Society's formulae for exchange of contracts and its Code for Completion by Post contain certain undertakings. Are you sure that you and your staff really know what undertakings they are giving in a normal conveyancing transaction?

- Make sure that each of your replies to requisitions on title concerning mortgages specifies exactly which mortgages or charges you intend to discharge. Vague replies will probably result in you being liable to discharge all charges − whether you know of them or not.

- Do not give unconditional undertakings without sufficient enquiry into the amount owed on prior charges − don't always rely on what your client tells you.

- If your ability to comply with an undertaking depends upon action to be taken by another solicitor, make sure that he or she will be able to comply, e.g. by obtaining an undertaking to a similar effect.

- Beware of bank "standard form" undertakings − they sometimes go beyond what is in your control − it may be necessary to amend them.

Good management

- Principals are responsible for undertakings given by staff. Clear guidance should be given to staff, specifying those permitted to give undertakings and prescribing the manner in which they can be given. Find out how safe you are by doing an "undertaking audit" − ask staff to check files for undischarged undertakings. Note how many have been given in a sloppy or negligent manner and calculate the size of the potential claims if things go wrong. Then introduce a system to put things right. This might be to:

- draw up standard undertakings for use, where possible, by all fee-earners, with any deviation from the norm to be authorised by a partner;

- have all undertakings checked by another fee-earner prior to being given (or at least those which amount to a financial obligation);

- confirm all telephone undertakings (given or received) in writing;

- make sure that undertakings are not overlooked by:

    - copying undertakings and attaching them to the file;

    - indicating on the file cover, using coloured labels, that an undertaking has been given and its date.

The Guide to the Professional Conduct of Solicitors has a chapter about undertakings which contains useful guidance — please read it!

BE SMART!

VII. FORMULAE

VII.1. The Law Society's formulae for exchanging contracts by telephone, fax or telex[1]

Introduction

It is essential that an agreed memorandum of the details and of any variations of the formula used should be made at the time and retained in the file. This would be very important if any question on the exchange were raised subsequently. Agreed variations should also be confirmed in writing. The serious risks of exchanging contracts without a deposit, unless the full implications are explained to and accepted by the seller client, are demonstrated in *Morris* v. *Duke-Cohan & Co.* [1975] 119 S.J. 826.

As those persons involved in the exchange will bind their firms to the undertakings in the formula used, solicitors should carefully consider who is to be authorised to exchange contracts by telephone or telex and should ensure that the use of the procedure is restricted to them. Since professional undertakings form the basis of the formulae, they are only recommended for use between firms of solicitors and licensed conveyancers.

Law Society telephone/telex exchange - Formula A (1986)

(for use where one solicitor holds both signed parts of the contract):

A completion date of   19   is agreed. The solicitor holding both parts of the contract confirms that he or she holds the part signed by his or her client(s), which is identical to the part he or she is also holding signed by the other solicitor's client(s) and will forthwith insert the agreed completion date in each part.

Solicitors mutually agree that exchange shall take place from that moment and the solicitor holding both parts confirms that, as of that moment, he or she holds the part signed by his or her client(s) to the order of the other. He or she undertakes that day by first class post, or where the other solicitor is a member of a document exchange (as to which the inclusion of a reference thereto in the solicitor's letterhead shall be conclusive evidence) by delivery to that or any other affiliated exchange, or by hand delivery direct to that solicitor's office, to send his or her signed part of the contract to the other solicitor, together, where he or she is the purchaser's solicitor, with a banker's draft or a solicitor's client account cheque for the deposit amounting to £..... .

Note:

1.   A memorandum should be prepared, after use of the formula, recording:

    (a)   date and time of exchange;

    (b)   the formula used and exact wording of agreed variations;

---

1. Formulae A and B: 9 July 1986, revised January 1996. Formula C: 15 March 1989, revised January 1996.

    (c)   the completion date;

    (d)   the (balance) deposit to be paid;

    (e)   the identities of those involved in any conversation.

Law Society telephone/telex exchange - Formula B (1986)

(for use where each solicitor holds his or her own client's signed part of the contract):

A completion date of   19   is agreed. Each solicitor confirms to the other that he or she holds a part contract in the agreed form signed by the client(s) and will forthwith insert the agreed completion date.

Each solicitor undertakes to the other thenceforth to hold the signed part of the contract to the other's order, so that contracts are exchanged at that moment. Each solicitor further undertakes that day by first class post, or, where the other solicitor is a member of a document exchange (as to which the inclusion of a reference thereto in the solicitor's letterhead shall be conclusive evidence) by delivery to that or any other affiliated exchange, or by hand delivery direct to that solicitor's office, to send his or her signed part of the contract to the other together, in the case of a purchaser's solicitor, with a banker's draft or a solicitor's client account cheque for the deposit amounting to £...... .

Notes:

1.   A memorandum should be prepared, after use of the formula, recording:

    (a)   date and time of exchange;

    (b)   the formula used and exact wording of agreed variations;

    (c)   the completion date;

    (d)   the (balance) deposit to be paid;

    (e)   the identities of those involved in any conversation.

2.   Those who are going to effect the exchange must first confirm the details in order to ensure that both parts are identical. This means in particular, that if either part of the contract has been amended since it was originally prepared, the solicitor who holds a part contract with the amendments must disclose them, so that it can be confirmed that the other part is similarly amended.

Law Society telephone/fax/telex exchange - Formula C (1989)

Part I

The following is agreed:

Final time for exchange: pm

Completion date: 19

Deposit to be paid to:

Each solicitor confirms that he or she holds a part of the contract in the agreed form signed by his or her client, or, if there is more than one client, by all of them. Each solicitor undertakes to the other that:

(a)   he or she will continue to hold that part of the contract until the final time for exchange on the date the formula is used, and

(b)   if the vendor's solicitor so notifies the purchaser's solicitor by fax, telephone or telex (whichever was previously agreed) by that time, they will both comply with part II of the formula.

The purchaser's solicitor further undertakes that either he or she or some other named person in his or her office will be available up to the final time for exchange to activate part II of the formula on receipt of the telephone call, fax or telex from the vendor's solicitors.

Part II

Each solicitor undertakes to the other henceforth to hold the part of the contract in his or her possession to the other's order, so that contracts are exchanged at that moment, and to despatch it to the other on that day. The purchaser's solicitor further undertakes to the vendor's solicitor to despatch on that day, or to arrange for the despatch on that day of, a banker's draft or a solicitor's client account cheque for the full deposit specified in the agreed form of contract (divided as the vendor's solicitor may have specified) to the vendor's solicitor and/or to some other solicitor whom the vendor's solicitor nominates, to be held on formula C terms.

'To despatch' means to send by first class post, or, where the other solicitor is a member of a document exchange (as to which the inclusion of a reference thereto in the solicitor's letterhead is to be conclusive evidence) by delivery to that or any other affiliated exchange, or by hand delivery direct to the recipient solicitor's office. 'Formula C terms' means that the deposit is held as stakeholder, or as agent for the vendor with authority to part with it only for the purpose of passing it to another solicitor as deposit in a related property purchase transaction on these terms.

Notes

1.   Two memoranda will be required when using formula C. One needs to record the use of part I, and a second needs to record the request of the vendor's solicitor to the purchaser's solicitor to activate part II.

2.   The first memorandum should record:

(a)   the date and time when it was agreed to use formula C;

(b)   the exact wording of any agreed variations;

(c)   the final time, later that day, for exchange;

(d)   the completion date;

(e)   the name of the solicitor to whom the deposit was to be paid, or details of amounts and names if it was to be split; and

(f)   the identities of those involved in any conversation.

3.   Formula C assumes the payment of a full contractual deposit (normally 10%).

4.   The contract term relating to the deposit must allow it to be passed on, with payment direct from payer to ultimate recipient, in the way in which the formula contemplates. The deposit must ultimately be held by a solicitor as stakeholder. Whilst some variation in the formula can be agreed this is a term of the formula which must *not* be varied, unless all the solicitors involved in the chain have agreed.

5.   If a buyer proposes to use a deposit guarantee policy, formula C will need substantial adaptation.

6.   It is essential prior to agreeing part I of formula C that those effecting the exchange ensure that both parts of the contract are identical.

7.   Using formula C involves a solicitor in giving a number of professional undertakings. These must be performed precisely. Any failure will be a serious breach of professional discipline. One of the undertakings may be to arrange that somone over whom the solicitor has no control will do something (i.e. to arrange for someone else to despatch the cheque or banker's draft in payment of the deposit). An undertaking is still binding even if it is to do something outside the solicitor's control [see **18.03,** p.314 of *The Guide to the Professional Conduct of Solicitors 1996*].

8.   Solicitors do not as a matter of law have an automatic authority to exchange contracts on a formula C basis, and should always ensure that they have the client's express authority to use formula C. A suggested form of authority is set out below. It should be adapted to cover any special circumstances:

> I/We............................ understand that my/our sale and purchase of .... are both part of a chain of linked property transactions, in which all parties want the security of contracts which become binding on the same day.

> I/We agree that you should make arrangements with the other solicitors or licensed conveyancers involved to achieve this.

> I/We understand that this involves each property-buyer offering, early on one day, to exchange contracts whenever, later that day, the seller so requests, and that the buyer's offer is on the basis that it cannot be withdrawn or varied during that day.

> I/We agree that when I/we authorise you to exchange contracts, you may agree to exchange contracts on the above basis and give any necessary undertakings to the other parties involved in the chain and that my/our authority to you cannot be revoked throughout the day on which the offer to exchange contracts is made.

VII.2.   The Law Society's Code for Completion by Post[1]

Preamble

The code provides a procedure for postal completion which practising solicitors may adopt by reference.

First, each solicitor must satisfy himself or herself that no circumstances exist that are likely to give rise to a conflict between this code and the interests of his or her own client (including where applicable a mortgagee client).

The code, where adopted, will apply without variation except so far as recorded in writing beforehand.

The Code

1.   Adoption hereof must be specifically agreed by all the solicitors concerned and preferably in writing.

2.   On completion the vendor's solicitor will act as agent for the purchaser's solicitor without fee or disbursements.

3.   The vendor's solicitor undertakes that on completion he or she:

    (1)   will have the vendor's authority to receive the purchase money; and

    (2)   will be the duly authorised agent of the proprietor of any charge upon the property to receive the part of the money paid to him or her which is needed to discharge such charge.

4.   The purchaser's solicitor shall send to the vendor's solicitor instructions as to:

    (1)   documents to be examined and marked;

    (2)   memoranda to be endorsed;

    (3)   deeds, documents, undertakings and authorities relating to rents, deposits, keys, etc; and

    (4)   any other relevant matters.

In default of instructions, the vendor's solicitor shall not be under any duty to examine, mark or endorse any documents.

5.   The purchaser's solicitor shall remit to the vendor's solicitor the balance due on completion specified in the vendor's solicitor's completion statement or with written notification; in default of either, the balance shown due by the contract. If the funds are remitted by transfer between banks, the vendor's solicitor shall instruct his bank to advise him or her by telephone immediately the funds are received. The vendor's solicitor shall hold such funds to the purchaser's solicitor's order pending completion.

6.   The vendor's solicitor, having received the items specified in paragraphs 4 and 5, shall forthwith, or at such later times as may have been agreed, complete. Thereupon he or she

---

1. 1984, revised January 1996.

shall hold all documents and other items to be sent to the purchaser's solicitor as agent for such solicitor.

7.   Once completion has taken place, the vendor's solicitor shall as soon as possible thereafter on the same day confirm the fact to the purchaser's solicitor by telephone, fax or telex and shall also as soon as possible send by first class post or document exchange written confirmation to the purchaser's solicitor, together with the enclosures referred to in paragraph 4 hereof. The vendor's solicitor shall ensure that such title deeds and any other items are correctly committed to the post or document exchange. Thereafter, they are at the risk of the purchaser's solicitor.

8.   If either the authorities specified in paragraph 3, or the instructions specified in paragraph 4, or the funds specified in paragraph 5, have not been received by the vendor's solicitor by the agreed completion date and time, he or she shall forthwith notify the purchaser's solicitor and request further instructions.

9.   Nothing herein shall override any rights and obligations of parties under the contract or otherwise.

10.   Any dispute or difference which may arise between solicitors that is directly referable to a completion agreed to be carried out in accordance herewith, whether or not amended or supplemented in any way, shall be referred to an arbitrator to be agreed, within one month of any such dispute or difference arising between the solicitors who are party thereto, and, in the default of such agreement, on the application of any such solicitor, to an arbitrator to be appointed by the President of the Law Society.

11.   Reference herein to vendor's solicitor and purchaser's solicitor shall, where appropriate, be deemed to include solicitors acting for parties other than vendor and purchaser.

Notes:

1.   The object of the code is to provide solicitors with a convenient means for completion, on an agency basis, that can be adopted for use, where they so agree beforehand, in completions where a representative of the purchaser's solicitors is not attending at the office of the vendor's solicitors for the purpose.

2.   As with the Law Society's formulae for exchange of contracts by telephone/telex/fax [See Appendix VII.1 above], the code embodies professional undertakings and is, in consequence, only recommended for adoption between solicitors.

3.   Clause 2 of the code expressly provides that the vendor's solicitor will act as agent for the purchaser's solicitor without fee or disbursements. It is envisaged that, in the usual case, the convenience of not having to make a specific appointment on the day of completion for the purchaser's solicitor to attend for the purpose will offset the agency work that the vendor's solicitor has to do and any postage payable in completing under the code, and on the basis that most solicitors will from time to time act both for the vendors and purchasers. If, nevertheless, a vendor's solicitor does consider that charges and/or disbursements are necessary in a particular case, as such an arrangement represents a variation in the code, it should be agreed in writing beforehand.

4.   Having regard to the decision in *Edward Wong Finance Co Ltd* v. *Johnson, Stokes & Master* [1984] A.C. 1296, clause 3 (2) of the code requires the vendor's solicitor to confirm, before agreeing to use the code, that he or she will be the duly authorised agent of the proprietor of any charge upon the property (typically but not exclusively the vendor's building society) to receive that part of the money paid which is needed to discharge such charge.

5. Clause 9 of the code provides that nothing therein shall override any rights and obligations of parties under the contract or otherwise.

The above notes refer only to some of the points that practitioners may wish to consider before agreeing to adopt the code. It is emphasised that it is a matter for the solicitors concerned to read the code in full, so that they can decide whether they will make use of it as it stands or with any variations agreed in writing beforehand, whether or not they are referred to in the above notes.

VIII. COSTS AND FEES

VIII.1. Solicitors' (Non-Contentious Business) Remuneration Order 1994 (S.I. 1994/2616)

1994 No. 2616

SOLICITORS

The Solicitors' (Non-Contentious Business) Remuneration Order 1994

Made	*5th October 1994*
Laid before Parliament	*10th October 1994*
Coming into force	*1st November 1994*

The Lord Chancellor, the Lord Chief Justice, the Master of the Rolls, the President of the Law Society, the president of Holborn law society and the Chief Land Registrar (in respect of business done under the Land Registration Act 1925(a)), together constituting the committee authorised to make orders under section 56 of the Solicitors Act 1974(b), in exercise of the powers conferred on them by that section and having complied with the requirements of section 56 (3), hereby make the following Order:

Citation, commencement and revocation

1. (1) This Order may be cited as the Solicitors' (Non-Contentious Business) Remuneration Order 1994.

(2) This Order shall come into force on 1st November 1994 and shall apply to all non-contentious business for which bills are delivered on or after that date.

(3) The Solicitors' Remuneration Order 1972(c) is hereby revoked except in its application to business for which bills are delivered before this Order comes into force.

Interpretation

2. In this Order:

"client" means the client of a solicitor;
"costs" means the amount charged in a solicitor's bill, exclusive of disbursements and value added tax, in respect of non-contentious business or common form probate business;
"entitled person" means a client or an entitled third party;
"entitled third party" means a residuary beneficiary absolutely and immediately (and not contingently) entitled to an inheritance, where a solicitor has charged the estate for his professional costs for acting in the administration of the estate, and *either*

(a) 1925 c.21.

(b) 1974 c.47, as modified by the Administration of Justice Act 1985 (c.61), Schedule 2, paragraphs 22 and 23.

(c) S.I. 1972/1139.

(a) the only personal representatives are solicitors (whether or not acting in a professional capacity); or

(b) the only personal representatives are solicitors acting jointly with partners or employees in a professional capacity;

"paid disbursements" means disbursements already paid by the solicitor;
"recognised body" means a body corporate recognised by the Council under section 9 of the Administration of Justice Act 1985**(d);**
"remuneration certificate" means a certificate issued by the Council pursuant to this Order;
"residuary beneficiary" includes a person entitled to all or part of the residue of an intestate estate;
"solicitor" includes a recognised body;
"the Council" means the Council of the Law Society.

Solicitors' costs

3. A solicitor's costs shall be such sum as may be fair and reasonable to both solicitor and entitled person, having regard to all the circumstances of the case and in particular to:

(a) the complexity of the matter or the difficulty or novelty of the questions raised;

(b) the skill, labour, specialised knowledge and responsibility involved;

(c) the time spent on the business;

(d) the number and importance of the documents prepared or perused, without regard to length;

(e) the place where and the circumstances in which the business or any part thereof is transacted;

(f) the amount or value of any money or property involved;

(g) whether any land involved is registered land;

(h) the importance of the matter to the client; and

(i) the approval (express or implied) of the entitled person or the express approval of the testator to:

(i) the solicitor undertaking all or any part of the work giving rise to the costs; or

(ii) the amount of the costs.

Right to certification

4. (1) Without prejudice to the provisions of sections 70, 71, and 72 of the Solicitors Act 1974 (which relate to taxation of costs), an entitled person may, subject to the provisions of this Order, require a solicitor to obtain a remuneration certificate from the Council in respect of a bill which has been delivered where the costs are not more than £50,000.

(2) The remuneration certificate must state what sum, in the opinion of the Council, would be a fair and reasonable charge for the business covered by the bill (whether it be the sum charged or a lesser sum). In the absence of taxation the sum payable in respect of such costs is the sum stated in the remuneration certificate.

(d) 1985 c.61.

Disciplinary and other measures

5. (1)   If on a taxation the taxing officer allows less than one half of the costs, he must bring the facts of the case to the attention of the Council.

(2)   The provisions of this Order are without prejudice to the general powers of the Council under the Solicitors Act 1974.

Commencement of proceedings against a client

6.   Before a solicitor brings proceedings to recover costs against a client on a bill for non-contentious business he must inform the client in writing of the matters specified in article 8, except where the bill has been taxed.

Costs paid by deduction

7. (1)   If a solicitor deducts his costs from monies held for or on behalf of a client or of an estate in satisfaction of a bill and an entitled person objects in writing to the amount of the bill within the prescribed time, the solicitor must immediately inform the entitled person in writing of the matters specified in article 8, unless he has already done so.

(2)   In this article and in article 10, "the prescribed time" means:

(a)   in respect of a client, three months after delivery of the relevant bill, or a lesser time (which may not be less than one month) specified in writing to the client at the time of delivery of the bill; or

(b)   in respect of an entitled third party, three months after delivery of notification to the entitled third party of the amount of the costs, or a lesser time (which may not be less than one month) specified in writing to the entitled third party at the time of such notification.

Information to be given in writing to entitled person

8.   When required by articles 6 or 7, a solicitor shall inform an entitled person in writing of the following matters:

(a)   where article 4(1) applies:

(i)   that the entitled person may, within one month of receiving from the solicitor the information specified in this article or (if later) of delivery of the bill or notification of the amount of the costs, require the solicitor to obtain a remuneration certificate; and

(ii)   that (unless the solicitor has agreed to do so) the Council may waive the requirements of article 11(1), if satisfied from the client's written application that exceptional circumstances exist to justify granting a waiver;

(b)   that sections 70, 71 and 72 of the Solicitors Act 1974 set out the entitled person's rights in relation to taxation;

(c)   that (where the whole of the bill has not been paid, by deduction or otherwise) the solicitor may charge interest on the outstanding amount of the bill in accordance with article 14.

Loss by client of right to certification

9.   A client may not require a solicitor to obtain a remuneration certificate:

    (a)   after a bill has been delivered and paid by the client, other than by deduction;

    (b)   where a bill has been delivered, after the expiry of one month from the date on which the client was informed in writing of the matters specified in article 8 or from delivery of the bill if later;

    (c)   after the solicitor and client have entered into a non-contentious business agreement in accordance with the provisions of section 57 of the Solicitors Act 1974;

    (d)   after a court has ordered the bill to be taxed.

Loss by entitled third party of right to certification

10.   An entitled third party may not require a solicitor to obtain a remuneration certificate:

    (a)   after the prescribed time (within the meaning of article 7(2)(b)) has elapsed without any objection being received to the amount of the costs;

    (b)   after the expiry of one month from the date on which the entitled third party was (in compliance with article 7) informed in writing of the matters specified in article 8 or from notification of the costs if later;

    (c)   after a court has ordered the bill to be taxed.

Requirement to pay a sum towards the costs

11. (1)   On requiring a solicitor to obtain a remuneration certificate a client must pay to the solicitor the paid disbursements and value added tax comprised in the bill together with 50% of the costs unless:

    (a)   the client has already paid the amount required under this article, by deduction from monies held or otherwise; or

    (b)   the solicitor or (if the solicitor refuses) the Council has agreed in writing to waive all or part of this requirement.

    (2)   The Council shall be under no obligation to provide a remuneration certificate, and the solicitor may take steps to obtain payment of his bill if the client, having been informed of his right to seek a waiver of the requirements of paragraph (1), has not:

    (a)   within one month of receipt of the information specified in article 8, either paid in accordance with paragraph (1) or applied to the Council in writing for a waiver of the requirements of paragraph (1); or

    (b)   made payment in accordance with the requirements of paragraph (1) within one month of written notification that he has been refused a waiver of those requirements by the Council.

Miscellaneous provisions

12.(1)   After an application has been made by a solicitor for a remuneration certificate the client may pay the bill in full without invalidating the application.

    (2)   A solicitor and entitled person may agree in writing to waive the provisions of sub-paragraphs (a) or (b) of articles 9 or 10.

(3) A solicitor may take from his client security for the payment of any costs, including the amount of any interest to which the solicitor may become entitled under article 14.

Refunds by solicitor

13. (1) If a solicitor has received payment of all or part of his costs and a remuneration certificate is issued for less than the sum already paid, the solicitor must immediately pay to the entitled person any refund which may be due (after taking into account any other sums which may properly be payable to the solicitor whether for costs, paid disbursements, value added tax or otherwise) unless the solicitor has applied for an order for taxation within one month of receipt by him of the remuneration certificate.

(2) Where a solicitor applies for taxation, his liability to pay any refund under paragraph (1) shall be suspended for so long as the taxation is still pending.

(3) The obligation of the solicitor to repay costs under paragraph (1) is without prejudice to any liability of the solicitor to pay interest on the repayment by virtue of any enactment, rule of law or professional rule.

Interest

14. (1) After the information specified in article 8 has been given to an entitled person in compliance with articles 6 or 7, a solicitor may charge interest on the unpaid amount of his costs plus any paid disbursements and value added tax, subject to paragraphs (2) and (3) below.

(2) Where an entitlement to interest arises under paragraph (1), and subject to any agreement made between a solicitor and client, the period for which interest may be charged may run from one month after the date of delivery of a bill, unless the solicitor fails to lodge an application within one month of receipt of a request for a remuneration certificate under article 4, in which case no interest is payable in respect of the period between one month after receiving the request and the actual date on which the application is lodged.

(3) Subject to any agreement made between a solicitor and client, the rate of interest must not exceed the rate for the time being payable on judgment debts.

(4) Interest charged under this article must be calculated, where applicable, by reference to the following:

(a) if a solicitor is required to obtain a remuneration certificate, the total amount of the costs certified by the Council to be fair and reasonable plus paid disbursements and value added tax;

(b) if an application is made for the bill to be taxed, the amount ascertained on taxation;

(c) if an application is made for the bill to be taxed or a solicitor is required to obtain a remuneration certificate and for any reason the taxation or application for a remuneration certificate does not proceed, the unpaid amount of the costs shown in the bill or such lesser sum as may be agreed between the solicitor and the client, plus paid disbursements and value added tax.

Application by solicitor

15. A solicitor, when making an application for a remuneration certificate in accordance with the provisions of this Order, must deliver to the Council the complete relevant file and working papers, and any other information or documentation which the Council may require for the purpose of providing a remuneration certificate.

EXPLANATORY NOTE

(This note is not part of the Order)

Section 56 of the Solicitors Act 1974 establishes a Committee with power to make general orders regulating the remuneration of solicitors in respect of non-contentious business. Paragraph 22(2) of Schedule 2 to the Administration of Justice Act 1985 modifies the section so that references to solicitors include references to recognised bodies (solicitors' incorporated practices recognised under section 9 of the Administration of Justice Act 1985). This Order sets out the rights of solicitors' clients and residuary beneficiaries of certain estates to require the solicitor charging the client or estate to obtain a certificate from the Law Society as to the reasonableness of his costs.The Order prescribes requirements in relation to information to be given in writing to clients and beneficiaries who are entitled to require a solicitor to obtain a certificate, and lays certain obligations on clients, beneficiaries and solicitors.

VIII.2. Table of *ad valorem* stamp duties

STAMP DUTY PAYABLE ON BUYING A FREEHOLD PROPERTY OR THE REMAINDER OF AN EXISTING LEASE

Where the purchase price is

* £60,000 or less
  and
* the sale is not part of a larger transaction or series of transactions

you will not need to pay Stamp Duty.

You will need to insert a statement * in the Land Registry Transfer or Conveyance document which says that the purchase is not part of a larger transaction or series of transactions for which the total purchase price is more than £60,000. If the document does not include such a statement duty becomes payable.

For purchase prices of over £60,000 the duty payable is as shown below.

Purchase Price	Duty
60,001 − 60,100	601
60,101 − 60,200	602
60,201 − 60,300	603
60,301 − 60,400	604
60,401 − 60,500	605
60,501 − 60,600	606
60,601 − 60,700	607
60,701 − 60,800	608
60,801 − 60,900	609
60,901 − 61,000	610
61,001 − 61,100	611
61,101 − 61,200	612
61,201 − 61,300	613
61,301 − 61,400	614
61,401 − 61,500	615
61,501 and above	£1 on each £100 (or part of £100)

STAMP DUTY PAYABLE ON BUYING A LEASEHOLD DOMESTIC PROPERTY WITH A NEW LEASE

Average Annual Rent	Duty on the Average Rent				Duty on the Premium
	7 years or less	More than 7 years and less than 35	More than 35 years and less than 100	Over 100 years	
		£	£	£	
Up to £5	nil	0.10	0.60	1.20	Premiums up to £60,000 where the rent does not exceed £600 a year (provided a statement* is inserted) no duty is payable
Over £5 " £10	nil	0.20	1.20	2.40	
" £10 " £15	nil	0.30	1.80	3.60	
" £15 " £20	nil	0.40	2.40	4.80	
" £20 " £25	nil	0.50	3.00	6.00	
" £25 " £50	nil	1.00	6.00	12.00	
" £50 " £75	nil	1.50	9.00	18.00	
" £75 " £100	nil	2.00	12.00	24.00	
" £100 " £150	nil	3.00	18.00	36.00	
" £150 " £200	nil	4.00	24.00	48.00	
" £200 " £250	nil	5.00	30.00	60.00	
" £250 " £300	nil	6.00	36.00	72.00	Premiums of £60,001 and over, £1 on each £100 (or part of £100).
" £300 " £350	nil	7.00	42.00	84.00	
" £350 " £400	nil	8.00	48.00	96.00	
" £400 " £450	nil	9.00	54.00	108.00	
" £450 " £500	nil	10.00	60.00	120.00	
Over £500	50p on each £50 (or part of £50)	£1 on each £50 (or part of £50)	£6 on each £50 (or part of £50)	£12 on each £50 (or part of £50)	

FURNISHED LETTINGS – A letting agreement for any definite term less than a year of any furnished dwelling house or apartment where the rent for the term exceeds £500 attracts a fixed duty of £1.

STAMP DUTY PAYABLE ON BUYING STOCKS AND SHARES

Purchase Price (Consideration Money)	Duty
	£.p
Up to £100	0.50
Over £100 " " £200	1.00
" £200 " " £300	1.50
" £300 " " £400	2.00
" £400 " " £500	2.50
" £500 " " £600	3.00
" £600 " " £700	3.50
" £700 " " £800	4.00
" £800 " " £900	4.50
" £900 " " £1000	5.00
" £1000 and above	50p on each £100 (or part of £100)

'Ad Valorem' means 'according to value', or those Stamp Duties which are graduated according to the value of the subject matter taxed.

WHERE SHOULD DOCUMENTS BE SENT FOR STAMPING?

Documents for stamping should be taken or sent to any one of the following Stamp Offices.

- **Belfast Stamp Office**
  Ground Floor
  Dorchester House
  52 – 58 Great Victoria St
  Belfast BT2 7QE
  Tel: 01232 – 314614
  DX: 2003 Belfast 2

- **Birmingham Stamp Office**
  Ground Floor
  City House
  140 – 146 Edmund Street
  Birmingham B3 2JG
  Tel: 0121 – 200 2616
  DX: 15001 Birmingham 1

- **Bristol Stamp Office**
  First Floor
  The Pithay
  All Saints Street
  Bristol BS1 2NY
  Tel: 0117 – 945 6874/75
  DX: 7899 Bristol 1

- **Edinburgh Stamp Office**
  Mulberry House
  16 Picardy Place
  Edinburgh EH1 3NF
  Tel: 0131 – 556 8511
  DX: ED 303 Edinburgh 1

- **London-Worthing Stamp Office**
  Personal callers:
  South West Wing
  Bush House
  Strand
  London WC2B 4QN
  Tel: 0171 – 438 7252/7452
  Postal applications:
  Ground Floor
  Durrington Bridge House
  Barrington Road
  Worthing
  West Sussex BN12 4SE
  Tel: 01903 – 701280
  DX: 3799 Worthing 1

- **Manchester Stamp Office**
  Alexandra House
  The Parsonage
  Manchester M60 9BT
  Tel: 0161 – 833 0413
  DX: 14430 Manchester 2

- **Newcastle Stamp Office**
  15th Floor
  Cale Cross House
  156 Pilgrim Street
  Newcastle upon Tyne
  NE1 6TF
  Tel: 0191 – 245 0200
  DX: 61021 Newcastle upon Tyne 1

DX mail for Edinburgh should be marked with a blue cross on both sides of the envelope.

Staff at these offices will be pleased to help you with any questions you may have concerning Stamp Duty.

VIII.3. Land Registration Fees Order 1997 (S.I. 1997/178)

1997 No. 178

LAND REGISTRATION, ENGLAND AND WALES

The Land Registration Fees Order 1997

Made	*27th January 1997*
Coming into force	*1st April 1997*

The Lord Chancellor, with the advice and assistance of the Rule Committee appointed in pursuance of section 144 of the Land Registration Act 1925(**a**), and the Treasury, in exercise of the powers conferred on them by section 145 of that Act, sections 2 and 3 of the Public Offices Fees Act 1879(**b**) and section 128 of the Finance Act 1990(**c**) hereby make and concur in the following Order:

PART I

GENERAL

Citation, commencement and interpretation

1. (1) This Order, which supersedes the Land Registration Fees Order 1996(**d**), may be cited as the Land Registration Fees Order 1997 and shall come into force on 1st April 1997.

(2) In this Order unless the context otherwise requires:
"account holder" means a person or firm holding a credit account;
"the Act" means the Land Registration Act 1925;
"charge" includes a sub-charge;
"credit account" means an account authorised by the Registrar under article 18(2);
"Index Map section" has the same meaning as in the Land Registration (Open Register) Rules 1991(**e**);
"licensed conveyancer" has the same meaning as in section 11(2) of the Administration of Justice Act 1985(**f**) and includes a recognised body within the meaning of section 32(2) of that Act;
"monetary consideration" means a consideration in money or money's worth (other than a nominal consideration or a consideration consisting solely of a covenant to pay money owing under a mortgage);

(**a**) 1925 c.21; section 144(1) was amended by the Administration of Justice Act 1982 (c.53), Schedule 5, paragraph (d). The reference to the Minister of Agriculture, Fisheries and Food was substituted by the Transfer of Functions (Ministry of Food) Order 1955 (S.I. 1955/554). Section 145 was amended by section 7 of the Land Registration Act 1936 (c.26).
(**b**) 1879 c.58.
(**c**) 1990 c.29.
(**d**) S.I. 1996/187.
(**e**) S.I. 1992/122, relevant amending instrument is S.I. 1993/3275.
(**f**) 1985 c.61.

"the principal rules" means the Land Registration Rules 1925(**g**);
"scale fee" means a fee payable in accordance with a scale set out in Schedule 1 or 2;
"scale fee application" means an application which attracts a scale fee, or which would attract such a fee but for the operation of article 6;
"Schedule" means a Schedule to this Order;
"share in registered land" means a share in the proceeds of sale of registered land held on trust for sale.

PART II

SCALE FEES

Applications for first registration

2. (1)   Subject to article 6 (large scale applications, etc.), the fee for an application for first registration (other than an application for first registration of title to a lease by an original lessee or his personal representative or an application for first registration of a rentcharge) shall be paid in accordance with Scale 1 in Schedule 1 on the value of the land comprised in the application determined in accordance with article 7.

(2)   Subject to paragraph (3), and to article 6 (large scale applications, etc.), the fee for an application for the first registration of a title to a lease (whether or not deriving from a registered freehold or leasehold title) by the original lessee or his personal representative shall be paid in accordance with Scale 1 in Schedule 1 on an amount calculated in accordance with the following formula:

$$A = P + (10 \times R)$$

where A is the amount on which the fee is to be paid, P is the amount or value of any monetary consideration given by the lessee as part of the same transaction by way of fine, premium or otherwise, and R is the largest ascertainable amount of annual rent reserved by the lease.

(3)   Where no monetary consideration is given by the lessee as part of the same transaction by way of fine, premium or otherwise and:

(a)   no annual rent is reserved; or

(b)   the annual rent reserved cannot be ascertained at the time the application is made,

a fee shall be paid in accordance with Scale 1 in Schedule 1 on the value of the lease determined in accordance with article 7, subject to the minimum fee being £40.

Transfers of registered land for monetary consideration, etc.

3. (1)   Subject to paragraphs (2) to (5), and to article 4(1)(i) (transfer of matrimonial home pursuant to an order of the Court) and article 6 (large scale applications, etc.), the fee for an application for the registration of:

(**g**) S.R. & O. 1925/1093 to which there are amendments not relevant to this Order.

(a) a transfer of registered land for monetary consideration;

(b) a transfer for the purpose of giving effect to a disposition for monetary consideration of a share in registered land;

(c) a surrender of a registered lease for monetary consideration (whether effected by deed or otherwise), except where the surrender is consideration or part consideration for the grant of a new lease to the registered proprietor for the registration of which a scale fee is paid;

shall be paid in accordance with Scale 1 in Schedule 1 on the amount or value of the consideration.

(2) Where a sale and sub-sale of land are effected by separate instruments of transfer, a separate fee shall be payable in respect of each transfer.

(3) Where a single instrument of transfer gives effect to a sale and a sub-sale of the same land a single fee shall be assessed upon the greater of the monetary consideration given by the purchaser or the monetary consideration given by the sub-purchaser in respect of that land.

(4) Where a single instrument of transfer gives effect to a sale, and a sub-sale of part only of the land comprised in the sale, the fee payable shall be the aggregate of:

(a) a fee assessed upon the monetary consideration given by the sub-purchaser in respect of the land comprised in the sub-sale; and

(b) a fee assessed upon the amount (if any) by which the monetary consideration given by the purchaser in respect of the land comprised in the sale exceeds the monetary consideration given by the sub-purchaser in respect of the land comprised in the sub-sale.

(5) Where an instrument gives effect to an exchange of registered land ("the first land") for other registered land ("the second land"), whether or not money is paid by way of equality it shall be treated for the purpose of assessing the fee payable for its registration as two separate transfers, being a transfer of the first land for monetary consideration equal to the value of the first land and a transfer of the second land for monetary consideration equal to the value of the second land.

(6) The fee for an application to cancel an entry in the register of notice of an unregistered lease which has determined on merger, surrender or otherwise shall be paid in accordance with Scale 1 in Schedule 1 on the value thereof immediately prior to its determination.

Transfers otherwise than for monetary considerations, etc.

4. (1) Subject to paragraphs (2) and (3), to article 6 (large scale applications, etc.) and to paragraph (8) of Schedule 4 (applications to which section 145(2) of the Act applies), the fee for an application for the registration of:

(a) a transfer of registered land otherwise than for monetary consideration;

(b) a surrender of a registered lease (whether effected by deed or otherwise) where the surrender is consideration or part consideration for the grant of a new lease to the registered proprietor for the registration of which a scale fee is paid;

(c) a surrender of a registered lease otherwise than for monetary consideration (whether effected by deed or otherwise);

(d) a transmission of registered land on death or bankruptcy;

(e)   an assent of registered land (including a vesting assent);

(f)   an appropriation of registered land;

(g)   a vesting order or declaration made under section 47 of the Act;

(h)   a rectification of the register;

(i)   a transfer of a matrimonial home (being registered land) made pursuant to an order of the Court;

shall be paid in accordance with Scale 2 in Schedule 2 on the value of the land which is the subject of the dealing, determined in accordance with article 8, but after deducting therefrom the amount secured upon the land by any charge subject to which the registration takes effect.

(2)   Where a transfer falling within paragraph (1)(a) is one for the purpose of giving effect to the disposition of a share in registered land the fee for an application for its registration shall be paid in accordance with Scale 2 in Schedule 2 on the value of that share.

(3)   Where, in the case of rectification of the register, the fee appears to the Registrar to be unreasonable or excessive he may reduce or waive it.

Charges of registered land

5. (1)   Subject to paragraphs (5) and (6), and to article 6 (large scale applications, etc.), the fee for an application for the registration of a charge shall be paid in accordance with Scale 2 in Schedule 2 on the amount of the charge determined in accordance with article 9.

(2)   Subject to article 6 (large scale applications, etc.), the fee for an application for the registration of:

(a)   the transfer of a charge for monetary consideration; or

(b)   a transfer for the purpose of giving effect to the disposition for monetary consideration of a share in a registered charge;

shall be paid in accordance with Scale 2 in Schedule 2 on the amount or value of the consideration.

(3)   Subject to article 6 (large scale applications, etc.), and to paragraph (8) of Schedule 4 (applications to which section 145(2) of the Act applies), the fee for an application for the registration of the transfer of a registered charge otherwise than for monetary consideration shall be paid in accordance with Scale 2 in Schedule 2 on the amount secured by the registered charge at the time of the transfer or, where the transfer relates to more than one charge, the aggregate of the amounts secured by the registered charges at the time of the transfer.

(4)   Subject to article 6 (large scale applications, etc.) and to paragraph (8) of Schedule 4 (applications to which section 145(2) of the Act applies), the fee for an application for the registration of a transfer for the purpose of giving effect to the disposition otherwise than for monetary consideration of a share in a registered charge shall be paid in accordance with Scale 2 in Schedule 2 on a proportionate part of the amount secured by the registered charge at the time of the transfer or, where the transfer relates to more than one charge, a proportionate part of the aggregate of the amounts secured by the registered charges at the time of the transfer.

(5)   Subject to paragraph (6), where a scale fee application ("the primary application") is made that will, when completed, result in a person ("the applicant") becoming registered as the proprietor of particular registered land or of one or more registered charges, no fee shall be payable for the registration of a charge by the applicant (or, where the primary application is for the first registration of title to land, by a predecessor in title of the applicant) which charges the registered land or the registered charge or charges which are the subject

of the primary application, provided the charge by the applicant either accompanies the primary application or is lodged for registration before the primary application is completed.

(6)   Where a charge by an applicant referred to in paragraph (5) also charges property ("the additional property") which comprises registered land or, as the case may be, one or more registered charges, not being property which is the subject of the primary application referred to in paragraph (5), that paragraph shall not extend to the additional property so that a fee shall be paid in accordance with Scale 2 in Schedule 2 for the registration of the charge by the applicant in respect of the additional property on an amount calculated in accordance with the following formula:

$$A = \frac{V_A \times C}{V_C}$$

where A is the amount on which the fee is payable, V_A is the value or amount of the additional property, V_C is the value of all the property comprised in the charge and C is the amount of the charge determined in accordance with article 9.

Large scale applications, etc.

6. (1)   In this article:

(a)   "large area application" means an application falling within article 2 (first registration of land; first registration of title to a lease) which comprises land having an area or aggregate area exceeding 100 hectares;

(b)   "large scale application" means a scale fee application which relates to not fewer than 20 land units, other than—

(i)   a large area application;

(ii)   a low value application; or

(iii)   an application to register a charge to which article 5(5) applies, except to the extent that it relates to additional land within the meaning of article 5(6);

(c)   "low value application" means a scale fee application, other than an application falling within article 2 (applications for first registration), where the value of the land, or the amount of the charge, to which it relates (as the case may be) does not exceed £30,000.

(d)   "land unit" means:

(i)   where the land is unregistered, a separate area of land not adjoining any other unregistered land comprised in the same application;

(ii)   where the land is registered, the land registered under a single title number.

(2)   The fee for a large scale application shall be whichever is the greater of:

(a)   the amount payable in respect of the application under article 2, 3, 4 or 5, as the case may be; or

(b)   a fee calculated on the following basis—

(i)   where the application relates to not more than 500 land units, £10 for each land unit to which it relates;

(ii)   where the application relates to more than 500 land units, £5,000 plus £5 for each land unit to which it relates in excess of 500 land units,

provided that the fee shall in no case exceed £40,000.

(3) If, having regard to the extent of the land comprised in a large area application, the Registrar considers that the cost of the work involved in dealing with that application would substantially exceed the scale fee otherwise payable such additional fee shall be payable as the Registrar shall direct as appropriate not exceeding the excess cost of the work involved.

PART III

VALUATION

Valuation (first registration)

7. (1) In the case of an application to which article 2(1) applies (first registration of title to land otherwise than by the original grantee under a lease or his personal representatives) made within one year of a sale (other than an exchange, whether or not money is paid for equality, or the sale of a share only in the proceeds of sale of such land) the value of the land shall be taken to be the amount of the monetary consideration given together with the amount outstanding at the time of the purchase under any charge or mortgage subject to which the land was purchased.

(2) In the case of an application:

    (a) to which article 2(1) applies, other than one falling within paragraph (1); or

    (b) to which article 2(3) applies,

the value of the land or lease (as the case may be) shall be ascertained by the Registrar at such sum as in his opinion it would fetch if sold in the open market at the date of the application free from any charge or mortgage.

(3) As evidence of such value the Registrar may require a statement in writing, signed by the applicant or his solicitor or licensed conveyancer or by any other person who, in the Registrar's opinion, is competent to make such a statement.

(4) Where an application for first registration is made on the purchase of a leasehold estate by the reversioner or of a reversion by the leaseholder or on any other like occasion and determination of an unregistered interest, by way of merger, surrender or otherwise, takes place, the value of the land shall be the combined value of the reversionary and determined interests assessed in accordance with paragraphs (1) to (3).

Valuation (registered land)

8. (1) Where the value of the land in a registered title falls to be determined under this Order it shall be ascertained by the Registrar at such sum as in his opinion the land would fetch if sold in the open market free from any charge or mortgage:

    (a) in the case of a surrender at a date immediately prior to the surrender;

    (b) in any other case at the date of the application.

(2) As evidence of such value the Registrar may require a statement in writing, signed by the applicant or his solicitor or licensed conveyancer or by any other person who, in the Registrar's opinion, is competent to make such a statement.

Valuation (charges)

9. (1) Subject to paragraph (5), where the amount of a charge falls to be determined under this Order it shall be taken to be:

(a) in the case of a charge to secure a fixed amount, the amount secured by the charge;

(b) in the case of a charge to secure further advances, where the total amount of the advances or of the money to be owing at any one time is in any way limited, the amount so limited;

(c) in the case of a charge to secure further advances, where the total amount of the advances or of the money to be owing at any one time is in no way limited, an amount equal to the value of the registered land comprised in the charge after deducting therefrom the amount secured on it by any prior registered charge.

(2) Where a charge of a kind referred to in paragraph (1)(a) or (1)(b) is secured on unregistered land or other property as well as on registered land, the fee in accordance with article 5 shall be payable on an amount calculated in accordance with the following formula:

$$A = \frac{V_R \times C}{V_C}$$

where A is the amount on which the fee is payable, V_R is the value of the registered land, V_C is the value of all the property comprised in the charge, and C is the amount of the charge determined in accordance with paragraph (1).

(3) The fee for the registration of a charge by way of additional or substituted security or by way of guarantee shall be payable on the lesser of:

(a) the amount secured or guaranteed; or

(b) the value of the land after deducting the amount secured on the land by any prior registered charge.

(4) Subject to paragraph (5), the fee for the registration of a charge to secure an obligation or liability which is contingent upon the happening of a future event (not being a charge falling within paragraph (3)) shall be payable on the value of the land after deducting the amount secured on the land by any prior registered charge.

(5) If in relation to a charge to which paragraph (4) applies, the maximum amount or value of the obligation or liability which may arise is in any way limited under the charge and is capable of being ascertained at the time of the application to register the charge then the fee shall be payable on that amount or value, if less than the value of the land after deducting the amount secured on the land by any prior registered charge.

(6) For the purpose of this Order, where two or more charges are contained in the same instrument and secure the same debt, the instrument shall be treated as creating a single charge by the chargor (or where there is more than one chargor, a single separate charge by each of the chargors) the amount of the charge (or the charge by each chargor) being equal to the lesser of:

(a) the whole debt; or

(b) the value of the registered land charged by that chargor after deducting therefrom the amount secured on it by any prior registered charge.

PART IV

FIXED FEES AND EXEMPTIONS

Fixed fees

10. (1) Subject to paragraphs (3) and (4), the fees for the applications and services specified in Schedule 3 shall be those set out in that schedule.

(2) The fee for an application in Form 112A, Form 112B or Form 112C in Schedule 1 to the Land Registration (Open Register) Rules 1991 shall be the aggregate of the fees payable for the services provided, save that the maximum fee for any one application shall be £200.

(3) The Registrar may, if he thinks fit, waive any fee or part of a fee or any category of fee payable under this article.

(4) If, having regard to the extent of the land to which an application for a search of the Index Map relates, the Registrar considers that the cost of the work involved in dealing with that application would substantially exceed any fee otherwise payable under this Order, such additional fee shall be payable as the Registrar shall direct as appropriate to cover the excess cost of the work involved.

(5) Notification of the additional fee shall be given to the applicant and, if he then elects to withdraw his application, no fee shall be payable.

Exemptions

11. No fee shall be payable in respect of any of the applications and services specified in Schedule 4.

PART V

GENERAL AND ADMINISTRATIVE PROVISIONS

Refund of fees

12. (1) Where an amount exceeding the prescribed fee has been paid, there shall be refunded any excess remaining after the deduction, if the Registrar so directs, of an amount not exceeding £10 in respect of the cost of repayment.

(2) Where the person or firm lodging the application is an account holder, any amount to be refunded under paragraph (1) may at the discretion of the Registrar be repaid to the account holder by crediting the amount to the account holder's credit account.

(3) Subject to article 10(5), if any application is cancelled or withdrawn no part of the fee thereof shall be refunded unless the Registrar so directs.

Cost of advertisements and special enquiries

13. If in the course of dealing with any application the Registrar directs publication of an advertisement or any other special enquiry, the costs so incurred shall be defrayed by the applicant unless the Registrar directs to the contrary.

Fixed boundaries

14. Where application is made for the boundaries of land to be noted on the register as fixed under rule 277 of the principal rules such fee shall be charged as the Registrar may consider necessary to cover the cost of any examination of title, enquiries, mapping, surveying, notices or other work involved.

Special expedition

15. Where application for special expedition in connection with an application is granted, such further fee, being not less than £40, shall be payable as the Registrar shall direct having regard to the special work involved.

Applications not otherwise referred to

16. Upon an application for which no other fee is payable under this Order and which is not exempt from payment, there shall be paid such fee (if any) not exceeding a fee in accordance with Scale 1 in Schedule 1 on the value of the land or on the amount of the charge as the Registrar shall direct having regard to the work involved.

Method of payment

17. Fees payable under this Order shall be collected in money and, subject to article 18:

   (a)   every fee shall, except where the Registrar otherwise permits, be paid by means of a cheque or postal order crossed and made payable to H.M. Land Registry;

   (b)   where the amount of the fee payable on an application is immediately ascertainable, the fee shall be payable on delivery of the application;

   (c)   where the amount of the fee payable on an application is not immediately ascertainable, on delivery of the application there shall be paid on account of the fee such sum, being not less than the minimum fee payable in accordance with Scale 1 in Schedule 1, as the applicant may reasonably estimate to be the fee payable and there shall be lodged therewith an undertaking to pay on demand the balance of the fee due, if any.

Credit accounts

18. (1) In this article "credit limit" in relation to a credit account authorised for use under paragraph (2) means the maximum amount (if any) which is to be due on the account at any time, as notified by the Registrar to the account holder from time to time, by such means of communication as the Registrar considers appropriate.

   (2) Any person or firm may, if authorised by the Registrar, use a credit account in accordance with this article for the purpose of the payment of fees for applications and services of such kind as the Registrar shall from time to time direct.

   (3) For the purpose of enabling the Registrar to consider whether or not a person or firm seeking to use a credit account may be authorised to use such an account, that person or firm shall furnish to the Registrar such information and evidence as the Registrar may require to satisfy him of the person or firm's fitness to hold a credit account and the ability of the person or firm to pay any amounts which may become due from time to time under a credit account, if authorised.

   (4) For the purpose of enabling the Registrar to consider from time to time whether or not an account holder may continue to be authorised to use a credit account, the account holder shall furnish to the Registrar from time to time, when requested to do so by the Registrar, such information and evidence as the Registrar may require to satisfy him of the account holder's continuing fitness to hold a credit account and the continuing ability of the account holder to pay any amounts which may become due from time to time under the account holder's credit account.

(5)   Where an account holder makes an application in respect of which credit facilities are available, he may make a request, in such manner as the Registrar shall direct, for the appropriate fee to be debited to the account holder's credit account, but the Registrar shall not be required to accept such a request where the amount due on the account exceeds the credit limit applicable to the credit account, or would exceed it if the request were to be accepted.

(6)   Where a person or firm having a credit account makes a application in respect of which credit facilities are available but which is not accompanied by any fee and does not contain a request for the fee to be debited to such account, the Registrar may debit the fee to that person's or that firm's credit account.

(7)   A statement of account shall be sent by the Registrar to each account holder at the end of each calendar month or such other period as the Registrar shall direct either in any particular case or generally.

(8)   On receipt of the statement the account holder shall pay by cheque any sum due on his credit account forthwith.

(9)   Cheques shall be crossed and made payable to H. M. Land Registry and sent to the Accounts Section, H.M. Land Registry, Burrington Way, Plymouth, PL5 3LP or at such other address as the Registrar shall direct.

(10)   The Registrar may at any time and without giving reasons terminate or suspend any or all authorisations given under paragraph (2).

Dated 16th January 1997   *Mackay of Clashfern*, C.

Patrick McLoughlin
Richard Ottaway
Dated 27th January 1997   Two of the Lords Commissioners
of Her Majesty's Treasury

SCHEDULE 1　　　　　　　Articles 2, 3, 5, 16 & 17

SCALE 1

NOTE: Where the amount or value is a figure which includes pence, it may be rounded down to the nearest £1.

Value or amount £	Fee £
0-30,000	40
30,001-40,000	50
40,001-50,000	70
50,001-60,000	90
60,001-70,000	110
70,001-80,000	130
80,001-90,000	160
90,001-100,000	190
100,001-150,000	220
150,001-200,000	260
200,001-300,000	300
300,001-500,000	400
500,001-700,000	500
700,001-1,000,000	600
1,000,001-2,000,000	900
2,000,001-5,000,000	1,200
5,000,001 and over	1,800

SCHEDULE 2　　　　　　　Articles 4 & 5

SCALE 2

NOTE: Where the amount or value is a figure which includes pence, it may be rounded down to the nearest £1.

Value or amount £	Fee £
0-100,000	40
100,001-200,000	50
200,001-500,000	70
500,001-1,000,000	100
1,000,001 and over	200

VIII

SCHEDULE 3   Article 10

PART I

FIXED FEE APPLICATIONS

Fee

(1)   To register or modify a caution, a restriction (other than a restriction to which paragraph (9) of Schedule 4 applies), a notice (including a priority notice), an inhibition, or a note for which no other provision is made by this Order and for which the Registrar considers a fee should be paid:

   − for the first title affected £40
   − for each subsequent title affected £20

Provided that no such fee shall be payable if, in relation to each registered title affected, the application is accompanied by a scale fee application or another application which attracts a fee under this paragraph.

(2)   To close or partly close a registered leasehold or rentcharge title other than on surrender (whether or not the surrender is for monetary consideration and whether effected by deed or otherwise) − for each title closed or partly closed £40

Provided that no such fee shall be payable if the application is accompanied by a scale fee application.

(3)   To convert from one class of title to another £40

Provided that no fee shall be payable if the application for conversion is accompanied by a scale fee application.

(4)   Application under rule 271 in relation to a lost or destroyed land certificate or charge certificate (in addition to the cost of any advertisement):

   (a)   where a replacement certificate is issued £40

   (b)   where a replacement certificate is not issued £20

(5)   First registration of a title to a rentcharge £40

(6)   To cancel an entry in the register of notice of an unregistered rentcharge which has determined on merger, redemption or otherwise − for each title affected . . .   £40

Provided that no such fee shall be payable if the application is accompanied by a scale fee application.

PART II

SERVICES − INSPECTION AND COPYING

(1)   Inspection of the register or any part of the register, to include the making of a copy of or extract from the register, on any one occasion when a person gains access to the Registrar's computer system by means of that person's remote terminal pursuant to the rule 4A of the Land Registration (Open Register) Rules 1991 − per title . .   £2

(2)   Inspection (otherwise than under paragraph (1) above):

   (a)   of the register or any part thereof − per title £4

   (b)   of the title plan − per title £4

(c) of any or all of the documents referred to in the register (other than documents referred to in paragraph (4) below) − per title ... £4

(3) Office copy in respect of a registered title:

    (a) of the register or any part thereof − per copy £4

    (b) of the title plan − per copy £4

    (c) of any or all of the documents referred to in the register (other than documents referred to in paragraph (4) below) − per copy or set .. £4

(4) Inspection or office copy (or both) in relation to:

    (a) a lease or mortgage referred to in the register, or a copy thereof; or

    (b) any document not referred to in a register −per document .. £8

(5) Application to the Registrar to ascertain the title number or numbers (if any) under which land is registered where the applicant seeks to inspect or to be supplied with an office copy of a register or part of a register or of a title plan and the applicant has not supplied a title number, or the title number supplied does not relate to any part of the land described by the applicant £4

PART III

SERVICES − SEARCHES

(1) An official search of the register or of a pending first registration application £4

(2) A search of the register made by telephone £4

(3) The issue of an official certificate of inspection of the title plan £4

(4) Subject to article 10(4), an official search of the Index Map:

    (a) where any part of the land to which the search relates is registered − per registered title in respect of which a result is given £4

    (b) where no part of the land to which the search relates is registered − per application £4

(5) Official search of index of proprietor's names − per name £10

PART IV

SERVICES − OTHER INFORMATION

(1) Application to be supplied with the name and address of the registered proprietor of land identified by its postal address − per application £4

(2) The supply by the Registrar of a copy of an Index Map section − per copy £40

(3) The supply of information under section 129 of the Act − per registered title in respect of which information is supplied £8

PART V

SERVICES – MISCELLANEOUS

(1)   To take an affidavit or declaration £5

(2)   To take exhibits to an affidavit or declaration – per exhibit £2

SCHEDULE 4   Article 11

EXEMPTIONS

No fee shall be payable in respect of:

(1)   making a land certificate or charge certificate correspond with the register;

(2)   changing the name, address or description of a registered proprietor or other person referred to on the register, or changing the description of a property;

(3)   giving effect on the register to a change of proprietor where the registered land or the registered charge, as the case may be, has become vested without further assurance (other than on the death or bankruptcy of a proprietor) in some person by the operation of any statute (other than the Act), statutory instrument or scheme taking effect under any statute or statutory instrument;

(4)   registering a discharge of a registered charge;

(5)   registering a notice or renewal of a caution or notice pursuant to the Matrimonial Homes Act 1983(a);

(6)   registering a withdrawal of a notice of deposit or intended deposit of a land certificate or charge certificate;

(7)   entering on the register the death of a joint proprietor;

(8)   registering a disposition to which section 145 (2) of the Act (dispositions otherwise than for valuable consideration by personal representatives of a deceased proprietor registered as such) applies;

(9)   registering a restriction which is obligatory under section 58(3) of the Act;

(10)   cancelling the registration of a notice (other than a notice in respect of an unregistered lease or unregistered rentcharge), caution, inhibition, restriction or note;

(11)   approving an estate layout plan or any draft document with or without a plan;

(12)   issuing of a summons under the seal of the Land Registry;

(13)   an order by the Registrar.

(a)   1983 c.19.

VIII.4. Stamp Duty Form 22: Apportionment of consideration under agreement for sale

A		B
Amount of consideration payable in Cash or Bills ...... £	Legal Estates in Freehold Property	£
Amount of consideration payable in Shares, Debentures etc ...... £	Fixed Plant and Machinery in Freehold Property	£
Liabilities assumed by the Purchaser:	Legal Estates in Leasehold Property	£
Amounts due on mortgages of Freeholds and/or Leaseholds, including interest to date of sale ...... £	Fixed Plant and Machinery in Leasehold Property	£
Hire Purchase Debts for Goods acquired ...... £	Equitable interests in Freehold or Leasehold Property ..	£
Other liabilities of the Vendor ...... £	Loose Plant and Machinery, Stock-in-Trade and other Chattels	£
Any other consideration ...... £	(Only Plant and Machinery in an actual state of severance, ie not fixed to the premises at the date of the Agreement for Sale, must be included in this figure)	
	Goods, Wares and Merchandise subject to Hire Purchase Agreements (Written Down Value)	£
	Goodwill and Benefit of Contracts	£
	Patents, Designs, Trade Marks, Licences, etc	£
	Book Debts	£
	Cash in Hand and at Bank on Current Account	£
	Cash on Deposit	£
	Shares, Debentures and other investments	£
	Other property viz	£
Please note that Column A should equal Column B. £		£

I hereby certify that the particulars shown in this form are in every respect fully and truly stated according to the best of my judgment and belief, and that the Loose Plant and Machinery included in the above apportionment were in a state of severance at the date of the sale agreement.

This certificate should be signed by the Vendor or Purchaser (the Secretary in the case of a Company) or by an Accountant or Solicitor acting in the sale.

Signed .... Address .... Date ....

VIII

VIII.5. Stamp Duty (Exempt Instruments) Regulations 1987 (S.I. 1987/516)

1987 No. 516

TAXES

The Stamp Duty (Exempt Instruments) Regulations 1987

Made	*24th March 1987*
Laid before the House of Commons	*26th March 1987*
Coming into force	*1st May 1987*

Note.—FA 1985, s. 87 (2) provides that instruments which would otherwise be chargeable with stamp duty of a fixed amount under any provision specified in regulations shall not be so charged if they are of a kind specified in regulations and certified to be instruments of that kind.

These regulations specify the provisions under which, subject to conditions, that duty shall not be charged; specify the instruments (executed on or after 1 May 1987) in relation to which the exemption is available; and provide for the certification requirements.

Regulation 1 provides the title and commencement date.

Regulation 2 provides the conditions for the exemption.

Regulation 3 provides for the requirements for the certificate and the conditions which have to be fulfilled.

Regulation 4 introduces the Schedule which specifies the instruments which may qualify for the exemption provided by regulation 2.

Regulation 5 dispenses with the requirement of adjudication in accordance with the Stamp Act 1891, s. 12 as required by FA 1985, ss. 82 (5) and 84 (9).

The Treasury, in exercise of the powers conferred on them by section 87 (2) of the Finance Act 1985, hereby make the following regulations:

1. These regulations may be cited as the Stamp Duty (Exempt Instruments) Regulations 1987 and shall come into force on 1st May 1987.

2. (1) An instrument which—

(a) is executed on or after 1st May 1987,

(b) is of a kind specified in the Schedule hereto for the purposes of this regulation, and

(c) is certified by a certificate which fulfils the conditions of regulation 3 to be an instrument of that kind,

shall be exempt from duty under the provisions specified in paragraph (2) of this regulation.

(2) The provisions specified are—

(a) the headings in Schedule 1 to the Stamp Act 1891—

"Conveyance or transfer of any kind not hereinbefore described";
or

"Disposition in Scotland of any property or of any right or interest therein not described in this Schedule";

(b) sections 83(2) and 84(8) of the Finance Act 1985.

3. The certificate—

    (a) shall be in writing and—

        (i) be included as part of the instrument, or

        (ii) be endorsed upon or, where separate, be physically attached to the instrument concerned;

    (b) shall contain a sufficient description of—

        (i) the instrument concerned where the certificate is separate but physically attached to the instrument, and

        (ii) the category in the Schedule hereto into which the instrument falls;

    (c) (i) shall be signed by the transferor or grantor or by his solicitor or duly authorised agent, and

        (ii) where it is not signed by the transferor or grantor or by his solicitor, it shall contain a statement by the signatory of the capacity in which he signs, that he is authorised so to sign and that he gives the certificate from his own knowledge of the facts stated in it.

4. The Schedule to these regulations shall have effect for the specification of instruments for the purposes of regulation 2.

5. An instrument which is certified in accordance with these regulations shall not be required under section 82 (5) or section 84 (9) of the Finance Act 1985 to be stamped in accordance with section 12 of the Stamp Act 1891 with a particular stamp denoting that it is duly stamped or that it is not chargeable with any duty.

VIII

SCHEDULE   Regulation 4

An instrument which effects any one or more of the following transactions only is an instrument specified for the purposes of regulation 2—

A. The vesting of property subject to a trust in the trustees of the trust on the appointment of a new trustee, or in the continuing trustees on the retirement of a trustee.

B. The conveyance or transfer of property the subject of a specific devise or legacy to the beneficiary named in the will (or his nominee).

C. The conveyance or transfer of property which forms part of an intestate's estate to the person entitled on intestacy (or his nominee).

D. The appropriation of property within section 84 (4) of the Finance Act 1985 (death: appropriation in satisfaction of a general legacy of money) or section 84 (5) or (7) of that Act (death: appropriation in satisfaction of any interest of surviving spouse and in Scotland also of any interest of issue).

E. The conveyance or transfer of property which forms part of the residuary estate of a testator to a beneficiary (or his nominee) entitled solely by virtue of his entitlement under the will.

F.   The conveyance or transfer of property out of a settlement in or towards satisfaction of a beneficiary's interest, not being an interest acquired for money or money's worth, being a conveyance or transfer constituting a distribution of property in accordance with the provisions of the settlement.

G.   The conveyance or transfer of property on and in consideration only of marriage to a party to the marriage (or his nominee) or to trustees to be held on the terms of a settlement made in consideration only of the marriage.

H.   The conveyance or transfer of property within section 83 (1) of the Finance Act 1985 (transfers in connection with divorce etc.).

I.   The conveyance or transfer by the liquidator of property which formed part of the assets of the company in liquidation to a shareholder of that company (or his nominee) in or towards satisfaction of the shareholder's rights on a winding-up.

J.   The grant in fee simple of an easement in or over land for no consideration in money or money's worth.

K.   The grant of a servitude for no consideration in money or money's worth.

L.   The conveyance or transfer of property operating as a voluntary disposition inter vivos for no consideration in money or money's worth nor any consideration referred to in section 57 of the Stamp Act 1891 (conveyance in consideration of a debt etc.).

M.   The conveyance or transfer of property by an instrument within section 84 (1) of the Finance Act 1985 (death: varying disposition).

IX.   LAND REGISTRY

IX.1   Land Registry Practice Leaflets

Practice Leaflet No. 1

Land Registration Rules 1925

Mergers and surrenders of leases affecting registered land

1.   Merger or surrender of a registered lease in a superior estate which is either already registered or is the subject of an application for first registration

a.   When a person is, or is about to be, registered, in the same capacity, as proprietor of both the leasehold and superior titles to a property, the Registry may treat the leasehold title as merged, unless the contrary appears to be intended (r.206). In practice, the leasehold title will rarely be merged unless the registered proprietor or his or her solicitor or licensed conveyancer has requested merger. When the superior title is already registered, the request may be made by letter. When the superior title is the subject of an application for first registration, the request is in the printed application form for first registration. Any incumbrances on the inferior title which would prevent merger must be removed.

b.   When the lease has been surrendered by deed, the surrender should be executed by the registered proprietor of the surrendered title and every person appearing by the register to be interested therein (r.200). The surrender must be in favour of the registered proprietor, or the person entitled to be registered as proprietor, of the superior title. It may take the form of a transfer in printed Form 19, adapted so that the actual words of transfer may be preceded by such words as "For the purpose of surrendering the term comprised in the registered title [and in consideration of . . . .]", or such other words as may be appropriate.

c.   When the surrender is not in writing, but takes effect by operation of law, evidence must be given of the acts which imply a surrender. This will be a simple matter if a surrender is implied by the grant of a new lease to an existing lessee. If the new lease was granted pursuant to s.14 of the Leasehold Reform Act 1967, this must be disclosed. If a surrender is to be implied by the parties having respectively given up and accepted possession, the supporting evidence must include a statutory declaration made by a reliable person with full knowledge of the facts and also the amount of the consideration paid for the surrender (if any). If the lessee was occupying the property and has given vacant possession to the lessor, the declaration should describe when and how the premises were vacated and the keys returned to the lessor. If an under-lessee was occupying the property, the landlord must prove that he or she is receiving the rent directly from that under-lessee. This may be done by producing, as exhibits to the declaration, the counterpart underlease and a copy of the authority requiring the under-lessee to pay the rent directly to the landlord. The registered proprietor of the surrendered title should, if possible, be persuaded to join in the application to close that title. Any incumbrances on the title being merged which would prevent merger must be discharged. Other evidence may be available (e.g. a receipt for money paid for the surrender, or an instrument of release of personal liability) and if so, it should be produced.

d.   In addition to the evidence mentioned above, an application to register a merger or surrender should be accompanied by the lease and any outstanding land certificate(s). When a legal charge has been registered on the title to be merged, the charge certificate must be produced together with a discharge of the charge. Similarly, when the land certificate of the title to be merged is subject to a notice of deposit, the withdrawal of that notice in printed Form 86 must be supplied. If the lease cannot be produced (e.g. the lease is not in the lessee's possession because it affects also other land) a short letter stating the reason why should be lodged.

e.   A fixed fee is payable for each registered title to be closed, wholly or partly, other than on surrender. This fee will include cancellation of notice of the lease from the register of the superior title. If, however, the application for merger is accompanied by another application that attracts a scale fee (e.g. a transfer of one or both estates) no fee is payable for the closure of the leasehold title (see Part I(2) Schedule 3 to the current Fees Order). If a leasehold title is closed, wholly or partly, on surrender, whether affected by deed or otherwise, the fee is assessed as follows:

(i)   If the surrender is for monetary consideration (except where the surrender is consideration or part consideration for the grant of a new lease to the registered proprietor — see (ii) below), the fee will be payable under Scale 1 on that consideration (see article 3(1)(c) of the Fees Order).

(ii)   If the surrender is consideration or part consideration for the grant of a new lease to the registered proprietor or if the surrender is not for monetary consideration, the fee will be payable under Scale 2 on the value of the land in the leasehold title (see articles 4(1)(b) and 4(1)(c) of the Fees Order). A statement of value should accompany the application.

f.   Inland Revenue Form L(A) 451 should be lodged if the application includes a deed of surrender for value which:

(i)   does not attract stamp duty, and

(ii)   pursuant to regulations made under the Finance Act 1985 does[1] not have to be produced to the Revenue first.

2.   Surrender of a registered lease in a superior estate which neither is registered nor is the subject of an application for first registration

a.   A surrender or other sufficient release executed by the registered proprietor and every person appearing by the register to be interested therein, is required (r.200). The surrender may take the form of a transfer in printed Form 19 adapted to fit the facts. If the surrender takes effect by operation of law, the evidence referred to in paragraph 1c above will be required.

b.   The application to register the surrender must be accompanied also by the land certificate or charge certificate (see paragraph 1d above), the lease and its counterpart together with prima facie evidence of the lessor's title, such as an examined abstract of title. When necessary, the application should also be accompanied by Inland Revenue Form L(A)451 (see paragraph 1f above).

c.   A fixed fee is payable for each registered title to be closed wholly or partly unless the application is based on a surrender, when a fee under Scale 1 or Scale 2 is payable, as in paragraph 1e above.

---

1. Stamp Duty (Exempt Instruments) Regulations 1985 (S.I. 1985/1688).

3. Merger or surrender of an unregistered lease noted against a registered superior estate

a. The application must be made in printed Form 92, supported by the land certificate of the superior title, the lease and all other deeds and documents relating to the leasehold title, as more particularly described in paragraph 4 of Form 92 (rr.201 and 202). When necessary, the application should also be accompanied by Inland Revenue Form L(A)451 (see paragraph 1f above).

b. A fee is payable under Scale 1 of the current Fees Order on the value of the leasehold estate immediately prior to its determination (see article 3(6) of the Order).

4. Determination of a lease by effluxion of time

a. Having regard to the provisions of the Landlord and Tenant Act 1954, the registration of a leasehold title or the notice of a lease on the registered title to the superior estate cannot be cancelled merely because the term for which the lease was granted has expired. An application to cancel the registration or notice of a time-expired leasehold term must be supported by a statement signed by the applicant's solicitor or licensed conveyancer either certifying that the provisions of the Landlord and Tenant Act 1954 do not apply to the lease, or specifying the statutory provisions in accordance with which the lease has been determined. The land or charge certificate should be lodged for official cancellation but the lease itself need not be produced.

b. In the case of a registered lease, a fixed fee is payable for each title to be closed wholly or partly. If, however, the application is accompanied by another that attracts a scale fee (such as a transfer of the registered superior estate or the first registration of that estate), no fee is payable for closure of the title to a time-expired lease (Part I(2) Schedule 3 to the current Fees Order). In the case of a noted lease, a fee is payable under Scale 1 on the value of that lease immediately prior to its determination (article 3(6) of the Order). This will usually be the minimum Scale 1 fee.

5. Application forms and fee orders

The various Land Registry printed forms referred to in this leaflet may be bought from any branch of HM Stationery Office or through a law stationer, as may the current Land Registration Fees Order.

6. Address of the district land registry to which an application is to be sent

The application should be sent to the district land registry serving the area in which the land is situated. The application is not deemed to be delivered until it is received at the proper office as shown in the current Land Registration (District Registries) Order. Since further changes in the distribution of records between the district land registries will need to be made from time to time it is not practicable to set out all the details in this leaflet. However, Explanatory Leaflet No. 9, which contains a complete list of all local government areas in England and Wales and indicates the district land registry currently serving each, is continually updated and is available free of charge from any district land registry.

N.B. Postage should be prepaid on all mail.

HM Land Registry   **John Manthorpe CB**
April 1996   **Chief Land Registrar**

Practice Leaflet No. 3

Land certificates and charge certificates lost or destroyed

(S.67(2) of the Land Registration Act 1925 and r.271 of the Land Registration Rules 1925)

A.   Steps to be taken immediately on discovery of loss

1.   *Search for missing certificate*

The Chief Land Registrar has to be satisfied that all reasonable steps have been taken to trace a missing land certificate or charge certificate before he is prepared to issue a replacement. In the case of a certificate that has recently been destroyed, it is usually easy to supply the necessary evidence. Difficulties may arise in trying to trace a missing certificate when there may have been no reason to refer to it for a number of years. If it is necessary to begin searching from the time when the certificate was last issued by the Land Registry, an initial enquiry by letter can be made of the appropriate district land registry (see Part F below) to find out when and to whom the certificate was issued.

2.   *Office copy of register*

Immediately the loss or destruction of a certificate is discovered, an application should be made on printed Form 109 to the appropriate district land registry for an office copy of the register. This office copy is admissible as legal evidence to the same extent as the register itself.

3.   *Address for service of registered proprietor and description of property*

If the office copy of the register shows that the address for service of the registered proprietor or the description of the property is out of date, please notify the appropriate district land registry so that the necessary amendment may be made on the register. This will ensure that any notice served by the Land Registry reaches the proprietor without delay and that any advertised description of the property is correct. No fee is payable for the registration of these changes and any application may be made by letter.

4.   *Precaution against fraud*

If the registered proprietor or the proprietor's solicitor or licensed conveyancer suspects that the land or charge certificate has been stolen to be used for fraudulent purposes, the appropriate district land registry should be consulted as to the desirability of entering an inhibition on the register as a safeguard against fraud.

B.   Application for new certificate

1.   An application to register a dealing with, or a transmission of, registered land or a registered charge, for which the production of the missing land or charge certificate is required, cannot be completed until an application for its replacement has been made to and approved by the appropriate district land registry.

2.   The application must be made by the registered proprietor of the land or the charge to which the missing certificate relates or on the proprietor's behalf or by a personal representative.

3.   The application should be supported by a statutory declaration made by a responsible person with full knowledge of the material facts (who will normally be the person in whose possession the missing certificate was last known to have been).

4.   The statutory declaration must:

(a) establish when, where, and the circumstances in which the loss or destruction occurred;

(b) in the case of loss, state the efforts made to trace the certificate;

(c) establish that the certificate was not deposited with any person as security for money;

(d) establish that no one other than the registered proprietor has any interest or claim;

(e) declare, if not made by the registered proprietor in person, that the proprietor has confirmed to the applicant that he/she was not in possession of the certificate;

(f) state, if the certificate has been lost or destroyed whilst in the solicitor's custody, whether the solicitor held it merely for safe custody or by way of lien.

5.   In the case of loss, the application must be supported by a written undertaking by, or on behalf of, the applicant proprietor(s) to surrender the certificate for official cancellation in the event of it being found at any future time.

6.   Where a replacement certificate is **not** required − in the case, for example, of a lost second or subsequent charge certificate when the registered charge is being discharged − evidence by way of the aforementioned statutory declaration (to account for the absence of the certificate) and an undertaking to surrender the missing certificate, if found, will still be required.

C.   Evidence of identity

1.   To safeguard against the risk of fraud, the Land Registry must verify the identity of an owner who alleges that a certificate has been lost or destroyed.

The applicant's solicitor or licensed conveyancer must provide the following:

● the applicant's permanent address, including the postcode;

● the applicant's date of birth;

● a passport size photograph of the applicant certified on the back by the solicitor or licensed conveyancer (**not** in the name of the firm) as being a photograph of the applicant; and

● a certified copy of the original of a utility bill (e.g. electricity or gas bill) not more than 3 months old, or a council tax bill relating to the current financial year.

The solicitor or licensed conveyancer must also certify in writing that they have verified the applicant's identity by inspecting the **original** of one or more of the following items and lodge with the application a certified copy of such of the following items as were provided:

● a current valid full passport;

● an armed forces identity card;

● an identity card issued by a well known employer which includes a photograph and signature;

- a full United Kingdom driving licence (not a provisional licence). (In this context a full Isle of Man or Channel Islands driving licence may be accepted).

2. In cases where the applicant is not the registered proprietor of the land or charge concerned, but claims to be entitled to represent the proprietor, evidence establishing their authority to do so must also be provided.

3. These requirements are normally waived where the certificate has been lost whilst in the custody of solicitors or licensed conveyancers and the application is lodged by that firm.

4. The registry will be pleased to provide guidance on these requirements and on any difficulty in complying with them.

D. Additional information

1. In considering particular applications, the Land Registry may call for further evidence or decide to advertise the loss by means of official notices in the press (see part E. below).

2. In certain circumstances notices will be served upon the registered proprietor and/or upon the proprietor of a registered or noted charge informing the recipient of the receipt of an application to replace the certificate. Such notices request information as to the whereabouts of the missing certificate and allow for objection to the issue of a replacement certificate to be made within a specified time.

E. Land Registry fees and advertising costs

1. A fee is payable under Part 1(4)(a) of Schedule 3 to the current Fees Order where a replacement land certificate or charge certificate is issued, and under Part 1(4)(b) of the same Schedule where a replacement certificate is not issued (see Part B, paragraph 6 above).

2. The appropriate fee should be sent with the application. On its receipt, the Chief Land Registrar may decide that he will advertise the loss of the particular certificate in the local and/or national press. The cost of advertising must be paid by the applicant who will be notified of the approximate costs before they are incurred and asked to give an undertaking to pay before the application proceeds any further. No sum to cover the advertising costs should thus be added to the standard fee sent with the application, unless the amount of that sum has been notified by the district land registry in earlier correspondence.

3. Fees may be paid by cheque or postal order drawn in favour of "HM Land Registry". Postage must be prepaid on all mail.

F. District Land Registries

Any enquiry or application should be addressed to the district land registry serving the area in which the registered property is situated. An application is not deemed to be delivered until it is received at the proper office as shown in the current Land Registration (District Registries) Order. Since further changes in the distribution of records between district land registries will have to be made from time to time, it is not practicable to set out all the details in this leaflet. However, Explanatory Leaflet No. 9 which contains a complete list of all areas of local government in England and Wales and indicates the district land registry serving each is continually updated and is available free of charge from any district land registry.

HM Land Registry
November 1996

Dr Stuart Hill
Chief Land Registrar

Practice Leaflet No. 4

First registration of title to land where the deeds have been lost or destroyed

1. Applications that can be entertained

First registration may be applied for if the title deeds have been lost or destroyed. Each application is treated on its merits but an absolute title or good leasehold title cannot be granted unless the loss or destruction of the deeds can be explained. Applications where the title deeds have been lost or destroyed (either totally or in part) by theft or whilst in the custody of (or in the post from) a solicitor, licensed conveyancer, building society or clearing bank are the most common. However, applications where the title deeds have been destroyed in some natural disaster (for example flood or fire) or by enemy action will be considered. Any application must be lodged using the appropriate application form:

- 1 B Application by solicitors or licensed conveyancers for first registration of freehold land;

- 2 B Application by solicitors or licensed conveyancers for first registration of leasehold land on behalf of other than an original lessee;

- 3 B Application by solicitors or licensed conveyancers for first registration of leasehold land on behalf of an original lessee;

and should be supported by evidence similar to that outlined in the following paragraphs so far as the circumstances permit. The requisite fee in accordance with Scale 1 of the current Land Registration Fees Order based on the current market value of the land will need to be lodged with the application.

2. Evidence of title

Whilst the Land Registry will consider each application sympathetically, the applicant must first establish that the deeds were lost or destroyed whilst in proper custody and must reconstruct the past history of the title as far as possible and also supply evidence of possession of the land.

3. Custody of deeds

In order to grant an absolute or good leasehold title, the Land Registry must be satisfied as to the custody of the deeds at the time of their loss or destruction. A fully factual statutory declaration made by a member of the firm or organisation in whose custody the deeds were held will normally be sufficient for this purpose if it establishes:

- a. who held the deeds and where they were held immediately before their loss or destruction;

- b. whether they were held for safe custody without any lien, charge or incumbrance or as a security for money owing; and

- c. when, where and how the deeds were lost or destroyed and the efforts made to recover them or their remains.

4. Reconstruction of title

The nature and quality of the secondary evidence of title available will vary but the applicant must submit the best available secondary evidence to show how the title has devolved. The following suggestions may help in preparing applications of this kind.

a. *Contents of deeds and execution*

The best possible secondary evidence of title would be a completed draft of the conveyance or assignment to the applicant (and, if there is a subsisting mortgage, of that too) coupled with completed drafts or examined abstracts of as much of the earlier title as can be reconstructed. It should be supported by a statutory declaration made by the solicitor or licensed conveyancer who acted when the applicant purchased the property:

     i.   proving that the title has been investigated in the normal way;

     ii.   indicating the source from which the documents lodged with the application were obtained; and

     iii.   confirming that the conveyance or assignment (and mortgage) were duly executed and adequately stamped.

If all drafts, abstracts and copy deeds held by the applicant's solicitor or licensed conveyancer have been lost or destroyed as well as all original deeds, it is sometimes possible to obtain like documents from the solicitor or licensed conveyancer who acted for the applicant's vendor, if his or her identity is known. A receipted schedule of deeds, if its source and origin are proved by statutory declaration, may afford some slight evidence of custody and title, as may copies of estate duty affidavits, receipts for rates and taxes, fire insurance policies and receipts for insurance premiums.

b. *Mortgaged property*

If the deeds were held by a mortgagee when they were lost or destroyed, a declaration by the solicitor or licensed conveyancer as to the investigation of title before the advance was made constitutes useful confirmatory evidence of the applicant's title. He or she should also either declare that the mortgage is subsisting or be able to give an account of its repayment.

c. *Unmortgaged property*

If the property was not in mortgage when the deeds were lost or destroyed, one or more of the supporting statutory declarations should state explicitly that at the time of the loss or destruction the owner had not created any mortgage, charge or lien on the property and had not deposited any of the title deeds with any person, firm or body as security for money.

d. *Leasehold property*

If an original lease has been lost or destroyed it is usually possible to obtain a certified copy of the counterpart lease. If the lease contains the usual provisions for the registration of assurances with the lessor's solicitor or licensed conveyancer, he or she may be in a position to make a declaration by reference to the record of documents produced by successive lessees or by reference to his or her knowledge of licences to assign that have been granted in the past. In any event, the present reversioner (or agent) will know who has paid the rent during the current period of ownership.

e. *Searching in the former deeds registries for Middlesex and Yorkshire*

If the land is situated within the area formerly covered by any one of these deeds registries, evidence by a solicitor or licensed conveyancer who has examined the memorials of deeds may establish or help to establish, a chain of title.

     i.   County of Middlesex

         Despite the closing of the Middlesex Deeds Registry, the registers of copy memorials 1709 to 1938 with covering indexes may be inspected at the Greater London Record Office, 40 Northampton Road, London EC1R 0HB, Monday to Friday 9.30 am to 4.45 pm with an extension until 7.30 pm on Tuesdays and Thursdays; for further information please telephone 0171 332 3820.

ii. East Riding of Yorkshire

The records of the former East Riding Registry of Deeds, to include memorials and indexes and covering the period 1708 to 1974, are now in the custody of the East Riding of Yorkshire Council, Archives and Records Service, County Hall, Beverley, East Riding of Yorkshire, HU17 9BA, where they are available for inspection upon prior application to the County Archivist, (telephone 01482 885007). Please state that you wish to inspect deeds when making an appointment.

iii. North Riding of Yorkshire

The North Riding Register of Deeds, which contains copies and memorials of deeds made between 1736 and 1970 is now in the custody of the North Yorkshire County Record Office and may be inspected at pre-arranged times during normal office hours if prior application is made to the County Archivist, whose address for correspondence is County Hall, Northallerton, North Yorkshire DL7 8AF. For further information please telephone 01609 777585.

The Register does not relate to land within the City of York or within the former West and East Ridings of Yorkshire.

The City of York did not fall within the areas formerly covered by the Yorkshire Deed's Registries.

iv. West Riding of Yorkshire

The records of the former West Riding Registry of Deeds, including copies and memorials of documents of title (freehold) for the period 1704 to 1970 are now in the custody of the West Yorkshire Archive Service at the Headquarters, Registry of Deeds Building, Newstead Road, Wakefield WF1 2DE, where they may be inspected. An appointment is necessary. The office is open Mondays 9.30 am−8.00 pm and Tuesdays and Wednesdays 9.30 am−5.00 pm. For further information, telephone 01924 295982. Please note, Wakefield Metropolitan District Council is now the lead authority for Archives in West Yorkshire.

f. *Undisclosed restrictive covenants*

If the applicant's solicitor or licensed conveyancer has not been able to reconstruct the title completely, the missing deeds may have contained or referred to restrictive covenants that are not disclosed in the application. This being so, the Land Registry will be obliged to make an entry on the charges register of the title to the effect that the land is subject to such restrictive covenants as may have been imposed thereon before the date of the destruction or loss of the deeds, so far as such covenants are subsisting and are capable of being enforced. It is particularly difficult to discover the existence of covenants entered into by a vendor, such as brewery covenants. The reason for the above entry is that if no notice of the possible existence of such covenants were to be entered on the register and subsequently the person entitled to their benefit were to succeed in obtaining rectification of the register or if they were to succeed in enforcing them, the registered proprietor would prima facie have a claim for indemnity. If, however, rectification were refused, the person entitled to the benefit of the covenants would probably be entitled to be indemnified. The Chief Land Registrar will, however, only make such an entry where he considers that there is some appreciable degree of risk.

Where an applicant had, as a purchaser, accepted a title of less than 15 years' duration or one which did not commence with a good root, again there may be undisclosed covenants affecting the land so that the Chief Land Registrar will need to consider whether notice needs to be entered. In particular, there may, in any such situation, be registrations in the Land Charges Department which will not have been revealed because the names of the former estate owners were not known. It is broadly the view of the Chief Land Registrar that he will not normally wish to make a protective entry in respect of possible registrations in the names of unknown estate owners where, if the title were not coming on to the register, compensation would be payable under section 25 of the Law of Property Act 1969. Accordingly, where he is supplied with a title of at least 15 years commencing with a good root, he will not make the entry referred to even though evidence of the results of Land Charges searches covering the period from the 1st January 1926 to the date of the commencement of the title is not available. Special considerations may, however, arise if the root of title consists of a mortgage or a specific device which is unlikely to refer to restrictive covenants to which the land is subject or if the application is a voluntary one.

g. Unverified copies of restrictive covenants

It may be that the only available copies of restrictive covenants are unverified.

Under the provisions of s.110(4), all copies and extracts of restrictive covenants that are set out on the register are assumed to be correct and a person who suffers loss by reason of any error or omission in the matter quoted is entitled to be indemnified. Every year the Registry receives numerous applications for first registration that are accompanied by unexamined particulars of restrictive covenants contained in old deeds and the Chief Land Registrar is consequently expected to guarantee the accuracy of such covenants by setting them out on the register. He will, however, only be prepared to do this if he considers that the risk of the abstract or copy being defective is so slight that it can safely be treated as sound evidence of the terms of the deed.

Thus, whilst each case must be treated on its merits, the Chief Land Registrar normally regards a printed abstract as satisfactory and in some cases a typed abstract will be accepted if it appears to be complete and carefully prepared, particularly when the area of land affected by the covenants is considerable (so that knowledge of the covenants is widespread).

Other factors which need to be taken into consideration are whether the later deeds are marked as examined, the nature of the covenants themselves and the value and situation of the land. In the case of old Middlesex or Yorkshire deeds, it may be possible to obtain corroborative evidence from the records of the old deeds registries. (See paragraph 4e above.)

In cases where unverified particulars of stipulations are lodged in the Registry and the Chief Land Registrar feels unable to guarantee their accuracy, an entry will be made to the effect that the relevant deed contained restrictive covenants but neither the original instrument nor a certified copy or an examined abstract thereof was produced on first registration.

However, as the result of representations made by The Law Society, the Chief Land Registrar has agreed that when, but only when, a solicitor so requests, the following form of non-guaranteed entry will be used:

> "A [Conveyance] of the land in this title [and other land] dated . . . .
> made between . . . . contains restrictive covenants but no
> verified particulars of them were produced on first registration. The details set out
> in the schedule of restrictive covenants hereto of what purport to be the said
> covenants were provided by Messrs. . . . ., solicitors acting
> for a vendor in [state year]."

However, the above requirements are not enforced so strictly in enemy action cases as they are in other applications.

h. *Undisclosed rentcharges*

A protective entry relating to rentcharges may similarly be made on the register when the land falls within an area where they abound.

5. Evidence of possession

The applicant will normally be expected to provide a statutory declaration establishing that, since the date of acquisition, the applicant has been either in actual occupation of the whole of the land or in receipt of specific rents from the land (particulars of which should be supplied), without any adverse claim being made. The declaration should include any other relevant facts.

6. Evidence of identity

To safeguard against the risk of fraud, the Land Registry must verify the identity of the applicant for first registration when they allege that the title deeds have been lost or destroyed.

The applicant's solicitor or licensed conveyancer must provide the following:

- the applicant's permanent address, including the postcode;

- the applicant's date of birth;

- a passport size photograph of the applicant certified on the back by the solicitor or licensed conveyancer (**not** in the name of the firm) as being a photograph of the applicant; and

- a certified copy of the original of a utility bill (e.g. electricity or gas bill) not more than 3 months old, or a council tax bill relating to the current financial year.

The solicitor or licensed conveyancer must also certify in writing that they have verified the applicant's identity by inspecting the **original** of one or more of the following items and lodge with the application a certified copy of such of the following items as were provided:

- a current valid full passport;

- an armed forces identity card;

- an identity card issued by a well known employer which includes a photograph and signature;

- a full United Kingdom driving licence (not a provisional licence). (In this context a full Isle of Man or Channel Islands driving licence may be accepted.)

In cases where the applicant is not the owner, but claims to represent the owner, evidence establishing their authority to do so must also be provided.

Should the applicant be a purchaser from a vendor who claims that the title deeds have been lost or destroyed then, in addition to the above, the applicant will need to satisfy him or herself, and in turn the Land Registry, that sufficient evidence has been produced to verify the identity of the vendor.

These requirements are normally waived where the deeds have been lost whilst in the custody of solicitors or licensed conveyancers and the application is lodged by that firm.

The registry will be pleased to provide guidance on these requirements and on any difficulty in complying with them.

7. Subsequent delivery

Where the title deeds have been lost, the applicant's solicitor or licensed conveyancer should enclose with the application for registration an undertaking to produce them to the Land Registry if they are subsequently discovered. If, after the date of first registration, further evidence of title comes to light, whether favourable or unfavourable to the registered proprietor it should be produced to the Land Registry with the land or charge certificate.

8. Additional information

Single copies of the following practice leaflets are obtainable without charge from any district land registry and may be useful.

Practice Leaflet	Subject
No. 3	Land certificates and charge certificates lost or destroyed
No. 5	First registration of title to land

The application should be sent to the district land registry serving the area in which the land is situated. The application is not deemed to be delivered until it is received at the proper office as shown in the current Land Registration (District Registries) Order. Since further changes in the distribution of records between the district land registries will need to be made from time to time it is not practicable to set out all the details in this leaflet. However, Explanatory Leaflet No. 9, which contains a complete list of all local government areas in England and Wales and indicates the district land registry currently serving each, is continually updated and is available free of charge from any district land registry.

N.B. Postage should be prepaid on all mail. Land Registry fees are payable by cheque or postal order made payable to "HM Land Registry". (As changes are made to Land Registry fees from time to time, please refer to the current Fees Order for the appropriate fee before making an application.)

HM Land Registry
November 1996

Dr Stuart Hill
Chief Land Registrar

Practice Leaflet No. 5
Land Registration Rules 1925

First registration of title to land

1. First registration

Throughout England and Wales[1] unregistered land must be registered following a sale. This is because a conveyance on sale of freehold land will become void, as regards the grant of the legal estate, on the expiration of two months from the date of the deed, unless the purchaser has, in the meantime, applied for registration of his title.[2] Since 1st January 1987, this has also applied, mutatis mutandis, to a grant of lease[3] for a term of more than 21 years or an assignment on sale of leasehold land held for a term with more than 21 years to run.

In referring to a conveyance or assignment on sale, the Land Registration Act 1925 does not define the word "sale", but it is generally taken to mean a sale by a vendor to a purchaser for money or money's worth. However, the Act does provide that the words "conveyance on sale" and "assignment on sale" include an exchange of land where money is paid for equality, but not an assignment or surrender of a lease to the reversioner containing a declaration of merger.[4]

If a purchaser or grantee who is obliged to apply for first registration fails to do so within the prescribed period of two months, an order granting an extension of the period may be applied for. Provided that he is given a reasonable explanation for the delay, the Chief Land Registrar will always make such an order. The order may be requested in a letter, which should also give the reasons for the delay. The letter should accompany the application for first registration, not precede it.

A lease for a term exceeding 21 years granted by the proprietor of registered land, is a disposition[5] of registered land. As such, it must be completed by the first registration of the title of the lessee,[6] as well as being noted against the lessor's title.[7] Unless this is done, the lessee will not obtain the legal estate. Furthermore, by using the official search procedure[8] and lodging the application for registration within 30 working days from the date of the certificate of the result of search, the lessee can secure priority for the entry of the lease on the register of the lessor's title.

On the first registration of a lease which is a disposition of registered land, production of the lessor's land certificate must be considered. If the lessor's title is subject to a legal mortgage, so that the land certificate is retained in the Land Registry,[9] clearly it cannot be produced although it is desirable that any outstanding charge certificate should be deposited for the lease to be noted thereon. If, however, the lessor's land certificate is outstanding, and the lessor takes a premium, the land certificate must be lodged in the Land Registry.[10]

1. Areas where registration was compulsory were first designated in 1898 and in December 1990 were finally extended to the whole of England and Wales. Explanatory Leaflet No. 9 (and supplemental leaflet) give details of the dates on which areas were made compulsory. (See paragraph 9 below.)
2. Land Registration Act 1925, s123(1) (as amended by the Land Registration Act 1986).
3. Throughout this leaflet, the word "lease" includes a sublease or underlease.
4. Land Registration Act 1925, s123(3).
5. Ibid; ss 18, 21.
6. Ibid; ss 19, 22.
7. Land Registration Rules 1925, r46. The application should take the form of a first registration.
8. See the current Land Registration (Official Searches) Rules and also Practice Advice Leaflet No. 5.
9. Land Registration Act 1925, s65.
10. Ibid; s64(1)(c).

If no premium is taken, production of the land certificate is desirable, but not essential. An assignee can find out whether the lease has already been noted against the lessor's registered title without the authority of the lessor by writing to the appropriate district land registry.

Application may also be made voluntarily at any time for first registration of the title to any freehold land or leasehold land which is held under a lease for a term with more than 21 years to run. [11]

The requirements for first registration where the deeds and documents of title are lost are set out in Practice Leaflet No. 4 (see paragraph 9 below).

2. Form of conveyance or assignment inducing first registration

On the purchase of freehold or leasehold land which is to be the subject of an application for first registration, it may be better to take a transfer following Land Registry form 19 [12] instead of the more usual conveyance or assignment in unregistered conveyancing form. However, there are certain difficulties in the preparation of such a transfer which do not arise in the case of a transfer of a registered title. The following points require particular attention:

a . the land transferred cannot be described as "the land comprised in the title above referred to" since the registered title has not yet been created. Instead, the precise extent of the land transferred by the instrument, if not capable of verbal description, must either be shown on a plan attached to the transfer or be identified by reference to the plan in an earlier deed which forms part of the title deduced. When the plan in an earlier conveyance is referred to, the possibility that part of the land in that conveyance was subsequently sold off must be considered;

b . all the rights and incumbrances incident to the land transferred must be specifically referred to in the transfer; and

c . the need to add to the simple statutory form such matters as indemnity covenants must not be overlooked.

3. Who can apply

The applicant for first registration must be the estate owner at the date of making the application. Where the owner has transferred the property before applying for first registration, the transferee must be named as the applicant in the application form.

4. Forms required

Application by a solicitor or licensed conveyancer for first registration should be made by post to the proper district land registry (see paragraph 10 below) using whichever of the following forms is appropriate. These forms may be bought from any branch of HM Stationery Office or through a law stationer.

Form No	Description
1B	For first registration of freehold land. (Replaces earlier editions of forms 1B, 1C, 1C(Co) and 1E)
2B	For first registration of leasehold land on behalf of other than an original lessee. (Replaces earlier editions of forms 2B, 2C, 2C(Co), 2E, 2F, and 2F(Co))

11. Land Registration Act 1925, s8.
12. Land Registration Rules 1925, r72.

3B   For first registration of leasehold land on behalf of an original
                                lessee. (Replaces earlier editions of forms 3B, 3E, 3F and 3F(Co))

The form must be properly completed and signed. An up-to-date address within the United
Kingdom of the applicant for entry on the register must be provided.

5. Documents which must accompany forms

The application in the appropriate form should be accompanied by:

a . All the original deeds and other documents of title which the applicant has or can
    oblige the holder to produce, including opinions of counsel, abstracts of title, copies
    of documents, contracts for sale, requisitions, replies and official certificates of
    the result of search at the Land Charges Department. Original documents need not
    usually be produced if they are held by a mortgagee under a subsisting mortgage
    entered into before the conveyance to the applicant, or they affect also other land,
    or their production would entail the applicant's paying a fee to the holder, provided
    that a sufficient abstract or certified copies are supplied. Where such documents
    are not produced, the name and address of the solicitor to the person who holds
    them should be stated. Abstracts should be marked by solicitors as having been
    examined with the original deeds and all particulars of wills, grants of probate or
    letters of administration, marriages and deaths set out therein as separate items
    should also be verified and marked accordingly.

b . A certified true copy of the conveyance, assignment, transfer or lease to the
    applicant and a similarly certified copy of any accompanying mortgage or charge
    which is to be registered.

c . An additional examined abstract or certified copy of any abstracted deed which
    contains restrictive covenants or stipulations, unless the original deed is also
    produced.

d . Sufficient particulars (if not contained in the conveyance or other assurance to the
    applicant), by plan or otherwise, to enable the position and extent of the land to
    be identified by the Land Registry on the Ordnance Survey Map.

e . A list in duplicate of all documents enclosed with the application.

f . The prescribed fee (see paragraph 8, below).

g . Inland Revenue form L(A)451 where the conveyance, transfer or assignment on
    sale to the applicant is executed on or after 1 January 1986, does not attract stamp
    duty and, pursuant to regulations[13] made under the Finance Act 1985, does not
    require to be produced to the Revenue first.

6. Evidence of title

Enquiries about Land Registry practice may be made at any district land registry before
making a formal application for first registration. However, until the formal application is
made, accompanied by the appropriate deeds and documents and the prescribed fee, the
Land Registry cannot express any opinion about a particular title. The title offered should
be such as a willing purchaser, acting under competent professional advice, could properly
be advised to accept and it should be prepared for first registration as if it were being prepared
for examination by a purchaser. In addition to a properly verified abstract of title, full
information should be given on any points regarding which a well-advised purchaser would

13. Stamp Duty (Exempt Instrument) Regulations 1985 (SI 1985/1688).

raise requisitions. The possibility that the title or any part of it is already known to the Land Registry should not be taken into account, unless the vendor can show written evidence of a special arrangement.

7. Charges

Any charge by the applicant must define the property charged. Since a Land Registry title number will not be issued until after the charge has been executed, it must describe the land charged in some other satisfactory manner, such as by full verbal description, reference to a plan, or reference to the conveyance or other assurance to the borrower. All material dates and particulars should be inserted in charges, especially in the blank spaces provided in printed forms of mortgage to building societies, insurance companies and the like.

8. Fees

The fees payable are set out in the current Land Registration Fees Order, which can be purchased from any branch of HM Stationery Office or through a law stationer.

A charge by the applicant which either accompanies an application for the first registration of the land (or is lodged before its completion) is registered without fee, under the current Fees Order.

Fees may be paid by postal order or cheque drawn in favour of "HM Land Registry" and postage must be prepaid on all mail.

9. Practice Leaflets

The Land Registry leaflets which have been mentioned are:

Explanatory Leaflet No. 9 "Areas served by District Registries".

Supplement to Explanatory Leaflet No. 9.

Practice Leaflet No. 4 "First Registration of Title to Land where the Deeds have been Lost or Destroyed".

Practice Advice Leaflet No. 5 "Searches of Registered Land and Land Subject to a Pending First Registration Application".

These leaflets are obtainable free of charge from any district land registry.

10. District Registries of HM Land Registry

The application should be sent to the district land registry serving the area in which the land is situated. The application is not deemed to be delivered until it is received at the proper office as shown in the current Land Registration (District Registries) Order. Since further changes in the distribution of records between the district land registries will need to be made from time to time it is not practicable to set out all the details in this leaflet. However, Explanatory Leaflet No. 9 referred to above, which contains a complete list of all local government areas in England and Wales and indicates the district land registry currently serving each, is continually updated and is available free of charge from any district land registry.

N.B.Postage should be prepaid on all mail.

HM Land Registry   **John Manthorpe CB**
January 1996   **Chief Land Registrar**

Practice Leaflet No. 6

Devolution on the death of a registered proprietor

1. Death of a sole proprietor

a. *Registration of the personal representatives*

An application to register the personal representative(s) of a sole proprietor of registered land or of a registered charge should be made in Form 82, accompanied by the relevant land certificate or charge certificate. Evidence of the grant of representation will be required and, in strictness, this should consist of the production of the original grant of probate or letters of administration. In practice, however, an official copy of the grant is acceptable. Even a plain copy is acceptable, provided that it has been certified as being a correct copy of the original grant. These documents may be conveniently submitted for registration under cover of form A4 which is the appropriate covering form for all dealings with the whole of the land in a registered title or registered charge.

The registration fee is payable under Scale 2 in the current Land Registration Fees Order on the value of the property. In respect of a transmission of registered land, the fee is assessed on the present value of the land in each registered title affected by the application after deducting the amount secured thereon by any registered charge. In respect of a transmission of a registered charge, the fee is assessed on the amount secured by the charge after deducting the amount secured thereon by any registered sub-charge of that charge.

b. *Registration of a disposition by the personal representatives*

The personal representatives of a deceased sole proprietor of registered land may, without first being registered themselves in that capacity, transfer the land by using Form 19, or dispose of it by way of assent or appropriation by using Form 56. Similarly, they may transfer any registered charge of which the deceased was registered as sole proprietor by using Form 54 or dispose of it by way of assent or appropriation by using Form 56. Any such application must be accompanied by the land certificate or charge certificate and by evidence of the grant of representation as stated in item a. above.

In the case of an assent or other disposition not for monetary consideration the fee payable is calculated under Scale 2 (see item a. above). However, where a registered proprietor has died and the personal representatives have already been registered as such, a disposition not for valuable consideration given by them is registrable without the payment of a fee (see Schedule 4(8) to the current Land Registration Fees Order).

In the case of a transfer or charge of the land for monetary consideration given by the personal representatives, whether or not they have already been registered, an ad valorem fee is payable under Scale 1 for the transfer, or under Scale 2 for the charge. On the registration of a transfer for monetary consideration of a registered charge given by the personal representatives, a fee is payable under Scale 2.

Note 1: Any transfer by the personal representative(s) to beneficiaries should contain, if appropriate, a certificate under the Stamp Duty (Exempt Instruments) Regulations 1987.
Note 2: The vesting of registered land in a tenant for life under the Settled Land Act 1925 is effected by means of a vesting assent in Form 57 but, in other respects, the application is the same as that to register an assent in Form 56. In the case of a continuing settlement, the special grant must be lodged.

c. *Liability to capital transfer tax*

The Finance Act 1975 abolished estate duty in respect of a death occurring after 12 March 1975 and, subject to certain exemptions, imposed capital transfer tax on all gifts of land occurring on death. This Act has now been replaced by the Capital Transfer Tax Act 1984, now called the Inheritance Tax Act 1984, which is a consolidation measure. Where Inheritance Tax is due to the Commissioners of Inland Revenue, a statutory charge in their favour is imposed upon the land subject of the gift. The Commissioners can, when they so wish, protect this charge by entering on the register the following notice under s.49 of the 1925 Act:

> "Notice of an Inland Revenue charge [Reference no.   ] in respect of such inheritance/capital transfer tax as may arise by reason of the death of A.B. of [address] who died on [date]."

Where appropriate, such an entry may also be made by the Chief Land Registrar at the time of first registration.

When such an entry has been made in the register, it will be cancelled only on production of a certificate in Land Registry Form 61 (CTT) given by the Commissioners of Inland Revenue. Land Registry Form 61 (CTT) is incorporated in Capital Taxes Office Form 31 (CTT) and the combined form is obtainable from the Controller, Inland Revenue, Capital Taxes Office, Ferrers House, P.O. Box 38, Castle Meadow Road, Nottingham NG2 1BB or from the bookshops of the Solicitors' Law Stationery Society Limited. The forms are not supplied by the Land Registry or Her Majesty's Stationery Office. If the certificate given in Form 61 (CTT) specifies that it is to take effect only upon the registration of a disposition to a purchaser, the entry in the register will be removed only when that certificate is produced accompanied by a proper application to register the transfer or other specified disposition in favour of the purchaser. The entry will remain on the register, even on the registration of a transfer on sale, until a certificate in Form 61 (CTT) is produced.

d. *Liability for death duties*

Where the proprietor of registered land died before 13 March 1975 and it appeared that the land was subject to a charge for death duties, the following entry was made in the register as a matter of course:

> "Until the registration of a disposition in favour of a purchaser for money or money's worth, the land is liable to such death duties as may be payable or arise by reason of the death of A.B. of [address] who died on [date]".

Upon the registration of a transfer of the land on sale or other disposition for value, this entry will be cancelled automatically. However, the entry will also be cancelled at any other time upon the production of a certificate in Land Registry Form 61 given by the Commissioners of Inland Revenue. That form is incorporated in Capital Taxes Office Form 31, obtainable as stated in item c. above. These forms are not supplied by the Land Registry or Her Majesty's Stationery Office.

2. Death of a joint proprietor

a. *Withdrawal of the name of the deceased from the register*

An application to withdraw from the register the name of a deceased joint proprietor of registered land or of a registered charge should be made in Form 83, accompanied by the relevant land certificate or charge certificate. Evidence of the death will be required and, in strictness, this should consist of the original death certificate or the grant of representation.

In practice, however, production of an official copy of one or other of these documents will suffice. Even a plain copy is acceptable, provided that it has been certified as being a correct copy of the original certificate or grant. The application may conveniently be submitted for registration under cover of Form A4. No fee is payable.

b. *Removal from the register of a restriction in Form 62*

If joint proprietors are registered in respect of land or a charge and there is no restriction entered in the register, a sole surviving proprietor is entitled to dispose of the registered property and give a valid receipt for the purchase money. However, a restriction often appears in the register, having been entered pursuant to s.58(3) of the Land Registration Act 1925, in the following or similar terms:

> "No disposition by a sole proprietor of the land (not being a trust corporation) under which capital money arises is to be registered except under an order of the Registrar or of the Court."

Nevertheless, whenever the above restriction has been registered and, as the result of an application (as described in item a. above), the number of joint proprietors has been reduced to one, the restriction will never be removed from the register as a matter of course. Nor, having regard to r.214 of the Land Registration Rules 1925, can it be removed merely upon a formal application by the survivor to do so. Hence, the printed form of application for the withdrawal of a restriction (Form 77) is not appropriate in this situation. The restriction can be removed on an application being made in Form A4 supported by adequate evidence of the equitable title, proving that the sole survivor can give a valid receipt for capital money arising on a disposition of the land. The kind of evidence usually accepted consists of a statutory declaration by the sole surviving proprietor that, in stated circumstances, such as by virtue of the terms of the will of the deceased joint proprietor, the declarant has become legally and beneficially entitled to the whole of the land in the registered title; has not incumbered his or her undivided share and that he or she has not received notice of any incumbrance on the undivided share(s) of the deceased joint proprietor(s). If the solicitor or licensed conveyancer acting for the survivor is able to speak from personal knowledge of the facts, a certificate by him or her is usually accepted in place of a sworn declaration by his or her client. The statutory declaration or certificate should be supported by any documentary evidence available, such as an assent in respect of the undivided share(s) of the deceased proprietor(s) in favour of the sole survivor. No fee is payable.

c. *Registration of the personal representative of the last survivor of joint proprietors or a disposition by such a personal representative*

When all the joint proprietors of registered land or a registered charge have died, the personal representative of the last survivor of them is normally entitled to apply for registration in that capacity or, without first being so registered, to dispose of the property by way of a transfer, assent, appropriation or vesting assent. Even when a restriction in Form 62 has been entered in the register against the joint proprietors, it is considered that this does not bind the personal representative of the last survivor of them so that it will be cancelled as a matter of course either on the registration of that personal representative or on the registration of a disposition by the personal representative. An application on similar lines to the appropriate one of those mentioned earlier in part 1 of this leaflet should be made according to the circumstances of the case. Evidence of the deaths of the other joint proprietors should be lodged if their deaths have not already been noted on the register (see item a. above). Fees will be payable as previously stated in this leaflet according to the nature of the particular applications.

3. Application forms and fees

a.   The several forms referred to in this leaflet (other than form 31/61 (CTT) and form 31/61 referred to in items c. and d. of part 1 above) may be bought from any branch of Her Majesty's Stationery Office or through a law stationer. So, too, may the current Land Registration Fees Order.

b.   Fees may be paid by cheque or postal order drawn in favour of "HM Land Registry".

4.   Address of the District Land Registry to which an application is to be sent

The application should be sent to the district land registry serving the area in which the land is situated. The application is not deemed to be delivered until it is received at the proper office as shown in the current Land Registration (District Registries) Order. Since further changes in the distribution of records between the district land registries will have to be made from time to time, it is not practicable to set out all the details in this leaflet. However, Explanatory Leaflet No. 9 which contains a complete list of all local government areas in England and Wales and indicates the district land registry currently serving each is continually updated and is available free of charge from any district land registry.

N.B. Postage should be prepaid on all mail.

HM Land Registry   **John Manthorpe CB**
April 1996   **Chief Land Registrar**

Practice Leaflet No. 10

Land Registration (Matrimonial Homes) Rules 1990

Applications to protect rights of occupation under the Matrimonial Homes Act 1983 affecting registered land

1. Rights of occupation

The purpose of the Matrimonial Homes Act 1983 (referred to in this leaflet as "the Act"), is to protect the right of a spouse to occupy the matrimonial home. This right is not an overriding interest but constitutes a charge on the matrimonial home which can be protected on the register by a notice in the circumstances described below. Prior to 14th February 1983, such charge could also be protected on the register by a caution (see paragraph 5 below). In this leaflet, reference is made to the wife as being the spouse whose rights of occupation in the dwellinghouse constituting the matrimonial home are in need of protection and the husband as being the owner of that dwellinghouse. This has been done because in most instances it is the wife who seeks protection. However, these notes apply equally when it is the husband who is seeking protection if the references to "husband" and "wife" are transposed throughout.

The charge arises on whichever is the latest of the following dates:

(a) the date when the husband acquires the home, or

(b) the date of marriage, or

(c) January 1 1968,

although it is not anticipated that protection for it will be sought until the wife has been deserted or the marriage appears to be in jeopardy. No protection under the Act is required in cases where the matrimonial home is held, both legally and beneficially, by husband and wife jointly.

2. Forms of application

The following printed forms of application have been prescribed by the Land Registration (Matrimonial Homes) Rules 1990 (S.I. 1990 No. 1360):

> Form 99. Application for Registration of a Notice of Rights of Occupation.

> Form 100. Application for Renewal of Registration of a Notice or Caution in respect of Rights of Occupation.

These Rules also prescribe:

> Form 106. Application by Mortgagee for Official Search in respect of Rights of Occupation. (See paragraph 12 below.)

The following printed form has been devised by the Registry to assist practitioners:

> Form 202. Application to Cancel Notice of Rights of Occupation under the Matrimonial Homes Acts.

3. Application for notice

When the title to the husband's estate or interest in the matrimonial home is registered under the Land Registration Acts and his wife has rights of occupation which are a charge on the property under the provisions of s.2(1) or 2(2) of the Act, application may be made in Form 99 to protect her charge by the entry of a notice on the registered title. The application for the entry of the notice does not require the production of the land certificate. No fee is payable.

4. Rights continued by order of court

A wife's rights of occupation under the Act will normally endure only during the subsistence of the marriage (see paragraph 6 below). However, s.2(4) of the Act provides that, in the event of a matrimonial dispute or estrangement, the court may, if it sees fit, make an order under s.1 of the Act, during the subsistence of the marriage, directing that the wife's rights of occupation shall continue even though the marriage may come to an end. If the court makes such an order and the wife's rights of occupation have not already been protected, application should be made as soon as possible to register a notice in accordance with s.5(3)(b) of the Act. The application should be made in printed Form 99. An official copy of the order must accompany the application and will be retained in the Land Registry. No fee is payable.

5. Renewal of protection

If the court makes an order under s.2(4) of the Act when the wife's rights of occupation are already protected on the register by means of a notice, or by means of a caution where that caution was registered before 14th February 1983, application should be made as soon as possible to renew the earlier protection in case the husband attempts to cancel it without disclosing the existence of the court order. The application should be made in printed Form 100 and must be accompanied by an official copy of the order. If the original protection was by way of notice, the land certificate need not be produced for the renewal of the registration. No fee is payable. The "renewal" will be effected on the register by means of the entry of a further notice or caution, as appropriate. This renewal of registration does not affect the priority of the original charge (see s.5(5) of the Act).

6. Cessation of rights

A wife's rights of occupation may be brought to an end in the following ways:

> (a) By the death of either party (s.5(1)(a) of the Act). But see paragraph 4 above as to the power of the court under s.2(4).
>
> (b) By the termination of the marriage otherwise than by death (s.5(1)(b) of the Act). But see paragraph 4 above as to the power of the court to make an order under s.2(4).
>
> (c) By an order of the court (s.5(1)(c) of the Act).
>
> (d) By the wife voluntarily releasing her rights in writing (s.6(1) of the Act).

7. Cancellation of a notice

An application to cancel a notice may be made by letter or in Form 202 accompanied by evidence proving the appropriate one of the events described in paragraph 6 above. Thus the evidence will consist of the death certificate, an official copy of the decree, an official copy of the court's order, Form 202 or a letter or other form of release signed by the wife. If the court has made an order under s.2(4) of the Act which is referred to on the register (see paragraphs 4 and 5 above), it will also be necessary for the applicant to satisfy the Chief Land Registrar that this order has ceased to have effect (see s.5(2) of the Act). No fee is payable.

8. Cancellation of a caution

An application to cancel a caution may be made in one of the following ways:

(a) By a letter accompanied by evidence proving the appropriate one of the events described in sub-paragraph (a), (b) or (c) of paragraph 6 above. See also paragraph 7 above if an order has been made under s.2(4) of the Act.

(b) By a withdrawal of the caution using printed Form 71, signed by the wife or her solicitors.

(c) By a request in the form of a letter to warn-off the caution under r.218 of the Land Registration Rules 1925. However, having regard to r.5 of the Land Registration (Matrimonial Homes) Rules 1990 the Chief Land Registrar will not be able to give effect to this application by serving a warning-off notice on the cautioner unless the application is accompanied by:

Either, a release in writing of the wife's rights of occupation protected by the caution, signed by her.

Or, a statutory declaration by the husband or some responsible person conversant with the facts, declaring that, as to the whole or any part of the land to which the caution relates, no charge under s.2(1) or 2(2) of the Act has ever arisen or, if such a charge has arisen, that it is no longer subsisting. This declaration should set out briefly the facts upon which the declarant relies.

No fee is payable on an application to cancel a caution.

9. Protection restricted to one house only

By virtue of s.3 of the Act, a wife is allowed to protect her rights of occupation in respect of only one house at any one time, whether the husband's interest in the house is held under a registered or unregistered title. A solicitor acting for an applicant must therefore ascertain from his client whether she already has any protection under the Act, and the position must then be disclosed on Form 99.

10. Is the estate or interest in the matrimonial home registered?

In all cases it is essential to know whether the husband's interest in the matrimonial home is held under a registered or an unregistered title. If it is a registered title then the registration of a land charge of Class F in the Land Charges Department is ineffective to protect the wife's rights of occupation. If it is not known, and cannot be discovered by any other means, whether any interest in the matrimonial home is held under a registered title an application to the appropriate district land registry (see paragraph 15 below) should be made by post in printed Form 96 for an official search of the public index map. The fee payable for an official search of the index map is prescribed in Part III(4) of Schedule 3 to the current Land Registration Fees Order. It is essential that the following note is written across the top of the form: − "This search is being made solely for the purposes of the Matrimonial Homes Act 1983. Please reveal details of any registered lease." This will enable the Land Registry to avoid raising any points as to the precise boundaries of the property which might otherwise arise and give particulars of any lease. The official certificate of the result of search will be sent by the district land registry within a day or two of the application being received, and will reveal which interest(s) (if any) in the land are registered. For further particulars see Practice Leaflet No. 15 referred to in paragraph 14 below.

11.　Charge securing further advances

For the purposes of s.30(1) of the Land Registration Act 1925, when a charge is already registered which secures further advances, the registration or renewal of registration of a notice or caution to protect a wife's rights of occupation under the Act is regarded as an entry which prejudicially affects the priority of any further advances which may be made under the registered charge. For the purpose of the Land Registration Act 1925, s.30(3), where a charge is already registered which contains an obligation to make further advances, the registration or renewal of registration of a notice or caution under the Act will be regarded as a subsequent registered charge which will take effect subject to any further advance made pursuant to that obligation. Accordingly, the statutory notice will be served by the Chief Land Registrar on the prior chargees in both these instances. It is emphasised, however, that in no circumstances will the Land Registry serve notice of the application upon the registered proprietor of the land.

12.　Official search by mortgagee

Under s.8(3) of the Matrimonial Homes Act 1983 a mortgagee of a dwellinghouse who brings an action for the enforcement of his security, must serve notice of the action on a spouse whose rights of occupation are protected at the relevant time by, in the case of unregistered land, a Class F land charge, and, in the case of registered land, by a notice or caution. A proprietor of a registered charge or a mortgagee of registered land may apply on Form 106 for an official certificate of the result of a search which will reveal if there is a notice or caution registered to protect a spouse's right of occupation. Form 106 must be delivered in duplicate at the appropriate district land registry. A fee prescribed in Part III(1) of Schedule 3 to the current Land Registration Fees Order is payable. This search will carry priority for the purposes of s. 8(4) for a period of 15 days. If the dwellinghouse is unregistered the mortgagee should make an official search at Land Charges Registry on Form K15.

13.　Rights of occupation of a bankrupt

A bankrupt who is entitled to occupy a dwellinghouse by virtue of a beneficial estate or interest has rights of occupation as against his trustee in bankruptcy in the circumstances outlined in the Insolvency Act 1986, s.337. This applies whether or not the bankrupt's spouse has any rights of occupation under the Matrimonial Homes Act 1983. A notice of his right of occupation may be entered on the register provided the application in Form 99 is amplified to state that the bankrupt applies under the Insolvency Act 1986, s.337 and that his interest in the property is now vested in his trustee in bankruptcy (who should be named).

14.　Application forms, etc.

The various Land Registry forms referred to in this leaflet may be bought from any branch of HM Stationery Office or through a law stationer.

Practice Leaflet No. 15 referred to is obtainable free of charge from any district land registry.

15.　Address of the District Land Registry to which an application is to be sent

The application should be sent to the district land registry serving the area in which the matrimonial home is situated. The application is not deemed to be delivered until it is received at the proper office as shown in the current Land Registration (District Registries) Order. Since further changes in the distribution of records between the district land registries will need to be made from time to time it is not practicable to set out all the details in this leaflet. However, Explanatory Leaflet No. 9, which contains a complete list of all areas of local government in England and Wales and indicates the district land registry currently serving each, is continually updated and is available free of charge from any district land registry.

16. Unregistered land

All applications under the Act in respect of unregistered land should be sent to:

> The Superintendent,
> Land Charges Department,
> Drakes Hill Court,
> Burrington Way,
> Plymouth PL5 3LP
> DX No 8249 Plymouth (3)
> (Telephone number: Plymouth (01752) 635600).

N.B. Postage must be prepaid on all mail, whether addressed to a district land registry or to the Land Charges Department.

HM Land Registry　　　　　　　　　　　　　　　　**John Manthorpe CB**
April 1996　　　　　　　　　　　　　　　　　　　**Chief Land Registrar**

Practice Leaflet No. 13

Inspection of the Register and Applications for Office Copies

1. Who may apply

Any person may apply to inspect the register or to be supplied with an office copy of the entries register and any document referred to in the register which is in the custody of the Registrar (other than a lease or charge or a copy or extract of a lease or charge) − s.112 Land Registration Act 1925 (as amended) and the Land Registration (Open Register) Rules 1991.

2. Applications for office copies

(i) What can be supplied

a.   An office copy of the **entries in the register** in respect of a particular title. This will automatically include any annexed schedule containing details of restrictive covenants, leases, rentcharges, etc.

b.   An office copy of the **title plan** in respect of a particular title. Where the title plan is either large or complex, information can be provided in the form of a simple certificate (see paragraph (v) below).

c.   Office copies of **any documents that are referred to in the register entries and which are in the custody of the Registrar** and office copies of **any personal covenants which are referred to but not set out in the register.**

d.   An office copy of a caution title. A caution title is prepared on each occasion that a caution against first registration is lodged. A caution title includes an official plan showing the extent of the land affected.

(ii) Exceptions

a.   Neither original **registered leases** nor original **registered mortgages** are filed in the Land Registry and, whilst copies of these documents may sometimes be filed, it should be noted that, subject to prescribed exceptions affecting the police and others, an office copy of a filed copy can only be issued if the Chief Land Registrar exercises his discretion in a particular case. Accordingly, any request for such an office copy should be in writing, setting out why it is considered that the Chief Land Registrar should exercise his discretion.

b.   The register of title is conclusive and the Chief Land Registrar is fully responsible for seeing that it contains all of the entries which it ought to contain. Where the text of a covenant, easement or other provision **is set out verbatim on the register,** an office copy of the document from which the extract is taken should not normally be necessary. This is because the object of setting out these verbatim extracts on the register is to avoid the expense entailed in obtaining an office copy of the whole of the document containing them. Moreover, where an entry has been made in this manner, it may well be that neither the original deed upon which the entry is founded nor a copy or abstract of it is held in the Land Registry.

c.   The Index of Proprietors' Names is not part of the Open Register. Rule 9 of the Land Registration Rules 1925 (as amended by the Land Registration Rules 1976) sets out the procedure for making a search of this index.

(iii) Authenticity

All office copies supplied by the Land Registry are prepared on paper water-marked with the letters "LR" in an oval surmounted by a crown.

(iv) The application forms: Form 109, Form 110 and Form 110A

a. Registers of title and title plans are normally held at the relevant district land registry. However, limited storage space means that documents referred to in registers as filed are, at many registries, stored in off-site repositories and can therefore take longer to retrieve. To prevent this holding up the early issue of office copy registers and title plans, a two stage process applies to the issue of office copies as a whole requiring the use of two separate forms, Form 109 and Form 110 (which replace the previous forms A44 and A44A).

b. Form 109 provides for requests for office copies of the register and title plan (or where appropriate a certificate in Form 102 — see paragraph (v) below). Form 110, which will usually only be needed where documents or copies of personal covenants are referred to in the register as filed, caters for requests for office copies of those documents or personal covenants as set out in form A54 annexed to the register. With regard to Form 110, it is a requirement that the deeds requested are listed specifically with their nature and dates being given. In addition, the title number under which the deeds are filed, as shown on the register, must be quoted and the number of copies required stated. Generalised requests for "all" or "any" deeds are not accepted. Form 109 and Form 110 may be submitted to the Registry at the same time. Form 110A is the form on which any person may apply for an office copy of a caution title, which includes the official plan.

c. Form 109, Form 110 and Form 110A are obtainable from Her Majesty's Stationery Office or any other law stationer. The use of the appropriate printed form is mandatory for applications made either in documentary form or by facsimile transmission. Paragraph 4 of this leaflet deals with applications by telephone and facsimile transmission (see the Land Registration (Open Register) Rules 1991, SI 1992 No. 122).

(v) Application for certificate of official inspection of the filed plan

When dealing with only part of the land in a registered title it is normally necessary to find out whether that part is in the title and which (if any) colour or other references shown on the title plan affect it. A simple certificate (Form 102) giving this information may be applied for using Form 109 under rule 2 of the Land Registration (Open Register) Rules 1991.

This procedure is particularly useful in the case of registered building developments where an estate layout plan has been approved by the Registry. In this case an application in Form 109 for a certificate in Form 102 may be made without an accompanying plan if the plot (and any separate garage or other parcel of land) can be identified by the plot number(s) shown on the approved layout plan. In any other case the application must be supported by an accurate plan in duplicate (at 1/2500 scale or greater) showing the precise position and extent of the land in relation to the detail shown on the title plan. A fee is payable (see paragraph (vii) below). These simple procedures are recommended. By using them practitioners avoid having to obtain and interpret plans which may be cumbersome and complicated. For a more detailed description of this procedure, see also Practice Advice Leaflet No. 5 and Practice Leaflet No. 7 referred to in paragraph 5 below.

(vi) Application for office copies where title number is not known

Where the property is known to be registered but the title number is not readily available, an application for office copies in Form 109 may be lodged with the words "Please supply the title number" written boldly at the head of the form. An additional fee is payable: see the next paragraph.

(vii) Land Registry fees

The fees payable under the current Fees Order are as follows:

Application for an office copy of the register	£5
Application for an office copy of the title plan or one official certificate of inspection of the title plan	£5
Application for an office copy of any or all of the documents referred to in the register other than a lease or mortgage − per title	£5
Office copy of a lease or mortgage referred to in the register (or a copy thereof) or any document not referred to in the register − per document	£10
Office copy of a caution title which includes the official plan	£10

In the case of an application for an office copy of the register or the title plan if no title number is quoted on the application form, or the title number quoted does not relate to any part of the land described in the application, an additional fee of £5 is payable.

Method of payment

A)   By credit account

The most convenient method of payment of fees for office copies is by a credit account. Credit facilities are available to any person or firm authorised to use a credit account. Any person or firm wishing to obtain such facilities should write to the Accounts Section, HM Land Registry, Burrington Way, Plymouth PL5 3LP for the necessary approval.

Forms 109, 110 and 110A contain fee panels for use by applicants with credit account facilities.

B)   By prepayment

An applicant who has no credit account should pay by enclosing a cheque or postal order made payable to "HM Land Registry".

APPLICATIONS LODGED WITHOUT A FEE OR WITHOUT THE APPROPRIATE DEBIT INSTRUCTIONS WILL BE REJECTED.

(viii) Sub-sales or re-sales

It sometimes happens that a registered proprietor ("A") sells part of his or her land to a purchaser ("B") who contracts to sell that land to a sub-purchaser ("C") before the registration of the transfer of part to B can be completed. In that event, the register of B's title will not have been brought into existence and B will not be able to prove title to C by producing the usual office copy of the register showing B as the registered proprietor of the land.

In this situation, it is possible for C to verify B's title by taking the following steps. C should first obtain from B an office copy of A's register. Upon receipt, C should at once apply in

Form 94C for a non-priority official search of A's register in order to bring the office copy completely up-to-date. Where appropriate the search application in Form 94C should be confined to the part of A's title in which C is interested. The search certificate will (a) disclose any alteration in A's register since the date of the office copy; (b) reveal the presence in the Land Registry of the pending application to register the transfer of part to B; and (c) indicate whether there are any other pending applications or official searches affecting B's land. Then, armed with this information, C should obtain from B a copy of the transfer to B. Finally, just before the completion of the sub-purchase, C will want to apply in the ordinary way for a purchaser's official search of the register, principally in order to secure the statutory priority period of thirty working days in which to register the latest transfer. By this time, the registration of B's transfer may well have been completed and C will be able to obtain an office copy of B's registration so that application can be made in printed Form 94A for a purchaser's search of B's register based on that office copy. But, should the registration of B's transfer still not be completed, C can apply on printed Form 94B for a purchaser's search of the relevant part of A's registered title based, as before, on the office copy of that title.

B should, however, bear in mind the provisions of section 110(5) Land Registration Act 1925.

This procedure can be adapted for a chargee who is proposing to make a loan to a sub-purchaser not yet entered on the register or where either of the two transactions is by way of lease instead of transfer.

3. **Personal inspection of the register, title plan and documents referred to on the register.**

(i)   District land registries are open to the public between the hours of 9 am and 4.30 pm Mondays to Fridays (excluding public holidays) during which time any person may apply to make a personal inspection of the register.

(ii)   A Form 111 must be completed in respect of each title to be inspected. Form 111 is obtainable from Her Majesty's Stationery Office or any other law stationer.

(iii) Under Part II(1) of Schedule 3 to the current Fees Order a separate fee is payable for each item inspected, ie. £5 for the register, £5 for the title plan and £5 for any or all of the documents referred to in the register (other than a lease or mortgage for which the fee is £10 per document).

(iv)   Where the title number is not known, or where the title number quoted does not relate to any part of the land described in the application Form 111, an additional fee of £5 will be payable under Part II(5) of Schedule 3 to the current Fees Order.

(v)   In order that the relevant records may be readily available it is always preferable for the applicant to give reasonable notice at the appropriate district land registry of his/her intention to make a personal inspection.

4. **Applications for office copies by telephone**

Land Registry credit account holders may obtain office copies by ringing the telephone services national number:-

(i)   **Croydon – (0171) 312 2332;**

(ii)   **Durham – (0191) 301 0019;**

(iii) **Gloucester – (01452) 511117;**

(iv)   **Lytham – (01253) 840011;**

(v)   **Stevenage – (01438)788887.**

The service covers all registered titles in England and Wales and is available from 9.30 am to 5.00 pm Mondays to Fridays (other than public holidays). The normal office copies fees are payable.

5. Applications for office copies by facsimile transmission

Credit account holders may also apply for office copies by fax. Details of this service can be obtained from the Enquiries Officer at any district land registry.

6. Other leaflets

The following leaflets may also be found useful and are available free of charge from any district land registry:

    a.   Practice Advice Leaflet No.5, entitled "Searches of Registered Land and Land Subject to a Pending First Registration Application".

    b.   Practice Leaflet No.7, entitled "Development of Registered Building Estates".

    c.   Explanatory Leaflet No.9, and supplement, entitled "Areas served by District Registries".

7. District land registries

Application for office copies should be sent to the correct district land registry serving the area in which the property is situated. The application is not deemed to be delivered until it is received at the proper office as shown in the current Land Registration (District Registries) Order. Since further changes in the distribution of records between the district land registries will need to be made from time to time it is not practicable to set out all the details in this leaflet. However, Explanatory Leaflet No. 9, which contains a complete list of all the local government areas of England and Wales and indicates the address of the district land registry currently serving each, is continually up-dated and is available free of charge from any district land registry.

N.B. Postage must be prepaid on all mail.

HM Land Registry   **Dr Stuart Hill**
October 1996   **Chief Land Registrar**

Practice Leaflet No. 17[1]

Form and execution of deeds

Definitions

In this leaflet:

"Section 1" means section 1 of the Law of Property (Miscellaneous Provisions) Act 1989 and references to particular parts of section 1 are to be interpreted accordingly;

"Section 36A" means section 36A of the Companies Act 1985 as inserted by section 130(2) of the Companies Act 1989 and references to particular parts of section 36A are to be interpreted accordingly;

"LRA 1925" means the Land Registration Act 1925;

"LPA 1925" means the Law of Property Act 1925;

"PAA 1971" means the Powers of Attorney Act 1971;

"EPAA 1985" means the Enduring Powers of Attorney Act 1985; and

"The 1925 Rules" means the Land Registration Rules 1925 (as amended) and reference to a rule by number means the rule of that number in the 1925 Rules.

Introduction

1.   Under the general law, most dispositions of land or interest in land, including conveyances, mortgages and leases, are void for the purpose of conveying or creating a legal estate unless made by deed. Accordingly, when such instruments are lodged for registration, the Registry must be satisfied from their form and execution that they have the necessary characteristics to constitute valid deeds (see paragraphs 3, 4 and 8 below). In the case of transfers of registered land and other dispositions for which the form is prescribed under the 1925 Rules similar considerations apply (see paragraphs 5 to 7, 15 and 16 below). This is because the principal form of transfer, Form 19 (substituted in the 1925 Rules by the Land Registration (Execution of Deeds) Rules 1990), prescribes forms of execution appropriate to deeds, and the other prescribed forms of transfer and disposition refer back to Form 19 for the purpose of execution.

2.   In view of the considerable changes which have been made to the law relating to the form and execution of such deeds by section 1 and section 36A, this practice leaflet seeks to give further guidance on the matters which need to be considered when deeds are prepared and executed for land registration purposes.

Paragraphs 5 and 15 below, in particular, set out the words of execution which should be used in relation to transfers of registered land.

General characteristics of a deed

3.   The necessary requirements of an instrument for it to constitute a valid deed are now set out in section 1, although other provisions also apply in relation to the execution of deeds by bodies corporate (see further paragraphs 8 to 21 below). The general requirements of a deed may be summarised as follows:

---

1. Practice Leaflet No. 17 is due to be replaced by Practice Advice Leaflet No. 6.

3.1   It must be in writing (see section 1(1)(a), which by implication carries forward this requirement from the previous common law);

3.2   It must make it clear on its face that it is intended to be a deed by the person making it, or the parties to it if more than one. This can be done by the instrument describing itself as a deed or expressing itself to be executed as a deed "or otherwise" (see section 1(2)(a)). So far as the Registry is concerned, it will look to see that the instrument uses the word "deed" in the body of it to describe itself, or that suitable words have been used in the execution clause (eg "Signed as a deed . . .", "Signed and delivered . . .", "Executed as a deed . . .", etc), or that it describes itself as a type of instrument which, by its nature, is required by law to be by deed (eg "This legal mortgage . . ." or "This Conveyance . . ."), or, in the case of registered land, it is in the appropriate form prescribed in the 1925 Rules.

3.3   It must be validly executed as a deed by the person making it, or one or more of the parties to it (see section 1(2)(b)). **The requirements for valid execution differ according to whether the person making the deed or the party to it is an individual, a company registered under the Companies Acts, or some other body corporate. These are dealt with in more detail below.**

Execution of deeds by individuals

4.   Section 1 lays down minimum requirements for the ways in which instruments are to be executed by **individuals** if they are to be valid deeds (see section 1(3)). The following are the points to be noted in relation to the execution of deeds generally:

4.1   In the usual case where the individual executes personally, it must be signed by him. Exceptionally, if for example through disability or illiteracy, the individual is unable to sign in the normal way, section 1 provides that "sign" in relation to an instrument includes making one's mark (normally this would be in the form of a cross). For obvious reasons, the signature or mark should be made in ink or using some other indelible means of writing and not in pencil. **Care should be taken to avoid the use of pens which are designed to produce writing capable of being erased after use.**

4.2   There is no longer any need for an individual to use a seal when executing a deed. Under section 1 this requirement was expressly abolished as from 31 July 1990. **However, should a deed executed after that date be lodged for registration bearing a seal, the Registry will simply ignore the seal as superfluous.**

4.3   The individual's signature must be witnessed by at least one person who attests the signature. Section 1 does not elaborate on what is required to attest a signature. However, since the purpose of attestation is to authenticate the original signature and to ensure that, if any question arises as to the validity of the execution, the witness can be traced for evidential purposes, **the Registry will look to see that the witness has also signed, that it is clear that the signature is by way of witnessing the execution of the party in question, and that the name and address of the witness appears on the deed.** Although not essential, it can be useful if, as has been the custom up to now, the witness also states his or her occupation.

4.4   Although no particular words of execution and attestation are required by section 1, the provision of suitable wording is highly desirable. This is to make clear that the signature of the individual who executes is intended to be by way of execution and that it is his or her signature which the subscribing witness intends to attest. Suitable wording which also makes it clear that the individual signs or executes the instrument "as a deed" will have the additional advantage that, even if the instrument does not make it clear elsewhere that it is intended to be a deed, the instrument will comply with the requirements of section 1 for a valid deed in this respect. An example of suitable wording which also accords with the requirements for execution of a transfer of registered land would be:

"Signed as a deed by
[name of individual]   )
in the presence of:)

Witness

Signature

Name

Address

4.5   Where it is appropriate, the wording should be adapted or expanded to explain any unusual feature of the execution. For example, if the individual executing is blind or illiterate is should be made clear that the contents of the deed were read over, and if necessary, explained to him or her before signature. In the case of someone who does not understand English (or Welsh in the case of a deed in Welsh) or whose grasp of the language is poor, the contents of the deed will need to be read over and explained in his or her native language before signature. Where this has been necessary, the facts should be briefly confirmed in the words of execution and attestation. In such cases, it is of advantage if the witness is a solicitor or licensed conveyancer who can be expected to ensure that the correct procedure has been followed. **Where an individual's name has clearly been signed in foreign characters, confirmation should be given to the Registry by the solicitor or licensed conveyancer acting either that the signatory nevertheless understands English, or that the deed was read over to him in his native language, and that he understood its effect.**

4.6   **If no, or insufficient, words of execution appear on the deed the Registry may raise requisitions to ensure that the deed has been duly executed.**

4.7   Section 1 also permits a deed to be executed by an individual arranging for it to be signed by someone else on his or her behalf (see section 1(3)(a)(ii)). Where this is done the person signing must do so at the direction of the individual, **in his physical presence and in the presence of two witnesses, both of whom must attest the signature** (see paragraph 4.3 and 4.4 above as to attestation of signatures). Again, the words of execution should be suitably modified to make clear how the deed has been signed (see paragraph 5 below as to the appropriate wording in the case of transfers of registered land).

4.8   As well as being signed, to be an effective deed an instrument must also be delivered as a deed by the individual who executes or by another person authorised to do so on his behalf (see section 1(3)(b)). Delivery here means legal delivery as distinct from physical delivery, ie some act generally (which may or may not include physical delivery) by which the deliverer evinces an intention to be bound by the deed. Until the coming into force of section 1, the individual had to deliver the deed personally. Another person could not deliver the deed on his or her behalf without authority, itself given by deed, to do so. This meant that a vendor executing a conveyance or transfer in advance of completion had to be presumed to have delivered the deed in escrow, which could have unexpected consequences.

4.9   However, the position is now that a person can be authorised by another to deliver a deed on his or her behalf without that authority having to be given by deed. In addition, if a solicitor or licensed conveyancer, or an agent or employee of either, purports to deliver a deed in the course of or in connection with a transaction involving the disposition or creation of an interest in land, on behalf of a party to the deed, a purchaser may presume without any investigation that the delivery was with the authority of the party in question.

So far as the Registry is concerned any deed lodged for registration will be presumed to have been delivered from the fact that, where it is lodged by the purchaser or other person taking the benefit of the deed, it has been released into the control of the applicant or, where it is lodged by the person making it, he or she has evinced an intention to be bound by it by seeking its registration.

Form and execution of transfers of registered land executed by individuals

5.   Transfers of registered land are required to be in one or other of the forms of transfer prescribed in the Schedule to the 1925 Rules "with such alterations and additions, if any, as are necessary or desired and the Registrar allows" (see Rule 74). As regards execution of transfers, Form 19 (transfer of freehold land (whole)) in the Schedule to the 1925 Rules (and therefore, by reference back each other prescribed form of deed) requires individuals to execute using one of the following execution clauses (AB being the party executing the instrument):

5.1   **Individuals in person**

Signed as a deed by AB   }
in the presence of: *(Signature of AB)*

(Signature, name and address of witness)

or

Signed and delivered by AB   }
in the presence of: *(Signature of AB)*

(Signature, name and address of witness)

5.2   **Individuals directing another to sign**

Signed as a deed by XY at
the direction and on behalf
of AB in [his **or** her] presence)   *(Signature of AB by XY)*
            and in the presence of:

(Signatures, names and addresses of two witnesses)

or

Signed and delivered by XY
at the direction and on
behalf of AB in [his **or** her]   *(Signature of AB by XY)*
presence and in the
presence of:

(Signatures, names and addresses of two witnesses)

6.   As with other deeds generally, these words may be amended if the transfer is executed under circumstances which require explanation (see paragraph 4.5 above). However, the prescribed wording should be followed as closely as the circumstances allow and, since variations to the forms of transfer generally require the Registrar's approval, **applicants may wish to take advantage of the Registry's draft approval of deeds service in advance of a transaction if it is proposed to adopt any unusual form of words which differ from the prescribed form.**

7.   Old forms of transfer, where the words of execution commence "Signed, sealed and delivered.....", will continue to be accepted for registration even though executed under

seal on or after 31 July 1990, on the basis that sealing is merely superfluous to the present requirements for a valid deed. **However, such forms can be readily amended to conform to the second of the forms of execution set out in paragraph 5 above by simple deletion of the word "sealed", and the Registry would encourage such practice where stocks of old forms need to be used on or after 31 July 1990.**

Execution of deeds by companies registered under the Companies Acts

8.   Following the bringing into force of section 36A, there are two principal methods by which a company registered under the Companies Act 1985, or one of the previous Companies Acts which it replaced, may execute deeds. First, as in the past, the company may execute under its common seal if it has one and chooses to use it (see further paragraphs 9 and 10 below). Second, if (as now permitted under section 36A(3)) it does not have a common seal, or if it has but chooses not to use it, the company may execute by the signatures of a director and its secretary, or of two directors, in accordance with section 36A (see further paragraphs 11 and 12 below).

9.   Where a company executes a deed under its common seal, the seal must be affixed and authenticated in accordance with its articles of association. The seal is normally affixed in the presence of a director and the secretary of the company, who attest the affixing of the seal by countersigning the deed and describing themselves by their respective offices of "Director" and "Secretary". This procedure ensures that the execution complies with section 74(1) LPA 1925 and therefore that, in favour of a purchaser, the deed is deemed to have been duly executed. No particular form of words of execution is prescribed for companies in relation to deeds generally (but see paragraph 15 below for the appropriate words of execution prescribed for transfers and other land registration deeds). **Where such a deed is lodged by a purchaser for registration and it is clear that section 74(1) LPA 1925 applies, the Registry will not raise any question as to due execution of the deed.**

10.   In some cases the articles of association permit the affixing of the company's common seal to a deed to be attested by some other person or persons than a director and the secretary. For example, article 101 of Table A in the Schedule to the Companies (Tables A to F) Regulations 1985 (S.I. No 1985/805), provides that "[t]he directors may determine who shall sign any instrument to which the seal is affixed and unless otherwise so determined it shall be signed by the director and by the secretary or by a second director". A company whose articles incorporate Table A in this respect may therefore arrange for two directors to attest the affixing of the company seal or, if the directors so determine, any other officer or officers of the company may do so. However, where the attestation is by persons other than a director and the secretary, section 74(1) LPA 1925 will not apply so as to deem the deed to have been duly executed (although section 74(6) LPA 1925 may serve to validate the execution if in accordance with the articles). **In such cases, therefore, unless the company executing is one with which the Registry is already familiar, the Registry reserves the right to call for further evidence that the person or persons attesting the seal are duly authorised by or under the company's articles to do so for the purpose of Rule 80.**

11.   The alternative mode of execution by a company, in accordance with section 36A, requires that the deed should be signed by a director and the secretary, or by two directors and expressed (in whatever form of words) to be executed by the company such signatures are then deemed to have the same effect as if the document were executed under the common seal (see section 36A(4)). In favour of a purchaser a document is deemed to have been duly executed by a company if it purports to be signed by a director and the secretary of the company, or by two of its directors (see paragraph 15 below for the appropriate words of execution prescribed for transfers and other land registration deeds). **The Registry will not**

therefore seek to question the due execution of a deed where this is lodged for registration by a purchaser and purports to have been signed by such officers by way of execution as a deed by the company in question.

12.   This method of executing deeds is by way of exception to the general rule of law that a document to constitute a valid deed must be executed under seal. Therefore, even though a company's articles permit the affixing of the seal, when used, to be attested by a person or persons other than a director and the secretary (or two directors) **this does not mean that such persons, because of their authority to countersign the seal, are able on that account to execute deeds on behalf of the company by means of their signatures alone.** If any document is lodged for registration which purports to be a deed executed by a company but which only purports to have been signed by such person or persons (eg where they are merely described as "authorised signatories") **the Registry will return the document with a requisition for it to be executed correctly, under seal or in accordance with section 36A.**

13.   A deed executed by a company, as with any deed, must also be delivered to be effective, but the process in this case is modified by the provisions of section 36A(5) and (6). Under section 36A(5), a deed is presumed to have been delivered upon its having been executed "unless a contrary intention is proved". This means that, in a typical case, where a solicitor or licensed conveyancer sends a deed relating to a conveyancing transaction to a client company for execution in advance of completion of the transactions, the deed must be taken to have been delivered at the point of execution, rather than later on completion following return of the deed to the practitioner. That is unless steps are taken to negate the presumption. In the absence of such steps, the position with regard to delivery of a deed executed by a company, and the need to treat the deed as executed in escrow, would appear to be similar to that of deeds generally before the coming into force of section 1 (see paragraph 4.8 above) notwithstanding the possibility of deeds being delivered by other persons (and solicitors or licensed conveyancers in particular) on behalf of the executing party under section 1.

14.   If it is desired to ensure that a deed executed by a company is not treated as delivered until a later date (such as completion of the relevant transaction) the solicitor or licensed conveyancer involved may wish to consider inviting the company client, when returning the executed deed prior to completion, to accompany it with a letter (the form of which the practitioner could suggest) in terms which negated section 36A(5) as to delivery. An example might be "the enclosed [Conveyance] has been executed but has not been delivered as a deed. You are authorised to deliver it as a deed on behalf of the company as and when [the sale of the property is completed]". This, it is suggested, should have the desired effect and provide the necessary proof to negate the operation of section 36A(5) without requiring the purchaser, or the Registry, to consider whether additional evidence as to intention and delivery is required as might be the case if the words of execution are amended to achieve this.

Execution of transfers by companies registered under the Companies Acts

15.   In relation to transfers of registered land, and other deeds prescribed by the Schedule to the 1925 Rules, Form 19 in the Schedule provides alternative methods of execution for companies registered under the Companies Acts. These are as follows (AB being the company executing the deed):

15.1 Companies using a seal

The common seal of AB was
affixed in the presence of   *(Common seal of AB)*

Director   _____

Secretary _____

15.2 Companies not using a seal

Signed as a deed by AB   } _____
acting by [a director and   Director
its secretary **or** two
directors]   _____
                                        [Secretary or Director]

or

Signed and delivered by AB } _____
acting by [a director and   Director
its secretary **or** two
directors]   _____
                                        [Secretary or Director]

16.   One or other of these forms of execution must be used in transfers and other prescribed forms of deed executed by a company except that, under Rule 80, the form of execution under seal may be modified to suit the case where persons other than a director and the secretary are empowered to attest the application of the company seal. **However where the form has been modified, unless the company is already familiar to the Registry, a certified copy of the company's articles of association will need to be lodged with the deed, together with any other evidence necessary to show that the persons who have attested the seal are authorised to do so.**

Unregistered companies

17.   Unregistered companies, for the purpose of section 718 of the Companies Act 1985, are those bodies corporate which are not registered under the Act but to which section 718 and Schedule 22 of the Act apply certain of its provisions, with or without modification under regulations made under section 718. There are relatively few unregistered companies, mainly certain companies incorporated under Royal Charter or Acts of Parliament other than Public General Acts. They are mostly utility and other companies of a local character but include some larger, more public enterprises such as insurance companies. In the case of such companies, new regulations under section 718 (the Companies (Unregistered Companies) (Amendment No. 2) Regulations 1990) provide that section 36A is to apply to them in the same way as it does to registered companies. An unregistered company may therefore continue to execute deeds under seal as hitherto in the manner provided for by its statute, charter or other document of constitution, but it may also now execute without using a seal provided it is arranged for a director and its secretary, or two directors to sign by way of execution on its behalf. It may be that, as a matter of its internal constitutional arrangements, the statute, charter or other document of constitution will need to be amended **but, in view of the purchaser protection provisions of section 36A, the Registry will not normally need to check on this point where execution accords with the section.**

18.   In practice, unregistered companies should use one or other of the alternative company execution clauses referred to in paragraph 15 above, modified if necessary in the case of execution under seal to reflect the provisions of its constitution, as permitted under Rule 80.

Foreign companies and corporations

19.   Although there is provision under section 130(6) of the Companies Act 1989 for regulations to be made applying, with any necessary modifications, section 36A to the case of companies incorporated outside Great Britain no such regulations have yet been made. Foreign companies and corporations must therefore continue to make such arrangements as they are able to ensure that transfers, conveyances and other documents effecting dispositions of land in England or Wales are executed as deeds in accordance with the law of England and Wales.

20.   To this end the following points should be borne in mind:

20.1   The possession of corporate seals is a feature of companies incorporated under some jurisdictions but not under others. Where this is so under the domestic law of a particular foreign company, arrangements should be made for execution by the company to comply with section 74(1) LPA 1925. In other words, the company seal should be affixed in the presence of, and countersigned by, the "clerk, secretary or other permanent officer or his deputy, and a member of the board of directors, council or other governing body of the corporation". The words of execution set out in paragraph 15.1 should be used, adapted if necessary to reflect the actual offices held by the countersignatories.

20.2   Where companies incorporated under the relevant domestic law do not normally possess common seals there is nevertheless the possibility (often neglected) of the particular foreign company, through a resolution of its board of directors, council or other governing body, or other appropriate decision making machinery, adopting a seal for the purpose of executing a deed in a manner which complies with English law. Where this is done (and there appears to be no reason why an embossed seal is required—a rubber stamp bearing the name of the company, for example, could suffice if adopted for this purpose) the deed can be executed as in paragraph 20.1 above. **However, appropriate evidence of such adoption should be lodged with the Registry in such cases.**

20.3   A deed which has been executed in a manner which complies with section 74(1) LPA 1925 is deemed, in favour of a purchaser, to be duly executed. **Therefore the Registry will not normally need any further evidence of due execution in such cases, other than as referred to in paragraph 20.2 above.**

20.4   The position is different however where section 74(1) LPA 1925 is not complied with and a common seal is not possessed or used. In general other modes of execution may be possible, depending upon the powers of the company under its constitution and its domestic law, **but the Registry will need to be satisfied that the mode of execution adopted is effective under section 74(6) LPA 1925.**

20.5   The very wide range of different foreign companies and corporations which exist, and from time to time deal with land in England and Wales, means that no one method of execution can be identified as appropriate to all cases. **However, the Registry will need to ascertain that the document complies with section 1 as to the formalities required of a deed. The Registry will also need to be supplied with a certified true and complete copy of the constitution of the company (including a notarial translation if it is not in English) and a letter from a lawyer practising within the country of incorporation confirming that the company or corporation remains in existence, has power under its constitution and under its domestic law to enter into the transaction for which registration is sought and that the mode of execution adopted is effective to bind the company under its domestic law.**

20.6   Where it is claimed that execution by a particular officer or officers of the company is effective execution on behalf of the company so as to bind it in relation to the transaction effected by the deed executed by them, **the Registry will further need to be satisfied as to the identity of the officers and the facts as to their appointment.** Appropriate evidence of such matters should be lodged with the application for registration such as relevant company or board resolutions (or the like), or extracts from relevant public registers translated as necessary, which may be required to show that the officers were duly appointed and invested with the necessary powers. Where by such evidence individual officers are shown to be empowered to execute on behalf of a foreign company or corporation section 1 will apply to dispense with the need for the individual to affix his or her own seal but the usual words of execution should be amended appropriately to show the capacity in which he or she signs the deed and the authority for the mode of execution adopted. Under Section 1 the signature of the individual will also need to be witnessed.

Other corporate bodies

21. Since section 36A and section 1 are in the nature of exceptions to the general requirement that a valid deed must be under seal, other corporate bodies must execute deeds under seal. This includes corporations sole (eg a bishop or the Official Custodian for Charities) because they are not individuals as such for the purposes of section 1 (see section 1(10)). In such cases the body or corporation should execute in accordance with the requirements of the statute, charter or other document or provision constituting or governing the particular body or corporation, and words of execution may be adapted to the circumstances of the case. In the case of deeds relating to registered land such adaptation is permitted by Rule 80, **but a copy of the relevant governing document should be lodged with the Registry.**

Powers of attorney

22. Under section 1 PAA 1971, powers of attorney are required to be by deed. Any individual, company or corporation appointing another person as attorney for the purpose of executing a transfer, conveyance or other deed of disposition of land in England or Wales must therefore execute the power as a deed in accordance with the appropriate paragraphs above. The power may be a general one, following the form in the Schedule to that Act, or it may be for specific purposes. Powers of attorney are interpreted strictly so that, in the latter case, it must be clear from its terms that the power permits the attorney to enter into the transaction which the instrument executed purports to effect.

23. Under section 10(2) PAA 1971, a person cannot delegate his function as trustee by way of a general power of attorney. This includes the case where a person is a trustee by virtue of holding land jointly with another or others (see *Walia v. Michael Naughton Limited* [1985] 3 WLR 1115). Subject to paragraph 24 below, trustees can only delegate their functions as trustees by a power which specifically delegates such functions in accordance with section 25 of the Trustee Act 1925 as amended by section 9 PAA 1971. Such delegation can only be for a maximum period of 12 months and the attorney is not permitted to be the only other co-trustee of the donor.

24. Generally, although a power of attorney (other than one which delegates trustee functions) can be granted for an indefinite period, it is revoked automatically by the mental incapacity of the donor. However, an enduring power of attorney under the EPAA 1985, executed in the form prescribed by the Enduring Powers of Attorney (Prescribed Form) Regulations 1990, including the prescribed explanatory notes (or until 31 July 1991 in the earlier form prescribed by the Enduring Powers of Attorney (Prescribed Form) Regulations

1987, including the earlier explanatory notes) will continue to have effect despite the mental incapacity of the donor. This is provided the requisite notices have been served on the appropriate near relatives and the power has been registered at the Court of Protection as required by the EPAA 1985. An enduring power of attorney is also capable of delegating trustee functions of the donor but a detailed analysis of the law relating to enduring powers of attorney is beyond the scope of this leaflet. However, as regards the execution of such powers, these must first be executed as a deed by the donor and then by the attorney if the power is to be an enduring power. (There is some argument that a power in the prescribed form may have some limited effect as an ordinary power of attorney if the donor only has executed, but the position is by no means clear and use of such powers is best avoided if possible). If there is more than one attorney under an enduring power then at least one of them, if they are appointed jointly and severally, or all of them, if they are appointed jointly, must execute as well if the power is to be an enduring power. Where there is more than one attorney appointed jointly and severally, only those attorneys who have executed the power can act once the donor has become mentally incapable.

25. The form of enduring power prescribed by the 1990 Regulations allows for the possibility of the donor, or any attorney, executing by arranging for another person to sign at his or her direction and in his or her presence, provided there are two witnesses both of whom attest, as now permitted by section 1. However, if the form prescribed by the 1987 Regulations is used (as permitted until 31 July 1991) only the donor can execute by direction, not any of the attorneys. Where the donor does this the words of execution may be modified accordingly.

26. Under Rule 82 (as substituted by the Land Registration (Powers of Attorney) Rules 1986) any deed lodged for registration which is executed under a power of attorney must be accompanied by the original power of attorney or "a copy by means of which its contents may be proved" under either section 3, PAA 1971, section 7(3), EPAA 1985, or a document which complies with section 4 of the Evidence and Powers of Attorney Act 1940. In practice, a complete copy of the power of attorney (including the explanatory notes attached to it in the case of an enduring power) certified on each page by a solicitor to be a true and complete copy of the original will suffice. If the power is an enduring power and has been registered with the Court of Protection under the EPAA 1985, appropriate evidence of such registration should be lodged with the copy power of attorney when application is made to register any instrument executed under it. (It may be noted that a donor may have sufficient mental capacity to execute an enduring power of attorney even though not otherwise capable of managing his affairs; see *In re K* and *In re F* [1988] 2 WLR 781).

27. It must also be clear that the power, if revocable, has not been revoked by the donor or some event such as the death or (except in the case of an enduring power) mental incapacity of the donor. In the case of a power of attorney which is not an enduring power it will be presumed in favour of a purchaser dealing with the donee that the power has not been revoked by the donor or by some supervening event where the purchaser has no notice of any such revocation or event. Where the duration of the power is not limited and the power is less than twelve months old lack of such notice is presumed under section 5 PAA 1971. Similar protection applies to purchasers in the case of enduring powers under the EPAA 1985.

28. Where the power of attorney is more than twelve months old at the date of execution of the transfer or other deed executed under it, evidence that the purchaser had no notice of such revocation or event must be lodged with the application for registration of the transfer or other deed in the form of a statutory declaration made by the person dealing with the donee of the power as required by Rule 82. **In the case of an enduring power in the prescribed form,** the declaration should be to the effect that the person dealing with the donee did not,

at the time of completion of the transaction:

(a)   know of any revocation of the power whether by the donor or by an Order of the Court of Protection;

(b)   know of the occurrence of any event (such as the death of the donor or the bankruptcy of the donor or of any donee or a direction by the Court of Protection on exercising its powers under Part VII of the Mental Health Act 1983) which had the effect of revoking the power;

(c)   know that the power was not a valid enduring power of attorney and had been revoked by the donor's mental incapacity.

In any other case, the declaration should be to the effect that the person dealing with the donee did not, at the time of the completion of the transaction:

(a)   know of any revocation of the power;

(b)   know of the occurrence of any event (such as the death, bankruptcy or other incapacity of the donor) which had the effect of revoking the power;

save that where the power was expressed to be irrevocable and given by way of security the statutory declaration must be to the effect that the declarant did not know that the power was not in fact given by way of security and did not know that the power had been revoked by the donor acting with the consent of the donee.

29.   As regards execution of the transfer or other instrument where an attorney is acting:

29.1   If the attorney is an individual, the donee may execute the deed on behalf of the donor (whether the donor is an individual or a corporation) by signing it with his or her own signature (see section 7 PAA 1971 as amended by section 1 and Schedule 1 of the Law of Property (Miscellaneous Provisions) Act 1989). Whether the attorney does this or signs with the name of the donor, the signature will need to be in the presence of a witness who attests it, in accordance with section 1. Suitable forms of attestation clause in such case might be:

Signed as a deed by XY
as attorney for AB   }   Signature – "XY as attorney for AB"
in the presence of

(Signature, name and address of witness)

or

Signed as a deed by AB acting
by [his **or** her] attorney XY   }   Signature – "AB by [his or her] attorney XY"
in the presence of:

(Signature, name and addres of witness)

29.2   In the case where the donor is a corporation and the attorney is an individual, the attorney is expressly empowered to execute the deed on behalf of the donor by signing it with the name of the corporation (see section 74(3) LPA 1925). Again the signature will need to be in the presence of a witness who attests it. A suitable form of attestation clause in this case might be:

Signed as a deed by AB
acting by its attorney   }   Signature – "AB by its attorney XY"
XY in the presence of:

(Signature, name and address of witness)

29.3 If the attorney is a corporation, whether the donor is an individual or a corporation, the attorney may execute under its seal (or now in accordance with section 36(A)) or the board of governors, council or other governing body of the attorney may, by resolution or otherwise, appoint one of its officers to execute the deed in the name of the donor (see section 74(4) LPA 1925). Suitable forms of attestation clause in this case might be:

The common seal of XY
acting as attorney for AB was }   *(Common seal of XY)*
affixed in the presence of:

Director of XY _____

Secretary of XY_____

or

Signed as a deed by XY   _____
acting by [a director and its   Director of XY
secretary **or** two directors] }
as attorney for AB   _____
                          [Secretary or Director] or XY

or

Signed as a deed by AB
acting by XY, duly appointed   Signature − "AB by XY, duly appointed
to execute as an officer of }   officer of [his, her or its]
[his, her **or**] attorney CD   attorney, CD"
in the presence of:

(Signature, name and address of witness)

HM Land Registry   **J. Manthorpe**
April 1991   **Chief Land Registrar**

IX.2. Land Registry Explanatory Leaflets

Explanatory Leaflet No. 5

Notes for the guidance of owners where an order of apportionment or a certificate of redemption of a rent or a rentcharge affects a registered title

1. General

These notes are issued for the guidance of property owners or of rentowners whose titles are registered at the Land Registry and whose property or rent is affected by an order of apportionment or certificate of redemption given by the Secretary of State for the Environment or the Secretary of State for Wales. In the case of a registered title, the owner should ensure that the apportionment order or redemption certificate is registered at the Land Registry. In this leaflet the term "property owner" is used to mean an owner of land subject to a rentcharge or a leaseholder, whilst the term "rentowner" means either an owner of a rentcharge or a landlord.

When a property owner's title is registered and the title is not subject to a registered mortgage, a land certificate is issued by the Land Registry as an official document giving evidence of ownership.

When a rentowner's title is registered and the title is not subject to a mortgage, a rentcharge certificate is issued as the official document providing evidence of ownership of the rent.

If it is not known whether a title is registered at the Land Registry, a property owner or a rentowner can find out by means of the enquiry described in paragraph 2 below. If the reply shows that neither the property owner's nor the rentowner's title is registered the apportionment or the redemption does not require registration at the Land Registry and paragraphs 3 to 6 below do not apply.

2. How to find out if the title is registered at the Land Registry

The property owner or rentowner can discover whether the title to the property or the rent is registered by applying on Land Registry Form 96 to the appropriate district land registry (see paragraph 7 below). Sufficient particulars should be given to enable the land to be identified by the Land Registry. A reply will be posted within a day or two of the enquiry being received. Land Registry forms can be purchased from HM Stationery Office or any law stationer. A fee (usually £5) is payable.

3. Procedure for registering an order of apportionment of a rent or a rentcharge (other than an order which is conditional on redemption − as to which, see paragraph 5 below)

Where the property owner's or the rentowner's title is registered, an official copy of the Secretary of State's order of apportionment should be sent to the appropriate district land registry (see paragraph 7) with the land and/or rentcharge certificate(s) of the title(s) affected. A covering letter should request that the necessary action be taken to enter notice of the apportionment on the register(s) of the title(s) concerned. A fee of £40 is payable for each title affected.

However, where the same application affects more than one title, the fee for each title after the first is £20 (see also paragraphs 6 and 8 below). After the appropriate entries have been made on the register, the copy order and the land and/or rentcharge certificate(s) will be returned. If the property owner's or the rentowner's title is subject to a registered mortgage, he will not have a land or rentcharge certificate, but the mortgagee will have a charge certificate and arrangements may be made for this to be lodged but this is not essential.

4. Procedure for registering a certificate of redemption of a rent or a rentcharge (other than a certificate given in pursuance of a conditional order of apportionment − as to which, see paragraph 5 below)

When the property owner's or the rentowner's title is registered, an official copy of the Secretary of State's certificate of redemption should be sent to the appropriate district land registry (see paragraph 7) with the land and/or rentcharge certificate(s) of the title(s) affected. A covering letter should request that the necessary action be taken to give effect to the redemption on the register(s) of the title(s) concerned. A fee of £40 is payable for each title affected, i.e. for either cancelling notice of a rentcharge on a property owner's title or closing (or partly closing) a rentowner's title (see also paragraphs 6 and 8 below).

After the registration has been completed, the copy order and the land certificate(s) will be returned. However, if the application results in a registered rentcharge title being closed, the land certificate will be retained in the district land registry but confirmation of the closure will be given when the copy certificate of redemption is returned.

If the property owner's or the rentowner's title is subject to a registered mortgage, he will not have a land or rentcharge certificate, but the mortgagee will have a charge certificate and arrangements should be made for this to be lodged.

5. Procedure for registering a certificate of redemption given in pursuance of a conditional order of apportionment

When an order of apportionment of a rent or rentcharge has been made which is conditional on redemption, no application should be made to the Land Registry until after the certificate of redemption has been obtained. Where the property owner's or the rentowner's title is registered, application should be made after redemption as is described in paragraph 4 above. The procedure will be the same except that an official copy of the Secretary of State's order of apportionment will need to be sent to the district land registry as well as an official copy of the certificate of redemption and the land and/or rentcharge certificate(s).

6. Procedure when a sale is contemplated

If the Secretary of State's order or certificate has been obtained in anticipation of a sale of the registered property or rent, the property owner or rentowner may well prefer to hand over the copy order or certificate to the purchaser and let him or his solicitor make the necessary application to the Land Registry when registering the transfer on sale. The fee payable for the registration of the transfer will cover the registration of the Secretary of State's order or certificate so neither the vendor nor the purchaser will incur a fee in that respect.

7. District Land Registries

Applications and enquiries made to the Land Registry must be addressed to the district land registry serving the area in which the property is situated. Because further changes in the distribution of records between the district land registries will need to be made from time to time it is not practicable to set out all the details in this leaflet. However, Explanatory Leaflet No. 9 contains a complete list of all local government areas in England and Wales and indicates the district land registry currently serving those areas.

8. Postage must be prepaid on all mail. Land Registry fees are payable by cheque or postal order made payable to "HM Land Registry". (As changes are made to Registry fees from time to time, enquiry should be made as to the appropriate fee before making an application.)

HM Land Registry
January 1996

John Manthorpe CB
Chief Land Registrar

IX

Explanatory Leaflet No. 12
Conversion of Title

1. Introduction

Where the title to land is registered at HM Land Registry there are seven possible kinds of title. There are three kinds of title for freehold and four for leasehold and they are set out below:

Freehold	Leasehold
Absolute	Absolute
Possessory	Good Leasehold
Qualified	Possessory
	Qualified

The best kind of title is an Absolute one and this is the title granted by the Chief Land Registrar in the vast majority of cases. Exceptionally, however, this may not be possible, for example, where some evidence is lacking or a defect in the title is apparent, so making it unsafe for the Chief Land Registrar to insure the owner absolutely against the risk of some other person claiming a right in the land. Also, there are many applications to register leasehold land where the title of the landlord to grant the lease which is being registered has not been produced so the Chief Land Registrar is not in a position to know if the landlord had the full and unrestricted power to make the grant or if any restrictive covenants or other incumbrances affect the property. In this case, provided that the title to the leasehold estate itself is satisfactory, he will give Good Leasehold title.

Possessory titles are usually (but not exclusively) granted where the owner claims to have acquired the land by adverse possession. These titles are rare.

Qualified titles, where there is some specific defect which has been identified and which is stated on the register, are even rarer.

There are provisions in the Land Registration Acts which entitle the registered proprietor to apply for conversion to a better class of title. Where the title is a possessory one, whether freehold or leasehold, the proprietor is entitled to claim conversion to either absolute freehold or good leasehold if the land has been registered for a certain time. The required period of time varies according to the circumstances and is dealt with in paragraph 2.

In other cases, conversation to absolute title will depend upon whether or not additional evidence to that produced on first registration can now be produced to the Chief Land Registrar. The evidence must be such as to demonstrate that the title is now suitable to be an absolute title. These applications may be made at any time after the land is registered and are dealt with in paragraph 3.

A fee may be payable, see paragraph 5 below.

2. Conversion of possessory titles

If a title is a possessory freehold or a possessory leasehold title, the registered proprietor, provided he is in possession, is entitled to require the Chief Land Registrar to convert the title provided that a certain number of years has passed since the date on which the title was first registered.

The class of title with which the property is registered is stated at the beginning of the proprietorship register. The date on which the title was first registered is stated in the property register or can be taken as the date on which the first proprietor was registered.

The law on these conversions is set out in section 77 of the Land Registration Act 1925 and section 1(2) of the Land Registration Act 1986. The provisions are complicated and the [following] chart shows when conversion is possible.

If conversion is possible an application can be made on Form 6 attached. The appropriate class of title box on the form should be ticked, as should box (a). Additionally, if the title is possessory leasehold then, if title to the freehold or any intermediate leasehold estate can be shown (see below, paragraph 3), box (b) should be ticked as well and absolute title requested as conversion can be direct from that class of title to absolute leasehold.

3. Other conversions

Application can also be made, at any time after the land is first registered, to convert:

a good leasehold title to absolute leasehold;

a qualified freehold or leasehold to absolute freehold or leasehold;

a possessory freehold to absolute freehold; or

a possessory leasehold to good leasehold or absolute leasehold title.

Before this can be done, however, the Chief Land Registrar must be satisfied that the proprietor has a good title to the land and that the defects in the title which the Chief Land Registrar identified on first registration of the land and which were the reason for the granting of other than an absolute title have been remedied. If such documentation can be produced, an application should be made on Form 6 enclosing all such documents of title (including the documents that were originally produced to the Chief Land Registrar). The Land or Charge Certificate and any appropriate fee should also be included. The Chief Land Registrar will then examine the title and, if he is satisfied that the title should be upgraded, he will convert the title. It is particularly important for title to be shown to any landlord's, and any superior landlord's title if conversion is to be from good leasehold to absolute leasehold.

Form 6 should be completed by ticking the appropriate class of title box and box (b).

4. Possessory titles registered before January 1909

When application is made to convert a possessory title which was originally registered before January 1909, the conveyance or assignment to the first registered proprietor should, if possible, be produced.

5. Fees

A fixed fee is normally payable for conversion from one class of title to another. However, if the application for conversion is accompanied by an application upon which a scale fee is payable, no fee is payable for conversion. Enquiries as to the fees currently payable may be made at any district land registry.

HM Land Registry   **John Manthorpe CB**
February 1996   **Chief Land Registrar**

Conversion of Possessory Title

made 10 or 15 years after registration (under the provisions of s.77(3)(b) of the Land Registration Act 1925 (as originally enacted − see s.1(2) of the Land Registration Act 1986))

Start here

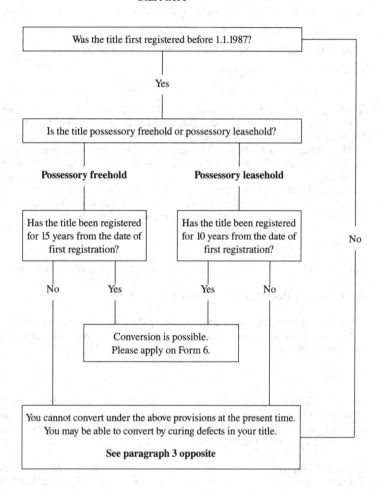

Application for Conversion of Title[1]

HM Land Registry

Form 6

(Section 77 Land Registration
Act 1925 and Section 1(2)
Land Registration Act 1986)

(1)Please complete
this form in typescript or in
BLOCK LETTERS
and in ink.

Title Number

Property

(2) Enter the full name(s) and
address(es) (including postcode)

I/We[2]

of

(3) Please see Explanatory Leaflet
No 12 – paragraphs 1 and 2 for an
explanation of the law on conversion
of title

being the registered proprietor(s) of the above title or
being entitled to be registered as such proprietor(s)
apply for the title to be converted to:

☐ Absolute[3]

☐ Good Leasehold[3]

because

(4) Please see Explanatory Leaflet
No 12 – paragraphs 2 and 3 for an
explanation of the required length of
possession

☐ (a) I am/We are in possession and the required time
has elapsed since first registration of the title[4]

☐ (b) I am/We are in possession and I/We enclose all
documents of title to support this application[4]

I/We confirm that no claim adverse to the title of the
property has been made.

Signature of applicant (or applicant's
solicitor or licensed conveyancer)

Date

Name and address of solicitor
or licensed conveyancer
(for correspondance)

Reference   Telephone No.

IX

Forms Leaflet No. 2

Land Registry forms: electronic reproduction of forms by applicants for registration and related services

Introduction

1. This leaflet sets out the Registry's requirements as to the electronic reproduction by computer of Land Registry forms by applicants. These requirements are necessary so as to ensure that any form received by the Registry is of a sufficient quality to allow the application to be dealt with correctly and efficiently. Reproduction using a word processor is unlikely to meet the required standard. Reproduction by software companies and by other means are dealt with at paragraphs 9 and 10 below. The Law Society has welcomed the practice set out in this leaflet.

2. In recent years advances in technology have meant that the facility to generate a form by computer and for the computer to complete the variable information, has become widely available. Some applicants are understandably anxious to be able to generate their own Land Registry application forms by this means.

3. Computerised form systems cannot readily provide hard copies of forms which feature colour on white, A3 size folded, print on both sides or perforations. In the past these features have been important in assisting both applicants and the Registry to efficiently and correctly complete and process the application. For example, the white boxes on the pink Form A44 (office copies) assisted completion by applicants, while its colour meant that this time sensitive application could be quickly identified and separated from the numerous other forms received at the Registry.

4. To assist users of computerised form systems; in order to reduce the cost of forms reproduction generally and in the light of the move towards being able to lodge certain applications by FAX, the Registry has redesigned its forms. It has switched to black on white, and, generally, single A4 size forms for preliminary applications, such as those for office copies or searches of the index map. However, to minimise the loss of key features and to speed up and simplify processing by the Registry, the layout of the forms has been altered radically. An important change to assist identification has been the use of much enlarged form numbers.

Crown copyright

5. Generally speaking there is Crown copyright in:

(a) the forms set out in the various Land Registration Rules and the Land Charges Rules 1974 ("prescribed forms");

(b) forms promulgated by the Chief Land Registrar under section 127 Land Registration Act 1925 ("promulgated forms");

(c) HMSO's printed versions of prescribed forms and promulgated forms.

Standard of reproduction

6. An applicant may reproduce on its in-house computer system any of the Land Registry forms set out in Appendix 1 to this leaflet if:

General requirements

(a)   the acknowledgement "Crown copyright forms are reproduced with the permission of the Controller of HMSO" appears on the entry screen each time the computer system is accessed;

(b)   the forms are only used by the applicant (and the Registry) and in particular are not sold in hard copy or machine-readable format;

(c)   the forms are not retransmitted electronically except in-house or, where the Land Registration or Land Charges Rules allow, by FAX;

(d)   once a form is out of date it is erased from the database.

Quality of forms

(e)   layout: the forms **must reproduce exactly the HMSO printed versions** and not those produced by other companies, but all HMSO official publishing and printing imprint must be omitted from the forms; only notes prescribed by the Rules need be produced and not other notes (e.g the instructions on the front of Form 109 must be reproduced but the notes for guidance and the "for official use only" on the reverse of the HMSO version of the form need not be reproduced);

(f)   paper quality: not less than 80 gsm. However, the Registry expects paper of at least 100 gsm to be used for transfers in Form 19 and similar documents;

(g)   paper size: International A4 size;

(h)   printing: this must be by a non-impact printer at a resolution of 300 dpi or an equivalent process. The print quality of the majority of word processors linked to dot matrix printers is unlikely to meet this standard.

(i)   duplicates: where the Rules require a form to be lodged in duplicate, the duplicate should be marked clearly as such.

If the above requirements are not met then Crown copyright is likely to be infringed. Further, it is regretted that any forms which do not comply with the relevant Land Registration Rules or Land Charges Rules will be rejected.

7.   Certain commonly used promulgated forms such as the dealings application Form (A4) are not included in the Appendix. These must **not** be reproduced because they must be printed in colour on white, A3 size folded paper and the majority of systems cannot reproduce the forms in this manner. Also certain Land Charges forms are not included because colour is still considered of crucial importance for the efficient working of the Land Charge Department which has to deal with over 5 million paper forms a year.

Enquiries from applicants

8.   Any enquiries concerning this leaflet should be addressed to: −

> The Forms Officer, The Forms Unit
> Practice & Legal Services Division
> HM Land Registry
> Lincoln's Inn Fields
> London WC2A 3PH
> DX: 1098 Lond/Chancery Ln WC2

Software companies

9. Software companies and others not covered by this leaflet **must not** reproduce Land Registry Forms by electronic means unless they hold a Crown copyright licence. Details of how such a licence may be obtained are set out in a free leaflet, Forms Leaflet No. 1 entitled "Land Registry Forms: Copyright Licences for electronic reproduction of forms by software companies", available from the Forms Officer at the address given in paragraph 8.

Reproduction other than electronically

10. Enquiries concerning reproduction of Land Registry Forms by means other than electronic (for example, by printing) or reproduction by electronic media to produce forms which are subsequently to be sold as printed copies should be directed to:–

> The Copyright Manager
> HMSO
> St Crispins
> Duke Street
> Norwich NR3 1PD

HM Land Registry **John Manthorpe**
September 1994 **Chief Land Registrar**

Appendix 1 to
Forms Leaflets Nos 1 and 2

The current HMSO version of the following forms may be reproduced electronically subject to the provisions of Forms Leaflets Nos. 1 and 2 above:

A. Registration of title forms

Form No.   Description

6   Application for conversion of title.

16   Withdrawal of a caution against first registration.

19   Transfer of whole.

19(CO)   Transfer of whole by a company or corporation.

19(JP)   Transfer of whole to joint proprietors.

20   Transfer of part.

20R2   Transfer of part informally apportioning an existing rentcharge.

20R3   Transfer of part subject to an existing apportionment of a rentcharge.

31   Transfer of whole in exercise of a power of sale contained in a registered charge.

43   Transfer of part imposing fresh restrictive covenants.

45A   Charge of whole.

45B   Charge of part.

45C   Charge of whole accompanying a first registration.

45D   Charge accompanying a transfer of part.

53   Discharge of registered charge.

53(CO)   Discharge of registered charge of which a company or corporation, including a building society, is the registered proprietor.

54   Transfer of charge.

55   Transfer and discharge of the whole.

56   Assent or appropriation.

57   Vesting assent (settled land).

63/14   Caution against dealings with registered land or charge.
(combined)

71   Withdrawal of a caution.

75   Application to register a restriction under section 58 of the 1925 Act.

77   Application to withdraw a restriction.

82   Application to register the personal representative(s) of a deceased sole proprietor.

83   Application to register the death of a joint proprietor.

Form No.	Description
84	Application to register notice of lease.
86	Withdrawal of a notice of deposit or intended deposit of land certificate or charge certificate.
92	Application to cancel notice of an unregistered lease.
92R	Application for cancellation of notice of an unregistered rentcharge.
94A	Application by purchaser for official search with priority in respect of the whole of the land in either a registered title or in a pending first registration.
94B*	Application by purchaser for official search with priority in respect of part of the land in a pending first registration application.
94C*	Application for official search without priority in respect of the land in a registered title.
96	Application for official search of the index map.
96B	Application for a copy of the index map section.
99	Application for registration of a notice of rights of occupation.
100	Application for renewal of registration of a notice or caution in respect of rights of occupation.
106*	Application for official search in respect of rights of occupation.
109	Application for office copies of register and title plan only.
110	Application for office copies of documents only.
110A	Application for office copies of a caution title including plan.
111	Application for a personal inspection of the register.
113	Application to note an obligation to make further advances.
202	Application to cancel notice of rights of occupation under the Matrimonial Homes Acts.
A13	List of documents sent to HM Land Registry.

* NOTE: The Rules require applications in forms marked with an asterisk to be submitted in duplicate to the Registry.

B. Land charges forms

Form No.	Description
K1	Application for registration of a land charge.
K7	Application for the renewal of a registration.
K9	Application for rectification of an entry in the register.
K10	Continuation of an application.
K14	Declaration in support of an application for registration or rectification.

HM Land Registry
September 1994

IX.3. Land Registration (Official Searches) Rules 1993 (S.I. 1993/3276)

1993 No. 3276

LAND REGISTRATION, ENGLAND AND WALES

The Land Registration (Official Searches) Rules 1993

Made	*14th December 1993*
Laid before Parliament	*11th January 1994*
Coming into force	*28th March 1994*

The Lord Chancellor, with the advice and assistance of the Rule Committee appointed in pursuance of section 144 of the Land Registration Act 1925(a), in exercise of the powers conferred on him by that section and section 112(2) of the said Act, hereby makes the following rules:

PART I

Citation and commencement

1. These rules may be cited as the Land Registration (Official Searches) Rules 1993 and shall come into force on 28th March 1994.

Interpretation

2. (1) In these rules, unless the context otherwise requires:

"the Act" means the Land Registration Act 1925;
"credit account" means an account authorised by the registrar under article 15(1) of the Land Registration Fees Order 1993(b);
"day" except in rule 14(1)(e), means a day when the Land Registry is open to the public;
"day list" means the record kept pursuant to rule 7A of the principal rules;
"designated plan" means a plan which is a copy or extract from the OrdnanceMap at the largest scale published for the area in which the land to which it relates is situated, such plan to have a length no greater than 297 mm and a width no greater than 210 mm (A4 paper size);

(a) 1925 c.21; section 8 was amended by the Land Registration Act 1986 (c.26), sections 2(2) and 3(1), and sections 112 and 144 were amended by the Land Registration Act 1988 (c.3), section 1 and Schedule. Section 144(1) was amended by the Administration of Justice Act 1982 (c.53), Schedule 5, paragraph (d) and the reference to the Minister of Agriculture, Fisheries and Food was substituted by the Transfer of Functions (Ministry of Food) Order 1955 (S.I. 1955/554).
(b) 1993/3229.

"official certificate of search" means a result of search issued in accordance with rule 4 or 10;

"pending first registration application" means an application made under section 4 or 8 of the Act and entered on the day list but where the registration has not yet been completed;

"the principal rules" means the Land Registration Rules 1925(c);

"priority period" means the period beginning at the time when an application for an official search is deemed by virtue of paragraph (3) below to have been delivered and ending immediately after 0930 hours on the thirtieth day thereafter;

"proper office" means the district land registry designated as the proper office by article 2(2) of the Land Registration (District Registries) Order 1991(d);[1],

"purchaser" means any person (including a lessee or chargee) who in good faith and for valuable consideration acquires or intends to acquire a legal estate in land and "purchase" has a corresponding meaning;

"search from date" means:

(a) (i) the date stated on an office copy (either issued in response to an application made under rule 2 of the Land Registration (Open Register) Rules 1991(e) or issued under rule 4(3) or rule 10(3) of these rules) of the register of the relevant registered title as the date on which the entries shown on the said office copy were subsisting, provided that the said office copy was issued by the registrar not more than twelve months before the day upon which the relevant application under these rules was delivered or, in the case of an application for an official search with priority, was deemed by virtue of paragraph (3) below to have been delivered;

(ii) the date stated at the time of an access by remote terminal, under rule 4A of the Land Registration (Open Register) Rules 1991, to the register of the relevant registered title as the date on which the entries accessed were subsisting, provided that the transmission by the registrar's computer system of the entries so accessed occurred not more than twelve months before the day upon which the relevant application under these rules was delivered or, in the case of an application for an official search with priority, was deemed by virtue of paragraph (3) below to have been delivered;

(b) where the term is used in Form 94C and at D of Part I of Schedule 3, either a date within (a) or the date (or most recent date, if more than one) stated in the land or a charge certificate of the relevant registered title as the date on which that certificate was officially examined with the register.

(2) In these rules a form referred to by number means the form so numbered in Schedule 1.

(3) (a) An application for an official search with priority made by a purchaser which is delivered under the provisions of rule 3(3)(a) or rule 3(3)(b)(ii) after 0930 hours on one day and before or at 0930 hours on the next day shall be deemed to have been delivered immediately before 0930 hours on the second day.

(c) S.R. & O. 1925/1093; relevant amending instruments are S.I. 1978/1601, 1986/1534, 1990/314.

(d) S.I. 1991/2634.

(e) S.I. 1991/122; amended by S.I. 1993/3275.

1. Revoked by the Land Registration (No.3) Rules 1995 (S.I.1995/3153).

(b) An application for an official search with priority made by a purchaser which is delivered under the provisions of rule 3(3)(b)(i) or rule 3(3)(b)(iii) shall be deemed to have been delivered at the time notice of it is entered on the day list.

(4) Expressions used in these rules have, unless the contrary intention appears, the meaning which they bear in the principal rules.

PART II

OFFICIAL SEARCHES WITH PRIORITY

Application for official search with priority by purchaser

3. (1) A purchaser may apply for an official search with priority of the register of the title to the land to which the purchase relates.

(2) Where land is subject to a pending first registration application a purchaser of such land may apply for an official search with priority in relation to that pending first registration application.

(3) An application for an official search with priority shall be made:

(a) by delivering in documentary form at the proper office an application on Form 94A or Form 94B, as appropriate; or

(b) during the currency of any relevant notice given pursuant to rule 14, and subject to and in accordance with the limitations contained in that notice, by delivering the application to the registrar, by any means of communication, other than that referred to in sub-paragraph (a) and:

(i) where the application is made by telephone or orally the purchaser shall provide, in such order as may be requested, such of the particulars as are appropriate and are required for an application for an official search with priority in Form 94A or Form 94B;

(ii) where the application is made by facsimile transmission the purchaser shall provide Form 94A or Form 94B, as appropriate, together with, where the application is in Form 94B (and the plot number or numbers of any relevant approved estate plan are not quoted), a designated plan of the land in respect of which the official search is to be made; and

(iii) in any other case the purchaser shall provide, in such order as may be required by that notice, such of the particulare as are appropriate and are required for an application for an official search with priority in Form 94A or Form 94B.

(4) Where the application is made on Form 94B under paragraph (3)(a), unless the registrar otherwise allows:

(a) Form 94B and any plan accompanying the application, shall be delivered in duplicate.

(b) the application shall be accompanied by Form 94B (Result) in duplicate.

(5) Where the application is made under paragraph (3)(b)(ii) in Form 94B, the purchaser shall provide, unless the registrar otherwise allows, Form 94B (Result).

Entry of application on day list and issue of official certificate of search with priority

4. (1)   If an application for an official search with priority is in order, notice of it shall be entered on the day list and upon completion of the official search with priority an official certificate of search shall be issued giving the result of the search as at the time and day it is deemed to have been delivered.

(2)   An official certificate of search with priority of a register or in relation to a pending first registration application may, at the registrar's discretion, be issued in one, or more than one, of the following ways:

(a)   in the form set out under the heading "Official Certificate of Result of Search" in Form 94B (Result);

(b)   in documentary form;

(c)   during the currency of any relevant notice given pursuant to rule 14, and subject to and in accordance with the limitations contained in that notice, by any means of communication, other than the means referred to in sub-paragraphs (a) and (b).

(3)   Subject to paragraphs (4) and (5), an official certificate of search issued under paragraph (2) shall include such information specified in Part I or Part II of Schedule 2 as the case may require and may be issued by reference to an office copy of the register.

(4)   Where the official certificate of search is issued in Form 94B (Result) or in documentary form, under paragraph (2), together with the relevant application form, or a copy of that application form, it need not include any of the information referred to in paragraph (3) which appears on that application form.

(5)   Where an official certificate of search is issued under paragraph (2)(c) and another official certificate of search is to be, or has been, issued under paragraph (2)(b) in respect of the same application, it need only include the information specified at A, F, G, and H, of Part I or A, H, and I of Part II of Schedule 2 as the case may require.

Inspection of applications for official searches with priority and official certificates of search with priority

5.   During the priority period details in a visible and legible form:

(a)   of the application for official search with priority; and

(b)   of the official certificate of search with priority;

shall be made available for inspection by any person.

Priority of applications protected by an official search with priority of a register

6.   Where a purchaser has applied for an official search with priority of a register, any entry which is made in that register during the priority period relating to that search shall be postponed to a subsequent application to register the instrument effecting the purchase and, if the purchase is dependent on a prior dealing, to a subsequent application to register the instrument effecting that dealing, provided each such subsequent application:

(a)   is deemed to have been delivered at the proper office within the priority period;

(b)   affects the same land or charge as the postponed entry; and

(c)   is in due course completed by registration.

Priority of applications protected by an official search with priority relating to a pending first registration application

7. (1)   Paragraph (2) has effect where, with respect to a purchase of land which is subject to a pending first registration application:

(a)   the purchaser has applied for an official search with priority in relation to the pending first registration application; and

(b)   the pending first registration application is subsequently completed by registration of all or any part of the land comprised in that purchase.

(2)   Any entry made in the register of title to the land pursuant to an application delivered or otherwise made during the priority period of the official search shall be postponed to any entry made pursuant to a subsequent application to register the instrument effecting the purchase and, if the purchase is dependent upon a prior dealing, a subsequent application to register the instrument effecting that dealing, provided each such subsequent application:

(a)   is deemed to have been delivered at the proper office within the priority period;

(b)   affects the same land or charge as the postponed entry; and

(c)   is in due course completed by registration.

Priority of concurrent applications for official searches with priority and concurrent official certificates of searches with priority

8. (1)   Where two or more official certificates of search with priority relating to the same land or the same charge have been issued and are in operation pursuant to these rules, such certificates shall, as far as relates to the priority thereby conferred, take effect, unless the applicants otherwise agree, in the order in which the applications for official search with priority were deemed to have been delivered.

(2)   Where two or more applications for official search with priority relating to the same land or the same charge are deemed to have been delivered at the same time the official certificates of search with priority shall, as far as relates to the priority thereby conferred, take effect in such order as may be agreed by the applicants or, failing agreement, as may be determined under rule 298 of the principal rules.

(3)   Where one transaction is dependent upon another the registrar may for the purposes of this rule assume (unless or until the contrary appears) that applicants for search with priority have agreed that their applications shall have priority as between each other so as to give effect to the sequence of the instruments effecting their transactions.

(4)   Where an official search with priority has been made in respect of a particular registered title and an application relating to that title is deemed, by virtue of rule 85 of the principal rules, to have been delivered at the same time as the expiry of the priority period relating to that search, the time of the delivery of the application shall be deemed to be within that priority period.

(5)   Where an official search with priority has been made in respect of a particular pending first registration application and a subsequent application relating to any land which is subject to the pending first registration application, or was so subject before completion of the registration of that land, is deemed, by virtue of rule 85 of the principal rules, to have been delivered at the same time as the expiry of the priority period relating to that search, the time of delivery of that subsequent application shall be deemed to be within that priority period.

PART III

OFFICIAL SEARCH WITHOUT PRIORITY

Application for official search without priority

9. (1)   A person (not being a purchaser requiring an official search with priority under Part II of these rules) may apply for an official search without priority of a register.

(2)   An application for an official search without priority may be made:

   (a)   by delivering in documentary form at the proper office an application on Form 94C; or

   (b)   during the currency of any relevant notice given pursuant to rule 14, and subject to and in accordance with the limitations contained in that notice, by delivering the application to the registrar, by any means of communication, other than that referred to in sub-paragraph (a) and:

     (i)   where the application is made by telephone or orally the applicant shall provide, in such order as may be requested, such of the particulars as are appropriate and are required by Form 94C;

     (ii)   where the application is made by facsimile transmission the applicant shall provide Form 94C and if the application is in respect of part of the land in a registered title and the plot number or numbers of any relevant approved estate plan are not quoted, the applicant shall also provide a designated plan of the land in respect of which the official search is to be made; and

     (iii)   in any other case the applicant shall provide, in such order as shall be required by that notice, such of the particulars as are appropriate and are required by Form 94C.

(3)   Where the application is made under paragraph (2)(a), unless the registrar otherwise allows –

   (a)   Form 94C and any plan accompanying the application, shall be delivered in duplicate;

   (b)   the application shall be accompanied by Form 94C (Result) in duplicate.

(4)   Where the application is made under paragraph (2)(b)(ii), the applicant shall provide, unless the registrar otherwise allows, Form 94C (Result).

Issue of official certificate of search without priority

10. (1)   On completion of the official search without priority an official certificate of search without priority shall be issued and such certificate shall not confer on the applicant priority for the registration of any dealing.

(2)   An official certificate of search without priority may, at the registrar's discretion, be issued in one, or more than one, of the following ways:

   (a)   in the form set out under the heading "Official Certificate of Result of Search" in Form 94C (Result);

   (b)   in documentary form;

(c) during the currency of any relevant notice given pursuant to rule 14, and subject to and in accordance with the limitations contained in that notice, by any means of communication, other than the means referred to in sub-paragraphs (a) and (b).

(3) Subject to paragraphs (4) and (5), an official certificate of search without priority issued under paragraph (2) shall include the information specified in Part I of Schedule 2 and may be issued by reference to an office copy of the register.

(4) Where the official certificate of search is issued in Form 94C (Result) or in documentary form, under paragraph (2), together with the relevant application form, or a copy of that application form, it need not include any of the information referred to in paragraph (3) which appears on that application form.

(5) Where an official certificate of search is issued under paragraph (2)(c) and another official certificate of search is to be, or has been, issued under paragraph (2)(b) in respect of the same application, it need only include the information specified at A, F, G, and H, of Part I of Schedule 2.

PART IV

REQUEST FOR INFORMATION AND SEARCHES WITHOUT PRIORITY

Information requested by applicant making a telephone or oral application under rule 3(3)(b)(i) or rule 9(2)(b)(i) or an application by remote terminal under rule 3(3)(b)(iii) or rule 9(2)(b)(iii)

11. (1) If so requested by an applicant who is making a telephone or oral application under rule 3(3)(b)(i) or rule 9(2)(b)(i), the registrar may at his discretion, before the official search has been completed in respect of such application, give to the applicant, by telephone or orally, details of:

(a) in the case of an application for a search of the whole of, or part of, the land in a registered title:

(i) any relevant adverse entry that has been made in the register since the search from date given in the application; and

(ii) any relevant entry subsisting in the day list made pursuant to rule 7A of the principal rules, rule 4 of the Land Registration (Official Searches) Rules 1990(f) or rule 4 of these rules; and

(b) in the case of an application for a search of the whole of, or part of, the land subject to a pending first registration application, any relevant entry subsisting on the day list made pursuant to rule 7A of the principal rules (and entered on the day list subsequent to the date upon which the pending first registration was deemed to be delivered), rule 4 of the Land Registration (Official Searches) Rules 1990 or rule 4 of these rules affecting the pending first registration application.

(2) If so requested by an applicant who is making an application to the registrar's computer system from a remote terminal under rule 3(3)(b)(iii) or rule 9(2)(b)(iii),

(f) S.I. 1990/1361.

the registrar may at his discretion, before the official search has been completed in respect of such application, inform the applicant, by a transmission to the remote terminal, whether or not there have been any relevant entries of the kind referred to in paragraph (1)(a) or (b), but the registrar need not provide the applicant with details of any relevant entries.

Search without priority by telephone

12. (1)   During the currency of any relevant notice given pursuant to rule 14, and subject to and in accordance with the limitations contained in that notice, a person may apply to the registrar by telephone for a search without priority of the whole of, or (where to search is in respect of one or more plots on an approved estate plan) part of, the land in a registered title to ascertain whether:

> (a)   any relevant adverse entry has been made in the register of the title since the search from date given in the application; and

> (b)   there is any relevant entry subsisting on the day list made pursuant to rule 7A of the principal rules, rule 4 of the Land Registration (Official Searches) Rules 1990 or rule 4 of these rules affecting the title.

(2)   Where an application is made under paragraph (1) the particulars set out in Part I of Schedule 3 shall be supplied in such order as may be required by the notice referred to in paragraph (1).

Result of search without priority by telephone

13. (1)   The result of a search given by telephone pursuant to an application under rule 12 shall include the information set out in Part II of Schedule 3.

(2)   A search made pursuant to an application under rule 12 shall not confer upon the applicant priority for the registration of any dealing.

PART V

Notice for the provision of additional arrangements for searches

14. (1)   If the registrar is satisfied that adequate arrangements have been or will be made for dealing with the applications for or results of search specified in paragraph (5) in accordance with this rule, he may, in such manner as he considers appropriate for informing persons who may wish to make applications under these rules, give notice to that effect specifying the class or classes of case covered by those arrangements; and such a notice may in particular, but without prejudice to the generality of the foregoing provision, specify the class or classes of case so covered by limiting them:

> (a)   to one or more of the types of application or result of search mentioned in paragraph (5);

> (b)   to applications for, or results in respect of, searches of the whole of the land in a registered title or the whole of the land subject to a pending first registration application;

> (c)   in the case of applications made as mentioned in paragraph (5), to applications made by a person maintaining a credit account;

> (d)   to applications which relate to land within specified counties, districts, London boroughs or other administrative areas;

> (e)   to applications made between specified hours and on specified days (which

need not be those between or on which the Land Registry is open to the public and may be different for applications of different types);

(f) where an application is made under rule 3(3)(b) or 9(2)(b) or a result is issued under rule 4(2)(c) or 10(2)(c), to delivery of such application or to the issue of such result by one or more means of communciation;

(g) where a result is issued under rule 4(2)(c) or rule 10(2)(c), to results of search which state, in the case of an official search of a register, that there are no adverse entries, no pending applications and no official searches which fall within paragraphs F, G or H of Part I of Schedule 2, or, in the case of an official search with priority in relation to a pending first registration application, that there are no pending applications and no official searches which fall within paragraphs H or I of Part II of Schedule 2;

(h) where an application is isn respect of part of the land in a registered title, to an application which provides the relevant plot number on the approved estate plan.

(2)   Subject to paragraph (3) and (4), a notice given pursuant to paragraph (1) shall be current from the time specified in that behalf in the notice either:

(a) until the time, if any, specified in that behalf in the notice; or

(b) if no time of ceasing to be current is specified in the notice, indefinitely.

(3)   A notice given pursuant to paragraph (1) may from time to time be varied, suspended, withdrawn, renewed or replaced by a further notice.

(4)   If and so long as owing to the breakdown or other unavailability of facilities or data involved in giving effect to the arrangements made for dealing with applications for or results of search covered by a notice given under paragraph (1) such arrangements cease, in whole or in part, to be effective, the notice shall cease, to the necessary extent, to be treated as current notwithstanding the absence of a variation, suspension or withdrawal thereof under paragraph (3).

(5)   The applications for or results of search referred to in paragraph (1) are:

(a) an application for an official search with priority made under rule 3(3)(b);

(b) an official certificate of search with priority issued under rule 4(2)(c);

(c) an application for an official search without priority made under rule 9(2)(b);

(d) an official certificate of search without priority issued under rule 10(2)(c);

(e) an application for a search without priority by telephone under rule 12.

(6)   Notwithstanding the provisions of rules 3(3)(b), 4(2)(c), 9(2)(b), 10(2)(b) and 12 the registrar may in his discretion refuse to accept an application made, or to issue a result, under any of those provisions in any individual case.

Revocation

15.   The Land Registration (Official Searches) Rules 1990 are hereby revoked.

Dated 14th December 1993   *Mackay of Clashfern*, C.

SCHEDULE 1   Rules 2, 3, 4, 9 and 10

Application by **Purchaser** for   **HM Land Registry**   **Form**
Official Search with priority
of the whole of the land in either a   # 94A
registered title or a pending first
registration application   Land Registration (Official
                                                            Searches) Rules 1993

_____ District Land Registry	**6** Enter the key number (if any) and the name and (DX) address of the person lodging the application (use BLOCK LETTERS).
	Key number:
	Name:
	DX No: DX Exchange:
	Address including postcode (if DX not used):

Please complete the numbered panels

Reference:

1 Title number (one only per form) - enter the title number of the registered land or that allotted to the pending first registration.

7 Enter, using BLOCK LETTERS, the name and either address (including postcode) OR (if applicable) the DX No and exchange of the person to whom the result is to be sent.(**Leave blank if result is to be sent to the address in panel 6.**)

2 Registered proprietor(s) / Applicant(s) for first registration - enter FULL name(s) either of the registered proprietor(s) of the land in the above title or of the person(s) applying for first registration of the land specified in panel 8.

SURNAME / COMPANY NAME:

FORENAME(S):

SURNAME / COMPANY NAME:

FORENAME(S):

Reference:

8 Property details
COUNTY AND DISTRICT / LONDON BOROUGH:

Address (including postcode) or short description:

3 Search from date - for a search of a registered title enter in the box a date falling within (a) of the definition of search from date in rule 2(1). Note: If the date entered is not such a date the application may be rejected. In the case of a pending first registration search, enter the letters 'FR'.

9 Type of search (enter X in the appropriate box)

☐ **Registered land search**
Application is made to ascertain whether any adverse entry has been made in the register or day list since the date shown in panel 3 above.

☐ **Pending first registration search**
Application is made to ascertain whether any adverse entry has been made in the day list since the date of the pending first registration application referred to above.

4 Applicant(s) - enter FULL name of each purchaser, or lessee or chargee.

10   **PAYMENT OF FEE**

Please enter X in the appropriate box.

☐ The Land Registry fee of **£** [____] accompanies this application; **or**

☐ Please debit the Credit Account mentioned in panel 6 with the appropriate fee payable under the current Land Registration Fees Order.

Note: If the fee is not paid by either of the above methods the application may be rejected.

5 Reason for application - I certify that the applicant(s) intend(s) to:- (enter X in the appropriate box)

☐ **P** purchase   ☐ **L** take a lease of   ☐ **C** take a registered charge on

(enter X in the appropriate box)

☐ the whole of the land in the above registered title   **or**

☐ the whole of the land in the pending first registration application referred to above.

Signature

Date   Telephone

SCHEDULE 1—*continued*

Application by
Purchaser for
Official Search with
Priority of part of the
Land in either a registered title or a
Pending first registration application

HM Land Registry

P R I O R I T Y S T A M P

Form

94B

Land Registration (Official
Searches) Rules 1993

_____ District Land Registry

Please complete the numbered panels

1 Title number (one only per form) - enter the title number of the registered land or that allotted to the pending first registration.

2 Registered proprietor(s) / Applicant(s) for first registration - enter FULL name(s) either of the registered proprietor(s) of the land in the above title or of the person(s) applying for first registration of the land specified in panel 12.

SURNAME / COMPANY NAME:

FORENAME(S):

SURNAME / COMPANY NAME:

FORENAME(S):

3 Search from date - for a search of a registered title enter in the box a date falling within (a) of the definition of search from date in rule 2(1). Note: If the date entered is not such a date the application may be rejected. In the case of a pending first registration search, enter the letters 'FR'.

4 Applicant(s) - enter FULL name of each purchaser, or lessee or chargee.

5 Reason for application - I certify that the applicant(s) intend(s) to: (enter X in the appropriate box)

| P | purchase | L | take a lease of | C | take a registered charge on |

the land described in panel 12, being part of the land in the above title.

6 Key No.

7 Enter, using BLOCK LETTERS, the name and either address (including postcode) OR (if applicable) the DX No. and exchange of the person lodging the application.

8 Reference:

9 Enter, using BLOCK LETTERS, the name and either address (including postcode) OR (if applicable) the DX No and exchange of the person to whom the result is to be sent. **(Leave this and panel 10 blank if result is to be sent to the address in panel 7.)**

10 Reference:

11 County and District / London Borough for land affected:

12 Details of land affected - complete either (a) or (b) below.

(a) Where an estate layout plan has been approved:

(i) the plot number(s) is/are

(ii) the date of approval of the estate plan is

OR

(b) Address (including postcode) or short description :-

as shown _____ on the attached plan

NB. A plan must be supplied when (a) above is not completed.

13 Type of search (enter X in the appropriate box)

Registered land search
Application is made to ascertain whether any adverse entry has been made in the register or day list since the date shown in panel 3 above.

Pending first registration search
Application is made to ascertain whether any adverse entry has been made in the day list since the date of the pending first registration application referred to above.

14 **PAYMENT OF FEE**

Please enter X in the appropriate box.

The Land Registry fee of £_____ accompanies this application; or

Please debit the Credit Account mentioned in panel 6 with the appropriate fee payable under the current Land Registration Fees Order.

Note: If the fee is not paid by either of the above methods the application may be rejected.

Signed

Date _____ Telephone

SCHEDULE 1—*continued*

FOR OFFICIAL USE ONLY

Form 94B (Result)

Official Certificate of Result of Search

It is certified that the official search applied for has been made with the following result :-

☐ **A** Registered land search

Since _____ 19 _____

☐ No adverse entries have been made.

☐ See Annex which forms part of this result.

☐ Entries have been made. Details of these and of pending applications (if any) are annexed to and form part of this result.

☐ No adverse entries have been made but there are pending applications details of which are annexed to and form part of this result.

☐ **B** Pending first registration search

☐ The property specified is the subject of a pending first registration application. Details are annexed to and form part of this result.

Note To obtain priority, the application for registration in respect of which this search is made must be delivered to the proper office at the latest by 0930 hours on the date when the priority expires.

SCHEDULE 1—*continued*

Application **for**
Official Search without priority
of the land in a registered title

HM Land Registry

Form

94C

Land Registration (Official
Searches) Rules 1993

Certificate Date

_____ District Land Registry

Please complete the numbered panels

Application is made to ascertain whether any adverse
entry has been made in the register or day list since the
date shown in panel 3 below.

1 Title number (one only per form) - enter the title number of the
registered land.

2 Registered proprietor(s) - enter FULL name(s) of the
registered proprietor(s) of the land in the above title.

3 Search from date - enter in the box a date falling within the definition
of search from date in rule 2(1).
Note: If the date entered is not such a date the application may be rejected.

4 Applicant(s) - enter FULL name(s) of applicant(s) if other than the
registered proprietor(s).

5 Key No. :

6 Enter, using BLOCK LETTERS, the name and
either address (including postcode) OR (if applicable)
the DX No. and exchange of the person lodging the
application.

7 Reference:

8 Enter, using BLOCK LETTERS, the name and either address
(including postcode) OR (if applicable) the DX No and exchange of
the person to whom the result is to be sent. (Leave this and panel 9 blank if
result is to be sent to the address in panel 6.)

9 Reference :

10 County and District / London Borough for land affected:

COMPLETE PANEL 11 or 12 AS APPROPRIATE
11 Search of WHOLE - enter address (including postcode) or short
description of land.

12 Search of PART - Complete either (a) **or** (b) below.
(a) Where an estate layout plan has been approved:

(i) the plot number(s) is/are

(ii) the date of approval of the estate plan is
OR
(b) Address (including postcode) or short description :-

as shown _____ on the attached plan.
NB. A plan must be supplied when (a) above is not completed.

13   **PAYMENT OF FEE**
Please enter X in the appropriate box.

☐ The Land Registry fee of **£**   accompanies this
application; or
☐ Please debit the Credit Account mentioned in panel 5 with the
appropriate fee payable under the current Land Registration
Fees Order.

Note: If the fee is not paid by either of the above methods the
application may be rejected.

Signed

Date   Telephone

SCHEDULE 1—*continued*

FOR OFFICIAL USE ONLY   Form 94C (Result)

Official Certificate of Result of Search

It is certified that the official search applied for has been made with the
following result :-

Since_____ 19 _____

☐   No adverse entries have been made.

☐   See Annex which forms part of this result.

☐   Entries have been made. Details of these and of pending applications
       (if any) are annexed to and form part of this result.

☐   No adverse entries have been made but there are pending applications
       details of which are annexed to and form part of this result.

Note: **This certificate confers no priority for the registration of any dealing.**

SCHEDULE 2

Rule 4(3)
Rule 10(3)

PART I

INFORMATION TO BE INCLUDED IN THE RESULT OF AN OFFICIAL SEARCH OF A REGISTER

A.   The title number
B.   The date of the official certificate of search
C.   If the official search is of part, a short description of the property or plot number on the approved estate plan
D.   The name of the person on whose behalf the application is made
E.   Applicant's reference (if any): limited to 25 digits including spaces, oblique strokes and punctuation
F.   Details of any relevant adverse entries made on the register since the date specified in the application as the search from date
G.   Notice of the entry of any relevant pending application affecting the title entered on the day list pursuant to rule 7A of the principal rules
H.   Notice of the entry of any relevant official search the priority period of which has not expired and which is entered on the day list pursuant to rule 4 of these rules or rule 4 of the Land Registration (Official Searches) Rules 1990
I.   If the official search is with priority, the date on which priority expires
J.   If the official search is without priority, a statement that the certificate shall not confer on the applicant priority for any dealing

PART II

INFORMATION TO BE INCLUDED IN THE RESULT OF AN OFFICIAL SEARCH WITH PRIORITY IN RELATION TO A PENDING FIRST REGISTRATION APPLICATION

A.   The title number allotted to the pending first registration application
B.   The date of the official certificate of search
C.   If the official search is of part, a short description of the property
D.   The name of the person on whose behalf the application was made
E.   Applicant's reference (if any): limited to 25 digits including spaces, oblique strokes and punctuation
F.   Full name of the person who has applied for first registration of the land
G.   The date upon which the pending first registration application is deemed to have been delivered at the proper office under rule 24 of the principal rules
H.   Notice of the entry of any relevant pending application affecting the land sought to be registered and entered on the day list subsequent to the date upon which the pending first registration application was deemed to have been delivered
I.   Notice of the entry of any relevant official search the priority period of which has not expired and which is entered on the day list pursuant to rule 4 of these rules or rule 4 of the Land Registration (Official Searches) Rules 1990 affecting the pending first registration application
J.   The date on which priority expires

SCHEDULE 3 Rule 12(2)
Rule 13(1)

PART I

PARTICULARS TO BE SUPPLIED WHEN A SEARCH IS MADE BY TELEPHONE UNDER RULE 12

A. The Credit Account number, name and telephone number of the person making the application together with the name of the person on whose behalf the application is being made
B. The title number
C. The full name of the proprietor of the land
D. The date from which the search is to be made being the search from date
E. In the case of a search of part of the land comprised in a registered title, the plot number on the approved estate plan against which the search is to be made

PART II

INFORMATION TO BE INCLUDED IN THE RESULT OF A SEARCH MADE BY TELEPHONE UNDER RULE 13

A. The title number
B. A statement whether the search has extended to the whole or been limited to a part of the land comprised in the registered title
C. The date from which the search has been made
D. The result given in accordance with paragraphs F, G and H of Part I of Schedule 2

IX.4. Land Charges Fees Rules 1990 (S.I. 1990/327)[1]

1990 No. 327

LAND CHARGES

The Land Charges Fees Rules 1990

Made	*21st February 1990*
Coming into force	*2nd April 1990*

The Lord Chancellor, with the concurrence of the Treasury, in exercise of the powers conferred on him by sections 9(1), 10(2), 16(1) and 17(1) of the Land Charges Act 1972**(a)** hereby makes in the following rules:

1. (1) These Rules may be cited as the Land Charges Fees Rules 1990 and shall come into force on 2nd April 1990.

(2) In these Rules, unless the context otherwise requires, –
"the Act" means the Land Charges Act 1972;
"credit account" means an account authorised by the Registrar for the purpose of providing credit facilities for the payment of fees;
"fee" means a fee specified in Schedule 1;
"Schedule" means a schedule to these Rules;
"written application" in Schedule 1 does not include an application made by teleprinter or facsimile transmission.

2. The fees specified in Schedule 1 shall be payable under the Act.

3. Every fee which accompanies an application is to be paid in money in accordance with the Land Charges (Fees) Order 1990**(b)** and shall, except as mentioned in Rule 4 or as the Registrar may otherwise allow, be paid in cash or by means of a postal order crossed and made payable to H.M. Land Registry.

4. (1) Any person or firm having a credit account may request the Registrar, on any application, to debit the requisite fee to that account.

(2) When a person or firm having a credit account makes an application which is not accompanied by any fee and does not contain a request for the fee to be debited to that account, the Registrar may, if he thinks fit, nevertheless accept the application and debit the fee to that person's or that firm's account.

(3) If the Registrar debits a fee to a credit account, this shall be treated as due payment of that fee.

(4) Credit accounts shall be authorised and maintained in accordance with the provisions set out in Schedule 2.

(a) 1972 c.61.
(b) S.I. 1990/323.

1. Incorporating amendments made by the Land Charges Fees (Amendment) Rules 1994 (S.I. 1994/286).

5. The Land Charges Fees Order 1985(c) so far as made under powers conferred by the Act is hereby revoked.

Dated 16th February 1990	*Mackay of Clashfern*, C.

We concur

David Lightbown
Stephen Dorrell

Dated 21st February 1990	Two of the Lord Commissioners of Her Majesty's Treasury

SCHEDULE 1	Rule 2

Service		*Amount of Fee*
1. Registration, renewal, rectification or cancellation of an entry in any register	per name	£1
2. Certificate of cancellation	per name	£1
3. Entry of priority notice	per name	£1
4. Inspection of an entry in the register	per entry	£1
5. Office copy of an entry in the register (including any plan) whether the application is made in writing or by telephone or teleprinter or facsimile transmission or to the registrar's computer system by means of the applicant's remote terminal	per copy	£1
6. Official search in the index (including issue of printed certificate of result): –		
written application	per name	£1
telephone application	per name	£2
teleprinter application	per name	£2
facsimile transmission application	per name	£2
Application made to the registrar's computer system by means of the applicant's remote terminal	per name	£2
7. Official search in the index (including visual display of result of search and issue of printed certificate of such result)	per name	£2

SCHEDULE 2	Rule 4(4)

PROVISION OF CREDIT ACCOUNTS

1. The Registrar may, as he thinks fit, authorise any person or firm to use a credit account for the purpose of the payment of fees but may withdraw or suspend any such authorisation at any time without giving any reason therefor.

2. The Registrar may also at any time terminate or suspend all credit accounting facilities generally.

(c) S.I. 1985/358.

3.   A statement of account shall be sent by the Registrar to each account holder at the end of each calendar month or at such other period as the Registrar shall direct either in any particular case or generally.

4.   On receipt of the statement and if no question arises thereon the account holder shall pay by cheque any sum due on his account promptly, and in any event within ten days of its receipt.

5.   Cheques shall be made payable to H.M. Land Registry and sent to the Accounts Section, Land Charges Department, Burrington Way, Plymouth, PL5 3LP or at such other address as the Registrar shall direct.

IX.5. Official searches against certain livery companies, colleges and schools

Land Charges Department
Practice Leaflet No. 2

The Practical Guide for Solicitors on the procedures which operate under computerisation in the Land Charges Department refers, at paragraph 23, to arrangements for searching certain special names. These include Livery Companies, the Colleges of Oxford and Cambridge Universities and certain other schools, colleges and institutions. Although, in strictness, the names of the bodies should be specified in extenso in any application, in order to simplify searching in these particular instances, the Chief Land Registrar undertakes to make a search against the full formal title whenever the commonly used shortened version of the name is given in the application, provided that the appropriate reference number set opposite the name is also quoted in the box in the left-hand margin (although it is headed "For Official Use Only").

The list is not exhaustive. It comprises bodies against which entries made under the Land Charges Act are known to exist.

Livery Companies

Ref. No.	Shortened Version of Name	Full Name
1001040	Society of Apothecaries	The Master, Wardens and Society of the Art and Mistery of Apothecaries of the City of London
1001137	Armourers' and Brasiers' Company	The Worshipful Company of Armourers and Brasiers in the City of London
1001234	Bakers' Company	The Master Wardens and Commonalty of the Mystery of Bakers of the City of London
1001331	Brewers' Company	The Master and Keepers or Wardens and Commonalty of the Mistery or Art of Brewers of the City of London
1001428	Carpenters' Company	The Master, Wardens and Commonalty of the Mistery of Freemen of the Carpentry of the City of London

Livery Companies/contd

Ref. No.	Shortened Version of Name	Full Name
1001525	Clothworkers' Company	The Master Wardens and Commonalty of Freemen of the Art or Mistery of Clothworkers of the City of London
1001622	Worshipful Company of Cooks	The Masters or Governors and Commonalty of the Mistery of Cooks of London
1001719	Coopers' Company	The Master Wardens or Keepers of the Commonalty of Freemen of the Mystery of Coopers of the City of London and the Suburbs of the Same City
1001816	Drapers' Company	The Master and Wardens and Brethren and Sisters of the Guild or Fraternity of the Blessed Mary the Virgin of the Mystery of Drapers of the City of London
1001913	Farriers' Company	The Worshipful Company of Farriers
1002010	Fishmongers' Company	The Wardens and Commonalty of the Mistery of Fishmongers of the City of London
1002107	Founders' Company	The Worshipful Company of Founders
1002204	Girdlers' Company	The Master and Wardens or Keepers of the Art or Mystery of Girdlers, London
1002301	Goldsmiths' Company	The Wardens and Commonalty of the Mystery of Goldsmiths of the City of London
1002495	Gold and Silver Wyre Drawers' Company	The Master Wardens Assistants and Commonalty of the Art and Mystery of Drawing and Flatting of Gold and Silver Wyre and making and spinning of Gold and Silver Thread Stuff
1002592	Grocers' Company	The Wardens and Commonalty of the Mistery of Grocers of the City of London
1002689	Haberdashers' Company	The Master and Four Wardens of the Fraternity of the Art or Mystery of Haberdashers in the City of London
1002786	Worshipful Company of Innholders	The Master, Wardens and Society of the Art of Mystery of Innholders of the City of London
1002883	Ironmongers' Company	The Master and Keepers or Wardens and Commonalty of the Mystery or Art of Ironmongers London
1002980	Leathersellers' Company	The Wardens and Society of the Mistery or Art of the Leathersellers of the City of London
1003077	Mercers' Company	The Wardens and Commonalty of the Mystery of Mercers of the City of London

IX

Livery Companies/contd

Ref. No.	Shortened Version of Name	Full Name
1003174	Merchant Taylors' Company	The Master and Wardens of the Merchant Taylors of the Fraternity of St John the Baptist in the City of London
1003271	Pewterers' Company	The Master and Wardens and Commonalty of the Mystery of Pewterers of the City of London
1003368	Poulters' Company	The Master Wardens and Assistants of Poulters of London
1003465	Saddlers' Company	The Wardens or Keepers and Commonalty of the Mystery or Art of Saddlers of the City of London
1003562	Salters' Company	The Master, Wardens and Commonalty of the Art or Mistery of Salters, London
1003659	Skinners' Company	The Master and Wardens of the Guild or Fraternity of the Body of Christ of the Skinners of London
1003756	Tallow Chandlers' Company	The Worshipful Company of Tallow Chandlers of the City of London or The Master, Wardens and Commonalty of the Mistery of Tallow Chandlers of the City of London
1003853	Tylers' and Bricklayers' Company	The Worshipful Company of Tylers and Bricklayers of London
1003950	Vintners' Company	The Master Wardens and Freemen and Commonalty of the Mystery of Vintners of the City of London

Cambridge University Colleges and Halls

Ref.No.	Shortened Version of Name	Full Name
1057785	Cambridge University	The Chancellor Master and Scholars of Cambridge University
1005017	Christ's College, Cambridge	The Master, Fellows and Scholars of Christ's College in the University of Cambridge
1005114	Clare College, Cambridge	The Master, Fellows and Scholars of Clare College in the University of Cambridge
1005308	Corpus Christi College Cambridge	The Master, Fellows and Scholars of the College of Corpus Christi and the Blessed Virgin Mary in the University of Cambridge

Cambridge University Colleges and Halls/contd

Ref. No.	Shortened Version of Name	Full Name
1005405	Downing College, Cambridge	The Master, Fellows and Scholars of Downing College in the University of Cambridge
1005502	Emmanuel College, Cambridge	The Master, Fellows and Scholars of Emmanuel College in the University of Cambridge
1005696	Fitzwilliam College, Cambridge	The Master, Fellows and Scholars of Fitzwilliam College in the University of Cambridge
1005793	Girton College, Cambridge	The Mistress, Fellows and Scholars of Girton College
1005890	Gonville and Caius College, Cambridge	The Master and Fellows of Gonville and Caius College in the University of Cambridge founded in honour of the Annunciation of Blessed Mary the Virgin
1005987	Jesus College, Cambridge	The Master or Keeper and Fellows and Scholars of the College of the Blessed Virgin Mary St John the Evangelist and the Glorious Virgin Saint Radegund Commonly called Jesus College in the University of Cambridge
1006084	King's College, Cambridge	The Provost and Scholars of the King's College of our Lady and Saint Nicholas in Cambridge
1006181	Magdalene College, Cambridge	The Master and Fellows of Magdalene College in the University of Cambridge founded in honour of St Mary Magdalene
1006278	New Hall, Cambridge	The President and Fellows of New Hall in the University of Cambridge
1006569	Pembroke College, Cambridge	The Master, Fellows and Scholars of the College or Hall of Valence-Mary, commonly called Pembroke College, in the University of Cambridge
1006666	Peterhouse, Cambridge	The Master, Fellows and Scholars of Peterhouse in the University of Cambridge
1006763	Queen's College, Cambridge	The President and Fellows of the Queen's College of St Margaret and St Bernard, commonly called Queen's College, in the University of Cambridge
1006860	St Catharine's College, Cambridge	The Master and Fellows of St Catharine's College or Hall in the University of Cambridge

IX

Cambridge University Colleges and Halls/contd

Ref. No.	Shortened Version of Name	Full Name
1006957	St John's College, Cambridge	The Master, Fellows and Scholars of the College of St John the Evangelist in the University of Cambridge
1007054	Selwyn College, Cambridge	The Master, Fellows and Scholars of Selwyn College
1007151	Sidney Sussex College, Cambridge	The Master, Fellows and Scholars of the College of the Lady Frances Sidney Sussex in the University of Cambridge
1007248	Trinity College, Cambridge	The Master, Fellows and Scholars of the College of the Holy and Undivided Trinity Within the Town and University of Cambridge of King Henry the Eighth's Foundation
1007345	Trinity Hall, Cambridge	The Master, Fellows and Scholars of the College or Hall of the Holy Trinity in the University of Cambridge

Oxford University Colleges and Halls

Ref. No.	Shortened Version of Name	Full Name
1029849	Oxford University	The Chancellor, Masters and Scholars of the University of Oxford
1008024	All Souls College, Oxford	The Warden and College of the Souls of All Faithful People Deceased in the University of Oxford
1008121	Balliol College, Oxford	The Master and Scholars of Balliol College in the University of Oxford
1008218	Brasenose College, Oxford	The Principal and Scholars of the Kings Hall and College of Brasenose in Oxford
1008315	Corpus Christi College, Oxford	The President and Scholars of Corpus Christi College in the University of Oxford
1008412	Exeter College, Oxford	The Rector and Scholars of Exeter College in the University of Oxford
1008509	Hertford College, Oxford	The Principal Fellows and Scholars of Hertford College in the University of Oxford
1008606	Jesus College, Oxford	The Principal, Fellows and Scholars of Jesus College, within the City and University of Oxford, of Queen Elizabeth's Foundation

Oxford University Colleges and Halls/contd

Ref.No.	Shortened Version of Name	Full Name
1008703	Keble College, Oxford	The Wardens, Fellows and Scholars of Keble College in the University of Oxford
1008897	Lady Margaret Hall, Oxford	The College of the Lady Margaret in Oxford Commonly known as Lady Margaret Hall
1008994	Lincoln College, Oxford	The Warden and Rector and Scholars of the College of the Blessed Mary and All Saints Lincoln in the University of Oxford commonly called Lincoln College
1009091	Magdalen College, Oxford	The President and Scholars of the College of St Mary Magdalen in the University of Oxford
1009188	Merton College, Oxford	The Warden and Scholars of the House or College of Scholars of Merton in the University of Oxford
1009285	New College, Oxford	The Warden and Scholars of St Mary College of Winchester in Oxford commonly called New College in Oxford
1009382	Oriel College, Oxford	The Provost and Scholars of the House of the Blessed Mary the Virgin in Oxford commonly called Oriel College of the Foundation of Edward the Second of Famous Memory sometime King of England
1009479	Pembroke College, Oxford	The Master, Fellows and Scholars of Pembroke College in the University of Oxford
1009576	Queen's College, Oxford	The Provost and Scholars of the Queen's College in the University of Oxford
1009673	St Catherine's College, Oxford	St Catherine's College in the University of Oxford
1009770	St Edmund Hall, Oxford	The Principal, Fellows and Scholars of Saint Edmund Hall in the University of Oxford
1009867	St John's College, Oxford	The President and Scholars of Saint John Baptist College in the University of Oxford
1009964	Somerville College, Oxford	The Principal and Fellows of Somerville College in the University of Oxford
1010061	Trinity College, Oxford	The President, Fellows and Scholars of the College of the Holy and Undivided Trinity in the University of Oxford of the Foundation of Sir Thomas Pope Knight Deceased
1010158	University College, Oxford	The Master and Fellows of the College of the Great Hall of the University commonly called University College in the University of Oxford

IX

Oxford University Colleges and Halls/contd

Ref. No.	Shortened Version of Name	Full Name
1010255	Wadham College, Oxford	The Warden, Fellows and Scholars of Wadham College in the University of Oxford of the Foundation of Nicholas Wadham, Esquire and Dorothy Wadham
1010352	Worcester College, Oxford	The Provost, Fellows and Scholars of Worcester College in the University of Oxford

Schools and Colleges

Ref. No.	Shortened Version of Name	Full Name
1011031	Christ's Hospital	The Mayor and Commonalty and Citizens of the City of London Governors of the Possessions Revenues and Goods of the Hospitals of Edward late King of England the Sixth of Christ Bridewell and St Thomas the Apostle as Governors of Christ's Hospital
1011128	Dulwich College	The Estate Governors of Alleyn's College of God's Gift at Dulwich
1011225	Eton College	The Provost of the College Royal of the Blessed Mary of Eton near unto Windsor in the County of Buckinghamshire commonly called The King's College of our Blessed Lady of Eton nigh or by Windsor in the said County of Buckinghamshire and the same college
1011322	Harrow School	The Keepers and Governors of the Possession Revenues and Goods of the Free Grammar School of John Lyon within the Town of Harrow on the Hill in the London Borough of Harrow (formerly in the County of Middlesex)
1011419	Highgate School	The Wardens and Governors of the possessions of the Free Grammar School of Sir Roger Cholmeley Knight in Highgate
1011516	Winchester College	Saint Mary College of Winchester near Winchester (the seal is referred to as "The , Common Seal of the Warden and Scholars Clerks of St Mary College of Winchester near Winchester")

Land Charges Department
August 1991

J Manthorpe
Chief Land Registrar

X. NEW PROPERTY

X.1. Inland Revenue Statement of Practice on the sale of new houses[1]

STAMP DUTY: NEW BUILDINGS

This Statement sets out the practice the Board of Inland Revenue will apply in relation to the stamp duty chargeable in certain circumstances on the conveyance or lease of a new or partly constructed building. It affects transactions where, at the date of the contract for sale or lease of a building plot, building work has not commenced or has been only partially completed on that site but where that work has started or has been completed at the time the conveyance or lease is executed.

This Statement reflects the advice the Board have received on this subject in the light of the decision in the case of **Prudential Assurance Company Limited v IRC ([1993] 1 WLR 211)**. The Statement does not apply to the common situation where the parties have entered into a contract for the sale of a new house and that contract is implemented by a conveyance of the whole property. This Statement replaces the Statements of Practice issued in 1957 and 1987 (SP 10/87) on this subject which are now withdrawn.

The Board are advised that, whilst each case will clearly depend on its own facts, the law is as follows:

1. **Two transactions/two contracts**

Where the purchaser or lessee is entitled under the terms of a contract to a conveyance or lease of land alone in consideration of the purchase price or rent of the site and a second genuine contract for building works is entered into as a separate transaction, the ad valorem duty on the conveyance or lease will be determined by the amount of the purchase price or rent which the purchaser or lessee is obliged to pay under the terms of the first contract. In these circumstances it does not matter whether any building work has commenced at the date of the conveyance or lease. The consideration chargeable to ad valorem duty will still be only that passing for the land.

2. **One transaction/two contracts**

Where there is one transaction between the parties but this is implemented by two contracts, one for the sale or lease of the building plot and one for the building works themselves, the amount of ad valorem duty charged on the instrument will depend on the amount of the consideration, which in turn will depend on whether those contracts can be shown to be genuinely independent of each other.

  (i) If the two contracts are so interlocked that they cannot be said to be genuinely capable of independent completion (and in particular where if default occurs on either contract, the other is then not enforceable) ad valorem duty will be charged

---

1. 12 July 1993.

on the total consideration for the land and buildings, whether completed or not, as if the parties had entered into only one contract.

(ii)   If the two contracts are shown to be genuinely independent of each other, ad valorem duty will be charged by reference to the consideration paid or payable for the land and any building works on that land at the date of execution of the instrument. It follows that, where the instrument is executed after the building works are completed, ad valorem duty will be charged on the consideration for the land and the completed building(s).

3. Sham or artificial transactions

This Statement does not apply to cases where the transaction concerned, or any part of it, involves a sham or artificial transaction.

4. Contracts already entered into

Where unconditional contracts have been entered into before or within 28 days of the date of this Statement and the duty payable on the resulting conveyance or lease would have been less under the earlier Statements of Practice, the Stamp Office will accept duty in the lesser amount. In such cases the instrument should be submitted together with all the evidence to support the claim that unconditional contracts were entered into within this transitional period.

5. Procedure for submitting documents

Where a person accepts that a conveyance or lease of a building plot is chargeable on the total price paid or payable for the land and the completed building, it should be submitted for stamping in the usual way together with a covering letter giving the aggregate price and a payment for the duty appropriate to that price.

Where the total price does not exceed the amount up to which the instrument is liable to nil duty (currently £60,000) and a certificate of value is included in the instrument, a conveyance may be sent direct to the Land Registry in England and Wales or, in Scotland, to the Keeper of the Registers of Scotland. A lease will need to be stamped in respect of the rent.

Where the total price exceeds the threshold at which duty becomes payable but the taxpayer takes the view that duty is payable on some smaller sum, the instrument should be submitted to the Stamp Office. This applies even where the taxpayer believes that the amount potentially chargeable to ad valorem duty is below the threshold and a certificate of value is included in the instrument. The instrument should be accompanied by a copy of the agreement(s) for sale etc. and a letter stating the amount which the taxpayer regards as chargeable consideration, identifying separately any amount attributable to building work. Details of any contractual arrangements not covered by the agreement(s) should also be given in the covering letter.

This Statement does not affect in any way a taxpayer's rights of appeal.

X.2. National House-Building Council Scheme[1]

The NHBC provides a scheme under which houses are designed and built to a set of standards by builders on its register. The NHBC Home Warranty scheme is split into two major parts:

1. the builder's obligations
2. NHBC's undertakings – the insurance policy

The builder's obligations are:

1. a general warranty to build in a good and workmanlike manner, and of proper materials so as to ensure that the home is fit for habitation.
2. to build in accordance with NHBC: Requirements.
3. to remedy any defect which results from a breach of NHBC's technical requirements during the two year initial guarantee period.

NHBC's undertakings are:

1. to cover loss resulting from the builder's insolvency prior to completion of the home.
2. to make good loss resulting from the builder's failure during the initial guarantee period to put right defects.
3. to cover loss resulting from defects or major damage to the structure or damage resulting from settlements, subsidence or heave or damage to the drainage system during the third to tenth years – structural guarantee period.

There are currently two different sets of documents in circulation.

1. The 1979 to 1986 Schemes

These schemes consisted of a House Purchaser's Agreement in duplicate, a page of explanatory notes and the House Purchaser's Insurance Policy and the Standard Notice of Insurance Cover.

The Standard Notice of Insurance Cover was issued following the final inspection of NHBC. This brings the principal benefits under the scheme into effect. Under the 1986 Scheme, both the builder and NHBC cover the cost of alternative accommodation, removals and storage where it was necessary for a home owner and his or her family to leave the home during repairs.

Under these Schemes, as with earlier schemes, the practice was to lodge the NHBC documents with the Title Deeds as evidence that the home was covered by the NHBC.

---

1. The material in this appendix is reproduced with the permission of the National House-Building Council.

2. The Buildmark Scheme (1988 to 1994)

The Buildmark Scheme consists of four principal documents:

- The Offer Form (NHBC code BM1)
- The Acceptance Form (NHBC code BM2)
- The Buildmark book
- The Ten Year Notice (and Common Parts Ten Year Notice in the case of flats, if applicable) (NHBC code BM4) or combined Ten Year Notice and Final Certificate.

Under the Buildmarks Scheme it is essential that the home owner receives the documents; they are not, with the exception of the lender's copy of the Ten Year Notice, sent to the Building Society. When the home receives its final inspection NHBC will issue the Ten Year Notice and the Common Parts Ten Year Notice if applicable (or Ten Year Notice and Final Certificate). This will be sent in duplicate direct to the home owner's solicitors provided the Acceptance Form has not been completed and returned to NHBC. One copy of the Ten Year Notice is sent to the purchaser for retention with the Buildmark book and Offer Form and the other copy is sent to the lender if applicable.

Cover under the Buildmark for pre-completion insolvency cover is now 10% of the contract sum or £10,000 whichever is the greater. Under the post-completion builders' liability period and the structural guarantee period cover is based upon the market value of the home as shown in the Acceptance Form or £500,000 whichever is the less. Under both schemes the builder must be a current member of the NHBC Register to be able to offer valid cover on exchange of contract.

In Spring 1995, the documents were redesigned and simplified: the Offer and Acceptance Forms are now combined, and there is no longer a Common Parts Ten Year Notice. Some minor amendments have been made to the scheme, for example conciliation is no longer compulsory.

NHBC has now introduced a variation of the Buildmark Scheme for Housing Associations called Buildmark Choice.

Claims

Claims are dealt with in regional offices. The regional office will arrange a conciliation meeting with the builder at the home where there are defects which are the responsibility of the builder having arisen during the two year initial guarantee period. Where a claim is made during the structural guarantee period an inspection will be carried out to ascertain if the claim is valid, and, if so, what work must be done by the NHBC. Disputes about insurance claims may be referred to the Insurance Ombudsman's Bureau.

Where building control is carried by NHBC a fourth element of insurance cover under Buildmark comes into operation. It covers the cost of work needed if there is a breach of the building regulations resulting in an imminent danger to the physical health and safety of an occupier. It is subject to a £200 index-linked excess.

Building control

A subsidiary company, NHBC Building Control Services Ltd, has been appointed by the Secretary of State for Environment as an Approved Inspector under Part II of the Building Act 1984. Under the Act a builder may opt to have his work inspected by the Building Control company for the purposes of compliance with the building regulations in substitution for the Local Authority. Supervision by the Building Control company will not affect the completion by the Local Authority of local searches and enquiries although many authorities note that an Initial Notice is in force.

NHBC can be contacted at its Head Office at Buildmark House, Chiltern Avenue, Amersham, Bucks HP6 5AP, DX 50712, tel: 01494 434477, fax: 01494 728521.

X.3. Foundation 15

Foundation 15 (F.15) is a New Home Structural Guarantee available from Municipal Mutual Insurance (MMI). It provides cover for a period of 15 years and is fully accepted by building societies, banks and other mortgage lenders. The guarantee is issued by builders and developers who are registered with F.15; the scheme as a whole consists of a set of Rules, Technical Standards and an Inspection Service, and the insurance policy entitled "Scheme Details".

The cover provided is in 3 stages:

   (i) *During Building:* the protection covers the deposit, or at the insurer's option, the cost of putting right defects when construction is not completed in accordance with the Requirements (e.g. if the developer becomes insolvent).

   (ii) *First 2 Years:* the primary responsibility is on the developer to correct Damage and Defects. However, if he fails to comply with this responsibility, the buyer may claim directly on the insurer.

   (iii) *Up to 15 Years:* MMI insures against Major Damage and Defects, generally relating to the structure of the new home.

The Scheme Details provide a glossary of all the terms used; the more important relate to the scope of cover and the insured. Included is damage caused by ground movement, and property covered includes common parts, separate or integral garage or other permanent building, footpath or drive, retaining or boundary wall and drainage system (including pipes, channels, gullies or inspection chambers for which the buyer is responsible). The insured is the original buyer (or successor in title), or any mortgagee in possession or lessor (other than the developer or builder).

When an F.15 registered builder commences work, the single premium is paid to MMI. The company immediately issues the policy (Scheme Details) together with an Initial Certificate which identifies the particular property covered; 3 Initial Certificates are produced – one each for the buyer, mortgagee and builder. All are sent to the builder to be distributed as required via a buyer's solicitor. Also produced at this time is a Buyer's Details form, to be completed on exchange of contracts. This information is used to produce the Final Certificate. The Initial Certificate is the evidence that a property is covered by the Scheme, and exchange of contracts can safely proceed in the knowledge that the protection "during building" is in place.

When construction is completed to the satisfaction of the F.15 surveyor, a Final Certificate is issued. This date commences the 15 year guarantee period. Again, this is produced as a set of 3. If contracts have been exchanged and the buyer details are known, then the buyer's name appears on the Final Certificate. If contracts are exchanged after physical completion, a revised Final Certificate can be issued, to include the buyer's details.

The Scheme is administered from the Head Office at Southwood, through a regional office network covering England, Wales and Scotland.

There is a telephone hot-line (01252-377474) dedicated to F.15 for urgent enquiries, otherwise enquiries should be addressed to the Administration Manager, Building Guarantee

Department, Municipal Mutual Insurance Ltd, Southwood Crescent, Farnborough, Hants, GU14 0NJ.

Note

Municipal Mutual Insurance ceased writing new business, including Foundation 15, on 1 October 1992. Consequently Foundation 15 is no longer available for new properties. Existing properties with an **Initial** Certificate dated prior to 1 October 1992 continue in force and are accepted by mortgagees generally. It should be noted that **Final** Certificates for these properties may well be dated after 1 October 1992 as these properties are physically completed, and such policies are all valid.

X.4. Zurich Insurance's range of building guarantees

Newbuild is a New Home Structural Guarantee from Zurich Insurance (ZI). It provides cover for a period of 10 years (extendable by the home owner at the end of the initial term for a further five years subject to additional premium and claims experience) and is fully acceptable by building societies, banks and other mortgage lenders. The guarantee is issued by builders and developers who are registered with ZI. The scheme as a whole consists of a set of Rules, Technical Standards and an Inspection Service, and the insurance policy entitled "Newbuild Guarantee".

The cover provided is in three stages:

(i)   During Building: the protection covers the deposit, or where so endorsed but not otherwise, the cost of putting right defects when construction is not completed in accordance with the Requirements due to the developer becoming insolvent or bankrupt.

(ii) First Two Years: the primary responsibility is on the developer to correct Damage and Defects. However, if he fails to comply with this responsibility, the buyer may claim directly on the insurer.

(iii) Up to 10 years: ZI insures against Major Damage and Defects, generally relating to the structure of the new home.

Newbuild provides a glossary of all the terms used; the more important relate to the scope of cover and the insured. Included is damage caused by ground movement, and property covered includes common parts, separate or integral garage or other permanent building, footpath or drive, retaining or boundary wall and drainage system (including pipes, channels, gullies or inspection chambers for which the buyer is responsible). The insured is the original buyer (or successor in title), or any mortgagee in possession or lessor (other than the developer or builder).

When a ZI registered builder commences work, the single premium is paid to Zurich Insurance. The company immediately issues the policy together with an Initial Certificate which identifies the particular property covered; three copies of Initial Certificates are produced – one each for the buyer, mortgagee and builder. All are sent to the builder to be distributed as required via a buyer's solicitor. Also produced at this time is a Buyer's Details form, which may be completed on exchange of contracts. The information can be included in the Final Certificate. The Initial Certificate is the evidence that a property is covered by the Scheme, and exchange of contracts can safely proceed in the knowledge that the protection "during building" is in place. Contract completion should not take place until the Final Certificate has been issued.

When construction is completed to the satisfaction of the ZI surveyor, a Final Certificate is issued. This date commences the 10 year guarantee period. Again, this is produced as as a set of three. If contracts have been exchanged and the buyer details are known, then the buyer's name appears on the Final Certificate. If contracts are exchanged after physical completion, a revised Final Certificate can be issued, to include the buyer's details. Cover runs with the property and so the buyer's details are optional rather than essential.

The Scheme is administered from the Head Office at Southwood, through a regional office network covering England, Wales and Scotland.

Newbuild is the policy which covers speculatively built homes. There are four other products in the Zurich range of guarantees and the insurance cover, Terms and Conditions vary according to the policy name;

Custom Build is applicable to a site owner who arranges for the building of his own home;

Rebuild is for speculatively converted properties and cover includes both new and existing structure;

Newstyle and Restyle are intended for the Housing Association or other rental markets, for newly built or converted properties respectively.

There is a telephone hot-line (01252 377474) dedicated to the Building Guarantee Department for urgent enquiries, otherwise enquiries should be addressed to the Administration Manager, Building Guarantee Department, Zurich Insurance, Southwood Crescent, Farnborough, Hants, GU14 0NJ.

XI.   MORTGAGES

XI.   Help lists from the Council of Mortgage Lenders

The help lists on the following pages are reproduced with the permission of the Council of Mortgage Lenders.

XI

BEFORE EXCHANGE OF CONTRACTS

Note: This information has been supplied by the Council of Mortgage Lenders and may alter from time to time. No warranty is given as to its accuracy. Any information supplied in this list may be overridden by the terms of engagement or mortgage instructions in any individual case.

Name of Lender	Request for deeds	Production fee (if any)	Acknowledgements required	Fee if borrower makes own insurance arrangements Freehold	Leasehold	Approximate time limit for returning deeds	Address of Head Office DX Number	Consent for letting obtained from	Date information supplied
Abbey National plc	Mortgage Service Centre holding account.	Nil.	No.	£25 for existing mortgages. No fee for new mortgages.	£25 for existing mortgages unless landlord insures due to obligation in lease. No fee for new mortgages.	4 months	DX 137000 Milton Keynes-2	Mortgage Centre holding account.	May 1997.
Alliance & Leicester Building Society	Mortgage Customer Services, Customer Services Centre, Carlton Park, Narborough, Leics LE9 5XX	£50.	No.	Yes, £25.	Yes, £25 unless landlord insures pursuant to obligation in lease.	6 months for a re-mortgage or purchase. Deeds sent out for all other purposes must be returned within 3 months.	Customer Services Centre, Carlton Park, Narborough Leics LE9 5XX DX 11000 Leicester	Mortgage Customer Services, Customer Services Centre, Carlton Park, Narborough Leics LE9 5XX DX 11000 Leicester	May 1997.

Lender									
Bank of Ireland Home Mortgages	Contact Customer Services	Included within redemption fee of £90 inc VAT. If redemption not proceeded with, fee is £40 inc VAT if deeds have been despatched.	Yes.	£25.	Nil.	6 months for sale or remortgage. For anything else return within 3 months.	Bridge St Plaza, West Bridge St, Reading DX 4029 Reading-1	Contact Customer Services	May 1997.
Barclays Bank PLC (See also Barclays Mortgages)	Send to account holding branch.	£25 + VAT.	Yes (branch will provide standard bank undertaking).	£25.	£25. Nil where landlord insures the property.	Negotiable.	54 Lombard Street London EC3P 3AH	Account holding branch.	May 1997.
Barclays Mortgages (See also Barclays Bank PLC branches)	P.O. Box HK444 Leeds LS11 8DD Tel: 0113 296 5000 DX 13947 Leeds Arlington	£25 + VAT.	Yes.	£25.	£25. Nil where landlord insures the property.	Registration to be effected following completion and the deeds to be returned immediately thereafter.	P.O. Box HK444 Leeds LS11 8DD Tel: 0113 296 5000 DX 13947 Leeds Arlington	P.O. Box HK444 Leeds LS11 8DD Tel: 0113 296 5000 DX 13947 Leeds Arlington	May 1997

XI

Name of Lender	Request for deeds	Production fee (if any)	Acknowledgements required	Fee if borrower makes own insurance arrangements		Approximate time limit for returning deeds	Address of Head Office DX Number	Consent for letting obtained from	Date information supplied
				Freehold	Leasehold				
Birmingham Midshires Building Society	Lending Services at principal office.	£40.	Yes.	£25.	£25 unless lease provides that landlord insures.	4 months.	DX 10401 Wolverhampton	Lending Services at principal office.	May 1997.
Bristol & West	Deeds Dept. H.O.	£37.50.	Yes.	£30.	No charge.	6 months.	DX 98850 Bristol-2	Deeds Dept. H.O.	May 1997.
Britannia Building Society	In writing to Mortgage Services (CO30). Panel solicitors only provided with title deeds.	£25 fee debited to mortgage account – solicitors notified requested to inform borrowers of deduction direct to enable borrower if so wishes to make payment to mortgage account.	Letter containing terms and conditions sent out, no acknowledgement will be necessary.	Fee charged £25 (form to be completed by insurance company (proposed) and borrower before insurance proposals accepted in freehold and leasehold cases).	If borrower required to insure under terms of lease – no charge. If borrower under no obligation to insure in the lease then a fee of £25 is charged if borrower wishes to make own insurance arrangements.	Sale/ redemption – 9 months. Transfer/ re-mortgage – 9 months. Boundary dispute/ inspection of deeds – 9 months.	Britannia House, Leek, Staffs. ST13 5RG DX 16351 Leek	Request in writing to Mortgage Services (CO15). Fee £80 each time consent is given (inclusive legal costs). On renewal refer to Commercial Lending (CO34). Fee £20 for same tenants or £80 if new tenants.	May 1997.
Cheltenham & Gloucester plc	Deeds Dept. Chief Office.	£20.	No.	No fee charged.	No fee charged.	This varies according to circumstances.	Chief Office Barnet Way Gloucester GL4 3RL DX 55251 Gloucester-2	Originating branch.	May 1997.

Halifax Building Society	Head Office Deeds Administration Department	£15. Debited to mortgage account. Solicitor should inform borrower.	None.	None.	None.	7 months for deeds on loan for a sale. 5 months for new title deeds following completion of mortgage.	Trinity Road Halifax West Yorkshire HX1 2RG DX 11896 Halifax	Application to be made to branch office where account is held. A fee may be charged each time a consent is given.	May 1997.
Midland Bank plc	Mortgage Service Centre (MSC) at Courtwood House in writing.	£17.62 inspection. £30 any other transaction.	Signed undertaking required.	Nil.	Nil.	4 months.	Midland Bank plc Courtwood House Silver Street Head Sheffield S1 2QA DX 10611 Sheffield-1	Midland Bank plc (Bank branch).	May 1997.

XI

Name of Lender	Request for deeds	Production fee (if any)	Acknowledgements required	Fee if borrower makes own insurance arrangements		Approximate time limit for returning deeds	Address of Head Office DX Number	Consent for letting obtained from	Date information supplied
				Freehold	Leasehold				
National Westminster Home Loans Limited	Head office.	£35.	Yes.	£25.	£25. No fee if insurance tied by lease.	Variable. Expected within about 16 weeks for new accounts.	PO Box 156, Priory House, Queensway, Birmingham B4 6AL DX 13200 Birmingham	Head office.	May 1997.
Nationwide Building Society	Securities Dept. Northampton Admin. Centre. DX 12499 Northampton	£25.	No.	£25.	No fee.	6 months.	For returning deeds: Securities Dept., Northampton Admin. Centre, King's Park Road, Moulton Park, Northampton NN3 6NW DX 12499 Northampton All others DX 12500 Northampton	Customer Service Teams, Northampton Admin. Centre, King's Park Road, Moulton Park Northampton NN3 1NL	May 1997.

Northern Rock Building Society	Securities Mortgage & Personal Lending Dept. Northern Rock House, Gosforth, Newcastle upon Tyne NE3 4PL	£40 charged to customer's account.	Yes.	£35.	£35.	3 months.	Northern Rock House, PO Box 2, Gosforth, Newcastle upon Tyne NE3 4PL DX 60350 Gosforth	Commercial Finance Dept., Northern Rock House	May 1997.
Paragon Finance plc	Deeds Administration, St. Catherine's Court.	£45 plus VAT.	Yes.	£25.	£25.	Inspection – 3 months. Alterations – 6 months.	Paragon Finance plc, St Catherine's Court, Herbert Rd, Solihull, West Midlands B91 3QE MDX 14031 Solihull-2	Mortgage admin., Account Management	May 1997.
Portman Building Society	Solicitors Department, Head Office.	£30	Yes.	£25.	£25 unless terms of lease require insurance to be arranged through a specific agency, when there is no fee.	3 months.	Portman House, Richmond Hill, Bournemouth, Dorset BH2 6EP DX 84300 Bournemouth-2	Customer Services Department, 25 High St, Marlborough, Wilts SN8 1NF DX 39455 Marlborough	May 1997.

XI

Name of Lender	Request for deeds	Production fee (if any)	Acknowledgements required	Fee if borrower makes own insurance arrangements		Approximate time limit for returning deeds	Address of Head Office DX Number	Consent for letting obtained from	Date information supplied
				Freehold	Leasehold				
TSB Bank plc	TSB Homeloans Ltd	£25.	No.	No.	No.	6 months.	TSB Homeloans Ltd., 2 Atlantic Quay, P.O. Box 6644 45 Robertson St., Glasgow G2 8JL DX 512000 Glasgow	TSB Homeloans Ltd	May 1997.
TSB Bank of Scotland plc	TSB Homeloans Ltd	£25.	No.	No.	No.	6 months.	TSB Homeloans Ltd., 2 Atlantic Quay, P.O. Box 6644, 45 Robertson St., Glasgow G2 8JL DX 512000 Glasgow	TSB Homeloans Ltd	May 1997.

The Mortgage Corporation Limited (TMC)	To be made by way of formal written request and undertaking to: 'The Securities Department'.	Only made in respect of photocopying charges. Not for the release of original title deeds.	Yes.	£25.	£25.	6 months.	Sir William Atkins House, Ashley Avenue Epsom, Surrey KT18 5AS DX 82550 Epsom 9	The Customer Services (General) Department – draft tenancy agreement must be forwarded for approval prior to commencement of the tenancy. Letting is not usually allowed for new mortgage applicants.	May 1997.
Woolwich Building Society	Deeds Services, Woolwich Building Society Corporate HQ. Watling St, Bexleyheath, Kent DA6 7RR DX 90000 Bexleyheath-2	£50.	Not required.	£25 admin fee.	No, unless lease provides for tenant to make own insurance arrangements – fee £25.	3 months after completion of the advance.	Corporate HQ, Watling Street, Bexleyheath, Kent DA6 7RR. DX 90000 Bexleyheath	Mortgage Services, Equitable Hse, Woolwich, London SE18 6AB or from the local branch.	May 1997.
Yorkshire Building Society	Securities Dept. – Deeds Control, Yorkshire House, Yorkshire Drive, Bradford BD5 8LJ DX 11899 Bradford	£38.50	No.	£25 one-off fee.	No charge if condition of lease.	6 months.	Yorkshire Hse, Yorkshire Drive Bradford BD5 8LJ DX 11899 Bradford. Legal Dept. DX 11762 Bradford	Mortgage Admin. Dept. Yorkshire Hse, Yorkshire Drive Bradford BD5 8LJ. £30 fee. Application obtained/submitted through branch.	May 1997.

XI

MORTGAGE OFFER – PURCHASE

Note: This information has been supplied by the Council of Mortgage Lenders and may alter from time to time. No warranty is given as to its accuracy. Any information supplied in this list may be overridden by the terms of engagement or mortgage instructions in any individual case.

Name of Lender	Queries on mortgage offer	Report on title to be sent to	Time for issue of cheque	Telegraphic transfer if available and fee charged	Delayed completion Return of cheque after ...... days	Interest charged from	Need to notify completion	Initial interest	Mortgage Guarantee premium deducted from mortgage advance
Abbey National plc	Mortgage service centre issuing offer.	Mortgage service centre issuing offer.	5 clear working days.	All advances over £125,000. No fee. (If ANMF issue offer then all advances. No fee.)	On next working day unless mortgage service centre agrees to funds being retained.	Completion.	No.	Yes.	A high loan to value fee is deducted from the mortgage advance, provided the loan does not exceed 100% of the purchase price or valuation, whichever is the lower.
Alliance & Leicester Building Society	Mortgage Unit issuing offer, or Carlton Park if it issued offer.	Mortgage Unit issuing offer, or Carlton Park if it issued offer.	4 clear working days.	Yes, fee is £30.	21 days.	Completion.	No.	Debited to mortgage account and payable by borrower with first monthly payment.	Yes.

Insurance from date of offer/exchange of contracts/ completion	How premium paid i.e. monthly/ annually	Loan includes further advances/ obligation to make a further advance	Need to approve terms of lease	Requirement for NHBC or Foundation 15 on purchase from original or subsequent buyer	Date infor-mation supplied	Name of Lender
Exchange of contracts.	Choice of either.	Deed includes further advances.	By solicitor.	Yes for new property on first purchase.	May 1997.	**Abbey National plc**
On risk from date of cheque for loan unless insurance requested from an earlier date.	Borrower can choose either monthly or annually.	See mortgage deeds and condi-tions as to whether mortgage secures further advance (always the case for deeds dated since 1986). No obligation to make further advances unless specifically indicated on front of the deed or specific instructions given in solicitor's instructions.	By solicitor on behalf of company.	Yes. Where NHBC/ Foundation 15 certificate is still valid, the certificate must be placed with the title deeds.	May 1997.	**Alliance & Leicester Building Society**

XI

Name of Lender	Queries on mortgage offer	Report on title to be sent to	Time for issue of cheque	Telegraphic transfer if available and fee charged	Delayed completion Return of cheque after ...... days	Interest charged from	Need to notify completion	Initial interest	Mortgage Guarantee premium deducted from mortgage advance
Bank of Ireland Home Mortgage	New Business Admin.	New Business Admin.	Normally 5 working days required.	Funds sent by T.T. Charge £20.	If after 1 day of sending out interest charged daily.	Date of release of funds.	No.	1st payment due 1 month after release of funds.	Yes.
Barclays Bank PLC (See also Barclays Mortgages)	Account holding branch.	Branch.	Arrange with branch method of payment.	Yes – £20.	Contact branch for instructions (interest running from date of request of funds).	Date of release of funds.	Yes.	Rate as negotiated and dependent on type of facility.	Added to loan but deducted from advance.
Barclays Mortgages (See also Barclays Bank PLC Branches)	To address on mortgage offer.	Barclays Mortgages DX 13947 Leeds, Arlington	N/A	Yes £20 deducted from advance.	1 day. Funds may be retained for a short period subject to interest running from date of release of funds	Date of release of funds.	Yes.	Dependent on type of loan and date of completion.	Added to loan but deducted from advance.
Birmingham Midshires Building Society	Lending New Business Dept. principal office.	Lending New Business Dept. Completion section at principal office.	5 working days from our receipt of R.O.T. 8 working days from our receipt of R.O.T. if an inspection is required.	Yes if requested. £20 – deducted from advance.	3 days after completion.	Date of release of mortgage advance.	No.	Date of release to end month.	Yes, except for loans which exceed 95% loan to value.

Insurance from date of offer/exchange of contracts/ completion	How premium paid i.e. monthly/ annually	Loan includes further advances/ obligation to make a further advance	Need to approve terms of lease	Requirement for NHBC or Foundation 15 on purchase from original or subsequent buyer	Date information supplied	Name of Lender
From date of completion unless otherwise advised.	Monthly automatically unless annual premium requested.	Deed includes further advances.	Legal representative to approve.	Yes.	May 1997.	**Bank of Ireland Home Mortgages**
Exchange of contracts.	Monthly (usually).	No.	Yes – submit draft to account holding branch.	Facilities will vary – contact branch.	May 1997.	**Barclays Bank PLC**
Buildings insurance on exchange of contracts. Life cover at exchange of contracts.	Monthly by direct debit.	Deferred and stabiliser products only.	Solicitors' obligation refer instructions given.	Yes – including architect's certificate.	May 1997.	**Barclays Mortgages** **(See also Barclays Bank PLC Branches)**
Exchange of contracts backdated at completion. Insurance set up from date of release of advance cheque and policy cover available from exchange of contracts.	Monthly.	Includes further advances. No obligation to make them.	Solicitors' obligation refer instructions given.	Solicitors to confirm documents exist and are in order.	May 1997.	**Birmingham Midshires Building Society**

Name of Lender	Queries on mortgage offer	Report on title to be sent to	Time for issue of cheque	Telegraphic transfer if available and fee charged	Delayed completion Return of cheque after ...... days	Interest charged from	Need to notify completion	Initial interest	Mortgage Guarantee premium deducted from mortgage advance
Bristol & West	Advances Dept. H.O.	Advances Dept. H.O.	3 working days from receipt of R.O.T. 7 working days if inspection required.	Restricted use only. £30 charge.	7 days.	Day after issue of cheque.	Yes.	Date after release of cheque to end of month prior to the first payment.	Yes.
Britannia Building Society	Completions DX 711041 Hanley 4 or PO Box 558 Hanley Stoke-on-Trent ST1 2BR	Completions DX 711041 Hanley 4 or PO Box 558 Hanley Stoke-on-Trent ST1 2BR	Report on title states 8 clear days' notice required.	The facility is not available. Exceptions may be made in extreme cases, e.g. where Society is to blame for delaying completion.	Return of cheque usually required unless lost. Cheque may be held by solicitors for a maximum of 7 days but only with Society's permission.	Interest is charged one day prior to the completion date as stated upon the report on title.	No need to notify of actual completion.	From date of release to end of month collected.	Yes.

Insurance from date of offer/exchange of contracts/ completion	How premium paid i.e. monthly/ annually	Loan includes further advances/ obligation to make a further advance	Need to approve terms of lease	Requirement for NHBC or Foundation 15 on purchase from original or subsequent buyer	Date infor- mation supplied	Name of Lender
Exchange of contracts or the date of the offer of advance whichever is later.	Monthly (+6% handling charge) or annually.	Loan includes further advances but no obligation to do so.	Solicitors' obligation refer to instructions given.	Yes.	May 1997.	**Bristol & West**
Insurance arranged on exchange of contracts if policy is with the Society.	Both buildings and buildings and contents combined may be paid monthly or annually as required. Monthly policies are arranged at no extra cost.	Deeds secures further advances (without obligation to make them).	The solicitors acting on behalf of the borrowers are instructed as Society's agents and must ensure the terms of the lease do not affect the Soc- iety's security and are therefore responsible to ensure the lease terms are approved.	If property is newly built an NHBC or Foundation 15 will be necessary or alternatively an architect's certificate.	May 1997.	**Britannia Building Society**

Name of Lender	Queries on mortgage offer	Report on title to be sent to	Time for issue of cheque	Telegraphic transfer if available and fee charged	Delayed completion Return of cheque after ...... days	Interest charged from	Need to notify completion	Initial interest	Mortgage Guarantee premium deducted from mortgage advance
Cheltenham & Gloucester plc	To the location specified on the report on title.	To the location specified on the report on title.	7 clear working days (14 if final inspection required).	This is the usual method. There is no fee.	1 day unless returning an unprecedented cheque (14 days).	Date on which funds are sent.	No — unless completion date changed.	Interest for period from issue of advance to first payment date payable with first monthly payment.	N/A.
Halifax Building Society (These procedures are for Halifax B.S. only. Any lending subsidiary of Halifax B.S. may have different procedures.)	Branch office where mortgage application made.	Head Office in envelope provided or by fax.	None specified.	Cheques normally despatched by first class post. In urgent cases only funds can be telegraphed for which the fee is £18.	Advance cheque to be returned if completion does not take place within 14 days of the completion date notified in the report on title.	The completion date notified in the report on title or the actual completion date notified by the conveyancer if different.	The Society must be notified of the actual completion date if different from that stated in the report on title.	Any interest charged in the first accounting year but not paid as part of the monthly payments in that year, will be payable on the date notified to the borrower on completion.	No. The premium is debited to the mortgage account on completion.

Insurance from date of offer/exchange of contracts/ completion	How premium paid i.e. monthly/ annually	Loan includes further advances/ obligation to make a further advance	Need to approve terms of lease	Requirement for NHBC or Foundation 15 on purchase from original or subsequent buyer	Date infor- mation supplied	Name of Lender
Where borrower elects to insure through C&G and assuming completion takes place, block cover commences on exchange of contracts except: 1. Where ex- cluded by special condi- tion or at borrower's request. 2. In stage advances or 'work to be completed' cases.	Monthly.	Deed secures further advances (without obliga- tion to make them). Each loan subject to separate loan agreement.	Conveyancer to approve in accordance with instructions.	Required in all cases whilst cover in existence.	May 1997.	**Chelten- ham & Glou- cester plc**
Insurance arranged from exchange of contracts on block policy where Society is arranging insurance. Premium only charged from completion unless a claim is made between exchange and completion.	The annual premium may be paid monthly with interest charged at the standard variable base rate.	The mortgage deed is security for further advances but there is no obligation to make further advances unless the mortgage deed states otherwise.	No. The conveyancer approves the lease on the Society's behalf.	Only required in respect of a new property to be occupied for the first time.	May 1997.	**Halifax Building Society**

Name of Lender	Queries on mortgage offer	Report on title to be sent to	Time for issue of cheque	Telegraphic transfer if available and fee charged	Delayed completion Return of cheque after ...... days	Interest charged from	Need to notify completion	Initial interest	Mortgage Guarantee premium deducted from mortgage advance
Midland Bank plc	Refer to Mortgage Department.	MSC at Courtwood House.	Variable according to circumstances.	CHAPS £17.50 fee.	3 days.	Date of advance of mortgage monies.	Yes.	Prevailing rate as at advance of mortgage monies.	MGP can be deducted from mortgage advance or, if the borrowers prefer, collected with the first payment.
National Westminster Home Loans Ltd	H.O. (Tel. no. as specified on offer letter.)	H.O.	7 days, not less than 14 if reinspection necessary, payment made by CHAPS.	Yes, £30.	Funds may be retained if completion is to take place within 5 days of date specified on R.O.T. Otherwise funds to be returned next working day by CHAPS.	Completion date as advised on R.O.T.	No.	Added to first full monthly payment.	Yes, although option to add to mortgage account exists.
Nationwide Building Society	Instructing Office.	Instructing Office.	3 working days below £300,000 and 5 working days above. 10 where final inspection required.	£15.	7 days.	T.T. – interest charged from day of transfer. Cheque – 2 working days after release.	Not unless delayed.	Added to full first monthly payment.	No.

Insurance from date of offer/exchange of contracts/ completion	How premium paid i.e. monthly/ annually	Loan includes further advances/ obligation to make a further advance	Need to approve terms of lease	Requirement for NHBC or Foundation 15 on purchase from original or subsequent buyer	Date infor- mation supplied	Name of Lender
Confirmation of building insurance required from completion. Life assurance required from completion. If advised to be from exchange, it will be done.	Either depend-ent on the insurance company being used.	N o .	Yes.	Required if property is still covered under either of the above.	May 1997.	**Midland Bank plc**
Exchange of contracts.	Annually although option to pay monthly exists.	Mortgage deed secures further advances but no obligation to make.	Acting solicitors' responsibility.	Yes. Architect's certificate may also be acceptable.	May. 1997.	**National Westmin-ster Home Loans Limited**
Exchange of contracts.	Monthly or annually dependent on contract.	Not obliged to make further advance. Deed secures further advances.	Solicitor should follow printed and other in-structions, and approve on Society's behalf. For further instructions specify items of concern in the lease, do not merely supply photocopy for approval. App-roach Instruct-ing Office who will make the appropriate enquiries.	Always one or the other when property is up to 2 years old (unless fully certificated by architect supervising construction).	May. 1997.	**Nation-wide Building Society**

Name of Lender	Queries on mortgage offer	Report on title to be sent to	Time for issue of cheque	Telegraphic transfer if available and fee charged	Delayed completion Return of cheque after ...... days	Interest charged from	Need to notify completion	Initial interest	Mortgage Guarantee premium deducted from mortgage advance
Northern Rock Building Society	Contact branch.	Completions Section, Mortgage Dept, Northern Rock Hse, PO Box 2, Gosforth, Newcastle.	4 days, not less than 14 if re-inspection required. Payment made by BACS.	Yes. £25 debited to borrower's a/c.	14 days.	Date of completion.	Completions Section.	Payable from date of completion to 1st of following month.	No.
Paragon Mortgages Ltd.	Underwriting.	Underwriting.	Minimum notice: 7 working days prior to completion.	All mortgage advances issued by T.T. Fee: £25 deducted from mortgage advance.	Advance to be returned by T.T. immediately.	Date of issue of advance monies by T.T.		Payable by direct debit.	Added to loan then deducted from advance.
Portman Building Society	Completions Dept, 25 High St, Marlborough, Wilts SN8 1NF. DX 39455 Marlborough.	Completions Department.	5 working days' notice required. All funds sent by CHAPS on day before completion.	All funds sent by CHAPS. £25.	Immediately to avoid interest charges.	Date of release of funds.	No.	Customer notified of amount payable in addition to first monthly instalment.	Yes.

Insurance from date of offer/exchange of contracts/ completion	How premium paid i.e. monthly/ annually	Loan includes further advances/ obligation to make a further advance	Need to approve terms of lease	Requirement for NHBC or Foundation 15 on purchase from original or subsequent buyer	Date infor- mation supplied	Name of Lender
From comple-tion unless otherwise requested.	Monthly within payment unless otherwise requested.	No obligation.	Acting solicitor to advise if conditions of lease materially affect the Society.	Yes.	May 1997.	**Northern Rock Building Society**
Buildings insurance from date of issue of advance unless otherwise agreed in writing.	Monthly. Collection by direct debit with monthly repayment.	Dependent on product/facilities requested. Where appropriate a specific mortgage deed is issued.	Solicitor to confirm terms of lease comply with the company's criteria detailed in: general offer condi-tions; special offer condi-tions; product conditions; instructions to solicitors.	Yes – if the property built within the last 10 years. Architect's certificate also acceptable.	May 1997.	**Paragon Mort-gages Ltd.**
Exchange of contracts.	Monthly.	The mortgage deed secures further advances but there is no obligation to make any unless the mortgage deed states otherwise.	Panel solicitor must approve the lease on the Society's behalf.	Yes.	May 1997.	**Portman Building Society**

XI

Name of Lender	Queries on mortgage offer	Report on title to be sent to	Time for issue of cheque	Telegraphic transfer if available and fee charged	Delayed completion Return of cheque after ...... days	Interest charged from	Need to notify completion	Initial interest	Mortgage Guarantee premium deducted from mortgage advance
TSB Bank plc	TSB Home-loans Ltd.	TSB Home-loans Ltd.	7 days.	T.T. not available. Use TSB speed-send or cheque. CHAPS.	7 days.	Date of release.	No.	For interest only loans interest from re-lease date includ-ed in first pay-ment.	No.
TSB Bank of Scotland plc	TSB Home-loans Ltd.	TSB Home-loans Ltd.	7 days.	T.T. not available. Use TSB speed-send or cheque. CHAPS.	7 days.	Date of reelease.	No.	For interest only loans interest from re-lease date includ-ed in first pay-ment.	No.
The Mortgage Corporation Limited (TMC)	'The Personal Mort-gage Consul-tant'. Our mort-gage refer-ence must always be quoted. Queries on title will be dealt with by our Legal Section.	As per Queries.	We only use T.T.	We only use T.T. Fee – £15. We require 5 days' notice of comple-tion.	1 day. We will look to our solicitor to account to us for interest accrued if the monies are not so returned in accord-ance with the Solici-tors' Ac-counts Rules.	The date of release of monies.	Yes.	As applic-able to the mort-gage on the date of com-pletion.	Yes. We can also add same to the gross mort-gage advance provided it does not exceed £6,000 or 1% of the GMA.

Insurance from date of offer/exchange of contracts/ completion	How premium paid i.e. monthly/ annually	Loan includes further advances/ obligation to make a further advance	Need to approve terms of lease	Requirement for NHBC or Foundation 15 on purchase from original or subsequent buyer	Date information supplied	Name of Lender
Date of exchange payable from date of completion.	Monthly.	The mortgage deed secures further advances but there is no obligation to make any.	No, unless non standard clauses.	Yes.	May 1997.	**TSB Bank plc**
Date of exchange payable from date of completion.	Monthly.	The mortgage deed secures further advances but there is no obligation to make any.	No, unless non standard clauses.	Yes.	May 1997.	**TSB Bank of Scotland plc**
Remortgage: date of completion. Purchase: date of exchange.	Our borrowers can elect to pay either monthly or annually.	We may grant further advances but are not under an obligation to do so, unless a deferred interest scheme.	Our requirements are laid out in our instructions to solicitors in some detail. Any queries thereon may be referred to our Legal Department.	Yes. An architect's certificate may be accepted in the absence of NHBC.	May 1997.	**The Mortgate Corporation Limited (TMC)**

Name of Lender	Queries on mortgage offer	Report on title to be sent to	Time for issue of cheque	Telegraphic transfer if available and fee charged	Delayed completion Return of cheque after ...... days	Interest charged from	Need to notify completion	Initial interest	Mortgage Guarantee premium deducted from mortgage advance
Woolwich Building Society	All queries to be referred to branch office named in mortgage offer.	Report to be sent to branch office named in mortgage offer.	Cheques up to £100,000 issued at branch office level. 8 days' notice is required. Cheque issued 4 days prior to completion.	Not available except if the advance is made by Woolwich Direct: fee £25.	7 days from issue.	Date of issue plus 1 day.	No.	Interest from the interest date (the day after despatch of advance moneys) to the end of the month in which interest date falls is added to the first payment.	Yes.
Yorkshire Building Society	In first instance, branch.	Branch.	8 working days before cheque required.	Yes (CHAPS) £20. 5 working days' notice needed for CHAPS transfer.	14 days after original completion date. If CHAPS must return within 24 hours.	Day prior to completion date.	If a completion has been delayed or if a further advance is linked then notification required.	Payable immediately on completion.	Yes, it will be deducted from loan on completion. However, it can be added onto mortgage if borrower has asked, subject to status, in order to avoid a separate payment on completion. It will then be interest bearing.

Insurance from date of offer/exchange of contracts/ completion	How premium paid i.e. monthly/ annually	Loan includes further advances/ obligation to make a further advance	Need to approve terms of lease	Requirement for NHBC or Foundation 15 on purchase from original or subsequent buyer	Date information supplied	Name of Lender
Insurance is effected upon request or on completion if no prior request.	Monthly — however this can be paid annually upon request.	The Society's mortgage deed provides for further advances.	Yes.	Yes.	May 1997.	**Woolwich Building Society**
Date of offer unless conveyancer informs Society when exchange of contracts takes place.	Monthly.	Mortgage deed secures further advances but there is no obligation to make them.	Conveyancer acts for Society and will be expected to advise the Society as to acceptance or rejection.	Yes or Zurich Insurance or architect's certificate (for properties up to 10 years old).	May 1997.	**York- shire Building Society**

AFTER EXCHANGE OF CONTRACTS – SALE

Note: This information has been supplied by the Council of Mortgage Lenders and may alter from time to time. No warranty is given as to its accuracy. Any information supplied in this list may be overridden by the terms of engagement or mortgage instructions in any individual case.

Name of Lender	Redemption statement obtained from	Interest charged on redemption i.e. to date of payment or end of month	Penalty for early redemption	Cheque to be sent to/ CHAPS: Sort Code and Client Account Number	Document to be sent to	Sealing fee (if any)	Insurance arranged by the lender continued/cancelled on redemption	Refund of insurance premium included in redemption statement	Date information supplied
Abbey National plc	Mortgage Service Centre holding account.	To date of payment.	Refer to mortgage conditions contained in mortgage offer for the individual loan.	Mortgage Service Centre holding account.	Mortgage Service Centre holding account.	£50 deeds handling charged in all cases unless enter into deed safe service.	Cancelled unless borrower requests otherwise.	No.	May 1997.
Alliance & Leicester Building Society	Mortgage Customer Services, Customer Services Centre, Carlton Park, Narborough Leics LE9 5XX.	Interest is normally charged to date of payment.	Please see mortgage deed and mortgage conditions incorporated in the deed.	Redemption cheque can be sent to either the local branch or Mortgage Customer Services, Carlton Park. TT goes to Girobank Bootle – Sort Code 72-52-52, A/N 80-00000000	Mortgage Customer Services, Carlton Park.	£60.	Cancelled unless borrower requests otherwise.	No.	May 1997.

Lender									
Bank of Ireland Home Mortgages	Customer Service Dept.	Interest charged to date of payment.	Standard penalty 3 months interest within 1st year. This may differ for individual products.	CHAPS Royal Bank of Scotland 16-29-25 A/C No: 11201986	Securities Dept.	Included within redemption fee of £90 inc. VAT.	If covered on block policy cancelled on redemption.	Yes. Based on whole months only.	May 1997.
Barclays PLC (See also **Barclays Mortgages**)	Account holding branch.	To date of payment.	On certain accounts – details available on request.	Contact branch for account details.	Branch.	None.	As required.	–	May 1997.
Barclays Mortgages (See also **Barclays Bank PLC branches**)	P.O. Box HK444 Leeds LS11 8DD Tel 0113 296 5000 DX 13947 Leeds, Arlington	To date of payment.	On certain accounts – details available on request.	Branch accts: Sort code: 20-19-14. Bank title: Barclays Mortgages. A/C name: BHMS AFTS Suspense A/C no: 88088306. Client's name. Client's mortgage ref. no. Third party accts: Sort code: 20-19-18. Bank title: Barclays Mortgages. A/C name: BHMS AFTS. Suspense A/C no: 68088306. Client's name. Client's mortgage ref. no.	P.O. Box HK444 Leeds LS11 8DD Tel 0113 296 5000 DX 13947 Leeds, Arlington	None.	Cancelled if account introduced through third party introducers. If introduced through branch network not cancelled.	Not applicable worked on % of month.	May 1997.

Name of Lender	Redemption statement obtained from	Interest charged on redemption i.e. to date of payment or end of month	Penalty for early redemption	Cheque to be sent to/ CHAPS: Sort Code and Client Account Number	Document to be sent to	Sealing fee (if any)	Insurance arranged by the lender continued/cancelled on redemption	Refund of insurance premium included in redemption statement	Date information supplied
Birmingham Midshires Building Society	Lending Services at principal office.	To the end of the month.	On fixed-rate and discount products various penalties. On ordinary mortgage penalty if redeemed in first year.	Lending Services at principal office. Cheque is preferred.	Lending Services at principal office.	£50.	We ask the customer what he wants. Will do either.	No. Refunded after redemption.	May 1997.
Bristol & West	Redemption Section H.O.	To end of month plus £50 fee.	Depends on type of loan as specified in the mortgage offer.	H.O. Redemption Section CHAPS Sort Code 57.14.62 A/C No. 53930037 N.W. Bank Corn Street Bristol Quote Mortgage No.	Redemption Section.	£50.	If annual, if no contrary instructions are received insurance is cancelled on redemption. If annual we automatically continue.	No.	May 1997.

Britannia Building Society	Branch office or Mortgage Services (CO15), Head Office.	Redemption statement calculated to a specific date and interest charged to that date, plus three days' additional interest unless specified otherwise in mortgage offer or conditions.	As specified in mortgage offer.	Cheque sent to Head Office, Mortgage Services Department (CO15) or the branch offices or CHAPS Nat West Bank plc, 24 Derby St., Leek, Staffs., Sort Code: 01-05-02 A/C No. 01871870	Mortgage Services (CO15).	£50.	Cancelled unless instructions received to continue.	No refunds included in redemption statement – any overpayment returned after redemption.	May 1997.
Cheltenham & Gloucester plc	Chief Office (Mortgage Support Dept).	End of month.	No. Fees are charged for special products (e.g. fixed rates and discounts) and some transferred Society loans.	Paid by cheque and sent to Chief Office (Mortgage Support Dept).	Chief Office (Mortgage Support Dept).	£35 per loan.	Cancelled at end of month in which redemption occurs.	No. Refunds are only applicable if insurance is paid annually and then only for the period unexpired.	May 1997.
Halifax Building Society	Branch office where the mortgage account is held.	Interest is charged to the date of redemption unless specified otherwise in the offer of mortgage.	None unless specified otherwise in the offer of mortgage.	Branch office where account is held.	Branch office where account is held.	£40.	Unless the borrower specifically requests cancellation or the issue of a private policy with the same company, the insurance will lapse at the next renewal date.	No. Any refund due is credited to an investment account or sent by cheque following cancellation.	May 1997.

XI

Name of Lender	Redemption statement obtained from	Interest charged on redemption i.e. to date of payment or end of month	Penalty for early redemption	Cheque to be sent to/ CHAPS: Sort Code and Client Account Number	Document to be sent to	Sealing fee (if any)	Insurance arranged by the lender continued/cancelled on redemption	Refund of insurance premium included in redemption statement	Date information supplied
Midland Bank plc	MSC at Courtwood House.	Interest charged at daily rate to date of payment.	Standard mortgage: £50 fee. Fixed mortgage: 6 mnths interest if more than 2 yrs of fixed term remaining or 3 mnths if less than 2 yrs + more than 5 yrs = 12 mnths' interest. Variable mortgage discounts: if loan redeemed within 3 yrs of draw-down and not replaced in whole or in part by further variable rate loan, a fee equivalent to the gross interest saved by the discount will be charged together with the amount of any cash incentive received.	Details to be advised in writing. CHAPS if possible – 40-41-42 quoting client's name and account no.	Mortgage Service Centre, Courtwood House, Redemptions.	None.	Up to customer to arrange, i.e. MSC send notice to insurers that MSC no longer interested in the policy.	No.	May 1997.

Lender									
National Westminster Home Loans Limited	H.O.	CHAPS settlement interest calculated to completion date. Cheque settlement 6 days' interest is charged after completion date.	Varies. Amount (if any) will be included with redemption statement.	Cheques: H.O. CHAPS: 60-05-00 78170087.	H.O.	£85.	Continued unless advised otherwise.	Customer or solicitor should contact insurance company.	May 1997.
Nationwide Building Society	Customer Service Teams, Northampton Admin. Centre, King's Park Rd, Moulton Park, Northampton NN3 6NW.	End of month unless taking new mortgage with Society in which case to date of redemption.	None except fixed-rate and variable discount rate products.	Customer Service Teams, Northampton Admin. Centre King's Pk Rd, Moulton Park, Northampton NN3 6NW. CHAPS: Sort Code 070093 Client A/C No. 333 333 34 (must quote customer name and A/C no. in ref. box).		£40.	Insurance cancelled unless borrower requires policy to be continued. If so proposal form sent to the borrower.	No – charged up to redemption month end.	May 1997.

Name of Lender	Redemption statement obtained from	Interest charged on redemption i.e. to date of payment or end of month	Penalty for early redemption	Cheque to be sent to/ CHAPS: Sort Code and Client Account Number	Document to be sent to	Sealing fee (if any)	Insurance arranged by the lender continued/cancelled on redemption	Refund of insurance premium included in redemption statement	Date information supplied
Northern Rock Building Society	Redemptions Section, Mortgage Dept, Northern Rock House, PO Box 2, Gosforth, Newcastle upon Tyne NE3 4PL	To end of month.	Variable where loans are part of special schemes.	CHAPS: 60655996 20-59-42. Cheque to Redemptions Section.	Redemptions Section.	£60.	Cancelled unless otherwise advised.	No – charged up to redemption month end.	May 1997.
Paragon Mortgages Ltd.	Redemption Section, Account Management.	Date of payment.	Yes. Penalty will vary dependent upon product.	CHAPS 40–05–30 40637432.	Deeds Section, Account Management.	No specific sealing fee. A £45 administration fee is charged.	Cancelled on redemption.	No refund buildings insurance charged to the date of redemption.	May 1997.

Portman Building Society	Redemptions Section DX: 39455 Marlborough Fax: 0202 414013	To the end of the month.	On certain products as specified in the offer of advance.	Redemptions Section CHAPS 20.71.71 Barclays Bank, 61 Old Christchurch Road, Bournemouth (please ensure that the customer name and account number are quoted).		Included in discharge fee of £55.	Borrower has the choice.	No.	May 1997.
TSB Bank plc	TSB Homeloans Ltd	Date of payment.	On all fixed rate and variable discount products, as specified in offer of advance. No penalty on standard variable rate loans.	TSB Homeloans Ltd	TSB Homeloans Ltd	£50.	Cancelled on redemption.	Yes.	May 1997.
TSB Bank Scotland plc	TSB Homeloans Ltd	Date of payment.	As for TSB Bank plc	TSB Homeloans Ltd	TSB Homeloans Ltd	£50.	Cancelled on redemption.	Yes.	May 1997.

XI

Name of Lender	Redemption statement obtained from	Interest charged on redemption i.e. to date of payment or end of month	Penalty for early redemption	Cheque to be sent to/ CHAPS: Sort Code and Client Account Number	Document to be sent to	Sealing fee (if any)	Insurance arranged by the lender continued/cancelled on redemption	Refund of insurance premium included in redemption statement	Date information supplied
The Mortgage Corporation Limited (TMC)	'The Redemption Department' – as per Head Office address	Up to the date of redemption. Solicitors should advise their clients not to cancel the direct debit mandate until the last monthly payment has been collected.	During the 1st year of the mortgage or in the case of most fixed-rate mortgages during the period for which the interest rate is fixed, an amount equivalent to ¼ of the annual amount of interest calculated at the applicable interest rate. Other specific mortgage products may specify a different penalty. Otherwise 30 days' notice or 30 days' interest in lieu of notice, except: 1st year of mortgage—90 days within fixed-rate period of the fixed-rate mortgage – please refer to special conditions.	We do not accept cheques. CHAPS details are as follows: Barclays Bank Plc, Cheapside Business Centre, Atlas House, 1-7 King's St, London, Sort Code: 20-19-90. Account details are given with the redemption statement since more than 1 is maintained.	'The Redemptions Department'.	£50.	Cancelled.	Yes. Part refund of buildings insurance if annual NOT IF MONTHLY.	May 1997.

		Date of payment	Redemption interest/penalty	Redemption payments paid into	Office	Fee	Insurance	Refund	Date
Woolwich Building Society	Mortgage Services, Redemption Section, Equitable House, Woolwich, London SE18 6AB.	Date of payment.	No, unless a special condition of mortgage offer.	Redemption payments can be paid into any branch of the Society or direct to Head Office, Mortgage Services, Redemption Section.	Mortgage Services, Redemption Section, Equitable House, Woolwich, London SE18 6AB.	None.	Insurance cover is cancelled on redemption unless otherwise requested.	No.	May 1997.
Yorkshire Building Society	Mortgage Administration Department, Yorkshire House, Yorkshire Drive, Bradford BD5 8LJ. DX 11762 Bradford-1.	Up to date of redemption	If mortgage is redeemed: (i) within the first 3 yrs. 1 mth's interest is charged; (ii) after the 3rd yr but within the first 5 yrs, 20 days' interest is charged; (iii) after the 5th yr no interest is charged. Specific mortgage products will have specific early redemption charges detailed in the special conditions on the mortgage offer.	Cheque to controlling branch. CHAPS: National Westminster Bank, Hustlergate, Bradford. Redemption funds to: Sort Code 56-00-36. A/C 4121377. Returned advance funds to: Sort Code 62.23.48. A/C 78735173. (Please ensure you quote mortgage A/C no./customer name as reference.)	Local branch or Mortgage Admin. Dept, Yorkshire House, Bradford.	£35.	Cancelled on redemption. If customer requests continuation insurer will quote for alternative cover.	No – most insurance monthly, so no refund required.	May 1997.

ENDOWMENT POLICY

Note: This information has been supplied by the Council of Mortgage Lenders and may alter from time to time. No warranty is given as to its accuracy. Any information supplied in this list may be overridden by the terms of engagement or mortgage instructions in any individual case.

Name of Lender	Solicitor to check policy on risk	Policy to be assigned	Policy to be deposited	Age to be admitted	Note of assignment/deposit/interest to be given by solicitor	Policy to be deposited with deeds	Policy to be sent to lender	Date information supplied
Abbey National plc	Abbey National life policies – no. Other assurance companies – yes.	No.	No.	Yes.	No.	No.	No.	May 1997.
Alliance & Leicester Building Society	Not required by Society as lender but solicitor encouraged to check on behalf of borrower.	Not required.	Not required.	Not required by Society but solicitor encouraged to check on behalf of borrower.	Not required.	Not required but can be lodged with deeds if borrower wishes to do so.	Not required.	May 1997.
Bank of Ireland Home Mortgages	Yes.	Yes.	No.	Yes.	Notice of assignment to be given.	Yes.	Policy to be sent with deeds.	May 1997.
Barclays Bank PLC (See also Barclays Mortgages)	Yes – at exchange of contracts.	No.	No.	Not insisted upon.	No – will be given by Bank.	Yes.	Yes.	May 1997.
Barclays Mortgages (See also Barclays Bank PLC Branches)	Yes – at exchange of contracts.	No.	No.	Not insisted upon.	Yes.	No.	No.	May 1997.

Birmingham Midshires Building Society	Yes.	Yes.	No.	Yes.	Yes.	Yes.	Yes.	May 1997.
Bristol & West	Yes.	No.	No.	Not insisted upon.	No.	No.	No.	May 1997.
Britannia Building Society	Not required.	No.	No.	No.	No.	No.	No.	May 1997.
Cheltenham & Gloucester Building Society plc	Not required.	No.	No.	No.	No.	No.	No.	May 1997.
Halifax Building Society	No, but conveyancer should check on behalf of borrower.	No.	No.	No.	No. Notice of the Society's interest in the policy is served on the Assurance Company by the Society.	No.	Yes, if policy is new or has not previously been used in conjunction with a mortgage to Halifax B.S., otherwise no. Policy will be returned to borrower or his conveyancer as appropriate. The policy should be sent to the branch office where the account is held within 6 months of completion of the mortgage.	May 1997.

XI

Name of Lender	Solicitor to check policy on risk	Policy to be assigned	Policy to be deposited	Age to be admitted	Note of assignment/deposit/interest to be given by solicitor	Policy to be deposited with deeds	Policy to be sent to lender	Date information supplied
Midland Bank plc	Yes – must check that policy on risk.	No.	Yes.	Desirable, not compulsory.	No.	Yes.	Yes.	May 1997.
National Westminster Home Loans Limited	No.	No.	Yes.	No.	No.	Yes.	Yes within 3 months of completion.	May 1997.
Nationwide Building Society	No.	No.	No.	No.	No.	No.	No.	May 1997.
Northern Rock Building Society	Yes.	Yes.	No.	Not insisted upon.	Yes.	Yes.	Yes.	May 1997.
Paragon Finance plc	Yes.	Yes.	No.	Yes.	Yes.	Yes.	Yes, only with deeds not separately.	May 1997.
Portman Building Society	Not required.	Not required.	Not required.	Not required.	Not required.	Not required.	Not required.	May 1997.

TSB Bank plc	Yes.	Yes.	Yes.	Yes, for non TSB policies. No, for TSB life policies.	Yes, for non TSB policies. No, for TSB life policies.	Yes.	Only as part of deed packet.	May 1997.
TSB Bank of Scotland plc	Yes.	Yes.	Yes.	Yes, for non TSB policies. No, for TSB life policies.	Yes, for non TSB policies. No, for TSB life policies.	Yes.	Only as part of deed packet.	May 1997.
The Mortgage Corporation Limited (TMC)	Yes.	Yes.		Yes.	Yes.	Yes.	Yes – with the rest of the deeds.	May 1997.
Woolwich Building Society	Yes.	No.	No.	Yes.	No.	No.	No.	May 1997.
Yorkshire Building Society	Yes.	No.	Yes.	Not compulsory.	No – only notice of re-assignment.	Yes.	Yes, within 3 months of completion to Securities Dept., Yorkshire House, Bradford.	May 1997.

GIFT / SALE / TRANSFER OF SHARE

Note: This information has been supplied by the Council of Mortgage Lenders and may alter from time to time. No warranty is given as to its accuracy. Any information supplied in this list may be overridden by the terms of engagement or mortgage instructions in any individual case.

Name of Lender	Application for consent	Fee charged	Lender to approve deed	Lender to join in deed	Release of original borrower	Deed to be sent for sealing to	Deed to be sealed or signed by attorney or authorised signatory	Date information supplied
Abbey National plc	Mortgage Service Centre holding account.	£95.	Solicitors are asked to approve this on behalf of Abbey National – standard guidelines issued.	Yes.	Yes if satisfied with status of new or remaining borrower.	Mortgage Service Centre holding account.	Yes – deed sealed.	May 1997.
Alliance & Leicester Building Society	Further Advance Unit, Halford House, Charles Street, Leicester.	Currently £85 (may be varied at a later date).	Solicitors are asked to approve on behalf of Alliance & Leicester: standard guidelines issued.	Alliance & Leicester is named as a party to deed but does not execute unless a party is being released. Consent is given by letter.	Yes, if satisfied with status of new or remaining borrower.	Mortgage Customer Services, Carlton Park.	Signed by authorised signatory.	May 1997.
Bank of Ireland Home Mortgages	New Business Administration.	£150 inc VAT.	Borrower's solicitor asked to act for B.I.H.M. Guidelines and precedents are supplied.	Yes.	Yes.	Securities Dept.	Yes.	May 1997.

Barclays Bank PLC (See also **Barclays Mortgages**)	Yes. Apply to account holding branch.	Yes. Branch will advise fee on request.	Yes.	Yes.	According to circumstances of each individual case.	Branch.	(Either.) Branch will advise at time of approval of draft.	May 1997.
Barclays Mortgages (See also **Barclays Bank PLC Branches**)	Yes.	Yes. Details available on request.	Yes.	Yes.	According to circumstances on each individual case.	P.O. Box HK444 Leeds LS11 8DD Tel: 0113 296 5000 DX 13947 Leeds Arlington	Either – Barclays Mortgages will advise on receipt of draft.	May 1997.
Birmingham Midshires Building Society	To Transfer Services team within Lending New Business at principal office.	£75 – split – £45 to consent; approval sealing £30.	Yes.	Where the Society agrees to do something or is expressed to do something, otherwise no need.	Yes. Except not released from covenants for title or further assurance contained in the original legal charge or from costs/claims arising from breaches of covenant prior to the date of the transfer and subject to income of new owner.	Transfer Services team within Lending New Business at principal office.	Authorised signatory seals.	May 1997.
Bristol & West	Yes. Branch of origin.	£100 to include deeds production fee.	No.	Yes.	Yes, if status of remaining borrower satisfactory.	Securities Dept.	Yes. Sealed by authority of the Board of Directors.	May 1997.

XI

Name of Lender	Application for consent	Fee charged	Lender to approve deed	Lender to join in deed	Release of original borrower	Deed to be sent for sealing to	Deed to be sealed or signed by attorney or authorised signatory	Date information supplied
Britannia Building Society	Mortgage Services Department (CO15) in writing.	£60 admin. fee.	Solicitors provided with Society standard conditions and must rely on their own expertise and act as Society agent.	Confirmed (to release a party to mortgage).	Society will release one borrower provided the account up to date and excess debt is cleared. Further indemnity guarantee on mortgage. Consent of insurance company will be required in some cases.	Mortgage Services Department (CO15).	Sealed and signed by authorised signatory.	May 1997.
Cheltenham & Gloucester plc	Local branch office.	No fee.	Yes.	Yes, where appropriate.	Yes, where appropriate.	Head Office (Legal Dept/ Dealings Section).	Sealed.	May 1997.
Halifax Building Society	Application to be made to branch office where the account is held.	£80.	No. The conveyancer will do this on the Society's behalf.	Only necessary where a party is being released from covenants unless a separate form of release is used.	The Society will agree to this in appropriate cases.	Head Office Mortgages Dept. for Halifax B.S. mortgages. Lending Services Lovell Park Leeds for former Leeds Permanent B.S. mortgages.	Where the Society is a party to the deed, it must be sealed by the Society.	May 1997.

Midland Bank plc	Bank branch.	£30 fee.	Yes.	Yes.	Yes.	MSC at Courtwood House.	Deed to be signed by hand under power of attorney.	May 1997.
National Westminster Home Loans Ltd	H.O.	Transfer of whole £90 inclusive of VAT. Add another party £45.	Yes, unless the wording supplied by the lender is used.	Yes.	Subject to lender's consent but reserves prior breaches.	H.O.	Yes.	May 1997.
Nationwide Building Society	Should be sent to local branch.	£50.	Society asks solicitor to act on its behalf in approving deed (precedent available).	Yes.	Subject to adequacy and status of new/ remaining covenant(s).	Customer Service Teams, Northampton Admin. Centre, King's Park Road, Moulton Park, Northampton NN3 1NL	Sealed and counter-signed.	May 1997.
Northern Rock Building Society	Transfers, Mortgages and Personal Lending Dept., N.R. House, Gosforth, Newcastle upon Tyne NE3 4PC.	£75.	No.	Yes.	Yes.	Yes.	Deeds Dept. Northern Rock House	May 1997.
Paragon Finance plc	Yes.	£125.	Yes.	Yes.	Contact: Account Management.	Contact: Account Management.	Yes.	May 1997.
Portman Building Society	Customer Services Dept. 25 High St. Marlborough, Wilts SN8 1NF DX: 39455 Marlborough.	£80.	Yes.	Yes, where necessary.	Yes, in appropriate cases.	Solicitors Depart. Head Office.	Sealed.	May 1997.

XI

Name of Lender	Application for consent	Fee charged	Lender to approve deed	Lender to join in deed	Release of original borrower	Deed to be sent for sealing to	Deed to be sealed or signed by attorney or authorised signatory	Date information supplied
TSB Bank plc	TSB Homeloans Ltd	£50.	Yes.	Yes.	Yes.	TSB Homeloans Ltd	Signed by attorney.	May 1997.
TSB Bank of Scotland plc	TSB Homeloans Ltd	£50. (Under review.)	Yes.	Yes.	Yes.	TSB Homeloans Ltd	Signed by attorney.	May 1997.
The Mortgage Corporation Limited (TMC)	Should be sent to Application Processing Dept.	£50 and legal fees where applicable. We may also require revaluation fee.	Yes. Sales of part – we may require solicitors to act on our behalf.	Yes.	Our conditions are applicable on application.	Application Processing Dept.	Usually deeds are sealed by TMC in the presence of two authorised signatories. There are occasions when the deed is executed by the duly appointed delegate attorney. Our solicitors will be advised of such cases.	May 1997.
Woolwich Building Society	The Society's local branch.	£80 administration fee.	Yes.	Yes, if necessary.	Yes.	Deeds Services Transfer of Equity Section.	Sealed.	May 1997.

Yorkshire Building Society	Mortgage Administration Department, Yorkshire Hse, Bradford.	£100 – transfer of equity plus £38.50 deeds production fee.	No.	Yes, where necessary.	Yes, in appropriate cases.	Mortgage Administration Department, Head Office.	Deed sealed and signed by authorised signatory.	May 1997.

DEED OF EASEMENT / ADJUSTMENT OF BOUNDARY / RELEASE OF PART SECURITY

Note: This information has been supplied by the Council of Mortgage Lenders and may alter from time to time. No warranty is given as to its accuracy. Any information supplied in this list may be overridden by the terms of engagement or mortgage instructions in any individual case.

Name of Lender	Application for consent	Fee charged	Lender to approve deed	Lender to join in deed	Deed to be sent for sealing to	Deed sealed/ signed by attorney or authorised signatory	Date information supplied
Abbey National plc	Mortage Service Centre holding account.	£50.	Solicitors are asked to approve on behalf of Abbey National – standard guidelines issued.	Yes.	Mortgage Service Centre holding account.	Yes. Deed sealed.	May 1997.
Alliance & Leicester Building Society	Mortgage Administration Service at Hove or Edinburgh.	£50. (May be varied at later date.)	Society asks solicitor to act on its behalf in approving deed.	Yes.	Deeds Service at Hove or Oadby.	Sealed in the presence of an authorised signatory.	May 1997.
Bank of Ireland Home Mortgages	To Customer Services Dept.	£40 to supply deeds.	Yes.	Yes.	Customer Services Dept.	Yes.	May 1997.
Barclays Bank plc (See also Barclays Mortgages)	Yes, to account holding branch.	Yes. Branch will advise fee on request.	Yes.	Yes.	Branch.	Either. Branch will advise at time of approval of draft.	May 1997.
Barclays Mortgages (See also Barclays Bank plc Branches)	Yes.	Yes. Details available on request.	Yes.	Yes.	P.O. Box HK444 Leeds LS11 8DD Tel 0113 296 5000 DX 13947 Leeds Arlington	Either. Barclays Mortgages will advise on receipt of draft.	May 1997.

Birmingham Midshires Building Society	Transfer Services Team within Lending New Business at principal office.	£50.	Yes.	Only where necessary to make the release.	Transfer Services Team within Lending New Business at principal office.	Authorised signatory seals.	May 1997.
Bristol & West	Deeds Dept.	£50 plus deeds production fee of £37.50 if applicable.	No. Solicitor acting on Society's behalf approves.	Yes.	Deeds Dept.	Yes. Sealed by authority of Board of Directors.	May 1997.
Britannia Building Society	Boundary disputes, easements/releases of part security – Mortgage Services Department (CO30).	£60.	Solicitors responsible to ensure Society's security not affected. Valuation necessary and any arrears/excess debt cleared – capital repayment may be required.	Confirmed.	Boundary disputes, easements/releases of part security – Mortgage Services Department (CO30).	Sealed by Society by authority of Board of Directors.	May 1997.
Cheltenham & Gloucester plc	Chief Office (Legal Dept/Dealings Section).	No.	Yes.	Yes – where appropriate.	Chief Office (Legal Dept/Dealings Section).	Sealed.	May 1997.
Halifax Building Society	To branch office where account is held for Halifax mortgages and Head Office Mortgages Dept. for former Leeds Permanent B.S. mortgages.	£50.	No. The conveyancer will do this on the Society's behalf.	Yes.	Head Office Mortgages Dept.	To be sealed by the Society.	May 1997.

XI

Name of Lender	Application for consent	Fee charged	Lender to approve deed	Lender to join in deed	Deed to be sent for sealing to	Deed sealed/ signed by attorney or authorised signatory	Date information supplied
Midland Bank plc	Yes, to MSC Courtwood House.	£15 + VAT re-release of deeds on inspection.	Yes.	Yes.	Mortgage Service Centre, Courtwood House.	Deeds to be signed by hand under power of attorney.	May 1997.
National Westminster Home Loans Ltd	Yes.	£45 – sale of part. £50 – others.	Yes.	Yes.	H.O.	Yes.	May 1997.
Nationwide Building Society	Customer Service Team, Northampton Admin. Centre, King's Park Road, Moulton Park, Northampton NN3 6NW.	£25 if Society to seal deed. £85 release of part security (inclusive of £25 sealing fee).	Society asks solicitor to act on its behalf in approving deed.	Yes, if instructed solicitor advises that this is appropriate.	Customer Service Team, Northampton Admin. Centre, King's Park Road, Moulton Park, Northampton NN3 6NW.	Sealed and counter-signed.	May 1997.
Northern Rock Building Society	Transfers, Mortgages and Personal Lending Dept., N.R. House, Gosforth, Newcastle upon Tyne NE3 4PC.	£90.	Yes.	Yes.	Transfers, Mortgage Dept, Northern Rock House, PO Box 2, Gosforth, Newcastle upon Tyne NE3 4PL.	Yes.	May 1997.
Paragon Finance plc	Yes.	£125	Yes.	Yes.	Account Management.	Yes.	May 1997.

Portman Building Society	Customer Services Dept. 25 High St. Marlborough Wilts SN8 1NF DX; 39455 Marlborough	£80 and any revaluation fee.	Yes.	Yes.	Solicitor's Dept, Head Office.	Sealed.	May 1997.
TSB Bank plc	TSB Homeloans Ltd	£50.	Yes.	Yes.	TSB Homeloans Ltd	Signed by attorney.	May 1997.
TSB Bank of Scotland plc	TSB Homeloans Ltd	£50. (Under review.)	Yes.	Yes.	TSB Homeloans Ltd	Signed by attorney.	May 1997.
The Mortgage Corporation Limited (TMC)	Yes.	£50.	Yes.	Yes.	'The Legal Department' – Head Office.	Deeds are sealed by TMC in the presence of two authorized signatories. As regards securitised loans, the deed is executed by a duly appointed delegate attorney of the trustee co. Our solicitor will be advised of such cases.	May 1997.
Woolwich Building Society	Lending Services, Corporate HQ, Watling Street Bexleyheath Kent DA6 7RR.	£50 production fee, if applicable.	Yes.	Yes, where necessary.	Lending Services.	Sealed.	May 1997.

XI

Name of Lender	Application for consent	Fee charged	Lender to approve deed	Lender to join in deed	Deed to be sent for sealing to	Deed sealed/ signed by attorney or authorised signatory	Date information supplied
Yorkshire Building Society	Yes.	£50 for release of land, plus £38.50 if deeds produced or £12.50 for copies of documents from deeds.	No.	Yes, if necessary.	Mortgage Administration Department, Yorkshire House, Bradford.	Deed sealed and signed by authorised signatory.	May. 1997.

XII. APACS AND CHAPS

XII.1. Association for Payment Clearing Services – an overview[1]

APACS – the Association for Payment Clearing Services – was set up by the major banks in 1985 to manage the payment clearing systems and oversee money transmission in the UK.

APACS has three operational clearing companies under its umbrella. These are:

- Cheque and Credit Clearing Company Limited, which operates the paper clearings.
- CHAPS Clearing Company Limited, which operates the high value same-day clearings.
- BACS Limited, which operates a bulk electronic clearing.

Membership of APACS and the clearing companies is open to any UK bank or building society, or credit institution from elsewhere in the EU, providing payment services and meeting the objective and published membership criteria.

APACS operates with a staff of about 100 people, under its Chief Executive, Christopher Pearson. Amongst the major responsibilities of APACS, in addition to overseeing the operations of the clearings mentioned above, are included: strategic studies and forecasting of payments matters and trends, formulating industry standards and maintaining comprehensive statistical data on money transmission activities.

APACS also speaks for and lobbies on behalf of the UK payments industry and has become the recognised authority on all matters relating to money transmission and payment clearing activities in this country.

Over recent years, APACS has also become the focus for payments industry co-operative activity to combat plastic card fraud. This involves putting in place a range of anti-fraud measures and, for the longer term, examining appropriate developments in plastic card technologies.

XII

---

1. The material in this appendix is reproduced with the permission of the Association for Payment Clearing Services.

MEMBERSHIP OF APACS AND THE CLEARING COMPANIES

MEMBERS	APACS	BACS	CHEQUE & CREDIT	CHAPS
Abbey National	X	X	X	–
Bank of England	X	X	X	X
Bank of Scotland	X	X	X	X
Barclays Bank	X	X	X	X
Citibank	X	–	–	X
Clydesdale Bank	X	X	–	X
Co-operative Bank	X	X	X	X
Coutts & Co	X	X	–	X
Crédit Lyonnais	X	–	–	X
Deutsche Bank	X	–	–	X
Girobank	X	X	X	X
Halifax Building Society	X	X	–	–
Lloyds Bank	X	X	X	X
Midland Bank	X	X	X	X
National Westminster Bank	X	X	X	X
Nationwide Building Society	X	X	X	–
Northern Bank	X	X	–	–
Royal Bank of Scotland	X	X	X	X
Standard Chartered Bank	X	–	–	X
TSB Bank	X	X	X	X
Yorkshire Bank	X	X	–	–

November 1996

XII.2. CHAPS
Clearing Company Ltd Banks

Bank of England
Banking Services
Threadneedle Street
London EC2R 8AH

Tel: 0171 601 4444
Fax: 0171 601 4771

Bank of Scotland
Accounting Division
PO Box No. 475
Teviot House
41 South Gyle Crescent
Edinburgh EH12 9DR

Tel: 0131 442 7777

Barclays Bank PLC
PO Box No. 120
Longwood Close
Westwood Business Park
Coventry CV4 8JN

Tel: 01203 694 242
Fax: 01203 532 467

Citibank N.A.
Financial Institutions &
    Transaction Services
    Group, Europe
Cottons Centre
PO Box No. 200
Hay's Lane
London SE1 2QT

Tel: 0181 318 8000
Fax: 0171 234 2438

Clydesdale Bank PLC
Payment Services
4th Floor
PO Box No. 43
150 Buchanan Street
Glasgow G1 2HL

Tel: 0141 221 8862
Fax: 0141 221 8397

Co-operative Bank PLC
Head of Transmissions (London)
9 Prescot Street
London E1 8AZ

Tel: 0171 480 5171
Fax: 0171 709 7295

Coutts & Co
440 Strand
London WC2R 0QS

Tel: 0171 753 1000
Fax: 0171 623 1185

Crédit Lyonnais SA
84-94 Queen Victoria Street
London EC4P 4LX

Tel: 0171 634 8000
Fax: 0171 489 1559

Deutsche Bank AG London
6 Bishopsgate
London EC2P 2AT

Tel: 0171 971 7000
Fax: 0171 971 7455

Girobank PLC
Carlton Park
Leicester LE9 5XX

Tel: 0116 272 6887
Fax: 0116 272 6917

Lloyds Bank PLC
Payment Services UKRB
3rd Floor
Hay's Lane House
1 Hay's Lane
London SE1 2HA

Tel: 0171 407 1000
Fax: 0171 357 4890

XII

Midland Bank PLC
PAYSOC
St Magnus House, 4th Floor
3 Lower Thames Street
London EC3R 6HA

Tel: 0171 260 5976
Fax: 0171 260 5713

National Westminster Bank PLC
Level 20
Drapers Gardens
12 Throgmorton Avenue
London EC2N 2DL

Tel: 0171 920 5555
Fax: 0171 920 1625

Royal Bank of Scotland PLC
Payment Services
Operations Division
Drummond House
PO Box No. 1727
1 Redheughs Avenue
Edinburgh EH12 9JN

Tel: 0131 556 8555
Fax: 0131 317 8609

Standard Chartered Bank PLC
London (City) Branch
37 Gracechurch Street
London EC3V 0BX

Tel: 0171 457 7500
Fax: 0171 280 6969

TSB Bank PLC
Retail Banking & Insurance
Transmission Services
TSB Clearing Centre
PO Box No. 3000
25 Lavington Street
London SE2 0NA

Tel: 0171 921 3000
Fax: 0171 921 3212

XIII. ADDRESSES
XIII.1. HM Land Registry

Head Office

32 Lincoln's Inn Fields
London WC2A 3PH

Tel: (0171) 917 8888
Fax: (0171) 955 0110
DX: 1098 Lond/Chancery Lane

District Registries

Birkenhead

*For titles in **Cheshire** and the London
Boroughs of **Kensington and Chelsea/
Hammersmith and Fulham***
The Birkenhead District Land Registry
Rosebrae Court
Woodside Ferry Approach
Birkenhead
Merseyside L41 6DU

Tel: (0151) 473 1110
Fax: (0151) 473 0366
DX: 24270 Birkenhead-4

*For titles in **Merseyside, Staffordshire**
and **Stoke-on-Trent***
The Birkenhead District Land Registry
Old Market House
Hamilton Street
Birkenhead
Merseyside L41 5FL

Tel: (0151) 473 1110
Fax: (0151) 473 0251
DX: 14300 Birkenhead-3

Coventry

The Coventry District Land Registry
Leigh Court
Torrington Avenue
Tile Hill
Coventry CV4 9XZ

Tel: (01203) 860860
Fax: (01203) 860021
DX: 18900 Coventry-3

Croydon

The Croydon District Land Registry
Sunley House
Bedford Park
Croydon CR9 3LE

Tel: (0181) 781 9100/9103
Fax: (0181) 781 9110
DX: 2699 Croydon-3

Durham

*For titles in **Cumbria** and **Surrey***
The Durham District Land Registry
Boldon House
Wheatlands Way
Pity Me
Durham DH1 5GJ

Tel: (0191) 301 3500
Fax: (0191) 301 3520
DX: 60860 Durham-6

*For titles in **Darlington, Durham,
Hartlepool, Middlesbrough,
Redcar and Cleveland,
Northumberland,
Stockton-on-Tees** and **Tyne & Wear***
The Durham District Land Registry
Southfield House
Southfield Way
Durham DH1 5TR

Tel: (0191) 301 3500
Fax: (0191) 301 0020
DX: 60200 Durham-3

Gloucester

The Gloucester District Land Registry
Twyver House
Bruton Way
Gloucester GL1 1DQ

Tel: (01452) 511111
Fax: (01452) 510050
DX: 7599 Gloucester-3

XIII

Harrow

The Harrow District Land Registry
Lyon House
Lyon Road
Harrow
Middlesex HA1 2EU

Tel: (0181) 235 1181
Fax: (0181) 862 0176
DX: 4299 Harrow-4

Kingston-Upon-Hull

The Kingston-Upon-Hull District Land
  Registry
Earle House
Portland Street
Hull HU2 8JN

Tel: (01482) 223244
Fax: (01482) 224278
DX: 26700 Hull-4

Leicester

The Leicester District Land Registry
Thames Tower
99 Burleys Way
Leicester LE1 3UB

Tel: (0116) 265 4000
Fax: (0116) 265 4008
DX: 11900 Leicester-5

Lytham

The Lytham District Land Registry
Birkenhead House, East Beach
Lytham St. Annes
Lancs FY8 5AB

Tel: (01253) 849849
Fax: (01253) 840013 (for Lancashire)
    (01253) 840001 (for Manchester,
    Salford, Stockport, Tameside and
    Trafford)
    (01253) 840002 (for Bolton, Bury,
    Oldham, Rochdale and Wigan)
DX: 14500 Lytham St. Annes-3

Nottingham

The Nottingham District Land Registry
Chalfont Drive
Nottingham NG8 3RN

Tel: (0115) 935 1166
Fax: (0115) 936 0036 (for Notts.)
    (0115) 935 0038 (other counties)
DX: 10298 Nottingham-3

Peterborough

The Peterborough District Land Registry
Touthill Close
City Road
Peterborough PE1 1XN

Tel: (01733) 288288
Fax: (01733) 280022
DX: 12598 Peterborough-4

Plymouth

The Plymouth District Land Registry
Plumer House
Tailyour Road
Crownhill
Plymouth PL6 5HY

Tel: (01752) 636000
Fax: (01752) 636161
DX: 8299 Plymouth-4

Portsmouth

The Portsmouth District Land Registry
St Andrew's Court
St Michael's Road
Portsmouth
Hampshire PO1 2JH

Tel: (01705) 768888
Fax: (01705) 768768
DX: 83550 Portsmouth-2

Stevenage

The Stevenage District Land Registry
Brickdale House
Swingate
Stevenage
Herts SG1 1XG

Tel: (01438) 788888
Fax: (01438) 780107
DX: 6099 Stevenage-2

Swansea

*For titles in the **Principality of Wales***
The Swansea District Land Registry
Tŷ Cwm Tawe
Phoenix Way
Llansamlet
Swansea SA7 9FQ

Tel: (01792) 458877
Fax: (01792) 458800
DX: 82800 Swansea-2

*For titles in **England** served by Swansea*
The Swansea District Land Registry
Tŷ Bryn Glas
High Street
Swansea SA1 1PW

Tel: (01792) 458877
Fax: (01792) 473236
DX: 33700 Swansea-2

Telford

The Telford District Land Registry
Parkside Court
Hall Park Way
Telford
Shropshire TF3 4LR

Tel: (01952) 290355
Fax: (01952) 290356
DX: 28100 Telford-2

Tunbridge Wells

The Tunbridge Wells District Land Registry
Curtis House
Forest Road
Hawkenbury
Tunbridge Wells
Kent TN2 5AQ

Tel: (01892) 510015
Fax: (01892) 510032
DX: 3999 Tunbridge Wells-2

Weymouth

The Weymouth District Land Registry
Melcombe Court
1 Cumberland Drive
Weymouth
Dorset DT4 9TT

Tel: (01305) 363636
Fax: (01305) 363646
DX: 8799 Weymouth-2

York

The York District Land Registry
James House
James Street
York YO1 3YZ

Tel: (01904) 450000
Fax: (01904) 450086
DX: 61599 York-2

XIII

XIII.2. Local authorities of England and Wales

Adur District Council
Civic Centre
Ham Road
Shoreham-by-Sea BN43 6PR

Tel: (01273) 455 566
Fax: (01273) 454 847

Allerdale Borough Council
Allerdale House
New Bridge Road
Workington CA14 3YJ

Tel: (01900) 604 351
Fax: (01900) 735 346

Alnwick District Council
Allerburn House
Denwick Lane
Alnwick NE66 1YY

Tel: (01665) 510 505
Fax: (01665) 605 099

Amber Valley Borough Council
PO Box 15
Town Hall
Ripley
Derbyshire DE5 3XE

Tel: (01773) 570 222
Fax: (01773) 841 616

Arun District Council
Civic Centre
Maltravers Road
Littlehampton BN17 5LF
West Sussex

Tel: (01903) 716 133
Fax: (01903) 730 442
DX: 57406 Littlehampton

Ashfield District Council
Council Offices
Urban Road
Kirkby-in-Ashfield NG17 8DA

Tel: (01623) 450 0000
Fax: (01623) 751 735

Ashford Borough Council
Civic Centre
Tannery Lane
Ashford TN23 1PL

Tel: (01233) 637 311
Fax: (01233) 645 654
DX: 30204 Ashford

Aylesbury Vale District Council
Bearbrook House
Oxford Road
Aylesbury
Berkshire HP19 3RJ

Tel: (01296) 555 555
Fax: (01296) 88887
DX: 4130 Aylesbury

Babergh District Council
Corks Lane
Hadleigh
Ipswich IP7 6SJ

Tel: (01473) 822 801
Fax: (01473) 823 594

Barnsley Borough Council
Town Hall
Church St
Barnsley S70 2TA

Tel: (01226) 770 770
Fax: (01226) 773 099
DX: 12266 Barnsley-1

Barrow-in-Furness Borough Council
Town Hall
Duke Street
Barrow-in-Furness LA14 2LD

Tel: (01229) 825 500
Fax: (01229) 842 499
DX: 63917 Barrow-in-Furness

Basildon District Council
Basildon Centre
Pagelmead
Basildon
Essex SS14 1DL

Tel: (01268) 533 333
Fax: (01268) 294 451
DX: 53008 Basildon

Basingstoke & Deane Borough Council
Civic Offices
London Road
Basingstoke RG21 4AH

Tel: (01256) 844 844
Fax: (01256) 841 945
DX: 3008 Basingstoke-1

Bassetlaw District Council
Queens Buildings
Potter Street
Worksop S80 2AH

Tel: (01909) 533 533
Fax: (01909) 482 622

Bath City Council
Guildhall
High Street
Bath BA1 5AW

Tel: (01225) 477 000
Fax: (01225) 477 489
DX: 8047 Bath

Bedford Borough Council
Town Hall
St Paul's Square
Bedford MK40 1SJ

Tel: (01234) 267 422
Fax: (01234) 221 606
DX: 2100 Bedford

Berwick upon Tweed Borough
    Council
Council Offices
Wallace Green
Berwick upon Tweed TD15 1ED

Tel: (01289) 330 044
Fax: (01289) 330 540

Birmingham City Council
The Council House
Birmingham B1 1BB

Tel: (0121) 235 9944
Fax: (0121) 235 1312
DX: 13053 Birmingham-1

Blaby District Council
Desford Road
Council Offices
Narborough LE9 5EP

Tel: (0116) 2750 555
Fax: (0116) 2750 368

Blackburn Borough Council
Town Hall
King William Street
Blackburn BB1 7DY

Tel: (01254) 585 585
Fax: (01254) 680 870

Blackpool Borough Council
Municipal Buildings
Corporation Street
Blackpool FY1 1NB

Tel: (01253) 25212
Fax: (01253) 751 163

Blaenau Gwent County
    Borough Council
Municipal Offices
Civic Centre
Ebbw Vale NP3 6XB

Tel: (01495) 350 555
Fax: (01495) 301255

Blyth Valley Borough Council
Civic Centre
Renwick Road
Blyth NE24 2BX

Tel: (01670) 542 000
Fax: (01670) 542 102

The District of Bolsover
Sherwood Lodge
Bolsover
Chesterfield
S44 6NF

Tel: (01246) 240 000
Fax: (01246) 242 424

Bolton Metropolitan Council
Town Hall
Civic Centre
Bolton BL1 1RU

Tel: (01204) 522 311
Fax: (01204) 392 808

Boothferry Borough Council
Council Offices
Church Street
Goole DN14 5BG

Tel: (0345) 887 7007
Fax: (01405) 767 256

XIII

Boston Borough Council
Municipal Buildings
West Street
Boston PE21 8QR

Tel: (01205) 314 200
Fax: (01205) 364 604

Bournemouth Borough Council
Town Hall
Bourne Avenue
Bournemouth BH2 6DY

Tel: (01202) 451 451
Fax: (01202) 451 001
DX: 7615 Bournemouth

Bracknell Forest Borough Council
Easthampstead House
Town Square
Bracknell RG12 1AQ

Tel: (01344) 424 642
Fax: (01344) 352 810
DX: 33611 Bracknell

Bradford Metropolitan Council
City Hall
Bradford BD1 1HY

Tel: (01274) 752 111
Fax: (01274) 752 065
DX: 11758 Bradford

Braintree District Council
Causeway House
Bocking End
Braintree CM7 9HB

Tel: (01376) 552 525
Fax: (01376) 552 626
DX: 56210 Braintree

Breckland District Council
Council Offices
Guildhall
Derham Norfolk NT19 1EE

Tel: (01362) 695 333
Fax: (01362) 690 821

Brecknock Borough Council
Cambrian Way
Brecon LD3 7HR

Tel: (01874) 624 141
Fax: (01874) 625 781

Brentwood Borough Council
Ingrave Road
Brentwood
Essex CM15 8AY

Tel: (01277) 261 111
Fax: (01277) 260 836
DX: 5001 Brentwood-1

Bridgend County Borough Council
PO Box 4
Civic Offices
Angel Street
Bridgend CF31 1LX

Tel: (01656) 643 643
Fax: (01656) 668 126

Bridgnorth District Council
Westgate
Bridgnorth WV16 5AA

Tel: (01746) 713 100
Fax: (01746) 764 414
DX: 23207 Bridgnorth

Brighton Borough Council
Town Hall
Bartholomews Square
Brighton BN1 1JA

Tel: (01273) 290 000
Fax: (01273) 712 011
DX: 2704 Brighton-1

Bristol City Council
Council House
College Green
Bristol BS1 5TR

Tel: (0117) 9222 000
Fax: (0117) 9224 330
DX: 7827 Bristol-1

Broadland District Council
Thorpe Lodge
Yarmouth Road
Norwich NR7 0DU

Tel: (01603) 431 133
Fax: (01603) 300 087

Bromsgrove District Council
Council Offices
Burcot Lane
Bromsgrove B60 1AA

Tel: (01527) 873 232
Fax: (01527) 875 660
DX: 17279 Bromsgrove

Broxbourne Borough Council
Borough Offices
Bishop's College
Churchgate
Cheshunt EN8 9XA

Tel: (01992) 631 921
Fax: (01992) 785 578

Broxtowe Borough Council
Town Hall
Foster Avenue
Beeston
Nottingham NG9 1AB

Tel: (0115) 9254 891
Fax: (0115) 9431 452

Burnley Borough Council
Town Hall, PO Box 17
Manchester Road
Burnley BB11 1JA

Tel: (01282) 425 011
Fax: (01282) 452 536

Bury Metropolitan Borough Council
Town Hall
Knowsley Street
Bury BL9 0SW

Tel: (0161) 253 5000
Fax: (0161) 705 5119

Caerphilly County Borough Council
Council Offices
Nelson Road
Tredomen
Ystrad Mynach
Hengoed CF82 7WF

Tel: (01443) 815 588
Fax: (01443) 864 211

Calderdale Metropolitan Borough Council
Town Hall
Crossby Street
Halifax HX1 1UJ

Tel: (01422) 357 257
Fax: (01422) 393 118

Cambridge City Council
The Guildhall
Market Square
Cambridge CB2 3QJ

Tel: (01223) 358 977
Fax: (01223) 463 364
DX: 5854 Cambridge

Cannock Chase Council
Civic Centre
PO Box 28
Beecroft Road
Cannock
Staffordshire WS11 1BG

Tel: (01543) 462 621
Fax: (01543) 462 317
DX: 16095 Cannock

Canterbury City Council
Council Office
Military Road
Canterbury CT1 1YW

Tel: (01227) 763 763
Fax: (01227) 763 727
DX: 5314 Canterbury

Caradon District Council
Luxstowe House
Liskeard
Cornwall PL14 3DZ

Tel: (01579) 341 000
Fax: (01579) 341 001

Cardiff City Council
County Hall
Atlantic Wharf
Cardiff CF1 5UW

Tel: (01222) 872 000
Fax: (01222) 872 462

Carlisle City Council
Civic Centre
Carlisle CA3 8QG

Tel: (01228) 23411
Fax: (01228) 511 216
DX: 63037 Carlisle

Carmarthenshire County Council
County Hall
Carmarthen SA31 1JP

Tel: (01267) 234 567
Fax: (01267) 222 097

Carrick District Council
Carrick House
Pydar Street
Truro TR1 1EB

Tel: (01872) 278 131
Fax: (01872) 42104
DX: 81232 Truro

Castle Morpeth Borough Council
Council Offices
The Kylins
Loansdean
Morpeth NE61 2EQ

Tel: (01670) 514 351
Fax: (01670) 510 348

Castle Point Borough Council
Council Offices
Kiln Road
Benfleet SS7 1TF

Tel: (01268) 792 711
Fax: (01268) 565 580
DX: 39603 Hadleigh

Ceredigion County Council
Neuadd Cyngor Ceredigion
Penmorfa
Aberaeron
Ceredigion SA46 0AP

Tel: (01545) 570 881
Fax: (01545) 572 009

Charnwood Borough Council
Southfields Road
Loughborough LE11 2TX

Tel: (01509) 263 151
Fax: (01509) 610 626
DX: 19628 Loughborough

Chelmsford Borough Council
Civic Centre
Duke Street
Chelmsford CM1 1JE

Tel: (01245) 490 490
Fax: (01245) 350 676
DX: 3318 Chelmsford-1

Cheltenham Borough Council
Municipal Offices
The Promenade
Cheltenham GL50 1PP

Tel: (01242) 262 626
Fax: (01242) 227 131
DX: 7406 Cheltenham-1

Cherwell District Council
Bodicote House
Bodicote
Banbury OX15 4AA

Tel: (01295) 252 535
Fax: (01295) 270 028
DX: 24224 Banbury

Chester City Council
The Forum
Chester CH1 2HS

Tel: (01244) 324 324
Fax: (01244) 324 338

Chester-le-Street District Council
Civic Centre
Newcastle Road
Chester-le-Street
County Durham DH3 3UT

Tel: (0191) 387 1919
Fax: (0191) 387 1583

Chesterfield Borough Council
Town Hall
Rose Hill
Chesterfield S40 1LP

Tel: (01246) 345 345
Fax: (01246) 345 252

Chichester District Council
East Pallant House
East Pallant
Chichester PO19 1TY

Tel: (01243) 785 166
Fax: (01243) 776 766
DX: 30340 Chichester

Chiltern District Council
Council Offices
King George V Road
Amersham HP6 5AW

Tel: (01494) 729 000
Fax: (01494) 729 332
DX: 50711 Amersham

Chorley Borough Council
Town Hall
Chorley PR7 1DP

Tel: (01257) 515 151
Fax: (01257) 241 066

Christchurch Borough Council
Civic Offices
Bridge Street
Christchurch BH23 1AZ

Tel: (01202) 486 321
Fax: (01202) 482 200

Colchester Borough Council
PO Box 884
Town Hall
Colchester CO1 1FR

Tel: (01206) 282 222
Fax: (01206) 282 288
DX: 3612 Colchester-1

Colwyn Borough Council
Civic Centre
Colwyn Bay LL29 8AR

Tel: (01492) 515 271
Fax: (01492) 512 637
DX: 20775 Old Colwyn

Congleton Borough Council
Westfields
Middlewich Road
Sandbach CW11 3IZ

Tel: (01270) 763 231
Fax: (01270) 768 460
DX: 15658 Sandbach

Conwy County Borough Council
Bodlondeb
Conwy LL32 8DU

Tel: (01492) 574 000
Fax: (01492) 592 114

Copeland Borough Council
PO Box 19
The Council Offices
Catherine Street
Whitehaven CA28 7NY

Tel: (01946) 693 111
Fax: (01946) 693 373

Corby Borough Council
Civic Centre
George Street
Corby NN17 1QB

Tel: (01536) 402 551
Fax: (01536) 400 200
DX: 12915 Corby

Cotswold District Council
Council Offices
Trinity Road
Cirencester
Gloucester GL7 1PX

Tel: (01285) 643 643
Fax: (01285) 657 334

Coventry City Council
Council House
Earl St
Coventry CV1 5RR

Tel: (01203) 833 333
Fax: (01203) 833 070

Craven District Council
Council Offices
Granville Street
Skipton BD23 1PS

Tel: (01756) 700 600
Fax: (01756) 700 658

Crawley Borough Council
Town Hall
The Boulevard
Crawley RH10 1UZ

Tel: (01293) 528 744
Fax: (01293) 511 803
DX: 57139 Crawley-1

Crewe & Nantwich Borough Council
Delamere House
Delamere Street
Crewe CW1 2JZ

Tel: (01270) 583 191
Fax: (01270) 537 759

Dacorum Borough Council
Civic Centre
Marlowes
Hemel Hempstead HP1 1MH

Tel: (01442) 60161
Fax: (01442) 228 995
DX: 8804 Hemel Hempstead

Darlington Borough Council
Town Hall
Darlington DL1 5QT

Tel: (01325) 380 651
Fax: (01325) 382 032

Dartford Borough Council
Civic Centre
Home Garden
Dartford DA1 1DR

Tel: (01322) 343 434
Fax: (01322) 343 422
DX: 31908 Dartford

Daventry District Council
Lodge Road
Daventry NN11 5AF

Tel: (01327) 871 100
Fax: (01327) 300 011
DX: 21965 Daventry

Denbighshire County Council
Council Offices
Wynnstay Road
Ruthin
Denbighshire LL15 1AT

Tel: (01824) 706 000
Fax: (01824) 707 446

Derbyshire Dales District Council
Town Hall
Bank Road
Matlock DE4 3NN

Tel: (01629) 580 580
Fax: (01629) 580 482
DX: 27259 Matlock

Derwentside District Council
Civic Centre
Medomsley Road
Consett DH8 5JA

Tel: (01207) 218 000
Fax: (01207) 580 156

Doncaster Borough Council
Copley House
Waterdale
Doncaster DN1 3EQ

Tel: (01302) 734 700
Fax: (01302) 734 665
DX: 12569 Doncaster-1

Dover District Council
Council Offices
White Cliffs Business Park
Dover
Kent CT16 3PE

Tel: (01304) 821 199
Fax: (01304) 824 917
DX: 6312 Dover

Dudley Metropolitan Borough Council
3 St. James's Road
Dudley DY1 1HZ

Tel: (01384) 818 181
Fax: (01384) 453 388
DX: 12767 Dudley

Durham City Council
Byland Lodge
Hawthorne Terrace
Durham DH1 4TD

Tel: (0191) 386 6111
Fax: (0191) 386 0625

Easington District Council
Council Offices
Seaside Lane
Easington
Peterlee SR8 3TN

Tel: (0191) 527 0501
Fax: (0191) 527 0076

East Cambridgeshire District Council
The Grange
Nutholt Lane
Ely CB7 4PL

Tel: (01353) 665 555
Fax: (01353) 665 240
DX: 41001 Ely

East Devon District Council
Knowle Station Road
Sidmouth
Devon EX10 8HL

Tel: (01395) 516 551
Fax: (01395) 577 853
DX: 48705 Sidmouth

East Dorset District Council
Council Offices
Furzehill
Wimborne BH21 4HN

Tel: (01202) 886 201
Fax: (01202) 841 390

East Hampshire District Council
Penns Place
Petersfield GU31 4EX

Tel: (01730) 266 551
Fax: (01730) 267 366
DX: 100403 Petersfield

East Hertfordshire District Council
2 The Causeway
Bishops Stortford CM23 2EN

Tel: (01279) 655 261
Fax: (01279) 757 582

East Lindsey District Council
Tedder Hall
Manby Park
Louth LN11 8UP

Tel: (01507) 601 111
Fax: (01507) 600 206

East Northamptonshire District
Council
East Northamptonshire House
Cedar Drive
Thrapston
Northants NN14 4LZ

Tel: (01832) 742 000
Fax: (01832) 734 839
DX: 701611 Thrapston

East Riding of Yorkshire Council
The Hall
Lairgate
Beverley HU17 8HL

Tel: (01482) 882 255
Fax: (01482) 883 913
DX: 28313 Beverley

East Riding of Yorkshire Council
(Legal Dept.)
County Hall
Beverley HU17 9BA

Tel: (01482) 887 700
Fax: (01482) 884 992

East Staffordshire Borough Council
Town Hall
Burton upon Trent DE14 2EB

Tel: (01283) 508 000
Fax: (01283) 535 412
DX: 700331 Burton-upon-Trent-2

Eastbourne Borough Council
Town Hall
Grove Road
Eastbourne BN21 4UG

Tel: (01323) 410 000
Fax: (01323) 410 322
DX: 6921 Eastbourne

Eastleigh Borough Council
Civic Offices
Leigh Road
Eastleigh SO50 9YN

Tel: (01703) 614 646
Fax: (01703) 643 952

Ellesmere Port & Neston Borough
Council
Council Offices
4 Civic Way
Ellesmere Port
South Wirral L65 0BE

Tel: (0151) 355 3665
Fax: (0151) 355 4305

Elmbridge Borough Council
Civic Centre
High Street
Esher KT10 9SD

Tel: (01372) 474 474
Fax: (01372) 474 972

Epping Forest District Council
Civic Offices
323 High Street
Epping CM16 4BZ

Tel: (01992) 564 000
Fax: (01992) 578 018
DX: 40409 Epping

Epsom & Ewell Borough Council
Town Hall
The Parade
Epsom KT18 5BY

Tel: (01372) 732 000
Fax: (01372) 732 109
DX: 30713 Epsom-1

Erewash Borough Council
Town Hall
Ilkeston
Derbyshire DE7 5RP

Tel: (0115) 9440 440
Fax: (0115) 9440 534

Exeter City Council
Civic Centre
Paris Street
Exeter EX1 1JN

Tel: (01392) 277 888
Fax: (01392) 265265
DX: 8323 Exeter

Fareham Borough Council
Civic Offices
Civic Way
Fareham PO16 7PP

Tel: (01329) 236 100
Fax: (01329) 822 732
DX: 40814 Fareham

Fenland District Council
Fenland Hall
County Road
March PE15 8NQ

Tel: (01354) 652471
Fax: (01354) 58271
DX: 30955 March

Flintshire County Council
County Hall
Mold
Flintshire CH7 6NB

Tel: (01352) 752 121
Fax: (01352) 755 910

Forest Heath District Council
College Heath Road
Mildenhall
Bury St Edmunds IP28 7EY

Tel: (01638) 719 000
Fax: (01638) 716 493

Forest of Dean District Council
High Street
Coleford
Glos GL16 8HG

Tel: (01594) 810 000
Fax: (01594) 810 134

Fylde Borough Council
Town Hall
Lytham St Annes FY8 1LW

Tel: (01253) 721 222
Fax: (01253) 713 113

Gateshead Borough Council
Civic Centre
Gateshead NE8 1HH

Tel: (0191) 477 1011
Fax: (0191) 478 3495

Gedling Borough Council
Civic Centre
Arnot Hill Park
Arnold
Nottingham NG5 6LU

Tel: (0115) 9670 067
Fax: (0115) 9670 014

Gillingham Borough Council
Municipal Buildings
Canterbury Street
Gillingham
Kent ME7 5LA

Tel: (01634) 281 414
Fax: (01634) 282 040
DX: 6654 Gillingham-2

Gloucester City Council
Council Offices
The Docks
Gloucester GL1 2EP

Tel: (01452) 522 232
Fax: (01452) 396 140

Gosport Borough Council
Town Hall
High Street
Gosport PO12 1EB

Tel: (01705) 584 242
Fax: (0105) 545 587

Gravesham Borough Council
Civic Centre
Windmill Street
Gravesend DA12 1AU

Tel: (01474) 564 422
Fax: (01474) 337 453
DX: 6804 Gravesend

Great Yarmouth Borough Council
Town Hall
Hall Quay
Great Yarmouth NR30 2QF

Tel: (01493) 856 100
Fax: (01493) 846 332
DX: 41121 Great Yarmouth

Guildford Borough Council
Millmead House
Millmead
Guildford GU2 5BB

Tel: (01483) 505 050
Fax: (01483) 444 444

Gwynedd Council
Council Offices
Caernarfon
Gwynedd LL55 1SH

Tel: (01286) 672 255
Fax: (01286) 673 993

Halton Borough Council
Municipal Buildings
Kingsway
Widnes WA8 7QF

Tel: (0151) 424 2061
Fax: (0151) 471 7301
DX: 24302 Widnes-1

Hambleton District Council
Civic Centre
Stone Cross
Northallerton DL6 2UU

Tel: (01609) 779 977
Fax: (01609) 780 017
DX: 61650 Northallerton

Harborough District Council
Council Offices
Adam & Eve Street
Market Harborough
Leicestershire LE16 7AG

Tel: (01858) 410 000
Fax: (01858) 462 766
DX: 27317 Market Harborough

Harlow District Council
Town Hall
Southgate
Harlow CM20 1HJ

Tel: (01279) 446 611
Fax: (01279) 446 767

Harrogate Borough Council
Council Offices
Crescent Gardens
Harrogate HG1 2SG

Tel: (01423) 568 954
Fax: (01423) 530 706
DX: 11962 Harrogate-1

Hart District Council
Civic Offices
Harlington Way
Fleet GU13 8AE

Tel: (01252) 622 122
Fax: (01252) 626 886

Hartlepool Borough Council
Civic Centre
Hartlepool TS24 8AY

Tel: (01429) 266 522
Fax: (01429) 523 005

Hastings Borough Council
Town Hall
Queens Road
Hastings TN34 1QR

Tel: (01424) 781 066
Fax: (01424) 781 743

Havant Borough Council
Civic Offices
Civic Centre Road
Havant PO9 2AX

Tel: (01705) 474 174
Fax: (01705) 480 263
DX: 50005 Havant

Hereford City Council
Town Hall
St Owen Street
Hereford HR1 2PJ

Tel: (01432) 364 500
Fax: (01432) 364 503
DX: 17231 Hereford

Hertsmere Borough Council
Civic Offices
Elstree Way
Borehamwood
Herts WD6 1WA

Tel: (0181) 207 2277
Fax: (0181) 207 2197
DX: 45602 Borehamwood

High Peak Borough Council
Council Offices
Hayfield Road
Chapel-en-le-Firth
Stockport SK12 6QJ

Tel: (01663) 751 751
Fax: (01663) 751 042

Hinckley & Bosworth Borough Council
Council Offices
Argents Mead
Hinckley LE10 1BZ

Tel: (01455) 238 141
Fax: (01455) 251 172
DX: 716429 Hinckley

XIII

Horsham District Council
Council Offices
Park House
North Street
Horsham
West Sussex RH12 1RL

Tel: (01403) 215 100
Fax: (01403) 262 985
DX: 57609 Horsham—1

Hove Borough Council
Town Hall
Norton Road
Hove BN3 4AH

Tel: (01273) 290 000
Fax: (01273) 207 277

Huntingdonshire District Council
Pathfinder House
St Mary's Street
Huntingdon PE18 6TN

Tel: (01480) 388 388
Fax: (01480) 388 099

Hyndburn Borough Council
Council Offices
Eagle Street
Accrington BB5 1LN

Tel: (01254) 388 111
Fax: (01254) 392 597

Ipswich Borough Council
Civic Centre
Civic Drive
Ipswich IP1 2EE

Tel: (01473) 262 626
Fax: (01473) 262 033
DX: 3225 Ipswich-1

Isle of Anglesey County Council
Swyddfeydd y Cyngor
Llangefni
Isle of Anglesey LL77 7TW

Tel: (01248) 750 057
Fax: (01248) 750 032

Isle of Wight Council
County Hall
Newport
Isle of Wight PO30 1UD

Tel: (01983) 821 000
Fax: (01983) 823 333

Kennet District Council
Browfort
Bath Road
Devizes SN10 2AT

Tel: (01380) 724 911
Fax: (01380) 729 146
DX: 42909 Devizes

Kerrier District Council
Council Offices
Dolcoath Avenue
Camborne TR14 8FX

Tel: (01209) 614 000
Fax: (01209) 713 369

Kettering Borough Council
Municipal Offices
Bowling Green Road
Kettering NN15 7QX

Tel: (01536) 410 333
Fax: (01536) 410 795
DX: 12816 Kettering

King's Lynn & West Norfolk Borough
   Council
King's Court
Chapel Street
King's Lynn PE30 1EX

Tel: (01553) 692 722
Fax: (01553) 691 663
DX: 57825 King's Lynn

Kingston upon Hull City Council
Guildhall
Kingston upon Hull HU1 2AA

Tel: (01482) 610 610
Fax: (01482) 615 062
DX: 11934 Hull-1

Kingswood Borough Council
Civic Centre
High Street
Kingswood BS15 2TR

Tel: (01454) 868 686
Fax: (01454) 863 099
DX: 43359 Kingswood

Kirklees Borough Council
PO Box 24
Civic Centre 3
Market Street
Huddersfield HD1 2TG

Tel: (01484) 422 133
Fax: (01484) 442 231
DX: 12986 Huddersfield

Knowsley Borough Council
PO Box 21
Legal Services
Municipal Buildings
Archway Road
Huyton
Knowsley L36 9YU

Tel: (0151) 489 6000
Fax: (0151) 443 3550

Lancaster City Council
Town Hall
Dalton Square
Lancaster LA1 1PJ

Tel: (01524) 582 000
Fax: (01524) 582 161

Leeds City Council
Civic Hall
Leeds LS1 1UR

Tel: (0113) 2348 080
Fax: (0113) 2474 651
DX: 12088 Leeds-1

Leicester City Council
New Walk Centre
Welford Place
Leicester LE1 6ZG

Tel: (0116) 2549 922
Fax: (0116) 2858 933

Leominster District Council
PO Box 3
Grange House
Leominster HR6 8LU

Tel: (01568) 611 100
Fax: (01568) 611 046
DX: 27038 Leominster

Lewes District Council
Lewes House
32 High Street
Lewes BN7 2LX

Tel: (01273) 471 600
Fax: (01273) 479 011

Lichfield District Council
Frog Lane
Lichfield WS13 6YY

Tel: (01543) 414 000
Fax: (01543) 250 673

Lincoln City Council
City Hall
Beaumont Fee
Lincoln LN1 1DD

Tel: (01522) 511 511
Fax: (01522) 521 736

Liverpool City Council
PO Box 88
Municipal Buildings
Dale Street
Liverpool L69 2DH

Tel: (0151) 227 3911
Fax: (0151) 225 2365
DX: 14206 Liverpool-1

Luton Borough Council
Town Hall
George Street
Luton LU1 2BQ

Tel: (01582) 746 000
Fax: (01582) 746 223
DX: 5926 Luton-1

Macclesfield Borough Council
Town Hall
Macclesfield SK10 1DX

Tel: (01625) 500 500
Fax: (01625) 504 203
DX: 25010 Macclesfield-2

Maidstone Borough Council
London House
5-11 London Road
Maidstone ME16 8HR

Tel: (01622) 602 000
Fax: (01622) 692 246
DX: 4819 Maidstone-1

Maldon District Council
District Council Offices
Princes Road
Maldon CM9 5DL

Tel: (01621) 854 477
Fax: (01621) 852 575

XIII

Malvern Hills District Council
Council House
Avenue Road
Malvern
Worcs WR14 3AF

Tel: (01684) 892 700
Fax: (01684) 862 473
DX: 17608 Malvern

Manchester City Council
Town Hall
Manchester M60 2LA

Tel: (0161) 234 5000
Fax: (0161) 234 3207
DX: 14376 Manchester-1

Mansfield District Council
Civic Centre
Chesterfield Road South
Mansfield NG19 7BH

Tel: (01623) 656 656
Fax: (01623) 420 197
DX: 10343 Mansfield

Melton Borough Council
Council Offices
Nottingham Road
Melton Mowbray LE13 0UL

Tel: (01664) 67771
Fax: (01664) 410 283
DX: 26764 Melton Mowbray

Mendip District Council
Council Offices
Cannards Grave Road
Shepton Mallet BA4 5BT

Tel: (01749) 343 399
Fax: (01749) 344 050
DX: 43001 Shepton Mallet

Merthyr Tydfil County
  Borough Council
Civic Centre
Merthyr Tydfil CF47 8AN

Tel: (01685) 725 000
Fax: (01685) 722 146

Mid Bedfordshire District Council
12 Dunstable Street
Ampthill
Bedford MK45 2JU

Tel: (01525) 402 051
Fax: (01525) 406 288
DX: 36903 Ampthill

Mid Devon District Council
The Great House
1 St Peter Street
Tiverton EX16 6NY

Tel: (01884) 255 255
Fax: (01884) 258 852

Mid Suffolk District Council
Council Offices
131 High Street
Needham Market IP6 8DL

Tel: (01449) 720 711
Fax: (01449) 727 345

Mid Sussex District Council
Oaklands
Oaklands Road
Haywards Heath
West Sussex RH16 1SS

Tel: (01444) 458 166
Fax: (01444) 450 027
DX: 300320 Haywards Heath-1

Middlesbrough Borough Council
PO Box 99A
Municipal Buildings
Middlesbrough TS1 2QQ

Tel: (01642) 245 432
Fax: (01642) 263 588
DX: 60532 Middlesbrough

Milton Keynes Borough Council
Civic Offices
1 Saxon Gate East
Milton Keynes MK9 3EJ

Tel: (01908) 691 691
Fax: (01908) 682 456
DX: 31406 Milton Keynes-1

Mole Valley District Council
Pippbrook
Dorking RH4 1SJ

Tel: (01306) 885 001
Fax: (01306) 876 821
DX: 57306 Dorking

Monmouthshire County Council
County Hall
Cwmbran NP44 2XH

Tel: (01633) 644 644
Fax: (01633) 832 990

Neath Port Talbot
  County Borough Council
Civic Centre
Port Talbot SA13 1PJ

Tel: (01639) 763 333
Fax: (01639) 763 444

New Forest District Council
Appletree Court
Lyndhurst SO43 7PA

Tel: (01703) 285 000
Fax: (01703) 285 555

Newark & Sherwood District Council
Kelham Hall
Newark NG23 5QX

Tel: (01636) 605 111
Fax: (01636) 708 486

Newbury District Council
Council Offices
Market Street
Newbury RG14 5LD

Tel: (01635) 42400
Fax: (01635) 519 431
DX: 30825 Newbury-1

Newcastle-under-Lyme Borough
  Council
Civic Offices
Merrial Street
Newcastle-under-Lyme ST5 2AG

Tel: (01782) 717 717
Fax: (01782) 711 032
DX: 20959 Newcastle-under-Lyme

Newcastle upon Tyne City Council
Civic Centre
St Mary's Place
Barras Bridge
Newcastle upon Tyne NE99 2BN

Tel: (0191) 232 8520
Fax: (0191) 232 3992

Newport County Borough Council
Civic Centre
Newport
South Wales NP9 4UR

Tel: (01633) 244 491
Fax: (01633) 244 721

North Cornwall District Council
The Council Offices
Higher Trenant Road
Weybridge PL27 6TW

Tel: (01208) 812 255
Fax: (01208) 893 255

North Devon District Council
Civic Centre
Barnstaple
Devon EX31 1EA

Tel: (01271) 327 711
Fax: (01271) 388 451

North Dorset District Council
Nordon
Salisbury Road
Blandford Forum DT11 7LL

Tel: (01258) 454 111
Fax: (01258) 480 179

North East Derbyshire
  District Council
Council House
Saltergate
Chesterfield S40 1LF

Tel: (01246) 231 111
Fax: (01246) 550 213

North East Lincolnshire District Council
Municipal Offices
Town Hall Square
Grimsby
Lincolnshire DN3 1HU

Tel: (01472) 313 131
Fax: (01472) 325 902
DX: 13536 Grimsby

North Hertfordshire District Council
Council Offices
Gernon Road
Letchworth SG6 3JF

Tel: (01462) 474 000
Fax: (01462) 474 227
DX: 31317 Letchworth

North Kesteven District Council
PO Box 3
District Council Offices
Kesteven Street
Sleaford Links NG34 7EF

Tel: (01522) 532 211
Fax: (01529) 413 956/305 808
DX: 26909 Sleaford

XIII

North Lincolnshire Council
Pittswood House
Civic Centre
Ashby Road
Scunthorpe DN16 1AB

Tel: (01724) 280 444
Fax: (01724) 296 219

North Norfolk District Council
Council Offices
Holt Road
Cromer NR27 9EL

Tel: (01263) 513 811
Fax: (01263) 515 042
DX: 31008 Cromer

North Somerset District Council
Town Hall
Weston-Super-Mare
North Somerset BS23 1UJ

Tel: (01934) 631 701
Fax: (01934) 418 194

North Shropshire District Council
Council Offices
Edinburgh House
New Street
Wem
Shropshire SY4 5DB

Tel: (01939) 232 771
Fax: (01939) 238 404
DX: 27386 Wem

North Tyneside Borough Council
14 Northumberland Square
North Shields
Tyne and Wear NE30 1PZ

Tel: (0191) 200 5151
Fax: (0191) 200 5858

North Warwickshire Borough Council
Council Offices
South Street
Atherstone CV9 1BD

Tel: (01827) 715 341
Fax: (01827) 719 225
DX: 23956 Atherstone

North West Leicestershire District
   Council
Council Offices
Coalville LE67 3FJ

Tel: (01530) 833 333
Fax: (01530) 510 290
DX: 23662 Coalville

North Wiltshire District Council
Monkton Park Offices
Monkton Park
Monkton Hill
Chippenham SN15 1ER

Tel: (01249) 443 322
Fax: (01249) 443 152
DX: 34208 Chippenham

Northampton Borough Council
Guildhall
Northampton NN1 1DA

Tel: (01604) 233 500
Fax: (01604) 238 723
DX: 18531 Northampton-2

Northavon District Council
Council Offices
Castle Street
Thornbury
Bristol BS12 1HF

Tel: (01454) 863 021
Fax: (01454) 863 060

Norwich City Council
City Hall
St. Peter Street
Norwich NR2 1NH

Tel: (01603) 622 233
Fax: (01603) 213 000
DX: 5278 Norwich-1

Nottingham City Council
The Guildhall
South Sherwood Street
Nottingham NG1 4BT

Tel: (0115) 915 5555
Fax: (0115) 9473 246

Nuneaton & Bedworth Borough Council
Council House
Coton Road
Nuneaton CV11 5AA

Tel: (01203) 376 376
Fax: (01203) 376 574

Oadby & Wigston Borough Council
Council Offices
Station Road
Wigston LE18 2DR

Tel: (0116) 2888 961
Fax: (0116) 2887 828

Oldham Borough Council
Civic Centre
West Street
Oldham OL1 1UL

Tel: (0161) 911 4812
Fax: (0161) 911 4826

Oswestry Borough Council
Council Offices
Castle View
Oswestry SY11 1JR

Tel: (01691) 671 111
Fax: (01691) 677 348
DX: 26610 Oswestry

Oxford City Council
St Aldate's Chambers
St Aldates
Oxford OX1 1DS

Tel: (01865) 249 811
Fax: (01865) 252 338
DX: 4309 Oxford

Pembrokeshire County Council
PO Box 27
Cambria House
Haverfordwest
Pembrokeshire SA61 1TP

Tel: (01437) 764 551
Fax: (01437) 760 703

Pendle Borough Council
Town Hall
Market Street
Nelson BB9 7LG

Tel: (01282) 661 661
Fax: (01282) 695 180

Penwith District Council
Council Offices
St Clare
Penzance TR18 3QW

Tel: (01736) 362 341
Fax: (01736) 64292

Peterborough City Council
Town Hall
Bridge Street
Peterborough PE1 1HG

Tel: (01733) 63141
Fax: (01733) 452 537
DX: 12310 Peterborough-1

Plymouth City Council
Civic Centre
Armada Way
Plymouth PL1 2EW

Tel: (01752) 668 000
Fax: (01752) 264 880
DX: 8278 Plymouth-2

Poole Borough Council
Civic Centre
Poole BH15 2RU

Tel: (01202) 633 633
Fax: (01202) 633 706
DX: 123820 Poole

Portsmouth City Council
Civic Offices
Guildhall Square
Portsmouth PO4 2AL

Tel: (01705) 822 251
Fax: (01705) 834 076
DX: 2244 Portsmouth-1

Powys County Council
County Hall
Spa Road
Llandrindod Wells
Powys LD1 5LG

Tel: (01597) 826 000
Fax: (01597) 826 230

Preston Borough Council
PO Box 10
Town Hall
Lancaster Road
Preston PR1 2RL

Tel: (01772) 254 881
Fax: (01772) 266 195

Purbeck District Council
Westport House
Worgret Rd
Wareham BH20 4PP

Tel: (01929) 556 561
Fax: (01929) 552 688

Reading Borough Council
Civic Offices
Civic Centre
Reading RG1 7TD

Tel: (01734) 575 911
Fax: (01734) 589 770
DX: 40124 Reading (Castle St)

XIII

Redcar and Cleveland Borough Council
Town Hall
Fabian Road
South Bank
Middlesbrough TS6 9AR

Tel: (01642) 444 000
Fax: (01642) 444 599
DX: 60041 Normanby

Redditch Borough Council
Town Hall
Alcester Street
Redditch B98 8AH

Tel: (01527) 64252
Fax: (01527) 65216
DX: 19106 Redditch

Reigate & Banstead Borough Council
Town Hall
Castlefield Road
Reigate RH2 0SH

Tel: (01737) 242 477
Fax: (01737) 247 698
DX: 54102 Reigate-2

Restormel Borough Council
39 Penwinnick Road
St Austell PL25 5DR

Tel: (01726) 74466
Fax: (01726) 68339

Rhondda-Cynon-Taff
   County Borough Council
The Pavilions
Cambrian Park
Clydach Vale
Tonypandy CF40 2XX

Tel: (01443) 424000
Fax: (01443) 424024

Ribble Valley Borough Council
Council Offices
Church Walk
Clitheroe BB7 2RA

Tel: (01200) 425 111
Fax: (01200) 26339
DX: 15157 Clitheroe

Richmondshire District Council
Swale House
Frenchgate
Richmond DL10 4JE

Tel: (01748) 850 222
Fax: (01748) 825 071

Rochdale Borough Council
Town Hall
Esplanade
Rochdale OL16 1AB

Tel: (01706) 47474
Fax: (01706) 59475

Rochester upon Medway City Council
Civic Centre
High Street
Strood
Rochester ME2 4AW

Tel: (01634) 727 777
Fax: (01634) 732 756
DX: 56006 Strood (Kent)

Rochford District Council
Council Offices
South Street
Rochford SS4 1BW

Tel: (01702) 546 366
Fax: (01702) 545 737
DX: 39751 Rochford

Rossendale Borough Council
Town Hall
Rawtenstall
Rossendale BB4 7LZ

Tel: (01706) 217 777
Fax: (01706) 224 958

Rother District Council
Town Hall
Town Hall Square
Bexhill-on-Sea TN39 3JX

Tel: (01424) 216 321
Fax: (01424) 217 869

Rotherham Borough Council
Civic Building
Walker Place
Rotherham S65 1UF

Tel: (01709) 382 121
Fax: (01709) 823 598
DX: 12606 Rotherham-1

Rugby Borough Council
Town Hall
Rugby CV21 2LA

Tel: (01788) 533 533
Fax: (01788) 533 577

Runnymede Borough Council
Civic Offices
Station Road
Addlestone KT15 2AH

Tel: (01932) 838 383
Fax: (01932) 855 135
DX: 46350 Addlestone

Rushcliffe Borough Council
The Civic Centre
Pavilion Road
West Bridgford
Nottingham NG2 5FE

Tel: (0115) 9819 911
Fax: (0115) 9455 882
DX: 19907 West Bridgford

Rushmoor Borough Council
Council Offices
Farnborough Road
Farnborough GU14 7JU

Tel: (01252) 516 222
Fax: (01252) 524 017

Rutland District Council
Council Offices
Catmose
Oakham LE15 6HP

Tel: (01572) 722 577
Fax: (01572) 758 307
DX: 28340 Oakham

Ryedale District Council
Ryedale House
Malton YO17 0HH

Tel: (01653) 600 666
Fax: (01653) 696 801

St Albans City & District Council
Civic Centre
St Peter's Street
St Albans AL1 3JE

Tel: (01727) 866 100
Fax: (01727) 843 167

St Edmundsbury Borough Council
Borough Offices
Angel Hill
Bury St Edmunds IP33 1XB

Tel: (01284) 763 233
Fax: (01284) 757 124
DX: 57223 Bury St Edmunds

St Helens Borough Council
Town Hall
Victoria Square
St Helens WA10 1HP

Tel: (01744) 456 000
Fax: (01744) 33337

Salford City Council
Civic Centre
Chorley Road
Swinton M27 5DA

Tel: (0161) 794 4711
Fax: (0161) 794 6595

Salisbury District Council
The Council House
Bourne Hill
Salisbury SP1 3UZ

Tel: (01722) 336 272
Fax: (01722) 434 500
DX: 58026 Salisbury

Sandwell Borough Council
The Sandwell Council House
Oldbury
Warley
West Midlands B69 3BE

Tel: (0121) 569 2200
Fax: (0121) 569 3245

Scarborough Borough Council
Town Hall
St Nicholas Street
Scarborough YO11 2HG

Tel: (01723) 372 351
Fax: (01723) 354 979

Sedgefield District Council
Council Offices
Spennymoor DL16 6JQ

Tel: (01388) 816166
Fax: (01388) 817 251

Sedgemoor District Council
Bridgwater House
King Square
Bridgwater TA6 3AR

Tel: (01278) 435 435
Fax: (01278) 446 412

XIII

Sefton Borough Council
Town Hall
Lord Street
Southport PR8 1DA

Tel: (01704) 533 133
Fax: (0151) 934 2256

Selby District Council
Civic Centre
Portholme Road
Selby YO8 0SB

Tel: (01757) 705 101
Fax: (01757) 292 020
DX: 27408 Selby

Sevenoaks District Council
Council Offices
Argyle Road
Sevenoaks TN13 1HG

Tel: (01732) 741 222
Fax: (01732) 740 693
DX: 30006 Sevenoaks

Sheffield City Council
Town Hall
Sheffield S1 2HH

Tel: (0114) 2726 444
Fax: (0114) 2735 003
DX: 10580 Sheffield-1

Shepway District Council
Civic Centre
Castle Hill Avenue
Folkestone CT20 2QY

Tel: (01303) 850 388
Fax: (01303) 245 978
DX: 4912 Folkestone

Shrewsbury & Atcham, Heading
  Borough Council
Guildhall
Dogpole
Shrewsbury SY1 1ER

Tel: (01743) 232 255
Fax: (01743) 271 594
DX: 19723 Shrewsbury

Slough Borough Council
Town Hall
Bath Road
Slough SL1 3UQ

Tel: (01753) 523 881
Fax: (01753) 692 499
DX: 3403 Slough

Solihull Borough Council
PO Box 18
Council House
Solihull B91 3QS

Tel: (0121) 704 6000
Fax: (0121) 704 6008

South Bedfordshire District Council
District Offices
High Street North
Dunstable LU6 1LF

Tel: (01582) 472 222
Fax: (01582) 474 009
DX: 57012 Dunstable

South Buckinghamshire District
  Council
Council Offices
Windsor Road
Slough SL1 2HN

Tel: (01753) 533 333
Fax: (01753) 529 841
DX: 42266 Slough West

South Cambridgeshire District
  Council
South Cambridgeshire Hall
9-11 Hills Road
Cambridge CB2 1PB

Tel: (01223) 443 000
Fax: (01223) 443 148
DX: 5848 Cambridge

South Derbyshire District Council
Civic Offices
Civic Way
Swadlincote DE11 0AH

Tel: (01283) 221 000
Fax: (01283) 550 128

South Hams District Council
Follaton House
Plymouth Road
Totnes TQ9 5NE

Tel: (01803) 861 234
Fax: (01803) 866 151

South Herefordshire District Council
Brockington
35 Hafod Road
Hereford HR1 1SH

Tel: (01432) 346 300
Fax: (01432) 340 189

South Holland District Council
Council Offices
Priory Road
Spalding PE11 2XE

Tel: (01775) 761 161
Fax: (01775) 711 253

South Kesteven District Council
Council Offices
St Peter's Hill
Grantham NG31 6PZ

Tel: (01476) 591 591
Fax: (01476) 591 810
DX: 27024 Grantham

South Lakeland District Council
South Lakeland House
Lowther Street
Kendal
Cumbria LA9 4UQ

Tel: (01539) 733 333
Fax: (01539) 740 300

South Norfolk District Council
South Norfolk House
Swan Lane
Long Stratton
Norwich NR15 2XE

Tel: (01508) 533 633
Fax: (01508) 533 695

South Northamptonshire Council
Springfields
Towcester NN12 6AE

Tel: (01327) 350 211
Fax: (01327) 359 219
DX: 16938 Towcester

South Oxfordshire District Council
PO Box 21
Council Offices
Crowmarsh
Wallingford
Oxford OX10 8HQ

Tel: (01491) 835 351
Fax: (01491) 833 390

South Ribble Borough Council
Civic Centre
West Paddock
Leyland PR5 1DH

Tel: (01772) 421 491
Fax: (01772) 622 287

South Shropshire District Council
Stone House
Corve Street
Ludlow SY8 1DG

Tel: (01584) 874 941
Fax: (01584) 872 971

South Somerset District Council
Council Offices
Brympton Way
Yeovil BA20 2HT

Tel: (01935) 462 462
Fax: (01935) 462 188

South Staffordshire District Council
Council Offices
Wolverhampton Road
Codsall
Wolverhampton WV8 1PX

Tel: (01902) 696 000
Fax: (0902) 847 124
DX: 18036 Codsall

South Tyneside Borough Council
Town Hall
South Shields NE33 2RL

Tel: (0191) 427 1717
Fax: (0191) 455 0208

Southampton City Council
Civic Centre
Southampton SO14 7PE

Tel: (01703) 223 855
Fax: (01703) 233 079
DX: 115710 Southampton-17

Southend-on-Sea Borough Council
Civic Centre
Victoria Avenue
Southend-on-Sea SS2 6ER

Tel: (01702) 215 000
Fax: (01702) 215 110
DX: 2812 Southend

Spelthorne
Borough Council
Knowle Green
Staines TW18 1XB

Tel: (01784) 453 222
Fax: (01784) 463 356
DX: 98044 Staines-2

XIII

Stafford Borough Council
Civic Offices
Riverside
Stafford ST16 3AQ

Tel: (01785) 223 181
Fax: (01785) 223 156

Staffordshire Moorlands District
    Council
Moorlands House
Stockwell Street
Leek ST13 6HQ

Tel: (01538) 399 181
Fax: (01538) 387 813
DX: 16361 Leek

Stevenage Borough Council
Daneshill House
Danestrete
Stevenage SG1 1HN

Tel: (01438) 356 177
Fax: (01438) 740 296/766 566

Stockport Metropolitan Council
Town Hall
Wellington Road South
Stockport SK1 3XE

Tel: (0161) 480 4949
Fax: (0161) 477 9530
DX: 22605 Stockport-2

Stockton-on-Tees Borough Council
Municipal Buildings
Church Road
Stockton-on-Tees TS18 1LD

Tel: (01642) 393 939
Fax: (01642) 393 092
DX: 60611 Stockton-on-Tees

Stoke-on-Trent City Council
Civic Centre
Glebe Street
Stoke-on-Trent ST4 1RN

Tel: (01782) 744 241
Fax: (01782) 404 592

Stratford-upon-Avon District Council
Elizabeth House
Church Street
Stratford-upon-Avon CV37 6HX

Tel: (01789) 267 575
Fax: (01789) 260 260
DX: 700739 Stratford-upon-Avon-2

Stroud District Council
Legal Administrative Department
Westwood Road
Stroud GL5 4UB

Tel: (01453) 766 321
Fax: (01453) 750 932

Suffolk Coastal District Council
Council Offices
Melton Hill
Woodbridge IP12 1AU

Tel: (01394) 383 789
Fax: (01394) 385 100
DX: 41400 Woodbridge

Sunderland Borough Council
Civic Centre
Burdon Road
Sunderland SR2 7DN

Tel: (0191) 553 1000
Fax: (0191) 553 1020
DX: 60729 Sunderland

Surrey Heath Borough Council
Surrey Heath House
Knoll Road
Camberley GU15 3HD

Tel: (01276) 686 252
Fax: (01276) 22277
DX: 32722 Camberley

Swale Borough Council
Swale House
East Street
Sittingbourne ME10 3HT

Tel: (01795) 424 341
Fax: (01795) 417 217
DX: 59900 Sittingbourne-2

Swansea City and County Council
County Hall
Ostermouth Road
Swansea SA1 3SN

Tel: (01792) 636 000
Fax: (01792) 636 340

Tameside Borough Council
Council Offices
Wellington Road
Ashton-under-Lyne
Lancs OL6 6DL

Tel: (0161) 342 8355
Fax: (0161) 342 3070

Tamworth Borough Council
Marmion House
Lichfield Street
Tamworth B79 7BZ

Tel: (01827) 311 222
Fax: (01827) 52769

Tandridge District Council
Council Offices
Station Road East
Oxted RH8 0BT

Tel: (01883) 722 000
Fax: (01883) 722 015
DX: 39359 Oxted

Taunton Deane Borough Council
The Deane House
Belvedere Road
Taunton TA1 1HE

Tel: (01823) 356 356
Fax: (01823) 356 329

Teesdale District Council
Council Offices
43 Galgate
Barnard Castle DL12 8EL

Tel: (01833) 690 000
Fax: (01833) 637 269

Teignbridge District Council
Forde House
Brunel Rd
Newton Abbot TQ12 4XX

Tel: (01626) 61101
Fax: (01626) 56803

Tendring District Council
23A Pier Avenue
Clacton-on-Sea CO15 1PN

Tel: (01255) 425 501
Fax: (01255) 221 660
DX: 34660 Clacton-1

Test Valley Borough Council
Beech Hurst
Weyhill Road
Andover SP10 3AJ

Tel: (01264) 364 144
Fax: (01264) 332 625

Tewkesbury Borough Council
Council Offices
Gloucester Road
Tewkesbury GL20 5TT

Tel: (01684) 295 010
Fax: (01684) 290 139
DX: 11406 Tewkesbury

Thamesdown Borough Council
Civic Offices
Euclid Street
Swindon SN1 2JH

Tel: (01793) 463 000
Fax: (01793) 490 420
DX: 6211 Swindon-1

Thanet District Council
Council Offices
Cecil Street
Margate CT9 1XZ

Tel: (01843) 225 511
Fax: (01843) 290 906
DX: 30555 Margate

Three Rivers District Council
Three Rivers House
Northway
Rickmansworth WD3 1RL

Tel: (01923) 776 611
Fax: (01923) 896 119
DX: 38271 Rickmansworth

Thurrock Council
Civic Offices
New Road
Grays RM17 6SL

Tel: (01375) 390 000
Fax: (01375) 652 782

Tonbridge & Malling Borough Council
Council Offices
Gibson Building
Gibson Drive
Kings Hill
West Malling ME19 4LZ

Tel: (01732) 844 522
Fax: (01732) 842 170
DX: 92854 West Malling

Torbay Borough Council
Town Hall
Torquay TQ1 3DR

Tel: (01803) 296 244
Fax: (01803) 292 677
DX: 59006 Torquay-1

Torfaen County Borough Council
Civic Centre
Pontypool NP4 6YB

Tel: (01495) 762 200
Fax: (01495) 755 513

Torridge District Council
Riverbank House
Bideford EX39 2QG

Tel: (01237) 476 711
Fax: (01237) 478 849

Trafford Borough Council
PO Box 11
Trafford Town Hall
Talbot Road
Stretford M32 0YU

Tel: (0161) 912 1212
Fax: (0161) 848 9738/875 0094

Tunbridge Wells Borough Council
Town Hall
Tunbridge Wells TN1 1RS

Tel: (01892) 526 121
Fax: (01892) 518 527
DX: 3929 Tunbridge Wells-1

Tynedale District Council
Council Offices
Hexham House
Hexham NE46 3NH

Tel: (01434) 652 200
Fax: (01434) 652 420
DX: 63216 Hexham

Uttlesford District Council
Council Offices
London Road
Saffron Walden CB11 4ER

Tel: (01799) 510 510
Fax: (01799) 510 550
DX: 200307 Saffron Walden

Vale of Glamorgan Council
Civic Offices
Holton Road
Barry CF63 4RU

Tel: (01446) 700 111
Fax: (01446) 421 479

Vale of White Horse District Council
The Abbey House
Abbey Close
Abingdon OX14 3JE

Tel: (01235) 520 202
Fax: (01235) 554 960
DX: 35863 Abingdon

Vale Royal Borough Council
Wyvern House
The Brumber
Winsford
Cheshire CW7 1AH

Tel: (01606) 862 862
Fax: (01606) 862 100

Wakefield District Council
Town Hall
Bond Street
Wakefield WF1 2HQ

Tel: (01924) 306 090
Fax: (01924) 305 243

Walsall Metropolitan Council
Civic Centre
Darwall Street
Walsall WS1 1TP

Tel: (01922) 650 000
Fax: (01922) 720 885

Wansbeck District Council
Wansbeck Square
Ashington NE63 9XL

Tel: (01670) 814 444
Fax: (01670) 520 136

Wansdyke District Council
Guildhall
High Street
Bath BA1 5AW

Tel: (01225) 477 000
Fax: (01225) 477 489

Warrington Borough Council
Town Hall
Sanky Street
Warrington WA1 1UH

Tel: (01925) 444 400
Fax: (01925) 413 449
DX: 17760 Warrington-1

Warwick District Council
Town Hall
The Parade
Leamington Spa CV32 4AT

Tel: (01926) 450 000
Fax: (01926) 451 602
DX: 29123 Leamington Spa-1

Watford Council
Town Hall
Watford WD1 3EX

Tel: (01923) 226 400
Fax: (01923) 226 133
DX: 4514 Watford-1

Waveney District Council
Town Hall
High Street
Lowestoft NR32 1HS

Tel: (01502) 562 111
Fax: (01502) 589 327
DX: 41220 Lowestoft

Waverley Borough Council
Council Offices
The Burys
Godalming GU7 1HR

Tel: (01483) 861 111
Fax: (01483) 426 337
DX: 58303 Godalming-1

Wealden District Council
Pine Grove
Crowborough TN6 1DH

Tel: (01892) 653 311
Fax: (01892) 602 222
DX: 36860 Crowborough

Wear Valley District Council
Civic Centre
Crook DL15 9ES

Tel: (01388) 765 555
Fax: (01388) 766 660

Wellingborough Borough Council
Council Offices
Swanspool
Wellingborough NN8 1BP

Tel: (01933) 229 777
Fax: (01933) 229 318
DX: 12865 Wellingborough

Welwyn Hatfield District Council
The Campus
Welwyn Garden City AL8 6AE

Tel: (01707) 331 212
Fax: (01707) 375 490

West Devon Borough Council
Kilworthy Park
Drake Road
Tavistock PL19 0BZ

Tel: (01822) 615 911
Fax: (01822) 614 840
DX: 82405 Tavistock

West Dorset District Council
Council Offices
58-60 High West Street
Dorchester DT1 1UZ

Tel: (01305) 251 010
Fax: (01305) 251 481
DX: 8724 Dorchester

West Lancashire District Council
Council Offices
52 Derby Street
Ormskirk L39 2DF

Tel: (01695) 577 177
Fax: (01695) 585 082

West Lindsey District Council
The Guildhall
Gainsborough DN21 2DH

Tel: (01427) 615 411
Fax: (01427) 810 622

West Oxfordshire District Council
Council Offices
Woodgreen
Witney OX8 6NB

Tel: (01993) 702 941
Fax: (01993) 770 255

West Somerset District Council
20 Fore Street
Williton
Taunton TA4 4QA

Tel: (01984) 632 291
Fax: (01984) 633 022

XIII

West Wiltshire District Council
Bradley Road
Trowbridge BA14 0RD

Tel: (01225) 776 655
Fax: (01225) 770 303
DX: 116891 Trowbridge-3

Weymouth & Portland Borough Council
Municipal Offices
North Quay
Weymouth DT4 8TA

Tel: (01305) 761 222
Fax: (01305) 760 971

Wigan Borough Council
New Town Hall
Library Street
Wigan WN1 1YN

Tel: (01942) 244991
Fax: (01942) 827 093

Winchester City Council
City Offices
Colebrook Street
Winchester SO23 9LJ

Tel: (01962) 840 222
Fax: (01962) 841 365

Windsor & Maidenhead Royal
   Borough Council
Town Hall
St Ives Road
Maidenhead SL6 1RF

Tel: (01628) 798 888
Fax: (01628) 796 408
DX: 6422 Maidenhead

Wirral Borough Council
Town Hall
Brighton Street
Wallasey L44 8ED

Tel: (0151) 638 7070
Fax: (0151) 691 8468

Woking Borough Council
Civic Offices
Gloucester Square
Woking GU21 1YL

Tel: (01483) 755 855
Fax: (01483) 768 746
DX: 2931 Woking-1

Wokingham District Council
PO Box 151
Wokingham RG40 1WH

Tel: (01734) 786 833
Fax: (01734) 789 078

Wolverhampton Metropolitan Borough
   Council
Civic Centre
St Peter's Square
Wolverhampton WV1 1RG

Tel: (01902) 556 556
Fax: (01902) 314 970

Worcester City Council
Guildhall
High Street
Worcester WR1 2EY

Tel: (01905) 723 471
Fax: (01905) 722 028
DX: 716287 Worcester-1

Worthing Borough Council
Town Hall
Chapel Road
Worthing BN11 1HA

Tel: (01903) 239 999
Fax: (01903) 236 552

Wrekin District Council
Civic Offices
Telford TF3 4LD

Tel: (01952) 202 100
Fax: (01952) 291 060

Wrexham County Borough Council
PO Box 1284
Guildhall
Wrexham LL11 1WF

Tel: (01978) 292 000
Fax: (01978) 292 106

Wychavon District Council
Civic Centre
Queen Elizabeth Drive
Pershore
Worcestershire WR10 1PT

Tel: (01386) 565 000
Fax: (01386) 561 089
DX: 25934 Pershore

Wycombe District Council
District Council Offices
Queen Victoria Road
High Wycombe HP11 1BB

Tel: (01494) 461 000
Fax: (01494) 421 333
DX: 4411 High Wycombe-1

Wyre Borough Council
Civic Centre
Breck Road
Poulton-le-Fylde FY6 7PU

Tel: (01253) 891 000
Fax: (01253) 899 000

Wyre Forest District Council
Civic Centre
Stourport-on-Severn DY13 8UJ

Tel: (01562) 820 505
Fax: (01299) 879 688

York City Council
Guildhall
York YO1 1QN

Tel: (01904) 613 161
Fax: (01904) 551 047

London Boroughs

Barking & Dagenham
Civic Centre
Dagenham
Essex RM10 7BN

Tel: (0181) 592 4500
Fax: (0181) 595 3758
DX: 8511 Barking

Barnet
Town Hall
The Burroughs
London NW9 4BG

Tel: (0181) 359 2000
Fax: (0181) 359 2680
DX: 59318 Hendon

Bexley
Civic Offices
Broadway
Bexleyheath
Kent DA6 7LB

Tel: (0181) 303 7777
Fax: (0181) 301 2661
DX: 31807 Bexleyheath-1

Brent
Town Hall
Forty Lane
Wembley
Middlesex HA9 9HD

Tel: (0181) 937 1234
Fax: (0181) 937 1313

Bromley
Civic Centre
Stockwell Close
Bromley
Kent BR1 3UH

Tel: (0181) 464 3333
Fax: (0181) 290 0608
DX: 5727 Bromley-1

Camden
Town Hall
Judd Street
London NW1 9JE

Tel: (0171) 278 4444
Fax: (0171) 860 5659

Corporation of London
Guildhall
PO Box 270
Basinghall Street
London EC2P 2EJ

Tel: (0171) 606 3030
Fax: (0171) 332 1119

Croydon
Taberner House
Park Lane
Croydon
Surrey CR9 3JS

Tel: (0181) 686 4433
Fax: (0181) 760 5679
DX: 2630 Croydon-1

Ealing
Town Hall
New Broadway
Ealing
London W5 2BY

Tel: (0181) 579 2424
Fax: (0181) 758 5965
DX: 5106 Ealing

Enfield
Civic Centre
Silver Street
Enfield
Middlesex EN1 3ES

Tel: (0181) 366 6565
Fax: (0181) 982 7291
DX: 90615 Enfield-1

Greenwich
29-37 Wellington Street
Woolwich
London SE18 6PW

Tel: (0181) 854 8888
Fax: (0181) 312 5284

Hackney
Town Hall
298 Mare Street
London E8 1HE

Tel: (0181) 986 3123
Fax: (0181) 986 3359

Hammersmith & Fulham
Town Hall
King Street
London W6 9JU

Tel: (0181) 748 3020
Fax: (0181) 741 8021

Haringey
Alexander House
10 Station Road
Wood Green
London N22 4TR

Tel: (0181) 975 9700
Fax: (0181) 849 5984
DX: 35651 Wood Green-1

Harrow
PO Box 2
Civic Centre
Station Road
Harrow
Middlesex HA1 2UH

Tel: (0181) 863 5611
Fax: (0181) 424 1557
DX: 30450 Harrow-3

Havering
Town Hall
Main Road
Romford
Essex RM1 3BD

Tel: (01708) 746 040
Fax: (01708) 772 482

Hillingdon
Civic Centre
High Street
Uxbridge
Middlesex UB8 1UW

Tel: (01895) 250 111
Fax: (01895) 250 784

Hounslow
Civic Centre
Lampton Road
Hounslow
Middlesex TW3 4DN

Tel: (0181) 570 7728
Fax: (0181) 572 4819/862 5008
DX: 3505 Hounslow

Islington
Town Hall
Upper Street
Islington
London N1 2UD

Tel: (0171) 226 1234
Fax: (0171) 477 3243

Kensington & Chelsea
Town Hall
Hornton Street
London W8 7NX

Tel: (0171) 937 5464
Fax: (0171) 361 3488

Kingston upon Thames
Guildhall
High Street
Kingston upon Thames
Surrey KT1 1EU

Tel: (0181) 546 2121
Fax: (0181) 547 5127

Lambeth
Acre House
10 Acre Lane
London SW2 5SG

Tel: (0171) 926 1000
Fax: (0171) 926 2361

Lewisham
Lewisham Town Hall
Catford
London SE6 4RU

Tel: (0181) 695 6000
Fax: (0181) 690 1044
DX: 34366 Lewisham

Merton
Merton Civic Centre
London Road
Morden
Surrey SM4 5DX

Tel: (0181) 543 2222
Fax: (0181) 543 7126
DX: 41650 Morden

Newham
Town Hall
Barking Road
East Ham
London E6 2RP

Tel: (0181) 472 1430
Fax: (0181) 470 0480
DX: 4706 East Ham

Redbridge
Town Hall
128-142 High Road
Ilford
Essex IG1 1DD

Tel: (0181) 478 3020
Fax: (0181) 478 7709

Richmond upon Thames
Regal House
London Road
Twickenham
Middlesex TW1 3QB

Tel: (0181) 891 1411
Fax: (0181) 891 7733

Southwark
Chatalaine House
186 Walworth Road
London SE17 1JJ

Tel: (0171) 237 6677
Fax: (0171) 525 7277

Sutton
Civic Offices
St Nicholas Way
Sutton
Surrey SM1 1EA

Tel: (0181) 770 5000
Fax: (0181) 770 5059
DX: 56408 Sutton-1

Tower Hamlets
Mulberry Place
5 Clare Crescent
Isle of Dogs
London E14 2BG

Tel: (0171) 364 5000
Fax: (0171) 364 9075
DX: 40905 Bethnal Green

Waltham Forest
Town Hall
Forest Road
Walthamstow
London E17 4JF

Tel: (0181) 527 5544
Fax: (0181) 523 4967

Wandsworth
Town Hall
Wandsworth
London SW18 2PU

Tel: (0181) 871 6000
Fax: (0181) 871 7506
DX: 59054 Wandsworth North

Westminster, City of
Westminster City Hall
64 Victoria Street
London SW1E 6QP

Tel: (0171) 828 8070
Fax: (0171) 798 3325
DX: 2310 Victoria SW1

XIII

XIII.3. Probate Registries – head and district registries

Principal Registry

Somerset House
Strand
London WC2R 1LP

Tel: (0171) 936 6000/6983
Fax: (0171) 936 6946
DX: 396 Lond/Chancery Ln WC2

Birmingham
The Priory Courts
33 Bull St
Birmingham B4 6DU

Tel: (0121) 681 3414
Fax: (0121) 681 3404
DX: 701990 Birmingham-7

Brighton
William Street
Brighton BN2 2LG

Tel: (01273) 684071
Fax: (01273) 688281
DX: 98073 Brighton-3

Bristol
The Crescent Centre
Temple Back
Bristol BS1 6EP

Tel: (0117) 927 3915/926 4619
Fax: (0117) 925 9377

Ipswich
Level 3
Haven House
17 Lower Brook Street
Ipswich
Suffolk IP4 1DN

Tel: (01473) 253 724
Fax: (01473) 280 889
DX: 3279 Ipswich

Sub-Registries

Bangor
1st Floor
Bron Castell
High Street
Bangor LL57 1YS

Tel: (01248) 362 410
DX: 23186 Bangor-2

Bodmin
Market Street
Bodmin
Cornwall PL31 2JW

Tel: (01208) 72279
DX: 81858 Bodmin

Cardiff
Probate Registry of Wales
PO Box 474
2 Park Street
Cardiff CF1 1TB

Tel: (01222) 376 479
Fax: (01222) 376 466
DX: 122782 Cardiff-13

Carlisle
Courts of Justice
Earl Street
Carlisle CA1 1DJ

Tel: (01228) 21751
DX: 63034 Carlisle

Carmarthen
14 King Street
Carmarthen
Dyfed SA31 1BL

Tel: (01267) 236 238
DX: 51420 Carmarthen

Chester
5th Floor
Hamilton House
Hamilton Place
Chester CH1 2DA

Tel: (01244) 345 082
DX: 22162 Chester (Northgate)

Exeter
Finance House
Barnfield Road
Exeter
Devon EX1 1QR

Tel: (01392) 274 515
DX: 8380 Exeter

Gloucester
2nd Floor
Combined Courts Building
Kimbrose Way
Gloucester GL1 2DG

Tel: (01452) 522 585
DX: 7537 Gloucester-1

Lancaster
Mitre House
Church Street
Lancaster LA1 1HE

Tel: (01524) 36625
DX: 63509 Lancaster

Leeds
3rd Floor
Coronet House
Queen Street
Leeds LS1 2BA

Tel: (0113) 243 1505
Fax: (0113) 244 8145
DX: 26451 Leeds Park Sq

Leicester
5th Floor
Leicester House
Lee Circle
Leicester LE1 3RE

Tel: (0116) 253 8558
Fax: (0116) 262 7796
DX: 13655 Leicester-4

Lincoln
Mill House
Brayford Side North
Lincoln LN1 1YW

Tel: (01522) 523 648
DX: 11048 Lincoln-1

Liverpool
The Queen Elizabeth II
  Law Courts
Derby Square
Liverpool L2 1XA

Tel: (0151) 236 8264
Fax: (0151) 236 5575
DX: 14246 Liverpool-1

Maidstone
Law Courts
Barker Road
Maidstone
Kent ME16 8EQ

Tel: (01622) 202 000
DX: 51972 Maidstone-2

Manchester
9th Floor, Astley House
23 Quay Street
Manchester M3 4AT

Tel: (0161) 834 4319
Fax: (0161) 834 5651
DX: 14387 Manchester-1

Middlesbrough
Teeside Combined
  Court Centre
Russell St,
Middlesbrough
Cleveland TS1 2AE

Tel: (01642) 340 001
DX: 60536 Middlesbrough

Newcastle upon Tyne
2nd Floor
Plummer House
Croft Street
Newcastle upon Tyne NE1 6NP

Tel: (0191) 261 8383
Fax: (0191) 233 0868
DX: 61081 Newcastle upon Tyne

Norwich
Combined Court Building
The Law Courts
Bishopsgate
Norwich NR3 1UR

Tel: (01603) 761 776
Fax: (01603) 760 863
DX: 5202 Norwich

Nottingham
Buttdyke House
33 Park Row
Nottingham NG1 6GR

Tel: (0115) 941 4288
Fax: (0115) 924 3374
DX: 10055 Nottingham

Oxford
10a New Road
Oxford OX1 1LY

Tel: (01865) 241 163
Fax: (01865) 204 402
DX: 4337 Oxford

Peterborough
1st Floor, Crown Building
Rivergate
Peterborough PE1 1EJ

Tel: (01733) 62802
DX: 12327 Peterborough-1

Sheffield
PO Box 832
The Law Courts
50 West Bar
Sheffield S3 8YR

Tel: (0114) 281 2596
Fax: (0114) 281 2425
DX: 26054 Sheffield-2

Stoke on Trent
Combined Court Centre
Bethesda Street
Hanley
Stoke on Trent ST1 3BP

Tel: (01782) 854 065
Fax: (01782) 201 944
DX: 20736 Hanley-1

Winchester
4th Floor
Cromwell House
Andover Road
Winchester
Hants SO23 7EW

Tel: (01962) 853 046
Fax: (01962) 877 371
DX: 96900 Winchester-2

York
Duncombe Place
York YO1 2EA

Tel: (01904) 624 210
Fax: (01904) 624 210
DX: 61543 York

XIII.4.   All other addresses

1.   **British Coal**

Charles House
5-11 Lower Regent Street
London SW1Y 4LR

Tel: (0171) 201 4141

2.   **British Gas**

Corporate Affairs

100 Thames Valley Park Drive
Reading
Berkshire RG6 7PT

Tel: (0171) 321 2880
Fax: (0171) 269 4945/6/7

3.   **BR Property Board (see also 44
below – Railtrack Property)**

Headquarters

1 Eversholt Street
London NW1 2DD

Tel: (0171) 214 9898
Fax: (0171) 214 9890

Regional Offices

London & South East
1 Eversholt Street
London NW1 2DD

Tel: (0171) 214 9898
Fax: (0171) 214 9890

Midlands
Stonier House
10 Holliday Street
PO Box 4482
Birmingham B1 1TR

Tel: (0121) 643 4444
Fax: (0121) 644 4447

North Eastern
Hudson House
Toft Green
York YO1 1HP

Tel: (01904) 524 848
Fax: (01904) 524 862

North Western
8th Floor
Tower Block
Piccadilly Station
Manchester M60 7BR

Tel: (0161) 228 5864
Fax: (0161) 228 4402

Scottish
Buchanan House
58 Port Dundos Road
Glasgow G4 0HG

Tel: (0141) 335 2424
Fax: (0141) 335 3524

South Western
Temple Gate House
Temple Gate
Bristol BS1 6PX

Tel: (0117) 934 8771
Fax: (0117) 934 8933

4.   **British Railways Board (see also
43 below – Railtrack Board)**

Euston House
24 Eversholt Street
London NW1 1DZ

Tel: (0171) 928 5151
Fax: (0171) 922 4131

5.   **British Sugar PLC**

Oundle Road
Peterborough PE2 9QU

Tel: (01733) 63171
Fax: (01733) 63068

XIII

6. **British Waterways Board (BWB)**

Willow Grange
Church Road
Watford
Herts WD1 3QA

Tel: (01923) 226 422
Fax: (01923) 226 081

7. **Charities Commissioners**

Central Register of Charities
St Albans House
57 Haymarket
London SW1Y 4QX

Tel: (0171) 210 3000
Fax: (0171) 210 4545

Northern Office
2nd Floor
20 King's Parade
Queen's Dock
Liverpool L3 4DQ

Tel: (0151) 703 1500
Fax: (0151) 703 1555

8. **Cheshire Brine Subsidence Compensation Board**

Chester County Council
Property Management Services
Richard House
80 Lower Bridge Street
Chester CH1 1SW

Tel: (01244) 602 576

9. **Church Commissioners for England**

1 Millbank
Westminster
London SW1P 3JZ

Tel: (0171) 222 7010
Fax: (0171) 976 8473

10. **Coal Authority**

200 Litchfield Lane
Mansfield
Nottingham NG18 4RG

Tel: (01623) 427 162
Fax: (01623) 22072

11. **Companies House**

Companies House
Crown Way
Cardiff CF4 3UZ

Tel: (01222) 388 588
Fax: (01222) 380 900

12. **Cornwall Consultants**

Gilberts Coombe
New Portreath Road
Redruth
Cornwall TR16 4HN

Tel: (01209) 313 511
Fax: (01209) 313 512

13. **Council for Licensed Conveyancers**

16 Glebe Road
Chelmsford
Essex CM1 1QG

Tel: (01245) 349 599
Fax: (01245) 348 380

14. **Council of Mortgage Lenders**

3 Savile Row
London W1X 1AF

Tel: (0171) 437 0655
Fax: (0171) 734 6416
DX: 81551 Savile Row W1

15. **Countrywide Legal Indemnities**

15 Riverside Road
Norwich NR1 1SN

Tel: (01603) 617 617
Fax: (01603) 622 933
DX: 5261 Norwich

16. **Court of Protection**

Protection Division
Stewart House
24 Kingsway
London WC2B 6JX

Tel: (0171) 664 7000
Fax: (0171) 664 7702
DX: 37965 Kingsway

17. **Duchy of Cornwall**

10 Buckingham Gate
London SW1E 6LA

Tel: (0171) 834 7346
Fax: (0171) 931 9541

18. **Duchy of Lancaster**

1, Lancaster Place
Strand
London WC2E 7ED

Tel: (0171) 836 8277
Fax: (0171) 836 3098

19. **Electricity Company Area Offices**

East Midlands Electricity
PO Box 444
Woollaton
NottinghM NG8 1EZ

Tel: (0115) 901 0101
Fax: (0115) 901 8200

Eastern Group
PO Box 40
Wherstead
Ipswich IP9 2AQ

Tel: (01473) 688 688
Fax: (01473) 601 036

London Electricity
81-87 High Holborn
London WC1V 6NU

Tel: (0171) 242 9050
Fax: (0171) 331 3108

MANWEB
Manweb House
Kingsfield Court
Chester Bus. Park
Chester CH4 9RF

Tel: (0345) 112 211
Fax: (01244) 653 507

Midlands Electricity PLC
Mucklow Hill
Halesowen
West Midlands B62 8BP

Tel: (0121) 423 2345
Fax: (0121) 422 3311

Northern Electricity
PO Box 1SE
Carliol House
Market Street
Newcastle upon Tyne NE1 6NE

Tel: (0191) 221 2000
Fax: (0191) 235 2109

North Western Electricity (NORWEB)
Talbot Road
Manchester M16 OHQ

Tel: (0161) 873 8000
Fax: (0161) 875 7360

South Eastern Electricity
Forest Gate
Brighton Road
Crawley
West Sussex RH11 9BH

Tel: (01293) 565 888
Fax: (01293) 657 327

South Wales Electricity
St Mellons
Cardiff CF3 9XW

Tel: (01222) 792 111
Fax: (01222) 777 759

South Western Electricity
800 Park Avenue
Aztec West
Almondsbury
Bristol BS12 4SE

Tel: (01454) 201 101
Fax: (01454) 452 238

Southern Electric PLC
Southern Electric House
Westacott Way
Littlewick Green
Maidenhead
Berks SL6 3QB

Tel: (01628) 822 166
Fax: (01628) 584 400

Yorkshire Electricity
Wetherby Road
Scarcroft
Leeds LS14 3HS

Tel: (0113) 289 2123
Fax: (0113) 289 5611

XIII

20. **English China Clays (Europe) PLC**

John Keay House
St Austell
Cornwall PL25 4DJ

Tel: (01726) 74482
Fax: (01726) 623 019

21. **Foundation 15**

Administration Manager
Building Guarantees Department
Municipal Mutual Insurance Ltd
Southwood Crescent
Farnborough
Hants GU14 0NJ

22. **Gas Consumer Councils**

Head Office

Abford House
15 Wilton Road
London SW1V 1LT

Tel: (0171) 931 0977
Fax: (0171) 630 9934

Regional Offices

East Midlands
Pennine House
31-33 Millstone Lane
Leicester LE1 5JN

Tel: (0116) 255 6611
Fax: (0116) 251 0946

Eastern
51 Station Road
Letchworth
Herts SG6 3BQ

Tel: (01462) 685 399
Fax: (01462) 480 902

London and South East
6th Floor
Abford House
15 Wilton Road
London SW1V 1LT

Tel: (0171) 931 9151
Fax: (0171) 931 9544

North East
3rd Floor
National Deposit House
1 Eastgate
Leeds LS2 7RL

Tel: (0113) 243 9961
Fax: (0113) 242 6935

North West
Boulton House
Chorlton Street
Manchester M1 3HY

Tel: (0161) 236 1926
Fax: (0161) 236 8896

Northern
Plummer House
Market Street East
Newcastle upon Tyne NE1 6NF

Tel: (0191) 261 9561
Fax: (0191) 222 0071

Scotland
86 George Street
Edinburgh EH2 3BU

Tel: (0131) 226 6523
Fax: (0131) 220 3732

Southern
3rd Floor
Roddis House
4-12 Old Christchurch Road
Bournemouth
Dorset BH1 1LG

Tel: (01202) 556 654
Fax: (01202) 291 080

Wales
Caradog House
St Andrews Place
Cardiff CF1 3BE

Tel: (01222) 226 547
Fax: (01222) 238 611

West Midlands
Broadway House
60 Calthorpe Road
Five Ways
Birmingham B15 1TH

Tel: (0121) 455 0285
Fax: (0121) 456 2976

23. **Inland Revenue Capital Taxes Office**

Ferrers House
PO Box 38
Castle Meadow Road
Nottingham NG2 1BB

Tel: (0115) 974 2400
Fax: (0115) 974 2649
DX: 701201 Nottingham 4

24. **Inland Revenue Stamp Offices**

Belfast Stamp Office
Ground Floor
Dorchester House
52–58 Great Victoria Street
Belfast BT2 7QE

Tel: (01232) 314 614
DX: 2003 Belfast 2

Birmingham Stamp Office
Ground Floor
City House
140–146 Edmund Street
Birmingham B3 2JG

Tel: (0121) 200 2616
DX: 15001 Birmingham 1

Bristol Stamp Office
First Floor
The Pithay
All Saints Street
Bristol BS1 2NY

Tel: (0117) 945 6874/75
DX: 7899 Bristol 1

Edinburgh Stamp Office
Mulberry House
16 Picardy Place
Edinburgh EH1 3NF

Tel: (0131) 556 8511
DX: ED 303 Edinburgh 1

London – Worthing Stamp Office
Personal callers
South West Wing
Bush House
Strand
London WC2B 4QN

Tel: (0171) 438 7452/7252

Postal applications
Ground Floor
Durrington Bridge House
Barrington Road
Worthing
West Sussex BN12 4SE

Tel: (01903) 701 280
DX: 3799 Worthing 1

Manchester Stamp Office
Alexandra House
The Parsonage
Manchester M60 9BT

Tel: (0161) 833 0413
DX: 14430 Manchester 2

Newcastle Stamp Office
15th Floor
Cale Cross House
156 Pilgrim Street
Newcastle upon Tyne
NE1 6TF

Tel: (0191) 245 0200
DX: 61021 Newcastle upon Tyne 1

25. **Insolvency Practitioners Control Unit**

Insolvency Service
2nd Floor
Ladywood House
45-46 Stephenson Street
Birmingham B2 4UZ

Tel: (0121) 698 4000
Fax: (0121) 698 4095

26. **Intervention Board Executive Agency**
Kings House
33 Kings Road
Reading RG1 3BU

Tel: (01734) 583 626
Fax: (01734) 531 370

27. **Land Charges Department (HM Land Registry)**

Drakes Hill Court
Burrington Way
Plymouth PL5 3LP

Tel: (01752) 635 600
Fax: (01752) 766 666
DX: 8249 Plymouth-3

XIII

28. **Land Registry (see above App.XIII.1.)**

29. **Lands Tribunal**

   48/49 Chancery Lane
   London WC2A 1JR

   Tel: (0171) 936 7200
   Fax: (0171) 404 0896
   DX: 44452 Strand

30. **Law Society of England and Wales**

   The Law Society's Hall
   113 Chancery Lane
   London WC2A 1PL

   Tel: (0171) 242 1222
   Fax: (0171) 831 0344
   DX: 56 Lond/Chancery Ln WC2

   Law Society House
   50 Chancery Lane
   London WC2A 1SX

   Tel: (0171) 242 1222
   Fax: (0171) 405 9522
   DX: 56 Lond/Chancery Ln WC2

   Ipsley Court
   Berrington Close
   Redditch
   Worcs B98 0TD

   Tel: (0171) 242 1222
   (local) (01527) 517 141
   Fax: (01527) 510 213
   DX: 19114 Redditch

31. **Leasehold Valuation Tribunal**

   Whittington House
   19-30 Alfred Place
   London WC1E 7LR

   Tel: (0171) 446 7738
   Fax: (0171) 637 1250

32. **Local authorities of England and Wales (see above App. XIII.2.)**

33. **Milk Marque**
   Cleeve House
   Lower Wick
   Worcester WR2 4YB

   Tel: (01905) 858 500
   Fax: (01905) 858 600

   (Agricultural land – milk quotas)
   The Brampton
   Newcastle-Under-Lyme
   Staffordshire ST5 0QS

   Tel: (01782) 580 580
   Fax: (01782) 582434/580 680

34. **National Association of Estate Agents**

   Arbon House
   21 Jury Street
   Warwick
   Warwickshire CV34 4EH

   Tel: (01926) 496 800
   Fax: (01926) 400 953

35. **National House-Building Council**

   Head Office
   Buildmark House
   Chiltern Avenue
   Amersham
   Bucks HP6 5AP

   Tel: (01494) 434 477
   Fax: (01494) 728 521
   DX: 50712 Amersham

   Regional Offices
   East
   Buildmark House
   Boycott Avenue
   Oldbrook
   Milton Keynes
   Bucks MK6 2RN

   Tel: (01908) 691 888
   Fax: (01908) 678 575
   DX: 54464 Milton Keynes-3
   North
   Buildmark House
   George Cayley Drive
   Clifton
   York YO3 4XE

   Tel: (01904) 691 666
   Fax: (01904) 690 474

Scotland
42 Colinton Road
Edinburgh EH10 5BT

Tel: (0131) 313 1001
Fax: (0131) 313 1211

South East
Buildmark House
London Road
Sevenoaks
Kent TN13 1DE

Tel: (01732) 740 177
Fax: (01732) 740 978
DX: 30023 Sevenoaks

South West
6/7 Clevedon Triangle Centre
Clevedon
Avon BS21 6HX

Tel: (01275) 875 676
Fax: (01275) 875 336
DX: 30356 Clevedon

West
Buildmark House
1-3 Roman Way
Business Centre
Droitwich
Worcs WR9 9AJ

Tel: (01905) 795 111
Fax: (01905) 795 116

36. **National Radiological Protection Board (NRPB)**

Radon Survey
Chilton
Didcot
Oxon OX11 0RQ

Tel: (01235) 831 600
Fax: (01235) 833 891
NRPB Radon Freephone:
0800 614529

37. **National Rivers Authority**
Headquarters
Rio House
Waterside Drive
Aztec West
Almondbury
Bristol BS12 4UD

Tel: (01454) 624 400
Fax: (01454) 624 409

38. **Office for the Supervision of Solicitors**

Victoria Court
8 Dormer Place
Leamington Spa
Warwickshire CV32 5AE

Tel: (01926) 8210 082
Fax: (01926) 431 435
DX: 292320 Leamington Spa 4

39. **Potato Marketing Board**

Broad Field House
4 Between Towns Road
Cowley
Oxford OX4 3NA

Tel: (01865) 782 200
Fax: (01865) 782 200

40. **Probate Registries (see above App. XIII.3.)**

41. **Public Records Office**

Ruskin Avenue
Kew
Richmond
Surrey TW9 4DU

Tel: (0181) 876 3444
Fax: (0181) 878 8905

Bourne Avenue
Hayes
Middlesex UB3 1RF

Tel: (0181) 573 3831
Fax: (0181) 569 2751

42. **Public Trust Office**

24 Kingsway
London WC2B 6JX

Tel: (0171) 664 7000
Fax: (0171) 831 0060

43. **Railtrack Board (see also 4 above – British Railways Board)**

40 Bernard St
London WC1N 1BY

Tel: (0171) 344 7100
Fax: (0171) 344 7101

XIII

44. **Railtrack Property (see also 3 above – BR Property Board)**

Headquarters

Fitzroy House
355 Euston Road
London NW1 3AG

Tel: (0171) 830 5500
Fax (0171) 830 5803

Regional Offices

London and South East
Fitzroy House
355 Euston Rd
London NW1 3AG

Tel: (0171) 830 5500
Fax: (0171) 830 5803

Midlands

7th Floor West
Stanier House
PO Box 4520
Birmingham B1 1SL

Tel: (0121) 654 4415
Fax: (0121) 654 3272

North Eastern
Hudson House
Toft Green
York YO1 1HP

Tel: (01904) 524 800
Fax: (01904) 524 803

North Western
Room 301
Rail House
Store St
Manchester M60 7RP

Tel: (0161) 228 4409
Fax: (0161) 228 4401

Scotland
Buchanan House
58 Port Dundos Rd
Glasgow G4 0LQ

Tel: (0141) 335 2424
Fax: (0141) 335 2365

South Western
Temple Gate House
Temple Gate
Bristol BS1 6PX

Tel: (0117) 934 8170
Fax: (0117) 934 8777

45. **Registry of Friendly Societies**

Victory House
30-36 Kingsway
London WC2B 6ES

Tel: (0171) 663 5000
Fax: (0171) 663 5060

46. **Rent Assessment Panels**

Great Eastern House
Tennison Road
Cambridge CB1 2TR

Tel: (01223) 505 112
Fax: (01223) 505 116

East Midlands
Chaddesden House
77 Talbot Street
Nottingham NG1 5GN

Tel: (0115) 947 3825
Fax: (0115) 947 4975

Greater Manchester & Lancashire
Alexandra House
14-22 The Parsonage
Manchester M3 2JA

Tel: (0161) 832 9661
Fax: (0161) 833 1438

London
Whittington House
19-30 Alfred Place
London WC1E 7LR

Tel: (0171) 446 7700
Fax: (0171) 637 1250

Merseyside & Cheshire
1st Floor
Port of Liverpool Building
Pier Head
Liverpool L3 1BY

Tel: (0151) 236 3521
Fax: (0151) 236 6238

Northern
4th Floor
Warwick House
Grantham Road
Newcastle upon Tyne NE2 1QX

Tel: (0191) 201 3795
Fax: (0191) 232 0584

South Eastern
6-7 Lovers Walk
Preston Road
Brighton
East Sussex BN1 6AH

Tel: (01273) 506 381
Fax: (01273) 558 830

South Western
Middlegate
Whitefriars
Lewins Mead
Bristol BS1 2AP

Tel: (0117) 929 9431
Fax: (0117) 929 3534

Southern
2nd Floor,
8 Ogle Road
Southampton SO4 7FB

Tel: (01703) 225 626
Fax: (01703) 633 179

Wales
1st Floor West Wing
Southgate House
Wood Street
Cardiff CF1 1EW

Tel: (01222) 231 687
Fax: (01222) 236 146

West Midlands
5th Floor
Somerset House
37 Temple Street
Birmingham B2 5DP

Tel: (0121) 643 8336
Fax: (0121) 693 8337

Yorkshire
Symons House
Belgrave St
Leeds LS2 8DD

Tel: (0113) 243 9744
Fax: (0113) 244 3102

47. **Royal Courts of Justice**

Strand
London WC2A 2LL

Tel: (0171) 936 6000

48. **Royal Institute of British Architects**

66 Portland Place
London W1N 4AD

Tel: (0171) 580 5533
Fax: (0171) 255 1541

49. **Royal Institution of Chartered Surveyors**

12 Great George Street
Parliament Square
London SW1P 3AD

Tel: (0171) 222 7000
Fax: (0171) 222 9430
DX: 2348 Victoria SW1

50. **Solicitors Financial Services**

50 Chancery Lane
London WC2A 1SX

Tel: (071) 242 1222
Fax: (071) 831 0170
DX: 56 Lond/Chancery Ln WC2

51. **Solicitors Property Group Ltd**

30 Station Road
Cuffley
Herts EN6 4HE

Tel: (01707) 873 126
Fax: (01707) 873 601
DX: 93801 Cuffley

XIII

52. **Sugar Bureau**

Duncan House
Dolphin Square
London SW1V 3PW

Tel: (0171) 828 9465
Fax: (0171) 821 5393

53. **Treasury Solicitor**

Dept. of HM Procurator General
and Treasury Solicitor
Queen Anne's Chambers
28 Broadway
London SW1H 9JX

Tel: (0171) 210 3000
Fax: (0171) 222 6006

54. **Water Service Companies**

Anglian Water
Anglian House
Ambury Road
Huntington PE18 6NZ

Tel: (01480) 443 000
Fax:(01480) 443 115

North West Water
Dawson House
Great Sankey
Warrington WA5 3LW

Tel: (01925) 234 000
Fax: (01925) 233 360

Northumbrian Water
Abbey Road
Pity Me
Durham DH1 5FJ

Tel: (0191) 383 2222
Fax: (0191) 384 1920

Severn Trent Water
2297 Coventry Road
Birmingham B26 3PU

Tel: (0121) 722 4000
Fax: (0121) 722 4800

South West Water
Peninsular House
Rydon Lane
Exeter EX2 7HR

Tel: (01392) 446 688
Fax: (01392) 434 966

Southern Water
Southern House
Yeoman Road
Worthing
West Sussex BN13 3NX

Tel: (01903) 264 444
Fax: (01903) 262 185

Thames Water Utilities Ltd
Nugent House
Vastern Road
Reading
Berks RG1 8DB

Tel: (01734) 591 159
Fax: (01734) 593 203

Welsh Water
Plas-y-Ffynnon
Cambrian Way
Brecon
Powys LD3 7HP

Tel: (01874) 623 181
Fax: (01874) 624 167

Wessex Water PLC
Wessex House
Passage Street
Bristol BS2 0JQ

Tel: (0117) 929 0611
Fax: (0117) 929 3137

Yorkshire Water
Broadacre House
Vicar Lane
Bradford BD1 5PZ

Tel: (01274) 306 063
Fax: (01274) 731 830

55. **Water Supply Companies**

Bournemouth & West Hampshire
Water PLC
George Jessel House
Francis Avenue
Bournemouth BH11 8NB

Tel: (01202) 590 059
Fax: (01202) 599 333

Bristol Water plc
P O Box 218
Bridgwater Road
Bristol BS99 7AU

Tel: (0117) 966 5881
Fax: (0117) 963 3755

Cambridge Water Company
41 Rustat Road
Cambridge CB1 3QS

Tel: (01223) 247 351
Fax: (01223) 214 052

Chester Waterworks Company
Aqua House
45 Boughton
Chester CH3 5AU

Tel: (01244) 320 501
Fax: (01244) 316 102

Cholderton & District Water
  Company
Estate Office
Cholderton
Salisbury
Wiltshire SP4 0DR

Tel: (01980) 629 203
Fax: (01980) 629 307

Sutton & East Surrey Water plc
London Road
Redhill
Surrey RH1 1LJ

Tel: (01737) 772 000
Fax: (01737) 766 807

Essex & Suffolk Water Company
Hall Street
Chelmsford
Essex CM2 0HH

Tel: (01245) 491 234
Fax: (01245) 212 345

Folkestone & Dover Water
  Services Ltd
The Cherry Garden
Cherry Garden Lane
Folkestone
Kent CT19 4QB

Tel: (01303) 276 951
Fax: (01303) 276 712

Hartlepool Water PLC
3 Lancaster Road
Hartlepool
Cleveland TS24 8LW

Tel: (01429) 868 555
Fax: (01429) 278 961

Mid Kent Water PLC
Rocport Road
Snodland
Kent ME6 5AH

Tel: (01634) 240 313
Fax: (01634) 242 764

Mid Southern Water PLC
22-30 Durk Road
Frimley Green
Camberley
Surrey GU16 6HZ

Tel: (01252) 835 031
Fax: (01252) 836 066

Northumbrian Water Ltd
PO Box 10
Allendale Road
Newcastle upon Tyne NE6 2SW

Tel: (0191) 265 4144
Fax: (0191) 276 6612

North Surrey Water Ltd
Millis House
The Causeway
Staines
Middlesex TW18 3BX

Tel: (01784) 455 464
Fax: (01784) 426 333

Portsmouth Water PLC
PO Box 8
West Street
Havant
Hants PO9 1LG

Tel: (01705) 499 888
Fax: (01705) 453 632

Severn Trent Water PLC
Bromwich Rd
Lower Wick
Worcester WR2 4BN

Tel: (01905) 424 300

South East Water Ltd
14 Upperton Road
Eastbourne
Sussex BN21 1EP

Tel: (01323) 411 411
Fax: (01323) 411 412

XIII

South Staffordshire Water PLC
Green Lane
Walsall
W Midlands WS2 7PD

Tel: (01922) 38282
Fax: (01922) 21968

Tendring Hundred Water
    Services Ltd
Mill Hill
Manningtree
Essex CO11 2AZ

Tel: (01206) 399 200
Fax: (01206) 399 210

Three Valleys Water plc
PO Box 48
Bishops Rise
Hatfield
Herts AL10 9HL

Tel: (01707) 268 111
Fax: (01707) 277 333

Wrexham Water plc
Packsattle
Wrexham Road
Rhostyllen
Wrexham
Clwyd LL14 4EH

Tel: (01978) 846 946
Fax: (01978) 846 888

York Waterworks plc
Lendal Tower
York YO1 2DL

Tel: (01904) 622 171
Fax: (01904) 611 667

56.   **Zurich Insurance**

Administration Manager
Building Guarantee Dept
Southwood Crescent
Farnborough
Hants GU14 0NL

Tel: (01252) 522 000
Fax: (01252) 372 989

XIV. The Law Society interest rate

Changes from September 1991

4 September 1991	14.5%
5 May 1992	14%
16 September 1992	16%
18 September 1992	14%
22 September 1992	13%
16 October 1992	12%
13 November 1992	11%
26 January 1993	10%
23 November 1993	9.5%
8 February 1994	9.25%
12 September 1994	9.75%
8 December 1994	10.25%
2 February 1995	10.75%
13 December 1995	10.5%
18 January 1996	10.25%
8 March 1996	10%
6 June 1996	9.75%
30 October 1996	10%
6 May 1997	10.25%

The Law Society rate is 4% above Barclays Bank base rate.

Index

Patients, execution of purchase deed E1.7.12
Payment
banker's draft *see* **Banker's draft payment**
cash payments, money laundering possibility F3.11
chain transactions
direct to ultimate destination F3.5.2, F3.6.1
time F3.5.2, F3.6.1
cheques F3.1.4
re-dated if completion delayed M1.3.3
cleared funds F3.4.1
clearing
CHAPS banks *App. XII. 2*
PACS *App. XII.1*
Clearing Company Ltd Banks *App. XII. 2*
coins F3.1.3
discharge of seller's mortgage F4.2.10
immediately after completion F3.7.1
separate cheques F3.7.2, F3.7.3
undertaking F4.2.10, F4.2.11
foreign currency F3.1.2
method F3.1
see also individual methods, e.g.
Banker's draft payment; cheques
notes F3.1.3
other than in contract F3.1.2
out of jurisdiction F3.1.2
release of deposit F4.2.14
agent for seller F3.9.1
stakeholder F3.9.2
retentions from purchase price F3.10.1
stamp duty *see* **Stamp duty**
Standard Conditions for method F3.1.1
telegraphic transfer *see* **Telegraphic transfer of funds**
time
by 2pm F1.2.4, F3.5.1, F4.6.1
chain of transactions F3.5.2
undertaking to remit funds
authority of client F3.8.1
binding F3.8.2
seller bound to complete F3.8.3
see also **Mortgage funds**
Periodic tenancies K5.2.6
Perpetuity rule
option to purchase reversion K13.2.1
option to renew K13.3.1, K13.3.2
Personal representatives
assent *see* **Assent**
capacity B7.5
registered land D2.8.2.1
unregistered land D2.8.2.2
conveyance to themselves
justified D2.7.2
voidable D2.7.1
covenants M9.3
joint powers in land B7.5.2
power during administration only B7.5.1
service of notice on E6.6.2

signature on contract C2.4.6
sole seller
service of notice to complete E6.2.4
wait for grant E6.2.1, E6.2.3
solicitor acting for A4.3.3
investment advice A4.3.4
solicitor who is trustee A4.3.1
investment advice A4.3.2
see also **Trustees for sale**
Photocopying *see* **Reproduction of standard forms**
Physical defects
disclosure B5.3.3
see also **New property**, defects
'Pink card' warning on undertakings *App. VI.3*
Pipelines B8.3.4, B8.10.1
survey of water supply pipes A13.4.8
Place of completion *see* **Completion place**
Planning
acting for buyer
alterations within last four years B24.3.2
authorised use B24.3.2
breach of planning B24.3.3
conditional contract B24.3.4
pre-contract enquiries B24.3.1
proposed alterations B24.3.2
required permission B24.3.4
acting for seller
disclosure B24.2.1
investigation B3.8.1
agricultural land
authorised use of land B8.4.1
change of use B8.4.2
alterations
proposed B24.3.2
within last four years B24.3.2
authorised use B24.3.2
breach of planning B24.3.3
Building Regulations B24.6.1
certificate of compliance B24.6.1
deposit of plans B24.6.1
service of notice B24.6.1
conditional contract B24.3.4
copies of decisions B24.2.3
development land B24.1.2
disclosure of matters B5.3.4
Enterprise Zone B24.5.1
environmental issues B24.7.1, B25.2.3
irregularities corrected by seller B24.2.2
listed buildings B24.4.2
matters not requiring permission
erection of fences B24.4.1
specifically excluded B24.4.1
new property I1.3.1
Property Information Form B24.2.1
required permission B24.3.4
restrictive covenants B24.1.1
Simplified Planning Zone B24.5.1
Special Development Order B24.5.1
'subject to planning permission' B13.7.3.4